ENCYCLOPEDIA OF CONTEMPORARY ITALIAN CULTURE

ENCYCLOPEDIA OF CONTEMPORARY ITALIAN CULTURE

Edited by
Gino Moliterno

London and New York

First published 2000
by Routledge
11 New Fetter Lane, London EC4P 4EE

Simultaneously published in the USA and Canada
by Routledge
29 West 35th Street, New York, NY 10001

Routledge is an imprint of the Taylor & Francis Group
© 2000 Routledge

Typeset in Baskerville by Taylor & Francis Books Ltd
Printed and bound in Great Britain by TJ International Ltd,
Padstow, Cornwall

British Library Cataloguing in Publication Data
A catalogue record for this book is available from the British Library

Library of Congress Cataloging in Publication Data
Encyclopedia of contemporary Italian culture / edited by Gino Moliterno
p. cm.
Includes bibliographical references and index.
1. Italy—Civilization—20th century—Encyclopedias. I. Moliterno,
Gino, 1951– .
DG450.E53 2000
945.09'03—dc21   99—38356
CIP

ISBN 0-415-14584-8

Contents

Editorial team

General editor
Gino Moliterno
Australian National University

Consultant editors
Camilla Bettoni
University of Verona, Italy

Richard Bosworth
University of Western Australia

Andrea Ciccarelli
Indiana University, Bloomington, USA

Millicent Marcus
University of Texas, USA

David Moss
Griffith University, Australia

Laurence Simmons
University of Auckland, New Zealand

Penny Sparke
Royal College of Art, London, UK

Max Staples
Charles Stuart University, Australia

List of contributors

Roger Absalom
Sheffield Hallam University, UK

Mauro Baracco
RMIT University, Australia

Jennifer Barnes
Royal College of Music, UK

Paolo Bartoloni
University of Sydney, Australia

Stefano Battilossi
London School of Economics, UK

Ian Bersten
Australia

Camilla Bettoni
University of Verona, Italy

Peter Bondanella
Indiana University, Bloomington, USA

Dorothée Bonnigal
France

RJB Bosworth
University of Western Australia

Pietro Cafaro
University of Turin, Italy

Piera Carroli
Australian National University

Enrico Cesaretti
University of Michigan, Ann Arbor, USA

Daniele Checchi
University of Milan, Italy

Andrea Ciccarelli
Indiana University, Bloomington, USA

Mirna Cicioni
Monash University, Australia

Alastair Davidson
Monash University, Australia

Olivia Dawson
UK

Cristina Degli-Esposti Reinert
University of Arizona, USA

Donatella della Porta
University of Florence, Italy

Mario Diani
University of Strathclyde, UK

John Dickie
University College London, UK

Mark Donovan
University of Wales, Cardiff, UK

Jeff Doyle
Australian Defence Force Academy

Joseph Farrell
University of Strathclyde, UK

Valerio Ferme
University of California, Berkeley, USA

Tim Fitzpatrick
The University of Sydney, Australia

John Foot
University College, London, UK

Antonella Francini
Syracuse University in Florence, Italy

John Gatt-Rutter
La Trobe University, Australia

Chiara Giaccardi
Catholic University, Milan, Italy

Manuela Gieri
University of Toronto, Canada

Eugenio Giusti
Vassar College, USA

Keith Green
University of Auckland, New Zealand

Stephen Gundle
University of London, UK

Hermann W. Haller
City University of New York, USA

John Jenkins
University of Canberra, Australia

Ross Jenner
University of Auckland, New Zealand

Thomas G. Kelso
USA

Claire Kennedy
Griffith University, Australia

John Kersey
Royal College of Music, UK

Suzanne Kiernan
University of Sydney, Australia

John Kinder
University of Western Australia

Gordana Kostich
University of Pennsylvania, USA

Jan Kurz
University of Bielefeld, Germany

Ben Lawton
Purdue University, USA

Ernesto Livorni
Yale University, USA

Bernadette Luciano
University of Auckland, New Zealand

Robert Lumley
University College London, UK

Giunio Luzzatto
University of Genoa, Italy

Franco Manai
University of Auckland, New Zealand

Millicent Marcus
University of Pennsylvania, USA

Anthony Masi
McGill University, Canada

Larry Mayer
Miami University, USA

Kitty Millet
San Francisco State University, USA

Gino Moliterno
Australian National University

Adriana Monti
Canada

David Moss
Griffith University, Australia

Elim Papadakis
Australian National University

Graziella Parati
Dartmouth College, USA

Simon Parker
University of York, UK

Francesca Parmeggiani
Fordham University, New York, USA

Virginia Picchietti
University of Scranton, USA

Emanuela Poli
Oxford University, UK

John Pollard
Anglia Polytechnic University, UK

Paolo Puppa
University Ca' Foscari, Venice, Italy

Claudio Radaelli
University of Bradford, UK

Marino Regini
University of Milan, Italy

Andrea Ricci
Indiana University, Bloomington, USA

Stephan Riedel
Monash University, Australia

Sherry Roush
Pennsylvania State University, USA

Antonia Rubino
University of Sydney, Australia

Laura Salsini
University of Delaware, Newark, USA

Andrew Schultz
Guildhall School of Music and Drama, UK

Achille Serrao
Italy

Laurence Simmons
University of Auckland, New Zealand

Glenda Sluga
University of Sydney, Australia

Penny Sparke
Royal College of Art, UK

Max Staples
Charles Stuart University, Australia

Paul Statham
University of Leeds, UK

Federica Sturani
Liverpool John Moores University, UK

Gianni Toniolo
Università de Roma Tor Vergata, Italy

Mariella Totaro Genevois
Monash University, Australia

Claudia Venditti
Italy

Riccardo Ventrella
DAMS, University of Bologna, Italy

Paolo Villa
Indiana University, Bloomington, USA

James Walston
American University of Rome, Italy

Bruno P.F. Wanrooij
Syracuse University in Florence, Italy

Dave Watson
University of New England, Armidale, Australia

William Van Watson
Illinois State University, USA

Nicola White
Kingston University, UK

Sharon Wood
University of Strathclyde, UK

Fassil Zewdou
University of Pennsylvania, USA

Giovanna Zincone
Italy

The entries by Paolo Puppa and Achille Serrau were translated by Gino Moliterno

Introduction

In the half century following the end of the Second World War Italy has been profoundly transformed from a predominantly rural and relatively provincial culture into a bustling, post-industrial, metropolitan society. This dramatic passage from almost pre-industrial to decisively postmodern in the space of only 50 years has been neither linear nor univocal and has not been achieved without costs. In fact, it would be no exaggeration to suggest that the keyword for this entire period has been the word 'crisis'. Nevertheless, at the end of the twentieth century the Italian success story goes on. A distinctive Italian style of design, fashion and cuisine continues to exert a strong influence in the international marketplace with the 'made in Italy' label remaining a mark of quality and prestige. In 1997 Italian actor-playwright Dario Fo won the Nobel prize for literature, and in 1999 Roberto Benigni's *La vita è bella* (Life is Beautiful) took the Oscar for Best Foreign Film, the third time an Italian film has done so in the last decade. More importantly, perhaps, as we enter the twenty-first century, the Italian lira has been allowed to join the common European currency and Italy has also been able to play a full particpatory role in NATO's intervention in the Kosovo war and other United Nations peacekeeping missions throughout the world.

At the same time, at a more academic level, there has also been a broadening of perspectives in the teaching of Italian Studies in the English-speaking world, with the focus now frequently moving beyond the traditional areas of literature, music and the fine arts to embrace many aspects of Italian life and culture previously ignored. Italian language courses, both at school and university, have also extended their scope beyond the confines of grammar in order to attempt to teach the language more effectively within its wider social and cultural contexts. At the same time, as Italy has come to be more closely integrated into the European Union, Italian politics and society have also been included in the curricula of courses on European Studies. This greater and more diversified interest in contemporary Italy has underlined the need for a comprehensive reference work in English which could offer accurate, concise and up-to-date information on a wide range of topics in a readily-accessible format. Routledge's *Encyclopedia of Contemporary Italian Culture* is an attempt to address that need.

In seeking to cater for both academic and more general readers we have interpreted the term 'contemporary Italian culture' in the broadest sense. We have assumed 'contemporary' to mean post-1945 since it was only with the founding of the First Republic at the end of the Second World War that Italy really embarked on its dramatic passage to modernity. Our historical reference, then, has been the postwar period. Nevertheless, it's clear that many aspects of Italian life and culture in the period following the War cannot be satisfactorily understood without at least some reference to earlier times, so reference to the prewar period has not been excluded where it could facilitate a better understanding of the topic at hand. 'Italy' and 'Italian' have been interpreted in a commonsense fashion to mean localized within the national borders. A certain amount of coverage of Italian culture outside the peninsula has also been provided in such entries as 'migration', 'literature of migration', 'Italian outside Italy' (referring to the language) and 'Italian-American Cinema', but limitations of space have prevented the inclusion of separate entries on all the 'little Italies' abroad, a task that would have required a volume on its own.

Although there has been much animated debate of late over the very notion of culture, in particular of 'culture' understood as a unitary phenomenon, we have avoided the temptation to become involved in a theoretical debate which is probably better conducted in the pages of more specialized journals. Here we have taken the opportunity offered by the Routledge series to interpret 'culture' in the very broadest sense as covering all social activities and institutions and all communicative and symbolic practices which might be considered as forming part of a distinctively Italian 'way of life'. The reader will thus find entries on all aspects of Italian postwar life, society and culture, ranging from food and religion to spas and sport. While not neglecting the traditional areas of 'high' culture this volume has also striven to present the more significant manifestations of Italian popular culture in the postwar period, by including entries on topics such as comics, *fotoromanzi*, detective fiction, pop music, and, of course, television. As Umberto Eco has noted, one of the most significant cultural achievements in the postwar period, namely the use of a standard Italian language throughout the peninsula, was finally brought about neither through literature nor the efforts of intellectuals but quite effortlessly by television. It is indeed significant that Italy is the only country in the world where a television magnate controlling three national networks has been elected, even if only briefly, to the office of Prime Minister, and our attention to television and television programmes in this volume attempts to pay due respect to this influence.

With over 900 entries covering every aspect of life and culture in the Italian First Republic, this encyclopedia seeks to offer both the academic and the more general reader the most extensive storehouse of information on contemporary Italy available in English today. The entries, ranging from short concise sketches of about two hundred words to the more substantial overview articles of around two thousand words, all attempt to present their factual information in a contextualized way so as to bring out the cultural relevance of each topic. Although each entry has been written to stand alone in order to facilitate quick consultation, internal cross-referencing is used extensively to help the reader make useful connections by turning to related topics. Wherever possible, entries also contain suggestions for further reading, usually annotated so as to guide the reader interested in pursuing further research to the most appropriate material. With an eye to serving readers who may not know Italian, an attempt has been made to refer to material in English but important texts in Italian have also been included where this seemed appropriate.

Having been created with the aim of meeting the needs of both the more specialized and the general reader, this Encyclopedia thus hopes to function both as an essential resource for teaching and learning as well as a valuable aid to further research.

Acknowledgements

The publication of this volume owes much to the willing collaboration of many individuals whose generous contribution I would like to acknowledge here.

My thanks go first to Professor Guido Almansi, Professor Luigi Bonaffini and Dr Jonathan White who offered valuable advice in the early stages of the project even if other commitments prevented them from contributing further to the volume.

A vote of thanks is due, of course, to all the writers but especially to Dr Stefano Battilossi, Dr Mark Donovan, Dr John Kersey and Fassil Zewdou who all willingly took on extra entries as the need arose. Professor Peter Bondanella and Professor Ben Lawton contributed more than is apparent on the surface and I express my gratitude to them. The consulting editors have all been invaluable in providing expert advice and helping to draw up the entry list but Dr Camilla Bettoni deserves special thanks for her meticulous organization and editing of all the language entries. A special vote of thanks, too, to Dr Max Staples and Professor Andrea Ciccarelli for always being available to answer my queries as well as taking on more entries as the need for them became apparent. Above all I would like to thank Professor

David Moss who for the past three years has generously shared his remarkable expertise in all things Italian with me and, with warmth and enthusiasm, has continually offered encouragement.

I thank the Australian National University for facilitating this project through the award of a research grant and a period of study leave. I would also like to warmly thank Professor Iain McCalman and the entire staff of the ANU Humanities Research Centre for their hospitality during my three months at the Centre as a Visiting Fellow.

Thanks also to Lucio Cavicchioli and Vivien Rubessa for their help in researching particular entries and to Patricia Werlemann and Alessandro Moliterno for their general support, especially in times of great difficulty.

Finally I would like to extend my warmest thanks to Professor Carol Sanders for having originally encouraged me to undertake the project and to Fiona Cairns, Denise Rea and all the Routledge staff who have consistently offered the most valuable editorial support and advice.

Gino Moliterno
Canberra, July 1999

How to use this book

The *Encyclopedia of Contemporary Italian Culture* contains over 900 signed entries, arranged alphabetically and ranging from concise thumbnail sketches to longer overview essays.

For readers with a particular interest, a thematic contents list on p. xiv groups entries according to subject (e.g. music or the visual arts). In the body of each entry direct cross-references, indicated in bold type, lead to other relevant articles in the volume. Where appropriate a 'see also' section at the end of an entry will indicate further related topics.

Biographical entries include dates and places of birth and death, followed by the profession of the subject. Wherever available, the exact day, month and year have been given. For the benefit of English speakers place-names have generally been anglicized.

Suggestions for further reading are given where appropriate and where relevant texts are easily accessible. All titles of books, plays and films are given both in their original and in English translation.

Thematic entry list

Architecture and design

Abitare
Albini, Franco
anti-design
architectural and design magazines
L'Architettura
Archizoom
Aulenti, Gae
Aymonino, Carlo
Bellini, Mario
Benevolo, Leonardo
BPR
Branzi, Andrea
Canella, Guido
Casabella
Castiglioni, Achille
Castiglioni, Pier Giacomo
Civiltà delle macchine
Colombo, Joe
Controspazio
De Carlo, Giancarlo
design education
Domus
Figini and Pollini
Gabetti and Isola
Gardella, Ignazio
Giacosa, Dante
Grassi, Giorgio
Gregotti, Vittorio
industrial design
interior design
IUAV
Libera, Adalberto
Magistretti, Vico
Mari, Enzo
Mendini, Alessandro
Michelucci, Giovanni
Milan Triennale
Modo
Mollino, Carlo
Moretti, Luigi Walter
Munari, Bruno
Muratori, Saverio
Natalini, Adolfo
Nervi, Pier Luigi
Piano, Renzo
Piccinato, Luigi
Ponti, Giò
Porcinai, Pietro
Portoghesi, Paolo
Purini, Franco
Quaroni, Ludovico
Ridolfi, Mario
Rogers, Ernesto N.
Rosselli, Alberto
Rossi, Aldo
Samonà, Giuseppe
Scarpa and Scarpa
Scarpa, Carlo
Sottsass, Ettore
Spazio e società
Stile Industria
Studio Alchimia
Studio Memphis
Superstudio
Tafuri, Manfredo
Thermes, Laura
urban planning
Valle, Gino
Venezia, Francesco
Viganò, Vittoriano

Zanuso, Marco
Zanussi
Zevi, Bruno

Cultural institutions/phenomena

arts festivals
Dante Alighieri Society
Istituti italiani di cultura
music festivals
music institutions
Spoleto Festival
tourism
Venice Biennale

Economy

Agnelli family
agriculture
Alitalia
Banca Commerciale Italiana
Banca d'Italia
banking and credit system
Carli, Guido
Cassa per il Mezzogiorno
Cefis, Eugenio
Ciampi, Carlo Azeglio
co-operatives
Confindustria
Cuccia, Enrico
De Benedetti, Carlo
economic miracle
economy
ENEL
ENI
Ferrari, Enzo Anselmo
Ferruzzi
Fiat
Fininvest
Finsider
Gemina
Ilva
industry
INPS
IRI
Italsider
Mattei, Enrico
Mediobanca
Menichella, Donato
Modigliani, Franco
Montedison

motor car industry
Olivetti
peasants
Pirelli
privatization/nationalization
Romiti, Cesare
STET
taxation
Third Italy
tourism
trade unions
unemployment
Vanoni, Ezio

Education and research

ASI
CENSIS
Consiglio Nazionale di Ricerche
education
ISTAT
Levi Montalcini, Rita
Rubbia, Carlo
universities

Fashion

Armani, Giorgio
Benetton
Biagiotti, Laura
Brioni
Capucci, Roberto
Dolce and Gabbana
fashion
Fendi, Paola
Ferragamo, Salvatore
Ferrè, Gianfranco
Fiorucci, Elio
Fontana
Gigli
Gucci
Krizia
Marzotto
MaxMara
Missoni
Moschino
Prada
Pucci, Emilio
Trussardi
Valentino
Versace

Film

Food and drink

bread
cheeses
coffee
olive oil
pasta
pizza
polenta
prosciutto
regional cooking
tartufo
tavola calda
wine

History

anti-fascism
emigration
environmental movement
European Union
Falcone, Giovanni
fascism/neofascism
foreign policy
feminism
gay movement
Giuliano, Salvatore
Gladio
historiography
immigration
Mani pulite
opening to the Left
postwar reconstruction
Resistance
strategia della tensione
student movement
Trieste

Intellectual life

Abbagnano, Nicola
Agamben, Giorgio
Alberoni, Francesco
alfabeta
Anceschi, Luciano
Asor Rosa, Alberto
Aut aut
Banfi, Antonio
Bobbio, Norberto
Cacciari, Massimo
Colletti, Lucio

Colli, Giorgio
Croce, Benedetto
De Felice, Renzo
De Martino, Ernesto
Della Volpe, Galvano
Eco, Umberto
Garin, Eugenio
Geymonat, Ludovico
Ginzburg, Carlo
Gramsci, Antonio
Gruppo 63
intellectuals
Momigliano, Arnaldo
Paci, Enzo
Pareyson, Luigi
Pensiero debole
Rinascita
semiotics
Severino, Emanuele
Vattimo, Gianni
il verri

Language

dialect usage
dialects
Italian and emigration
Italian language
Italian lexicon
Italian morphology
Italian outside Italy
Italian phonology
Italian syntax
language attitudes
language education
language institutions
language policy
minority languages
sectorial languages
sexism in language
varieties of Italian

Literature and criticism

Agosti, Stefano
Asor Rosa, Alberto
Barilli, Renato
Bo, Carlo
Branca, Vittore
Cecchi, Emilio
Ceserani, Remo

Mass media and publishing

Religion

Pope John Paul I
Pope John Paul II
Pope John XXIII
Pope Paul VI
Pope Pius XII
Ruini, Cardinal
Second Vatican Council
Sorge, Bartolomeo
Vatican

Society

abortion
American influence
armed forces
autostrada network
bureaucracy
carabinieri
censorship
Church, state and society
Cicciolina
citizenship
clientelism
consumerism
crime
divorce
drug culture
earthquakes
emigration
environmental movement
environmental policy
Falcone, Giovanni
family
feminism
flag
friendship
gay movement
Harry's Bar
health services
HIV/AIDS
housing policy
legal system
local administration
lotteries
mafia
marriage
motor scooters
national anthem
P2
patron saints

police
population
pornography
postal services
presepe
psychoanalysis/psychiatry
railway system
regions
salotti
sexual mores
social welfare
Southern Question
spas
sport and society
student movement
Ustica

Sport

ARCI
athletics
Bartali, Gino
basketball
boxing
Brera, Gianni
Coppi, Fausto
cycling
football
motor racing
Olympics
sport and society
sports broadcasting
sports publications
tennis
Tomba, Alberto
Touring Club Italiano
volleyball
winter sports

Visual arts

Accardi, Carla
Adami, Valerio
Anselmo, Giovanni
Argan, Giulio Carlo
art criticism
art movements
arte concreta
arte povera
Azimuth
Baj, Enrico

Writers

Cancogni, Manlio
Capriolo, Paola
Caproni, Giorgio
Cassola, Carlo
Cavalli, Patrizia
Castellaneta, Carlo
Cederna, Camilla
Celati, Gianni
Ceronetti, Guido
Chiara, Piero
Chohra, Nassera
Cima, Annalisa
Citati, Pietro
Consolo, Vincenzo
Cucchi, Maurizio
D'Arrigo, Stefano
D'Eramo, Luce
De Carlo, Andrea
De Cespedes, Alba
Del Giudice, Daniele
Duranti, Francesca
Erba, Luciano
Fabbri, Diego
Fallaci, Oriana
Fenoglio, Beppe
Ferrucci, Franco
Flaiano, Ennio
Fontanella, Luigi
Fortini, Franco
Frabotta, Biancamaria
Fruttero e Lucentini
Gadda, Carlo Emilio
Ginzburg, Natalia
Giudici, Giovanni
Giuliani, Alfredo
Guareschi, Giovanni
Jaeggy, Fleur
Jewish writers
Jovine, Francesco
La Capria, Raffaele
Lagorio, Gina
Lampedusa, Giuseppe Tomasi di
Landolfi, Tommaso
Levi, Carlo
Levi, Primo
Liala
literature in dialect
Loy, Rosetta
Luzi, Mario

Magrelli, Vallerio
Majorino, Giancarlo
Malaparte, Curzio
Malerba, Luigi
Manganelli, Giorgio
Maraini, Dacia
Meneghello, Luigi
Merini, Alda
Methnani, Salah
Montale, Eugenio
Morante, Elsa
Moravia, Alberto
Morselli, Guido
Moussa Ba, Saidou
Orelli, Giorgio
Orengo, Nico
Ortese, Anna Maria
Ottieri, Ottiero
Pagliarani, Elio
Palazzeschi, Aldo
Parise, Goffredo
Pavese, Cesare
Pazzi, Roberto
Penna, Sandro
Piovene, Guido
Pomilio, Mario
Pontiggia, Giuseppe
Porta, Antonio
Pratolini, Vasco
Pressburger, Giorgio
Quasimodo, Salvatore
Raboni, Giovanni
Rasy, Elisabetta
Rea, Domenico
Rimanelli, Giose
Risi, Nelo
Romano, Lalla
Rosselli, Amelia
Roversi, Roberto
Saba, Umberto
Sanguineti, Edoardo
Santucci, Luigi
Saviane, Giorgio
Sciascia, Leonardo
Sereni, Vittorio
Sgorlon, Carlo
Siciliano, Enzo
Silone, Ignazio
Sinisgalli, Leonardo

A

Abbado, Claudio

b. 26 June 1933, Milan

Conductor

Born into a musical family, Abbado began to study piano with his father. After further piano studies at the Milan Conservatoire he turned to conducting, becoming a student of Swarowsky in Vienna and winning the Koussevitsky Prize in 1958. He won the Mitropoulos Prize in 1963, and the consequent engagements with the New York Philharmonic launched his international career. In 1969 he was appointed conductor at **La Scala**, becoming its musical director from 1971–80. His period of office saw a notable broadening of the repertoire and lifting of standards. He served as principal conductor of the Vienna Philharmonic from 1971, and of the London Symphony Orchestra from 1979–88. In 1986 he was appointed director of the Vienna State Opera, and in 1989 succeeded Karajan at the Berlin Philharmonic. Abbado's conducting is distinguished by his attention to detail and his robust rhythmic grasp. His repertoire is impressively wide, with particular strengths in the Germanic and Italian twentieth-century traditions.

JOHN KERSEY

Abbagnano, Nicola

b. 15 July 1901, Salerno; d. 9 September 1990, Milan

Philosopher

Nicola Abbagnano was Italy's first existentialist philosopher. His early works (from the 1920s) opposed the idealism of **Croce** and Gentile by arguing that thought was not as central to the life of the mind as the will, meaningful action and the immediate experience of life itself. In 1939 he published *La struttura dell'esistenza* (The Structure of Existence), which Enzo **Paci** recognized as the work that would define Italian existentialism and put Abbagnano in the league of Heidegger and Jaspers. Abbagnano subsequently differentiated his philosophy from both ontological and theistic existentialisms by insisting that possibility should neither be doomed to failure, nor guaranteed by Being (identified with God). Abbagnano taught from 1936 to 1976 at the University of Turin, where his students included Umberto **Eco** and Gianni **Vattimo**, and he is also well-known for his reference books on the history of philosophy.

Further reading

Langiulli, N. (1992) *Possibility, Necessity, and Existence: Abbagnano and His Predecessors*, Philadelphia:

Temple University Press (a careful analysis and contextualization of Abbagnano's philosophy).

THOMAS KELSO

Abitare

A Milan-based, fully-bilingual, international monthly magazine for contemporary architecture, design, art and interior decoration, *Abitare* first appeared in 1960. Its editorial policy has been to 'present the latest projects and trends through in-depth articles on industrial and graphic design, furniture and artifact production around the world'. Although it concentrates on craft design and traditionally devotes much space to product advertising, it also incorporates a genuine intersec-tion of the 'home, town and environment living' as well as certain exclusively architectural themes, especially in its monographic presentations of architects and particular projects and trends. *Abitare* played an important role in making the sumptu-ousness of Italian neo-modern interiors known internationally. It targets not only those profession-ally and commercially interested in design issues, but also a larger, informed readership concerned with all aspects of the quality of the living environment. The magazine was acquired by Milan's Segesta Publishing group in 1976 and has most recently been edited by Maria Giulia Zunino.

See also: architectural and design magazines

GORDANA KOSTICH

abortion

The campaign for abortion during the 1970s was the single issue which united the many and varied strands of feminist opinion in Italy, turning Italian **feminism** into a mass movement which mobilized on a national scale. The huge pro-abortion rallies of the mid-1970s, attended by hundreds of thousands of women, marked feminism as a significant radical force which cut across traditional class and political lines. While the misery of clandestine abortion was more endured by the poor who could not afford to travel abroad, the politicization of women's real experience, at such variance from the powerful ideologies promulgated by both church and state, revealed the gulf between rhetoric and reality in the lives of all Italian women.

Under Italian law, clandestine abortion – usually the only available form of birth control – was punishable by up to five years' imprisonment. Campaigning for abortion was initiated in the early 1970s by the **MLD**, the Movement for Liberation of Woman, affiliated with the **Radical Party** which, with its loose structure, was able to accommodate pressure group and single-issue politics. The 500,000 signatures needed to initiate a referendum under the Italian constitution was well exceeded, and the collection of signatures was accompanied by a campaign of civil disobedience which recalled the direct action of the 1960s. Information networks on safe abortion procedures were set up, and women organized clandestine abortions which they then defiantly announced in public; many women 'confessed' to having had an abortion themselves. Indeed, surveys suggested that almost all Italian women had either had an abortion themselves or knew of someone who had. No party could thus continue to ignore the issue now forced onto the political agenda.

However, despite women's public demonstration of support, the bill which was finally put before **Parliament** in 1978 (Law 194) was severely compromised by right-wing interests and the failure of the Left to fully embrace women's issues. While abortion within ninety days of conception now became legal, there were numerous clauses limiting the woman's right to choose: a doctor had to confirm that continued pregnancy would be prejudicial to a woman's physical or psychological health; women under the age of eighteen were required to seek parental permission; a seven-day 'reflection' period was established; and abortions could take place only in authorized medical establishments in which medical staff could refuse to carry out abortions on the grounds of con-science. The latter clause in particular caused much bitterness, with some observers suspecting collusion and shared vested interests between the medical establishment and the state. Some areas of the South registered up to a 90 per cent conscientious objection rate, making abortion within the legislated time limits extremely difficult.

Many were left disappointed, and women still faced numerous difficulties in seeking an abortion. One practical consequence of this weakness of the law was the setting up of women-only clinics by female health practitioners.

In 1980 there were 220,000 abortions, though the figure had dropped to just over 160,000 in 1990. The most likely causes of this decline were improved contraception facilities, more readily available information on women's health and, possibly, a response to the spread of **HIV/AIDS**. The biggest decrease in recourse to abortion was registered in the North, where one-parent families and children born outside marriage were possibly more socially acceptable than in other parts of the country. A dual referendum in 1981 seeking on the one hand to overturn, and on the other hand considerably to widen, the legislation was defeated and, despite attacks from the Right to undermine it, Law 194 remains on the statute books.

Further reading

Bono, P. and Kemp, S. (1990) *Italian Feminist Thought: A Reader*, Oxford: Blackwell (see especially pp. 211–34 for documents related to the abortion law).

Cazzola, A. (1996) *Aborto e fecondità: gli effetti di breve periodo indotti dall'aborto legale sulle nascite in Italia* (Abortion and Fertility; Short-Term Effects of Legal Abortion on the Birthrate in Italy) Milan: F. Angeli (studies the impact of abortion legislation on birth-rate and family life within changing social and economic context of women's lives).

Gatta, G. (1997) *Aborto: una storia dimenticata* (Abortion: A Forgotten Story) Bologna: Il parallelo (history of the struggle to pass legislation on abortion in Italy).

SHARON WOOD

Accardi, Carla

b. 19 October 1924, Trapani, Sicily

Artist

Carla Accardi was a central figure in the develop-

ment of Italian abstraction. In 1947 she was a founding member of Forma (Form), a group which announced itself to be both formalist in art and Marxist in politics. She thus distanced herself from the social realism approved by the Communist Party (**PCI**), believing it was possible to produce abstract art and still support the cause of class struggle. Her style at this time was a dynamic, French-influenced neo-cubism. From 1961 Accardi was a member of the **Continuità** (Continuity) group. She experimented with the optical effects of colours, and produced works on transparent plastic. *Stella*, a work from the 1960s, wittily shows her knowledge of the American abstractionist Frank Stella. Later works, while still abstract, are decorative and suggest organic forms. In 1964 and 1988, Accardi was chosen to represent Italy at **Venice Biennale** and in 1997 she was honoured by the Italian State with the title of 'cavaliere' (knight).

MAX STAPLES

Adami, Valerio

b. 17 March 1935, Bologna

Artist

Adami's early work was abstract, but a gradual drift from abstraction to more formal figuration began to occur in the late 1960s. In his paintings of this period, the often ironical use of a dislocated imagery displays pop art influences and affinities with the work of Emilio **Tadini**. Adami also examined the relationship between the photographic and the painted image. His compositions of public spaces like swimming pools and waiting rooms painted from photographs he had himself taken conveyed a strong sense of suspense and immobilization. He maintained a consistent style of strong uniform colours, black outlines and shattered perspectives. Fragments of written text figure significantly in Adami's later work, which draws heavily upon literary and mythological subject matter. Adami has mostly lived in Paris. His work has been the subject of an important essay by

French post-structuralist philosopher, Jacques Derrida.

LAURENCE SIMMONS

Adelphi

One of Italy's most prestigious publishing houses, Adelphi was founded in 1962 by Roberto Bazlen and Luciano Foà. They was soon joined by Roberto **Calasso** who became, and thereafter remained, Adelphi's managing editor and major driving force. Adopting a Chinese pictogram of the dance of life and death as its emblem and light pastel colours for its simple but elegant cover designs, Adelphi sought to promote an ideal of literary culture as spiritual enlightenment. Some of its most successful titles have been, in fact, the orientalising novels of Herman Hesse and other spiritual manuals such as Pirsig's *Zen and the Art of Motorcycle Maintenance*. This taste for arcane and sometimes obscure gnostic texts has always attracted criticism from some quarters, but Adelphi has undoubtedly also been responsible for introducing Italians to important Central European writers like Joseph Roth, Karl Kraus and Milan Kundera, amongst others. During the 1980s it reissued the work of Italian idealist philosopher Benedetto **Croce** as well as continuing to promote fine Italian novelists such as Anna Maria **Ortese**, Leonardo **Sciascia** and Calasso himself. Arguably, one of Adelphi's most significant cultural contribution has been its publication of a critical edition of the complete works of Nietzsche, under the scholarly editorship of Giorgio **Colli** and Mazzino Montinari.

GINO MOLITERNO

advertising

In Italy, as in many other Western countries, advertising has privileged different media in different periods. While posters, press, cinema and radio were the dominant media in the immediate postwar era, from the 1950s onwards television became the most preferred medium for advertisers. Two other aspects of advertising in Italy are especially notable: the role of the artistic avantgarde (especially futurism) in advertising posters and the peculiar relationship between cinema and television.

Avantgarde

A number of artists (mainly painters and graphic designers, but also writers and poets) contributed to the birth of advertising in Italy, creating a marriage between advertising and art. This became rarer in later years when advertising came to be viewed with suspicion, especially by *intellectuals* and the educated class, but its original role was nevertheless significant.

In order to understand the situation in the postwar period, it is necessary to go back to the years between 1910 and 1930, when avantgarde movements like dadaism, surrealism and futurism were flourishing. The latter in particular merged high and low culture, by expanding the scope of aesthetics to include aspects of everyday life like technology and machines. Advertising was thus seen as a form of popular culture which could bring aesthetic principles to a large public. The merger between art and advertising proceeded along two main paths: advertising became a common 'quotation' in painting, and painters became creators of advertisements. A visual or a verbal style was established, based on the creative principle of *parole in libertà* (free-floating words), a free and expressive use of language and lettering. Some of the most important artists of that period such as S. Pozzati (Sepo), M. Nizzoli, G. Boccasile and F. Seneca invented brand images that in some cases are still in existence (for example, Seneca's trade mark for the Italian petrol industry Agip).

The merging of art and advertising also included verbal aspects: authors and poets were involved in the creation of brand names and slogans (the oldest and most famous was D'Annunzio's invention of the name for the first Italian department store, La Rinascente). This avantgarde influence continued throughout the 1930s with futurist artists like Depero and Marinetti writing catchy slogans for Campari and other Italian brands, and well into the 1950s and 1960s when writers such as **Soldati**, Tofano and M. Marchesi invented long-lasting slogans for television advertising.

Carosello

The entry of advertising into Italian television in 1957 was very restrained, due to the rather paternalistic attitude of the **RAI**'s single national channel of the time. The management was mostly made up of intellectuals (**Eco** and **Vattimo** were among the youngest) who were very wary of introducing commercials into a state channel whose main function was pedagogical (and for which the public was paying licence fees). The result was a strictly regimented programme: SACIS, a committee from the RAI in charge of gathering and controlling advertising and the Ministero delle Poste (Ministry for Post), under whose jurisdiction the RAI fell, drew up an agreement according to which advertising could only be broadcast if it conformed to a suitable format and quality which could ensure that the rest of the RAI's programmes would not fall into disrepute. Thus *Carosello* was born.

Broadcast daily from 3 February 1957 to 1 January 1977, *Carosello* (Carousel) was a fifteen-minute nightly segment composed of commercial messages of two minutes and fifteen seconds each. The rules dictated that no product could be seen, mentioned or alluded to during the first one minute and forty seconds of the film. During this time a 'show' had to be offered to the viewers, a story based on creative and original ideas and produced according to the style and principles of mainstream broadcasting. Only during the last thirty seconds (called a *codino* or 'little tail') was it possible to introduce the product, and the attempts to justify its presence led to a series of puns and nonsense that came to characterize the language of advertising at the time. The fact that advertising had to enter households in the most unnoticeable and 'delicate' way was a sign of the anti-industrial and anti-modern bias of a very traditional society. Moreover, the ads were quite expensive for the firms to produce since each story could be repeated only twice and during *Carosello*'s twenty years some 30,000 different stories were broadcast.

Well-known theatre and cinema actors, amongst them Nino **Manfredi**, Ugo **Tognazzi**, Alberto **Sordi**, Eduardo **De Filippo**, and radio and television personalities such as Mike **Bongiorno** and Renzo **Arbore** starred in *Carosello*'s short

stories, many of which were directed by famous film-makers like **Fellini**, **Leone**, **Olmi** and the **Taviani brothers**. However the most popular and long-lived heroes of Italian commercials were probably cartoon characters and animated puppets like Calimero and Pippo the Hippopotamus.

Significantly, *Carosello* was shot in **Cinecittà**, at the heart of Italian film industry in Rome, whilst the main advertising agencies (which with only a few exceptions were all branches of American and British firms) were in Milan. Consequently, while the main agencies were applying marketing strategies and motivational research, *Carosello*'s creative staff were left to their own imagination, and were thus able to produce ideas and witty exchanges closer to the improvisational techniques of *Commedia dell'arte* than to modern advertising. Many phrases thus coined for *Carosello* became so popular as to pass into the everyday language of Italian viewers.

The four or five short stories which made up the programme were always framed by a series of drop-scenes. From the 1960s onwards, they depicted four famous Italian squares in Venice, Siena, Naples and Rome, drawn by the painter Manfredi, (another demonstration of the tradition of 'marriage' between art and advertising that characterized the postwar period) whilst the sound-track consisted of an arrangement of an old *tarantella*, a jingle that has remained part of Italian television history.

Variously defined as a fascinating aberration of Italian television advertising, the best product of Italian cinema, as French film-maker Jean-Luc Godard once remarked, or as the most original contribution offered by Italy to the history of television (by *Le Figaro*, commenting on the end of the programme in 1997), *Carosello* was certainly the most characteristic expression of advertising made in Italy. Becoming virtually synonymous with publicity itself, it contributed to setting the evening ritual of most of the Italian viewers. Coming after the news, it marked the beginning of the 'light' part of the evening's viewing and the time for children to go to bed: 'after *Carosello*' became the proper time for a whole generation to go to bed.

The cancellation of the enormously popular programme was due to a number of factors linked to the cultural climate of the 1970s – political terrorism, youth protest, criticism of consumer culture, economic recession in Italy – as well as to the end of RAI's monopoly on broadcasting in 1976. If the change in cultural climate forced advertising to become more rational, informative and product-oriented, and also less expensive, the end of the RAI's monopoly and the advent of **private television** produced a true revolution of the television system itself, within which advertising came to play a leading role, particularly during the 1980s.

The 1970s witnessed three other major innovations: the birth of social advertising (called *Pubblicità Progresso* or Progressive Advertising), the beginning of sponsorship (especially in sports programmes), and the introduction of colour, which allowed for a wider exploration of audiovisual language.

Advertising in the age of competition

The advent of commercial channels during the late 1970s and 1980s produced a major change in the role of television: from a primarily informative and educational medium under state control, it became a source of diversion and entertainment more along the lines of the American model. The birth of commercial television was a business decision: there was a demand for advertising time on television which exceeded what the RAI could supply, and it was this source of revenue that the new broadcasters – with **Berlusconi** in the lead – sought to tap in order to finance their various enterprises, using even highly unconventional and unscrupulous methods such as special offers and free broadcast time which brought confusion to the market. The result was an overcrowding of advertisements and sponsorship on the commercial channels, as well as a huge increase in the number of ads on the public channels.

For a time in the 1980s the situation was almost grotesque: advertising revenues rose from 911 billion lira in 1979 to 4,640 billion in 1986, and the commercial channels themselves recognized the need to reduce the amount of advertising in order to avoid counterproductive effects such as saturation, rejection and zapping. A brilliant depiction of the situation was given in Fellini's 1986 film *Ginger e Fred*, where the hyperbole of television advertising is represented in a range of different formats: huge posters with sexy images,

televisual screens everywhere, and enormous gadgets advertising Italian products, especially food. Television has become merely a container for advertising, and the old fashioned show (represented by the two dancers) is reduced to a sort of introduction (paradoxically, a 'publicity' role) for the 'modern' show, a mix of personal stories and spots, where all distinctions are erased (for example, a Dante Alighieri puppet advertises a watch). All this is set against the background of a physically and socially degraded metropolis, suggesting that the 'hyperrealistic' images of ads draw attention away from reality, and finally destroy it.

It is significant that during the 1980s, unlike preceding decades, advertising campaigns were primarily television campaigns, and press advertisements and posters were largely considered as a kind of backup for the television commercials. The exception to this general rule was the press and poster campaign for **Benetton** orchestrated by Oliviero **Toscani**, a photographer who used provocative and sometimes shocking images in the style of reportage, such as a new-born baby, a **mafia** killing, or a man dying of AIDS (see also **HIV/AIDS**), to attract the consumer's attention in a world overcrowded with advertising.

Advertising in the age of globalization

From its beginnings, advertising played a key role in popular culture by creating a repertoire of social situations and suggesting a range of codes of good manners to apply in different circumstances. It thus helped overcome some of the resistance to new domestic and technical products by framing them within appropriate settings and contexts of use. Even though most of the advertising agencies in Italy are now branches of international firms (apart from few exceptions such as the A. Testa agency in Turin, which started in 1946 as a graphic studio, became an agency in 1956 and was the first Italian agency to open in New York in the 1960s), advertising campaigns tend to be sensitive to the cultural context in which they are received. There are themes and representations that appear to be culturally specific to Italian advertising and which have endured for decades: the overwhelming presence of the family; a focus on interpersonal (mainly conjugal) relationships and on faithfulness and indissolubility as attributes of the male–female relationship that are transferred to the woman-product relationship; a sharp distinction between male and female characters; an outspoken, redundant style in which the verbal track often duplicates the visual one. Nevertheless, the international flow of images, products and people on the one hand and the fragmentation of Italian society and the cultural differences between the North and the South of the country on the other appear to have weakened the core values upon which cultural and national identities were grounded and these changes have become visible in the way advertising itself has changed.

Further reading

Abruzzese, A. and Colombo, F. (eds) (1994) *Dizionario della Pubblicità* (Dictionary of Advertising), Bologna: Zanichelli.

Barbella, P. *et al.* (eds) (1983) *Creative Advertising: The Best Italian Advertising*, Milan: Electa (a good selection of Italian print ads, with text in both English and Italian).

Ceserani, G. (1988) *Storia della pubblicità in Italia* (History of Advertising in Italy), Bari: Laterza.

Giaccardi, C. (1995) 'Television Advertising and the Representation of Social Reality: A Comparative Study', *Theory, Culture and Society* 12: 109–31.

Valeri, A. (1986) *Pubblicità italiana. Storia, protagonisti e tendenze di cento anni di comunicazione* (Italian Advertising: History, Protagonists and Tendencies in One Hundred Years of Communication), Milan: Edizioni del Sole 24 Ore (an informative and well-illustrated history).

CHIARA GIACCARDI

Agamben, Giorgio

b. 1942, Rome

Philosopher

Professor of philosophy at the University of Macerata and later at the University of Verona, Agamben was also for some time Director of the Philosophy Programme at the Collège Interna-

tional de Philosophie in Paris. He attended Martin Heidegger's seminars in Le Thor in 1966–8 and, beginning in 1982, produced the Italian edition of the collected works of Walter Benjamin. Associated with the magazine *Aut aut*, Agamben came to be one of the most widely read and influential of the new Italian philosophers. His works include *Stanze* (Stanzas) (1977) on the problem of representation; *Infanzia e storia* (Infancy and History) (1979) on the relationship between experience and knowledge; *Il linguaggio e la morte* (Language and Death) (1982), an analysis of the place of negativity in philosophical discourse; and *La communità che viene* (The Coming Community) (1990) on the contemporary forms of sociality. *Homo sacer* (1995) and *Mezzi senza fine* (Means Without End) (1996) are a rethinking of political categories in a period of crisis for the nation-state. Agamben writes in an erudite and epigrammatic style, and his work is a mixture of philology and contemporary linguistics imbued with references to medieval scholars and theorists of Judeo-Christian scripture.

LAURENCE SIMMONS

Age and Scarpelli

Perhaps the most famous and versatile scriptwriting team of Italian postwar cinema, Age (Agenore Incrocci, b. 1919, Brescia) and Scarpelli (Furio Scarpelli, b. 1919, Rome) began their long partnership by writing some of the **Totò** movies. However their real triumph was to bring Italian film comedy out of **neorealism** and into the so-called comedy Italian style (**commedia all'Italiana**). Eventually they also played an instrumental role in the major transformation of the genre in the 1970s. They scripted many of the early classics of the genre: **Monicelli**'s *I soliti ignoti* (Big Deal on Madonna Street) (1958) and *La grande guerra* (The Great War) (1959), Dino **Risi**'s *I mostri* (The Monsters) (1963) and **Germi**'s *Sedotta e abbandonata* (Seduced and Abandoned) (1964). In the 1970s they wrote some of **Scola**'s best films, from *C'eravamo tanto amati* (We All Loved Each Other So Much) (1974) to *La terrazza* (The Terrace) (1980), a caustic and self-reflexive critique of both comedy Italian style and the society it portrayed and perhaps produced. In the mid-1980s their fertile collaboration came to an end.

MANUELA GIERI

Agnelli family

The most famous entrepreneurial dynasty of Italy, owners of **Fiat** and Juventus, a popular Italian football team, the Agnelli are the very emblem of private family-based capitalism, Italian style. In spite of the tremendous growth of Fiat in the century since its foundation, the family has succeeded in retaining control of the company through financial holdings whose exclusive share-holders have always been members of the family and by solid alliances with other entrepreneurial families such as the **Pirelli**. Nevertheless, what might be called 'the Buddenbrook syndrome' – that is, the fear of the extinction of the dynasty and its vocation for business – has surfaced as a recurring threat in the family's history, obliging it to face the choice of either continuing their entrepreneurial tradition or becoming simple rentiers.

Management, in fact, has been quite a demand-ing inheritance, and transmission of it has never turned out to be smooth. In 1945, Giovanni Agnelli, the founder and, until then, absolute ruler died with no heirs to take his place, since Edoardo, his only son, had been killed in 1935 in an air crash, and Gianni, his elder nephew, was still too young. The family thus appointed Vittorio Valletta, a powerful manager who had been the founder's right hand, as chairman of the group. After Valletta's exit in 1966, Gianni (a cosmopolitan figure, then considered a golden boy of the international jet-set) and his younger brother Umberto felt obliged to take a leading role, but soon neglected their managerial responsibilities. Gianni, nicknamed the Lawyer, (*l'avvocato*), became leader of the **Confindustria** (the Employers' Association), while Umberto, pursuing political ambitions, was elected a senator for the Christian Democrat party. One of the Agnelli sisters, Susanna, also followed a political career in the Italian Republican Party (**PRI**) which culminated in her becoming Minister of Foreign Affairs in the **Dini** government (1995–6). During the 1970s,

even Gianni was unable to disguise his ambition to achieve prestigious public office such as Italy's ambassador to the United States. Moreover Edoardo, Gianni's son, showed no entrepreneurial vocation at all, declaring himself deeply distrustful of science and technology and rather fond of Eastern philosophy. No wonder that in the harsh crisis of the mid-1970s, rumours spread that the Agnelli were about to abandon business.

The dilemma was again resolved by hiring dynamic external managers such as Cesare **Romiti** and Vittorio Ghidella, who succeeded in relaunching Fiat's fortunes. Finally in the 1990s, the Agnelli had to prepare the succession in view of Gianni's (and Romiti's) exit, though this could no longer be only a family affair since external shareholders (such as foreign banks) had gained a large influence and Fiat needed strong interna-tional alliances to cope with the challenge of global markets. All the family's hopes were placed in Giovanni, Umberto's son, a promising young manager educated in the United States, who had already successfully run Piaggio (the motorbike company which produces the famous Vespa); moreover he was also a strong believer in promoting social progress and a fervent supporter of planning and innovation. Unfortunately, losing the fight against a rare form of cancer in December 1997, he died at only 33 and, as a result the dynasty's entrepreneurial continuity became un-predictable once more.

Further reading

Friedman, A. (1988) *Agnelli and The Network of Italian Power*, London: Harrap (an unauthorized and caustic portrayal of Agnelli's large economic, financial and political influence in the recent history of Italy).

STEFANO BATTILOSSI

Agosti, Stefano

b. 1930, Caprino Veronese, Verona

Academic and critic

Professor of French literature at the University of

Venice, Agosti has published extensively on French and Italian poetry and narrative (notably on Stephan Mallarmé, Gustave Flaubert, Francesco Petrarca, Pier Paolo **Pasolini** and Andrea **Zanzotto**) and on literary theory. Regarded as one of the most distinguished Italian scholars, Agosti views literature from a comparative perspective, with particular sensitivity to the most recent debates in contemporary literary theory. His textual analyses display his interest in psychoanalysis and linguistics, always supported by a solid philological competence.

Further reading

Agosti, S. (1972) *Il testo poetico. Teoria e pratiche d'analisi*, (The Poetic Text: Theory and Practices of Analysis), Milan: Rizzoli.
—— (1987) *Modelli psicanalitici e teoria del testo*, (Psychoanalytic Models and Textual Theory), Bologna: Il Mulino.

FRANCESCA PARMEGGIANI

agriculture

In the past half-century, the place of agriculture in Italian society has been utterly transformed. Many of the practices, values and social relations of a rural world less than two generations away have been dispatched into history by the combined forces of the industrial economic miracle, massive **emigration** from the countryside of the South and Northeast, the impact of the **European Union**'s Common Agricultural Policy and contemporary agribusiness. The disappearance of that world has, however, been far from uniform or complete: in the South, the proportion of the workforce in agriculture is still double that in the North, and one in seven Italian households still owns agricultural land. Moreover, the residue of a society built around the power of landed property and the deference of peasants includes a prolonged, often deeply ambivalent, afterglow in contemporary Italian culture: see, among many examples, Bernardo **Bertolucci**'s film *1900* (1976) and Ermanno **Olmi**'s *The Tree of Wooden Clogs* (1978).

Yesterday's world

In 1951 almost half (42 per cent) of Italy's workforce derived its primary livelihood from agriculture. The poorer South was more dependent on agriculture than the North, but systems of tenure, land use and rural family relations could vary widely within regions. Large capitalist enterprises using wage-labour for industrial crops were found mainly in the Po Valley; sharecropping farms, with returns divided in fixed proportions between landlord and tenant, dominated the **Third Italy**; and peasant cultivation of cereals, olives and vines by family labour was characteristic of the Alpine regions and South, where it existed alongside large extensively-farmed estates (*latifundi*). Ownership of land was very unevenly distributed everywhere. Fewer than 5 per cent of owners held half of Italy's privately-owned land, most peasant households had barely sufficient land of their own to ensure subsistence, and many of the usually underemployed rural workers had no land at all: herding animals – sheep in the hills and mountains, cattle on the plains – offered better returns but greater risks. One-quarter of all households, and a much higher proportion of those dependent on agriculture, were officially classified as in hardship or destitute. Protest followed by emigration – repeating the pattern of the late nineteenth century – was the immediate postwar response to such levels of deprivation and insecurity.

Between 1944 and 1950, mass occupations of large estates across Italy forced the government to concede a land reform which, despite the 700,000 hectares distributed to 121,000 families, offered too little to too few. The urgent task of modernizing the technologically backward rural sector was entrusted to state agencies, Federconsorzi, **Cassa per il Mezzogiorno** (Fund for the South) and producer associations (Coldiretti), which, however, did as much to press farmers into voting for the governing parties as to provide them with financial support and technical assistance. Many peasants and day labourers chose to leave, preferring industrial work in northwest Italy or abroad, while others sought white-collar jobs in cities and the offices of Italy's expanding welfare state. Despite the Green Plans of the 1960s and a series of laws improving the contractual rights of tenants, agriculture came to seem one of the least attractive occupations. Areas where few alternatives to agriculture existed became seriously depopulated, and already by 1970, making a living solely from ownership of land or livestock remained the aspiration of a declining and disproportionately aged minority almost everywhere.

Contemporary agriculture

By the mid-1990s, agriculture accounted for only 6 per cent of all workers, and the number of farms and area of land under cultivation had both been reduced by about 15 per cent since 1970. Share-cropper farms, which in 1961 numbered nearly half a million and covered 4 million hectares, had all but disappeared, taking with them the distinctive rural culture of central and northeast Italy. Agricultural production had become more diverse, greatly reducing the importance of wheat in favour of fruit, flowers and industrial crops. Cattle numbers had fallen steadily while sheep increased, especially in Sardinia, which accounted for about half the national total. Specialization within and between regions developed strongly. In Tuscany, Piedmont and the Veneto, emphasis came to be placed on the extremely localized identification of quality products such as **wine** and **olive oil**, with substantial foreign investment: poorer qualities for mass domestic consumption were produced in the South. More mechanized farms – two-thirds now had tractors – could rely solely on individual or family labour and on services contracted from other farmers. Wage labour still remained significant in the South, however, where African immigrants were able to take on seasonal and poorly paid work in the tomato industry which had become one of Italy's major agricultural exporters. Yet, despite rapid gains in productivity and substantial support from Europe's Common Agricultural Policy and structural funds, Italian agricultural and livestock production remained unable to meet domestic demand: the appetite for meat, in particular, could only be satisfied by imports from Germany. The national deficit was closely associated with the persisting importance of small farms and part-time work. Average farm size (6 hectares) remained half the European average and was almost unchanged since the 1960s: within

Europe, Italy remained uniquely polarized between very large and very small enterprises. One in four farmers also had a non-agricultural job which kept families on the land, in line with the EU encouragement of ecologically beneficial strategies for rural areas, but inhibited productivity, capital investment and the ability to compete with larger farms in Northern Europe. Technologically and ecologically, Italian agriculture remains incompletely modernized.

See also: economic miracle; peasants; regions; Southern Question

Further reading

Davis, J. (1973) *Land and Family in Pisticci*, London: Athlone Press (the best account in English of peasant life in the South in the mid-1960s).

Fabiani, G. (1995) 'L'agricoltura italiana nello sviluppo dell'Europa comunitaria' (Italian Agriculture in the Context of EU Development') in AA.VV, *Storia dell'Italia repubblicana* (History of Republican Italy) vol. 2, 'La trasformazione dell'Italia: sviluppo e squilibri' (The Transformation of Italy: Development and Unbalance) part 1, Turin: Einaudi (a survey of postwar trends in Italian agriculture, with particular emphasis on the impact of EU farm policies).

Lanza, O. (1979) 'Gli enti del settore agricolo' (The Institutions of the Rural Sector), in F. Cazzola (ed.) *Anatomia del potere DC* (Anatomy of Christian Democrat Power), Bari: De Donato (description of the political role played by state agencies for rural development).

Pratt, J. (1994) *The Rationality of Rural Life: Economic and Cultural Change in Tuscany*, Amsterdam: Harwood Academic Publishers (analysis of the social and production relations of post-sharecropping agribusiness in Montalcino, celebrated for its Brunello wine).

White, C. (1980) *Patrons and Partisans*, Cambridge: Cambridge University Press (comparison between developments in agricultural and ideological relations in neighbouring villages in the Fucino plain since the late nineteenth century).

DAVID MOSS

Alberoni, Francesco

b. 8 December 1929, Piacenza

Sociologist

In Italy, Alberoni has become the country's best-known sociologist, less through his academic works than his regular columns in *Il Corriere della sera* and the great success of his short books on big themes (love, good and evil, ethics). Trained in medicine and psychology, influenced by Ernst Bloch, Teilhard de Chardin and Ilya Prygogine, Alberoni's work explores the dynamics of social relations. In various styles, he tries to capture the fleetingly successful attempts by individuals and social groups to institutionalize meanings and values. His sociological writings range widely: modernization in Sardinia, **immigration**, consumption, classes and generations, the star system and party activists. He also played a notable role at the Istituto Superiore di Scienze Sociali (University of Trento) at the time of the **student movement**.

Further reading

Alberoni, F. (1977) *Movimento e istituzioni* (Movement and Institutions), Milan: Franco Angeli.
– (1997) *Il primo amore* (First Love), Milan: Rizzoli.

DAVID MOSS

Albertazzi, Giorgio

b. 8 August 1923, Fiesole, Florence

Actor and director

After growing up in the Florentine circle around Luchino **Visconti**, Albertazzi achieved prominence in the early 1950s as a star performer both on the stage and in televised plays as well as appearing in Alain Resnais' landmark film, *L'année dernière à Marienbad* (Last Year at Marienbad) (1960). For many years he carried on both an artistic and personal relationship with Anna Proclemer, with whom in 1965, after several years of delay due to problems with censorship, he produced *La governante* (The Housekeeper), written by Vitaliano **Brancati**. As an actor, he was a brilliant and

magnetic Hamlet in 1963, a thorough neurotic in **Brusati**'s 1967 *Pietà di novembre* (Pity of November) and threatening and unpredictable in a 1981 production of Pirandello's *Enrico IV* (Henry IV) . He has often modified scripts to suit his own purposes, and directs himself on stage. The results are always culturally refined but often tinged with a certain mannerism, with sometimes a lack of strong direction of the other actors, in spite of his own claims to achieving an almost trance-like state.

PAOLO PUPPA

Albini, Franco

b. 17 October 1905, Robbiate, Como;
   d. 1977, Milan

Architect

Albini's design, ranging from fittings and furniture to town planning, found its highest expression in the fields of restoration and exhibition, where his unmistakable stylistic traits were elegance of design, refinement of detail and technical virtuosity. His most influential works are in Genoa, and include two reconstructed Renaissance palaces, the Palazzo Bianco (White Palace) and the Palazzo Rosso (Red Palace), a series of dramatically-lit underground circular rooms adjacent to the cathedral, built to house the Treasury of the Cathedral of San Lorenzo, and the Sant'Agostino Museum restoration and addition. Other outstanding works include La Rinascente department store in Rome, the Linea 1 stations of the Milan subway and the Thermal Bath Building at Salsomaggiore, Terme.

Further reading

Leet, S. (1990) *Franco Albini: Architecture and Design 1934–1977*, New York: Princeton Architectural Press (the most comprehensive survey of his work in English).

ROSS JENNER

alfabeta

The most important cultural magazine to appear in Italy during the 1980s, *alfabeta* was founded in Milan in May 1979 by Nanni **Balestrini**, who assembled an eleven-member editorial committee bringing together some of the most illustrious names of Italian postwar culture, amongst them Maria **Corti**, Umberto **Eco**, Antonio **Porta**, Pier Aldo Rovatti and Paolo **Volponi**. The magazine, in tabloid format similar to the *New York Review of Books* and the *Times Literary Supplement*, appeared monthly until 1988 and, as well as major articles by members of the editorial board, also hosted a wide range of contributions on all aspects of modern culture from Italian writers and intellectuals such as **Cacciari**, **Vattimo** and **Calvino** as well as prestigious foreign names like Habermas and Lyotard. Although it never sold more than 15,000 copies, the magazine became a major point of reference for cultural discussion and critical reflection during those years, not least on the difficult topic of terrorism.

Further reading

Bossaglia, R. *et al.* (1996) *alfabeta 1979–1988. Antologia della rivista*, Milan: Bompiani (a selected anthology which illustrates the depth and scope of the magazine).

GINO MOLITERNO

Alitalia

Established in 1946 as Aerolinee Italiane Internazionali but soon merged with Linee Aeree Internazionali in 1947, Alitalia became Italy's national airline. Originally operating thirty-seven planes over a network of 49,000 km, it carried fewer than 120,000 passengers a year. However, it modernized rapidly, and by 1968 Alitalia had an all-jet fleet, subsequently updated further by the acquisition two- and three-engined Boeing and McDonnell-Douglas jets. At the same time, it developed a wide network of international and intercontinental routes over Europe, the USA and South America, while national routes were left to its subsidiary ATI (Aero-Trasporti Italiani), which was merged with the parent company in 1994. By the late 1990s Alitalia was flying 144 jets over a network of 200,000 km, covering 130 destinations in 60 countries around the globe and moving 25 million passengers a year. However, from the 1980s it came under increasing pressure from international competition, and began incurring greater losses. In 1996 a reorganization was undertaken in order to reduce debts, cut down operating costs and improve economic performance. Alitalia also established co-operative agreements with a number of American and European airlines, and in 1998 entered a strategic partnership with KLM, a Dutch carrier, in order to better confront increasingly keen competition both internationally and domestically.

STEFANO BATTILOSSI

L'altra domenica

L'altra domenica (Another Side of Sunday) is regarded as a monument in Italian television history. Largely modelled on his popular radio program *Alto gradimento* (High Appreciation), in March 1976 Renzo **Arbore** invented a new format for weekend TV entertainment on the second RAI channel. By mixing classic Sunday afternoon football fever with other games and music, and using the telephone for the first time ever in live television events – people would ring from home with answers to a silly quiz – Arbore was able to create a interesting and bizarre climate of cultural mayhem. Roberto **Benigni** as a surrealistic cinematographic critic, Andy Luotto, the strange American cousin, the cartoons of Maurizio **Nichetti**, Isabella Rossellini on the phone live from the United States and the trans-gender musical group *Sorelle Bandiera* (The Flag Sisters), all became familiar acts in a crazy circus. A world away from the subdued programs on the RAI's other channel, *L'altra domenica* represented a breath of fresh air for the intelligent and the curious so from 1976 to 1979, it attracted a devoted public who made it into something of a cult programme.

RICCARDO VENTRELLA

Amato, Giuliano

b. 13 May 1938, Turin

Politician and professor of constitutional law

Known as 'Doctor Subtilis' (Doctor Subtle) for his diplomatic and political skills, Amato graduated in jurisprudence and subsequently taught constitutional law at Rome University. Speaking impeccable English and well regarded in international circles, he has also held visiting professorships at several prestigious American institutes and universities.

A convinced socialist, Amato joined the **PSI** in 1958 and was an elected member of the Chamber of Deputies from 1983–94 (see also **Parliament**). Undersecretary to the Prime Minister in 1983–7, he became Deputy Prime Minister in 1987–8 and Treasury Minister in 1988–9 as well as deputy secretary of the PSI between 1989–92. A close associate of Bettino **Craxi**, Amato was appointed Prime Minister in 1992 in Craxi's place. In March 1993 the Amato government attempted to pass a decree law which would have retrospectively decriminalized illegal financing of political parties, but President **Scalfaro** refused to sign the law and Amato resigned. He subsequently served as president of the Anti-Trust Authority between 1994–7. He returned to government as Minister for Institutional Reform under **Prodi** in 1998 and Treasury Minister under **D'Alema** in 1999.

JAMES WALSTON

Amelio, Gianni

b. 20 January 1945, San Pietro Magisano, Catanzaro

Film director

One of the most impressive directors of the 'new' generation, Amelio achieved international acclaim with his 1992 film *Ladro di bambini* (The Stolen Children). He came to be regarded as the leading representative of a cinema committed to a realistic reflection of, and commentary upon, pressing historical, social and political issues.

After being abandoned by his father, who emigrated permanently to South America, Amelio grew up in a poor town of the South. In 1965 he moved to Rome and had the chance to work as an assistant to director Vittorio **De Seta** on his *Un uomo a metà* (A Man in Half) (1966). For several years he collaborated on a wide variety of filmic ventures including spaghetti westerns, musicals and advertising. His first film as director was *La fine del gioco* (The End of the Game), a 1970 low-budget black and white film shown on Italian public television as part of a series titled *Programmi sperimentali* (Experimental Programmes). In 1976, Amelio revealed one of the main influences on his own film-making by shooting a documentary on the making of Bernardo **Bertolucci**'s *Novecento* (1900). Indeed, the lesson of the 'masters' of Italian cinematic **neorealism** is filtered through Bertolucci in many of Amelio's films, such as *Colpire al cuore* (Aim at the Heart) (1982), *I ragazzi di Via Panisperna* (The Boys in Panisperna Road) (1988) and *Porte aperte* (Open Doors) (1990). In these films, Amelio freely borrowed images and rhythms from Bertolucci's filmography. It was only with *Ladro di bambini*, a gripping portrayal of the dismal reality of contemporary Italy where children are physically exploited, dispossessed of their innocence, and then abandoned in morally and emotionally deserted territories, that Amelio found his own personal way of retrieving and reactivating the neorealist mandate for a cinema committed to a realistic portrayal and a thorough critique of social and political injustice.

Amelio's films were often powerful premonitions of things to come, as in the case of *Lamerica* (1994), which deals with the devastating situation in Albania at the close of the twentieth century. The project was prompted by the devastating events of 1991, when Italians watched on national television the desperate exodus of thousands of Albanians trying to find a refuge and a home in Italy. After several trips to post-communist Albania, Amelio conceived of a story which draws impressive parallels between contemporary Albania and the Italy of the 1940s, where morally and economically impoverished people nourish the desperate dream of emigrating to a foreign country as the land of plenty (see **emigration**). The conclusion leaves the audience speechless and disturbed as the story develops a relentless critique of Western culture built on exploitation and imperialism, a disturbing critique of ourselves.

See also: New Italian Cinema

Further reading

Crowdus, G. and Porton, R. (eds) (1995) 'Beyond Neorealism: Preserving a Cinema of Social Conscience/An Interview with Gianni Amelio', *Cineaste* 21(4): 6–13.

MANUELA GIERI

Amendola, Giorgio

b. 21 November 1907, Rome; d. 5 June 1980, Rome

Politician

The son of socialist leader Giovanni Amendola, Giorgio joined the **PCI** in 1929 but was soon arrested and sent into internal exile. He subsequently went to France in 1937 as a representative of the party, and then to Tunisia where he organized the party underground. Expelled from Tunisia, he returned to France and then to Italy in April 1943, becoming a leading member of the CLN (Committee of National Liberation). At war's end he served as undersecretary to the Prime Minister under Parri and **De Gasperi** from June 1945 to June 1946. Elected to the **Constituent Assembly**, he remained a parliamentary deputy from 1946 to his death, and was also elected to the European Parliament in 1975. He was a member of the PCI's Central Committee and party executive from the Fifth Congress. After Palmiro **Togliatti**'s death in 1964, Amendola led the PCI's reformist wing which proposed a new type of party of the Left, neither completely Marxist nor completely social democrat.

JAMES WALSTON

American influence

The image of the United States in Italy in 1945 could almost be summed up in three terms:

chocolate, chewing gum and boogie-woogie. The fabled destination of so many poor emigrants at the end of the nineteenth century had now also become the instrument of liberation from Nazi occupation. As the initial glow subsided, however, the question arose: would American influence receive cautious acceptance, or would it be regarded as colonization?

Given Italy's geopolitical position, there was an active American presence in Italian politics throughout the Cold War period in order to guard against the threat of Communism. Marshall Plan aid helped to feed a starving Italy but it also came with certain conditions, and Clare Boothe Luce, American ambassador to Italy during this period, played a key role in maintaining Italy's place on the Western side of the Iron Curtain. Culturally, however – and in spite of the importance that would later be given to **neorealism** – the main focus of the invasion was through the cinema: American movies, prohibited by the Fascist regime, were now everywhere and John Wayne, James Dean and Marilyn Monroe became matinee idols for Italians just as they were for American audiences. '*Tu vuo, fa l'americano*' (You Wanna be American), sang Renato Carosone in 1957 in an ironic way; but the phrase came to be repeated with approval, especially by the younger set, on Italian piazzas and from Italian jukeboxes everywhere.

The attitude of Communist intellectuals remained ambivalent. There had already been the discovery and popularization of authors like Ernest Hemingway and William Faulkner by left-leaning writers such as Elio **Vittorini** and Cesare **Pavese**, and a similar popularity was later afforded to Jack Kerouac and the Beat Generation. In 1950 the **Venice Biennale** officially welcomed and hosted the first exhibition of Jackson Pollock and Action Painting. Yet the official attitude of the Communist Party (**PCI**) was to continue to characterize American culture as a sort of social degeneration.

The end of the 1950s saw two different mythologies arise. The first looked to John F. Kennedy and aspired to world peace through a different relationship with the USSR. The other looked to Elvis Presley and rock'n'roll music, with blue jeans becoming the most desired American import as the first signs of a youth culture began to appear. Soon, imitating American rock singers, young Italian 'shouters' like Adriano **Celentano** scandalized lovers of the melodic tradition with hit songs like *24 mila baci* (Twenty-Four Thousand Kisses).

Paradoxically, in spite of the leftist politics of the 1968 movement, it too was influenced by American models, especially by the student agitation at American universities. The war in Vietnam provoked similar opposition from the younger generation in Italy as in America, and it become one of the movement's main points of reference. The 'summer of love' and American hippie ideals also found a place in Italy, as did the music of Bob Dylan and psychedelic rock groups like Jefferson Airplane.

The renewed growth of the Communist Party in the 1970s again prompted an active role for the United States in Italian politics, and the CIA was widely believed to have played some part in the terrorist activities of those years. If all youth movements after 1977 openly criticized America as the kingdom of capitalism and economic exploitation, American influence nevertheless continued to spread in Italy in the 1980s through cinema, literature, music, fashion and sports. Steven Spielberg, Woody Allen and Quentin Tarantino all came to occupy a place in the imagination of Italian movie-goers and, at the beginning of the 1990s, grunge-style flannel shirts and the music of Nirvana also invaded Italy. American novelists like Stephen King and John Grisham are bestsellers at the newsstands and **private television** has constructed much of its success on American serials like *Beverly Hills 90210*, and *Melrose Place*. As the world shrinks into an ever-smaller global electronic village at the end of the twentieth century, American influence in Italy has never been greater.

See also: pop and rock music

Further reading

Brunetta, G.P. (1995) *Cent'anni di cinema italiano* (One Hundred Years of Italian Cinema), Bari: Laterza (volume 2 discusses American cinema in Italy).

Castaldo, G. (1994) *La terra promessa. Quarant'anni di cultura rock (1954–1994)* (The Promised Land: Forty Years of Rock Culture 1954–1994), Milan: Feltrinelli (on rock'n'roll music in Italy).

D'Attorre, P.P. (ed.) (1991) *Nemici per la pelle. Sogno americano e mito sovietico nell'Italia contemporanea* (Enemies Through the Skin: The American Dream and the Soviet Myth in Contemporary Italy), Milan: F. Angeli.

Gundle, S. (1995) *I comunisti italiani fra Hollywood e Mosca. La sfida della cultura di massa* (Italian Communists Between Hollywood and Moscow: The Challenge of Mass Culture) Florence: Giunti (on the relationship between the PCI and communist intellectuals with American culture).

Wollemborg, L.J. (1983) *Stelle, strisce e tricolore. Trent'anni di vicende politiche fra Roma e Washington* (Stars, Stripes and the Tricolour: Thirty Years of Political Events between Rome and Washington), Milan.

RICCARDO VENTRELLA

Anceschi, Luciano

b. 20 February 1911, Milan; d. May 1995, Bologna

Literary critic and philosopher

Lecturer in aesthetics and specialist in the theory of literary criticism at the University of Bologna, Anceschi was a pupil of Antonio **Banfi** and interested in the phenomenology of artistic forms. He believed that the analysis of poetic structures was the first stage towards ascertaining transcendental aesthetic structures. His study of poetry focused on the baroque and the twentieth century as periods of crisis and experimentation, which he explored in critical essays and also by publishing influential anthologies of poetry such as *Lirici nuovi* (New Lyricists) (1942). He was one of the first critics to respond positively to the work of the hermetic poets, and was actively involved in promoting avantgarde movements in the 1960s. Anceschi was also editor-in-chief of the important periodical *il verri* which he founded in 1956 and which soon became a focus for the publication of experimental poetry as well as a vehicle for introducing the work of foreign poets such as T.S. Eliot to Italy. He won the Feltrinelli Prize for Literary Criticism in 1992.

See also: Gruppo 63; poetry

LAURENCE SIMMONS

Andreotti, Giulio

b. 14 January 1919, Rome

Politician

The curriculum vitae of Andreotti – devout Catholic, Christian Democrat leader, seven times Prime Minister, life senator, alleged associate of the **mafia** – is often taken to display both the inspiration and instincts of Italy's postwar governing class. Similarly, his ecclesiastical connections, his apparently interminable occupation of high office and his ability to pass unscathed through scandal have given him the status of the quintessential Christian Democrat. Yet in several respects – a limited power base in his party, a chilly reluctance to play either the populist or the intellectual, an independence from the social groups and institutions providing his firmest support – he has also been anomalous among **DC** leaders. His retort to observations about the pernicious consequences of long-term occupation of power – 'il potere logora chi non ce l'ha' (power corrodes those without it) – neatly summarizes his emphasis on power as an end rather than a means. Indeed, despite an uninterruptedly successful political career, his name cannot be linked to any distinctive political vision or notable public achievement. Significantly, his diaries covering the dramatic years 1976–9 are the least informative that any politician of comparable seniority can ever have authored.

Andreotti's interest in politics was aroused in 1938 by Alcide **De Gasperi**, an early mentor. In 1942, Andreotti replaced **Moro** as President of the Catholic university student organization (FUCI), in which many DC leaders began their careers, alongside the 'Communist–Christians' who would later facilitate his acceptability to the **PCI** to lead 'national solidarity' governments between 1976 and 1979. In 1947 he was appointed to his first government position: for the following forty-five years, until the close of his seventh and final term as Prime Minister in 1992, he was rarely out of government office. His career took him principally

to Defence (1959–66) and Foreign Affairs (1980s), which enabled him to acquire valuable knowledge of the activities of the unreliable security services (see **terrorism**) and to establish firm links with the United States.

Like Moro, Andreotti achieved political success without the support of a large party faction. His group, Primavera (1954–64), was tiny, its support confined to Rome and its hinterland where, thanks to his links in church and state bureaucracies, Andreotti enjoyed a vast personal following. After 1968, his role in the DC was strengthened by the allegiance of the Sicilian DC leader Salvo Lima (mayor of Palermo, national and Euro-MP, linked to the **mafia**, and murdered in 1992). In the 1980s Andreotti established a close political alliance with the **PSI** leader and Prime Minister, Bettino **Craxi**. In 1994, evidence from **pentiti** ended Andreotti's charmed life among dubious associates, when he was charged with using his power to protect mafia interests in return for political support.

Further reading

Allum, P. (1997) 'Statesman or Godfather? The Andreotti Trials', in R. d'Alimonte and D. Nelken (eds), *Italian Politics: A Review*, vol. 12, Oxford: Westview Press.

Andreotti, G. (1964) *De Gasperi e il suo tempo* (De Gasperi and His Era), Milan: Mondadori.

Della Chiesa, N. (1996) *La politica della doppiezza. Da Andreotti a Berlusconi* (The Politics of Duplicity: From Andreotti to Berlusconi), Turin: Einaudi.

Orfei, R. (1975) *Andreotti*, Milan, Feltrinelli.

Stille, A. (1995) *Excellent Cadavers. The Mafia and the Death of the First Italian Republic*, London: Jonathan Cape (judicial investigations of the mafia in the 1980s and the eventual incrimination of Andreotti.)

DAVID MOSS

Ansa (Agenzia nazionale stampa associata)

Founded in January 1945 by the leading Italian newspapers as a private co-operative, Ansa (National Agency of Associated Press) soon became the country's leading news agency. Although, beginning in the 1960s, it greatly extended its scope and upgraded its technological capacities to now be on par with other international information agencies, it has remained a co-operative with the participation of some forty-five daily newspapers, although it now also supplies news services and information to other private and commercial entities.

Ansa's headquarters are located in Rome, from which are administered eighteen regional offices in Italy and ninety bureaux throughout the world, employing 600 full-time journalists and 500 foreign correspondents. Ansa's DEA archive contains all Ansa news reports since 1 January 1981, and since 1998 Ansa has also offered a public access news page on the Internet.

See also: information agencies

GINO MOLITERNO

Anselmo, Giovanni

b. 5 August, 1934, Borgofranco d'Ivrea, Turin

Artist

Anselmo shares with Gilberto **Zorio** a fascination with energy. His *La struttura che mangia* (The Structure that Eats) (1968) has fresh lettuce being 'consumed' between slabs of granite, while his *Torsione* (Torsion) (1968) consists of cowhide twisted by a piece of wood. He explains: 'My work really consists of making physical the force of an action or the energy of a situation ... I know of no other way of being at the heart of reality; my work becomes an extension of my living, my thinking, my acting'. This approach to materials and the idea of bringing art closer to life made Anselmo a key figure in *arte povera*. Since the mid-1980s, he has explored our relationship to gravity using large triangles of granite held upright by cables, in which the stone, pointing northwards, seems about to take off.

Further reading

Giovanni Anselmo, (1989) Florence: Hopefulmonster.

ROBERT LUMLEY

anti-design

Anti-design was a radical movement of architects and designers which, in the late 1960s and early 1970s, set out to challenge the direction in which design had been moving in the previous two decades. Also called 'contro-design' (counter-design) or radical design, the name was given to the collective efforts of a number of groups of young architects, based for the most part based in Florence; among them were **Archizoom**, **Super-studio**, UFO and Gruppo NNNN (in addition to the individual designer, Ugo La Pietra). They rejected the idea of designers working as the handmaidens of industry, intent on producing goods which encouraged conspicuous consumption within the context of late capitalism, and favoured a more idealistic and radical engagement with the concepts of design and architecture. They also rejected the 'chic' image of the designed artefact which had characterized Italian design in the international arena in the years of the **economic miracle**.

Linked to radical student politics in these years, and inspired by the humour and irony of the American Pop artists who, in turn, looked back to the tactics of the surrealists to create an art of provocation, these young designers presented writings, photographs and images of idealized monuments and artefacts, among them Super-studio's *Twelve Ideal Cities* of 1971 and Archizoom's *No-stop City* of the previous year, which set out to challenge the non-involvement of the Italian architect and designer with political life and urban issues.

The movement had its first manifestations in 1966 and was strongly influenced by the work of the older architect/designer Ettore **Sottsass**, who had an exhibition of highly personal furniture propositions in Milan in that year. Sottsass was the first of his generation to stand outside the relentless direction of the design/industry alliance and to project idealized designs which suggested a questioning of the status quo.

While the vast majority of Anti-design statements remained on the level of idealized propositions, a few were directed at the marketplace. Notable among these were two furniture items manufactured by the Zanotta company, which had established a tradition of working with radical designers. The 'Sacco', a bag of polyeurathane pellets designed by Gatti, Paolini and Teodoro and produced in 1969, quickly became a classic 'anti-design' object, standing as it did for formlessness and a flexible, youthful lifestyle. Lomazzi, D'Ubino and De Pas's 'Joe' sofa of the following year, a giant leather baseball glove for sitting in, was a design version of a Claes Oldenburg sculpture.

Anti-design made its impact on the architectural and design world through the exhibitions which promoted it, among them *Superarchitecture* at Pistoia and Modena in 1966 and 1967; the magazines which documented their activities, among them *Casabella* and *IN*; and through shared projects such as the 'Separate School for Expanded Conceptual Architecture' (1970); and 'Global Tools' (1973). By the mid-1970s, however, the movement had faded from view.

See also: interior design

Further reading

Raggi, F. (1973) 'Radical Story', in *Casabella* 382, p. 39.
Sparke, P. (1988) *Italian Design: 1870 to the Present*, London: Thames & Hudson (see especially pp.182–95).

PENNY SPARKE

anti-fascism

ideology

The military humiliations of the Second World War, the experience of **Resistance**, occupation and bombing, and the revelations of Fascist collaboration in the Holocaust left Mussolini's regime with few supporters after 1945. The Italian **Republic** was thus created not only to replace the dictatorship but with anti-fascism as its essential ideology. The dictatorship had emphasized hierarchy and one-man rule; the Republic would be parliamentary and democratic. Fascism had privileged the wealthier sections of society; the Republic would be based on labour. Mussolini had held women in contempt; the Republic would at once

give them the vote and would aim at their further liberation. The Fascist regime had stood for centralization and for war; the anti-fascist Republic would recognize the **regions** and would be pledged to a peaceful **foreign policy**. Committed to anti-fascism, Italy would at last become a place of liberty, equality, fraternity and happy gender relations.

The purity of these ideals was, however, soon compromised by political practice, both national and international. As the Cold War descended over Europe, anti-communism challenged anti-fascism as Italy's governing ideology. In the elections of 1948, it became clear that Italy was indeed to be part of the liberal capitalist and anti-communist 'West'. In these circumstances, during the 1950s, a decade dominated by anti-communism, anti-fascism became largely associated with the political and cultural opposition both to Christian Democrat and to American hegemony. For anti-fascists, the injuries done to the Italian people by Fascism had not been altogether amended by the fall of the regime. Its harmful legacy in, for example, the continuing harsh treatment of trade unionists, the failure to carry through regional reform, the survival of such reactionary social policies as the ban on **divorce** and the retention of an unpurged police and bureaucracy, needed still to be expunged. Thus until the 1980s, most programmes of political reform in Italy took anti-fascism as their starting point. Although Italy was a place of many political parties and even more social variation, in the world of ideas the essential contest from 1945 to about 1990 was fought out between conservatives who maintained that communism was the greatest evil of the twentieth century and, given its continued presence in Italy, the greatest threat there, and leftists who believed that Nazism and Fascism were the greater evil and that a vigilance against those ideas must be exercised continually.

With the thaw in the First Cold War from the 1960s onwards, anti-communism for a time weakened while anti-fascism took on renewed vigour. By the 1970s anti-fascism appeared to have become the dominant ideology in Italian public culture and was especially exemplified in cinema and literature. Anti-fascism was also evoked in the political sphere as long overdue social reforms were enacted, the union movement blossomed, and the legitimization of the PCI by entry into national government appeared imminent. A Christian Democrat leader like Benigno **Zaccagnini**, who had been a Resistance fighter near his home town of Ravenna, seemed to embody the possibilities of the '**historic compromise**' and to demonstrate that Italy's governing classes were now more committed to anti-fascism than to anti-communism.

However, the onset of the 'Second Cold War' between the USA of Ronald Reagan (President 1981–9) and the USSR, in what was its terminal decline, coincided with Italy's recoil from the radicalism of the 1970s, and with the marginalization of left-wing terrorists who had claimed to be the 'New Resistance' and thus the genuine anti-fascists. It became clear that much of conservative Italy, as assembled in the **P2** Masonic Lodge or as organized in Operation **Gladio**, had retained a visceral anti-communism.

In 1978, Sandro **Pertini**, an independent socialist and old Resistance fighter, became President of the Republic. His record of active opposition to Mussolini and the political causes which he had favoured since 1945 seemed to incarnate anti-fascism in its purest sense. As if to demonstrate a mass consensus for the ideals of anti-fascism Pertini became more popular than any other president, before or since. However, Pertini's purism might be better defined as naivety. His term of office coincided with the rise of a newly rapacious politics typified by Pertini's fellow socialist, Bettino **Craxi**. For this member of the new generation (born 1934) memories of the Fascist dictatorship lacked relevance in the world of Thatcher, Reagan and Silvio **Berlusconi**.

Italian culture was similarly switching its focus. A good example of this change can be seen in the work of the film directors the **Taviani brothers**, Paolo and Vittorio. Although in the 1970s they had appeared 'anti-Fascists like everyone else', by the time of *La notte di San Lorenzo* (The Night of the Shooting Stars) (1982) they had drifted into a postmodernist construction of the past in which history had no definite lessons. Then, in *Good Morning Babilonia* (1987) and *Fiorile* (1993), they expressed a cosy populism in which culture lay in the blood of Italians and the soil of Italy. Such a revised culture duly fitted Berlusconi's announcement on Liberation Day (25 April 1994) that the conflict between Fascism and anti-fascism was over and that Italy had moved into an entirely new era. In the eyes of Berlusconi and his supporters, anti-anti-fascism had then become the governing ideology.

The defeat of Berlusconi in the 1996 elections brought the Left to national political power. Supporters of the **Ulivo** coalition on occasion still express the ideas and attitudes of anti-fascism. However, the ambiguous metaphor of the olive is a good indication of how current Italian politics have lost their old certainties. Anti-fascism is the most evident of these weakened ideals.

See also: Gramsci; intellectuals

Further reading

Ginsborg, P. (1990) *A History of Contemporary Italy: Society and Politics 1943–1988*, Harmondsworth: Penguin (the best anti-fascist history of postwar Italy).

R.J.B. BOSWORTH

Antonacci, Anna

b. 5 April 1961, Ferrara

Soprano

Anna Antonacci's passionate stage presence and dark-hued voice have ensured her success as one of Italy's leading **opera** singers. After initial studies in Bologna she gave an accomplished stage debut as Rosina in Arezzo in 1986. In 1988 she was the winner of the Pavarotti Prize, and subsequently launched a career that has centred on the eighteenth- and early nineteenth-century repertoire, with especial strengths in Rossini. She has performed in all the leading Italian opera houses, returning regularly to Rome, Bologna and Catania, and has also appeared with success in Philadelphia and London. Notable roles include Semiramide, Ermione, Elizabeth (*Maria Stuarda*), Elfrida (*Paisiello*) and Fiordiligi. She has been active in the revival of lesser-known operas, taking the part of Horatia in Cimarosa's *Gli Orazi ed i Curiazi* which was given at Rome and Lisbon in 1989.

JOHN KERSEY

Antonioni, Michelangelo

b. 29 September 1912, Ferrara

Film director, scriptwriter, short story
   writer and critic

Considered one of the principal *auteurs* of the
modernist movement, Antonioni is known in Italy
for a string of early films in the realist style. From
the 1960s onwards he made more formalist films
both in Italian and in English, with international
casts. His reputation as one of the leading directors
of world repute grew as his subject matter shifted
increasingly towards a representation of individual
alienation within a context of global politics.

Educated in economics and business at the
University of Bologna, he worked as a film critic for
Corriere Padano before moving to Rome in 1938 and
joining the journal *Cinema*, while also briefly
studying film-making at the **Centro Sperimentale di Cinematografia**. In the early 1940s he
collaborated on the screenplays of **Rossellini**'s *Un
pilota ritorna* (A Pilot Returns) (1942) and Marcel
Carné's *Les Visiteurs du soir* (Evening Visitors) (1942).
His first film, *Gente del Po* (People of the Po), a
documentary on the Po valley, was begun in 1943
but, hindered by Fascist censorship and the war,
was not released until 1947. In the immediate
postwar period he made several more documentaries and collaborated on the screenplays of
De Santis's *Caccia tragica* (Tragic Hunt) (1947),
and **Fellini**'s *Lo sceicco bianco* (The White Sheik)
(1952). Finally in 1950 he released his first feature,
Cronaca di un amore (Story of a Love Affair), a
conventional narrative involving love and adultery
but already strongly marked by his formal style.

At a time when Italy was rebuilding from the war
(see **postwar reconstruction**) and **neorealism**
was propelling directors such as Rossellini to
international status, Antonioni took the neorealist
interest in characters at the edge to extremes which,
while earning critical respect – although often
voiced with a certain puzzlement at the lack of clear
meanings – at the same time also attracted
occasional official censure and disdain within the
industry itself. His 1952 film *I vinti* (The Van-
quished) presented criminal behaviour in too
graphic a manner for both the Italian government
and the French authorities, who refused to allow the

film to be shown in France for the next ten years. In
his next film, *La signora senza camelie* (The Lady
Without Camelias) (1953), Antonioni focussed on
the industry's own exploitative treatment of women,
a theme which would recur throughout his career.
An early manifestation of his later preoccupation
with the theme of alienation appeared in his
characterization of the working class in his native
Po valley in *Il grido* (The Cry) of 1957.

By the end of the 1950s his neorealist style was
evolving towards films with more disjointed
narratives. Rejecting the superficial imposed coherence of Hollywood-style composition, plot and
editing, he produced what would remain his most
successful films: *L'avventura* (The Adventure) (1960),
La notte (The Night) (1961), *L'eclisse* (The Eclipse)
(1962), and his first film in colour, *Deserto rosso* (The
Red Desert) (1964), which marked his maturation
as a major film-maker. As he continued to explore
the failure, or indeed the impossibility, of human
intimacy and a deepening sense of social alienation, particularly that of women, within postwar
Europe, Antonioni developed a personal and
highly formal style to match his disjointed and
alienated subject matter. Thus, in spite of an
increasing international reputation and good box
office success, his films continued to strike most
critics as ambiguous and uncertain.

In 1966 he made *Blow-Up*, set in the mid-1960s
Carnaby Street and depicting life in the hip
London of British photographer David Bailey.
His first film in English, it made the reputations
of its English actors, Vanessa Redgrave and David
Hemmings, and brought Antonioni himself into
the international spotlight. It set the trend for the
next decade or so, and from 1967 to 1982
Antonioni made his films outside Italy. Existential
alienation gave way to more specific themes of late
twentieth-century life, in particular a preoccupation with surveillance and the epistemology of
vision. 'How is it that we know the real?' became
an increasingly dominant subtext in films that
concerned themselves with the problems of seeing
and knowing, and of how the artist represents them
within their political context. Critical acclaim,
though often still puzzled, followed and there were
more box office successes. Major films from this
period are *Zabriskie Point* (1969), set in California,
and *Professione: Reporter* (1975, titled for English

audiences as *The Passenger*), which starred Jack Nicholson, both of which attempt to explore the problems of middle-class identity allied to political action.

In 1972 he returned to documentary, shooting *Chung-Kuo Cina* in China for the **RAI**. Admired in the West, it earned him yet more political flak, this time from the Chinese government which did not appreciate its openness. Experimentation with colour and video technology resulted in *Il mistero di Oberwald* (The Oberwald Mystery) (1980) but he soon returned to his earlier subjects of middle-class social alienation and the problems of intimacy in his *Identificazione di una donna* (Identification of a Woman) (1982). Other projects were planned, but from the mid-1980s his health began failing and most remained unrealized. A stroke in the late 1980s left him without speech, but in 1995, with the assistance of German film-maker Wim Wenders, he made *Par-delà des nuages* (Beyond the Clouds), a film based on some of his own short stories. Among many awards, including Cannes (1982) and Venice (1983), he was awarded an Oscar for lifetime achievement in 1995.

Further reading

Antonioni, M. (1996) *The Architecture of Vision: Writings and Interviews on Cinema*, ed. M. Cottino-Jones, New York: Marsilio Publishers.

Arrowsmith, W. (1995) *Antonioni: The Poet of Images*, New York: Oxford University Press (critical readings of the major films).

Bondanella, P. (1990) *Italian Cinema: From Neorealism to the Present*, New York: Continuum, 2nd revised edn (a survey of postwar film in Italy placing Antonioni, among others, in a national context).

Brunette, P. (1998) *The Films of Michelangelo Antonioni*, Cambridge: Cambridge University Press (an overview which closely examines six of the major films including *La Notte* and *The Passenger*).

Rohdie, S. (1990) *Antonioni*, London: British Film Institute (a basic introductory biography).

Sorlin, P. (1996) *Italian National Cinema 1896–1996*, London and New York: Routledge (another survey with a strong emphasis on a cultural studies reading of nationalism).

JEFF DOYLE

Arbasino, Alberto

b. 22 January 1930, Voghera, Pavia

Writer and cultural critic

Among the most versatile intellectuals and caustic critics of Italy's cultural, political and social life – see such essay collections as *Fantasmi italiani* (Italian Ghosts) (1977) and *Un paese senza* (A Country Without) (1980) – Arbasino was also a founding and prominent member of the neoavantgarde Gruppo 63. He left his professorship at the University of Rome to devote himself to literature, journalism (regularly contributing to **La Repubblica**) and to politics (he sat in **Parliament** as a deputy for the Republican Party from 1983 to 1987). In his numerous novels – parodies and pastiches such as *L'anonimo lombardo* (The Anonymous Lombard) (1959), *Specchio delle mie brame* (Mirror of My Yearnings) (1974) and *Fratelli d'Italia* (Brothers of Italy) (2nd revised edition, 1993) – Arbasino inventively plays with language to both record and sarcastically comment on the chaotic reality of contemporary Italy.

See also: narrative

FRANCESCA PARMEGGIANI

Arbore, Renzo

b. 24 June 1937, Foggia

Musician, film-maker, radio and
    television presenter

Italy's most famous and multi-talented showman, Lorenzo (Renzo) Arbore began his showbusiness career playing clarinet with the South Railway Travellers, a group that performed dixieland music for American soldiers in Naples immediately after the War. After having moved to Rome in the 1960s, he began to work for **RAI** Radio and created the first of his many innovative and extremely popular music programmes, *Bandiera gialla* (Yellow Flag), in 1965. This was followed in 1970 by *Alto Gradimento* (High Approval), a show that was similarly successful and which ran uninterruptedly until 1980. By this time Arbore had already moved into television and had achieved even greater popularity with the legendary Sunday variety programme, *L'altra domenica* (Another Side of Sunday). After trying his hand at cinema and directing several amusing films which, although not spectacularly successful, nevertheless showcased a number of rising young talents including Diego Abatantuono, Roberto **Benigni** and writer Luciano De Crescenzo, Arbore returned to radio with *Radio anche noi* (We're Also Radio) in 1981. Already something of a showbusiness legend among the initiated, Arbore would become a household name throughout Italy in 1985 with **Quelli della notte** (The Night Crowd), a zany late-night music and talk show which ran five nights a week for only two and a half months but which profoundly changed the face of Italian television and marked something of a revolution in Italian popular culture. At its height, the programme achieved an unprecedented 51 per cent share of the total television viewing audience and many of the oddball characters who regularly appeared on the show achieved enough fame to subsequently host their own programmes as part of the diaspora of what became known the 'Arbore tribe'.

The clever parody of television shows which had made *Quelli della notte* such a hit was repeated in a new guise in several new programmes that followed, the most famous of which was *Indietro Tutta* (All Behind) in 1988. At the same time Arbore continued to pursue his musical career, competing with his clarinet at the **Sanremo Festival** in 1986 where he was placed second. After touring Italy with the Balilla Boogie Band in the late 1980s, he achieved a much wider international recognition in the early 1990s when he toured Australia and the Americas with his Orchestra Italiana (The Italian Orchestra), a large and eclectic ensemble which played unusual but ingenious arrangements of well-known Italian popular songs. In the mid-1990s he became artistic director of RAI International and became even better known worldwide as the public face of the RAI's satellite broadcasts.

GINO MOLITERNO

Arca, Paolo

b. 12 May 1953, Rome

Composer

Arca studied at the Rome Conservatory with Irma Ravinale and subsequently with Donatoni in Rome and Siena. His compositional style is direct and accessible and shows a strong theatrical instinct. He won a composition prize at Avignon in 1982, and has since been noted for his dramatic collaborations with the librettist Giovanni Carli Ballola. This partnership yielded the one-act opera, *Angelica e la luna* (Angelica and the Moon) (1985), based on an Italian folk-tale, and its successor *Il Carillon del Gesuita* (The Jesuit's Carillon) (1989), written to commemorate the bicentenary of the French Revolution. This latter work is concerned with the fate of the boy Dauphin (the son of Louis XVI) and develops from a realistic treatment of the drama to one of increasing magic and fantasy. At the 1990 Munich Festival, Arca was commissioned by Henze to write an opera for marionettes. The resulting work, *Lucius, Asinus Aureus* (to a libretto based on Apuleius) shows Arca's commitment to the perpetuation of established forms while renewing their intellectual and musical language.

JOHN KERSEY

Archibugi, Francesca

b. 16 May 1960, Rome

Scriptwriter and film director

Archibugi studied film-making at **Olmi**'s school at Bassano and later at the **Centro Sperimentale di Cinematografia** in Rome. The few short films she directed there brought her to the critics' attention as one of the most interesting minimalist directors of the 1980s. In 1988 she reached a larger audience with her first feature *Mignon è partita* (Mignon Has Gone), a delicately wrought film about the first-love experiences of a sensitive, middle-class Roman teenager.

A keen observer and a subtle psychologist, Archibugi conserves the strong influence of her mentors Ermanno Olmi, Gianni Amico and Furio

Scarpelli (see **Age and Scarpelli**) in both her scriptwriting and direction. Feature films such as *Verso sera* (In the Evening) (1990), the highly-praised *Il grande cocomero* (The Great Pumpkin) (1992) and more recently *L'albero delle pere* (The Pear Tree) (1998) all confirm her ability to hold the audience while dealing with unusual and intimate themes.

ADRIANA MONTI

architectural and design magazines

The uniqueness of the Italian postwar architectural and design scene was fully reflected in the proliferation of magazines dealing with design-related themes. Architectural training underpinned so many areas alongside urban and architectural design, including product and fashion design, furniture, transport, packaging and graphic design, that it came to constitute the major characteristic of Italian design culture, and this situation inevitably manifested itself in the magazines. Although it was the scarcity of architectural work, combined with the overproduction of architectural graduates, that drove architects to explore other areas during this early period, architect-designers would continue to be the leading figures in Italian design from the First Generation onwards.

There were few architectural and design magazines in the prewar period. Marcello Piacentini's *L'Architettura* (1921–41) was founded in Rome as a conservative architectural history magazine, but soon developed into a mouthpiece of Fascist architecture. With the advent of **Domus** (1928) followed by **Casabella**, *Poligono*, *Edilizia Moderna* (1939) and later *Quadrante* (1933–5), which all regularly reviewed new projects and materials, Milan was established as the main centre of both design studios and related publishing activities. In fact, the founding of *Domus* and *Casabella* signals a new era in the history of modern Italian design. Passing through various directors and editorial policies, they nevertheless always maintained the highest standard as leading magazines of the profession and set the tone for the resulting professional debates. Members of the First Generation of designers such as Giò **Ponti**, the **BPR**

Studio and Carlo **Mollino** established themselves in the first half of the century and would continue to make an impact in the postwar period but, in general, the war years themselves saw very little design magazine production. The exceptions were *Lo stile* (full title: *Lo stile nella casa e nell'arredamento* (Style in House and Furnishings), which Ponti founded in 1941 and edited until resuming the directorship of *Domus* from **Rogers** in 1947 (*Lo stile* itself dissolved in 1967) and the antifascist *Quaderni italiani* which, beginning in 1942, was edited by Bruno **Zevi** and published in London and then smuggled into Italy.

Among the magazines founded immediately after the war, a central role was taken by Rome-based *Metron*, which became the mouthpiece of Zevi's APAO (Association for Organic Architecture) and a focal point for intellectuals like **Piccinato**, Musatti and Radiconcini and architects such as **Ridolfi**, Figini, Peressuti and Tedeschi. Programmatically directed towards the promotion of organicism and the international style, it was formed in opposition to the old elites and consequently advocated the uncompromising erasure of all traces of the rationalist aesthetic and its politics. It continued from 1955 onwards as **l'Architettura, cronache e storia**, and in the 1980s became equally critical of postmodernism. Postwar *Casabella* published special issues subtitled 'Costruzioni' (Constructions), directed by **Albini** and Palanti: the first (no. 193) was on the theme of Reconstruction, the second (no.194) was on the 'Piano AR' (The AR Plan) and the last one (no. 195–98) was devoted to Pagano. However the series was soon discontinued as unprofitable. Guided by the enlightened social thinker and industrialist Adriano **Olivetti**, *Comunità* (1946) and the Turin-based *Urbanistica* (1949) attempted to address a professional audience whilst at the same time widening the scope of discussion by calling attention to the underdeveloped South and advocating intervention at the urban level inspired by English Garden Cities and Mumford's ideas. The late 1940s were generally characterized by a number of smaller, ephemeral periodicals of differing ideological stances. Elio **Vittorini**'s influential leftist **Il Politecnico**, graphically designed by Albe Steiner in the neo-constructivist style, led a brief but notorious existence between

September 1945 and December 1947. In Florence, beginning in 1945, **Michelucci** edited *La nuova città*, focusing particularly on the problems of urbanism. *Pirelli*, promoted by Linoleum, came out from 1947 to 1972 as a monthly review of cultural information. Also worthy of mention is *A, Cultura della Vita*, a weekly popularized by Zevi, Pagani and Lina Bò, which however for only lasted a few issues in 1946. There also appeared De Finetti's *La città, architettura e politica* and *Cantieri*, which dealt with technical themes and building policies.

The years of reconstruction, the 1950s, saw a vast multiplication of magazines, some highly specialized, attesting to the existence of a sophisticated audience both professional and lay. This also reflected the strengthening of the economy as well as a stratification within the field of design itself. In Rome, Luigi **Moretti** started the sadly short-lived yet beautiful *Spazio* in 1950. *Edilizia Moderna*, although a mouthpiece of the Linoleum Pirelli from 1929, was also 'refounded' in Milan in 1950. *Prospettive*, launched a year later, and *Architetti* were both addressed to professional architects. Promoted by the glass manufacture Saint-Gobain, the specialized *Vitrum* also started in 1950. ***Civiltà delle macchine***, edited by Leonardo **Sinisgalli**, appeared in Turin in 1953 as a house organ of the Finmeccanica company. Together with *Edilizia Moderna*, it expressed the critical views of the design intelligentsia of the time. Alberto **Rosselli** started the enormously influential bilingual (Italian/English) ***Stile Industria***, completely dedicated to the promotion of mass-produced object design. It only ran from 1954 to 1963, but was re-issued in June 1997. Its concentration on visual detail helped to raise the most banal utilitarian objects to the status of art, and was a vital force in establishing the international reputation of Italian design both aesthetically and theoretically. *Rivista dell'arredamento* was launched in 1954; under the direction of Antonello Vincenti, it became *Interni* in 1967. *Zodiac* was another periodical with a high cultural impact, originally founded by Adriano Olivetti in 1957 and then revived in 1989. *Il Mobile Italiano* (1957–60) and *Ideal Standard* (Milan, 1959) focused on interiors, while *La Casa* (Rome, 1955–61), directed by Pio Montesi, was a monographic magazine of architectural criticism which provided

some of the first studies of twentieth-century Italian architecture with themes such as 'Quartiere' (urban block) and 'Italian Modern Architecture'. Many other journals dealing with private, interior and exterior spaces came out in Gorlich editions. *Ville e giardini*, from 1956, was directed at a larger, non-specialized audience.

The **Milan Triennale**, the **Venice Biennale** and *la Mostra del Cinema*, now elevated to high culture, were closely followed and debated as major seasonal cultural events in many periodicals that promoted design as a cultural force, especially *Stile Industria*.

The production of design periodicals continued to flourish throughout the 1960s when a whole range of new magazines appeared. ***Abitare*** (Milan, 1960) and *Interni* (1967) exhibited the sumptuousness of Italian neo-modern interiors while *Casa Vogue* (Milan, 1968), edited until 1993 by Isa Vercelloni, was the first magazine dealing with the radical and the postmodern not addressed exclusively to professionals. *Ottagono* (Milan, 1966) was issued as a general design magazine supported by such major design manufacturers as Artemide, Bernini, Boffi, Cassina, Flos and Tecno. *Rassegna* (Milan, 1966) published important issues under the editorship first of Adalberto De Lago (from 1968) and then, after moving to Bologna, under Vittorio **Gregotti** (1979). ***Controspazio*** (Milan, 1969) led by Paolo **Portoghesi**, *Contropiano* (Rome, 1968) and *Lotus* (Milan, 1964–5), and later *Lotus International* (winter 1970–1), directed by Pierluigi Nicolin, provided valuable alternatives to the hegemony of *Domus* and redirected attention to the interrelation of architecture, urbanism and social issues. Many of the 'house organs' appeared, including *Marmo*, a beautiful magazine sponsored by S. Henreaux SpA and directed by Bruno Alfieri from 1963; *Caleidoscopio* (1965), a house organ of Gruppo Industriale Busnelli; and *Qualità* of Kartell. *Pianeta Fresco* came out with two issues in 1967, edited by Ettore **Sottsass** and Fernanda Pivano, dealing with pop art and beat culture. Of the other magazines, the most popular were *La Mia Casa, Shop Casa & Giardino, Forme, Humus, Ufficio Stile, Ville Giardini, Marcatrè, Metro, Argomenti di Architettura, Il Quadrifoglio* and *Stile Auto*.

The political and social upheaval of the late 1960s resulted in a disillusionment with the social power of design on the part of both younger and older generations of designers and the crisis carried on into the 1970s. At the same time, this fostered a new architectural awareness in the profession and important theoretical works were produced. The tension between the social context and the aesthetics of isolated and idealized objects needed redefinition, but much of the resulting critical 'radicalness' and 'newness' represented highly intellectualized and conceptualized diagnoses of problems rather than their solutions. Probably the most influential magazine of those years was *Modo* (Milan, 1977), directed first by **Mendini**, then by Franco Raggi, Andrea **Branzi** and Cristina Morozzi. It proposed repositioning design within a larger technical and social milieu by connecting it with anthropology, social customs, industrial techniques and craftsmanship. Another journal aiming to shift architectural, design and social co-ordinates was ***Spazio e società*** (Milan, 1978) edited and directed by Giancarlo **De Carlo**. *IN: Argomenti e Immagini del Design* (Milan, 1971–4) was a review dedicated to radical design, as was *Op Cit*, a quarterly edited in Naples by Renato de Fusco and supported by Alessi, the Neapolitan Chamber of Commerce, Drieade, Golden Shave and Sabatini. The Paduan *Quaderni del Progetto*, with two issues (1974, 1979) financed by Paolo Deganello, debated the relationship between politics and design. A number of journals like *L'ambiente cucina* (1970) and *Il bagno oggi e domani* (1973) initiated a series of similarly specialized periodicals which included *In più* and *Psicon*.

The 1980s brought another crisis in design but also a further diversification of architecture and design periodicals which mirrored the growing complexity of Italian society. Florentine Radical design, embodied in **Studio Alchimia** (1978) and the Memphis movement (1981–87) (see **Studio Memphis**, capitalized on the notion of design as figurative communication, and the magazines formed around them expressed the theories and aesthetics of the New Design. Exemplary is *Terrazzo* (1988), directed by Barbara Radice (in consultation with Ettore Sottsass), in many ways a refined mirror of the cultural movements that followed design, anthropology, history and the post-industrial metropolis. *Ollo*, a house organ of Mendini, was issued as a quarterly. *Area, L'arca, Arredo Urbano*

and *CAD* all came out in 1981, followed by *Gapcasa, Recuperare, Abacus, Habitat Ufficio* and *Vetro spazio* (1985) and *Disegno* (1986). *Quaderni*, a quarterly on architecture culture founded in 1989, attracted the collaboration of Bruno **Munari** while *Materia* (1989), a quarterly of architecture and design, appeared as a house organ of Graniti delle Fiandre.

The Fourth Generation of architect-designers developed from diverse influences of the Third Generation. From the Sottsass/Mendini 'school' come Aldo Cibic, De Lucchi, Thun, Zanini and Christoph Radl; Luca Scacchetti shares a sensibility with **Rossi**; Maurizio Peregalli represents the word of high fashion, primarily **Armani**; Denis Santachiara, Luigi Serafini and Mario Conventino are inspired by visual arts; Capelli, Ranzo and Giuseppe D'Amore (based in Naples) find inspiration in 'Mediterranean design'; Laura de Santillana cultivates the crafts approach; Alberto Meda stands for the poetics of engineering in design; furniture and industrial/artisan traditions groomed Antonio Citterio, Forcolani and Paolo Pallucco. The Bolidist Movement, which appeared in 1986, is recognizable by its streamlined forms and computerized cartoon images (as in work of Massimo Iosa-Ghini and Maurizio Corrado). Its celebration of speed and smoothness of technology, as well as of mental and physical mobility, brings it close to the futurist inspiration.

In the 1990s, Italian design inevitably became more 'global'. As both design and architecture became obsessed with computerization, the magazines became 'intelligent', computerized and 'virtual', in both their 'packaging' and their themes. Although the greater number of leading Fourth Generation Italian designers still have an architectural degree, architecture seems to have lost its privileged cultural status. New titles appeared, including *Elle Decor, Axa, Progex, Exporre, d'A* and *Polaris*. Needless to say, by the mid-1990s every 'self-respecting' magazine had a homepage on the World Wide Web.

See also: design education; industrial design; interior design; Movimento di Comunità

Further reading

Albera, G. and Monti, N. (1989) *Italian Modern: A*

Design Heritage, New York: Rizzoli (a good survey of postwar Italian design).

Bellati, N. (1990) *New Italian Design*, New York: Rizzoli (a review of the fourth generation Italian designers).

Branzi, A. (ed.) (1996) *Il Design Italiano 1964–1990*, Milan: Electa (a series of essays that situate the phenomenon of Italian design in relation to different aspects of Italian social, economic and political life).

Branzi, A. and De Lucci, M. (eds) (1985) *Centrokappa, Il design italiano degli anni 50* (Centrokappa: Italian Design in the Fifties), Milan: RDE (in-depth presentation of the 1950s designers and their artefacts).

Eco, U. (1982) 'Phenomena of This Sort Must Also be Included in any Panorama of Italian Design', in P. Sartogo (ed.), *Italian Re-evolution: Design in Italian Society in the 80s*, Montreal: La Jolla Museum of Contemporary Art/Musée d'art contemporaine (thoughts on the development of Italian postwar design from the renowned intellectual and semiotician).

Sparke, P. (1988) *Design in Italy: 1870 to the Present*, New York: Abbeville Press (a historical, economic and social review of the phenomenon of Italian design presented through six distinct periods).

GORDANA KOSTICH

L'Architettura, cronache e storia

The architectural journal *L'Architettura, cronache e storia* (Architecture, Chronicles and History) was widely regarded as an extension of the Roman journal *Metron*, the mouthpiece of the APAO (Association for Organic Architecture) founded by Bruno **Zevi** in 1944. *L'Architettura* itself was launched by Zevi in Rome in 1955 as a magazine 'for the history of art and architecture'. It continues to be published under his direction, although it has lost some of its original enthusiasm for a radical socio-political transformation of architecture. As well as regularly documenting building activities in Italy and abroad, *L'Architettura*'s programme has aspired to present the widest range of architectural interests including matters political and artistic,

professional and historical, contemporary and traditional. It has constantly attempted to bridge the gap between modern architecture and architectural historiography, an issue it addressed in its inaugural editorial and which it characterized as a schism that had already proved disastrous from a cultural point of view.

See also: architectural and design magazines

GORDANA KOSTICH

Archizoom

An experimental, avantgarde design studio, Archizoom Associati specialized in industrial and architectural design and in **urban planning**, creating a number of visionary environments and fantasy furniture designs. Established in Florence in 1966 by architects Andrea **Branzi**– the theoretical leader – Gilberto Coretti, Paolo Deganello and Massimo Morozzi, the studio was joined two years later by industrial designers Dario and Lucia Bartolini. The group was similar to another Florentine studio, **Superstudio**, founded around the same time on similar principles and led by Adolfo **Natalini**. Like Superstudio, Archizoom was partly inspired by British Conceptual Design and *Archigram*. Its aesthetics demanded a reform of design that would enhance consumers' awareness of both objects and architecture; to achieve this goal, members often produced ironical and mischievous projects, especially in their furniture designs, with playful allusions to the modern movement as well as to kitsch, pop and stylistic revivalism. Archizoom's project for the standard polyurethane foam sofa, *Superonda* (1966), a two-piece sectional divan with a sinusoidal silhouette, was a paradigm of 'counter-design'. As an ironic response to Le Corbusier's famous injunction to clean up lounges and lives, Archizoom proposed a Safari sofa and palm-shaped Sanremo standing lamp with illuminating leaves (1968). The 'Mies chair', produced by Poltranova in 1969, was their commentary on the classical modernist armchair, and consisted of a stretch-rubber membrane supported by a triangular chromium frame. Their 'dream bed' *Presagio di Rose* (Presage of Roses) (1967) challenged the traditional understanding of good taste with its wilful and hard-edged, neo-kitsch vulgarity.

Archizoom's involvement with architecture was equally radical, and here too the studio argued against tradition, familiarity and comfort, and what they regarded as the 'anti-humanism of modernism'. Together with Superstudio, Archizoom organized the 'Superarchitecture' exhibition in Pistoia and in Modena in 1966–7. They also exhibited at Eurodomus in Turin and Theatro Domani in Modena (1968), in the 'Center for Eclectic Conspiracy' at the 14th **Milan Triennale**, at Milan's Salone del Mobile (Furniture Showroom). In 1970 they presented their famous 'No-stop City', which extended the idea of a city into infinity. In 1972, the exhibition 'Italy: The New Domestic Landscape' at New York's MoMA, brought international attention to Italian radical design and, with typical bravura, in the 'Counter-design as Postulation' section, Archizoom presented an empty, grey room in which a female voice vividly described a wonderful, illuminated and colourful house which the audience was left to imagine for itself.

Archizoom dissolved in 1974, and Branzi went to work in **Studio Alchimia** with Ettore **Sottsass**, Alessandro **Mendini** and the UFO group, and later, for the more commercial **Studio Memphis**, again with Mendini. The spirit of Archizoom and its anti-design postulates thus continued to influence design aesthetics well into the 1980s and 1990s. The Archizoom archives are housed at the University of Parma's Institute for the History of Art.

See also: industrial design

Further reading

Branzi, A. (1994) *The Hot House: Italian New Wave Design*, London: Thames & Hudson (a wide-ranging illustrated study of twentieth-century Italian design with special emphasis on the postwar period and on the role of groups such as Archizoom and Superstudio).

GORDANA KOSTICH

ARCI

A non-profit organization which operates primarily at the local level, ARCI (Associazione Ricreativa Culturale Italiana, the Italian Recreational and Cultural Association) works in conjunction with local administrations to provide Italians with leisure activities. In its statement of purpose, ARCI promotes 'the values of tolerance, brotherhood, solidarity and community, to foster the growth of each individual through active participation within society'.

The association is particularly active in the field of culture and entertainment, where its principal activity is the promotion of books, movies and music which might otherwise be neglected by mainstream mass-media. It organizes physical education and sporting events that encourage participation rather than competition, and strives to provide environments for group activities for young people that are safe and intellectually stimulating. ARCI was also one of the first organizations to openly discuss and advocate homosexual rights in Italy.

PAOLO VILLA

Argan, Giulio Carlo

17 May 1909, Turin; d. 12 November 1992, Rome

Art historian and critic

Argan was interested in art as a form of social engagement, integral and necessary to life. He identified architecture and **urban planning** as areas where the community has a particularly strong interaction with culture. His major works, which tend to emphasize the social context of art, range from studies of Renaissance painters and architects, including Botticelli, Fra Angelico, Michelangelo, Serlio and Palladio, through the Baroque to modern sculpture and abstract art. He stimulated much debate in 1963 with his discussion of the 'death of art', by which he meant the end of the creative autonomy of the individual.

Argan moved from academic posts at Palermo and the University of Rome to the world of politics, first serving as Mayor of Rome between 1976 and 1979 and later becoming a senator for the Communist Party.

Further reading

Argan, G.C. (1970) *The Renaissance City*, trans. S.E. Bassnett, New York: G. Braziller (looks at the city in its social context, including the role of princes and architects).

—— (1988) *Storia dell'arte italiana* (The History of Italian Art), revised edn, Florence: Sansoni (one of Argan's best-known works, widely used as a standard school text in Italy).

MAX STAPLES

Argento, Dario

b. 7 September 1940, Rome

Film director

The son of a film producer, Argento began his career as a film critic and a scriptwriter for Bernardo **Bertolucci** and then Sergio **Leone**, co-writing the internationally successful spaghetti Western *C'era una volta il West* (Once Upon a Time in the West) (1968). With films like *L'uccello dalle piume di cristallo* (The Gallery Murders) (1970) and *Profondo rosso* (Deep Red) (1975), Argento contributed significantly to the revival of the Italian B-movie horror genre, which is highly original and strongly influenced by local adventure film and Italian comic book traditions (see **comics**). Argento's *Suspiria* (1977) with its breakdown of conventional narrative and elements of baroque sensibility, represented a turning point for the genre.

Argento has been a producer and a mentor for younger directors working in the horror genre (such as Lamberto Bava's daughter Asia, who starred in his American production *Trauma* (1993), and has become a successful screen actress).

LAURENCE SIMMONS

Armani, Giorgio

b. 11 July 1934, Piacenza

Fashion designer

Armani is acclaimed both for establishing power dressing for executive women and for the unstructured aesthetic of the 1980s, which simultaneously offered simplicity, flexibility and elegance for both men and women. He did this using luxurious fabrics in muted tones, while resisting abrupt fashion change.

Armani began his career as a stylist for Rinascente stores, before becoming a designer at Cerruti in 1960 and then a freelance designer in 1970. He produced his own men's wear line in 1974, followed by a women's collection a year later, to international acclaim. Emporio Armani and Armani Jeans came in 1981, and diffusion ranges, accessories and an extensive network of retail outlets followed. Armani has been central to the rise of Italian fashion in the international marketplace, and has continued to expand his business and to exert a strong influence on the cosmopolitan wardrobe.

See also: fashion

NICOLA WHITE

armed forces

After the Second World War, the role of the armed forces in Italy was drastically reduced. A number of factors contributed to this reduction, including the prior involvement of the armed forces with Fascism (see also **fascism and neo-fascism**), the total collapse of the Royal Army after the fall of Mussolini, the legacy of a lost war, the hostility of the main **political parties** towards nationalism and militarism, and above all the rejection of war as a means of settling international disputes explicitly written into the **constitution** of 1948. At the same time, the armed forces retained their special status as a separate body, and although the constitution called in very general terms for their 'democratization', their integration into the democratic process has remained incomplete. The armed forces have remained under the jurisdiction of a separate military judiciary, which has continued to enforce autonomous military laws even in peace time. The Ministry of Defence – which gradually co-ordinated the three formerly divided forces of army, air force and navy – has continued to enjoy a relative autonomy from both government and the **Parliament**, and the Consiglio Supremo di Difesa (Supreme Defence Council), established in 1950 as a joint political body, has never exercised any effective power. Even the military budget is usually drafted in relative secrecy and has remained virtually free from control of Parliament.

The main source of legitimization of the armed forces has thus been international rather than national. After Italy joined NATO in 1949, the Italian army was permitted to rearm and to station a number of contingents within the Atlantic security forces. The USA was granted military bases on Italian soil, where, since 1958, the Italian government has allowed the deployment of nuclear missiles. Military industry was also relaunched by both state and private concerns (such as **Fiat** and **IRI**), which developed successful joint ventures in high-tech sectors with both US and European industrial groups.

Doubts about the Army's commitment to the democratic process arose during the 1960s and 1970s, when high-ranking military personnel were discovered to have been involved in a series of destabilising plots jointly carried out by subversive right-wing groups and sectors of the **intelligence services** (see **strategia della tensione**), a mistrust increased by the large number of generals revealed to have been members of the secret Masonic Lodge **P2** in 1981 and the uncovering of the **Gladio** affair in 1990. Further severe damage to the public image of the armed forces resulted when a commercial airliner was shot down on 27 June 1980 above the island of **Ustica** in the Tyrrhenian sea, with the loss of eighty-one lives. In spite of strong suspicions that the plane had become unwittingly caught up in an air battle – allegedly between NATO or French forces and Libyan aircraft – and accidentally hit by a missile, the Italian Air Force refused to release information and tampered with radar records, thus actively obstructing investigations and leading to a number

of charges being laid against some Chiefs of the General Staff and several other officers in 1990.

All of these events further eroded public trust in the armed forces. Moreover, the army is almost unanimously considered to be a gigantic and extremely costly bureaucratic machine, plagued by inefficiency and, as a number of judicial enquiries have uncovered, in some cases corruption. A military career is commonly regarded as an opportunity for occupational security, another form of safe bureaucratic employment, and the number of both officers and non-commissioned officers has continued to increase, reaching almost 90,000 in the early 1990s; only 20,000 of these are on active duty. Military service has continued to be compulsory for all persons of age (18 years at present) and the armed forces continue to call up a very large number of conscripts (up to 300,000 at the mid-1970s, gradually reduced to 210,000 twenty years later), although the period of service has been progressively shortened from two years to fifteen months in 1964, then to one year in 1975 and finally to ten months in the mid-1990s. Compulsory service for men – women were never conscripted, though recently a small number have been allowed into military training at their own request – was once considered a duty which contributed to the maintenance of the democratic process. However, military service is now largely regarded, especially by young people, as a waste of time and a meaningless obligation. A high number of suicides and revelations of the widespread use of intimidation and violence against recruits have further weakened the army's reputation to the point where increasingly a larger number of young people have opted to carry out their duty for national service through civilian service, either under social service organizations or in public administrations. This alternative, allowed for the first time in 1978, originally sought to deter many so-called 'obiettori di coscienza' (conscientious objectors) by obliging them to serve for twenty months, but the term was eventually brought into line with the period of military service.

Nevertheless, there is also wide acknowledgement of the socially useful functions performed by the army in providing support during natural disasters such as **earthquakes** or floods or a military presence in some southern towns (such as

Naples and Palermo) as a deterrent against **mafia** and other organized crime. Some argue, however, that this merely highlights the absence of a proper civil defence and the chronic shortage of police personnel. Moreover, since the 1970s both the air force and the navy – along with some specialized corps of the army – have largely benefited from larger investments for modernization of equipment and armaments and gained greater technological expertise. Italian special contingents also took part successfully in some peacekeeping and peace-enforcing missions of the United Nations, such as those in the Sinai, Lebanon and the Persian Gulf during the 1980s, and more recently in Somalia (1992), the former Yugoslavia (1996) and Kosovo (1999). The Italian Air Force also participated in the Gulf War in 1990–1, the first time Italian armed forces have been deployed in military operations since the end of the Second World War, and in the air strikes on Serbia in 1999. As a result the idea of a professional army made up exclusively of volunteers has gained momentum in recent years, to such an extent that a bill to abolish military service and create a professional army was announced by the D'Alema government in early 1999, with the proposal receiving widespread public support.

Further reading

Barrera, P. (1988) 'Crisis in the Military: Rethinking Conscription and the Military Code', in R.Y. Nanetti, R. Leonardi and P. Corbetta (eds), *Italian Politics: A Review*, vol. 2, London: Pinter.

STEFANO BATTILOSSI

Arpino, Giovanni

b. 27 January 1927, Pola; d. 10 December 1987, Turin

Novelist and editorial adviser

Giovanni Arpino first appeared on the literary scene in 1952 with the novel *Sei stato felice, Giovanni* (You Have Been Happy, Giovanni), followed by *La suora giovane* (The Young Nun) (1959). This successful novel – the diary of a middle-aged man recounting his love for a religious novice – was highly praised by the poet Eugenio **Montale** as one of the finest examples of Italian realist narrative.

Arpino investigated social and psychological themes in all his works, from *L'ombra delle colline* (Shadow of the Hill) – which was awarded the Strega Prize in 1964 (see **literary prizes**) – to his later *Il fratello italiano* (The Italian Brother) (1980) and the posthumously published *La trappola amorosa* (The Love Trap) (1988). Besides writing fiction (including children's literature) and several plays, Arpino contributed to a number of periodicals and was also editorial adviser for the publishing houses **Einaudi**, Zanichelli and **Mondadori**. His writing always displays a penetrating insight into reality while preserving political autonomy and freedom of thought.

See also: narrative

FRANCESCA PARMEGGIANI

art criticism

The function of the art critic is in part journalistic – to record what is happening in the art world like any other news – and in part commercial – to give an opinion which serves to advise the reader about attending exhibitions, or buying artworks. In Italy, the art market and the exhibition and museum structure are vast. Government plays a substantial role in the presentation, conservation and promotion of the visual arts in recognition of their economic and social importance, and many people visit Italy specifically to look at works of art. However, most of the attention is on the art of the past. There is no 'arts council' type of government financial support for contemporary artists, and few tourists travel to Italy with the intention of viewing recent works. This is reflected in Italian newspapers and magazines, which carry regular sections on literature, music, and cinema but deal much more sporadically with the visual arts; when they do, Italian contemporary art is the poor relation which must jostle for attention with more popular art of the past or from other countries. If one also considers that artists are in commercial competition with each other, the intense nature of much postwar art criticism, with critics attempting to direct a limited limelight upon their own favoured players, becomes understandable, and it is significant that much art criticism has appeared outside the regular press, in the form of manifestos, catalogue essays or books.

Until the Second World War, Italian art criticism was philosophical and largely grounded in aesthetics. Fascism discouraged discussion of the content and meaning of works unless they happened to accord with government programmes. After the war there was intense debate about whether art should serve party political purposes and whether progressive styles implied progressive politics. At its crudest, this took the form of an argument between realists and abstractionists, with Communist Party leader Palmiro **Togliatti** condemning modern styles. Lionello **Venturi**, one of a number of writers who had originally made their mark as art historians, took the opposite view. One might have expected a political conservative to support a realist style, but Venturi's distaste for the state, and his belief in the individual, caused him to favour experimental forms of contemporary art. He was happy to trace a line of progress from his own beloved artists of the Renaissance through to the modernists of the 1950s, thus conferring artistic legitimacy on the latter.

Another concern, given the poor domestic economy at the time, was with seeking international attention and markets, which raised the question of whether this could best be done by employing a regional, a national or an international style. Venturi contributed to the international marketing of the unremarkable **Gruppo degli otto** by describing them as independents, free of petty political influence. Giulio Carlo **Argan**, on the other hand, argued for the need for Italian artists to replace their native traditions with a generic European modernity, while Cesare Brandi clung to the idea of a regional art, deriving from the characteristics of the northern Italian landscape.

Since modernism implies the idea of the avantgarde and a decisive break with the past, the attempts by historians-turned-critics to relate modern art to the past were not always successful. Furthermore, the styles of the 1950s and 1960s brought new values and techniques which could

not be described in terms of traditional art history. If art did not aspire to 'beauty', but instead claimed to be descriptive of the artists and society that produced it, then art criticism needed the vocabularies of disciplines such as sociology, psychoanalysis and semiotics, and the next generation of Italian critics were, in fact, imaginative writers familiar with these languages.

The semiotic critics did not seek to judge the technical quality of an artwork, or describe its links to tradition. Instead, they sought to explain its semiotic functioning and levels of meaning. The *critica militante* ('militant' or 'engaged' criticism) was progressive criticism intent on social change, and judged works on the basis of their political message. Critics again became personal sponsors of artists and movements. In 1961 Argan organized **Continuità** (Continuity); in 1967 Germano **Celant** recognized *arte povera*; and in 1979 Achille **Bonito Oliva** coined the term '**transavantgarde**'. In each case their criticism was unashamedly partizan, designed to promote the movement they had described.

After the 1960s the language of art criticism became more 'artistic' and harder to understand, in part because of its blending of a variety of discourses. At times it overshadowed the artwork itself. Post-structuralism recognized critical writing itself as an art, valuing the explanation in place of the thing. Certainly, critics seemed in no way beholden to the artist, or of lesser status. The journal *Flash Art* gave ample space to obscure metaphor, such as Bonito Oliva's tortuous pronouncement:

> The initial precept is that of art as the production of a catastrophe, a discontinuity that destroys the tectonic balance of language to favor a precipitation into the substance of the [imaginary], neither as a nostalgic return, nor as a reflux, but a flowing that drags inside itself the sedimentation of many things which exceed a simple return to the private and the simple.
>
> (Bonito Oliva, 1990: 62)

Other critics have spoken out against the dubious morality of the partizan review and the unintelligibility of much 'artistic' writing. Renato **Barilli** has noted that the *critica militante* leads to poor writing, because the critic is too close to the subject, is writing in haste and in brevity for a particular occasion, and too often takes on the role of defending the artist. Gillo **Dorfles** believes that Germano Celant concentrates on an explanation of the semiotic functioning of the work, at the expense of any judgements of value or taste. Federico **Zeri** has spoken of the need to balance formal, contextual, and aesthetic judgements of the work of art. In seeming to promote art, critics such as Celant and Bonito Oliva have succeeded in promoting themselves, to a point where they are far better known today than most living Italian artists.

Further reading

Bonito Oliva, A. (1979) 'The Italian Transavant-garde', trans. M. Moore in G. Politi and H. Kontova (eds), *Flash Art: Two Decades of History: XXI years*, Cambridge, MA: MIT Press, 1990.

Gonzalez-Palacios, A. (1988) 'The Flight From Boredom: Italian Writing on Art Since the War', *Apollo*, May: 342–5.

Vetrocqu, M.E. (1989) 'National Style and the Agenda for Abstract Painting in Post-War Italy', *Art History* 12 (4): 448–71.

MAX STAPLES

art movements

In the postwar period, art in Italy has followed a course parallel to the developments in art elsewhere in Europe and the United States but with some unique features. Immediately after the Second World War, the USA eagerly embraced abstract expressionism. In Italy, however, realism had never achieved an official status under Fascism, and so it still retained some attraction and credibility. As a result, Italian art generally retained closer links with figuration and with the figurative tradition, and this provided it with a basis for moving beyond modernism in the 1980s through the innovations of the **transavantgarde**.

Art and Italy

In the second half of the twentieth century, art has tended to be international with the same styles appearing everywhere throughout the developed world and enjoying much the same fortunes. Museums of modern art, wherever they are situated, have all developed similar collections.

Italy, with close economic and cultural links to Europe and the Americas, has reflected international trends in the visual arts much more than it has driven them. The broad outline of the international history of art since the Second World War – abstract expressionism, minimalism, pop, conceptual art, neo-expressionism – applies to Italy as well, despite some minor difference in labels. There are, however, some important features specific to contemporary Italian art. One is the unavoidable influence of Italy's unique artistic heritage. Another is the extraordinary proliferation of artists' groups. In fact, it seems that little artistic action took place in Italy without those involved first forming a group and issuing a manifesto, although often this was all that the group did as a unit before its members quickly went their separate ways. A third unique feature is the importance of critics and curators in assembling groups of artists, giving them a title and explanation, and mounting an exhibition or writing a book about them. Lionello **Venturi** and Astratto-Concreto, Gillo **Dorfles** and the MAC, Carlo **Argan** and **Continuità**, Germano **Celant** and *arte povera*, and Achille **Bonito Oliva** and the transavant-garde are all examples of the crucial intervention of art historians and critics in the creation of the artistic phenomenon that they claimed to be discovering.

Unique artistic heritage

Italy has an artistic patrimony unlike that of any other country. It is a highly-developed country but it is also riddled with the remains of the past in the form of architectural ruins, museums such as the Uffizi and the Vatican, churches filled with sculpture, painting, and mosaic, and sculptures and fountains in public places. No Italian could avoid acquaintance with other periods and styles. This might be seen as both an advantage and a disadvantage. While it provides artists and the population at large with a wide education in art history, it also makes the country itself into a sort of museum, and some artists have felt the past to be a dead weight from which it was necessary to escape in order to develop their own particular talents. Reacting to this dead weight of the past, in the early part of the twentieth century the Futurists suggested nothing less than the destruction of all museums and all art of the past.

Struggle of the styles

Postwar Italian art might be considered in terms of two broad styles, figurative and non-figurative, each of which may be further sub-divided. Figurative art uses recognizable shapes which represent objects, be they real or imaginary. In its realist mode, figurative art combines real objects in a naturalistic setting. Other figurative forms, such as surrealism or expressionism, may depict objects, but in a way which is not intended to be a representation of physical nature. They may be stylized or made partially abstract by devices such as unnatural colours, distortion of shapes, unnatural perspective or bizarre combinations of elements. Non-figurative art (often called abstract art) does not represent physical objects. Instead, it explores the expressive possibilities of colour and shape. It can be formal, in the sense that it uses regular shapes and composition, or informal, that is, free-flowing and spontaneous.

Broadly speaking, modern art abandoned realism, regarding straightforward representation as 'artless' or more properly the domain of photography. Instead it oscillated between non-figurative styles, which tended to quickly exhaust themselves, and stylized figurative styles, which placed some importance on subject matter.

In Russia, Germany, and the Americas, realism came to be poorly regarded after the 1930s, when it was used by governments of various hues for propaganda purposes. Its simple, easy-to-read style was regarded as the ideal means for communicating political messages to the masses. Hitler – to take only the most obvious example – openly derided abstract art and its complexity, characterizing it as the work of degenerate perverts and, in reaction, most politically progressive artists came to identify with modernism. There was, however, no such reaction in Italy. Under Fascism there was an official style of monumental architecture, and the Fascist government encouraged a great deal of

vaguely neoclassical sculpture, exerting its influence through assigning commissions and organising art exhibitions. Significantly, however, Fascism never attempted to gain total control over art and various different artistic currents persisted under it so that, after the war, Italians did not automatically associate social realism with the art of the totalitarian state and modernism with freedom (see also **fascism and neo-fascism**). In Italy, both forms were available for use by 'progressive' artists, and it was individual artists who had enjoyed established careers under the Fascists, such as **de Chirico** and **Morandi**, who were somewhat discredited, rather than any particular styles.

The 1940s

The 1940s were marked by debate between the figurative and non-figurative camps. In the first years after the Second World War, artists in Rome, Milan, and Venice banded together in the Fronte nuovo delle arti (New Front of the Arts) which included such diverse figures as Renato **Guttuso**, Emilio **Vedova**, Renato Birolli and Giulio Turcato, who represented quite different artistic trends. The only common denominator of the group was a past opposition to Fascism.

Argument soon arose, reflecting political orientations, and carried out in a spate of newspaper articles, pamphlets and books. Guttuso, the leading exponent of realism, was a staunch member of the Communist Party (see **PCI**) and followed the official party line which decreed that art should serve the class struggle. Other artists argued that art should be detached from politics, or that realism was not the best way to achieve socialist ends. Carla **Accardi**, Piero Dorazio and Giulio Turcato established the abstract Forma (Form) Group in Rome in 1947. In their manifesto, they claimed freedom for the individual to believe in Marxism, but without rigid adherence to the Party line. They styled themselves 'formalists *and* Marxists', and condemned realism as spent and conformist, all of which made confrontation with the Party inevitable. Writer Elio **Vittorini**, himself a sort of symbolic realist, suggested that artists should be free to at least pretend they were autonomous, and not be obliged to 'suonare il piffero per la rivoluzione' (play the pipe for the revolution).

At the **Venice Biennale** of 1948 came the definitive break between realists and abstract art. What seemed the golden years of neorealism turned out to be its last hurrah, as abstract groups began to proliferate. Renewed artistic contact with France encouraged a formalist style, variously described as concrete art, geometric abstraction or post-cubist. In Milan, MAC (the Movement of Concrete Art) was developed in 1948 under the influence of critic Gillo Dorfles, with artists Bruno **Munari** and Atanasio Soldati. Lucio **Fontana**, in the same city, began *spazialismo* (spatialism). In Rome, *Arti Visive* (Visual Arts), a magazine dealing with abstraction, was founded, as were Gruppo Origine with Ettore **Colla**, Alberto **Burri** and Giuseppe Capogrossi, and the Fondazione Origine gallery, which exhibited abstract works.

The 1950s

Throughout the 1950s, while older artists such as Guttuso and **Marini** continued to work in a figurative vein, the major developments took place in non-figurative art, on the fault line between formal and informal abstraction. Critic Lionello Venturi oversaw the formation of the **Gruppo degli otto** pittori Italiani (Group of Eight Italian Artists) in 1952, coining the term 'abstract-concrete' to describe their work. The group was in fact quite varied, although Afro, Birolli and Santomaso certainly had formalist qualities. As American influences became dominant, there was a shift towards informalism. For the sake of clarity, we should note that whilst some Italian critics distinguish between abstract expressionism, action painting and *arte informale* (or '*informel*' as it is called in France), others use them quite interchangeably. However, despite differences between artists and countries, all these terms generally refer to an art that is gestural, which reveals the mark of the artist in creating the work. The artwork is thus a spontaneous record rather than a premeditated outcome. This was characteristic of Burri, Vedova and Fontana, and also of Sergio Romiti and Mario Mafai.

Sculpture in the 1950s, such as the work of **Colla** and the **Pomodoro** brothers, also tended

toward abstraction, though here the distinction between formal and informal is less valid since, by virtue of its medium, it is difficult for sculpture to be purely gestural or devoid of intended form.

The 1960s and 1970s

By the 1960s, the limitations of the wilful individualism of informalism had become obvious. While Vedova continued in this vein, other artists turned back to exploring the possibilities of pattern making and optical effects. The spirit of MAC was revived in 1960 by the Concrete Art exhibition in Zurich which included works by Dorazio, **Manzoni** and Castellani. The idea that the work was something beyond merely the process carried out by the artist dovetailed with the writings of Umberto **Eco** on the open work and the role of the reader. The notion of art as research and therefore a group activity with logical components took hold to the extent that a plethora of new groups appeared: Gruppo T in Milan and Gruppo N in Padua, Gruppo I, Sperimentale P and Gruppo Operativo R in Rome, Tempo 3 in Genoa, Gruppo Atoma in Livorno and Gruppo V in Rimini.

In 1961, as a more specific reaction to *informale*, the group **Continuità** (Continuity) was formed, championed by critic Carlo Argan and advocating formal abstraction with a return to the values of composition and reference to the artistic past rather than spontaneity and the fragmentation of informalism. Argan also spoke of 'the sign', a recognizable, considered element specific to a certain artist. The group included Consagra, Dorazio, Turcato and the Pomodoro brothers.

During the 1960s the real appeared in art in two unusual ways. The first was pop, which used representation of real things and objects themselves, sometimes of the most banal sort, such as everyday bits and pieces and advertising. **Baj** used collage to achieve political satire, while **Schifano** reproduced street signage and television screens. The second was through *arte povera*. The works produced by this loose-knit movement did not necessarily stand for anything else. They drew attention to the qualities of the material itself, at times raw and at other times already elaborated, such as Pascali's *Due metri cubi di terra* (Two Cubic

Metres of Earth), which was just that, Prini's *Perimetro d'aria* (Perimeter of Air), and the parrot of **Kounellis**.

Arte povera signalled an attempt to move away from the production of individual items for an elite art market, in response to a growing disillusionment with consumer society and the Italian state. The social and political upheaval of 1968–9 marked a watershed in the production of art, after which many artists declared easel painting to be dead and took to forms of conceptual art and performance, which placed strong emphasis on delivering a message. **Merz**, **Boetti** and **Fabro** produced conceptual work; **Pistoletto** progressed from his painted mirrors to live street theatre.

Despite the claims of some of its exponents, art turned out to be a rather ineffective weapon for social change. The political and economic traumas of the 1970s played themselves out without obvious assistance from artists. What appeal remained in the old ideologies was finally exhausted, and with them, the myth of the value of the avantgarde and experimentation.

The return of figuration

The stage was set for the revival of the processes and traditions of art by a group of painters whom Bonito Oliva labelled the transavantgarde. **Clemente**, **Paladino**, **Cucchi** and **Chia** led a return to a figurative art of personal expression, which made reference to the art of the past. It was an 'untopical' art, which did not attempt to comment on the events of the day. Whereas movements of the 1960s had eschewed technique and argued that everyone was, or could be, an artist, the transavantgarde was elitist, elevating the artist to the position of a hero gifted with extraordinary technical skills and imagination, an attitude which polarized other artists.

Despite Bonito Oliva's claims for its uniqueness, the transavantgarde has proved to be the rule rather than the exception. It is part of a much larger trend by artists to return to the figurative styles and motifs of the past. **De Chirico**, who had worked in the same style for fifty years and been increasingly derided for it, came back into fashion. **Mariani** produced polished works in the style of David and Mengs, albeit with more surreal subject matter. Ubaldo Bartolini's landscapes are uncanny imitations of Claude and Poussin. These revivalists have been given a swag of names: new romantics, *anacronisti*, *pittura colta* painters, *ipermanieristi*. However, their work is not mere copying. It is informed and enriched by the entire course of modern art, so it is abstract and conceptual, as well as having aesthetic and representational values.

See also: art criticism

Further reading

Braun, E. (ed.) (1989) *Italian Art in the 20th Century: Painting and Sculpture 1900–1988*, Munich: Prestel Verlag (exhibition catalogue, chronological articles and many colour illustrations).

Celant, G. (ed.) (1994) *The Italian Metamorphosis, 1943–1968*, New York: Guggenheim Museum (exhibition catalogue, wide-ranging coverage of art, photography, cinema, design and fashion; valuable for colour and black and white illustrations and reproduction of documents).

MAX STAPLES

arte concreta (concrete art)

In very broad terms, non-figurative abstract art can be divided into two tendencies: one is expressive and spontaneous (see **L'Informale**) whilst the other is a calculated art which is non-representational and non-illusory, and which explores instead the properties of its own materials and forms, thus representing only itself. Although this distinction is not absolute, and some artists produced works in both categories, it was the latter tendency, strongly under the influence of cubism, which was the dominant form of abstraction in Italy in the 1940s and early 1950s.

In 1947 the Forma group, which included Carla **Accardi**, Pietro **Consagra** and Giulio Turcato, declared itself both formalist and Marxist. In declaring that pure form is all that exists, it not only directed itself against realism, which it described as spent and conformist, but also against any art with expressive or psychological qualities. Furthermore, its condemnation of all arbitrary elements in art, such as reliance on the subconscious, placed it in direct opposition to that aspect of surrealism that would later become central to abstract expressionism.

The Movimento per l'arte concreta (MAC), formed in 1948 by critic Gillo **Dorfles** and artists Atanasio Soldati and Bruno **Munari**, claimed still greater purity by rejecting any social or political programme for their art. Gruppo Origine, founded in Rome by Ettore **Colla**, Alberto **Burri** and Giuseppe Capogrossi, called for a reduction of art to elementary forms with a complete renunciation of decorative and illusionistic effects, although it did concede an expressive function for the artist.

The mid- to late 1950s came to be strongly influenced by *L'Informale* and abstract expressionism. However, of the two abstract tendencies – one expressive and the other geometrical – it was the more ordered variety that eventually won out, and led to the movements of the 1960s. One reason was the rise of the idea of art as a form of research, to be carried out by groups. A number of groups appeared, all claiming to be engaged in 'research' into abstract design: Gruppo T in Milan, Gruppo N in Padua, Gruppo I, Operativo R and Sperimentale P in Rome, Tempo 3 in Genoa, Gruppo Atoma in Livorno and Gruppo V in Rimini.

In 1961 the group **Continuità** (Continuity) was formed by the artists **Consagra**, Dorazio, **Turcato** and the brothers **Pomodoro**. The name was a reference to the need for a link with the past, in a formal abstraction that showed a return to composition. The group's champion, the critic Giulio Carlo **Argan**, held these up as positive values in opposition to the fragmentary and spontaneous nature of informalism. There was also interest in 'the sign' as a recognizable considered motif, as in the regular, non-representational shapes created by sculptor Arnaldo Pomodoro.

Piero **Manzoni**'s 'achromes' were intended to be completely devoid of expressive or representational qualities. A picture, he said famously, says nothing. Thus, in spite of the overwhelming force of personality that abstract expressionism imposed on the viewer, concrete art moved ineluctably towards the notion of the 'open work' (see Umberto **Eco**).

Further reading

'Manifestos' (1994) in G. Celant, *The Italian Metamorphosis, 1943-1968*, New York: Guggenheim Museum, 708–25.

MAX STAPLES

arte povera

A loosely associated art movement of the late 1960s and early 1970s, *arte povera* (poor art) presented all sorts of objects as art. Exponents included Pino Pascali, Gilberto **Zorio**, Mario **Merz**, Luciano **Fabro**, Michelangelo **Pistoletto**, Alighiero **Boetti**, Emilio Prini, Giovanni **Anselmo**, Jannis **Kounellis**, Giuseppe Penone and Giulio **Paolini**.

The name was coined in 1967 for a group exhibition in Genoa, Arte povera-Im spazio, curated by Germano **Celant**. By 'poor', Celant meant works which were not necessarily highly elaborated, and which could well be things already existing in the world. The exhibition demonstrated a new interest in materials themselves, such as Pascali's *Due metri cubi di terra* (Two Cubic Metres of Earth). Prini articulated an empty space with lights in the corners and centre in his *Perimetro d'aria* (Perimeter of Air). Soon after, Kounellis exhibited a parrot.

The 'poor' was also intended politically. In the heightened political atmosphere of the day, Celant positioned the movement as anti-capitalist, anti-consumerist and opposed to the creation of unique masterpieces for a small elite. In a boisterous manifesto in *Flash Art* of November 1967, Celant described *arte povera* as guerrilla art, and praised its freedom and energy. The critic Achille **Bonito Oliva** also championed the movement as an art of social protest, opposed to the status quo and to 'the System'.

Over the next few years, in exhibitions in Italy and throughout Europe, *arte povera* manifested a freedom of materials and influences, a renewed interest in the personal and subjective, and a willingness to evoke attitudes and moods without precise meanings. It tended toward installation and untitled works which were abstract and non-figurative even when composed of natural materials. Bonito Oliva described the artist as organizer rather than creator, bringing forward natural elements which could include the artist's own actions without judgement or manipulation. In this respect, *arte povera* differed from the formal concerns of minimalism.

Celant's manifestos were written as programmes rather than description, so it is hardly surprising that in reality the works of the *arte povera* artists are sometimes more refined than he suggested. Furthermore, although they may have been subversive of the accepted definition of art at the time, they never made direct statements, nor did they have any discernible impact on the contemporary political situation.

By the 1980s, the movement had been superseded by the return to figurative art and painting. The claim that art could change the world now seemed naive and outdated, and Celant and Bonita Oliva moved on to champion other, more fashionable concerns.

Further reading

Celant, G. (1967) '*Arte Povera*: Notes for a Guerrilla War', in G. Politi, G. Kontova and H. Kontova (eds), *Flash Art: Two Decades of History: XXI years*, Cambridge, MA: MIT Press, 1990.

—— (1969) *Arte Povera: Conceptual, Actual or Impossible Art*, London: Studio Vista.

MAX STAPLES

arts festivals

Italy's arts festivals are numerous and widespread. They include international exhibitions such as the **Venice Biennale**, the contemporary arts extravaganza held every odd-numbered year in the numerous pavilions of the Giardini Pubblici in Venice, and the annual **Spoleto Festival** of the Two Worlds, a two-month long festival of classical concerts, films, ballet, street theatre and performing arts.

Many of Italy's arts festivals are held during the summer months in major cities, resort areas or smaller provincial towns. The venues for many of these festivals are often historical and monumental settings. For example, Rome offers open air opera at the Baths of Caracalla and concerts at the Campidoglio in July. The Sferisterio in Macerata in the Marche region and the Roman arena in Verona also become music venues every year during the summer months, and the Panatenee Pompeiane is a music festival held in the ruins of Pompeii during the last week in August. In Siracusa, the ancient theatre becomes the site for Greek drama in May and June.

Summer brings special programmes of music and culture to Milan, the Milano d'estate in July and Vacanza a Milano in August. In nearby Brescia from June to September, the Estate Aperta offers an impressive array of concerts, theatrical performances and films in churches, courtyards and piazze. Sabbioneta, a town close to Mantova, holds a summer music festival. Music, theatre and dance are offered in Turin in the month of June when the city invites international companies to the Sere d'Estate festival. Settembre Musica in Turin is a month-long extravaganza of classical concerts performed in various venues in the city. The Asti Teatro, which is held during the last two weeks of June and the first week of July, presents theatrical productions from medieval to modern and includes jazz, drama and dance. Bologna's newest night-time summer entertainment is the city-sponsored Bologna Sogna series, which features shows and concerts in the city's piazza and museums in July and August. In the same months, Ferrara hosts Ferrara Estate, a music and theatre festival that brings a diverse number of performances to the city's piazze. For one week at the end of June or the beginning of July, the Settimana Estense features at Modena with special exhibits, art shows and an authentic historic parade. During July and August the city sponsors a summer music, ballet, and theatre series called Sipario in Piazza. The city of Parma sponsors a summer music festival called Concerti nei chiostri, which features classical music in the local churches and cloisters. From the last week in June to the last week in August, the Church of San Francesco in Ravenna sponsors Ravenna in Festival featuring operas, concerts, folk music and drama.

The last half of July offers an opera and theatre festival at Barga near Lucca, and the Estate Fiesolana is a summer festival held from mid-June to August featuring music, cinema, ballet and theatre in the Tuscan town which overlooks Florence. Siena and Stresa both offer a Settimana musicale in August. The Estate Musicale Lucchese stretches from July to September, and the September period is taken up with a combination of artistic, athletic and folkloric presentations.

In July and August, Estate a Perugia offers a series of musical, cinematic and dance performances. Macerata, a little-known provincial capital in the Marche region, hosts an annual Stagione Lirica offering opera and ballet performances in an open air venue. Amandola, a hill village in the Marche, hosts a week-long international theatre festival in the first week of September. Focusing on participation, the festival overcomes language barriers through mime and movement performances and workshops. Viterbo hosts a baroque music festival from mid-June to July. The village of Scanno in Abruzzo is a well-preserved medieval village surrounded by mountains, which holds a classical musical festival every August. Martina Franca in the Puglia region puts on the Festival della Valle d'Itria, an opera, classical and jazz festival at the end of July and the first week in August. The city of Lecce comes alive in July and August with the Estate Musicale Leccese a festival of music and dance.

In Sicily, from July to September the city of Cefalu hosts Incontri d'estate, outdoor concerts of classical, contemporary and Sicilian folk music as well as opera. The city of Taormina hosts Taormina Arte, an international festival of theatre, music and film in its Greek theatre from July through September.

In Sardinia, the city of Cagliari hosts an arts festival in its amphitheatre which includes concerts, operas and classical plays. In Alghero in July and August the classical music of the Estate musicale internazionale fills the cloisters of the Church of San Francesco.

Some of Italy's festivals celebrate composers who achieved international fame. For example, the music of Puccini is performed in an annual celebration from the end of July to mid-August in his home town of Torre del Lago, and Rossini's music is celebrated in Pesaro from mid-August to September. In September, Bergamo celebrates its renowned native-born composer with a festival of Gaetano Donizetti's lesser known works. The

Festival Vivaldi takes place in Venice in early September, and in summer Vivaldi's music is featured in a concert series in the church of Santa Maria della Pietà, where he was choirmaster.

There are a number of other well-known music festivals in Italy. Florence itself offers Maggio Musicale, one of the most famous festivals of opera and classical music in Italy. Contrary to what the name suggests, it occurs not exclusively in May but continuously from late April to early July with additional offerings in October and November. Events are staged at the Teatro Comunale, the Teatro della Pergola, the Palazzo dei Congressi and occasionally in the Boboli Gardens.

There is a chamber music festival in Città di Castello every August and September. In Brescia, there is a universally acclaimed two-month International Piano Festival. Ravello's numerous classical music festivals are held the weeks of New Year's Day, Easter and during parts of June, July and September. These concerts are held in the cathedral and in the gardens of the Villa Rufolo, usually hosting musicians of international renown.

In addition to classical music, a number of other musical genres are also represented in Italian festivals. Jazz is celebrated at the Riva di Garda International Jazz and Folklore festival. The Umbria Jazz Festival is held in Perugia every July and August, and the Siena Jazz festival also takes place in August. Pistoia attracts European visitors during the last weekend of June for the Pistoia Blues concert series, and Salerno hosts an International Blues festival in July. There is also an International Music Festival in the last half of May in Naples and a Neapolitan song contest at Piedigrotta in the first half of September. The city of Umbertide hosts an annual summer rock festival.

Naturally enough, Italy also boasts a number of important film festivals. In addition to the Venice Film Festival – the oldest international film festival in the world – international film festivals are held in Taormina, Messina, Salerno and Verona. Sorrento hosts an international cinema convention in October. Pesaro hosts the International Festival of New Films during the second and third weeks of June in an effort to show rarely screened films, new and old, commercially and independently produced.

Though not technically a festival, Italy's **opera** season also looms large in the cultural calendar, beginning in December and running through to May or June. The main opera houses in Italy are **La Scala** in Milan, the Teatro dell'Opera in Rome, the Teatro Comunale in Florence and the Teatro San Carlo in Naples. Other major cities also have opera houses with regular seasons. Bergamo's opera season lasts from September to November. Trieste's regular opera season in the Teatro Verdi runs from November to May, but also features a six-week operetta season in June and July. There are also countless other lesser known venues with regular opera performances and, in addition to opera, many Italian cities also run regular theatre and ballet seasons.

See also: music festivals; opera

BERNADETTE LUCIANO

Agenzia Spaziale Italiana

The Agenzia Spaziale Italiana (ASI) or Italian Space Agency was instituted in 1988 with responsibility for managing and co-ordinating all Italian participation in space exploration and research. With an annual budget of around 700 million dollars, the Agency is responsible for preparing and implementing recurrent national five-year plans of research and development in the areas of space technology, earth sciences and telecommunications. ASI is also charged with co-ordinating all Italian participation in the programmes of the European Space Agency (ESA), which Italy helped to found in 1975 and to which it contributes financially. Both as part of ESA and independently, ASI co-operates with other national and international space agencies such as NASA on collaborative projects such as the permanent International Space Station (ISS), which Italy is helping to build and on which it will have allocated space and resources for ongoing research.

GINO MOLITERNO

Asor Rosa, Alberto

b. 23 September 1933, Rome

Literary historian and politician

Professor of Italian Literature at the University of Rome, 'La Sapienza' and a pupil of Natalino **Sapegno**, Asor Rosa was a long-time member of the **PCI** (Italian Communist Party) and from 1989–90 directed the party weekly *Rinascita*. In the early 1960s Asor Rosa edited two influential journals on the Left, *Classe operaia* (Working Class) and *Quaderni Rossi* (Red Notebooks). His most important works have treated political and social issues as well as literary and cultural topics. In *Scrittori e popolo* (Writers and the People) (1985) he traces the thread of populism in Italian literature from the Risorgimento through to **Pasolini**, while questioning **Gramsci**'s notion of a 'national-popular literature'. Asor Rosa has also written extensively on seventeenth-century literature and society. In 1979 he was elected a member of the Chamber of Deputies, only to resign a year later (see also **Parliament**). Since 1982 he has been editor-in-chief of *Letteratura italiana* (Italian Literature), published by **Einaudi**.

LAURENCE SIMMONS

athletics

The efforts of CONI (the Italian Olympic Committee) and FIDAL (the Italian Track and Field Federation) have consistently put Italy among the world's top competitors (see **Olympics**). Italian teams excel in disciplines such as indoor cycling, fencing and shooting. In track and field, special mention should go to Pietro Mennea, whose record for the 200 metres was unbeaten for more than sixteen years, high-jumper Sara Simeoni, and long-distance runner Alberto Cova. Many victories have come from marathon-runners: Orlando Pizzolato won the New York City marathon in 1984 and 1985, and later winners have included Gianni Poli in 1986, Giacomo Leone in 1996 and Franca Fiacconi in 1998.

Gelindo Bordin became Italy's first marathon gold medalist in Seoul in 1988, and won the Boston marathon in 1990. The most important Italian annual meet is at Sestriere, in the northwestern Alps, where the prize for anyone setting a new world record is a **Ferrari** car. In September 1996, after extensive renovations, the historic Arena of Milan was re-opened for the Grand Prix, the competition that determines the best athlete in each class.

PAOLO VILLA

Auditel

Following an agreement in 1984 between **RAI** (state television) and the **private television** networks which had emerged in the wake of the deregulation of television broadcasting in 1975 (see **broadcasting**), Auditel was instituted as an independent research organization for monitoring the viewing habits of 'typical' Italians by a system of electronic meters attached to the television sets of anonymous 'average' families. Monitoring began in December 1985 and television programming soon came to be almost completely determined by the Auditel ratings, especially during the 'television wars' of the late 1980s. The credibility of the agency's figures was often widely contested, particularly on the grounds of too limited a sample (originally there were 633 meters for all of Italy, later increased to 1,300 and finally in 1997 to 8,000 meters, monitoring 5,000 families) but Auditel ratings continued to be the touchstone for television programming well into the 1990s. By this time the agency had expanded its survey methods to include regular personal interviews and also began to publish its data on the World Wide Web.

GINO MOLITERNO

Aulenti, Gaetana

b. 4 December 1927, Palazzolo della Stella, Udine

Architect and designer

Gae Aulenti belongs to the second wave of Milanese postwar designers. A frequent contributor to **Casabella** after graduating from the Milan Politecnico in 1954, she developed fastidious furniture designs in the 1950s and 1960s. She also contributed considerably to the European art museum design genre, her first project being the Musée d'Orsay, involving the transformation of a Parisian railway station into a museum (completed 1986), a feat which earned her international renown. There followed the Palazzo Grassi in Venice, the Catalonian Art museum and the Greater Istanbul Municipality Art Museum. She designed exhibitions for **Olivetti** and **Fiat**. Whether working on integrating theatre and regional landscape (Laboratorio teatrale in Prato, 1975–79), on the church of Santa Maria Novella and **Michelucci**'s train station in Florence, or just providing a new setting within an existing structure (the Beaubourg's Modern Art Museum), Aulenti's solutions always demonstrate unusual clarity but often provoke controversy.

See also: interior design

Further reading

Petranzan, M. (1997) *Gae Aulenti*, New York: Rizzoli (a well-referenced, comprehensive review of Aulenti's opus).

GORDANA KOSTICH

Aut aut

One of the more important Italian philosophical periodicals, *Aut aut* (its Latin title alludes to existential choice and, in particular, Soren Kierkegaard's 'Either/Or') was founded by Enzo **Paci** (1911–76), one of the major exponents of existentialism in Italy. Often using *Aut aut* as his vehicle, Paci examined the existential links between subjectivity and historical materialism and also spearheaded an influential 'return' to the phenomenology of Edmund Husserl in the 1960s. In recent decades, *Aut aut* has been important for the introduction of French post-structuralist thought to Italy including the writings of Foucault, Lacan, Derrida, Lyotard and Deleuze, as well as furnishing a forum for contemporary re-readings of Marx, Freud and Nietzsche. *Aut aut* has also provided a focus for philosophers of the pensiero debole (Weak Thought) school, and Gianni **Vattimo**, Remo Bodei and Giorgio **Agamben** are frequent contributors.

LAURENCE SIMMONS

autonomia

Autonomia (autonomy) was an influential topic for debate among a dissident Marxist intelligentsia in the 1960s, and a practical aspiration among variegated components of left-wing youth culture in the 1970s. The theoretical development of the term, offering a new analysis of the developmental trends in capitalist society, owes most to the writings of Raniero Panzieri in **Quaderni Rossi**. Panzieri's emphasis on the factory as a key site in the struggle for a Communist society, retrieved from **Gramsci**'s then largely-ignored early writings on the worker councils of 1919–21, was elaborated in particular by Mario Tronti. The notion of 'autonomy' was hailed as marking a decisive advance for Marxist-Leninist theory in two respects. First, the development of capitalist work organization generated simultaneously capacities for subordination and insubordination: it created the social knowledge, relations and needs among workers which undermined its own power. This argument resisted any suggestion that capitalist society tended progressively to integrate the working-class and narcotize its interest in, and capacity for, socialist revolution. Second, emphasis on the overriding significance of conflicts in the workplace devalued the importance of working-class political organization and the conquest of state power. Left-wing parties and trade unions naturally regarded with suspicion a school of thought which implied a substantial reduction in the historical importance of their own role as agents of political enlightenment and collective mobilization.

Until the 1970s, interest in 'autonomy' remained confined to the fields of theory and to historical investigations of its hitherto unnoticed existence among subordinate classes. Its translation into active extreme left-wing politics in the 1970s derived mainly from three sources. First, the groups of the extraparliamentary Left found the notion of 'autonomy' a useful basis for their distinctive political genealogies and a ready framework for criticism of 'reformist' **PCI** and **trade unions**, mired in capitalist rationality. Second, the emergence of dissident youth and feminist cultures suggested that an increasingly heterogeneous society had outrun capitalism's ability to satisfy its needs. Third, the expansion of exploitative 'informal economies' presaged the replacement of a disciplined workforce built around stable careers and job satisfaction by a disaffected marginal proletariat with Luddite predilections.

Such diverse ideas found equally loosely-organized expression in the many-hued *autonomia* movement of 1973–77, built around 'proletarian youth circles' and 'social centres', with its cultural capital in Bologna and its political strongholds in Milan (the broadsheet *Rosso*), Rome and Padua (Radio Sherwood). Political leadership was claimed mainly by academics (Negri, Piperno) who detected proof of the growth of 'autonomy' in political violence and industrial sabotage. Support waned following deaths in confrontations with police provoked by *autonomia* groups in 1977, disappearing altogether in 1979 after the arrest of its leading figures on charges of involvement in violence, followed by their long pre-trial imprisonment, conviction and flight abroad.

See also: Radio Alice; Red Brigades; extraparliamentary Left; terrorism

Further reading

Lotringer, S. and Marazzi, C. (eds) (1980) *Italy: Autonomia. Post-Political Politics*, special edition of *Semiotext(e)* 3 (3) (an extensive series of readings by both protagonists and antagonists of *autonomia*).

Lumley, R. (1990) *States of Emergency: Cultures of Revolt in Italy from 1968 to 1978*, London, Verso.

Tronti, M. (1966) *Operai e capitale* (Workers and Capital), Turin: Einaudi (major work of influential theorist).

DAVID MOSS

autostrada network

In the interwar period, Italy had by comparison with other European countries only a very small, non-integrated network of highways (less than 500 km in 1945, built up by private companies and almost exclusively centred on Milan and the northwest regions). The gap began to be bridged only in the 1960s–1970s, when both mass motorization and tourism gained momentum and the development of a national highway system became one of the main goals of the economic planners.

At that time **IRI**, through its affiliate Società Autostrade, made massive investments and played a leading role in boosting the growth of the network, but private companies also received concessions from the state and the highway system rapidly expanded from 1,500 to nearly 5,000 km. The industrialized regions of northern and central Italy came to be increasingly connected by high-speed motorways which also linked to northern Europe through long tunnels passing under the Alps, and for the first time the network was also extended southwards through long-distance highways along both the Adriatic and Tyrrhenian coasts. The Mezzogiorno (southern Italy) was thus brought nearer to the rest of Italy, but it nevertheless continued to suffer a wide gap in comparison with the rest of the country, while the main legs – the north–south motorway Milan to Rome, the so-called Autostrada del Sole (Sun Highway), and the west–east leg Turin to Trieste – became increasingly congested. This situation provoked widespread public dissatisfaction, as traffic by both private cars and trucks grew dramatically (the vehicles per km ratio increased from about 15,000 a year in 1970 to over 55,000 in the early 1990s) and conditions, especially in peak holiday periods, deteriorated. In fact, public investments were stopped in the mid-1970s and the autostrada network has remained practically at a standstill ever since (there were 5,550 km of toll highways and tunnels in mid-1990s, plus some 900 km of non-toll routes). Subsequently, both Società Autostrade and private concessionaire companies submitted a cluster of new plans to the Ministry for Public Works, related mainly to projects for the building of 1,000 km of new highways in the industrialized northern regions, but none of these have been carried out. Another project for doubling the 90 km Florence to Bologna leg across the Apennine mountains (actually the most crowded highway in Italy, with up to 50,000 vehicles a day and daily traffic jams) provoked fierce opposition from environmentalist organizations, not to mention wearisome bargaining between national and local governments, and so exists only on paper. Plans for a badly needed refurbishment of the southern route from Salerno to Reggio Calabria (a non-toll and thus unprofitable highway) were also pigeonholed.

Yet managing autostradas has been a remarkable source of profits in recent years, as both traffic and tolls have continued to increase; it is not by chance that concerns such as **Fiat** (through its affiliate Fiatimpresit) and other large building companies have enlarged their shareholdings in private concessionaires, which already run nearly 45 per cent of the toll highways network. Large cash flow and high profitability were expected to aid the privatization of Società Autostrade, which was announced in 1997 by the **Prodi** government, but this venture suddenly faded. As the expected extension of the state concession's expiry date from 2018 to 2038 was rejected by the Corte dei Conti (Court of Accounts), Autostrade's shares plummeted on the stock market and the interest of would-be private shareholders declined. A new programme of privatization was announced by the D'Alema government in 1999. Nevertheless, whatever the future of Società Autostrade, the highway system is in need of action. Northern industry – responsible for 50 per cent of GDP and 65 per cent of all exports – has been expressing alarm at the loss of competitiveness caused by a transport system on the verge of a collapse both domestically and in terms of international links, especially in the northeast where Austria frequently denies transit permission to Italian trucks for environmental reasons. A massive effort to modernize the transport network as a whole (not only motorways but also the **railway system** and ports) is still badly needed in order to avoid serious economic shortcomings in the future.

See also: tourism

STEFANO BATTILOSSI

avantgarde theatre

The immediate postwar era opened the Italian stage to works of American realism, Brechtian epic theatre and French absurdist drama previously banned under Fascism. American realism informs the early wordy drama of writers such as Giuseppe **Patroni Griffi** and Natalia **Ginzburg**, while Giorgio **Strehler** disseminated Brecht's politically conscious theatre throughout Italy from his Piccolo Teatro in Milan. With its own roots in the theatre of Luigi Pirandello, French absurdism in turn influenced the dramatic output of Dino **Buzzati**, Mario Fratti and Enzo **Siciliano**, while French absurdism itself found a precarious haven for production within Italy with the opening of Aldo **Trionfo**'s theatre La Borsa di Arlecchino (Arlecchino's Bag) in Genoa in 1957.

Trionfo, Carmelo **Bene** and Luca **Ronconi** approached dramatic texts critically, each developing different strategies in order to expose and undermine the bourgeois ideological assumptions of the traditional repertoire. Texts were contaminated by extraneous and dialectical elements which allowed their context to be both read and critically deconstructed. Trionfo subjected works of French absurdism to a process of parody and pastiche, peppering them with gags, poems, songs, sketches and striptease in the cabaret tradition. Following the theories of Edoardo **Sanguineti** and the **Gruppo 63**, Ronconi sought to sabotage plays at the metalinguistic level by denaturalizing their language. Ronconi established his reputation with a theatrical production of Ariosto's epic *Orlando Furioso* performed at the **Spoleto Festival** in 1969 by staging different parts of the poem concurrently on separate wagons, thus forcing the audience to choose which portion they wished to follow. Ronconi extended Brechtian dramaturgy by emphasizing an episodic vertical structure over a linear dramatic one, and Brechtian alienation by having his actors serve simultaneously both as narrators and protagonists of the action. In 1977 Ronconi set up his Prato Theatre Workshop, where he has continued his experiments with both new and traditional texts. Bene attacked canonized texts by paring them down in a minimalist manner to what he deemed their ideological bare essentials. He furthered Brechtian estrangement by his use of intrusive dialectical soundtracks, the alienation of the actor's voice, and his evasion of empathetic interpretations and performance techniques.

Italian performance groups of the late 1960s and early 1970s sought to combine the experimentation of their futurist heritage with leftist revolutionary politics, but the utilization of dramatic texts for bringing about sociopolitical transformation bowed to much more aesthetic concerns in the work of Giuliano Vasilicò and Memè Perlini. Based at Teatro Beat '72 in Rome, Vasilicò deployed a parade of theatre pictures, tableaux vivants, slow repetitive movements, suggestive sounds and brief snatches of dialogue to evoke the consciousness of each of his chosen protagonists of different works, namely Marcel Proust, the Marquise de Sade and Shakespeare's Hamlet. Vasilicò left sense perception unmediated by intellectual explanation, so that the audience was left to actively interpret the performances in the manner of 'open works' (see Umberto **Eco**). Perlini's *Pirandello, chi?* (Pirandello, Who?) catapulted him to prominence in 1973. Using only fragments of dialogue from *Sei personaggi in cerca d'autore* (Six Characters in Search of an Author), the piece was an exercise in the intersection of choreographed movements with highly calculated lighting techniques used to decompose and recompose theatrical space and spatial relationships. Perlini's later work continued this preference for spectacle over representation. Postmodern performance groups of the late 1970s and 1980s, such as **La Gaia Scienza** in Rome and Il Carrozzone in Florence (see **Magazzini Criminali**), expanded upon the work of Vasilicò and Perlini by focusing on the semiotics of theatrical language in a more analytical manner. Together with groups such as **Falso Movimento**, Krypton, Stran'amore and Trademark, they rejected literary-dramatic texts in favor of electronic media, surrealistic imagery, pantomime, music and eventually computerization.

Pier Paolo **Pasolini**'s 'Manifesto for a New Theatre' (1968) divided postwar Italian theatre into the Theatre of Chatter and the Theatre of Gesture or Howl. The former designates the talky realist drawing-room plays favoured by the bourgeois *stabili* (state-run theatres), while the latter refers to the tendency of the Italian theatrical avantgarde to discard the verbal in pursuit of anarchic

experimentation emphasizing the visual and ki-
netic. In response to this denigration of the verbal,
Pasolini proposed his own 'Theatre of the Word'
by writing a number of verse dramas between
1968 and 1975. As the plays both aspire to and, at
the same time despair of, political engagement,
they risk the linguistic hermeticism of the dramatic
work of Sanguineti. However, the challenge of
Pasolini's texts provoked innovative and diverse
production techniques from such artists as Vittorio
Gassman, Ronconi and Strehler.

In Milan, Dario **Fo** developed a comically
agitational, politically engaged theatre under his
aegis as autocratic *mattatore* (showman), while his
wife Franca **Rame** created feminist works whose
populist-activist aims corresponded closely to those
of her husband. In Rome, the Teatro della
Maddalena served as the primary venue for
feminist theatre during the 1970s and 1980s,
providing a forum for the plays of Dacia **Maraini**.
Maraini's work ranges from a recurrent preoccupation with the prostitute as icon of female
subjugation in a capitalist society to biting feminist
pastiches of works by Friedrich Schiller and
Aeschylus. In a Shavian manner, Maraini deploys
wit, dialogue and reason to expose the absurdity of
the presuppositions of a male-biased culture.

Beginning in 1971, the Teatro dell'Elfo in Milan
dedicated itself to the representation and address of
youth and urban subcultures. Also in Milan, the
Centro Ricerca per il Teatro (Centre for Theatrical
Research) promoted traditional popular forms of
theatre such as mime, ritual, and street performance, and continued to sponsor various community festivals in accordance with the ideas of
Eugenio **Barba** who, like Pasolini, sought to avoid
the simplistic division of theatre into either
institutional or avantgarde categories. The Piccolo
Teatro di Pontedera and the Teatro all'Orologio in
Rome also served as venues for avantgarde theatre,
the former mounting innovative productions of
canonized texts, while the latter provided a forum
for experimental plays, political satire, cabaret
performance and improvisation.

See also: theatre directors

Further reading

Kirby, M. (1978) 'Italian Theatre Issue,' *The Drama
Review* 22 (1) (a useful 'special issue', contains a
number of articles examining both general
avantgarde tendencies as well as specific performers such as Fo, Perlini, Vasilicò, Gaia Scienza
and others).

Ponte di Pino, O. (1988) *Il nuovo teatro italiano 1975–
1988* (The New Italian Theatre 1975–1988),
Milan: Usher (a rich compilation of material,
photographs, interviews and exhaustive performance lists of all the major protagonists of
avantgarde and postmodern theatre from the
mid-1970s to the late 1980s).

Quadri, F. (ed.) (1977) *L'avanguardia teatrale in Italia*
(The Theatrical Avantgarde in Italy), 2 vols,
Turin: Einaudi (a comprehensive survey of the
theatrical avantgarde movement which includes
essays as well as manifestos and materials).

WILLIAM VAN WATSON

Avati, Giuseppe (Pupi)

b. 3 November 1938, Bologna

Film director

Avati belongs to that generation of the **New
Italian Cinema** that in the 1970s began a search
for new ways to represent the emerging multiple
identities in contemporary Italy while not rejecting
the need for a memory of the past that could be a
bridge to the future. After numerous failed
attempts to get a university degree of some sort,
Avati followed his passion for music and travelled
all over Europe playing clarinet with the Reno-Jazz
Band. In the late 1960s he began directing, and
then produced a long and unending cinematic tale
of the provinces in his region, Emilia-Romagna,
characterized by jazzy tempos as well as by an
often oneiric and mythic dimension. His most
impressive films to date are *Aiutami a sognare* (Help
Me to Dream) (1981), *Regalo di Natale* (Christmas
Present) (1986) and *Storie di ragazzi e ragazze* (*Stories of
Boys and Girls*) (1989).

MANUELA GIERI

Aymonino, Carlo

b. 18 July 1926, Rome

Architect, educator and theoretician

Co-founder of Studio AYDE (1960), Aymonino taught at the University of Rome from 1963 and then at Venice, where he was Dean of Architecture from 1973–79. A member of the editorial board of *Casabella-Continuità* from 1959, he has focused, both in his projects and his theoretical writings, on the relationship between architecture and town planning. As a member of the Associazione per l'Architettura Organica (Association for Organic Architecture), he worked on housing projects for INA-Casa, first with Mario **Ridolfi** and Ludovico **Quaroni** on the Tiburtino development, and later in Matera, Foggia and Brindisi. His building opus is large and diverse. He is also a prolific author with publications ranging from architectural monographs and studies of building typology to a comparison of nineteenth-century Paris and Vienna and a discussion of the 'Utopia of Reality'.

Further reading

Carlo Aymonino (1996), London: Academy Editions (well illustrated and referenced review of his whole work).

GORDANA KOSTICH

Azimut and Azimuth

Azimut, the Italian word for 'azimuth', meaning 'the arc of the horizon', was the name given by Enrico Castellani and Piero **Manzoni** to a gallery they founded in Milan in 1960, which played a key part in showing contemporary art. It held an important exhibition devoted to Lucio **Fontana**, whose work had been strangely overlooked, and hosted path-breaking work by Manzoni, such as his *Lines, Breath of the Artist* and *Living Statues*. It also opened its doors to new work from Klein, Mack, Holweck and other Europeans who, instead of the label 'painters', preferred to think of themselves as 'artists' for whom performances too were works. *Azimuth* was the name of the review, of which there were only three issues: the first was largely historical in content, the second included pieces by Manzoni and Castellani, and the third was a **Fiat** 500, considered equally useful as a vehicle for contacting contemporary artists. The short-livedness of the experience belied its significance for the invention of a new artistic language.

ROBERT LUMLEY

B

Baget Bozzo, Gianni

b. 8 March 1925, Savona

Priest, author, journalist and politician

After graduating from the Gregorian University, Bozzo was ordained in 1949. A contributor to various newspapers, including **La Repubblica**, he is also author of several books, amongst them *Il Partito cristiano al potere: il DC di De Gasperi e Dossetti, 1945–54* (The Christian Party in Power: the DC of De Gasperi and Dossetti, 1945–54) (1974), and *I cattolici e la lettera di Berlinguer* (Catholics and Berlinguer's Letter) (1978). In 1983, with Giovanni Tanassini, he co-authored *Aldo Moro: il politico nella crisi 1962–1973* (Aldo Moro: A Politician in Crisis 1962–1973). During the early 1970s Baget Bozzo had been moving closer to the Socialist Party (**PSI**) and eventually became a strong supporter of Bettino **Craxi**. He was suspended *a divinis* from the priesthood after his election as a Euro MP in 1984. In 1993 he transferred his allegiance to Silvio **Berlusconi**, and has since remained one of his counsellors and speechwriters. He was readmitted to the priesthood after leaving the European Parliament in 1994.

JOHN POLLARD

Baj, Enrico

b. 31 October 1924, Milan

Artist

After a period in the abstract vanguard of the 1950s, Baj developed a strong figurative, satirical vein. His *Generale* (General) of 1961 pokes fun at a fat, pompous military leader, in the spirit of Dada collage. His style is kitsch, as he readily admits, but he argues this is an effective mode for serious themes, from nuclear holocaust to the population explosion. His painted figures are cartoonish, adorned with stuck-on pieces of cloth, sequinned patches, tassels, braid and costume jewellery. In the 1960s he used meccano to construct humorous, life-size figures, later returning to this material for a series of marionettes for a production of Alfred Jarry's play, *Ubu Roi*. While not always appreciated by the critics, Baj has achieved a financial success which suggests that, ironically, his social satire has found a broad acceptance and wide appeal.

MAX STAPLES

Balestrini, Nanni

b. 2 July 1935, Milan

Poet, writer and political activist

Like most writers who became active in the late 1950s, Balestrini reconciled his poetic vocation with cultural engagement by contributing to journals and newspapers and working as an editor for **Feltrinelli**. His poetry, first launched by Alfredo **Giuliani**'s anthology *I novissimi*, is highly representative of the iconoclastic mood of the neoavantgarde movement. Rejecting traditional poetry, Balestrini utilized a language drawn mainly from newspapers to turn poetry into a nonsensical accumulation of words or the simple juxtaposition of statements.

In the late 1960s he founded the extreme-left group Potere Operaio but subsequently, charged with participation in armed violence, he left Italy until charges were dropped in 1985. The novels he produced in the 1970s – transcriptions of tape-recorded speeches and articles obtained from the official and the underground press – proved both his continuing political engagement and his strong commitment to faithfully documenting Italy's social reality of that period. In the 1987 novel *Gli invisibili* (The Unseen), Balestrini reconsidered the political and intellectual activism of the 1960s and 1970s and finally discussed the reasons of its failure.

See also: Gruppo 63; narrative; poetry

FRANCESCA PARMEGGIANI

Banca Commerciale Italiana

The Banca Commerciale Italiana (Italian Commercial Bank), established in 1894 as German-type universal bank, played an important role in promoting Italy's rapid industrialization between 1896–1928, soon becoming the leading financial institution of the country and the most internationally oriented one. It suffered from severe liquidity problems during the banking crisis of the early 1930s, but was rescued by the state and put under **IRI**'s wing in 1934.

From the mid-1930s to the early 1970s, the Banca Commerciale Italiana was led by Raffaele Mattioli, an extraordinary example of a humanist banker. He upheld the domestic and international prestige of the bank and its independence from the state, even though its market share was shrinking. Formally forbidden by law to engage in industrial banking, Banca Commerciale was nevertheless able to long maintain its leadership as provider of credit and financial services to the largest Italian corporations. It was privatized in 1994.

See also: banking and credit system

GIANNI TONIOLO

Banca d'Italia

The Banca d' Italia (Bank of Italy) is Italy's central bank. It was established in 1893 from the amalgamation of four previously existing banks of issue, and was granted the monopoly of bank note issue in 1926, together with supervisory powers over the banking system. Such powers were extended and made more effective by the Banking Act of 1936. After the Second World War, while monetary policy rested formally in the hands of the Treasury, the Banca d'Italia enjoyed a broad *de facto* independence based upon its prestige and technical skills, thereby playing a most substantial role in shaping Italy's economic policy.

The Banca d'Italia is headed by the governor, appointed for life by the government, and is assisted by a Direttorio (Directorate) made up of the general director and the two vice-general directors. A Consiglio Superiore (Board of Administration) makes the main administrative decisions but has no power over monetary and supervisory policies. The budget of the Bank is approved by its shareholders (public-owned banks and financial institutions) at their annual assembly. In opening the latter, the governor traditionally reads his *Considerazioni finali*, a most influential assessment of the country's economic conditions and policies.

The first postwar governor was Luigi Einaudi (1945–7) who later became **President** of the Republic. He and his successor, Donato **Menichella** (1947–60), successfully fought runaway inflation and stabilized the exchange rate in 1947–8. Menichella consistently pursued monetary stability during the 1950s and established full convertibility of the lira by the end of the decade. The next governors were Guido **Carli** (1960–75), Paolo Baffi (1975–80) and Carlo Azeglio **Ciampi** (1980–92). The current governor is Antonio Fazio.

During the 1970s the Banca d'Italia had no choice but to accommodate an increasing demand for money made by the successive governments in times of social unrest and outright terrorism. This resulted in double-digit inflation. In the years after 1978, when the decision was made to join the European Monetary System (see **European Union**), the Banca d'Italia played a crucial role both in controlling inflation – brought down to record low levels by 1996–7 – and in pushing for more competition in the banking system. In 1981 a measure was passed freeing the Banca d'Italia from the obligation of buying government securities that remained unsold at auctions. This measure – nicknamed 'the divorce' – was a first step made towards granting the Bank formal independence from the government. The second major step in the same direction was taken ten years later in January 1992 when an Act of Parliament was passed granting the Bank, not the Treasury, the power to set the official discount rate; in November of the same year, compulsory lending by the Bank to the government was abolished. The existing legislation thus gave the Banca d'Italia the degree of *de jure* independence required by the Maastricht Treaty.

Due to the stature of its governors and top managers, and to the high technical profile of its staff, the Bank has traditionally played a major role in economic policy making both directly in managing monetary policy and indirectly in providing advice and technical support to several branches of the administration. Its national standing was highlighted when, after the collapse of the party system in the early 1990s, so-called 'technical governments' were formed first by Ciampi (a governor of the Bank) and then by Lamberto **Dini** (who had been Ciampi's deputy at the Bank).

See also: banking and credit system

GIANNI TONIOLO

Banfi, Antonio

b. 30 September 1886, Vicamerate; d. 20 July 1957, Milan

Philosopher

After graduating from Milan in 1910, Banfi spent a year studying in Berlin, and enjoyed a close relationship with Georg Simmel. He was thus heavily influenced by German philosophy, particularly Husserl, though Husserl's appeal to the originary evidence of self-consciousness appeared to Banfi to anchor reason in a moment of intuition, and hence dogmatism. Banfi perceived the negative results of this unreasoned moment particularly in the works of Heidegger and Max Scheler. In

1940, Banfi founded *Studi Filosofici*, a journal that became an important forum for debates on existentialism. Although long nurturing socialist sympathies, Banfi became a Marxist during the Second World War through participation in the Resistance with the **PCI**. After the war, he remained in the party and contributed to *L'Unità*. These commitments led him to see personhood not as a self-sufficient state, but rather as the product of the individual's enmeshment in the social responsibilities of humanity as a whole.

Further reading

Erbetta, A. (1978) *L'umanesimo critico di Antonio Banfi*, (The Critical Humanism of Antonio Banfi), Milan: Marzorati.

THOMAS KELSO

banking and credit system

Since the beginning of 'modern economic growth' in the nineteenth century, Italy's financial system has been heavily 'bank oriented'. In the absence of well-developed capital markets (stock exchanges), 'universal' (or 'mixed') banks typically provided both long-term and short-term credit as well as investment banking services. During the 1920s, the largest banks acquired control of an important share of manufacturing and utilities companies, a situation that led to instability and eventually to a major bank and industrial crisis during the Great Depression. In the early 1930s the government stepped in to save the largest banks, an operation that resulted in the state's control of a huge share of Italy's big business, later (1933) put under the aegis of the **IRI**. The 1936 Banking Act (*legge bancaria*) radically altered the existing institutional setting of the banking system by allowing deposit banks to engage only in short-term lending and limiting the extent to which they would be allowed to own shares in non-financial companies. At the same time, between 1936 and 1947 the **Banca d'Italia** (Bank of Italy) was given extensive supervisory powers aimed at providing stability and promoting efficiency in the credit system. In 1947 an amended Banking Act was passed to provide the framework for the postwar development of Italy's banking system which continued to the early 1990s.

The banking system that emerged from the banking crisis of the 1930s and the Second World War was almost entirely owned by the state or other public bodies, in various – and ingenious – institutional settings for ownership that reflected the history of individual banks or type of banks. Deposit banks (whose operations were limited by law to short-term lending) that were owned or controlled by public institutions could be divided into three broad categories. First, there were the Istituti di credito di diritto pubblico – such as the Banco di Napoli, the Banco di Sicilia, the Banco di Sardegna, the Banca Nazionale del Lavoro – all owned directly by the Treasury and/or by regional governments and enjoying a special legal status. Second, there were the so-called *banche di interesse nazionale* (banks of national interest) such as the Banca Commerciale, Credito Italiano and Banco di Roma that had been acquired by IRI as the result of the banking crisis of 1931 (they retained their previous legal status of public companies and, for long periods of time, were listed on the Milan stock exchange). Third, there were the Casse di Risparmio (savings banks), whose origins in some cases dated back to the first part of the nineteenth century and were controlled by local institutions such as city halls, provincial governments and chambers of commerce. With some exceptions (the most notable one being the Cassa di Risparmio delle Provincie Lombarde), savings banks were mostly medium-sized or small credit institutions deeply rooted in the local economies, particularly where the latter were dominated by small-size companies.

Among the largest private deposits banks were the Banca Nazionale dell'Agricoltura, Banca Cattolica del Veneto and the Banco Ambrosiano. Privately owned but heavily regulated by the state were the co-operative banks (*banche popolari* and *casse rurali e artigiane*), while long-term credit was the business of the so-called Istituti di Credito Speciale such as IMI, Mediocredito centrale, Crediop and several others. **Mediobanca**, Italy's most important investment bank, had a special role all of its own.

Until the 1920s, the Italian banking system appeared well organized, shaped as it was in a clearly defined pyramidal fashion with the Bank of Italy at its pinnacle, a few large branch banks enjoying a substantial share of the market and a number of medium and small-sized banks providing for the needs of the local economy. This system was shattered by the banking crises of the late 1920s (involving a number of regional banks) and of 1931–34 (involving the largest ones). After the Second World War, no conscious attempt was made to restore the old pyramidal system: both governments and monetary authorities favoured the development of local banking (particularly of savings and co-operative banks) on the one hand and of the special (medium- and long-term) credit institutions on the other. Italy's banking system, sheltered from foreign competition, coped well with the financial needs of the high-growth years (1950–73). From the mid-1960s onward, however, huge amounts of credit were extended to both public and private companies investing in capital intensive sectors such as steel-making, heavy engineering and basic chemicals, particularly in the South. Overinvestment and underestimation of risk produced a hidden but serious crisis of several special credit institutions during the 1970s when domestic growth slowed.

Some of the largest banks were involved in the industrial restructuring of the late 1970s and early 1980s, and new links were formed between banks and non-financial companies. At the same time, the increasing globalization of financial markets and the new drive towards Europe's single market confronted both monetary authorities and individual banks with the new reality of international competition. In these circumstances, the institutional setting created in 1936–47 showed signs of obsolescence and was slowly reformed: banks were again allowed to be 'universal', the savings banks were transformed into limited liability companies, competition was favoured, and regulation was scaled down and reformed.

Since the mid-1990s, privatizations, mergers and acquisitions have been slowly but steadily changing the traditional state-owned and fragmented Italian banking system. Banca Commerciale and Credito Italiano were the first to be privatized. The Cassa di Risparmio delle Provincie Lombarde, the largest European savings bank merged in 1998 with the largest Italian private bank (Banco

Ambroveneto). The Banca Nazionale del Lavoro and INA (a formerly state-owned insurance company) have taken over the ailing Banco di Napoli and are planning a merger that will create the largest Italian banking company. Savings banks are selling their shares to the public as well as proceeding to mergers and consolidations at regional level.

GIANNI TONIOLO

Barba, Eugenio

b. 1936, Gallipoli

Theatre director

Eugenio Barba ranks as one of the great visionaries of modern theatre and one of the most inspirational directors of the postwar period. He was deeply indebted to Stanislavsky and Meyerhold and, in spite of occasional disagreements, had a close affinity with such other innovators as Jerzy Grotowski. Dissatisfied with traditional Western theatre, he turned to the noh, kabuki and kathakali theatres of Asia and came to see theatre in quasi-religious terms as a means to self-fulfilment and an arena for individual and collective transformation. His ideal theatre was based on the figure of the actor, on anti-naturalism, on dissatisfaction with narrative and on the search for some form of communication deeper than that based on conventional notions of 'meaning' in theatre.

Although born in the South of Italy, Barba moved to Norway in his youth, where he worked as a sailor and studied religions before joining forces in 1960 with Grotowski at his Theatre Laboratory in Poland. He travelled widely, visiting Kerala to study kathakali at first hand, and in 1964 established with a group of Norwegian actors his Odin Teatret, which moved two years later to the Danish town of Holstrebro.

The company lived in semi-monastic conditions, dedicated to professional, almost athletic 'training' in the arts of the theatre. Barba's prime desire was to experiment with physical theatre, gestures, visual ritual and non-verbal techniques of communication. Lighting effects were outlawed, as was any distinct stage which might set a barrier between performer and spectator. The spectator was invited to identify with the drive of the piece and open his emotions to its spirit. Improvisation, requiring of the actor 'total trust in the director', assumed a central role in theatre making.

Unlike subsequent productions, the group's first work, *Ferai* (1965), followed a script, written by Jens Björneboe. *Min Fars Hus* (1972), on the other hand, was conceived as a biography of Dostoievsky, but changed in rehearsal to an exploration of the encounter between Dostoievsky and the inner being of the Odin group. Self-scrutiny provided material for other works.

In 1974 the company decamped to Carpignano, near Barba's birthplace, but after an initial period of mutual incomprehension, Barba realized he could not impose his own outlook on the host community and established a system of 'barter' in which the theatre-producing group traded with the traditional culture. In 1976, Barba developed the concept of Third Theatre, viewed as an alternative both to traditional theatre and the established avantgarde, and in 1979, following a convention in Belgrade, set up the ISTA (International School of Theatre Anthropology), a travelling series of conventions which brings together various disciplines and acts as point of reference for the 'floating islands', the associated theatre troupes inspired by Barba's philosophy. These groups, or islands, are to *be* rather than 'produce' culture, yet to have no fixed roots and limited contact with the mainland, which they will visit spasmodically to explain and expose the culture they themselves embody. Barba has resolutely remained outside any mainstream, but his influence on experimental theatre has been profound.

See also: theatre directors

Further reading

Barba, E. (1995) *The Paper Canoe: A Guide to Theatre Anthropology*, New York: Routledge, 1995 (a recent and comprehensive volume representative of Barba's thought).

—— (1997) 'An Amulet Made of Memory: The Significance of Exercises in the Actor's Dramaturgy', *The Drama Review* 41 (4): 127–32 (details some of Barba's most recent experimentation with theatrical practice).

Watson, I. (1993) *Towards a Third Theatre: Eugenio Barba and the Odin Teatret*, London: Routledge (an in-depth study of Barba's history, theory and methods).

JOSEPH FARRELL

Baricco, Alessandro

b. 1958, Turin

Novelist, critic and playwright

After his early beginnings as a music columnist for the Italian newspapers **La Repubblica** and **La Stampa**, Baricco has interspersed his career with experiences in different creative fields. After two experimental and at the same time divulgative television projects, respectively dedicated to opera and to literature, he published the novels *Castelli di rabbia* (Castles of Anger) and *Oceano Mare* (Ocean Sea), both of which received prestigious literary prizes. In 1994 he published a theatrical monologue, *Novecento* (Nineteen Hundred), and then *Seta* (Silk), the first of his novels to be translated into English. A constant concern with the analysis and investigation of different kinds of media make Baricco a figure very much tied to contemporary industrial culture, although he also yearns for a solitary and craftsman-like dimension to his writing and displays a strong interest in oral culture.

ANDREA RICCI

Barilli, Renato

b. 18 August 1935, Bologna

Academic and critic

A pupil of Luciano **Anceschi** and a member of the **Gruppo 63**, Renato Barilli taught at the University of Bologna while contributing widely to cultural journals such as **il verri**, *Quindici*, *Rivista di estetica* and **alfabeta**, and to newspapers and magazines such as **Il Giorno**, **Il Corriere della sera** and **L'Espresso**. His intense interest in aesthetics, poetics and rhetoric resulted in a number of impressive studies of nineteenth- and twentieth-century European literature, among them *La barriera del naturalismo* (The Barrier of Naturalism) (1964) and *Tra presenza e assenza* (Between Presence and Absence) (1974). He has published close analyses of the linguistic microdynamics of contemporary Italian poetry, and also provided an informed and detailed history of the postwar neoavantgarde movement in his *La neoavanguardia italiana: dalla nascita del 'Verri' alla fine di 'Quindici'* (The Italian Neoavantgarde: From the Birth of *Il Verri* to the End of *Quindici*) (1995).

FRANCESCA PARMEGGIANI

Bartali, Gino

b. 18 July 1914, Ponte a Ema, Florence

Cyclist

Bartali is one of Italy's cycling legends along with Fausto **Coppi**. Bartali's major victories were in the Giro d'Italia in 1936, 1937 and 1946, the Milan–San Remo in 1939–40, 1947 and 1950, and the Tour de France in 1938 and 1948. Bartali's accomplishments in the Tour de France, the hardest race of all, are truly impressive. His two victories came ten years apart, one before and one after the Second World War. In 1938 he also became the first rider ever to concomitantly win the Tour de France and to finish as 'King of the Mountains', the title reserved to the best *scalatore* (a rider particularly strong on uphill courses); he repeated this exploit in 1948. To his three victories in the Giro d'Italia, Bartali added four second place finishes, and he won the prize for best *scalatore* a total of seven times (1935–7, 1939–40 and 1946–7).

See also: cycling

PAOLO VILLA

Bartoli, Cecilia

b. 4 June 1966, Rome

Mezzo-soprano

The recordings which Cecilia Bartoli made for

Decca in the early 1990s brought her to wide international recognition as one of the most musically and dramatically gifted singers of her generation. She studied at the Accademia di S. Cecilia in Rome, but had already made her stage debut at the age of nine as the Shepherd Boy in *Tosca*. Her mature debut occurred in 1987 at the Teatro Filarmonico in Verona. She attracted the patronage of Katia **Ricciarelli** and other influential musical figures, and her appearance at a memorial concert for Maria Callas at the Paris Opéra soon led to engagements at the major European opera houses as Rosina and Cherubino. She made her Covent Garden debut in 1992 in *Le Comte Ory* (under Chailly). Since then, the undoubted beauty of her voice has attracted widespread critical praise in her key repertoire of Rossini and Mozart.

JOHN KERSEY

Bartolini, Luciano

b. 1948, Fiesole; d. 1994, Milan

Installation artist, painter and collagist

Emerging as a young artist in the 1970s, Bartolini was influenced by Alberto **Burri** and *arte povera* (poor art). From early conceptual pieces in kleenex and cardboard, he moved to installations of similarly modest materials, evoking dream images and mythological themes. In the early 1980s he turned to painting and developed a vocabulary of archetypal forms that included labyrinths, tantric motifs and a mysterious pseudo-alphabet of angular shapes. Subsequently, during a stay in Berlin he shifted into a more expressionistic mode, with agitated brushwork and murky colours that lacked the refinement and the suggestive quality of his earlier work. His ongoing fascination with the aesthetic qualities of paper and calligraphy also took the form of publishing books, beginning in 1974 with a book entitled *Soft*.

Bartolini exhibited consistently throughout the 1970s and 1980s in Italy and abroad, taking part in the 1980 **Venice Biennale**, in the 'Printed Art' exhibition at the MoMA in New York in 1979 and

in 'Arte Italiana 1960–82' (Italian Art 1960–82) at the Hayward Gallery in London in 1982.

OLIVIA DAWSON

basketball

Basketball only became a popular sport in Italy in the late 1960s when, after a six-year ban, American players were again allowed to play for Italian teams. The most successful teams are Pallacanestro Olympia Milano, which dominated the European scene in the late 1980s; Pallacanestro Varese, which played a record ten consecutive European Champion's Cup finals in the1960s and 1970s; and Pallacanestro Trieste, Virtus Bologna and Pallacanestro Cantù. The Italian national team took the silver medal at the 1980 Moscow Olympics and also won one European championship. The greatest Italian player of all times is considered to be Dino Meneghin, with 836 games played in a career of almost thirty years. A peculiar feature of Italian basketball is that the name of the current sponsor becomes the name of the team. Thus, Pallacanestro Olympia has been known as Borletti, Simmenthal, Simac, Philips, and so on (see also **volleyball**).

PAOLO VILLA

Bassani, Giorgio

b. 4 March 1916, Bologna

Novelist and editor

A member of the Italian Jewish community and a passionate anti-fascist, Bassani spent his youth in Ferrara and later moved to Rome, where he published his most important novels while contributing to several prestigious journals and periodicals. In his novels and short stories, from *Gli occhiali d'oro* (The Gold-Rimmed Spectacles) (1958) and *Il giardino dei Finzi-Contini* (The Garden of the Finzi-Continis) (1962) – both made into successful movies by, respectively, Giuliano **Montaldo** (1987) and Vittorio **De Sica** (1971) – to *L'odore del fieno* (The Smell of Hay) (1972), Bassani tells stories of human and socio-political marginalization, often inspired by his own youthful experiences in the war years and mainly set in the provincial microcosm of Ferrara.

A pervasive sense of death, the melancholia of remembrance, the stillness of nature in the Po valley and the familiar architecture of the city where his characters – and the writer with them – endure history, are the constants of Bassani's writing. Literature is the metaphorical space in which reality can be experienced and where both the sense of the inexorable passage of time and the disappointment of unfulfilled expectations in the present can be mitigated. In fact, Bassani's style has been characterized as 'lyric realism', and despite the common appearance of themes such as the war, the Fascist persecution of the Jews and the **Resistance**, is very different from the neorealist representation of factual reality where 'facts' are assumed to speak for themselves (see **neorealism**). Reality is always filtered through the inner world of the narrator, though this lyrical screening does not soften its harshness; indeed, Bassani's central characters are all, to varying degrees, doomed to moral loneliness, social isolation and death. In *Il giardino dei Finzi-Contini*, for instance, the distinctiveness of the Finzi-Contini family degenerates into racial isolation. In *Gli occhiali d'oro*, the two main characters – the young Jewish narrator and an old homosexual doctor – both symbolize political and psychological marginalization and the doctor's suicide, brought about by his painful experience of his own 'diversity', also foreshadows the deaths of the Jews in the Second World War. In *L'airone* (The Heron) (1968), Bassani recounts the last day in the life of a landowner who, searching for an absolute, non-transient existence, realizes the emptiness of his earthly experience and resolves to end it. In 1974, Bassani collected his major narrative works in *Il romanzo di Ferrara* (The Novel of Ferrara), in which he refined his metaphor of the human condition by also giving an editorial consistency and an enclosed form to the sense of a unique and self-contained world where individual existence and collective destiny intertwine.

Besides writing fiction, which was both popular and critically acclaimed (he won the coveted Strega in 1956 and the Viareggio in 1962), Bassani also published several collections of poetry and critical essays. From 1958 to 1963 he directed the series 'Biblioteca di letteratura' for **Feltrinelli**, promoting the controversial publication of Tomasi di **Lampedusa**'s novel *Il gattopardo* (The Leopard) (1958).

See also: Jewish writers

Further reading

Radcliff-Umstead, D. (1987) *The Exile into Eternity: A Study of the Narrative Writings of Giorgio Bassani*, Cranbury: Associated University Presses.

Schneider, M. (1986) *Vengeance of the Victim: History and Symbol in Giorgio Bassani's Fiction*, Minneapolis, MN: University of Minnesota Press.

FRANCESCA PARMEGGIANI

Battisti, Lucio

b. 5 March 1943, Poggio Bustone, Rieti; d. 9 September 1998, Milan

Singer-songwriter

Regarded as one of the most influential singer-songwriters of postwar Italy (see **cantautori**), Battisti grew up in Rome where he taught himself the guitar. He soon moved to Milan, where his talents began to be recognized when some of his songs were performed by the Dik Dik and Equipe 84. His career really blossomed, however, when he teamed up with lyricist Mogol (Giulio Rapetti) in 1966, and together they produced over twenty best-selling albums, many of which are still regarded as landmarks of Italian popular music. However, unlike many of the other *cantautori*, Battisti wrote songs which were exclusively personal and apolitical and far removed from the protest movement of 1968. This led some in the early 1970s to accuse him of reactionary leanings. Deeply offended by these accusations, he retired from public view in 1976. His artistic partnership with Mogol was abruptly terminated in 1980, and from then on his songs were co-written with his wife Grazia Letizia and, later, with Pasquale Panella. He continued to release an album regularly every two years but, by the time of his premature death in 1998, Battisti had completely withdrawn from the Italian musical scene and not performed or appeared in public for over twenty years.

GINO MOLITERNO

Baudo, Giuseppe (Pippo)

b. 7 June 1936, Militello, Catania

Television presenter

From the mid-1970s, Pippo Baudo became one of the most important public faces of Italian television. A reliable and utterly unflappable host of numerous editions of the Saturday evening variety show *Fantastico*, as well as *Domenica In*, the **Sanremo festival** and quiz shows, he spent most of his working life at the **RAI**. A Christian Democrat until the dissolution of the party (see **DC**), he began his career in the 1960s and quickly won a reputation for civility, cordiality and conformity. With his slicked-back black hair and dark suits, the tall and thin Baudo resembled nothing so much as a slightly too-jovial undertaker. In the mid-1990s he became, for a brief period, artistic director of RAI-TV, but resigned when it became clear that the old-style variety formulas had had their day. In 1986 he married the opera singer Katia **Ricciarelli**.

See also: Canzonissima

Further reading

Calabrese, O. (1984) 'Pippo Baudo', in N. Ajello *et al.*, *Perche lui?* (Why Him?), Bari: Laterza.

STEPHEN GUNDLE

Bellezza, Dario

b. 5 September 1944; d. 1996, Rome

Novelist and poet

A passionate non-conformist and something of a *poète maudit*, in all his works Bellezza explores the limiting effects of a totalling mass culture. In earlier works, such as the 1971 poetry collection *Invettive e licenze* (Invectives and Licences) and the 1970 novel *L'innocenza* (Innocence), he offers an embittered response to the restrictions of social conformity. In his predominantly autobiographical narratives, many of which continue to deal with this issue, he investigates questions of alterity and the status of the poet in Italy. These works include the novel *Lettere da Sodoma* (Letters from Sodom) (1972), the first Italian work to deal openly with homosexuality and *Morte di Pasolini* (Pasolini's Death) (1981), a personal and literary inquiry into the tragic death of his close friend and mentor, Pier Paolo **Pasolini**. Among Bellezza's autobiographical works are the novels *Angelo* (Angel) (1979) and *L'amore felice* (Happy Love) (1987), both about his relationship with the author Elsa **Morante**. In 1976 Bellezza received the prestigious Viareggio Prize (see **literary prizes**) for his poetry collection *Morte segreta* (Secret Death). Ironically, five months after his death from AIDS, he was awarded a government pension for his contributions to Italian culture.

VIRGINIA PICCHIETTI

Bellini, Mario

b. November 1935, Milan

Architect and industrial designer

Bellini trained in the School of Architecture at the Politecnico of Milan. He received his doctorate in 1959 and soon gained a wide reputation, first in the areas of furniture and **industrial design** and later in architecture and **urban planning**. His subsequent professional career falls into three main phases.

In his formative period during the 1960s, Bellini became very active in industrial and **interior design**, engaging imaginatively with the new technologies and rapid developments in micro-electronics. During this time he achieved renown with his furniture designs for leading firms such as Cassina, B & B Italia, and Vitra, and earned the first of his seven Golden Compass Awards from Rinascente-UPIM in 1962. He also served as vice-president of the ADI (Association for Industrial Design) and was awarded numerous other prizes. In 1963, he began what would be a long and fruitful collaboration with the **Olivetti** Company as its chief industrial design consultant and subsequently created some of his best work in designing Olivetti's microcomputers, typewriters, calculators and copying machines.

Bellini's second phase, during the 1970s, was marked by a strong interest in flexibility. This was the maturing of an interest he had already developed whilst working on a prototype car in 1962–3, an innovative design that attempted to meet the needs of the rapidly changing dynamics of modern life. With its modular design, the car was expandable so as to hold twelve passengers while still supplying the essential features of a house. This interest continued in his numerous designs for **Fiat** and Renault, and in his proposal for 'Kar-a-Sutra', a vehicle he designed for an exhibition held at MoMA in New York in 1972 which aimed at re-enacting the basic domestic rites (sleeping, entertaining, etc.) in a moving urban setting. Throughout the 1970s Bellini continued to explore the notion of flexibility, as in the numerous office electronic machines he designed for Olivetti.

Bellini's formal training in architecture came to the fore in the 1980s, the third phase of his career, which included a period as editor-in-chief of **Domus** (1986–91). During this time he designed numerous buildings and urban projects in Italy, Japan and the Middle East. In these projects, as well as in his theoretical essays, he confronted the major problems besetting the contemporary architect and his designs often proposed poetic solutions which allowed essential elements to express themselves in a composite image.

Bellini's special approach to design as a poetic means of expression has continued to earn him international renown. His work was given special prominence in an exhibition held at The Museum of Modern Art of New York in 1987, where his innovative designs were exhibited and where over two dozen of his works are now permanently housed. Bellini lectures and practises internationally, while maintaining a special place in the history of modern Italian design.

Further reading

McCarty, C. (1987) *Mario Bellini: Designer*, New York: The Museum of Modern Art (extended essay and illustrated catalogue of the exhibition held at MoMA, June 24–September 15, 1987, presenting some of Bellini's most accomplished work in industrial design).

Ranzani, E. (1996) *Mario Bellini, architecture 1984–1995*, Berlin: Birkhäuser (an illustrated anthology of Bellini's architectural work in the years shown. Also contains a general biography and an extensive bibliography).

FASSIL ZEWDOU

Bellocchio, Marco

b. 9 November 1939, Piacenza

Film director

A virtuoso provocateur, Bellocchio belongs to the generation of ideologically oriented film-makers whose highly politicized cinema participated in the social revolution associated with 1968. Graduating from Rome's **Centro Sperimentale di Cinematografia** in 1962 and later attending London's Slade School of Fine Arts, Bellocchio combines a solid professional training with a sharp eye for the incongruities of the Italian body politic. Pursuing an engagement in radical politics, Bellocchio's films are dedicated to the caustic denunciation of the corruption and repression of Italian social institutions. His controversial first film, *I pugni in tasca* (Fists in the Pocket) (1965) explores in a tragic mode the moral decadence of the family, while *La Cina è vicina* (China is Near) (1967) and *Nel nome del padre* (In the Name of the Father) (1971) utilize a more sarcastic tone in order to attack education and patriarchy generally. His later films draw more openly on psychoanalysis and his *Diavolo in corpo* (Devil in the Flesh) (1986) is one of very few Italian films which deal with terrorism.

DOROTHÉE BONNIGAL

Bene, Carmelo

b. 1 September 1937, Campi Salentina, Puglia

Actor, director and writer

The irrepressible *enfant terrible* of Italian postwar theatre, Bene has often provoked a negative reaction from conservative critics, but he is nevertheless widely regarded as one of the most powerful and innovative presences on the Italian stage in the postwar period. Typically, Bene himself has suggested that Italian theatre can be divided into 'Before Bene' and 'After Bene', and most critics tend to agree.

Born in a small town in southern Italy where he was educated by the Jesuits, Bene moved to Rome and in 1957 enrolled in the Academy of Dramatic Arts. Abandoning the Academy without graduating, he made his stage debut in 1959 in a production of Camus's *Caligula* at the Arts Theatre of Rome. Although the production itself was fairly conservative, Bene's acting already displayed what would become the signature of his theatrical style: an intense, almost maniacal egocentrism and exhibitionism whereby the actor violently took over his character and confronted the audience with an experience close to madness. Continuing in this direction during the next five years, Bene developed his own version of Artaud's 'theatre of cruelty', writing, directing and acting in a series of provocative spectacles which became the spearhead of the great wave of experimental theatre of the 1960s. These included, amongst others, *Spettacolo Majakovskij* (Majakovskij Spectacle) in 1960, with music provided by that other *enfant terrible*, Sylvano **Bussotti**; an adaptation of *Doctor Jekyll and Mr Hyde* in 1961, together with an eroticized *Pinocchio* and a disturbing *Amleto* (Hamlet); a desecratory *Cristo '63* in 1963 (immediately blocked by censorship); and in 1964, a version of Oscar Wilde's *Salomé*. All these fully manifested what would remain the characteristic features of Bene's unique theatrical method: an extreme deformation and deconstruction of the original text (in effect, a reduction of it to mere 'pre-text') and a strongly physicalized stage presence with a major role given to the human voice. The voice became and remained the nucleus of Bene's provocative theatrical practice, and all his productions sought to explore its possibilities to their ultimate limit, orchestrating everything from blood-curdling screeches, screams and howls to low murmurs, sighs, yelps and whimpers.

In 1965 Bene published *Nostra Signora dei Turchi* (Our Lady of the Turks), a 'scandalous' semi-autobiographical novel which he subsequently staged. In 1967, after acting in **Pasolini**'s *Edipo re* (Oedipus, the King), Bene became attracted to the cinema and directed himself in a number of films – including a version of *Nostra Signora* which received the special jury prize at Cannes in 1968 – before returning to the stage in the mid-1970s. In the 1980s, while continuing to work on the stage, he also acted and directed a number of his own plays for television as well as performing several oratorios with full orchestra and singers. At the same time he became the theatrical director of the **Venice Biennale**, although ongoing disputes with the administration eventually led to his resignation in 1990.

After having been, wilfully and provocatively, the thorn in the side of the bourgeois establishment for over three decades, Bene's significance for postwar Italian culture was underlined in 1995 when his collected works began to be published by Bompiani in its series of literary classics.

Further reading

Baiardo, E. and De Lucis, F. (1997) *La moralità dei sette veli: La Salomé di Carmelo Bene* (The Morality of the Seven Veils: Carmelo Bene's Salomé), Genoa: Erga Edizioni (an analysis of one of Bene's most intense obsessions and a text which he produced on the stage, in film, for the radio and also for television).

Prosperi, M. (1978) 'Contemporary Italian Theatre', *The Drama Review* 22(1): 17–32 (Bene in the context of other Italian experimental theatre).

GINO MOLITERNO

Benedetti, Arrigo

b. 1 June 1910, Lucca; d. 26 October 1976, Rome

Novelist and journalist

A journalist of particular importance – he was variously editor of and contributor to prestigious newspapers and magazines such as *L'Europeo*, *L'Espresso*, *Il Mondo* and *Paese Sera* – Benedetti's narrative style is, not surprisingly, characterized by a realistic and immediate language. His meticulous attention to everyday reality is manifest in all his novels from *I misteri della città* (The Mysteries of the City) (1941) to *Gli occhi* (Eyes) (1970). In *Rosso al vento* (Red in the Wind), his last book of fiction, the representation of aspects of life in Italy during the Second World War is so vivid that a comparison with neorealist cinema (see **neorealism**) becomes inevitable. The polyphonic nature of the narrative in this last novel, where myriads of voices intermingle constantly so as to enhance the sense of fear and uncertainty gripping the characters, is also reminiscent of other fictional representations of human tragedy, such as Manzoni's portrayal of the plague in Milan in *I promessi sposi* (The Betrothed).

PAOLO BARTOLONI

Benedetti Michelangeli, Arturo

b. 5 January 1920, Brescia; d. 12 June 1995, Lugano, Switzerland

Widely regarded as the greatest Italian pianist of the twentieth century, Benedetti Michelangeli began playing violin at the age of three but soon turned to the piano, which he studied first at the Venturi Musical Institute at Brescia and then at the Milan Conservatory. He graduated with full honours in 1933, aged fourteen. Six years later, he achieved worldwide renown when he won the International Piano Competition at Geneva, being favourably compared to Liszt. A volatile and eccentric personality who avoided interviews and always cultivated an air of reserve, he was totally devoted to his instrument, although in younger days he had nurtured a passion for racing cars. A virtuoso and a perfectionist who stunned audiences with his exquisite technique and startling interpretations, he was also well-known for unexpectedly cancelling performances or interrupting recitals if he suspected conditions to be less than optimal. After being an enthusiastic and inspiring teacher who had created new courses and summer schools during the 1960s, Benedetti Michelangeli abandoned Italy for Switzerland in 1968, following an incident in which his two pianos were confiscated by authorities in a bankruptcy suit. He returned to Italy on only three occasions, twice

to play in the Vatican and once in his native Brescia.

GINO MOLITERNO

Benetton

Legend has it that a yellow sweater knitted for Luciano Benetton by his sister Giuliana was responsible for the birth of the clothing empire. The response the sweater generated in a still predominantly black and white world motivated Luciano and Giuliana Benetton to embark on a coloured wool venture with the assistance of their two brothers, Gilberto and Carlo. The business, featuring colourful and reasonably priced knitwear, expanded quickly from the initial shop in Belluno (1969) to the opening of a Paris store in 1970. The key factor to the company's rapid success was the technique of dying wool after, rather than before, producing the sweaters, which allowed the Benettons to adjust the colours to rapidly changing fashion trends. By the end of the 1970s, Benetton's three factories in and around Ponzano were the largest consumers of pure virgin wool in the world.

Motivated by internationalization and diversification, Benetton labels targeted distinct groups, including children, young adults and women. While initially appealing to popular taste, Benetton colours made a splash in high society as well. Sylvester Stallone, Dustin Hoffman, Sally Field and Jackie Onassis became regular customers of the New York store on East 57th Street. When Diana, Princess of Wales was photographed coming out of Benetton's London store, a British newspaper ran the headline 'Benetton dresses both queens and housewives'. But Benetton did not limit itself to clothing. It entered the shoe business with yet another label, Tip-Top, and began sponsoring sports teams, starting with a rugby team in 1978, then basketball, Formula 1 and volleyball teams.

Luciano Benetton, formerly a senator for the Republican Party (see **PRI**), abandoned politics and has dedicated himself to an empire which now operates in 120 different countries and has moved into many sectors. Benetton sports manages the sports labels it has acquired, which include Killer Loop Prince and Rollerblade. Benetton-owned major distribution and fast food industries include the Euromercato, Supermercati GS and Autogrill and, most recently, a multiple restaurant along the lines of a multiplex cinema, with slow food and fast food co-existing with bars and even a **Feltrinelli** bookstore in the Galleria Vittorio Emanuele in Milan, a true monument to the family's diversification.

Other areas of investment are small companies specialising in hydra massage showers and tubs, the produce industry, multimedia firms, ice cream and olive oil. With plans in place to buy airports, highways and railroad stations, Luciano Benetton claims he is not buying Italy but supporting a sort of privatization which will improve services in Italy by providing faster highways and more punctual trains.

Sometimes labelled the McDonald's of the fashion industry, Benetton owes at least part its huge international success to Oliviero **Toscani**, the mastermind behind the advertising campaigns that have turned Benetton into a phenomenon studied in business schools the world over. In 1989, Benetton ads replaced their products with powerful and controversial images of AIDS sufferers, environmental disasters, terrorism and racism. While some have accused him of commodifying social issues, Toscani sees his ads as heightening social consciousness. In 1999, the Benetton and UN logos appeared side by side in a newspaper advertisement featuring an image of a red blood-stain on a white field. Explaining it as a response to the crisis in Kosovo, Toscani claims the ad is an antiwar message meant to 'stain' the pages of newspapers with the very images that advertising attempts to wipe from the human conscience.

BERNADETTE LUCIANO

Benevolo, Leonardo

b. 1923, Orta, Novara

Architect, urbanist and historian

One of Italy's most internationally renowned architectural and urban historians, Benevolo is a prolific author whose numerous books on urban history, theory, planning and design have been widely translated into English and are now standard reading in academic programmes of urban and regional planning. He has taught at the Universities of Rome, Florence, Venice and Palermo as well as being visiting professor at the Universities of Yale, Columbia, Caracas, Rio de Janeiro and Tokyo. He has contributed extensively to architectural magazines, participated in planning debates and been a consultant for the planning of cities such as Brescia, Urbino and Ferrara. Although Benevolo's 'clean continuity' approach has been criticized, he is highly respected for his method of interconnecting architectural production and professional tendencies, and presenting them within their socioeconomic and political contexts.

See also: urban planning

Further reading

Benevolo, L. (1985) *The History of the City*, trans. G. Culverwell, Cambridge, MA: MIT Press (numerous and detailed case studies of various urban patterns and evolution, extensively illustrated).

GORDANA KOSTICH

Benigni, Roberto

b. 27 October 1952, Castiglion Fiorentino (Arezzo)

Comedian, actor and film director

The most popular and critically-acclaimed of the 'new comedians' who emerged in Italy during the early 1980s, Benigni began performing theatrical monologues in the 1970s before moving to film and television. Giuseppe **Bertolucci**, who wrote some of his material, also directed him in his first film, *Berlinguer ti voglio bene* (I Love You, Berlinguer) in 1977. While continuing to perform his manic and surreal humour on stage and television, Benigni also began to direct himself in his own films in the 1980s, most of which achieved significant box-office success and made him into something of a cult figure. The clever and enormously popular *Non ci resta che piangere* (Nothing Left to Do but Cry)

(1986), made with fellow comedian Massimo **Troisi**, was followed by *Il piccolo diavolo* (The Little Devil) in 1989 and the even more popular *Johnny Stecchino* in 1991. At the same time Benigni also achieved international renown by playing major roles in Jim Jarmusch's *Down By Law* (1985) and the less successful *The Son of the Pink Panther* (Blake Edwards, 1993). With Benigni's international popularity still growing, his holocaust comedy *La vita è bella* (Life is Beautiful) was awarded the grand prize at Cannes in 1998 and went on to win the Oscar as Best Foreign Film in 1999, with Benigni also winning a personal Oscar as best actor.

GINO MOLITERNO

Benni, Stefano

b. 12 August 1947, Bologna

Novelist and journalist

Benni's first appearance dates to the 1970s, when he contributed to magazines and newspapers such as **Panorama**, *Il Mago* and **il manifesto**, and published several books of political and cultural satire. While continuing to vent his polemical humour on contemporary society, Benni turned ever more to literature, proving to be an inventive and unpredictable storyteller. His rich, often invented language registers the unceasing motion of a fertile and fantastic imagination which is nevertheless well grounded in reality, since the author maintains his leading role of witnessing – often in a cynical manner – his own times. His successful novels and surreal short stories range from science fiction (*Terra!* 1981) to mystery (*Comici spaventati guerrieri*) (Funny Frightened Warriors) (1986), and foresee a world where the 'human' eventually reconciles itself with the automatism of a technological society. Mirroring both the curiosity and the consternation of the post-1968 generation, his books have consistently met with the public's bemused appreciation.

Further reading

Degli-Esposti, C. (1995) 'Interview with Stefano Benni: A Postmodern *Moraliste*', *Italian Quarterly*,

Winter–Spring, 99–105 (a wide-ranging interview with bibliographical references).

FRANCESCA PARMEGGIANI

Berio, Luciano

b. 24 October 1925, Oneglia

Composer

Widely regarded as Italy's foremost postwar composer, Berio draws extensively on ideas from contemporary culture and musical tradition in order to create a unique and sophisticated synthesis. Coming from a musical family, he had lessons on the organ with Ernesto Berio from an early age. He then attended the Conservatorium Giuseppe Verdi in Milan (1945–50), where he studied composition with Giorgio Ghedini and conducting with Carlo Maria Giulini. He subsequently studied with compatriot Luigi **Dallapiccola** at the Berkshire Music Centre, Tanglewood, Massachusetts. While in the USA in 1950, he married soprano Cathy Berberian, who inspired him to produce innovative vocal music including *Circles* and *Folk Songs*. In 1954 he undertook study at the Ferienkurse für Neue Musik (New Music Masterclass) in Darmstadt, and developed contacts with other leaders of the European avantgarde such as Pierre Boulez and Karlheinz Stockhausen.

Following his studies, Berio taught at a number of schools including the Berkshire Music Centre, Tanglewood, the Dartington Summer School (England), Mills College (Oakland, California) and the Juilliard School of Music in New York. With Bruno **Maderna**, he founded the electronic music studio 'Studio Fonologia Musicale' at the **RAI** in Milan in 1955, and later collaborated on the television series *C'è musica e musica* (There's Music and Music) (1971).

Berio worked with Pierre Boulez at the studios of IRCAM (Institut de Recherche et de Coordination Acoustique/Musique) (Institute for Acoustic and Musical Research and Coordination) in Paris in 1974–80, and has been Artistic Director of a number of orchestras and music institutions including the Israel Chamber Orchestra (1975), the Accademia Filarmonica Romana, (1976) the

Orchestra Regionale Toscana (1982), the Maggio Musicale Fiorentino (1984) and Tempo Reale in Florence (1987). He received an Honorary Doctorate in Music from City University, London, in 1980 and was awarded the 34th Premio Italia (Italia Prize) in 1982.

Key features of Berio's work are the distinctive and experimental use of texts by contemporaries such as Beckett, **Eco** and **Sanguineti** (for example, *Opera* and *Laborintus II*), demandingly complex virtuoso writing for instruments and voices (as in the *Sequenza* series of works for soloists), a tendency to re-use and expand ideas – and even whole works – in subsequent compositions (for example, the *Chemins* series) and the use of quotation and stylistic references to music by other composers. His five-movement work for orchestra and voices, *Sinfonia* (1967–68), was written for the New York Philharmonic and the Swingle Singers, and stands as a landmark in twentieth-century music. The work draws on a diverse range of texts including anthropological writings by Claude Lévi-Strauss and, in its celebrated third movement, presents an exhilarating collage of musical quotations.

Further reading

Osmond-Smith, D. (1991) *Berio*, Oxford: Oxford University Press (a detailed study of the composer).

Steinitz, R. (1992) 'Luciano Berio', in B. Morton and P. Collins (eds), *Contemporary Composers*, Chicago: St James Press (for a comprehensive list and a discussion of Berio's works).

ANDREW SCHULTZ

Berlinguer, Enrico

b. 15 May 1922, Sassari; d. 11 June 1984, Brescia

Politician

Enrico Berlinguer was the most popular and controversial postwar leader of the Italian Communist Party (**PCI**). One and a half million people attended his funeral after his untimely death in 1984, a tribute to his rare mix of conviction, tolerance and integrity. Yet his political strategy – increasingly explicit recognition of the constraints of West European economic and political institutions – aroused strong opposition within the party. Likewise, the overall balance sheet concerning his leadership – which covered both the single greatest electoral advance in the party's history in 1976 and the calamitous loss of political direction in the early 1980s – remains fiercely contested.

Berlinguer came from a Sardinian family, ennobled in 1777, which produced a stream of political and academic figures. His brother Giovanni was a leading Communist MP and public health specialist; and his cousins include a rector of the University of Siena (Luigi), a minister in **Berlusconi**'s government of 1994 (Sergio) and a President of the Republic (Francesco **Cossiga**). Berlinguer's uninterrupted rise through the PCI hierarchy prompted his colleague Giancarlo **Pajetta** to observe that '[he] enrolled very young in the leadership of the PCI' (Gorresio 1976: 5). He started as secretary of the Sassari youth section in 1943, joined the Central Committee in 1945 and became an MP in 1968. In 1972, as the most prominent representative of the post-**Resistance** generation, he succeeded Luigi **Longo** as general-secretary, a position he held until his death.

A moderate within his party, Berlinguer took charge of the PCI in extreme circumstances. The **extraparliamentary Left** had rejected its claims to be a force for genuine change; the turbulent 'Hot Autumn', and the independent political role demanded by **trade unions** had weakened its links with working-class supporters, and the growth of **terrorism** and economic crises of the 1970s confronted the party with difficult political choices. Berlinguer's reputation varies according to whether his responses – the **historic compromise**, mass mobilization to defend against violence a state in the hands of his political opponents, and acceptance of economic sacrifices by the working class – are regarded as necessary in the circumstances, insufficiently revisionist or a fatal capitulation to **DC** power. Their unpopularity certainly cost the party dearly in the 1979 elections. This spurred Berlinguer, largely on his own initiative, to switch to open confrontation with the DC, an emphasis on the 'moral distinctiveness' of the PCI, and erratic support for shopfloor radicalism. None of these changes revived the PCI's fortunes, nor did Berlinguer's completion of the PCI's detachment from the Soviet Union and corresponding enthusiasm for an evanescent 'Eurocommunism' in the mid-1970s, and a blunt statement in 1981 that the October Revolution had exhausted its innovative potential. A decade after his death, post-communists remained deeply divided over their lost leader's role in the evolution of Italian communism.

Further reading

Gorresio, V. (1976) *Berlinguer*, Milan: Feltrinelli.

Hellman, S. (1988) *Italian Communism in Transition: The Rise and Fall of the Historic Compromise in Turin, 1975–1980*, New York: Oxford University Press (the Historic Compromise in theory and practice).

Tatò, A. (ed.) (1984) *Conversazioni con Berlinguer* (Conversations with Berlinguer), Rome: Editori Riuniti.

Valentini, C. (1987) *Berlinguer il segretario* (Secretary Berlinguer), Milan: Mondadori.

DAVID MOSS

Berlusconi, Silvio

b. 29 September 1936, Milan

Entrepreneur and politician

Of lower middle-class origins, Silvio Berlusconi had by the beginning of the 1990s become one of the richest of Italian entrepreneurs and owner of the second largest Italian business group, **Fininvest**. In 1994, he entered politics with spectacular success, and as the leader of a newly-formed political movement called **Forza Italia**, he became for a short time the **President of the Council of Ministers** of Italy.

Berlusconi began in the late 1960s in the construction sector with a number of real estate projects, including the construction of the satellite cities Milano 2 and Milano 3. At the beginning of the 1980s he turned his attention to the **private television** sector, which was at the time still largely unregulated. He developed his first televi-

sion network, **Canale Cinque**, in 1980, and subsequently bought the networks **Italia Uno** (1982) and **Rete Quattro** (1984) from other private owners. By the mid-1980s, Berlusconi's control over the Italian private television system was largely consolidated and his three channels directly challenged the public-service broadcaster **RAI** in a daily battle for audiences and advertising revenue. Fininvest's broadcasting strategy was a blend of consumerism and glamour, modernity and family values, and focused on movies and telefilms imported from the USA, Brazilian **telenovelas**, Japanese cartoons, variety and quiz shows, and endless advertising.

During the 1980s Berlusconi expanded into other sectors of the industry of popular culture and entertainment, such as cinema and music. Furthermore, through the acquisition of the Milanese conservative daily *Il Giornale* (1979), the foundation of the publishing house Silvio Berlusconi Editore (1986), and the acquisition of *Mondadori* (1991), Berlusconi's presence was also established in the publishing sector. Between weekly and monthly magazines, Berlusconi's two publishing houses marketed around twenty-five of the best-sold Italian periodicals, including the television guide *TV Sorrisi e Canzoni*, with a readership of more than 13 million. With the acquisition of the soccer team AC Milan in 1986, and the ongoing series of successes the team enjoyed afterwards, Berlusconi crowned his career as entrepreneur in the field of mass entertainment and added the final touches to his public image of self-made, all-powerful winner.

On 26 January 1994, on the eve of the national elections, Berlusconi suddenly resigned from the position of President of Fininvest (which, however, remained a family-held company) and entered the political field at the head of Forza Italia, a brand new political party – with a name, significantly, culled from a football slogan – which he had been covertly organizing during the previous six months. The outcome of an intense two-month electoral campaign, which saw Forza Italia employing the most advanced techniques of political marketing and fully exploiting all the potential of Fininvest's media, was a 21 per cent share of the vote and the elevation of Berlusconi to the presidency of the Council of Ministers. However, due to the withdrawal of the Northern League from the governing coalition, Berlusconi's presidency lasted only seven months (10 May 1994–22 December 1994), and the subsequent national election of April 1996 saw him relegated to the role of leader of the opposition.

Having entered politics, Berlusconi was accused of concentrating excessive economic and political resources in his hands, thus creating a great number of potential conflicts of interest. Nevertheless, in June 1995, three referenda concerning the private television system – which, if passed, would have reduced Berlusconi's concentration of ownership as well as the revenue of his media empire – were defeated by the majority of the Italian voters. The problem of the potential conflict of interest seemed to find a partial solution one year later with the entry into the stock market of Mediaset, the holding company of the Berlusconi's three televisions, even if Berlusconi himself retained the majority of the shares.

Despite having been convicted of corruption while president of Fininvest, Berlusconi remained a national political figure and the symbol of the postmodern erosion of the demarcation between business, politics, media and popular culture.

See also: broadcasting; private television

Further reading

Fiori, G. (1995) *Il venditore. Storia di Silvio Berlusconi e della Fininvest* (The Salesman: The History of Silvio Berlusconi and Fininvest), Milan: Garzanti.

Schlesinger, P. (1990) 'The Berlusconi Phenomenon', in Z. Baranski and R. Lumley (eds), *Culture and Conflict in Postwar Italy*, London: Macmillan.

EMANUELA POLI

Bernabei, Ettore

b. 16 May 1921, Florence

Politician and manager

After being editor of the Christian Democrat newspaper *Il Popolo* from 1956–60, Bernabei was appointed general manager of the **RAI** by Amintore **Fanfani**. He directed the national broadcaster until 1974 – in effect throughout the entire period of its monopoly (see **broadcasting**) – and thus left such an indelible stamp on Italian television culture that the period is often called simply the 'Bernabei era'. With Italian television still in its infancy, he established the idea of regular daily programming with the aim of making television the new hearth of the Italian family. Throughout the 1960s, while firmly exercising **DC** power, he increased progressive cultural programming in order to weaken opposition from the Communists. Subsequently judged as something of an enlightened despot, he kept tight control of the organization but greatly expanded its scope and professionalism, although this eventually led to huge budget deficits. After leaving the RAI in 1974 he became active in producing films for television, his best-known to date being the mega-production *La Sacra Bibbia* (The Holy Bible).

RICCARDO VENTRELLA

Berto, Giuseppe

b. 27 December 1914, Mogliano, Veneto;
    d. 1 November 1978, Rome

Novelist and scriptwriter

A volunteer in the African campaign during the Second World War, Berto was captured by the Allies and taken to a prisoner-of-war camp in Hereford, Texas, where he began to write short stories and the novel *Il cielo è rosso* (The Sky is Red), published upon his return to Italy in 1946. From the neorealist mode of his 1940s and 1950s narrative, Berto turned to psychoanalysis, which became the theoretical frame for his more introspective novels such as *Il male oscuro* (Incubus) (1964), a narrative based on his own experience and consisting in the breathless monologue of a main character tracing the reasons of his neurosis. In his later fiction, Berto discussed environmental issues (*Oh Serafina!*, 1973) and explored religious themes (*La gloria* (Glory), 1978).

Further reading

Artico, E. and Lepri, L. (eds) (1989) *Giuseppe Berto: la sua opera, il suo tempo* (Giuseppe Berto: His Work and Times), Florence: Olschki.

FRANCESCA PARMEGGIANI

Bertolucci, Attilio

b. 18 November 1911, San Lazzaro, Parma

Poet, critic and translator

Father of film director Bernardo **Bertolucci**, Attilio Bertolucci is recognized as one of Italy's finest poets. His early poetry, published in the 1930s, was immediately hailed by fellow poet Eugenio **Montale**, and explores elegiac themes and the languid portrayal of seasonal rhythms that characterize all his work. After the Second World War, Bertolucci moved to Rome where he taught art history and became a consultant for Garzanti and for **RAI** (state television). In 1951, he was awarded the prestigious Premio Viareggio (see **literary prizes**) for his collection *La capanna indiana* (The Indian Hut). With *Viaggio d'inverno* (Winter Voyage), published in 1971, Bertolucci modernized his language and prosody without losing the elegiac tone of his verse. A regular contributor to the national daily *La Repubblica*, he has also published collected essays in *Viaggi fotografici di Giuseppe Michelini (1873–1951)* (Photographic Voyages of Giuseppe Michelini 1873–1951) (1981) and *Aritmie* (Arrhythmias) (1991), volumes that underscore his continuing interest in mass media and the cinema.

Further reading

Bertolucci, A. (1997) *Opere*, Milan: Mondadori (collected poems with a bibliography and an introductory essay on the poet's work).

VALERIO FERME

Bertolucci, Bernardo

b. 16 March 1941, Parma

Film director

The son of the celebrated poet Attilio **Bertolucci**, Bernardo first followed in his father's footsteps and began his artistic career as a poet. Because of obvious oedipal conflicts, he soon abandoned poetry and turned to film-making. The oedipal paradigm is in fact particularly suited to an exploration of Bertolucci's career, and how to relate to patriarchy and tradition is one of the central issues raised by Bertolucci's filmography, in both artistic and personal terms. Bertolucci's investment in psychoanalysis suffuses his films and gives them a psychological density admirably enhanced by the use of symbolism.

It was probably Bertolucci's first guide, Pier Paolo **Pasolini**, who inspired the young film student to have faith in 'the poetic world of his own vital experiences', to borrow Pasolini's own words. It is to Pasolini indeed that Bertolucci owes both his first job as an assistant on *Accattone* (1961) and the material for his first film, *La commare secca* (The Grim Reaper) (1962). The subject of *La commare secca*, the Roman underworld, the brutal murder of a prostitute in a park peopled with thieves and psychopaths, is very Pasolinian and reminiscent of *Accattone*, but the treatment is already unmistakably Bertoluccian in the smoothness of the shifts in point of view and the round elegance of the images. *La commare secca* almost unwillingly kills off Bertolucci's first cinematic father, for it has nothing of the 'sacrality' of Pasolini's imagery but rather all the slick asymmetry to become typical of the Bertoluccian style.

With *Prima della rivoluzione* (Before the Revolution) (1964), Bertolucci confirms his commitment to political cinema and expresses his faith in Marxist ideology. A quote from the French statesman Talleyrand is the premise of the film – 'Whoever has not known life before the Revolution does not know the sweetness of life' – an acknowledgement that in the most revolutionary desire for radical change, there remains an irrepressible nostalgia for the past. This is what Fabrizio, the film's protagonist, demonstrates in the dissolution of his short-lived commitment to Marxism. First rebelling against the rigid bourgeoisie to which he belongs, Fabrizio ends up espousing the old order by ultimately wedding the upper middle-class fiancée he had originally left behind.

Working on television documentaries and other short projects, Bertolucci waited four years before making his next feature film, *Partner*. A free adaptation of Dostoievski's short story, 'The Double,' *Partner* echoes the 1968 movement in its reflection on life, art and revolution. The film's elitist aesthetics mark the unresolved influence of the French New Wave on Bertolucci's style, and more particularly of the French director Jean-Luc Godard, Bertolucci's second cinematic father.

In *La strategia del ragno* (The Spider's Stratagem) (1970), Bertolucci turns to psychoanalysis to interweave aesthetic and personal inquiries for the first time. A young man visits the small town that made his father a hero of the **Resistance**. As he attempts to elucidate the murder of his father at the request of the hero's aged mistress, he is led to question the integrity of the Resistance hero, until he chooses to rehabilitate him through a personal understanding of the man's betrayal.

After revisiting the aftermath of Fascism, Bertolucci explores 'the heart of the beast' with *Il conformista* (The Conformist) (1970), a penetrating investigation of the neuroses that sustain fascist ideology. As always building upon literary references, the film is an adaptation of Alberto **Moravia**'s 1951 novel, *Il conformista*. Thanks to the collaboration of the gifted cinematographer Vittorio **Storaro**, the film is a feat of technical virtuosity. Distorted by long lenses, layered with screens, windows, mirrors or curtains, Bertolucci's images powerfully convey the mendacity of fascist rhetoric. The director's own fear of conformism is exorcized by the fascist protagonist's descent into a monstrous 'normality' leading to murder and betrayal. The film culminates in a dazzling dance scene that leads to the protagonist's loss of self and to the film's 'journey to the end of fascism'. Bertolucci's films almost always include a momentous dance scene, perhaps the film-maker's aesthetic signature.

Ultimo tango a Parigi (Last Tango in Paris) certainly centres on a dance, but it is a lethal one. Still stamped by the scandalous aura that surrounded the film when it came out in 1972, *Ultima tango* is openly controversial, but certainly less so in the explicitness of its sexual representations than in its aesthetic ambition to coin a new cinematic language. Breaking with Jean-Luc Godard and the New Wave that it denounces as falsely radical, it addresses the tragic failure of communication in a world neurotically entrapped in pre-established identities and roles.

The controversy over *Ultimo tango* brought Bertolucci to the attention of Hollywood. Putting the capitalist dream machine at the service of his ideology, Bertolucci made *Novecento* (1900) in 1976, a magnificently photographed two-act epic encapsulating the history of the twentieth century in four seasons from 1900 to 1945. Set near Parma, the film documents the revival of the peasantry's political consciousness in the long confrontation between fascism and communism in Italy. Overlong (originally over 300 minutes, it was reduced to 240 minutes for commercial distribution) and excessively romantic, the film was visually stunning but on the whole failed to live up to its original conception.

The failure of *Novecento* led Bertolucci to reconsider the present. With *La luna* (Luna) in 1978, the incest taboo is revisited on an intimate mode. The patent Freudian academism of the film fortunately does not undermine the authenticity of the explored relationships. *La tragedia di un uomo ridicolo* (Tragedy of a Ridiculous Man) (1981), on the other hand, marks Bertolucci's return to politics. *La tragedia* furthers the film-maker's ongoing examination of power relations through a reflection on the incongruities that plague the contemporary Italian body politic, including terrorism.

L'ultimo imperatore (The Last Emperor) (1987) is perhaps the most impressive manifestation of Bertolucci's meditation on power. Portraying the end of the Manchu dynasty, *The Last Emperor* is a political parable with the dimensions of an epic. In spite of its historical setting, it can be regarded as the metaphorical continuation of Bertolucci's reflection on the sociopolitical problems uncovered in *La tragedia di un uomo ridicolo*.

Staying with the epic genre, once *The Last Emperor* had definitively conquered Hollywood, Bertolucci adapted a novel by Paul Bowles in *The*

Sheltering Sky, a 1990 film that marks a departure from the director's commitment to the present and its problems. Bertolucci's own 'stay in the desert' (the film takes place in North Africa), *The Sheltering Sky* is an existential meditation on death which exudes a certain nihilism. It was followed by *Piccolo Buddha* (Little Buddha) Bertolucci's 1992 quest for spiritual solutions, though the technical brilliance and the stylistic enthusiasm of the film do not camouflage its essential emptiness and Bertolucci's creative anxieties.

It is perhaps this fear of aesthetic impotence that *Io ballo da sola* (Stolen Beauty) best assesses in 1995. However intrusive Bertolucci's camera tries to be, it never captures nor penetrates the beauty on the screen. As such, the film is an admission of the paradox that representing beauty necessarily deflowers it.

Further reading

Michalczyk, J. (1986) *The Italian Political Filmmakers*, London and Toronto: Fairleigh Dickinson University Press (see especially ch. 3: 'Bernardo Bertolucci: The Strategy of a Freudian Marxist').

Pasolini, P.P. (1988) *Heretical Empiricism*, trans. B. Lawton and L.K. Barnett, Bloomington, IN: Indiana University Press, 167–86 (see 'The Cinema of Poetry' (1965) and more particularly Pasolini's visionary discussion of Bertolucci's *Prima della rivoluzione*, 180–1).

DOROTHÉE BONNIGAL

Bertolucci, Giuseppe

b. 27 February 1947, Parma

Film director

Son of poet Attilio **Bertolucci** and younger and less well-known than his more famous brother Bernardo **Bertolucci**, Giuseppe Bertolucci has nevertheless carved out a successful career for himself as one of the directors of the so-called **New Italian Cinema**. After collaborating with Bernardo on the scripts of both *Last Tango in Paris* (1972) and *Novecento* (1976), and some work for television, Giuseppe directed *Berlinguer ti voglio bene*

(I Love You Berlinguer) (1977), the feature that launched the film career of the popular comedian and later director Roberto **Benigni**. Bertolucci continued to work with Benigni, directing *Tuttobenigni* (All of Benigni) for **RAI** television in 1986. There have followed a number of interesting films, including a zany road movie *I cammelli* (Camels) (1989) which featured the talents of another of the most popular new Italian comics, Paolo Rossi.

GINO MOLITERNO

Betocchi, Carlo

b. 23 January 1899, Turin; d. 25 May 1986, Florence

Poet and editor

Athough born in Turin, Betocchi grew up and spent most of his long life in Florence. With Piero Bargellini he directed *Il Frontespizio*, the Fascist era's most influential Italian Catholic journal, in which he published his first poems. Completely immune to the influence of *ermetismo* (formally elegant poetry, enigmatic in meaning but often tinged with existential pessimism), Betocchi's poetry celebrates man's daily interaction with God's creation in the Tuscan landscape through language that is at once precise and humble, concrete and spiritual. His later work, from *Estate di San Martino* (Indian Summer) (1961) to *Prime e ultimissime* (First and Latest Ones) (1974), while formally more experimental, continues in its thankful praise of God and earned Betocchi numerous accolades as the bard of contented old age.

Further reading

Betocchi, C. (1964) Poems, New York: Clarke and Way (selected poems in English).

—— (1996) *Tutte le poesie* (Complete Poems), Milan: Garzanti (includes a bibliography of Betocchi's work).

VALERIO FERME

Betti, Ugo

b. 4 February 1892, Camerino
   (Macerata); d. 9 June 1953, Rome

Magistrate, playwright

The most prominent Italian playwright in the immediate postwar years and, according to many, second only to Pirandello, Betti centred his works on one major theme; the nature of evil and the ambiguous attitude that men have towards it. His experience as a magistrate gave him a particular insight into the nature of human relationships, around which the plot of his plays often revolved. Many of the issues investigated in his works, like predestination, free will and sexual morality, represented the same beliefs that drew him away from organized religion. However, they are also symbolic of his hunger for a justice which was above human fallibility, a search which would eventually reconcile him with the Catholic Church.

Although he began his career as a dramatist in the mid-1920s with *La Padrona* (The Mistress of the House) (1926) and wrote several plays during the Fascist period, which he never rejected, his most famous works were written in the 1940s. *Ispezione* (Inspection) (1947), and *Corruzione al Palazzo di Giustizia* (Corruption in the Palace of Justice) (1949) are among his best.

Further reading

Betti, U. (1964) *Three Plays on Justice*, trans. with introduction by G.H. McWilliam, San Francisco: Chandler (comprehensive introduction and translation of *Frana allo Scalo Nord*, *Lotta fino all'alba* and *La fuggitiva*).

FEDERICA STURANI

Bettiza, Enzo

b. 1927, Spalato, Croatia

Journalist, essayist and novelist

A journalist who has covered the recent historical events in Eastern Europe, Bettiza has also developed a marked personal style which reflects his disbelief in a clearcut distinction between chronicle and fiction and all his writing strives for a prose that contains the complexities of a novel. Discovered by Guido **Piovene** in the 1950s and strongly influenced by the Russian novelist tradition, Bettiza could be located in the neorealist milieu, although his ideological position is complicated by moral and existential issues. Amongst his best novels are *La campagna elettorale* (The Electoral Campaign) (1953), *Il fantasma di Trieste* (The Ghost of Trieste) (1958) and *I fantasmi di Mosca* (The Ghosts of Moscow) (1993). One of his finest essays is *Mito e realtà di Trieste* (Myth and Reality in Trieste) (1966).

ANDREA RICCI

Bevilacqua, Alberto

b. 27 June 1934, Parma

Novelist, poet and film-maker

While Bevilacqua's first collection of short stories, entitled *La polvere sull'erba* (Dust on the Grass) (1955), reflected his early idyllic years in Parma, the author soon turned to more penetrating themes after he moved to Rome. Responding to the tumultuous cultural changes taking place in Italy in the 1960s, Bevilacqua used the novel as a way of exploring the psychological and philosophical crises facing contemporary society. His numerous works, which received both critical acclaim and public recognition, include *Questa specie d'amore* (This Kind of Love), which won the Campiello Prize in 1966, and *L'occhio del gatto* (Cat's Eye), which was awarded the prestigious Strega Prize in 1968. Bevilacqua's style is noted for its lyrical blend of linguistic experimentation and autobiographical elements. His poetry has been anthologized in two volumes, *Immagine e somiglianza* (Images and Similarities) (1982) and *Vita mia* (My Life) (1985). He has also successfully directed several films adapted from his own books, among them *La califfa* (The Female Caliph) (1970) and *Gialloparma* (Crime in Parma) (1998).

LAURA A. SALSINI

Biagi, Enzo

b. 9 August 1920, Lizzano, Bologna

Journalist

One of the most popular journalists in Italy, Biagi, unlike Giorgio **Bocca**, is more loved by the public than respected by his colleagues. His productivity is comparable to that of a successful small business of his native Emilia-Romagna: he has been a columnist for **Il Corriere della sera** and then for **La Repubblica** ('*Strettamente personale*', Strictly Personal), a travel writer with books on Russia, China and America, a biographer of Gianni Agnelli (see **Agnelli family**), an autobiographer (*Disonora il padre*) (Dishonour Thy Father) (1975), a newspaper editor (**Il Resto del Carlino**) and television presenter. His recipe is a mild populism stuffed with anecdotes reminiscent of **Fellini**'s *Amarcord*. He speaks for the common man, spicing his stories with personal experiences, and he has consistently shown scepticism towards the political class, something that perhaps dates back to his involvement with the **Partito d'Azione** (Action Party) in the **Resistance**. He takes pride in writing straightforward prose with a humorous touch.

See also: newspapers

Further reading

Biagi, E. (1984) *Diciamoci tutto* (Let's Tell Each Other Everything), Milan: Mondadori.

ROBERT LUMLEY

Biagiotti, Laura

b. 4 August 1943, Rome

Fashion designer

Later renowned as the 'Queen of Cashmere', Biagiotti began her career in fashion design in her mother's dressmaking business. Her personal brand of women's ready-to-wear clothes was launched in 1972 with a soft and loose Biagiotti line, which typically sought to strike a balance between elegance and practicality. Biagiotti expanded from women's clothing into a men's line in 1987 and then into a large women's line (Laura Più) as well as one for children (Biagiotti Junior). Among the Biagiotti licences are her well-known sunglasses. In a crowded and competitive environment, Biagiotti managed to achieve some remarkable 'firsts': she was the first Italian designer to present a collection in China and also the first to stage a fashion show inside the walls of the Kremlin in Moscow, where Biagiotti clothes seem to be very popular in a climate that welcomes the warm and elegant embrace of cashmere. The distinctive Biagiotti logo features the towers of the fifteenth-century medieval fortress outside Rome which Biagiotti restored and turned into her headquarters.

BERNADETTE LUCIANO

Bigongiari, Piero

b. 15 October 1914, Navacchio, Pisa; d. October 1998, Florence

Poet and essayist

Professor of contemporary literature at the University of Florence, Bigongiari wrote a number of influential critical works on modern Italian poetry and in particular on Giacomo Leopardi. As an expression of Florentine *ermetismo* (see also Mario **Luzi**), Bigongiari's early poetry, collected in the 1968 anthology *Stato di cose* (The State of Things), is linguistically polished but revolves almost obsessively around the hermetic themes of absence and expectation. In the 1970s, Bigongiari abandoned the formal rigidity of his early verse and reduced its lyrical introspection. His later work, from *Anti-materia* (Anti-Matter) onward, juxtaposes rational and fantastical elements to become an open meditation on the process of writing as the only reality truly accessible to the poet.

Further reading

Bigongiari, R. (1994) *Tutte le poesie* (Complete Poems), Florence: Le Lettere (with bibliographical references).

Macrì, O. (1988) *Studi sull'ermetismo: l'enigma della poesia di Bigongiari* (Studies on Hermeticism: The Enigma of the Poetry of Bigongiari), Lecce:

Milella (a comprehensive study of Bigongiari's poetry covering his entire career).

VALERIO FERME

Bilenchi, Romano

b. 9 November 1909, Colle Val d'Elsa, Siena; d. 17 November 1989, Florence

Journalist and novelist

Although Bilenchi began his career as a journalist by working for early proto-fascist periodicals in Tuscany, he soon rejected all allegiance to right-wing politics. As the Fascist regime became more repressive, Bilenchi's political philosophy turned to the Left, and he not only joined the Italian Communist Party (see **PCI**) but also took part in **Resistance** activities in Florence during the Second World War. After the war he founded the daily newspaper *Il Nuovo Corriere* (The New Courier), and remained its editor until 1956. Bilenchi's novels, which manifest his view of literature as a psychological evocation of memory and lived events, often focus on the psychic development of young characters as they confront adult expectations. His works include the novels *Il conservatorio di Santa Teresa* (The Conservatory of Santa Theresa) (1940) and *Il bottone di Stalingrado* (The Stalingrad Button), which was awarded the 1972 Viareggio Prize; several long stories including *La siccità* (Drought) (1941) and *Il Gelo* (The Frost) (1982) and a memoir, *Amici* (Friends) (1976), recalling twentieth-century intellectual life.

LAURA A. SALSINI

Blasetti, Alessandro

b. 3 July 1900; d. 2 February 1987, Rome

Film director

Blasetti began as a film critic. In 1927, together with a number of other young enthusiasts, he founded the film company Augustus through which, in 1929, with no real directing experience, he produced and directed his first film *Sole* (Sun), based on the reclaiming of the Pontine Marshes.

The film received a very mixed response and Augustus folded, but Blasetti moved on to direct films for the Cines company. A grandiose monumental style, borrowed from successful epics of the 1910s, became a characteristic of his films which conformed, more on the formal level than on the level of subject matter, to the policy of the Fascist regime. Although he remained somewhat tainted by his Fascist associations, *Vecchia guardia* (The Old Guard) (1934) was the only film which explicitly expressed Fascist ideology; his other films relied mainly on literary sources, like *Ettore Fieramosca* (1938), adapted from a novel by Massimo D'Azeglio, or mythic situations that hover between history and legend like *La corona di ferro* (The Iron Crown) (1941). He made several films in collaboration with **Zavattini**, beginning with *Quattro passi fra le nuvole* (A Walk through the Clouds) (1942) and then continued to produce popular well-made films into the late 1970s, including two films starring Sophia **Loren** and Marcello **Mastroianni**. His best works remain *1860* (1934) and *Il cappello a tre punte* (The Three-Cornered Hat) (1935).

CRISTINA DEGLI-ESPOSTI REINERT

Bo, Carlo

b. 25 January 1911, Sestri Levante, Genoa

Literary critic and academic

While pursuing a successful academic career as professor of French literature, and since 1947 as *rettore* (vice-chancellor) at the University of Urbino, Carlo Bo actively participated in the cultural life of prewar and postwar Italy. Originating from the existential notion of literature as he described it in the 1930s essay *Letteratura come vita* (Literature as Life), Bo's critical discourse focused mainly on the significance of ethical and religious motifs in contemporary poetry and narrative. In addition to countless articles published in literary journals, newspapers and magazines, Bo wrote seminal essays on hermeticism, surrealism and **neorealism** and on such authors as Giacomo Leopardi, Renato Serra, Massimo Bontempelli and Tommaso Landolfi. Highly respected as an academic and intellectual, he has presided over several committees for literary prizes, and in 1984 he was nominated life senator by the then President of the Republic, Sandro **Pertini**.

FRANCESCA PARMEGGIANI

Bobbio, Norberto

b. 18 October 1909, Turin

Political and legal philosopher

A liberal philosopher and one of the foremost public intellectuals of the First **Republic**, Bobbio is a keen analyst, critic and defender of the civil state. He has held chairs of jurisprudence at the Universities of Siena, Padua and Turin and has shown an enduring concern with the role of philosophy in relation to religion and to science. A public figure of note, he has used the mass media to expound his insight that the growth of democracy in Italy has been matched by an apparent vocation on the part of the intellectual class for the antidemocratic and the irrational, a strong parallel, he has suggested, to the undermining of the achievements of the 'liberal age' of Giolitti by fascism.

Chief amongst the figures to whom he publicly paid tribute in 1984, when he was made a life senator, was Benedetto **Croce**, valued for his individualistic and determined anti-fascism. Bobbio's autobiography was published in 1997.

Further reading

Bobbio, N. (1995) *Ideological Profile of Twentieth-Century Italy*, trans. L.G. Cochrane, Princeton, NJ: Princeton University Press.

SUZANNE KIERNAN

Bocca, Giorgio

b. 18 August 1920, Cuneo

Journalist

A leading member of the generation that fought in the **Resistance** as young men, Bocca began his journalistic apprenticeship with the party paper of *Giustizia e Libertà* (Justice and Liberty). After an initial sojourn in Turin he moved to Milan, where he remained. His investigative articles for *Il Giorno* in the early 1960s established his reputation as a new breed of journalist bent on discovering the real Italy of unbridled capitalism and social malaise. He became a regular columnist for *L'Europeo* and then for *La Repubblica* and *L'Espresso*. His politics made him an uncomfortable figure for both the ruling Christian Democrats (see **DC**) and for the Italian Communist Party (see **PCI**). His *Palmiro Togliatti* (1973) stressed the Stalinism of this leader, while his *Il caso 7 aprile* (1980) attacked the distortions of the Italian system of justice resulting from its battle against terrorism. Freedom of speech and opinion remained Bocca's watchwords. His *Il provinciale* (1991) provides autobiographical insights, but his books tend to be extended versions of his more succinct newspaper articles.

See also: newspapers

ROBERT LUMLEY

Bocelli, Andrea

b. 22 September 1959, Lajatico, Tuscany

Tenor

Blind from the age of twelve, Andrea Bocelli rose to international fame in the mid-1990s, building a career with equal strengths in the classical and popular repertoires. After graduating in law he began serious vocal studies under Franco Corelli, and supported himself by singing in clubs and bars. He auditioned for **Zucchero**, who invited him to join his 1993 European tour and later performed in **Pavarotti**'s annual charity galas. In 1996 he achieved major chart success with his single 'Con te partirò' (Time to Say Goodbye), which was re-recorded as a duet with soprano Sarah Brightman. Bocelli's album *Romanza* (1997) sold several million copies worldwide, and was swiftly followed by the classically oriented *Aria* (1998). His detractors have questioned both his technique and his musicianship, but his popular appeal is beyond doubt. His appearance on the American Rosie O'Donnell show in April 1998 attracted an unprecedented 24 million viewers.

JOHN KERSEY

Boetti, Alighiero

b. 16 December 1940, Turin; d. April 1994, Rome

Artist

Boetti was always intensely interested in the idea of order and disorder, and he used his art to suggest unexpected relationships between ordinary things. In semiotic terms, Boetti transforms a conventional relation into a causal one, as when he writes a word so as to form the shape of the object it represents. Working in a style related to the ideas of *arte povera*, pop and **conceptual art**, Boetti conceived works which he then had manufactured by Afghan embroiderers.

L'albero delle ore (The Tree of the Hours), from 1979, uses the idea of church bells which sound on the hour and quarter hours, and converts them to visual signs which form a large Christmas Tree, linking tree and time. *Arazzo* (Tapestry), from 1980, is a map of the world which shows each country in the colours and design of its flag. These connecting protocols are of no practical use, but they do create surprise and wonderment.

In the early 1970s, Boetti changed his name to 'Alighiero e Boetti', suggesting a duplication of his personality.

MAX STAPLES

Bolognini, Mauro

b. 28 June 1922, Pistoia

Film director

Trained in architecture and with an interest in painting, Bolognini became known for the formal beauty and pictorial composition of his films. An uneven collaboration matched his elegant direction with Pier Paolo **Pasolini**'s raw screenplays about the subproletariat. Concluding their working relationship with a successful film version of Vitaliano

Brancati's *Il bell'Antonio* (1960), Bolognini continued adapting classics of modern Italian literature to the screen, creating films in which he demonstrated his skill at recreating the ambience of Italy's various regions in bygone eras. Bolognini defended his work against accusations of ideological vacuity by claiming that, like Luchino **Visconti**, he studied the dynamics of familial power relationships as a microcosm for the political operations of society at large.

Further reading

Montezemola, V.C. (ed.) (1977) *Bolognini*, Rome: Istituto Poligrafo dello Stato (text in English, French and Italian; includes an extended interview with Bolognini and an important essay on his adaptation of literary works by the film critic/historian Gian Piero Brunetta).

Witcombe, R.T. (1982) 'Form as Fatherscape: Bolognini and Bertolucci,' in *The New Italian Cinema*, New York: Oxford (explores the theme of family conflict in the work of both directors).

WILLIAM VAN WATSON

Bongiorno, Mike

b. 26 May 1924, New York, USA

Television presenter and broadcaster

The name of Mike Bongiorno is synonymous with Italian television. Having been present at its inauguration as one of the two interviewers on *Arrivi e partenze* (Arrivals and Departures), the **RAI**'s first public television programme broadcast on 3 January 1954, Bongiorno has gone on to appear uninterruptedly on Italian television for almost half a century, continuing to exercise his role of high priest of quiz with all the resilience and confidence of a national institution.

Born in New York of an American father and Italian mother, Bongiorno was in Italy during the Second World War but returned to America in 1945 and began his broadcasting career as the presenter of a radio programme called *Voci nuove dall'Italia* (New Voices from Italy). In 1953 he returned to Italy and began to work for the RAI, first in radio and then in television. Although he made his television debut in 1954, his first real success came in 1956 with the now legendary *Lascia o raddoppia* (Double or Nothing), a weekly quiz show modelled on the American *The $64,000 Dollar Question*, which ran for 191 consecutive weeks and marked a milestone in Italian television culture. The programme's overwhelming popularity not only served to rapidly increase licences and sales of television sets but even forced cinemas to interrupt film screenings on Thursday nights, sometimes showing the programme themselves. Bongiorno thus became a household name, and in the years that followed he consolidated his position as grand quizmaster with new shows that attempted to rejuvenate a familiar formula: *Caccia al numero* (Hunt the Number) (1962), *La fiera dei sogni* (The Dream Fair) (1963), *Giochi in famiglia* (Family Games) (1966), *Rischiatutto* (Risk All) (1970), *Scommettiamo* (Let's Bet) (1978) and *Flash* in 1980.

By 1981, however, Silvio **Berlusconi** was preparing his own entry into Italian television, and Bongiorno was drawn away from the RAI to work for Berlusconi's **Canale Cinque**, where he has remained to preside forever over much-watched quiz shows like *Superflash*, *Telemike* and *La ruota della fortuna* (The Wheel of Fortune). Over the years he has also been called upon to host the **Sanremo Festival** eleven times, his most recent appearance being in 1997 with sexy soubrette Valeria Marini at his side. His popularity undiminished and having finally and formally achieved the status of a living legend – in 1997 he entered the Guinness Book of Records for the length of his career in television – Bongiorno has continued to shrug off accusations of mediocrity and venality levelled at him by more intellectual critics, and reasserted his eternal willingness to continue being the extraordinary incarnation of the ordinary televisual Italian.

See also: broadcasting; private television

Further reading

Eco, U. (1963) 'Fenomenologia di Mike Bongiorno' (Phenomenology of Mike Bongiorno), *Diario minimo* (Miniature Diary), Milan: Mondadori (a classic study of Bongiorno as a significant cultural phenomenon by the famous Italian

semiotician who himself worked briefly on Bongiorno's *Lascia or raddoppia*).

GINO MOLITERNO

Bonino, Emma

b. 9 March 1948, Bra, Cuneo

Social activist and politician

With a degree in foreign languages from the prestigious Bocconi University of Milan, Bonino began her political career during the 1970s as militant feminist, vocal and active in the campaign for the legalization of **abortion**. She was jailed for her pro-abortion activities in 1975, but in 1976 was elected to Parliament as a deputy for the **Radical Party**. From 1979 onwards she also served as a member of the European Parliament, and in 1994 became European Commissioner for Humanitarian Aid, Consumer Rights and Fishing. Highly respected internationally for her passionate support for the environment, equality and human rights, she was named European of the Year in 1996. Equally popular at home, in 1999 she became a strong contender for the Presidency of the Republic, the first time a woman had even been considered for the position. In the event she lost the Presidential contest to **Ciampi**, but proved herself again in June 1999 when she led a strong team of Radicals to success in the elections for the European Parliament.

GINO MOLITERNO

Bonito Oliva, Achille

b. 4 November 1939, Caggiano, Salerno

Art critic and curator

Bonito Oliva has curated numerous art exhibitions since 1969, and has written over twenty books. In 1979 he coined the term **transavantgarde**, and the next year he achieved prominence by launching the artists of this grouping in the open section of the **Venice Biennale**.

Because of the markedly partizan nature of his writing, Bonito Oliva has been regarded more as a promoter than a researcher. His strongly opinionated judgements have often provoked harsh reactions as, for example, when he characterized **arte povera** as repressive and masochistic and the 1992 *Documenta* as a mere waste of money by uninformed organizers.

In 1993 he returned to the Venice Biennale as Artistic Director, an appointment which tends to reflect political influence. In fact, the actual title of Director was denied him, as in the meantime his Socialist sponsors had fallen from grace.

See also: art criticism

Further reading

Bonito Oliva, A. (1982) *Transavantgarde international*, Milan: Giancarlo Politi Editore (a sample of Bonito Oliva's writings on art).

MAX STAPLES

Bossi, Umberto

b. 19 September 1941, Cassano Magnano, Varese

Political leader

A medical student at Pavia in the 1960s, Umberto Bossi joined the student movement becoming, a member of, successively, **il manifesto**, PDUP (the Democratic Party of Proletarian Unity) and the Greens (see **Verdi**). In 1982 Bossi founded the Lombard Autonomous League, and in 1987 he was elected Senator of the Lombard League. Success in the European and regional elections of 1989 and 1990 respectively led to his establishing and leading the **Lega Nord** (Northern League), which triumphed in the 1992 national elections with 80 MPs elected. Bossi's blunt, even crude, rhetorical style and his political ability in mobilizing a mass movement had thus helped break the mould of Italian politics. In 1994, a tactical alliance with **Berlusconi** put the League briefly in government, but Bossi quickly re-established the League's oppositional character, which proved electorally successful in 1996. A populist rather than a statesman, his movement nevertheless put state reform, and specifically federalism, firmly on the national political agenda.

MARK DONOVAN

boxing

The 1960s were the golden age of Italian boxing. Duilio Loi was the world junior welterweight champion in 1960–2, and Sandro Lopopolo held the same title in 1965–6. Italy won five gold medals in the **Olympics** of 1960 and 1964. Among the medallists was Giovanni (Nino) Benvenuti, who dominated the welterweight division at the 1960 Rome Olympics and then advanced to the light middleweights, taking the world title in 1965–6. He then defeated Emil Griffith to become the middleweight champion of the world in what *Ring* magazine declared the best fight of 1967. Benvenuti was the only Italian to triumph in different weight categories. He retained his middleweight title until 1970, when he lost it to Carlos Monzon.

After Benvenuti, the only Italian boxing champions to gain international recognition were middleweight Vito Antuofermo, who attained a brief moment of glory in 1979, and Michele Piccirillo, who took the welterweight crown in 1998.

PAOLO VILLA

BPR

Officially refounded in 1947, the architectural studio BPR had initially been established in 1937 as Studio architetti BBPR, a name formed from the initials of its four partners: Gian Luigi Banfi (1910–45), Lodovico Belgiojoso (1909), Enrico Peressutti (1908–45) and its principal Ernesto Nathan **Rogers** (1909–69). The studio served as a personal and intellectual association for its founding members, and maintained its original form even after Banfi's death in the concentration camp of Mauthausen, though postwar events did prompt a slight change of name to signify the group's maturity. The members drew much of their inspiration and guidance from older architects such as Giuseppe Pagano (who had also died at Mauthausen), and sought to introduce modern ideas about architecture into the Politecnico of Milan, an institute then directed by Gaetano Moretti with a long-established conservative curriculum against which the nascent **BBPR** reacted. Their work continued to be grounded in considerations about the wider social and cultural context, and the group maintained a reputation for attempting to rescue Italian architecture from a stifling formalism.

FASSIL ZEWDOU

Branca, Vittore

b. 9 July 1913, Savona

Literary critic and essayist

Branca's long and illustrious career has been marked by an ability to combine the more scientific and philological aspects of literary research with the more openly interpretative aspects of criticism, an approach which is exemplified in the volume he co-authored with Jean Starobinski, *Filologia e critica* (Philology and Literary Criticism) (1977). Branca's critical method is best represented by his fundamental studies devoted to Boccaccio, culminating in his *Boccaccio medievale* (1959, revised 1981) and in his critical edition of the *Decameron* in 1976. A tireless and hardworking scholar, author, organizer and promoter of cultural events, Branca is the editor (with Carlo **Ossola**) of the journal *Lettere Italiane*, and also currently president of one of the most active and prestigious Italian cultural institutes, the Giorgio Cini Foundation of Venice. Besides his lifelong works on Boccaccio, Branca has written extensively on humanism and on the eighteenth century. He contributes to several major newspaper such as *Il sole Ventiquattore*.

ANDREA CICCARELLI

Brancati, Vitaliano

b. 24 July 1907, Pachino; d. 25 September 1954, Turin

Novelist, playwright and critic

Although Brancati lived for many years in Rome,

he remained tied to the people and customs of Sicily, often using his native land as a backdrop for his novels and plays. His early plays reflected fascist leanings, but Brancati eventually repudiated his earlier politics and his later work deals with themes such as the relationship between men and women, and provincial life in Sicily. Frequently focussing on social and sexual situations, these works tend to satirize the traditional male Sicilian code of honour. Brancati's novels, generally infused with tragicomic undertones, include *Gli anni perduti* (The Lost Years) (1941), *Don Giovanni in Sicilia* (Don Juan in Sicily) (1942) and *Paolo il caldo* (Paolo the Hot) (1955). His *Il Bell'Antonio* (1949), later adapted for the cinema by Mauro **Bolognini** and starring Marcello **Mastroianni** and Claudia **Cardinale**, depicts a stereotypical Don Juan type whose philanderings are eventually revealed as merely a ruse to hide his sexual insecurity and impotence.

LAURA A. SALSINI

Branzi, Andrea

b. March 1938, Florence

Architect

Often called the godfather of Italian New Design, Branzi regarded design and architecture as privileged forms of expression, joining functionality and artistry and transforming the real into the imaginary. In 1968, Branzi became involved in 'radical' design, and in the late 1970s he emphatically rejected the current preoccupation with pure functionality and proposed a novel aesthetics built on symbolism and allegory. A founding member of **Archizoom** Associati, he advocated an alternative architectural language, proposing natural materials for new architectural expression. He joined **Studio Alchimia** and **Studio Memphis**, and in 1983 he founded the exclusive post-graduate Domus Academy in Milan. In 1986, he joined the EEC Commission to develop and promote design in Europe, and in 1987 he received the Golden Compass Award for theory and design. Branzi provided an important contribution to the post-functional design that, after the 1980s, was to become decisive in Italy's design culture.

See also: anti-design; design education; interior design

Further reading

Branzi, A. (1992) *Luoghi Andrea Branzi: The Complete Works*, introduction by G. Celant, London: Thames & Hudson (an illustrated anthology of Branzi's work assembled from several exhibition catalogues).

FASSIL ZEWDOU

Brass, Tinto (Giovanni)

b. 26 March 1933, Milan

Film director

After studying in France in the 1950s and working for a period at the Paris Cinémathèque, Brass served as assistant director to Rossellini on *India* (1958) and *Il generale Della Rovere* (General Della Rovere) (1959). His first feature film as director, *Chi lavora è perduto* (Whoever Works is Doomed), made in 1963, was an anarchic and semi-autobiographical work strongly influenced by the French New Wave. There followed a number of other films in the late 1960s that manifested a strong degree of originality and caustic anti-conformism, but from the mid-1970s the explicit sexual content of his films became ever more pronounced. This tendency continued through the 1980s and 1990s to become something of a trademark, leading many to regard Brass as the great Italian master of cinematic eroticism while others dismiss these later films as commercial soft porn thinly disguised as cultural provocation.

GINO MOLITERNO

bread

Directly derived from the Latin word *panis*, the Italian term for bread is *pane*. This fundamental component of the Italian diet is made from a dough obtained using wheat flour, water, yeast and salt. After leavening, it is cooked in an oven.

In Italy, as in many other countries, bread has always carried symbolic and religious connotations. For Catholics in particular, bread is the fundamental component of the Eucharist, where believers achieve communion with Christ by eating it as spiritual nourishment; the fundamental prayer of the Christian liturgy, the 'Our Father', begins with a request to 'give us this day our daily bread'. This religious legacy explains many deeply rooted Italian habits such as the reluctance to throw away bread, perceived as an expression of food wasting, or the aversion for resting bread upside down, interpreted as a sign of disrespect towards a holy food. One might have expected that, with the almost total disappearance of peasant culture in the later postwar period, the reverential attitude to bread may have faded. However, as a cultural habit touching on both religion and superstition, it still survives to a certain extent, at least at a subconscious level. The term *pane*, used as a synonym for food, also appears in countless expressions with metaphoric value: *buono come il pane*, as good as bread; *rendere pan per focaccia*, to exchange tit for tat; *mangiare pane a ufo*, to scrounge a living.

Bread is an integral component of the Italian daily diet, and is included in most main meals. Italians eat it for breakfast with *caffellatte*, and it is likely to be omnipresent on the table at lunch and the evening meal. In contrast to the widespread habit elsewhere, Italians do not normally spread butter on their bread, which falls into two main categories. The first or common one, *pane comune*, is made with the basic ingredients indicated above. According to the type of flour used, it is called *casareccio* (homemade) or *integrale* (wholemeal), and *pane bianco* (white bread) where the whiteness of the flour characterizes the product itself. To make *pane speciale* (special bread), additional ingredients – oil, potatoes, herbs, milk – may be used and different kinds of flour (corn, rye, soya flours) may be added. Under the generic labels of *pane bianco* and *pane nero* there proliferate a large number of bread types, with regional differences playing a role in three distinct ways: flavour, names and shapes of the product. Across internal regional boundaries, bread varieties have migrated far from their place of origin, so that, for example, Neapolitan bread is popular also in Milan and Tuscan bread (without salt) is sold in most northern and southern towns.

For toast lovers, *pane a cassetta* (sliced bread) is the required element, while *panini* (bread rolls) in countless forms, consistency and flavours are available everywhere on the peninsula. Bread sticks or *grissini* (born in Turin and named after its dialect) are a popular alternative to bread for those worried about gaining weight. No one likes *pane raffermo* (stale bread), while *pan grattato* (bread crumbs) is an essential ingredient of many dishes. Typical of central Italy is *bruschetta*, a generous slice of roasted bread on which garlic is rubbed before adding salt and virgin olive oil; the southern variation includes pieces of fresh, ripe tomatoes.

Internationally renowned *focaccia* is a close relation of bread, in fact a variation on the bread theme. It consists of a flattened layer of bread dough, cooked in a large baking tin and covered with a variety of ingredients. *Focaccia* in its simplest version was known in Roman times. The delicious combination of ingredients used as a topping have become more elaborate in recent years, giving origin to a wide range of different specialities in each region (see **regional cooking**).

MARIELLA TOTARO GENEVOIS

Brera, Giovanni Luigi (Gianni)

8 September 1919, San Zenone al Po; d. 19 December 1992, Codogno

Journalist and writer

The most famous and influential Italian sports journalist of all time, Gianni Brera wrote for *La Gazzetta dello Sport*, *Il Guerin Sportivo*, **Il Giorno** and **La Repubblica**. Brera willingly voiced his often provocative opinions on a variety of subjects ranging from his lifelong passion for food and wine to politics, literature and Italian history. However, his main professional interests remained **football** (*calcio*) and **cycling**.

Studies of Brera's distinctive use of the Italian language have highlighted his resourceful combination of erudite and vernacular idiom, and he coined many neologisms that subsequently became standard elements of Italian sports vocabulary (such as *libero* to designate the defensive soccer player who does not guard a specific opponent). A

prolific writer, Brera published several collections of essays and articles, a history of the World Cup, soccer manuals and novels.

Further reading

Brera, G. (1993) *L'Arcimatto 1960–1966*, ed. A. Maietti, Milan: Baldini & Castoldi (a collection of articles selected from the weekly feature of the same name that appeared in *Il Guerin Sportivo*).

PAOLO VILLA

Brioni

Fashion designer Gaetano Savini and tailor Nazareno Fonticoli inaugurated the Brioni men's fashion house in Rome in 1945, naming it after an elegant Adriatic resort. Brioni's new way of dressing men seemed to appeal to Hollywood actors such as Clark Gable and Gary Cooper, who flocked to Rome with the great success of Italian cinema in the 1950s. Brioni's reputation spread around the world with award-winning fashion shows in New York and other American cities Eventually Brioni branched out from its hand-sewn jackets and trousers to a shirt factory, a leather fashion house and a women's line. Quality has always been a trademark of Brioni, with each garment requiring at least eighteen hours of work. 'Your suit will be pressed no less than 184 times in a two-month period, the time you'll need to wait for it to be finished' says Mr Savini-Brioni. Apparently the wait is not a problem for the elite clientele of 25,000 customers, who order two or three garments per season.

BERNADETTE LUCIANO

broadcasting

Broadcasting in Italy is dominated by the state corporation Radiotelevisione Italiana (**RAI**) and a commercial sector that is principally controlled by Silvio **Berlusconi**'s **Fininvest** corporation. There are seven national terrestrial television networks, with three public channels – Rai Uno, Rai Due and Rai Tre – and four private channels,

Rete Quattro, **Canale Cinque** and **Italia Uno** which are part of the Mediaset group in which Fininvest holds a controlling stake, and **Telemontecarlo**, purchased in 1995 by cinema producer Vittorio Cecchi Gori. There are no cable networks, though Mediaset offers entertainment (Tele+1) and sport (Tele+2) oriented 'pay-per-view' channels. News programmes are a legal requirement for national channels. The state broadcaster provides five national radio stations – Radiouno, Radiodue, Radiotre, Stereo Rai and Radio Verde Rai – and regional and local stations, and also broadcasts overseas. There are many commercial local radio stations.

At the national level, the coverage of public affairs is supplied by a virtual 'duopoly' of the Rai state channels and Fininvest private channels. Since Berlusconi's entrance into politics at the helm of the Fininvest-created **Forza Italia** party, there have been a series of conflicts between the political alliances of centre–left and centre–right over the issue of *par condicio* (the fair balance of political coverage and control over resources). Public office has not dampened Berlusconi's enthusiasm for utilizing his communication resources for political self-promotion. It should be noted, however, that broadcasting was also a field for political conflict in the 'First' **Republic**.

The broadcasting system has been a slow developer relative to its European counterparts. Before the mid-1970s it remained trapped, like many aspects of Italian culture and society, within an incomplete process of modernization. Television was the only 'mass' medium in the sense that it addressed the entire population. People turned to newspapers for political commentary, as broadcast news was rather unsophisticated and limited in appeal. News coverage tended to report uncritically the activities of the government of the day, provided little space for opposing views and excluded the Communists (**PCI**) from representation. The sole supplier was the state broadcasting monopoly RAI. In most Western democracies, established regulatory norms and institutional codes of conduct ensure that the media coverage of politics maintains accepted standards of impartiality, and that a plurality of political opinions are available to the electorate. The Italian media system has been exceptional in that it has been traditionally dominated by a state corporation under the control of the ruling political parties.

Between 1975 and 1990, the broadcasting system developed within a legislative vacuum but under the influence and control of the political parties. In the early 1970s a **Constitutional Court** ruling ended the public monopoly of broadcasting by asserting the need for a more pluralist mass media. This triggered internal reform within the RAI organization and facilitated the establishment of private local television networks. Party control of state broadcasting was strengthened and institutionalized by the legislative reforms. An administrative council was created, whose members were nominated by Parliament on a 'representative' basis in proportion to the number of seats held by each party. Subsequently, the RAI became subject to the practice of *lottizzazione* (party political division of spoils and state resources). The ruling political parties divided the state broadcasting institution into 'pillars' of control, each party controlling a 'pillar' of the network. They had effective patronage over appointment to all levels of the organization (see **clientelism**). Competition between the channels reflected party political competition: the major channel Rai Uno became a fiefdom of the Christian Democrats (**DC**), Rai Due under the patronage of the Socialists (**PSI**), and Rai Tre, a channel initiated to offer a wider and more 'plural' coverage, to the Communists (**PCI**). The only three national television news programmes, TG1, TG2 and TG3, supported the political lines of the DC, PSI and PCI respectively. The control of the political parties over the state broadcasting media was institutionalized and remained intact until the 'old' party political system fell apart in 1993.

RAI operated according to public service criteria that were established by Law no. 103 in 1975, but the public broadcaster's ability to innovate and engage in commercial activities was constrained by an organizational logic that prioritized the interests of the political parties. This left significant commercial opportunities open to the private sector. After a 1974 Constitutional Court ruling stating that it was legitimate for private interests to set up transmitting equipment for radio and television within a defined local territory, the commercial broadcasting sector blossomed, initially at local levels. It provided a service based almost exclusively on entertainment. Operating in a regulatory vacuum and building on advertising revenues, entrepreneurs soon built up networks of local stations which tacitly challenged the ruling against a national level commercial network. One such attempt to establish a national commercial network came from the Rizzoli publishing group. However, the first national commercial network was Berlusconi's Canale Cinque, a group of local channels that broadcast simultaneously. Such an example of selective myopia towards the statute book was a common feature of Italian business in the First Republic. It also provided an opportunity for commercial business in a rapidly changing sector to innovate in the face of legislative stagnation. Implementing a market strategy for importing expensive foreign entertainment to attract high audiences and generate high advertising revenues, Berlusconi's Fininvest group of publishing and publicity interests took control of the commercial television and advertising market. By 1984, Fininvest had bought Italia Uno from the Rusconi publishing group and Rete Quattro from **Mondadori**. In October 1984, public prosecutors challenged the legality of Berlusconi's national television network and confiscated broadcasting equipment in Turin, Rome and Pescara. When the plugs were pulled on the commercial networks, Socialist Prime Minister **Craxi** was forced to issue an emergency decree that effectively authorized national commercial broadcasting. This established the RAI/Fininvest 'duopoly' which has been the hallmark of the rather unusual Italian broadcasting system ever since.

The RAI/Fininvest 'duopoly' was legitimated by the so-called Mammì law, the 1990 Broadcasting Act (no. 223). The Mammì law sidestepped the serious structural and financial problems faced by the state broadcasting organization, which were rendered impossible to negotiate because of the 'pillarization' of party interests. Instead, the Mammì law focused on commercial broadcasting, establishing a 'guarantor' to keep a register of stations, rule on libel controversies, report to **Parliament**, meet with a viewers' advisory council and set up minimal regulations on accepted standards of decency in programming and scheduling.

In the intervening years, commercial television had transformed the medium and the context of operation for the RAI. Crippled by organizational inefficiency and financial crisis, the RAI tried to compete with the entertainment-based transmissions of Fininvest and lost distinctiveness and credibility as a public service. In contrast, Berlusconi's introduction of popular programmes challenged the hierarchy and stifled the cultural elitism of Italian society that was embodied by the RAI. Given the nickname 'Sua Emittenza' (His Broadcastingship), he was prepared to use his public profile and mass popularity as a resource for backing politicians to defend his commercial interests. Furthermore, unlike many media moguls, Berlusconi always took an active personal control of editorial decisions for his media outlets.

In the 1990s, the RAI state television channels came increasingly under competition for the provision of information relating to public affairs from the Fininvest commercial channels. Kick-started by the legal requirement to provide news, the private channels increasingly developed a commercial strategy for covering public affairs. This came at a time when public attention for news and editorial freedom were emerging in response to the **Tangentopoli** scandals. High advertising revenues that accrued from peak viewing figures for public affairs programmes brought the Fininvest channels into competition with the RAI channels. Prior to 1992, the RAI channels maintained a virtual monopoly of television news broadcasting. After starting to broadcast national news in 1992, the Fininvest channels rapidly developed their news programming. By 1994 they supplied a total of 2,961 hours of news (13.7 per cent of net programming) in comparison to the 3,136 (12.8 per cent) supplied by the RAI channels. The viewing figures for the prime editions of the television news show that in a short time the Fininvest channels emerged from the shadow of the RAI as the provider of news.

The data on shifts in programming indicate a convergence between the public and commercial broadcasting sectors, due to competition and the need to respond to a changing set of public demands. The Tangentopoli crisis bore the seeds of a more active civil society in which the media have a greater role to play. In 1989, the Fininvest channels supplied a net programming of 92 per cent entertainment, 4.6 per cent cultural programmes and 3.4 per cent news and current affairs. By 1993, Fininvest programming had shifted to 75 per cent entertainment, 8 per cent cultural programmes and 16.4 per cent news and current affairs, which compared with the RAI breakdown of 50.7 per cent, 22.6 per cent and 26.7 per cent for the same categories. Such trends were indicative of broader changes in the broadcasting system which brought RAI and Fininvest into closer competition for supplying programmes to similar types of audience. In 1987, 23 per cent of Fininvest transmissions were produced and 77 per cent were bought; by 1993, the organization produced 46 per cent of its own transmissions, buying in only 54 per cent. Over the same time span, 1987–93, the proportion of transmissions bought in by RAI channels increased from 25 per cent to 37 per cent. This indicates that the 'convergence' of the quality of private and public supplies of information over time has consisted of a shift in programming by both the state and commercial broadcasters, rather than simply constituting a downgrading of the public service to the commercial one.

After the political crisis of Tangentopoli, the cosy Rai/Fininvest 'duopoly' was challenged by the needs of a renewed political system. Reform of the RAI and regulatory standards for media ownership became high-profile political conflicts. Berlusconi entered politics as an entrepreneur enters the marketplace, effectively breaking the established norms of political communication. His personal control over the commercial sector of the media industry brought charges of a conflict of interests with his leading political role.

This issue was complicated by the fact that at a crucial time for politics, it would appear that the broadcasting system may have been unable to provide 'fair play' to the competing political parties in the vital function of supplying information. One Fininvest television channel, Rete Quattro, operated as a vehicle of propaganda for Forza Italia, supplying a coverage which not only attacked the political opposition, but also discredited the judiciary for the Berlusconi cause. Suffice it to say that the editor of TG 4, Emilio Fede, considered standing as a candidate for Forza Italia in the 1996 elections, but was deemed more useful to the party at the editorial helm of Rete Quattro's news.

Control over media resources became a field of political conflict, precisely at a time when the media discourse was itself the forum through which political conflicts were waged. This further threatened an already 'weak' tradition for editorial independence in Italian broadcasting. A major legislative initiative was required to meet the needs of the industry, but attempts were politically 'hamstrung'. The undefined nature of the regulatory system, high value of public information to political parties, and emergence of the Fininvest owner as a political leader, ensured that the long-running uncertainty concerning the balance and roles of public and private sectors within Italian broadcasting was a structural problem for which it would remain difficult to find political agreement.

See also: private television; radio

Further reading

Mazzoleni, G. (1994) 'Italy', in J. Mitchell and J.G. Blumler (eds), *Television and the Viewer Interest: Explorations in the Responsiveness of European Broadcasters*, Media Monograph no.18, London: John Libbey (an account of the development of the regulatory system for broadcasting in Italy).

—— (1995) 'Towards a "Videocracy"? Italian Political Communication at a Turning Point', *European Journal of Communication* 10 (3): 291–319 (an account of history of media and politics in Italy with 'videocracy' thesis that media may be increasingly controlling politics).

Statham, P. (1996) 'Berlusconi, The Media and the New Right in Italy', *The Harvard International Journal of Press/Politics* 1 (1): 87–105 (an account of the role of media resources in Berlusconi's entrance into politics).

—— (1996) 'Television News and the Public Sphere in Italy: Conflicts at the Media/Politics Interface', *European Journal of Communication* 11 (4): 509–54 (an account of the history of the 'politicization' of broadcasting with comparative data on public/private television news coverage of public affairs prior to 1996 election).

PAUL STATHAM

Bruck, Edith

b. 1932, Tiszabhrcel, Hungary

Novelist and poet

Bruck, pen-name of Edith Steinschreiber, survived the holocaust and after the Second World War lived in different countries, including Israel, before moving finally to Italy in 1954. Bruck's literary works are mostly inspired by her childhood experiences and by the haunted memory of the concentration camps, as well as by an existential and anthropological analysis of human life. One fundamental characteristic of her writing is her deliberate choice to write in Italian, a language that reflects neither her mother tongue (Hungarian) nor the learned language of her ethnic background (Hebrew), as a sign, perhaps, of her need to find a linguistic and cultural inner equilibrium to counterbalance the painful memories of forced migrations. Bruck's books are often candidly autobiographical and do not hide the still-fresh scars etched forever into the author's memory. Among her works are *Chi ti ama così* (Who Loves You in This Way) (1959), *Transit* (1978), *Lettera alla madre* (Letter To the Mother) (1988), *Nuda proprietà* (Naked Property) (1992).

See also: Jewish writers

ANDREA CICCARELLI

Brusati, Franco

b. 4 August 1922, Milan; d. 28 February 1993, Rome

Scriptwriter, film and theatre director

With a degree in political science and a background in journalism, Brusati began his career in cinema as assistant director to Renato **Castellani**. He also worked as scriptwriter for many films including **Rossellini**'s *La macchina ammazzacattivi* (The Machine for killing Bad People) (1948) and **Lattuada**'s *Anna* (1951) before making his first feature, *Il padrone sono me* (The Boss is Me) in 1956. Regarded as a talented but minor director, his best-known and most successful film remains *Pane e cioccolata* (Bread and Chocolate), made in 1974 and

featuring Nino **Manfredi** in a bittersweet comedy about an Italian migrant worker in Switzerland.

GINO MOLITERNO

Bufalino, Gesualdo

b. 15 November 1920, Comiso, Ragusa; d. 14 June 1996, Comiso

Poet, novelist and essayist

Sicilian by birth, Bufalino first appeared on the literary scene at the age of sixty with the autobiographical novel *Diceria dell'untore* (The Plague-Sower) (1980), winning much critical praise for his baroque prose and subject matter. In subsequent novels and short stories – from *Argo il cieco* (Blind Argus) (1984) to *Tommaso e il fotografo cieco* (Tommaso and the Blind Photographer) (1996) – Bufalino employs a highly literary language and skilful rhetorical technique to represent, with tragic humour, the relativity of human existence, devoid of any metaphysical consolation. Bufalino also translated from several French authors, among others Victor Hugo and Charles Baudelaire, and collected his poems in the much-praised *L'amaro miele* (Bitter Honey) (1989, 2nd expanded edition). His spirited contributions to newspapers such as *Il Giornale* and *Il Messaggero* were collected in *Cere perse* (Cires Perdues) (1985) and *La luce e il tutto* (Light and Everything) (1988).

FRANCESCA PARMEGGIANI

bureaucracy

Burocrazia has a more pejorative connotation in Italian than in most other European languages. This is because the average Italian often sees the state administration as a daily obstacle which has to be overcome in order to acquire even the most rudimentary of services.

The origins of the unhappy relationship between the Italian public and the representatives of its government can be traced back to the period of unification. In 1853, Count Cavour reorganized the state administration of Piedmont into a series of ministries to which all public offices and agencies were to be accountable. Cavour's reforms aimed at the unification of administrative functions by establishing the primacy of government ministries to which the entire civil service would be subordinate. Under Prime Minister Crispi in the 1880s, a measure of autonomy was granted to the civil service by the creation of ministerial under-secretaries who represented the minister in Parliament and enjoyed delegate authority as executive heads of their respective departments. Nevertheless, the political initiative afforded to senior public officials was limited and this lack of political power was compensated for by the guarantee of job security, eventual promotion, and generous salaries and conditions. This relationship between politicians and senior bureaucrats altered little in subsequent years making for a hierarchical, inflexible and politically unresponsive administrative apparatus.

Mussolini attempted to 'fascistize' the civil service, and it became compulsory for all public employees to carry the Fascist Party card. However, the *stato di diritto* or 'legal state' continued to function with little interference from the executive. Mussolini was conscious of the need to reward the loyalty of bureaucratic elites who had become increasingly important as agents for the transformation of Italy in a corporatist and statist direction. The founding of the Institute for the Reconstruction of Industry (**IRI**) in 1934 and the major public works projects in the South created thousands of jobs in the public sector and extended the reach of the state throughout the national territory. This state-aggrandizing process continued unabated under a succession of Christian Democratic governments after the Second World War, transforming the public administration into a major source of patronage and providing vast opportunities for illicit exchange (see **clientelism**).

It is estimated that there are over 40,000 non-departmental state agencies in Italy all with their own budgets and administrative structures. Many agencies enjoy special statutory powers which makes it difficult if not impossible to streamline or to coordinate their activities more effectively. Central government ministries range from tiny bureaux such as the environment ministry which employed only 226 officials in 1990 to vast empires such as the Ministry of the Interior which in the

same year employed nearly 140,000 personnel (compared to just over 42,000 in the UK Home Office). If armed forces personnel and teachers are included, there were just over 2 million employees on the central government payroll in 1990 (of which approximately 640,000 were civil servants). The lower levels of social security personnel in Italy (as compared to the UK or France) and the higher level of 'state participation' jobs are explained by a relatively undeveloped welfare state (in north European terms) and the larger 'footprint' of the Italian public sector in the national economy. Yet with the continuing need to maintain a strict fiscal regime in line with European Monetary Union conditions and the collapse of the clientelistic party system of the First **Republic**, it is likely that the remote and underemployed state bureaucrat will soon be a thing of the past.

Further reading

Cassese, S. (ed.) (1984) *L'amministrazione centrale* (The Central Administration), vol. 9, *Storia della società italiana dall'Unità a oggi* (A History of Italian Society from Unification to the Present day), Bologna: UTET (the most authoritative history of Italy's civil administration).

Hine, D. (1993) *Governing Italy: The Politics of Bargained Pluralism*, Oxford: Oxford University Press, ch. 8, 'The Administrative System' (a clear and informative guide to modern Italian governance).

SIMON PARKER

Burri, Alberto

b. 12 March 1915, Città di Castello, Perugia; d. 13 February 1995, Nice

Artist

Self-taught as an artist, Burri's early experiences as a doctor, handling blood-stained bandages and sewing up wounds on the Italian front in North Africa during the Second World War, provided the inspiration for much of his later work. Burri began his artistic activity during his period as a prisoner of war in Texas and his works display a fascination with surface texture and use different media such as torn sacking, charred wood, iron plates and plastic sheets with gaping holes burnt by a blowtorch. Fissures, like coagulated streams of lava, and bubbling irruptions or 'wounds' are the predominant features of a later major series of works in Cellotex (a compound derived from cellulose). Burri's work reflects the philosophy of the *Informale* movement and it also has strong links to the work of Spanish artist Antoni Tapies. Today, a foundation which exhibits and documents Burri's work is located in his birthplace of Città di Castello.

LAURENCE SIMMONS

Busi, Aldo

b. 5 February 1948, Montichiari, Brescia

Novelist and cultural critic

Aldo Busi's appearance on the cultural scene dates back to 1984 when he published his first successful novel *Seminario sulla gioventù* (Seminar on Youth), which was to be followed by a number of other comic and provocative narratives. In his highly controversial writings, characterized by outrageous humour, explicit sexual imagery, the cutting exhibition of his homosexuality and, in general, the blatant exposure of his self, Busi displays skilful literary technique and a masterly use of the Italian language. Besides writing fiction, translating from English and German and constantly turning himself into a public figure in order to shake up the intellectual establishment, Busi has continued to promote himself by contributing playful commentaries to a number of popular newspapers and magazines such as *Epoca* and *IoDonna*.

Further reading

Busi, A. (1994) *Cazzi e canguri: pochissimi i canguri* (Dicks and Kangaroos: Very Few Kangaroos), Milan: Frassinelli (one of his later novels).

FRANCESCA PARMEGGIANI

Bussotti, Sylvano

b. 1 October 1931, Florence

Composer, painter, film and stage director

A radical and experimental composer and visual artist specializing in multidisciplinary art and multimedia works, Bussotti is one of Italy's most controversial composers. His works often portray violent, erotic and homoerotic themes, leading critics to sometimes describe his works as indulgently self-referential and libertine. Performers of his music are often faced with the daunting task of deciphering complex scores and presenting dense and confronting works.

Bussotti entered the Conservatorium Luigi Cherubini in Florence in 1940 after early lessons on the violin. During this time he studied piano with Luigi **Dallapiccola** and music theory with Roberta Lupi. There followed a number of years abroad, studying composition in Paris, Darmstadt, the United States (with the assistance of a Rockefeller Foundation grant) and Berlin (with the assistance of a DAAD award) and a number of prizes including the All'Amelia Prize (**Venice Biennale**, 1967), Toscani d'Oggi (Golden Olive Branch, 1974), and the Psacaropulo Prize (Turin, 1979).

A painter like his uncle and brother, Bussotti has exhibited in galleries in Italy, Japan, the United States, Germany and France. He has also been successful as a director and designer of stage works and as consultant to a number of theatres including La Fenice in Venice and the Puccini Festival at Torre del Lago. He has held two teaching positions, that of teacher of music drama at the Academy L'Aquila, and teacher of composition and musical analysis at the Fiesole School of Music.

Bussotti's early works were influenced by serialism, but he later rejected the strictness of this method and delved instead into the notation of indeterminacy. However, his abiding interest has been in multidisciplinary art forms, always tending towards the theatrical. He has thus been composer, designer and director of stage works such as his *La passion selon Sade* (Passion According to Sade) (1965) and *Lorenzaccio* (1972) and has introduced extra-musical, theatrical devices into his works, such as pianists wearing thick gloves in the *5 Pieces for David*

Tudor of 1959. Interested in exploring the boundaries of sound production and sound combinations, he has allowed performers the freedom to use fragments and repetitions of music at will and has introduced unusual vocalizations and instrumental techniques into his scores, which themselves often use a highly graphic form of notation, including fragments of musical score joined together with performing instructions and odd illustrations.

Something of a musical *agent provocateur* and not unlike that other *enfant terrible* of the Italian stage, Carmelo **Bene**, with whom he sometimes collaborated in the 1960s, Bussotti has always created works that have exploited fantasy and imagination to the limit, resulting in highly theatrical events that have never failed to arouse strong audience reaction.

Further reading

Morris, M. (1996) *A Guide to 20th-century Music Composers*, London: Methuen (a biographical discussion of Bussotti's work in the context of other Italian and twentieth-century composers).

Scarpone, G. (1992) 'Sylvano Bussotti', in B. Morton and P. Collins (eds), *Contemporary Composers*, Chicago: St James Press (for a comprehensive list of works and a discussion of Bussotti's compositional intent).

ANDREW SCHULTZ

Buzzati (Traverso), Dino

b. 16 October 1906, San Pellegrino, Belluno; d. 28 January 1972, Milan

Journalist, narrator, painter and mountaineer

Born into an educated and affluent milieu in the northern Alpine region of Belluno – a mountainous setting that would return often in his fictional works – Buzzati graduated in law from the University of Milan. In 1928, after two years of military service, he joined *Il Corriere della sera* where he would continue to work for the next forty years, first as reporter and then as war correspondent, editor, sports writer and finally, in the 1960s,

as art critic. His first forays into fiction, *Barnabo delle montagne* (Barnabo of the Mountains) (1933) and *Il segreto del Bosco Vecchio* (The Secret of the Old Wood) (1935), two fantastic tales permeated by an eerie air of mystery and foreboding, went largely unnoticed, but *Il Deserto dei Tartari* (The Desert of the Tartars), a longer novel published in 1940 when Buzzati himself was already in Africa as a war correspondent, brought him national and international acclaim. Set in an unnamed border region in an undefined time, the novel recounts the story of a diligent young lieutenant, Giovanni Drogo, as he and his companions spend a lifetime awaiting the predicted attack of the mysterious enemy Tartars. The assault only appears to eventuate when Drogo is too old and sick to participate, which makes the novel into a typically Buzzatian allegory for human life as a series of inevitable disappointments, spent in the vain hope of a great moment of fulfilment which never arrives except in the form of death.

In the postwar period, Buzzati became ever more drawn to the theatre and wrote numerous plays, most of which were produced in Italy and several also abroad; his *Un caso clinico* (A Clinical Case) was staged both in Berlin in 1954 and in Paris in 1955 in a translation by Albert Camus. However, despite his great desire to achieve fame in the theatre, for which he would also design sets and compose operatic *libretti*, Buzzati's greatest successes would be in the genre of the short story, the form in which he really excelled. In all he would publish eight collections of short stories, with the anthology *Sessanta racconti* (Sixty Stories) winning him the prestigious Strega prize in 1958 (see **literary prizes**).

In 1960 he experimented with science fiction in the short novel *Il grande ritratto* (The Great Portrait), while also continuing to develop a talent for painting and drawing which had already become manifest in the self-illustration of earlier narrative works. As well as a number of full-scale painting exhibitions, this led to the publication of *Poema a fumetti* (Poem in Comics) (1969), a modern recounting of the classical journey of Orpheus to the underworld, with Orpheus in the guise of a modern guitar player and the story told through a series of brilliantly coloured comic strip vignettes, creatively mixing elements of surrealist and expressionist painting and imagery from horror films and pop art. This powerful and disquieting visual style, which reproduced visually the unsettling surrealism of his short stories, was continued in a series of paintings exhibited in Venice in 1970 and subsequently published in book form as *I miracoli di Val Morel* (The Miracles of Morel Valley).

A collection of Buzzati's best journalistic pieces was published posthumously as *Cronache terrestri* (Earthly Chronicles) (1972) which was followed in 1973 by a revealing long interview which Buzzati had recorded with Yves Panafieu titled *Dino Buzzati: un autoritratto* (Dino Buzzati: A Self-Portrait). In 1976 Buzzati's finest novel, *Il Deserto dei Tartari*, was made into an equally fine film by the Italian director, Valerio **Zurlini**.

Further reading

Buzzati, D. (1984) *Restless Nights: Selected Stories*, chosen and trans. L. Venuti, Manchester: Carcanet Press (a representative selection of Buzzati's short stories)

Rawson, J. (1984) 'Dino Buzzati', in M. Caesar and P. Hainsworth (eds), *Writers and Society in Contemporary Italy*, New York: St. Martin's Press (a brief but comprehensive survey of Buzzati's fiction).

GINO MOLITERNO

C

Cacciari, Massimo

b. 5 June 1944, Venice

Philosopher and politician

A disciple of architectural historian Manfredo **Tafuri**, Cacciari came to occupy the chair of Aesthetics at the University of Venice. One of Italy's most influential social philosophers associated with the critical trend known as *pensiero debole* (negative thought), Cacciari's philosophy should be placed within the milieu of the political activism of the 1960s in which, as a member of the Italian Communist Party (see **PCI**), he participated vigorously. He served as a Communist deputy in **Parliament** from 1979 to 1984, and was then briefly associated with the Democratic Party of the Left (**PDS**).

The concept of 'crisis' informs Cacciari's work, and he argues that although crisis is fundamental to capitalist development, it may also be made to function for the working class. He wrote extensively on the relation between philosophy and modern architecture in *Architecture and Nihilism* (1993) and in *Dallo Steinhoff* (Posthumous People) (1980) on the concentration of intellectual and philosophical activity in Vienna at the end of the nineteenth century. His *Dell'inizio* (On the Beginning) (1990) is a mystical and religious meditation inspired by Heidegger, blending together mystical and Marxist elements reminiscent of one of Cacciari's favourite authors, Walter Benjamin. Cacciari was elected mayor of Venice of 1993, and re-elected in 1997.

LAURENCE SIMMONS

Calasso, Roberto

b. 1941, Florence

Writer, essayist and chief editor

A graduate in English literature from the University of Rome, Roberto Calasso has published various articles on philosophy and literature, important translations of Nietzsche and Karl Kraus and three essay-novels, *La rovina di Kasch* (The Ruins of Kasch) (1983) and *Le nozze di Cadmo e Armonia* (The Marriage of Cadmus and Harmony) (1988) and *Ka* (1996) which have been critically acclaimed both in Italy and abroad. In his creative writing, Calasso challenges his reader to undertake a highly intellectual, philosophical and spiritual journey through time. His narrative originates from and develops the notion of storytelling as a strategy for tracking history to its mythical beginnings. Calasso has also been for many years the chief editor of the prestigious Milanese publishing house, **Adelphi**.

FRANCESCA PARMEGGIANI

Calvesi, Maurizio

b. 18 September 1927, Rome

Art historian and critic

A student of Lionello **Venturi** and a supporter of Carlo **Argan**, Calvesi has attempted to explore the links between art and social history, and the relationship between past and present.

After an early career as an arts administrator and then a teacher, Calvesi was appointed to the University of Rome in 1976. In the 1980s and 1990s he held positions with the **Venice Biennale**. He has also been art critic for *L'Espresso* and *Il Corriere della sera*, and has curated numerous exhibitions of historical and modern art.

Like many other eminent Italian art historians, Calvesi has published books and catalogue articles on a multitude of subjects, including Dürer, Giorgione, Michelangelo, Francesco Colonna, the Carracci, Titian, Correggio, Futurism, Dada, Duchamp, **de Chirico**, the avantgarde, Renato **Guttuso**, Alberto **Burri** and Pop Art, crowned by the inevitable monograph on Caravaggio. Of particular note is his work on *L'Informale*, which, he insists, had peculiar characteristics in Italy because of the late development of the avantgarde.

See also: art criticism

Further reading

Calvesi, Maurizio (1981) *Le due avanguardie. Dal futurismo alla Pop Art* (The Two Avantgardes: From Futurism to Pop Art), Bari: Laterza.
—— (1990) *Le realtà del Caravaggio* (The Reality of Caravaggio), Turin: Einaudi.

MAX STAPLES

Calvino, Italo

b. 15 October 1923, Santiago de las Vegas, Cuba; d. 19 September 1985, Siena

Novelist, essayist and critic

Widely regarded as the greatest Italian fiction writer of the second half of the twentieth-century, Calvino's reputation and popularity in Italy was matched by wide international renown, with his work appearing extensively in translation and exercising a strong influence over the so-called 'postmodern' and 'magic realist' schools in both the USA and the UK.

Born in Cuba while his parents were on scientific fieldwork there, Calvino returned with his family to Italy in 1925 to live in the northern town of San Remo on the Ligurian Riviera. The family background in science – his father was a noted agronomist, his mother a botanist and his maternal uncle and aunt both chemists – would leave its mark on Calvino's fiction, not least in his fascination with organizing principles and with the processes of close observation.

Between 1943 and 1945 he took part in the **Resistance** movement, fighting with the partizans in the area around San Remo. He was captured and briefly imprisoned by the Fascists, but managed to escape and take refuge in the Alps with Communist groups. In 1945 he joined the **PCI** and continued to be an active member of the party until the Russian invasion of Hungary in 1956, after which he resigned.

Having begun his university studies in Turin in 1941, originally following in his father's footsteps by enrolling in agronomy, he eventually graduated in letters in 1947 with a dissertation on the work of Joseph Conrad. In the same year he joined the **Einaudi** publishing house, for which he would continue to work in various editorial and advisory capacities for most of his professional life. At Einaudi, Calvino soon became part of a close-knit group of writers and intellectuals around Cesare **Pavese** and Elio **Vittorini**, with whom Calvino collaborated on a number of literary and cultural magazines including the short-lived but highly influential *Il Politecnico* and, in the late 1950s, *il menabò*. Later, Calvino himself edited a major collection of Pavese's letters in 1966 and wrote a critical study on Vittorini in 1968.

A productive year, 1947 also saw the publication of Calvino's first novel, *Il sentiero dei nidi di ragno* (The Path to the Nest of Spiders). Already displaying the poetically precise but nimble style that would characterize all his subsequent writing, the novel recounted Calvino's own experiences of the war through the eyes of a street-urchin named Pin, continually transforming what had been real events into elements of a fabulous adventure story. The novel nevertheless also strove to conform to the aesthetic and political tenets of **neorealism** which dominated literature and cinema during this period (see also **narrative**). Reviewed favourably by Pavese, who declared it the work of one of Italy's most promising novelists, *Il sentiero* was awarded the

Riccione Prize. While continuing his political miltancy and contributing articles to **L'Unità** and **Rinascita**, Calvino next published *Ultimo viene il corvo* (Adam, One Afternoon) (1949), a collection of short stories written in a realist mode, again centred on wartime experiences. During the 1950s, however, the tendency towards fable and fantasy in his fictional writing became more pronounced. Of major importance, and marking a decisive break with the realist genre, was the trilogy *I nostri antenati* (Our Ancestors) (1960), which brought together *Il cavaliere inesistente* (The Non-Existent Knight) (1952), *Il visconte dimezzato* (The Cloven Viscount) (1957) and *Il barone rampante* (The Baron in the Trees) (1959), three parables that unashamedly used fable and fantasy in order to explore profound ethical and philosophical questions. With this group of works, Calvino confirmed his commitment to the fairy tale and to non-realist writing, a commitment already made manifest by his magnificent collection of folk tales and fables, *Fiabe italiane* (1956) (partially translated into English as *Italian Fables* in 1959 and then in a fuller version as *Italian Folktales* in 1975). This fantastic/fabulative trend culminated in the later 1960s with *Le cosmicomiche* (Cosmicomics) (1965) and *Ti con zero* (T Zero) (1967), collections of short stories which effortlessly mix fable and science fiction in order to explore modern cosmological notions and molecular aspects of the physical universe.

During the 1970s, Calvino's fascination with the actual processes of fabulation – the making of stories – produced several outstanding international successes. These highly structured fictions, which insistently foreground the very process of narrative construction, remain among his most important works: *Le città invisibili* (Invisible Cities) (1972); *Il castello dei destini incrociati* (The Castle of Crossed Destinies) (1969/73), which uses readings of a deck of tarot cards as a structural narrative principle; and, arguably his single most famous and important novel, *Se una notte d'inverno un viaggiatore* (If on a Winter's Night a Traveller) (1979), a highly self-reflexive work that fictionally presents itself as the incompletely-bound set of ten different chapters from ten other (fictional) novels. Immediately translated into numerous other languages, *If on a Winter's Night a Traveller* deservedly became a runaway bestseller and reconfirmed Calvino's

international standing. His last major work proved to be the less spectacular but nevertheless brilliant *Palomar* (Mr Palomar) (1983), a work which succeeds in fusing all his concerns with narrative and observation into a study of the nature of knowledge.

From the late 1960s onwards, Calvino lived in Paris where he associated with intellectuals such as Roland Barthes and French experimental writers such as Raymond Queneau and Georges Perec, both members of the famed Oulipo group (*L'Ouvoir de Littérature Potentielle* (Workshop of Potential Literature)). By the time he returned to live in Rome in 1980, Calvino's national and international status had been amply recognized through such awards as the Asti Prize (1972), the Premio Feltrinelli (1973), honorary membership of the American Academy and Institute of Arts and Letters (1975) and the Oesterrischiches Staatspreis für Europeische Literatur (1976).

A prolific writer of essays, criticism and other occasional pieces, Calvino also collected his non-fictional writings in a number of volumes, the most important being *Una pietra sopra* (The Uses of Literature) (1980). At the time of his death in 1985 he was preparing to give the Charles Eliot Norton lectures at Harvard, the unfinished text of which was published as *Six Memos for the Next Millennium* (1988). As the American writer Robert Coover suggested, in his extended review of the *Memos* in the *New York Times Book Review* (20 March 1988), Calvino's limpid musings in these pages on the art of imaginative fiction are really a profound reflection by the master himself on what was best in his own work.

Further reading

Brink, A. (1998) *The Novel: Language and Narrative from Cervantes to Calvino*, London: Macmillan (places Calvino in a long tradition of European literature and devotes its last chapter to *If on a Winter's Night a Traveller*).

Calvino, I. (1988) *Six Memos for the Next Millennium*, Cambridge, MA: Harvard University Press.

Carter, A.H. (1987) *Italo Calvino: Metamorphoses of Fantasy*, Ann Arbor, MI: UMI Research Press (a detailed study of Calvino's use of fantasy for serious intellectual exploration).

Hume, K. (1992) *Calvino's Fictions: Cogito and Cosmos*, Oxford: Clarendon Press (a comprehensive monograph devoted to the major works).

Nash, C. (1987) *World Games: The Tradition of Anti-Realist Revolt*, London: Methuen (an extensive survey with substantial comments throughout on Calvino's habits and styles, and his status within the tradition).

Ricci, F. (ed.) (1989) *Calvino Revisited*, Ottawa: Dovehouse (fourteen essays by leading critics dealing with specific works and important aspects of Calvino's writing).

Rushdie, S. (1991) *Imaginary Homelands*, London: Granta Books (contains an important essay by one great novelist on the other).

JEFF DOYLE
GINO MOLITERNO

Camerini, Mario

b. 6 February 1895, Rome; d. 5 February 1981, Gardone Riviera

Film director

The subdued style and the minimalism of many of Camerini's most characteristic films manifest an ironic and sentimental sense of existence, with middle-class characters portrayed in situations that indirectly address social and political issues. His most popular work was done between 1929, when he directed his first film *Rotaie* (Rails) and the end of the War. Several of his best films from this period such as *Gli uomini, che mascalzoni!* (Men, What Rascals!) (1932) and *Il signor Max* (Mr Max) (1937) starred the young Vittorio **De Sica** at the beginning of his career. During the 1940s, when the genre of the sentimental comedy appeared exhausted, Camerini turned to the historical novel with two rather conventional films: *I promessi sposi* (The Betrothed) (1941), adapted from Alessandro Manzoni and *La figlia del capitano* (The Captain's Daughter) (1949) from Pushkin. With *Suor Letizia* (Sister Letizia) (1957), Camerini went back to his early, less sweet portrayal of life but his last work was to be *Don Camillo e i giovani d'oggi* (Don Camillo and today's Young People) (1972).

CRISTINA DEGLI-ESPOSTI REINERT

Camon, Ferdinando

b. 14 November 1935, S. Salvaro d'Urbana (Padua)

Poet, critic and novelist

Camon's childhood in an economically-depressed region near Padova is reflected in his lifelong project of giving voice to the marginalized and the poor. His early poetry (Viareggio Prize in 1973) and a trilogy of novels trace the cultural, political and social isolation of these people while denouncing the conditions giving rise to such economic misery. The trilogy, called the *ciclo degli ultimi* (cycle of the last) includes *Il quinto stato* (The Fifth State) (1970), *La vita eterna* (Life Everlasting) (1973), and *Un altare per la madre* (An Altar for the Mother) (1978). His later novels examine more contemporary social issues such as the youth and women's movements of the 1960s and 1970s in *La malattia chiamata uomo* (The Illness Called Man), drugs in *Storia di Sirio* (The Story of Sirio) (1984), and psychoanalysis in *La donna dei fili* (The Woman of the Threads) (1986). His critical works include collections of interviews with twentieth-century poets and novelists.

LAURA A. SALSINI

Campanile, Achille

b. 28 September 1900, Rome; d. 4 January 1977, Velletri

Journalist, playwright and novelist

A renowned journalist, Campanile contributed articles to *Il Corriere della sera*, *Fiera letteraria*, *900* and *Omnibus*. He was also editor of *La Tribuna* and for some years television critic for *L'Europeo*. Although more widely known for his essays, Campanile also wrote plays and novels. Among his stage comedies are *L'inventore del cavallo* (The Inventor of the Horse) and *Centocinquanta la gallina canta* (One Hundred and Fifty, the Chicken Sings) and his novels include *Ma che cos'è questo amore?* (What Is This Love?), *Se la luna mi porta fortuna* (If the Moon Brings Me Luck), and *Il diario di Gino Cornabò* (Gino Cornabò's Diary). In 1933 he was awarded the Viareggio Prize (see **literary prizes**) for *Cantasilena all'angolo della strada* (Cantasilena on the Side of the Road), a collection of editorial essays, and in 1973 he received the prize again for *Manuale di conversazione* (Conversational Manual).

VIRGINIA PICCHIETTI

Canale Cinque

Soon to become the cornerstone of the media empire of Silvio **Berlusconi**, private television channel *Canale Cinque* was born in 1980 in Milan by bringing together five private channels, thus inaugurating the era of commercial television in Italy. Its first coup was in 1981 with the purchase of rights to the football event *Mundialito*, which was followed by success in poaching from the **RAI** some of the national broadcaster's best-known faces, amongst them personalities like Mike **Bongiorno**. Changing all the rules of television programming, *Cinque* exploited neglected time bands, like the morning period, and scheduled its daily programs strategically so as to draw viewers from the RAI. Presenting itself as a lively channel for the whole family with films, quizzes and variety shows, *Cinque* consolidated its success by screening the American serial 'Dallas' which became one of the most-watched shows on Italian television. In 1987, in another victory in the 'television wars', Pippo **Baudo** also abandoned the RAI for *Cinque*. With his flagship thus firmly established, Berlusconi tried – though, as it turned out, in vain – to export *Canale Cinque* to France (*La Cinq*) and to Spain (*Telecinco*). Following a law permitting live broadcasts in 1992, *Cinque* initiated its own national news program, TG5, thus confirming its status as alternative to the RAI.

Further reading

Doyle, W. (1988) 'Why Dallas was able to conquer Italy', *Altro Polo*, edited I. Grossart and S. Trambaiolo, Sydney: Frederick May Foundation.

RICCARDO VENTRELLA

Cancogni, Manlio

b. 6 July 1916, Bologna

Novelist and journalist

After contributing short stories to literary journals before the War, Cancogni became a journalist in the immediate postwar period and wrote for weeklies such as ***L'Europeo*** and ***l'Espresso***. Since the mid-1950s he has published numerous novels and been recipient of several of the most prestigious literary prizes including the Bagutta prize in 1965 for *La linea del Tomori* (The Tomori Line), the Campiello for *Il ritorno* (The Return) in 1971 and the Strega in 1973 for his *Allegri, gioventù* (Happy, Youth).

Cancogni's fiction generally concerns itself with the search for a deeper truth within the individual, a psychological excavation which is often undertaken in a broader historical context. In *Il ritorno*, for example, the life of a group of soldiers is investigated against the backdrop of the occupation of Croatia by Italian troops during 1943. The latent sense of danger hovering around the soldiers assigned to defend an indefensible position is well-rendered by a nervous, syncopated writing.

Cancogni has also published several volumes of critical essays and a work on the Renaissance painter, Guido Reni.

PAOLO BARTOLONI

Canella, Guido

b. 19 July 1931, Bucharest, Romania

Architect, designer, academic and editor

After graduating from the Milan Politecnico where he studied under Ernesto **Rogers**, Canella joined the project for ***Casabella***-*Continuità* (1957–64). Whilst practising professionally he also taught architectural composition at the **IUAV** (replacing **Samonà**), and at the Milan Politecnico from 1962 onwards, taking over the chair from Rogers in 1970 and becoming a Director in 1982. During the 1950s and 1960s he published a number of important studies on national schools in Europe, such as Russian Constructivism, the Amsterdam

School and Milanese Liberty, all of which had been marginalized by the orthodox Modern movement. Since 1989 he has been editor of the series *Architettura e città* (Architecture and the City). The Civic Center of Piave Emanuele (1971–81) remains the epitome of Canella's perpetual aspiration to extract a shape from a landscape that he regards determined more by history than geography.

Further reading

'Guido Canella' (1995) *Zodiac*, 13: 216–27 (overview of Canella's professional work).

GORDANA KOSTICH

Cantafora, Arduino

b. 1945, Milan

Architectural draughtsman and figurative artist

After studying architecture under Aldo **Rossi**, Cantafora became part of Tendenza, a group which, in the 1970s, was at the centre of debate on the subject of architecture and the split between theory and practice. Tendenza, which sought to question the myth of historical progress, was anti-modernist and part of a tradition which pursued architectural drawings as an end in themselves, independently of construction. For Tendenza the city, a discontinuous place, achieves unity in the Monument, which is a synthesis, a focus of meaning for all its surroundings. Drawn architecture serves to create an imaginary context for monuments, a cultural place without consumers, deserted stage-sets inhabited only by architecture with no need of people.

Cantafora's drawings are full of references ranging from the Renaissance to Sironi, from **de Chirico** to mediocre Fascist theatre sets. They show cities crowded with deserted monuments, like Piranesi's Fori Imperiali, where eclecticism plunders history, aligning its masterpieces in a large cemetery-setting.

OLIVIA DAWSON

Cantautori

In the first half of the twentieth century the Italian popular music tradition generally made a radical distinction between the songwriter and the performer. Great songwriters and great singers could both be famous although they were seldom the same person and singers like Alberto Rabagliati tended to be better known than songwriters like Cesare Bixio. After 1960, however, following the birth of modern **pop and rock music**, a new tendency of singer–songwriters developed, inspired in its early phase by the example of French 'chansonniers' like Jacques Brel and Gilbert Becaud.

The most important city in the early phase of this development was Genoa, close to the French border, and the first two singers to emerge were Luigi Tenco and Gino Paoli.

Tenco, afflicted with a troubled personal life, is generally considered the founder of this new tradition and melancholic songs like 'Mi sono innamorato di te' (I Fell in Love With You) (1962) and 'Lontano, lontano' (So Faraway) accompanied the growing pains of an entire generation of young Italians. Usually beginning with the theme of love, Tenco's songs often developed into deeper reflections on the meaning of life. This existential depth became all the more poignant following his unexpected (and still mysterious) suicide after he had been eliminated from the **Sanremo Festival** in 1967. Following his tragic death a 'Club Tenco' was established at Sanremo which has continued to host and encourage new songwriters quite outside the glare of the more commercial official annual festival.

Gino Paoli, on the other hand, with a decidedly romantic touch, was closer to a more traditional form of love song ('Il cielo in una stanza' (The Sky In a Room), or 'Senza fine' (Without an End)), as were Bruno Lauzi and Sergio Endrigo, who won the Sanremo Festival in 1968 with 'Canzone per te' (A Song For You). Also from Genoa emerged the talent of Fabrizio **De Andrè**, who gradually overcame the dominant love theme of songs like 'La canzone di Marinella' (The Song of Marinella), by introducing bits of 'pure' poetry from sources as different as Edgar Lee Masters and the Four Gospels.

Around the same time in Milan there was a coming together of the theatre and music scene.

The crazy art of Enzo **Jannacci** emerged from an aggressive and iconoclastic approach to the audience as in his 'Vengo anch'io no tu no!', (I'll come too! No, you won't). Giorgio Gaber, after a debut as a melodic singer ('Grazie tante' (Thank You Very Much)), proposed his own brand of irony in songs like 'Torpedo Blu' (Blue Torpedo) and 'Porta Romana', recalling an older style from the 1920s and 1930s, and, later, a touch of surrealism in songs like 'La libertà' (Freedom) (1972). A new source of inspiration came from the American folksingers and from the hippy movement. The 'Summer of Love' inspired a new freedom in songwriters like Gian Pieretti ('Il vento dell'Est' (The Wind of East)), Riki Maiocchi ('C'è chi spera' (There Are Some Who Hope)) and Mauro Lusini, author of 'C'era un ragazzo che come me amava i Beatles e i Rolling Stones' (There Was a Boy Who, Like Me, Loved the Beatles and Rolling Stones), a song which later became a hit for Gianni **Morandi**. The example of Bob Dylan and Joan Baez was fundamental to the development of the protest song especially during the 1968 **student movement**. Paolo **Pietrangeli** sang his 'Contessa' (Countess) on the barricades and Ivan Della Mea, in his 'Cara moglie' (Dear Wife), celebrated the heartaches of the working-class. As ballads accompanied the winds of change, strongly under the influence of Bob Dylan and Leonard Cohen, a new generation of '*cantautori*' – a neologism coined, in fact, in the early 1970s – was in the wings.

In Rome, Francesco De Gregori and Antonello Venditti emerged from the Folkstudio club and in 1973 recorded an LP together, *Theorius Campus*. De Gregori's approach to lyrics was intimate and poetic as in songs like 'Alice' (1973), 'Rimmel' (1975), 'Generale' (General) (1978) and 'La donna cannone' (Cannonball Woman) (1983) and won him a large following. Venditti, a pianist, moved from a more popular and melodic inspiration, creating fascinating atmospheres in 'Roma capoccia' (Hardheaded Rome) (1974), 'Lilly' (1975) and 'Notte prima degli esami' (The Night Before the Exams) (1984).

In Bologna, Francesco Guccini, who had previously written provocative songs like 'Dio è morto' (God Is Dead), which was censored by **RAI** when sung by the rock group I Nomadi, returned to more traditional values but from an introspective point of view, and couched his protest in a more refined language. In 'La locomotiva' (The Locomotive) (1972), he created a working-class epic, and in 'L'avvelenata' (The Poisoned) (1978) ironically painted a self-portrait. Meanwhile Claudio Baglioni and Riccardo Cocciante ruled over the love song: romantics, with powerful voices, they conquered their audiences with 'Questo piccolo grande amore' (This Small Great Love) (1972) and 'Margherita' (1974). Teacher Roberto Vecchioni sang of the bitter taste of love ('Stranamore' (Strangelove)) while Eugenio Finardi rode the 1977 protest wave with angry songs like 'La musica ribelle' (Rebel Music). Ivano Fossati, former leader of the group Delirium, celebrated the more sophisticated dimension of pop music in his 'Panama', while Alberto Fortis (*Milano e Vincenzo*) indulged in the crazier side. In Naples, the picturesque dialect came to be freely and creatively mixed with other influences with Edoardo Bennato choosing the rock idiom and the magic world of fables (the figure of Pinocchio, for example, in *Burattino senza fili* (Puppet Without Strings) (1977)), while Pino Daniele developed a genuinely Neapolitan version of the blues ('Je so'pazzo' (I'm Crazy), 1977).

Two *cantautori* who have occupied a unique place of their own are Paolo Conte and Rino Gaetano. Conte, a lawyer by profession, has created a very distinctive personal style by fusing elements from the Italian melodic tradition with the French chansonniers and South-American influences, achieving a very strong international reputation. Gaetano, with his humorous 'Gianna', was the new discovery of the 1978 Sanremo Festival, although his death in a car accident in 1981 tragically deprived Italian music of his talent.

The 1980s witnessed the great success of Franco Battiato (from avantgarde compositions to pop music), the rock ballads of Gianna **Nannini** and the daredevil life of Vasco Rossi. **Zucchero** continued to develop a personal style from within a blues tradition from 'Donne' (Women, 1984), to the 1987 album *Blue's* which thrust him into international stardom. On the model of Bruce Springsteen, Luciano Ligabue wrote songs in which the Emilia Romagna region figured as a sort of Italian far-west with storylines that mixed on-the-road culture, racing cars, wine and love.

The 1990s saw a continuation of the popularity of many of the established names, although two of the most renowned of the older generation, Lucio **Battisti** and De Andrè, died in the latter part of the decade. There also emerged a new generation of songwriters, balanced between aspirations to love and acknowledgement of harsh reality, the most significant of these being Samuele Bersani, Massimo Di Cataldo, Biagio Antonacci and Daniele Silvestri.

See also: rock and pop music

Further reading

Borgna, G. (1992) *Storia della canzone italiana* (History of Italian Song), Milan: Mondadori.

Castaldo, G. (1994) *La terra promessa. Quarant'anni di cultura rock (1954–1994)* (The Promised Land: Forty Years of Rock Culture 1954–1994), Milan: Feltrinelli.

De Andrè, F. and Gennari A. (1996) *Un destino ridicolo* (A Ridiculous Destiny), Turin: Einaudi.

Gentile, E. (1990) *Guida critica ai cantautori italiani* (Critical Guide to Italian Singer-songwriters), Milan: Gammalibri.

Jachia, P. (1998) *La canzone d'autore italiana 1958–1997* (Italian authored songs 1958–1997), Milan: Feltrinelli.

Rizzi, C. (1993) *Enciclopedia del rock italiano* (Encyclopedia of Italian Rock), Milan: Arcana.

RICCARDO VENTRELLA

Canzonissima

From its inception Italian state television (**RAI**) dedicated its Saturday evening to a variety show which for over fifteen years was called *Canzonissima* and which in later years became *Fantastico*.

The basic idea of *Canzonissima*, i.e. a big budget show linked to the New Year lottery, drew on ideas from Broadway and the Hollywood musical, but it also incorporated the Italian revue tradition. Presented by Enzo Tortora, Johnny Dorelli or Pippo **Baudo** (amongst others), the show always included a careful mix of international stars, Italian singers, comics and imitators as well as one or two soubrettes and a scantily-dressed *corps de ballet*. Song

and dance, rapid-fire gags and pure escapism were the show's stock in trade, the aim being to offer something that would please everyone, without distinction of class, region or education. Nevertheless the show did have its controversial moments as, for example, in 1962 when the relatively light satire of Dario **Fo** and Franca **Rame** caused a veritable scandal, resulting in the couple being banished from the RAI for many years.

Further reading

Veltroni, W. (1992) *I programmi che hanno cambiato l'Italia* (The Programmes that Changed Italy), Milan: Feltrinelli (see pp. 37–46, 'Canzonissima' and pp. 90–8 'Fantastico').

STEPHEN GUNDLE

Capriolo, Paola

1962, Milano

Novelist, short story writer and translator

A philosopher by training, in her narratives Capriolo investigates the relationship between myth and reality, exploring the notion of reality as an inaccessible absolute which nevertheless can be glimpsed in the artificial structures and forms people use to define their lives. These issues give shape to her first collection of short stories *La grande Eulalia* (The Great Eulalia) (1988), winner of the Giuseppe Berto Prize, her novel *Il nocchiere* (The Helmsman) (1989), winner of the *Rapallo* and *Campiello* Prizes and the collection of fables, *La ragazza della stella d'oro* (The Girl of the Golden Star). Capriolo's inquiry into the nature of reality and art also informs her revision of Puccini's romantic opera *Tosca*, *Vissi d'amore* (*Floria Tosca*). As well as writing fiction, Capriolo contributes to *Il Corriere della sera* and works as a translator.

Further reading

Wood, S. (1995) *Italian Women's Writing 1860–1994*, London: Athlone Press.

VIRGINIA PICCHIETTI

Caproni, Giorgio

b. 7 January 1912, Leghorn;
d. 22 January 1990, Rome

Poet, novelist and journalist

Trained as a violinist, Caproni abandoned his instrument to become a school teacher and writer. After the War, having fought in the **Resistance**, Caproni returned to teaching and wrote for *L'Unità* and *Avanti!*. Whilst his early poetry betrays the influence of Giuseppe **Ungaretti** and Umberto **Saba**, his postwar collections are closer to the traditional metres and hermetic themes of Mario **Luzi**. Especially important are, in the 1950s, *Il Passaggio di Enea* (Aeneas' Passage), where Caproni depicts the struggle of human beings to understand the rapidly changing modern world, and the collection of short stories *Il gelo della mattina* (Morning Frost), heavily influenced by the destruction of the Second World War. Caproni's later poetry is pervaded by a sense of isolation and solitude, only occasionally mediated by consoling memory.

Further reading

Caproni, G. (1998) *L'opera in versi* (Complete Poems), Milan: Mondadori (a comprehensive collection of Caproni's poetry with selected bibliography).
—— (1992) *The Wall of the Earth: 1964–1975*, trans. P. Verdicchio, Montreal: Guernica (selected poems in English).

VALERIO FERME

Capucci, Roberto

b. 2 December 1930, Rome

Fashion designer

Capucci began his career as an assistant to Italian fashion designer Emilio Schuberth, before opening his own business in Rome in 1950, followed by a Paris studio between 1962–8. Known as one of Italy's most creative *haute couturiers*, he has consistently rejected adherence to fashionable change, and has tended to present only occasional small collections to his select and devoted clientele. His approach has been essentially architectural and sculptural, involving a particular commitment to volume, line, texture and colour, in relation to the human body. Capucci has also stressed the importance of natural forms in his search for proportion and unity. This extraordinary approach to design can be seen most clearly in his celebrated grand evening dresses, where dramatically coloured silks are juxtaposed to emphasize curvilinear effects.

See also: fashion

NICOLA WHITE

carabinieri

Police force

The most prominent of the police bodies operating in Italy, the *Carabinieri* are also the oldest, having been founded in 1814 by King Victor Emanuel I as a crack unit for civil protection and the maintenance of law and order. Just as their name derives from the carbines with which they were first armed, so their specific orientation is military, being officially part of the army and coming under the jurisdiction of the Ministry for Defence rather than the Interior.

Numbering some 120,000, the corps is divided into three divisions with headquarters in Milan, Rome and Naples, further divided into 24 Legions, 100 Groups and 498 Companies which, through a network of 4,700 outposts, cover the entire national territory.

Highly visible in their colourful traditional uniforms, *carabinieri* are also much respected for their frontline action in the battles against **terrorism** and the **mafia**, but their autonomous jurisdiction with respect to other state police forces and a consequent rivalry and general lack of coordination between them continues to be a problem for Italian crime-fighting.

See also: Dalla Chiesa; police

Further reading

Collin, R.O. (1999) 'Italy: A Tale of Two Police Forces', *History Today* 49(9): 27–33.

GINO MOLITERNO

Cardinale, Claudia

b. 15 April 1939, Tunis (Tunisia)

Film-actress

Born and raised in Tunisia but destined to become one of the most renowned actresses of Italian postwar cinema, Cardinale moved to Rome in 1958 and enrolled in the acting school of the *Centro Sperimentale di Cinematografia*. In the same year, she made her first Italian film, Mario **Monicelli**'s *I soliti ignoti* (Big Deal on Madonna Street). In 1960, she earned fame thanks to her performance in Francesco Maselli's *I delfini* (The Dolphins), a film produced by Franco Cristaldi, by then her husband and one of the most audacious producers of his generation.

In the 1960s, Cardinale's collaborations with Luchino **Visconti** and Federico **Fellini** confirmed her star status and resulted in some of Italian cinema's most celebrated moments, as *Otto e mezzo* (8½) and *Il gattopardo* (The Leopard) illustrate.

In the latter part of her career, her maturity particularly suited the strong women she often portrayed, as in **Comencini**'s *La storia* (The History) or in *Sous les pieds des femmes* (Under the Feet of Women), a 1997 film by Algerian female director Rachida Krim.

DOROTHÉE BONNIGAL.

Carli, Guido

b. 1914, Brescia; d. 1993, Rome

Economist

A central banker with political ambitions, Carli was governor of the **Banco d'Italia** from 1960 to 1975, thus holding strategic office during both the happiest period of the **economic miracle** and the worst years of high inflation and increasing unemployment. A figure of high international standing, Carli was managing director of the European Payment Union during the 1950s and later played a major role in the G-10 Group, aimed at fostering international monetary cooperation among the main Western countries. Both a lucid analyst of the weaknesses of Italian capitalism and a firm supporter of the market economy, he was keen to reform the Italian financial system and to reshape it according to the Anglo-Saxon market-oriented model. Paradoxically, however, he ended up leaving his successors an extremely rigid banking system, mainly based on bureaucratic command and market segmentation. After leaving the Bank of Italy, he became chairman of **Confindustria** (the employers' association) in 1976–80, was elected as a **DC** senator in 1983 and crowned his outstanding career as Minister of the Treasury in 1989–92.

STEFANO BATTILOSSI

Carrà, Raffaella

b. 18 June 1943, Bellaria, Rimini

Entertainer and television presenter

Singer, dancer, actress and presenter, Carrà (real name Raffaella Pelloni) appeared in films and on television from the early 1960s. With her trademark platinum blond hair – cut in a helmet style which remained unchanged for thirty years – she became one of the most popular faces on Italian television in the 1980s. Although ridiculed for its banality ('how many beans do you think are in the jar, signora?'), her lunchtime phone-in show *Pronto, Raffaella?* successfully exploited **RAI**-TV's monopoly on live broadcasting and won back the housewife audience from **Canale Cinque**. A vivacious, down-to-earth personality whose low-voltage sex appeal perfectly matched the requirements of Italian public television, she was seen as an archetype by almost every woman in entertainment broadcasting. Following the success of her evening show, *Buonasera Raffaella*, she was recruited by **Berlusconi** in 1987 in his ratings war with the RAI. As in other cases, the transfer did not meet expectations. After a period in exile in Spain,

Carrà returned to RAI-TV in the mid-1990s to host *Carramba!*, a shamelessly emotional show reuniting long-separated friends and families.

Futher reading

Calabrese, O. (1985) 'Raffaella Carrà' in G. Ascoli *et al.*, *Perche lei?* (Why her?), Bari: Laterza.

STEPHEN GUNDLE

Casabella

A journal of architecture and related arts, *Casabella* (House Beautiful) was founded in Milan in 1928. By 1933 *Casabella* had become an established polemical vehicle for Italian 'Rationalist' architecture under the editorial direction of Giuseppe Pagano and Edoardo Persico. Suppressed by the Fascists in 1943, the journal only resumed continuous publication in 1953 under the influential editorship of Ernesto N. **Rogers**. Re-titled *Casabella continuità* (Casabella-continuity), it now sought to promote a contextual approach to design that emphasized pre-existing local conditions of building, site and culture. To help articulate this position, Rogers assembled a group of younger architects who would soon become significant in their own right: Giancarlo **De Carlo**, Aldo **Rossi**, Gae **Aulenti**, Marco **Zanuso**, and Vittorio **Gregotti**. Among the subsequent editors of *Casabella* perhaps the most influential has been Gregotti.

See also: architectural and design magazines

Further reading

'Casabella 1928–1978' (1978) *Casabella* October/November, 440/441.

KEITH EVAN GREEN

Cassa per il Mezzogiorno

The Cassa per il Mezzogiorno (Southern Development Fund) was created in August 1950 as both a specific government response to a series of violent protests by farmers in the South demanding agrarian reform and as a decisive measure for finally resolving the **Southern Question** by ending the economic and social backwardness of the South and the islands. Originally projected to last 10 years, it was extended several times until July 1984 when it was officially closed and some of its functions were taken over by the Fondo nazionale per lo sviluppo del Mezzogiorno (National Fund for the Development of the South), itself terminated in 1993.

During the Fund's thirty-five-year history an enormous amount of money was spent (some credible estimates put it at around 200,000 billion lira) but although there were undoubted improvements in the South's infrastructure in terms of roads, land reclamation and water supply, it is generally agreed that the Fund's aims to industrialize the South and to bring it to the level of economic productivity of the North failed miserably.

The fears originally expressed by the Socialists and Communists who opposed the law instituting the Fund on the grounds that it would sideline agrarian reform and serve 'other' interests than those of the southern poor proved well-founded since the Fund effectively became a huge reservoir of resources which could be traded by politicians of the governing parties in return for votes and general political support.

See also: agriculture; clientelism; peasants

GINO MOLITERNO

Cassola, Carlo

b. 17 March 1917, Rome; d. 29 January 1987, Montecarlo di Lucca

Novelist and journalist

Cassola's experience with the partizan movement during the Second World War was perhaps the primary thematic influence on his work, as many of his novels explore the lives of those in the **Resistance**. The novels *Fausto e Anna* (*Fausto and Anna*) (1952) and *La ragazza di Bube* (translated as *Bebo's Girl*) (1960) reflect Cassola's belief that the Resistance failed to achieve completely its moral and political goals. Indeed in *La ragazza di Bube*, his best-known and most popular novel, and for which he received the Strega prize, the young partizan, Bube, becomes involved in a murder, and it is his girlfriend who embodies the virtues of the movement. Cassola returned to his earlier experiments with existential writings in the 1961 novel *Un cuore arido* (*An Arid Heart*), which traces in its quotidian details the gradual shrivelling of one woman's soul. A convinced environmentalist and anti-nuclear activist in later years, Cassola's last novels focus on topics such as the threat of nuclear holocaust, animal protection and antimilitarism.

Further reading

Moss, H.K. (1977) 'The Existentialism of Carlo Cassola', *Italica* 54: 381–98.

LAURA A. SALSINI

Castellaneta, Carlo

b. 8 February 1930, Milan

Novelist, short story writer and journalist

In his numerous fictional works Castellaneta explores social and class issues arising from personal experiences, his family and his work as editor and director of the journal *Storia Illustrata* (Illustrated History). In novels such as *Viaggio col padre* (Voyage with My Father) (1958) and *L'età del desidero* (The Age of Desire) (1990), he deals with themes from his family background while in the novel *Una lunga rabbia* (A Long Rage) (1991), he examines his own work experiences. He also explores passionate love in novels such as *Passione d'amore* (Passion of Love) (1987) and the emotions more generally in his guide *Dizionario dei sentimenti* (Dictionary of Feelings) (1980). From his many years as a reporter and his editorial work for *Storia illustrata*, Castellaneta developed a narrative style that privileges a journalistic observation of his times. Love of his native city and an attention to social issues shape the collections of essays *Storia di Milano* (History of Milan) (1975) and *La mia Milano* (My Milan) (1998).

VIRGINIA PICCHIETTI

Castellani, Renato

b. 4 September 1913, Finale Ligure;
   d. 28 December 1985, Rome

Film director

Castellani's debut feature, *Un colpo di pistola* (A Pistol Shot), was released in 1941; but it was only after the Second World War that he made the 'trilogy of the poor people' for which he will be remembered: *Sotto il sole di Roma* (Under the Sun of Rome) (1948), *È primavera* (Springtime) (1949) and his most successful work, *Due soldi di speranza* (Two Cents' Worth of Hope) (1951). Like other neorealist directors, Castellani used authentic settings and non-professional actors, but his moralistic insistence on happy endings caused Giuseppe **De Santis** to label him a 'calligraphist', an uncommitted formalist (see also **neorealism**). While Castellani's skills remain undisputed, he has been branded a 'pink neorealist', whose films, even the prison drama *Nella città l'inferno* (And the Wild, Wild Women) (1959), have more in common with the Italian-style comedies of the late 1950s than with the early films of **Rossellini** and **De Sica**.

See also: neorealism

Further reading

Trasatti, S. (1984) *Renato Castellani*, Florence: La Nuova Italia.

DAVE WATSON

Castiglioni, Achille

b. 16 February 1918, Milan

Architect and designer

The younger brother of the designers Luigi and Pier Giacomo **Castiglioni**, Achille Castiglioni set up a design practice with Pier Giacomo in 1945. They played an important role in the postwar Italian design movement, working primarily on exhibition and product design. Together, they created the 'Turbino' desk lamp, produced by Arredoluce in 1949, the 'Spalter' vacuum cleaner produced by Rem in 1956, and the 'Arco' lamp produced in 1962. Following his brother's death in 1968, Achille went on to work on oil and vinegar flasks for Alessi (1980) and the 'Gibigiana' light for Flos in 1980. He remains one of Italy's leading designers and continues to work in Milan in a modest studio.

See also: interior design

Further reading

Gregotti, V. (1984) *Achille Castiglioni*, Milan: Electa.

PENNY SPARKE

Castiglioni, Pier Giacomo

b. 22 April 1913, Milan; d. 27 November 1968, Milan

Exhibition and product designer

Pier Giacomo Castiglioni worked first with his elder brother Livio before the Second World War, and then subsequently with his younger brother Achille. In 1938, Livio and Pier Giacomo Castiglioni opened a design studio with Luigi Caccia Dominione. Together they designed the first Italian bakelite radio (Model 547), just before the studio was closed in 1940. Following the war, Pier Giacomo joined forces with Achille and together they worked on exhibitions and products from 1945 onwards. Their work of the 1940s and 1950s rates among the best Italian design from the period, including the 'Turbino' desk lamp produced by Arredoluce in 1949, the 'Spalter' vacuum cleaner produced by Rem in 1956 and the 'Arco' lamp of 1962. Working alone, Pier Giacomo designed the 'Mezzandro' stool for Zanotta in 1957, based on Marcel Duchamp's idea of the 'ready-made'. It was not produced until 1971, after his death.

See also: interior design

Further reading

Pica, A. (1969) 'Piergiacomo Castiglioni', *Domus*, 470, January, 1–2.

PENNY SPARKE

Castri, Massimo

b. 25 May 1943, Cortona, Arezzo

Director

Strongly influenced by both Artaud and Brecht, on whom he published a study in 1973, Castri began as an actor but soon abandoned acting in favour of directing. Driven by an intense ideological commitment, in his early productions he aggressively deconstructed texts, using a psychoanalytical approach to bring their latent contents to the surface. Exemplary in this sense was the Pirandellian triptych *Vestire gli ignudi* (Clothe the Naked), *La vita che ti diedi* (The Life I Gave You) and *Così è (se vi pare)* (Right You Are! If You Think So), produced between 1976 and 1979, as well as his series of Ibsen plays. The results were dark, brooding spectacles, sometimes bizarre ironic pastiches, as in his approaches to Euripidean tragedy. In his later work he became more restrained, abandoning the accumulation of signs and intellectual metaphors in performance as well as moving into the mainstream of publicly financed spaces which allowed him more time and resources to prepare shows. In the later period he relied more on the intensity of actors and the disquieting spaces created by scenographer, Massimo Balò, as in the Goldoni cycle which went from *I rusteghi* (The Rustics) in 1992 to *La trilogia della villeggiatura* (The Holiday Trilogy) of 1996.

Further reading

Innamorati, I. (1993) *Massimo Castri e il suo teatro* (Massimo Castri and His Theatre), Rome: Bulzoni.

PAOLO PUPPA

Catholic Action

The sole surviving non-fascist organization under Mussolini's regime, thanks to Article 43 of the Concordat of 1929, Catholic Action became the most powerful, lay 'long arm' of the Church in the immediate postwar period. From its inception, the fundamental and stated purpose of Catholic Action remained to ensure the permeation of civil society by Catholic moral and social principles, most especially in relation to the importance of the family, the sanctity of human life and solidarity, and the defence of the Church's interests in the broadest sense. To this end it provided instruction and training of Catholics as 'active' members of society. Essentially a complex of different associations, male and female, young and old, students and graduates, in 1954 it had a total affiliated membership of 2,700,000, and it provided a vast network of recreational and sports facilities. Catholic Action was always a national association, though its effectiveness on the ground varied according to the strength of the Church in the localities; it was weaker in the 'red belt' and central Italy generally, and in some parishes in the South it was almost non-existent.

As a result of the reforms of Pius XI in the 1930s, leadership of Catholic Action was highly centralized in its Rome headquarters, under the direct control of the Vatican. Its national president, Luigi Gedda, was therefore a power in the land. As the crucial general elections of April 1948 approached, Gedda set up the 'Civic Committees' to mobilize the Catholic vote on behalf of the Christian Democratic Party (see **DC**). Catholic Action was forbidden to directly involve itself in politics by the 1929 Concordat, but in many parishes it was Catholic Action which effectively operated as the Catholic party, and it provided the essential training ground for DC cadres over several decades.

Catholic Action went into decline in the 1960s, and by 1970 membership had fallen by over half. Young people in particular abandoned the organization in droves, some ending up as militants in the Communist Party or extraparliamentary left-wing 'groupuscules', or even occasionally as members of left-wing terrorist groupings.

Since the 1970s, Catholic Action has held a much lower profile in the Church's life, partly because of the increasing autonomy of the Christian Democratic Party and partly because of the defeat in the **divorce** referendum of 1974. Nevertheless, it retains a crucial role as the organ co-ordinating the Church's activities in Italian civil society. This centrality may be judged by the standing of just two of its recent national presidents, Alberto Monticone, historian and now parliamentarian of the Popular Party (see **PPI**) and Mario Agnes, editor of the Vatican newspaper *L'Osservatore Romano*.

See also: Catholic associations; church, state and society; Vatican

Further reading

Poggi, G. (1967) *Catholic Action in Italy*, Stanford University Press (the classic sociological study of Catholic Action before Vatican II).

JOHN POLLARD

Catholic associations

The influence of Catholic associationalism has been a major feature of Italian civil society since the Risorgimento, and its emergence in that period was a sign of the defensive posture which the Church adopted towards the liberal state. Nevertheless, the heyday of Catholic associationalism was undoubtedly the fifteen years following the end of the Second World War when, by some estimates, as many as 10 out of the 45 million Italians belonged to one Catholic association or another.

Catholic associations have covered almost the whole gamut of human activity, from the obviously spiritual, such as the Children of Mary and the more traditional pious, parish confraternities, to the political and economic spheres, trade unionism, youth (including a Catholic Boy Scouts group), sport, leisure and culture. The Church has sought to control them through a direct clerical presence – the so-called 'ecclesiastical assistants' at every level internally – as well as through their affiliation and subordination to a succession of umbrella organizations – the Opera Dei Congressi, down to 1904; the economic–social, electoral and popular *unioni* until 1914, and thereafter through an intensely centralized **Catholic Action** organization. Pius XI's attempt in the 1920s and 1930s to 're-Christianize' Italian society led to the creation of a network of Catholic associations, most of which survived the fascistization of Italy by Mussolini's regime.

In the post-Second World War period, it was possible for most Italian Catholics to live through both childhood and adult life in a series of Catholic associations and organizations attached to the parish in much the same way as Dutch Catholics did in their ghetto-like 'pillar'. The only influences on their lives that were not under direct Catholic control were the state school system and the electronic media. Furthermore, as the Cold War intensified, this ghettoization of Catholic life became more pronounced. Apart from Catholic Action itself, four Catholic associations had the most influence in Italian civil society: ACLI, the Italian Catholic Workers' Associations; Coldiretti, the peasant farmers' organization; CISL, the Catholic trade union; and CFI, the Catholic women's organization. All four worked in unison with Catholic Action and, to a certain extent, with the Christian Democratic Party (see **DC**), until the mid-1960s. Lesser but still influential associations were FUCI (the students' organization), Movimento Laureati (Graduates' Movement) and UCID, the Catholic employers' and managers' association.

Catholic associationalism has changed since the crisis and decline of the later 1960s and the early 1970s. New forms of associationalism, chiefly spiritual and even charismatic in inspiration, the most notable being the Focolare movement, **Communione e Liberazione** and Opus Dei, have emerged to replace or supplement the old. Some four million people are now estimated to be involved in Catholic associations.

See also: church, state and society

Further reading

Allum, P.A. (1973) *Italy: Republic Without Government?*, London: Weidenfeld & Nicolson (good on Catholic associations as 'interest groups' in Italian politics).

Garelli, F. (1991) *Religione e Chiesa in Italia* (Religion and Church in Italy), Bologna: Il Mulino (standard work on the Church's presence in civil society).

Riccardi, A. (1994) 'La vita religiosa' (Religious Life), in P. Ginsborg (ed.), *Stato Dell'Italia* (State

of Italy), Milan: Mondadori (a more up to date account of Catholic associations and activism).

JOHN POLLARD

Catholic press and publishing

Whereas in the pre-Fascist period the strength of the Catholic press lay in a network of daily newspapers, especially in northern and central Italy, today it lies with the popular, weekly and monthly publications like **Famiglia Cristiana** (one million readers) and *Il Messaggero di Sant'Antonio* (900,000), as well as with a network of diocesan weeklies having a total readership of about 1,200,000. It is these publications which really penetrate to the Catholic faithful in town and country. In fact, only *L'Eco di Bergamo*, *Il cittadino* of Lodi (both diocesan controlled) and *L'Avvenire* (owned by the Italian Bishops' Conference) survive as dailies, but with small circulations: **L'Osservatore Romano**, the semi-official organ of the Vatican Secretariat of State, has even fewer regular readers.

There is also a variety of more intellectually 'heavyweight' periodical publications which manifest the extreme complexity and diversity of the Italian Catholic world. The most notable of these are *La Civiltà Cattolica*, run by the Jesuits and closely supervised by the Vatican, *Jesus* (Edizioni Paoline) which deals exclusively with political and theological issues, *Il Regno*, published by Dehoniane, and *Il Sabato* and *Trenta Giorni*, both aligned to **Communione e Liberazione**, the latter edited by Giulio **Andreotti**. In 1995 a new magazine, **Liberal**, was born under the joint editorship of two 'lay' intellectuals, Ernesto Galli Della Loggia and Ferdinando Adornato, and the Catholic historian Giorgio Rumi as a meeting point between liberal conservatives of both a Catholic and a secular stamp. In addition, there is an independent Catholic news agency, Adista, based in Rome, which publishes news of Catholic 'dissidence' of all kinds, all over the world.

There are over one hundred avowedly 'Catholic' publishing houses, large and small, the most important of which are Ancora and AVE (Rome), Dehoniane and the Edizioni Paoline (Bologna),

Editrice La Scuola and Editrice Morcelliania (Brescia), Edizioni Piemme (Turin), Jaca Books (Milan), and Libreria Editrice Vaticana and Vita e Pensiero, the press of the Catholic University of Milan. In the last two years, a number of Catholic publishers have begun to move out of the restricted network of Catholic bookshops, seeking a wider readership for their books.

While the bulk of the Catholic press and publishing sector is directly or indirectly under the control of the Church authorities or religious orders, the presence of a strong lay element testifies to the continuing vitality of Italian Catholicism.

See also: Catholic associations; church, state and society; the Vatican

Further reading

Riccardi, A. (1994) 'La vita religiosa', in P. Ginsborg (ed.), *Stato dell'Italia* (The State of Italy), Milan: Bruno Mondadori (includes a full list of publications and publishing houses).

JOHN POLLARD

Cavalli, Patrizia

b. 1947, Todi, Perugia

Poet, novelist and translator

Proficient as a translator as well as poet, Cavalli has contributed to many literary magazines and her poetry has appeared in prestigious journals such as *Paragone*, *Linea d'ombra* and *Nuovi Argomenti*. Her strikingly individualistic style, betraying in places the influence of Sandro Penna, struggles to render the passions of both the human body and the soul, although beneath the pulsing rhythm of her compositions there seems to lie a profound disenchantment and discontent with the human condition. Her most important poems are in the collections *Le mie poesie non cambieranno il mondo* (My Poetry Will not Change the World) (1981) and *Il Cielo* (The Sky) (1981). She has also published a short novel, *Ritratto* (Portrait) (1992).

ANDREA RICCI

Cavani, Liliana

b. 1 January 1933, Carpi, Modena

Film director

One of the very few Italian female directors to have achieved international renown, Cavani has constantly offered new points of view on controversial historical figures and on the extremes of human behaviour. It is this search for hidden truths, combined with a refined style and a disregard for social conventions, that makes Cavani's body of work one of the most daring in Italian cinema. Although she had already directed a number of interesting films in the 1960s (*Francesco d'Assisi*, 1966; *Galileo*, 1968; *I cannibali* (The Cannibals), 1969) she first came to international attention in 1974 with *Il portiere di notte* (The Night Porter) followed by *Al di là del bene e del male* (Beyond Good and Evil) (1977), a film about the strange *ménage à trois* between the proto-feminist Lou Salomé, the poet Paul Rée and the philosopher Friedrich Nietzsche. Amongst her numerous subsequent films is also a striking adaptation of Curzio Malaparte's novel *La pelle* (The Skin) (1981), starring Burt Lancaster and Marcello **Mastroianni**. Although her frequently confrontational films are not universally liked, Cavani has undoubtedly made important contributions to Italian cultural and political debate. In 1996 she served as council member of **RAI**.

Further reading

Tiso, C. (1975) *Liliana Cavani*, Florence: La Nuova Italia (a general survey of Cavani's work to the mid-1970s).

ADRIANA MONTI

CCD

The CCD (Centro Cristiano Democratico, or Democratic Christian Centre) was born out of the split which followed the attempt to re-found the Christian Democratic Party (see **DC**) in January 1994. A group of centre–right DC parliamentarians led by Casini, Fumagalli, D'Onofrio and

Mastella founded the CCD and joined forces with **Berlusconi**'s **Polo della Libertà** in order to preserve a Catholic political presence under the new electoral regime. They won 6 per cent of the proportional representation vote in the 1994 elections, and established an influential presence in the ensuing Berlusconi government through ministers like D'Onofrio, who took the prestigious justice ministry. Though they stayed loyal to Berlusconi following the collapse of his government in December 1994, they did less well in the elections of 1996.

Further reading

Fontana, S. (1995) *Il destino politico dei cattolici* (The Political Destiny of the Catholics), Milan: Arnaldo Mondadori.

Wertman, D. (1995) 'The Last Year of the Christian Democratic Party', in C. Mershon and G. Pasquino (eds), *Italy: Ending the First Republic*, Boulder, CO: Westview Press.

JOHN POLLARD

CDU

The CDU (Cristiani Democratici Uniti, or United Democratic Christians) was formed by Rocco Buttiglione during the March 1995 split in the Popular Party (see **PPI**) provoked by the debate over future electoral alliances, specifically as to whether to join the **PDS** and Progressives or **Berlusconi**'s **Polo della Libertà**, which Buttiglione preferred. Buttiglione, a philosophy professor who has been a counsellor of Pope John Paul II, ensured that the CDU retained close links with **Communione e Liberazione**: in fact, Roberto Formigoni, one of the leading lights of the latter, is also CDU president of the Lombard regional government.

In alliance with Berlusconi's Polo, the CDU won seats in the Senate and Chamber of Deputies in the 1996 elections. It subsequently worked closely with the **CCD** and there was much talk of reconstructing the old Christian democratic party around them, perhaps even of reunification with the PPI, but this did not happen. However, following the fall of the Prodi government in 1998, the CDU merged with the newly formed **UDR**, which became part of D'Alema's centre–left government.

JOHN POLLARD

Cecchi, Carlo

b. 25 January 1939, Florence

Theatre director and actor

Cecchi's acting is characterized by the use of Neapolitan dialectal cadences acquired during his youthful apprenticeship with Eduardo **De Filippo**. His friendship with Elsa **Morante** and an encounter with the Living Theatre which pushed him in the direction of alternative performance were also perhaps influential in his vaunted autonomy from the system of *stabili* or established public theatres. His repertoire includes both classic and modern works, amongst them Majakovski whose *The Bath* (1971) and *The Flea* (1975) were presented in an expressionist style; Büchner's *Woyzech* (1969), where the protagonist spoke in Calabrian dialect; Pirandello's *L'Uomo, la bestia e la virtù* (Man, Beast and Virtue), produced in 1978 with animal masks; and other plays by Molière, Pinter and Bernhardt. The directorial approach alternates with singular efficacy between popular tradition and Brechtian alienation, and there is an unusual rigour in the guidance of the actors with an almost maniacal attention to gesture and pauses. More recently Cecchi has achieved a greater popularity due to his fascinating roles in the films of Mario **Martone**.

PAOLO PUPPA

Cecchi, Emilio

b. 17 July 1884, Florence; d. 5 September 1966, Rome

Journalist, critic and translator

Amongst the most prolific and influential Italian intellectuals of the twentieth century, Cecchi contributed to influential journals and newspapers (*Il Leonardo, La Voce, La Critica, **Il Corriere della*** *sera* among others) and was a founding member of the literary journal *La Ronda* (1919–23), which after Futurism's artistic iconoclasm, urged writers to return to a classical style modelled on Leopardi and Manzoni. His prose collections during this period exemplify his lyrical, yet ironic, narrative style characterized as *prosa d'arte* (artistic prose).

While continuing a journalistic career, Cecchi also taught Italian literature and culture at the University of California, Berkeley (1930–1), collaborated with the Italian film company Cines (1932–58) and co-edited a nine-volume history of Italian literature with Dante scholar Natalino **Sapegno**. Never having completed his university studies, Cecchi was nevertheless awarded an honorary degree in Letters in 1958. His interests ranged from English and American literatures to twentieth-century Italian poetry and prose, and included American culture, which he described in his travel books, particularly in *Messico* (Mexico) (1932) and *America amara* (Bitter America) (1932).

FRANCESCA PARMEGGIANI

Cecchi D'Amico, Suso (Giovanna)

b. 21 July 1914, Rome

Scriptwriter

One of the most respected and prolific scriptwriters in postwar Italian cinema, Cecchi D'Amico has worked with all the major directors including **Antonioni**, **Bolognini**, **Blasetti**, **Comencini**, **Monicelli**, **Rosi**, **Zeffirelli** and **De Sica**, for whom she co-wrote *Ladri di biciclette* (Bicycle Thieves) (1948). Her most constant collaboration, however, was with **Visconti** and she was scriptwriter for all his most famous films including *Senso* (1953), *Rocco e i suoi fratelli* (Rocco and His Brothers) (1960), *Il gattopardo* (The Leopard) (1962) and *Morte a Venezia* (Death in Venice) (1970). She has received numerous awards including the Nastro d'Argento (Silver Ribbon) six times and an honorary degree in letters from the University of Bari, as well as being made Commander and Grand Officer of the Order of Merit of the Italian Republic. Her enormous contribution to Italian cinema was officially recognized with a

Golden Lion for lifetime achievement at the Venice International Film Festival in 1994.

Further reading

Cecchi D'Amico, S. (1996) 'Writing Rocco and his Brothers', in J. Boorman and W. Donohue (eds), *Projections 6: Filmmakers on Filmmaking*, London: Faber & Faber (an extended interview in which the scriptwriter discusses her work with Visconti).

GINO MOLITERNO

Cederna, Camilla

b. 21 January 1911, Milan; d. 9 November 1997, Rome

Writer and editor

Cederna, whose writings span the mid-1940s to the 1990s, began her career as a journalist. She was among the founders of the weekly *L'Europeo*, and later contributed regularly to other news and cultural magazines such as *L'Espresso* and *Panorama*. In her many books she depicted all the major aspects and personalities of Italian society, from the Milanese upper classes in *Noi siamo le signore* (We are The Ladies) (1958) to **Fellini** in *La voce dei padroni* (The Voice of the Bosses) (1962). In subsequent publications such as *Pinelli: Una finestra sulla strage* (Pinelli: A Window on the Carnage) (1971) and *Sparare a vista. Come la polizia del regime DC mantiene l'ordine pubblico* (Shooting on Sight: How the Police of the Christian Democratic Government Maintains Public Order) (1975), she publicly accused the government of political oppression and of backing police violence. With her ironic and spirited writing style, Cederna captured the changing trends, the tragedies and the comedies of Italian society over a period of five decades.

PIERA CARROLI

Cefis, Eugenio

b. 21 July, 1921, Cividale, Friuli

Industrial manager

Originally a member of Enrico **Mattei**'s team at

ENI, Cefis succeeded Mattei as chairman of the group and, with remarkable business acumen, successfully steered the state-owned oil company through the 1960s and early 1970s, a most difficult period for the world oil market. Drawing upon strong support from his political patrons within the **DC**, he made ENI an outstanding power in the Italian economy. He nevertheless preferred to rule rather than be ruled, and so pressed ENI to acquire control over **Montedison**, a leading chemical company, attempting to transform it into his own independent realm. A silent, enigmatic figure, Cefis's outstanding managerial skill was overshadowed by his fame as an unscrupulous adventurer who systematically bribed parties and used his public office to carry on his personal business. As the emblem of an entire generation of rapacious public managers, Cefis is reputedly the model for one of the main characters in *Petrolio* (Oil), the last, unfinished novel of Pier Paolo **Pasolini**.

STEFANO BATTILOSSI

Celant, Germano

b. 1940, Genoa

art critic and curator

Celant studied Futurism at the University of Puerto Rico, so it is perhaps not surprising that he believes in a strong relationship between critic, manifesto and art movement. In 1967 he coined the term *arte povera* for an exhibition he was curating, and promoted the group with a manifesto in *Flash Art*. He also wrote for *Forma Nuova*, *Casabella* and *Marcatrè*, and taught at the University of Genoa. His many publications include lavishly illustrated catalogues for shows he has curated on individual artists such as Mario **Merz**, Claes Oldenburg and Robert Mapplethorpe. In 1994–5, as Curator of Contemporary Art at the Guggenheim Museum in New York, he organized the major exhibition 'The Italian Metamorphosis: 1943–1968.' Celant's signature catalogue essay is non-factual, a stream of consciousness exploration of an extended metaphor, at times with a classical flavour.

In 1997 he returned to Italy as the director of a wilfully eclectic **Venice Biennale**. He remains enormously influential.

See also: art criticism

Further reading

Celant, G. (1994) *The Italian Metamorphosis: 1943–1968*, New York: Guggenheim Museum.

MAX STAPLES

Celati, Gianni

b. 10 January 1937, Sondrio

Novelist, translator and academic

During the 1960s Celati was an active member of the avantgarde movement (see **Gruppo 63**) and his writings, especially earlier works such as *Comiche* (Comics) (1971), *Le avventure di Guizzardi* (The Adventures of Guizzardi) (1973) and *Lunario del paradiso* (Moonscape of Paradise) (1978), subvert and renegotiate traditional notions of literature and its function in society by jettisoning the elitist distinction between 'high' and 'popular' culture and adopting instead a style which is an intriguing amalgam of popular jargon and everyday language. The iconoclastic stance taken in the 1970s gives way to a more relaxed prose in his subsequent narratives from *Narratori delle pianure* (Voices from the Plains) (1985) to *Quattro novelle sulle apparenze* (Appearances) (1987). Here Celati's writing is dominated more by the theme of wandering and the observation of nature and human reaction to it. Celati, who teaches American literature at the University of Bologna, has also translated works by Swift, Twain, Céline, London and Melville.

PAOLO BARTOLONI

Celentano, Adriano

b. 6 January 1938, Milan

Singer, actor and film director

Italy's most famous and most enduring rock'n'roll

singer, Celentano was born in Milan of southern parents. While working at various jobs, including as a plumber and a watchmaker, he began doing imitations of Jerry Lewis and Bill Haley at the Santa Tecla Club. In May 1957, backed by the Rock Boys – a group that included, amongst others, Giorgio **Gaber** and Enzo **Jannacci** – he sang at the first National Festival of Rock'n'Roll at the Palazzo di Ghiaccio (Ice Palace) in Milan. He proved to be an overwhelming success and was immediately offered a recording contract. His singing career on the rise – and by now becoming notorious as 'il molleggiato' (the sprung one) because of the way he moved his body – he performed at the second Italian National Rock'n'Roll Festival in 1958 and was soon also appearing in films, including being featured in a segment of **Fellini**'s *La dolce vita* (1960). In 1961 he was inducted into military service but was nevertheless able to continue his singing career, competing in the Sanremo festival that year to perform his now legendary '24,000 baci' (24,000 Kisses). He scandalized the judges by turning his back on the audience and so failed to win, but his song immediately leapt to the top of the hit parade and sold over a million copies, making him the most popular rock'n'roll artist in Italy.

In the following years, having founded his own recording company, the Clan Celentano, he continued to produce a long string of hits in Italy, and performed in rock festivals abroad, thereby acquiring an international reputation. By the mid-1970s, having already appeared in films by **Lattuada** and Dario **Argento**, he also began writing, directing and acting in several of his own films. During the next decade, as well as touring intensely both in Italy and abroad, he also appeared in over fifteen films as well as directing himself in *Joan Lui* (1985), a film in which he played Jesus Christ returning to the earth for the second time.

In 1987 he was invited to host a season of the RAI's long-running and extremely popular Saturday evening variety programme *Fantastico* (see **Canzonissima**) where he caused a furore (as well as increasing the ratings) with his assorted, improvised and often contradictory opinions on everything from consumerism and television advertising to hunting and environmental issues.

Regarded as something of a dinosaur by the younger generation in the 1990s, he nevertheless manages to maintain considerable popularity amongst a more mature audience by regularly releasing new albums, the most recent being a CD recorded in collaboration with another classic rock star, **Mina**, and an album of new songs written with the lyricist Mogol (see Lucio **Battisti**) in 1999.

GINO MOLITERNO

CENSIS

Originally founded in 1964 as a private institute for socioeconomic research, the CENSIS (Centro Studi Investimenti Sociali, or Centre for the Study of Social Investments) received official recognition for the high standard of its work in 1973 when it was granted the legal status of a state foundation. As such, it has since carried out a wide range of studies and research into all aspects of economic and social developments in Italy, and in 1989 was placed under the direction of the newly-instituted Ministry for Universities and Scientific and Technological Research (MURST). While conducting specific surveys on commission for other national agencies or private firms, the CENSIS also publishes an authoritative annual report on the state of Italian society, which since 1984 has also appeared in English as *Italy Today*.

GINO MOLITERNO

censorship

Notwithstanding a new **constitution** which sanctified the principle of freedom of expression, censorship did not disappear with the fall of Fascism and continued to be used in postwar Italy for both political and moral reasons. Together with the legislation against **pornography**, norms regarding offences to the **Republic** and its institutions, to the **armed forces**, to the nation, to the **flag**, to state religion and to its clergy, to public servants, magistrates and to foreign heads of state have survived and legitimated censorial interventions.

During the second half of the 1940s and throughout the 1950s, censorship was particularly severe because the political and social leadership was convinced of the necessity to defend Italy against a concerted attack by Marxists, free-thinkers and pornographers. In 1947 prefects, acting on behalf of the government, ordered the confiscation of numerous books, including *La Romana* (The Woman of Rome) by Alberto **Moravia**. Even well-known works of classical art were censored. Again in 1947, a Roman Court declared that the reproduction of famous nudes by Goya and Allori in a popular magazine was a criminal offence, because these paintings could arouse sexual desires when isolated from their 'proper' cultural context.

Political censorship was also common in this period. During the campaign for the pivotal elections of April 1948, the prefects often prohibited the posting of political manifestos. Newspapers were forbidden to publish information about strikes and social unrest because this was considered a threat to public order. The situation did not change greatly after the victory of the **DC**. The new government, dominated by Catholic forces, seriously restricted opportunity for political discussion, and was particularly severe about presumed offences to the institutions and state religion. A famous case involved Guido Aristarco and Renzo Renzi, who were arrested in 1953 and condemned by a military court for having offended the army by publishing a film script dealing with sexual relations between Italian soldiers and Greek women during the Second World War.

Film directors needed to be very careful if they wanted to avoid cuts ordered by the Board of Censors. The social criticism of neorealist films could be interpreted as offensive to national dignity, while any reference to **divorce** or adultery was presumed to offend public decency and family order. In 1947, many prominent directors signed a letter denouncing the attempt to reintroduce preventive censorship of films, rather than on viewing the final product. In 1952 Vitaliano **Brancati** added his voice to protests against the censors who had prohibited even the staging of Machiavelli's sixteenth-century classic *La Mandragola*, to say nothing about Feydeau's plays which made fun of adultery, or the politically disturbing

plays by Bertold Brecht. However, the Catholic organizations which campaigned in favour of 'moral rearmament' found a strong ally in the Minister of Internal Affairs, who characterized as *culturame* (cultural trash) all those who disagreed with his frequent use of censorship.

Catholic censorship played an important role in integrating and reinforcing state censorship. In 1949, the last *Index librorum prohibitorum* was published. Among the new entries were books by the idealist philosopher Benedetto **Croce** and the popular novels of Guido Da Verona. However, as it proved impossible to review the never-ending stream of new books, the *Index* was officially abolished in 1965.

More important were the activities of the Catholic Centre for Cinema, which was created in 1935 with the precise purpose of 'moralizing' the film industry and which published short descriptions of all films together with a moral classification. This publication was patently intended to orient the public, but it also served to pressure film producers and distributors since no film labelled 'for adults only' or worse could be shown in cinemas controlled by the clergy.

During the 1950s, state censorship continued to limit the freedom of expression of journalists, writers and film directors. Danilo **Dolci** was accused of obscenity for some pages of his investigations of poverty in Palermo. Manlio **Cancogni** was condemned for libel after having published his famous denunciation of illegal speculation in the building industry in Rome. Both Moravia and Pier Paolo **Pasolini** had to fight off the censors for almost all their books and films. Under these circumstances, even the attempts of the Viareggio carnival to satirize political leaders were unwelcome and the legal authorities prohibited the more caustic elements, threatening to confiscate the carnival floats.

The relatively more tolerant attitude which was gradually becoming more common among magistrates during the 1960s did not exclude occasional upsurges of repression, often based on the personal initiatives of local attorneys such as Pietro Trombi and Carmelo Spagnuolo. **RAI** television continued to be regulated by a strict moral code which excluded anything controversial. A special committee was nominated to draw up guidelines and exercise control. However, self-censorship and conformism normally prevailed, and authoritarian interventions were rarely necessary. Only with the rise of private **radio** and television stations in the 1970s did a more critical attitude became common. At the same time, eroticism became a common ingredient of television shows.

During the period of political unrest following 1968, censorship was used against the **extraparliamentary Left** press. In 1969, Francesco Tolin was condemned to prison for having exalted political violence on the pages of *Potere operaio* (Workers' Power). Other newspapers were also denounced for inciting and defending what was regarded as criminal behaviour.

In the 1980s, censorship more often took the form of self-censorship: the authors or producers avoided interventions by legal authorities, popular protests and financial losses by omitting what might be considered illegal, immoral or offensive. However, in 1986 the Ministry of Internal Affairs was still instructing the police to use all available legal and administrative rules to combat obscenity. As most magistrates adhered to a relativistic interpretation of the notion of public morality, police efforts often did not lead to a conviction. Significantly, in 1986 the Penal Court of Rome declared that the film *Ultimo tango a Parigi* (Last Tango in Paris) by Bernardo **Bertolucci** could no longer be considered obscene because the sensibility of the general public had changed.

In the 1990s, the uncertain rules of commercial culture often substituted formal censorship, which continued, however, to be applied against the more extreme forms of pornography. Furthermore, the attempts in the late 1990s to introduce legislation for the protection of privacy and a number of proposals aiming at protecting minors against the negative influence of mass media may nevertheless lead to new limitations to the freedom of expression.

See also: sexual mores

Further reading

Cesari, M. (1982) *La censura in Italia oggi (1944–1980)* (Censorship in Italy Today

(1944–1980)), Napoli: Liguori (a general overview of censorship in postwar Italy).

Liggeri, D. (1997) *Mani di forbice. La censura cinematografica in Italia* (Scissor Hands: Film Censorship in Italy), Alessandria: Falsopiano (a much updated discussion of more recent developments in film censorship in Italy).

BRUNO P.F. WANROOIJ

Centro Sperimentale di Cinematografia

Italy's most prestigious national film institute, the Centro Sperimentale di Cinematografia was founded in 1935 by a group of respected filmmakers and critics including Umberto Barbaro, Luigi **Chiarini** and Alessandro **Blasetti**, in order to promote all aspects of film culture and production. Although nominally under the control of the Fascist government, the Centre always managed to exercise a large degree of autonomy. Throughout its many years it has seen most of the important figures of Italian postwar cinema pass through its doors, either as students or as teachers or as both. In addition to the film school itself, which offers professional courses on all aspects of film production to selected students (access is severely limited), the Centre also houses extensive libraries holding books, journals, scripts, posters, photographs and other documentation related to Italian cinema, as well as the national cinetheque which contains a copy of every film produced in Italy.

GINO MOLITERNO

Ceronetti, Guido

b. 24 August 1927, Turin

Poet, translator and literary critic

An acclaimed and widely renowned translator of biblical as well as classical and modern works, Ceronetti has provided fine Italian translations of Latin poets such as Martial and Catullus, contemporary French authors such as Blanchot and several biblical books, among them the Psalms, the

Song of Songs, and the Book of Job, the latter many times reprinted by the prestigious publisher **Adelphi**. A tireless and vocal opponent of mass consumer culture, Ceronetti has also been a political contributor and a literary critic for the newspaper **La Stampa**, later collecting his articles in *Difesa della luna* (In Defense of the Moon) (1971), *Un viaggio in Italia* (A Trip Through Italy) (1983) and *L'occhio malinconico* (The Melancholy Eye) (1988). He was awarded the Viareggio Prize for poetry in 1969 and later collected his poems in *Compassioni e disperazioni: Tutte le poesie, 1946–1987* (Compassions and Despairs: Complete Poems 1946–1987). In more recent years, Ceronetti has attempted to revive the tradition of street performers, and has toured many Italian cities with his marionette theatre. He lives in the small Sienese town of Cetona.

VIRGINIA PICCHIETTI

Ceserani, Remo

b. 1933, Soresina, Cremona

Literary critic and essayist

After many years as Professor of Theory of Literature at the University of Pisa, Ceserani is currently Professor of Comparative Literature at the University of Bologna. One of the most profound and well-versed Italian scholars of the last decades, he has produced learned editions of many Italian literary classics such as Ariosto's *Orlando Furioso*, has written extensively on modern and contemporary Italian literature and has also produced many critical works of literary theory extending to topics related to American, English, German and French, as well as Italian, culture. His intense scholarship has gone hand in hand with a vocation for teaching and a broad journalistic production, and he has also recently published a novel, *Viaggio in Italia del Dottor Dappertutto* (Dr. Everywhere's Voyage to Italy) (1996), which surveys Italian academia and society at large with an acute satirical eye.

ANDREA CICCARELLI

cheese

The Italian for cheese, *formaggio*, derives from the medieval Latin word *formaticum*, itself stemming from *forma* (shape), because of the wicker baskets in which these dairy products were moulded and reached maturation. Cheese has always been part of the Italian diet, both in rural and urban cultures, and this fondness for cheese has not abated within the consumer culture of the late twentieth century when fine cheeses have become ever easier to produce and obtain.

In Italy, cheeses are firstly classified according to the type of milk used: cow's milk is the most common, but goat and sheep milk are also widely used, *pecorino* being an example of a cheese made with the latter. The lapse of time between production and usage further determines the classification of cheeses into *formaggi freschi* (fresh cheeses), to be consumed immediately after preparation; *formaggi molli* (soft cheeses) that can be eaten within approximately two months; and *formaggi secchi* (dry cheeses) which last and improve in flavour over time. Other categories of cheese are those that grow mouldy (such as gorgonzola). Processed cheeses correspond to the Italian *formaggi fusi*, whose preparation implies a melting process. Other classifications take into account the percentage of fat contained in the milk utilized; thus the terms *formaggi grassi* (fat cheeses) for those obtained from whole milk and *semi-grassi* for those made with skim milk. Hot cheeses are qualified as *piccanti* (for example, *provolone piccante*).

Italian cheeses are eaten on their own or as part of a meal; however, they are not served with coffee and would never follow dessert. Cheeses are primarily consumed with bread: the expression *essere pane e cacio* (to be like bread and cheese) refers metaphorically to an enduring bond of friendship. Another sought-after combination is cheese with pears, which appears in the proverb: 'Al contadino non devi far sapere quanto è buono il formaggio con le pere' (Don't let the peasant know how good cheese tastes with pears), the assumption being that peasants should be left to eat less delicate foods or, perhaps, not given an excuse to raise the price of their products.

As well as being a popular food, cheeses are used in many renowned Italian dishes. **Pizza** is topped with *mozzarella* cheese, while calzone is stuffed with it. **Polenta** is served in a variety of recipes which almost always include abundant cheese. As well as being generously sprinkled with grated cheese, several **pasta** dishes also include it in their recipe especially when they are oven baked. Dry, tasty cheeses such as *parmigiano*, or alternatively *romano* or *pecorino*, are all suitable for grating. The internationally renowned risottos (rice dishes), in particular the classic recipes such as *risotto alla milanese*, are generally topped with freshly ground parmesan cheese.

Most Italian **regions** are famed for the production of specific cheeses. This is the case for *parmigiano* from the town of Parma in Emilia. *Mozzarella*, of Neapolitan origin, was originally made with buffalo milk but later came to be industrially produced with cow's milk. *Pecorino* from Sardinia is one of the most sought-after varieties. Val d'Aosta prides itself on the mild but richly-flavoured *fontina* which is also used in a famous Piedmontese specialty, *fonduta* (a cream of *fontina*, milk, butter and eggs, served hot and sprinkled with white **tartufo** thinly sliced). *Gorgonzola*, one of the most renowned Italian cheeses, has been produced in Lombardy since medieval times and is used also in delicious pasta dishes.

See also: regional cooking

MARIELLA TOTARO GENEVOIS

Chia, Sandro

b. 20 April 1946, Florence

Painter

Chia began exhibiting in 1971, achieving wider prominence in 1979 when **Bonito Oliva** identified him as part of the Italian **transavantgarde**. He has been featured at the **Venice Biennale** and is widely represented in art museums around the world.

Chia's work is figurative and expressionist. He uses thick, visible brushstrokes and high-keyed tonings to present human figures with inflated bodies and massive shoulders in dramatic, even mock heroic poses, brought out from the background with black outlines and rough chiaroscuro. He draws on a wide range of sources, from the old masters to European modernists including **de Chirico** and Picasso, and many of these influences are clearly visible in his paintings. He himself has described his work as graffiti, a characterization borne out by the sketchy, scribbled quality of paintings such as *Rabbit for Dinner* and *Speed Boy* (both 1981).

Further reading

Di Corato, L. (ed.) (1997) *Sandro Chia: opere scelte, 1975–1996*, Milan: Leonardo arte (exhibition catalogue in Italian and English, with colour illustrations and bibliography).

MAX STAPLES

Chiara, Piero

b. 23 March 1913, Luino;
   d. 31 December 1986, Varese

Writer

Chiara's exuberant prose and memorable characters have made him a favourite with Italian readers. After early experiments with poetry and biography, Chiara turned to prose, often using his native town as a setting for his novels. A thread of eroticism is woven through his works, including *Il piatto piange* (The Pot Is Empty) (1962), which discusses the amorous adventures of a group of poker players, and *La spartizione* (The Division) (1964), in which three unmarried, excessively pious sisters destroy a young clerk. Many of Chiara's works have been adapted for cinema, including *Venga a prendere il caffè ... da noi* (Come Have Coffee With Us), directed by Alberto **Lattuada** in 1970 and based on *La spartizione* and *Il cappotto di Astrakan*, published in 1978. Other novels by Chiara include *Il balordo* (The Foolish One) (1967), *I giovedì della signora Giulia* (Mrs Giulia's Thursdays) (1970), *La stanza del vescovo* (The Bishop's Room) (1976) and *Una spina nel cuore* (A Thorn in the Heart) (1979).

LAURA A. SALSINI

Chiarini, Luigi

b. 20 July 1900, Rome; d. 12 November 1975, Rome

Film theorist, critic and director

One of the most respected names in Italian cinema history, Chiarini began his career as a film critic. In 1935 he was co-founder of the **Centro Sperimentale di Cinematografia**, becoming its director until 1943 as well as editing and contributing to the Centre's prestigious theoretical journal, *Bianco e nero*. He published widely on theoretical and aesthetic aspects of cinema – his best-known books are *Arte e tecnica del film* (Art and Technique of Film) (1952) and *Cinema quinto potere* (Film, the Fifth Estate) (1954) – and later taught film history at the University of Pisa as well as being director of the Venice Film Festival from 1964–8. In spite of his great love of film and his influential position in Italian cinema, he only directed a handful of films, all during the 1940s; most were sophisticated adaptations of literary works such as *Via delle Cinque Lune* (Five Moons Street) (1941), admired for their formal qualities but with little popular appeal.

GINO MOLITERNO

Chohra, Nassera

b. 1963, Marseilles, France

Writer

Born into an Algerian family in France, Chohra came to Italy in the late 1980s. Her autobiography, *Volevo diventare bianca* (I Wanted to Become White), edited by Alessandra Atti di Sarro, is the result of a difficult collaboration between an immigrant writer and a linguistic expert and translates into Italian Chohra's experience as a *beur* (a second generation Algerian) in Marseilles. Chohra describes the isolation and marginalization of growing up in an immigrant ghetto, and recounts her childhood desire to assimilate, to 'become white'. Not until the final chapter does Chohra turn to her experiences in Italy, which she originally visited as a tourist but to which she subsequently immigrated after marrying an Italian. Chohra thus directly connects migration experiences in two different cultural and national contexts, and creates a link between her second-generation migration experience and the numerous first-generation testimonies published in Italy in the early 1990s.

See also: immigrant literature

Further reading

Chohra, N. (1993) *Volevo diventare bianca*, Rome: Edizioni e/o.

GRAZIELLA PARATI

church, state and society

The peculiarities of the relationship between Church, state and society in Italy, the home of the Papacy, form a very traditional part of the country's culture, and the historical tensions are reflected in the writings of both Dante and Machiavelli. Since 1945, the legal framework has been set by the terms of the Lateran Pacts of 1929. This treaty, which resolved the sixty-nine-year-old 'Roman Question' – the conflict between the Papacy and the Italian liberal state over the loss of the Papal States – by setting up the State of the Vatican City, also reiterated the declaration in the Piedmontese *Statuto* (constitution) of 1848 that Roman Catholicism was the sole religion of the state, while the Concordat restored to the Italian Church most of the property, legal privileges and social influence which it had lost during the Risorgimento. The collapse of Fascism, Catholic participation in the armed **Resistance** against the German occupation and the Fascist Social Republic from September 1943 to April 1945, and the subsequent abolition of the monarchy in June 1946, left the Church as one of the strongest forces in Italian civil society and a powerful influence on its politics. The strength of the Church's influence at this time was demonstrated by the decision of Palmiro **Togliatti** and the Communist deputies in the **Constituent Assembly** to support the insertion into the Republican **constitution** of Article 7, which effectively incorporated the Pacts into the overall constitutional structure by stating that: 'Church and State are each in their own sphere sovereign and independent. Their relations are regulated by the Lateran Pacts of 1929.'

The overwhelming dominance exercised over immediate postwar Italy by the Church and by the Church-sponsored Christian Democratic party (see **DC**) led one American historian to dub it 'The Papal State of the Twentieth Century' (Webster, 1960). Certainly, Catholic 'triumphalism' in the face of a narrowly averted Communist–Socialist victory in the 1948 national elections created a repressive atmosphere in which not only were **trade union** and political opponents in the Cold War situation marginalized, but so also were the Protestant minorities, non-believers and anyone else who challenged the new 'Catholic' order. In reality, **Pope Pius XII** had only limited tolerance for **De Gasperi**'s democratic pluralism, and would have prefered an integralist, authoritarian Catholic state on the lines of Salazar's Portugal or Franco's Spain.

Catholic cultural and political dominance of Italy began to be undermined in the 1950s and 1960s as a result of three 'revolutionary' forces: the so-called **economic miracle**, the **Second Vatican Council** and the Anglo-American cultural invasion which took place in that period. Industrialization, urbanization and mass migration – from country to town and from South to North – and the influences of cinema and television strained the bonds between organized religion and Italian society. The Second Vatican Council's stress on religious liberty and the autonomous role of the laity contributed enormously to a dramatic change in the nature of Italian Catholic culture which had hitherto been based on conservative and rural or small town values.

The effects of these changes in Italian society manifested themselves in a number of ways. Between 1956 and 1967, attendance at Sunday mass fell from 69 per cent to 48 per cent of the population. As late as 1970, civil marriages were almost unknown outside of the big cities and the 'red belt' (roughly the Emilia-Romagna region) and stood at a national average of just over 2 per cent of all marriages. By 1988 they had risen to over 16 per cent of all marriages, with much higher rates in northern and central cities. There was a dramatic decline in religious vocations and a fall in the number of priests: between 1978 and 1988 numbers fell by 7 per cent, with a consequent ageing of the clergy. All this was accompanied by a veritable crisis in support for Catholic association-alism. These changes also had 'knock-on' effects for the Catholic party: the Catholic 'sub-culture' of northern and eastern Italy, on which the Christian Democratic electorate was originally based, began to shrink, forcing a shift in party strength to the South.

In 1974, against the declared wishes of the pope and the episcopal hierarchy, Italians voted by a majority of 59 per cent in a referendum to retain the **divorce** law which had been introduced in 1970, and in 1981 67 per cent supported a law permitting **abortion**. Such was the strength of the perception that religion had dramatically declined in Italy that in 1975 the Italian Bishops' Conference declared the country a 'mission territory'. Nine years later the *de facto* secularization of Italy was recognized by the negotiation of a new concordat between the Holy See and Italy to replace that of 1929. The most striking feature of the new arrangements was the omission of the phrase 'Roman Catholicism is the sole religion of the Italian State'. The Italian Church had thus been effectively dis-established, but some legal and financial ties between Church and state still remain. The Church took over the endowment funds formerly administered by the state for the benefit of the clergy, and income from this fund is supplemented by covenanted offerings by the faithful and a system modelled on the German 'church tax'. Italians can elect to have .008 of their income tax assigned to the Catholic Church, or alternatively to other religious communities or specified charities. Parents now have to 'opt in' rather than 'opt out' of religious instruction in state schools.

On the other hand, the legal reordering of the relationship between church and state has certainly not eliminated anti-clericalism as a force in Italian society and politics: indeed, women's and **gay movements** born out of the social and political tumult of the late 1960s and early 1970s have continued to add their voice to those deeply concerned about the Church's tendency to 'interfere' in Italian politics, especially on matters affecting sexual freedom (see **sexual mores**, **censorship**).

The collapse of the Church-sponsored Christian Democratic party in 1993 has also substantially altered the relationship between church and state in Italy. No party can now claim the 'sponsorship' of the Church although Catholics are still to be found amongst the leadership and electorate of nearly all of Italy's political parties and groupings, even the Northern League, against whom the Church at a grassroots level has often taken a strong stand on the issue of the unity of Italy, the continuing necessity of the welfare state and the need for special assistance to the South on the basis of the Catholic doctrine of 'social solidarity'. In the absence of a major governing party which is exclusively Catholic in inspiration and leadership, the Church, and more precisely the Italian Bishops' Conference (CEI), has entered into a direct dialogue with government. Since 1994, the major issues that have concerned the Church are abortion, bioethics, the protection of the family – especially against the European Parliament motion on gay marriages – and the financing of church schools. As far as the latter is concerned, a joint commission has been instituted to produce a compromise solution.

Despite the depredations of secularization, the Catholic Church remains a major force in Italian civil society. At 30 per cent, Italy's rate of Sunday mass attendance is still one of the highest in Europe and the figure has been stable for over a decade. Adherence to and practice of the faith firmly transcends class: Italian Catholicism is emphatically not a middle-class phenomenon. Admittedly there are several geographical black spots, notably the Emilia-Romagna region, the former so-called 'red belt', which in 1995 was described by Cardinal Oddi, perhaps slightly tongue in cheek, as 'Sodom and Gomorrah'. However, during the last three decades there has also been a significant revitalization of the Church in the South, where leading bishops including Cardinal Giordano of Naples have given public warnings about the need to preserve welfare provision for the poorest and most vulnerable groups. The Italian Bishops' Conference as a whole has campaigned against organized crime, economic decline and the resulting disintegration of southern urban society, and the heroism of anti-mafia priests has resulted in two of their number being murdered (see **mafia**). Thus Italian Catholicism remains a national religion in geographical terms, even if it is no longer officially the religion of the state.

There is also still an extensive network of Catholic newspapers, periodicals and publishing houses which testifies to the intellectual vitality of Italian Catholicism. And if traditional Catholic associationalism is somewhat in decline, support for such movements as Focolare, **Communione e Liberazione**, the St Egidio Community in Rome and the voluntary organizations generally demonstrates the continuing idealism and commitment of Catholic young people. Significantly, despite secularization, the Church remains a major provider of health, welfare and educational facilities, and is in the forefront of action to meet the twin evils of drugs (see **drug culture**) and **HIV/AIDS** and to meet the needs of Italy's rapidly growing immigrant populations (see **immigration**). Taking all these factors into account, it is clear that the Catholic Church remains a major cultural, social, economic and, in a somewhat reduced form, political influence in Italy at the end of the 1990s.

See also: Catholic Action; Catholic associations; Catholic press and publishing; Vatican

Further reading

Allum, P.A. (1990) 'Uniformity Undone: Aspects of Catholic Culture in Post-war Italy', in Z. Baranski and R. Lumley (eds), *Conflict and Culture in Post-war Italy: Essays on Mass and Popular Culture*, Basingstoke: Macmillan (provides excellent insight into the Italian Catholic mentality in an age of 'triumphalism').

Bedani, G. (1994) 'Church and State in Italian History: Origins of the Present Crisis', in M. Donovan (ed.), *Italy*, Aldershot: Ashgate, vol. 1 (a useful overview).

Garelli, F. (1991) *Religione e Chiesa in Italia* (Religion and Church in Italy), Bologna: Il Mulino (the standard work on Catholic religious behaviour).

Iadanza, M. (ed.) (1992) *Chiesa e Società Civile nel Mezzogiorno* (Church and Civil Society in the South), Rome: Borla (Catholic discussion of the role of the Church in the South).

Pollard, J.F. (1989) 'Post-war Italy: the Papal State of the Twentieth Century', in E.A. Millar (ed.), *The Legacy of Fascism*, Glasgow: Glasgow University Press (a brief study of the impact of the Lateran Pacts on postwar Italy).

Riccardi, A. (1994) 'La vita religiosa' (Religious Life), in P. Ginsborg (ed.), *Stato Dell'Italia* (State of Italy), Milan: Bruno Mondadori (the best short survey of religious activity and the Catholic Church in Italy).

Webster, R.A. (1960) *The Cross and the Fasces: Christian Democracy and Fascism in Italy*, Stanford, CA: Stanford University Press.

JOHN POLLARD

Ciampi, Carlo Azeglio

b. 9 December 1920, Livorno

Economist

A central banker who entered politics at a late age (although in his youth he had actively supported the *Partito d'Azione*, a small left-wing party), Ciampi played an outstanding role in promoting economic and financial recovery in Italy in the 1980s and 1990s. As governor of the **Bank of Italy** between 1979 and 1993, he fostered major reform of the Italian financial system and won greater independence for the Bank from the Treasury. A believer in European monetary integration (see **European Union**), he strongly supported Italy joining the European Monetary System in 1979 and played a significant role in the long negotiations which finally led to the signing of the Maastricht Treaty in the early 1990s. Thanks to both his international standing in financial circles and his independence from political parties, he was appointed prime minister of a so-called 'technical' government in April 1993, after the **Tangentopoli** inquiries had taken the political system to the verge of collapse. Following the victory of the Olive Tree coalition (see **l'Ulivo**) in the 1996 elections, he became Minister of the Treasury in the **Prodi** government; in fact, he was a sort of super-Minister of the Economy, since he not only fought inflation successfully, improved the national budget and finally led Italy into the European single currency in 1998, but also played a critical role in the privatization of large state-owned companies (see **privatization and nationalization**) such as **ENI** and Telecom (see **STET**) and the preparation a new set of general rules for corporate governance.

A fervent Catholic but strongly opposed to any confessionalism – an attitude that provoked a certain coldness towards him in some Catholic circles – he was elected **President of the Republic** in 1999 on the first ballot on the basis of a wide agreement between the ruling centre–left parliamentary majority and the centre–right opposition, a unanimous acknowledgement of both his meritorious services to the country and his high international reputation.

STEFANO BATTILOSSI

Cicciolina

b. 1950, Hungary

Porn queen and politician

Ilona Staller, better known by her stage name 'Cicciolina', became Italy's most famous porn queen in the postwar period and, from the 1970s onward, achieved a reputation throughout Europe for explicit sex shows on stage and screen. Her ultimate exploit was to be elected to the Chamber of Deputies in 1987 as a member of the **Radical Party**, subsequently serving on a parliamentary committee for defence (see also **Parliament**). She also contested the 1992 national elections at the head of her own 'Party of Love', but this time proved unsuccessful. Meanwhile she had married American sculptor Jeff Koons and had a son by him. Koons fanned his own notoriety with provocative paintings and sculptures of Cicciolina but eventually filed for divorce, which he was granted in 1994, together with custody of the child. Cicciolina appealed long and vehemently against the decision but was unsuccessful in having it reversed.

GINO MOLITERNO

Cima, Annalisa

b. 20 January 1941, Milan

Poet and painter

Cima began as a painter in the early 1960s, and published her first book of poetry, *Terzo Modo* (Third Way), in 1969. Her poetry springs from an investigation of two main themes of the Western tradition: love and time. Through a lyrical exploration of human will and desire, Cima comes to the conclusion that only love can make sense of the chaotic and magmatic mutations of life. Love becomes, therefore, the sentiment which offers to the poet the opportunity to identify the only moments in which life is not subjected to the incessant passage of time, which Cima defines as a 'predator'. This confrontation between time and love is well represented in Cima's best poetry collection, *Ipotesi d'amore* (Hypotheses on Love) (1984) where love becomes indeed a 'hypothesis' or theorem that needs to be proven by the very existence of poetry, the artistic medium which challenges the omnipotence of time.

Cima's poetic works have been translated into many languages, and a bilingual anthology, in Italian and English, has been published in Milan by Scheiwiller.

ANDREA CICCARELLI

Cinecittà

With nineteen modern and well-equipped studios spread over an area of 400,000 square metres, Cinecittà or 'Cinema City' is the largest film studio complex in Italy. Constructed in record time on the outskirts of Rome as a replacement for the Cines studios, which had burnt down in mysterious circumstances in September 1935, the complex was privately built but generously subsidized by the state, and was officially inaugurated by Mussolini on 27 April 1937 as proof of the strong commitment of the Fascist regime to the renewed development of the Italian film industry. Two hundred and ninety-seven films – more than half of them light comedies or what would later come to be called 'white telephone' films – were made at

the studios between 1937 and 1943 before Allied bombings extensively damaged the buildings and much of the equipment was looted by retreating German troops. Following the liberation of Rome the complex came to be used as a camp for refugees, and it only began functioning as a film studio again in 1947.

However, by the 1950s all facilities had been fully restored and new Italian government regulations obliging foreign film companies to reinvest part of their profits in Italy led to filming at Cinecittà becoming an attractive option for many of the American companies. This led to a decade of major American films being made in Rome with Cinecittà crowded with American directors and stars and thus deservedly earning the sobriquet 'Hollywood on the Tiber'. By the late 1950s Italian directors like **Rossellini** and **Visconti** also returned to Cinecittà, and from 1959 **Fellini** almost took up residence there, making all his subsequent films in Studio 5 (which would be named in his honour after his death in 1993).

By the late 1970s, however, as part of the general crisis that overtook the Italian film industry at the time, film production at Cinecittà fell disastrously, prompting suggestions that the complex might be closed altogether in order to make way for residential housing. Fortunately the mid-1980s brought a reprieve, largely with an increase of production for television.

In the early 1990s an effort was made to revive the fortunes of both the studios and the Italian industry with the establishment of Cinettà International, a state-owned company meant to promote Italian film interests abroad. However, the company lost money and appeared to achieve very little, and it was liquidated in 1996. In July 1998, under the **Prodi** centre–left government, Cinecittà itself was finally privatized, allowing the Cecchi Gori Group and De Laurentis to take an 11.5 per cent share each but with a 40 per cent share firmly held by Cinecittà Holding, a company controlled by the State Treasury and headed by veteran filmmaker Gillo **Pontecorvo**.

See also: film industry

GINO MOLITERNO

cinematographers

Giuseppe **Rotunno**, Italy's most eminent specialist in colour film photography, once pointed out that it is the cinematographer who provides the vital link between a director's inner vision and its materialization on the screen, and postwar Italian directors have been well-served by a number of great artists in this field. Rotunno himself is one of Italy's prominent cinematographers and has had a long and fruitful collaboration with Federico **Fellini**. In fact, much of what viewers normally identify as the baroque idiosyncrasies of the Fellinian universe are in large part the result of the brazenness of Rotunno's framing and lighting strategies.

Fellini's first feature-length colour film, *Giulietta degli spiriti* (Juliet of the Spirits) (1965) was nonetheless photographed by Gianni **Di Venanzo** (1920–66). Paradoxically, however, it is primarily Di Venanzo's black and white photography that led the former neorealist cameraman to collaborate with some of the most distinctive Italian film directors (**Antonioni**, Fellini). His prestigious career was tragically ended by premature death in 1966.

Di Venanzo's former assistant, Pasqualino **De Santis**, the younger brother of film-maker Giuseppe **De Santis**, quickly carved out a name of his own, especially thanks to his lasting collaboration with Francesco **Rosi**. His uniform talent for improvisation and stylization made him as equipped for hand-held camerawork, as in Rosi's *Il caso Mattei* (The Mattei Affair) (1972) as for the polished sophistication of **Visconti**'s *La caduta degli Dei* (The Damned) (1969), *Morte a Venezia* (Death in Venice) (1971) or *L'innocente* (The Innocent) (1976). Interestingly, the De Santis brothers never collaborated.

It is instead Otello Martelli (1903–) who is most closely associated with the cinema of Giuseppe De Santis and with the tragic purity of the neorealist image in films such as *Caccia tragica* (Tragic Pursuit) (1947) and the more notorious *Riso amaro* (Bitter Rice) (1949). In fact, although Martelli is well remembered for his luminous participation in Anita Ekberg's midnight ablution in Fellini's *La dolce vita* (1960), the Roman cinematographer was inseparable from the neorealist movement. With Roberto **Rossellini**, Martelli participated in the birth of **neorealism**, along with the other major cinematographer of neorealism, Aldo Tonti (1910–), who photographed Visconti's *Ossessione* (1942), **Lattuada**'s *Senza Pietà* (Without Pity) (1948) and Rossellini's *Il miracolo* (The Miracle) (1948).

Also starting his career in the aftermath of the Second World War, Tonino **Delli Colli** later established himself as Pier Paolo **Pasolini**'s cinematographer, giving life, thanks to the classical perfection of his photography, to the innovative plasticity and the sense of the sacred in Pasolini's vision. Equally capable of conveying Sergio **Leone**'s epic humour, Delli Colli also photographed Fellini's last three films.

Representing the new generation of Italian cinematographers, Vittorio **Storaro** is known as a maverick conjurer who combines a high degree of technical expertise with a virtuosity that at once explores and renews the art of cinematography. Such gifts led him to become the partner of Bernardo **Bertolucci** in the 1970s. Capitalizing on his collaboration with Francis Ford Coppola on *Apocalypse Now*, Storaro has been working exclusively in Hollywood since 1980.

Further reading

Masi, S. (1983) *Storie della luce nel cinema* (Stories of Light in the Cinema), Rome: Savelli/Gaumont (a detailed study of Italy's major cinematographers).

Prédal, R. (1985) *La photo de cinéma* (Photography in the Cinema), Paris: Éditions du Cerf (a general study of cinematography with a useful appendix listing 100 prominent cinematographers).

DOROTHÉE BONNIGAL.

Citati, Pietro

b. 20 February 1930, Florence

Critic, essayist and translator

Pietro Citati distinguished himself in the mid-1950s as translator of the French author Marivaux. In addition to his countless contributions to such literary journals as *L'Approdo* and *Paragone*, and to the widely-circulated newspapers *Il Corriere della sera* and *La Repubblica*, his literary achievements include numerous essay collections on classical and modern literature, and the fictionalized biographies of Goethe, Manzoni, Katherine Mansfield, Tolstoy, Kafka and Proust. An intellectually subtle, linguistically refined and stylistically versatile writer, Citati also published a book on humour with the poet Attilio **Bertolucci** (*Gli umoristi moderni* (The Modern Humorists), 1961). Particularly successful was his 1989 novel *Storia prima felice, poi dolentissima e funesta* (Story, Happy at First, Then Very Sorrowful and Fatal), in which Citati retraces the story of his great-grandparents' love and death as documented in his family's letters.

FRANCESCA PARMEGGIANI

citizenship

Citizenship has both formal and substantive dimensions: on one hand, there is the definition of who is, and can become, a citizen and the civil, political and social rights legally attached to that status; on the other hand, there is the distribution and exercise of those rights in practice, which usually produce invidious distinctions between citizens who are formally equal. The development of citizenship in Italy as an idea and practice has historically been hampered by the political and cultural barriers to features which have underpinned the growth of citizenship elsewhere: a sense of nationhood, thriving economy and confidence in state institutions. However, the emergence of Italy as an increasingly multicultural and Europeanized society in the 1990s has made the definition and content of citizenship a renewed concern.

The definition of citizenship

For most of the twentieth century, the attribution and acquisition of citizenship were regulated by Law no. 555 of 1912. Citizenship was transmitted by men (women by default), dual citizenship was largely excluded, and a residence period of ten years in Italy was established for any foreigner to qualify for citizenship. Children of the many

emigrants who had already renounced Italian citizenship in favour of their new state were nonetheless considered citizens. Special categories of citizenship were later added to cover Italy's colonial empire in North and East Africa and the Dodecanese. In 1983 the disparities as transmitters of citizenship between men and women married to foreigners were reduced. Overall revision of the 1912 law was not undertaken until 1992 when – in response to increasing **immigration**, the creation of a European citizenship and the pursuit of closer links with the descendants of former Italian citizens who had emigrated after 1870 (see **emigration**) – new criteria for citizenship were established. The new regulations eliminated the remaining disparity between genders, shortened the residence requirements for descendants of former citizens and for EU citizens, and facilitated both the recovery of citizenship and the acquisition of dual citizenship. The importance of residence (*jus soli*) was thus reduced for all except non-European immigrants, and the significance of descent (*jus sanguinis*) was enhanced. Italy shifted towards a cultural rather than territorial definition of formal citizenship.

The substance of citizenship

The content of the political and social rights available to those who share the common status of 'Italian citizen' has been extremely uneven. Until 1945, state provision of universal social and economic protection was limited by a backward **economy** and by the deliberate creation of space for Church initiatives and institutions. After 1945, when women acquired political rights for the first time and began to demolish the legal barriers to levels of participation available to men (see **feminism**), rapid economic development supplied the resources to expand the content of citizenship. However, its expansion followed a highly particularistic route, rewarding social and occupational groups differently according to their bargaining power and political importance and producing a patchwork of highly unequal rights and privileges. In general, the distribution of resources available as citizenship rights – favouring cash subsidies rather than universally accessible services – tended to mirror rather than modify the individual and regional inequalities produced by the market economy (see **Southern Question**). In the 1970s efforts were made to respond to demands for greater political and industrial participation and to standardize basic levels of citizen entitlement (see **health service**). However, these efforts to offer common substantive citizenship to all Italians have had to combat the increasing financial pressures on the state to curtail social protection and the devolution of many health and welfare responsibilities to regional authorities of unequal wealth and institutional capacity. In addition, the persistence of a sizeable informal economy, swollen by immigrants who since 1992 must wait ten years before becoming eligible for formal citizenship, simultaneously deprives its participants of rights and the state of taxes. At the close of the twentieth century, the content of substantive citizenship continues to vary considerably across Italy; the extent of social protection remains heavily dependent on place of residence, the local weight of private initiatives and religious institutions, and the support of the family.

Further reading

Ascoli, U. (1997) 'Volunteering for Human Service Provisions: Lessons from Italy and the USA', *Social Indicators Research* 40: 299–327.

Ferrera, M. (1986) 'Italy', in P. Flora (ed.), *Growth to Limits: The Western European Welfare States Since World War II*, vol. 2, Berlin: Walter de Gruyter.

Zampaglione, G. and Guglielman, P. (1995) *La cittadinanza. Diritto e pratica consolari*, vol. 3, Rome: Stamperia Reale.

DAVID MOSS

Civiltà delle macchine

Established originally as a bi-monthly house magazine for the **IRI**-owned Finmeccanica, *Civiltà* rapidly became one of the most important Italian postwar design magazines. Together with other more established and reputable journals such as **Casabella**, **Domus** and **Stile Industria**, it helped to foster a healthy debate on design issues. Edited until 1959 by the poet, writer and engineer, Leonardo **Sinisgalli**, it often hosted articles on

mathematics, poetry and industrial design. It thus elevated design to the status of 'high culture', while also often taking sides on fundamental design issues such as the conflict between needs and production.

While some magazines focused on updating styles and some, like *Stile industria*, maintained neutrality on ideological questions of design, *Civiltà* approached design and industry as vectors of contemporary cultural values. This attitude allowed it to compensate for the lack of a national plan regarding the transformation of contemporary design methods until it ceased publication in 1978.

See also: architectural and design magazines; industrial design

FASSIL ZEWDOU

Clemente, Francesco
b. 23 March 1952, Naples

Artist

With little formal training and always regarding himself as a dilettante, Clemente has contributed much to the rejuvenation of Italian art following the conceptual dead end of modernism. In 1979 he was named as part of a new grouping called the **transavantgarde**, but his use of figurative elements in a imaginative, non-realist way leads him to be more often placed within neo-expressionism, an identification he makes himself.

With the financial support of his family, Clemente was able to practise as an artist from the age of eighteen. He did not attend art school, but chose rather to train himself by producing thousands of drawings between 1971 and 1978. Although self-taught, or possibly because of this – given the radical nature of art schools in the 1960s and 1970s – Clemente was strongly influenced by traditional art and looked to the Italian masters as well as the art of ancient Egypt, Greece and Rome.

After an early association with **arte povera** and **conceptual art**, his drawings began to suggest a way forward in their use of both figurative and abstract forms. Clemente sought something more personal than the political art then in vogue. The big breakthrough occurred in 1980, when he exhibited as part of the transavantgarde at the

Venice Biennale. These artists signalled a rejection of modernism and the myth of constant progress by revisiting and reusing the art of the past, and returning to traditional techniques of painting. For inspiration, they looked back to some of the more wayward figures in art history. Clemente found inspiration in the sixteenth-century mannerists, and in **de Chirico** and his brother Alberto Savinio with their kitsch combination of classical and contemporary motifs. He also studied the Quattrocento Italian frescoists, with their flat areas of colour and simple, monumental figures.

This marked eclecticism is the most prominent feature of Clemente's art. He consumes not just fragments and pieces but entire iconographies, which is what gives his work its richness. He finds inspiration in the juxtaposition of cultures, and travels regularly between studios in Rome, Madras and New York. The influence of Indian art can be seen in *India*, a book chronicling 'the working life of the artist' during 1985, with its black outlines around figures, flat areas of colour, patterned backgrounds, stylized landscapes and decorative symbols. His 'Three Worlds Exhibition' of 1990–1 was devoted to works on paper, including watercolours, drawings, lithographs and pastels, which use imagery derived from the cultures of Italy, India and the United States.

Clemente's work often presents strong elements of autobiography and self-investigation. His subject matter includes plants and animals, the female form, the face and the hand, and also his own image. He takes his themes from the life processes, including procreation. The 'Black Paintings' of 1994 are an example of what has been called Clemente's sexual mysticism.

India, he explains, is in some ways like ancient Italy: 'The gods who left us thousands of years ago in Naples are still in India, so it's like going home for me' (Percy, 1990: 50). In India, he uses local craftsmen to paint the backgrounds of his works, such as the *Indian Miniatures* of 1980–1. Prolific and internationally appreciated, Clemente is widely represented in collections around the world.

Further reading:

Percy, A. and Foye, R. (eds) (1990) *Francesco Clemente: Three Worlds*, Philadelphia Museum of Art (includes articles, illustrations and bibliography).

Politi, G. (1984) 'Francesco Clemente', *Flash Art* 117: 12–21 (interview).

MAX STAPLES

Clementi, Aldo

b. 25 May 1925, Catania

Composer

Clementi is one of the leading figures of the postwar Italian avantgarde. His initial studies under Sangiorgi in Catania led to an interest in twelve-tone techniques, an interest further developed in the directions of advanced serialism and electronics under the guidance of **Petrassi** (1952–4), **Maderna** (1956–7) and Stockhausen (1961–2). Clementi's early style is characterized by a strict concern with form and structure bordering on terseness (for example, *Concertino* (1956) or *Compozitione no.1* (1957)), and it was only gradually that other influences combined to mitigate this acerbity. The discourse of contemporary non-figurative painting was to prove important in *Collage* (1961), a collaboration with artist Achille Perilli, in which scenic elements were introduced for the first time, and also in the aleatoricism of the three *Informels* (1961–3). The pursuit of varying techniques of indeterminacy is the key to Clementi's work during the 1960s and 1970s. *Collage 3 (Dies irae)* (1966–7) subjects four Beatles' songs to a radical electronic metamorphosis, whilst the action of *Blitz* (1973) is dependent on the moves of eight chess players. Clementi teaches at the Milan Conservatory and at the University of Bologna.

Further reading

(1970) 'Scheda 10: Aldo Clementi', *Collage* 9: 77 (contains biography, worklist, writings, discography and bibliography).

JOHN KERSEY

clientelism

Clientelism (also called patronage) is the self-interested distribution of state resources (jobs, pensions, licences, subsidies) by political parties to citizens in return for their votes. Party allegiance therefore comes to depend more on gratitude for personal benefits received or anticipated than on disinterested endorsement of programmes or policies. Clientelist politics rest mainly on the social ties and obligations of **family**, kinship and **friendship** through which the powerful distribute resources, build their individual clienteles and mobilize electoral support. Obtaining privileges by loyal service to patrons usually appears more desirable and secure than claiming rights attached to **citizenship**.

In postwar Italy, the confrontation with communism encouraged the recently established and weakly organized governing parties – in particular the **DC** – to bolster their own positions by using for private advantage the public resources which the **economic miracle** placed at the disposal of governments and new welfare state agencies (see **social welfare**). Party and factional struggles over the occupation of ministerial and managerial offices with control over lavish budgets frequently engaged more passion than disputes over policy, which were in any case devalued by the high turnover rate of postwar governments. Since the **PCI** was not regarded as a democratically reliable alternative government, real pressure for accountability in the use of public funds declined, which permitted the unrestrained growth of the public debt and encouraged widespread corruption (see **Tangentopoli**).

Clientelism has generally been regarded as having damaging consequences for both society and the economy in postwar Italy. Deference towards the powerful is always conservative, demeaning and anti-egalitarian; attachment to individual patrons has hampered collective action by clients to achieve social reform and has undermined respect for the law; and the relentless pursuit of party advantage has eclipsed economic efficiency and social justice in determining how state resources should be allocated. The difficulty of achieving sustained development in the South, where clientelism is especially widespread, is often attributed to such features. Nonetheless, a positive case for clientelism has also been argued in terms of its role in reducing the sense of social exclusion, attracting resources to otherwise powerless groups and regions, providing a means of bypassing the inefficient workings of an archaic state, and stabilizing a society marked by deep ideological and economic conflicts.

See also: Mani pulite

Further reading

Allum, P. (1997) '"From Two into One": The Faces of the Italian Christian Democrat Party', *Party Politics* 3 (1): 23–52 (the postwar organization of clientelism in Naples and the Veneto).

Chubb, J. (1982) *Patronage, Power and Poverty in Southern Italy*, Cambridge: Cambridge University Press (on how state resources are used to recruit support).

Moss, D. (1995) 'Patronage revisited: the dynamics of information and reputation', *Journal of Modern Italian Studies* 1 (1): 58–93 (re-examination of patronage in the light of evidence on corruption).

Mutti, A. (1994) 'Il particolarismo come risorsa: politica ed economia nello sviluppo abruzzese' (Particularism as a Resource: Politics and Economy in the Development of the Abruzzi), *Rassegna italiana di sociologia* 35 (4): 451–518 (the contribution of clientelism to development in the Abruzzi).

Putnam, R. (1993) *Making Democracy Work: Civic Traditions in Modern Italy*, Princeton, NJ: Princeton University Press (controversial analysis of the causes and consequences of clientelism in different regions).

DAVID MOSS

Codice Rocco

From 1931, both Italy's criminal code and the code of criminal procedure were those drafted by Alfredo Rocco, Minister for Justice between 1925 and 1932 (hence reference to the 'Codice Rocco' or 'Rocco Code', usually referring to the latter). While the code's pre-Fascist roots and technical sophistication were used after the fall of Fascism to distinguish it from the regime (see also **fascism and neo-fascism**), its architect was a leading authoritarian nationalist intellectual who became a prominent state technocrat, and the Rocco code was undeniably repressive of associational and individual rights, not least those of women. The code aimed above all to defend the state, and while major amendments were made in 1944–5, it was also used to repress opposition in the new democracy. Despite reform being pushed forward by the **Constitutional Court** from the 1960s, wholesale replacement was blocked in the 1970s by the terrorist crisis. The Rocco code (of criminal procedure) was replaced in 1989 as part of the sharp conflict between parts of the judiciary and the political class.

See also: legal system; police

MARK DONOVAN

coffee

Ever since the first coffee shop in Europe opened in Venice in 1615, Italians have written and talked about coffee. Nevertheless, when compared to the rest of Europe, coffee consumption in Italy during the nineteenth century was very low and was confined mostly to the wealthy classes, who drank it in small cups. The only real Italian contribution to coffee technology during this period was the 'napoletana', a reversible drip-filter machine which, as its name implies, probably had its origins in Naples in the middle of the eighteenth century and which remained a common way to make coffee in Italy until the espresso revolution arrived.

Espresso was the great advance in coffee technology in the twentieth century, and it came to be uniquely associated with Italy. When the first steam espresso machines appeared in 1906, tall, impressive constructions with eagles, valves and spouts, they soon became the centrepiece of Italian coffee shops. The machines themselves were expensive and the clients were still aristocrats and wealthy businessmen who came for coffee and liqueurs, a luxury to which the rest of the population could only aspire. As Italy developed economically, however, more ordinary people were

able to afford coffee and so going to the 'bar' – the Italian coffee shop sells alcohol as well as cakes and sandwiches – became the norm. For many Italians, in fact, breakfast became simply a coffee and brioche in a 'bar' on the way to work and the local bar might be visited several times in one day, providing a social space equivalent to that of an English pub.

The first espresso coffee machines were not very efficient nor did they make a good espresso coffee – the beans had to be burnt to give any flavour at all from the quick brewing process – so the custom arose to add a little frothed milk or several sugars to make a small but hot, delicious and strongly flavoured mixture. The Italian drinker was thus forced to choose from the beginning between many variations of strength and combinations with hot milk as, for example, 'macchiato' (spotted), which is espresso coffee with only a spot of milk, or 'cappuccino', where the strong coffee is covered ('cappuccino' is a small hat or hood) with a layer of hot frothy milk topped with a dash of chocolate powder, 'caffelatte' (milk coffee), usually half coffee and half milk in a large cup or glass, and a wide range of other variants, among them the so-called 'caffe corretto' where the coffee is 'corrected' by the addition of spirits and liqueurs. Thus over time, an Italian's preference for one coffee over another became as much an expression of character and personal flair as the simple choice of a hot drink.

Foreigners visiting Italy were delighted with the coffee, which was very different to the large cups of diluted coffee common elsewhere, and thus the international reputations of Italians and their coffee grew. Italian espresso machines began to be exported all over the world even before the Second World War. After the war, new machines with levers and, later, with more efficient electric pumps which extracted even more flavour were invented and developed in Italy and were again exported in large numbers to the rest of the world, thus continuing to nurture the association between good, strong and delicious coffee with Italy and Italian culture.

Further reading

Bersten, I. (1993) *Coffee Floats, Tea Sinks: Through History and Technology to a Complete Understanding,*

Roseville, NSW: Helian Books (a comprehensive international history).

IAN BERSTEN

Colla, Ettore

b. 13 April 1896, Parma; d. 27 December 1968, Rome

Sculptor

After a long formation as a figurative artist, including a period on the Victor Emanuel monument in Rome, Colla began to produce abstract sculpture in the early 1950s. Along with **Burri** and Capogrossi, he was a founding member of Gruppo Origine (the Origin Group), which favoured an expressive art without figuration or decorative elements. His works were constructed from found materials, such as gear wheels, manhole covers, grills and rusty pieces of metal. Colla disregarded their previous functions, looking instead to their basic geometric forms and the aesthetic possibilities for their recombination. *Genesi* (Genesis) (1955), with its stark surfaces and menacing spikes, looks like a diabolical machine.

By the 1960s, Colla had an international reputation for his mechanical looking figures such as the *Dioscuri* of 1961, and what have been termed his 'immobilized machines'. His work suggests that art can be created from what industrial society has thrown out, and that expressive intent can transform even apparent junk into art.

See also: sculpture

MAX STAPLES

Colletti, Lucio

b. 8 December 1924, Rome

Philosopher

After studying with Galvano **Della Volpe**, Colletti came to teach philosophy at the University of Rome, La Sapienza, where he remained for the rest of his career. Having joined the **PCI** in 1949, he soon became part of the editorial committee of the party's cultural journal, *Società*. He officially left the party in 1964 but went on to publish a number of major studies of Hegel and Marx, and of Marxism and ideology, which were widely read and translated and which became extremely influential in leftist circles during the 1970s, both in Italy and abroad. With the passing of time, however, his political position gradually shifted towards the centre. In the 1980s he manifested strong sympathies for **Craxi**'s **PSI**, and in the 1990s he was elected as a deputy for **Forza Italia**, thereafter being regularly numbered among the 'professors' who formed **Berlusconi**'s intellectual brigade.

Further reading

Colletti, L. (1974) 'A Political and Philosophical Interview', *New Left Review*, 86: 3–28 (an in-depth interview in which Colletti traces his own history and discusses his place within Marxist thought).

GINO MOLITERNO

Colli, Giorgio

b. 1918, Turin; d. 6 January 1979, Florence

Philosopher

Together with Mazzino Montinari, Giorgio Colli produced the definitive critical edition of Friedrich Nietzsche's complete works and correspondence. These volumes were published simultaneously in Germany, France, Italy and Japan. Colli also produced critical editions of Aristotle's *Organon* and Kant's *Critique of Pure Reason*, and a compendium of ancient Greek thinkers. In addition to these accomplishments as an editor and translator, Colli taught ancient philosophy at the University of Pisa from 1948 onwards, and wrote a number of original philosophical studies on the philosophy of expression, Nietzsche, and the origins of the philosophical impulse in ancient Greece. He opposed rationalism with a conception of philosophy that valorized the mysterious power of thought, and that saw the relationship between politics and (intellectual) culture as one of mutual dependency.

Although he is indisputably a very important figure in Italian intellectual life, there has been little serious discussion of his works since his premature death.

Further reading

Colli, G. (1975) *La nascita della filosofia* (The Birth of Philosophy), Milan: Adelphi.

THOMAS KELSO

Colombo, Joe

b. 30 July 1930, Milan; d. 30 July 1971, Milan

Painter, sculptor and designer

Joe Colombo was among the most internationally celebrated Italian designers of the 1960s. He was known best for his futuristic items of furniture and interior designs, which came to epitomize the modern image of itself that Italy projected on to the rest of the world in the middle of that decade.

Unlike many of his contemporaries, Colombo was not trained as an architect in the tradition of rationalism but as a painter and sculptor, and he practised as such from 1951–5. He was allied to the **Movimento Nucleare** (Nuclear Movement), and to the movement known as 'concrete art' (see **arte concreta**). His first experience of design came with a scheme for the 10th Triennale of 1954, where he worked on three open-air rest areas which contained benches and television sets. In 1956 he designed his first piece of architecture, a condominium. These early projects were followed by a radical change of direction in 1959 when he took over the family electrical equipment company and, in 1962, opened a design office in Milan.

From then on he worked on a range of designed artefacts, including furniture, lighting, pottery and electrical appliances. Notable among them were his Acrilica lamp (O-luce, 1963), his Mini-kitchen (Boffi, 1963), his Roll chair (1962), his Elda armchair (1963) and his Spider lamp (1965), all of which were stamped by the same rigorous approach which derived from functionalist ideas. Colombo was deeply committed to the aesthetic of the modern object being a rational result of the

materials and production techniques employed, in addition to the use to which it is to be put. His exercises in plastics reflect this openly, resulting in classic designs such as his famous 1965 Chair 4860, manufactured by Kartell, the main body of which was a single piece of injection-moulded plastic. Not only did this break new ground technologically but it did so aesthetically as well, since it introduced a luxurious image for plastic products which was linked to ideas of 'quality' and 'modernity' rather than, as hitherto, with 'cheapness' and 'nastiness'. The bright primary colours and severe black and white used by Colombo in so many of his designs reinforced their overtly synthetic appearance thus breaking any links with the idea of 'craft' within Italian design of these years.

Colombo died prematurely at the peak of his career. His work has been exhibited and published widely, both during his life and afterwards, notably at the 'New Domestic Landscape' exhibition which was held at the Museum of Modern Art in New York in 1972. He retains the reputation of being one of the most innovative of his generation of Italian designers.

See also: interior design

Further reading

Favata, I. (1988) *Joe Colombo, Designer 1930–1971*, Milan: Idea.
Hiesinger, K.B. and Marcus, G.H. (eds) (1983) *Design Since 1945*, Philadelphia: Philadelphia Museum of Art.
Valota, M.P. (1971) 'Joe C. Colombo', *Casabella* 35 (358): 46–8.

PENNY SPARKE

Comencini, Cristina

b. 19 August 1956, Rome

Screenwriter, director and writer

Eldest daughter of veteran film-maker Luigi **Comencini**, Cristina originally graduated in economics but soon came to work with renowned scriptwriter Suso **Cecchi D'Amico**, thus refining her scriptwriting skills considerably. A gifted storyteller, Cristina later worked as scriptwriter on her father's productions of *Cuore* (Heart) (1984) from Edmondo de Amicis' novel, and *La Storia* (History) (1986), adapted from Elsa **Morante**.

After her first critically acclaimed features *Zoo* (1988) and *I divertimenti della vita privata* (The Pleasures of Private Life) (1990), she attracted a larger audience in 1992 with *La fine è nota* (The End is Known), a daring adaptation of the eponymous novel by G. Holiday Hall but, interestingly, placed within the context of Italian **terrorism**. After also publishing a number of novels with **Feltrinelli**, she returned to feature film-making in 1995 with an adaptation of Suzanna **Tamaro**'s bestselling novel, *Va dove ti porta il cuore* (Follow your Heart), followed in 1998 by another film about intimate relations, *Matrimoni* (Marriages), which starred Stefania **Sandrelli** and two of the most popular younger actors of the 1990s, Diego Abatantuono and Francesca Neri.

ADRIANA MONTI

Comencini, Luigi

b. 8 June 1916, Salò

Film director

Comencini is best known for his prominent role in the establishment and development of the *commedia all'italiana* (comedy Italian style), a genre inscribed in the aftermath of **neorealism** and which, especially in the decade 1958–68, produced highly popular comedies. As one of the pioneers in this new comic tradition, Comencini distinguished himself through the combination of a realist concern for the postwar wasteland and a humorous bias aimed at assuaging social problems with comic relief and entertainment. Such is the recipe presiding over the 'bread and love' formula that the 'poor but happy' protagonists of Comencini's *Pane, amore e fantasia* (Bread, Love, and Fantasy) (1953) and its sequel *Pane, amore e gelosia* (Bread, Love, and Jealousy) (1954) successfully put into practice. Comencini's dedication to a cinema pairing social commitment and popular entertainment is also illustrated by his adaptation of Giacomo Puccini's *La bohème* in 1988.

Further reading

Gili, J. (1981) *Luigi Comencini*, Paris: Edilig (a detailed study in French of Comencini's film production).

Marcus, M. (1986) *Italian Cinema in the Light of Neorealism*, Princeton, NJ: Princeton University Press (see ch. 5, 'Comencini's Bread, Love, and Fantasy: Consumable Realism').

DOROTHÉE BONNIGAL

comics

Originating in the United States at the end of the nineteenth century, comics first came to Italy in 1908 through a **Corriere della sera** supplement for children, *Corriere dei piccoli*. Over time they became a vehicle for expression and diffusion of the collective imagination although, given the relatively poor organization of cultural production in Italy, comics remained in an incubation phase up until the early 1960s.

Many Italian cartoonists drew for the *Corriere dei piccoli*, which achieved a daily circulation of approximately 40,000. It carried translated versions of American classics, stimulating a proliferation of imitations. These were usually individual panels with captions written in rhyming couplets. The weekly *L'Avventuroso* (The Adventurer), founded in 1934, aimed at a readership of teenagers and adults. With sales oscillating between 300,000 to half a million copies, it offered readers stories from American comics, which had developed sophisticated procedures of script writing. The subsequent development of equivalent writing techniques in Italy during the 1930s and 1940s allowed Italian authors of comics to popularize photography, cinema and especially adventure stories and fantasy literature ranging from Salgari to Stevenson and from Ariosto to Goethe. This happened under the constrictions of Fascist censorship, which banned cultural importation from the USA and imposed a specific policy of prioritizing written text over images. All of these developments occurred despite the negative role played by schools, which had control of the popularization of literature. After the war, comics were freed from these restrictive norms and became an integral part of urban consumer culture. The Italian cultural industry, through the development of serialization, catered increasingly for a public that fed on the collective imagination. Consequently, production formulas were standardized and the public's competence in the field was developed and exploited.

Certain publishing ventures spearheaded the evolution of comics. One was connected to the Disney world, and centred on **Topolino** (Mickey Mouse). Another concerned the Bonelli publishing house, which exploited the western adventure genre through ever wider offerings, sensitive to demands of the markets. The serials *Tex Willer*, *Zagor*, *Il comandante Mark* (Commander Mark) and *Il piccolo Ranger* (The Little Ranger), in which the basic structure of the western genre was supplemented by elements from fantasy, horror, detective and science fiction, humour and magic, were followed in time by many other serials which emphasized one or another of these different elements. Examples include *Ken Parker*, a highly sophisticated version of Wild West colonization; *Martin Mystere*, an experiment in archaeological science fiction; and *Dylan Dog*, a horror detective fiction. Another leading role was provided by the periodicals with very high circulations aimed at adolescents: *Il Giornalino* and *Vitt*, under Catholic auspices, were distributed in schools and parishes as well as through newsagents. They offered, along with a generally mediocre range of adventure stories, works of great authors like Hugo **Pratt** and Massimo Mattioli (who later was published also in avantgarde magazines such as *Corto Maltese* and *Frigidaire*). Having to adapt to necessarily rigid content rules, these cartoonists experimented with original and sophisticated graphics. Less rigid were the weekly *L'intrepido* (The Intrepid) and *Il monello* (The Rascal) which appeared in the 1950s and were followed by *Lancio Story* and *Skorpio* in the 1970s. Along with comics based on scenarios incorporating romantic adventure, realism and melodrama, these also published articles on topical subjects from show business to sports and society news.

The American superheroes also had great editorial success including the DC Comics classics, Batman and Superman and the more 'human' heroes of Marvel Comics who had to face the superproblems of everyday life. However, the most interesting phenomenon in the history of Italian comics was the sudden appearance on the scene of the *fumetto nero* (crime comics) in the early 1960s. This genre imposed itself strongly on the market. It had a profound influence not only on the comic book world but also on society through its violent critique of middle-class myths, taboos and values. As a genre, it was well in tune with the tendency to question everything which characterized many cultural manifestations of that period. The first *fumetto nero* was *Diabolik*, which appeared in 1962. It was based on the adventures of a sort of anti-hero of the same name who, unlike the American superheroes, was a violent and vengeful criminal, always triumphing and never getting caught. His actions were a statement of self-affirmation and antisocial individualism in the face of the hypocrisy of middle-class false morality and repectability. *Kriminal* and *Satanik*, which appeared in 1964, were modelled on *Diabolik* but tended to be more extreme, with new and more shocking elements. They adopted an expressionistic drawing style bordering on caricature, with audacious close-ups and faster paced narrative. The dialogue was drier, vulgar and often truculent. These *fumetti* introduced a powerful erotic and sadistic content along with horror and magical moods.

Within a short time, newsagents' stalls were filled with crime comics utilizing the basic formula and emphasizing one or another element. They were published on cheap paper, often poorly inked and drawn, by small-time editors who wanted to get a foothold in the new and promising market niche. The whole phenomenon was spontaneous and responded to the public's expectations and changes in taste. The pornographic line was particularly successful and explored all perversions parodying all literary genres. Both fictitious characters and real personages appeared in these magazines, which interpreted the collective imagination from a purely pornographic perspective. The reader was presented with a total disregard for social inhibitions and taboos, as the *fumetto nero* left behind the passive conformism of traditional comics and made a frontal attack on every principle of authority. However, the spontaneity of the crime comic was also the cause of its early decay and disappearance for, apart from the tendency of the general readership to accept rather than question social norms, minor editors could not compete with larger publishing houses which were offering more standardized products. By the end of the 1970s *Diabolik* was the only one still surviving. Its original formula, which once seemed so shockingly extreme, proved able to weather the ups and downs of the market.

It was in the scene set by the *fumetto nero* that the *fumetto d'autore* (auteur comics) found a favourable ground for development. The middle 1960s also saw the appearance of the specialized periodicals which upgraded comics and promoted theoretical studies on the cultural industry. These gave legitimacy to the authors' professional work, published old and new foreign cartoonists, and welcomed Italian authors who would not have being given space in large and standardized editorial enterprises. The first of these were ***Linus*** and *Eureka*, and they were followed in time by many others: *Sgt. Kirk*, where Hugo Pratt published the cult comic 'Corto Maltese'; *Horror*; the sophisticated *Sorry*; *Il Mago*; *Cannibale*; *Frigidaire*; *Corto Maltese*; and *Comic Art*. Among Italian authors, Vittorio Giardino, Milo Manara, Attilio Micheluzzi, Andrea Pazienza and Sergio Toppi were published.

In the 1980s and 1990s, a major change in the distribution of comics occurred with the appearance of specialized shops which abetted the passage of the medium from a mass readership to a more selective one. Competition from television and the spread of video games combining the imagery of electronics and genetics led to a crisis in the sales of comics, but also provided a stimulus for a renewal of the medium's language. The monthly *Cyborg* and the Bonelli series *Nathan Never*, both focusing on technological science fiction and cyberpunk imagery, were an answer to that crisis.

Further reading

Brancato, S. (1994) *Fumetti. Guida ai comics nel sistema dei media* (Comics: A Guide to Comics in the Media System), Rome: Datanews (a clear and well-informed treatment of the relationship between Italian comics and other media).

Frezza, G. (1989) 'Il fumetto' (Comics), in A. Asor Rosa (ed.), *Letteratura italiana. Storia e Geografia* (Italian Literature: History and Geography), Turin: Einaudi, 1244–68 (a short history of Italian comics with critical comment on major authors).

FRANCO MANAI

commedia all'Italiana

Although Italian popular cinema probably became better known abroad in the guise of more spectacular genres such as the **spaghetti western** or the mythological sword and sandal epic, in Italy itself the most prolific, popular and characteristic genre of the postwar period was that which became known as *commedia all'italiana*, or comedy Italian style.

Generally regarded as first making its full appearance in 1958 with Mario **Monicelli**'s *I soliti ignoti* (Big Deal on Madonna Street), the new comedy's roots lay, at least in part, in the more traditional theatrical forms of the variety theatre and stage review. It also re-elaborated many elements of earlier Italian film comedy such as the films of **Totò** and the 'pink neorealist' films of the immediate postwar years, but adopting a much darker and more cynical attitude which completely undermined the fundamental optimism of these earlier comedies. Flourishing mainly during the 'golden age' of Italian cinema (approximately 1958–68), which itself developed in parallel with the so-called **economic miracle**, it was essentially a form of 'tragicomedy bordering on the grotesque', which, with its laughter always tinged with a sense of desperation, brought to the surface all the painful contradictions and the undercurrent of social malaise of a culture undergoing rapid transformation (Bondanella, 1983: 145).

The genre thus accurately reflected Italy's profound social and cultural changes while at the same time fiercely satirizing the pretensions of the 'new Italian', a character type explored in all its possible variations in the many, but essentially similar, characters played by the four actors who most came to exemplify this sort of comedy: Alberto **Sordi**, Vittorio **Gassman**, Ugo **Tognazzi** and Nino **Manfredi**. The most frequent themes of these bittersweet farces were the very obsessions and concerns which were agitating the new Italy: greater sexual freedom (see **sexual mores**), a scramble for status through its new symbols such as cars and expensive holidays, and the greater selfishness and individualism promoted by increased affluence. With films such as *Divorzio all'italiana* (Divorce Italian Style) (1961) and *Sedotta e abbandonata* (Seduced and Abandoned) (1964) Pietro **Germi** also developed a southern version of the genre which hilariously exposed the dark underside of traditional notions of male honour and the proper place of women, themes that would also be taken up by one of the few female practitioners of the genre, Lina **Wertmüller**, in many of her films featuring Giancarlo Giannini and Mariangela Melato.

The overwhelming success of the genre is generally credited not only to its reflection of contemporary society but also to the combined talents of a number of scriptwriters, actors and directors who often worked together during this period. Foremost among the scriptwriters were **Age and Scarpelli**, Rodolfo Sonego, Ruggero Maccari, Stefano **Vanzina** (Steno) and Ettore **Scola**, who also came to feature alongside Monicelli, Dino **Risi**, Luigi **Comencini** and Alberto **Lattuada** as one of the main directors of the genre. After contributing to numerous comedies Italian-style in the 1960s, it was Scola who, with *C'eravamo tanto amati* (We All Loved Each Other So Much) (1973), not only summed up the previous twenty years of Italian social history but also created the last great masterpiece and effective swansong of the genre.

Further reading

Bondanella, P. (1983) *Italian Cinema: From Neorealism to the Present*, New York: Ungar (see all of ch. 5, 'A Decisive Decade: Commedia all'italiana, Neorealism's Legacy, and a New Generation').

Giacovelli, E. (1995) *La commedia all'italiana. La storia, i luoghi, gli autori, gli attori, i film* (Comedy Italian Style: Its History, Settings, Authors, Actors, Films), Rome: Gremese (an indispensable tool for understanding the genre in all its aspects, with a detailed history plus appendices on all the major directors, scriptwriters and actors).

GINO MOLITERNO

La Comune

La Comune is an extreme left-wing political theatre company formed by Dario **Fo** and Franca **Rame** in 1970 after the breakdown of their partnership with the Italian Communist Party (**PCI**), which had provided the performance venues for their previous company, Associazione Nuova Scena (New Scene Association).

When Fo and Rame left the mainstream theatre circuit in the wake of the 1968 student uprising, they performed for working-class audiences in factories and in the workers' clubs run by the cultural arm of the PCI. However, their criticisms of the party's revisionist policies led to an inevitable falling-out, and the company split: Fo and Rame and a number of other actors then formed La Comune. Throughout the 1970s the company toured incessantly, invited by striking workers to perform at rallies and in occupied factories. They were continually harassed by authorities, and Fo was even arrested at one point. Nevertheless, some of Fo's most inventive plays were written during this period, and the company achieved an enormous popular following, providing the workers with what Fo called 'counter-information' on the real state of Italian political and social affairs.

Further reading

Mitchell, T. (1984) *Dario Fo: People's Court Jester*, London and New York: Methuen (an overview of the careers of Fo and Rame, including discussion of the political dimension of their collective theatre work).

TIM FITZPATRICK

Comunione e Liberazione

Founded by Don Giussani in Lombardy in the 1960s, Comunione e Liberazione became one of the most influential 'inspired' movements at work in the Italian Church, with privileged access to **Pope John Paul II**. It has been particularly strong among young people, especially in schools and universities, with highly successful rallies at Rimini in the summer and on Catholic World Youth Days.

An integralist and conservative organization, Comunione e Liberazione has tended to be intolerant of even its Catholic critics, describing them as 'neo-pelagians' or 'crypto-Protestants'. *Il Sabato* and *Trenta giorni* form its journalistic arm, and its Compagnie delle Opere (Companies of works) run manufacturing and service industries and social welfare organizations valued at 2 billion pounds sterling worldwide.

Through the Movimento Popolare (Popular Movement), Comunione e Liberazione exerted a powerful influence on the **DC**. Its present political point of reference is the **CDU**. One of the leaders of Comunione e Liberazione, Roberto Formigoni, is also president of the Lombardy region.

See also: Catholic associations

Further reading

Urquhart, G. (1996) *The Pope's Armada: Unlocking the Secrets and Mysteries of Powerful New Sects in the Church*, London: Corgi.

JOHN POLLARD

conceptual art

Conceptual art is an approach to art, widespread in the 1960s and 1970s, which placed more emphasis on the idea or 'concept' being expressed, than on the physical art object which carried the meaning. The art object thus became a mere vessel for the message, and manifested no aesthetic qualities. Significantly, this approach coincided with the liberalization of art education, and the spread of the notion that anyone can be an artist, and that technical expertise is not necessary.

Conceptual art is neither movement nor style, but rather a tendency in which works may participate to a greater or lesser degree. While the term was coined by American Sol Le Witt in 1967, the tendency goes back at least to 1917, when French artist Marcel Duchamp took a porcelain urinal, titled it *Fountain*, and attempted to enter it in an exhibition. Duchamp argued that the new title and point of view superseded the original use.

Duchamp's *Fountain* delineates some of the possibilities: conceptual art may consist of pre-existing objects or it may be purpose-built; in either event it requires little skill. It may comment on the nature of art and the production and consumption of art, or it may bear some clear political message.

This approach was ideal in the social context of the 1960s. Traditional art, despite being 'beautiful', seemed not to have effected any positive social changes. Produced at high cost in individual examples, it could only be bought by the wealthy or the state, which became anathema at a time of increasing social protest against consumerism and state control. Traditional art thus came to symbolize all that was wrong with capitalist society. It was aesthetically pleasing but served the oppressors. Conceptual art, on the other hand, questioned and educated.

The great Italian precursor of conceptualism is Piero **Manzoni**. Like Duchamp, his taste tended to the scatological. By canning his own excrement, in a limited and numbered edition, Manzoni is not asking us to admire the colour and consistency of his stools. Instead, in *Merda d'artista* (Artist's Shit), from 1961, he is commenting on artistic production and the effrontery of his peers. Artists produce excrement, yet they pass it off as gold and expect us to receive it with admiration. Manzoni is also dealing with authenticity. This is real and personal, and literally produced by the artist.

Conceptual art spills over into installation and performance art and is also related to ***arte povera***, notwithstanding the latter's attention to physicality and materials. Italian critics have categorized the distinction in various ways: implosive and explosive; synthetic and analytical; process and behavioural. Both, however, work against the traditional ideas of painting and technique. Examples include Mario **Merz**, with his use of the Fibonacci series, sometimes as numbers scrawled in chalk on existing objects; Jannis **Kounellis**, who exhibited a live parrot, as well as live horses, which, while real, are somehow prosaic; Giulio **Paolini**, whose plaster pairs of classical sculptures are intended to raise the question of perception; Luciano **Fabro**, whose titles and materials are intended to comment on the state of Italy; and Emilio **Isgrò**, who in 1970 crossed out all the words in Volume XXXII of the *Encyclopedia Treccani*.

Further reading

Migliorini, E. (1979) *Conceptual Art*, 2nd edn, Florence: Il fiorino (in Italian; gives Italian examples, with illustrations).

Smith, R. (1994) 'Conceptual Art', in N. Stangos (ed.), *Concepts of Modern Art*, 3rd edn, London: Thames & Hudson (gives description and international history, with some illustrations; this chapter was written in 1980).

MAX STAPLES

Confindustria

As the national association of employers, the Confindustria (Confederazione generale dell'industria italiana) has been an important player in the Italian political arena. Since 1945, when it was re-established as a free association, the Confindustria has always proclaimed itself independent of parties and sometimes aspired to direct political leadership, but rarely achieved either. The period of **postwar reconstruction** was its golden age. At this time it rejected the legacy of Fascist period, when it had become a bureaucratic arm of the state, but maintained a strong centralized organization and tight links with the state **bureaucracy**. Chaired by Angelo Costa, a Catholic family entrepreneur of Genoa close to the Church hierarchy, the Confindustria generously funded all centre and right-wing parties and developed a tight alliance with centrist governments and particularly with the Christian Democratic Party (**DC**). Through close ties with **De Gasperi**, Costa deeply influenced government economic policy though this proved short-lived. The alliance went through a crisis when the DC began to colonize old and new state-owned enterprises, thus enforcing itself as an economic power. A Ministry of State shareholding was established and state-owned enterprises, which had been members of the Confindustria until 1958, created their own association, Intersind, and instituted a more flexible policy towards unions. The Confindustria suffered more major setbacks in the early 1960s when it unsuccessfully opposed the birth of a centre–left government, the nationalization of electricity and the launching of economic planning.

A further challenge came from workers whose struggles since the *autunno caldo* ('Hot Autumn') of 1969 had strengthened the unions' political influence. Finally, the emergence of the small enterprises of the so-called '**Third Italy**', in the regions of northeast and central Italy, widened an already existing cleavage, since the Confindustria was traditionally ruled by representatives of north-west big business.

All this required a change of strategy and organization, and so in 1970 the so-called 'Pirelli Project' was launched. Drawn up by a committee chaired by Leopoldo **Pirelli**, this became a sort of manifesto of Italian neo-capitalism, stressing that fighting unions and maintaining a patronage over moderate parties could no longer suffice. As a result, under the leadership of Gianni Agnelli (see **Agnelli family**) and later of Guido **Carli**, entrepreneurs joined government and unions in negotiating economic planning and goals. The Confindustria also attempted to improve its own democracy and to strengthen internal cohesion by involving all members in the decision-making process and making an effort to improve its public image by promoting better relations with the mass media and the cultural elites. The public standing of Italian entrepreneurs was thus improved and their social role was eventually legitimated, leading to a major change in the country's culture throughout 1980s. Nevertheless, the political influence of the Confindustria declined, and in fact big business became more dependent on state support in order to overcome the crises of the 1970s and early 1980s. Even organizational problems proved difficult to solve: new intermediate associations of small enterprises and young entrepreneurs arose and representatives of small and medium-sized enterprises, such as Luigi Lucchini, Sergio Pininfarina, Luigi Abete and Giorgio Fossa, were appointed as chairmen. However, the gap between big business and small enterprises persisted, thus weakening Confindustria's claim to represent all Italian entrepreneurs.

Further reading

Mattina, L. (1993) 'Abete's Confindustria: From Alliance With the DC to Multiparty Appeal', in S. Hellman and G. Pasquino (eds), *Italian Politics:*

A Review, vol. 8, London: Pinter, 151–64 (an examination of the Confindustria in the early 1990s).

STEFANO BATTILOSSI

Consagra, Pietro

b. 4 October 1920, Mazzara del Vallo, Sicily

Sculptor and writer

Consagra studied at the Academy of Fine Arts (1941–4) in Palermo before moving to Rome, where he met Renato **Guttuso**. He became a founder member of the group Forma (1947) and by 1948 he had produced his first abstract sculptures (such as *Homage to Christian Zervos*, bronze). He participated in the **Venice Biennale** in 1956, 1960 and 1972, with individual exhibitions on each occasion. In 1961 he co-founded the group **Continuità**.

Consagra had numerous public commissions such as the bronze sculpture for the Foreign Ministry in Rome (1966) and the cemetery gates in Gibellina (1977). His main preoccupation remained the investigation of humanity's place within a changing world, a subject that dominates his work, from the abstract spatial figures known as *Dialogues* (1954–62) to the larger environmental projects such as *Frontal City* (1968). He also experimented with colour in works such as the *Planets* series (1987). His writings include *Necessità della scultura* (The Need for Sculpture), a polemical response to Arturo Martini's *La scultura lingua morta* (Sculpture, a Dead Language) (1945).

Further reading

Consagra, P. (1952) *Necessità della scultura*, Rome: Lentini.

OLIVIA DAWSON

Consiglio Nazionale di Ricerca

Originally founded in 1923 as an agency to represent Italian scientific interests internationally, the Consiglio Nazionale di Ricerca (National Research Council) was reorganized in 1945 as an autonomous governmental body within the department of the President of the Coucil of Ministers. It was assigned responsibility for promoting, undertaking and co-ordinating scientific research in Italy, as well as supplying technical and scientific support to the government and helping to define proper standards and practices in scientific and technological areas. In 1989 the CNR was merged with other public research institutions through the creation of MURST (the Ministry for Universities and Scientific and Technological Research), but this produced a number of organizational problems which hampered its efficient functioning. In July 1998, with the aim of facilitating the CNR's functions and in the context of a major re-definition of national objectives in the area of scientific research, the **Prodi** government restructured the Council so as to give it more financial autonomy and greater organizational flexibility.

GINO MOLITERNO

Consolo, Vincenzo

b. 18 February 1933, Sant'Agata di Militello, Messina

Lawyer, novelist, playwright and essayist

A lawyer by profession who practises in Milan, Consolo uses his professional training to research issues which he then explores in writings which focus on his native Sicily. The rich linguistic and stylistic experimentalism of his literary works has been likened by some to that of **Gadda**. The novel *Il sorriso dell'ignoto marinaio* (The Smile of the Unknown Mariner) (1976), for example, is based on archival documents of the 1860 Sicilian uprisings, while its linguistic style is forged out of a fusion of language and dialect. Consolo's concern with social activism is an underlying theme of many of his works, including the collection of essays and short stories *Le pietre di Pantalica* (The Stones of Pantalica) (1988). He was awarded the prestigious Pirandello Prize for his play *Lunaria* (1985), and the Grinzane Cavour Prize for his novel *Retablo* (The Altar Piece) (1987). He has also published several collections of sociological essays, including *Il barocco in Sicilia: La rinascita della Val di Noto* (The Baroque in Sicily: The Rebirth of the Val di Noto) (1991).

VIRGINIA PICCHIETTI

Constituent Assembly

On 2 June 1946, Italians voted in the first free elections since 1922. Before them was a choice between the old monarchy, strongly implicated with the fallen Fascist regime, or a new republican form of government. In addition, they were to elect of a single-chamber legislature which would guide the country through the necessary **postwar reconstruction**. For the first time in Italian history women were given the vote, and almost 90 per cent of the 25 million qualified voters participated. A majority of 12.7 million voters chose the **Republic** (as against 10.7 million for the monarchy) and the elected assembly of 556 therefore set to work for the next eighteen months in order to draw up a new republican constitution.

The new women's vote undoubtedly contributed to the **DC**'s relative majority (35.2 per cent) in the Assembly. The Left was represented by the Socialists (**PSIUP**) who won 20.7 per cent and the Communists (**PCI**) who received 19 per cent. On the Right was the quasi-Fascist Qualunquista movement (see **L'Uomo Qualunque**) led by Guglielmo Giannini, which polled 5.3 per cent, while the secular and liberal parties were split and polled poorly compared to the pre-1922 Parliament. The **constitution** which was produced – and eventually approved on 22 December 1947 by 453 votes to 62 – reflected the Assembly's political composition, with strong collectivist elements coming not only from the Left but also from part of the Catholic sector.

The draft constitution was drawn up by a committee of seventy-five nominated by the Assembly's president, Giuseppe Saragat, on the recommendation of the various parties. They presented their work in January, and it was debated in the Assembly from March to December. The **Vatican** pressured for an American-style presi-

dent, but **De Gasperi** and the Assembly resisted. The Vatican also pressed for inclusion of the 1929 Lateran Pacts in the constitution; surprisingly, this became Article 7 when **Togliatti** decided that the PCI should support the measure against its secular and socialist allies, and all but one PCI deputy agreed to support the party line. An amendment proposed by another Communist, Giovanni Grilli, prevented the indissolubility of marriage from being written into the constitution, thereby making the passage of a **divorce** law twenty years later much easier.

In practice, however, many of the more innovatory elements of the constitution were not applied and many existing Fascist laws remained on the books after a verdict of the Court of Cassation in February 1948 divided the constitution's articles into those to be immediately implemented and those which could de delayed.

Apart from purely constitutional matters, the Constitutional Assembly also witnessed, in January 1947, the split of the Socialist Party (PSIUP) into the left wing **PSI** and the centrist **PSDI**, and later that month De Gasperi visited the USA preparing the ground for the expulsion of the PCI and PSI from executive government, a move he put into action in May. Soon Italy began to receive the aid and benefits that came as part of the Marshall Plan.

The Assembly, and the republican constitution that it produced, have often been criticized for their many compromises. Nevertheless, given the division between East and West, and consequently between Christian Democrat and Communist, which became increasingly bitter during the Assembly's time, it was a remarkable achievement to have drafted, approved and implemented a constitution which has lasted largely intact for fifty years.

See also: church, state and society; political parties

JAMES WALSTON

constitution

Drafted by the **Constituent Assembly** over a period of eighteen months and 'often criticized for its "studied imprecision" ' (Hine, 1993: 147), the constitution of the Italian **Republic** came into force on 1 January 1948. It is made up of 139 articles divided into two sections: the first (articles 1–54) covers 'basic principles', the aims of the state, the nature of citizenship and citizens' rights and duties, and the second part (articles 55–139) deals with institutional arrangements.

Given the political makeup of the Constituent Assembly which produced it, the constitution is a compromise between Catholic, Marxist and secular ideology. It thus includes nineteenth-century liberal (negative) rights and guarantees, together with twentieth-century collectivist and positive rights. Institutionally, given the recent experience of fascism, it aimed above all to prevent a concentration of power, to weaken the executive and to make the **Parliament** and the parties the centre of power.

Most of the first section makes statements of aims rather than describing rights which can be implemented. There is the right to work (article 4) and the protection of linguistic minorities (article 6); the 'Republic promotes the development of culture and scientific and technical research' (article 9). These and other clauses needed normal legislation to actually take effect. By contrast, relations between Church and state (see **church, state and society**) are regulated by the 1929 Lateran Pacts which become an integral part of the constitution (article 7). After the basic principles, the constitution outlines civil liberties (13–28), ethical and social relations (29–34), economic relations (35–47) and political relations (48–54).

The second section describes the institutions. There is a symmetrical bicameral legislature (articles 55–82). The **President of the Republic**'s powers are defined (83–91) along with the powers of government (92–100), a **Constitutional Court** and the governance of the magistrature through a High council of the Magistrature (CSM) (101–13). There is some regional autonomy (114–15) and there is provision for **referenda** to repeal certain types of legislation (75). Modification of the constitution is only possible by passage of the proposal through both houses twice on occasions at least three months apart. A referendum is necessary if the second majority is less than two-thirds.

In practice, implementation of much of the constitution was a slow process; the Constitutional Court only came into operation in 1956, and the CSM in 1958. The ordinary regions elected their first assemblies in 1970 while the first referendum (to repeal the **divorce** law) was held in 1974. The twenty-five constitutional laws passed up to 1999 and the Constitutional Court verdicts have only produced minor revisions.

By the late 1970s there were strong calls to revise the constitution in the name of 'governability', although these calls were led by Bettino **Craxi** who saw himself as the potential president of a new system. Old fears of fascism coupled with a fundamental inertia prevented any real reform until the early 1990s when first, the electoral laws were changed through normal legislation (see **electoral systems**) and then a series of bicameral commissions put forward proposals for constitutional reform regarding presidential powers, relations between the two chambers of Parliament, federalism and administration of Justice. In 1997 Massimo **D'Alema** was elected to the chair of the Third Bicameral Commission with high hopes of reforming the constitution, but the Commission concluded its work a year later without agreeing to any change.

Further reading

Hine, D. (1993) *Governing Italy*, Oxford: Oxford University Press.

Neppi Modona, G. (ed.) (1995) *Lo stato della costituzione* (The State of the Constitution), Milan: Il Saggiatore.

Pasquino, G. (1998) 'Reforming the Italian Constitution', *Journal of Modern Italian Studies* 3 (1): 42–54.

Vercellone, P. (1972) 'The Italian Constitution of 1947–48', in S.J. Woolf (ed.), *The Rebirth of Italy 1943–50*, New York: Humanities Press.

JAMES WALSTON

Constitutional Court

The creation of a Constitutional Court envisaged in the 1948 **constitution** was Italy's first experiment with judicial review. That such a Court did not come into existence until 1956 and that the election of its fifteen judges is shared equally by the **President of the Republic**, **Parliament** and the highest judicial bodies testify to the extreme wariness among the political class that its own decisions might be subjected to critical review by a partizan power centre free from all accountability. In fact, those worries have been largely groundless. The Court has shown itself to be essentially conservative in relation to the established political order, protecting the secular and centralized nature of the postwar state and preferring to prompt Parliament into action or revision rather than risk open dispute. On the other hand, it has been progressive in regard to issues of individual freedoms, extending the rights of citizens against the overmighty state and thus ensuring that the Court itself has remained largely exempt from the widespread distrust of other parts of the judicial system.

The Court responds to queries raised by lower courts over the constitutionality of particular laws and resolves disputes between different branches or levels of government. Its field of intervention has therefore been exceptionally wide, and by 1990 it was receiving nearly one thousand demands for adjudication each year.

The most significant sets of issues that it has been involved in are essentially four. First, it has extended civil liberties by regularly striking out illiberal or discriminatory fascist laws in conflict with the 1948 constitution. The Court was also instrumental in expanding freedom of speech by forcing change to the **RAI**'s monopoly on public broadcasting in the mid-1970s (see **broadcasting**). Second, in its judgements on religious freedom, the status of the Catholic Church and the constitutionality of **divorce**, the Court has played an important role in resisting attempts to limit the state's authority in the name of religion. Third, by virtue of its substantial and largely self-defined powers to approve or block referendum proposals, the Court has become an important filter for the pressures to force major changes on a reluctant Parliament, especially because the referendum has been repeatedly used as an instrument of political mobilization since 1970 (see **referenda**). Fourth, this political involvement has been accentuated by the establishment of regional governments in 1970 and the subsequent demand to define the constitutional limits of national and regional authorities (see **regions**; **regional government**). Here too, however, the Court has been

essentially conservative: its decisions have tended to frustrate efforts to devolve greater legislative powers to the regions and convert Italy into a federal state.

See also: legal system

Further reading

De Franciscis, M.E. and Zannini, R. (1992) 'Judicial Policy-Making in Italy: The Constitutional Court', *West European Politics* 15 (3): 68–79.

Volcansek, M. (1994) 'Political Power and Judicial Review in Italy', *Comparative Political Studies* 26 (4): 492–509.

DAVID MOSS

consumerism

There was little to consume in Italy in 1945, as the war receded to leave Italians cold, hungry and unemployed. The imperative of 'autarchy' or self-sufficiency, imposed by the Fascist regime during the 1930s, had practically cancelled the very idea of consumerism and replaced it with the modest dream of just 'mille lire al mese' (a thousand lire a month) and a peaceful life. In 1950, over 70 per cent of an Italian family's expenditure was on food, housing and clothing. By the mid-1950s, however, three major factors began to effect a profound change on Italian spending patterns: rapid economic expansion (the so-called **economic miracle**), mass motorization and television.

With much of the population in work by this time, increased wages offered new possibilities for allocating a greater part of income to other than basic expenses. As damage to infrastructure and transport systems was repaired (see **postwar reconstruction**), the country was brought back together. The first part of the motorway between Milan and Rome was opened in 1958, connecting different parts of the country as never before (see **autostrada network**). The introduction of the Vespa motor scooter made personal transport easy and economical, although it was the motor car that now arose as the new object of desire. The mass production of small, affordable cars like the **Fiat** Cinquecento and Seicento soon put most Italians on four wheels, signalling the beginning of consumerist behaviour. This was energetically fanned by the introduction of television in 1954, as advertisements for consumer products were now able to reach a larger audience through the new medium. *Carosello*, the advertising segment introduced on public television in 1957 which showcased an attractive carousel of consumer products, thus encouraging a new standard of living and a new ideal of consumption, immediately became – and for many years remained – the most watched programme on Italian television. As children were allowed to stay up late to watch the barrage of ads, the first consumerist generation born without memories of lack and deprivation matured.

Nevertheless, the new affluence was not uniform and there were great disparities: the economic 'boom' clearly favoured the North over the South. So, from the early 1950s on, southern labourers flocked to the northern factories of Turin and Milan, chasing the utopia of economic well-being (see **Southern Question**). At the same time, the new consumerism began to be criticized by the Catholic Church, alarmed by the progressive loss of ethics and the reduction in religious observance. Some intellectuals also voiced their criticism. Writers like Luciano Bianciardi, in his novel *La vita agra* (Sour Life), and Valerio Mastronardi, in *Il maestro di Vigevano* (The Teacher of Vigevano), both written in 1962 at the peak of the boom period, highlighted the dramatic contradictions of a rapidly changing society. Louder than most, filmmaker and writer Pier Paolo **Pasolini** passionately criticized the new mass society created in the image of television commercials, although he was to remain largely a voice in the wilderness.

Although the economic boom was all but over by 1965, consumerism had become firmly established as a standard of life and the measure of well-being. A concerted attack on consumerism was mounted by the 1968 student movement, but this had little practical effect until the 'oil crisis' of 1973–4 imposed on Italians another real period of austerity. The subsequent double-digit inflation and economic downturn coupled with political terrorism to make the late 1970s the *anni di piombo* (years of lead). Beginning in 1983, however, the 'Craxi era' seemed to renew the myth of the Italian economic prosperity and to encourage, more than

ever, an ethos of unfettered consumerism. A decade later the explosion of **Tangentopoli** and the **Mani pulite** investigations again introduced a more sober note of restraint as they uncovered the unscrupulous way in which the wealth had been accumulated. Nevertheless, by this stage Italians had become, and now remain, inveterate consumers although the object of greatest desire of the 1990s is no longer the refrigerator or the sports car but the ubiquitous mobile phone.

See also: advertising

Further reading

Crainz, G. (1996) *Storia del miracolo italiano* (History of the Italian Economic Miracle), Rome: Donzelli (for a new interpretation of the 'boom' phenomenon).

Lanaro, S. (1992) *Storia dell'Italia repubblicana* (History of Republican Italy), Venice: Marsilio (see ch. 5 'Consumi e costumi' (Consumption and Customs)).

Mastronardi, L. (1962) *Il maestro di Vigevano* (The Teacher of Vigevano), Milan: Einaudi (a novel about the darker aspects of consumerist culture).

RICCARDO VENTRELLA

Contini, Gianfranco

b. 4 January 1912; d. 1 February 1990, Domodossola, Novara

Academic and literary critic

Widely regarded as one of Italy's foremost literary scholars, Contini was professor of Romance Philology at the universities of Freiburg and Florence and later at the Scuola Normale of Pisa from 1938–52. A life member of the elite Lincei and Crusca academies, he also served as president of the Società Dantesca Italiana (Italian Dante Society, 1956–68) and director of the journal *Studi Danteschi* (Dante Studies).

Contini's critical methodology, most characteristic in his studies of Dante and Montale, rests on a close philological analysis of textual variations which allows him to meticulously reconstruct the historical, stylistic and aesthetic dimensions of the text's composition and progressive development. Contini produced numerous seminal studies of medieval poets and of Petrarch, Ariosto, Leopardi, Croce and **Gadda**, as well as important critical editions of thirteenth-century poets and of Petrarch's *Canzoniere*. Editor of some of the most authoritative and fundamental scholarly editions of Italian literary historiography, Contini also published a number of sensitive translations of the poetry of Hölderlin.

SHERRY ROUSH

Continuità

Founded in Rome in 1961, Continuità included Carla **Accardi**, Pietro **Consagra**, Piero Dorazio, Gastone Novelli, Achille Perilli and Giulio Turcato among its founder members. Some had previously been members of Forma, founded in 1947 to promote abstract art. The original members were soon joined by Lucio **Fontana**, Arnaldo and Giò **Pomodoro** and the art critic Giulio Carlo **Argan**, who became the group's main spokesman.

Inherent to the group's general aim was the notion of continuity – to regenerate the traditional greatness of Italian art – and an ideal for specific works of art, each painting or sculpture reflecting the order and continuity of its creation. This was in opposition both to the social realists, such as Renato **Guttuso** and Armando Pizzicato, and to the informalist trends among artists of the Fronte Nuovo delle Arti (New Front of the Arts) and the **Gruppo degli otto** pittori Italiani, which had come out of the immediate postwar years. Some members of the group, Turcato in particular, went through many phases, from expressionism in the 1930s to geometrical abstraction in the 1960s. Accardi, Perilli and Novelli incorporated geometrical writings or 'signs' into their work. After going through an intense abstract phase, Accardi broke almost programmatically with painting as such. Her coloured plastic tents (1965) were intended as a rejection of the passive role of the spectator with regards to painting, and an attempt to create a situation which would surround and involve the spectator in a more active relationship with the work. Fontana, the most influential and

openly abstract artist to be associated with the group, developed a further side to Continuità, the idea of continuity of a work within its surroundings, as for example in his *Spatial Environment* (1949), which was a precursor of environmental art. From the late 1950s onwards he also suggested continuity with space behind the paintings in his slit canvases known as *Tagli* (Slashes). Among the sculptors, Giò Pomodoro made cast bronze reliefs with irregular surfaces, creating a sense of integration with the surrounding wall or floor. Continuità, like Forma, before it, represented a convergence of artists with similar aims rather than a definitive or programmatic movement.

Further reading

(1971) *New Italian Art 1953–71*, Liverpool: Walker AG (exhibition catalogue, introduction by G. Caradente).

OLIVIA DAWSON

Controspazio

A magazine of 'architecture, urbanism, technology and design', *Controspazio* was founded by Paolo **Portoghesi** in Milan in 1969 and was explicitly intended as an alternative to **Ponti**'s *Domus*, which had begun with a focus on contemporary product design but had eventually come to dominate the entire architectural scene. The manifesto of Controspazio, published in the first issue, declared an uncompromising, critical position 'regarding both research and action', and the magazine sought to provide a venue for different theoretical views, thus helping to reactivate discussion regarding the relationship between architecture, urbanism and wider social issues. It hosted contributions from architects such as Massimo Scolari, Enzo Bonfanti and Virgilio Vercelloni (members of the initial editorial board) as well as Sergio Petrini and Marcello Fabri, whose interests lay in the wider cultural and social milieu of architecture. The magazine continued its active involvement in all important architectural debates. In 1983 the directorship passed to Marcello Fabri.

See also: architectural and design magazines

GORDANA KOSTICH

Convegno per un Nuovo Teatro

A landmark event in the history of Italian neoavantgarde theatre, the Convention for a New Theatre was held at Ivrea between 9 and 12 June 1967, sponsored in part by the **Olivetti** foundation and attended by most of the leading practitioners and sympathizers of what was regarded as the new or experimental theatre. Following on from a polemical manifesto previously printed in the prestigious theatrical journal *Sipario* (Curtain) and signed by many of the participants, the convention sought to sanction a new direction for Italian theatre which included a thorough reform of the major training institutes and the *stabili* (state-financed repertory theatres), an emphasis on theatrical experimentation especially in the direction of group work and a broadening of the social scope of theatre by moving it into public spaces in the form of communal *feste* or festivals.

Much theatrical activity during the next five years did indeed follow this more experimental line although theatre historians are divided in estimating the extent to which the convention was responsible for such developments rather than merely bearing witness to them. What is generally agreed, however, is that the convention's open rejection of the theatrical status quo contributed to a renewal of Italian theatre.

GINO MOLITERNO

co-operatives

The evolution of the co-operative system in Italy has closely followed developments in the country's **economy** as a whole. After some pioneering moves in the mid-nineteenth century, the real beginning of Italian co-operatives coincided with the economic depression at the turn of the century, consolidating during the Giolitti era and then slowing during the Fascist period. After the Second World War, during both the economic boom years of the 1960s and in the twenty years that followed, the movement generally strengthened and consolidated its position in order to become the biggest in Europe.

Among the historical peculiarities of Italian co-operatives, when compared to similar experiences in other European countries, is the lack of a leading sector for the movement as a whole. Neither the consumer co-operative (as in Great Britain) nor the credit co-operative (as in Germany) or the co-operative society for work and production (as in France) constituted the absolute point of reference for the whole system. In the Italian case, all sectors were present from the very beginning but no single form prevailed upon the others. Another important feature of the movement in Italy was the division of the various co-operatives according to political ideology, an element obvious in the federal structure of the base co-operatives. During the Fascist years, there was an attempt to reorganize the whole movement on a unified basis, but this came at the cost of an authoritarian imposition which in reality modified the movement's most profound ideals. On the eve of the Second World War there were around 12,000 co-operatives with three million members in Italy.

After the war, a number of organizations similar to those of the pre-Fascist period were re-created. Among these, uniting the so-called 'red co-operatives', was the National League of Co-operatives and Mutual Aid which was socialist and communist inspired; the Confederation of the Italian Co-operatives, which was supported by the Christian Democrat Party (see DC) and brought together the 'white' or Catholic co-operatives; and the General Association of Italian Co-operatives, of a more generic social democratic character, united the so-called 'green co-operatives' and was supported by the Social Democrats and the Republican Party (see **PRI**). Later, a newer organization, the National Union of Italian Co-operatives, also joined the three historical groups but there nevertheless remained a considerable number of independent co-operatives not affiliated to any of these larger umbrella organizations.

In the postwar years the co-operative movement expanded rapidly. During the 1950s development followed the traditional pattern, but from the 1960s there was a re-consideration of both the economic organization of the system and the organization of its basic units at the level of the firm, which led to strategic choices being made in the sectors of finance and credit, consumer goods and building construction, all of which facilitated the strong consolidation and development of the movement during the 1970s. The 1980s saw the beginning of co-operatives in areas until then untried, such as the advanced tertiary sector and social solidarity.

Overall, during the years following the Second World War, the co-operative movement developed more – as it had always done – in the centre and the North, being almost non-existent in the south of Italy; a credit co-operative in Sicily was the only real exception to this general trend. However, in the 1980s a modification of legal regulations and in particular the passing of a law aimed at encouraging entrepreneurial activity by young people began to redress this imbalance in favour of the South.

In the early 1990s the Italian co-operative movement embraced 160,000 companies which employed about 500,000 people, with the total number of co-operative members estimated to be at almost ten million.

Further reading

Earle, J. (1986) *The Italian Co-operative Movement: A Portrait of the Lega Nazionale delle Co-operative e Mutue,* London: Allen & Unwin (centred on the Lega but discusses the other co-operative organizations as well).

Holmström, M. (1989) *Industrial Democracy in Italy: Workers' Co-ops and the Self-Management Debate,* Aldershot: Avebury (a comparative study, with focus on Italy).

Thornley, J. (1981) *Workers' Co-operatives: Jobs and Dreams,* London: Heinemann (see ch. 8 for a brief but comprehensive overview of the nature and development of the Italian movement).

PIETRO CAFARO

Coppi, Fausto

b. 15 September 1919, Alessandria;
d. 2 January 1960, Tortona

Cyclist

Coppi began his string of victories in 1940 by winning the Giro d'Italia (see **cycling**) at age twenty-one. In the Milan velodrome two years later, before leaving to fight in the war, he set the new mark of 45.871 km for the Hour Record, a race against the clock. When cycling resumed in 1946 he won the Milan–San Remo, but was placed second after **Bartali** in the Giro. The next year Coppi bounced back, and this time it was Bartali's turn to be runner-up. In 1948, Coppi won his second Milan–San Remo.

In 1949 Coppi began a remarkable season by winning the Milan–San Remo, and went on to first place in both the Giro and the Tour de France, a feat no other rider had accomplished before. Switching from road to velodrome, he then became World Pursuit Champion. In 1952, Coppi again won both the Giro d'Italia and the Tour de France. In 1953 he added the World Road Race Championship to his record-equalling fifth victory in the Giro.

Coppi died prematurely of undiagnosed malaria in 1960, but the memory of the *campionissimo* (the champion of champions), lives on: in his honour, the highest peak of the Giro now bears the official name of Cima Coppi.

PAOLO VILLA

Il Corriere della sera

With an average daily circulation of around 700,000 at the end of the 1990s, *Il Corriere della sera* was, for almost a century, the closest Italy came to having a national newspaper. Founded in Milan in March 1876 by Eugenio Torelli Viollier as an afternoon daily (hence its name, 'Evening Courier'), it always expressed an attitude of firm but enlightened conservatism and, from 1900 onwards under the directorship of Luigi Albertini, came to be closely modelled on the London *Times.* Its prestige and leadership continued to grow during the immediate postwar years, but in the mid-1970s it faced both a series of severe financial crises, which led to a number of disruptive changes in ownership and direction, and a direct challenge from the new Roman daily *La Repubblica.* Its reputation was further damaged in 1981 by revelations of its association with the Masonic **P2** Lodge, and in 1986 the unthinkable happened and it was overtaken in sales by *La Repubblica*. However, greater financial stability and able leadership during the 1990s enabled it to regain its lead in sales and its influential voice in public affairs.

See also: newspapers

GINO MOLITERNO

Corti, Maria

b. 7 September 1915, Milan

Academic, writer and critic

Corti was born in Milan, where she currently resides after retiring from a long and successful career as a university professor first in Lecce and then in Pavia. For many years she taught philology and the history of the Italian language, and gained an international reputation as a linguist and semiotic critic. She is still active in the research center she established Pavia, which collects manuscript material of contemporary authors. Her academic publications are wide-ranging and include annotated editions of Cavalcanti, Dante, Leopardi, **Vittorini** and **Fenoglio**. While primarily a literary critic, Corti is also a writer of fiction, a testament to her belief that the best critics are also themselves writers. Throughout her career Corti has been recognized for the high quality of her fiction, winning the Crotone prize in 1963 for her first work, *L'ora di tutti* (Everyone's Time) and the Pavese Prize for *Il canto delle sirene* (The Sirens' Song) (1989). In 1990 she received the Premio della Presidenza del Consiglio dei ministri (Prime Minister's Prize) for literature. She has served as editor and co-director of important literary journals, has contributed to periodicals such as *alfabeta* and *Strumenti critici* and has also occasionally written for national newspapers such as *Il Giornale* and *La Repubblica*.

BERNADETTE LUCIANO

Corto Maltese

Corto Maltese is the best-known fictional character created by Italian cartoonist and illustrator, Hugo

Pratt. An intrepid adventurer and wandering seaman, reminiscent of characters in Joseph Conrad's novels, Corto first emerges (quite literally from the sea) in the *Ballad of the Salt Sea*, a story Pratt published in 1967 in the Genoese illustrated magazine *Sgt. Kirk*. In this early story, however, Corto plays a largely supporting role, sharing the limelight with the ruthless pirate captain Rasputin, the mysterious criminal boss 'Monk' and the Pacific Ocean itself. He becomes the more suave and elegant sea captain, and the major protagonist of his stories, only in 1970 in the pages of the French magazine *Pif Gadget*. In subsequent stories we find him indulging his wanderlust, confidently roaming the world in the early twentieth century, becoming entangled in real historical events and crossing paths with both fictional and historical figures. By 1983 he had become famous enough to appear in an illustrated travel and adventure magazine named in his honour.

A recent re-issue of the *Ballad of the Salt Sea* in English bears a perhaps apocryphal but significant quote from Umberto **Eco** which illustrates the overwhelming respect which Pratt's character and the magazine had achieved in the 1980s: 'When I want to relax I read an essay by Engels; when I want something more serious I read Corto Maltese'.

Further reading

Pratt, H. (1996) *The Celts: A Corto Maltese Adventure*, trans. from the French by I. Monk, London: The Harvill Press (contains six stories that recount Corto's adventures between 1917 and 1918).

GINO MOLITERNO

Cossiga, Francesco

b. 26 July 1928, Sassari

Politician and statesman

An expert in constitutional law and a Catholic activist, Francesco Cossiga joined the **DC** in 1945. Elected as a deputy in 1958, he became a junior minister in 1966. As Interior Minister between 1976–8, he oversaw the establishment of Italy's anti-terrorist squads and was responsible for handling the **Moro** crisis. Moro's assassination provoked his immediate resignation. Prime Minister in 1979–80, he was regarded with extreme suspicion by the Left yet was elected **President of the Republic** at the first ballot in 1985 thanks to **PCI** support. From 1990, as he was drawn into the **Gladio** scandal, he adopted a highly controversial and outspoken political stance, supporting those seeking major institutional reform and attacking even his own party, which he left. His resignation from the presidency in April 1992 influenced the process of government formation during a critical phase of political developments. Appointed a life senator in 1992, he later became a vitriolic critic of Silvio **Berlusconi** in particular and the Freedom Alliance more generally (see **Polo della Libertà**). His formation of the **UDR** in 1998 may have been intended to encourage the 'Europeanization' of Italy's apparently enduringly anomalous Right.

MARK DONOVAN

Costanzo, Maurizio

b. 28 August 1938, Rome

Television presenter

Host of his own nightly chat show on **Canale Cinque** – and still portly despite a drastic diet undertaken in 1997 – Costanzo is a familiar companion to insomniacs. His show offers a sly mixture of the topical, the salacious, the curious and the obvious: typical guests might include a politician, an author, several showgirls, a psychologist and an aspirant comic. Costanzo himself wanders between his guests posing questions in a confidential, understated way, raising his voice and rudely interrupting them only when an opportunity arises to play on the sympathies of his live audience. A political chameleon who supported the Olive Tree coalition in 1996 after having been associated in turn with the **DC**, the **Radical Party**, the Socialists and the 'lay' area, as well as Gelli's **P2** Lodge, he became the only prominent **Berlusconi** employee not to publicly back **Forza Italia**. Nevertheless, he is in no way a marginal figure. In addition to his own show, he presents the

Saturday afternoon show *Buona Domenica* and, in late 1997, he became director of Canale Cinque.

See also: private television; television talk shows

Further reading

Veltroni, W. (1992) *I programmi che hanno cambiato l'Italia* (The Programmes That Changed Italy), Milan: Feltrinelli (see pp. 60–3, Maurizio Costanzo show).

STEPHEN GUNDLE

Cottafavi, Vittorio

b. 30 January 1914, Modena;
d. 14 December 1998, Anzio

Film and television director

A versatile and refined director with a background in law, literature and philosophy, Cottafavi is unfortunately most remembered for 'sword and sandal epics' like *La rivolta dei gladiatori* (The Revolt of the Gladiators) (1958) and *Ercole alla conquista di Atlantide* (Hercules Conquers Atlantis) (1961). After graduating from the **Centro Sperimentale di Cinematografia** in 1938, Cottafavi worked as scriptwriter and then as assistant director to Vergano, **Blasetti** and **De Sica**. His first solo direction was in 1943 with *I nostri sogni* (Our Dreams), from a play by Ugo Betti, followed in the early 1950s by a number of films that led French cinephiles to compare him to **Antonioni**. In the late 1950s he directed several popular mythological and pseudo-historical epics in the genre that became known as the 'peplum', but from 1965 chose to work almost exclusively in television, directing numerous literary adaptations ranging from Ibsen's *A Doll's House* to works by Dostoievsky, Lorca and Tennessee Williams. His adaptation of **Pavese**'s *Il diavolo nelle colline* (The Devil in the Hills) was shown at Cannes in 1985 to much critical acclaim.

GINO MOLITERNO

Council of Ministers

The Council of Ministers is the cabinet of the Italian government, which has varied in number from 18 to 32 members. According to the **constitution** (article 92), the Council of Ministers is nominated by the **President of the Republic** on the advice of the Prime Minister (that is, the **President of the Council of Ministers**). In practice, in the 'First' **Republic**, ministries and junior ministries were a reflection not only of the strength of the parties who made up the coalition but, above all, of the factions within the **DC**. There are three specifically economic ministries (Treasury, Finance and Budget). The size of the various ministries varies from over a million employees (Education) to less than 500, which has led to considerable fragmentation. In contrast to the Westminster system, there is no doctrine of cabinet responsibility and very little collegiality or policy co-ordination; it was thus a first when, in May 1996, Romano **Prodi** declared that his cabinet would work in unison in pursuit of **L'Ulivo**'s electoral programme, although there have been examples of ministers breaking ranks since then.

JAMES WALSTON

Craxi, Bettino

b. 24 February 1934, Milan; d. 19
   January 2000, Hammamet, Tunisia

Politician

Having 'modernized' the **PSI** and created a relatively factionless party, Craxi's intention was to lead it to victory on the 'long wave' of socialist success. In the event, he became the very symbol of the political corruption of the so-called 'First' **Republic** and, in the process, brought about the complete demise of the Socialist Party.

Craxi began his political career in 1956 as a PSI town councillor; he became a member of the party's Central Committee in 1957 and of the executive in 1965. He was a councillor and member of local government in Milan from 1960–70, a deputy in the national **Parliament** from 1968–94 and a member of the European Parliament in 1979. Most impor-

tantly, he was party secretary between 1976–93 and Prime Minister from 1983–7.

After the PSI's disappointing results in the June 1976 elections, Craxi was elected secretary at a meeting at the Midas Hotel in Rome. At the time he led a minority faction, and was seen as a compromise candidate rather than effecting a dramatic change of direction for the party. However Craxi began to reorganize the party and, for the first time in the PSI's history, he succeeded in uniting it. He also changed the party symbol from the hammer and sickle to the red carnation, and brought the PSI into the mainstream of European socialism.

Craxi maintained the party's support for the governments of national unity against the threats of **terrorism**, but emphasized the PSI's distance from the **PCI**. When the national solidarity governments failed and the **historic compromise** was shelved, Craxi again put the PSI forward as the **DC**'s only possible interlocutor on the left. With a socialist as **President of the Republic** (**Pertini**) and the DC in electoral decline, Craxi became Prime Minister in 1983 and held the post for almost four years (the longest prime ministership in the history of the Republic). His government introduced a new Concordat with the **Vatican** (see **church, state and society**) and removed the *scala mobile* (index-linked wage increases). The party's electoral shares increased, even if only gradually, and it became increasingly southern.

Both as Prime Minister and subsequently, Craxi grew ever more authoritarian, putting forward the doctrine of *decisionismo* – whereby he felt empowered to take decisions without consultation with other party members – and 'governability', a buzzword for giving more power to the executive in some sort of presidential system, obviously with Craxi as president. His growing authoritarianism was well-portrayed by the political cartoonist Forattini, who always showed him in black shirt and jackboots. From 1989–92, and in spite of his no longer being the Prime Minister, Craxi still effectively controlled all public resources, sharing these with the Christian Democrat powerbrokers Giulio **Andreotti** and Arnaldo Forlani, in an ominous clientelistic triumvirate known as the CAF.

As a result, the Socialist party and its secretary became closely identified with a high-spending system based almost entirely on *tangenti* or kickbacks, most for the parties but some for the individual leaders (see **Mani pulite**; **Tangentopoli**). Craxi's high profile, especially in Milan where the Tangentopoli investigations began, meant that he and the PSI took even more responsibility for the corruption than they probably deserved. In 1993, Craxi abandoned the secretariat of his party and then the country, refusing to stand trial in person. Since then, he has lived in gilded exile in Hammamet in Tunisia, while some of his faithful have tried to rehabilitate him. His first definitive conviction for corruption was handed down in 1996. A number of trials were still pending when he died in Hammamet in January 2000.

Further reading

Gundle, S. (1996) 'The Rise and Fall of Craxi's Socialist Party', in S. Gundle and S. Parker (eds), *The New Italian Republic: From the Fall of the Berlin Wall to Berlusconi*, London: Routledge.

Hine, D. (1986) 'The Craxi Premiership', in R. Leonardi and R.Y. Nanetti (eds), *Italian Politics: A Review*, vol. 1, London: Pinter.

JAMES WALSTON

crime

Like most countries, Italy is afflicted with a range of socially deviant and legally delinquent behaviour that comes under the heading of crime, understood as non-conformity to a given set of norms accepted by a significant number of people in a community. However, even if the international notoriety achieved by the **mafia** has tended to suggest that Italy is a country controlled by criminals, and in spite of Italy being undoubtedly afflicted with its own share of political corruption, white-collar crime, street delinquency and property crime, comparative statistics suggest that the incidence of crime in Italy is slightly below average for comparable countries of the European Union and the Western world. In 1994 the international crime statistics of Interpol relegated Italy to fourteenth place, with about 4,000 crimes committed per 100,000 population, well behind countries like

Sweden (over 12,000), Denmark, Canada, the Netherlands (each about 10,000), Germany, France and the United States (each between 6,000 and 8,000). However, the systematic comparison of crimes like murder, theft, burglary and sexual deviance remains unreliable due to different methods of making inquiries and different forms of calculation as well as changes in the reference period. Nevertheless, crime in Italy might be considered under the following headings.

Organized crime

Organized crime refers both to the activity and to the formal structure of interactions between individuals involved. Although the Sicilian mafia is the best-known organized criminal association in Italy – and with good reason since, as the **Mani pulite** (Clean Hands) investigations showed, there were very strong and extensive links between the mafia and the political class during the First **Republic** – there are other equally formidable organizations, such as the Neapolitan Camorra, the Calabrian 'Ndrangheta and the Puglia-based Società Onorata (Honoured Society).

In earlier times, loosely organized gangs of brigands were not unusual in the Italian countryside. *Banditismo* (brigandism) was often a form of collective self-defence and a protest against political or economic oppression. Gangs of brigands were still active in Sicily, Sardinia and Calabria after the Second World War (see Salvatore **Giuliano**), although brigandism was largely stamped out or became incorporated into the mafia in Sicily and Calabria by the late 1940s.

The expansion of the mafia after the Second World War led to a diffusion of what had traditionally been a rural organization into urban areas, targeting largely the public money which the government was devoting to developing the South (see **Cassa per il Mezzogiorno**). The mafia's infiltration of the public bureaucracy, legal authorities and the political parties all date from this time. In addition, some of the Sardinian gangs had been able to survive and also expanded their activities to the mainland, especially to Tuscany, in the 1960s. The 'Anonima sarda' (Anonymous Sardinian) or, alternatively, 'Società anonima' (Anonymous Society), with its ironic reference to a legally constituted limited company, became notorious for its kidnapping and blackmailing activities in cities.

Such criminal organizations do at times collaborate, but what most unites them is their similar organizational structure and their value system. They also appear similar in their history as responses, at the end of the nineteenth century, to the unwillingness or inability of the Italian state to enforce the executive power against existing social oppression and economic exploitation. Thus, in the absence of a strong state, for a long time the activity in family-bound mafia networks was regarded as honourable and prestigious. Honour and the imposed silence of *omertà* are, in fact, two basic values traditionally connected with historic brigandism in Italy, and both still play a relatively important role in rural areas where forms of the traditional *vendetta* (revenge) between families can even today lead to bloody showdowns. Family and territory are further traditional elements crucial for understanding historical brigandism and the roots of modern organized crime in Italy.

Yet if the threat of mafia violence continues to worry foreigners and Italians alike, there is no doubt that the effective influence of organized crime has been reduced in recent times. This has been in part due to the activities of judges like **Falcone** and Borsellino and the gradual uncoupling of the links between crime, government and the judiciary. At the same time, and perhaps more importantly, the public itself has turned against the 'men of honour'. A large proportion of the Italian population now openly condemns organized crime and is more willing to mobilize against it, a dramatic shift in attitude towards crime which is itself an sign of profound social change.

White-collar crime

Despite comparative statistics, it is likely that the incidence of white-collar crime in Italy may be above the level of comparable countries, since in Italy many infringements of the law are commonly regarded as peccadilloes, that is, punishable but not defamatory. The major forms of this sort of crime include political corruption, financial embezzlement, tax evasion, illegal marketing and environmental crime.

The *Mani pulite* investigations demonstrated a vast network of exchange between organized crime, finance and industry and the political class, amounting to a very high incidence of white-collar crime. Tax fraud or evasion (*evasione fiscale*) is also high. In 1991, for example, more than 240,000 individual cases of tax evasion were discovered and approximately 261,000 billion lire of earnings were estimated to have not been declared (see **taxation**). In order to limit tax evasion the government has from time to time declared tax amnesties, although the most significant counter-measure has been the strict imposition of the *scontrino fiscale* (tax receipt) whereby every financial transaction requires a *scontrino* to be issued and kept by both seller and customer, under pain of criminal prosecution.

Illegal marketing, the sale of dangerous products and working under illegal conditions constitute another group of common white-collar crime. The building industry in postwar Italy became proverbial for permitting poor working conditions, using illicit labour and undertaking construction work without any permits (for example, an estimated 61 per cent of all new buildings between 1971 and 1981 were erected without building permits). Better legal regulations and controls were introduced at the end of the 1970s but, just as tax evasion could be legalized through an amnesty, so illegal construction could be legalized through a *condono edilizio* (building amnesty), with the result that most illegal constructions have become legalized through amnesties over the years.

Illegal environmental practices such as the indiscriminate dumping of waste materials were also long accepted in Italy and committed by private individuals as well as by major companies. The most tragic symbol of this criminal behaviour was the accident at Seveso, although on the positive side, the incident dramatically demonstrated the dangers of such criminal behaviour towards the environment and led to a decreasing tolerance of such practices as well as to calls for a stricter and better enforced **environmental policy** (see also **environmental movement**; **Verdi**).

Other crimes

New forms of delinquency such as throwing rocks from overpasses at cars and a high rate of minor crimes like theft and pickpocketing are often juvenile behaviour motivated by boredom and a number of other factors which Italian society shares with other Western countries. Thus, although theft of bags by youths on motorcycles, the so-called *scippi*, came for a time to be strongly associated with Italy, subsequent research showed that this was a widespread activity in tourist centres of other countries as well.

The age of criminal responsibility in Italy is eighteen years, as in comparable countries. A relatively high rate of unemployment draws many young Italians into a criminal career or into the large underground economy which offers illicit work. Over four million Italians and an increasing number of immigrants (see **immigration**) now earn their living illegally in activities such as child labour, drug trafficking, prostitution or smuggling. Street crimes such as theft, drug trafficking and assault as well as burglary and organized robbery are, in recent times, more often carried out by illegal migrants exploited by other groups. Since no way has been found to effectively stem this influx of illegals, this sort of criminality seems destined to grow.

As with the total number of crimes, the Italian incidence of murder is relatively modest. With an average yearly rate of 4 murders per 100,000 population between 1985 and 1995, Italy is close to France and Germany and remains well below the official rate of the United States (9 per 100,000). The average annual rate of thefts of private cars between 1985 and 1995 at 524 per 100,000 is lower than in France (595) and the United States (650) but higher than in Germany (173).

Due to the varying definition of drug offences in different countries and the variety of social attitudes against people involved in drug-related crimes, comparable statistics may again be unreliable, but countries like the Netherlands show an average rate of less than 100 cases a year per 100,000 inhabitants, while Sweden and Denmark easily reach average numbers between 300 and 400 cases. The number of drug offences prosecuted in Italy is lower than in France or Germany.

A similar unreliability regarding comparative statistics is likely to apply in the case of sexual offences, which show European countries like Denmark, Germany, the Netherlands and Sweden in leading positions with their rates of about 50 to 70 per annum per 100,000, surpassed only by Canada with over 100. With an average of 1 case per annum per 100,000, Italy is behind Japan (4 cases) and thus statistically among the countries with the lowest rate of sexual crime in the world. However, this encouraging but rather surprising result may depend more on the deficiencies of Italian laws than on an actual low incidence of sexual violence. It is important to note that until September 1995, when the Chamber of Deputies (see **Parliament**) finally passed a law which the women's movement had been advocating for over fifteen years, sexual violence was still legally an offence against public morality rather than against a person and thus more a form of disorderly conduct than assault (see also **feminism**). A number of other cultural factors would also have served to mask the incidence of sexual crime. According to Church law, for example, rape within marriage was impossible since it was the women's duty to obey her husband in every respect. Furthermore, rape could only be denounced by the raped woman who thus risked 'losing her honour' and suffering shame, all of which would have undoubtedly contributed to such crimes not coming to light. Significantly, the late 1990s have seen a rise in the incidence of denunciations of sexual violence.

Further reading

Centorrino, M. (1995) *Economia assistita da mafia* (Economy Helped by the Mafia), Messina: Rubbettino.

Ginsborg, P. (1994) *Stato dell'Italia* (The State of Italy), Milan: Mondadori.

Violante, L. (1997) *Storia della criminalità in Italia* (History of Criminality in Italy), Turin: Einaudi.

JAN KURZ

critical currents

In order to understand the specific developments of critical currents in Italy after the Second World War, it is necessary to recall the overwhelming influence exercised over almost every aspect of Italian culture during the first part of the century by Benedetto **Croce**. Croce's dominant hold over the Italian critical scene in the early 1900s was to have an ambivalent effect on Italian culture as a whole. His magisterial authority originally blocked any fruitful exchanges between Italian criticism and that of other European cultures, although it is undeniable that his critical theory, revised and modernized, later opened the way to some of the major critical approaches which have flourished in the second part of this century.

Croce's idealist philosophical method focused both on the clear identification of the quality and purity of the poetic form within the works of an author as well as on the definition of literary criticism as a means of reconstructing the paths of the creative inner life. For Croce, this twofold approach was needed to isolate that which was to be considered genuine 'poetry' from the merely dogmatic or propagandistic aspects of a work of art and to decide if the artistic world of an author – feelings, intellectual beliefs, literary images and creations – should be regarded as poetic at all. Without reopening the debate on the Crocean consistency of Italian culture, which is well closed by now, one needs to note that Croce's system, while prone to idealism, offers the possibility of exploiting either one of its components depending on one's own ideological and cultural interests and intellectual formation. In fact, Croce's theory supports both a critical approach which privileges the close reading of the text as well as one centred more on the author's ideological intent. In other words, one aspect of his theory selects the literary text as the main object of the critical survey, the other promotes the context (historically, sociologically, ideologically) as a major component of the critic's interest.

After the Second World War and in the wake of the work of scholars such as Natalino **Sapegno** (1901–90) and Luigi Russo (1892–1961), who had merged Croce's hermeneutical ideas with the nineteenth-century historical current founded by Francesco De Sanctis (1817–83), Italian literary criticism took a dramatic ideological turn, in parallel with the rise of **neorealism** in literature, art and cinema. The sociological line of scholarship, which developed in the first two decades after the war, split essentially into three branches. One, anchored to the teachings of Marx and Engels, is best represented by Carlo Salinari (1919–77),

whose works, especially those on Italian postwar narrative, explore the possibility of defining the realistic current of Italian culture. Another aspect of this strongly sociological approach to literature was represented by Carlo Muscetta (b. 1912) and Sebastiano Timpanaro (b. 1923), the latter favouring a solid philological approach while Muscetta wanted to join more concretely the Crocean approach with Marxist ideology to construct a broader historical interpretation of Italian literature. Finally, a third stream sprang from a better understanding and knowledge of new sociological theories, such as those of the Frankfurt School or Marxist scholars such as Georgy Lukacs. This third current, open to an anthropological perception of the literary events, found one of its best promoters in Alberto **Asor Rosa**, whose critical works are centred on the connection between ideology and literary forms, an approach exemplified in his recent multi-volume *History of Italian Literature* published by **Einaudi**. Other active and influential scholars belonging to this current are Cesare Cases (born in 1920), Romano Luperini (born in 1940), who has recently flanked his ideological approach with a more psychoanalytical one, and poet-critic Franco **Fortini**, whose essays display a sharp and insightful combination of textual analysis and sociological interpretation.

The other component of Croce's cultural inheritance, the attention to the form of the literary text, was also extensively developed in the second part of the century, following the examples already set by Crocean scholars such as Attilio Momigliano (1883–1952), and independent intellectuals like Giuseppe De Robertis (1888–1963). Two major currents came from this more openly textual approach, one philological and the other 'stylistic'. The first saw philology not only as a basic instrument for grasping the genesis of a text but also as an indispensable critical tool for exploring its artistic form. This approach in the 1950s and 1960s was strongly fostered by Vittore **Branca**, whose studies of Boccaccio and humanism are a conspicuous and convincing example of how philology and literary analysis can be successfully combined to achieve a balanced critical insight into specific authors and subjects. The stylistic approach, according to the lesson of famous foreign scholars of Italian culture such as Leo Spitzer

(1887–1960) and Erich Auerbach (1892–1957), is solidly based on indispensable philological critical skills but is more openly interested in scrutinizing the stylistic elements of a literary work in order to understand the creative dynamics an author uses to achieve aesthetic goals. Besides the cornerstone works on stylistic criticism by scholars of different backgrounds such as Mario **Fubini** (1900–70), Benvenuto Terracini (1886–1968) and Alfredo Schiaffini (1895–1971), it is imperative to remember Gianfranco **Contini**'s robust and profound stylistic surveys of both medieval and modern romance literatures. Contini's ability to penetrate a text and an author's creative process has pointed the way for generations of scholars and has marked the rediscovery and re-evaluation of the experimental current of Italian literature from Dante to the present. The work of other important scholars also moved freely between philology, stylistics and linguistics such as Gianfranco Folena's (1920–90) studies on eighteenth-century language and literature, Aurelio Roncaglia's (b. 1917) works on medieval literature, or Pier Vincenzo Mengaldo's (b. 1936) publications on twentieth-century Italian poetry.

While many stylistic analyses led to psychoanalytic approaches (already in Spitzer, for instance) and despite the active presence of a scholar of the calibre of Giacomo **Debenedetti** (1901–67), a direct psychoanalytic criterion never really found a fertile current in Italian criticism. The stylistic method was further revitalized in the 1960s and 1970s by a series of cultural events which brought Italian criticism into close contact with other cultures and ideas, in particular by the rediscovery of the Russian formalists of the 1920s, whose theories on the importance of closely analysing texts in order to fully reconstruct the ideological itinerary of the literary work had a deep impact on Italian scholarship. Other major critical steps were the translation of Ferdinand De Saussure's 1916 *Treatise of General Linguistics*, the circulation of the works of Roman Jakobson on the importance of the phono-symbolic structures of a text, the spread of works by other prominent structuralists such as Juri Lotman and, finally, the reception of new ideas coming from other disciplines such as anthropology and psychoanalysis, in particular the works of Lévi-Strauss and of

Lacan. All these new (at least for Italy) critical assumptions and information on how to read literary texts generated a genuine and strong interest in new methods and theories such as structuralism and **semiotics**. Scholarly attention began to switch more and more from an ideological and contextual approach to methods which would focus on the relationship between the phonetic and the semantic structures of literary texts aimed at identifying their own special linguistic code. It is not a coincidence that some of the most innovative scholars who introduced structuralism and semiotics to Italy and who actually proposed an original school of Italian structuralism were also well versed in philological studies. Cesare **Segre**, Maria **Corti** (co-editors of a seminal work on the subject, *I metodi attuali della critica in Italia* (The Current Critical Methods in Italy), 1970), D'Arco Silvio Avalle and Dante Isella are the four founders of the journal *Strumenti critici* (see **literary journals**), devoted mainly to studies of a semiotic nature. Amongst the many scholars who have, in different ways, pursued a semiotic and structuralistic approach are Stefano **Agosti**, Marcello Pagnini and the linguist Gian Luigi Beccaria. The continued and vital presence in the Italian academic world and in the Italian publishing industry of Umberto **Eco**, one of the major thinkers in contemporary semiotics as a critical means of literary and artistic interpretation, has been of fundamental importance in the growth of the discipline.

In recent years, in part because of the fading or the rethinking of philosophical currents developed in the last decades, such as Derrida's deconstructionism or **Vattimo**'s *pensiero debole* (weak thought), and also as a result of the rediscovery of literary theories such as that of Bakhtin's 'dialogism', there has been a more controlled meditation on some of the new scholarly theories. Especially with the development of interdisciplinary studies which have changed previous conceptions regarding entire cultural periods (for example, the intensification of studies on the relationship between literature and art during the Renaissance or the relationship between cinema and literature) and of cultural studies themselves (gender, ethnic, popular culture and so on), scholars have felt the need to confront literary texts with more open and flexible critical tools. In a few noticeable cases, some critical tendencies have pointed to new roads which combine the phonosemantic and phonosymbolic values of a text with more traditional sociological and philological approaches. The contact between deep textual analysis and the recuperation of the aesthetic world expressed by the author allows for a more thorough definition and interpretation of literary works. In this direction, we can recall the works of Ezio **Raimondi** whose critical tendency falls somewhere between a sociological, an anthropological and a symbolic approach. Raimondi, moving from the perspective that literary works' special linguistic codes are part of the rhetorical universe, opens his scholarship to the most modern and varied critical experiences continuously rediscussing them in his publications. Other active scholars whose works, in these last few years, tend to combine textual analysis with either anthropological or sociological methods more suitable for exploring various topics across a number of disciplines and cultures are Remo **Ceserani**, Carlo **Ossola**, Giulio **Ferroni**, Paolo **Valesio**, Mario Lavagetto, Andrea Battistini and Bruno Basile.

One should note the fundamental distinction between the critical currents as proposed by academic scholarship and those promoted directly by the authors themselves and expressed through articles and essays in specific literary journals or debates. Since the early years of **neorealism**, the idea of literature propounded by most authors and most scholars did not always coincide (one could think of the polemic between Muscetta's idea of realism on one side and **Pratolini**'s and Salinari's on the other). There were even moments in which a specific literary movement openly proposed critical theories which differed from any of the preceding scholarly tendencies. This was the case, for instance, with the neoavantgarde period, when young writers such as **Arbasino**, **Porta**, **Balestrini** and others, exploiting the critical methodology proposed a few years earlier by Luciano **Anceschi**, sustained a critical current which minimized the difference between the creative act and its critical interpretation. Many authors, on the other hand, were and are also successful and highly influential scholars (and vice versa, one famous example being Umberto Eco), and have often directed the cultural debate of their times toward an idea of literature which in their minds corresponded to a specific critical theory or current. Witness, for example, the decisive effect on the theoretical currents of the time of **Pasolini**'s 1950s writings in favour of expressiveness in literature or, on the other side, of Mario **Luzi**'s essays in defence of the existential current which was under attack precisely because of the position of more realistic writers like Pasolini himself. It is no mere coincidence that their intellectual debate in the 1950s solicited, on the one hand, major critical regard for expressiveness and realistic style different from the neorealistic one, and on the other, more hermeneutic attention for the existential and lyrical quest proposed by the former hermetic poets (see **poetry**).

One last and final consideration would be the inevitable relationship between cultural trends (and therefore critical currents), and the social, political and economic situation of the country. It is fair to say that Italian culture has shown that the critical currents which prevail are usually those more compatible with the social and cultural status of the nation. It is not by chance, for instance, that the importance of the once prevailing sociological current has substantially diminished during the last two decades, during which Italy has slowly but steadily blossomed to the status of an economic power in the West.

See also: literary journals; narrative

Further reading

Cecchi, O. and Ghidetti, E. (eds) (1983) *Sette modi di fare critica* (Seven Ways of Conducting Criticism), Rome: Editori Riuniti (a reconstruction, in the form of review articles written by different scholars, of various critical approaches and debates; includes a bibliographical guide).

Corti, M. (1978) *An Introduction to Literary Semiotics*, Bloomington, IN: Indiana University Press.

Corti, M. and Segre, C. (eds) (1980) *I metodi attuali della critica in Italia* (Present Critical Methods in Italy), Turino: ERI (a landmark volume, published originally in 1970, subdivided into a number of sections, each devoted to a specific critical current – sociological, symbolic, psycho-analytic, stylistic, philological, formalistic, structuralistic, semiotic – introduced by a specialist, and followed by selected readings).

Lucente, G. (ed.) (1996) *Italian Criticism: Literature and Culture*, Ann Arbor, MI: Michigan Romance Studies.

Segre, C. (1988) *Introduction to the Analysis of the Literary Text*, trans. J. Meddemen, Bloomington, IN: Indiana University Press.

ANDREA CICCARELLI

Croce, Benedetto

b. 25 February 1866, Pescassèroli, Abruzzo; d. 20 November 1952, Naples

Philosopher, historian and literary critic

From the 1960s until recent years, Croce's reputation was in eclipse and his philosophical and critical methodology often maligned. Yet for the entire first half of the twentieth century, Croce had been the most important and most imposing presence in many aspects of Italian life and culture. An eclectic philosopher in the tradition of Western idealism who developed and articulated his own highly individual system, Croce was also a wide-ranging historian and an erudite literary scholar whose approach to literature influenced several generations of writers and literary critics.

In public life, Croce was made a senator in 1910, and was Minister for Education in 1920–21 in the last pre-Fascist government of the so-called 'Giolitti era'. As a public intellectual, he took his distance equally from the universities, the Catholic church, and a post-Enlightenment 'liberal humanism' in so far as this could be considered part of any system of received ideas. Following the murder of socialist deputy Giacomo Matteotti in May 1925, however, Croce abandoned the studied neutrality he had observed towards fascism as both doctrine and regime, and issued a counter-manifesto to Giovanni Gentile's 'Fascist(ic) Intellectuals' Manifesto', thus taking on the mantle of leader of the anti-fascist intellectuals, a role he continued to play until the end of the war.

As a scholar and a researcher, he cultivated the solitary demeanour that he so admired in the eighteenth-century thinker Giambattista Vico. Enabled by independent means, he founded the influential journal *La Critica* (1903–44) which was to remain a touchstone of Italian cultural life for four decades. He was antithetical alike to D'Annunzio's debased romanticism, to the inherent irrationalism of Marinetti's futurism, and to the prevalent positivism, whose attempt to apply the methodologies of the natural sciences to human affairs in their historical reality he believed to be mistaken.

Historicism was Croce's alternative to both the positivism of science and the irrationalism of religion. Conceived as the 'science of history', historicism was a guarantee of certain knowledge, though of a different kind from that yielded by the 'hard' natural sciences, and on an equal footing with its 'consort', philosophy. Significantly, Croce was, together with another equally anti-positivist thinker, Antonio Labriola (1843–1904), one of first Italian intellectuals to make use of the writings of Karl Marx, even if Croce was never a Marxist.

Croce's presence in Italian culture for almost five decades has meant that his influence and importance have been matters for debate. Some, like Norberto **Bobbio**, acknowledge Croce's example and influence in terms of **anti-fascism**, but believe his thought is to be identified more with a method or an 'approach' than with any systematic doctrine. Literary critics such as Giorgio Bárberi Squarotti, however, suggest that Croce's ahistorical theory of the 'lyric' wellspring of art did Italian culture more harm than good by preventing any understanding of literary modernity. Some have further argued that, in insisting that the practice of historiography is 'by its very nature' liberal, Croce had put fascism outside history and therefore beyond explanation or understanding, a dangerous position for any historian. And yet, Croce's famous statements in *History as the Story of Liberty* (1938) that 'all history is contemporary history', and that 'universal histories are always particular histories', continue to have epigraphic value for historians of widely differing schools.

Croce has also sometimes been assimilated to a resurgent culture of the Right in the 1970s, a co-option perhaps affirmed in more recent years by the reissue of fourteen of Croce's books by **Adelphi**, a publisher considered to have cultural affiliations to the right wing in Italy. Croce's works have also been reissued in recent times by his original publisher, Laterza, many of them in new editions, while since 1989 the publisher Bibliopolis has been issuing the national critical edition of Croce's voluminous and varied works.

Further reading

Roberts, D.D. (1987) *Benedetto Croce and the Uses of Historicism*, Berkeley, CA: University of California Press.

SUZANNE KIERNAN

Cucchi, Enzo

b. 20 September 1949, Morro d'Alba, Ancona

Artist

During the 1970s Cucchi experimented with conceptual art, although by 1980 he was working in a figurative, neo-expressionist style and being identified with the new **transavantgarde**. Since then his themes have broadened: roosters have made way for other birds and animals, human heads, arms, and feet, skulls, landscapes and townscapes. Critics profess to see a dialogue with nature in his imagery, an ethical concern to return a sense of meaning to things, and an apocalyptic vision. Cucchi has himself described light, or flame, as the central element in painting, and indeed used a flame in his *Untitled–Roma* (1990).

Cucchi now works in many media. He has produced bronze fountains, frescoes, mosaics and marble reliefs, artist's books, and innumerable small drawings. He has a penchant for innovative gallery installations, such as suspending works from steel wires like so much washing.

Further reading

Turner, J. (1993) 'Painting with Fire', *ARTnews* 92 (10): 96–9 (a summary of Cucchi's career).

MAX STAPLES

Cucchi, Maurizio

b. 20 September 1945, Milan

Poet and editor

Maurizio Cucchi lives in Milan and worked as editor of the prestigious series 'Quaderni della Fenice' at the Guanda publishing company house, before becoming editor at **Mondadori**. He published his first collection of poems, *Paradossalmente e con affanno* (Paradoxically and With Anguish), privately in 1970, and followed it with *Il disperso* (The Lost One) in 1976.

The great novelty of Cucchi's poetry lies in its continuous elaboration of a language in which speech reveals itself only in terms of a fragmented discourse. The reflective monologues of his poems are presented in their raw existence, as they actually occur in the quotidian, mechanical and meaningless activities of the day. Therefore, the thoughts of the subject are offered as they surface in the interstices between one daily activity and another. It is this sense of deranged relief that Cucchi's poetry depicts, leaving the impression of a natural, spontaneous process which reconciles the speaker and the reader with an otherwise 'dispersed' reality.

Further reading

Cucchi, M. (1993) *Poesia della fonte* (Poetry of the Fount), Milan: Mondadori.

ERNESTO LIVORNI

Cuccia, Enrico

b. 24 November 1907, Rome

Banker and financier

Born in Rome of Sicilian descent but adopting Milan as his real home, Cuccia is universally recognized as the undisputed grand master – some would say puppet-master – of Italian finance for the entire postwar period.

After an apprenticeship with the **Bank of Italy**, **IRI** and the **Banca Commerciale Italiana** in the 1930s and early 1940s, Cuccia created **Mediobanca** in 1946 and became its chairman. From then on, practically every major financial deal in Italy passed through the hands of Cuccia and Mediobanca which, though nominally a public credit institution set up to provide venture capital for industry and development, was ingeniously used by its chairman to safeguard the position of the big families in Italian capitalism – Agnelli and **Pirelli** first and foremost – thus effectively utilizing public money to strengthen the private sector (see also **Agnelli family**). Forced to resign formally as Mediobanca chairman when the institution was 'privatized' in 1988, Cuccia nevertheless engineered a way to stay on as 'honorary chairman' and continued to exercise an overwhelming influence.

An otherwise intensely secretive man who has always avoided the public spotlight, Cuccia's other declared interests are philosophy and mysticism and he is said to be a lover of James Joyce.

Further reading

McCarthy, P. (1995) *The Crisis of the Italian State: From the Origins of the Cold War to the Fall of Berlusconi and Beyond*, New York: St Martin's Press (see especially 'Enrico Cuccia: A Dirigist against the State', pp. 86–91).

GINO MOLITERNO

Cuore

Born in January 1989 as a weekly six-page comic supplement of *l'Unità*, *Cuore* (Heart) proved popular enough to be published as an independent satirical journal beginning in February 1991 under the direction of writer and journalist Michele Serra. Subtitled 'Settimanale di resistenza umana' (A Weekly of Human Resistance), it hosted the work of many cartoonists and collaborators of the earlier and more controversial comic insert of *l'Unità*, **Tango**, many of whom, like Vincino, had originally been part of the legendary **Il Male**. With much fuel for its satirical fire provided by the **Tangentopoli** revelations, the magazine, in its familiar green newspaper-size format, achieved sales of 140,000 in 1992 but by 1994 had fallen back to less than 80,000. As the political climate changed it continued to lose ground until, in 1997, with national sales at 30,000 and still falling, it was declared bankrupt. In 1998, under a new owner-publisher, an attempt was made to relaunch it, but initial results were far from promising and its future remains extremely doubtful.

GINO MOLITERNO

Curcio, Renato

b. 23 September 1941, Monterotondo

The only child of single mother from Apulia, Curcio was brought up in Piedmont (with the family of an uncle, who had been killed in the **Resistance**), Rome (where he was attracted to the cinema world of another uncle, Luigi **Zampa**), and Liguria (where his schooling was completed with a chemistry diploma). In 1963 he enrolled in the new sociology programme at Trento University, directed by **Alberoni**, and married fellow student Margherita Cagol in 1969. Joining the worker and **student movement** in Milan, Curcio and Cagol invented the **Red Brigades** in 1970. Arrested in 1974, Curcio escaped with help from Cagol (who was killed in 1975) but was recaptured in 1976. Publicly unrepentant, publishing texts that grew more baffling but less political (for example, *Wkhy* (1988)), he played out the years of **terrorism** and his accumulating prison sentences as 'leader' of the Red Brigades. After President **Cossiga**'s botched attempt to pardon him as a sign of national reconciliation, he was granted work release in 1993.

Further reading

Curcio, R. (1993) *A viso aperto* (Openly), Milan: Mondadori.

Franceschini, A. (1988) *Mara, Renato e io* (Mara, Renato and I), Milan: Mondadori (insider account of the Red Brigades by Curcio's closest associate.)

DAVID MOSS

cycling

Since the inception of the sport of bicycle racing, Italian athletes have numbered among the world's best. It is not uncommon during late winter and early spring to encounter professional teams out training on Italy's backroads. This visibility keeps the top athletes in close contact with their fans, and enthusiasm for the sport is consequently very high even at the recreational level. Big groups of amateur cyclists take to the roads, especially on the weekends, many equipped with the latest gear and riding elite bicycles often bearing the names of current or former champions. Due to the high quality of Italian products, the bicycle industry itself also flourishes and owning an Italian-made racing bicycle is the dream of every devoted rider.

The two most important road races held in Italy are the Giro d'Italia and the Milan–San Remo. The Milan–San Remo, held in mid-March, traditionally marks the start of the professional cycling season, and is one the longest single-day races.

Organized by *La Gazzetta dello Sport* (see **sports publications**), the Giro is a three-week tour of the peninsula. Held in a period when the other main sports are idle, the Giro enjoys the media's undivided attention. In addition to exhaustive reports in *La Gazzetta*, public and private television channels broadcast the race daily to an audience of millions. Italian fans crowd the roads where the Giro passes and paint the asphalt with messages of support for their favourite champions.

Cycling greats Gino **Bartali** and Fausto **Coppi** won the Giro d'Italia, the Milan–San Remo and the Tour de France several times each, despite the fact that both their professional cycling careers were temporarily interrupted by the Second World War. Bartali and Coppi were the protagonists of many a battle, often finishing first and second. The rivalry between these two athletes still divides Italy's cycling fans into two camps, 'bartaliani' and 'coppiani'.

In 1965, Felice Gimondi emerged to win the Tour de France in his first attempt. Gimondi, the World Champion in 1973, was the first Italian to win all three major tours (Spain, Italy and France), proving to be the best Italian rider of his generation.

In 1977, Francesco Moser became the sixth Italian to claim the World Championship. He followed with three consecutive victories in the Paris–Roubaix, 1978–80. However, Moser's golden year was 1984, when he won the Milan–San Remo and the Giro after having set two new marks for the Hour Record in Mexico City. After Moser, Italian world road champions include Giuseppe Saronni (1982), Moreno Argentin (1986), Maurizio Fondriest (1988) and Gianni Bugno, winner in 1991–2. Bugno, Italy's top rider of the early 1990s, also triumphed at the Milan–San Remo and at the Giro in 1990. Ivan Gotti won the Giro in 1997, followed by Marco Pantani in 1998. In 1998, Pantani also triumphed at the Tour de France, ending a thirty-three-year-long drought and becoming the first Italian rider to win both competitions in the same year since 1952. Pantani, who had to overcome two career-threatening injuries, has now emerged as the new front runner of Italian cycling

Women's cycling became popular only in the 1970s and 1980s (the first Tour de France and Olympic women's road race were held in 1984). Maria Canins took the second edition of the Tour in 1985 and repeated her success in 1986. In 1988, Canins won the first edition of the women's Giro d'Italia. In 1995, Fabiana Luperini won both the

Giro d'Italia and the Tour de France. At the Atlanta Olympic games in 1996, Paola Pezzo took the gold medal in the first women's mountain-bike Olympic race ever held, and Imelda Chiappa finished second in the road race. In the velodrome, Antonella Bellutti won the women's pursuit. In Atlanta, two other gold medals for cycling came from the velodrome: Alessandro Collinelli won the men's pursuit, and Silvio Martinello secured the men's individual points race, continuing an established winning tradition.

See also: Olympics

PAOLO VILLA

D

D'Alema, Massimo

b. 20 April 1949, Rome

Politician

D'Alema has spent all his life in left-wing politics. Coming from a communist family, he joined the Communist party's youth section, the FGCI, in 1963 and became its secretary in 1975. Elected a **PCI** Parliamentary deputy in 1987, he also edited the party daily, ***L'Unità***, between 1988 and 1990 and worked closely with then party secretary, Achille **Occhetto** in transforming the PCI into the **PDS**. Following Occhetto's resignation after the 1994 elections, D'Alema was elected party secretary. In the 1996 elections, the PDS was the largest party in the winning **Ulivo** coalition and D'Alema supported the **Prodi** government. He was elected president of the important Parliamentary Bicameral Commission for Constitutional Reform (see **constitution**) and re-confirmed as secretary of the PDS at its second Congress in February 1997. Ironically, when the Prodi government fell due to the desertion of Rifondazione Comunista (see **RC**) from the Ulivo Alliance in mid-1998, D'Alema had enough support to be appointed Prime Minister at the head of a centre–left government, thus becoming the first Italian Prime Minister who had begun his career as a communist.

Further reading

D'Alema, M. (1997) *La Sinistra nell'Italia che cambia* (The Left in a Changing Italy), Milan: Feltrinelli.

Gilbert, M. (1998) 'In Search of Normality: The Political Strategy of Massimo D'Alema', *Journal of Modern Italian Studies* 3 (3): 307–17.

JAMES WALSTON

Dalla, Lucio

b. 4 March 1943, Bologna

Singer-songwriter

One of Italy's foremost singer-songwriters (see *cantautori*), Dalla began his musical career in 1959, abandoning school in order to play clarinet with the Roma New Orleans Jazz Band. Encouraged by Gino Paoli, whom he met in 1963, Dalla started singing but was markedly unsuccessful until appearing at the **Sanremo Festival** in 1965. His first big hit, however, was '4 marzo '43' (4 March 1943), which became a best-selling single in 1971. In 1974 he struck up a fertile partnership with poet, Roberto **Roversi**, which resulted in three major albums and a more theatrical style of live performance with a greater commitment to social criticism.

Dalla's own songwriting talents first came to be fully recognized with the extremely popular 1977 album, *Com'è profondo il mare* (How Deep the Ocean Is), which effectively marked the beginning of his rise to superstardom. In the late 1970s, his popularity still steadily increasing, Dalla toured with Francesco De Gregori and soon set up his own record company, Pressing, of which he remains managing director. Continuing to tour extensively and to release best-selling albums in the late 1980s and 1990s, Dalla has also written musical scores for a number of films, the most recent being for **Antonioni**'s *Al di là delle nuvole* (Beyond the Clouds) (1996), for which he received a Golden Ribbon.

GINO MOLITERNO

Dalla Chiesa, Carlo Alberto

b. 27 September 1920, Saluzzo, Cuneo;
  d. 3 September 1982, Palermo

General of the Carabinieri

When Dalla Chiesa was posted to Palermo in May 1982, he was a symbol of the victory of the Italian State over the political **terrorism** of the previous decade. In 1977, with terrorist activity at its height, he had been appointed security co-ordinator for prisons and in 1978 overall co-ordinator of police forces against terrorism. In both high-profile jobs he had been largely successful, and his appointment to Palermo was clearly made in the hope that he would repeat his success, this time against the **mafia**. Having already commanded the *carabinieri* in Palermo between 1966–73 he now returned there as prefect although, curiously, without special powers of co-ordination. In an interview in August 1982 he implied that he did not have the full support of the government, and in September he was gunned down, together with his wife and bodyguard.

Parliament immediately passed a bill which introduced the crime of 'mafia association', and subsequent prefects were given powers of co-ordination. Nevertheless, disquiet over his death and suspicion regarding those responsible has continued, with one possible scenario shown in Giuseppe Ferrara's film *Cento giorni a Palermo* (100 days in Palermo) (1984).

Further reading

Arlacchi, P. *et al.* (1982) *Morte di un generale* (Death of a General), Milan: Mondadori.

JAMES WALSTON

Dallapiccola, Luigi

b. 3 February 1904, Pisino;
  d. 19 February 1975, Florence

Composer

A composer of high international standing, Dallapiccola is noted for his large volume of vocal works. After early schooling in Pisino, Dallapiccola moved to Florence and undertook studies at the Conservatorium Luigi Cherubini. He was appointed to the staff of that institution in 1934 and worked there until 1967, occasionally taking leave to lecture in the USA.

Dallapiccola's compositional style can best be described as serial or twelve-tone, although he is particularly renowned for the beauty of his vocal lines while working within a strict compositional style. His most notable compositions are his vocal works, which cover half a century and which include the memorable wartime work, *Canti di prigionia* (Prison Songs) (1938–41).

Further reading

Morris, M. (1996) *A Guide to 20th-Century Composers*, London: Methuen (contains a concise but informative guide to Dallapiccola and his work).

ANDREW SCHULTZ

Damiani, Damiano

b. 23 July 1922, Pordenone

Film director and actor

A versatile director who has worked in many genres in both cinema and television, Damiani studied painting at the Brera Fine Arts Academy in Milan before beginning his film career in 1946. While working as a scriptwriter and director's assistant he also made a large number of short documentaries before directing his first feature film, *Il rossetto* (The Lipstick), in 1960. His subsequent production varied greatly from literary adaptations such as **Moravia**'s *La noia* (The Empty Canvas) (1963) to **spaghetti westerns** like *Quien sabe?* (A Bullet for the General) (1967). After 1968, his films addressed more political and social themes such as high-level corruption and the problem of the mafia, although this did not prevent him from directing a sensational horror thriller like *Amityville II: The Possession* in the USA in 1982. In 1984 he wrote and directed *La piovra* (The Octopus), a popular television series on the mafia which became one of the great success stories of Italian television and continued for over a decade. In the mid-1990s he also worked as scene and costume designer for opera, and in 1997 received the Order of Merit of the Italian Republic.

GINO MOLITERNO

Dante Alighieri Society

The Dante Alighieri Society was founded in July 1889 with the aim of helping Italians outside Italy to maintain their Italian language and culture and thus preserve a sense of Italian identity (Article 1 of the Society's Constitution). Originally this took the modest form of Italian classes for intending migrants, but a greater awareness of the problems faced by migrants soon led to the founding of chapters in host countries from which to more effectively promote both retention of the language and the spread of Italian culture by the provision of funds, teaching materials, books and libraries.

The Society strove to maintain some independence under Fascism, but was inevitably associated with the regime and thus suffered a decline during the war years. After the war the Society went through a phase of renewed vigour, concentrating more on social support and cultural activities and minimising appeals to nationalism. Throughout the 1970s and 1980s, it sought greater co-ordination with other cultural associations abroad and in 1989, the year of its centenary, it was recognized officially by the Italian state as an integral part of its National Commission for the promotion of Italian Culture abroad.

GINO MOLITERNO

D'Arrigo, Stefano

b. 10 October 1919, Alì, Messina, Sicily;
d. 2 May 1992, Rome

Novelist and poet

Having previously produced only one volume of poetry, in 1958 D'Arrigo presented two chapters of a novel in progress in **il menabò**, the prestigious literary journal edited by **Vittorini** and **Calvino**. He received a warm critical response and subsequently spent the next fifteen years writing the massive novel which was finally published in 1975 under the title of *Horcynus Orca*. Although the work proved unequal to the extreme expectations generated by the massive publicity campaign just before its publication, it is a vast and complex fresco of human life and passion, dominated by the theme of the journey, a journey not only in space but also in time, in literature and in language. The writing is an intriguing amalgam of dialect, neologisms and archaisms woven through a narrative that combines contemporary references and mythological symbols. The journey as a literary and existential metaphor appears again in D'Arrigo' s subsequent fiction, *Cima delle nobildonne* (Highest of the Noblewomen) (1985), which is largely an interrogation of the mystery of creation that relies on the rich cosmogony provided by classical writings, Egyptian texts and above all by Ovid's *Metamorphoses* whose echoes resound constantly in D'Arrigo's tale of the surgical transformation of an effeminate boy into a young woman.

PAOLO BARTOLONI

DC

The Democrazia Cristiana (Christian Democrat) party ruled Italy, usually in coalition with other centre–left or centre–right parties, for nearly fifty years from June 1944 until April 1994, and held the prime ministership for nearly forty-two years. This Christian Democratic 'regime' was thus in power twice as long as the Fascists.

The DC created in 1943 by Alcide **De Gasperi** was largely a reconstruction of the Partito Popolare Italiano (Italian Popular Party), Italy's first 'Catholic' party founded in 1918 and dissolved by the Fascists in 1926. De Gasperi was the natural 'historic' leader of the DC and was supported by ex-*popolare* MPs in Milan and Rome. They were joined by younger groups with different priorities: the Guelfisti, the only Catholic anti-Fascist group to openly resist the Regime; Enrico **Mattei** and Catholic participants in the **Resistance**; the Dossettiani (see **Dossetti**), and leaders of the Catholic students' movement, **Andreotti**, Colombo and **Moro**.

Ideological diversity of the new party was matched by poor organizational structures so that the DC was heavily indebted to **Catholic Action** and the Church for its electoral successes in the 1940s. This was a mixed blessing for De Gasperi, who sought to escape the suffocating, authoritarian embrace of **Pius XII** by coalitions with small parties of the centre such as the Social Democrats (**PSDI**), the Republicans (**PRI**) and the Liberals (**PLI**).

Strong American support played an important role in the DC's victory in the Cold War setting of 1948, but within Italy the DC's electoral success was made possible by the support of women (60 per cent of their electorate), the southern middle and upper classes, and even of organized crime. Ironically, the DC's commitment to resolving the '**Southern Question**' through land reform and the institution of the **Cassa per il Mezzogiorno** (Southern Development Fund), alienated many of its newfound supporters, and by 1953 it was clear that the centrist coalition would lose the election. De Gasperi passed an electoral reform law, dubbed the 'swindle law' by its opponents, which gave two-thirds of the seats to the grouping of parties that won more than 50 per cent of the votes. It did not work; the DC and its allies lost 10 per cent of the vote compared to 1948 and De Gasperi resigned, dying in 1954.

The DC was never again to have an overall majority or an authoritative leader like De Gasperi. Amintore **Fanfani** sought to step into his shoes but failed, and the DC henceforth remained an uneasy and unstable alliance of faction leaders until its demise in 1994. Fanfani did, however, succeed in making the party independent of the financial support of the **Confindustria** (the Italian employers' organization) and the electoral support of the Church and **Catholic Action**, by extending the

clientelistic networks in the South (see **clientelism**), colonizing the huge state sector and creating a mass organizational base for the party.

Thereafter, the DC became an increasingly clientelistic and middle-class party and, as the effects of the **Second Vatican Council** and the secularization process induced by the '**economic miracle**' and American cultural influences made themselves felt from the 1960s onwards, the party's electoral centre of gravity steadily shifted from the heartlands of the Catholic sub-culture in northern and eastern Italy to the South and the islands. Shrewd tactical manoeuvring also helped the party and its allies to stay in power. In the early 1960s an '**opening to the Left**' brought the Socialist Party into the coalition, and in the mid-1970s a temporary ''historic compromise' with the Communists ensured stability despite a very serious terrorist threat (see **terrorism**).

Ironically, the fear of communism had always been the DC's major electoral card and, given Italy's geopolitical position, the DC was, as Aldo **Moro** – later to be abducted and killed by the **Red Brigades** – once put it, 'condemned' to govern. However, by the mid-1980s the DC's hold on power had become less secure. Under the dynamic Bettino **Craxi**, the Socialists had moved to take a bigger share of patronage and were playing a bigger role in government; indeed, in 1983 Craxi became prime minister. Due to an increasing dependence on clientelism and sometimes outright corruption, the DC regime was heading into decline. In the North, the Leagues developed into a mass protest movement against precisely these evils (see **Lega Nord**); in the South, the La Rete movement campaigned against the DC's links with organized crime (see **mafia**), and inside the DC itself, Mario Segni led the campaign to abolish the very proportional representation on which the *partitocrazia* (party dominance) was based (see **electoral systems**).

The 1992 general elections marked a turning point, with the DC winning only 29 per cent of the vote. The results demonstrated the growing weakness of the DC and of its regime, emboldening the judiciary to strike at the heart of corruption in government through the *Mani pulite* (Clean Hands) investigations. Beginning in Milan in the Spring of 1992, the *Tangentopoli* (literally,

'Bribesville') scandals soon engulfed politicians of all the governing parties, but especially the Socialists and DC, a crisis exacerbated by the indictment a year later of Giulio Andreotti, the longest-serving DC politician of all, on charges of collusion in mafia crime.

In 1991, Mino Martinazzoli (Party Secretary) and Rosa Russo Jervolino (President) had initiated an attempt to drastically reform the DC, but the 'Bribesville' scandals and defeats in the local elections of 1993 undermined these efforts. In January 1994, in an attempted break with the past, the party was 're-founded' as the **PPI** (Partito Popolare Italiano – Italian Popular Party), with the support of the Church, expressed in an open letter from the pope invoking the principle of the 'political unity of Catholics'. In spite of this, the move was unsuccessful; the party split and there was a 'diaspora' of Catholic politicians in every direction. Left-wing ex-DC MPs led by Pierre Carniti created a group of Cristiani Sociali (Social Christians) allied with the **PDS**, Publio Fiori and Antonio Selva joined the ex-neo-fascist Alleanza Nazionale (see **National Alliance**), another group formed the **CCD**, and only about 30 per cent of the former DC entered the **PPI**.

Further reading

Allum, P.A. (1994) '"From Two into One", The Faces of The Italian Christian Democratic Party', in M. Donovan (ed.), *Italy*, vol. 1, Aldershot: Ashgate.

Donovan, M. (1994) '*Democrazia Cristiana*: party of government', in D. Hanley (ed.), *Christian Democracy in Europe: A Comparative Perspective*, London: Pinter (probably the best short account of the 'DC phenomenon' in English).

Furlong, P. (1996) 'Political Catholicism and the Strange Death of the Christian Democrats', in S. Gundle and S. Parker (eds), *The New Italian Republic: From the Fall of the Berlin Wall to Berlusconi*, London: Routledge (a key text on the collapse of the DC and its 'regime').

Leonardi, R. and Wertman, F. (eds) (1989) *Christian Democracy in Italy: The Politics of Domination*, Basingstoke: Macmillan (a detailed analysis of the origins and development of the DC).

Pollard, J. (1996) 'Italy', in T. Buchanan and M. Conway (eds), *Political Catholicism in Italy, 1918–1968*, Oxford: Oxford University Press (a useful short history of the DC and its precursor the Partito Popolare, 1919–1926).

Scoppola, P. (1995) 'The Christian Democrats and the Political Crisis', *Modern Italy* 1 (1): 18–29 (an interesting overview of the history of the DC by a Catholic academic who was briefly one of its senators).

JOHN POLLARD

De Andrè, Fabrizio

b. 18 February 1940, Genoa;
d. 11 January 1999, Milan

Singer-songwriter

One of the most popular and highly-respected singer-songwriters of the first-generation (see **cantautori**), De Andrè abandoned a comfortable middle-class background and an almost-completed degree in Law in order to pursue a passion for music and poetry. Fascinated by anarchist thinkers like Bakunin, he also came to be influenced by the French *chansonnier* tradition and his lyrics often incorporated numerous poetic allusions ranging from medieval poets like Cecco Angiolieri and Francois Villon to moderns like Edgar Lee Masters.

Although he had already established a presence on the popular music scene with a number of singles in the late 1950s, De Andrè's success really began in 1968 when **Mina** recorded his charming fable, *La Canzone di Marinella* (Marinella's Song) and it became a runaway bestseller. The strong and genuine social commitment expressed in so many of his compositions aligned him quite naturally with the social protests of 1968 and he soon became one of the leading voices of the **student movement**. His popularity continued to increase throughout the 1970s during which time he produced many innovative albums whose songs were united by a central theme.

At the height of his success and following the birth of his second child he retired to live and work on a property he had bought in Sardinia. However in August 1979 he and his wife were kidnapped by a local gang and held for ransom for four months before being eventually released unharmed. Characteristically, the experience prompted no recriminations on his part but rather an album of songs about Sardinia and its problems. This was followed in 1984 by what many critics judged one of his very best albums, *Creuza de ma* (Muletrack by the Sea), composed and sung in the Genoese dialect.

After several years of relative silence in the early 1990s De Andrè returned to prominence in 1996 with *Anime Salve*, a bestselling album which again united the critics in praise. In the same year, together with Alessandro Gennari, he also co-authored a novel *Un destino ridicolo* (1996, A Ridiculous Destiny). He was still writing and performing and on the crest of popularity at the time of his untimely death in early 1999.

Further reading

Meacci, G., Di Roberto, M., Serafini, F. and Vendettuoli, G. (1994) 'Fabrizio De Andrè' in *La Lingua Cantata: L'Italiano nella canzone dagli anni Trenta ad oggi* (The Language of Song in Italy from the Thirties to Today), eds G. Borgna and L. Seriani, Rome: Garamond (an illuminating and detailed stylistic analysis of the poetic mechanisms of De Andrè's compositions).

GINO MOLITERNO

De Benedetti, Carlo

b. 14 November 1934, Turin

Entrepreneur and industrial manager

De Benedetti has always depicted himself as the only Italian practitioner of American-style capitalism. Since 1976, when he was ousted as managing director of **Fiat** after only three months in the position, his aggressiveness and proverbial immodesty have set him at odds with Cesare **Romiti**, and later with Enrico **Cuccia**, who became his fiercest enemy. As head of **Olivetti** from 1978 to 1996, De Benedetti boasts a few ephemeral successes but many strategic defeats. In 1981 he unwisely accepted becoming shareholder and vice-chairman of the Banco Ambrosiano, a private bank run by Roberto Calvi (a banker linked to the

mafia) only to withdraw with a considerable profit two months later, just before the bank's bankruptcy, thus provoking a trial and a loss of public prestige. Declaring himself averse to politics, he nonetheless used his close ties with the publishing group ***L'Espresso-La Repubblica*** to support Ciriaco **De Mita**, thereby attracting the enmity of Bettino **Craxi**. Even his ambition to win international stature for CIR (the mixed conglomerate he owns) faded after the failure of his hostile takeover bid for the Société Genérale de Belgique in 1988. A controversial performer as an entrepreneur, De Benedetti has nevertheless succeeded in assembling, dismantling and trading companies, thus demonstrating his capacities as a financial alchemist.

STEFANO BATTILOSSI

de Berardinis, Leo

b. 3 January 1940, Gioj, Salerno

Actor, playwright and director

Generally regarded as one of the protagonists of the 'new' generation of Italian neoavantgarde theatre, Leo de Berardinis forged a career based on radical and controversial adaptations of classic texts. In the 1960s he teamed up with Perla Peragallo, and throughout the 1970s worked on an experimental community theatre project involving amateur actors in a working-class town near Naples. In the mid-1980s he worked in Bologna with professional actors on an improvisational and collaborative approach to Shakespeare. He subsequently established his own company and continued the line of experimental exploration that characterized his entire career, using classical texts and improvisation to explore form and meaning in the theatre, both through collaborative projects with other actors and as a solo performer. His unswerving dedication to research into performance and its potential for self-knowledge mark him as an outstanding representative of the Italian theatre tradition of the actor–author–director.

See also: theatre directors

Further reading

De Marinis, M. (1991) 'From Shakespeare to Shakespeare: the Theatre Transcended', *New Theatre Quarterly* 7: 49–63 (an informative interview with Leo de Berardinis).

TIM FITZPATRICK

De Carlo, Andrea

b. 11 December 1952, Milan

Novelist, scriptwriter and director

After travelling in Australia and the United States and working as a waiter, musician, teacher and photographer, De Carlo devoted himself to literature and cinema. He published critically acclaimed novels, amongst them *Treno di panna* (Train of Cream) (1981) – prefaced by Italo **Calvino** and later made into a movie by the author himself – and also worked as assistant to Federico **Fellini** in the making of *E la nave va* (And the Ship Sails On) (1983). By employing a cinematic narrative technique to express his characters' perception of the surface of things, De Carlo represented Italian youth culture from the 1960s onwards, and its easy manipulation by the media. In later novels such as *Tecniche di seduzione* (Techniques of Seduction) (1991) and *Uto* (1995), there is an increasing interest in psychological themes and environmental issues to document both the individual and collective search for social and political identity.

FRANCESCA PARMEGGIANI

De Carlo, Giancarlo

b. 12 December 1919, Genoa

Architect, engineer and urban planner

Although De Carlo's libertarian socialism has undoubtedly limited his portfolio, his beliefs have never been compromised by fashion, as witness the consistent stance taken by his journal **Spazio e società** and his persistent support for his colleagues in Team X. Devoted to developing a place for regionalism within the modern movement, he voiced the need for building rehabilitation already in the 1950s, making this a major preoccupation of his programme at the International Laboratory of Architecture and Urban Design. Ideological dissentions caused his 'noisy' resignation from **Casabella** in 1956. De Carlo has had especially close ties with Urbino, having authored its master plan and having built extensively for the university. His Matteotti quarter in Terni, and later Mazzorbo housing complex near Venice are examples of the most successful architectural 'participatory democracies'. He taught at his alma mater, the **IUAV**, as well as at Genoa and in the USA.

Further reading

Zucchi, B. (1992) *Giancarlo De Carlo*, Oxford/Boston: Butterworth Architecture (a thorough presentation of De Carlo's credo and projects; includes an interview, biographic and bibliographic data and a translation of 'Architecture's Public' (1970)).

GORDANA KOSTICH

de Céspedes, Alba Carla Laurita

b. 11 March 1911, Rome; d. 14 November 1997, Paris

Writer

De Céspedes, who began her career as a journalist in the 1930s, became famous in 1938 with *Nessuno torna indietro* (There is No Turning Back). The book, like her following novels *Dalla parte di lei* (The Best of Husbands) (1949), *Quaderno proibito* (The Secret) (1952) and *Il rimorso* (Remorse) (1963), was translated into twenty languages. In German-occupied Italy, de Céspedes crossed the lines into Allied territory to collaborate with the Bari partizan Radio under the pseudonym of Clorinda, and later founded *Mercurio*, the first cultural review to be published in Italy after the war. She was the first woman to be elected President of the International Council for Literary Authors (CISAC) and among the first authors to highlight women's difficult path to economic, legal and intellectual independence.

Further reading

Carroli, P. (1993) *Esperienza e narrazione nella scrittura di Alba de Céspedes* (Levels of Experience and Narrative Form in the Writings of Alba de Céspedes), Ravenna: Longo (a comprehensive survey of the author's narrative works).

PIERA CARROLI

de Chirico, Giorgio

b. 10 July 1888, Volos, Greece;
d. 20 November 1978, Rome

Painter

Born in Greece to Italian parents, de Chirico succeeded, throughout a long and varied career, in proving himself possibly the most influential Italian artist of the twentieth century. His reputation was established by his *pittura metafisica* (metaphysical painting) of 1910–18, depictions of mannequins and threatening shadows in modern city squares. Unlike most of his contemporaries, who were moving toward abstraction, de Chirico continued to use figurative elements, combining them in striking ways which drew attention to the mystery of being. His interest in heightened perceptions and a reality which lies beyond physical objects made him a crucial model for the surrealists.

Critical and commercial consensus is that de Chirico then suffered a very long period of decline, when he repeated, plagiarized and even faked his own works. At the same time he took legal action against art museums which owned earlier versions of his work, claiming that these apparently genuine examples were forgeries. In his 'Baroque' style, which lasted from the 1930s into the 1960s, there is much evidence of the brushstroke, tacky mock-heroic references to mythology, and extensive white highlighting, giving an overall feeling of kitsch. Nevertheless, his works from the Fascist period and later inspired the **transavantgarde**, who saw his rather idealized realism as a bridge between traditional and contemporary art. His all-over style, with attention to the spaces as well as objects, his simple modelling and his use of black outlines reappear in their work.

In the 1960s and 1970s de Chirico returned to the smoother brushwork and bizarre juxtaposition of elements of his metaphysical style. *The Return of Ulysses* (1968), for example, shows an effete hero paddling a small dinghy across his living room floor.

De Chirico's most timeless feature is irony, amply manifested, for example, in his 1950 advertisement for the **Fiat** 1400, which displays the car in classical grandeur with a young god leading a prancing Pegasus. The god is gesturing towards the Fiat as if pointing out its virtues to his steed, perhaps even suggesting that the automobile will eventually supplant him. More generally in de Chirico's work, there is an implied irony in the perspective used to construct pictorial space, which is intentionally 'not quite right'. De Chirico anticipates that, to an eye attuned to Renaissance art, such proportions will cause unease and discomfort.

De Chirico's eclecticism and his taste for pastiche and the recycling of styles put him completely at odds with the modernist notion of the avantgarde in vogue at mid-century, but it was precisely these elements that made him the outstanding precursor of postmodernity.

Further reading

Calvesi, M. and Ursino, M. (1996) *De Chirico: The New Metaphysics*, trans. M. Eaton and F. Lutz, Rome: Edizioni De Luca/Craftsman House (concentrates on the later work from the 1960s and 1970s, with colour illustrations).

Far, I. (1968) *De Chirico*, trans. J. Bernstein, New York: H.N. Abrams (substantial illustrations but basic and uncritical text, by the artist's wife).

Lista, G. (1991) *De Chirico*, trans. E. Crockett, Paris: Hazan (small format; deals intelligently with philosophical underpinnings of works; illustrated).

MAX STAPLES

De Felice, Renzo

b. 8 April 1929, Rieti; d. 25 May 1996, Rome

Historian

Renzo De Felice's early academic career as a Marx-inspired historian of late eighteenth-century Italian revolutionaries offered few hints of the furore he would provoke when he turned his prodigious research and publication energies to the apparently sympathetic study of fascism. The appearance of each volume of his *magnum opus*, an eight-volume biography of Mussolini inaugurated in 1965 and still unfinished thirty years later, became the occasion for controversy far beyond university halls. Political opponents accused him of making Mussolini a progressive figure, inventing a mass consensus for his regime and diminishing the value of the **Resistance**; fellow historians deplored his lack of methodological rigour, conceptual clarity and interpretative perspective. De Felice retorted that it was time to jettison the ideological straitjacket inhibiting the serious study of fascism and that his conclusions were directly based on the vast array of hitherto unknown documents he had unearthed. The bitter dispute was fuelled by often provocative interviews given in the years of **terrorism**, when any threat to the historical and moral distinctions between fascism and anti-fascism had immediate political reverberations. Beyond the polemics, the significance of De Felice's work seems more likely to rest on his accumulation of the documentary evidence necessary to assess fascism than on his interpretations of the details he uncovered.

See also: historiography

Further reading

De Felice, R. (1977) *Interpretations of Fascism*, trans. B.H. Everett, Cambridge, MA: Harvard University Press.

Gentile, E. (1997) 'Renzo De Felice: A Tribute', *Journal of Contemporary History* 32 (2): 139–51 (contains details of his major publications, interviews and historiographical credo).

DAVID MOSS

De Filippo, Eduardo

b. 24 May 1900, Naples; d. 31 October 1984, Rome

Actor, playwright and poet

The son of actor and playwright Eduardo Scarpetta and Luisa De Filippo, Eduardo (as he came to be affectionately known by public and critics alike) devoted his entire life to the theatre, which he regarded as the most powerful means to represent the plight of the humble individual in a rapidly changing society. Through a large number of plays, which he wrote, acted and directed for theatre, film and television, Eduardo left his stamp on Italian culture as one of the greatest playwrights and actors in Italian twentieth-century theatre.

Eduardo began his theatrical apprenticeship as a child, being assigned a small role in a play by Scarpetta in 1906, and soon became a seasoned performer. While continuing to perform and direct in theatre productions, he also wrote short sketches, among them his first successful one-act play *Sik-Sik, l'artefice magico* (Sik-Sik, The Magician) (1929). In 1931 he founded the theatre company Teatro Umoristico De Filippo with his brother Peppino and his sister Titina, mainly proposing a comic repertoire which combined the farcical characters and vital dialect of the Neapolitan tradition with Luigi Pirandello's bourgeois drama.

From the 1940s onwards Eduardo wrote and staged his most famous plays, including *Napoli milionaria!* (Millionaire Naples) (1945), *Ouesti fantasmi* (Oh, These Ghosts!) (1946), *Filumena Marturano* (1946), *Le voci di dentro* (The Inner Voices) (1948), *Il sindaco del Rione Sanità* (The Local Authority) (1960), *Gli esami non finiscono mai* (Exams Never End) (1973) which were later collected in the three-volume *Cantata dei giorni dispari* (Cantata of the Odd Days) (1979). Eduardo's intense acting, a unique combination of comic verve and dramatic expressiveness, his ability to charm any audience, earned him an enthusiastic appreciation both in Italy and abroad. In recognition of his artistic achievements, the University of Birmingham (1977) and the University of Rome (1980) awarded him honorary degrees. In Rome he started a drama school and in 1981 was appointed senator for life by President **Pertini**. Physically frail in the 1980s, he nevertheless continued to teach and to perform until a few months before his death.

Although mostly set in Naples, Eduardo's plays cross local boundaries to become emblematic of the human condition. In his drama, he represents the individual's despair when forcefully confronted with reality. The characters' charming *candore* (innocence), their anachronistic attachment to noble sentiments and old family values, their obliviousness to the greed for richness characterising the world they live in, provoke the audience to hearty laughter which soon turns into the bitter acknowledgement of a tragic human defeat.

Further reading

Barsotti, A. (1992) *Introduzione a Eduardo* (Introduction to Eduardo), Rome-Bari: Laterza.

Ciolli, M. (1993) *The Theatre of Eduardo De Filippo*, New York: Vantage.

Di Franco, F. (1984) *Le commedie di Eduardo* (Eduardo's Plays), Rome-Bari: Laterza (an introductory study of De Filippo's theatre providing brief analyses of all his plays).

Giammusso, M. (1994) *Eduardo: da Napoli al mondo* (Eduardo: From Naples to the World), Milan: Mondadori (a comprehensive survey of all De Filippo's work, richly illustrated, with details of all the plays, a filmography and a list of shows and performances abroad).

FRANCESCA PARMEGGIANI

De Gasperi, Alcide

b. 3 April 1881, Pieve Tesino, Trento;
   d. August 1954, Sella Valsugana

Politician and prime minister

Born in the Trentino region, part of the Austro-Hungarian Empire until 1919, De Gasperi served in the Vienna Parliament as a Christian Social MP from 1911 to 1919, a fact used against him by the fascists in the early 1920s. After 1919 he became a prominent member of the Partito Popolare, succeeding Don Luigi **Sturzo** as leader in 1923. Following the forced dissolution of the PPI in 1926, he tried to escape Italy but was caught; he was eventually released on a Vatican guarantee of his good behaviour.

In 1943, De Gasperi set about rebuilding a Catholic party but the newly-formed **DC** was more than a mere reconstitution of the PPI, as it came to include younger elements from the neo-Guelf movement, members of the **Resistance** and **Catholic Action** organizations. Furthermore, from the very beginning De Gasperi faced strong opposition from the left wing of the party led by **Dossetti** and La Pira. Nevertheless, in December 1945, De Gasperi became prime minister.

For the next three years, De Gasperi successfully steered the party through difficult terrain. During the referendum on the monarchy in 1946, he wisely insisted on DC neutrality. In early 1947 he managed to gain approval from even the communists in the **Constituent Assembly** for the inclusion in the new Republican **constitution** of Article 7 which confirmed the 1929 Lateran Pacts between the Church and Fascism (see **church, state and society**). Later in the same year he succeeded in expelling the **PCI** and **PSI** from the government and in the general elections of April 1948, the first under the new constitution, he led the DC to an overwhelming victory against the Left. In the following years he continued to follow a political middle way, seeking to minimize the influence of **Vatican** by retaining coalitions with small centre parties, despite the DC's absolute majority. In 1952, however, he only narrowly escaped Vatican pressure to enter into an alliance with neo-fascists in the Rome local elections.

De Gasperi's achievements during the longest premiership in postwar Italian history were considerable. He presided over the postwar political settlement and Italy's economic reconstruction, in the latter case with the assistance of Luigi Einaudi. Aided by Carlo Sforza, he also had considerable foreign policy successes. He brought Italy out of the diplomatic isolation caused by the disasters of the Fascist period. The establishment of an understanding with the USA meant a mitigation of the original terms of the Peace Treaty of 1947, and eventually saved **Trieste** from falling into the hands of Tito's Yugoslavia. In 1949 Italy was firmly aligned with the West by means of entry into NATO, and De Gasperi had helped lay the foundations of Italy's participation in European integration.

Nevertheless, his critics have argued that his failures were also considerable. Under his leadership, the DC failed to carry out the deep economic and social reforms which Italy needed or to implement much of the 1948 constitution. He also failed to develop the DC into a mass, organized political party. In 1953 the DC and its allies lost heavily, and De Gasperi was unable to form a new government. He died a year later.

Further reading

Ginsborg, P. (1990) *A History of Contemporary Italy: Society and Politics 1943–1988*, London: Penguin (chaps 3, 4 and 5).

Scoppola, P. (1977) *La proposta politica di De Gasperi* (The Political Proposal of De Gasperi), Bologna: Il Mulino (a comprehensive analysis of De Gasperi's historical role).

JOHN POLLARD

De Maria, Nicola

b. 6 September 1954, Foglianise, Campania

Painter

Born in Southern Italy, De Maria has lived and worked in Turin since the age of twelve. He participated in his first group exhibition in 1973 (Turin, Galleria Il Punto). In 1975 he had his first one-man show (in Naples and Genoa), and in the 1980s he was associated with the *Transavanguardia* group. His paintings, on canvas, paper and velvet, are extremely colourful and lyrical, incorporating symbolic writing that enhances their poetic effect. Some are highly abstracted (for example, *Song of Heavenly Sea*, 1990), while others are more obviously figurative but imbued with a strong metaphorical significance (such as the *Slaughter-House Poetry*, 1980–1). Although much of his work is small-scale, he was also asked to decorate whole rooms of the Kaiser Wilhelm Museum in Krefeld (1983), and the Castello Rivoli in Turin (1985) where some of his paintings were hung.

Further reading

Bonito Oliva, A. (1982) *Transavantgarde International*, Milan: Giancarlo Politi (especially pp. 94–8).

De Maria, N. (1992) *Musica del mare* (Music of the Sea), introduction by G. Raillard, Paris: Gal. Lelong (exhibition catalogue representative of his later work).

OLIVIA DAWSON

De Martino, Ernesto

b. 1908, Naples; d. 1965, Rome

Ethnologist

Ernesto De Martino's scholarly enterprise spanned the fields of philosophy, folklore, history and anthropology. Although De Martino was a member of Benedetto **Croce**'s intellectual circle, he was also influenced by Heidegger, Hegel, Marx and **Gramsci**. These influences prompted him to contest Croce's ideas by attempting to historicize cultures that Croce considered to be 'without history'. Anti-fascist and socialist tendencies oriented his postwar work, but rather than ascribing a progressive role to popular culture, he maintained that the popular culture of Italy's subaltern classes led, through superstition and mystification, to their unwitting participation in their own exploitation. His studies of ritual mourning, the evil eye, and tarantism reflect this perspective, but they also critically analyse the dominant culture's misunderstandings of these phenomena. His work continues to influence both discussions of the **Southern Question** and studies of Italian popular culture.

Further reading

Saunders, G. (1993) 'Critical Ethnocentrism and the Ethnology of Ernesto De Martino', *American Anthropologist* 95 (4): 875–93 (an analysis of De Martino's contribution to anthropology).

THOMAS KELSO

De Martino, Francesco

b. 31 May 1907, Naples

Politician

A classical scholar and author of works on the Roman constitution and economy, De Martino fought in the **Resistance** with the **Partito d'Azione** (Action Party). After the war he joined the **PSI** (Italian Socialist party), rose to its national leadership and served as general secretary for much of the period from 1964 to 1976. Deputy-President of the **Council of Ministers** in **DC**–PSI governments from 1970 to 1972, he subsequently adopted a more pro-communist stance, promoting **PCI**–PSI alliances in local and regional councils after gains by both parties at administrative elections in 1975. He also favoured the left-wing alternative at national level, where the PCI however preferred its **historic compromise** with the DC. De Martino instigated a government crisis in 1976, which led to a general election at which the PCI's vote increased greatly while the PSI's remained unchanged. He was then ousted from the PSI leadership by Bettino **Craxi**, who set the party definitively on a course of competition with the PCI. After a long career as an elected member, De Martino was appointed a life senator in 1991.

Further reading

Zavoli, S. (1998) *De Martino: Intervista sulla sinistra italiana* (Interview on the Italian Left), Bari: Laterza.

CLAIRE KENNEDY

De Mita, Ciriaco

b. 2 February 1928, Nusco, Avellino

Politician

A Catholic university graduate, De Mita joined the **DC** in 1950. He became a deputy in 1963, serving both as a minister and then briefly, in 1988–9, as prime minister, although his career in the party was more important. A member of the faction which had favoured the **opening to the Left** in the early

1960s, he became party vice-secretary in 1969 but failed in his attempt to facilitate political reform by encouraging recognition of the **PCI** as a legitimate opposition. As party secretary from 1982–9, he again sought vainly to legitimize the PCI while personally countering **Craxi**'s bid to turn the **PSI** into the DC's principal competitor. Although partially successful in modernizing the party's management of the state, he was nevertheless unable to end the oligarchic clientelism of his party. Himself a southern notable, with Avellino as something of a personal fiefdom, he returned to **Parliament** in 1996 via a stand-down arrangement with the **Ulivo** (Olive Tree). Thus, despite his exclusion from Parliament in 1994–6, he again became influential in the **PPI**.

MARK DONOVAN

De Santis, Giuseppe

b. 11 February 1917, Fondi; d. 19 June 1997, Sant'Ivo

Film critic and director

Now generally acknowledged as one of the 'fathers' of **neorealism**, De Santis studied at the **Centro Sperimentale di Cinematografia** in the late 1930s and, together with **Visconti** and **Antonioni**, was one of the militant critics writing for the journal *Cinema* who advocated a greater sense of realism in Italian films. In 1942 he helped write and direct the film regarded as the landmark of neorealism, Visconti's *Ossessione*. His first feature film, *Caccia Tragica* (Tragic Hunt) (1946), was critically well-received but his next film, *Riso Amaro* (Bitter Rice) (1948), although hugely successful at the box office – it was even nominated for an Oscar – was almost unanimously and ferociously attacked, especially by left-wing critics, for mingling social criticism and eroticism. De Santis succeeded in making several other films during the 1950s and early 1960s, but continued to be ostracized and, in spite of many scripts and projects, was unable to make any major film after his *Italiani brava gente* (Good People the Italians) in 1964. Somewhat belatedly, in 1995 he was awarded a Golden Lion at Venice for his career in cinema.

GINO MOLITERNO

De Santis, Pasqualino

b. 24 April 1927, Fondi; d. 23 June 1996, Rome

Cinematographer

Younger brother of the **neorealist** film-maker Giuseppe **De Santis**, Pasqualino De Santis started his career as the assistant of Piero Portalupi in the 1950s. In the 1960s he became the assistant of Gianni **Di Venanzo**, one of Italy's most eminent cinematographers. The tragedy of Di Venanzo's death in 1966 led De Santis to take over his mentor's position for Mankiewicz's *The Honey Pot* and thus pursue his career as a full-fledged cinematographer.

De Santis's uniform talent for both improvisation and stylization made him as equipped for the polished sophistication of Luchino **Visconti**'s films (*La caduta degli Dei* (The Damned), 1969, amongst others), the stark realism of Robert Bresson (*Lancelot du Lac*, 1974), or hand-held camerawork as in **Rosi**'s *Il caso Mattei* (The Mattei Affair) (1972). De Santis is especially famous for his lasting collaboration with Rosi, for whom he photographed almost a dozen films. De Santis died while working on Rosi's 1996 film, *La Tregua* (The Truce).

DOROTHÉE BONNIGAL.

De Seta, Vittorio

b. 15 October 1923, Palermo

Film-maker

In spite of making only a very limited number of films, De Seta is widely regarded as one of the best Italian documentary film-makers of the postwar period. Born into an aristocratic Sicilian family, he studied architecture in Rome before turning to cinema. After a brief apprenticeship as assistant director to J-P. Le Chanois on *Le village magique* (1954), he made nine short but impressive docu-

mentaries between 1954 and 1960, all depicting harsh aspects of life in Sicily and Sardinia and all written, produced, directed and photographed by himself. His first feature film, *Banditi a Orgosolo* (Bandits at Orgosolo), explored the phenomenon of Sardinian banditry by using genuine Sardinian shepherds to play the roles and received wide acclaim when it was shown at the Venice Film Festival in 1961. After only two more films in the 1960s, *Un uomo a metà* (Half a Man) (1966) and *L'invitata* (The Guest) (1969), in the 1970s De Seta made several documentaries for the RAI, the best known being his *Diario di un maestro* (A Teacher's Diary) in 1973.

GINO MOLITERNO

De Sica, Vittorio

b. 7 July 1901, Sora; d. 13 November 1974, Neuilly-sur-Seine, France

Actor and film director

Born into a very poor family in Southern Italy, De Sica grew up in Naples. He began acting on the stage when he was still a teenager, and by 1918 had appeared in his first film. However, it was his starring role in **Camerini**'s *Gli uomini, che mascalzoni!* (Men! What Scoundrels!) (1932) that transformed him into Italy's most popular matinee idol of the 1930s. In these early 'white telephone' films he generally played the role of the *bravo ragazzo* (nice guy), and was thus immensely popular with female audiences.

In his long career he acted in over one hundred films, often using the proceeds to finance his own productions. The first films he directed were mostly adaptations of stage plays but his fourth, *I bambini ci guardano* (The Children Are Watching Us) (1942), was to be the key to his postwar films. The film uses a child's perspective on an adult adulterous affair to elicit a sentimental response from its viewers and, in directing it, De Sica teamed up with screenwriter Cesare **Zavattini** in a partnership that would be the most significant of his career. With Zavattini as scriptwriter, general assistant and often uncredited co-director, De Sica went on after the war to make a series of films which would define the neorealist canon: *Sciuscià* (Shoeshine) (1946), *Ladri di biciclette* (Bicycle Thieves) (1948), *Miracolo a Milano* (Miracle in Milan) (1951) and *Umberto D* (1952). Each of these films dealt with a particular social problem (crime, unemployment, homelessness) using the vehicle of a powerfully emotive personalized story. However, despite being hailed by film critics like Andrè Bazin as a cinematic masterpiece, *Umberto D* was a box office failure and is now often regarded as the last great neorealist film.

De Sica had already been wooed by Hollywood when David O. Selznick had offered to produce *Bicycle Thieves* if Cary Grant would be allowed to play the leading role. On that occasion De Sica refused, but eventually in 1953 he succumbed and moved to Hollywood to make *Stazioni termini* (released as *Indiscretions of an American Wife*), which showcased Selznick's wife Jennifer Jones in the main role. De Sica turned out eight films for the lucrative American market in the 1960s, of which *Ieri, oggi, domani* (Yesterday, Today and Tomorrow) (1963) and *Matrimonio all'italiana* (Marriage Italian Style) (1964), both starring Sophia **Loren** and Marcello **Mastroianni**, are by far the best.

De Sica also continued to act for other directors. He appeared in Luigi **Comencini**'s extremely successful *Pane, amore e fantasia* (Bread, Love and Dreams) (1953), and gave a striking performance in Roberto **Rossellini**'s *Il generale Della Rovere* (General Della Rovere) (1959). After his lacklustre commercial films of the 1960s (the so-called 'rose-tinted comedies'), De Sica returned in the early 1970s to a more committed style of film-making with *Il giardino dei Finzi-Contini* (The Garden of the Finzi Contini) (1970), adapted from the novel by Giorgio **Bassani** and dealing with the incarceration of Italian Jews during the Second World War. This last film succeeded in creating a renewed interest in his work as a film-maker.

Further reading

Daretta, J. (1983) *Vittorio De Sica: A Guide to References and Resources*, Boston: Hall and Co. (a comprehensive guide to materials on De Sica which includes a compact biography and list of films).

Pecori, F. (1980) *Vittorio De Sica*, Florence: La Nuova Italia (a history of De Sica as director

with analyses of individual films and a full filmography).

LAURENCE SIMMONS

Debenedetti, Giacomo

b. 25 June 1901, Biella; d. 20 January 1967, Rome

Literary critic and essayist

After formative years spent under the influence of **Croce**'s philosophy, Debenedetti became attracted by psychoanalysis, sociology, phenomenology and anthropology. As a result, his critical approach betrayed a wide range of interests that could not be restricted to a single methodology and his analysis of authors was based to a large extent on his own personal experience. He founded the literary journal *Primo tempo* and worked for several Italian cultural magazines. During Fascism, due to his Jewish origins, he was forced to work as a ghost-writer for numerous film scripts. He also wrote several books on the Second World War experience such as *Otto ebrei* (Eight Jews) (1944) and *16 Ottobre 1943* (October 16, 1943) (1944). Most of his critical works were collected under the title *Saggi critici* (Critical Essays) and published in three different series. Many other important works were published posthumously, amongst them *Il romanzo del Novecento* (The Twentieth Century Novel) (1971), *Poesia italiana del Novecento* (Twentieth Century Italian Poetry) (1974) and *Pascoli: la 'rivoluzione inconsapevole'* (Pascoli: the Unconscious Revolution) (1979).

ANDREA RICCI

Del Giudice, Daniele

b. 11 January 1949, Rome

Writer

Part of the 'new generation' of Italian novelists and regarded by many critics as the heir to Italo **Calvino**, Del Giudice's prose is characterized by measure, control and meticulous description, using very precise and often scientific language. Several of his novels and short stories confirm a fascination with flying and aircraft. His first novel, *Lo stadio di Wimbledon* (Wimbledon Stadium) (1983), recounts a young writer's attempt to piece together the life of a mysterious literary figure long dead whilst his second, *Atlante occidentale* (translated as *Lines of Light*, 1985) deals with the opposition between science and literature. *Nel museo di Reims* (In the Reims Museum) (1988), a text accompanied by the paintings of Nereo Rotelli, examines themes of vision whereby its central character, who is losing his sight, has a young woman describe to him the paintings in a museum he visits. *Staccando l'ombra da terra* (Takeoff) (1994) contains a series of pieces on the theme of flying and *Mania* (1997) continues this format of thematically connected stories with six pieces on the themes of violence and war.

LAURENCE SIMMONS

Del Monte, Peter

b. 29 July 1943, San Francisco, California

Film director

Peter Del Monte stands out among the film-makers of his generation as an auteur of cinema made of feelings and emotions, removed from realism. Del Monte grew up between the United States and Italy, where he graduated in literature from the University of Rome in 1965. In 1969 he received his diploma from the **Centro Sperimentale di Cinematografia** by presenting the short film *Fuori campo* (Off Screen) which defined his style and his interest in exploring characters' psychology. After working for television for several years, he entered the film industry in 1975 with *Irene, Irene*, which confirmed his preference for a non-realistic, almost abstract, cinema. He became more widely known with *Piso Pisello* in 1981 and *Giulia e Giulia* (Julia and Julia) in 1987, the first high-definition feature-length film. In 1990 Del Monte produced the fourteen-episode film *Tracce di vita amorosa* (Traces of Love Life), followed in 1995 by *Compagna di viaggio* (Travel Companion).

ANTONELLA FRANCINI

Della Volpe, Galvano

b. 24 September 1895, Imola; d. 13 July 1968, Rome

Philosopher

Professor of the History of Philosophy at the University of Messina and the most influential postwar Italian Marxist philosopher, Della Volpe was formed within the neo-idealist tradition associated with Giovanni Gentile and Benedetto **Croce**, but soon rejected their idealist position in *Critica dei principi logici* (Critique of Logical Principles) (1942). He joined the **PCI** (Italian Communist Party) in 1944, and in the immediate postwar years explored the relationship between Marxism and the work of Hegel, culminating in his first major Marxist work, *Logica come scienza positiva* (Logic as Positive Science) (1950). Della Volpe helped form a generation of younger Marxist philosophers, of whom the best-known is Lucio **Colletti**. His most widely-read work, *Rousseau e Marx e altri saggi di critica materialistica* (Rousseau and Marx and Other Essays on Materialist Criticism) (1957) traces the two strands of modern democracy – civil liberty and social liberty – back to their eighteenth-century origins. Della Volpe then argues that only the 'socialist legality' of communism can provide an effective historical synthesis of these two traditions. Nevertheless, Della Volpe's most influential book remains a work of aesthetic theory. In *Critica del gusto* (Critique of Taste) (1960) he attempts to develop a 'rational poetics' by demonstrating that conceptual meaning cannot be separated from aesthetic effect.

Further reading

Fraser, J. (1977) *An Introduction to the Thought of Galvano della Volpe*, London: Lawrence & Wishart.

LAURENCE SIMMONS

Delli Colli, Tonino

b. 20 November 1923, Rome

Cinematographer

With over seventy feature films to his credit, Tonino Delli Colli is one of Italy's most prominent and versatile cinematographers. His eclectic talents, combining a taste for classical simplicity with a sophisticated and innovative approach, especially served the cinema of Pier Paolo **Pasolini**. As early as Pasolini's first two films, *Accattone* (1961) and *Mamma Roma* (1962), Delli Colli wholeheartedly embarked upon Pasolini's aesthetic project, agreeing to subvert the rules of photography so as to show the sacred side of gritty realities or, conversely, to recall the human scope of myths and religions, as *Il Vangelo secondo Matteo* (The Gospel According to Saint Matthew) (1964) best epitomizes.

Delli Colli also collaborated with many other major European film-makers: Mario **Monicelli** and Dino **Risi** with whom he made many comedies, Louis Malle (*Lacombe Lucien*, 1974), Sergio **Leone** (*C'era una volta in America* (Once Upon a Time in America), 1969), Federico **Fellini** (on the director's last three films), Marco **Ferreri** (*Storie di ordinaria follia* (Tales of Ordinary Madness), 1983, and *Il futuro è donna* (The Future is Woman), 1984) and Polanski (*Lune de Fiel*, 1992 and *Death and the Maiden* 1994).

DOROTHÉE BONNIGAL.

Democrazia Proletaria

Democrazia Proletaria (Proletarian Democracy) was an umbrella organization formed by a variety of small parties and organizations to the left of the Communist Party in order to contest the national elections of 1976. In spite of what had originally appeared to be a groundswell of popular support for its various component groups, the organization itself failed to draw votes away from the **PCI** and only polled 1.5 per cent of the vote. In the wake of this defeat, several of the organizations left and some, like Lotta Continua (Continuous Struggle; see **extraparliamentary Left**) actually dissolved. The DP nevertheless continued, as a deeply divided and rather mixed party, to contest national elections in subsequent years but never achieved more than 1.7 per cent of the vote. In June 1991, after **Rifondazione Comunista** (Communist Refoundation) split from the newly formed **PDS**, Democrazia Proletaria decided to dissolve itself and merge with Rifondazione which, ironically, was carrying on staunchly the old traditions of the very PCI which Democrazia Proletaria had been founded to oppose.

GINO MOLITERNO

D'Eramo, Luce

b. 17 June 1925, Rheims, France

Novelist and essayist

The daughter of an officer of the Fascist party, D'Eramo grew up in Paris and moved with her family to Italy in 1939. After the fall of Mussolini, she decided to investigate first-hand revelations of Nazi atrocities. She went to Germany in 1944, worked in a factory in Frankfurt and joined Todt, an organization created to bring foreign workers to Germany. During this period, she also volunteered to work in the concentration camp at Dachau. However, after discovering the reality of Nazi atrocities, she escaped to Magonza. While assisting bombing victims there, she suffered wounds that left her permanently paralysed. She returned to Rome in 1945, and earned degrees in Italian literature, history and philosophy. Her early publications were the collections of essays *Raskolinov e il marxismo* (Raskolinov and Marxism), *L'opera di Ignazio Silone* (The Works of Ignazio Silone) (1971) and *Cruciverba politico* (Political Crossword Puzzle) (1974). In her fictional narratives, D'Eramo explores political themes and focuses on the marginalized. Among these are *Deviazione* (Deviation) (1979), an autobiographical account of her experiences in Germany, and *Nucleo zero* (Zero Nucleus) (1980), one of the first novels to deal with Italian terrorism.

VIRGINIA PICCHIETTI

design education

Given the reputation of Italian design in the international arena it is perhaps surprising that, unlike Great Britain and a number of other countries, Italy did not until fairly recently have a very extensive design educational system. There is no equivalent in Italy of Germany's 'Bauhaus' or 'Hochschule fur Gestaltung' at Ulm, or of Great Britain's Royal College of Art, schools which have produced leading designers for industry through this century. Most of Italy's designers were trained as architects, many of them graduating, in the interwar years and beyond, from the polytechnics of Milan and Turin where they were trained in the tenets of European modernism.

Many of the anti-design protagonists of the 1960s – members of **Superstudio** and **Archizoom** among them – received their education in the architectural department at the University of Florence where, among others, Adolfo **Natalini** was a key teacher of those years. Michele de Lucchi was among the many to emerge from this hothouse, bringing his background to Milan when he moved there in the 1970s. Architecture provided then, and to a great extent still provides, the pedagogic framework for Italian industrial designers, allowing them to move freely across objects and media.

The first school to concentrate on training designers, the Domus Academy, was established in Milan in 1982 by Maria Grazia Mazzochi, Valerio Castelli and Alessandro Guerriero (the last having also been the force behind the radical **Studio Alchimia** which had been in operation since 1979). Andrea **Branzi**, a leading member of Studio Alchimia, was appointed as the first director of the Academy and he instantly made it a landmark within international design education.

A private institution, Domus Academy attracts young designers from around the world and invites them to Milan, the design centre of Europe. It provides a postgraduate education for these young people in what it calls the 'New Design', in which the emphasis falls less upon the finished object than on the experiential process of designing. In the 1980s, Branzi encouraged the students to concentrate on the sensorial qualities of design. With the assistance of Clino Trini Castelli, who had been working since the early 1970s on what he called the 'reactive

surface', and Massimo Morozzi, who worked in the area of 'soft design', the school encouraged a move away from formalism towards a more appropriate design for the late twentieth century.

Much of a student's time at the Domus Academy is spent studying the context within which design fits, from its socioeconomic to its technological framework. Ezio Manzini has also played an important role there as a teacher, developing new projects with plastics and formulating his ideas about 'semantic pollution'. Other teachers have included Carlo Alfonso, Valerio Castelli, Michele de Lucchi, Gian Franco Ferre, Alberta Meda, Francesco Morace, Gianni Pettena, Daniela Puppa and Pierre Restany. More recently, possibilities for design education have expanded in Italy, and the Polytechnic of Milan now offers a course in **industrial design** as well as architecture.

See also: anti-design; interior design

Further reading

Branzi, A. (1984) *The Hot-House: Italian New Wave Design*, London: Thames and Hudson.

PENNY SPARKE

detective fiction

Detective fiction is also known as *giallo* (yellow), from the yellow covers of the **Mondadori** series that launched the genre in Italy in 1929, importing the classics – from Edgar Wallace and Robert Louis Stevenson to Agatha Christie and Rex Stout – and creating a readership for this genre of popular literature.

The first Italian *giallo*, *Il settebello* (The Seven of Diamonds) by Alessandro Varaldo, appeared in 1931 and introduced the first Italian detective, Police Commissioner Ascanio Bonichi, a down-to-earth character from the countryside who solved his cases by chance rather than by using Holmesian scientific rigour. Other prewar detective writers included Alessandro De Stefani, Giorgio Spini and Ezio D'Arrico (creator of an Italian version of Simenon's Maigret, Commissioner Emilio Richard). Augusto De Angelis provided the Italian tradition with a complex and well-defined character in Commissioner De Vincenzi: educated and pessimistic, he carried out his investigations utilizing psychological analysis.

In the late 1930s the Fascist Ministry of Popular Culture banned detective fiction, and it was only after the war that the genre once again became widely diffused. The classic detective novel, based on detection, continued to have a readership but the model of the American hard-boiled school, which focused on chasing and capturing the criminal in a metropolitan jungle where the investigator uses the same methods as the criminal, became more popular. Franco Enna and Sergio Donati were two authors of the period who imitated this model. A series of authentic and original Italian detective novels were published by Giorgio Scerbanenco between 1966 and 1969. Novels such as *Venere privata* (Private Venus), *Traditori di tutti* (Traitors of Everybody) and *I ragazzi del massacro* (The Guys of the Massacre) used a successful recipe, mixing features of the classic detective genre with those of the hard-boiled school and the sentimental novel. The protagonist, Duca Lamberti, who works in a sadistically violent Milan, is a tough cynic like some of Hammett's or Chandler's characters, but the impossibility of changing the surrounding moral squalor infuriates rather than saddens him. A physician struck off the register and jailed for three years for practising euthanasia, he has no ethical attachment to his job but feels sorry for himself and for innocent victims, and passionately hates all 'criminals', who for him include homosexuals, prostitutes, drug addicts, women who undergo abortion, *capelloni* (hippies with long hair), corrupt lawyers and exploiters of all kinds. His job is not to re-educate them but to punish them violently and to expose the details of their horrible crimes. His Manichaean moralism appealed to an urban middle-class readership which, in the late 1960s, was demanding law and order. However, the author added other main characters who came from the society's lower ranks, thus expanding his readership.

Scerbanenco's success has not been repeated in the history of the Italian detective novel in its true form. In 1972, Carlo Fruttero and Franco Lucentini published *La donna della domenica* (The Sunday Woman), a bestseller which, while remaining within the convention of a classic detective novel, included references to many other literary genres, thus becoming a detective novel of manners. The technique of mixing genres and quoting other books has been fully explored by Umberto **Eco** in his 1980 international bestseller *Il nome della rosa* (The Name of the Rose), a genuinely postmodern combination of medieval whodunnit, gothic novel, allegory and *roman-à-clè*.

Italian detective stories by such writers as Massimo Felisatti, Fabio Pittorru, Loriano Macchiavelli, Nicoletta Bellotti, Luciano Anselmi, Laura Grimaldi and Luciano Secchi have continued to find a popular audience, and in the late 1990s the novels of Giuseppe Ferrandino and Andrea Camilleri have become bestsellers. Detective fiction has also had its high-brow authors, in particular Carlo Emilio **Gadda** and Leonardo **Sciascia**. Gadda's *Quer pasticciaccio brutto de Via Merulana* (That Ugly Mess in Merulana Street) is an experimental avantgarde text of 1946 which uses the detective genre brilliantly in order to explore language in a way that has drawn frequent comparison with James Joyce. In Sciascia's *Il giorno della civetta* (The Day of the Owl) (1961) and *A ciascuno il suo* (To Each His Own) (1966), we also find an original utilization of the traditional structures of detective fiction for the purposes of social commentary.

Further reading

Carloni, M. (1985) 'Storia e geografia di un genere letterario: il romanzo poliziesco italiano contemporaneo' (History and Geography of a Literary Genre: The Contemporary Italian Detective Novel), *Critica letteraria* 13 (46): 167–87 (a useful history of the genre with interesting exploration of the relationship between the novels and their setting).

FRANCO MANAI

Di Pietro, Antonio

b. 2 October 1950, Montenero di Bisaccia, Campobasso

Magistrate

A relatively unknown magistrate, Antonio Di

Pietro found himself thrown abruptly into the limelight on 17 February 1992 with the arrest of Mario Chiesa, the first move in the anti-corruption drive codenamed **Mani pulite** (Clean Hands). Thereafter Di Pietro's name was inextricably linked to the campaign whose aim was to dismantle the system of public corruption, subsequently nicknamed **Tangentopoli** (Bribesville), and which contributed significantly to the fall of the First **Republic**.

Born into a peasant family in the Southern region of Molise, Di Pietro emigrated as a young man to Germany to find work. In 1974 he enrolled in the Law Faculty in Milan, graduating in 1979. His first employment was with the **police** force, and only in 1981 was he taken on as magistrate in Bergamo. The experience was not a happy one. He was dismissed as 'unfit to undertake the work of a magistrate', and reinstated only after appeals to the Supreme Council of the Magistracy.

In 1986 he transferred to Milan and began working with a pool of magistrates who became convinced of the existence of a widespread network of corruption linking the worlds of business and politics. Di Pietro's adroit use of computer technology enabled him to track what he suspected were illegal payments, until a complaint against Mario Chiesa, who was employed by a philanthropic trust but was closely involved with the Milanese Socialist Party, gave him the opportunity he needed. Chiesa was caught red-handed, and after a period of imprisonment provided information which incriminated other public officials and politicians.

Subsequent suspects were equally willing to talk. Di Pietro revealed himself a relentless interrogator, but he attracted criticism in some quarters for his willingness to use preventive detention as a means of persuading suspects to collaborate. Investigations widened out from Milan, and it came to seem that the entire system of government which had ruled Italy since the war was on trial. Local and national politicians, cabinet ministers, civil servants, financiers and businessmen found themselves under investigation for giving or receiving bribes. The Socialist leader and ex-Prime Minister, Bettino **Craxi**, was probably the most celebrated casualty, while the televised trial of the financier Sergio Cusani in 1993–4 revealed to the nation both the forensic skills of Di Pietro and the sheer scale of the political–financial intrigue involved. Silvio **Berlusconi**, the first Prime Minister of the supposed 'new' order, was also incriminated over the activities of his industrial empire, **Fininvest**.

Di Pietro was now lionized by ordinary Italians, but was increasingly vilified by the Berlusconi press and embroiled in the machinations of his many enemies. He resigned from the magistracy in 1994 in mysterious circumstances, amid allegations that he had been blackmailed. Having expressed interest in a political career, he was courted by several parties. His own political allegiances, although unclear, seemed to lie with the Right, but perhaps because the right-wing coalition was headed by Berlusconi, from whom he was divided by deep personal antipathy, he refused all Rightist affiliations and in May 1996 accepted Romano Prodi's invitation to become Minister for Public Works in his centre–left cabinet. His period in office was undistinguished, and he resigned in November of the same year when under inquiry by Brescia magistrates for alleged receipt of illegal payments. He was completely exonerated, and in November 1997 was elected to the Senate as a member of the Olive Tree coalition (see **Ulivo**).

See also: legal system

JOSEPH FARRELL

Di Venanzo, Gianni

b. 18 December 1920, Teramo;
d. 3 January 1966, Rome

Cinematographer

At the time of his premature death at the age of forty-five, Di Venanzo was widely regarded as Italy's leading cinematographer. After serving as a young camera assistant under Otello Martelli and G.R. Aldo on many of the classic neorealist films, including Visconti's *La Terra Trema* (The Earth Trembles) (1948) and Rossellini's *Paisà* (Paisan) (1946), he became director of photography for **Lizzani**'s *Achtung! Banditi!* (Halt! Bandits!) (1951). He subsequently worked on over forty films with most of the major Italian directors including **Monicelli**, **Fellini**, **Comencini** and Lina **Wert-**

müller. He developed a particularly strong partnership with **Antonioni**, for whom he photographed all of the early films with the exception of *L'avventura* (The Adventure) (1960), and with Francesco **Rosi**, with whom he made all the films up to and including *Le mani sulla città* (Hands over the City) (1963). An innovative and creative photographer, he experimented with lighting and pioneered new techniques, thereby developing a distinctive personal style which was nevertheless flexible enough to serve both the austerity of Antonioni's *La notte* (The Night) (1961) and the sumptuousness of Fellini's *8½*.

See also: cinematographers

GINO MOLITERNO

Diabolik

A comic book series first appearing in 1962, *Diabolik* was created by Angela and Luciana Giussani, who modelled their stories on those of the criminal hero of French popular literature, **Fantomas**, and added a touch of romance. Each episode presents the thief, Diabolik, dressed in a black catsuit and assuming different disguises, performing the most sensational and atrocious crimes, with no other aim than self-affirmation. He always escapes the implacable pursuit of his almost as ingenious nemesis, Police Commissioner Ginko, through his exceptional intelligence, audacity and the indispensable help of his lover Eva Kant. Diabolik's victims come from the aristocracy and upper middle classes, and are shown as evildoers who hide their own crimes behind their false morality and respectability.

In direct contrast to the American superheroes who put their powers in the service of the law, Diabolik appealed to a transgressive and anti-conformist teenage and adult readership. Its format was also attractive, pocket-size like **Topolino** (Mickey Mouse), while its cover carried the label 'For adults only'. Its drawings were suggestive in black and white, and its narrative was easy to read. Diabolik's great success generated the phenomenon of the *fumetto nero* (crime comic), but it also survived the demise of the latter by adapting to change in public taste while remaining fundamentally faithful to its original formula.

See also: comics

FRANCO MANAI

dialect usage

Dialects are widely used in Italy. While the percentage of dialect monolinguals is very low (around 7 per cent), and that of Italian monolinguals is somewhat higher (around 30 per cent), the vast majority of Italians are bilingual and alternate the use of both languages in a complex and interesting way. Dialects are used more within the home than outside, more in informal situations than in formal ones, and more in the northeast area, the South and the islands than in the northwest and the centre of Italy. Older people use them more than younger people, and men more than women; younger interlocutors, in particular children, elicit minimal use of dialect, whereas maximal use occurs in addressing older people. Furthermore, dialects are used more (1) among the lower classes; (2) by people with lower levels of education but also, interestingly, by graduates more than by people with high school diplomas; (3) in rural areas; and (4) in smaller towns, particularly those with less than 2,000 inhabitants. Besides everyday communication, they are used in other areas such as music and literature.

Use of dialects has been decreasing considerably since the Second World War as a result of the spreading of the **Italian language**, and this may raise the question of their disappearance in the near future. However, although dialects enjoy a lower prestige than Italian, they are still a vital part of the repertoire of Italians, and today it is not so much a matter of disappearance as of transformation, as the dialects increasingly become more similar to Italian.

The changes that have occurred in dialect use at the national level were particularly rapid in the decades 1950–90, concurrent with the rapid social and economic transformations of postwar Italy. However, throughout the 1990s the decrease in dialect usage seems to have slowed down. In 1951 more than 60 per cent of the Italian population still

used only dialect in most circumstances. Subsequent changes in use have been recorded by a
series of surveys conducted by Doxa, a public
opinion poll research institute. These surveys
included questions on language use inside and
outside the home environment (with friends and
work mates). Table 1 shows that use of dialect (1) is
constantly higher within the home than outside; (2)
is higher among older people, men and in the
northeast, the South and the islands, within the
home but more markedly so outside; and (3) has

constantly decreased from 1974 to 1991 while
increasing slightly outside the home throughout the
1990s.

Table 2 shows the incidence of the interlocutor's
age. Minimal use of dialect occurs in talking to
children, and the more so by young speakers,
whereas maximal use occurs in addressing older
people, the more so by speakers of the same age or
older.

Table 3 shows that, although the use of Italian
only is on the increase, in the Doxa surveys more

Table 1 Use of dialect in Italy according to age, gender and geographical area (Doxa surveys)

	1974	1982	1988	1991	1996[1]
	At home				
Total Italy	51.3%	46.7%	39.6%	35.9%	33.9%
age					
up to 34 yrs	46.0%	37.9%	31.2%	28.6%	24.7%
35–54 yrs	46.7%	46.7%	32.7%	32.9%	27.9%
beyond 54 yrs	64.0%	58.1%	57.1%	48.4%	48.0%
gender					
women	49.3%	47.4%	36.2%	32.7%	31.9%
men	53.4%	46.0%	43.4%	39.4%	35.9%
geogr. area					
Northwest	39.0%	37.2%	25.0%	20.2%	18.6%
Northeast	61.3%	59.6%	50.5%	51.0%	47.5%
Centre	33.2%	24.7%	24.1%	22.0%	24.0%
South & Islands	66.8%	60.6%	53.7%	48.5%	44.2%
	Outside the home[2]				
Total Italy	42.3%	36.1%	33.2%	22.8%	28.2%
age					
up to 34 yrs	31.4%	23.8%	22.3%	11.6%	18.0%
35–54 yrs	42.1%	37.5%	32.1%	24.6%	31.0%
beyond 54 yrs	55.7%	50.3%	48.7%	35.4%	53.0%
gender					
women	40.3%	36.6%	29.0%	19.6%	25.6%
men	44.4%	35.6%	37.8%	26.3%	31.0%
geogr. area					
Northwest	34.8%	29.0%	19.2%	12.9%	20.9%
Northeast	55.2%	53.2%	51.0%	37.7%	38.9%
Centre	23.7%	14.7%	19.0%	12.2%	19.2%
South and Islands	52.2%	45.2%	42.2%	29.1%	33.2%

Notes:
1 For 1996, the percentages against the age brackets have been calculated by collapsing the six age brackets provided by
   Doxa.
2 These percentages include both the respondents who 'always use dialect' and those who 'use more dialect than Italian'.

Table 2 Use of dialect outside the home in Italy, 1996 (Doxa survey)

| subjects | interlocutors | | | |
	children	younger	same age	older
15–24 years	6.8%	13.1%	17.3%	20.7%
25–34 years	5.6%	9.3%	12.7%	21.9%
35–44 years	10.5%	14.1%	21.2%	29.9%
45–54 years	10.9%	19.6%	32.6%	39.6%
55–64 years	18.6%	26.6%	45.5%	49.2%
beyond 64 years	21.4%	31.6%	58.7%	60.7%

Table 3 Use of dialect and Italian in Italy (Doxa Survey)

| | Language use at home | | | | |
	1974	1982	1988	1991	1996
Dialect with all family members	51.3%	46.7%	39.6%	35.9%	33.9%
Italian with all family members	25.0%	29.4%	34.4%	33.6%	33.7%
Dialect with some, Italian with others	23.7%	23.9%	26.0%	30.5%	32.4%

| | Language use outside the home | | | | |
	1974	1982	1988	1991	1996
Always uses dialect	28.9%	23.0%	23.3%	12.8%	15.3%
Always uses Italian	22.7%	26.7%	31.0%	29.9%	32.6%
Uses both Italian and dialect	22.1%	22.0%	19.5%	29.1%	22.2%
Uses more dialect than Italian	13.4%	13.1%	9.9%	10.0%	12.9%
Uses more Italian than dialect	12.9%	15.2%	16.3%	18.2%	17.0%

than one quarter of the subjects within the home and more than half outside still declare they use both the dialect and Italian.

The division in the use of dialect and Italian is not clearcut, as the shift away from dialect has been occurring not so much in the direction of the exclusive use of Italian, but more commonly of the alternate use of the two languages also within conversation. The alternation of dialect and Italian in conversation, or 'code switching', has not yet been researched extensively. It seems however that it occurs more in rural areas than in urban ones, and more frequently and in a wider range of social situations in some regions (for example, Veneto and Sicily) than in others. Patterns of switching also seem to vary, as in rural areas it tends to be from a dialect base into Italian, whereas in urban areas it is often limited to the insertion of dialect words in Italian-based discourse. The latter is more evident in the speech of younger generations and may be due to their inadequate competence of dialect.

Switching between dialect and Italian can also be connected to situational factors, among which interlocutor and topic tend to play a prominent role. Typically, interlocutors belonging to the same network and more personal topics elicit switches towards dialect. However, asymmetrical conversations, where one participant uses dialect and the other Italian, are also very frequent. Switching can also be linked to (1) the organization of discourse, for example to reformulate, to add a side comment or to signal a quotation; (2) the speaker's language preferences or competence; or (3) specific conversational functions, such as switches to dialect for special emphasis, for expressive or emotive reasons, or jokingly. However, the frequent bi-directionality of switching indicates that often it is the contrastive use of the two languages to be meaningful, rather than the single switch into either language. Furthermore, dialect–Italian switching generally occurs in a smooth way, without any signalling to the interlocutor. This has been attributed to the fact that, since in Italy speaker and interlocutor belong to the same bilingual community, they do not need to negotiate the linguistic rules of their behaviour.

As extensively used in everyday conversation as switching is dialect–Italian mixing, where forms from each language alternate within the same utterance in an often inextricable way: for example, *None quedda. Sta ancora questa. Sai ce d-è? quiddu magglione bianco, quiddu grande che comprai io* (Sobrero 1988) ('Not that one. There is still this one. You know what is it? That white jumper, the big one that I bought' (my translation)). This excerpt shows mixing between dialect and regional Italian, with dialect affecting Italian in terms of sounds, grammar and word choice. Mixing is favoured by the structural similarity between dialects and Italian and by the reciprocal interference caused by their intense contact, whereby dialect forms become Italianized and Italian forms take on dialectal features. For example, words can be made up by lexical morphemes of one language and grammatical morphemes of the other, so that it can be difficult to assign them to either language: for example, Sicilian *appizzare* with the Sicilian meaning of *perdere*, 'to miss out', and the Italian verbal ending -*are*. Due to the structural similarity, the occurrence of mixed words and the high number of homophones, dialect–Italian switching and mixing tend to occur freely without any structural restriction.

Another area where dialect is used is in literature. Interestingly, after the Second World War, poetry in dialect has developed considerably, possibly as a reaction against the levelling of the Italian language, and is particularly thriving in some regions like the Veneto, with such poets as Noventa and **Zanzotto**. On the other hand, the general decline of dialects in Italian society seems to have determined also their decline in narrative, where today they have a rather marginal role. However, many contemporary writers still make use of some dialect in their works, particularly at the lexical and syntactic levels (for example, Mastronardi or **Sciascia**).

Dialect is not much used in the cinema, probably because it would not be understood by the wider audience. However, Italian–dialect mixing is fairly common, and has become the distinctive speech style of some actors, such as the Neapolitan of Massimo **Troisi** or the Florentine of Roberto **Benigni**. Some dialect is used in advertising, often to link the product to past ages and thus underline its high quality. Dialect is also used in music, by groups that perform traditional folk songs, for example **Nuova Compagnia di Canto Popolare**, as well as by other singers or songwriters. A more recent phenomenon is the formation of rock bands that choose to sing in dialect, such as Pitura Freska in the Veneto or the 99 Posse in Naples (see **rap music**).

Dialects are also used outside of Italy, for example in some parts of Switzerland (Lombard) or of Corsica (Tuscan), and in the numerous communities of Italian migrants. The secessionist movements such as **Lega Nord** use dialect as a symbol of their struggle for autonomy, but they do not seem to have been particularly effective in reversing the shift away from dialect, particularly among the younger generations. The impact of these movements, however, has yet to be investigated systematically.

See also: *cantautori*; dialects; Italian language; Italian outside Italy; Italian and emigration; language attitudes; language education; language policy; literature in dialect; varieties of Italian

Further reading

Anonymous (1996) 'L'uso del dialetto' (The Use of Dialect), in *Bollettino della Doxa* 50 (16–17), 17 September.

Alfonzetti, G. (1992) *Il discorso bilingue. Italiano e dialetto a Catania*, (Bilingual Discourse: Italian and Dialect in Catania), Milan: Franco Angeli (a study of Italian–Sicilian code switching in a range of social situations; see chaps 2 and 3).

Giacalone Ramat, A. (1995) 'Code-Switching in the Context of Dialect/Standard Language Relations', in L. Milroy and P. Muysken (eds), *One Speaker, Two Languages: Cross-disciplinary Per-*

spectives on Code-switching, Cambridge: Cambridge University Press (an in-depth discussion of the issues raised by code switching in the light of the specific Italian situation).

Sobrero, A.A. (1988) 'Villages and Towns in Salento: The Way Code Switching Switches', in N. Dittmar and P. Schlobinski (eds), *The Socio-linguistics of Urban Vernaculars: Case Studies and Their Evaluation*, Berlin and New York: de Gruyter.

—— (1994) 'Code Switching in Dialectal Communities in Italy', *Rivista di Linguistica* 6 (1): 39–55 (an overview of the major sociolinguistic variables of Italian–dialect code switching).

ANTONIA RUBINO

dialects

Italian dialects are separate languages geographically distributed throughout the peninsula, which differ from each other to the extent of being mutually unintelligible if they belong to non-adjacent areas. The reason for such profound diversity is to be found initially in a different evolution of spoken Latin in the various parts of Italy during the Middle Ages, and in the following centuries of political fragmentation before final unification in 1861. In relation to the **Italian language** – the national language – today the dialects are 'low languages' in the sense that they are used mainly orally in a narrower geographical area (**dialect usage**). Although they are still very vital, in the last decades they have been undergoing a process of Italianization as a result of their intense contact with Italian and the latter's increasing use nationwide. Consequently, dialects are tending to become more uniform throughout their region or province as they are losing their more local features. At the same time, they also influence the way Italian is used in the various regions, particularly at the level of pronunciation and vocabulary (see **varieties of Italian**).

The formation of dialects dates from the last centuries of the Roman empire, when the central power started to decline and cultural and linguistic models began to weaken. The already existing difference between literary and spoken Latin increased remarkably, particularly when Italy was split into separate areas after the fall of the empire. Political autonomy favoured linguistic fragmentation, and thus many distinct languages developed. The first documents which prove the existence in Italy of languages significantly different from Latin date back to the end of the first millennium. From approximately the year 1000, these languages developed considerably, particularly as spoken languages but also in writing. Some of them were especially prestigious in that they were the languages of important and thriving towns, such as Milan, Bologna, Florence and Palermo, where the first literary works were also written.

This situation of polycentrism changed from the fourteenth century onwards as a result of the increasing importance of Florence as the major economic, political, cultural and literary centre. The fact that three eminent writers – Dante Alighieri, Francesco Petrarca (Petrarch) and Giovanni Boccaccio – wrote in Florentine gave high prestige to this language, while Florence's status as a major commercial centre contributed to promoting it. Between the fourteenth and fifteenth centuries, Florentine continued to spread as a written language next to Latin well outside Tuscany, and became the basis of the national literary language, Italian. From this point onwards Italian was the high language, and all the others began to be considered dialects.

In the following four centuries, the various dialects were used practically by the whole population for speaking purposes, while a narrow elite also used Italian (or Latin and French) for writing. However, on a much smaller scale, some dialects were also used for literary works (for example, Venetian in Goldoni's plays). This gap between speech and writing continued until the country was unified (1861) as well as throughout several decades after unification, due to the poor socioeconomic conditions of the new state and continuing high levels of illiteracy. In spite of their widespread use, dialects were stigmatized as an obstacle to the learning of 'correct' Italian, particularly by schoolchildren, and thus to the spreading of a single national language. The repression of dialects reached its climax during Fascism, when they were seen as counter to the nationalism and centralism that were essential to the Fascist regime. Thus, publications in dialect were banned (1931) and dialects were excluded from schools (1934). In spite of the absence of such prohibitions after the fall of Fascism, the use of dialects continued to decrease in the postwar period.

Geographically, Italian dialects form a continuum, such that those of adjacent areas differ only minimally while more distant ones differ to a greater extent. The traditional classification divides them into three main groups: Northern, Central and Southern dialects, separated by two lines: La Spezia–Rimini and Ancona–Rome.

The La Spezia–Rimini line divides Northern from Central (more specifically, Tuscan) dialects. Some of the phonetic features distinguishing the two groups are the following: (1) voiced intervocalic consonants to the north versus voiceless ones to the south of the line (for example, [d] versus [t], as in [fra'dɛl] instead of *fratello*, 'brother'); (2) single intervocalic consonants to the north versus double ones to the south of the line (for example ['fato] for *fatto*, 'fact'; (3) deletion of unstressed final vowels to the north of the line (for example, [ka'val] for *cavallo*, 'horse'). At the grammatical level, Northern dialects substitute subject pronouns *io* ('I') and *tu* ('you'), with the equivalent object forms *mi* ('me') and *ti* ('you').

The Ancona–Rome line separates Central from Southern dialects. At the phonetic level, Southern dialects are distinguished by particular consonant groups: -nd- instead of -nt- (e.g., *quanto*, 'how much', becomes ['kwando]); -nn- instead of -nd- (e.g., *manda*, 'send', becomes ['manna]); and -mm- instead of -mb- (e.g., *gamba*, 'leg', becomes ['gamma]). A second important feature of Southern dialects compared with the Central ones, and Tuscan in particular, is metaphony, that is, a process of assimilation between non-adjacent vowels in a word; in Southern dialects this is often triggered by final unstressed [i] and [u] which cause changes in the preceding stressed vowels (e.g., Southern Latium *niru* for the masculine singular *nero* 'black', and *niri* for the masculine plural *neri*, given that [e] becomes [i] under the influence of final [u] and [i] respectively, versus the feminine singular *nera* which maintains [e]). At the grammatical level, Southern dialects are characterized by possessive adjectives postposed and attached to the nouns they refer to (e.g., *matrima* for *mia madre*, 'my mother'). Furthermore, a number of words distinguish Central from

Southern dialects, such as *donna* versus *femmina* for 'woman', or *fratello* versus *frate* for 'brother'.

Within the three main groups of dialects, some further subdivisions can be identified. Among the Northern dialects, the so-called Gallo-Italian dialects (in Piedmont, Lombardy, Liguria and Emilia-Romagna) are distinguished from those of the Veneto region. Some of the main features of the Gallo-Italian dialects are the following: rounded vowels [ö] [ü] (e.g., ['lüm] for *lume*, 'lamp'); palatalization of [a] into either [ɛ] or [e] (e.g., ['sɛl] for *sale*, 'salt'); and deletion of unstressed vowels, either in final position or preceding stressed vowels (e.g., *man* for *mano*, 'hand', or *fnestra* for *finestra*, 'window'). Furthermore, the Latin consonant group -kt- has developed into -jt- in parts of Piedmont and into [tʃ] in Lombardy: for example, Latin 'noctem' has become ['nojt] and ['notʃ] respectively for the Italian *notte*, 'night'. On the other hand, in the dialects from the Veneto region, the same consonant group -kt- has developed into [t], so that the word is ['note].

In Central dialects, important differences exist between dialects from Tuscany and Corsica, and those from nearby regions (such as Marche, Umbria and Lazio). A major feature of Tuscan dialects is the so-called *gorgia* whereby intervocalic [k], [t] and [p] are converted into fricatives: for example, *la casa*, 'the house', becomes [la 'hasa]. The other Central dialects share many features with Southern dialects. Within this group, Roman speech deserves a mention for its particular history. While up until the Middle Ages it was strongly influenced by Southern dialects, after the fifteenth and sixteenth centuries such factors as the presence of popes from Tuscany and a strong influx of migrants from all over Italy spread the use of Florentine and of Italian as a *lingua franca*. Hence at the time of the unification of Italy, the population of Rome was the most Italian-speaking outside Tuscany.

Southern dialects are further divided between a northern and a southern group with a line splitting Calabria into two parts. In the southern group are included the dialects from southern Calabria and the area of Salento (Apulia), together with the Sicilian dialects. Some of the specific features of this southern group are (1) a system of five (rather than seven) stressed vowels, as [i] and [e] have converged into [i], and [u] and [o] into [u] (e.g., *neve,* 'snow', is ['nivi], and *sole,* 'sun', is ['suli]); and (2) retroflex pronunciation of [d], [r], and of [t] and [d] in consonant groups -tr-, -dr- and -str-. Also, in contrast to the other Southern dialects, parts of this southern group have kept the consonant groups -nd- and -mb-: for example, Calabrian *quandu,* 'when', and Salento *palumbu,* 'pigeon'.

The linguistic distance of Sardinian and Friulian from the other dialects together with other factors (such as their high number of speakers and a long written tradition) has allowed them to be classified as separate languages rather than dialects, with important consequences in terms of legislation protecting **minority languages**.

The process of Italianization of dialects which has been occurring in recent decades is taking place in varying degrees in different regions. It has caused the loss or reduction of the most distinctive features of local dialects and given greater uniformity at the regional level. It is generally believed that such factors as speaker's age, socioeconomic position and aspirations, conversational topic and situational context may be important variables in this process, and that Italian forms and rules penetrate into dialects more readily via younger, middle-class and more educated speakers, and via cities and towns more than villages. However empirical studies have shown that this is not always the case.

Italianization occurs particularly at the phonological and lexical levels. Dialectal sounds may be substituted with Italian ones: for example, in Sicilian, *cavallu,* 'horse', replaces *cavaddu,* with the substitution of Sicilian retroflex [d] with [l]. This can occur even when the sound is unknown to the dialect: the Venetian [s] shifts to [ts] in words such as *canzone,* 'song'. At the word level, (1) terms connected with the context of rural societies tend to disappear; (2) traditional dialectal words may coexist with terms taken from Italian (e.g., Calabrian *custuréri* alternates with *sartu* from the Italian *sarto,* 'tailor'); (3) local and often more specific terms may be substituted with Italian ones (e.g., Sicilian *visulatu,* 'tile floor', is replaced by *pavimentu,* 'floor', from the Italian *pavimento*); and (4) words may be borrowed from Italian to express notions previously unknown to the dialects, such as Calabrian *delegazziòni,* 'delegation'.

While some may argue that both the reduced use of the dialects and their Italianization may cause them to disappear completely, others maintain that it is this very Italianization that shows not only flexibility but also resilience.

See also: dialect usage; Italian language; Italian and emigration; language attitudes; language education; language policy; minority languages; varieties of Italian

Further reading

Bruni, F. (1984) *Elementi di storia della lingua e della cultura* (Elements of the History of Language and Culture), Turin: Utet, ch. 6 (a concise profile of dialects, in their historical and linguistic aspects).

Devoto, G. and Giacomelli, G. (1972) *I dialetti delle regioni d'Italia* (The Dialects of the Regions of Italy), Florence: Sansoni (a clear description of dialects, region by region).

Grassi, C. (1993) 'Italiano e dialetti' (Italian and dialects), in A.A. Sobrero (ed.), *Introduzione all'italiano contemporaneo. La variazione e gli usi* (Introduction to Contemporary Italian: Variation and Usage), Bari: Laterza (an account of the impact of Italian on dialects).

Lepschy, A.L. and Lepschy, G. (1988) *The Italian Language Today,* 2nd edn, London: Hutchinson, ch. 3 (a discussion of the main linguistic features of the dialect groups).

Maiden, M. and Parry, M. (eds) (1997) *The Dialects of Italy,* London and New York: Routledge (a collection of essays on dialects by specialist scholars; see part II on the dialect areas with separate chapters on each region).

Rohlfs, G. (1966–9) *Grammatica storica della lingua italiana e dei suoi dialetti* (Historical Grammar of the Italian Language and its Dialects), Italian translation, Turin: Einaudi (a complete linguistic history of dialects).

ANTONIA RUBINO

Dini, Lamberto

b. 1 March 1931, Florence

Economist and politician

After graduating in economics from the university of Florence, Dini studied in America as a Fullbright scholar. He joined the International Monetary Fund in 1959 and in 1976 he was elected its Executive Director. From October 1979 to May 1994 he was director-general of the **Bank of Italy** as well as holding other high economic posts. Between May 1994 and January 1995 he served as Minister for the Treasury in the **Berlusconi** government. After the fall of Berlusconi, Dini was appointed Prime Minister in January 1995 and remained in the office until the May 1996 elections. Highly respected for his administrative capacities and as the leader of Rinnovamento italiano (Italian Renewal), a small moderate-liberal political party which he founded in 1996, Dini became Minister for Foreign Affairs in the first **Ulivo** (Olive Tree) government. His negotiating skills proved useful during a number of severe international crises which included the flood of illegal immigrants into Italy from the North African countries and the dispute with Turkey over its demands for the extradition of rebel Kurdish leader, Abdullah Ocalan.

GINO MOLITERNO

Dionisotti, Carlo

b. 9 June 1908, Turin; d. 22 February 1998, London

Academic and literary critic

Regarded by many as among the finest Italianists of the second half of the twentieth century, Dionisotti held minor positions at the universities of Turin and Rome before becoming lecturer in Italian Literature at the University of Oxford, and then Professor of Italian at Bedford College, London, where he remained until his death.

Dionisotti's historical and philological studies focussed primarily on the Renaissance period and in particular on the works of Pietro Bembo. His essays on Machiavelli were collected in 1980 in a lively polemical book, and his later critical studies addressed some authors and themes of intellectual history of the last two centuries. Perhaps his most original historiographical research is the *Geografia e storia della letteratura italiana* (The Geography and History of Italian Literature) (1967), a work which

showcases Dionisotti's skilful integration of rigorous philological study and vast cultural erudition with a solid civil sensibility in order to read Italian literature in terms of the larger picture of Italy's history and its *passione politica* (political passion).

An influential teacher with a strong cultural presence, Dionisotti was a prolific author and actively contributed to many critical journals, especially to the *Giornale storico della letteratura italiana* and to *Italia medioevale e umanistica*, for which he served as an editor and as co-director respectively.

SHERRY ROUSH

divorce

Calls for legislation on divorce had been heard in Italy since Unification and the Civil Code of 1865. While civil marriage was now possible in Italy, despite the bitter opposition of the Church, most political parties took an anti-divorce stance in order to appease the clerics and guarantee their support against the growing tide of socialism. Women continued to be denied the right to administer their own property or finances, while the husband could dispose of his wife's income and goods at will. However, while civil divorce was out of the question, the provisions of the Lateran Pacts, later confirmed in the Republican **constitution** of 1946, incorporated Catholic doctrine into the Fundamental Law, and marriages could be annulled by the Church where the wife turned out not to be a virgin.

The divorce law was first introduced into the Italian Parliament in 1965 by the Socialist deputy, Loris Fortuna, but, although extremely moderate in its formulation, it was effectively blocked by the ruling Christian Democrats (see **DC**). By 1969, however, in part due to the effective publicity of the Lega Italiana per l'Istituzione del Divorzio (Italian League for the Introduction of Divorce), public opinion had changed and the bill, with a number of amendments proposed by Liberal deputy Antonio Bislini, was again put before the Parliament and was passed with broad support, being opposed only by the Christian Democrats and the neo-fascist MSI. Pope Paul VI remained aloof from the heated debates and the more progressive areas of the Church admitted the need for change, but immediately after the law was passed various militant Catholic organizations decided to call for a referendum on the issue and were soon able to collect the necessary 500,000 signatures.

Originally scheduled for 1972, the referendum was not held until 1974 but it proved to be a significant moment in postwar Italy since it was the first of several pieces of progressive legislation to be brought in and upheld over the course of the 1970s through the use of the referendum, confirming an abyss both between post-1968 public opinion and a stagnant political culture, and between civil and religious society. The referendum also marked the first serious defeat for the Christian Democrat party. Set against the background of a number of economic scandals rocking the ruling Christian Democrats, the referendum was seen by Amintore **Fanfani** as a means of restoring credibility to his party through a turn to the Right, a move encouraged by the results of the 1972 elections from which anti-divorce parties had emerged well. Furthermore, while the socialist and lay centre parties were in favour of divorce, the communists, although finally acceding to the need for change, were more tentative both in their estimation of public readiness for a programme of radical civil liberties and in their desire not to disrupt the growing understanding between Catholics and communists which was supposed to lead to the **historic compromise**. The result, however, proved that public opinion was in advance of the ruling elite, and the divorce law was upheld by an unexpectedly high 59.1 per cent of the vote.

Despite hard-won legislation, Italy still has one of the lowest divorce rates in Europe, together with Greece. There is considerable regional variation, with Italians in the South and the islands of Sardinia and Sicily less likely to divorce than their northern counterparts. Factors implicit in the relative reluctance to divorce in these areas include social opprobrium in cultural contexts which continue to value the family unit above all, and traditional working patterns which militate against financial independence for women.

See also: family; feminism

Further reading

De Rose, A. (1992) 'Socio-Economic Factors and Family Size as Determinants of Marital Dissolution in Italy', *European Sociological Review* 8 (1): 71–91.

Maggioni, G. (1990) *Il divorzio in Italia: storia dell'applicazione di una legge nuova* (Divorce in Italy: the History of the Application of a New Law), Milan: F. Angeli (study of the effect of the divorce law on family life with reference to regional variation).

SHARON WOOD

Dolce and Gabbana

After working for Marzotto for several years, Sicilian Domenico Dolce and Milan-born Stefano Gabbana joined forces in 1982 to open their own design studio. In 1985 they presented their collections in a 'new talents' category in Milan, and their name became associated with a new era of Italian design. Using lace, wool and silk, Dolce and Gabbana appeared to want to dress 'real' women, not just supermodels, and this contributed to their international success. They expanded into knitwear design in 1987, into lingerie and summerwear in 1989 and to a men's wear collection in 1990. Other lines include the Dolce and Gabbana Basic and a youthful line. In 1988 they began distributing their designs in Japan, and later opened a number of boutiques in Hong Kong, Singapore, Taipei and Seoul. Dolce and Gabbana also won an international award for best female fragrance in 1993.

Among the designers' most famous clients are 'unreal' women like the pop star Madonna (for whom they designed a number of outfits for a world tour) and actress Demi Moore. In a recent show in Milan, their style was labelled 'rude and ironic' as the two self-proclaimed deeply Catholic men displayed silk-lined cellophane dresses and a top veiling an embroidered reproduction of Murillo's Madonna and Child.

BERNADETTE LUCIANO

Dolci, Danilo

b. 28 June 1924, Sesana, Yugoslavia;
   d. 30 December 1997, Palermo

Writer, poet, sociologist, educator and
social worker

A rather unique figure in postwar Italian culture,
Dolci was a talented poet and writer as well as a
committed social worker, an educator and an
internationally respected social theorist. Although
brought up in a middle-class environment in
Northern Italy, in 1952 he moved to Trappeto,
one of the poorest and most underdeveloped areas
of Palermo, to help the local people improve their
lives. One of his first actions was a hunger strike to
publicize the high rate of infant mortality due to
malnutrition, a strategy he used often in the next
forty years to draw official attention to the poverty
and exploitation of the underprivileged in Sicily
and elsewhere. His effective use of non-violence led
to his being known as the Gandhi of Sicily, and his
achievements came to be admired and recognized
internationally, with a large number of his works
being translated into many languages. A passionate
supporter of community and self-determination, he
was also active in the International Peace Movement.

GINO MOLITERNO

Domus

Founded in 1928 by Milanese architect Giò **Ponti**,
Domus (Home) presented itself as a journal of
architecture and related arts committed to discovering the quintessential 'home'. Ceasing publication in
1941 when Ponti initiated *Stile* (Style), an alternative
journal of arts, crafts and culture, it was revived in
1946 with Ponti appointing Ernesto **Rogers** as
editor. To *Domus*, Rogers added the subtitle *Casa
dell'uomo* (House of Man), to indicate an architecture
that aimed at accommodating the functional,
cultural and spiritual needs of both individuals and
the collective. Dismissed after only two year as
editor, Rogers nevertheless realized his polemical
intentions in a revitalized ***Casabella*** while Ponti
again took over Domus and edited it until his death

in 1979. The editorship passed first to Mario
Bellini, then to Vittorio Magnago Lampugnani
and, in 1996, to the Swiss critic François Burkhardt.

See also: architectural and design magazines

KEITH EVAN GREEN

Donatoni, Franco

b. 9 June 1927, Verona

Composer

Donatoni's fertile imagination and constant recourse to experiment have maintained his position
at the forefront of the Italian avantgarde. He
initially qualified as an accountant, but concurrently pursued musical studies with such figures as
Liviabella, Pizzetti and **Maderna**. From 1954–61
he attended the summer courses at Darmstadt, and
in 1969 was appointed professor of composition at
the Milan Conservatory. Donatoni enjoyed early
success with works such as the cantata *Il libro dei
sette sigilli* (The Book of the Seven Seals) (1951),
which shows the influence of **Petrassi**, but in 1955
turned wholeheartedly towards advanced serialism
as pioneered by Boulez. Serialism was to prove a
transitional phase, however, and in 1961 *Puppenspiel*
introduced the concept of indeterminacy that was
to provide the foundation for Donatoni's work in
the 1960s and 1970s. His subsequent compositions
have continued to demonstrate a constantly
impressive level of craftsmanship, often within
structures of great complexity.

Further reading

Collage (1968) 'Scheda 9: Franco Donatoni', *Collage*
   8: 27, Palermo (contains biography, discography,
   bibliography, worklist and essays by A. Genti-
   lucci and P. Castaldi).

JOHN KERSEY

Dorfles, Gillo

b. 12 April 1910, Trieste

Art critic, academic and painter

Dorfles grew up in **Trieste** in a vibrant intellectual milieu which included the novelist Italo Svevo. In 1948, as a practising artist, he helped to form MAC, the Movimento Arte Concreta (see **arte concreta**). He subsequently taught aesthetics at Italian and foreign universities and in 1995 participated in the organization of the **Venice Biennale**.

In his *Il divenire della critica* (The Coming-To-Be of Criticism) (1976), Dorfles provided some of the more reflective and informed writing on the state of Italian art criticism of the postwar period. He meticulously charted the change from prewar criticism, which was historicist, content-based, even romantic, to the later *critica militante* (militant criticism) and postmodern writing which borrowed its language from a range of disciplines. The critic, Dorfles concluded, has little real effect on artistic production. The best the critic can do is to explore the links between art, the artist's epoch and the broader cultural context.

Dorfles strongly criticized fellow-critic Germano **Celant** for restricting his attention to the semiotic functioning of the artwork, emphasising instead the need for a return to a discussion of content and to making judgements of value and taste, something Dorfles himself practised in his teaching and writings. Dorfles thus helped to revive the discipline of aesthetics as a way of looking at art and culture by focussing on the notion of taste and the way things go in and out of fashion. In opposition to the cultural pluralism which developed in the 1960s and 1970s, Dorfles developed the concept of 'kitsch', which he defined as absolute bad taste. Dorfles described kitsch as the product of an intellectually lazy consumer society: inferior, false and sentimental artwork intended to give pleasure while not placing any demands on the viewer.

In his 1997 work, *Conformisti* (Conformists), Dorfles expands his topic to cover the way we live our daily lives. He suggests that many people conform to a bland middle-class mediocrity, based on what they judge to be common sense and common usage, because of a mistaken obsession with what other people think. Examples of needless conformist behaviour and the desire to run with the herd range from the innocuous, such as using verbal clichés, to the dangerous tendency to fascism, a connection which was also proposed by Alberto **Moravia** in some of his novels.

Further reading

Dorfles, G. (1969) *Kitsch: An Anthology of Bad Taste*, London: Studio Vista (an illustrated anthology of what Dorfles regarded as representative examples of kitsch, with essays by various authors).

—— (1976) *Il divenire della critica*, Turin: Einaudi.

—— (1997) *Conformisti*, Rome: Donzelli.

MAX STAPLES

Dorotei

A leading faction of the Christian Democrat Party (see **DC**) which took its name from the convent of Saint Dorotea in which it was founded in 1959, the Dorotei occupied a powerful pivotal position in the party for the next decade, conditioning the party's leadership and political choices. Led by Mariano Rumor, Emilio Russo, Emilio Colombo and Paolo Emilio Taviani, the group's main aim was to oppose the then party secretary and prime minister, Amintore **Fanfani** and his policy of an '**opening to the Left**'. For a time the faction was supported by Aldo **Moro**, until he founded his own group (the so-called 'Morotei'). By 1964 the Dorotei controlled around 46 per cent of the party's national congress delegates, but they also embodied the worst aspects of Christian Democrat **clientelism** and power-grabbing. The faction split in the early 1970s and became identified more directly with various leaders such as Colombo, Rumor and Piccoli. The term *doroteismo*, or sometimes *neo-doroteismo*, was used until the late 1980s to describe the centre of the DC.

JAMES WALSTON

Dossetti, Giuseppe

b. 13 February 1913, Genoa;
   d. 15 December 1996, Oliveto,
   Bologna

Catholic politician, ideologue and priest

After having taken part in the **Resistance** movement during the Second World War, Dossetti
became the deputy secretary of the newly-formed
Christian Democrat Party. As charismatic leader of
the integralist wing of the party organized around
the journal *Cronache Sociali* (Social Chronicles), he
was **De Gasperi**'s main party opponent until
1951 when, despairing of the DC's ability to ever
carry through any serious reforms, he abandoned
politics in favour of the religious life. He subsequently lived a monastic existence, and a number
religious communities and families developed
around him. He returned to politics briefly in
1994 in order to oppose the rise of Silvio
Berlusconi, whom he regarded as Italy's 'public
enemy number one', and, as guru of the left wing
of the former DC, Dossetti expressed his strong
support for both Leoluca Orlando's new anti-mafia
party, La Rete (see **mafia**) and for Romano **Prodi**
and the **Ulivo** coalition.

See also: DC

Further reading

Leonardi, R. and Wertman, D. (1989) *Italian
   Christian Democracy: The Politics of Dominance*,
   Basingstoke: Macmillan.

JOHN POLLARD

drug culture

The close association of intravenous drug use and
AIDS in Italy, the role of the **mafia** in drug
trafficking and regular party political confrontations
between 1989 and 1993 on the question of
legalization have given the topic of illicit drugs and
their associated social problems substantial publicity
since the 1980s. As a result, much less attention has
been paid to the disparity between even the worst
postwar figure for drug-related deaths (1,383 in

1991) and the 35,000 deaths annually from the
immediate or long-term consequences of alcohol
consumption, especially liver cirrhosis.

Among illicit drugs, cannabis is the most
widespread: up to one-third of high school students
even in provincial centres have probably tried it.
Cocaine and synthetic drugs remain minority
choices, but police seizures of drugs suggest rapid
expansion since 1990. The estimates of heroin
consumption suggest a large increase in users
during the 1970s, followed by substantial containment between 1984 (100,000–240,000 regular
injectors) and 1992 (195,000–313,000). Regular
users are likely to have begun injecting in their
early teens, to live in a city in north or central Italy
and to be men: only one in five injectors are
women. Since illicit drugs lost their early countercultural associations in the early 1980s, injectors
are also increasingly likely to be enrolled in
treatment programmes: 50 per cent of programme
participants manage to combine their addiction
with full-time employment. Another feature of the
institutionalization of drug culture is that regular
users have come to constitute a significant segment
of the prison population, up from 8 per cent in
1980 to 31 per cent by 1992. Both forms of
institutionalization derive largely from changes in
drug policies. In 1975, as part of a general
expansion of civil liberties, possession of small
quantities of drugs for personal use was legalized.
Consumption increased, but was overshadowed as
a social problem by the more urgent issue of youth
involvement in political violence (see **terrorism**).
By the mid-1980s the anticipated treatment centres
had finally been established by the new **health
service**, flanked by increasing numbers of private
lay and religious 'therapeutic communities' and
associations (notably Gruppo Abele, Comunità
Incontro, San Patrignano). Participation in their
programmes grew tenfold, doubling each centre's
average caseload and shifting treatment emphasis
away from methadone towards psychotherapeutic
and social rehabilitation. In 1990 this success was
put at risk by the political grandstanding of the
Socialist Party, which forced its coalition government partners to accept recriminalization of all
drug possession and a shift in emphasis from
treatment to repression. Imprisonment of users,
increasing slowly in the 1980s, rose sharply. In

1993, the law's opponents, led by the heirs of the **Radical Party**, submitted its key feature to a referendum in which it was narrowly overturned, leaving management of drug culture to the local discretion of police and judges (see also **referenda**).

Further reading

Journal of Drug Issues 24 (1994) (4), special issue on Italy (survey of epidemiological, social and legal aspects of drug use).

Moss, D. (1991) 'Combating Drug Use in the AIDS Decade: The 1989 Campaign in Context', in F. Sabetti and R. Catanzaro (eds), *Italian Politics: A Review. Vol. 5*, London: Pinter (drug use and policy from 1975 to1990).

DAVID MOSS

Duranti, Francesca

b. 2 January 1935, Genoa

Writer

Originally trained as a lawyer, Duranti started writing in the 1970s. Her first novel, *La bambina* (The Little Girl), published in 1976, immediately became a popular bestseller. There followed *Piazza, mia bella piazza* (Piazza, My Beautiful Piazza) (1978) which relates the breakup of Duranti's marriage caused by her husband's opposition to her writing, and *La casa sul lago della luna* (The House on Moonlake) (1984), which was translated into several other languages and which won Duranti international renown. In this stylistically refined novel, which was awarded several prizes, including the prestigious Bagutta (see **literary prizes**), the boundaries between fiction and reality, and the writer and the translator, become blurred. In *Effetti personali* (Personal Effects), Duranti's next novel and winner of the Campiello prize in 1989, the protagonist's quest for an independent identity after her husband leaves her is extended to the search for an ideal social system. Duranti has continued to publish and now has an international readership.

Further reading

Vinall, S.W. (1993) 'Francesca Duranti: Reflections and Inventions', in Z.G. Baranski and L. Pertile (eds), *The New Italian Novel*, Edinburgh: Edinburgh University Press.

PIERA CARROLI

Dylan Dog

Created in 1986 by novelist and poet Tiziano Sclavi for the veteran comic-book publisher Sergio Bonelli, and subsequently written by Sclavi but drawn by a number of different illustrators, *Dylan Dog* became the publishing success of the decade. By the time sales peaked in the mid-1990s, the comic was selling over 1,200,000 copies a month, although sales fell thereafter to settle at about 450,000 in the late 1990s.

The overwhelming popularity of the comic book, which appealed both to younger pre-teen readers as well as to a more mature audience, seemed largely to derive from its clever marrying of the private detective and the supernatural horror genres, but always with a strong dose of irony and self-conscious humour. The young and handsome Dylan ('Mr Dog', as he's often addressed by strangers or mere acquaintances) is modelled on English actor Rupert Everett, lives in London at 7 Craven Road and is a professional 'investigator of nightmares'. As such, he fearlessly takes on all sorts of cases which involve him in gruesome and deadly battle with ghosts and vampires, werewolves and aliens, but he is also openly terrified of flying and of dentists, suffers from vertigo and claustrophobia and in between cases is shown relaxing at home doing nothing more exciting than practising his clarinet or eternally attempting to assemble a model boat. A further touch of oddball and self-conscious humour is provided by the ubiquitous presence of a butler called Groucho, who not only physically resembles the vaudeville comedian Groucho Marx, but is also continually making quips and banter in the Marx Brothers style.

All these quirky features, presented in a visual style clearly influenced by the language of film, are further enhanced by a marked propensity for postmodern pastiche and citation. Frequent intertextual allusions to everything from Hitchcock films to Umberto **Eco** contribute a higher cultural and literary dimension for the benefit of more educated readers, while the younger set probably remain more drawn by its splatter visuals and its gothic atmospherics.

After increasing meteorically for almost a decade, sales began to fall in the mid-1990s, but by then *Dylan Dog* had become so familiar to Italians that in 1996 the character was used in a concerted advertising campaign to convince young people to wear seat belts in cars.

GINO MOLITERNO

E

earthquakes

Due to its position above the convergence of African and Eurasian tectonic plates, Italy is, together with Greece, the European country most exposed to the risk of earthquakes and nearly half the Italian territory is regularly subjected to shakes. Scientists use a magnitude scale to measure the size of earthquakes ranging from a magnitude of 1.0, roughly equivalent of breaking a rock the size of a bus, to magnitude 9.0, the equivalent of a fault rupturing through hundreds of kilometres of continental rock. Strong Italian earthquakes are usually in the magnitude range of 5.0 to 7.0. A complete catalogue of the earthquakes that have occurred in Italy in the last 2,000 years has now been compiled by the Italian National Institute for Geophysics (ING), but recognition of the role played by the tectonic faults in earthquakes has been slow, with a result that the need for preventative measures has only recently come to be addressed.

Italy has suffered several strong earthquakes since 1945, and this has led to greater research into earthquake generation and hazard assessment. In 1979, an earthquake of magnitude 5.9 struck Norcia, in the Apennines, and was believed to form a small fault scarp. The formation of a fault scarp, the place where a fault rock rupture reaches the ground surface, pointed to a connection between faults and earthquakes. That connection was dramatically driven home by the 1980 earthquake in Irpinia in southern Italy, which registered a magnitude of 6.9, originating 3–15 km below ground but breaking all the way to the surface and causing a long meter-high fault scarp. Given the severity of the Irpinia earthquake, which killed 3,000 people and completely levelled a number of small towns, the Italian government finally moved not only to provide earthquake relief but also, through a new law promulgated in January 1986, to establish appropriate and compulsory building codes in areas of seismic hazard.

Since the Irpinia earthquake, several more strong earthquakes have occurred including at Valcomino in 1984, a quake of magnitude 5.5, and at Potenza in 1990, with a quake of magnitude 5.2 centred on the southeast end of the Irpinia fault. Then in 1997 in Colfiorito, located in the central Apennines, a magnitude 6.0 tremor occurred 10 km below ground, shaking the surface strongly enough to kill twelve people and leave 80,000 homeless throughout Umbria and the Marches region. With strong aftershocks that lasted for several weeks, the Colfiorito earthquake left in its wake extensive damage to a large number of historic and artistic sites, including the 800-year old Basilica of Saint Francis at Assisi. The Department of Civil Protection was called upon to assist over 38,000 people in the first three days following the earthquake, and total reconstruction costs were estimated at about 10 trillion lira.

Current research suggests that 45 per cent of the Italian territory should be classified as 'seismic' and so subject to certain strict regulations for new construction. However, 86 per cent of all of Italian dwellings were built before earthquake codes were developed and thus remain at risk. Furthermore, although there are three categories of 'seismic' classification related to needs for increased level of regulation, zoning in the country takes into account only the definition of broad seismic source zones and does not factor in surface faulting. This is further complicated by the fact that the enforcement of seismic codes is the responsibility of the communes (see **local administration**), which themselves determine what criteria new construction must meet. In addition, although there has developed a tradition of fully supporting the victims of natural disasters with state funding, Italy still has no earthquake insurance.

On the positive side, the government has instituted the Department of Civil Protection and the National Seismic Survey of Italy, a division of the National Technical Surveys, which has among its missions the conducting of seismic risk assessment and the collection of information on the effects of strong earthquakes. The National Seismic Survey provides information about earthquakes to the public by mailing information along with electrical bills as well as from a web site.

LARRY MAYER

Eco, Umberto

b. 5 January 1932, Alessandria

Novelist, semiotician and theorist of
narrative and popular culture

After beginning a traditional academic career with a dissertation on the aesthetics of St Thomas Aquinas at the University of Turin supervised by Luigi **Pareyson** in 1954, Eco began working for Italian state television (**RAI**). In 1959 Eco also began his long association with the Bompiani publishing house in Milan. After obtaining his degree in aesthetics in 1961, he received the Chair of Visual Communications at the Faculty of Architecture of the University of Florence. In 1971 he moved to the University of Bologna in a new experimental faculty and was later awarded Italy's first chair in semiotics. In 1993, he became the chairman of a new department at the university devoted to the sciences of communication.

Few if any contemporary Italian writers have enjoyed the international fame that Eco has earned from his critical theory and fiction. *Opera aperta*

(The Open Work) gained him national renown in 1962 with his novel and original aesthetic theory which distinguished between traditional 'closed' art and the truly avantgarde art which Eco defined with a particularly felicitous term as 'open': examples are Joyce's *Finnegans Wake*, the mobiles of Alexander Calder or the music of Luciano **Berio**. With *Diario minimo* (Misreadings) in the following year, Eco added a popular audience to the academic public he had won through his scholarship with witty, humorous parodies and satirical essays; the book became a bestseller and a classic overnight.

Fascinated by the problem of devising a critical theory capable of analysing both manifestations of high culture and those of mass or popular culture, Eco turned his attention to popular culture in the 1960s and 1970s, producing a number of seminal works in what he calls his 'pre-semiotic' stage. In 1964, in *Apocalittici e integrati: comunicazioni di massa e teorie della cultura di massa* (partially translated as *Apocalypse Postponed*), Eco provided a brilliant discussion of the ways in which intellectuals approach popular culture. A number of essays in journals or anthologies – eventually published in 1976 as *Il superuomo di massa: retorica e ideologia nel romanzo popolare* (partially translated as *The Role of the Reader*) – confirmed Eco's original theoretical approach to popular culture. The book included Eco's single most famous essay, 'Narrative Structures in Fleming', a study of Ian Fleming's character James Bond, which would lead Eco toward the adoption of semiotics as a master discipline encompassing all forms of human culture. The 1976 publication of a major semiotic treatise, *Trattato di semiologia generale* (A Theory of Semiotics), established Eco as Italy's foremost semiotician, a rival to Roland Barthes in popularity and originality.

Eco's fiction combines all his intellectual interests – popular culture, medievalism, the detective novel, literary and semiotic theory – and may be said to embody the most innovative aspects of literary **postmodernism**. His first novel in 1980, *Il nome della rosa* (The Name of the Rose) earned numerous Italian and foreign literary prizes and sold tens of millions of copies all over the world. No single Italian book in the twentieth century has enjoyed such commercial or critical acclaim. Eco provided every possible audience with something of interest: for the mass market reader, he offered a 'whodunit' complete with a Sherlock Holmes surrogate, a monk named William of Baskerville, who attempts to solve a series of murders in an abbey; for the intellectual or academic audience, the book was filled with history, arcane information and medieval philosophy that was thinly disguised contemporary semiotic theory. Eco's own assessment of his novel in *Postille al 'Nome della rosa'* (Postscript to 'The Name of the Rose') in 1983 was subsequently hailed by critics as one of the most intelligent and persuasive definitions of the term 'postmodern'.

Eco's two subsequent works of fiction continued his postmodernist, pastiche style, combining the most erudite forms of literary theory and arcane lore about the past with other generic traits of the thriller, the adventure story and the mystery novel. In 1988, *Il pendolo di Foucault* (Foucault's Pendulum) detailed the adventures of a group of friends working for Milanese publishers who stumble upon (and help to create) a plot to take over the world. In the process, Eco pokes fun at deconstructionism and cranks who view the world through paranoid eyes. *L'isola del giorno prima* (The Island of the Day Before) (1994) represents a cross between *Robinson Crusoe, Treasure Island* and the swashbuckling historical romances of Alexandre Dumas: it proposes a fascinating and original parallel between only apparently bizarre ideas typical of Baroque culture in the seventeenth century and similar concepts accepted today as exemplary notions of postmodern thought.

Eco's witty and learned ruminations on the nature of fiction are found in what may be his most charming work of literary theory, originally presented as the prestigious Norton lectures at Harvard University in 1992–3, then published as *Sei passeggiate nei boschi narrativi* (Six Walks in the Fictional Woods).

Further reading

Bondanella, P. (1997) *Umberto Eco and the Open Text: Semiotics, Fiction, Popular Culture*, Cambridge: Cambridge University Press (a survey of Eco's entire career, his novels and his writings on popular culture).

Bouchard, N. and Pravadelli, D. (eds) (1998) *The Politics of Culture and the Ambiguities of Interpretation: Essays on Umberto Eco*, New York: Peter Lang (a collection of essays treating Eco's literary and theoretical writings).

Capozzi, R. (ed.) (1997) *Reading Eco*, Bloomington, IN: Indiana University Press (an anthology of studies of Eco's works).

Coletti, T. (1988) *Naming the Rose: Eco, Medieval Signs, and Modern Theory*, Ithaca, NY: Cornell University Press (a useful approach to *The Name of the Rose* and its combination of medieval erudition and contemporary literary theory).

Eco, U. (1989) *The Open Work*, trans. A. Cancogni, Cambridge, MA: Harvard University Press.

—— (1979) *The Role of the Reader: Explorations in the Semiotics of Texts*, Bloomington, IN: Indiana University Press.

—— (1994) *The Name of the Rose* (including the Author's Postscript), trans. W. Weaver, New York: Harvest Books.

—— (1988) *Foucault's Pendulum*, trans. W. Weaver, New York: Harcourt Brace Jovanovich.

—— (1994) *Six Walks in the Fictional Woods*, Cambridge, MA: Harvard University Press.

PETER BONDANELLA

economic miracle

While the first period of high economic growth in postwar Italy extended from the early 1950s up to 1973, the 'economic miracle' or 'boom' is commonly placed in the period 1958–1963. The 'miracle' was characterized by extremely rapid cultural, social and economic change. Italy became an industrialized nation, at least in parts of the north and centre, and centuries-old social categories – the rural day labourer, the sharecropper – all but disappeared across much of the country (see **peasants**; **agriculture**). Mass migration (10 million Italians moved from one region to another in a ten-year period, and more than seventeen million moved home) was the most striking effect of, and catalyst for, change, throwing together different cultures, dialects and customs in the urban environment. With increasing prosperity, many Italians were able to purchase consumer goods for the first time (usually on credit), including televisions (broadcasting began in 1954), cars (the cheap symbols of the boom were the **Fiat** 500 (1957) and 600 (1955) and the Topolino), scooters (the Vespa and the Lambretta), fridges and washing machines. The number of private cars in Italy rose from 364,000 in 1950 to 4.67 million in 1964. **Advertising** became a permanent feature in Italian homes, especially in the form of *Carosello*, which began transmission in 1957. Mass schooling and urbanization transformed the literacy and cultural outlook of a new generation.

The cultural effects of this 'great transformation' have been the subject of extensive debate. **Pasolini**'s influential analysis identified a process of cultural homologation whereby the popular classes had simply accepted the mass cultural consumerist values of neocapitalism. In reality, this 'anthropological revolution' was far more complicated and less linear than Pasolini believed, as Umberto **Eco** first argued in his classic *Apocalittici e integrati* (1964), partially translated as *Apocalypse Postponed*.

Within the traditional 'cultural industries', the view of the boom was an overwhelmingly negative one. Dino **Risi**'s *Il sorpasso* (The Easy Life) (1962) – a bittersweet road movie starring Vittorio **Gassman** and his spyder car – became the film symbol of the boom, but Risi's *I mostri* (The Monsters) (1963) was a ferocious portrait of the miracle generation of the early 1960s. In Vittorio **De Sica**'s *Il boom* (1963), Alberto **Sordi** sells his eye to pay off the debts of his greedy wife. Mario **Monicelli**'s 'Il frigorifero' (The Refrigerator, an episode of *Le coppie* (The Couples)) (1970) depicts how Sardinian immigrant Monica **Vitti** becomes a prostitute to meet the payments on an enormous fridge. In 1960 **Fellini** (*La dolce vita*), **Visconti** (*Rocco e i suoi fratelli* (Rocco and His Brothers), 1960) and **Antonioni** (*L'avventura*) all released films which presented a negative image of the Italy of the miracle. The first two movies were also enormous box office hits.

Television was far more caught up in the 'fever' of the boom. Game shows became national events, especially *Lascia o raddoppia* (1954–9) (see **Bongiorno**), *Il musichiere* (1957–60) and *Campanile sera* (1959–61). It was at this time that television began to replace other cultural forms, especially cinema, as a more privatized cultural form, for use above all

(at a later stage) in the home. The boom also saw the tentative birth of Italian sociology, with the opening of a first department at Trento University, and of cultural studies, through the work of Eco and others. Architects, historians and writers collaborated at institutions like the **Milan Triennale** on a series of innovative exhibitions. The **Gruppo 63** was formed in many ways to provide a collective critique of the boom. Certain individual novels stand out for their depiction of the period, especially Luciano Bianciardi's *La vita agra* (Sour Life) (1962) for its elegant but savage critique of boomtown Milan. Ottiero **Ottieri**'s *Donnarumma all'assalto* (Donnarumma on the Attack) (1959) vividly describes the shock effect of industrialization in the South. **Calvino**'s *La speculazione edilizia* (Building Speculation) (1957) shows how the whole Italian landscape was being transformed, and for the worse. Alberto **Arbasino**'s *Fratelli d'Italia* (Brothers of Italy) (1963) is a vivid road novel of a country on the move.

The 'miracle' also coincided with new forms of newspaper production and journalism, either local 'tabloids' (such as *Il Corriere Lombardo*) or national weeklies and dailies such as *Il Mondo*, *L'Espresso* (1955), *Il Giorno* (1956) and the right-wing *Il Borghese*. Left-wing publisher **Feltrinelli** had best-sellers with Pasternak's *Doctor Zhivago* (1957) and Tomasi Di **Lampedusa**'s *Il Gattopardo* (The Leopard) (1958). In general, the boom was a period of intense and contradictory cultural change in every sphere, whose effects are still being felt today.

Further reading

Crainz, G. (1996) *Storia del miracolo italiano. Culture, identità, trasformazioni* (History of the Italian Miracle: Cultures, Identity, Transformations), Rome: Donzelli.

Foot, J. (1995) 'The Family and the "Economic Miracle": Social Transformation, Work, Leisure and Development at Bovisa and Comasina (Milan), 1950–1970', *Contemporary European History* 4 (3): 315–38.

Ginsborg, P. (1990) *A History of Contemporary Italy*, London: Penguin (see ch. 7, 'The "Economic Miracle", Rural Exodus and Social Transformation, 1958–63').

Pasolini, P.P. (1975) *Scritti corsari* (Pirate Writings), Milan: Garzanti.

Piccone Stella, S. (1993) *La prima generazione. Ragazze e ragazzi nel miracolo economico italiano* (The First Generation: Girls and Boys of the Italian Economic Miracle), Milan: Franco Angeli.

JOHN FOOT

economy

Italy's postwar economy proved to be a great success. As unlikely as it must have seemed at the immediate end of the Second World War, between 1950 and 1973 Italy's production per capita grew on average by about 5 per cent per year, a rate as high as the German 'miracle' and higher than that of all the other large European countries. Although Italy's growth rate slowed in the period 1973–92, together with the rest of the industrial countries, it still remained the highest in Europe with the exception of small, oil-rich Norway. Italy's per capita GDP now stands at about 73 per cent of that of the United States, and the average Italian is about 3 per cent better off than the average Briton. Italy's success story is, however, in need of severe qualification since the mass of unsolved problems are all too apparent: the North–South income gap has remained almost as wide as ever; the productivity of the service sector (both public and private) is below that of Italy's competitors; financial intervention is less than satisfactory; and public expenditure threatens future growth with income distribution worsening.

Postwar reconstruction

In 1945 the Italian economic system lay in ruins, its per capita GDP having fallen to 1909 levels, down 40 per cent relative to 1939, the best prewar year. However, material reconstruction was swift and prewar income levels were reached sometime between 1949 and 1950. High inflation was successfully brought under control in 1947–8, the financial infrastructure almost entirely repaired and the domestic market reunified.

The main economic decisions affecting the long-run economic prospects of the country taken during the reconstruction years were closely connected with political moves, in particular with the irrevocable commitment to remain in the Western camp by signing the North Atlantic Treaty. As early as 1947 Italy joined the International Monetary Fund, a bold resolution for a country virtually deprived of hard currency reserves and saddled with an array of quotas, import duties and foreign exchange controls inherited from the autarkic and wartime policies. Participation in the European Payment Union and the European Coal and Steel Community followed (see **European Union**). In terms of international economic relations, an irrevocable decision was made in favour of free market and free trade. Credit for these crucial choices should be given more to farsighted politicians than to the main social actors, for both the employers and the trade unions favoured the old growth pattern based upon protection of the domestic market or, at best, advised prudence in the new course.

Domestic economic policy making was not nearly as favourable to a free market economy. State intervention in the economy remained both cumbersome and inefficient. Rather than being privatized, public companies were fostered as tools of economic development and their number was increased. Government subsidies to the South were made permanent with the establishment in 1950 of the **Cassa per il Mezzogiorno**. Thus from the early postwar years, Italy's policy making was torn between two conflicting camps: the first supporting trade liberalization and competition in the international arena, the second tied to state intervention and protection of a large number of (often petty) vested interests on the domestic front.

The 'miracle'

Production and aggregate productivity growth grew so rapidly between 1950 and 1963 (on average by 5.9 and 3.7 per cent per annum, respectively) that most observers, taken by surprise, spoke of an 'Italian miracle'. In fact, it is hardly necessary to resort to supernatural forces to account for Italy's excellent economic performance in these years. Current explanations draw on various combinations of the following factors: (1) the advantages of borrowed foreign technology to a country endowed with a well-educated, well-disciplined labour force, (2) the productivity gains implicit in the rapid reallocation to manufacturing of a low-productivity agricultural labour force, (3) the effects of public investments on the productivity of private capital, (4) the benefits of newly found domestic and international stability, (5) a rapidly growing domestic demand deriving from both the private and the public sector, (6) a booming world-wide demand for goods (such as consumer durables) in the production of which Italy enjoyed a comparative advantage, and (7) an orthodox monetary and fiscal policy aimed at maintaining low inflation and stable exchange rates. All of these factors together created an enormously positive environment for entrepreneurial skills and creativity.

1963–73: increased growth

In 1962, for the first time in its long history, Italy reached full employment of its labour force. This new and extraordinary situation was to severely test both the Italian ruling classes and the institutions created, or consolidated, in the immediate postwar years. Both entrepreneurs and trade unionists found themselves unprepared for a full employment economy that placed a new stress on productivity growth, deepening rather than widening investments and requiring new industrial relations both at the shopfloor and at the industrial level. As for public institutions, they proved unable to lead or even to broker the transition.

Alarmed by a sudden rise in wages and by ill-advised government policies such as the nationalization of the electrical power industry (see **ENEL**), capital fled abroad or took refuge outside the factory (for example, in real estate). The resulting downturn in private industrial investment was only partly compensated for by much needed public capital expenditure. In the medium term – after a brief, if rather severe, recession in 1963–4 – growth continued at a steady pace, driven by buoyant international demand and by the introduction of labour-saving techniques. In the longer term, however, the half-hearted response to the challenge of full employment in the 1960s only postponed the institutional and cultural adjustments that were needed for the Italian economy to fully develop its considerable productive potential.

Oil

An effective reaction to the shock caused by the sudden increase in oil prices in 1973–4 would have required a stronger social fabric and bolder political leadership than Italy enjoyed in the first part of the 1970s. A succession of particularly weak governments chose to follow what appeared to be the easiest way out of the doldrums, at least in the short run: devaluation of the currency with the attendant double digit inflation. **Terrorism**, while further undermining international confidence in the Italian system, seemed to justify the fear that any change in economic policy might tip the balance of a social equilibrium which, rightly or wrongly, politicians perceived to be extremely precarious.

It was only after the formation of the so-called 'national unity parliamentary majority' that the decision was made to join the European Monetary System and therefore to effectively tackle inflation. Moreover, during the early 1980s the state itself promoted a process of industrial restructuring by helping large companies to reduce excessive labour force.

Growth, deficit spending and income inequality

A high growth rate resumed for approximately five years after 1983, reaching 4.1 per cent in 1987. Private consumption grew even more rapidly, and inflation fell to an average of about 6 per cent per annum. For a time, it seemed as if political stability might feed economic prosperity. Unfortunately, the governments of the time did little to tackle the causes of low productivity, while at the same time they created longer term problems by expanding government deficits. As it turned out, in Italy as in other countries including the United States, in spite of much lip service being paid to 'supply side policies', it was precisely old-fashioned deficit spending that, for a while, propelled the economy upward. The ratio of outstanding government debt to GDP rose from 51 per cent in 1982 to 102 per cent in 1990.

During the expansion of the 1980s income distribution deteriorated, thereby ending a thirty-year period of slow but steady movement towards a more egalitarian society. At the same time, unemployment remained stubbornly around 9 per cent from 1982 to the end of the decade.

Little was done to remedy the 'structural' weaknesses of the system, including an inefficient public administration, the low quality of services (notably those in the modern network sectors), poor research and development, and education. Some improvements were introduced in the financial sector, which was cautiously deregulated and slowly opened to privatization.

The European Monetary Union

At the time of the collapse of the party system in 1992, ever-growing government deficits and spiralling debt seriously threatened both future growth and Italy's participation in the European Monetary Union as envisaged by the Maastricht Treaty. Successive governments, the so-called 'technical' governments of **Amato**, **Ciampi** and **Dini** and then the 'political' governments of **Berlusconi** and **Prodi** were therefore engaged in a race against the clock to get Italy to meet the main criteria set forth by the Treaty for participation in the EMU as of 1 January 1999.

Each annual budget strove to cut expenses and/ or increase taxation in order to curb the deficit and reduce it from about 9 per cent of GDP to the required 3 per cent. After decades of careless budget management this was not an easy task, since so many sectors of the economy and of society had become accustomed to shifting to the future the costs of their large immediate benefits. At the same time, high inflation forecasts needed to be reversed.

In 1992, the lira was forced out of the European Monetary System. This time, however, inflation did not follow the sharp (almost 20 per cent) devaluation of the exchange rate. Demonstrating a high sense of responsibility for the future of the economy, a pact to freeze wages was brokered by the government between employers and the unions. The economy was given a much needed edge on export markets and prices were kept remarkably under control. In later years, thanks also to tight monetary policy by the **Banca d'Italia**, inflation rates were reduced to a level close to the European average.

The combination of low inflation and narrowing government deficit reduced the risk on government debt, and interest rates began to converge to those of the 'bund', Germany's state bond. Thus, after risking serious derailment, the Italian economy was brought back on track in order to join the European Monetary Union.

The North–South divide and high unemployment

Italy's postwar economic success story is far from unqualified. The North–South income gap and continuing high levels of unemployment amply manifest the main weaknesses of Italy's remarkable overall economic performance. While economic theory predicts a convergence of the levels of productivity among regions and while the South has made considerable progress since the end of the war, Italy still remains a country of two economies. Regional value-added per labour unit in the South was equal to 82 per cent of national average in 1951 and to 78 per cent in 1989. Today, while the regions in the Po valley are amongst the richest in Europe, the Mezzogiorno still ranks as one of the poorest. Unemployment in the North is about 6 per cent (roughly half the European average), but reaches 20 per cent in the South, a fact that underlines the close connection of the **'Southern Question'** with the unemployment issue.

Explanations of the relative underdevelopment of the South range from national economic policy failures to poor Southern financial institutions, from cultural differences between North and South to the social costs of organized crime. Its high unemployment is also explained by a variety of factors: rigid labour markets, welfare state failures and outdated education system. While changes in all these areas have been very slow in coming, nevertheless the spread of a buoyant small enterprise system from the northeast down the Adriatic coast all the way to Apulia bodes well for the future of the southern economy. Today, the Mezzogiorno is far from being just one homogeneous zone of underdevelopment, as it incorporates ever increasing patches of rapidly developing and modernizing areas.

Further reading

Barca, F. (ed.) (1997) *Storia del capitalismo italiano dal dopoguerra a oggi*, Rome: Donzelli.

Rossi, N. and Toniolo, G. (1996) 'Italy', in N. Crafts and G. Toniolo (eds), *Economic Growth in Europe Since 1945*, Cambridge: Cambridge University Press, 427–54.

GIANNI TONIOLO

education

For Italy, the end of the war in 1945 meant also a recovery from more than twenty years of fascist rule. In the educational system two kinds of changes were supposed to follow the return to democracy. First, the ideological contents of the curricula, often permeated by nationalistic and illiberal views, had to be modified. This was done immediately, while the Allied troops still were occupying part of the country; an important contribution came from Carleton Washburne, who was at the same time a member of the Allied Control Commission and a prestigious scholar in education. Second, the whole structure of the school system had to be revised: in fact, even in the pre-fascist era emphasis had always been placed upon a selective curriculum, one based on the humanities and reserved for the happy few, rather than on mass education (in 1951, 12.9 per cent of the population aged over six years was illiterate). Thus, the **constitution** of the new-born **Republic** asserted the right to education of all citizens and called for positive action by the state to overcome difficulties due to social inequalities. However, the implementation of the constitutional principle remained extremely slow, mainly due to the conservative nature of the Christian Democrat Party (**DC**) which, as the ruling party, effectively controlled the Ministero della Pubblica Istruzione (Ministry of Education). Given the extremely centralized nature of the school system until very recent times, the Education Ministry provided excellent opportunities for expanding the influence of the Party (see **clientelism**), which thus discouraged the implementation of any major reforms.

The structure of the educational system inherited by the Republic dates back to the Gentile reform of 1923. Excepting higher education (see **universities**), it is divided into four sectors, called cycles: infant school, age 3–6; elementary school, 6–11; lower secondary, 11–14; and upper secondary, 14–19. This overall structure has been retained well into the late 1990s though significant changes have taken place at the infant and secondary level; the elementary sector has remained more stable, since from the beginning it was the only one attended almost universally by the corresponding age group.

The infant school, though not compulsory, is extremely well attended (in 1996, by 97 per cent of children, compared with 35 per cent in 1945). It has undergone a radical transformation, since it used to be a mainly socially oriented institution, receiving children whose families could not care for them during the day, whereas it has now acquired a high pedagogical value. Originally it was not included in the state educational system: the public schools were run by the local authorities (*comuni*), the private ones mainly by Church institutions. However in 1968, after a long struggle against those who were protecting the dominance of the private sector, the infant school was added to the state system and the results have been quite positive. In all recent international reports, the Italian Infant School has ranked high; a school run by the Municipality of Reggio Emilia recently won first prize in a comparative test, and the average value is not much lower.

Table 1 shows the huge quantitative development of the secondary school system during the decades from the 1950s – the years of the **economic miracle** – to the late 1970s, reaching a plateau around the beginning of the 1990s as the increase in schooling rate began to be counterbalanced by a decrease in the birth rate. Around the middle of the 1990s, the ratio of upper secondary students to the general population in the corresponding age group was above 75 per cent, whereas the degree (*maturità*) was taken by 65 per cent of the nineteen-year-old population; both figures were still slowly increasing.

Compulsory schooling till the age of fourteen, as established by the constitution, became effective in 1962 when a centre–left coalition government instituted the Scuola Media Unica, a unified lower secondary school. Thus, the age for choosing between a general education, a technical education, vocational training or school leaving was shifted from eleven to fourteen or fifteen years; after being in place for a third of a century, there is now a general consensus that the Scuola Media open to all children has turned out to be a very effective instrument for homogenising Italian society.

On the other hand, no structural reforms accompanied the expansion of the upper secondary school. It still includes separate channels called Licei (general education), Istituti Tecnici (technical education), Istituti professionali (vocational training), and other specialized institutions mainly in the fields of art and music. Of course, some curricula have been more or less modernized; but this has been done independently, inside each channel, without a global strategy. Such a strategy would have been required for at least three reasons: the impact of the change from a school system aimed at the ruling class to a system for everybody; the presence of the Scuola Media Unica (previously, the various upper secondary institutions were connected to different lower secondary schools); the admission of all secondary school graduates to higher education, as decreed by the 1969 law concerning the university.

This last factor in particular, which could not help but deeply influence the very mission of technical and professional establishments, led to repeated calls for a general secondary school reform. Although a number of legislative proposals were introduced into the Parliament, none came to fruition. The continual blocking of this reform has often been taken as the typical, and perhaps most dramatic, example of a general weakness in the decision-making process of Italian political institutions.

Another complication of the Italian educational system is that vocational education takes place also outside the state school system, namely in centres, or in more flexible training programmes, administered by the **regions**. The regional system, being more directly connected with the labour market, is rather important with regard to adult education and re-training; it is less relevant for the age group 14–18 years, as the percentage of students proportional to the total in the school system is only 6 per cent, and even the proportion relative to the state Istituti professionali is less than 30 per cent. In spite of this limited weight, the very existence of two completely different public institutions in charge of the same activities, without a clearcut distinction of goals and responsibilities, leads to conflicts and to financial waste; moreover, it makes it extremely difficult to plan coherently the development of the whole system.

Consequently, in the late 1990s there are a number of major issues which are on the education agenda, both at the political and administrative level as well as within the ambit of education professionals. Uppermost is an insistent demand for a decentralization of the system, relating to two separate aspects of the present situation. The first is the need for an increase in school autonomy, and some initial steps in that direction have already been taken. Schools are becoming more directly responsible for their day-to-day running (previously managed by state bureaucracy) and moreover, the national curriculum, embedded in the Napoleonic tradition which was absorbed by the Italian administration upon unification, is strongly under pressure to change. A compromise curriculum is partly operating in a large number of experimental situations: a few subjects, and some kind of 'core chapters' within each subject, are uniform all over Italy but other subjects and chapters are decided locally and teachers have more scope for individual choice. One should note, however, a strong perceived need to retain some common core to the curriculum in order to ensure a reasonable national homogeneity and also as a cultural reply to the separatism that circulates in the North of Italy in the wake of the successes of the **Lega Nord**.

A second aspect of decentralization requires crucial political resolution since it involves the very structure of the Republic. Present proposals for major constitutional reform suggest a movement towards an almost federal state; consequently, only the fundamental choices concerning education would remain national, whereas the regions and other local authorities would be responsible for decisions not directly devolved to the responsibility of individual schools. The exact location of the borders between state responsibilities and regional jurisdiction, and of those between regions and schools, is, of course, extremely controversial. Furthermore, for some political parties, and for a part of public opinion, autonomy for individual schools should also involve a change of the rules concerning private schools (almost all Catholic), making them fully equivalent to public ones; up to now, according to the constitution private schools may be authorized to award certification having full legal value but they may not be publicly financed. In fact, the number of students in private schools is rather small (it only exceeds 10 per cent for infant school), whereas Catholic ideas and teachers are widely present inside the public schools (for those who do not refuse it, Catholic religion is a compulsory subject, taught by priests or other catechists appointed by the bishop and paid by the state). Consequently, the call to finance private schools has been in the past rather weak, coming only from clericalist movements, and received little political support even when the Christian Democratic Party was in power.

Instead, there is general consensus about a radical change in pre-service training of all teachers; after a long delay, the implementation of a 1990 law is beginning. It provides that elementary and infant school teachers should have a university qualification, whereas previously the *maturità* at the end of secondary school was sufficient. Furthermore, it provides for attendance of a postgraduate pedagogical specialization school by secondary school teachers-to-be, whereas previously the subject qualification (*laurea*) was sufficient without any further competence or pedagogical training.

Finally, with a new centre–left majority in government since 1996 and with a good chance that the Parliament will run its five-year course, the possibility of a general school reform has been put forward. There is widespread agreement about some points: the end of secondary school should be reached at the age of eighteen instead of nineteen, as in almost all European countries; school attendance should be compulsory at least up to the age of fifteen or sixteen, not necessarily according to a unified curriculum; the system should become much more flexible, without insurmountable barriers between different curri-

cula; and programmes integrating general and vocational education need to be made available.

A legislative proposal submitted by the government to the Parliament in 1997 addresses these points, integrating them into a major transformation of the cycles which presently form the structure of the school system. The text passed by one house of the Parliament, the Chamber of Deputies, but still under scrutiny by the Senate as of the autumn of 1999, unifies elementary and lower secondary schools in a seven-year cycle (*scuola di base*), and thus sets the five-year secondary school ending at the age of 18; the final outcome is however difficult to predict.

At the same time, further debate is taking place concerning the weight that each subject, and topics inside each subject, should have in the curricula. In general education, the Italian school tradition has always granted a predominant role to the humanities: even the Liceo Scientifico has Latin at its centre. Modern subjects like sociology or cinematography, and even economics, are absent. Moreover, in each subject the contemporary aspects are treated only marginally. However, some changes are occurring: computer science has been receiving considerable attention and in history the last year of each cycle has been devoted to the twentieth century. However, there has been strong dispute even about these limited novelties; the road to real modernization of the Italian education system is still a long one. There are official proposals to have English as a compulsory language in all schools, and to have science strongly present for its fundamental cultural values (and not only as technology, in the technical schools). A real struggle about these innovations is going on, and the quality of Italian education will ultimately depend on the results of this struggle.

See also: student movement; universities

Further reading

Cives, G. (ed.) (1990) *La scuola italiana dall'Unità ai nostri giorni* (The Italian School from Unification to the Present), Florence: La Nuova Italia (a general history).

Gattullo, M. and Visalberghi, A. (eds) (1986) *La scuola italiana dal 1945 al 1983* (School in Italy

Table 1

	Lower secondary schools (since 1962, Scuola Media Unica)	Upper secondary schools
Year	Number of students	Number of students
1945–6	508,418	370,575
1950–1	718,604	391,987
1955–6	905,768	593,796
1960–1	1,414,177	768,205
1965–6	1,795,214	1,258,758
1970–1	2,167,539	1,656,117
1975–6	2,778,597	2,096,582
1980–1	2,884,759	2,423,230
1985–6	2,764,635	2,607,749
1990–1	2,261,569	2,860,983
1995–6	1,901,208	2,693,328
1996–7	1,893,476	2,644,291

Source: yearbooks by ISTAT (Istituto nazionale di Statistica)

from 1945 to 1983), Florence: La Nuova Italia (essays on various aspects of postwar Italian education).

Moscati, R. (1998) 'The Changing Policies of Education in Italy', *Journal of Modern Italian Studies* 3 (1): 55–72.

Ricuperati, G. (1995) 'La politica scolastica' (The Politics of the School), in *Storia dell'Italia repubblicana* (History of Republican Italy), vol. II, *La trasformazione dell' Italia: sviluppo e squilibri* (The Transformation of Italy: Developments and Lack of Balance), Turin: Einaudi (education policies in postwar Italy).

Soldani, S. and Turi, G. (eds) (1993) *Fare gli Italiani. Scuola e cultura nell'Italia contemporanea* (Creating Italians: School and Culture in Contemporary Italy), Bologna: Il Mulino, 2 vols (essays about education and culture in Italy 1920–90).

Visalberghi, A. (1994) 'Italy: a system of education', in *The International Encyclopedia of Education*, 2nd edn, Oxford: Pergamon, vol. 5, 302836.

GIUNIO LUZZATTO

Einaudi

Founded in 1933 by Giulio Einaudi, son of the senator Luigi Einaudi, this publishing house soon became the most prestigious in Italy. Giulio Einaudi's first collaborators included Leone Ginzburg, and the initial anti-fascist leanings bore fruit after the war when **Pavese**, **Vittorini** and **Calvino** worked with Einaudi to open Italian culture to the latest international developments. *Il Politecnico*, which led the way in translating American and English novels banned under Fascism, was published by Einaudi, whose subsequent list of writers reads like a who's who of Italian literary talent: Beppe **Fenoglio**, Lalla **Romano**, Carlo **Cassola**, Leonardo **Sciascia**, Italo **Calvino** and Natalia **Ginzburg**. It also played a major role in introducing new currents in Marxism, such as Theodor Adorno and Herbert Marcuse. However by the end of the 1970s Einaudi was in serious financial trouble, and even Calvino moved to **Adelphi** shortly before his death. In 1989 Einaudi was taken over by Elemond, part of the **Berlusconi**-controlled **Mondadori** group, and faced the difficult task of maintaining an authoritative name and addressing new emergent readerships.

Further reading

Cinquant'anni di un editore. Le edizioni Einaudi negli anni 1933–1983 (Fifty Years of a Publisher: Einaudi

Publications in the Years 1933–1983) (1983), Turin: Einaudi.

ROBERT LUMLEY

electoral systems

Since 1861, Italy has experimented with many variations on both types of electoral system – plurality and proportional representation – in the hope of solving political problems. Their history falls into five periods. Between 1861 and 1919, variations on the plurality system – giving victory to candidates with 50 per cent plus one of votes cast – were tried. In 1919 proportional representation (PR) – matching party representation in Parliament to the percentage of votes received – was introduced. In 1923 this system was greatly modified by the Fascist Party to reward the most successful party, provided it gained at least one-quarter of valid votes. After 1946 a particularly pure form of PR was established for most levels of election in order to provide the fairest system for a deeply divided society. Finally, between 1991 and 1995 widespread disillusion with the apparent consequences of PR led to its replacement everywhere by variations on the plurality system which nonetheless retained a PR component. The full 'electoral system' also contains, *inter alia*, the rules which regulate the funding and activities permitted to parties during election campaigns (Fusaro, 1995): here, too, major changes were made in the 1990s as the *Mani pulite* (Clean Hands) investigations revealed the extent of political corruption, and the successful entry into politics of the media magnate Silvio **Berlusconi** made the issue of fair access to the press and television during election campaigns a central concern.

The pre-1991 electoral system and the need for reform

The postwar PR system for national elections established multi-member constituencies, preferential voting for up to four candidates from party lists, and a very low threshold for party representation in Parliament. Even small parties were therefore assured of representation and bargaining power,

and no party was likely to win an outright majority. Governments thus came to consist of unstable multi-party coalitions. In 1953 the **DC** tried to make governments stronger, and improve its own position, by the *Legge Truffa* (Swindle Law) which assigned two-thirds of seats in Parliament to the party or party alliance that had received 50 per cent plus one of votes cast. In the ensuing election, however, the DC-led list narrowly failed to reach the necessary threshold and the law, strongly opposed by the **PCI** and **PSI**, was repealed. PR was subsequently extended to municipal elections in all towns with more than 5,000 inhabitants (from 1964), regional elections (from 1970) and European Parliament elections (from 1979), reproducing at every level many of the features of weak central government and creating popular resentment by placing ever more power in the hands of the political parties. Multiple preference voting enabled local political bosses to determine the winning combinations of candidates, and faction-driven party leaders, not policy-scrutinising electors, made and unmade governments. How much blame for the associated **clientelism** and corruption (see *Tangentopoli*) of the postwar political system should actually be attributed to the electoral rules rather than political culture, party organization or institutions poorly designed to cope with rapid social and economic change remains controversial. However, since electoral systems can be altered more easily than culture or institutions, reform began there.

The reforms of 1991–5 and their consequences

In 1991, after years of inconclusive Parliamentary discussion, renegade MPs led by Mario Segni from the DC harnessed popular pressure for political change by organising a **referendum** to reduce preference choices. Overwhelming success encouraged bolder initiatives. In 1993 a further referendum established a plurality system for the election of the Senate, which in turn forced change to the PR rules for the Chamber of Deputies in order to avoid the possibility of different rules producing different political majorities in the two branches of Parliament. The resulting Mixed Member Proportional System (MMPS) provided for the election of three-quarters of MPs by plurality voting and one-quarter by PR, ostensibly retained to protect minority voices. Also in 1993, a plurality system with direct election of mayors was introduced for municipal elections, and a new mix of plurality and PR was later created for regional elections. By 1995 seven different systems for elections, ranging from neighbourhood to European levels, were in use.

High expectations accompanied the shift from PR to plurality voting. Party identification would matter less to candidates than individual reputation; electoral alliances between parties would give voters a direct choice between alternative governments; new composite parties would emerge from the alliances, eliminating coalitions and guaranteeing government stability (Gambetta and Warner, 1996). Such hopes were not immediately realized. The complexity of the rules for aggregating votes made it difficult for electors to predict the consequences of their choices and thus reduced the desired transparency of the electoral process. Small parties, protected by the partial retention of PR, refused to dissolve into more inclusive groupings. Furthermore, the first post-reform Berlusconi government, elected in 1994, had an even shorter life than most of its PR-based predecessors and, like many of them, was forced out of office by the defection of a coalition member rather than by popular vote. The failure of the new electoral system to deliver fundamental change by itself should have come as no surprise. Under the plurality system of 1861–1919, fifty-two governments had held office with an average life of thirteen months, only a marginally better record than the forty-nine governments with an average twelve-month life under PR between 1946 and 1994. By the late 1990s, therefore, reform of the recently reformed electoral system was already under Parliamentary consideration.

Further reading

D'Alimonte, R. and Bartolini, S. (1997) '"Electoral Transition" and Party System Change in Italy', *West European Politics* 20 (1): 110–34 (how electoral reform influenced the Italian party system in the 1990s).

Donovan, M. (1995) 'The Referendum and the Transformation of the Party System', *Modern Italy* 1 (1): 53–69 (the context for the 1991 referendum).

Fusaro, C. (1995) *Le regole della transizione* (The Rules of the Transition), Bologna: Il Mulino (detailed account of Italy's twentieth-century electoral systems).

Gambetta, D. and Warner, S. (1996) 'The Rhetoric of Reform Revealed (or: If You Bite the Ballot, It May Bite Back)', *Journal of Modern Italian Studies* 1 (3): 357–76 (review of the aims and outcomes of the 1993 electoral reform).

Hine, D. (1993) *Governing Italy*, Oxford: Oxford University Press (the structure and working of the Italian political system until 1991).

Parker, S. (1996) 'Electoral Reform and Political Change, 1991–1994', in S. Gundle and S. Parker (eds), *The New Italian Republic: From the Fall of the Berlin Wall to Berlusconi*, London: Routledge.

Sani, G. and Radaelli, C. (1992) 'Preference Voting: Before and After the 1991 Referendum', *Il Politico* 57 (2): 193–203.

DAVID MOSS

emigration

Emigration is one of the great themes of the first century of national Italian history after 1860. Already before 1914 Italians had moved in great numbers, mostly to North and South America but also to many other parts of the world. The Fascist regime, however, restricted emigration on both opportunist and ideological grounds and, on one occasion, boasted that it had removed the word 'emigration' from Italian vocabularies. However, as soon as the Second World War was over, emigration resumed in a way which bore strong similarities to the situation in Liberal Italy, except that entry to the USA had by now become difficult. For twenty years after the war the United States preserved most of the restrictions which it had originally applied against Italian immigration in 1921 and 1924, although it did make some exceptions for migrants from **Trieste** and the border territories lost to communist Yugoslavia as a result of the war. In the three decades after 1945, only 15,000 immigrants entered the USA each year.

Given these restrictions, at first Argentina became the most favoured destination for Italian migrants after 1945: in 1949, almost 100,000 Italians flocked there. But in the 1950s and 1960s, Canada and Australia, in the past relatively minor sites of Italian immigration, also attracted tens of thousands of immigrants. However, extra-continental emigration was rapidly supplanted by migration to Western Europe, where the long postwar economic boom had begun. The peak year for European migration was 1961 when almost 330,000 Italians emigrated, more than 140,000 to Switzerland and 114,000 to West Germany.

At the same time, a huge migration process was occurring within Italy itself as workers, especially from the South, moved to the industrial centres of the North. Indeed Italy's own economy began growing at such a rate that emigration outside the national borders, first to overseas countries and then to Europe itself, soon dwindled to a trickle. In 1952, 17,000 had left for Brazil, but in 1964 there were only 233; Canada was the choice for 28,000 emigrants in 1958, but only 3,600 went there in 1976. In that year, even the United States received only 6,000 Italian immigrants. The number going to Switzerland reached its maximum in 1962 at 143,000; by 1975 only 30,000 went there. Indeed, from the mid-1970s Italy became a country both of return migration and of active **immigration**, a situation that was to continue throughout the 1990s. Nonetheless, by this time millions of people of Italian origin were residing outside the borders of the nation state.

An appropriate policy towards these emigrants has remained a matter of debate in Italy itself. In the period of mass departure up to the mid-1960s, the parties of both the far Left and the Right tended to object to emigration, while the parties of the centre, namely those which were governing Italy, tended to favour it. For the **PCI**, migration was the 'international capitalist exploitation of the subaltern classes'. The neo-fascists of the **MSI** continued to inveigh against what they perceived as the loss of Italian 'blood' and increased their complaints about the surrender of the East African colonies which had been one of the results of Italy's defeat in the Second World War. The Christian

Democrats (see **DC**) and their allies, by contrast, regarded emigration as a 'safety valve', a hard necessity which would bring material benefit both to the emigrants themselves and to Italy as a country burdened with excess population.

These political differences in turn favoured regional distinctions in the pattern of emigration. Calabria, Sicily, Campania and the Veneto (this last not yet having experienced its eventual extraordinary economic development), all 'white', socially conservative and politically Christian Democrat regions, became (or remained) the classic sites of exodus of postwar emigration. By contrast, 'red' regions such as the Emilia-Romagna, Umbria and Tuscany, experienced very little emigration. Thus 67,000 left the area around Naples in 1961, while only 8,800 moved out of the Emilia-Romagna. Men were still much more likely to emigrate than women. In the decade from 1956 to 1965, for example, an average of 240,000 men left each year, as against 77,000 women. This pattern did begin to vary in countries like Australia and Canada, where the motivation to increase the population was as great as the need for economic development and policies of family reunion gradually increased female immigration.

Nonetheless, migration remained what it had always been for most emigrants, a matter of temporary sojourn. The overwhelming majority first defined themselves as 'birds of passage' and envisaged an early return to Italy, or rather, to their village, town or city of origin. Vast numbers did indeed return. From 1955 to 1975, more than 140,000 emigrants repatriated each year and at least one-third of those who had departed to continents beyond Europe now returned. By the 1970s Italy was regularly receiving more returnees from such countries than the number of migrants it was sending out.

The most vexed question about the emigrant experience, wherever it occurred, was the extent to which the emigrants remained, or became, 'Italian'. In the first decades after 1945, most countries outside Europe accepted immigrants on the condition that they would 'assimilate', that is, they would abandon their 'old ways' in order to adopt the national characteristics of their 'new world'. In the 'melting pot' of their new life, they would shed their Italian-ness. Within Europe, by contrast, immigrants were usually received as 'guest work-ers', obliged to fulfil a work contract and not envisaged as ever acquiring full citizenship. Ger-many and Switzerland were notably rigorous in denying their immigrants such basic rights as the vote. Quite often immigrants were also not given access to much welfare, and local unions typically did little for them, whether out of racial prejudice or a fear that the guest workers were, as leftist theory held, the playthings of a ruthless interna-tional capitalism.

Gradually, however, it became clear that plan-ners of all types – planning had seemed another of the undisputedly good results of the Second World War – were not always achieving what they had initially predicted, and that migrants were an evident example of human beings who stubbornly took agency for their own lives in ways that neither governments nor employers had foreseen. In countries of migration settlement, assimilationism was gradually ousted by integrationism; the melting pot then transmogrified into the 'salad bowl'. By the late 1960s and early 1970s, integrationism was in turn being replaced by 'multiculturalism', a somewhat ambiguous concept which nonetheless did entail the acceptance that immigrants were likely to maintain some version of their 'culture' or 'heritage'. A good index of this change, certainly in nomenclature and perhaps in practice, was the Roman Catholic Church. *Exsul Familia*, an allocu-tion of Pope **Pius XII** in 1952, urged host societies to show charity to migrants but had little doubt that Italians had to go and that, having gone, there was no special reason for them not to assimilate. By contrast, in the encyclical *Cura pastoralis migrantorum* of **Pope Paul VI** in 1969, the Church favoured the retention of an emigrant's 'roots' and spelled out the emigrants' right to retain their own language, culture and spiritual patrimony, both religious and national. Certain Catholic orders, and especially the Scalabrinians, had fought for the cause of *religione e patria* (religion and homeland) from the beginning of the century and the Scalabrinians' Centro Studi Emigrazione (Centre for Emigration Studies) in Rome became the most active and effective scholarly centre for the study both of Italian emigration and of immigration into Italy.

How the culture or spiritual patrimony of emigrants might be defined has remained a difficult and debated issue. The institutions of the **Republic** have found it too complex to resolve and have never worked out a serious way to bring emigrants, especially those gone outside Europe, within the national political process. The Republic saved face by a network of consulates and by the half-hearted subsidizing of the teaching of an official national culture, notably Dante studies, in Saturday schools, through 'Institutes of Culture' (see **Istituti italiani de cultura**) and branches of the **Dante Alighieri Society**. The consulates do offer information about welfare, but the 'culture' of this side of the diplomatic service is a world away from the emigrants themselves and a comprehen-sion gap frequently exists.

Emigrant 'Italians' of course vary in many ways, even if today host societies, in their multicultural-ism, will usually be proud of possessing an Italian 'community'. Once 'Italian' signified poor peasants and the odour of garlic; now it implies **Benetton**, **Ferrari** and the guaranteed health of a 'Medi-terranean diet'. The idea of a community, however, remains a slippery one. Emigrants typically vary by class, gender and age and by their individual history, as reflected in the precise moment and circumstance of their departure. Often they better reflect the 'Italies' than Italy, and Italians in emigration are much more likely to assemble in regional associations (the Tuscan club, the Trina-cria society, Club Vastese and so on) than in national bodies. Anthropologists have similarly observed that, in emigration, intermarriage will occur most frequently with spouses from the same original region or *paese* (town) and least frequently with Italians from other parts of the peninsula.

Host societies will nonetheless emphasize the existence of an 'Italian community', and such a community is likely to have certain features. Italian language newspapers exist in many foreign cities. They will usually be socially and culturally conservative in tone and often politically conserva-tive as well (even while claiming to have 'no politics'). They will work in close harness with the local institutions of the Catholic church, which, by the 1990s, will have forgotten the old quarrels between Italian Catholics and earlier immigrant ones (typically Irish or Polish). They will preach the cause of the 'Italian family', with ideas about gender relations, the treatment of the old and many other aspects of human behaviour which may well not be identical with what is presently occurring in Italy itself. These papers are likely to sponsor, or even be owned by, a community 'leader', who will not have been elected but may act as a 'padrone figure', that is, a patron with certain rights and responsibilities. Whether or not bolstered by a newspaper, a 'community leadership' will seek good ties with both the government of Italy and that of the host society and will, to some extent, act as a conduit between humbler migrants and the local authorities.

These practicalities of emigrant life will sometimes enhance the *italianità* (Italian-ness) of emigrants who may gradually replace regional or local identifications with a version of a national Italian one, just as, in their daily speech, they can move from use of dialect to standard Italian (see **dialects**). By the 1990s Italians abroad are usually members of a second, third, fourth or even fifth generation. Though some of them will have lost all contact with Italy, many will retain, refurbish or re-invent an Italian-ness. A typical ritual is the return visit in which the children of emigrant families go back to 'Italy', by which is meant the *paese* and the surviving family, and the international tourist beat of Rome, Florence and Venice. Cases can even be found in which an *italianità* survives after the loss of the Italian language, and thus where it is possible to be an Italian in English, for example. All these matters indicate what a fluid concept identity is and, indeed, how multiple and flexible are the possibilities of any individual's culture. In their diaspora, Italians, like other emigrants, demonstrate that nationality is only one of the factors which constitutes humankind.

See also: literature of emigration

Further reading

Bosworth, R.J.B. (1996) *Italy and the Wider World 1860–1960*, London: Routledge (a general survey of Italy's place in the world, see especially chapters 6 and 7).

Rosoli, G. (1978) *Un secolo di emigrazione italiana: 1876–1976*, Rome: Centro Studi Emigrazione (a thorough factual introduction to the subject).

R.J.B. BOSWORTH

ENEL

Established in 1962, in the wake of the nationalization of electrical energy (see **privatization and nationalization**), ENEL (Ente Nazionale Energia Elettrica, or National Electrical Energy Agency) came to effectively exercise a monopoly over the production and distribution of electricity throughout Italy (it accounted for 75 per cent of production and 93 per cent of distribution at the end of the 1990s), although marginal quotas were retained for large industrial groups which produced electricity for their own use and for a large number of municipal companies which served local markets. In the two decades following its inception, ENEL achieved some remarkable successes including the creation of an integrated national grid (until then fragmented into a number of inefficient regional systems), a shift from hydropower to thermopower, the elimination of the North–South electricity gap and unified tariffs which reduced large disparities between users. However – and at the same time – it also suffered from consistently poor economic performance and heavy financial imbalances as well as slow growth of tariffs in comparison with inflation.

ENEL also failed to develop nuclear power. Although a number of plans, all stressing the need to diversify energy sources, were proposed by successive governments and passed by the Parliament, by the mid-1980s Italy had only four nuclear plants which contributed no more than 4 per cent to the total national production. The nuclear option was definitively abandoned in the wake of the Chernobyl disaster of 1986, and the strongly supported referendum organized by environmentalist associations against nuclear energy in 1987.

Italy's heavy dependence on thermopower turned out to be a serious disadvantage after the 1973–4 and 1979–80 oil shocks and the consequent steep increase in oil prices. In spite of this, research on projects utilizing renewable energy sources remained underdeveloped and Italy continued to depend largely on foreign sources for its energy needs.

In 1992 ENEL was transformed into a limited company with the Italian Treasury as its sole shareholder and was also considered eligible for privatization, although any decision was postponed after the enforcement of the liberalization of the electricity market required by European authorities. In view of this, an independent Authority for Electricity and Gas was established in 1995 and, after much debate, at the beginning of 1999 the ruling centre–left government took another major step by setting production, import and export and purchase and sale of electricity totally free. A state monopoly on transmission and distribution was maintained under a concession regime which enables the government to appoint a single operator of both the national transmission grid (which continued being owned by ENEL) and the wholesale market, and a multiplicity of regional distributors. ENEL was also required to sell out a substantial share of its generating plants in four years' time and to split into specialized operating companies to perform separate activities (from production and transmission to sale and distribution). This is likely to ease both its partial privatization (launched in 1999) and the establishment of joint ventures with private partners, and is expected to lead in the near future to a liberalization of 40 per cent of the market.

STEFANO BATTILOSSI

ENI

Founded by Enrico **Mattei** in 1953 as a state-owned agency for research, refinery and distribution of petroleum and gas, ENI (Ente Nazionale Idrocarburi) became the world's seventh largest publicly traded oil group. Its history is emblematic of the way the **DC** used state power. At first ENI was completely under Mattei's control, as he built up first its gas and then petroleum and petrochemical interests and then diversified (into textiles, engineering, financial sectors and the Milanese daily *Il Giorno*). Mattei ably manipulated the DC and other parties into supporting a massive growth of the power and influence of the agency, and after his death in a plane crash in 1962 the agency became part of the process of *lottizzazione* (spoil-sharing) in internal politics and also strongly influenced Italian foreign policy towards oil-producing countries. ENI eventually absorbed AGIP, SNAM (natural gas distribution company)

and ANIC (chemical and petrochemicals). Privatization of the agency began in 1995, and by 1999 the state share was down to 36.3 per cent although the Treasury retained a so-called golden share with special voting rights, thus maintaining a strong influence in the appointment of directors and the orientation of strategy (see also **privatization and nationalization**).

JAMES WALSTON

environmental movement

The development of the Italian environmental movement in the postwar period was determined, at least in part, by characteristics peculiar to Italian society and politics. First, the relative backwardness of the country until the late 1950s and the extreme speed and depth of the subsequent economic transformation militated against a shift in value priorities – from issues of personal security and material wealth to self-realization and quality of life – which are usually regarded as the most conducive to environmental action. Second, the dominant political culture in the country did not help such a move either. The persistence of a division between the Left and the Right slowed down the spread of environmental ideas and associations in at least three ways: it reduced opportunities for forms of collective action like the environmental one, which did not align with the major division but rather cut across it; it left little room for cultural perspectives which were not founded on the anthropocentric worldview shared by both Marxist and Catholic ideologies and, by assigning priority to collective identities based on social classes and/or ideological groups, rather than on membership of the national community, it reproduced the traditional shortage of civic values in the country. Admittedly, it may be unfair to blame the major postwar political actors for a state of affairs which long pre-dated them, since one could argue that class and religious ideologies simply occupied a ground which had been left void by the inept and corrupted political elites of the recently unified Italian state. Whatever the case, the pervasive presence of these factors slowed the spread of any collective action targeting public goods, and environmentalist action proved no exception to this general pattern. Even the radical social movements which developed in the late 1960s and early 1970s were in the beginning quite indifferent to environmental perspectives, being as they were closely tied to a Marxist-Leninist model of political organization, and largely untouched – despite significant minorities – by the countercultural styles influential elsewhere, particularly in the USA. For all these reasons, the time for a breakthrough of environmental organizations came only in the early 1980s, when the significance of the Left–Right divide drastically decreased. Even by the mid-1990s the overall strength of the movement remained relatively low compared to its northern European and American counterparts.

It is important to recall these peculiarities because otherwise, in its broad lines at least, the history of the Italian environmental movement does not differ significantly from that in other countries. Associations with an interest in the preservation of natural and historical heritage were founded between 1894 (Touring Club Italiano) and 1914 (the National League for the Protection of Natural Monuments). Their impact did not usually go beyond the most enlightened sectors of the elites, and this also applies to the early conservation groups established several decades later, such as Italia Nostra (1955) and Pro Natura (1959).

In the 1960s and early 1970s, opportunities for environmental action increased. Scientific publications denouncing environmental risks (in particular the celebrated, albeit controversial, MIT–Club of Rome report on the 'Limits to Growth') fuelled environmental concerns among the elites and the educated public. The costs to the natural and urban environment of the unprecedented economic growth experienced by the country since the late 1950s also became increasingly evident. These developments were reflected in the creation of new associations which would play a major role in the following decades: the League for the Protection of Birds (1964) and the Italian branch of WWF (1966).

From a different perspective, the radicalization of political life and the participatory attitudes spurred by 1968 created a globally favourable climate for collective action. Some left-wing groups, in particular radical working class organi-

zations (see **extraparliamentary Left**), started to address issues related to the environmental question, such as industrial pollution inside and outside the factory. Cooperations developed on this ground between working-class activists and radical scientists; radical journals were founded (*Sapere*, *Ecologia*) and new organizations were created (Democratic Geology in 1973, Democratic Medicine in 1976). Mobilizations were promoted by left-wing groups in response to the Seveso accident in 1976. The foundations for the development of a political ecology perspective, and for regarding environmental problems as a byproduct of mechanisms of capitalist domination, were thus laid.

The crisis of the post-1968, class-oriented left-wing movements liberated a significant mobilization potential which partially turned to the environment when the Italian government announced its nuclear energy plan in 1975. Opposition to the proposed plants spread across the country and peaked in Montalto di Castro, North of Rome, between 1977 and 1978. However, the anti-nuclear coalitions were inherently unstable, consisting as they did of local – and often conservative – residents, extreme left autonomous groups, action committees set up by concerned members of the scientific community (for example, the Committee for Popular Control over Energy Policies) and new environmental groups like the Italian branch of Friends of Earth (created in 1977 under the auspices – but not the control – of leading figures of the **Radical Party**).

While the anti-nuclear campaigns were instrumental in setting the conditions for the growth of an environmental movement, they did not result directly in the emergence of a network of organizations capable of sustained, coordinated action at the national level. Barriers created by ideological differences and disagreements regarding strategies proved still too strong to overcome. Nevertheless, the late 1970s left some permanent legacies in that some new organizations were created in addition to those mentioned above. These included leading animal rights groups LAV (Anti-Vivisection League, established 1977) and LAC (Anti-Hunting League, 1978), what was to become the most influential political ecology group in the country, Legambiente (1980), and the right-wing organization Gruppi di Ricerca Ecologica (Ecological Research Groups, or

GRE, 1978). Although some regarded it, especially in its early years, as a covert attempt by the Communist Party to hegemonize environmental activism, Legambiente played an important role in linking local groups all over the country. It also brought together early political ecology campaigners, mostly from the new Left but also from the traditional Left. As for GRE, they played no significant role in the environmental movement, mainly due to their links to the neo-fascist party (**MSI**), although it remains to be seen whether the momentous changes in the Italian political system of the early 1990s may not have increased opportunities for collaboration between right-wing and mainstream environmentalists.

Interest in environmental issues grew dramatically during the 1980s, affecting both lifestyles (outdoor activities, natural food and interest in the body all boomed) and political choices (Green lists became a significant presence in the mid-1980s). Membership of the major environmental groups rose by about 250 per cent between 1983 and 1991, and the number of independent local groups active on small projects was estimated at 2,000. That Greenpeace opened its Italian branch in 1986 also testifies to the growing visibility of environmental activism in that period. Many political ecology groups were also involved in the peace movement which mobilized in 1983 and 1984 against plans to install cruise missiles in the country. Organizational growth and the declining salience of the Left–Right cleavage rendered the emergence of a national environmental movement easier during this time, and an occasion for action was provided by the Chernobyl accident in 1986. Major organizations in the conservationist and political ecology tradition joined forces and acted as the backbone of a heterogeneous coalition which eventually obtained consent to a referendum. Held in November, 1987, the referendum sanctioned the virtual demise of the nuclear energy programme in the country. Mobilization spread in the following years to invoke the closure of other types of high-risk factories, including the Montedison-controlled Farmoplant in Tuscany and Acna in Piedmont.

By contrast, the 1990s started rather inauspiciously as in May 1990 two new referenda, targeting hunting and the use of pesticides in agriculture, were not validated due to the low turnout. Later, a number of important campaigns were launched on issues ranging from high-speed trains and urban traffic to the impact of affluent economies over the environment in the Third World. Despite securing some media coverage, however, none of them matched the emotional and political impact of the anti-nuclear mobilizations of the 1980s.

Nevertheless, it would be wrong to interpret this as a complete withering of environmental political action. On the one hand, the network of cooperation between environmental groups stayed in place, and they remained an established presence in Italian society. If still small by international standards, they represented nonetheless the largest component of the voluntary sector in Italy (although estimates of their actual size varied considerably, from 350,000 to 550,000 in the mid-1990s, and up to 1,500,000 if organizations promoting environment-friendly leisure-time activities, like the Touring Club or the Alpine Club, are included). The major difference from the previous phases was that environmental associations in the 1990s relied overwhelmingly on traditional pressure group tactics rather than on confrontational protest. They frequently operated as watchdogs on behalf of the public, regularly monitoring the state of natural resources like air and water. Their status as a routine source of information and commentary for the media also facilitated their gradual abandonment of direct action.

One the other hand, the 1990s also witnessed the spread of protest activities, promoted at neighbourhood or city level by small, independent residents' action groups. These targeted any project perceived as threatening the quality of life of the local communities, from garbage incinerators to new roads, railways, car parks and so on. Protests were conducted for the most part independently of major organizations, even though the latter were frequently involved in them. Local actions also sometimes took a distinctive 'not-in-my-backyard' flavour, or linked up with other non-environmental protest activities on sensitive urban issues such as immigration or law and order. How the established environmental organizations and these new forms of local action might be able to develop some systematic co-operation remained a complicated problem with no immediate solution.

An evaluation of the results of the environmental movement is similarly complex, even leaving aside its indirect impact on the party system. In terms of formal recognition, there were undeniably positive results. Environmental organizations came to have a formal consultative status at the Environment Ministry, and former environmental leaders were appointed – albeit still occasionally – to senior positions in the government or in public agencies. However, concrete policy outcomes were only partially achieved. Important innovations were implemented in several municipalities on matters ranging from recycling to experiments of time management meant to reduce air pollution. Similarly significant policy measures in areas such as energy savings were passed, and the complex of laws regulating environmental matters in Italy became comparable to that of other Western countries. However, even if one attributed most of the credit for such innovations to the environmentalists – in all likelihood an overstatement of their effective impact – their actual implementation has been far less systematic. The well-known weakness of Italian public administration and the strong influence of vested interests over policy makers have inevitably contributed to limiting this success.

See also: environmental policy

Further reading

Biorcio, R. and Lodi, G. (eds) (1988) *La sfida verde* (The Green Challenge), Padua: Liviana.

Diani, M. (1995) *Green Networks: A Structural Analysis of the Italian Environmental Movement*, Edinburgh: Edinburgh University Press.

Farro, A. (1991) *La Lente verde* (The Green Frame), Milan: Angeli.

Poggio, A. (1996) *Ambientalismo* (Environmentalism), Milan: Editrice Bibliografica.

MARIO DIANI

environmental policy

It took almost thirty years for an autonomous environmental policy to develop in Italy. Three distinct phases in the evolution of environmental policies can actually be identified. The first phase lasted approximately from 1966 to 1975, its most important result being the passing of the air pollution act in 1966, the so called 'legge anti-smog'. The second phase started in the mid-1970s and ended about ten years later. In that decade, systematic regulations were passed providing adequate legal instruments to cope with major environmental problems. The water pollution act (319/76), also known as 'legge Merli', was passed in 1976, while in 1985 the so called 'legge Galasso' (431/85) set new and stricter limitations on the possibility of building in environmentally sensitive areas. The third phase of environmental policy started with the creation of the Ministry for the Environment in 1986. The new ministry gave further stimulus to legislative action and attempted to better co-ordinate activities which had been previously fragmented between a number of other departments and public agencies. The act which established the Environmental Ministry also formalized a consultative role for major environmental organizations.

During the 1980s, policy and institutional innovation also spread at the local level. Environmental departments (*assessorati*) were created in most local administrations, and local issues became a major area of consideration for the formation of environmental policy. In the late 1990s, the Environmental Agency was established to promote environmental research, to better circulate relevant information to policy makers and the public and to monitor high risk plants and other potential sources of environmental damage.

The timing of the active development of environmental policy in Italy was slow in comparison to other West European countries, where, for example, environmental ministries had, in some cases, already been established in the early 1970s. By the late 1990s, however, the Italian legislative and administrative apparatus did not differ substantially from that of other countries. What still differed was the capacity to implement environmental policy decisions. On the whole, Italy has failed to anticipate problems of environmental degradation and has done no more than react to them. Even the implementation of EEC and, later, EU directives on environmental issues has been quite slow, even reluctant (by December 1991, Italy had implemented only 59 per cent of European regulations, although the picture improved over the 1990s). Italian environmental legislation was also criticized for its lack of unifying principles, for the enormous number of laws and regulations dealing with environmental problems (over 1,400 according to some 1992 estimates) and for its uneven emphasis, with some areas (such as waste disposal) being overregulated and others (such as acoustic pollution) still not properly controlled. These shortcomings have increased the difficulties of the public administration to mediate between divergent interests and to set clear guidelines for action.

See also: environmental movement; Verdi

Further reading

Alexander, D. (1991) 'Pollution, Policies and Politics: The Italian Environment', in F. Sabetti and R. Catanzaro (eds), *Italian Politics: A Review*, vol. 5, London: Pinter (an analysis of the state of the Italian environment in the early 1990s and of governmental response to the growing pollution).

Bulsei, G.L. (1990) *Le politiche ambientali* (Environmental Policies), Turin: Rosenberg & Sellier.

Lewanski, R. (1997) *Governare l'ambiente* (Regulating the Environment), Bologna: il Mulino.

MARIO DIANI

Epoca

Modelled closely on the American magazine *Life* and the French *Paris Match*, *Epoca* began publication in October 1950, edited by Alberto Mondadori. After an initial lacklustre performance, in 1953 editorship passed to Enzo **Biagi**, a talented journalist who was able to assemble an impressive team of collaborators including Cesare **Zavattini**, Luigi Barzini Jr, Indro **Montanelli** and Oreste del Buono. With an elegant, glossy format featuring spectacular photographs and consciously presented as 'the magazine for the Italian family', by 1955 it had established itself firmly and reached sales of 500,000. While continuing to focus on current affairs and changing social attitudes, the magazine also introduced a television column among other

novel features and thus soon overtook all its rivals. For political reasons, Biagi was forced to leave the magazine in 1960 and from then emphasis shifted to travel reportage and well photographed nature and scientific features. This divulgative role was inevitably undermined by television and from the mid-1970s sales began to fall. In spite of several attempts to change the format, the magazine's fate was sealed and it closed in January 1997.

GINO MOLITERNO

Erba, Luciano

b. 18 September 1922, Milan

University professor, poet and translator

Erba received a degree in letters from the Catholic University of Milan in 1947, where he later taught French literature while also contributing to various Italian and foreign literary magazines, among them *il verri*, *Officina*, *La Fiera letteraria*, *Botteghe oscure*, *Poetry* and *The Western Review*. He began to write in the years following the end of the Second World War, and is usually situated in the so-called *Linea lombarda* (Lombard Line), a group of poets who, borrowing from the tradition Pascoli–Gozzano–**Montale**, write a kind of poetry characterized by concrete images and moral tension but also, as in Erba's case, by a subtle allusivity and a balanced irony.

See also: poetry

Further reading

Luzzi, G. (1978) 'La poesia di Luciano Erba da "Il male minore" a "Il Prato più verde"' (The Poetry of Luciano Erba from 'The Lesser Evil' to 'The Greenest Field'), *Paragone* 29 (340): 83–96 (an informative essay covering twenty years of Erba's earlier poetry).

ENRICO CESARETTI

L'Espresso

One of Italy's foremost newsmagazines, *L'Espresso* was founded in October 1955 by Arrigo **Benedetti** and Eugenio **Scalfari**. Originally in large newspaper format but restyled in 1974 to a small, glossy magazine, it was characterized from the beginning by an aggressive investigative journalism strongly focussed on **DC** (and later Socialist Party) corruption and **clientelism**. In the 1950s it uncovered major scandals in the health and housing industries, in 1964 it revealed the attempted *coup d'état* by General Di Lorenzo and in 1976 it conducted a strong campaign against the then President of the Republic, Giovanni Leone, for his alleged involvement in the Lockheed scandal. During the 1970s and 1980s it critically confronted all the major current issues including **terrorism** and strongly supported the campaigns for **divorce** and **abortion**. However, from the mid-1970s onwards it became engaged in fierce competition with Italy's other major news magazine, *Panorama*, a rivalry that increased dramatically in the early 1990s when **Berlusconi**, having already taken control of *Panorama*, attempted to also absorb *L'Espresso* but narrowly failed. Since then the two magazines, ever more similar in format and coverage, are distinguished by and large by their consistent stance pro or contra Berlusconi.

GINO MOLITERNO

European Union

The European dimension of Italian government is a long-standing factor in the evolution of the **Republic**. At critical junctures, European integration has shaped economic and political dynamics in Italy. By contrast, the Italian contribution to the dynamics of European integration, although hardly negligible, has been overshadowed by the pivotal role of other countries, most notably by the Franco–German axis in European affairs.

In the postwar period, joining the European Coal and Steel Community (1951) and the European Economic Community (1957) was part of a national strategy. At the international level, this secured legitimacy, status and credibility for a country which had come out of the war as a loser. Internally, European membership contributed to the consolidation of the newborn Italian democracy and strengthened the solidity of the Republic against the risk of a breakdown of democratic processes. The choice was not without its own risks, as Italy was the only founding member of the Community with such serious problems of poverty and illiteracy and with pronounced regional disparities between the North and the South (see **Southern Question**). Ultimately, however, integration did produce more benefits than costs.

Being – in terms of population – a large founding member of the European Community, Italy gained the same formal status as the most important members, such as France and Germany, in terms of voting power and numerical presence within the European institutions. Yet the Italian influence on European policies remained limited. Indeed, even under the best circumstances Italy merely played the role of mediator and not of leader (Sbragia, 1992). Governmental instability and poor administrative resources also severely constrained the capability of Italian negotiators to make a profound impact on the trajectory of European integration. Italy as a country had a poor record of implementation of European decisions, decidedly at odds with the Euro-enthusiasm of both Italian public opinion and policy makers. In fact, European integration had always been strongly supported by Italians and even the Italian Communist Party (**PCI**), after an initial period of opposition to the European Community, came to share in the general enthusiasm for Europeanism. The pro-European attitude was only mildly challenged by the **Berlusconi** government in 1994. All the same, it seems paradoxical that Italy often agreed to European decisions which later were difficult to implement, although Italian politicians were always able to capitalize on an Italian consensus which could be taken for granted. The latter, in fact, proved to be a positive political investment of goodwill and reputation at the table of European decisions, and Italian policy makers were able to cash in the return on this investment when asking their European partners for more leniency on pressing domestic problems, such as the closure of steel plants (see **Ilva**), excessive milk production and state aids to ailing industries (Giuliani, 1996).

Notwithstanding the deficit in implementation and the difficulties in playing a purposive role in European affairs, Italy was able to defend the national interest in crucial episodes of European integration. Italy was at the margins of the Franco-German scheme leading to the European Coal and Steel Community, but **De Gasperi** obtained subsidies for the Sardinian mines, access to Algerian iron ore and, most crucially, free movement of workers. In a country where the 'Piano **Vanoni**' (Vanoni Plan) assumed that 800,000 workers would leave Italy each year, free movement of labour within the Community was indispensable. Hence this fundamental concession was a typical Italian mark on the shape of European integration. Italy was also instrumental in the creation of the European Social Fund and the European Investment Bank, two instruments of the Community designed to tackle the problems of unemployment and regional disparities, and Italian industry also gained from the progressive establishment of the single market. By contrast, Italian interests in the Common Agricultural Policy yielded to those of central and northern countries: fruit and vegetables, the typical Italian products, were far less protected by the Common Agricultural Policy than cereals and meat.

European monetary policy positively transformed the Italian state. In December 1978 the **Andreotti** government decided to join the European Monetary System in spite of the glaring gulf between the Italian rate of inflation and the European average. This decision inaugurated the policy of tying Italy's hands in advance to European rules, which proved to have an impressive disciplinary force. The provisions regarding the single currency, enshrined in the Treaty on the European Union signed at Maastricht, came to be the most powerful mechanism for discipline on Italian public finance in the 1990s. In conjunction with domestic political upheavals, they also transformed the Italian state by assigning more political power to the Treasury, the Bank of Italy and the technocrats in government, while curbing the power of the *partitocrazia* (rule by the parties).

Nevertheless, in the late 1990s, as Italy prepared to join the Economic and Monetary Union, the problems relating to the welfare state, the **taxation** system and, most importantly, socioeconomic disparities across regions seemed likely to be exacerbated (Radaelli and Bruni, 1998). If, in the postwar era, the European Union had been able to provide an 'external constraint' on Italian economic policy, at this point the structural problems of the Italian economy remained solely in the hands of Italians.

See also: foreign policy

Further reading

Dyson, K. and Featherstone, K. (1996) 'Italy and EMU as a "Vincolo Esterno": Empowering the Technocrats, Transforming the State', *South European Society and Politics* 1 (2): 272–99 (an accurate analysis of the political impact of the European external constraint).

Giuliani, M. (1996) 'Italy', in D. Rometsch and W. Wessels (eds), *The EU and Member States. Towards Institutional Fusion?*, Manchester: Manchester University Press, 105–33.

Hine, D. (1993) *Governing Italy: The Politics of Bargained Pluralism*, Oxford: Clarendon (see ch. 10 on the European Community dimension of Italian government, a plain introduction to the main issues).

Radaelli, C. and Bruni, M. (1998) 'Beyond Charlemagne's Europe: A Sub-National Examination of Italy Within EMU', *Regional and Federal Studies* 8 (2).

Sbragia, A. (1992) 'Italy–EEC: An Undervalued Partnership', *Relazioni Internazionali* 2 (June): 78–86.

CLAUDIO M. RADAELLI

L'Europeo

Originally a large format news and culture weekly, *L'Europeo* first appeared in November 1945 and was edited for its first ten years by Arrigo **Benedetti**. Largely under his influence, it cultivated an elegant but sober look, being well-written and illustrated with impeccable care and taste. Directed mainly at a middle-class and family readership but slightly more culturally elevated than its popular rival,

Epoca, it was politically centrist but was also one of the few magazines at the time willing to openly have dialogue with the Communist Party. Focussing for the most part on news and current affairs, the magazine achieved some impressive scoops, one of the most memorable being Tommaso Besozzi's investigative report on the death of Salvatore **Giuliano**, which convincingly disproved official accounts of how the bandit had died. Some of the great names of Italian journalism passed through its pages, including Giorgio **Bocca** and Enzo **Biagi** as well as writers like Oriana **Fallaci** and photographers such as Federico Scianna (see **photography**) and Oliviero **Toscani**. Under pressure from falling sales during the late 1970s, the magazine changed to a small format in 1981. By the early 1990s it had managed to regain some ground but it was eventually forced to close in 1995.

GINO MOLITERNO

Evola, Giulio Cesare Andrea (Julius)

b. 19 May 1898, Rome; d. 11 June 1974, Rome

Philosopher, writer and painter

Evola was the principal figure in the not over-crowded cultural world of the post-1945 extreme Right. Of aristocratic descent, Evola began his creative life as a futurist painter under Marinetti's influence. An encounter with dadaism marked both his paintings and his poetic production (1916–22) from which he embarked on a parallel exploration of the world of Eastern thought and the decadence of the modern West. His racial theories brought him popularity in Germany and Italy in the 1930s and the offer (declined) of a personal Chair in Racism at the University of Rome in 1939.

In postwar Italy, Evola's mandarin contempt for democracy and equality – symptoms of the ideological and political ruin in which modern man was now living – made him a natural reference point for the violent groups of the neo-fascist Right (see **fascism and neo-fascism**). His

numerous and arcane writings featured on their reading lists for militants, and he was hailed by Giorgio Almirante, leader of the **MSI** (Movimento Sociale Italiano, or Italian Social Movement) as 'our Marcuse (only better)'.

Further reading

Evola, J. (1996) *Revolt against the Modern World*, trans. G. Stucco, Rochester, VT: Inner Traditions International (extended exposition, originally published in 1934, of Evola's basic doctrines).

Ferraresi, F. (1987) 'Julius Evola: Tradition, Reaction and the Radical Right', *Archives européennes de sociologie* 28 (1): 107–51 (discussion of Evola's intellectual origins, main themes and postwar influence).

DAVID MOSS

extraparliamentary Left

As a significant political force, the extraparliamentary Left in Italy covered the period 1969–76. However, its intellectual inspirations predate 1969 and its political legacies can be traced beyond the mid-1970s. An unstable collage of distinct political traditions and experiences, its impact was both benign and destructive. On one hand, the pressures exercised by its militants helped to demolish some of the most archaic and authoritarian features of schools and workplaces: its groups played a vital role in the cultural revolution of 1968–9 in which Italy struggled, with partial success, to modernize its politics and institutions and to absorb the social consequences of the **economic miracle**. On the other hand, pursuit of the mirage of revolution eventually alienated many prospective future leaders from all political involvement and led some of the more disillusioned rank and file members into **terrorism** once mass protest had subsided and the extraparliamentary groups themselves had disintegrated.

Before the revolution: pre-1968 origins

After 1945, a variety of voices in the communist tradition, inspired in particular by Trotsky and

Mao Zedong, continued to criticize the strategy and tactics of the **PCI** from the Left. However, only in the 1960s did these isolated voices start to make an impact outside a limited circle. The appearance of ***Quaderni Rossi*** (1961), ***Quaderni piacentini*** (1962) and *Classe operaia* (1963) greatly expanded the systematic application of renovated Marxist theory to features of contemporary Italian society and culture, and the hitherto barely known works of the young **Gramsci** were scrutinized for political guidance. Except for the tiny Partito Comunista d'Italia (marxisti-leninisti), whose reverence for the Chinese and Albanian experiments in socialism was as profound as the party's cohesion was shallow, the gap between Marxist theory and revolutionary practice remained great. The unexpected opportunity to try to close it was provided by the **student movement** of 1967–8, immediately followed by the worker revolt across northern and central Italy in the 'Hot Autumn' of 1969.

Revolution at hand? 1968–73

Between 1968 and 1970 the principal organizations of the extraparliamentary Left were created, including Lotta Continua (Continuous Struggle), Potere Operaio (Worker Power), Avanguardia Operaia (Worker Avantgarde) and **il manifesto**. With the exception of the last (a group of intellectuals expelled from the PCI in 1969), each organization remained strongly marked by the city in which it had originated, although each attracted at least a few members in most major cities. Lotta Continua, the most iconoclastic and least disciplined group, was a product mainly of Turin and the leadership of Adriano Sofri, Luigi Bobbio and Guido Viale. Events at **Fiat**, particularly in the ungovernable megafactory of Mirafiori, therefore tended to loom large in shaping its views on the state of revolutionary progress in Italy generally. Potere Operaio, directed by Toni Negri, Franco Piperno and Oreste Scalzone, had an especially strong presence in the Veneto and Rome, both largely non-industrial contexts which encouraged the group's distinctive combination of mandarin intellectual acrobatics and political sectarianism. Avanguardia Operaia, among whose leaders Silverio Corvisieri stood out, had a grassroots

presence in the so-called CUB (Comitati unitari di base, or unified base committees) in factories around Milan but found recruitment elsewhere difficult. As well as struggling for change in workplaces, schools and universities, the extraparliamentary groups were active in conflicts over housing which were especially marked in the northern cities swollen by **emigration** from east and south Italy in the 1960s.

Local pressures and ideological differences made relations between the groups unstable. Competition for the allegiance of a fairly limited number of activists (Milan, the largest concentration, had an estimated 8,000 irregular participants in extreme Left activities) was intense, especially among secondary school students who represented the largest single category of members. With their broadsheets, cultural events, political activism and self-defence against the extreme Right, the groups came to form exclusive, often mutually hostile, local sub-cultures, increasingly detached from the world of the working class whose interests they claimed to advance. Moreover, the leaders, sharing a dissatisfaction with the insufficiently radical PCI but divided by endless disputes over genuinely revolutionary strategy and tactics, also became estranged from the generally younger grassroots activists, especially after the widespread industrial and educational protest had peaked by 1975 and the prospects of socialist revolution or military reaction, to be respectively accelerated and resisted by the extraparliamentary Left as its political rationale, had both faded.

Towards violence, parliamentary politics and feminism: 1974–6

Adoption of an extraparliamentary identity inspired by Leninism forced all groups to define their attitude to the antithesis of parliamentary democracy: political violence. Most were deeply equivocal, talking up the need for violence but deploring specific violent acts. As splinter groups (see **Red Brigades**) embarked in 1970 on campaigns of deliberate destruction in the workplace and physical injury of political enemies, the boundary between politics and violence became blurred and the tensions within each group more severe. Minority groups in the major cities became open advocates of political violence: the self-defence squads of Lotta Continua, trained to respond to the now-waning extreme Right violence, provided recruits for terrorist organizations such as Prima Linea (Front Line); members of Potere Operaio, which dissolved itself in 1973, passed into **Autonomia** and supported low-level factory and neighbourhood violence. Some of the leaders of Potere Operaio (Negri, Piperno, Scalzone) were later convicted of direct involvement in terrorism. However, the overwhelming majority of the extraparliamentary Left was opposed to violence and favoured a partial return to parliamentary politics. An effort to organize a joint group cartel to contest the 1976 national elections achieved only very disappointing results (see **Democrazia Proletaria**) which led directly to the dissolution of the largest remaining group, Lotta Continua. Many activists then abandoned politics altogether. Some who did not joined the resurgent **Radical Party** (see Marco **Pannella**) with its focus on civil rights such as **divorce**. Prominent female members, however, dissatisfied with their experiences as subordinates in the male-dominated politics of the extraparliamentary Left, provided the leadership of the distinctive Italian feminist movement (see **feminism**).

Further reading

Bobbio, L. (1979) *Lotta Continua: storia di una organizzazione rivoluzionaria* (Lotta Continua: The History of a Revolutionary Organization), Rome: Savelli (history of LC by a prominent Turin leader).

Corvisieri, S. (1979) *Il mio viaggio nella sinistra* (My Journey Through the Left), Rome: Editoriale l'Espresso (perceptive account by leader of Avanguardia Operaia).

Lumley, R. (1990) *States of Emergency: Cultures of Revolt in Italy from 1967 to 1978*, London: Verso (cultures and ideologies in the emergence of student and worker movements).

Tarrow, S. (1989) *Democracy and Disorder: Protest and Politics in Italy 1965–1975*, Oxford: Clarendon Press (fundamental study of grassroots antiauthoritarian protest, secular and religious).

Vettori, G. (1973) *La sinistra extraparlamentare in Italia* (The Extraparliamentary Left in Italy), Rome: Newton Compton (history and documents of major groups).

DAVID MOSS

F

Fabbri, Diego

b. 1911, Forlì; d. 1980, Riccione

Playwright

One of the few playwrights of the postwar years with a strong Catholic background and inspiration, Fabbri created a body of work which revolved around the theme of the relationship between God and men, and the values of faith. He was interested particularly in the capacity of these values to give answers to human needs while at the same time portraying human weaknesses and contradictions.

Fabbri started his career in theatre during the 1940s when he wrote a number of 'intimist' plays of a psychological nature. His major theatrical works, however, were written during the 1950s and include *Inquisizione* (Inquisition) (1950) and *Processo a Gesù* (The Trial of Christ) (1955) which are characterized by a more religious inspiration and *Il Seduttore* (The Seducer) (1951) and *La Bugiarda* (The Deceitful Woman) (1956) which focus more on social values and corruption.

From the early 1960s Fabbri also began to write for television, with successful screenplays adapted from major European novels. Amongst the most popular were *Le inchieste del Commissario Maigret* (Inspector Maigret's Inquiries) (four series from 1964 to 1972), *I fratelli Karamazov* (The Brothers Karamazov) (1969) and *Il Segreto di Luca* (Luca's Secret) (1969).

FEDERICA STURANI

Fabro, Luciano

b. 20 November 1936, Turin

Sculptor

Usually associated with **arte povera**, Fabro regards art as a process for heightening the viewer's awareness. The artwork is built as a site for seeing and sensing, not in order to reduce something to a single image or solution. While interested in abstract elements, such as space, which can be seen in his constructed cubes and habitats, Fabro tends to use figurative elements in a novel way. The *Piedi* (Feet) series of 1968–72 has a number of bronze, glass and marble paws protruding from giant, silken trouser legs suspended above them. *Sisifo* (Sisyphus) (1994) consists of a large onyx roller which has been rolled across a bed of flour, suggestive of the mythological futile labours.

Fabro's best-known works are the *Italia* series, produced since 1968. These are large, upside down representations of the Italian peninsula, using a variety of materials such as iron, leather, glass and fur, each making a comment on the nature of contemporary Italy.

MAX STAPLES

Falcone, Giovanni

b. 18 May 1939, Palermo; d. 23 May
1992, Capaci

Magistrate

Giovanni Falcone was the key member of a team of
magistrates in Palermo (the 'antimafia pool', which
was directed by Antonino Caponnetto and included the equally respected Paolo Borsellino)
whose investigations between 1983 and 1988
secured the convictions of many **mafia** bosses.

Falcone's unprecedented feat of obtaining firm
evidence which could survive courtroom contests
and mafia pressure on judges, jurors and witnesses
at every level of the legal process rested principally
on three novel elements: scrutiny of financial
transactions, confessions elicited from *pentiti* such
as ex-boss Tommaso Buscetta, and identification of
the mafia as a centrally directed organization. An
upbringing in a mafia-saturated neighbourhood,
the financial knowledge gained from his early work
as a magistrate in the bankruptcy court and a
capacity for unrelenting attention to hard-won
detail in a pre-computerized judiciary, enabled
Falcone to win the respect and collaboration of
mafia turncoats and to follow the intricate detail of
the organization's business transactions far beyond
Sicily. To overcome the rigid jurisdictional limits to
investigations, he created a network of collaborators among police and magistrates in northern
Italy, France and the USA which enabled him to
track the movements of mafiosi and money more
accurately than any previous magistrate.

However, investigative success and the accompanying public renown exposed him to both
professional jealousies and to mafia revenge. The
anti-mafia team was dismantled, and Falcone –
failing to win election to the judiciary's governing
body, the CSM – moved to the Ministry of Justice
in Rome. A mafia car bomb killed him as he made
a brief return to Palermo in 1992, and two months
later his closest colleague, Paolo Borsellino, was
killed in similar fashion. In Sicily the murders
provoked unprecedented public demonstrations
against the mafia and the political system that
allowed it to thrive. The brutal murders also
created disorientation and defection within the
organization over the wisdom of challenging a
long-tolerant state so directly. Within a few months
the mafia boss responsible for these and many
other murders, Totò Riina, had been arrested after
twenty-two years on the run and Falcone had
become a powerful and enduring symbol of the
commitment of Sicilians themselves to the elimination of the mafia.

See also: legal system; *Mani pulite*

Further reading

Caponnetto, A. (1992) *I miei giorni a Palermo*
(My Days in Palermo), Milan: Garzanti (the
creation of the anti-mafia team of judges
described by its senior member).

Falcone, G. (1992) *Men of Honour*, trans. E. Farrelly,
London: Fourth Estate (Falcone's interpretation
of mafia).

La Licata, F. (1995) *La storia di Giovanni Falcone* (The
Story of Giovanni Falcone), Milan: Fabbri.

Stille, A. (1996) *Excellent Cadavers: The Mafia and the
Death of the First Italian Republic*, London: Vintage
(mafiosi, judges and politicians in Italy since
1980).

DAVID MOSS

Fallaci, Oriana

b. 30 June 1930, Florence

Writer and journalist

Fallaci's childhood experience in the Florentine
Resistance imprinted on her an uncompromising
commitment to heroic libertarian individualism.
This runs through all her work from her early
reportages on Hollywood (1958) and the state of
women around the world to her massive novel
about war-torn Beirut, *InsciAllah* (1990). It dominates her accounts of the US space programme
and the Vietnam War, with herself as the site of
conflict, as well as her interviews with world
celebrities and political leaders. The international
success of her informatively titled *Lettera a un
bambino mai nato* (Letter to a Child Never Born)
(1975), about the anguishing dilemmas of expec-
tant motherhood in an oppressive world, coincided
with the mass feminism of the **divorce** and

abortion referendum debates, but was surpassed with *Un uomo* (A Man) (1979), a second-person biography addressed to her dead companion the Greek freedom fighter, Alexandros Panagoulis. Fallaci continued to exemplify the highest values of the Italian Resistance, but intellectuals generally failed to do justice to her originality as a writer.

Further reading

Gatt-Rutter, J. (1996) *Oriana Fallaci: The Rhetoric of Freedom*, Oxford: Berg (a detailed and in-depth study).

JOHN GATT-RUTTER

Falso Movimento

Formed in 1977 by a group of Neapolitan teenagers, the Falso Movimento (False Movement) company produced some of the most exciting experimental performances in the late 1970s and early 1980s. They saw theatre as a meeting place for the various interests of the group members (music, visual arts, cinema), and the loose structure of their performances reflected the collective nature of their collaboration.

Their productions (for example, their reworking of Verdi's *Otello* in 1982–3) typify a further shift in Italian experimental theatre (after the mid-1970s development from 'avantgarde' to 'post-avant-garde' exemplified in the **Magazzini Criminali**) moving towards what has been described as a new interest in spectacle (*nuova spettacolarità*) and a greater emphasis on the expressive force of the constitutive elements or media in the moment of performance. Mario **Martone**, the most prominent member of the group, went on to direct cinema.

Further reading

Sinisi, S. (1983) *Dalla parte dell'occhio* (From the Eye's Point of View), Rome: Kappa, 185–95 (a detailed description of the group's productions).

TIM FITZPATRICK

Famiglia Cristiana

With a steady readership of close to one million, *Famiglia Cristiana* (The Christian Family) is the largest weekly magazine in Italy. With its reassuring mixture of popular piety, feature articles, recipes, fashion and music reviews, an 'agony column' and lots of glossy advertising, it has exerted a powerful influence on the Catholic laity since the mid-1950s. However, since 1996 it has found itself in serious difficulty. Apart from a battle inside the Society of Paulist Fathers, who own it, its support of the **Ulivo** alliance of the **PDS** and the Popolari in the 1996 elections alienated some of its readers, including many parish priests. At the end of 1996, the editor was summoned before both Cardinal Ratzinger, head of the Congregation for the Doctrine of the Faith, and Cardinal **Ruini**, the Vicar of Rome and president of the Bishops' Conference, and taken to task for discussing topics such as communion for divorced persons, homosexuality, adultery, masturbation and nudity. Despite putting up some strong resistance, the magazine now faces direct censorship as a result of the takeover of the Paulist Society in Italy by a Vatican-nominated delegate.

See also: Catholic press and publishing

JOHN POLLARD

family

The role of the family in Italy has always been judged ambivalently. In the late 1950s the American sociologist Edward Banfield notoriously criticized the 'amoral familism' he noted amongst peasants in the South, their inability to transcend their immediate interests for the wider good of the community. Other sociologists and anthropologists have similarly regarded the traditional, individualistic structures of the Italian family as inimical to social and economic progress. Catholic ideology in the new united Italy also set the family in opposition to the collective, a view hardly surprising given parlous church–state relations. Later, the family was, in the Catholic view, to be the bulwark against the rising tide of communism.

The traditional nature of the family in Italy was

radically transformed in the postwar period by a series of economic and cultural developments. Family structures already modified and broken up first by the war and then by the rapidly increasing industrialization, urbanization and **emigration** associated with the so-called **economic miracle**, were further unsettled by economic and political developments. The situation, however, was startlingly different across the country: families in the South, often deprived of their main breadwinner, depended on money sent from the North or abroad for survival, while in the North competition from migrant male workers led to a dramatic reduction in work opportunities for women and young men. Increasing unemployment led young people to stay at home longer before marriage, while university studies, albeit sporadic and part-time for many, were one of the few alternatives to unemployment. Even in the 1990s young people still tend to stay in the parental home far longer in Italy than elsewhere. The absence of a mortgage market in Italy leaves younger people more dependent on parents for accommodation; and an inadequate social security system encourages those with low incomes to stay under the same roof. This combination of enforced contact and increased educational opportunities for young people led to a generation gap phenomenon more deeply felt in Italy than in most comparable countries.

The decline of collective values and movements in recent years has led to the reassertion of the family as the principal object of allegiance for the vast majority of Italians, old and young. Families are smaller and, in the North at least, much more prosperous, while reforms of the 1970s guaranteed improved state medical and social provisions. If, as some claim, the introspective nature of family life in the South has fed into the structure of the mafia family, it is equally true that the enormous number of successful and flourishing family enterprises and businesses in the North is without parallel elsewhere in Europe (see **Third Italy**).

There are nonetheless symptoms of radical change. As elsewhere in Europe, there are increasing numbers of one-parent families, of couples who decide not to marry and of adults who choose to live alone, although Italian levels remain far below the European average. The decrease of the birth rate in Italy has accelerated and Italy now has the lowest birth rate of any major European country, with an average of just 1.3 children per woman of child-bearing age. Nonetheless the family unit in Italy remains, on the whole, cohesive if diverse across the country. Even while the family in Italy has seen dramatic and sweeping changes in recent years, it retains its status as the core source of identity for the majority of Italians.

See also: divorce; feminism; marriage

Further reading

Barbagli, M. and Saraceno, C. (1997) *Lo stato delle famiglie in Italia* (The State of Families in Italy), Bologna: Il Mulino.

Foot, J. (1995) 'The Family and the "Economic Miracle": Social Transformation, Work, Leisure and Development at Bovisa and Comasina (Milan), 1950–1970', *Contemporary European History* 4 (3): 315–37 (one of several useful essays in this issue dedicated to the theme of the European family).

Ginsborg, P. (1990) 'Family, Culture and Politics in Contemporary Italy', in Z.G. Baranski and R. Lumley (eds), *Culture and Conflict in Postwar Italy*, London: Macmillan (a brief but comprehensive survey of the postwar Italian family).

Livraghi, R. (ed.) (1994) *Economia della famiglia ed economia del lavoro* (Economy of the Family and Economy of Work), Milan: F. Angeli.

Saraceno, C. (1996) *Sociologia della famiglia* (Sociology of the Family), Bologna: Il Mulino.

SHARON WOOD

Fanfani, Amintore

b. 6 February 1908, Arezzo;
   d. 20 November 1999, Rome

Politician

A leading figure of postwar Italian politics, Fanfani entered **Parliament** in 1946 and remained there for life. He served in the **Constituent Assembly** from 1946–8, was a deputy from 1948–63, senator from 1968–72, and was appointed life senator in 1972. He was prime minister six times between 1954 and 1987, and held many other cabinet posts including Interior and Foreign Affairs between 1947 and 1989. In 1958 he was simultaneously Prime Minister, Foreign Minister and General Secretary of the Christian Democrat Party (see **DC**). As party secretary he carried out far-reaching reforms, making the DC more independent of the Church and then, in the late 1950s, began the process of '**opening to the Left**', later completed by Aldo **Moro**. In 1974, probably against his better judgement, Fanfani led the unsuccessful referendum campaign to repeal the **divorce** law. Like many Italian politicians, Fanfani also held academic positions and taught economic history at the Catholic University of Milan 1936–55 and Rome 1955–83.

JAMES WALSTON

Fantomas

Fantomas is a character belonging to the large group of heroes of French serial novels known as *roman noir* (crime novel) where the protagonist is a criminal. A typical story presents a series of ingenious, atrocious and often gratuitous crimes performed by Fantomas who, thanks to extraordinary physical strength and agility, always escapes the implacable pursuit of the almost equally cunning police Commissioner Juve. Pierre Souvestre and Marcel Allain published the first Fantomas story in 1911, and its immediate success led them to write another thirty-one sequels in the following four years. The character became an international myth through the films of Louise Feuillade. Fantomas is known as a criminal genius, an elusive master of fear who constantly changes his identity, an extraordinary actor who triumphs in all his roles. The novels were published in Italy one year after the French edition and republished with some success in 1963. But it is in the comic book field that the influence of Fantomas was paramount, helping to generate the character of **Diabolik**, founder of the *fumetto nero*.

See also: comics

Further reading

Riccomini, F. (1979) *Fantomas. Un mito* (Fantomas: A

Myth), Prato: Azienda autonoma di Turismo (an illuminating discussion of the mythological features of Fantomas and their natural attractions for an Italian audience).

FRANCO MANAI

fascism and neo-fascism

Despite the terrible nature of the Second World War, the utter defeat suffered militarily, socially and psychologically by Fascist Italy and its participation in the horror of Auschwitz, fascists or neo-fascists have constituted an important part of postwar political life. Even before the conflict ended, those social forces which had underpinned Mussolini's regime rallied to the **Uomo Qualunque** movement of Guglielmo Giannini, with its battle cry of 'Abbasso tutti!' (down with everyone). Only in 1947 would it become clear that the Christian Democrats and not the Uomo Qualunque were to be the catch-all party of the Right in the Italian **Republic**. By this time, ex-Fascists led by Arturo Michelini had set up the **MSI** (Movimento Sociale Italiano, or Italian Social Movement) which, until the 1990s, officially embodied postwar fascism. The MSI's electoral record was mixed, but generally it polled fourth in national elections behind the Christian Democrats, the **PCI** and the **PSI**.

Like other Italian parties, the MSI was itself a coalition, socially, regionally and ideologically. In terms of ideology, debates were at their most heated in the party's early days when a radical fascism which still evoked the social policies enunciated, if not carried through, in the Salò Republic (1943–5) had as its spokesperson, Giorgio Almirante (d. 1988). In 1950, however, the party settled down under the moderate secretariat of Augusto De Marsanich, for whom fascism meant a general authoritarianism which could associate the MSI with the more conservative elements of the Christian Democrat Republic. Radical fascism found its durable champion in Pino Rauti who, typically, proclaimed that fascism stood for a revolutionary third way, separate from both capitalism and socialism, systems which, in Rauti's eyes, were incompatible with the best side of national life. From 1950, Rauti headed an extra-parliamentary group called Ordine Nuovo (New Order) and drew intellectual sustenance from the international far Right, praising Nazism and the cloudy ideas of Romanian fascist C.Z. Codreanu (whose battle cry had been 'Long live death!'), as well as the less revolutionary and more straight-forwardly authoritarian regimes of Franco in Spain and Salazar in Portugal.

In 1954 Michelini was returned as MSI secretary and favoured, at least in the public arena, the non-revolutionary aspects of fascism. He died in 1969, to be replaced by Giorgio Almirante, who although seeming more radical (Rauti then re-joined the party), soon pursued similar compromise policies. After 1987, when Almirante himself retired, the story repeated itself again and, in a leadership battle, the moderate Gianfranco **Fini** overcame Rauti. In 1994–5 Fini took the neo-fascists into coalition with Silvio **Berlusconi**, bringing fascists into Italian government for the first time in fifty years. Fini now explained that he stood for a 'post-fascism', of uncertain character. In 1995 he dissolved the MSI into a new grouping called Alleanza Nazionale (AN; see **National Alliance**). For the 1996 elections the AN joined Berlusconi's losing **Polo della Libertà** centre–right coalition. It was still challenged by a recalcitrant rump, the 'MSI Fiamma' led by Rauti. Such recalcitrance is not surprising given that fascism, an ideology committed to a powerful state and to a version of welfare, is doubtfully compatible with contemporary conservatism's free market economics. Moreover, the South, which with its system of patron–client networks (see **clientelism**) and its widespread 'corruption' has provided the main pool of neo-fascist votes, is scarcely a society to be endorsed by a literal follower of Friedrich Hayek or Milton Friedman.

The formal political activities of the neo-fascists are, however, only part of their history, though the most visible and the best documented part. In many senses, the MSI was merely the public and respectable face of believers in an ideology committed to terrorism, murder and their own version of revolution. Even in the era of the **Red Brigades**, a tradition of right-wing action flourished, though fascists preferred the indiscriminate effect of a bomb to the more targeted killing practised by leftist terrorists. The bombs placed in the **Piazza Fontana** in Milan in December 1969, in the Piazza della Loggia in Brescia in May 1974, on the 'Italicus' express (August 1974) and on another train stopped at Bologna station in August 1980, and further incidents (notably the riots in Reggio Calabria during the summer and autumn of 1970), ensured that neo-fascist terror took a terrible toll.

The intention behind such acts was to dismay fascism's opponents and critics, and to prompt some sort of armed intervention from fascism's friends against the ambiguities and confusions of the existing political order. This last hope was the greater because pockets of a residual sympathy for some variety of fascism survived in many sections of the ruling elite. Italy's multiple secret services, despite their constant internecine warfare, were notorious in this regard, with dark figures like General De Lorenzo (involved in a possible coup attempt in 1964) surfacing time and again in the Republic's complex political history. Revelations about the Masonic Lodge **P2** and about 'Operazione **Gladio**' (Operation Gladio) similarly confirm the unsurprising reality that Italian anti-communism could easily embrace philo-fascism. The emigrant Italies, too (see **emigration**) were frequently places in which neo-fascism retained sympathizers and fund-raisers.

From the 1980s, the neo-fascists were able to make their presence more overt, and in 1987 Bettino **Craxi**, showing his characteristic realism, formally met the young MSI secretary Gianfranco Fini. This meeting presaged that process, outlined above, which has led to 'post-fascism' and to the eclipse of the view that the essence of the Italian Republic is its **anti-fascism**. Among many others, Fini, Rauti and Mussolini's own grand-daughter Alessandra Mussolini possess voices, helping to compose the babel of that 1990s Italy which no longer possesses a reliable past and whose future may or may not be 'post-fascist'.

See also: strategia della tensione; terrorism

Further reading

Ferraresi, F. (1996) *Threats to Democracy: The Radical Right in Italy after the War*, Princeton, NJ:

Princeton University Press (a detailed and comprehensive study of neo-fascism and the radical Right in postwar Italy).

Ignazi, P. (1989) *Il polo escluso: profilo del Movimento Sociale Italiano* (The Excluded Pole: A Profile of the Italian Social Movement), Bologna: Il Mulino (the most scholarly history of the MSI).

R.J.B. BOSWORTH

fashion

Women's wear

Italy is seen as one of the foremost fashion centres in the contemporary world, yet the story of Italian fashion is essentially a postwar tale. Production and presentation centres around Milanese high quality ready-to-wear, led by international names such as **Prada**, **Armani**, **Versace** and **Dolce and Gabbana**. Famous for its use of colour and fabric, the essence of Italian style is casual elegance.

Before the Second World War, there was little innovative couture and no fashionable women's ready-to-wear industry in Italy. As in the rest of the Western world, wealthy Italian women looked to Paris for style. However, Italian textile production was already industrialized and supplying a growing international market, and Italy also enjoyed a reputation for excellent craftsmanship in apparel and accessories, with names such as **Ferragamo**. Very soon after the war, there was a conscious effort to move away from Paris, and a discernible Italian style emerged.

The first collective international fashion show of made-to-measure 'haute couture', which took place on 12 February 1951, is hailed as the birth of this style. The event was organized by Giovan Battista Giorgini at the splendid Villa Torrignani in Florence and included presentations by Simonetta, Schuberth, **Fontana**, Veneziani and Marucelli. There were also two 'boutique' or 'exclusive casual ready-to-wear' collections by **Pucci** and Tessitrice. Although the couture was not highly innovative and still took its lead from Paris, it was notable for its imaginatively decorated evening wear and the quality of both the workmanship and the Italian fabrics used. However, it was the 'new and exciting' boutique collections which particularly impressed the audience. The presentations flourished, and in January 1953 moved to the more spacious Sala Bianca (White Room) at the Florentine Pitti Palace.

Italian culture, the Italian upper classes and their media representation were fundamental to the international perception of Italian fashion. The Italians were renowned for their careful appearance and for their vitality, which was related to Italy's climate and culture. Moreover, a high proportion of Italian designers were stylish aristocrats, and the appeal of this fact was not ignored. Fashion buyers and journalists were entertained with lavish parties at ancestral palaces, and both the nobility and historical locations were widely used by the foreign press for fashion shoots. American films made in Italy from the early 1950s also helped to create an aura of elegance for Italian fashion. Shot in captivating locations, films such as *Roman Holiday* (1953) portrayed a carefree and simple Italy which was, at the same time, full of high culture and sophistication. Ateliers generated publicity for themselves by dressing the most famous Italian and American stars when they were in Rome, including Ava Gardner and Sophia **Loren**.

Italian fashion soon became internationally known for both quality and ease. Boutique, in particular, was seen to be well-suited for the more relaxed modern lifestyle. The international fashion press described the boutique as sensual, young, liberating, colourful and fresh, but at the same time comfortable, sleek, well-fitting and flattering. From the early 1950s, boutique clothes were not only produced by exclusive ready-to-wear designers. Certain luxury knitwear designers, such as Mirsa, were also included in this category, and Italian knitwear was seen as an integral element of Italian fashion. Moreover, couturiers began to show boutique collections alongside their couture at the Florence presentations. The global market for exclusive ready-to-wear expanded and exports of Italian clothes increased dramatically, notably to the USA, Germany and Great Britain.

However, rivalry between Florence and Rome for the title of Italy's fashion capital led to a potentially disastrous geographical fragmentation of the industry. In 1967 a compromise was reached, whereby Florence continued to show accessories and boutique while the couture presentations moved to Rome. As yet, quality mass production at the level below boutique was seen as 'unworthy' and was not considered in the negotiations.

Mass market production of women's apparel had been slow to take off in Italy compared to many other Western nations. Ready-to-wear manufacturers in the north of Italy, such as **MaxMara** and Gruppo Finanzario Tessile (GFT) were the first to mass produce smart fashionable garments for women in Italy, in the first half of the 1950s. By the second half of the decade, there was an important group of manufacturers with modern factories, producing quality garments using predominantly Italian fabrics. The international reputation of Italian textiles for quality and innovation continued to grow, and the close and flexible relationship between the two industries was central to the expansion of the Italian garment industry. From 1958–63, Italy experienced an unprecedented economic boom (see **economic miracle**). The standard of living rose substantially and the domestic market for women's ready-to-wear expanded rapidly as the presentation of a smart appearance, or *fare bella figura*, grew more widespread. By the mid-1960s, quality ready-to-wear manufacturers had established themselves in the Italian market and many were exporting to the USA and other European nations.

In the late 1960s growth in domestic consumption slowed and this, coupled with industrial unrest, had a marked effect on the industry. At the same time, the international competitiveness of Italian products waned as rivals in developing countries emerged. The first half of the 1970s are known as the 'crisis period' of Italian fashion, as many Italian ready-to-wear companies of varying sizes came to grief. Thereafter, clothing manufacturers realized the importance of technology and began to invest in computer-controlled production.

The 1970s saw two very important steps on the path towards Italy's future international success in luxury off-the-peg clothing. The first came in April 1972 when leading ready-to-wear designers **Albini**, Cadette and Ken Scott seceded from the Florentine presentations and staged a show in Milan, which was already seen as the centre of the Italian ready-to-wear industry, and was close to the hub of Italian textile production. Over the next few years they were joined by more and more top ready-to-wear names, including **Krizia**, **Versace**, **Ferrè** and **Missoni**, and by the mid-1970s the focus of Italian fashion had shifted firmly from Florence to Milan.

The second significant move came when GFT agreed to produce collections for both **Valentino** and Armani, successfully marrying designer labels to mass production. This example, together with the 'crisis' of the early 1970s, dissuaded designers from establishing their own factories and encouraged them to have their lines manufactured by existing producers. Alongside these collections sold under their own names, designers also worked anonymously under contract for manufacturers. Such arrangements grew more and more common at both top and middle range ready-to-wear. At the top, for example, Versace was contracted to Genny, Albini to Basile and French designer Montana to Complice. In the middle market, manufacturers relied increasingly on innovative design, led by MaxMara, using predominantly French designers. Significantly, although many of the designers employed in Italian fashion were foreigners, the designs they produced were seen as Italian.

Italy's reputation for high-quality, fashionable yet wearable garments burgeoned as the focus of global fashion production shifted further away from made-to-measure. From 1960–70 a number of Italian couture houses closed. With the exception of **Capucci**, the rest stopped presenting their clothes in collective fashion shows and concentrated on designing accessories which were produced under licence. Italian couture garments grew richer and more elaborate in search of new markets in the Middle East, and a clearer stylistic distinction emerged between Italian couture and Italian ready-to-wear, which continued to be known for its understated elegance.

These developments transformed the Italian fashion industry and were confirmed in 1978 with the establishment of the 'Milan Collezioni' by Beppe Modenese as an international showcase for the best Italian ready-to-wear. By the end of the 1970s, most of the important brand names were established, the Milan fashion industry had settled into a relatively stable pattern and the city's position secured as Italy's fashion capital. Ready-to-wear production escalated, and although the domestic market remained strong, exports represented an increasingly high proportion of turnover.

Furthermore, during the 1970s Italian industry earned foreign respect for its marketing skills and this was also crucial to the subsequent expansion of Italian fashion. **Benetton**'s enormous global success since the late 1970s in the mid and lower ready-to-wear market is a pertinent example of this. Despite its franchise basis, Benetton developed a conspicuous and unified corporate identity worldwide. Image-conscious marketing is seen as a key factor in the continuing good fortunes of the Italian fashion industry. By the early 1980s Milan was one of the top three destinations on the international fashion circuit, challenging the stylistic dominance of Paris. Italian fashion production was widely perceived to be both technologically innovative and of an excellent standard, and leading designers from around the world sought to have their collections manufactured in Italy, often in Italian fabrics. All Italian manufacturers and designers continued to acknowledge the significance of the support of the innovative and flexible Italian textile industry to their sustained success.

New names emerged on the Milan scene in the 1980s, including **Gigli**, Moschino, and Dolce and Gabbana. Despite the global recession of the late 1980s and early 1990s which hit the luxury Italian fashion industry particularly hard, none of the big manufacturers or designer labels went out of business. In the early 1990s, **Gucci** and Prada hit fashion headlines with modern streamlined designs, which became the 'must-haves' of the world's fashion cognoscenti. Around this time a certain amount of interest shifted to Florence, largely as a result of more aggressive marketing for the Florence shows but Milan remains the unchallenged centre of Italian fashion. The essence of Italian fashion is still a combination of luxury and ease, and it clear with hindsight that Italian ready-to-wear has been profoundly influential in the development of international postwar fashion.

Men's wear

Italian men's wear is well-known worldwide for its high quality, yet while the expertise of Italian tailors was widely acknowledged, there was no identifiable 'Italian style' in men's wear until the mid-1950s. The most obvious unifying factor in the dress of Italian men was a tendency to conform to the traditional British model. However, in the immediate postwar years visitors to Italy noted a careful elegant vitality in the dress of Italian men, at odds with the restrained attitude associated with British style. There was an emerging distinction between a select elite who remained faithful to the British tailoring tradition, and a predominantly middle-class group who preferred the 'American style' they saw in films. This centred on a vigorous new masculine ideal, symbolized by the *abito a sacchetto* or 'baggy suit'.

This look remained fashionable until the early 1950s, when a distinct 'Italian style' emerged. Instead of a long, spacious double-breasted suit with its wide, turned-up trousers, the Italian suit, with its short, straight jacket and narrow trousers, was seen as 'modern'. The association with modernity, together with the quality reputation of Italian products and relatively low prices combined to make the Italian look alluring. The look was an amalgamation of Italy's desire to join the 'modern world' and the slim off-duty wear of American GIs who occupied Italy at the end of the war, and by the mid-1950s it became internationally influential.

Also in the 1950s, Italian tailoring experienced a golden age, with names such as **Brioni** and Caraceni achieving international renown. By the early 1960s, Italy's postwar economic recovery had produced a moderate degree of prosperity and a broader range of consumers. The growing ready-to-wear industry with its two leading manufacturers, Lanerossi and **Marzotto**, offered a viable alternative to made-to-measure for the masses, and tailoring declined. Throughout these years Italian clothing manufacturers built a strong relationship with the Italian textile industry. The interaction was fundamental to the success of Italian fashion, particularly from the late 1960s, when textile houses began making fabrics to meet the demands of individual designers and manufacturers.

In 1969, men's wear presentations were introduced alongside women's luxury ready-to-wear at the Pitti Palace in Florence. Twelve men's ready-to-wear houses of the highest quality, including Litrico and **Pucci** (by Zegna) were very well received internationally because they filled a gap between ready-to-wear and made-to-measure. Pitti Uomo was launched in Florence in 1972, for the exclusive presentation of quality men's wear, and was soon seen as the most important men's wear show in the world. However, in the late 1970s a number of designers, such as Albini, Basile and Armani, moved to Milan to present their collections and the city became the unchallenged centre of Italian fashion for both men and women. Henceforth, the unstructured, luxurious aesthetic of Italian men's wear became a universal symbol of the successful male and contributed to a transformation of the businessman's wardrobe.

Further reading

Bianchino, G. *et al.* (eds) (1987) *Italian Fashion*, 2 vols, Milan: Electa.

Chenoune, F. (1993) '"Tempo di Roma", Europe, Italian-style', in *A History of Men's Fashion*, Paris: Flammarion.

NICOLA WHITE

Fellini, Federico

b. 20 January 1920, Rimini;
d. 31 October 1993, Rome

Film director, scriptwriter and cartoonist

Renowned worldwide and both loved and respected in Italy, Federico Fellini is universally regarded as perhaps the greatest of Italian film directors. Indeed, during a long and fruitful career that saw him continually present in half a century of film production, Fellini's name came to be simply synonymous with Italian cinema itself.

After an uneventful provincial childhood in Romagna where the future director showed his talent as a cartoonist, the young Fellini moved to Rome in 1939, working on the humour magazine *Marc'Aurelio*, a periodical with an enormous circulation that included many journalists working in the cinema. Fellini contributed comic gags, cartoons, serial narratives and humorous vignettes. In 1943 he married Giulietta **Masina**, began scriptwriting in earnest, and in the following year met Roberto **Rossellini**, who engaged him as one

of a team of writers who created *Roma, città aperta* (Open City). Its release in 1945 heralded the rebirth of postwar cinema, was the occasion for the rise of Italian cinematic **neorealism**, and garnered the young Fellini his first Oscar nomination for scriptwriting. After collaborating with Rossellini, Pietro **Germi**, Alberto **Lattuada** and Luigi **Comencini** on a number of scripts, Fellini made his debut as director, collaborating with Lattuada on *Luci del varietà* (Variety Lights) in 1951, initiating that trilogy of character analysis that would continue with *Lo sceicco bianco* (The White Sheik) (1951) and *I vitelloni* (1953), his first critically successful work that also scored at the box office.

Fellini's career assumed international dimensions with the subsequent trilogy of grace or salvation: of the three films dealing with the nature of innocence in a cruel and unsentimental world, two – *La strada* (1954) and *Le notti di Cabiria* (The Nights of Cabiria) (1956) – both won successive Oscars for Best Foreign Language Film in 1956 and 1957. This critical success was followed by the stupendous commercial success of *La dolce vita* in 1959, which began his long collaboration with Marcello **Mastroianni**. The film's title became synonymous everywhere and in numerous languages with the society life depicted by Rome's gossip-column photographers or *paparazzi*, a word that Fellini contributed to the English language. The film critics regard Fellini's masterpiece to be *8½*, made in 1963 with Mastroianni as a film director and perhaps Fellini's alter ego, which earned Fellini his third Oscar. The high modernist aesthetics of *8½* has become emblematic of the very notion of free, uninhibited artistic creativity.

In the wake of *8½* Fellini's name would become forever linked to the vogue of the postwar European art film, even though he was one of the few non-American directors who could be counted on by his producers to score at the box office. Nevertheless, his post-*8½* production would include a number of brilliant films but also a number which were commercial disappointments. Many of them dealt with the myth of Rome, the cinema, and consequently with Fellini's own subjective fantasy world. *Fellini Satyricon* (1969) demonstrated his mastery of a dreamlike cinematic language in an original adaptation of Petronius's Latin classic; *Roma* (1971) provided a personal portrait of the Eternal City, including much autobiographical material; and *Amarcord* (awarded Fellini's fourth Oscar in 1974) offered a nostalgic portrait of Fellini's provincial adolescence during the Fascist period. Other films of his late period, however, encountered both critical objections and commercial difficulties: the sumptuous sets of *Casanova* in 1976 somehow failed to mesmerize audiences except, perhaps, in Japan; *La città delle donne* (The City of Women) (1980) offended every feminist except Germaine Greer. Other films – such as *E la nave va* (And the Ship Sails on) in 1983, *Ginger e Fred* (Ginger and Fred) in 1985, *Intervista* (Interview) in 1987 and his last work in 1989, *La voce della luna* (The Voice of the Moon), are still being evaluated following Fellini's death, as film historians attempt to come to grips with the complex evolution of Fellini's cinematic style over a period of forty years.

During the last years of his life, Fellini made commercials for a number of companies (Barilla pasta, Campari Soda, the Banco di Roma), exhibited his sketches and cartoons all over the world with great success, and received numerous honours – including the Golden Lion at the **Venice Biennale**'s Film Festival in 1985 and the fifth Oscar for his career in 1993. In 1987, a panel of professionals from eighteen European nations named *8½* the best European film of all time and Fellini Europe's greatest director. In 1992 this verdict was confirmed in another poll of international film directors conducted by *Sight and Sound*, which ranked Fellini as the most significant film director of all time. These directors also cited two of Fellini's works (*La Strada* and *8½*) in a list of ten masterpieces which had the most profound influence upon them and the history of the cinema.

Fellini's funeral in Rome was a national event, with throngs of people in attendance at the church and thousands more filing by his coffin to pay him their last respects in the huge Studio 5 of his beloved **Cinecittà**, afterward renamed Studio Fellini in his honor. A foundation was subsequently established in Rimini to support the study and further dissemination of his work.

Further reading

Bondanella, P. (1990) *Italian Cinema: From Neorealism to the Present*, New York, Continuum, 2nd revised edn (a survey of postwar film in Italy that places Fellini in a national context).

—— (1992) *The Cinema of Federico Fellini*, Princeton, NJ: Princeton University Press (a detailed account of Fellini's life using archival sources).

Bondanella, P. and Degli-Esposti, C. (eds) (1993) *Perspectives on Federico Fellini*, New York: G.K. Hall (an anthology of critical interpretations of Fellini's cinema from a wide variety of theoretical perspectives).

Costantini, C. (ed.) (1995) *Conversations with Fellini*, trans. Sohrab Sorooshian, London: Faber & Faber (a very useful series of interviews with Fellini covering his entire career).

Kezich, T. (1987) *Fellini*, Milan: Camunia (the indispensable, classic biography by Italy's best film critic).

PETER BONDANELLA

Feltrinelli

Founded by Giangiacomo Feltrinelli (1926–72), then aged twenty-nine, the publishing house was one aspect of an ambitious project of promoting left-wing and antifascist culture in Italy. In 1949 Feltrinelli set up what later became the Institute, while book publishing followed on from the experience of a co-operative producing popular editions. The bookshops were launched in the late 1960s, and by the firm's thirtieth anniversary there was a chain of fourteen outlets. The publishing activity took off in 1957 with the world's first edition of Boris Pasternak's *Doctor Zhivago*, and this success was consolidated with Tomasi Di **Lampedusa**'s *The Leopard* and García Marquez's *One Hundred Years of Solitude*. The company created an impressive fiction list, consisting not least of innovative young writers, both Italian and foreign. The non-fiction list under Giangiacomo Feltrinelli included works representative of political movements in Latin America (a famous photograph shows him with Fidel Castro) and the Third World, not to mention New Left writings in Europe. Mystery still surrounds the publisher's death (he was found dead in 1972 at the foot of a pylon outside Milan, apparently the victim of his own bomb) but it seems that his fears of a *coup d'état* drove him to espouse the armed struggle. His memory and legacy is still honoured in a company that continues to combine capitalist organization with ideas critical of capitalism.

ROBERT LUMLEY

feminism

Of all the social and civil movements which swept across the nation in the 1960s and 1970s, it was arguably feminism which had the most substantial and long-term impact on personal, family and economic life in Italy. New wave feminism emerged amidst the political fervor of the late 1960s, but went on to challenge all aspects – legal, financial, moral, cultural – of women's lives in Italy.

This feminism represented a dramatically new phenomenon in its refusal to separate private life from the public and the political, and in its ability to undercut and disrupt traditional forms of politics by appealing to a constituency unlimited by age or class. New wave feminism also marked a radical break from older forms of feminist organization such as the suffrage campaign at the turn of the century or the reformist, emancipationist movements after the Second World War, which had failed to achieve mass support and which had sought to enter, rather than to challenge, existing forms of civic politics. These earlier demands for women's rights had tacitly and implicitly recognized the legitimacy of the state in their demand to participate in the political process on equal terms but feminism in the 1970s, while campaigning vigorously for legal and civic reform, also came to question emancipation and equality as ultimate goals, seeing in them an erasure of sexual difference. While remaining rooted in political activism, demanding equality in family law and fighting for **divorce** and the right to **abortion**, the new feminism also sought to understand ways in which women remained oppressed by linguistic structures and philosophical categories as well as by ideology and legislation.

By the late 1960s, rapid urbanization and increased educational opportunities had radically transformed the expectations of Italian women; no longer content with their traditional role, they sought professional employment and equal status. Women were active in trade union agitation in the factories, but the egalitarian rhetoric of left-wing activism was undermined by a continuing stereotype of women's roles. Women were deemed politically immature and strategically naive, and their contribution to the revolution was held by all too many to be sexual rather than intellectual. Once again the political parties of the Left – as in the days of Anna Kuliscioff's struggle within the Socialist party at the turn of the century, or as in the period immediately following the Second World War and the drama of the **Resistance** – refused to acknowledge the dimension of gender within radical politics.

From 1970 onwards, feminist groups began to emerge in the larger cities. The increase in their education and the decrease in the birth rate gave women the time and means to consider events around them, while the increased complexity of women's lives, their 'double presence' in the home and in the workplace, made this imperative. The American influence was decisive in a nation where traditional politics was alien ground to most women. Women began to practise their own form of consciousness raising, or *autocoscienza*, a movement which established numerous informal contacts and elaborated the inseparability of personal experience from ideological structures. Women analysed both Catholic ideology, which characterized women exclusively as home-makers, and, more bitingly, left-wing politics which replicated the patriarchal structures of the Catholic party. This move marked a significant break from the more moderate reformism of organizations such as the **UDI** (Unione donne italiane), which was affiliated with the Communist Party (see **PCI**) and which, despite the influence of **Togliatti** and **Gramsci**, continued to seek alliances between social classes. Class-based political analysis was soon dismissed as inadequate and hostile to women's interests. Many of the earlier feminists emerged from the student movement appalled by its reactionary mode of organization. Carla Lonzi, one of the most influential thinkers of these early years, in the *Demau* (Demystification of Authority) manifesto of 1966, denounced Marxism for its occlusion of women's perspectives, for its failure to

address the patriarchal dimension of social structures and for its continuing blinkered obsession
with a class analysis which, unable to deal with the
different positions of men and women, effectively
eliminated gender difference. The oppression of
women could thus no longer be understood purely
in terms of class.

Women rapidly organized into local and regional groups, thus reflecting the continuing regional
nature of cultural life in Italy. These groups
constituted a loose federal structure, so that, in
the case of Italy, it would certainly be more correct
to speak of 'feminisms' rather than 'feminism': they
included the Libreria delle donne (Women's Bookshop) and Rivolta Femminile (Female Revolt) in
Milan, the Movimento Femminista Romano (Roman Feminist Movement), Diotima in Verona and
Transizione (Transition) in Naples. Autonomous
women's research and study centres were set up, as
well as numerous feminist journals and magazines
such as *Effe* and *Quotidiano Donna* (Woman Daily).
Feminism began to elaborate a new politics based
on the transformation of everyday social relations
and sought women's liberation not through
external structures but through a revolution in
the sphere of the private, the subjective and the
personal. The group Lotta Femminista (Feminist
Struggle), for example, campaigned for wages for
housework. While their approach was criticized for
a sterile economic reductionism which would have
logically required state intervention in every area of
family life, they did succeed in bringing into the
open the question of women's domestic labour, as
well as pointing out the wage gap suffered by
women in paid employment.

The 1970s saw a wave of reforming legislation
covering all aspects of family and personal life. The
MLD (Movimento di Liberazione della Donna
(Movement for the Liberation of Woman)),
affiliated to the **Radical Party**, demanded contraception, abortion, free medical services, legal
equality, the end of economic exploitation and
the end of discrimination on grounds of sex. In
1970, a divorce bill finally went through Parliament and was upheld by referendum in 1974
despite the opposition of the Catholics. This was a
serious defeat for the Christian Democrats (see
DC), since it was women themselves who were
decisive in the campaign to defeat the referendum.

In 1975, the Christian Democrats and the Communists united to pass a reform of family law which
finally abolished adultery (by women) as a criminal
offence and gave illegitimate children equal civil
rights. However, the campaign which saw the
greatest cohesion of all the disparate and local
women's groups was that for abortion, finally
legalized in 1978 and upheld overwhelmingly by
referendum three years later. Feminists turned the
issue from a matter of civil rights to a question of
ownership and control of women's bodies, analysing and exposing the exercise of coercive power
over women's lives. With the achievement of these
major pieces of legislation, the women's movement
returned largely to its former loose, fragmented
and local forms of organization, integrating into
the municipal, provincial and regional administrative structures (see **regional government**;
local administration). Nonetheless, these campaigns had powerfully demonstrated the extent to
which feminism cut across traditional class and
political lines in its challenge to the traditional
political, and moral, status quo.

As well as achieving significant legal reform,
feminists also sought to challenge wider cultural
and literary codes and expectations. The new
feminist presses published new work by women
writers and reprints of long-discarded works as well
as translations of key foreign texts, while women's
study and research centres, such as the Centro
Virginia Woolf (Virginia Woolf Centre) in Rome,
were set up in order to provide an alternative
syllabus to that offered by the universities. Women
writers challenged the supposed neutrality of art
and explored both women's access to artistic
discourse and their representation by the dominant
cultural forms. Novelists and poets sought to
produce accounts of women's lives rather than
high art, and set themselves the task of investigating
female subjectivity and sexual identity. In the
decade of the 1970s, aesthetics became a branch
of politics.

The successful campaigns for legal reform
marked a transitional moment. By the end of the
1970s women had made real gains, while sending
an effective challenge to the organization of politics
and the dominance of the traditional parties. The
end of the mass campaigning by women – for
abortion, for divorce and for an end to sexual

violence – coincided with the fragmentation of other political and grassroots movements in Italy following the Communists' '**historic compromise**' and a general weariness with struggles and ideologies. Feminism lost its ability to mobilize on a mass scale and turned in the 1980s from the streets and squares, and from a demand for radical changes in the civic and legal status of women, to a more reflective theoretical and political consideration of questions of sexual difference. Here Italian feminism showed its eclecticism, influenced not only by the militant radicalism and pressure group politics of the United States, but also by the philosophical and theoretical traditions of French feminism. Italian feminism, after emerging from women's movements formed in the hothouse atmosphere of Italian political life in the 1960s and early 1970s and engaging in protracted political and legislative campaigns, was markedly successful in bridging the gap between theory and praxis, between an academic, theoretical analysis and an engagement with those issues which affected all women.

Italian feminism's most significant and original theoretical contributions are its elaboration of theories of sexual difference, and its strategies for new forms of sociality between women. Sexual difference can be mapped neither onto biological determinism nor onto the social construction of gender. The demand for equality is set aside as foreshadowing the assimilation of women into orthodox male conceptualizations and the annihilation of difference. The philosophical elaboration of sexual difference requires a shift in thought and discourse to accommodate a multiple perspective on the world. The philosophical perspective on sexual difference has unravelled somewhat, however, on legislation dealing with equal opportunities. The practice of *affidamento*, or entrustment, on the other hand, sought to connect women of different levels of knowledge and experience in a form of network mentoring, focussing on the other woman as reference point. *Affidamento* was closely related to the analysis of maternity which led to the rejection not only of motherhood but of the figure of the mother as oppressive and static, and the adoption of another woman in the search for more dynamic and open-ended relationships between women. While the success of both these theoretical

enterprises may be open to question, the Italian emphasis on relations between women, and on the figure of the mother, is striking, a reflection perhaps of the feminist challenge to the dominance of traditional cultural accounts, whether Catholic or communist, of women's lives.

Two decades of feminism saw women active in all areas of work and cultural and political life, but still in a minority. Women were largely silent spectators of the collapse of the First **Republic**. Since first achieving the vote in 1946 the percentage of women in parliament has not risen above 10 per cent. Quota systems were introduced in the 1993 local elections, guaranteeing 30 per cent representation by women, but this controversial measure has only been partly successful and vociferously opposed by some women as well as by parties such as the **Lega Nord**, despite its strong base among women voters. Indeed, in recent years the few women to have caught the public eye in politics have been on the Right rather than the Left, in Catholic rather than progressive parties; generally, social, political and cultural structures remain irreducibly male-dominated. There have been some changes: the 1991 equal opportunities law clarified the 1977 law on equality, and there are moves towards a law on sexual harassment, and a growing debate on violence, as well as a new willingness among professional women to organize and debate issues, a move perhaps more productive than the idea of *affidamento*. While feminism in the 1990s finds itself somewhat adrift politically, with few clear and tangible objectives in pursuit of which women can come together, there has nonetheless been a transformation of women's personal and family life not registered by orthodox politics.

See also: sexism in language

Further reading

Beccalli, B. (1994) 'The Modern Women's Movement in Italy', *New Left Review* 204: 86–112 (an overview of the movement).

Bono, O. and Kemp, S. (eds) (1991) *Italian Feminist Thought: A Reader*, Oxford: Blackwell (a comprehensive volume drawing together in English translation all the most important documents of

Italian feminism together with rigorous chron-
ology and bibliography).

Doria, M.R. (ed.) (1987) *La ricerca delle donne: studi
femministi in Italia* (Women's Research: Feminist
Studies in Italy), Turin: Rosenberg & Sellier (an
interdisciplinary survey of feminist research in
Italy, including chapters on history, anthropology, economics, psychoanalysis and philosophy).

Ergas, Y. (1986) *Nelle maglie della politica: femminismo,
istituzioni e politiche sociali nell'Italia degli anni '70*
(In the Weave of Politics: Feminism, Social and
Political Institutions in Italy in the 1970s),
Milan: F. Angeli (studies the relationship of the
feminist movement to political parties in Italy).

Kaplan, G (1992) *Contemporary Western European
Feminism*, London: UCL Press (see especially
pp. 229–58 for a general but comprehensive
overview of the strategies and achievements of
Italian feminism).

SHARON WOOD

feminist cinema

Before the emergence of what might be termed
feminist cinema in Italy in the 1970s, only two
women had gained a reputation in the predominantly male world of Italian cinema: Lina **Wertmüller** and Liliana **Cavani**. Wertmüller replied
to **Scola**'s film *Se permettete parliamo di donne* (Let's
Talk About Women) (1964) with the successful
commercial film *Questa volta parliamo di uomini* (This
Time We Talk About Men) (1965), while Cavani
confronted the delicate issue of the **Resistance** in
Le donne nella Resistenza (Women in the Resistance)
(1963) and reinterpreted the legend of Antigone in
I cannibali (The Cannibals) (1969).

Of course, many women already worked in the
film industry as scriptwriters and assistants to male
directors. However, with the rise of **feminism**,
women began to produce, write and direct their
own feature films. In 1972 Elda Tattoli's *Il pianeta
Venere* (The Venus Planet), the first Italian film
about a woman under class and gender oppression,
was presented at the **Venice Biennale**. In 1977
Lù Leone wrote and produced *Io sono mia* (I Am
Mine), a film adapted from Dacia **Maraini**'s novel
Donne in Guerra (Women in War) and directed by

Sofia Scandurra with an all female crew. Loredana
Dordi, Marina Tartara and Tilde Capomazza
produced two series for the **RAI**, entitled *La donna
e la salute* (Women and Health) (1975) and *Si dice
donna* (It's Called Woman) (1977), both completely
written and directed by women.

Both feminism and feminist cinema began
during the 1968 student protest. There were many
analogies between the two movements: the demonstrations, the endless meetings, the congresses,
the propaganda, the occupations and the militant
cinema documenting the struggle. Women started
discussing gender and sexual relations, as well as
the institution of the **family** and 'Il privato è
politico' (The personal is political) became their
slogan. Acts of violence, oppression and abuse
came to light, and women tried to document them.
Thus, in those years feminist cinema was largely
the mirror of the women's movement. Painfully
aware of the complex nature of reality, women
nevertheless attempted to document their political
struggle and tell their private stories. They
reinterpreted Greek mythology from a feminist
perspective and narcissism became a means of
escaping the traditionally imposed male point of
view on women. The film titles during this period
are eloquent: *Destino casalinga* (Housewife's Fate) by
Armenia Balducci, *La madre della sposa* (The Bride's
Mother) by Alessandra Bocchetti, *Essere madre a 40
anni* (Being a Mother at 40) by Loredana Dordi,
Aborto: parlano le donne (Abortion: The Women
Speak) by Dacia **Maraini**, *Il rischio di vivere* (The
Risk of Living) by Anna Carini and Annabella
Miscuglio, *8 marzo, giornata di festa e di lotta* (8 March,
Day of Celebration and Struggle) by the Arcoba-
leno co-operative, *Euridice* by Valentina Berardi-
none, *Medea* by Pia Epremian and *Cenerentola,
psicofavola femminista* (Cinderella, Psychological Feminist Fairy Tale) by Lina Mangiacapre.

Generally, however, the new women's cinema
alluded to actions rather than showing them. It
observed reality rather than commenting upon it,
as exemplified in *Processo per stupro* (The Rape Trial)
(1978) by Rony Daopoulo, Annabella Miscuglio
and Maria Grazia Belmonti, a television documentation of the first open-doors rape trial and a
documentary well received and screened internationally. Daopoulo and Miscuglio also co-directed a
number of historical feminist films, such as *La lotta*

non è finita (The Struggle Is Not Over) (1972), a 16mm short which documented the police charge at the first women's movement demonstration in Rome; *A.A.A. Offresi* (1979) a video recording a prostitute's work and shot with a hidden camera (this documentary was censored and eventually withdrawn by **RAI** itself in spite of women's demonstrations demanding a public screening); and *I fantasmi del fallo* (The Phantasms of the Phallus) (1980), a documentary about the shooting of a porno film. This documentary was screened in 1984 at the New York University seminar, 'Italian and American Directions: Women's Film Theory and Practice', and was favourably received by American feminists and critics alike.

Italian feminists also focused on the problem of sexuality and the rediscovery of the body, with a high value placed on alternative lifestyles, a new way of living among women and a withdrawal from the male world. Fiorella **Infascelli** shot a psychoanalytic session in *Ritratto di donna distesa* (Portrait of a Reclining Woman) (1980), Liliana Cavani presented Lou Andreas Salomé in *Al di là del bene e del male* (Beyond Good and Evil) (1978) and Giovanna Gagliardo directed a film inspired by Luce Irigaray's work, *Maternale* (Motherhood) (1978).

During the 1980s, comedy and irony entered women's films, and the label feminist cinema became outdated. The struggle for equal opportunities achieved some major successes and several women were able to make their directorial debut even if only a few managed to continue, among them Francesca **Archibugi**, Cinzia **Torrini**, Cristina **Comencini** and Giuliana Gamba, the only woman director of erotic films. Largely unknown to a wider public but occupying an important position in the development of Italian feminist cinema were directors such as Gabriella Rosaleva with *Processo a Caterina Ross* (The Caterina Ross Trial) (1984), Adriana Monti with *Gentili Signore* (Kind Ladies) (1988) and Emanuela Piovano with *Le rose blu* (The Blue Roses) (1990).

The lack of interest in women's cinema displayed by producers and distributors was paralleled by a lack of critical interest which continued to put women film-makers at a disadvantage. Significantly, until the late 1990s no woman held a chair of film studies in any Italian public university. The female public took refuge in the reassuring romantic image given by the male perspective, film critics discovered trash and B-grade movies and even feminists themselves came to prefer investigating the female imagination in Hollywood films. The definition of women's cinema itself became largely obsolete. However, there are now two Women's Film Festivals, one in Florence and one in Sorrento, several Lesbian Film Festivals and some film schools for women.

The most significant phenomenon during the 1990s was the appearance of vibrant, new generation of female directors represented by Roberta Torre, a Milanese working in Sicily, who graduated from the Milan Film School and subsequently co-ordinated several collective projects such as *Femmine Folli* (Mad Women) (1991), a practice typical of both feminism and feminist cinema during the 1970s. At the 1997 Venice Biennale she presented her first fiction film, *Tano da morire*, a **mafia** musical starring an international porn star.

Further reading

Bruno, G. and Nadotti, M. (eds) (1988) *Off Screen: Women and Film in Italy*, London and New York: Routledge.

ADRIANA MONTI

Fendi

In Italian fashion, the Fendi name dates back to 1925 when Eduardo and Adele Fendi opened a leather and fur store and workshop in the centre of Rome. Eventually the couple's daughters, Paola, Carla, Anna, Franca and Alda, all went to work for the family business, which moved to an old movie theatre in via Borgognona, the very same street that today houses five Fendi shops. The business grew in status through its alliance with German designer Karl Lagerfeld, who inspired new ways to work with fur and invented the Fendi logo, the inverted FF. In 1969 Fendi presented a ready-to-wear fur collection at the Palazzo Pitti in Florence. In addition to its innovation and creativity, the collection offered furs at more accessible prices. The Fendi sisters expanded their repertoire to include clothing to be worn underneath their furs and the more youthful Fendissime lines as well as other licences. Today Fendi boutiques can be found all over the world.

BERNADETTE LUCIANO

Fenoglio, Beppe

b. 1 March 1922, Alba, Cuneo;
   d. 18 February 1963, Turin

Novelist

Fenoglio's experience in the Piedmont **Resistance** during the Second World War formed the nucleus for most of his works, with the partizan movement symbolizing an existential as well as a political crisis. *Il partigiano Johnny* (Johnny the Partizan), Fenoglio's most famous novel, although not published until after his death, portrays the protagonist's struggles with both internal doubts and the more immediate threat of death. Fenoglio's rendering of the material and his focus on the disenfranchised led to his being regarded as a neorealist writer, though he was very much a loner and his talent remained under-appreciated. One of his few sponsors was Elio **Vittorini**, who published Fenoglio's collection of short stories *I ventitré giorni della città di Alba* (The Twenty-Three Days of the City of Alba) for **Einaudi** in 1952. Having taught himself English, Fenoglio read and translated many authors from Shakespeare to Coleridge and his later novels, most published posthumously, reflect the strong influence of such American authors as Hemingway and Dos Passos. After several decades of relative neglect, Fenoglio's work and reputation have more recently been re-evaluated.

Further reading

Ioli, G. (ed.) (1991) *Beppe Fenoglio Oggi* (Beppe Fenoglio Today), Milan: Mursia (a re-evaluation of his works).

O'Healy, A. (1990) 'Four Critics and Fenoglio', *Italica* 67 (1): 42–52.

Saccone, E. (1996) 'War and Peace in Beppe Fenoglio's Partizan Novels', *MLN* 111 (1): 31–7.

LAURA A. SALSINI

Ferragamo, Salvatore

b. 1898, Naples; d. 1960, Fiumetto

Footwear designer

Ferragamo served an apprenticeship in Italy before establishing a shop in California in 1914, where he attracted the patronage of Hollywood for his exclusive handmade designs. He returned to Italy in 1927, and established himself in Florence two years later. Despite bankruptcy in 1933, he was soon serving the international jet-set. While in America, he had scrutinized mass production techniques, as well as studying anatomy and balance, and he applied this knowledge to the creation of many glamorous and graceful styles. Some of Ferragamo's most innovative work was produced during the war, when severe shortages inspired him to work with unconventional materials such as fish skins and cellophane. His most famous designs include the 'platform' (1938), and the 'invisible' shoe (1947). After his death his family expanded production internationally and added clothing ranges, while maintaining a reputation for quality.

See also: fashion

NICOLA WHITE

Ferrari, Enzo Anselmo

b. 18 February 1898, Modena;
   d. 14 August 1988, Modena

Racing driver and industrialist

Enzo Ferrari's extraordinary career in the automobile industry began in 1918. At the end of the First World War he moved to Turin, seeking employment with **Fiat**. Having been turned down, Ferrari went to work as a test driver for light trucks. He soon moved to Milan, where he started working as a test driver for CMN (Costruzioni Meccaniche Nazionali (National Mechanical Constructions)) and also began racing cars. He entered several races, including the famous Targa Florio. In 1920 he began working for Alfa Romeo (see **motor racing**), and eventually became the man in charge of Alfa Romeo's racing operations. Ferrari immediately surrounded himself with the best engineers he could find; Luigi Bazzi and Vittorio Jano, who would later design many of the most famous Ferrari models, joined him in 1923 and remained with Ferrari for the rest of their lives.

It was during his years with Alfa Romeo that Ferrari established the Scuderia Ferrari in Modena. When he left Alfa Romeo in 1940, Ferrari returned to Modena and started an independent company, Auto-Avio Costruzioni Ferrari (Ferrari Auto and Aviation Constructions). The company built a car for the 1940 edition of the Mille Miglia race, which it called simply the 815.

The first car to bear the Ferrari name was built in 1946 in Maranello, a small town close to Modena which remains the site of the company's main plant to this day. The cars bearing the symbol of the *cavallino rampante* (rampant horse) symbol were highly competitive and successful from the very beginning, and throughout the years have continued to outperform all other makes. No other car company can match the number of victories obtained by *le rosse* – red being the distinctive Ferrari colour – and no single owner has achieved as much as Enzo Ferrari.

Ferrari's professional success was unfortunately marred by personal tragedy, in particular the death of his first son Alfredo, known as Dino, at the age of twenty-four. Dino was also involved in the family company, and an engine he had helped design was first used in a race a few months after his death.

In 1969 Ferrari agreed to a joint participation with Fiat; ironically, the giant company that had originally turned away the young Enzo now became his business partner. In 1979 Enzo Ferrari received the Italian Cavalierato di Gran Croce (Italian Knighthood of the Great Cross), the highest decoration of the Italian **Republic**.

PAOLO VILLA

Ferrè, Gianfranco

b. 15 August 1944, Legnano, Milano

Fashion designer

Now a byword for Italian fashion, Gianfranco Ferrè's background was in architecture and he began his career in furniture and accessory design. His first collection of Ferrè ready-to-wear clothes for women appeared in 1978. The standard white blouse with creative touches became the Ferrè trademark, and he became popular in the United States for elegant and sophisticated executive dressing, appealing above all to women who wore suits by day but welcomed the rebirth of the grand ball gown by night. His first perfume for women was launched in 1984, with a men's fragrance following in 1986. The first high fashion collection designed by Ferrè met with an enthusiastic response in Rome in 1986, and in 1989 he was selected as chief designer for the prestigious French House of Dior. After eight years with the French company Ferrè left Paris to return home to work at the centre of Italian fashion in Milan. His international appeal, however, continues to spread with boutiques now on every continent.

BERNADETTE LUCIANO

Ferreri, Marco

b. 11 May 1928, Milan; d. 9 May 1997, Paris

Film director

One of Italy's most eccentric comic directors, Ferreri addressed the shortcomings and absurdities of the white, capitalist and patriarchal world in an outrageous cocktail of surrealism and black humour reminiscent of Luis Bunuel's social satires. Ferreri's cinema is caustically ideological and inscribed in the post-1968 overthrow of petit bourgeois institutions and values. Especially memorable is his 1973 attack on excessive consumerism in *La grande abbuffata* (*La Grande Bouffe*), the story of a weekend-long orgy climaxing in cannibalistic annihilation. From the bizarre parody of the Western genre in *Non toccare la donna bianca* (Don't Touch the White Woman) (1975) to the deconstruction of masculinity which culminates in the male protagonist's self-castration with an electric knife in *L'ultima donna* (The Last Woman) (1976), Ferreri's films are always provocatively excessive in their representation and denunciation of Western society's dehumanizing materialism.

Further reading

Mahéo, M. (1986) *Marco Ferreri*, Paris: Edilig (a detailed study in French of Ferreri's films).

DOROTHéE BONNIGAL

Ferrero, Lorenzo

b. 17 November 1951, Turin

Composer

Lorenzo Ferrero's fusion of classical and pop traditions has made him one of the most widely acclaimed opera composers of his generation. Initially self-taught, he went on to study with Massimo Bruni and Enore Zaffiri before conducting research into electronic music at Bourges (1972–3). His involvement in multimedia composition began in 1974 when he began collaborating with the Musik-Dia-Licht Film Galerie in Munich. The chamber opera *Rimbaud* (1978) shows the crystallization of the increasingly eclectic elements of Ferrero's mature style, which is unashamedly neo-tonal and employs ostinato techniques derived from rock music. This was to lay the foundations for his success with *Marilyn* (1980), which focuses on scenes from the private and public lives of Marilyn Monroe. During the 1980s Ferrero embarked on a series of imaginative works for the stage, notable among which are the children's opera *La figlia del mago* (The Magician's Daughter) (1981) and the operas *Mare nostro* (Our Sea) (1985) and *Charlotte Corday* (1989). He has served as artistic director of the Puccini Festival in Torre del Lago (1980–4), and of the Arena di Verona (1991–4).

Further reading

Gerhatz, L.K. (1982) 'Auch die Avantgarde steht in Entwicklungsprozessen ... Gesprach mit dem italienischen Komponisten Lorenzo Ferrero' (On the Development Processes of the Avant-garde: Conversation with Lorenzo Ferrero), *Neue Zeitschrift für Musik* 9: 4–7.

JOHN KERSEY

Ferroni, Giulio

b. 1943, Rome

Literary critic and essayist

Ferroni's first critical works were close analyses of developments in Italian theatre both during the Renaissance and in the twentieth century, after which his attention shifted to a variety of topics from Romanticism to the current state of narrative in Italy. He has devoted his attention particularly to an intelligent and lively discussion of both contemporary criticism and fiction writing, a discussion carried out in scholarly journals as well as in major newspapers such as *Il Corriere della sera*. Ferroni has also been involved with pedagogic publications such as an authoritative *History of Italian Literature* published in 1991 by Einaudi. The distinctive characteristic of his acute analysis of contemporary literary theory and practice has been that of distinguishing literary works which carry a broad ethical and universal message behind their complex stylistic structures from those deriving merely from fashionable trends.

ANDREA CICCARELLI

Ferrucci, Franco

b. 1936, Pisa

Writer and literary critic

Ferrucci has been living in the Unites States for many years and is Professor of Italian at Rutgers University in New Jersey. As a scholar, he has concentrated mostly on Italian authors of the Enlightenment and of Romanticism, and on the concept of myth throughout western culture. He has written numerous novels, amongst them *Il cappello di Panama* (The Panama Hat) (1973), *Il Mondo creato* (1986), translated as *The World according to God*, and *Lontano da casa* (Far Away from Home) (1996). Ferrucci's narrative is characterized by a search – often within the broader context of a cosmological pessimism – for a stable and positive existential condition, the possibility of which is usually only glimpsed or barely guessed by the characters of his books.

ANDREA CICCARELLI

Ferruzzi

A family-owned industrial group based in Ravenna with international trade in cereals and sugar at its core, Ferruzzi was a shooting star of Italian big business. In 1986, thanks to **Mediobanca**'s blessing, Ferruzzi – then ruled by Raul Gardini, son-in-law of Serafino Ferruzzi, the group's founder – became the main shareholder of **Montedison**, a chemical group then in grave financial crisis. However Gardini's ambition of relaunching the Italian chemical industry through ENIMONT, a joint venture with **ENI**, failed because of strong political interference and furious disputes between the prospective partners. Ferruzzi consequently sold its major interest in the Montedison chemical plants to ENI, making a very large profit, but paid massive bribes to the ruling parties. Business turned into tragedy when Gardini broke off with Ferruzzi and finally in 1993, after *Tangentopoli* inquiries, preferred to commit suicide rather than face trial for corruption. Of fiery temperament and a charismatic leader, Gardini became very popular in the early 1990s thanks to his sailing boat, *Il Moro*, which successfully competed in the America's Cup. He was the only real entrepreneur of the family, and after his death Ferruzzi had to be rescued and fell under the control of Mediobanca and other banks.

STEFANO BATTILOSSI

Festa dell'Unità

One of the most important social events in the **PCI** calendar, the Festa dell'Unità (Festival of Unity) was instituted by a group of party militants in Milan in September 1945 to celebrate class solidarity and collect money for the party's newspaper, *l'Unità*. Originally functioning largely as communal picnics for party members and their families concluding with a few political speeches, the *feste* soon became important annual occasions for spreading the faith,

both at the local and the national level. During the 1950s, when tension between communist and centre–right forces was at its height, the festivals came to include noisy parades with placards and banners as well as fervent political speeches, often leading to violent clashes with police. The festivals changed during the 1960s, becoming progressively less stridently political and more broadly cultural events, thus inviting and attracting a much wider public participation from non-party members. This trend towards a more pluralist political orientation and an increasing focus on culture and entertainment continued throughout the 1970s and 1980s, and when in 1991 the PCI transformed itself into the **PDS**, it was feared the festivals might disappear altogether. However this fear proved to be unfounded and, at the end of the 1990s, the national Festa dell'Unità still featured as a major media event in the Italian calendar.

GINO MOLITERNO

Fiat

Probably the best-known industrial group in Italy, with a large multinational network, Fiat played an extraordinary role as promoter of postwar mass motorization. The Fiat 500, a popular economy car, was a symbol of the '**economic miracle**' of the 1960s, and Fiat itself has always been synonymous with the **motor car industry**, although its actual identity has become far more complex. One of the oldest Italian enterprises – established in Turin in 1899 by Giovanni Agnelli, founder of the dynasty – Fiat is also the largest, and Enrico **Cuccia** once justifiably referred to it as the Mont Blanc of Italian capitalism, surrounded by hills but no comparable mountains.

While continuing its traditional core business of motorcars and industrial vehicles, Fiat widely diversified its activities towards a number of unrelated sectors such as aircraft, railway systems, telecommunications, construction and civil engineering, cement, insurance and chains of department stores. Consequently, motor cars, which accounted for 65 per cent of group's total sales in 1970, declined to 40 per cent just ten years later. Facing a grave crisis in the late 1970s, when car sales fell both in Italy and abroad and costs and debts rose with no restraint, Fiat undertook an effective restructuring plan and regained a successful position in international motor car markets. Under a new management, led by Cesare **Romiti** and Vittorio Ghidella, workers' opposition was crushed, employment was heavily reduced (from 139,000 to 78,000 employees in the motor car division alone), the introduction of new automated technologies was accelerated, production was partly decentralized, new cars were planned (the Uno proved the most successful) and debt was reduced thanks to new Libyan shareholders (a striking financial operation managed by **Mediobanca**). The dramatic 1980 dispute between Fiat and the unions proved to be not simply a company affair but rather represented an epoch-making struggle with a nationwide impact, since it marked a general decline of union power and the beginnings of the 'entrepreneurial revenge' of the 1980s. For its own part, Fiat stuck to its traditional bureaucratic organization, which relied upon a rigorous vertical hierarchy, an extreme centralization of decision making and a marginalization of unions. Fiat's top managers subsequently attempted to make the organization more flexible by launching a 'total quality' programme in 1989, vaguely echoing Japanese managerial doctrines; this was supposed to improve products by actively involving workers but remained largely bombast.

Nevertheless, Fiat changed greatly in the 1990s. After Ghidella's exit, Fiat gave up its 'motor car-centred' strategy, which involved an alliance with Ford to block Japanese penetration into Europe, and heavily diversified towards hi-tech sectors (electronics and space industry, biotechnology), finance (banks and insurance) and other activities such as the food and drink industry through an alliance between IFIL, a financial holding owned by the Agnelli, and the French group BSN Danone. A further reduction of labour was carried out in 1992–3 which affected 12,000 employees, mostly middle managers and white-collar workers in the motor car division. Production was mostly moved towards new factories in southern Italy (such as Melfi) and abroad, so that Turin was no longer considered a core location. The large conglomerate thus enters its second century of life under a cloud of uncertainty, more than ever in need of a strong

alliance with a leading foreign car maker in order to compete in global markets.

See also: Agnelli family

Further reading

Bonazzi, G. (1993) *Il tubo di cristallo. Modello giapponese e fabbrica integrata alla Fiat auto* (The Glass Tube: The Japanese Model and Integrated Factory at Fiat Auto), Bologna: Il Mulino (a study of the attempt to adapt Japanese managerial doctrines to Fiat's car making division).

Enrietti, A. and Fornengo, G. (1989) *Il gruppo Fiat: dall'inizio degli anni Ottanta alle prospettive del mercato unificato del 1992* (The Fiat Group: From the Early 1980s to the Prospect of the Single Market in 1992), Rome: Nuova Italia Scientifica (a detailed and well-informed analysis of the Fiat group's structure).

Lerner, G. (1988) *Operai: viaggio all'interno della Fiat* (Workers: A Journey Inside Fiat), Milan: Feltrinelli (a journalistic inquest on the impact of the technological changes of the 1980s on Fiat's workers).

STEFANO BATTILOSSI

Figini and Pollini

Luigi Figini (b. 27 January 1903, Milan; d. 1984, Milan) and Gino Pollini (b. 13 January 1903, Rovereto; d. 1991, Milan) were founding members of Gruppo 7, which initiated 'rationalist' architecture in Italy in 1927. After the war they continued their collaboration with Adriano **Olivetti**, for whom they designed a whole sequence of works at Ivrea, including the Olivetti factory in various stages, 1934–57. A summation of their earlier elegance is found in the Apartment and Office Building in the Via Broletto, Milan (1947–8), but their works subsequently became more textured in surface and complex in geometry. Of these, probably the most significant was the Church of the Madonna of the Poor (1952–4) on the outskirts of Milan. A translation of early Christian basilical form into industrialized materials, tough, introverted yet deeply penetrated by light filtered through blocks of randomly laid stone, its gritty 'unfinished' state is characteristic of the postwar climate.

Further reading

Gregotti, V. and Marzari, G. (eds) (1996) *Luigi Figini, Gino Pollini Opera Completa*, Milan: Electa (the most comprehensive catalogue and analysis to date).

ROSS JENNER

film actors

In part because of the popularity of Italian cinema itself and in part because of the strength of their on-screen personae as well as the assumed glamour of jet-setting lifestyles, Italian actors and actresses achieved international renown in the postwar period. Sophia **Loren** and Marcello **Mastroianni** became household names even in the depths of middle America, connoting both Italian cinema and stardom. Furthermore, although many Italian film actors came from the theatre – as, for instance, Mastroianni and **Gassman**, who started their careers side by side under **Visconti**'s artistic direction – many also became so vitally associated with the directors who used them to express their highly individualistic vision as to function as alter egos. It is indeed impossible to separate Roberto **Rossellini** and Anna **Magnani**, Michelangelo **Antonioni** and Monica **Vitti**, Mariangela Melato or Giancarlo Giannini and Lina **Wertmüller** and, of course, **Fellini** and Mastroianni.

Neorealism first celebrated what Rossellini called the 'spontaneous creations of the actors'. Such faith and trust in actorial inventiveness elicited brilliant performances from non-professionals such as Lamberto Maggiorani and Enzo Staiola, the forgotten protagonists of Vittorio **De Sica**'s *Ladri di biciclette* (Bicycle Thieves) (1948) or Carlo Battisti, better known as *Umberto D* (1952). But neorealism also gave great scope to the talents of professionals like Fabrizi and Magnani, who were able to transform themselves from comic vaudevillians to serious dramatic stars.

The 1960s marked the heyday of Italian postwar cinema and the rise of big stars such as Claudia **Cardinale**, Vittorio Gassman, Sophia Loren and Marcello Mastroianni. A very strong tradition of comic actors simultaneously bred huge names like Ugo **Tognazzi** or even **Totò**, who, though a national star for some time, only became internationally known in 1966 with Pier Paolo **Pasolini**'s political parable, *Uccellacci e uccellini* (Hawks and Sparrows). The political cinema of the **Taviani brothers**, Francesco **Rosi** or Elio **Petri** likewise consecrated actors like Gian Maria **Volonté** who also owed his renown to the very popular **spaghetti westerns**.

The actor-star system declined in the days of the so-called **New Italian Cinema** of the 1980s and 1990s, which gravitated more towards the figure of the actor-director epitomized by Carlo **Verdone**, Massimo **Troisi**, Roberto **Benigni** and, most of all, Nanni **Moretti**. However, as evidenced by Diego Abatantuono's numerous collaborations with Gabriele **Salvatores**, or Enrico Lo Verso's work with Gianni **Amelio**, character actors remained important mediators in the expression of a director's vision even though the growing internationalization of Italian film productions predictably lessened the importance of the national identification of particular actors.

DOROTHÉE BONNIGAL

film composers

During the first decades of the cinema, Italian composers like Pietro Mascagni and Ildebrando Pizzetti (*Cabiria*, 1915) contributed to the success of the new medium by composing either musical guide lines or original music scores to accompany silent films. The introduction of sound opened up a new and more essential role for music and for the film composer. The first Italian film with sound, Giovanni Gennaro's *La canzone dell'amore* (The Song of Love) (1930) used Nino Bixio's composition 'Solo per te, Lucia' (Lucia, Only For You) both as leitmotiv and as commentary on the narrative. In general, however, the carefree world of the *telefoni bianchi* (white telephone) films did not expand the potential of film music, which remained largely anchored to the idea of pleasing the audience with easy listening and often amusing tunes. Such light and unremarkable musical scores were flanked by the highly rhetorical and bombastic scores of heroic pseudo-historical epics so dear to the Fascist regime.

Although film scores still remained illustrative in the 1940s, during the neorealist period composers such as Fernando Previdali, Franco Ferrara, Enzo Masetti, Giovanni Fusco and Nino **Rota** were able to introduce the fundamental notion that the film's psychological element should also be appropriately explored and expressed through its music. However, it was only with the advent of a finer and often more complex correlation between image and music, such as in Rota's collaboration with Federico Fellini and Fusco's scores for the early Antonioni films, that film music began to approach its full potential.

This new approach was also carried on in the 1950s by other composers such as Mario Nascimbene and Ennio **Morricone**, who were willing to experiment and thus succeeded in creating interesting and unusual relationships between image and sound. New paths were also explored by composers who had been active earlier but who had remained more conservative in their music, such as Piero Piccioni who worked extensively with Francesco **Rosi**, and Armando Trovajoli who later worked on many of the films of Ettore **Scola**. Such composers introduced jazz into Italy, both in film scores and more widely in the *musica leggera* (light, popular music). Trovajoli was particularly influential as orchestra director for some of the **Sanremo Festivals**.

In the panorama of contemporary film music, Morricone deserves a place of his own. His music has become known throughout the world, especially since the mid-1960s when his name became closely associated with the phenomenon of the 'spaghetti western'. However, he has worked with most of the major Italian directors such as Elio **Petri**, Gillo **Pontecorvo**, Bernardo **Bertolucci** and Pier Paolo **Pasolini** as well as with many international names such as Roman Polanski, Brian De Palma, Roland Joffè, and more recently Pedro Almodovar. At ease with all film genres, Morricone has even worked with Italian horror film master Dario **Argento**, in *L'uccello dalle piume di cristallo* (The Bird With Crystal Feathers) (1969).

The other outstanding film composer of the postwar period was undoubtedly Nino Rota, whose memorable musical themes and compositions became indissolubly wedded to some of Fellini's most striking images in a collaboration that lasted twenty-seven years, from *Lo sceicco bianco* (The White Sheik) (1952) to *Prova d'orchestra* (Orchestra Rehearsal) (1978). Rota's work with directors outside Italy included his scores for Coppola's *Godfather* films, with *Godfather II* winning him an Oscar in 1974.

In Fellini's last films, *Intervista* (Interview) (1988) and *La voce della luna* (The Voice of the Moon) (1990), Rota's place was taken by the talented Nicola Piovani, who tried to maintain Rota's distinctive touch. Piovani had started his composing career with the young generation of the 1970s, achieving notable success with his work for the **Taviani brothers** on *La notte di San Lorenzo* (The Night of the Shooting Stars) (1982) and *Kaos* (1984). More recently he has worked with Nanni **Moretti** on *La messa è finita* (Mass is Over) (1985) and *Palombella rossa* (Small Red Dove) (1989).

In the most recent Italian cinema, the music has often been composed by singer-writers such as De Gregori, Antonello Venditti, Lucio **Dalla**, Edoardo Bennato and Gianna **Nannini**.

Further reading

Comuzio, E. (1992) *Colonna sonora. Dizionario ragionato dei musicisti cinematografici* (Sound Track: Annotated Dictionary of Film Musicians), Rome: Ente dello spettacolo.

CRISTINA DEGLI-ESPOSTI REINERT

film industry

At the end of the Second World War, the Italian film industry was in tatters. Most of the country's movie theatres had been destroyed during the war years, and in 1945 **Cinecittà** itself had been requisitioned by the Americans as a refugee camp with much of its equipment having already been looted by the retreating Germans and Fascists.

Nevertheless the industry slowly started to function again and, in spite of crushing difficulties, twenty-five films were made in 1945, many of them landmarks of not only Italian but of world cinema.

The situation clearly demanded a great deal of improvisation and ingenuity, such as the ability to film outside studios and to stretch limited budgets by using non-professional actors. The result of such measures was an experimental documentaristic look which came to be known as **neorealism**. Films like **Rossellini**'s *Roma città aperta* (Open City) (1945) and **De Sica**'s *Sciuscià* (Shoeshine) (1946) reflected, both in their themes and in their production, the severe hardship of the time. Although they would later be recognized as masterpieces, when these films were first released they received little or no attention since the Italian audience was, at the time, in need of more escapist fare.

From 1945 to 1946 Italnoleggio, **Istituto Nazionale LUCE** and Cinecittà were the production companies that, under the protection of the Ente Gestione per il Cinema (Film Development Board), sustained and defended the Italian film industry. By 1946 the number of films produced reached sixty-two, and it increased slowly in the following years (in 1950 there were 100) until the explosion of the economic boom. Gradually the Istituto Luce was able to produce and distribute films that found favour with the public, such as **De Santis**'s *Riso amaro* (Bitter Rice) (1949) and Pietro Germi's *In nome della legge* (In the Name of the Law) (1949). The profit share of national films in 1946 was only 13 per cent, but by the end of 1950s it reached 34 per cent. Furthermore, by the end of the 1950s Italian cinema was living through a new period of creative ferment. Enjoying great success abroad, films like **Fellini**'s *La dolce vita* (1960) and **Antonioni**'s *L'avventura* (1960) helped to renew a sense of the cinema a form of art.

Supported by a series of regulating laws, the production of Italian films increased throughout the 1960s. The great box office success, first domestic then international, of films like De Sica's *La ciociara* (Two Women) (1960) and Visconti's *Rocco e i suoi fratelli* (Rocco and His Brothers) (1960) led new patterns of production and distribution, especially of the *cinema d'autore* or 'art film', which could now be exported. Furthermore as new

genres developed – the ***commedia all'italiana*** (comedy Italian style), the **spaghetti western**, the *peplum* and so on – more production companies came into being; by 1970 they numbered almost 400.

Yet the history of the industry in the 1970s is indissolubly tied to television, which had begun to take an active part in the production or co-production of films since 1968, when the RAI public television network had joined Italnoleggio in the process of making films. Positive in some ways, this partnership would nevertheless in the long run lead to a slow decline of cinema at all its levels. Among the positive results were films like **Bertolucci**'s *La strategia del ragno* (The Spider's Stratagem) (1972), **Olmi**'s *L'albero degli zoccoli* (The Tree of the Wooden Clogs) (1978) and the Tavianis' *Padre padrone* (My Father, My Master) (1977), but by the late 1970s the industry faced a major crisis, provoked to a great extent by the increasing dominance of television and above all by the private networks (see **private television**) which sometimes broadcast up to five (often foreign) films a day. If this contributed on the one hand to a fall in cinema attendance, on the other hand it also led to a decline in quality since many films of little value were made programmatically in order to meet demand.

By the beginning of the 1980s, most of the successful models and genres of the previous two decades had become exhausted and many of the directors of this generation began to look back nostalgically to the tradition of neorealism and that of a committed cinema. Furthermore, during the 1980s, as the RAI and Berlusconi's **Fininvest** increasingly replaced the old distributors in financing films, the final product came to look more like television and less like cinema. Consequently, a number of new production companies were started which eventually produced some of the best films of the following period: Colorado Film Production was founded in 1986 by producer Maurizio Totti, director Gabriele **Salvatores**, and actor Diego Abatantuono, and Sacher Film was founded by Angelo Barbagallo and director Nanni **Moretti**, with Sacher also running a movie theatre in Rome.

In 1996 there were some 175 active production societies which had produced at least three successful films. Perhaps the most significant large producer is the Cecchi-Gori Group, which began in the boom years of the 1950s but which continues to play an important role in both finance and distribution. Cecchi-Gori has produced many of the most significant films of recent years including Salvatores' Oscar-winning *Mediterraneo* (1991), Fellini's *La voce della luna* (The Voice of the Moon) (1990), **Mazzacurati**'s *Il toro* (The Bull) (1994), Michelangelo Antonioni and Wim Wenders's *Al di là delle nuvole* (Beyond the Clouds) (1995) and Leonardo Pieraccioni's *I laureati* (The Graduates) (1995).

At the end of the 1990s the number of movie houses and the volume of moviegoers is about a fifth that of the 1960s and 1970s. National production during this decade has varied from 12 to 30 per cent of the total Italian market. Responsible for emptying the cinemas, television has nevertheless also provided substantial economic support to the film industry ranging from advertising on private television channels to direct financing.

By creating a new market, home video actually expanded the consumption of domestic films in the 1980s, although since 1994 the trend has slowed considerably. Television co-production as well as computer technology appear to be fundamental for cinema in the near future. As cinema and the Italian industry enter the new century it is clear that creative drive, cyber technology and choices of production will all have to work together in order to keep the Italian film industry alive.

Further reading

Bondanella, P. (1983) *Italian Cinema: From Neorealism to the Present*, New York: Ungar.

Liehm, M. (1984) *Passion and Defiance: Film in Italy from 1942 to the Present*, Berkeley, CA: University of California Press.

Sorlin, P. (1996) *Italian National Cinema. 1896–1996*, London and New York: Routledge.

Wagstaff, C. (1996) 'Il cinema Italiano nel mercato internazionale' (Italian Cinema in the International Market) in G.P. Brunetta (ed.), *Identità italiana e identità europea nel cinema italiano del 1945 al miracolo economico* (Italian Identity and European Identity in Italian Cinema from 1945 to the Economic Miracle), Turin: Fondazione Giovanni Agnelli.

CRISTINA DEGLI-ESPOSTI REINERT

film journals

The first Italian schedule of travelling cinematographic screenings appeared in Bologna in 1889 and continued until 1914. Soon other film publications appeared: *Il cinematografo* (1907, Rome), *Lux* (1908, Rome), *La cinematografia italiana* (1908, Milan), *Film* (1914, Naples), *Iride* (1914, Genoa), *La rivista cinematografica* (1921, Turin) and *Scenario* (1932–43, Rome). These mostly originated to satisfy advertising needs but soon began to include essays concerning the educational and cultural possibilities of cinema.

This trend continued into the 1920s when some of the more significant film journals began. The earliest of these was *Il cinema italiano* (1924, Rome), the official publication of the National Film Trade and Film Dealers. *Cinematografo* (1927, Rome), edited by Alessandro **Blasetti**, included informed essays on Italian cinema as it went from silent to sound, providing valuable information on the conditions of Italian cinema in late 1920s and the birth of the first cinematographic corporations. In 1935 *Intercine* appeared in Rome as the publication of the Istituto Internazionale per la Cinematografia Educativa (International Institute for Educational Cinema). Special issues were devoted to the Venice Film Festival, television and other related areas. It also published Ferdinando Chiarelli's fundamental article 'Pirandello e il cinema' (Pirandello and the Cinema) before closing, after only 12 issues, in December 1935.

Bianco e nero (1937, Rome), edited by Luigi **Chiarini**, originated at the **Centro Sperimentale di Cinematografia**. It is still published today and remains one of the most prestigious academic journals which examines the theoretical and aesthetic aspects of cinema. *Filmcritica*, the monthly review of the Italian Cinema Clubs begun in Rome in 1950, also continues to be published and is now directed by Edoardo Bruno. It presents interviews, festival reports, book reviews and articles on Italian and foreign cinema while also addressing general questions of film theory and aesthetics. *Cinema Nuovo* (1952, Milan, Genoa, Florence), originally directed by Guido Aristarco, is still published bi-monthly, offering panoramic overviews on the condition of cinema in Italy and abroad as well as interviews and articles on scriptwriters and on particular aspects of the history of the cinema.

Cineforum (Quaderno della Federazione Italiana dei Cineforum) first appeared in 1960 in Venice. Edited by Sandro Zambetti, it is still published monthly. It presents essays on special topics and films, as well as a substantial number of film reviews. *Segno Cinema* (1970, Vicenza) is published every two months and is directed by Paolo Cherchi-Usai. Like *Cineforum*, it resembles the British journal *Sight and Sound* in presenting specialized essays combined with a considerable number of film reviews. *Cinema e cinema* (1973, Bologna) a quarterly founded by Adelio Ferrero, tackles issues of film theory and aesthetics as well as questions related to the restoration of old films.

The 1990s have seen an increasing number of reviews such as *Cinema/Studio* (1990, Rome), published every three months and edited by Orio Caldison. Some of them also appear on Internet, like *Voci Off* (1995, Bologna) which has articles, reviews and interviews. *Cine Critica* appeared in January 1996 (Rome); it is a quarterly of film culture edited by the National Union of Italian Cinematographic Critics (SNCCI). The first number of *Close Up* appeared in March 1997 (Rome). Directed by Giovanni Spagnoletti, it is similar in format and look to *Bianco e nero*, offering dossiers, interviews, and historiographic reviews.

On a non-academic level there is *Ciak* (1984, Rome), edited by Roberto Briglia. The journal appears monthly and parallels the format, content and brief overview of coming events of *Premiere* (the French, British, and American editions). *Film. Tutti i film della stagione* (1992, Rome) is a bi-monthly which presents an exhaustive list of film summaries and comments.

CRISTINA DEGLI-ESPOSTI REINERT

Fini, Gianfranco

b. 3 January 1952, Bologna

Political leader

While a student at Rome university, Fini joined the neo-fascist **MSI**, deeming it Italy's only real anti-Communist party. By 1977 he was national secretary of the party's youth movement (FDG), and in 1983 he was elected as a deputy. Backed by the party's historic leader, Giorgio Almirante, Fini became party secretary in 1987. Briefly pushed aside by the radical Pino Rauti in 1990–1, Fini thereafter successfully led his party into the 'Second' **Republic**. He appeared regularly on television, and was liked for his clarity and especially his commentary on President **Cossiga**'s controversial interventions, which helped legitimize the MSI's presidentialism. In 1993 Fini exploited the **DC**'s collapse to launch the AN (**National Alliance**) and in 1994, allied to Silvio **Berlusconi**, he broke the taboo on 'fascist' participation in government. Thereafter he was Berlusconi's rival for leadership of the Liberty Alliance (see **Polo della Libertà**), although his legitimacy as an eventual prime ministerial candidate was questioned by many.

MARK DONOVAN

Fininvest

Founded by Silvio **Berlusconi** in 1978 as a consolidation of his building and other interests into a single holding company, Fininvest soon moved into television, taking over **Canale Cinque** and the publicity agency Publitalia in 1980, **Italia Uno** in 1982, **Retequattro** in 1984 and then the AC Milan football club in 1986. By the late 1990s its main fields of activities were in media (grouped together into Mediaset), publishing (**Mondadori**), retail (Standa and others), and insurance and financial services (Mediolanum and others). Berlusconi's close relationship with Milan gave the group the nickname 'il biscione', alluding to the snake on the city's crest.

Accusations of a conflict of interest and anti-trust legislation have forced Berlusconi to gradually give up personal control of Fininvest. However, despite his relinquishing of company posts in 1994 when he founded **Forza Italia**, and Mediaset and Mediolanum being traded on the Milan stock exchange from 1996, the family has retained control with Berlusconi's children, Marina and Piersilvio, as executives on the board.

JAMES WALSTON

Finsider

A financial holding company founded in 1937 under the auspices of **IRI** to manage state participation in the steel sector, Finsider's major task in the postwar period became the reorganization of crude steel production in Italy by modernizing the three existing centres at Bagnoli (Naples), Piombino (Livorno) and Cornigliano (Genoa), and constructing a fourth one at Taranto. Together with several more specialized plants – for stainless steel at Terni (Perugia) and for large diameter pipes at Dalmine (Bergamo) – the productive enterprises formed the company called **Italsider**. These efforts saw Italy become Europe's second-largest steel producer (behind Germany) and guaranteed a strong position for Italian crude steel on domestic, European and international markets. In subsequent reorganizations of the steel sector, several Finsider plants and mills were decommissioned, and the financial holding itself was officially liquidated in 1989.

Further reading

Balconi, M. (1991) *La siderurgia italiana (1945–1990): Tra controllo pubblico e incentivi del mercato*, (Italian Steel-Making (1945–1990): Between Public Control and Market Incentives), Bologna: Il Mulino (a detailed discussion of all aspects of the Italian steel industry in the postwar period).

ANTHONY C. MASI

Fiorucci, Elio

b. 10 June 1935, Milan

Fashion designer

The son of the owner of an elegant shoe shop in Milan, Elio Fiorucci made a bold statement in 1962 by taking three pairs of bright plastic galoshes to a Milan fashion magazine to be photographed. The famous photo speaks for the alternative youthful look that Fiorucci has represented from then on. Mass and contemporary trends from rock music to political issues have been reflected and parodied in the Fiorucci look, which flaunts colourful parachute cloth jumpsuits, plastic and metal lunchbox 'purses', fishnet stockings, fake animal fabrics, spandex and military clothing. Above all it has been jeans which have defined the Fiorucci look, preferably in colours that are not blue but fuschia, jade or the colour of those galoshes which first made Fiorucci a fashion industry name. Today Fiorucci stores can be found worldwide and continue to provide an alternative to the more conservative trends in Italian fashion.

BERNADETTE LUCIANO

flag

The Italian national flag is composed of three equivalent vertical bands of green, white and red. The colours first appeared in Italy under Napoleon, and were immediately adopted by the Cispadane, and then the Cisalpine, Republics. Disappearing with the fall of Napoleon, the 'tricolour' resurfaced in the 1830s with the Giovine Italia (Young Italy) movement of Giuseppe Mazzini, and was prominent in the revolutionary uprisings of 1848. Having become a popular emblem of Italian aspirations, it was reluctantly accepted by Charles Albert of Savoy alongside his own flag, was flown in the wars of liberation against Austria and was subsequently adopted – with the Savoy coat of arms at its centre – as the flag of the United Kingdom of Italy. With the fall of the monarchy in 1946 and the referendum and the consequent establishment of the Italian **Republic**, the Savoy coat of arms was removed but the tricolour was reconfirmed as the flag of Italy and its place enshrined by Article 12 of the **constitution**.

GINO MOLITERNO

Flaiano, Ennio

b. 5 March 1910, Pescara; d. 20 November 1972, Rome

Writer, critic, journalist and screenwriter

Flaiano's literary activity was linked to his decision to move to Rome, where he soon came to contribute short stories and theatre and film reviews to the weekly magazines *Oggi* and *Il Mondo*. In the meantime he began writing screenplays for films, some of which were destined to mark the history of Italian cinema: he collaborated with Federico **Fellini** on many films including *La dolce vita*, and he also worked with Michelangelo **Antonioni**. Flaiano's novels and plays, however, were written in the immediate postwar period.

The late publication of Flaiano's creative works gave him time to refine his moral attitude and to sharpen it in the light of his own satirical temperament. One of the main themes of his writings is the solitude of the intellect in an era in which the arts are definitively separated from reality. All that is left to the artist is a noble, albeit fruitless, consumption in the fire of his own efforts to acquire knowledge. Flaiano achieves his best results in the epigrammatic, often allegorical tale, as in his first novel, *Tempo di uccidere* (Time to Kill), winner of the Strega Prize in 1947. In this respect, Flaiano finds his literary niche between the scepticism of a man of faith such as Vitaliano **Brancati** and the fantastic tales of Dino **Buzzati**.

Further reading

Flaiano, E. (1992) *Time to Kill*, trans. and introduction S. Hood, London: Quartet.

ERNESTO LIVORNI

Flash Art

Flash Art is a journal of discussion and review of contemporary art, edited and published by Giancarlo Politi. Appearing first in Rome in 1967 as *Flash*, it moved to Milan in 1971 and since 1979 the international edition has been published in English, separate from the Italian edition, in approximately six issues per year. The masthead declares it to be 'the world's leading art magazine'.

Flash Art pursues the latest trends in style and theory, and is not afraid of influencing them. It has been vigorously postmodern (see **postmodernism**) and post-structuralist, with long texts by artists and articles by European intellectuals and critics such as **Celant** and **Bonito Oliva**. Politi claims some credit for the development of *arte povera*, **conceptual art**, minimalism, performance art, the **transavantgarde** and neo-geo. *Flash Art* also makes a point of recognizing different cultures and ethnic groups, with its coverage of art extending to Eastern Europe, Asia and the Americas.

Given that illustrated art journals can be potent instruments of cultural imperialism, *Flash Art* has at least provided an alternative to the American models.

Further reading

Politi, G. and Kontova, H. (1990) *Flash Art: Two Decades of History: XXI years*, Cambridge, MA: MIT Press (selection of articles).

MAX STAPLES

Fo, Dario

b. 24 March 1926, Leggiuno, Varese

Actor, playwright and director

The most famous and notorious figure in contemporary Italian theatre, and 1997 winner of the Nobel Prize for Literature, Dario Fo (together with his wife Franca **Rame** and their company **La Comune**) terrorized the Italian bureaucratic and political establishment throughout the 1970s with their unique brand of political theatre which aimed primarily to provide the working class with 'counter-information' on the real state of national and international affairs. This left-wing theatre for a class deprived of critical viewpoints on current affairs by the state-owned media monopoly had its roots in the 1968 student uprisings, but Fo and Rame had since the early 1960s been running foul of state censorship for their irreverent and anti-Catholic positions on current affairs. In 1962 they were thrown off a popular national television variety show, *Canzonissima*, over objectionable material in some of their skits.

Fo absorbed the riches of the Italian popular performance tradition, which goes back at least as far as the Commedia dell'Arte, and developed into a prolific playwright and talented performer, creating his own physical performance style based on mime, storytelling in dialect, gibberish or 'grammelot' derived from medieval performance, and folk music.

Immediately after the Second World War he began an architecture degree, but quickly became involved in theatre. His earliest performance experiences were in musical reviews, but his marriage to Franca Rame, a member of a family touring company, gave him the opportunity to extend his skills as a playwright to the point where by the late 1960s he was premiering a new play each year and touring it in Italy on the main commercial circuits. The political upheaval of these years prompted Fo and Rame to shift radically away from their role as entertainers of the middle classes; they set up Associazione Nuova Scena, which toured their productions on an alternative circuit of communist workers' clubs. A subsequent break with the Italian Communist Party (**PCI**) led to the formation of the theatrical collective La Comune, an extreme left-wing 'theatrical flying squad' which travelled rapidly and incessantly from one political hot spot to the next, performing in popular venues and for workers in occupied factories. This work was done at considerable personal cost and risk; at one point Rame was abducted by neo-fascists, and in Sardignia Fo was arrested while performing a play on the *coup d'état* by the military against the democratically elected communist government of Salvatore Allende in Chile. Despite difficulties even with the hiring of venues during this period (due to theatre managers'

fear of the violence that was threatened by his political opponents), Fo's best-known play, *Morte accidentale di un anarchico* (Accidental Death of an Anarchist), was so popular that the company was hiring indoor sports stadia and performing it to audiences of 10,000 or more at a time. Its function as 'counter-intelligence', to inform the working class of the 'frame-up' of left-wing activists by the forces of law and order, gave a pungent political immediacy to its farcical surface (an immediacy lost in subsequent productions outside Italy, which tended to stress the farcical elements). Perhaps Fo's most theatrically innovative work occurred in this period, as the shoestring conditions in which he worked necessitated great simplicity of production. *Mistero Buffo* (Funny Mystery), a series of monologues based on Bible stories, and *Storia della Tigre* (Tiger Story), an account of one man's experience of Mao's Long March, relied entirely on Fo's acting skills: dressed in simple black and wearing a radio microphone, he narrated and enacted the events of the story, employing extraordinarily inventive mime to delight the audience. The performances were always framed in political terms to ensure their didactic impact, as were a series of monologues he wrote with and for Franca Rame on women's issues.

The 1980s saw a return to favour by the mainstream media, and Fo began to reappear on television (a priceless series of demonstrations of his acting techniques was screened on the third national television network, **RAI** 3). As his plays began to be produced in translation outside Italy, he toured and lectured in Europe, England and America, and began to direct mainstream theatre.

In 1997, Fo was awarded the Nobel Prize for Literature (he had been shortlisted in 1975), an award which immediately provoked negative reactions from certain sectors of Italian political and cultural life. The objections of right-wing politicians were predictable – Fo's fame in Italy was more as a performer than as a writer – and some members of the literary establishment made clear their displeasure and incomprehension at the Nobel committee's implicit broadening of the definition of 'literature' to include performance works such as those by Fo. Playwrights are not highly regarded within literary culture in contemporary Italy, and while a playwright like Luigi

Pirandello had previously received the Nobel Prize, his plays are unmistakably literary and stand beside a substantial narrative output. The same cannot be said for Fo: many of the published texts of his plays of the 1970s, such as *Morte accidentale* and *Mistero Buffo*, cited by the committee as high points of his *oeuvre*, are little more than transcripts of performance, and his cultural significance is undoubtedly through his performances and his public persona rather than through the influence of his published works. Nevertheless, as the Nobel award seemed to testify, Fo's reinvention and political adaptation of medieval oral-based story-telling techniques of performance is a most valuable technical contribution to both theatre and literature and, as such, is an important contribution to international culture as a whole.

Further reading

Fo, D. (1991) *The Tricks of the Trade*, trans. J. Farrell, London: Methuen.

Fo, D. and Rame, F. (1983) *Theatre Workshops at Riverside Studios*, London: Red Notes (valuable outlines of their working processes).

Mitchell, T. (1984) *Dario Fo: People's Court Jester*, London and New York: Methuen (an overview of Fo's theatrical career and successes both in Italy and Europe).

TIM FITZPATRICK

Fontana

The three sisters Zoe, Micol and Giovanna Fontana were introduced to their craft in their home town of Parma by their great-grandmother, Zeide. Zoe was the first to leave the provincial town for Rome in 1937, where she went to work for a large fashion house. She was soon joined by her sisters, and together they set up their own shop on the corner of the fashionable Via Veneto where they attracted famous and influential women as customers. Their designs also appealed to foreign actresses who had come to Italy's film capital. Among the personalities adorned in Fontana styles were Princes Grace of Monaco, Jacqueline Kennedy, Audrey Hepburn, Elizabeth Taylor, Ava

Gardner and Barbara Stanwyck. The sisters went on to conquer the world, exporting their designs to United States as well as to other European countries, Africa and Asia. While their clothes belong mostly to the world of high fashion, they have also produced a ready-to-wear line, a leather line and bridal wear.

BERNADETTE LUCIANO

Fontana, Lucio

b. 19 February 1899, Rosario de Santa Fe, Argentina; d. 7 September 1968, Milan

Artist

Fontana's early work was figurative and influenced by fascist artistic themes, but he soon moved towards abstraction. In 1948 he founded spatialism (see **spazialismo**) which stressed that space, movement and time were as important as colour, perspective and form, and he would subsequently refer to his paintings as *concetti spaziali* (spatial concepts). Fontana's lacerated canvases of the 1950s, created by cutting the surface of the painted canvas with a blade thus allowing the viewer to see through to the space behind, challenged accepted notions of pictorial space and brought him notoriety within and outside Italy. Fontana also experimented with *ambienti spaziali* (spatial environments), often neon installations in which he attempted to extend his painting practice into a specific environmental space. He is one of the postwar Italian artists whose work has had a genuine influence outside of Italy and an enduring relevance to contemporary painting.

LAURENCE SIMMONS

Fontanella, Luigi

b. 1943, San Severino, Salerno

Critic and poet

Fontanella lives in the USA, where he teaches literature at the State University of New York at Stony Brook. He has published critical essays, poetry and novels and also edits the journal *Gradiva*.

In 1996 he founded IPSA, the Italian Poetry Society of America.

At the basis of Fontanella's poetry is a sense of the dissolution of human relationships, rapidly consumed by the flames of the quotidian. Salvation is only offered by the chance of daily encounters, transformed into mythical occasions by the poet's artistry. Fontanella's poetic idiom tends to adhere as much as possible to everyday language, while the self of this poetry appears to be writing a sort of masked autobiography, fluctuating between two different realities: his native Italy, left behind and rescued in fragments of past memories or conscious efforts in the present, and the United States where daily existence flows out of the self and forces the poet to find new linguistic tracks in order to unite the languages of the mind.

Further reading

Fontanella, L. (1991) *Round Trip. Diario in versi*, Udine: Campanotto (collection of poetry which received the Premio Ragusa).

ERNESTO LIVORNI

football

Football (*calcio* in Italian) is unquestionably Italy's favourite sport, an intense passion that engages great numbers of active participants and spectators. It began towards the end of the nineteenth century with the formation of the first Italian football teams, Genoa football club being the first in 1893. The first official Italian championship, played according to the English rules of football association, took place in 1898 and was won by Genoa FC. The FIGC (Federazione Italiana Gioco Calcio) was founded 1898 and has remained Italian football's governing body.

Professional teams are divided into different leagues (*serie* in Italian), called Serie A, B, C-1 and C-2. The other leagues, including all the women's teams, are officially considered amateur ones, although in some cases the salaries paid to the players of these leagues make them true professionals. In the course of a season, which typically lasts from September to May, each team plays all the other teams in its category twice. Serie A is the top league: the team that wins the Serie A becomes Italy's football champion for the year and secures the chance to represent the country in the Champions' League (formerly Champions' Cup), the most prestigious of the European competitions for clubs. Inclusion in a given category is determined by the results obtained in a single season. For example, the teams with the four worst records at the end of the Serie A season play the next year in Serie B, while the best four teams of Serie B move up to Serie A.

Although not lucrative *per se*, mostly due to the high salaries paid to the players, owning a Serie A team is a sign of prestige and provides much publicity. Many Serie A teams are under the control of Italy's prominent business entrepreneurs, such as **Fiat**'s **Agnelli family** (in charge of Juventus FC) and television tycoon Silvio **Berlusconi** (AC Milan). Most of Italy's major urban areas are home to a team competing in one of the professional leagues. Cities such as Rome, Milan, Turin and Genoa each host two major football teams, and these have traditionally been the main competitors for the title of Italian champions. Juventus FC of Turin leads the pack with twenty-five championships, followed by AC Milan with fifteen, Internazionale FC (also of Milan) with thirteen, Genoa FC with nine and AC Turin with eight. AC Milan was the first Italian team to triumph in the Champions' League in 1963, followed by Internazionale FC in 1964–5 and then AC Milan again in 1969. Between 1985 and 1996, Italian teams have participated in eight of the twelve finals of the Champions' League, winning five of them. AC Milan's record between 1989 and 1995 was especially impressive, with three victories out of five attempts.

A factor which contributed to these renewed accomplishments on the part of Italian club teams was the lifting of the ban on foreign players. Italy has in fact long been home to one of the most competitive and lucrative football leagues, attracting many international star players. However, in 1966, after the disastrous expedition to the World Cup held in England, a law was passed to stop the influx of foreign players. This measure was aimed at increasing the playing possibilities of young Italian players, who might otherwise be prevented from developing their talent by the their team's reliance on more famous and experienced foreign stars. Foreign players were allowed to return in 1980, initially only one player per team and then two beginning in 1982. Today, European Community laws overrule those of the Italian football federation, and as a consequence there no longer is a limitation on the number of foreign players who can come from countries belonging to the European Community. Since the mid-1990s players from African nations have started to be considered by Italian teams, which traditionally have looked to South America and northern Europe as the main sources for their foreign players. This pattern of global trading of players has finally influenced Italian players as well, who in the past rarely played in other countries. When this happened, it was usually an end of career move to one of those countries where the level of play was somewhat inferior to that of Italy, thus providing the chance to still compete in the main leagues, as opposed to accepting a descent to one of Italy's lower categories. The trend was reversed in the 1990s when players still in their prime, including some members of the national team, began accepting offers to play abroad.

Italy's national team has consistently been among the world's best. Among its major accomplishments are the victories in the World Cup in 1934, 1938 and 1982 and the success at the European championships of 1968. On two other occasions, 1970 and 1994, Italy reached the World Cup's final match, both times losing to Brazil. Televized matches of the national team can attract audiences in excess of ten million people. Important victories of the *azzurri* (*azzurro* means 'blue', the team's nickname from the colour of the jersey) usually prompt spontaneous celebration by the Italian *tifosi* (fans) who fill the country's streets with long parades of cars, honking and displaying the national flag. This enthusiasm can sometimes escalate into riots between fans of opposing teams. Certain sectors of Italian football stadiums are closely guarded by police and are practically off limits for the regular spectators.

Media coverage of football is extensive and is not limited to the broadcasting of matches. Three nationally distributed sport dailies (see **sports publications**) and many television programmes

are dedicated to pre- and post-game reports and interviews. CONI (the Italian Olympic Committee) has been able to take advantage of football's great popularity through two betting games called Totocalcio and Totogol, which are based on the week's results and scores. The huge profits made through these games are used by CONI to support less popular Olympic sports.

PAOLO VILLA

foreign policy

From 1860 to 1945, much of Italy's history was influenced by the fact that it was 'the least of the Great Powers'. However, the disastrous nature of defeat in the Second World War gave the newborn Italian **Republic** the blessing of no longer being a state which must aim to possess an empire or which would automatically demand recognition as a major player in every diplomatic crisis. After 1945, international affairs were rarely an immediately decisive factor in Italians' lives. This diminished importance of foreign policy paradoxically brought tremendous advantages. Having lost its empire under Fascism, Italy avoided those pains of decolonization which so marked the postwar histories of Britain and France and which still afflict Russia. In its happy powerlessness, Italy could avoid going nuclear. When Italy did spend money on 'defence', it was largely directed into the domestic economy without that waste on international technological competition which was rapidly reducing Britain to the poorest of the major Western European states. Italy was able to avoid being directly involved in the Korean and Vietnam wars and even membership of the United Nations brought few burdensome responsibilities.

Some commentators have alleged that Republican Italy has been a country of 'limited sovereignty', forced to follow the greater powers in all international dealings. Certainly, as arranged at Yalta in February 1945, Italy became part of 'the West' and by 1949 had been inducted into NATO, the military alliance of the liberal capitalist nations, led by the United States. Situated, as it was, on the western edge of the communist world, Italy would become an important (and well-rewarded) American military base. Italy's domestic politics, with the permanent non-legitimation of the **PCI** (Italian Communist Party) and, therefore, the system of *bipartitismo imperfetto* (imperfect bipartisanship) were severely circumscribed by American power. Idiosyncratic Italian politics might be; anti-Western they could never become, or even seem to become.

Nonetheless, a certain continuity can be traced between the foreign policy of Italy, the middle-ranking European Republic and Italy, the Liberal and then Fascist aspirant Great Power. Dino Grandi, who had served as Fascist Foreign Minister, had once emphasized Italy's intention of being the *peso determinante* or 'determining weight' in the Great Power balance. This idea that Italy should do its best not to be committed too heavily or too naively to one side or the other in any dispute frequently reappeared in postwar policy making. Thus, the creation of the European Common Market, solemnized in the Treaty of Rome of 1957, owed something to the belief of **De Gasperi** and other Christian Democrats (see **DC**) that both their political Catholicism and 'Europe' offered a third way between the rigours of American capitalism and those of Soviet 'socialism'. Similarly, in the Middle East, the traditions of Italy, of Christian Democracy and of Catholicism, suggested an openness to the Arab world and thus a less than total endorsement of Israel, the USA's essential ally in the region. In the 1950s Enrico **Mattei**, in his negotiation of oil contracts, and in the 1970s and 1980s Giulio **Andreotti**, in his multifarious commercial and political dealings, would similarly seek a certain independence for Italy in a bipolar world.

An aversion to bipolarity was also evident in Italy's relations with the communist bloc. The presence within Italy of a powerful Communist Party undoubtedly assisted Italy's successful trade and investment policy in the USSR and in other parts of Eastern Europe. It was recognized that in any eventual conflict Italy would side with the West but until that final moment was reached, contacts in the East could remain and Italy pursued policies there that were less hostile than demanded by ardent enthusiasts of the Cold War.

Occasional voices were heard protesting that this lack of status and of a public exercise of power was demeaning to the Italian nation. The signature of the peace treaty of Paris in 1947 was accompanied by nationalist complaint from such diverse sources as the liberal philosopher, Benedetto **Croce**, who talked carelessly of the 'Paris diktat' and the leadership of the Communist Party. Until 1954, the **Trieste** issue inflamed irredentist and patriotic sentiments, and few in the political world granted that Yugoslavia had a case there. The return of Trieste within the national borders did, however, end irredentism as a serious factor in political life, though Italian diplomatists have continued to fight off suggestions that the Brenner border with the Germanic world, agreed in 1919 and confirmed in 1945, is not a just one.

In more recent times **intellectuals**, generally but not always conservative in their ideological preference, have complained that the worst sin of the Republic is its loss of national sense. It is true that opinion polls have regularly demonstrated that Italians are anxious to define themselves as Europeans and that they trust the institutions of the **European Union** more than they do those of the Italian nation state. At the same time, this flaunted 'good Europeanness' is somewhat counterbalanced by the fact that European legislation is regularly ignored by Italian governments at the same time as European subsidies are digested.

Another unresolved issue in foreign relations is what might be called Italy's missing 'world policy'. **Emigration** dispersed Italians all over the world, but governments in Rome have preferred to focus on Europe rather than becoming closely involved with, for example, South American affairs. In this, as in other aspects of international dealing, Italian politicians have taken advantage when it has been offered, but have sought to avoid the expense of unnecessary involvement.

During the 1990s there have been occasional flutters of a revived nationalism, the most menacing being from that lunatic fringe who would meddle 'patriotically' in the fate of ex-Yugoslavia. More moderate forces have acknowledged an alleged responsibility to engage in international peacekeeping efforts in Somalia and Albania, with decidedly uneven results. But in most questions of international diplomacy Italy prefers both to keep a low profile, and to favour the sales of **Benetton** and the rest of the nation's export industries.

Foreign policy remains the least of its preoccupations.

Further reading

Santoro, C.M. (1991) *La politica estera di una media potenza: L'Italia dall'Unità ad oggi* (The Foreign Policy of a Middle Power: Italy from Unification to the Present), Bologna: Il Mulino (a stimulating structural approach to the subject).

R.J.B. BOSWORTH

Forlani, Arnaldo

b. 8 December 1925, Pesaro

Politician

Arnaldo Forlani entered Parliament in 1958. In a generational coup in 1969, aided by Ciriaco **De Mita**, he became **DC** party secretary despite his own politics being based, quite unlike De Mita's, on rigid anti-communism. Forlani remained party leader until 1973. Several times a senior minister, he became prime minister between 1980 and 1981 but was forced to resign by the **P2** Lodge scandal. He returned to the party leadership in 1989–92, becoming part of the so-called CAF triumvirate whereby **Craxi**, **Andreotti** and Forlani, as the united heads of the DC and the **PSI**, divided up all the spoils of the 'First' **Republic** in a thick network of **clientelism** which encapsulated all its worst features. The disastrous 1992 parliamentary election and Forlani's failure to be elected **President** led to his resignation. In December 1993 he was humiliated by television coverage of his cross-examination by Antonio **Di Pietro** in the Cusani corruption trial, thus abruptly ending his political career.

MARK DONOVAN

Forma Group

The Forma group, an art collective, was founded in Rome in 1947, and its original members included Pietro **Consagra**, Giulio Turcato, Piero Dorazio, Achille Perilli, Antonio Sanfilippo, Carla **Accardi**, Ugo Attardi, Mino Guerrini and Concetto Maugeri, all artists who played an important role in the development of Italian abstract art during the late 1940s and the 1950s.

As the name of the group and the title of its magazine makes clear, the artists' main interests were focussed on the question of form. A manifesto was published in the first edition of its eponymous magazine. The opening paragraph stated:

> We declare ourselves Formalists and Marxists, convinced that the terms Marxism and formalism are not unreconcilable, particularly today when progressive individuals in our society must maintain a revolutionary and avantgarde position, and not make the mistake of falling into the blandness and conformism of realism which, in its most recent attempts in painting and sculpture has shown what a limited and narrow road it is. The necessity of bringing Italian art to the level of contemporary European artistic language forces us to take a clear and resolute position against any foolish nationalistic ambition and against the provincial and pointless gossip of Italian culture today.
>
> (*Forma* 1, Rome, 15 March 1947; my translation)

The fight against artistic torpor taken up in Rome by the artists of Forma had a decisive influence in those years immediately after the war. The fact that a common manifesto united artists whose work was so divergent, if not diametrically opposed, was an indication that the said group of artists believed that in order to develop, Italian art had to conquer certain essentially formal values while at the same time pushing the individual values of each artist to their extreme.

Although generally influenced by contemporary Art Informel (see **L'Informale**), the work of Forma cannot be limited to any one stylistic definition. Turcato, Dorazio and Accardi experimented at this time with geometric abstraction, influenced in particular by the work of the futurist Giacomo Balla. Turcato's paintings tended towards a stronger narrative element, as can be seen from *Political Gathering* (1950), in which the bright red triangles have an obvious political significance. Dorazio's work consisted of rhythmic, sometimes calligraphic patterns of interlocking shapes and lines, whilst Accardi's canvases were more boldly geometric. On the other hand, Accardi and other painters such as Sanfilippo and the sculptor Consagra moved towards creating freer, more expressive works. During the 1950s, Turcato too moved towards a more lyrical form of abstraction.

As well as organizing its own exhibitions (for example, at the Art Club in Rome in 1947), Forma was involved in important international events, including the **Venice Biennale** of 1948 and the exhibition 'Arte astratta e concreta in Italia' (Abstract and Concrete Art in Italy) held at the Galleria d'Arte Moderna in Rome in 1951. The group also made an important contribution to debate on art through its magazine. Its successor was the group **Continuità** (founded in 1961), which included Accardi, Consagra, Dorazio, Perilli and Turcato.

Further reading

Merchiori, G. (1948) 'Il Fronte Nuovo delle Arti' (The New Front of the Arts), in *XXIV Biennale di Venezia, Catalogo*, Venice: La Serenissima Edizioni (exhibition catalogue).

Venturi, L. and Turcato, G. (1957) *Painting in Postwar Italy 1945–1957*, New York: Columbia University Press (exhibition catalogue).

OLIVIA DAWSON

Fortini, Franco

b. 10 September 1917, Florence;
d. 28 November 1994, Milan

Poet and literary critic

Having earned first a law degree in 1939, then one in art history in 1940 from the University of Florence, Fortini (real name Franco Lattes) taught history of criticism at the University of Siena. He was co-editor of *Il Politecnico* and among the founders of the political-literary journal *Ragionamenti*. A prolific and versatile writer, Fortini published collections of poetry, narrative works, translations from German and French (Brecht, Goethe, Eluard) and war memoirs, and engaged in militant literary criticism from the pages of important periodicals such as *Nuovi Argomenti* and

Paragone and daily newspapers like *Il Corriere della sera* and *il manifesto*.

Described alternately as post-hermetic or anti-hermetic poetry and as 'neo-realist', Fortini's verse represents a reaction against what was seen as a divorce between words and their referents in symbolist and neoavantgarde poetics, while maintaining a distance from formalist lyricism. Fortini's strong political commitment and his dedication to art as a means of furthering social and moral values earned him the Montale poetry prize in 1985.

Further reading

Forgàcs, D. (1984) 'Franco Fortini', in M. Caesar and P. Hainsworth (eds), *Writers and Society in Contemporary Italy*, Warwickshire: Berg Publishers.

SHERRY ROUSH

Forza Italia

Officially founded by businessman Silvio **Berlusconi** in January 1994 and modelled on a football slogan (meaning roughly 'Go, Italy!'), Forza Italia (FI) achieved immediate success in the national elections of March 1994, gaining 21.4 per cent of the vote, establishing itself as the largest party in the electorate and elevating its leader to the premiership. In April 1996, having in the meantime lost government and contesting its second national election, FI's performance was again strong (it won 20.6 per cent of the vote) but not enough to regain government.

The basis of FI's 1994 success lay in the timing of its appearance on the electoral market, the innovativeness of its alliance strategy, its campaigning techniques and its organizational arrangements. Berlusconi and a small team drawn mainly from his media corporation, **Fininvest**, began organizing, more or less secretly, in the autumn of 1993. Berlusconi's idea was of a very lightly structured but highly centralized party, supported by a loose network of 'clubs' operating as electoral committees open to citizens' volunteer participation, presenting candidates with no previous political experience but with a strong professional (generally self-employed) background and solid social status. In the post Cold

War and post-***Tangentopoli*** context of the time – characterized by displaced electoral identities, a widespread desire for renovation of the political class, growing anti-party sentiments and an inexorable weakening of the old subcultural belongings – Berlusconi indeed succeeded in presenting himself and Forza Italia as the new, non-political answer to the crisis of Italy's old politics. In addition, he was able to create a new system of alliances using FI to bridge two regionalized and divided electorates: that of the right-wing and southern-based **National Alliance** (AN) and that of the separatist and northern-based Northern League (see **Lega Nord**), thus creating a brand new national centre–right pole.

The campaign for FI's electoral launch, organized by Fininvest's experts in marketing and communication, was first prepared by mass opinion polls and focus groups and then developed through a bombardment of political advertisement on Fininvest's televisions and on a skilful construction and communication of Berlusconi's image. FI's campaign was highly personalized and centred on the figure of the leader. Berlusconi's invariable smile, elegant clothes, polite and non-confrontational manners, self-confidence, reassuring discourse and 'man of the street' language (rich in sporting but also biblical metaphors) were all elements which contributed to the projection into politics of the myth of the successful modern entrepreneur, able to create wealth and deliver prosperity, thus legitimizing Berlusconi as a trustworthy politician.

FI''s neo-liberal programme (pro-religion, pro-family, pro-market economics, pro-privatization, anti-mismanagement, anti-bureaucracy, anti-Left) attracted wide electoral support across all social classes and across the spectrum of the traditional Catholic and lay centrist parties. The average socioeconomic profile of FI voters and their values did not differ very much from the average profile and values of the whole Italian electorate, and it was precisely on such an 'average society' that FI constructed its identity.

After the extraordinary electoral performance in 1994, however, FI encountered serious difficulties as a governing party, particularly with its recalcitrant ally the Northern League. In December 1994 the League abandoned the coalition, causing the fall of the Berlusconi government. The subsequent months were difficult for Forza Italia, especially from an organizational point of view. Its light organizational arrangements, initially appealing to voters because of their anti-party connotations, proved inadequate to the long months in opposition. In January 1997, in response to internal discontent further fuelled by electoral defeat at the national elections of April 1996, FI adopted a new statute, eventually instituting a diffused and structured territorial organization, collegial deliberative and executive bodies at national and local level, and a membership empowered to elect local and national party managers.

At the end of 1997, Forza Italia, with its almost 5,000 elected representatives (at the various levels), its 150,000 members, 3,500 supporting clubs involving around 100,000 activists, its local headquarters run by party secretaries and its associated youth and women organizations, seemed to have become rather similar to a traditional mass party and to be undergoing a phase of organizational institutionalization. Whether this will prove sufficient to guarantee FI a long term political life remains to be seen.

Further reading

Lyttelton, A. (1994) 'Italy: The Triumph of TV', *The New York Review,* 11 August.

McCarthy, P. (1996) 'Forza Italia. The New Politics and Old Values of a Changing Italy', in S. Gundle and S. Parker (eds), *The New Italian Republic: From the Fall of the Wall to Berlusconi,* London: Routledge.

Seisselberg, J. (1996) 'Conditions of Success and Political Problems of a "Media-Mediated Personality-Party": The Case of Forza Italia', *West European Politics* 19 (4): 715–43.

EMANUELA POLI

fotoromanzo

The *fotoromanzo* (photo romance) is love story, published episodically or as a single issue. The plot is narrated through a series of photos, a narrative beneath them and a dialogue which is contained in speech balloons within the frame. It is similar to comics, but here photographs replace drawings. *Fotoromanzi* are directed primarily to a female readership from the lower middle and lower socioeconomic classes. They have been enormously successful in Italy and have been widely exported, especially to Latin American countries. They first appeared in 1947 when two major publishing houses, Rizzoli and **Mondadori**, published the two weekly magazines *Sogno* (Dream) and *Bolero Film*. These followed in the wake of **Grand Hotel**, which had very successfully published love stories in comic book format the previous year, selling hundreds of thousands of copies per issue. Other publishing houses copied the formula, which consisted of sixteen pages in black and white, the cover often in colour, two or three *fotoromanzi* and a love story or a literary classic in instalments.

The typical *fotoromanzo* story has the structure of the classic fairy tale and uses techniques of the serial novel, namely a complicated plot and the continual succession of revelations. It is usually the story of a troubled union of social unequals (she is poor and he is very rich) which ends up happily as pure love triumphs over social barriers. Men are always given an active role as opposed to the passive one attributed to women who, however, are rewarded at the end for their resignation and faith. The moral of the story is clear: women need only follow their hearts and Providence will make their dream of a happy marriage and upward social mobility come true. In the *fotoromanzo*, the visual element is used to impart veracity to the fairy tale: the characters are beautiful but not excessively so. They are clean-cut and fashionably dressed but they are not far removed from ordinary people. Landscapes and interiors are usually easily recognizable and urban. The characters are portrayed psychologically in a simple yet consistent fashion, their attitudes and gestures are plausible and symbols are usually avoided. Conversely the language of the speech balloons and the narrative is pompous as it attempts to lift the story from its overly prosaic reality.

Fotoromanzi exhibit primitive figurative realism, rooted in romantic melodrama. They provide erotic escapism and are concerned with private feelings, avoiding comment on anything that touches on the relation between the individual and society. Their themes are always the family, honour (which is actually masculine honour and feminine virginity) and conflict between love and duty. From the outset, the *fotoromanzo* magazines were integrated into an urban system of communication, connected to show business, fashion news and the media. Their humble style interacted with that of the cinema and weekly news magazines, and there was also some experimentation with **detective fiction** and adventure stories.

The production and language of *fotoromanzi* changed over time but the stories kept their basic structure and techniques. In the mid-1960s, when Italy changed from being a backward agricultural country to an advanced industrial one, the publishing house Lancio had great success with its monthly magazines printed on laminated paper. These presented previously unpublished stories in full, featuring characters modelled on the urban youth of the new consumer society. With the diffusion of consumerism, the need for long-running sagas and popular heroes was accentuated. Lancio responded with the two magazines, *Le avventure di Lucky Martin* (Lucky Martin's Adventures) and *Le avventure di Jacques Douglas* (Jacques Douglas's Adventures), which became extremely popular.

During the 1980s and 1990s the *fotoromanzo* went through a crisis due to socioeconomic and structural changes: rising costs, the advent of colour, the need for a greater standardization and intensive marketing brought about the end of the proliferation of production houses and a decrease in sales. The irreversible crisis in the cinema and television's success in differentiating and stratifying the public also had a negative influence on the *fotoromanzo*, which withdrew more and more into itself. It continued to be interested only in the private world, in fashion and in love relationships, repressing any historical reference or admitting it only when it could be linked to basic emotions.

See also: comics

Further reading

Abruzzese, A. (1989) 'Fotoromanzo', in A. Asor Rosa (ed.), *Letteratura italiana. Storia e Geografia* (Italian Literature: History and Geography), Turin: Einaudi (an acute critical analysis of the genre).

Detti, E. (1990) *Le carte rosa. Storia del fotoromanzo e della narrativa popolare* (The Pink Papers: A History of the Photo Romances and of Popular Fiction), Florence: La nuova Italia (a short, popular history of the photo romances with numerous interesting illustrations from the early issues).

FRANCO MANAI

Frabotta, Biancamaria

b. 11 June 1946, Rome

Literary critic, feminist and poet

Professor of Twentieth-Century Italian Literature at the University of Rome, La Sapienza, Frabotta contributes to various publications, including *Nuovi argomenti*, **Aut aut** and **La Repubblica**. In the 1970s she became one of the leading voices of the women's movement and the principal organizer of the Marxist branch of the Roman feminist movement. She drew on these experiences to write *Femminismo e lotta di classe* (Feminism and Class Struggle) (1973) and *La politica del femminismo: 1973–1976* (The Politics of Feminism) (1976). Later, her attention turned to more literary concerns. In *Letteratura al femminile* (Literature in the Feminine) (1980), for example, she explores the relationship between women's writing and women's place in literary history, while in the edited collection *Donne in poesia* (Women in Poetry) (1976), she showcases postwar Italian women's poetry. Her experiences as a feminist and as a woman writer also form the basis of her more introspective works, including the poetry collection, *Appunti di volo* (Flight Notes) (1985), and the novel, *Velocità di fuga* (Speed of Flight) (1989).

See also: feminism; women's writing

VIRGINIA PICCHIETTI

Fracci, Carla

b. 20 August 1936, Milan

Dancer

Perhaps the most renowned of Italian postwar dancers, Fracci studied at the ballet school of the Teatro alla Scala where she soon achieved the status of *prima ballerina* (principal dancer). She subsequently performed as guest ballerina at London's Festival Ballet, the Ballet Festival of Nervi, the **Spoleto Festival** of Two Worlds, the Royal Ballet and the American Ballet Theatre. Her reputation was consolidated in *From Taglioni to Fracci*, a ballet devised by her husband, Beppe Menegatti, in which she displayed her extraordinary versatility as a dancer by playing six different characters from the history of dance, ranging from *La Sylphides, La Pèri, Spectre de la Rose, L'Après Midi d'un Faune* and *Les Sylphide*, and by her performance in *Medea*, a ballet created for Fracci by Mikhail Baryshnykov. She remains best-known, however, for her very personal interpretation of the central character in the romantic ballet *Giselle*.

CLAUDIA VENDITTI

friendship

In a society where relations of kinship, **family** and **marriage** claim so many of the resources for sociability, the ties of friendship (*amicizia*) might be expected to have only a limited importance. Yet friendship is a relationship recognized in an unusually wide range of public and private contexts in Italy. In politics, the former Christian Democrat party invented annual 'Festivals of Friendship' for its supporters in 1976, and its smaller factions identified themselves collectively as the 'friends' of a particular leader. Mass **clientelism** is built out of the exploitation of reciprocally acknowledged 'friendships' between powerful patrons and loyal clients and, in Sicily, members of the **mafia** may be colloquially referred to as 'friends of friends'. Friendships can thus link people otherwise widely separated by differences of wealth and social position, since it is not a relationship which requires equality of status or material contributions on both sides.

In the private domain, friendship is an important relationship right through the life cycle. Italians seem less likely than some other European peoples to shed friends as they get older, and the practice of shoring up friendships by converting them into bonds of unbreakable ritual kinship (*comparaggio*) is common. However, the details of the kinds of commitments that friends assume, or expect to assume, towards each other have not been a focus for study and the best available data come from cross-national comparative surveys. Among the 85 per cent of Italians who claim to have friends at all, the majority in all age groups say they have between one and four. Contact is frequent: most (56 per cent) meet their best friends several times a week, by comparison with only one-third (36 per cent) of Britons (who probably use the telephone and the post more frequently). Surprisingly few differences exist between the patterns of friendships among Italian men and women, except that Italian women are more likely than men to claim a best friend of the opposite sex. Unusually among Europeans, very few Italians establish friendships in the workplace: only 3 per cent claim to have made friends at work, as against 60 per cent of Hungarians and 23 per cent of Britons. Italians are also less likely than other Europeans to make friends with neighbours, so that two-thirds of friends are neither from work nor from the neighbourhood. The content of friendships obviously varies greatly. The limited survey evidence suggests that Italians are less likely to turn to friends for instrumental reasons (financial help, domestic tasks) than other Europeans, but rather more likely to find emotional support from them.

Further reading

Bruckner, E. and Knaup, K. (1993) 'Women's and Men's Friendships in Comparative Perspective', *European Sociological Review* 9 (3): 249–65.

Hollinger, F. and Haller, M. (1990) 'Kinship and Social Networks in Modern Societies: A Cross-Cultural Comparison Among Seven Nations', *European Sociological Review* 6 (2): 103–24.

DAVID MOSS

Fruttero and Lucentini

Under the single name 'Fruttero and Lucentini', these two authors (Carlo Fruttero, b. 1926, Turin;

Franco Lucentini, b. 1920, Rome) have collaborated on a myriad of articles, satirical essays and a number of bestselling novels which employ an ironic tone and a rich narrative style. Most of their novels are loosely based on the *giallo* or detective format (see **detective fiction**) but are sophisticated and polished works which have achieved both critical and popular success. Among these are *La donna della domenica* (The Sunday Woman) (1972) and *Enigma in luogo di mare* (An Enigma by the Sea) (1991). Together, Fruttero and Lucentini also edit the science fiction magazine *Urania*, and have edited an anthology of translations of English tales of the supernatural called *Storie di fantasmi* (Ghost Stories) (1960). Lucentini, as well as being a literary translator, has explored neorealist themes and style in his own novels *La porta* (The Door) (1947) and *Notizie degli scavi* (News of the Excavations) (1964), while Fruttero has co-edited with Sergio **Solmi** an anthology of science fiction tales titled *Le meraviglie del possibile* (The Marvels of the Possible) (1959).

LAURA A. SALSINI

Fubini, Mario

b. 18 March 1900, Turin; d. 29 June 1977, Turin

Academic and literary critic

Fubini taught Italian literature at the universities of Turin, Palermo, Trieste and Milan before the Second World War, when he was forced to seek asylum in Switzerland in order to avoid racial persecution. He returned after the war to teach history of criticism at the Scuola Normale Superiore of Pisa. A member of the Accademia dei Lincei, he served as editorial director of the *Giornale storico della letteratura italiana* (Historical Journal of Italian Literature) and the Utet series of *Classici italiani* (Italian Classics), as well as being president of the committee for the national edition of the works of Ugo Foscolo. He made numerous contributions to the study of French literature in Italy (especially on de Vigny and Racine), as well as studies of Giambattista Vico, Giuseppe Parini and Vittorio Alfieri, but the bulk of his critical energies were dedicated to Foscolo. Into what was fundamentally a Crocean, historicist methodology, Fubini integrated a careful attention to stylistics, which became the basis of his works on criticism, metrics and poetry.

SHERRY ROUSH

G

Gaber, Giorgio

b. 25 January 1939, Milan

Singer-songwriter and performer

One of Italy's most accomplished stage performers, Gaber (real name Giorgio Gaberscik) began his long showbusiness career in the mid-1950s, attempting unsuccessfully to become a rock musician. Eventually, in the thriving cabaret milieu of Milan, he teamed up with Enzo **Jannacci** in *I due corsari* (the Two Buccaneers), an act which featured iconoclastic and irreverent songs permeated by a surrealist sense of humour. In the early 1960s he achieved national exposure by presenting the **RAI**'s *Canzoniere Minimo* (Miniature Songbook) and *Le nostre serate* (Our Evenings), television programmes which showcased the new popular music. Throughout the 1960s he also competed repeatedly but with little success in the **Sanremo Festival**. His career took a decisive turn in 1970 when he re-created himself as *Il signor G* (Mr G), a new stage persona which became the basis of numerous one-man shows which integrated elements of theatre, cabaret and song in an exploration of the major themes of the day. Having dealt with the protest movement during the 1970s, Gaber's reviews during the 1980s became more centred on the individual while in the 1990s shows such as *E pensare che c'era il pensiero* (And to Think There Was Once Thought) (1996) have tended to articulate a sense of dismay at the loss of community spirit and increasing social isolation.

GINO MOLITERNO

Gabetti and Isola

Professors of architectural composition at the Turin Faculty of Architecture, Roberto Gabetti (b. 1925, Turin) and Aimaro Oreglia d'Isola (b. 1928, Turin) generally worked as a duo. Their professional craftsmanship is especially manifest in their furniture designs. They also built the Turin Stock Exchange (1952–6, with Giorgio and Giuseppe Raineri) and the Bottega d'Erasmo (1953–6), a fine example of neoliberty architecture which was regarded as something of a 'scandal' at the time because it appeared to be a retreat from the modern movement. Best known among their numerous residential and public buildings, mostly in Turin and the Piedmont area, are the headquarters of the Turin Equestrian Society (1962), the 'crescent in curtain-wall' **Olivetti** housing centre at Ivrea (1969–70), and a refined residential building on the via Sant'Agostino in Turin. The LIS bookshop built in 1992 is another example of their 'total design' (architecture and furniture), in this case a masterfully illuminated high-tech 'shelter'. Their approach to the landscape is unobtrusive and delicate.

Further reading

Guerra, A. and Morresi, M. (1996) *Gabetti e Isola: opere di architettura* (Gabetti and Isola: Architectural Works), Milan: Electa.

GORDANA KOSTICH

Gadda, Carlo Emilio

b. 14 November 1893, Milan; d. 21 May
1973, Rome

Electronics engineer, essayist and novelist

Carlo Emilio Gadda is unanimously considered
among the most influential writers of the twentieth
century. By exploring and carrying to extreme the
expressive and communicative potential of language, his narrative lays bare the existential illness
that affects the individual in contemporary society
and drives him to neurosis and depression.

Born into a Lombard bourgeois family left in
difficult straits by the father's death, Gadda
enrolled in the Polytechnic of Milan in 1912 to
study engineering. After fighting as a volunteer in
the First World War, he graduated in 1920 and
worked as an engineer both in Italy (1920–2) and
in Argentina (1922–4). On his return to Italy in
1924, he taught mathematics and physics to high
school students and enrolled in the University of
Milan to study philosophy without ever completing
his degree. Meanwhile, he began to contribute to
the Florentine literary journal *Solaria* with short
prose works and the important essay *Apologia
manzoniana* (Apology of Manzoni) (1927), which
documented his interest in the nineteenth-century
novelistic tradition, particularly in Alessandro
Manzoni's narrative and linguistic theory, and also
his revisionist perspective on the genre which he
was already experimenting. In the 1920s and 1930s
Gadda worked at his first novel, *Racconto di ignoto del
Novecento* (An Italian Tale by an Unknown Author
of the Twentieth Century), posthumously published in 1983, on several texts that were to remain
unfinished – the philosophical treatise *Meditazione
milanese* (Milanese Meditation) and the novel *La
meccanica* (The Mechanic) – and on several collections of short stories: *La Madonna dei filosofi* (The
Madonna of the Philosophers) (1931), *Il castello di
Udine* (The Castle of Udine) (1934) and *Le meraviglie
d'Italia* (Italy's Wonders) (1939). The significance of
these early writings lies in Gadda's ability to mix
Italian, dialect and varieties of jargon in order to
masterfully represent human psychology and social
dynamics.

In the late 1930s and 1940s, after having long
divided himself between his engineering profession

and literary activity for economic reasons, Gadda
turned definitively to literature and moved to
Florence where he met intellectuals such as
Gianfranco **Contini** and Roberto **Longhi**, and
the poets Umberto **Saba** and Eugenio **Montale**.
He also published the short story collections
L'Adalgisa. Disegni milanesi (Adalgisa: Milanese
Sketches) (1944) – a colourful description and a
sarcastic critique of the Milanese bourgeoisie – and
excerpts from his autobiographical novel *La
cognizione del dolore* (Acquainted with Grief) (1938–
41), which he was later to publish again in two
expanded yet unfinished versions in 1963 and 1970.
In this novel, set in a non-existent South American
city (a disguised postwar Italy), Gadda recounts
Gonzalo Pirobutirro's solitary life with his mother,
progressively focalizing the character's psychological illness, obscure in its essence but tragically
affecting his relationship with his self, his mother
and the surrounding community. Besides its penetrating analysis of the complexity of the human
psyche and its subtle insights into the contradictions
of contemporary society, Gadda's narrative offers a
unique sample of stylistic inventiveness and linguistic richness, as it mixes Italian and Spanish and
interweaves different linguistic levels.

In 1950 Gadda settled in Rome, where he
collaborated with **RAI** to produce cultural radio
programmes (1950–4). He published a new short
story collection, *Novelle del Ducato in fiamme* (Stories
of the Duchy in Flames) (1953), which earned him
the Viareggio Prize in 1953, and the autobiographical *Giornale di guerra e di prigionia* (Journal of War
and Captivity) (1955, expanded in 1965), based on
his experiences in the First World War. The
publisher Livio Garzanti urged him to resume
writing his detective story *Quer pasticciaccio brutto de
via Merulana* (That Awful Mess on Via Merulana),
which had partially appeared in the journal
Letteratura in 1946. In this intricate novel, adapted
into a movie by Pietro **Germi** in 1960, Gadda tells
of superintendent Ciccio Ingravallo's investigations
on the brutal murder of a woman in Rome. As the
story unfolds, the mystery becomes more obscure
and the reader is plunged into an inextricable
pasticcio (pastiche, mess) or *groviglio* (entanglement)
of contrasting perspectives on the case. In Gadda's
view, reality is a multifaceted human theatre, the
hilarious set for the confused emergence of multiple

voices among which is the author's, each speaking its own language be it Italian, dialect – from Tuscan to Romanesque, from Neapolitan to Venetian – professional jargon or literary or scientific language.

Like Gadda's critical essays and previous fiction, *Quer pasticciaccio brutto de via Merulana* originates from a notion of language and literature as the means to explore and represent reality as a process of constant metamorphosis, where one term and its opposite co-exist and no centre is given to ground them. Aiming at the most completed and systematic representation of the various aspects of the world, Gadda registered as many voices, languages and objects as possible, endlessly accumulating. Yet the logical consequence of such an obsessive desire to transcribe each detail of reality was the impossibility of any completion. In fact, Gadda never came to the end of his stories; his major novels, *La cognizione* and *Pasticciaccio*, (both masterfully translated into English by William Weaver), have no conclusion: the former ends with the unsolved murder of the protagonist's mother, the latter with the ongoing police search for Liliana Balducci's murderer.

In his later years, although withdrawing from the cultural scene, Gadda continued to revise his previous works and published the collections of essays *I viaggi la morte* (Voyages of Death) (1958) and *Verso la Certosa* (To the Certosa) (1961), as well as *Eros e Priapo* (Eros and Priapus) (1967), a fierce pamphlet against fascism and its rhetoric. Gadda's ingenious linguistic expressionism and the unfinished feature of his works proved an inspiration to many postwar writers who attempted in their narratives to represent a sense of irreversible existential and historical fragmentation characterising late twentieth-century society.

Further reading

Bertone, R. and Dombroski, R. (1997) *Carlo Emilio Gadda: Contemporary Perspectives*, Toronto: University of Toronto Press.

Dombroski, R. (1974) *Introduzione allo studio di Carlo Emilio Gadda* (Introduction to the Study of Carlo Emilio Gadda), Florence: Vallecchi.

Roscioni, G.C. (1969) *La disarmonia prestabilita: studio su Gadda* (A Pre-Established Disharmony: Study on Gadda), Turin: Einaudi.

Sbragia, A. (1996) *Carlo Emilio Gadda and the Modern Macaronic*, Gainsville, FL: University Press of Florida.

FRANCESCA PARMEGGIANI

Gardella, Ignazio

b. 30 March 1905, Milan; d. 1999, Oleggio

Architect and civil engineer

After graduating from the Milan Politecnico in 1930, Gardella adhered to Pagano's **Casabella** architectural group from 1931–49 and then taught at the **IUAV** from 1949 to 1975. His early work exemplifies the genuine spirit of rationalism and is manifested in the Anti-Tuberculosis Dispensary at Alessandria (1938). One of the leading figures of modern Italian architecture, Gardella was the first recipient of the **Olivetti** National Prize for Architecture in 1955 for his Recreational Centre Complex at Ivrea. His 1950s masterpieces are characterized by elegance and purity of composition, deriving their inspiration from the specifics and culture of place, such as the Thermal Baths at Ischia and the Borsalino corporate building at Alessandria. The house on the Zattere in Venice became a symbol of the Italian deviation from the rules of the Modern movement. The postmodernist slant of his later years is evident in his reconstruction of the Carlo Felice theatre in Genoa (1981–3, with Aldo **Rossi**).

Further reading

Fera, S. (1996) 'Ignazio Gardella: la grammatica dello spazio', (Ignazio Gardella: The Grammar of Space), *Abitare* 347: 57–9 (profile of Gardella in Italian and English).

GORDANA KOSTICH

Garin, Eugenio

b. 9 May 1909, Rieti

Academic and historian of ideas

For many years Professor of the History of Philosophy at the Scuola Normale Superiore of Pisa, Garin published numerous studies on Italian Humanism, the Renaissance, the English Enlightenment and nineteenth- and twentieth-century Italian intellectual and cultural history. As a cultural historian, Garin stresses the transmission and continuity of ideas and values, initially disputing the widely held assumption of the total 'overthrow' of medieval culture by Renaissance humanism, and emphasizing the contribution made by late medieval *Studia humanitatis* to the early modern ethical, political and economic disciplines. He similarly posits a continuity between humanistic culture and modern – specifically, Enlightenment – ideological and cultural tendencies. In the mid-1960s he engaged in what was a highly divisive question for Italian **historiography**, namely the continuity or discontinuity of pre-fascist, fascist and post-fascist culture. In the mid-1980s his interests engaged with more contemporary issues.

SUZANNE KIERNAN

Gassman, Vittorio

b. 1 September 1922, Genoa

Actor

Widely regarded as one of the leading actors of stage and screen in postwar Italy, Gassman studied at the National Academy of Dramatic Arts in Rome during the war years and later opened his own theatre school in Florence. Establishing a reputation for intelligent bravado and keen attention to language in his interpretation of classical texts, Gassman devoted much of his theatrical career to ancient Greek drama and to the tragedies of playwrights such as Shakespeare, Alfieri, Manzoni, Ugo Betti and Pier Paolo **Pasolini**. Although much of his earlier work in film – in Italy and in America – saw him cast as the crafty villain,

Monicelli's *I soliti ignoti* (Big Deal on Madonna Street) (1958) revealed a considerable talent for comedy which was subsequently given scope in many of the later films of Monicelli, Dino **Risi** and Ettore **Scola**.

Further reading

Lucignani, L. (ed.) (1982) *Vittorio Gassman: intervista sul teatro* (Vittorio Gassman: Interview on the theatre), Rome-Bari: Laterza.

WILLIAM VAN WATSON

gay movement

The Italian gay movement was born in Milan in May 1971 founded by a group of leftist militants from Turin, Rome and Milan. Originally called the Italian Revolutionary Homosexual Front (FUORI, a word which means 'out'), it published a magazine under the same name from June 1972 until 1976. The Front's ideology was anti-capitalist and against bourgeois morality but, confronted with the 'machismo' of the new communist organizations, it sought and found political support in the **Radical Party**. In 1974, FUORI's decision to officially join the Radical Party led to the secession of the Milanese branch, which became the ancestor of the autonomous groups of the late 1970s.

During the 1976 national elections, FUORI decided to come to terms with the bourgeois institutions and, as a result, its leader Angelo Pezzana was the first openly gay member in the Italian Parliament. Pezzana's reformist ideology was not shared by the movement's left-wing groups, whose common denominator was the practice of self-awareness under the slogan of 'what is private is political'. The activity by these groups culminated in the 1977 student revolt, centred in Rome and Bologna.

In 1978 FUORI's new magazine, *Lambda*, became the voice of the movement, which also had its first national gathering in Bologna on May 26–8. Felix Cossolo had been responsible for the magazine's political transformation, and he also became the organizer of the first Italian gay camp in the summer of 1979, an event which then became the major annual gay gathering for the following ten years.

In the early 1980s, significant changes gave the movement its present configuration. By 1981 FUORI was no longer a national organization, *Lambda* had ceased publication, and a new gay group was born within the ranks of the Italian Cultural and Recreational Association (**ARCI**), whose political referents were the communist and socialist parties. In 1982 the city of Bologna gave the local gay organization an official headquarters, called 'Il Cassero'. In Milan, Felix Cossolo and Ivan Teobaldelli became the editors of *Babilonia*, which remains the only national gay and lesbian magazine. In 1983, all the Roman groups were unified and renamed Circolo Culturale Mario Mieli after the most famous theorist of the gay movement who had recently died.

During the following years the movement had to fight for its rights as well as its life. By 1986 the movement had founded the AIDS Solidarity Association (ASA) and the Italian League for the Fight against AIDS (LILA). It was only in 1988 that the health ministry financed a prevention campaign, and health emergency funds were not allocated until 1990.

On the electoral front, ARCI-gay, which had recently become national, successfully campaigned for Paolo Rutter, an independent candidate for the Communist Party, who became Milan's first gay town councillor in 1985. After the 1990 administrative elections, six gay representatives were members of town, provincial and regional councils. The ARCI-gay's constant efforts to legalize domestic partnership were also partially rewarded by the European Parliament's recognition of gay and lesbian rights in 1994. Two years earlier, Paolo Rutter had publicly married eight gay couples and one lesbian couple. Among them was Gianni Delle Foglie, co-owner with Francesco Ingargiola of Libreria Babele, the only gay and lesbian Italian bookstore.

During the 1990s, a series of specialized groups were born. As well as a number of religious organizations that appeared during the 1980s such as Il Guado, Davide e Gionata and the Collettivo assistenza pastorale omosessuali e transessuali, there now also exist Gay Bears (Orsi), Gay Swimmers (Collettivo pesce) Cybergays and Par-

ents of Gays (AGEDO). The cultural environment has changed, and gay and lesbian people are more visible than ever. For three consecutive years (1994–6) Rome, Bologna and Naples have respectively seen large demonstrations of gay and lesbian pride, but fragmentation is still the movement's major internal problem. In 1996 ARCI-lesbica, which, contrary to the separatist lesbian tradition, had shared the leadership of the organization since 1988, decided to go its own way. At the same time in 1997 political and personal conflicts between ARCI-gay and the Circolo Mario Mieli produced two separate gay pride parades, one in Venice and the other in Rome, with limited participation.

Further reading

Mieli, M. (1980) *Homosexuality and Liberation: Elements of a Gay Critique*, trans. D. Fernbach, London: Gay Men's Press (the major text on 1970s queer theory in Italy).

Rossi-Barilli, G. (1997) *Storia del movimento gay italiano* (History of the Italian Gay Movement), Milan: Babilonia edizioni.

EUGENIO GIUSTI

gay writing

Much postwar homosexual writing in Italy reflects the ambiguities and tensions of a prevailing anti-homosexual ethos within Italian culture. Lesbian or woman-identified literature, a very recent phenomenon, needs to be placed in the context of second-wave feminism, while writing by gay males is less easy to categorize within the political framework of the gay liberation movement.

Until the 1980s the lesbian literary tradition in Italy was, with only minor exceptions, a tradition of reading and not of writing. A substantial corpus of work attempted to theorize lesbianism as a socio-political phenomenon, but purely literary representations were scarce. At the literary level, Anglo-American texts and writers, from Radclyffe Hall and Virginia Woolf to Rita Mae Brown and Adrienne Rich, dominated the scene. There are some examples in modern Italian literature of texts in which lesbians are seen as minor characters providing marginal storylines, but very few which deal with the specificity of the lesbian experience. Annamaria Borgonovo's *La gabbia* (The Cage) (1964), in which the lesbian protagonist eventually commits suicide, and Bibi Tommasi's *La sproporzione* (Disproportion) (1980) are of only historic interest. Dacia **Maraini**'s important *Lettere a Marina* (Letters to Marina), a feminist meditation in epistolary form published in 1981, seems to mark a turning point for lesbian writing in Italy. It is from this point that the woman-identified *weltanschauung*, for the first time, becomes privileged. For Italian lesbians, 1981 was indeed a watershed, a year which saw the first national lesbian conference and the formation of the first Italian lesbian organization, the CLI (Collegamento Lesbiche Italiane). These two factors, together with the publication in 1980 of a collection of interviews with Italian lesbians, functioned to focus public attention on lesbianism as a phenomenon distinct from its gay male counterpart.

Two other writers, Fiorella Cagnoni and Liana Borghi, are worthy of note. Borghi's *Tenda con vista* (Tent With a View) (1987) is a lesbian subversion of the Scheherazade tale, a modern *conte philosophique*. Cagnoni's two lesbian feminist thrillers, *Questione di tempo* (A Matter of Time) (1985) and *Incauto acquisto* (Imprudent Purchase) (1992), feature a lesbian amateur sleuth.

While the 1980s marked a flowering of the literature of lesbian experience, male homosexuality had been a consistent thematic of postwar literature. In the works of many mainstream heterosexual writers, Alberto **Moravia** (*Agostino, The Conformist*), Elsa **Morante** (*Arturo's Island*), Vasco **Pratolini** (*Tale of Santa Croce*) and Giorgio **Bassani** (*The Gold-Rimmed Spectacles*), homosexuality is unfailingly situated within a poetics of difference and the homosexual experience is loaded with negative connotations.

This negative position is also evident in the work of certain gay writers like Pier Paolo **Pasolini** and Dario **Bellezza**. In Pasolini, two homosexual types can be identified: the gay and the male prostitute. *Ragazzi di vita* (The Ragazzi) (1955) and *Una vita violenta* (A Violent Life) (1959) describe the world of the sub-proletarian street kids in Rome who prostitute themselves out of sheer economic necessity. The truly gay characters are stereotypi-cally drawn as the simpering and impotent victims of an almost acceptable persecution, whereas the *ragazzi di vita* with their mercenary indifference to gay sexual relations evoke a degree of sympathy from Pasolini, who sees in them a lost Eden of sexuality.

In Bellezza's first novel, *L'innocenza* (Innocence) (1971), Nino, the protagonist, consciously chooses the perdition and corruption of a living homo-sexual hell. In Bellezza's infernal world, homo-sexuality can be nothing else but prostitution and neurotically masochistic obsessions: in *Lettere da Sodoma* (Letters from Sodom) (1972), his conclusion is that everything is Hell and that the only salvation is the systematic refusal of the self.

For other writers homosexual guilt was exor-cised, either on the model of Forster's posthu-mously published *Maurice* in works like Umberto **Saba**'s *Ernesto*, or on the model of an essentially heterosexual transfiguration of the lived homo-sexual experience which one finds in Giovanni Comisso and Aldo **Palazzeschi**. Palazzeschi managed to leave not a single trace of his homosexuality in anything he wrote except for a vague, ephemeral homoeroticism in his epistolary novel, *Allegoria di novembre* (A November Allegory) (1958). Comisso, like Saba, left a posthumous homosexual novel, *Giochi d'infanzia* (Childhood games) (1969), but, like Saba, reads homosexuality as a state of arrested adolescence in the autoerotic–homosexual–heterosexual continuum common in much contemporary psychoanalytic practice.

A number of writers were primarily concerned with the reconciliation of their homosexuality with their Christian faith, hardly surprising in Catholic Italy. Of these, perhaps the best-known, and certainly the most widely translated, is Carlo Coccioli, whose *Fabrizio Lupo*, printed for the first time in Italy in 1978, had been a classic for twenty-five years in Latin America. Coccioli seeks to condemn the attitudes of the Catholic church to homosexuality but without seeking at the same time to deconstruct its phobic position. Public intellectuals like Alberto **Arbasino**, Giuseppe **Patroni Griffi**, Goffredo **Parise** and Gian Piero Bona offer an aristocratic, often snobbish view of the homosexual world, a world where the proletar-iat is seen as homosexually available but projected out of history.

Pier Vittorio **Tondelli**'s debut text, *Altri libertini* (Other Libertines), was banned for a short period immediately after publication in 1980 on the grounds of obscenity. *Altri Libertini* treated old taboos aggressively and with a deep sense of irony which was not to extend into subsequent works. His last and only truly homosexual novel, *Camere separate* (Separate Rooms) (1989) displays all of the standard canonically internalized attitudes to relationships between males. Like Alberto Arbasino (*L'Anonimo Lombardo* (The Anonymous Lombard) 1959), Tondelli's homosexual protagonists are a cultured and cosmopolitan group whose playground is Europe and whose concerns are far removed from the reality of what it is to be homosexual in contemporary Italy.

Aldo **Busi** is perhaps the most difficult of all Italian writers to categorize. A truly postmodern figure, his output reflects a deep concern for the minutiae of that construct which is Italy. In novels like *Vita standard di un venditore provvisorio di collant* (The Standard Life of a Temporary Pantyhose Salesman) and *Sodomie in corpo 11* (Sodomies in Elevenpoint), Busi dazzles with the baroque richness of his language, shocks with his defiant approach to the often explicit nature of his descriptions of gay sexual relations and stimulates with his postmodern reflections on the very nature of literature itself.

Further reading

Dall'Orto, G. (1984) *Leggere omosessuale. Bibliografia* (Reading Homosexuality: Bibliography), Turin: Edizioni Gruppo Abele (a comprehensive bibliographic study of all works with homosexual content, both Italian and foreign, published in Italy).

Gnerre, F. (1981) *L'eroe negato. Il personaggio omossessuale nella narrativa contemporanea* (The Denied Hero: The Homosexual Character in Contemporary Narrative), Milan: Gammalibri (a detailed study of the homosexual protagonist in works by Italian homosexual authors).

Mieli, M. (1977) *Elementi di critica omosessuale* (Elements of Homosexual Critique), Milan: Einaudi (the major theoretical contribution of the Italian gay liberation movement).

STEPHAN RIEDEL

Gemina

Once a share parking of **Montedison** (then owned by **ENI**), in 1981 Gemina (Generale Mobiliare Interessenze Azionarie) passed under joint control of **Mediobanca** and **Fiat** and bought a large parcel of Montedison shares from **ENI**, thus giving Enrico **Cuccia** and his allies control of the chemical giant. Led by Cesare **Romiti** and later by Giampiero Pesenti, during the 1980s Gemina abandoned Montedison (which was nationalized again) but bought Rizzoli-**Corriere della sera**, a giant publishing group then on the verge of bankruptcy, became a shareholder in AmbroVeneto, a Catholic banking group, and eventually turned itself into a holding of merchant banking and insurance activities. In 1995 Mediobanca planned to transform it into a giant chemical conglomerate, SuperGemina, which had to amalgamate Montedison (in deep crisis after **Ferruzzi**'s collapse) and chemical companies of the Fiat group. The project was given up after an enormous loss in Rizzoli's balance sheet was discovered and Gemina's managers were prosecuted. More recently, Gemina has given up control of Rizzoli to HDP (Holding di Partecipazioni), a financial holding of which Gemina itself is a shareholder, has abandoned the financial services business and has focused on merchant banking in favour of emerging middle-size companies.

STEFANO BATTILOSSI

Germanà, Mimmo

b. 1944, Catania, Sicily; d. 1992, Milan

Painter

Germanà studied at the Accademia d'Arte in Rome at the same time as Sandro **Chia**. He completed his studies in 1970 and in 1980 he moved to Milan. His first solo exhibition was in 1970 at the Galleria L'Attico in Rome. His paintings are representational, vibrantly coloured and strongly expressionistic. From 1977 to the mid-1980s, Germanà was one of the artists included in the broad current known as the **transavant-**

garde, although by the late 1980s he was no longer numbered amongst its active members.

OLIVIA DAWSON

Germi, Pietro

b. 14 September 1914, Genoa;
d. 5 December 1974, Rome

Film director

Once characterized by **Fellini** as 'il grande falegname' (the great carpenter), Germi was undoubtedly one of the best artisans of Italian postwar cinema. Having begun his directorial career with dramatic films, he nevertheless became one of the undisputed masters of the comic genre with films which, for all their comedy, offered some of the most mordant and incisive critiques of contemporary Italian society.

Germi studied acting and film-making at the **Centro Sperimentale di Cinematografia** in Rome under Alessandro **Blasetti**, and then started by making neorealistic films marked by a visibly dramatic vein. In 1948 he made *In nome della legge* (In the Name of the Law), a gripping story about the Sicilian **mafia**. This was followed by his neorealist masterpiece *Il cammino della speranza* (The Path of Hope) (1950) which narrated the epic journey of a group of Sicilian workers to France in search of a better life, a film which patently reflected the influence of **Visconti**'s *La terra trema* (The Earth Trembles) (1948) as well as being a stylized reprise of the narrative patterns of the classical Hollywood Western as exemplified in the films of John Ford. In fact, the narrative rhythm of Germi's films would always owe much to American cinema, and he was much loved in the USA, especially by Billy Wilder.

In 1961, Germi moved suddenly to comedy with *Divorzio all'italiana* (Divorce Italian Style). *Divorzio* was slightly removed from the then traditional 'comedy Italian style' in theme, but similar to it in terms of its satirical intent. The film marked the birth of the so-called 'Southern comedy' which became a genre in itself because the economic boom was taking place well away from the South where human beings were not being faced with a fast-paced, industrialized society, but rather with the ancestral southern civilization. However, in spite of their difference from the so-called 'comedies Italian style', Germi's comedies were quite as aggressive and ferocious. In fact, *Divorce Italian Style* was initially meant to be a dramatic film, and yet, at the completion of the script, Germi realized that in the backward Sicily that served as the setting for the story, even the most dramatic events, such as the *delitto d'onore* (crime of honour), then still sanctioned by the penal code, could easily take on farcical tones.

In 1964 Germi directed *Sedotta e abbandonata* (Seduced and Abandoned), in which he portrays a monstrous society caught up in an almost medieval and tribal culture. The film is nearly an anthropological documentary on a barbaric world where an archaic penal code allows, and almost encourages, the use of matrimony to repair the ills caused by sexual violence and exploitation. The same kind of remoteness which characterizes Germi's Sicily qualifies his Veneto in *Signore e signori* (Ladies and Gentlemen) (1966) where Germi again investigates backward sexual and social behaviours. With *Le castagne sono buone* (Chestnuts Are Good) (1970), *Alfredo, Alfredo* (Alfred, Alfred) (1973) and his last but unfinished film, *Amici miei* (My Friends) (1975), completed by his friend Mario **Monicelli**, Germi returned to comedy to express bewilderment at the new and nostalgia for the past.

A fairly isolated but important figure in the history of postwar Italian cinema, Germi constantly attempted to combine two apparently opposing tasks: cinema as entertainment and cinema as commitment to social and political commentary.

Further reading

Giacovelli, E. (1991) *Pietro Germi*, Milan: Il Castoro (a concise and useful survey of Germi's career and his films, with a complete filmography and selected bibliography on individual films).

MANUELA GIERI

Geymonat, Ludovico

b. 11 May 1908, Turin; d. 29 November
1991, Passirana di Rho

Philosopher and historian of science

Appointed in1956 to Italy's first chair of Philosophy
of Science at the State University of Milan,
Geymonat was the foremost Italian representative
of empiricist or logical positivist thought, although
Geymonat himself often preferred the term 'neo-
positivist'. In his many publications, Geymonat's
chief concern was to bridge the gulf he saw between
science and philosophy in Italy since the Counter-
Reformation. At times locked in fierce debate with
his coeval, Norberto **Bobbio**, Geymonat also had a
long history of anti-fascist political activism, including participation in the armed **Resistance** and
membership of the Communist Party in the
immediate postwar years. Having abandoned the
PCI in the 1970s, he stood as an independent
candidate for **Democrazia Proletaria** (Proletarian Democracy) in the national elections of 1983. In
1985 he was awarded the Feltrinelli prize by the
national Accademia dei Lincei.

SUZANNE KIERNAN

Giacosa, Dante

b. 3 January 1905, Rome; d. 31 March
1996, Turin

Engineer and industrial designer

After graduating from the Milan Polytechnic in
1927, Giacosa joined the **Fiat** motor company.
Displaying much talent and promise, he was soon
given the pressing task of designing a car for the
mass Italian market which would be small, cheap
and economical to run. Giacosa's solution, un-
veiled in 1936, was the legendary 500cc economy
car which came to be universally known as the
Topolino (little mouse) because of its look and
diminutive size. Although successful, the model
remained out of the reach of most Italians and was
eventually discontinued in the early 1950s to be
replaced by a 600cc model and a new 500cc, both
also designed by Giacosa. The new 500cc, a tiny

but efficient two-door sedan with a foldback
sunroof, affectionately known as the Bambina
(little one), proved to be *the* car of the Italian
economic miracle, and 3.7 million were produced
before it too was discontinued in 1973.

Giacosa also designed many of Fiat's other
successful models and became head of its Research
and Development Division before retiring in 1975.
He later recounted his remarkable career in *I miei
40 anni di progettazione alla Fiat* (My 40 Years of
Designing for Fiat), published in Milan by Auto-
mobilia in 1979.

GINO MOLITERNO

Gigli, Romeo

b. 12 December 1949, Castelbolognese,
Faenza

Fashion designer

Defined as the 'minimalist' of fashion and a
'romantic' intellectual whose look has been labelled
pre-Raphaelite, Romeo Gigli's designs contrast
dramatically with the business look created for the
new executive woman. His designs aim to be soft and
fluid, often opting for muted but rich colours, and
are inspired by the Empress Theodora of Byzantium
and the women depicted in the mosaics of Ravenna's
Byzantine churches. A very private man, Gigli set up
his own label in 1983, and in 1991 he broke with his
former partners to establish his new 'Romeo World'.
His preferred fabrics are linen, chiffon, gauze, wool,
cashmere and silk. He also works in crushed velvet
and designs embroidered scarves. In 1991, England's Bath Costume Museum selected one of his
outfits (a midnight blue velvet pantsuit, a striped-
sunset blouse, and a gilt-embroidered cummerbund)
as its Outfit of the Year.

BERNADETTE LUCIANO

Ginzburg, Carlo

b. 1939, Turin

Cultural historian

Carlo Ginzburg (son of Leone and Natalia

Ginzburg) studied at the Normale Superiore of Pisa and at the Warburg Institute in London. He now teaches history at the University of Bologna and several universities in the United States. One of the foremost Italian practitioners of the so-called 'new erudition' characterized by 'interdisciplinary incursion' (his term), Ginzburg ranges from structural anthropology, ethnography and sociology to literary studies, art history and stylistic analysis. A practitioner of 'microhistory', he employs novelistic techniques to recount the mental life of individuals in the past reconstituted from evidence that is not exclusively documentary. One of his books, *The Cheese and the Worms*, has garnered a readership beyond the scholarly community, becoming an international bestseller.

Further reading

Ginzburg, C. (1976) *The Cheese and the Worms: The Cosmos of a Sixteenth-Century Miller*, London: Routledge and Kegan Paul.

SUZANNE KIERNAN

Ginzburg, Natalia

b. 14 July 1916, Palermo; d. 7 October 1991

Writer

Ginzburg (born Natalia Levi) was born in Palermo but grew up in Turin where, as a young writer, she befriended anti-fascist intellectuals such as Cesare **Pavese**, Primo **Levi** and Leone Ginzburg, whom she married and whose name she kept after his death at the hands of the regime. Her novels, short stories and plays are populated with mediocre characters often defined by their indecision, their inconsistency and their inability to extricate themselves from unhappy family situations. In fact, family relationships and domestic life have been the constant themes in Ginzburg's literary and dramatic production. The play *Ti ho sposato per allegria* (I Married You for Fun), published in 1966 and soon adapted for the cinema, focuses on a newly-wed couple struggling to make sense of their recent marriage. With this text Ginzburg captures the

uneasiness and insecurity of the 1960s generation, eager to discard traditional family values in an attempt to establish new means of relating. In this as in so many of her other works, the writer's compassionate irony accompanies the portrayal of the characters' failures, endearing them to the reader.

See also: Jewish writers

PIERA CARROLI

Il Giorno

Il Giorno (The Day) is a daily **newspaper**, published by Sogedit in Milan, with a circulation of approximately 170,000 copies (1992 figures). Launched on 21 March 1956, the paper broke with the traditional old-style format of Italian dailies by inventing a quality newspaper with headline banners, brief articles and a new eye-catching layout. It thus appeared to be making history as the first truly modern newspaper in Italy. The paper was initially under the dominant financial control of Enrico **Mattei** who, as president of the state-owned **ENI** and a prominent member of the **DC**, exerted a decisive influence. Following Mattei's death and a wave of concentrations, ENI took over 99 per cent of the capital and became the paper's publisher. Significantly, in 1963 *Il Giorno* became the first newspaper to hail the centre–left government (see **opening to the Left**). However, having openly supported Bettino **Craxi** and the **PSI** in the 1970s and 1980s, *Il Giorno* was hit particularly hard by Craxi's fall from grace and after 1992 it underwent a crisis from which it never fully recovered. It closed in 1997.

See also: newspapers

JAN KURZ

Giudici, Giovanni

b. 26 June 1924, Le Grazie di Portovenere, La Spezia

Poet and essayist

Giudici grew up in Rome and worked in Ivrea and

Turin before settling in Milan as copyright editor for **Olivetti** from 1958 onward. Up to the late 1960s his poetry juxtaposes autobiographical elements and the ironic description of everyday minutiae in an essentially prosaic style. Frequent in his collections is a jocose fascination with the grotesque – uncommon in Italian contemporary poetry – that serves to counterbalance the evident conflict between the poet's Catholic and Marxist personae. Giudici's later poetry develops lyrically around an identity crisis engendered by his refusal to accept the monotonous repetitions of daily existence. As a result, the poems acquire a linguistic sobriety and meditative tone that contrasts with the poet's earlier playfulness, and the autobiographical elements often displace the previous work's social concerns.

Further reading

Giudici, G. (1991) *Poesie 1953–1990* (Poems 1953–1990), Milan: Garzanti (selected poems with bibliographical references).

VALERIO FERME

Giuliani, Alfredo

b. 23 November 1924, Pesaro

Poet and critic

Professor of Contemporary Italian Literature at the University of Chieti, Giuliani is one of the chief promoters of the neoavantgarde movement. He edited the groundbreaking poetic anthology *I novissimi* (The Very New) in 1961, organized the first historic meeting of the **Gruppo 63** in Palermo and, together with Nanni **Balestrini**, also edited the proceedings of that meeting. In the 1960s and 1970s he edited the anthology *Poeti di 'Tel Quel'* (Poets of the Tel Quel) and also published in journals such as *il verri*, *Quindici* and *Grammatica*.

The first important tenet of the neoavantgarde movement is that to regard language as an accurate reflection of the world is to become complicit with a political, economic and ideological system. For Giuliani, as for the entire neoavantgarde movement, poetry should refuse the functional use of language to recount the experiences of one's life and instead should attempt to dramatize the difference between language and reality by generating an incongruous grammar. The work of poetry thus becomes a continual challenge to conventional truths. This leads Giuliani to a sort of schizophrenic or schizomorphic writing which highlights all the inconsistencies of grammar. In this respect, Giuliani's poetry can be considered the heir of Theodor Adorno's negative dialectics.

Further reading

Smith, L.R. (1990) 'Alfredo Giuliani: The Poetics of Schizophrenia', *La Fusta: Journal of Literature and Culture* 5: 136–57.

ERNESTO LIVORNI

Giuliano, Salvatore

b. 16 November 1922, Montelepre, Sicily;
d. 5 July 1950, Castelvetrano

Bandit

Giuliano, or the 'King of Montelepre', as he was also known, was the most famous bandit in postwar Italy. A small-time black marketeer who in September 1943 killed a policeman to avoid being arrested with contraband, Giuliano soon achieved a Robin Hood reputation as leader of the most notorious bandit gang in Western Sicily. What came to distinguish Giuliano from other bandits, however, was his willing participation in the Sicilian Separatist Movement; by 1945 he had become a colonel in EVIS, the Voluntary Army for Sicilian Independence. When the movement eventually collapsed Giuliano came under the influence of a reactionary grouping of local monarchists, landowners and possibly the mafia, that feared the rise of the Left. Giuliano's band then fired indiscriminately on a May Day celebration in 1947, killing 11 people and injuring 27. Giuliano himself was killed in July 1950 in mysterious circumstances. The official version reported that he had died in a gun battle with police but eventually Gaspare Pisciotta, Giuliano's brother-in-law and lieutenant, confessed to having shot him while he was sleeping as part of a deal with police and others. Soon after Pisciotta was poisoned in his prison cell, leaving many questions unanswered, making the case of Giuliano the first of many dark skeletons in the closet of the 'First' Republic.

Further reading

Candler, B.J. (1988) *King of the Mountain: The Life and Death of Giuliano the Bandit*, DeKalb, IL: Northern Illinois University Press (an illuminating and thorough examination of all aspects of the Giuliano case).

GINO MOLITERNO

Gladio

The existence of a secret military organization codenamed 'Gladio', set up in the mid-1950s as part of what the Americans called their 'stay behind network' in Europe and administered from within the Italian secret services, was reluctantly revealed in **Parliament** in 1990 by Prime Minister **Andreotti** and subsequently confirmed by then President of the Republic, Francesco **Cossiga**. Originally declaring that the organization had been disbanded in 1972, Andreotti was later forced to admit that it was still in place.

The network, consisting of some 620 covert operatives divided into forty commando units and five rapid action forces, with access to weapons and ammunition in 140 arms caches hidden throughout the country, was designed to be able to offer armed resistance to any Warsaw Pact invasion or attempted communist takeover. Following controversy and a great deal of public outcry, the government officially dissolved the organization in October 1993, but the existence of such a structure has continued to cause disquiet, not least regarding the possible participation of the 'gladiators' and their arms in Italian right-wing terrorist activities especially during the 1960s and 1970s.

Further reading

Ferraresi, F. (1992) 'A Secret Structure Codenamed

Gladio', in S. Hellman and G. Pasquino (eds), *Italian Politics: A Review*, vol. 7, London: Pinter.

GINO MOLITERNO

Gramsci, Antonio
b. 22 January 1891, Ales; d. 27 April 1937, Quisisana, Rome

Communist Party leader and Marxist theorist

A founder member of the Italian Communist Party (1921), its second leader (1923–37) and a leading Marxist theorist, Gramsci was born in Sardinia to a petty-bourgeois landowning family. His father, Francesco, worked in the land registry and his mother, Giuseppina, was the daughter of the local tax collector.

Gramsci developed a hunchback in infancy and, when his father was jailed for fraud, became the butt of the mockery of peasant children. As the child of the hated local landowning notables, he had a miserable youth. After a secondary education at the *liceo* Giovanni Maria Dettori in Cagliari, he won a scholarship to the University of Turin (1911) and studied letters.

After a brilliant academic start he abandoned the university, joined the Italian Socialist party (1913) and became a journalist for *Avanti* and *Il Grido del Popolo*, writing a regular theatre column. With his colleagues, Angelo Tasca, Umberto Terracini and Palmiro **Togliatti**, he conducted educational campaigns in the working class, setting up the *club di vita morale* (clubs for moral living). All were greatly influenced by the Russian revolutions of 1917 and thereafter supported a revolutionary end to Italy's disastrous participation in the First World War. Together, they established the newspaper *Ordine Nuovo* (1919), which promoted the creation of factory councils which would teach workers how to manage economic production.

Joining with other groups, notably Il Soviet led by the Neapolitan, Amedeo Bordiga, they split from the Socialist party and set up the Italian Communist Party (**PCI**). Gramsci was soon marginalized by his Neapolitan rival, who continued to advocate violent revolutionary policies despite the rise of fascism and the defeat of socialist forces in 1921–3. He was sent as delegate to the Communist International in Moscow in 1922–4 and while there he met and married Giulia Schucht, with whom he had two sons. In 1924 he returned to Italy to organize a new leading group to replace Bordiga, and was elected for the Veneto.

The political triumph of the Fascists redirected Gramsci's attention to an investigation of the reasons for its success and how best to organize opposition to such a movement. Before any concrete opposition could be mounted he was jailed for twenty years, five months and four days, under the Exceptional Laws of 1926 which banned all opposition political parties. These laws effectively crippled the Communist Party, which was condemned to illegality and reduced to a few thousand disorganized members until 1943. Gramsci spent his jail sentence in many Fascist jails, mainly at Turi di Bari but also in Ustica, Formia and various clinics. The difficult conditions, poor diet and constant harassment progressively destroyed his health and ultimately led to an early death.

Gramsci had opposed Comintern policies from 1922 onwards, as he was too much to the Left. He refused to openly criticize Trotsky, and broke with Togliatti on the issue in 1926. From 1931 onwards he also opposed Stalin's policies, which added to his isolation and made his leadership of the Communist Party little more than nominal after his imprisonment.

While in prison he wrote a series of letters (*Lettere dal carcere* (Letters From Prison)), short stories for his sons (*l'Albero del Riccio* (The Tree of the Hedgehog)) and filled numerous exercise books with notes on history, politics, literature, political theory and philosophy. These were smuggled out of Italy and published after the war as *Quaderni del carcere* (Prison Notebooks). It is largely these notebooks that established him as one of the greatest Marxist theorists and philosophers of the twentieth century.

The themes of the notes have provoked much debate and controversy, since Gramsci wrote them in different forms and used codes to avoid censorship. Nevertheless, Gramsci clearly declared his initial intention in 1927 as the undertaking of an enquiry into the creative popular mind, in its various phases and levels of development. He also made clear that the notes constituted an investigation into how that mind was formed, educated and controlled and could be freed from such hegemonies. In turn, this focus was prompted by a consideration of the basis for the success of fascism, particularly how and why it had won the support of the peasantry and middle classes whose role had been neglected by communists and Marxists more generally, despite their being a majority of Italians.

In a debate with Vico, Machiavelli and **Croce**, Gramsci asks what explains the way the ideas of **intellectuals** are taken up by the great masses of people to become forces for historical change? How do ideologies like fascism become 'hegemonic' and sustain particular arrangements of political forces? Gramsci's study was informed by his vast reading of European sources, and his reflection on the peasant culture he had grown up in and which had provided crucial support for fascism, while Communists ignored peasants and their middle-class leaders. These reflections prevented the fascist plan to 'stop this mind working for twenty years' becoming reality. Instead, his notes were successfully written 'fur ewig' (forever), as he had hoped.

Gramsci's critique of economic determinist Marxism, his emphasis on an optimism of the will and his radical emphasis on democratic mass organization for change has made his theory a fruitful source for research. The notes are still used extensively by literary theorists, geographers, sociologists, historians and political scientists of the post-Marxist generation.

Further reading

Buittigieg, J. (ed.) (1995) *Antonio Gramsci Prison Notebooks*, New York: Columbia University Press.

Davidson, A. (1977) *Antonio Gramsci Towards an Intellectual Biography*, London, Merlin.

Golding, S. (1992) *Gramsci's Democratic Theory: Contributions to a Post-Liberal Democracy*, Toronto: University of Toronto Press.

Holub, R. (1992) *Antonio Gramsci: Beyond Marxism and Postmodernism*, London: Routledge.

ALASTAIR DAVIDSON

Grand Hotel

Probably the best-known *fotoromanzo* magazine, *Grand Hotel* was the first to launch the love story in comic book form. The first issue appeared on 26 July 1946, published by Editoriale Universo. Its cover was melodramatic: an elegantly dressed couple smiling in the foreground, while the background featured the lobby of the 'Grand Hotel' and a movie theatre, crowded with more elegant people waiting to see *Anime incatenate* (Chained Souls), a film produced by a fictional film studio, the Edituniverso. The sixteen-page magazine introduced the first episode of the love story, *Anime incatenate*, and the last page was dedicated to letters from readers and an illustrated news item under the title 'It Happened'. The aim of *Grand Hotel* was to entertain and educate a young female readership who did not even have the right to vote. It was instantly successful and continues to be so, having survived the market's ups and downs by adapting to changes in fashion and behavioural norms while adhering to its original format.

FRANCO MANAI

Grassi, Giorgio

b. June 1937, Milan

Architect and teacher

From his student years at the Politecnico of Milan, Grassi displayed an interest in bridging architectural theory and practice, imagination and pragmatism, tradition and invention. He expressed his views in the journal **Casabella** while engaged in a long and uninterrupted teaching career. After the mid-1960s, Grassi combined design and research with teaching architectural composition at Pescara University and the Politecnico of Milan. In 1967 he published *La costruzione logica dell'architettura* (Principles and Axioms in Architecture), elaborating views on contemporary architectural theory first expressed in 1961 in a long article in *Casabella*. Drawing on a series of historical and critical studies, he argued that logic and rationality can overcome the accidental rules and obstacles of architectural design. His own architectural projects

demonstrate how cultural and historical properties can be translated into a new architectural form. He maintained a critical attitude towards much of the modern movement, not only towards those trends that developed from a rationalistic origin to functionalism, but also towards those that measured the rationality of architecture by the purity of its form.

See also: architecture and design magazines

Further reading

Crespi, G. and Pierini, S. (eds) (1996) *Giorgio Grassi: I progetti, le opere e gli scritti* (Giorgio Grassi: Projects, Built Works and Writings), Milan: Electa (an illustrated anthology of Grassi's built and unbuilt architectural works in the years 1961–95, also contains unabridged versions of his important writings as well as a complete list of his projects, exhibitions of his work and an extensive bibliography).

FASSIL ZEWDOU

Greco, Emilio

b. 11 October 1913, Catania; d. 5 April 1995, Rome

Sculptor

Initally Greco worked as a funerary stone mason and then studied at the Palermo Academy of Art. He had his first one-man show in Rome in 1946 and began to examine the realist origins of his sculpture in his series of *Omoni* (Big Men) and *Teste virili* (Virile Heads). From the 1950s onwards he worked mainly in bronze, producing portrait busts and life-size female nudes, often figures of bathers and ice skaters. These works, though still in a realistic vein, nevertheless contain parodic elements of classical statues and represent an emphatic confrontation with sculptural tradition. An important example of this later work is *La grande bagnante* (Large Bather) (1956), a figure of a standing woman with her torso twisted in mannerist fashion like a column, for which Greco was awarded the sculpture prize of the 18th **Venice Biennale**. In the early 1960s he was commissioned to sculpt panels for the doors of the Duomo of Orvieto. Greco went on to exhibit internationally and his work has been collected around the world.

LAURENCE SIMMONS

Gregotti, Vittorio

b. 10 August 1927, Novara

Architect, designer, editor and theoretician

A prominent member of the 'second postwar generation' of architects, Gregotti graduated from the Milan Politecnico in 1952. Except between 1969 to 1974 when he worked alone, Gregotti preferred the teamwork of the Gregotti Associati, first founded in 1953, then a second team assembled in 1974 and finally the current one, founded in 1981. Professor of architecture at the University of Venice since 1971, Gregotti has also taught in other European and American universities. As an editor and writer, he has been actively engaged with current problems and ideas in architecture since the early 1950s. His editorial involvement has included **Casabella**, *Edilizia moderna*, **il verri**, *Lotus* and *Rassegna* while his books, *Inside Architecture* (1991) and *La Città Visibile* (The Visible City) (1995) offer clear statements of his theoretical positions. Gregotti's most recurrent theme is a dialogue between architecture and its situation: its place, history and environment. Urban design, installations, industrial and graphic design are all active elements in Gregotti's architectural experimentation. He has built throughout Italy and internationally.

Further reading

Rykwert, J. (1995) *Gregotti Associati*, Milan: Rizzoli (a thorough review of all Gregotti Associati projects, with extensive bibliography).

GORDANA KOSTICH

Grillo, Giuseppe

b. 21 July 1948, Savignone, Genoa

Comedian and actor

One of the new generation of comedians to emerge in the late 1970s, Giuseppe 'Beppe' Grillo began in cabaret theatre and soon graduated to television. Despite a rising popularity, his tendency to fire biting satirical broadsides against Christian Democrat and Socialist politicians led to his being largely ostracized from the **RAI** in the 1980s. His strongly environmental and anti-capitalist sentiments have continued to made him an uncomfortable presence for the entire Italian establishment in the 1990s, although this has only served to increase his popular appeal. He has also appeared in a number of films, notably in **Comencini**'s *Cercarsi Gesù* (Looking for Christ) in 1981 and Laudadio's *Topo Galileo* (Galileo and the Mouse) in 1988 but, unlike fellow comics like **Benigni** and **Troisi**, Grillo has not managed to successfully transfer his comic verve to the big screen. In 1997, however, he was commissioned by the European Union to prepare and act in an environmental video for wide distribution to schools.

GINO MOLITERNO

Gruppo 63

A loose configuration of self-consciously experimental painters, musicians, writers and cultural critics, Gruppo 63 first came together at a conference in Palermo in 1963 (hence its name). Its membership varied during its brief existence, but its nucleus remained the five 'experimental' poets already launched by the influential anthology *I novissimi* (Alfredo **Giuliani**, Edoardo **Sanguineti**, Nanni **Balestrini**, Antonio **Porta** and Elio **Pagliarani**) together with other emerging young writers, musicians and cultural critics of the immediate postwar generation such as Alberto **Arbasino**, Renato **Barilli**, Umberto **Eco**, Enrico Filippini, Francesco Leonetti, Giancarlo Marmori and Adriano **Spatola**, many of whom had already been published in the prestigious cultural journal *il verri*. The group also included figures such as Angelo Guglielmi who worked in the recently established television industry.

Several members of the group held important positions in the major publishing houses and this, together with a consummate skill in utilizing all the modern techniques of advertising and marketing, helped to keep the group in the public eye and to foster the perception of a common identity. However, the group only held one further public meeting, another conference in Palermo in 1965 which discussed the so-called 'experimental novel'. During this meeting the serious divergence of opinion which had already been evident at the first conference became even more pronounced. Two years later some members of the group initiated a cultural journal called *Quindici*, but this closed after only two years due mainly to the contrasting responses of its key members to the student protests of 1968. The journal's closure signalled the definitive dissolution of the group, whose members then went their separate ways. Giuliani and Guglielmi withdrew ever more into the closed world of poetry, while Balestrini moved to the left-wing publisher **Feltrinelli** where he took up publishing documents of the working-class movement. Sanguineti continued to experiment with poetry but became more deeply involved with the Italian Communist Party (see **PCI**) and began practising the very parliamentary politics which the group had previously scorned. Eco took up a chair at the university of Bologna and continued to chart his course to intellectual superstardom. In 1993, a commemorative conference at Reggio Emilia was organized to mark the twentieth anniversary of the first Palermo conference, but some original members of the group had died and other founding members such as Riva and Eco refused to attend, branding the event an exercise in 'instant nostalgia'.

Judgements on the group have varied enormously. Poet and critic Franco **Fortini** dismissed it all as an odd mixture of techno-rationalism and instinctual irrationalism, and there was also a great deal of criticism regarding the way in which the conference was lavishly co-financed by **Feltrinelli** and the local council. Eco reportedly characterized the group as 'an avantgarde that only travels first-

class', and clearly the group was not a 'traditional' avantgarde made up of struggling bohemian artists but rather a self-conscious grouping of professional intellectuals holding prominent – and influential – positions in the universities, the publishing industry and in the other mass media.

However, as some commentators have pointed out, it was precisely the middle-brow make-up of the group and the influential position of its members inside the cultural establishment that allowed them to evaluate more accurately the enormous changes that were being wrought by the Italian '**economic miracle**' and the challenges that were being presented to a culture which, in spite of its postwar opening to European ideas, was still rather provincial. In fact, despite the wide divergence of opinion amongst its members on a range of issues, the group's most important contribution was undoubtedly its clear and commonly voiced recognition that the economic boom of the late 1950s, and the unprecedented consumeristic ethos that came with it, were changing fundamentally the nature of Italian society. In the process, for better or for worse, new social subjects were being created within a culture no longer linked exclusively to the time-honoured figures of poets and artists, but rather produced and reproduced *en masse* by the media industry itself. In the great marketplace of mass culture which advanced capitalism had thus opened up, political, social and cultural values all became messages and products to be produced and consumed like everything else. Within such an environment, the group argued, artists, writers and intellectuals simply could not refuse the industrial role of cultural 'producer', but they could, and should, explore new possibilities for 'political' action by using all the techniques of the mass media to subvert the easy consumption of prefabricated messages and attempt to generate instead ironic, ambiguous, 'open' meanings.

In this sense, Eco's *Opera aperta* (The Open Work), published a year before the founding conference and presenting for the first time a modern aesthetic built on the idea of unfinished or 'open' interpretations, could be regarded as something like the gravitational centre of an otherwise highly differentiated intellectual cluster. Furthermore, with the innovative idea that all cultural activity presents the possibility for political struggle, the group seemed uncannily to anticipate the war cry of the 1968 student movement: 'everything is political'. Ironically, however, once such notions became not only acceptable but common currency, both within the **student movement** and in the society at large, the group had no more reason for existing and so, quite appropriately, dissolved. Consequently, in spite of its brief duration, Gruppo 63 is justly celebrated as perhaps the first moment when contemporary Italian culture became self-conscious of its own modernity.

See also: poetry

Further reading

Alexander, G. (1978) 'Poetry and Politics: Sanguineti and the *Novissimi*', *Altro Polo*, 193–214 (a discussion of the nexus between poetry and politics in the *novissimi* poets and in the Gruppo 63 generally).

Balestrini, N. (1964) *Gruppo 63: la nuova letteratura*, Milan: Feltrinelli (a presentation of the protagonists of the first Palermo conference).

Eco, U. (1989) *The Open Work*, trans. A. Cancogni, Cambridge, MA: Harvard University Press.

Ferretti, G.C. (1978) 'Italy and the New Avant-garde', *Yale Italian Studies* 2 (3): 233–41 (general considerations on the importance of the Gruppo 63).

GINO MOLITERNO

Gruppo degli otto

The Gruppo degli otto (Group of Eight) were eight Italian artists – Afro, Birolli, Corpora, Moreni, Morletti, Santomaso, Turcato and **Vedova** – who joined together for the purposes of commercially promoting their work and invited the eminent art historian Lionello **Venturi** to be their spokesman. Keen to promote contemporary Italian art and recognizing the importance of international markets, Venturi produced a brief catalogue, *Otto Pittori Italiani* (Eight Italian Painters), with parallel French and English translations, to accompany the group's exhibition at the Venice Biennale of 1952.

Venturi argued that the members of the group were independent and autonomous artists who stood above the petty squabbles between abstraction and realism and were free of the taint of political association. After exhibitions in Rome and Hanover in 1953, the group dissolved in 1954 and the members went their various ways, Morlotti to seek a style expressive of national identity and Vedova to embrace the gestural.

See also: art movements

Further reading

Somaini, L. (1986) *Otto Pittori Italiani 1952–1954* (Eight Italian Painters 1952–1954), Rome: De Luca/Mondadori (the most exhaustive treatment of the group).

MAX STAPLES

Guareschi, Giovanni

b. 1 May 1908, Fontanelle di Roccabianca; d. 22 July 1968, Cervia

Editor, cartoonist and novelist

Consistently ignored, when not openly reviled, by the literary establishment, Guareschi nevertheless found an immense public following with his series of bestselling novels recounting the humorous exploits of Don Camillo, a high-spirited parish priest, and his tussles with the town's communist mayor, Peppone. The first novel, *Don Camillo* (1948), managed to portray through these two contrasting characters all the ideological Cold War battles being waged in postwar Italy. The book's huge success led to a series of sequels with the same characters in situations which closely reflected the social and political changes occurring in the country, as well as a number of popular films starring Gino Cervi and Fernandel in the lead roles. Guareschi edited *Bertoldo*, a weekly satirical magazine and, together with Giovanni Mosa, founded with another satirical periodical entitled *Candido* in which, at one stage, he libelled **Togliatti** and as a consequence spent several months in prison.

Long ostracized in cultural circles as a writer of conservative politics and little literary value, Guareschi and his work have been recently reassessed and in 1998 Rizzoli published *Tutto Don Camillo* (All Don Camillo), in three large volumes.

LAURA A. SALSINI

Gucci

The internationally-recognized inverted 'G' logo designates a family dynasty whose name was once synonymous with Italian fashion. Guccio Gucci, who learned about style and aesthetic sophistication in Paris and London, returned to Italy and opened the first Gucci leather goods shop in Florence in 1920. By the 1940s Gucci shops had sprung up in most major Italian cities. Guccio, patriarch and artisan, bequeathed his business to his five sons in 1953. With that passage came international expansion, with stores opening in New York, Great Britain, France, Hong Kong and Japan. Along with expansion came diversification into shoes, silk scarves, ties, leather clothing, bamboo-handle handbags and watches. In the late 1960s the Gucci logo became a status symbol appealing to celebrities such as Audrey Hepburn and Jackie Onassis.

By the late 1980s, however, the Gucci label had lost some its appeal. The company itself was caught up in family infighting and lawsuits, and Maurizio, Guccio's grandson, was named to head the family empire at the age of forty-seven. Maurizio began downsizing and focusing on those articles which reflected Gucci's artisan traditions and which had been responsible for the company's success: the famous handbag, suitcases, shoes and the foulard. Maurizio also closed a number of boutiques. In 1993 he sold the remainder of his own holdings in the company to Investcorp, an Arab multinational, which thereby became sole stockholder of the Gucci Group.

On 27 March 1995 tragedy struck as Maurizio, the last heir of the Gucci dynasty, was shot and killed on his way to work. Two years of investigation led to nothing. Motives were initially linked to the enemies Maurizio had made in negotiating the sale of the Gucci label. Finally Maurizio's ex-wife, Patrizia Reggiani, was charged and convicted of ordering the murder, together with her fortune-teller friend and a night porter, who were responsible for hiring the assassin and the getaway driver. While admitting she often wished her ex-husband dead, Patrizia Reggiani continued to deny her involvement in the murder but the prosecution claimed her resentment over their divorce, Maurizio's plans to remarry and a reduction in alimony payments had motivated her to order the killing.

In spite of personal tragedy, the 1990s have seen the Gucci Group bounce back from the slump of the previous decade. The positive turnaround has been attributed to CEO Domenico de Sole and creative director Tom Ford, a Texan who is considered responsible for saving Gucci from bankruptcy. His designs, promoting classic elegance combined with innovative twists, led to a sudden leap in sales and inspired the name of a new fragrance, 'Envy', in 1996. His more recent designs include a return to the 1970s: bellbottomed trousers, fringes, and suits with floral colours and the 'Jackie O' purse revived in bright colours such as turquoise, yellow and orange. The 1980s also feature in his designs for the end of the millennium which celebrate 'maximalism' as opposed to minimalism. Finally, to spite the animal rights group, he advocates a return to furs of all types in all forms including fur jackets, fur coats and fur vests.

Despite Gucci's revival, Ford and Domenico de Sole have other worries, mainly the ongoing battle for financial control of the company. They have triumphed in the latest round, with a Dutch court ruling in Gucci's favour in the most recent hostile takeover bid by LVMH. Ironically, all this might have been avoided had Gucci stuck to its motto: 'Stay small to remain great'.

BERNADETTE LUCIANO

Guccione, Piero

b. 1935, Scicli, Ragusa, Sicily

Painter

A significant artist who has exhibited widely both

in Italy and internationally (several times at the **Venice Biennale**), Guccione depicts scenes from the physical world, such as landscapes, seascapes, fences and buildings, with an almost photo-realist technique, but he composes and colours his work so as to highlight abstract patterns in a way that is reminiscent of 1960s minimalism and colour-field painting. After a period in Rome, Guccione returned to Sicily in 1980, which he used as subject matter in much of his subsequent work. *Study of the Sea* (1982–3), for example, depicts a Mediterranean seascape but also plays with the interaction between horizontal and diagonal patterns.

Further reading

Siciliano, E. and Sontag, S. (1989) *Guccione*, Milan: Fabbri Editori (an informative illustrated monograph).

MAX STAPLES

Guttuso, Renato

b. 2 January 1912, Bagheria, Sicily;
   d. 18 January 1987, Rome

Painter

Despite disagreement about his quality as an artist, Guttuso remains the best-known exponent of Italian social realist, or neorealist, art (see **realism**). He participated in the **Resistance** as a member of the Italian Communist Party (**PCI**) and after the war responded to the communist demands for programmatic and realist art by depicting the things and events around him: common people, interiors of ordinary homes and scenes of class struggle. Nevertheless, his realism is not extreme and his paintings do not attempt to dissemble their painterly nature. With its swirling line, thick black outlines and sombre shadows, his style is figurative but perhaps better described as expressionist. The *Crucifixion* (1941), for example, used a religious theme to suggest the repression experienced under fascism. Condemned by the Church and the pro-fascist press, it showed a nude Magdalene cleaning the wounds of a Christ whose face is obscured while the surrounding chaos of horses and weeping figures echoes Picasso's *Guernica*.

Remaining loyal to the Communist Party, Guttuso achieved high office, becoming a senator of the **Republic** in 1976–83 and receiving the Lenin Peace Prize in 1972.

Further reading

(1996) *Guttuso*, London: Thames & Hudson/ Palermo: Novecento Editore (exhibition catalogue with a number of illuminating essays, colour reproductions, detailed biography and extensive bibliography).

MAX STAPLES

Harry's Bar

Opened by Giuseppe Cipriani in 1931 and later managed by his son Arrigo, who was named after it, Harry's Bar is a Venetian landmark, an international meeting place and a bar/restaurant famous for its drinks.

The original Harry was Harry Pickering, a rich young American who advanced Cipriani the original stake of 40,000 lire to open a bar. Located at the end of the Calle Vallaresso, beside the gondolas bobbing on the Grand Canal, from the outside it hardly seems a bar at all. Its frosted-glass windows make it difficult to peer in and there is no sign advertising its presence. Inside is a smallish, cosy room decorated in art deco style and an elegant first floor dining room. Harry's Bar is famous for its carpaccio, its risottos and its Bellinis, a cocktail invented in the 1930s and made from white peach juice mixed with prosecco, an Italian version of champagne.

The guest book of Harry's Bar records such names as Noel Coward, Ernest Hemingway, Arturo Toscanini, Charlie Chaplin, Orson Welles, Humphrey Bogart and Lauren Bacall, as well as countless members of European royalty. There have been attempts to clone Harry's Bar in other parts of Italy and around the world, but none have managed to recreate the unique personality of the Venetian original.

LAURENCE SIMMONS

health services

In European surveys, Italians have regularly shown the least satisfaction with their own health and the greatest discontent with the state services designed to protect it. The two dissatisfactions are probably related.

Italians go to the doctor more frequently than other Europeans and make more use of pharmaceuticals. As emigrants and travellers, many Italians have experience of health care abroad and are well placed to compare their own system with others. Their views are unequivocal. First, complaints about long waiting times, bureaucratic formalities, hospital hygiene and uncooperative personnel are voiced by most respondents in all surveys. Second, since 1980, previously insignificant private health schemes have expanded more rapidly in Italy than elsewhere as Italians seek an alternative route to adequate care. The high levels of dissatisfaction by European standards cannot, however, be directly related to low levels of health expenditure. Italy spends roughly the same proportion of its GDP on health as other European societies; specialists and GPs receive comparable salaries; hospital bed occupancy rates have been much lower than in Germany, France and the UK; and – until cutbacks in 1994 – up to one-third of Italians have been exempted from rising prescription charges and have used their exemption to consume nine times as many pharmaceuticals as the non-exempt. Moreover, doctors and nurses complain as vociferously about the health service as their patients do.

Its basic structure – the National Health System (SSN) – was created in 1978, replacing about one hundred uncoordinated health insurance funds which protected their different memberships very unevenly. The new system was intended to reduce social and regional differences in the quality of health services and to evade the financial crisis of the funds. Local health boards (USL) were established, managed by committees under the supervision of the new regional health authorities. The reform's defects soon appeared. First, funding was provided at national level, but expenditure was decided locally: effective monitoring of spending and services became impossible. Second, the USL management committees were staffed by party political nominees, anxious to use the new resources for **clientelism**. Third, doctors' commitment to the public sector was discouraged by their right to maintain private practice, and low pay led to a shortage of paramedical staff: 30,000 extra nurses, about 14 per cent of total nursing employment, were needed by 1991. Widespread dissatisfaction, unsustainable increases in costs and revelations of inefficient and corrupt management – prompting the arrest of politicians, public health officials and doctors in many cities – led to drastic reforms in 1991–4. The number of USL was reduced by two-thirds, professional managers replaced politically-appointed committees and consumers were required to pay a larger share of treatment and pharmaceutical costs. Pressures for an efficient, user-friendly service will continue to be exerted by the greater determination to increase the substantive content of citizenship and by the needs of an ageing population.

See also: social welfare

Further reading

Ferrera, M. (1996) 'The Partitocracy of Health: Towards a New Welfare Politics in Italy?', in M. Donovan (ed.), *Italy*, vol. II, Aldershot: Ashgate.

Granaglia, E. (1996) 'The Italian National Health Service and the Challenge of Privatisation', *Southern European Society and Politics* 1 (3): 155–71.

DAVID MOSS

historic compromise

The term 'historic compromise' was coined by Communist leader Enrico **Berlinguer** in 1973 to indicate a possible governing coalition between the **DC** and the **PCI**. After the military takeover of Chile in September 1973, Berlinguer proposed collaboration with the Christian Democrats in order to prevent a similar response from the Italian Right. It thus began as a defensive policy but soon developed into a grand strategy by which Catholics and communists could work together. In practical terms – and during a time when **terrorism** appeared a real threat – it produced governments of 'national solidarity' (summer 1976–spring 1979). By 1978, the PCI was drawing up programmes and voting with the government. In effect, however, the historic compromise became a policy of co-optation and neutralization of the PCI by the DC, who appeared the ultimate winner. The idea was eventually abandoned, partly due to the assassination of its strongest DC supporters, Aldo **Moro**, by the **Red Brigades** in 1977, and partly because many in the PCI vehemently opposed it.

Further reading

McCarthy, P. (1995) *The Crisis of the Italian State: From the Origins of the Cold War to the Fall of Berlusconi and Beyond*, New York: St. Martin's Press (see ch. 6, 'Enrico Berlinguer and the Historic Compromise').

JAMES WALSTON

historiography

In 1945 the Italian historical profession emerged from the dictatorship in an ambiguous condition. The regime had given great attention to history – Mussolini himself often asserted the need to be part of it – but Italian historians had, arguably, not linked their discipline to fascism in the same servile way that so many German historians had done with Nazism (see also **fascism and neo-fascism**). In particular, Benedetto **Croce** could be depicted, and depicted himself, as an anti-fascist who, in his palace in Naples, had clung to liberalism and to the ideals of the humanities even while fascism was proclaiming its 'totalitarian' state. In 1945, Croce rapidly interpreted fascism as a 'parenthesis' in the general progress of united Italy, and implied that the writing of history too was now back on its naturally liberal course. In this atmosphere of forgive and forget, few Italian historians, with the exception of Gioacchino Volpe, were purged from their jobs as Italy was declared a republic.

One of Croce's most tenacious beliefs was 'idealism', that is, the view that ideas are the chief instruments of historical change and, consequently, that intellectuals are the key element in any society. This idealism had never been renounced in fascist Italy, and in the **Republic** it remained the strongest implicit notion in all history writing and indeed in most intellectual life. Croce himself died in 1954. By then, the leader of the historical profession was Federico Chabod (1901–60). Like Croce, Chabod was a liberal, but from 1943–4 he also became an active partizan, joining the **Partito d'Azione** and taking on the fighting name of 'Lazzaro' (Lazarus). A cynic might say that Chabod needed to rise from the dead because, in the 1930s, he had actively served the Fascist regime. His most celebrated book, *Storia della politica estera italiana dal 1870–1896* (History of Italian Foreign Policy from 1870–1896) (1951) – a pioneering account of the 'unspoken assumptions' which lie behind the words of politicians and diplomatists – had been begun under the aegis of the fascist Volpe. Despite these equivocations, Chabod was hailed by the 'West' as a great historian and, in demonstration of the return of Italy to historiographical respectability, in 1955 the Tenth International Congress of Historical Sciences assembled in Rome with Chabod occupying the presidential chair. Meanwhile, the great journals of liberal Italian historiography, *Rivista Storica Italiana* (from 1884), *Rassegna Storica del Risorgimento* (from 1914), *Nuova Rivista Storica* (from 1917), all of which had been founded before fascism, simply shrugged off their editorial fellow-travelling with fascism and continued publication.

Another guarantor of Italy's commitment to a liberal and 'Western' approach to history was the patriotic radical, Gaetano Salvemini (1873–1957), an anti-fascist who had chosen exile during the regime. He took sanctuary in the United States and taught at Harvard, where he inspired a generation of American Italianists. The book which best sums up his school is A.W. Salomone's *Italy in the Giolittian era: Italian Democracy in the Making, 1900–1914* (1945, revised edn 1960). As the title suggests, Salomone's thesis was that Italy was moving inexorably and happily towards a liberal capitalist democracy before it was hit by the difficulties of the First World War and fascism. Salomone shared Croce's belief that, after 1945, progress would once again resume. Having freed itself in 1860, and having overcome the 'sickness' of fascism, Italy would again become a vehicle for liberty.

Italy's process of unification in the nineteenth century soon became the epicentre of historiographical debate for both liberals and their critics, not least because between 1948 and 1961 a series of centenaries of the Risorgimento fell due. Under **Togliatti**'s leadership, the Communist Party (**PCI**) was itself a rather idealist body in the Crocean sense, and it remained interested in finding itself a culture, indeed a national culture. Until the collapse of the USSR, Italian historiography therefore became a battleground of 'Marxists' – often the definition of this term was decidedly loose – and anti-Marxists in much the same way that its politics were fought out between 'anti-fascists' and anti-communists (see **anti-fascism**). The great symbol of a humane and 'national popular' Marxist reading of the Italian past was Antonio **Gramsci** (1891–1937). A martyr to fascism, Gramsci was a highly saleable product for the PCI, defined sardonically by the American Jackson Lears as, 'the Marxist you can take home to mother'.

Gramsci's interpretation of the Risorgimento became the starting point of a Marxist meta-narrative running from past to future. In his wonderfully wide-ranging *Prison Notebooks*, Gramsci had reflected on the process of national unification which he assessed as a *rivoluzione mancata* (a missed revolution). In his eyes, the forging of the Italian nation state had occasioned a political but not a social revolution. The consequent task of Italian politicians and of Italian culture generally was to bring the people in, as it were, from the cold, to create a national polity of sufficient social justice to embrace both the southern peasantry and the working-class North.

Gramsci's splendid breadth of intellectual interests and his insistent emphasis both on history in general and on national Italian history in particular gave inspiration and justification to a generation of Marxist scholars. It was appropriate that the most orthodox of PCI historical journals, *Studi storici*, should from 1959 be published by the Istituto Gramsci in Rome. In turn the events of 1968, both in Italy and in the rest of Europe, gave impulse to fresh ideas and an enhanced sense of self-importance among the so-called 'New Left'. The historiographical result was that other Marxist and Gramsci-influenced historical journals commenced publication, retailing a critical view of the Italian past which challenged liberal complacency about the inevitability of national progress. Especially notable were the *Rivista di Storia contemporanea* (first issue, 1972) and *Passato e presente* (from 1982). Also important was the journal *Quaderni storici*, modelled to some extent on the French *Annales*, which became a special place of publication for 'structural' histories, whether of recent times or the remote past.

The most extreme of the New Left histories was Renzo Del Carria's *Proletari senza rivoluzione* (Proletarians Without Revolution) (2 volumes, 1970). More scholarly was the work of such varied leftist historians as Guido Quazza, Claudio Pavone and Nicola Tranfaglia. Probably the most internationally celebrated modern historian from this background, however, was Luisa Passerini (b. 1941), whose history of 'passive dissent' in Turin has been translated into English as *Fascism in Popular Memory* (1987). Passerini also wrote a fascinating personal account in *Autoritratto di gruppo* (Group Self-Portrait) (1988), there speaking with three 'voices': one as a historian of her generation, the second as autobiographer and, last, as herself under psychoanalysis. In this and other works, Passerini helped to import into Italian historiography crucial ideas from French theory.

Ironically, however, the most influential, critical, historical account of Italy's past, published in the Republic after 1946, was written by a foreigner, the Oxbridgean gentleman-radical Denis Mack Smith. In 1959, Mack Smith brought out the first edition of *Italy: A Modern History*. The book was swiftly translated by Laterza and made available in a cheap paperback edition. Though there is no strong evidence that Mack Smith had read Gramsci, the theses of his book matched a Gramscian comprehension of the past. In Mack Smith's account, fascism became the 'revelation' of a continuity in national history, which ran from the sins of the Risorgimento to the greater evil of Mussolini's regime.

The book gave Mack Smith lasting fame which he would renew in the 1970s with a study of Fascist foreign policy (*Mussolini's Roman Empire*) (1976) and a biography of Mussolini (1981). Then and thereafter he was regularly summoned by the Italian media to comment on Italian historiographical disputes. His career is a reminder that much Italian history at the time was being written outside Italy, in France and Germany and especially in the Anglo-Saxon world. There, a number of British historians were likely to review the Italian past in critical vein. In the United States, by contrast, perhaps because many Italianists came from emigrant families, the critique tended to be more muted. Readers who wish to pursue this matter might contrast Paul Ginsborg's *A History of Contemporary Italy* (1990) or Roger Absalom's *Italy Since 1800* (1995) with the Italo-American Spencer Di Scala's *Italy: From Revolution to Republic* (1995).

Radical readings of the history of the Italian nation were also countered within Italy itself. Technically the most impressive conservative historian was Rosario Romeo (1924–87), the biographer of Cavour. Already in the 1950s Romeo led those determined to rebut the Gramscian interpretation of the Risorgimento and he remained a consistent foe of Mack Smith. Romeo argued that a unification 'from above' had been 'necessary' for industrialization and modernity to reach Italy. He avoided much discussion of Fascism, but regretted what he viewed as the absence of a proper national spirit in the Republic.

More renowned than Romeo was his friend Renzo **De Felice** (b. 1929), the biographer of Mussolini. Indeed, by the time of his death in 1996, De Felice seemed to many to be Italy's leading modern historian. A dedicated researcher, De Felice kept close to the archives, too close as far as his critics were concerned. After the 1970s, when his cause was taken up by anti-Communist academics in the USA, De Felice developed a neo-Rankean approach to the past. Fascism, he argued, should be investigated on its own terms and without any 'journalistic' propensity to moralizing. In any case, he increasingly implied, Mussolini's regime was neither worse nor better than any other. It should, however, be clearly distinguished from Nazism. Fascism was not responsible for 'Auschwitz'. Its defeat in the Second World War was as much the result of the madness of Hitler and the lack of national spirit of too many Italians as it was the fault of fascism, while the period of '**Resistance**' from 1943 to 1945 was best defined as one of civil war.

These decidedly contentious theses were treated by De Felice as self-evident truths. He and his followers, especially in their journal, *Storia contemporanea* (from 1970), preached a party line that was at least as intolerant of their critics as vulgar Marxists had been before them. De Felice and his intellectual heir, Emilio Gentile, both professors at Rome University and each elevated to the editorial board of the important *American Journal of Contemporary History*, constructed an account of Italy's travails in the twentieth century which well fitted the nation's conservative turn after 1978 and the general international 'end of history' as Fukuyama has called it. By the 1990s new conservatives, though not unchallenged, were the dominant influence in Italian history writing.

Just as much modern Italian history was composed outside Italy, so quite a lot of the research and writing of history under the Italian Republic has focused on periods before the invention of the nation state. The Renaissance remains of considerable historiographical interest and both Italian and international writing on that subject has flourished mightily, with a special emphasis, over the last two or three decades, on social history. If one book had to be selected to represent the historiography of the Republic it would, however, be Carlo **Ginzburg**'s *The Cheese and the Worms: The Cosmos of a Sixteenth Century Miller* (Italian edition, 1976; English, 1980). In his microcosmic account of the Friulian miller Menocchio, Ginzburg recounts the stubborn survival of humanist values in an unlikely person, at a difficult time, and in the cruel circumstances of the Inquisition. Doubtless Menocchio's tale was origin-ally a parable for the 1970s, but its lessons remained pertinent for later times.

See also: intellectuals

Further reading

Bosworth, R.J.B. (1993) *Explaining Auschwitz and Hiroshima: History Writing and the Second World War 1945–1990*, London: Routledge (an attempt to place Italian history writing in a comparative perspective).

Ginzburg, C. (1980) *The Cheese and the Worms: The Cosmos of a Sixteenth-Century Miller*, trans. J. Tedeschi and A. Tedeschi, London: Routledge and Kegan Paul (the most brilliant example of postwar Italian history writing).

R.J.B. BOSWORTH

HIV/AIDS

Italy's first AIDS case was diagnosed in June 1982, and the first instance of HIV was later traced to Milan in 1979. By the mid-1990s the cumulative Italian total of 30,447 reported cases showed one of the highest levels of infection in Europe. HIV/AIDS has remained largely concentrated in the major urban areas of north and central Italy, especially Milan, Rome and Bologna, where higher standards of treatment and care attract virus-carriers from other regions.

Although the first Italians with AIDS were gay, they were soon rapidly outnumbered by injecting drug users, who accounted for about 75 per cent of cases by 1990. This unusual early dominance of heterosexual drug users had three consequences. First, women and infants made up an especially significant minority (about 20 per cent) of people infected. Second, the recriminalization of drug use in 1990 ensured exceptionally high rates of infection in prison populations; approximately one-third of all prisoners were seropositive by the mid-1990s. Fierce but inconclusive conflicts therefore raged over whether testing should be imposed on all new prisoners and whether prisoners with HIV/AIDS should be housed in special sections or given non-custodial sentences. Third, since drug users are not easily organized on their own behalf to demand action from others, pressure for policy initiatives was weak; needle exchange programmes, for example, were rarely even a topic for public debate. Policy making on HIV/AIDS therefore remained under the control of politicians, health bureaucracies and the medical scientific establishment, and none of the public controversies in other societies – testing, patient confidentiality, public funding – occurred in Italy.

When the virus first appeared, homosexual acts and the possession of drugs and syringes were legal, although widely disapproved. Relieved from difficult debates about the urgency of decriminalizing high-risk activities, the government limited itself mainly to providing guidelines on infection control. Active intervention was left to regional health authorities who responded, where they responded at all, to uneven local pressures. The most significant practical initiatives in sex education, support and care for HIV-carriers fell to the private sector, including gay organizations (**ARCI** Gay in Bologna, the Circolo Mario Mieli in Rome, and the Associazione Solidarietà Aids in Milan), treatment centres for drug users, and welfare work by the Church. Between 1987 and 1990, however, central direction was established. A national advisory committee (CNLA) and research centre (COA) were set up, blood donation and transfusion were more strictly regulated, the first mass education campaign was launched and all forms of discrimination, including clandestine or testing without consent, were outlawed by law 135/90. Sex education in schools remained very poor, however, and the crucial coordination of policy making for AIDS and illicit drugs was no better than in other areas of the **health services**.

See also: drug culture

Further reading

Moss, D. (1990) 'AIDS in Italy: Emergency in Slow Motion', in B.A. Misztal and D. Moss (eds), *Action on AIDS: National Policies in Comparative Perspective*, New York: Greenwood.

Steffen, M. (1996) *The Fight Against AIDS*, Grenoble: Presses Universitaires de Grenoble (comparison of policy responses in Italy, France, Britain and Germany).

DAVID MOSS

housing policy

The Second World War left many of Italy's cities devastated: 1.2 million homes had been destroyed in the big cities, and in Naples alone 200,000 people were homeless. Inhabited shacks were still to be found in Milan and Turin in the late 1950s, while the institutionalized *borgate* (shanty towns) still housed a fifth of Rome's population in the 1970s. The immediate needs of the Reconstruction period were therefore to build as many houses as possible in a short time.

The most important public programme was that of the INA-Casa (Istituto Nazionale Abitazioni, National Institute for Housing) launched by **Fanfani** in 1949. This provided funds for large-scale public housing on the urban peripheries. For many of the first occupants of these houses, the prospect of space, light, electricity and hot water was a miracle. Of course, as in all European countries, the clearing of the slums and shanty towns also implied a destruction of whole communities, although this process was never as straightforward and negative as it has been painted. Many of the early neighbourhoods built under the INA-Casa scheme were notable examples of collective planning by architects, urbanists and politicians. The celebrated Tiburtino district in Rome remains the most important example. Ten years after its construction, the architect Lodovico **Quaroni** subjected his own work at Tiburtino to a savage self-critique in the pages of *Casabella*: 'In the push towards the "city"', he wrote, 'we stopped at the "village"' (Quaroni, 1957: 24).

Other important neighbourhoods were constructed at Matera – to house those who had lived in caves – the Sassi – under the influence of Adriano **Olivetti** – and at Milan (for example, the Comasina quarter). Many of these quarters were mixed developments, intended to be 'self-sufficient' and to create (artificially) public communities. In reality, although the situation on these estates varied greatly and there were important internal divisions between single housing blocks, self-sufficiency proved to be a chimera. The phrase 'dormitory quarter' was quickly and rightly applied although it is important to understand that many people chose to 'retreat' within the home, as values such as privacy became more important than 'sociability'. **Pasolini** captured some of the aspects both of the 'old *borgata*' and of the new neighbourhoods in his *Una vita violenta* (A Violent Life) (1959) and his films *Accattone* (1961) and *Mamma Roma* (1962).

The **economic miracle** blew the cosy world of the INA-Casa (replaced by GESCAL in 1963) wide open. Millions of immigrants arrived in the cities, especially Milan and Turin. A real building boom occurred: three times as many houses were built in 1961 as in 1951. Cities became virtual building sites. Most of these houses were not for the new arrivals to live in, but to work on. At Milan, many immigrants constructed their own rudimentary homes in the extreme urban periphery. These micro-neighbourhoods – built without any rational criteria and completely lacking in basic services – became known as *coree*. At Turin, the immigrants were housed either in the city centre, in attics or cellars or squalid hotels, or in new out-of-town developments. The latter were classic ghettos, almost entirely inhabited by southerners and built to very low specifications and standards. The situation was no better around Rome or Naples, where innovative plans were ruined by corrupt politicians, builders and the **mafia**. Speculators continued to build millions of homes (450,000 houses in 1964) largely outside of planning regulations, and the attempts to rectify the situation were blocked by political campaigns (such as that against the 1962 Sullo laws) or criminal influence. One extreme example will suffice here: the peripheral neighbourhoods at Palermo. **Gregotti**'s designs for housing based on African villages have been criticized as utopian, but the whole saga of the infamous ZEN neighbourhood, which has never been finished, remains the supreme example of urban mismanagement in Italy. The failure to rehouse those who lost their homes in the Belice earthquake in 1968 is even more tragic. Thousands were still living in prefabricated huts in the 1980s.

The 1970s and 1980s saw housing hit the centre of the political debate. Italy was one of the first and only countries to see a general strike in favour of cheaper housing (in November 1969). Better housing was a key demand in 1968 and afterwards, and occupied houses became a common sight in Italian cities. In Milan, an occupied hotel in the city centre became one of the symbols of the **student movement**, and the slogan 'let us retake the city' was a potent one. Many occupations were collective, and the authorities were often powerless to intervene. Other forms of struggle included rent strikes and, later, 'auto-reduction'. This pressure forced the governments to pass a law in favour of public housing in 1971 and another enforcing extremely strict rent controls in 1978 – the *equo canone* – which linked rent to wages and made eviction extremely difficult. A ten-year plan for residential housing was presented in the same year. The effects of this legislation have been contradictory. On the one hand, many poor tenants have been given security in the face of the threat of eviction and are able to meet rent payments. However, the rent market dried up in the major cities – with flats only available to 'foreigners', for 'businesses' or through illegal contracts. This situation encourages young people to stay at home for much longer than in other European countries, and has helped diminish labour mobility, in contrast with the 1950s and 1960s. The relaxation of this law in 1992–3 helped to relaunch a dead rental market. In the South, the problem of illegal house-building is endemic and by now is a permanent feature of the landscape; 2.7 million illegal houses are estimated to have been built between 1971 and 1984. Politicians appear powerless to halt this open lawlessness, and a series of amnesties have only made the problem worse.

By 1992, an astonishing 70 per cent of Italians owned their own homes. Many were weighed down by bank mortgages (Italy has very few building societies, although there are important co-operatives, especially in central Italy). In addition, more Italians owned a second home than in any other European country (there were 1.26 dwellings per person in 1991). The market was as static as it has ever been, but prices continue to rise in the major cities, with calculations being done by the square metre. The contrast between these trends and the thousands of immigrants who were sleeping in disused factories and under bridges in Milan, Turin and Rome in the 1990s only underlines the urban problems faced by a society with high living standards but poor levels of civic pride and public services.

See also: architecture and design magazines; urban planning

Further reading

Ginsborg, P. (1990) *A History of Contemporary Italy*, London: Penguin.

Padovani, L. (1996) 'Italy', in P. Balchin (ed.), *Housing Policy in Europe*, London: Routledge, 188–209.

Quaroni, L. (1957) 'Il paese dei Barocchi', *Casabella* 215 (April–May).

Rochat, G., Sateriale, G. and Spano, L. (eds) (1980) *La casa in Italia* (Housing in Italy), Bologna: Zanichelli (a good general anthology.)

JOHN FOOT

I

Ilva

Ilva was the name given in 1987 to the reorganized public sector steel-operating company after the liquidation of **Finsider** and Nuova **Italsider**. The original operating arm of Finsider from 1937 until the formation of Italsider in 1959 was also called Ilva. Ilva is also the Latin name for Elba, the island facing the Piombino integrated plant in Tuscany. The island had Italy's only substantial iron ore deposits upon which the earliest steel efforts were based. Ilva originally had plants at Piombino and Bagnoli (Naples) but ironically, in the restructuring that saw the re-emergence of the name Ilva, neither of these two plants was included. The company was again reorganized as Ilva Laminati Piani (flat-rolled products) in 1994, in a form ready for privatization (see **privatization and nationalization**) but there was considerable controversy surrounding this restructuring as the **European Union**'s Commission and the Italian government fought over the size of the required trade-off of state aids for a substantial reduction in productive capacity. In 1996 the company was finally sold to the Riva group.

See also: industry

Further reading

Masi, A.C. (1996) 'Steel', in H. Kassim and A. Menon (eds), *The European Union and National Industrial Policy*, London: Routledge (a compre-

hensive survey of restructuring and privatization efforts of the Italian steel industry in the 1990s).

ANTHONY C. MASI

immigrant literature

1990 marks an important moment in the development of immigrant literature in Italy for in that year the Martelli Law gave a large number of undocumented immigrants legal status in Italy. Subsequently, many immigrants began to make their stories public, some even achieving publication by major Italian publishers. The resulting Italophone literature – in this context, literature written in Italian by immigrants – tells of the complex lives of people from many different countries and cultures who migrated to Europe for economic and political reasons.

The first group of Italophone writers, mainly male, originated largely in the Francophone areas of Africa and created autobiographical texts written in collaboration with a linguistic expert. However, this co-authoring was often problematic, being an uneasy collaboration between Western and non-Western writers. An example is Salah **Methnani** and Mario Fortunato's *Immigrato* (Immigrant), written in 1990, which tells of a man from Tunisia as he struggles to find work and eventually turns to drugs.

Published in 1990, Pap Khouma's *Io venditore di elefanti* (I, Elephant Seller) became a bestseller in Italy. Written in collaboration with Italian writer and journalist Oreste Pivetta, Khouma's autobiography supplies a model of immigrants' life stories in Italian. Khouma came to Italy from Senegal and began to write his life story while simultaneously teaching himself Italian with a French–Italian grammar. Thus French, the colonial language, became for Khouma, as for many other immigrants, the element of mediation that allowed the acquisition of a new language which, in turn, allowed Khouma to reject his ex-motherland and choose another country of migration.

This ideological motivation behind the choice of another country and another romance language is shared by Saidou **Moussa Ba**, another Senegalese writer living in Italy, who expressed his resentment against the ex-motherland in a 1995 short story entitled *Nel cuore di un clandestino* (In the Heart of an Illegal Immigrant). In *La promessa di Hamadi* (Hamadi's Promise), written in 1991 in collaboration with Alessandro Micheletti, Ba experimented with the genre of autobiographical narrative. His semi-autobiographical text recounts the fictional story of two brothers who migrate to Italy, where one of them is killed. The book begins with a chant that connects Western and non-Western traditions; in this way, Ba narrates the hybridizing effects that migration has both on the mother/father culture and on the culture of the country of migration.

Mohsen Melliti's *Pantanella: Canto lungo la strada* (Pantanella: A Song along the Road) narrates community life in the Pantanella, an immigrant squatter community living in an abandoned pasta factory in Rome. Where Khouma's *Io venditore* offers an optimistic vision of the future that finds redemption in the very act of narration, by contrast Melliti's novel ends with the suicide of one of the main characters and the destruction of the Pantanella, strongly suggesting the impossibility of constructing a future within Italian culture and society.

With his 1995 novel *I bambini delle rose* (The Rose Children), Melliti moves from autobiographical writing to a fictional narrative that focuses on immigration but places at its centre other immigrants, in this case two children. This is an example of the second phase of Italophone literature, which contains fewer autobiographical texts and is rarely written in collaboration with a linguistic expert. These narratives often look at the future and at the concerns of other generations.

Tahar Lamri's *Solo allora, sono certo, potrò capire* (Only Then, I'm Certain, I'll Understand) tells of a second-generation Algerian man who returns to Algeria to discover the culture and language that his father had always tried to repress in the name of assimilation.

Second-generation concerns are also at the centre of Nassera **Chohra**'s *Volevo diventare bianca* (I Wanted to Become White) (1993). In this autobiography, Chohra narrates her second-generation Algerian childhood in Marseilles and her eventual migration to Italy. This text, which tells of repeated migrations, is the first autobiography in Italian by an immigrant woman published in Italy, and epitomizes the fact that women's testimonies surface later than men's. Immigrant women's texts, always in a minority with respect to men's, also discuss gender issues. The Somalian Shirin Ramzanali Fazel's *Lontano da Mogadiscio* (Far From Mogadishu) (1994) is, together with the Eritrean Ribka Sibhatu's *Aulò*, one of the few texts to mention Italy's colonial past and to discuss the deliberately repressed memory of colonialism in Italy.

Cristiana de Caldas Brito's *Ana de Jesus* (Ana of Jesus) was published in the anthology *Le voci dell'arcobaleno* (The Voices of the Rainbow), a collection of the pieces submitted to the first literary prize for immigrant writers held in 1995. Brito's *Ana* is not an autobiographical short story: a deliberately grammarless monologue, it introduces the grammar of immigration, the grammar of silence that fills the domestic space in which Ana, the protagonist, is trapped.

The volumes, *Le voci dell'arcobaleno* (The Voices of the Rainbow), *Mosaici d'inchiostro* (Mosaics of Ink), *Memorie in valigia* (Memories in a Suitcase), *Destini sospesi di volti in cammino* (Uncertain Destinies of Transient Faces) and *Parole oltre i confini* (Words Beyond Borders), collect the short stories and poems presented at the subsequent 1996, 1997 and 1998 literary awards in Rimini. These collections allow a plurality of voices to become published and therefore public, documenting both the history of immigration and the history of immigrant literature in Italy. Published by a small company, Fara editore, these anthologies are just one example of the role that small publishers are playing in the dissemination of immigrant writings. Another publishing company, Sensibili alle Foglie (Sensitive to Leaves) has published a number of controversial texts such as Fernanda Farias de Albuquerque and Maurizio Jannelli's *Princesa*, an account of Fernanda's experience as a transsexual prostitute in Italy, her incarceration and her discovery that she has AIDS.

This wealth of first-hand testimonies of the immigrant experience have been echoed by a number of texts by Italian writers about immigrants in Italy, such as Marco Lodoli's *I fannulloni* (The Layabouts), Giulio Angioni's *Una ignota compagnia* (An Unknown Company), Emilio **Tadini**'s *La tempesta* (The Tempest) and Giorgio Saponaro's *Il ragazzo di Tirana* (The Boy from Tirana). The considerable, and growing, number of texts exploring the migrant condition in contemporary Italy have succeeded in establishing a dialogue between the self-representation of immigrants and the portrayal of otherness by established Italian writers. Such a dialogue is profoundly significant, and is likely to revise fundamentally the very concept of Italian culture at the end of the millennium.

Further reading

Parati, G. (1997a) 'Strangers in Paradise: Foreigners and Shadows in Italian Literature', in B. Allen and M. Russo (eds), *Revisioning Italy: National Identity and Global Culture*, Minneapolis, MN: Minnesota University Press, 169–90.
—— (1997b) 'Looking Through Non-Western Eyes: Immigrant Women's Autobiographical Narratives in Italian', in G. Brinker-Gabler and S. Smith (eds), *Writing New Identities: Gender, Nation, and Immigration in Contemporary Europe*, Minneapolis, MN: Minnesota University Press, 118–42.

GRAZIELLA PARATI

immigration

Historically, Italy has been a country of outward migration, but by the mid-1990s foreign residents in Italy numbered more than one million, representing nearly 2 per cent of the Italian population (see also **emmigration**). Such a figure may both overstate and understate the actual volume of Italian immigration, if 'immigrant' is interpreted in the most narrow sense of persons seeking to establish themselves in a foreign country for economic reasons or for safety. In fact, nearly 14 per cent of foreigners residing in Italy come from other countries in the **European Union**, and more than 8 per cent of those origination from non-EU countries come from developed economic areas. US citizens, for example, represent the fourth foreign national group. On the other hand, the official figures cannot give any account of the overwhelming presence of undocumented people, who may represent a further 30 to 50 per cent of the legal resident population.

The disproportionate percentage of undocumented foreigners is one of the peculiar features of Italian immigration. This peculiarity derives from two other specific characteristics of Italy as a country of immigration: the fact that it was for a long time a country of emigration, and the fact that the immigration process started quite late. Italy still has more emigrants abroad than foreigners at home; four and a half million Italians live abroad, and Italians still represent the third largest foreign national community in Europe and Japan, and fourth largest in Oceania and America. The net migration flow was reversed at the beginning of the 1970s, but the perception of Italy as a country of emigration continued. This misperception explains why, for a long period, immigration caught Italian policy makers unprepared. They tended to be deeply understanding of immigrants' reasons for coming to Italy, and even turned a benevolent blind eye to clandestine entries and overstaying. The latecomer position of Italy and its role as a subsidiary destination of flows diverted from economically more appealing European countries such as France, which shut their borders after the second oil shock, saw the peak of Italian migratory inflows in the mid-1980s coincide with high rates of unemployment in the country. Residence permits issued by the Home Office totalled 298,749 in 1980, 423,004 in 1985, 781,138 in 1990 and 991,419 in 1995.

By contrast with Italian emigration to Central and Northern Europe during the 1950s and 1960s, or with southern Italians moving to the industrial triangle of northern Italian cities during the '**economic miracle**', foreign immigration into Italy from the 1970s onward was not drawn by economic growth and job opportunities in the 'visible' labour market. In fact, since the 1980s Italian unemployment rates have been relatively high (see **unemployment**), with a resulting high unemployment rate for foreign workers as well. Thus it is likely that increasing immigration flows have been pushed more simply by the increasing economic and demographic gap between developed and developing countries, namely between the northern Mediterranean countries on the one hand and those of the south and east Mediterranean on the other. Some of these flows are undoubtedly also due to administative collapse, political turmoil and civil war in Eastern Europe after the fall of the communist regimes. The largest foreign community in 1996 was the Moroccan (10.91 per cent), while the second largest was the Albanian (5.84 per cent). Residents from the former Yugoslavia numbered 67,850 in 1993, and 89,444 in 1994, though numbers dropped to 51,973 in 1995 and 44,821 in 1996 after the peace process. Since 1990, flows from Eastern Europe have begun to overtake those from North Africa.

There have been few pull factors on Italian immigration. At least until the mid-1990s, Italian policies treated immigrants largely as foreign workers. The first substantial immigration law (December 1986) gave priority to Italians and EU citizens in placement while introducing the principle of equal pay and equal access to social rights for national and foreign workers. The second important law, the so-called 'Martelli Law' (February 1990), named after the deputy prime minister and minister responsible for immigration policy at the time, confirmed the mild and 'labour'-oriented attitude of the Italian government. To overcome the positive discrimination in favour of national labour and to respond to a lack of specific types of labour, in 1993 a special provision made it legal to hire housekeepers individually from abroad. Domestic labour is one of the main components of foreign employment (40 per cent of undocumented aliens legalized by the 1996 provision were domestic workers), made up largely of Filipinos and, increasingly, Peruvians. Nevertheless, the overall national composition of Italian immigration

is extremely fragmented, and many communities only comprise around 1–2 per cent of the total. According to a typical 'globalized' syndrome, recent flows tend to both reinforce regional character (with the top two sources of immigration being Mediterranean countries) and to widen the scope of flows (Filipinos are now the third largest immigrant community).

The prohibition against hiring foreign labour when national or EU labour is available (with the exception of domestic workers mentioned above) was reaffirmed by law in 1998 but is likely to have little effect given the extent of the 'submerged' economy. A survey by the Ministry of Labour in 1995 of a large sample of Italian firms showed the presence of 2.2 per cent of foreign workers, 37 per cent of whom were hired illegally. Besides a consistent demand for domestic servants (Italy is the Western country that makes the greatest use of this kind of labour) and some gap in the availability of labour in areas like agriculture, the building industry and health services, it is the huge submerged economy, especially in southern Italy, that functions as the most relevant pull factor in an immigration process which, all things considered, is mainly driven by push factors.

The three most important immigration laws (1986, 1990 and 1995) also included measures for the legalization of undocumented foreigners. 118,349 aliens were made legal after the 1986 law, 234,841 after 1990. The 1995 decree resulted in 248,501 requests for legalization. However, the third legislation provision was inspired by a new and more severe political attitude towards illegal entry and overstaying.

In fact, Italian policies of immigration had begun to change as early as 1993. This change was mainly due to the necessity of complying with the requirements of stricter border controls and more active repression of international crime imposed by the European partners for Italy's participation in the free circulation space defined by the Schengen Treaty of 1985. Italy signed the Schengen Treaty in November 1990 and ratified it in September 1993, but was only allowed to join the free circulation area in October 1997. In addition to the pressure exerted by the European partners, Italian governments also faced a growing intolerance on the part of Italian public opinion towards petty crime and illegal stays, which in the minds of many Italians were closely associated with each other. According to surveys conducted in the late 1990s, Italians scored highest among European populations in believing that immigrants in their own country were 'too many' (in spite of Italy having one of the lowest ratios of immigrants to total population of any European country), and they were in the middle rank among European countries in terms of racist attitudes.

These converging pressures from the European partners and domestic public opinion for border control and repression were able to influence Italian policies, although these were never guided merely by repressive goals nor simply followed the severe pattern prevailing abroad. The first bill of the 'new wave' was prepared by the Contri Committee, named for the then Minister of Social Affairs, Fernanda Contri. Appointed in October 1993, the committee presented a complete immigration reform bill by the end of February 1994. Because of the fall of the **Ciampi** government in March 1994 the bill was not passed, but eventually the 'technical' government led by **Dini** (January 1995–April 1996) introduced part of the Contri proposals by decree. Livia Turco, Minister for Social Affairs in the **Prodi** Centre–Left government (April 1996–October 1998), appointed more or less the same experts that had served on the Contri Committee and these presented a new bill in February 1997, which became law in 1998. The strategy of all these bills consisted of two parallel strands: implementing repression of illegal and criminal behaviour on one hand, and improving immigrant rights on the other hand. Expulsion of illegal immigrants was facilitated by introducing the possibility of confining them in ad hoc buildings. By the same token, illegal immigrants who cannot be expelled will not be deprived of all rights. In particular, public health facilities (emergencies, maternity, prevention and basic care) as well as education are also made available by law to undocumented immigrants.

Italian immigration policy also diverges from the prevailing European trend with respect to political rights. The 1998 law originally made provision for voting rights in local elections to be extended to immigrants holding a regular permit for five years. Although this article was subsequently expunged because it appeared likely to create constitutional problems, articles 2 and 7 of the 1998 law still refer to political participation and the local vote 'in accordance with our legal system', thus devolving the provision to a constitutional reform. Also in contrast with official attitudes in other European countries, family reunification is facilitated and reunited relatives are allowed to work. The measure is not only aimed at providing immigrants with basic living conditions and the possibility of integration, but also at the elimination of those legal constraints and prohibitions that can force immigrants to break the law. To prevent overstaying and to make employment in the submerged economy less convenient, the 1998 law also allows a six-month legal residence in Italy to foreigners who can rely on a sponsor, a documented immigrant or an Italian citizen, who will support them while they are searching for employment. According to Italian policy makers, detaching the residence permit from employment will also make the immigrant labour market more flexible and able to respond to unforecast needs.

However, the most recent law regarding **citizenship** (February 1992) does not follow the universalistic pattern of other laws. It is more generous towards foreigners of Italian origin and EU citizens, but less generous than before towards other categories of foreigners. Previously, the period of residence required was five years for all, but the 1992 law raised it to ten years for non-EU citizens and reduced it four years for EU citizens and three years for people of Italian origin. In this respect, Italy is now in step with other European countries.

Thus by the late 1990s, Italian immigration policies are converging with European and other traditional countries of immigration like the USA and Australia on the one hand (repression of criminal and illegal behaviour, more strict border control) but also diverging to the extent that Italy is actually increasing immigrants' rights. The more liberal attitude towards immigrant rights has so far been made possible by several specific factors, including the near-uninterrupted stay in government of Centre–Left coalitions and the responsible attitude of the main right-wing party, the Alleanza Nazionale (**National Alliance**). However, both these factors are susceptible to change, and accordingly Italian immigration policy may become less liberal in the future.

Further reading

Birindelli, A.M. and Bonifazi, C. (1993) 'Italy', in L.A. Kosinski (ed.), *Impact of Migration in the Receiving Countries*, Geneva: CICRED.

Heckmann, F. and Bosswick, W. (eds) (1994) 'Immigration Policies in Italy', in *Migration Policies: A Comparative Perspective*, Stuttgart: Enke.

Perlumtter, T. (1996) 'Immigrant Politics Italian Style: The Paradoxical Behaviour of Mainstream and Populist Parties', *South European Society and Politics* 1 (2).

Veuglers, J.W.P. (1994) 'Recent Immigration Politics in Italy: A Short Story', *West European Politics* 17 (2): 33–49.

Zincone, G. (1983) 'Immigrants in Italy: The Three Dimensions of Political Rights', *New Community* 20 (1): 131–45.

GIOVANNA ZINCONE

L'Indice dei libri del mese

Disillusioned with the widespread Italian practice of parochial and partisan book reviewing, a group of intellectuals turned to the *New York Review of Books* as their model, underlining the shift in cultural gravity that had taken place as English replaced French as the principal foreign language of the Italian intelligentsia. The founding editor of *L'Indice dei libri del mese* (Index of Books of the Month), Gian Giacomo Migone, was himself an Americanist, and the declared wider mission of *L'Indice* was to create a critical culture based on pluralism and accountability. At the outset it presented itself as an astringent voice, with elegant layout and reviews of fiction and non-fiction, arts and sciences that cut across genres normally kept segregated. However, in spite of firmly establishing itself as an indispensable and authoritative source of information about publishing in Italy, its circulation never rose above 15,000 and its readership has remained limited mainly to the academic community.

See also: literary journals

ROBERT LUMLEY

industrial design

In contemporary Italy, the concept of industrial design has had a relatively short history. For the most part it originated from the pioneering efforts of the large-scale manufacturers of the 1930s, notable among them being **Olivetti** and **Fiat**. These were among the first Italian producers of modern goods – namely office furniture and automobiles – to look to the USA not only for ideas about how to rationalize their production lines and standardize their products but also about how to sell their mass-produced goods on the basis of their appearance. Thus when Adriano Olivetti employed the graphic designer Marcello Nizzoli in the late 1930s to remodel the company's adding machines and later their typewriters, this was in direct imitation of companies such as Gestetner which had hired the US-based pioneer industrial designer Raymond Loewy to restyle its duplicator and transform it into an icon of modernity.

Instances such as these were relatively rare in the prewar period, but after 1945 they increased considerably as Italian industry, influenced by the presence of American money and expertise, began to adopt a more modern approach to its manufacture. By the end of the 1940s, Italy had evolved its own modern industrial design movement as well as a product style which owed much to American streamlining but which was subtly different at the same time. This was epitomized in a group of objects which collectively exhibited what was called the 'Italian line'. They included Piaggio's new 'Vespa' motorscooter of 1947, which was covered with a bulbous body shell made of pressed metal; Marcello Nizzoli's 'Lexicon 80' typewriter for Olivetti of 1949, which was designed in a 'stripped streamlined' style, noticeably unadorned compared with the chromed detailing of its transatlantic equivalents; the architect Gio **Ponti**'s espresso coffee machine for La Pavoni of 1948, another dramatic exercise with a shiny steel shell; and Pininfarina's 'Cisitalia' automobile of 1951 which, perhaps even more than the others, showed how

Italian designers combined the excitement of streamlining in its American incarnation with a simpler, more sculptural and, by implication, high cultural approach towards the mass-manufactured object, in a quite unique way.

The advances that were made in metal goods in the late 1940s were paralleled soon afterwards in furniture design as that industry was also modernized and transformed. From its craft base in the prewar years, it turned to the international marketplace with highly styled modern products in new materials which represented the new postwar, industrialized Italy to the rest of the world. To do this, furniture designers needed a new profession of industrial designers who could envisage the new aesthetic and apply it to the new goods. While the USA had found its industrial design profession in the ranks of the advertisers and graphic designers who were already skilled in selling goods to a mass audience, Italy took another route and used the services of a new generation of creative individuals who had been trained as architects in the tradition of rationalism but for whom there were very few architectural projects to work on after 1945.

Thus a new group of 'designers for industry' appeared on Italian soil, among them Carlo de Carli, Vico **Magistretti**, Marco **Zanuso**, Roberto Menghi, Ettore **Sottsass** and several others, who all applied their visualizing skills to a whole spectrum of goods, thereby echoing the multidisciplinary approach of their American colleagues. Their background in architecture, however, meant that they took a more purist, less overtly commercial approach. The result was a range of highly innovative products, especially items of furniture but also increasingly electrical goods as well, which helped to establish Italy as an important modern force to be reckoned with in the international arena.

The Olivetti company continued to take an active lead in this area through the 1950s. Marcello Nizzoli designed a range of items for them and also a sewing machine for the Necchi company, among other innovative projects. In 1958, Ettore Sottsass took over the responsibility for the design input into Olivetti's computer division and made a radical impact with his colourful scheme for the Elea 9003, launched in the following year. In the area of furniture and lighting, companies such as Cassina, Artemide, Arteluce, Flos and others brought in the new architect designers to transform their products by providing a modern image for them thereby making them highly desirable to an international marketplace with sophisticated, discerning taste and a commitment to modernity. For Cassina, for example, first Franco **Albini** and later Giò **Ponti** proposed designs which gave the company a very high profile. For Artemide, Marco Zanuso experimented with new synthetic fabrics to create new expressive furniture forms which had no antecedents.

Unlike the American industrial designers who worked with very large commercial offices to support them, the Italian architect designers worked in small groups in modest studios. The furniture companies also remained relatively small, for the most part supplying goods to a wealthy niche market rather than to a mass one. The Italian model of industrial design was more 'fine art' oriented than its American equivalent, and the term *l'estetica industriale* (the industrial aesthetic) was used widely in the 1950s to denote the distinctive Italian phenomenon. However the term *design industriale* gradually came to replace it, as it became increasingly international in nature. In 1956, as a mark of the 'coming of age' of the new profession, the ADI – the Association of Industrial Designers – was formed, and from that date onwards it played a crucial role within Italian economic and cultural life.

See also: architecture and design magazines; design education; interior design

Further reading

Ambasz, E. (ed.) (1972) *Italy: The New Domestic Landscape*, New York: Museum of Modern Art.

Branzi, A. (1984) *The Hot House: Italian New Wave Design*, London: Thames & Hudson.

Fossati, P. (1972) *Il Design in Italia 1945–72* (Design in Italy), Turin: Einaudi.

Gregotti, V. (1982) *Il Disegno industriale italiano: Italia 1880–1980* (Italian Industrial Design, 1880–1980), Milna: Electa.

Sparke, P. (1988) *Italian Design: 1870 to the Present*, London: Thames & Hudson.

PENNY SPARKE

industry

Italy underwent a late and uneven industrial development, and its relative backwardness in the process led the state to play a much more direct and active role than was the case among most other countries in Western Europe. One of the most decisive factors in establishing its pattern of industrial development in the period after the Second World War was the role played by one of fascism's 'leftovers', namely, the State Participation System. Banks, of course, financed industrial growth in the boom after the First World War (see **banking and credit system**). In an early example of a 'bubble economy', banks took equity in productive enterprises as collateral for loans, but when the depression forced firms into bankruptcy, Italian banks were left holding these companies' paper. When the banks themselves were threatened with failure, the Italian state, under Mussolini's Fascist dictatorship, nationalized several important banks (in the name of national interest), and therefore found itself as the 'owner' of a considerable industrial base. These holdings were organized and reorganized under **IRI** (the Institute for Industrial Reconstruction) and its various financial holding companies. Originally viewed as temporary institutions, these soon became permanent. IRI usually organized its financial holding companies by type of enterprise. After 1945, these enterprises played a vital, and in some cases decisive, role in Italy's reconstruction and its emergence as a world-class industrial economy.

The process of late industrialization in Italy had two other important contributors to its industrial patrimony. On the one hand, a series of entrepreneurs, mostly from the northwestern regions, founded large firms in a broad spectrum of sectors that to this day continue to be dominated by family capital. The **Fiat** motor company of the **Agnelli family**, **Pirelli** rubber and tyres, **Olivetti** office machinery and electronics are the best known. The appearance of these firms guaranteed that Italy's growing internal market would be provided with modern goods. On the other hand, the north-eastern and central regions of Italy came to be dominated by a patchwork of small to medium-sized enterprises that developed around textiles, clothing, and footwear as well as in precision machining operations and mini-mills in the steel sector. An important characteristic of the small to medium-sized firms was that their growth depended on exports in highly competitive world markets. In the reconstruction period following the Second World War, the three mainstays of Italian industrialization came together. The state participation sector provided valuable input into both of the other 'pillars' of Italian industry, thus laying the groundwork for the country's '**economic miracle**' and its continued growth to become, by the end of the 1980s, the world's fifth largest economy.

From its very beginnings, however, industrialization was not evenly distributed across Italy's regions (King, 1986). Early recognition of the disadvantages to the South that either resulted from, or were exacerbated by, the unification process led to national inquiries and state attempts to address the problem. It was not until the early 1950s, however, that systematic efforts were undertaken to close the gap in productivity and living standards between the two Italies. The most significant programmes, under the auspices of the **Cassa per il Mezzogiorno** (Southern Development Fund) followed a tripartite logic. First, they called for the establishment of infrastructures that would lay the groundwork for industrial development. Next, incentives and subsidies designed to encourage plant and factory location in the South were implemented. Finally, state participation firms were required to locate specific percentages of new and total investments in the depressed regions. One of the consequences of these initiatives was that the South found itself with a considerable proportion of Italy's heavy and/or capital-intensive industries (such as steel and petrochemicals). Unfortunately, the South also had very few firms that could actually use the products of these so-called 'cathedrals in the desert' in the manufacture of final goods.

Insofar as the state's investments in productive enterprises almost always involved heavy industry, the industrial geography of Italy began to change noticeably after the 1960s. The heavy industries owned by the State, particularly steel (IRI) and petrochemicals (**ENI**, the national hydrocarbons firm), came to dominate investment, employment and output in the previously underdeveloped South. At the same time, inputs from these firms fed into the large-scale mass production enterprises of the northwest, which were mainly in the hands of family capital that had begun to realize the advantages of stock market shares for expanding their enterprises. The small and medium-sized firms of the northeast and central parts of Italy benefited from tax incentives and export subsidies, but had to remain flexibly specialized in order to compete on world markets. This situation has been defined as the phenomenon of the 'Three Italies'.

Even though investments in the South had been quite high through the 1980s, a fundamental flaw in the mechanisms chosen for national and regional economic growth was that the Mezzogiorno did not achieve an autonomous capacity for sustained industrial development. Ironically, at the very time that certain areas in southern Italy were becoming used to the idea of being industrial, a process of tertiarization of the economy, if not a full-blown deindustrialization, had begun. Simultaneously, the weak equity market in Italy made it difficult for the large-scale family firms in the northwest to float financial offerings to raise capital, and globalization made the going tougher for the export-led growth sector of the northeast and centre. Industrial restructuring and readjustment programmes, often painful for entire regions, were decisively implemented, and thus by the mid-1990s a whole new pattern of industrial development was underway.

The new model saw massive privatization, some closures of state participation enterprises, a restructuring of the mass production sector, an invigoration of the competitive drive of flexibly specialized firms through the elimination of export subsidies, and an opening up of the Italian market to more foreign products (see also **privatization and nationalization**). But privatization was only in part a response to industrial problems; there was also a political dimension (albeit with economic overtones). The **European Union**, via its commissions, had come to question the role played by state enterprises in inhibiting trade and competition among the firms of member states (see Masi, 1996). While Italy was not the only country with such holdings, in the 1980s its state participation sector was by far the largest in Europe outside of the then communist bloc. In fact, in its heyday the state participation sector employed nearly three quarters of a million people and was engaged in activities that covered iron and steel, cement, engineering, shipbuilding, hydrocarbons, chemicals, textiles and other manufacturing. The holdings also extended into the service sector, including airlines, highways, shipping, radio and telephones.

Privatization of the state participation sector was supposed to be an ongoing effort. In the original mandate of the IRI, for example, individual firms, once placed back on a solid financial and productive footing, were to be returned to private hands. Occasionally this was done, but for the most part, until the mid-1980s, the state participation sector grew rapidly, sometimes by continuing 'salvaging' operations and sometimes by creating wholly new enterprises. The latter involved sectors into which private capital either could not venture, because of high costs or simply would not, due to perceived high risks. While these firms for the most part did exactly what they were supposed to do, political pressures to absorb local labour eventually led many to require state aid. Given the sectors in which they operated, especially steel, restructuring efforts involving such aid had to be approved by the European Commission in Brussels. The trade-off demanded for supplying funds for restructuring was a reduction in productive capacity, and a consequence of this was often a withdrawal of the state from ownership altogether in order to avoid aid being funnelled illegally to such enterprises. The first major privatization effort involved the sale of the Alfa Romeo automotive division to Fiat, and this established a pattern of the sale of 'national champions' to local industrialists rather than through a process of large-scale public offerings of stocks. By far the largest privatization was the absorption of the old **Finsider–Italsider–Ilva** integrated steel-making centres (whose most important productive activities were in Taranto, in Italy's southeastern region) to mini-mill operators Lucchini and Riva from Lombardy (in the northwest, mainly centred near Brescia).

Three key factors in Italy's successful reconstruction after the Second World War and its overtaking of the United Kingdom in terms of gross domestic product by the end of the 1980s were modern technology, flexible specialization and the production of high value-added goods (Locke, 1995). In the transformation of its steel industry from a minor competitor to the second largest producer in the European Union (after Germany), Italy's state participation sector invested heavily in the latest metallurgical engineering advances. Its flagship operation was the integrated steel complex at Taranto, which in the 1980s was Europe's largest. While the principal product of the state sector was basic or crude steel (with some specialized items for the automotive, oil and gas industries), mini-mill operators in Italy's North specialized in single products, most notably concrete reinforcement bars. Indeed, they practically cornered that market, to the dismay of the Coal and Steel Commission of the European Union. The industrial districts of the centre and northeast combined new technologies with a highly skilled labour force and dense networks of social and commercial relations to produce goods to exacting standards and customer specifications. In fact, the clothing industry in Italy has firms that are based as much on advanced manufacturing techniques as on high fashion design.

The tight linkages between textile and garment producers in Italy have allowed Italian firms to dominate some sectors (women's stockings, for example) or be market leaders in others (such as luxury men's clothing). Recently, however, there has been some movement toward vertical integration rather than on the more traditional co-operative efforts. At the same time, the large manufacturers of the northwest have begun a process of decentralization of their productive enterprises. Indeed, years after the incentive programmes for the industrialization of the Mezzogiorno ceased, many large manufacturers have discovered the advantages of locating in Italy's South. Fiat now has its largest manufacturing plant outside of Melfi in Basilicata, but has also located smaller components factories in adjacent regions as well. At the end of the 1990s, the Melfi plant had one of the world's best productivity records. Fiat itself is the world's fifth largest automotive producer, second in Europe only to Volkswagen. In general, while Italian enterprises have emphasized the importance of competitiveness in the global market, they have generally chosen to compete on quality rather than on price.

Insofar as Italy is heavily dependent on the import of petroleum, its industries suffered considerably from the oil shocks of the 1970s. The subsequent restructuring process saw an interesting mixture of adaptive strategies on the national level involving government policies, national business associations and the trade union movement, and on the local level involving stakeholders and interest groups.

The transformation of the Italian economy and in particular of its manufacturing sector in the postwar period has been accompanied by abrupt shifts in government policies, political alignments and the country's industrial relations system. Eventually, however, Italy moved from policies that favoured a form of planning to those that merely fostered a good business climate. In so doing, it also moved dramatically to privatize its state participation holdings, some of which were its national champions, in its successful effort to compete on a world scale and become an integral member of the European Union. As Italy's Communist Party (**PCI**) became the Democratic Party of the Left (**PDS**), its traditional strong alliance with the largest left-wing trade union (CGIL) weakened and the latter, together with its more moderate trade union partners, began pursuing national level negotiations directly with government and the employers' association (**Confindustria**).

The distribution of product and labour force by industrial sector in Italy continues to change as the country's economy responds to both internal institutional pressures and external pressures based on tighter economic and monetary union with European partners and greater global competition in more open markets. Significant regional differences continue to characterize Italian industrial geography, but seem not to have worsened as the state has withdrawn from direct subsidization of the poorer areas of the South. Italian firms are increasingly present on foreign markets both in terms of the sale of goods produced in Italy and as owners or partners of enterprises located in other countries. Italy's equity markets are expanding rapidly, and thus new avenues for financing productive enterprises are also developing. The continued emphasis on high value-added products, technological innovation, integration via networks or acquisitions, and flexible specialization should allow Italy's industrial structure to adapt successfully to emerging and ever-changing world markets.

See also: postwar reconstruction; Third Italy; trade unions

Further reading

King, R. (1985) *The Industrial Geography of Italy,* London: Croom Helm.

Locke, R.M. (1995) *Remaking the Italian Economy,* Ithaca, NY: Cornell University Press.

Masi, A.C. (1989) 'Deindustrialization, Economic Performance, and Industrial Policy: British and American Theories Applied to Italy,' in R.E. Foglesong and J.D. Wolfe (eds), *The Politics of Economic Adjustment: Pluralism, Corporatism, and Privatisation,* New York: Greenwood Press.

Pichierri, A. (ed.) (1986) *Il declino industriale* (Industrial Decline), Turin: Rosenberg & Sellier (a collection of essays dealing with the erosion of the manufacturing base in areas of traditional industrial development).

ANTHONY C. MASI

Infascelli, Fiorella

b. 29 October 1952, Rome

Film director

Widely acknowledged as one of Italy's most interesting female directors, Fiorella Infascelli began her career in advertising and later worked as assistant director to Pier Paolo **Pasolini**, Giuseppe **Bertolucci** and Bernardo **Bertolucci**. In 1980 she directed *Ritratto di donna distesa* (Portrait of Reclining Woman) for the **RAI**, a short video about a psychoanalytic session which was well received in several film festivals. Soon after she shot a series of interview portraits which included Luciano **Pavarotti** and Roberto **Benigni**. In 1987 she wrote and directed *La maschera* (The Mask), an abstract and symbolic tale of seduction set in the eighteenth century starring Helena Bonham Carter, and in 1991 the more realistic *Zuppa di pesce* (Fish Soup), an account of Infascelli's youth set in her family's seaside villa (her father Carlo, here played by Philippe Noiret, was a major

film producer). These two divergent features demonstrate Infascelli's various and contrasting talents as both sophisticated auteur and commercial director.

ADRIANA MONTI

L'Informale

Derived from the French *art informel,* a term widely used to describe non-figurative abstract art which is spontaneous and improvisational, the concept has also sometimes been translated into Italian as *informalismo,* and into English as 'informalism' and 'art without form'. To confuse matters further, it has also been called 'lyrical abstraction' and 'Tachism'.

Essentially, the term is applied to art in which the creative process is controlled by the subconscious and not by a preconceived plan. The art produced may at times resemble depictions of objects, but it is not intended to do so and in fact is meant more as the visual record of the process of its own making. In its use of the subconscious, *L'Informale* relates back to surrealism. In its display of the mark of the artist at the moment of creation it is gestural, and thus closely related to American abstract expressionism and action painting, though the closeness of this relation continues to be the subject of critical debate. The relationship is sometimes described as one of parallel development.

The style was rare in Italy until the early 1950s, at which time it came to dominate abstract art. In part this reflected a change from the influence of Picasso and post-cubism to the adoption of new American models such as Jackson Pollock (a tendency encouraged, it has been suggested, by American agencies eager to provide an alternative to left-wing culture in Italy during the Cold War). Nevertheless, it was never a movement with a fixed membership. Artists moved in and out of *L'Informale,* and some works are difficult to classify. In 1952 Michel Tapié, the French critic who had originally coined the term, identified some Italian artists as having 'informal' qualities, particularly Giuseppe Capogrossi, Gianni Dova, Mario Sironi, and Marino **Marini**, though this related more to a gestural quality perceivable in their work than to their overall style.

Fontana's rendering of the surface of canvases, leaving holes and tears, is not a pattern or a representation but the result of the process of the artist's breaking through and physically violating the surface, an action which painters are usually at pains not to do. Hence his work is gestural. Alberto **Burri** was similarly expressive in his undisguised use of raw materials such as sacks, wood and iron.

After 1956, devices such as the dripping of paint on the surface became more commonplace, as with Toti **Scialoja**. Typical are the works of Emilio **Vedova**. His canvases from the late 1950s are great gestural action paintings, like the works of the American abstract expressionists, with all the inventive grace of a tornado in a soup kitchen. At the same time the 'nuclear artists', including Enrico **Baj**, Giò **Pomodoro** and Piero **Manzoni**, experimented with *informel* techniques, and condemned the right angle and the cold mechanical qualities of geometrical abstraction.

After this period of romantic individualism and freedom of expression, there was a return to objectivity and finite forms, marked by the *Possibilità di relazione* exhibition in Rome in 1960. Pop and minimalism each signalled a subsequent turning away from spontaneous expressiveness to a more calculated art.

See also: art movements

Further reading

Calvesi, M. (1989) 'Informel and Abstraction in Italian Art of the Fifties', in E. Braun (ed.), *Italian Art in the 20th Century: Painting and Sculpture, 1900–1988*, Munich: Prestel Verlag.

MAX STAPLES

information agencies

Information agencies are regulated by the Italian Press Law (law 47/1948) and officially controlled by the **President of the Republic**. Their task is to collect and distribute news, mainly to established clients.

Agenzie di Stampa (press agencies) and Agenzie d'Informazione (information agencies) are distinguishable by the type of information they supply and their mode of distribution. While the former work on a continuous basis (see examples below), the latter provide information to their clients only periodically. The latter are also normally linked to certain pressure or lobby groups (for example, AGA, founded in 1953 as an agency of the employers' organization, the **Confindustria**, or ASCA, founded by the **DC** politician Flaminio Piccoli to service the newspaper *L'Osservatore Romano*). Their clients are generally the mass media as well as financial institutions and industrial or political groups (parties, interest groups, trade unions).

Founded in Rome as a co-operative in 1945, the Agenzia Nazionale Stampa Associata (**Ansa**) is the most important Italian information agency. The structure of Ansa, with its eighteen regional and ninety offices worldwide, assures its dominant position. Forty-three publishing companies participate in the co-operative, and it is associated with other major international news agencies such as AFP, Reuters and UPI. The Italian and English news services cover all domestic and international political, economic and cultural events. Each day more than 100 national newspapers,100 national radio stations and nearly 100 international newspapers receive news items from Ansa.

AGI (Agenzia Italia; after 1960, Agenzia Giornalistica Italia) is the second largest information agency. Founded in 1950, AGI became part of the **ENI** Group in 1960 when it was completely restructured. The agency was traditionally classified as politically left-wing. At present it belongs to the publishing group of the newspaper *Il Giorno* and has a strong reputation for its reporting in the economic area. Collaboration with international news agencies (AP, Dow Jones, Associated Press, ITAR-TASS) provides AGI with up-to-the-minute information on world politics, arts and general news.

AdnKronos is the third important information agency. It resulted from the merger of two agencies, ADN and Kronos, in 1960. Under its president and editor-in-chief, Giuseppe Marra, the AdnKronos Group was influenced by socialist thinking. In alliance with international agencies such DPA, USA Today, Times, JIJI Press and Xian Hua, it provides its subscribers with national and international news items as well as offering special services such as developing and managing communication plans and strategies. In 1994 the AdnKronos Group was expanded to include the AdnKronos Salute (Health) agency

On the initiative of some independent private radio stations, the agency Area was founded in 1983. Area delivers news programmes to more than 150 private stations and is linked with the broadcasting network Sper and the radio network Rete 105. During the Gulf Crisis of 1991, Area entered into a contract with CNN and still broadcasts CNN news.

JAN KURZ

Ingrao, Pietro

b. 30 March 1915, Lenola, Latina

Politician

Editor of *L'Unità* from 1947 to 1957, Ingrao became the charismatic unofficial leader of the **PCI**'s left wing and a strong proponent of direct democracy. The clash between Ingrao and right-wing leader **Amendola** dominated party debate in the 1960s. Fearful that the Right's strategy of political alliances would lead to working-class integration into the system, Ingrao called instead for class-based alliances across party lines and greater internal party democracy. He responded to repeated defeats by accepting the majority line and working to restore unity. His election as the first communist president of the lower house in 1976 reflected the wide respect he enjoyed. True to form, after unsuccessfully opposing **Occhetto**'s plan for transforming the party with a counter-proposal for refounding communism, Ingrao nevertheless remained in Occhetto's **PDS** for the next two years.

Further reading

Amyot, G. (1981) *The Italian Communist Party,* London: Croom Helm (discusses Ingrao's popular front strategy).

CLAIRE KENNEDY

INPS

By far the most important agency for social security in Italy, INPS (Istituto Nazionale della Previdenza Sociale, or National Social Security Institute) was created in 1933 by the merger of a number of existing insurance funds. Hand in hand with the widening of social welfare provisions during the following sixty years, INPS has administered the collection of compulsory contributions from employers and employees and the distribution of pensions to both employees of private firms and autonomous workers (farmers and sharecroppers, craftsmen, shopkeepers and all the professions). A bureaucratic and financial giant, at the beginning of the 1990s it insured 19 million workers (85 per cent of total national employment) and distributed 14.2 million pensions, which accounted for over 45 per cent of social security expenditure (thus equalling 10 per cent of gross national product). However, the role of INPS became even more extensive since, as well administering retirement and disability pensions, it was appointed to manage all the main social security services: on behalf of the state, it now collects tax deductions and contributions to the National Health Service, distributes 'social pensions', a wide number of grants (family allowances, illness and unemployment benefits), and administers the Cassa Integrazione Guadagni (a fund which pays a benefit to the temporary unemployed) and severance payouts.

From the early 1980s onwards, INPS recorded large deficits as contributions proved inadequate to cover the surging amount of expenditures. This forced governments to subsidize it, thus contributing to an increasing deficit in the national budget. Affected by all the inefficiencies typical of giant bureaucratic organizations, it was reorganized in 1989 in order to make both collection and distribution more effective and timely. New directors were appointed to improve managerial standards and its budget was relieved of a number of undue burdens, all of which led to a remarkable recovery in economic performance. Thanks also to the 1994–5 reform of the pension system, INPS ceased to be a time bomb under the public purse.

See also: health services; social welfare

STEFANO BATTILOSSI

intellectuals

The social and political role of Italian intellectuals, and in particular the related ethics and obligations of such a role, came into dramatic crisis in the 1990s due to new factors such as globalization, information technology and the influence of the media (see **Berlusconi**). Such factors diminished the position of intellectuals in the 1990s, whereas for most of the postwar period they had been accorded a central role in Italian society. This privileged position was fostered above all by Benedetto **Croce** in 1902–45, then expressed most of all in the works of Antonio **Gramsci** and only gradually challenged after the 1970s by the views of Norberto **Bobbio** and more particularly by Umberto **Eco**.

In the nineteenth century, only a tiny proportion of the Italian middle class had either secondary or tertiary education. Moreover, the self-appointed intellectual and idealist middle-class leaders of the Risorgimento, men like Mazzini, the fratelli Bandiera and others belonging to the movement of the Giovane Italia (Young Italy) all failed disastrously to achieve their aims. In the end it was practical men, politicians and administrators, who succeeded in creating a united Italy and even a figure like Garibaldi 'obeyed'. This resulted in a particular conception of the intellectual becoming dominant between 1902 and 1945. It was promoted above all by the influential Neapolitan historian, literary critic and philosopher Benedetto Croce, the 'lay pope' of Italy, in the pages of the journal *Critica* and through the activity of the Laterza publishing house in Bari. Despite his open opposition to fascism, expressed in his *Appeal to the Intellectuals* of 1925, Croce's idealist notion of intellectuals distanced from life and politics strongly influenced Italian thinkers throughout the interwar period and continued to be promoted

after 1945 by the journal *Belfagor*, edited by Luigi Russo. In the 1960s and 1970s many Italians, even those on the Left like Giovanni Saragat, President of Italy, acknowledged that Croce's ideas dominated their sense of themselves.

Croce made Liberty into a sort of religion to rival that of the Roman Catholic church. Taking stock of the failures of his romantic predecessors and the success in politics of practical men of positivist persuasion, Croce stated that the task of intellectuals was to remain 'above the struggle' and to engage in a serene search for the truth through a free exchange of ideas. Despite his own neo-Hegelian historicism, and his admiration for nationalistic figures such as Spaventa and de Sanctis, Croce was not himself a strong nationalist and he identified Liberty with the development of Europe as a whole, a view he expressed most forcefully in his *Storia d'Europa*, published in 1932 in the heyday of fascism. Croce's ivory tower notion of intellectual work, his contempt for politics and for democracy, his disdain for folklore and for the common man and in particular his sharp separation of art and philosophy all made his ideas increasingly unpalatable to the postwar anti-fascist generation that had been educated in the Crocean mould during the fascist period.

After 1950 the pre-eminence of this notion of the intellectual was replaced by one based on the prison notebooks of Antonio Gramsci (published posthumously 1946–52). Gramsci described the intellectual class as all those who gave theoretical and practical organization to the different practices of social reproduction, like technicians, economists, trade union and party leaders. This view expanded the role accorded to the intellectual in polemical contrast to the Crocean view. As its publication corresponded with an explosion in education and the transformation of Italy from a peasant to an industrial economy, it became enormously popular.

Gramsci's view stressed the necessary involvement of the intellectuals in politics and in everyday life, suggesting that, through their organizational work, intellectuals could construct a more human and progressive national culture. Gramsci believed that Croce's focus on the universal and the cosmopolitan had led Italian intellectuals to ignore the sufferings of the Italian people and so Gramsci denied the cosmopolitan aspect of the intellectual in favour of the national. He stressed that only when the views of the populace ('those who feel') complemented those of the intellectuals ('those who know') could a national popular culture emerge. Where Croce's intellectual stayed at home in the study and read the great works of European culture, the Gramscian intellectual entered politics to defeat the hegemony of such bourgeois ideas using the national cultural icons as a starting point.

This Gramscian conception was strongly promulgated by the communist journal **Rinascita** (1944–) and through the publishing houses of **Einaudi** and Riuniti. Huge numbers of 'intellectuals' became communists after 1945 as young Croceans defected and rival parties of intellectuals collapsed. Other major points of reference for Gramscian intellectuals were the journals *Società* (1945) and **Il Politecnico** (1945–7) which attracted figures as different as Ranuccio Bianchi Bandinelli, the musician Igor Markevitch, and the writer Elio **Vittorini**. An entire neo-realist generation of the cinema including Luchino **Visconti**, Roberto **Rossellini** and Vittorio **de Sica** adopted the communist/Gramscian intellectual role as their own, as did painters like Renato **Guttuso**, writers like Carlo **Levi** and the later writer, poet and filmmaker Pier Paolo **Pasolini**.

Communist insistence that the intellectuals 'go to school' with the working classes and learn from them provoked continuing tension in the 1950s and 1960s. Led by its national general secretary, Palmiro **Togliatti**, the Communist Party (see **PCI**) insisted that all its new intellectual members and supporters accept its understanding of what was artistically and intellectually progressive. This developed into a struggle for the patrimony of Gramsci's ideas which was only resolved in the late 1960s by which time he had become the 'Gramsci di tutti' (Gramsci belonging to all).

Where Croce had demanded a position of 'au dessus de la mêlée' (above the fray) and Gramsci one of actively building a counter-hegemony of ideas to those which justified an unjust social order built on class exploitation, a third view now started to win ground. This had grown out of ideas developed in the **Resistance** against fascism by Giustizia e Libertà, (Justice and Freedom) but which went back to the nineteenth-century traditions of liberal socialism whose first leaders were Piero Gobetti and Carlo Rosselli. This view suggested that the intellectual should oppose received truths with an activism which, while political, was not party political. The leading spokesman for this was Norberto Bobbio, whose opinions remained marginal until the 1980s when Italian communism went into crisis.

All three positions outlined above shared a common Eurocentrism and a strong sense of national and coherent intellectual history. Gramsci, whose preferred interlocutors were Vico, Machiavelli and Labriola, merely enlarged upon the Crocean pantheon. Bobbio added Cattaneo and Salvemini. All three shared an affection for Gobetti, and all their sources of inspiration consequently also became inspirations for the Italian intellectual. Clearly, however, all three focused much more on where Italians had come from than on where they were going, regardless of their differing assessments of that national history. They looked back to an Italy where most people were **peasants**, where the educated lived in small regional towns and where the tiny class of educated to which they belonged were known familiarly as intellectuals and *did* provide leadership. If Croce had snarled that he could not 'take his ways from proverbs', Gramsci had thought good sense could be found in the common sense of the masses and Bobbio had believed that a sparrow's view was more useful than that of an eagle, all were nevertheless concerned about the middle class from which they came since in fact, until 1945, it had been the only 'national class'.

All three knew little about the USA and the non-European world, or what industrialization and post-industrial society might mean. The Gramscian view was still dominant when *Time* magazine wrote that California started in Milan. The communists resisted bitterly any such suggestion, and opposed those who suggested American literature should be studied as a way of throwing light on Italy's future. Intellectuals like Vittorini and **Pavese** (and by the 1960s, the big-screen epic cineastes), were decried for their openness to the new world.

Umberto Eco and the **Gruppo 63**, although once communist in orientation, replied by insisting on the reality that Italy was an industrial society and that US sociology and literature were signposts to what that would mean. As the 1960s passed, their view that the intellectual's role was much more limited than that ascribed by Gramsci gained support. After 1968, large numbers of young communist intellectuals left the party and joined small parties like Potere operaio and Giovane critica (Negri, Tronti) and a very much less unified notion of the intellectual became current in Italy.

The 1970s were a watershed, as the sons and daughters of the intellectuals turned on their fathers in the student, and then the terrorist, movements. While the Communist Party made common cause with others in defence of liberal democracy, the failure to return to the direct democratic tradition of Italy's medieval and Renaissance past, which was tried in the 1970s, led to widespread disillusionment with politics. The resort to **terrorism** and the denial of the role of reason and ideas in changing society for the better greatly discredited the Gramscian position, which privileged intellectuals as the leaders of social change. Bobbio's famous condemnation of the relevance of deeply held beliefs in direct democracy, which went back via Gramsci to communal traditions, marked a reorientation in Italian politics in favour of liberal democracy.

The 1980s were a period when even the originally vital women's movement came to a halt before the obdurate and uncontrollable nature of economics and capitalist society. An ever more unpopular Communist Party sought solutions in Eurocommunism, leaving behind the notion that enlightened masses could remake the world in a gigantic effort of will. For the first time, the humanist Italian philosophies started to give way to structuralist views, mainly of French origin. Their pessimism of the will contrasted totally with the celebrated Gramscian dictum: 'Pessimism of the intellect, optimism of the will'. The world as a prison of language started to win over even the women's movement.

In the 1990s, the notion of a lay pope or of a leading intellectual as ethical spokesman lingers on only in octogenarians like Bobbio. The Italian intellectual of the decade is much more a person who plays with ideas on the one hand and acts as a technician in a limited realm on the other, without laying any claim to interpret the way the world works. The literary/legal middle-class intellectual

about whom the great theorists wrote has been replaced by a new technical, service specialist, frequently a computer specialist. Italy, where the state once controlled all audio-visual media, has become a place of myriad private conflicting voices in radio, television and even the press, complemented by a few private monopolies like those of Berlusconi which manipulate political images. To this proliferation of voices from below correspond new intellectual concerns with neglected subjects like **psychoanalysis**, **feminism**, **semiotics** and cybernetics.

Further reading

Ajello, N. (1979) *Intelletuali e PCI 1944/1958* (Intellectuals and the PCI 1944–1958), Bari: Laterza.

Bobbio, N. (1995a) *Ideological Profile of Twentieth Century Italy*, Princeton, NJ: Princeton University Press.

—— (1995b) 'Intellectual Biography', trans. T. Chatway, *Political Expressions* 1 (1): 51–65.

Bosworth, R. and Rizzo, G. (eds) (1983) *Altro Polo: Intellectuals and their Ideas in Contemporary Italy*, Sydney: May Foundation, University of Sydney.

Davidson, A. (1998) 'Norberto Bobbio, Liberal Socialism and the Problem of Language', *Citizenship Studies* 2 (1): 223–45.

ALASTAIR DAVIDSON

intelligence services

In the post-1945 world, dominated by the Cold War, the secret services evolved rapidly from their traditional role in espionage and counter-espionage towards a much wider and more complex position in both information and national security, thus gaining an unprecedented political relevance. Nowhere was this more true than in Italy.

As with most areas of state administration, the intelligence services of the Italian Republic maintained a strong continuity with the past. The civilian intelligence, the Ufficio Affari Riservati (Confidential Affairs Office) under the Ministry of Home Affairs – first established in 1919 and transformed by the Fascist regime into an arm of social control and political repression – emerged virtually unchanged, both in its structure and staff, to continue to serve successive Republican governments. The reorganization of military intelligence was slower but eventually led in 1949 to the establishment of SIFAR (Servizio Informazioni Forze Armate, or Armed Forces Information Service) under the Ministry of Defence. SIFAR's main task was to integrate and co-ordinate the activities of the individual information services of the army, navy and air force. A number of links were also established with the American CIA and the secret services of other European countries, shielded by the NATO treaty. Soon, however, SIFAR also undertook the surveillance of the activities of unions, parties and politicians within Italy.

Neither civilian nor military intelligence were under any effective parliamentary control. Moreover, during the hard times of the Cold War, the proliferation of 'parallel' units within the intelligence services led to looser control by the government and by even by the ministers in charge. Among these 'parallel' units was '**Gladio**', a secret organization established in 1956 whose existence, long denied, was finally officially admitted by the government in 1990. This paramilitary organization was based on an agreement between CIA and SIFAR within the so-called 'stay behind' operation – a secret network established by America in several European countries, officially in order to counteract any hostile invasion or communist insurrection. Gladio's activities, however, were never open to public scrutiny and in spite of the alleged legitimacy and 'patriotism' later claimed for it by high dignitaries like Giulio **Andreotti** and Francesco **Cossiga**, the organization appears to have been involved in a wide range of illegal activities, such as retention of arms and explosives and the secret gathering of information on politicians.

Other sectors of the Italian intelligence services also proved to have ambivalent loyalties to the democratic process. This emerged for the first time in 1966, when investigation by the press and a parliamentary commission of enquiry revealed the existence of secret plans devised by the Carabinieri corps, led by General Giovanni De Lorenzo (former head of SIFAR), to arrest a number of

politicians and union leaders in a sort of *coup d'état*. The plans had been dangerously close to being put into action in June 1964, during a crisis of the centre–left government. Some years later, judicial enquiries into the so-called 'strategy of tension' – a long series of bloody bomb attacks, including one in Milan's **Piazza Fontana** in 1969 and one at a union meeting at Brescia's Piazza della Loggia in 1975 – brought to light suspicious links between sectors of the military secret service – renamed SID (Servizio Informazioni Difesa, or Defence Information Service) in 1965 after harsh internal conflicts had led to a semblance of reform – and terrorist groups of the radical Right. In 1974 the head of the SID, Vito Miceli, was even charged with complicity (though in the end acquitted by a controversial sentence) with other generals and neo-fascist activists, in the farcical *coup d'état* attempted in 1970 by Prince Junio Valerio Borghese (a former commander of Fascist troops during the Republic of Salò in 1944–5). In the same year, senior officers of the SID were also proven to be members of a neo-fascist organization the Rosa dei Venti (Wind Rose), which the judiciary held responsible for a range of terrorist activities. In most cases the intelligence services were shown to be responsible for misleading the judicial enquiries by tampering with evidence or providing false evidence.

The disclosure of such 'parallel' networks within the SID led to heated political confrontations, and public alarm at the lack of democratic accountability of the intelligence services finally prompted **Parliament** to pass a reform bill in 1977. The bill established a supervisory parliamentary commission and placed the secret services under the stricter and more systematic control of the prime minister. SID was also replaced by SISMI (Servizio per le Informazioni e la Sicurezza Militare, or Information and Military Security Service), while a new civilian Intelligence, SISDE (Servizio per le Informazioni e la Sicurezza Democratica, or Service for Information and Democratic Security) was created particularly in order to co-ordinate the activities of a wide range of anti-terrorist bodies. Both SISMI and SISDE were put under the co-ordination of a joint structure, CESIS (Comitato Esecutivo per i Servizi di Informazione e di Sicurezza, or Information and Security Services

Executive Committee). In the event, the results of the reform proved rather disappointing. The parliamentary commission was only given limited powers, and the reorganization of the reformed intelligence services proved to be slow and sometimes only partial. Judicial enquiries, endless trials and a parliamentary commission of enquiry repeatedly questioned the role of SISDE during the kidnapping of Aldo **Moro** by the **Red Brigades** in 1978, and disturbing evidence of misleading activities and links with the extreme Right were also uncovered by the judiciary during its investigation of the terrorist bomb attack at the Bologna railway station of 2 August 1980. All the senior officers in charge in SISMI, SISDE and CESIS also later proved to be members of the secret masonic lodge **P2**, which many considered a subversive organization.

The discovery of such ambivalent allegiances resulted, between 1982 and 1984, in the most massive turnover of officers in the history of the intelligence services. Since then, control by both the government and the Parliament has been successfully enforced, officers of assured democratic loyalty have been appointed and 'parallel' units have been gradually dismantled. After the end of the Cold War and the collapse of traditional parties, political control of the intelligence services has withered to the point where, once the political consequences of the Gladio affair faded away, the services largely stopped being used as an arm in battles between party factions and state bodies. The one exception appeared to be in 1993–4 at a judicial enquiry relating to secret funds allegedly used by SISDE to assure the support of politicians and which attempted to involved Oscar Luigi **Scalfaro**, the President of the Republic. The allegations raised much controversy but in the end remained unproven. Thus in more recent times, the Italian intelligence services have been able to claim a more legitimate function in a democratic society, and have become a more efficient organization performing a decisive role in supporting the state in its struggle against both **terrorism** and organized crime.

Further reading

De Lutiis G. (1991) *Storia dei servizi segreti in Italia* (A History of the Secret Services in Italy), Rome: Editori Riuniti (a well-informed, but ideologically biased history of the Italian intelligence services and their role in the political life of postwar Italy; updated to 1990).

STEFANO BATTILOSSI

interior design

Italian interior design flourished in the 1950s and 1960s as one aspect of the work of the architect-designers who came to the fore in that decade. All the key Italian designers who made a name for themselves in the postwar period – among them Vico **Magistretti**, Marco **Zanuso**, Giò **Ponti**, Ettore **Sottsass**, Achile **Castiglioni**, Alberto **Rosselli** and others – were trained as architects in the years prior to the Second World War. The dominant architectural ideology of that period was that of rationalism, Italy's version of the modern movement which dominated avantgarde European activity through the work of such key individuals as Le Corbusier, Walter Gropius and Mies van der Rohe. A number of significant architectural projects, among them Piero Bottoni's Electric House of 1930 and Luciano Baldessari's Craja Bar of the same year, were realized in Italy at this time, demonstrating the strong, typically modernist links between the inside and outside of the building and a creative use of space, and light and minimal geometric decoration with primary colours used to accentuate the internal structure and the intersection of planes within the interiors.

This dramatically modern approach towards the interior moved into the postwar period as the new architect-designers attempted to set up their practices in the new climate. Much of their attention was devoted to exhibition design, an important facet of modernist interior design of these years. Back in the mid-1930s Marcello Nizzoli had designed a structure for the Aeronautical Exhibition in Milan's Galleria Vittorio Emmanuele, which had consisted of a complex grid crossed in the form of an aeroplane. This innovative approach to exhibition design, based on modernist principles, moved into the postwar period. It was especially obvious in the **Milan**

Triennales where the designers created not only the objects on display but the display itself. Ettore Sottsass's setting for the room of Italian glass at the 1957 Triennale was a case in point, where the drama of the grid-like structure that he created competed with the glass itself for attention.

The **Castiglioni** brothers, Livio, Pier Giacomo and Achille, were well versed in exhibition design and Achille was later to work on a number of notable interiors and spaces, among them the lighting for the 10th Triennale of 1954 and a *sala espressioni* (expressive room) in 1964 for Ideal Standard in Milan. In 1962 he worked on an interior for the Gavina showroom in Milan, while a few years earlier he had been responsible for the design of the Splugen Brau restaurant, also in Milan.

All the architect-designers who set up their practices in the decade following the Second World War worked on private interiors as a means of making a living in a period when there were very few architectural commissions in evidence. Many of them, Carlo de Carli, Ignazio **Gardella** and Vico Magistretti among them, worked on furniture for the new mass housing, concentrating on minimal, flexible forms destined for modest living spaces. They developed a range of chairs, bookshelves and other small items which could constitute the essential furnishings for the new apartment dwellings. While they also worked on more luxurious interiors for the wealthy inhabitants of Milan who wanted to show that they participated in the new style – among them, for instance, Ettore Sottsass's interior for Signor Ghedini of 1953 in which he used paintings on the wall to decorative effect – it was the restaurants, shop interiors and showrooms which attracted international attention and filled the pages of the glossy magazines. For example, Igazio Gardella's Olivetti showroom in Dusseldorf, designed in 1960, was a minimal setting with typewriters and adding machines placed on plinths as in an art gallery. Carlo **Scarpa**'s showroom in Venice was an even more severe space, relieved only by the grain of the marble he used.

By the 1960s the modern Italian interior had become associated with the idea of 'Italian chic'. No sophisticated interior was complete without an 'Arco' light designed by Achille Castiglioni, hovering over a white sofa and a glass and chrome coffee table. Lighting objects in fact played a key role within the spaces that were envisaged, creating dramatic effects and acting as sculptural forms in the elegant settings in which they were placed. Countless 'B' Italian movies boasted such interiors, a mark of modern sophistication and wealth. The democratic ideals of the early postwar years were replaced by signs of conspicuous consumption. The brightly coloured plastic chairs, designed by Marco Zanuso, Vico Magistretti and Joe **Colombo**, were not democratic statements but an attempt to show that even that material could be made to look chic and expensive.

Colombo was responsible for a number of interior settings as well as for individual furniture items which became icons of Italian modernity. His striking spatial compositions used intersecting planes, lighting and colour to dramatic effect, and he used objects he had designed himself to provide sophisticated details. He found minimal, technological solutions to the problem of illumination in lights such as his 1965 'Spider' for O'Luce, which could be attached to a wall or positioned on a flat surface.

By the early 1970s, the idea of Italian design had become synonymous with that of the sophisticated, modern interior and Italian furniture items, used sparingly, with a creative use of lighting and strong colours, played a key role in these spaces. In 1972, the exhibition held at New York's Museum of Modern Art, entitled 'Italy: the New Domestic Landscape' developed this theme and contained a series of what were described as 'micro environments', a cross between architecture and interior design.

See also: architectural and design magazines

Further reading

Aloi, R. (1956) *L'arredamento moderno* (Modern Interior Design), Milan: Hoepli.

Baroni, D. (1981) *L'oggetto lampada: forma e funzione* (The Object Lamp: Form and Function), Milan: Electa.

Massoni, L. (1986) *Made in Italy: Mobili, illuminazione, complementi di arredamento* (Made in Italy:

Furniture, Lighting, Interior Furnishings), Milan: Mondadori.

PENNY SPARKE

IRI

During the Great Depression of the 1930s, the government and the **Banca d'Italia** (Bank of Italy) provided large amounts of last-resort cash to the three largest Italian banks in order to save from bankruptcy both the banks themselves and the industrial companies they controlled. As a result of this operation, the state came to own a large share (about 45 per cent) of the companies listed in Italy's stock exchanges. To manage these companies, IRI (Istituto per la Ricostruzione Industriale, Institute for Industrial reconstruction) was established in January 1933. Thus the peculiar Italian experience of state-owned and state-managed industrial companies did not originate from any precise design or 'plan', but resulted from the failure of private capitalists to develop sound financial bases and corporate control institutions for their enterprises.

After the war, as policy makers were unwilling to allow banks to resume the control of industrial companies, it proved impossible to privatize state-owned ones. IRI, and later **ENI**, were thus given a number of tasks regarded as relevant to their brief from a public policy point of view: (1) to invest in infrastructures and high-tech projects, that is, in sectors crucial for the development of the country but considered too risky by private capitalists; (2) to contrast the establishment of monopolies in the private sector; and (3) to promote the industrialization of the South. A law in 1957 stipulated that 40 per cent of all new investment by IRI should be in the Mezzogiorno (the South).

In spite of IRI's size and importance, the government's attitude to it in the first decade after the war might best be described as one of benign neglect, leaving all the relevant decisions to company managers. It was during this period that the so-called Senigaglia Plan succeeded in creating, for the first time in Italy's history, a large and efficient iron and steel **industry**. In 1956, a Ministry for State-Owned Companies was created, signalling the end of benign neglect and inaugurat-

ing a long era of increasing political interference in IRI. In 1967, during the heyday of the 'economic planning' ideology, control over IRI was transferred to a ministerial committee, and as a result the dividing line between political and managerial tasks became increasingly blurred, paving the way for exchanges of favours and payments yet to be fully known and documented.

By the late 1970s, both IRI and large private sector companies were uncompetitive, overmanned and in desperate financial condition. However, while the private sector undertook, at least in part, the necessary restructuring, reform in the state-owned industrial sector was delayed by several years. When it finally took place, it was of necessity both difficult and painful. Between 1980 and 1995, the number of IRI employees fell by 45 per cent to 263,000, and by the early 1990s a slow but irreversible process of privatization had been inaugurated (see also **privatization and nationalization**).

Further reading

Barca, F. and Trento, S. (1997) 'La parabola delle partecipazioni statali' (The Rise and Fall of State Participation), in F. Barca (ed.), *Storia del capitalismo italiano dal dopoguerra a oggi* (History of Italian Capitalism from the Postwar to the Present), Bari: Laterza.

GIANNI TONIOLO

Isgrò, Emilio

b. 1937, Barcellona, Messina

Artist and writer

Born in Sicily, Isgrò lived and worked in Milan from 1957 onwards, gaining notoriety in the 1960s with his famous *cancellature* (cancelled books) in which he cancelled out by hand the entire printed text of various volumes including a copy of the Bible. In these works language was being erased because it was already worn out by use and tradition. Subsequently, he became a well-known exponent of *poesia visiva*, producing 'concrete poetry' by joining visual images with the written word and he came to use the term *scrittura semiotica* (semiotic writing) to describe his work in poetry and prose. Isgrò has exhibited frequently in the **Venice Biennale**, and in 1977 won first prize at the Biennale of San Paulo. He has also written experimental novels, including a fictional 'auto-biography', as well as volumes of poetry and verse plays.

LAURENCE SIMMONS

ISTAT

Officially instituted in July 1926, ISTAT (Istituto Nazionale di Statistica, or National Statistics Institute) is the national agency responsible for the collection and publication of all national statistics. Since its inception, it has published monthly bulletins and, with the exception of 1941 when wartime conditions prevented it, it has carried out a population census every ten years. From the late 1960s the Institute has also initiated specific surveys of changing Italian social habits and demographic patterns. Since the mid-1980s it has become more open to the public by making much of its information and data banks available electronically. In 1989 ISTAT was restructured so as to manage and co-ordinate Sistan (Sistema Statistico Nazionale), a national network of data collecting agencies, and since 1993 it has published an annual report on the state of the nation, thus remaining the chief and most up-to-date source of information regarding the current state of Italy.

GINO MOLITERNO

Istituti italiani di cultura

Founded in 1926 under Fascism, the Istituti italiani di cultura (Italian Cultural Institutes) were first intended as foreign outposts of Italian culture throughout the world. A new law in 1940 organized them even more explicitly as centres for the spread of Fascist propaganda. After the war, the function of the Institutes was changed to a less strident promotion of Italian culture abroad, and administrative control of the Institutes was vested with the Ministry for Foreign Affairs while personnel was recruited from the Education Ministry. This situation often proved unsatisfactory and generally led to bureaucratic immobility. In spite of several attempts to redefine the Institutes' role and function in 1978 and 1982, they continued, with a few exceptions, to function poorly. A further attempt was made in the early 1990s to improve the situation by defining more clearly the role of the Institutes and in particular by appointing, for the first time, high-profile cultural figures as directors of some of the more important centres. The measure was moderately successful, but inadequate funding continued to hamper proper functioning of the Institutes well into the late 1990s.

GINO MOLITERNO

Istituto Nazionale LUCE

The Istituto Nazionale LUCE was originally a private association of documentary film-makers. In 1924 it was appropriated by Mussolini, who gave it a new name (the acronym is for L'Unione Cinematografica Educativa, Union of Educational Cinema) and responsibility for producing and co-ordinating all non-fictional and educational cinema in Italy. In effect, through its highly professional but often politically biased newsreels and documen-taries – the screening of which was made compulsory in all cinemas by law from 1927 onwards – LUCE became the strongest arm of the regime's propaganda machine. After the war, given its association with Fascism, the Institute was provisionally liquidated in 1947, but was re-established in 1949 with roughly the same aim of producing documentaries, newsreels and educa-tional films though within a democratic context. The organization was restructured several times from the mid-1960s, and in 1982 it was merged with Italnoleggio Cinematografico, a state com-pany for film distribution. As such, it continued to produce and distribute documentaries and films for educational purposes. In the 1990s, it was granted greater autonomy to collaborate on projects funded by private investments.

GINO MOLITERNO

Italia Uno

A private television channel founded in early 1982 by the publisher Rusconi, Italia Uno was soon acquired by media magnate, Silvio **Berlusconi**. Targeting a younger audience, it broadcast a steady stream of successful American serials such as *The A-Team* and *Beverly Hills 90210*, as well as cartoons and action movies, but it also developed an innovative approach to the variety show as in the popular *Drive-In*. In 1991, Italia Uno began broadcasting **Fininvest**'s first regular news programme, *Studio aperto* (Open Studio), directed by Emilio Fede and later by Paolo Liguori. Another important part of the regular programming came to be in the sports area, particularly football, with live shows such as *Pressing* and the satirical programme *Mai dire goal* (Never Say Goal Again). In 1996, the much-respected journalist Michele **Santoro** migrated from the **RAI** to host his political talk show *Moby Dick*, the first to appear on a private channel and thus marking another coup for Berlusconi.

RICCARDO VENTRELLA

Italian and emigration

In the communities of Italian migrants outside Italy, the use of Italian and of dialects is still widespread, although it tends to decrease in the transition from the first generation, that is, Italians born in Italy, to the subsequent generations, those born in the country of migration. At the community level, Italian and dialects are generally spoken in the more informal social domains, whereas the host language is dominant in the formal ones (such as work, education and government offices). More specifically, dialect tends to be used more in the family and with friends from the same region, while Italian is the language of the wider ethnic community (clubs and associations, Italian cafes and restaurants, radio and television programmes). Due to this reduced use across generations and domains, and to the continual pressure from the host language, Italian and dialects abroad undergo formal changes. These occur differently in each generation, as levels of competence and preference in the various languages are also different. In general, the impact of the host language on the speech of the first generation is limited to the insertion of single words into their Italian or dialect discourse. Its impact on Italian and dialect spoken by the second generation can be much stronger, and affects also sounds and intonation patterns and rules about word order in the sentence and about contextual use of the language. Another feature of the Italian or dialect speech of second generation is code switching, that is, the alternate use of the host language with Italian or dialect in conversation, particularly due to a lack of competence in these latter two languages.

In general, levels of linguistic competence tend to be higher in the migrant communities in Europe than in the transoceanic ones, due to the much more frequent contact with Italy of the former. With regard to language attitudes, studies conducted in Australia and in the United States have shown that among Italian migrants (1) the host language is considered the more prestigious one as it is associated with success and high socioeconomic status; (2) language mixtures, particularly those with a dialect base, are strongly censored as they are associated with low socioeconomic conditions; (3) Italian tends to elicit positive attitudes but is associated with likeability and solidarity rather than prestige and success; and (4) in some cases (for example, in Australia) dialects elicit negative attitudes. Interestingly, second-generation Italians hold more favourable attitudes than the first generation towards mixtures, dialects and Italian.

Due to lack of empirical studies, it is difficult to establish whether Italian or dialect is better maintained in a migration context. However, considering (1) a possible process of Italianization favoured by postwar migration, which brought into contact Italians from different regions; (2) the more favourable attitudes towards Italian; (3) the perception among some migrants that Italian is more vital than dialect; (4) the higher maintenance of Italian rather than dialect by second generation, at least in European countries; and (5) the widespread opinion among migrants that Italian rather than dialect is the language to teach and transmit to younger generations, it can be stated that Italian has a better chance of survival among descendants of Italian migrants.

The total number of Italian migrants and their descendants who speak Italian and/or dialect is unknown. However, figures are available for some countries that include a specific language question in the census: for example, in the United States in 1990, out of almost fifteen million people of Italian origin, over 1.3 million declared they speak Italian at home, and in Australia in 1996 the figure was over 375,000 out of almost one million people of Italian origin. Census data, however, do not distinguish between Italian and dialects.

As to the rate of shift towards use of the host language, the Italian communities (particularly in transoceanic countries) are generally in an intermediate position between migrant groups displaying very high rates (such as the Dutch) and those displaying much lower ones (such as the Greeks). Factors that can promote maintenance of Italian and dialect include high levels of urban concentration (often a consequence of chain migration), endogamy and a relatively strong family cohesion. On the other hand, factors that can play against their maintenance are a relatively high degree of integration within the host country, the dearth of new monolinguals migrating from Italy, the secondary role played by language in maintaining a sense of community amongst Italians, and the unfavourable attitudes towards dialects held by many first-generation migrants.

With regard to the gradual shift from Italian and dialect across generations, some of the demographic variables that affect the process include age, as use of the two languages (particularly dialect) tends to increase with increased age within the first generation, and to decrease with increased age within the second generation; gender, as first-generation women use more Italian and dialect than the men; and type of marriage, as the second generation maintains Italian and dialect more if both parents rather than only one (particularly the mother) are first-generation Italians.

At the community level, analyses of language use across domains as well as across generations have shown that the second generation uses Italian and dialects in fewer domains than the first: for example, with Italo-Australian friends, second generation Italo-Australians use predominantly English. Furthermore, the distinction between domains becomes gradually less clearcut as the host language begins to penetrate those domains where Italian and dialect were previously spoken. This typically occurs within the family when the first child starts attending school, becomes dominant in the host language and starts using it to address their younger siblings as well as their parents. Consequently, the use of Italian and dialect becomes more and more restricted to older family members.

With regard to the formal changes occurring in the Italian and dialect speech of the first generation, it has been noted that initially, words from the host language may be borrowed to express concepts that are unique to the host country or that have been acquired there: for example, *fenza*, from 'fence', to refer to the typical barrier separating Australian backyards, or *cecco*, for 'cheque', probably unknown before migrating. However, with the passing of time, even words that do exist in Italian or dialect tend to be transferred; the process can be favoured by such factors as the resemblance with an Italian word: an example is *cappa*, 'cup', instead of *tazza*, under the influence of the English word but also because the same word exists in Italian with the meaning of 'kitchen hood'. Nouns and interjections are the most frequently transferred words, whereas adjectives, verbs, pronouns or conjunctions tend to be carried over much less frequently. Transferred words are generally pronounced with Italian (or dialect) sounds and are given Italian (or dialect) grammatical endings, as in the examples above. However, a great deal of variation can be found in this process, particularly with regard to nouns: 'computer' may become a feminine or a masculine noun, *la computa* or *il computa*. Also, the amount and type of transferred words tend to vary with the level of formality of the situation as well as with individual variables, such as levels of education or length of stay abroad.

In the Italian and dialect speech of the second generation, some instances of the stronger impact of the host language may be, for the English-speaking countries, (1) the aspirated pronunciation of [t] and [p] under the influence of the English sounds, (2) a phrase like *una rossa macchina*, 'a red car', with the wrong position of the Italian adjective, or (3) the widespread use of the informal *tu* at the expense of the formal *lei* under the influence of the generalized 'you'. Furthermore, words from the host language may be used in the Italian speech with the original sounds and grammatical structures. With regard to code switching (*l'ho visto proprio lì* in the middle of the shopping centre, 'I saw him right there', where the first part of the sentence is Italian, the second English), it has been observed that it can also be used by more competent second-generation Italians to express or negotiate particular meanings or values, for example, to reaffirm their Italian identity.

Overall, the Italian and dialect speech of the second generation displays a high level of variation, not just between these two languages and the host language but also between Italian and dialect. While the more competent speakers may be able to control the shift between these two languages, for the less competent ones it is a case of not being able to keep them apart. Another major trait shown by the least competent speakers is the simplification of Italian grammatical endings.

The levels of Italian and dialect competence among second-generation Italians tend to vary a great deal, from a limited passive knowledge displayed by the subjects in studies conducted in Australia or Canada, to the almost native-speaker competence in popular regional Italian and in dialect which has been observed in Switzerland. Besides the geographical distance, some of the factors that can account for such variability include parents' length of stay in the host country (especially for transoceanic migration); number of children in the family, with an only child maintaining the languages better than a child with siblings; and birth order in the family, with the first child maintaining the languages better than younger siblings. More specifically, knowledge of Italian rather than of dialect seems to increase with increased contact with Italy and with Italian relatives abroad, or if parents are from different regions and therefore do not use the dialect in talking to each other, or through instruction at school.

With regard to the first generation, given the rapid changes in the Italian sociolinguistic context from the 1950s onwards (see **dialect usage**), competence of Italian tends to be higher among postwar than prewar migrants even though a dialect is still the first language. Thus, the *lingua franca* of prewar migrants was often a common dialect which was formed either by the levelling out of differences among the various dialects or by the spreading of the dialect spoken by the dominant regional group (such as the Venetian dialect in Rio Grande do Sul, Brazil). Among postwar migrants, on the other hand, a popular regional variety of Italian (see **varieties of Italian**) is used as the language of the community.

Italian migrant communities outside Italy can boast of a considerable production of literary as well as more broadly artistic works (such as films), which often deal with various aspects of the migration experience. In many of these works, the language used aims to reflect and highlight the linguistic phenomena in progress in the community, in particular the different preferences and competencies across generations.

See also: dialects; dialect usage; emigration; Istituti italiani di cultura; Italian language; Italian outside Italy; language policy

Further reading

Bettoni, C. (ed.) (1986) *Altro Polo. Italian Abroad: Studies on Language Contact in English-Speaking Countries*, Sydney: University of Sydney, F. May Foundation for Italian Studies (essays on various sociolinguistic aspects of Italian migration in Australia, Canada, Great Britain, New Zealand and USA).

—— (1993) 'Italiano fuori d'Italia', in A.A. Sobrero (ed.), *Introduzione all'italiano contemporaneo. La variazione e gli usi* (Introduction to Contemporary Italian: Variation and Usages), Bari: Laterza (a discussion of the main issues affecting Italian and dialects in postwar migrant communities).

Bettoni, C. and Rubino, A. (1996) *Emigrazione e comportamento linguistico. Un'indagine sul trilinguismo dei siciliani e dei veneti in Australia* (Emigration and Linguistic Behaviour: An Investigation of the Trilingualism of Sicilians and Venetians in Australia), Galatina: Congedo (a detailed study on the use of Italian, dialect and English in a range of social domains among first- and second-generation subjects in Australia, with comparative data from other host countries).

Haller, H. (1993) *Una lingua perduta e ritrovata. L'italiano degli italo-americani* (A Language Lost and Rediscovered: The Italian of Italo-Americans), Florence: La Nuova Italia (a collection of essays on the presence of Italian and dialects in the language of migrants, the media and English itself in the USA).

Lo Cascio, V. (ed.) (1987) *L'italiano in America Latina* (Italian in Latin America), Florence: Le Monnier (various essays on language shift in the Italian communities in South and Central American countries).

ANTONIA RUBINO

Italian language

Italian is the official language of Italy, now spoken by almost all Italians within the national borders, and outside them by several groups of different peoples and by Italian emigrants.

Italian is a Romance language within the Indo-European family. It derives its formal characteristics from the evolution of Latin as shaped by Italy's cultural history. Compared to other Romance languages, Italian is more conservative in the sense that, although it came about somewhat later in the Middle Ages, it was from its beginnings closer to Latin and then changed less dramatically throughout the following centuries. Yet in another sense, it can be considered younger and now more unstable, since it was only in the twentieth century that the majority of Italians, who had previously spoken only their **dialects**, began to use it and thus to weaken the elitist forces that had kept it stable for so long. Once undeniably Florentine-based in its standard form, it is now represented by numerous **varieties of Italian** which are both regionally and socially marked, and of which the standard form is but one, arguably not even the most appreciated one (see **language attitudes**). According to how we see the Italian language, we might assign to it three very different dates of birth: the Middle Ages, the sixteenth century and the twentieth century.

First, we can use the label 'Italian' retrospectively for Florentine, that is, for one of the new Romance languages that came about from the gradual evolution of Vulgar Latin in the second half of the first millennium. Strictly speaking, until the sixteenth century there was no 'Italian': in the Middle Ages there was classical Latin, the learned international language of high culture, acquired by study and used for writing by the very few who were literate, and there were numerous local native languages, acquired in infancy and used in everyday speech. These new languages gradually consolidated into a written form and enjoyed varying prestige according to the political and economic power of their area and the excellence of their literature. At the beginning of the fourteenth century, in his *De Vulgari Eloquentia* (About the Vulgar Tongue), Dante distinguished fourteen of them. As there was no unitary state, Dante also stressed the lack of a common new language for the whole of Italy. Among these languages, Florentine was undoubtedly the language of a powerful, wealthy and cultured small state spreading its influence well beyond its city borders.

Secondly, as a national language, Italian came about in the sixteenth century when Florentine came to be largely accepted outside Tuscany. Although Italy was still politically fragmented into regional states, the need for a common language became overwhelming in the new world of the courtiers' *Signorie*. Latin was still of course widely known and used by the literate elites, but paradoxically the humanists' revival of Latin in the fifteenth century had shown the widening gap between the ancient or medieval worlds and the modern one. Latin could therefore still be used (and was in fact used for at least a further two centuries) in the domains where little was changing, such as the Church and the law, but it needed replacement in the new domains, especially the literary one. The absence of a strong national centre in early sixteenth-century Italy, analogous to Paris in French cultural life or London in the English, meant that there was no obvious choice for its national language. Various proposals were put forward, but since the strongest need for a common language was elitist, cultural and literary, the choice ultimately fell on the old Florentine which two centuries before had reached its highest glory with Dante, Petrarch and Boccaccio. Other factors also contributed to this choice: the central geographic location of the Tuscan language; its linguistic forms, often intermediate between the southern and northern ones; its conservatism, that had kept it somewhat closer to Latin; and the cultural and commercial vitality of the region, whose merchants and bankers were active nationally.

With the promotion of Florentine to the status of national Italian, all the other local languages found themselves in the position of dialects, that is, of 'low', less prestigious languages compared to the 'high' national one, even if no changes had occurred in their formal characteristics. On the other hand, the newly promoted Italian begun to lose some of its most provincial Tuscanisms and to shape itself into the language we know today. From the sixteenth century onwards, the diffusion of printing, the careful watch of an authoritative academy (the Accademia della Crusca in Florence; see **language institutions**), the compliance of non-Tuscan writers of great prestige, and more generally the stagnation of Italian cultural life all contributed to the remarkable stability of Italian well into this century. In fact, contemporary Italians can read their sixteenth-century texts, and indeed even their fourteenth-century literature (Petrarch in particular), with far greater ease than the English, French or Germans can read theirs of the same periods.

While the high position enjoyed by Italian assured its stability and status, it did not assure its liveliness. In fact, all Italians, irrespective of rank and education, continued to speak in their local dialects, which were often used also for written texts, particularly those dealing with practical matters and the lower literary genres (such as comedy), and those produced in the larger, most powerful states (such as the Venetian Republic). On the basis of census and literacy figures, the linguist Tullio De Mauro has estimated that at the time of Italy's unification in 1861, the number of Italians able to use Italian could not have amounted to more than 600,000, representing 2.5 per cent of the total population. Since this figure includes 400,000 Tuscans and 70,000 Romans, and refers only to *the ability* to use it rather than to its everyday use, Italian can hardly be considered a national language in the popular sense. In linguistic matters, in fact, the **intellectuals** rather than contemporary usage were the arbiters, and constant campaigns were fought to preserve a high literary model from the corrupting influences coming from outside (French and English) and from below (the dialects). The *questione della lingua* (language question) is a four-century-long debate which periodically deals with deeply controversial issues relating to purist principles and rebellion against them. This complex controversy cannot always be resolved simplistically by equating the purists with the reactionary and wrong, and their more innovative enemies with the progressive and correct, since purism at certain times could also represent progressive patriotic attitudes. In any case, the aspirations to perfection and detachment from ordinary life which characterized the debate on the Italian language deeply affected the literary production in favour of the genres that escape further from reality, such as lyric poetry, to the detriment of those that more closely reflect it, such as the theatre and the novel. They also distanced the Italian-speaking intellectuals from the common people who spoke only the dialects.

Thirdly, as a truly national and popular language used also by the masses throughout the Italian nation, Italian only began its fully fledged life in the twentieth century, at first timidly and then more forcefully after the Second World War. Many factors contributed to its spread from the upper to the lower classes. At unification in 1861, the *questione della lingua* became a political and social issue for the new Italian state, and although little was achieved in practice, various solutions to the problem of educating Italians and teaching them their national language were at least debated. During the century that followed, **emigration** abroad taught illiterate people the value of literacy for securing better jobs and communicating with distant relatives. Especially after the Second World War, emigration from the South to the industrial North, and from rural areas to the cities, also brought people with different dialects into contact; increased urbanization led to wider attendance at school and more frequent occasions requiring the use of Italian (visits to administrative offices, and so on). The rapid industrialization of the so-called **economic miracle** encouraged not only geographical homogenization but also more education and greater dialogue between social classes. The new national bureaucracy imposed a uniform language, and compulsory military service brought together young men from all parts of the country. The growth of mass media, especially radio, first introduced in 1924, and then television which began broadcasting in 1954 (see **RAI**), also played an important role. Finally, even the Church began celebrating mass in Italian, abandoning the use of Latin after the **Second Vatican Council** in 1962–5. In this progressive spread of the Italian language, fascism, contrary to its intentions, contributed very little (see also **fascism and neo-fascism**). While rhetorically it promoted a language policy in favour of the strong, glorious and pure national language and violently repressed the dialects, in practice it did nothing to create the conditions for a wider use of the former, and succeeded only in discrediting the latter.

The recent widespread use of Italian by most Italians for a great variety of purposes, both oral and written, has brought about important formal changes. Freed from the normative canons of the academies and the straitjackets of the literary models, Italian is rapidly evolving in two main directions. On the one hand, there is a development towards a common mass language adjusted to middle-level tastes, which, given the elitist past, is more of a welcome simplification and search for more effective clarity than a banalization; on the other, in reaction against this mass language, geographical and social varieties of Italian are being maintained more strongly, and **sectorial languages** are being created in an attempt to express special interests, such as those of the sciences, the media and sports. The interplay among all these varieties, including the old dialects, far from constituting a weakness, represents the vitality and richness of the national culture.

See also: Italian and emigration; Italian lexicon; Italian morphology; Italian outside Italy; Italian syntax; Italian phonology; language attitudes; language education; language policy; minority languages

Further reading

Lepschy, A.L. and Lepschy, G. (1977) *The Italian Language Today*, London: Hutchinson (a description of contemporary Italian preceded by a long introduction examining 'some aspects of its history which have often led people to wonder whether an "Italian" language really existed').

Migliorini, B. and Griffith, T.G. (1984) *The Italian Language*, 2nd edn, London: Faber & Faber (on the history of Italian, a basic work is still Migliorini's *Storia della Lingua Italiana*, Florence: Sansoni, 1960, which stops at 1915; a 1964 abridged edition was extended to the 1960s by I. Baldelli, as *Breve storia della Lingua Italiana*, Florence: Sansoni; this was abridged and re-edited in English by T. Griffith in 1966).

Sobrero, A.A. (ed.) (1993) *Introduzione all'italiano contemporaneo. Vol. I: Le strutture. Vol. II: La variazione e gli usi* (Introduction to Contemporary Italian, Vol. I: The Structures, Vol. II: Variation and Usage), Bari: Laterza (an excellent two-volume collection of essays written by specialists covering the main areas of contemporary forms and usage).

Vincent, N. (1988) 'Italian', in M. Harris and N. Vincent (eds), *The Romance Languages*, London: Routledge (an excellent introduction, including the historical dimension and an eye to the future).

CAMILLA BETTONI

Italian lexicon

The vocabulary of a language is an accurate, if complex, record of the history of the society in which the language is spoken. As a member of the Romance family of languages, Italian draws the vast majority of its vocabulary from Latin. The base vocabulary of Italian is derived from Vulgar Latin, the informal register of colloquial Latin which evolved into the various Romance languages. So-called Classical Latin, the formal register of Roman times and the international language of high culture during medieval and Renaissance times, also provided a layer of learned input. These two Latin sources can be seen in different words relating to the same object – *cavallo* 'horse' and *equestre* 'equestrian' – and in different outcomes of the same Latin word – *piazza* 'square' and *platea* 'stall in a theatre', both from Latin *platea*.

The historical vicissitudes of the country appear

in the various strands of the lexicon. During the late Roman Empire, Greek words were adopted in Christian Latin and thence into Italian: the Greek *ecclesia* produced *chiesa* (church), and also the (learned) adjective *ecclesiastico*. The barbarian invasions left behind words of Germanic origin such as *guerra* 'war' and *bianco* 'white', and the Arab domination of the Mediterranean (and Sicily) also left its mark with *dogana* 'customs' and *albicocca* 'apricot'. The later ascendancy of Spain and of France produced considerable new vocabulary: from the former came *etichetta* 'etiquette' and *posate* 'cutlery', and from the latter came *ragù* 'ragout' and *parruca* 'wig'.

In describing the development of the Italian lexicon in more recent times, it is useful to distinguish between two modes of lexical enrichment: borrowings which enter the language from some other source, and 'neologisms', derived from pre-existing words.

Italian has borrowed internally and externally. Internal sources are the **dialects** and the **sectorial languages**. The variety of vocabulary items among the dialects is legendary. As the dialect-speaking population acquired Italian as a second language, many dialect words have entered the regional vocabularies of Italian, usually undergoing some Italianization in the process. A 1951 survey asked 124 persons from 54 provinces what name they used for 242 different concepts: only one, 'strong black coffee served in a bar', was given the same name by all informants (*espresso*). Such rich geographical variation is still a major feature of spoken Italian.

The sectorial languages are a rich source of new vocabulary. Technical meanings are applied to common vocabulary (examples are *scaricare* 'download' and *motore di ricerca* 'search engine'); old metaphors are reworked to fit new technologies as in the extension of the language of maritime navigation to space travel to produce *astronauta* 'astronaut', and later to hypertextuality to produce *navigare* 'navigate'. New words from styles such as youth language usually enter colloquial or non-standard varieties of Italian. Youth slang is somewhat Janus-faced in deriving new lexicon from international (mostly English-language) youth culture and also from local dialects, as well as from free creativity.

Italian has also absorbed words from other languages. The international status of English makes it the primary donor of foreign words to Italian, although other languages appear according to circumstances, such as the Brazilian *goleador* 'goal-scorer (in soccer)', the Iranian *khomeinista* and the Russian *glasnost*. Anglicisms enter the language through all aspects of social life. They tend not to be integrated morphologically and to conserve their original meaning and spelling until well accepted in common parlance, though some show unpredictable changes in meaning, such as the classic *footing* 'jogging', *mister* 'soccer coach', or *box*, which may mean 'shower cubicle', 'garage' or 'baby's playpen' (*boxe* is French and means the sport of boxing), and others present interesting formal features: *fans* (as well as *fan*) is the *singular* word for a 'fan' or 'supporter'.

Attitudes to foreign words in Italian are in general relaxed, and their use is sometimes associated with positive attributes such as travel and education. The attempt by the Fascists to legislate in this area was mostly a failure, except for a few creations which have remained to this day: *calcio d'angolo* for 'corner kick'; *rete* alternates with *goal* (or *gol*). Newspaper columnists and letter writers occasionally muse on the extent of English usage (usually in newspapers themselves) and the consequent danger to the vitality of the Italian language itself. Research suggests, however, that in everyday spoken language the presence of foreign words is of the order of one per thousand words (De Mauro, 1993).

Even more telling is the expansion of the lexicon through the creation of neologisms, by means of the processes of derivational morphology (see **Italian morphology**). These affect words originating in Italian itself, sectorial languages, dialects or foreign languages: examples include *interpiattaforma* 'cross-platform', *manageriale* 'managerial', and *managerialità* (the root *manager* is ultimately of Latin origin, so the 'borrowing' from English is actually a return), *sviluppatore* '(software) developer', *malavitoso*, from *malavita* 'underworld', *interfaccia* 'interface' (and the verb *interfacciare*), *Palasport*, a contraction of *Palazzo dello Sport*, 'sports stadium' and *scuolabus* 'school bus'. What is significant here is not so much the new words themselves as the processes which create them and the new confidence with which

Italian speakers are experimenting with the lexicon. Many of the derivational processes are well documented in the history of Italian, but their creative potential is only now being released. They are at the same time bringing the lexicon of Italian into line with trends observed in the other languages of Europe.

In the opposite direction, a number of words of Italian origin have become international words, usually via American English, for example *ciao*, from the Venetian dialect form of the salutation (*vostro*) *schiavo* 'your servant'; *jeans*, from *Gênes*, the French name for Genova (Genoa); or *baloney/polony*, from *Bologna*.

An interesting phenomenon of the 1980s was the commercial success of dictionaries, which were published in large numbers and often appeared in bestseller lists. These could be seen as a sign of renewed interest in linguistic matters, of delight among literate Italians at the expanding riches of the language or, perhaps, of insecurity in the face of so many changes in such a short time.

See also: Italian language; Italian morphology; varieties of Italian

Further reading

De Mauro, T. *et al.* (1993) *Lessico di frequenza dell'italiano parlato*, Milan: Etas Libri.

Sobrero, A.A. (ed.) (1993) *Introduzione all'italiano contemporaneo*, Bari: Laterza (see M. Dardano, 'Lessico e semantica'; A.A. Sobrero, 'Lingue speciali'; E. Radtke, 'Lingue giovanili'; and P. Ramat, 'L'italiano lingua d'Europa').

Vincent, N. (1988) 'Italian', in M. Harris and N. Vincent (eds), *The Romance Languages*, London: Routledge (has a section on the history of Italian lexicon and current trends).

JOHN J. KINDER

Italian morphology

The **Italian language** has a rich morphology. Words change their form much more frequently than in English. They do so in two main ways. Inflectional morphology creates different forms of the 'same word' according to its grammatical function; and derivational morphology derives 'new words' from others.

Inflectional morphology affects nouns (and related parts of speech, adjectives, pronouns and articles) and verbs. Noun morphology shows distinctions of number (singular and plural) and gender (masculine and feminine); verb morphology carries information on number, tense, aspect and mood. Invariable parts of speech, which do not change their form, are prepositions (unless they combine with articles), adverbs and conjunctions. The morphological distinctions are usually made through word endings and are clearly marked, since Italian has retained, from its Latin heritage, clear vowel sounds at the end of words which carry the morphological information.

Italian morphology has in general remained richer than that of the other Romance languages, in part because as a primarily written language it was, until recent times, protected from the natural effects of widespread use in speech.

Derivational morphology is the process of forming nouns, adjectives and verbs from other nouns, adjectives and verbs. This is achieved by the use of prefixes and suffixes and through composition. Prefixes produce words of the same class as the base – *nazionale* (national), *internazionale* (international) – while suffixes can produce words of the same class or of another class, such as *nazione* (noun), *nazionale* (adjective), *nazionalizzare* (verb), *nazionalizzazione* (noun). Composition is the process of combining two or more words, from the same or different classes: *portaborse* 'bagman' (literally 'bag carrier'), *telecomando* 'remote control device', or *pastasciutta*, literally 'dry pasta', i.e. not in broth (see **pasta**).

Italian also has a rich repertoire of affective derivational suffixes which express the qualities of the object in question, especially size, and the speaker's attitude to it. They express subtle shades of intensity: *caldo–calduccio* 'hot–quite hot', *sudato–sudaticcio* 'sweaty–a little sweaty', *febbre–febbrone* 'fever–strong fever'; and complex ranges of emotional attachment, including endearment (*mamma–mammina* 'mummy–darling mummy'), irony (*furbo–furbacchione* 'cunning person–crafty so-and-so') or censure (*vita–vitaccia* 'life–rotten life'). In many cases the suffixed word acquires a distinct meaning:

cucchiaio 'spoon', *cucchiaino* 'teaspoon'; *orso* 'bear', *orsacchiotto* 'teddy bear'.

All Italian words end in a vowel, except for a few prepositions – *con* 'with', *per* 'for' – and unintegrated words of Latin origin, such as *ribes* 'blackcurrant'. This basic principle of morphological structure is now coexisting with modern borrowings from other languages such as *sport* and *box*, and with acronyms such as **Fiat** and USL. Foreign words tend to be assigned to masculine gender if nouns and to the first, unmarked, conjugation -*are* if verbs. Anglicisms tend to remain invariable: *la star – le star.*

The most conspicuous effect of the recent history of Italian has been the rationalization of several morphological sub-systems, for example, the reduction in the pronouns and in the number of verb tenses in general use, which implies that the categories in use are being exploited to express a richer range of meanings.

See also: Italian language; Italian lexicon; Italian syntax; Italian phonology

Further reading

Sobrero, A.A. (ed.) (1993) *Introduzione all'italiano contemporaneo*, Bari: Laterza (see M. Berretta, 'Morfologia'; R. Simone, 'Stabilità e instabilità nei caratteri originali dell'italiano').

Vincent, N. (1988) 'Italian', in M. Harris and N. Vincent (eds), *The Romance Languages*, London: Routledge (a comprehensive description with a historical dimension and an eye to future developments).

JOHN J. KINDER

Italian outside Italy

Outside the confines of Italy, the Italian language is used both as one of the four national and three official languages of Switzerland, and is also spoken in regional varieties along its immediate border areas to the west, as well as to the east (Istria). Historically, Italian had a strong linguistic tradition in the islands of Corsica, where it continues to flourish as a dialectal substratum in the new Corsican language, and in Malta, as well as along the Dalmatian coast. In addition to its fundamental role as a language of culture in Europe principally from the sixteenth to the eighteenth centuries, as a language of **emigration** throughout the world particularly since the industrial age, and as a language studied by a population of about one million, Italian was also brought to northern and eastern Africa as a colonial language during Fascist rule. Where it is spoken as an autochthonous idiom outside Switzerland, Italian tends to be exposed to the pressures, language shifts and attritions that typify the fate of minority languages. On the other hand, due to the modern mass media, Italian as a spoken second language is alive in many countries of the Mediterranean rim (for example, in Northern Africa, Albania, Greece).

Italian is the language of a population of 250,000 in the Canton Ticino; at 4 per cent, it ranks as the third language of Switzerland, behind German and French. The region, south of the Swiss Alps and at the doorsteps of Lombardy and Milan, became independent and part of the plurilingual Swiss confederation in 1803. With the opening of the Gotthard railway in 1882, the region became a crossroads between North and South, and gained economic prosperity especially after the Second World War. The economic boom led to the migration of people from remote valleys to the urban areas of Lugano and Chiasso. Today, the Ticinese dialects, which generally share linguistic features of the Lombard system, tend to lose ground to Italian, not unlike the **dialects** of Italy's regions. At the same time German language presence is considerable, and many Ticinese regionalisms can be explained by this language contact (for example, *azione* from German *Aktion* 'sales promotion'; *organizzazione tetto* from German *Dachorganization* 'umbrella organization'). North of the Alps, one comes across a bureaucratic variety of Italian – which Berruto (1984) called Helvetic Italian, with calques such as *vuotatura* from German *Leerung* 'mail collection' – as well as the use of Italian as a structurally simplified *lingua franca* among foreign workers (due to the large numbers of Italian immigrants in the 1960s). Italian is also spoken in the Mesolcina, Calanca, Poschiavo and Bregaglia valleys of the neighbouring Grisons, where German and Rhaetoromansh are the major languages. Unlike the dynamic sociolinguistic situation of the Ticino, the triple minority status of Italian in this region contributes to steady erosion.

Italian also had in the past a strong presence in Corsica, one of the largest Mediterranean islands north of Sardinia. The seven-century Pisan and Genoese rule in Corsica was replaced in 1754 by the establishment of an autonomous yet short-lived government under Pasquale Paoli, crushed in 1768 when Corsica became French. While French became gradually the island's official language, the former Italian dialects – with a Tuscan base in the north and a south–central foundation in the south – were gradually moulded into Corsican, with a written standard that was introduced as an optional school subject in 1974. Corsican is recognized today by France as one of its languages. Among the island's 240,000 speakers, Italian tends by now to be but a remote echo.

In the multilingual Mediterranean island of Malta, located some fifty miles South of Sicily, at the crossroad of East and West and of Christian and Islamic cultures, Italian became the official language along with English during the political reorganization in the nineteenth century. However, the British colonial rule was successful in assigning Italian to secondary status, and in the 1932 constitution Maltese, a Siculo-Tunisian dialect based on indigenous Arabic speech, was declared the official language together with English, a contact situation resulting in strong interference from the latter.

See also: Italian language; Italian and emigration; minority languages

Further reading

Berruto, G. (1984) 'Appunti sull'italiano elvetico', *Studi linguistici italiani* 10: 76–108.

Bianconi, S. (1989) *I due linguaggi. Storia linguistica della Lombardia dal '400 ai nostri giorni* (The Two Tongues: A Linguistic History of Lombardy from the Fifteenth Century to Today), Bellinzona: Casagrande.

Goebl, H. (1988) 'Korsisch, Italienisch und Französisch auf Korsika' (Corsican, Italian and French in Corsica), in G. Holtus, M. Metzeltin and C. Schmitt (eds), *Lexikon der romantischen Linguistik* (Lexicon of Romance Linguistics), vol. 4, Tübingen: Niemeyer.

Hull, G. (1994) 'Maltese from Arabic Dialect to European Language', in I. Fodor and C. Hagège (eds), *Language Reform: History and Future*, Hamburg: Buske.

Lurati, O. (1992) 'Il Canton Ticino' (The Canton Ticino), in F. Bruni (ed.), *L'italiano delle regioni* (Italian in the Regions), Turin: UTET.

HERMANN W. HALLER

Italian phonology

The phonology of the Italian language consists of thirty generally agreed phonemes (sounds which are capable of distinguishing pairs of words). There are seven vowels: i e ɛ a ç o u. There are no nasal vowels. There are twenty-one consonants: p b m t d n ɲ k g ts dz tʃ dʒ f v s z ʃ r l ʎ. There are two semi-consonants: j w. Stress usually falls on the penultimate syllable but may occur in any other position and is distinctive, *pàpa* 'pope' versus *papà* 'daddy'; *càpito* 'I turn up' versus *capìto* 'understood' versus *capitò* 'he turned up'. Consonant length is also distinctive: between vowels, all but six consonants (z which is always short and ɲ ts dz ʃ ʎ which are always long) may be pronounced short or long, *pala* 'spade' versus *palla* 'ball'; *cade* 'it falls' versus *cadde* 'it fell'. Vowel length depends on these two features: vowels are short if unstressed or followed by a consonant in their syllable; vowels in stressed, open syllables are long. Stressed syllables are pronounced roughly twice as long as unstressed syllables. Intonation is also distinctive, for example, the usual way of turning a statement into a question is simply to use an interrogative intonation pattern.

Syllables in Italian are centred on a single vowel. All vowels are given their full phonetic value: *aereo* 'aeroplane' contains four syllables (diphthongs combine a vowel with a semi-consonant: *più* [pju], *qui* [kwi]). Syllable structure is given by (CCC)V(C): syllables may end in a vowel or a consonant, and may begin with the vowel or up to three consonants, but usually one or two, as there are severe restrictions on consonant clustering; for example, the only possible three-consonant groups all have 's' as the first element.

Italian phonology includes a number of features which cross word boundaries. For example, elision is the fall of an unstressed vowel at the end of a word when the following word also begins with a vowel: *la Italia* > *l'Italia* 'Italy', and truncation, the fall of a final vowel: *dolce fare niente* > *dolce far niente* 'sweet idleness'. Syntactic doubling is the doubling of the initial consonant of a word when that word follows one of a particular set of words; this is not normally seen in writing but appears in certain historically established forms: *cosiddetto* 'so-called', *dimmi* 'tell me'.

Italian is often said to be a 'phonetic' language, an inaccurate description which does however refer to the fact there is a very high degree of correspondence between the spelling conventions of the language and the sounds. Its reputation as a 'musical' language is based on the clear vowel sounds, the paucity of harsh consonant sounds and of consonant groups, the predominance of vowels in syllable structure and the alternation of long and short syllables.

The above description is based on the notion of standard Italian, founded on educated Florentine. From a sociolinguistic point of view, the most striking feature of Italian phonology, compared to English, is that there is no agreed national standard which is actually spoken by any one social group. There is no Italian equivalent to English 'Received Pronunciation', which is to say that even the social elites in Italy show their regional origin by their accent.

See also: Italian language; Italian lexicon; Italian morphology; Italian syntax; language attitudes; varieties of Italian

Further reading

Mioni, A.M. (1993) 'Fonetica e fonologia', in A.A. Sobrero (ed.), *Introduzione all'italiano contemporaneo*, Bari: Laterza.

Vincent, N. (1988) 'Italian', in M. Harris and N. Vincent (eds), *The Romance Languages*, London: Routledge (a comprehensive description with a historical dimension and an eye to future developments).

JOHN J. KINDER

Italian syntax

The basic structure of the Italian sentence is SVO (Subject–Verb–Object). Whereas in Latin the grammatical function of the elements in a sentence was shown by the inflectional morphology of the words, in Italian and the other Romance languages the functions of, especially, subject and object are identified by their position in the sentence. Compared to the other Romance languages, however, the morphology of Italian is relatively transparent; that is, the endings of words convey grammatical information clearly (and audibly). This permits a wide choice of variations on the standard SVO word order. Groups of words can be moved from their normal position with great freedom in order to express emphasis or some stylistic nuance. The word order of Italian is somewhat freer than the other Romance languages (although less free than its parent language Latin), and is considerably freer than Germanic languages like English.

The most frequent of the expressive word orders is known as 'left dislocation': *Le pizze le compri tu questa volta* (The pizzas *you* buy them this time), but there are many possible variations on the theme, such as *Le compri tu, le pizze, questa volta*; *Sei tu che compri le pizze questa volta*. Compared to English, we may say that Italian makes greater use of grammatical variation to emphasize certain elements in a sentence, while English relies much more on using the voice.

These word orders have to do with the fact that the focus of new or important information tends to be at the end of the Italian sentence: *Rispondo io* 'I'll get it (the telephone)'. This sentence also shows how subject pronouns are often used for emphasis or contrast, although in Italian they are not obligatory since the verb ending shows clearly who the subject is.

Grammatical freedom also expresses nuances of meaning in the case of adjectives. Usually they come after nouns (and agree with them): *l'enciclo-*

pedia italiana, le enciclopedie italiane. But they may come before the noun, if the information they provide is not crucial to defining the object in question but rhetorical, emotive or metaphorical. In some cases, the difference in position effects a drastic change in meaning: in *un amico vecchio* 'an old friend', the adjective refers to the age of the friend, while in *un vecchio amico* it refers to the length of the friendship.

In the case of verbs, Italian has a number of compound tenses, formed by the past participle of the verb and an auxiliary, either *avere* 'to have' or *essere* 'to be'. Italian makes greater use of alternation between the two auxiliaries than the other Romance languages: the list of verbs which always require *essere* is long (they are all intransitive), and in some cases the choice of auxiliary can convey important information: *il negozio è chiuso a mezzogiorno* 'the shop closed at midday (until it reopens)', *il negozio ha chiuso a mezzogiorno* 'the shop closed down at midday'.

As for complex sentences, Italian has a rich repertoire of subordinating conjunctions and strict rules for use of verb tenses and moods in main and subordinate clauses. The subjunctive mood (alive and well in written Italian at least) allows meaning distinctions to be made: *cerchiamo il ristorante che è aperto* 'we are looking for the restaurant that is open'; *cerchiamo un ristorante che sia aperto* 'we are looking for a restaurant (any) that is (may be) open'.

See also: Italian language; Italian morphology; Italian phonology; varieties of Italian

Further reading

Sobrero, A.A. (ed.) (1993) *Introduzione all'italiano contemporaneo*, Bari: Laterza (see R. Simone, 'Stabilità e instabilità nei caratteri originali dell'italiano'; P. Benincà, 'Sintassi').

Vincent, N. (1988) 'Italian', in M. Harris and N. Vincent (eds), *The Romance Languages*, London: Routledge (a comprehensive description with a historical dimension and an eye to future developments).

JOHN J. KINDER

Italian-American cinema

Italian-American cinema might be defined as a genre of films made by Italian Americans about the still evolving Italian-American immigrant experience in the United States. The Italian-American experience has been depicted in many films made both in Italy and the United States, by both Italian film-makers and American film-makers of various nationalities and ethnic origins, but these films, ranging from Giuliano **Montaldo**'s *Sacco and Vanzetti* (1970), Francesco **Rosi**'s *Lucky Luciano* (1973), Sergio **Leone**'s *Once Upon a Time in America* (1983) and the **Taviani brothers**' *Good Morning, Babylon* (1986) to John Huston's *Prizzi's Honour* and Norman Jewison's *Moonstruck*, are generally not considered to be 'Italian-American' films. By the same token, over the years many Italian-Americans have been involved in every aspect of film-making in the United States although, for the most part, their work was not concerned with the Italian-American experience. This was particularly true for the directors and actors of what might be defined as the first generation such as Frank Capra, Vincente Minnelli, Ida Lupino and others.

It has been the film-makers of the second generation who created what has generally come to be known as Italian-American cinema: Francis Ford Coppola, Martin Scorsese, and to a lesser degree, Brian De Palma and Michael Cimino. Coppola and Scorsese in particular have not only dealt extensively, albeit not exclusively, with their Italian-American heritages in their films, but they have also spoken openly of the importance of their heritages in their personal lives. The Italian-American films of the members of this generation (Coppola's *Godfather* films, Scorsese's *Mean Streets* and *Raging Bull*, De Palma's *Wise Guys*), deal explicitly with themes, issues, locales, customs and traditions that may in some way be described as 'Italian-American' and thus either function as metaphors for the Italian-American immigrant experience or reappropriate an Italian heritage, be it historical, literary or cinematic. For example, Cimino's *The Sicilian* is based on Mario Puzo's (admittedly wildly inaccurate) rendition of the life of Sicilian revolutionary/bandit Salvatore **Giuliano**; De Palma's *Obsession* is loosely inspired by Dante's *Vita Nuova*; and Coppola's *The Conversation* and De Palma's *Blow-Out* derive from Michelangelo **Antonioni**'s *Blow-Up*.

Following the Italian literary and filmic tradition of national self-criticism – a tradition which may be traced from Dante to **Fellini** – Scorsese is harshly critical of the maschilist aspects of the Italian-American heritage while Coppola uses his *Godfather* epic to create an Italian-American mythology, to condemn its criminal manifestations and to reveal the parallels between organized crime and the WASP establishment of the United States. The parallels between the methods of organized crime and of the government are reiterated in De Palma's *The Untouchables*, while Cimino attempts to destroy the myth of the West in *Heaven's Gate* by revealing the truth about the criminal collusion between the government and capital.

When the public failed to perceive that organized crime, as depicted in the *Godfather* films, was not exclusively an Italian-American phenomenon, Coppola went to some lengths to show in *Cotton Club* that organized crime in the United States pre-existed the rise to power of the **mafia**. De Palma continued and expanded this process by revealing the advent of new ethnic criminal organizations in *Scarface* and in *Carlito's Way*. Cimino might be seen to be making a similar point in *Year of the Dragon*.

Film-makers of the third generation such as Abel Ferrara, Quentin Tarentino, Stanley Tucci, Tom Di Cillo, Steve Buscemi and James Merendino have achieved some popular and critical success in the United States and to a greater degree abroad, but while they may be perceived as Italian-American in terms of parentage, they have not established an identity as Italian-American film-makers, as have the exponents of the second generation. For the most part, their films do not reflect the classical Italian-American concerns and themes. Even Tucci's *Big Night* is, at most, an attempt to describe an Italian immigrant experience, rather than a specifically Italian-American experience.

The Italian-American women film-makers, Nancy Savoca (*True Love, Dog Fight, Household Saints*) and Helen De Michiel (*Tarantella*) are the only members of the third generation who would appear to be making films that focus programmatically, albeit subversively, on the Italian-American experience. While the concern with food and family continues, organized crime, that mainstay of the second generation, is absent, and maschilist males are revealed as weak and pathetic.

Italian-American actors, while not always necessarily restricted to ethnic roles, do seem to be indispensable for the making of Italian-American cinema. Amongst the most connected with Italian-American cinema one would include Al Pacino, Robert De Niro, Danny DeVito, Joe Pesci, Paul and Mira Sorvino, Sylvester Stallone, John Travolta and John Turturro.

Further reading

Casillo, R. (1991) 'Moments in Italian-American Cinema: From "Little Caesar" to Coppola and Scorsese', in A.J. Tamburri, P.A. Giordano and F.L. Gardaphè (eds), *From the Margin: Writings in Italian Americana*, West Lafayette, IN: Purdue University Press, 374–96 (comes both to praise Italian-American film and to bury 'this twilight of ethnicity').

Cortes, C.E. (1987) 'Italian-Americans in Film: From Immigrants to Icons', *Melus* 14 (3–4): 108–26 (a somewhat optimistic study of the evolving representation of Italian-Americans on screen).

Golden, D.S. (1980) 'The Fate of *La Famiglia*: Italian Images in American Film', in R.M. Miller (ed.), *The Kaleidoskopic Lens: How Hollywood Views Ethnic Groups*, Englewood Cliffs, NJ: Jerome S. Ozer, 73–97 (the conflict between the old ways and assimilation).

Lawton, B.R. (1995) 'What is "Italian American" Cinema?', *Voices in Italian Americana* 6 (1): 23, 27–51 (an attempt to identify the key features of Italian-American cinema).

Sautman, F.C. (1994) 'Women of the Shadows: Italian American Women, Ethnicity and Racism in American Cinema', *Differentia* 6/7: 219–46 (an intelligent feminist study of the caricatures of Italian-American women in American cinema).

Tamburri, A.J., Gardaphè, F.L., Giunta, E. and Bona, M.J. (eds) (1997) *Italian/American Literature and Film: A Select Critical Bibliography*, West Lafayette, IN: Bordighera (the best single source for further reading on Italian-American film).

BEN LAWTON

Italsider

The operating company of the **Finsider** state participation holding for the steel sector in the period from 1959 to 1987, Italsider became known as Nuova Italsider in the 1980s after a restructuring of its operating facilities and debt. Its principal operating plants were in Genoa, Piombino, Naples and Taranto. The last, Italy's only greenfield integrated site built after the Second World War, was initially designed to produce approximately three million tonnes of crude steel, but was doubled and redoubled again giving it a capacity of nearly 11.5 million tonnes, thus becoming Europe's largest integrated facility and one of the three largest in the world. In 1989, Nuova Italsider decommissioned the Bagnoli works in Naples. In 1987, a second major restructuring saw remaining holdings being either privatized or restructured into a new company called **Ilva**.

See also: industry

Further reading

Masi, A.C. (1987), 'Nuova Italsider-Taranto and the Steel Crisis: Problems, Innovations, and Prospects', in Y. Mény and V. Wright (eds), *The Politics of Steel: Western Europe and the Steel Industry in the Crisis Years (1974–1984)*, New York: Walter de Gruyter.

ANTHONY C. MASI

IUAV

The IUAV (Istituto Universitario di Architettura di Venezia, or Venice University Institute of Architecture) is one of the oldest and most important schools of architecture in Europe. Under the directorship of **Samonà** from 1945–71, the liveliest protagonists of architectural culture in Italy were called to teach there – amongst them **Albini**, Belgiojoso, **De Carlo**, **Gardella**, **Muratori** and **Scarpa** (who became director from 1972–8) – and it achieved prominence as a refuge for restless non-academic intellectuals. Later, figures such as **Gregotti**, **Aymonino**, **Rossi**, **Tafuri** (who was director of the Department of History of Architecture) and Massimo **Cacciari** also taught there.

The Institute was renowned for the innovative analyses which it developed in an attempt to refound architectural theory both as an extension and as a critique of modernism. Its particular concerns remained the areas of the city in history, the relationship of building to region, building typology, and figuration and drawing.

Further reading

Semerani, L. (ed.) (1985) *The Venice School*, London: Architectural Design/New York: St. Martin's Press (a concise and illustrated review of the School's scope).

ROSS JENNER

J

Jaeggy, Fleur

b. 1940, Zurich

Novelist and translator

Fleur Jaeggy lives and works in Milan. In addition to a number of critical essays on and translations from De Quincey and Schwob among others, she published short novels such as *Il dito in bocca* (The Finger in the Mouth) (1968), *L'angelo custode* (The Guardian Angel) (1971) and *Le statue d'acqua* (The Water Statues) (1980). Childhood and education, madness and solitude are the recurrent motifs of her narrative characterized by a clear and aphoristic style. Her novel *I beati anni del castigo* (Sweet Days of Discipline) (1989), the story of a female friendship set in a girls' boarding school in Switzerland, was awarded the Rapallo prize in 1990 and translated into several languages. With this novel and her latest collection of short stories *La paura del cielo* (Last Vanities) (1995), Jaeggy's introspective narrative finally won the critics' recognition and the public's favour, both in Italy and abroad.

FRANCESCA PARMEGGIANI

Jannacci, Enzo

b. 3 June 1935, Milan

Singer-songwriter and physician

A bizarre mixture of contrasting talents, Vincenzo 'Enzo' Jannacci is both a practising cardiologist who holds a black belt in karate and one of Italy's most respected songwriters and cabaret performers. He began singing in clubs at night while studying medicine in Milan in the 1950s, and soon formed a comic duo with Giorgio **Gaber** called I due corsari (The Two Buccaneers). In the 1960s, often using the Milanese dialect, he further developed his particular brand of surreal humour in songs such as 'El purtav i scarp de tennis' (He Wore Tennis Shoes) (1964) while at the same time performing political songs with Dario **Fo**. In 1968 he achieved national notoriety with a rather demented composition titled 'Vengo anch'io; no, tu no' (I'll Come Too; No You Won't) and since then he has released over twenty albums to remain one of the most genial and iconoclastic musical figures in Italy.

A consummate performer who uses mime and the body as well as voice, in 1994 Jannacci instituted a cabaret school in Milan at his own cabaret restaurant, the Bolgia Umana (The Human Ditch). He has also composed material for other artists, amongst them **Milva** for whom he wrote an entire album, *La rossa* (The Redhead), in 1980.

See also: cantautori

GINO MOLITERNO

Jewish writers

Any discussion of contemporary Jewish writing in Italy needs to begin with the historical fact that Jews in Italy have never represented a very visible

Other. They have remained a very small proportion of the population (approximately 0.1 per cent), and it is well known that until the first anti-Semitic laws were passed in November 1938, the Jews were integrated into Italian society almost to the point of assimilation.

The shock of discrimination, and later the experiences of the war and deportation, forced many Italian Jews to rethink the notions of 'integration' and 'identity' and to take active steps to oppose fascism. It is significant that the proportion of Italian Jews who joined the **Resistance** was higher than both the numerical proportion of Jews in Italy and the proportion of non-Jewish Resistance fighters within the Italian population.

It is not surprising, therefore, that recurrent themes in the works of the generation of Italian Jewish writers born between 1910 and 1930 should be the alienation resulting from being declared 'other', the growing commitment to anti-fascism, and the experience of going into hiding, losing loved ones or surviving deportation. Many of them have written autobiographical narratives which contain reflections on family history, on the symbolic role of words and expressions from the Hebrew–Italian dialects, and on the way the men and women of their generation learned to redefine themselves in terms of their difference. The first, and one of the most important, of such works is Natalia **Ginzburg**'s *Lessico Famigliare* (Things We Used To Say) (1963), a reconstruction of the life and anti-fascist activities of her family and friends in the period between the end of the First World War and the early 1950s. Jewish culture is specifically present only in a few, lighthearted references and in the occasional use of jargon, but it is implicit in every page, and is identified with the intellectual pursuits and the opposition to fascism which permeate every detail of personal daily life, often in humorous juxtapositions. Primo **Levi**'s *Il sistema periodico* (The Periodic Table) (1975) starts with a succession of anecdotes about Levi's ancestors, outlining their gradual merging into Piedmontese society through their Hebrew–Piedmontese dialect. The author's autobiographical persona is presented as being gradually forced by the anti-Semitic laws to see the meaning, and the value, of difference as he returns from deportation with a lifelong commitment to memory and witness.

Family anecdotes and sayings, anti-fascism, alienation and the duty to pass on historical memories are also interwoven in Giacoma Limentani's *Dentro la D* (Inside the D) (1992), Gaia Servadio's *Un'infanzia diversa* (A Different Childhood) (1988) and Aldo Zargani's *Per violino solo* (For Solo Violin) (1995). These narratives, published in the 1980s and 1990s, deal with childhood experiences between the 1930s and the end of the Second World War. Limentani is also comparatively well-known as the author of non-fiction works on Jewish culture and collections of stories which retell traditional legends and *midrash* parables.

Of the same generation is also Edith **Bruck**, who must be considered an Italian writer because, although born in Hungary, she has lived in Italy since the 1950s and writes in Italian. The dominant theme of many of her numerous stories and novels – the most important of which are *Due stanze vuote* (Two Empty Rooms) (1974), *Lettera alla madre* (Letter to My Mother) (1988) and *Nuda proprietà* (Bare Property) (1993) – is the pain felt by a middle-aged woman who survived deportation as a child but must come to terms daily with the irretrievable loss of family members and of a whole way of life. Bruck's *Chi ti ama così* (Who Can Love You Like This) (1958) is, with Giuliana Tedeschi's *Questo povero corpo* (This Poor Body) (1946), one of the best-known Italian texts of Holocaust testimony, the most powerful of which is undoubtedly Levi's *Se questo è un uomo* (If This Is a Man) (1947).

The writings of Giorgio **Bassani**, while fictional rather than directly autobiographical, are directly connected to the themes of alienation, estrangement and identity. Many of them – most notably *Gli occhiali d'oro* (The Gold-rimmed Spectacles) (1958), *Il giardino dei Finzi-Contini* (The Garden of the Finzi-Continis) (1962) and *Dietro la porta* (Behind the Door) (1964) – share the same first-person narrator, a young intellectual who describes the lives of the members of the Jewish community in the microcosm of pre-Second World War Ferrara, together with their progressive marginalization from mainstream society. In *Gli occhiali d'oro* and *Il giardino dei Finzi-Contini*, the narrator distances himself from his father's relative optimism about the more 'benign' nature of

Mussolini's Italy as opposed to Nazi Germany, and from any attempt to define Jews in terms of their past traditions. Yet the overall perspective offered in Bassani's fiction is that all the Jewish characters, including the narrator, are unable or unwilling to formulate a coherent, autonomous discourse based on their present oppression, and are therefore ultimately ineffectual and doomed to defeat.

The following generation has been led by the collapse of political ideologies from the late 1970s onward to question the notion of a homogeneous Jewish 'identity' and to focus instead on retrieving fragments of individual and family pasts, which can be connected and contextualized in a constant process of redefinition. In the semi-autobiographical fiction of Alain Elkann – particularly *Piazza Carignano* (1985) and *Vendita all'asta* (Auction Sale) (1993) – Jewishness is represented mainly as the cosmopolitan, multilingual heritage of an extended family network. In Clara Sereni's *Casalinghitudine* (Picking Up Domestic Pieces) (1987) and *Il Gioco dei regni* (The Kingdom Game) (1993), the family history and the life of the author's autobiographical persona are reconstructed through fragmented recollections: recipes in the first text, letters, diaries and archival material in the second. The narrating self strives to reconcile family conflicts, cultural and religious tradition, history and politics, all the 'pieces' of her roots, with all the contradictions that this process entails.

After the Holocaust, it has become impossible for Jewish writers to represent 'Jewishness' as a coherent whole of family, faith and history. The unifying factors in the works of postwar Italian Jewish writers are the retrieval of whatever fragments of the past are meaningful in the present, and the effort to situate them into the context of their changing world.

Further reading

Hughes, H.S. (1983) *Prisoners of Hope: The Silver Age of Italian Jews (1924–1974)*, Cambridge, MA: Harvard University Press (a general survey of twentieth-century Jewish writing in Italy).

MIRNA CICIONI

Jotti, Nilde (Leonilde)

b. 10 April 1920, Reggio Emilia;
  d. 3 December 1999, Rome

Politician

Perhaps Italy's most prominent and respected female politician, Jotti graduated from the Catholic University of Milan and became a teacher. Under Fascism she was an underground member of the Italian Communist Party (see **PCI**) and during the war was an active member of the **Resistance** movement, setting up and leading the Women's Defence Groups. After the war she was elected to the **Constituent Assembly** and was one of the seventy-five members who drafted the **constitution**. Since 1948 she has been a member of the House of Deputies (see **Parliament**) and in June 1979 was elected speaker of the House, a position she held continuously until 1992. In 1956 she became a member of the central committee of the PCI and from 1962 onwards was an integral part of the party leadership. In 1991 she supported the transformation of the PCI, became a leading member of the **PDS**; as such, she was again elected to the House of Deputies in the 1992, 1994 and 1996 elections. When she retired in November 1999 due to ill-health she had served continuously in the Italian Parliament for 53 years.

BERNADETTE LUCIANO

Jovine, Francesco

b. 9 October 1902, Guardialfiera;
  d. 30 April 1950, Rome

Writer

Jovine overcame his humble beginnings to become a teacher and a headmaster, and the figure of a poor, self-taught student achieving success is a common motif in his writings. Moreover, a strong commitment to social justice and a belief that artistic endeavours should be guided by a moral framework informs all his works, which are usually set in his native Southern Italy and illustrate the entire spectrum of human virtues and shortcomings. Several of his early works, including the novel

Un uomo provvisorio (A Temporary Man) (1934), were criticized by the Fascist regime for their anti-government stance, a political position which Jovine would develop further by participating in the **Resistance** during the Second World War and working with the Communist Party (see **PCI**). His major works include the posthumous novel *Le terre del Sacramento* (The Estate in Abruzzi), which was awarded the 1950 Viareggio Prize, and the short story collections *Tutti i miei peccati* (All My Sins) (1948) and *Ladro di galline* (Chicken Thief) (1940).

LAURA A. SALSINI

K

Kounellis, Jannis

b. 21 March 1936, Piraeus, Greece

Artist

Kounellis settled in Rome in 1956, where he studied art and began painting monochromes decorated with stencilled letters. From 1967 he abandoned painting in favour of installation, and his interest in pre-existing materials and objects naturally allied him with the **arte povera** movement. The use of ephemeral and changeable elements gave his work the nature of performance, as when he set fires and displayed live animals. *Cavalli* (Horses), of 1969, consisted of eleven live horses. Later displays using caged birds provoked opposition from animal rights activists. In 1994 he transformed the interior of the cargo ship *Ionion* by welding metal works to the walls as a retrospective. As with other artists of *arte povera*, Kounellis has sought to draw attention to the aesthetic qualities of existing objects and actions, rather than trying to add to the sum of things already in the world.

MAX STAPLES

Krizia

Born in Bergamo in 1933, Mariuccia Mandelli (Krizia) opened her first design studio with a friend, Flora Dolci, in two rented rooms in Milan in 1955. Beginning with a line of skirts, they moved to dresses with fitted sleeves and a flat smooth line. Her first public exhibit in 1957 paraded a series of fruit-print dresses, and this was followed by a black and white collection shown in the Pitti Palace in 1964. Today Krizia is among the most successful and wealthiest of Italian fashion designers, an 'iron woman' in a world of men. She designs for active women like herself who, in her own words, 'like to look good in practical clothes which are comfortable and pleasant to wear but also fun'. The numerous Krizia labels include men's wear, children's wear, knitwear and licenses for glasses, purses, ties, perfumes and kitchen furniture. The Krizia empire sells worldwide, and a microcosm of the Krizia world thrives in the Barbuda resort which she developed and for which she designed everything down to the maids' uniforms. Having no heirs, she 'invests' her fortune in altruistic activities, which include a scholarship for a deserving Barbudan islander and a women's publishing house.

BERNADETTE LUCIANO

L

La Capria, Raffaele

b. 8 October 1922, Naples

Novelist and screenwriter

After graduating in law, La Capria turned to journalism and screenwriting. His first novel, *Un giorno d'impazienza* (A Day of Impatience) (1952), was followed at ten-year intervals by *Ferito a morte* (The Mortal Wound) (1961), which won the Strega Prize, and *Amore e Psiche* (Eros and Psyche) (1973). The novels chart the angst of the same protagonist, at different times of life and in different situations, but always in a Neapolitan setting. Of socio-historical interest are several volumes of his collected essays, while his *L'armonia perduta* (Lost Harmony) (1986) traces the transformation of Naples from a community at one with nature to a city in continual crisis. His 1996 essay *La mosca nella bottiglia* (The Fly in the Bottle) attacks the cult of modernity and the sectorialization of knowledge.

Further reading

Gaglianone, P. (ed.) (1995) *Conversazione con Raffaele La Capria* (Conversation with Raffaele La Capria), Rome: Omicron.

DAVE WATSON

La Gaia Scienza

Together with **Magazzini Criminali** and **Falso Movimento**, La Gaia Scienza represented the leading edge of experimental post-avantgarde theatre in Italy in the 1970s and 1980s. The company was formed in Rome in 1975 by Giorgio Barberio Corsetti, Marco Solari and Alessandra Vanzi, who remained its performing nucleus and chief animators. Its first productions were presented at Beat '72 in Rome, a performing space which was home to a great deal of the theatrical experimentation of those years, although the group soon moved outside to create their spectacles in various public locations throughout the city, as well as taking their productions to many other national and international festivals.

Characteristic of its exuberant and energetic performance style, which was constantly renewed and extended with each new production, was a mobile configuration of the stage space in order to permit an effective co-penetration between the sets and other stage properties and the actors' bodies. This interpenetration of animate and inanimate on the stage, when coupled with an emphasis on partly improvised rhythmic body movements, accompanied but never regimented by music, created a richly poetic theatrical writing made up of gestures and sounds, patterns and repetitions, presenting fragments of stories through striking visual and sound images but with no reference to any pre-existing literary or dramatic text. The overall effect, however, was always of an extreme lightness and freedom, with the actors' bodies often appearing to defy gravity as they found their place almost casually in breathtaking visual tableaux.

Following their brilliant *Cuori strappati* (Torn Hearts) of 1983, tensions began to develop and the company presented itself at the 1984 Venice

Biennale with two completely separate works, *Il ladro di anime* (The Thief of Souls), created by Barberio Corsetti, and *Notturni diamanti* (Nocturnal Diamonds), by Solari and Vanzi. A year later the original name was abandoned and the company split into the Compagnia Giorgio Barberio Corsetti and the Compagnia Solari–Vanzi, with both companies building on their earlier experiments to courageously explore new theatrical possibilities. An interesting development for both companies in the 1990s was a return to the use of an existing literary text as the basis for performance, with Barberio Corsetti drawing much inspiration from, amongst others, the works of Goethe and Franz Kafka, and the Solari–Vanzi company more recently exploring the ritual roots of Euripides' *The Bacchae*.

Further reading

Pasquini, M. (ed.) (1983) 'La Gaia Scienza', *Frigidaire*, July–August, 62–71 (notes on *Cuori strappati*; well-illustrated with colour photographs and set designs).

Ponte di Pino, O. (1988) *Il nuovo teatro italiano 1975–1988* (The New Italian Theatre 1975–1988), Florence: La casa Usher (see pp. 71–89 for extended interviews with Barberio Corsetti, Solari and Vanzi on their work).

Solari, M. and Infante, C. (eds) (1992) *Percorsi Cifrati: Navigazioni nel teatro della compagnia Solari Vanzi* (Cyphered Paths: Navigations Through the Theatre of the Solari–Vanzi Company), CD-ROM produced by Solari–Vanzi and Impronte Digitali for CARL and ETI (a thorough digital documentation of, and interactive journey through, all the work of both La Gaia Scienza and the subsequent Compagnia Solari–Vanzi).

GINO MOLITERNO

Lagorio, Gina

b. 6 January 1922, Bra, Cuneo

Novelist, short story writer and essayist

Lagorio grew up in Piedmont, including the Langhe region, and has lived in Savona and Milan. These geographic landscapes provided the setting for her artistic growth and personal expression and constitute recurring motifs in her narratives. The notion that sense of self can be discovered through a sense of place recurs in works such as the short story collection *Il polline* (Pollen) (1966), and the novels *Tosca dei gatti* (Tosca with the Cats) (1983), winner of the Viareggio Prize, and *Tra le mura stellate* (Among the Starry Walls) (1991), a Strega Prize finalist. Another central theme in Lagorio's works is the experience of women, as for example the novel *Un ciclone chiamato Titti* (A Cyclone Named Titti) (1969) which focuses on motherhood. Lagorio has also written children's stories and critical works, amongst them *Sbarbaro: un modo spoglio di esistere* (Sbarbaro: A Bleak Existence) (1981), winner of the Città Messina Prize, and *Il bastardo* (The Bastard) (1996), a historical reconstruction of the life of Emmanuel of Savoy. In 1987 Lagorio entered Parliament as a representative of the independent Left.

Further reading

Pietralunga, M.F. (1990) 'Gina Lagorio and the Courage of Women', in S.L. Aricò (ed.), *Contemporary Women Writers in Italy: A Modern Renaissance*, Amherst, MA: University of Massachusetts Press.

VIRGINIA PICCHIETTI

Lampedusa, Giuseppe Tomasi di

b. 23 December 1896, Palermo; d. 23 July 1957, Rome

Writer

Giuseppe Tomasi was the last Prince of Lampedusa. His life was dominated by his acute awareness of his place in history at the end of a long line of Sicilian noblemen, and by his love for Sicily despite what he saw as her present decadence. Lampedusa's legal studies were interrupted by the First World War and he never resumed them. Indeed, excepting his appointment as President of the Red Cross in Palermo (1944–6) he pursued no career, and lived in impoverished gentility. Shy and introverted by nature, Lampedusa was exceptionally widely read, but wrote nothing save several articles before the last two and a half years of his life. Out of this late burst of creativity came the novel *Il Gattopardo* (The Leopard) and a number of shorter narrative works. None of these were published in his lifetime, but after his death *Il Gattopardo* won the 1959 Strega Prize (see **literary prizes**) and went on to be acclaimed as one of the greatest Italian literary works of the century.

Further reading

Gilmour, D. (1988) *The Last Leopard: A Life of Giuseppe di Lampedusa*, London: Quartet Books.

JOHN KERSEY

Landolfi, Tommaso

b. 7 August 1908, Pico, Frosinone;
d. 8 July 1979, Rome

Novelist, poet and critic

Landolfi's belief in the futility of literature led to forays into increasingly experimental narrative styles whose very wit and inventiveness undermined the author's thesis. He straddled two worlds of literature, that stemming from the highly disciplined rhetorical nineteenth-century French and Russian Schools (whose authors he translated), and that of the innovative Hermetic movement whose adherents called for radical reworking of both literary structures and themes. Yet Landolfi's narrative style was always uniquely his own, whether he employed a diary format, linguistic tricks or surrealistic characters. Often his female characters are the repository of a mysterious essence that illustrates the slippery boundary between reality and unreality. Amongst Landolfi's numerous works are the poetry collection, *Breve canzoniere* (Short Songbook) (1971), the novel *Ottavio de Saint-Vincent* (1958) which won the Viareggio Prize, and *A caso* (By Chance), the collection of short stories that was awarded the Premio Strega in 1975.

LAURA A. SALSINI

language attitudes

The term 'language attitudes' indicates the attitudes held by Italians towards varieties of the Italian language and its dialects. Overall, with regard to Italian, Italians seem to be torn between loyalty towards the variety that they actually speak (regional Italian) and the aspiration towards a standard norm; with considerable uncertainty, however, about what this norm actually is. With regard to the dialects, they tend to hold positive attitudes towards their users in terms of personal traits, as they consider them nice and reliable, but negative ones in terms of socioeconomic position, as they consider them little educated and poor.

In terms of accent, a comparison between standard (non-regionally accented) Italian and regional (regionally accented) Italian shows that the former, which is far less widespread than the latter, is associated with high socioeconomic and educational levels and is considered the most prestigious variety, according to studies conducted in various cities (Padua, Catania, Milan, Bologna and Rome). However, the standard accent is generally not much liked, as it is seen as somehow unnatural: people speaking without a regional accent are judged cold, distant and to some extent also as show-offs. On the other hand, regionally accented Italian elicits a more negative evaluation from a socioeconomic point of view but a more positive one in personality terms: people speaking it are viewed as less affected and more friendly. This positive evaluation, however, tends to decrease with a marked increase of dialectal traits in the regional variety.

Within these general tendencies, striking differences occur among the various regions. In particular, southern varieties enjoy lower prestige than the northern or central ones, and the Florentine variety has definitely lost the privileged status it enjoyed in the past. The following are some of the most important results from several detailed studies using both direct questioning and indirect techniques (for example, matched-guise tests, where judgements on language are elicited by asking for judgements on the actual speakers). While Milanese people associate a Sicilian accent with low socioeconomic and educational levels only, Venetians give it a negative evaluation also in personality terms, as they consider speakers with a Venetian accent more likeable and reliable than those with a Sicilian accent. Interestingly, this prejudice is also found among Sicilians themselves, from both the socioeconomic and personal points of view, as Sicilians living in Padua consider speakers with a Venetian accent to be more educated, more successful, more beautiful and richer than they themselves are, thus showing a general low self-image. An even lower self-image is shown by Sicilians living in Sicily, who give Venetians more positive judgements on the socioeconomic level than the ones expressed by their co-regionals residing in the Veneto. Like the Milanese, Romans and Florentines also generally claim to prefer their own accent most of all and to wish it for their children as well; in particular, the Milanese variety enjoys high prestige, given that even the Florentines opt for it as their second preferred one. The Florentine accent, although it is never the preferred one outside Tuscany, still retains some prestige, as it is the second preferred accent by both Milanese and Roman people; on the other hand, the Florentines do not reciprocate the favour to the Romans, as a Roman accent is not much liked in Florence.

With regard to dialects, negative attitudes towards them tend to become stronger in connection with women. In fact, women are both harsher judges of the dialects than the men, and targets of harsher judgements when they speak them themselves. Furthermore, certain regional groups stigmatize their own dialect more than others do; for example, the Sicilians seem to favour their own dialect least. As well as gender and region, other variables have been investigated such as age, level of education, and socioeconomic status. A comparison between younger and older Venetians of similar socioeconomic background, for example, shows major differences in their perception of their own dialect, with the older group displaying much more favourable attitudes towards it, to the preference even of locally accented Italian. In Sicily, on the other hand, the younger the age of the people expressing their attitudes, the milder appear their reactions in terms of both the directions of maximum dislike and maximum favour of dialect. Furthermore, the most severe judgements on the dialect are expressed by older

women, with limited education, living in smaller towns.

See also: dialects; Italian language; Italian phonology; varieties of Italian

Further reading

Baroni, M.R. (1983) *Il linguaggio trasparente* (Transparent Language), Bologna: Il Mulino (a detailed study of attitudes towards dialect, regionally accented and non-accented Italian among Sicilians, Venetians and Milanese, elicited through indirect techniques).

Galli de' Paratesi, N. (1985) *Lingua toscana in bocca ambrosiana* (Tuscan Language in Ambrosian Mouth), Bologna: Il Mulino, part 2, ch. 3 (a survey on attitudes towards regionally accented and non-accented Italian in Rome, Florence and Milan, in response to direct questions).

Vecchio, S. (1990) 'Una mappa dell'ideologia linguistica' (A Map of Linguistic Ideology), in F. Lo Piparo (ed.), *La Sicilia linguistica oggi* (Language in Sicily Today), Palermo: Centro di Studi Filologici e Linguistici Siciliani (a study of judgements on Sicilian by a wide sample of Sicilians, through responses to a series of statements).

Volkart-Rey, R. (1990) *Atteggiamenti linguistici e stratificazione sociale* (Linguistic Attitudes and Social Stratification), Rome: Bonacci (a detailed survey of attitudes towards regionally accented and non-accented Italian in Catania and in Rome, through indirect techniques).

ANTONIA RUBINO

language education

In the process of postwar reconstruction, the curricula of Italian schools were redrafted in 1945. The approach to language rejected the fascist ideology of the previous programmes but at the same time returned to earlier, prescriptive conceptions of language education. The model of Italian offered to school students for study and imitation was a literary one, and paid scant regard to the **dialects** which were the first language of the vast majority of students. Subsequent policy reviews in 1955 and 1963 repeated this approach, instructing primary teachers not to use dialect while speaking to their pupils and to discourage use of dialect or of colloquial expressions.

The economic and social developments of the 1950s and 1960s and their linguistic consequences led to reflection among groups of teachers who led the process of change in education policy. The Centro d'Iniziativa Democratica degli Insegnanti (Teachers' Democratic Initiative Centre) drew up a policy document in 1975, the *Dieci tesi per l'educazione linguistica democratica* (Ten theses for democratic language education). The choice of the word *educazione* is noteworthy, since it suggests a more holistic vision than the more usual *istruzione*. This document was adopted by the Gruppi di Intervento e di Studio nel Campo nell'Educazione Linguistica (GISCEL), formed in 1978 within the Società di Linguistica Italiana (see **language institutions**), and had significant influence on the reform of the *scuola media* (intermediate schools) promulgated in 1979.

The 1979 programmes set the study of language at the centre of the educational process:

L'acquisizione di una sempre più sicura padronanza del linguaggio in tutte le sue funzioni è un diritto dell'uomo e, di conseguenza, uno degli obiettivi fondamentali della scuola la quale, con la varietà dei suoi interventi, si propone di promuovere nell'alunno la capacità di esprimere una più ricca realtà interiore ossia il suo pensiero, i suoi sentimenti, come segno di una crescente presa di coscienza di sé, degli altri e del mondo (The acquisition of an ever more secure mastery of language in all its functions is a human right and consequently one of the basic aims of the school which, in its various interventions, aims to promote in the pupil the ability to express a richer interior reality, i.e. her/his thoughts and feelings, as a sign of a growing awareness of self, others and world).

The programmes combine a descriptive study of the linguistic universe from which the students have come and into which they will eventually move (including the historical context of the **Italian language** and the dialects, contemporary **varieties of Italian** and theoretical reflection on the study of language), with the prescription of a model which is considerably more flexible and eclectic than previous models of standard Italian.

In the primary schools, there has been some experimentation and progress in developing contrastive methods of teaching Italian, which involve systematic comparison between Italian and the native dialects of the pupils. This is aimed at encouraging effective bilingualism and at maintaining children's contact with their home cultural environment while introducing them to wider contexts.

From the late 1980s the study of a foreign language has been compulsory for all children from primary to lower secondary school. However, in practice not every Italian school, particularly in the South, has complied with the legislation. In the border regions of Italy, where **minority languages** are spoken, there are, thanks to the autonomous status of those regions, numbers of 'bilingual schools' which offer tuition in Italian and/or a second language. In Valle D'Aosta the second language is French; in the province of Bolzano in the region of Trentino Alto-Adige, the second languages are German and, in certain valleys, Ladin; in Friuli Venezia-Giulia, the second languages are Slovene and, in a small number of schools, Friulian. In Sardinia, the regional government has been considering proposals to introduce bilingual education in Italian and Sardinian, but no programmes have as yet begun.

One dimension of language education which has come to the fore since the 1980s has arisen because of the new **immigration** into Italy. The immigrants themselves need to be provided with effective tuition in Italian to enable them to contribute to their host society and gain maximum (human as well as economic) benefit from it; and, even more pressing and difficult, is the presence of the children of immigrants in Italian classrooms. Official measures are inadequate, but there is a good deal of informed debate among specialists on how best to teach Italian to the second generation of migrants, on whether schools should take on the responsibility of maintaining the migrants' first languages, and on how best to educate Italian children to learn from the experience of the new 'multiculturalism'.

See also: dialects; dialect usage; education; immigrant literature; language policy

Further reading

De Mauro, T. and Lodi, M. (1979) *Lingua e dialetti*, Rome: Editori Riuniti (a comprehensive and accessible guide for teachers, written by two of the protagonists of the changes described).

JOHN J. KINDER

language institutions

Italy has a number of learned academies and other institutions, all of which play a role in the development and promotion of Italian in Italy and abroad, but without any single institution having an official status comparable to the Académie Française in France or the Real Academia de la Lengua in Spain.

The Accademia della Crusca (Crusca Academy) is the most famous linguistic Academy. It was founded in Florence in 1583 to keep Dante Alighieri's fourteenth-century Italian alive and free from contamination (*crusca* means 'chaff', and the Academy's emblem, the sieve, represents its mission of separating good linguistic usage from bad). The Crusca's 1612 Dictionary was a monument to that linguistic ideal. Subsequent editions have broadened the scope of acceptable Italian usage to words in common usage in other parts of Italy and to technical vocabulary, and new editions are continually in preparation. The Crusca is also active in academic publishing, in hosting philological studies and in promoting debate on the current state of Italian.

The Istituto dell'Enciclopedia Italiana, founded in Rome in 1931 by Giovanni Treccani, published the monumental *Enciclopedia Italiana* (1929–39, plus later *Appendici*) and many other works of reference and culture. Since the 1980s the Institute has been active in promoting the teaching of Italian language and culture abroad, through the publication of didactic and teacher training materials and organs of cultural and scientific information.

The Società Dante Alighieri (**Dante Alighieri Society**) was founded in 1899 'for the protection and diffusion of the Italian language and culture'. The Society runs Italian language schools in Italy and has branches in very many countries which organize language classes and various cultural activities. In 1984 the Society opened the Università per Stranieri 'Dante Alighieri' in Reggio Calabria.

A number of institutions specialize in teaching Italian to foreigners in Italy. The oldest public institutions are the Università Italiana per Stranieri in Perugia (1925) and the Università per Stranieri di Siena (founded 1917, a public university since 1992). Similar courses are offered in many other universities and innumerable private colleges. The Universities for Foreigners in Perugia and Siena, and the 'Università di Roma Tre' have all developed 'Certificates of Competence' in the Italian language. The three Certificates have rather different emphases, and are all recognized by the Ministero degli Affari Esteri. In some cases it is possible to sit the Certification tests in other countries, at the local consulate, Istituti Italiani di cultura (Italian Institutes of Culture) or at designated universities.

A number of professional bodies are active in fostering informed debate among language professionals as the basis for action on language matters. These include the Società di Linguistica Italiana (SLI, founded 1967) and the Società Italiana di Glottologia (SIG), with memberships mostly from the universities, and the Gruppi di Intervento e Studio nel Campo dell'Educazione Linguistica (1978), founded within the SLI, which focus on the school system.

See also: Italian language; language education; scholarly publishers

JOHN J. KINDER

language policy

Modern Italy has not had a clearly articulated policy on language, but has rather produced broad statements on language as a human right without however specific provisions for implementation. Much responsibility for language policy is devolved from the central government to the **regions**.

Attempts to formulate a language policy had been made by the Fascist regime (see also **fascism and neo-fascism**). Fascism did not produce a coherent set of policies on language, and often showed ambivalent attitudes. Initially, the 1923 Gentile reform of the school curriculum urged teachers to encourage use of dialect by their pupils, as a stepping stone to Italian. Thereafter, the regime became increasingly committed to centralized policies based on 'autarchy' (self-sufficiency) and growing xenophobia under the more general ideological principle, inherited ultimately from the French Revolution, of 'one nation, one language', as seen also in Hitler's ideal of 'ein Volk, eine Sprache, ein Führer' (one people, one language, one leader). Thus **dialects** and **minority languages** were officially banned from public life – schools, the press, theatre and so on – even while they continued to be the everyday spoken language of most Italians. The Italian language was purified, by legislation, of items believed to be of foreign origin (the *Lei* form of address was considered of Spanish origin and banned in 1938), and a rhetorically rich but communicatively ineffective model of the language was offered by the regime through its official organs. Much of the official language policy of Fascism did not leave lasting effects, except for negative views of the dialects and minority languages. In particular, the claim that dialects and illiteracy were linked in a vicious circle was to leave its mark in the **language attitudes** of the next generation, in Italy and abroad.

The 1948 **constitution** ushered in a new official attitude of tolerance and respect. It contains two explicit statements of principle on linguistic matters. Article 3 reads in part: 'Tutti i cittadini hanno pari dignità sociale e sono eguali davanti alla legge, senza distinzione di sesso, di razza, di lingua, di religione, di opinioni pubbliche, di condizioni personali e sociali' (all citizens have equal social dignity and are equal before the law without distinction of sex, race, language, religion, public opinions, personal and social circumstances). Article 6 reads: 'La Repubblica tutela con apposite norme le minoranze linguistiche' (the Republic protects the linguistic minorities through appropriate regulations).

The decentralized system of regional government has allowed much of the responsibility for support for dialect cultural production to be devolved from central to regional and even local authorities. Many **regional governments** have responded to local initiatives in promoting and funding a wide variety of activities aimed at keeping alive local dialect-based traditions. The space conceded to local linguistic legislation was particularly great in the five geographically peripheral regions, Sicily, Sardinia, Trentino-Alto Adige, Friuli-Venezia-Giulia and Valle d'Aosta, declared 'autonomous' by the constitution. In these regions, support for Italian–dialect bilingualism is strong, and there is flourishing production of newspapers, radio programmes, theatre and poetry in dialect (see **literature in dialect**). The Italian state has adopted a non-interventionist, passive stance in relation to the question of dialect usage and maintenance and minority languages, concentrating its resources on combating illiteracy, spreading Italian through the school system and after hours adult education.

The major forces which shaped linguistic developments were the social changes in Italy, rather than any 'top down' policy provisions. These changes included **emigration**, the spread of the national **bureaucracy**, national military service, the **economic miracle** and associated urbanization, the mass media (especially television), and the decision by the **Second Vatican Council** to adopt Italian instead of Latin as the language of the Catholic liturgy. It was these developments that led to the effective Italianization of the population. They also determined the nature of the Italianization, since the **varieties of Italian** which grew out of these changes were not derived from the literary-based model of Italian being offered by the school system, but from the communicative needs of everyday life, which dialect speakers now found they had to meet in Italian. The new varieties of Italian were at once a source of problems and opportunities for change for the school system, which began to respond to these challenges in the 1970s (see **language education**).

The mass emigration of the postwar period led the Italian state to address the question of a language policy towards the Italian communities abroad. The *scuole italiane all'estero* (Italian schools abroad), founded in 1889, had always operated mostly in Europe and Latin America providing an

Italian education to Italian and non-Italian students (12,000 students in 1986). The postwar emigration produced a new type of policy, expressed in the famous 'Law 153' of 1971 (when emigration had almost ceased as a mass phenomenon), which aimed to provide tuition in Italian language and culture to the emigrants and to their children. Other policy initiatives to promote Italian abroad include the activities of the Institutes of Culture (see **Istituti italiani di cultura**); the many scholarships for teachers and students of Italian abroad, provided under the bilateral cultural agreements between Italy and several other countries; and the Italian government 'lettori' sent to teach Italian in selected foreign universities. The number of those studying Italian worldwide, at all educational levels, is estimated at between 1 million and 1.5 million. The regions have also played an important role in offering various forms of contact with Italian and with Italy, to the children of migrants around the world through scholarships and a variety of exchange programmes.

On matters of the form of the Italian language in Italy, there has been little direct intervention at the political level. Attention began to be given in the 1980s to the issue of **sexism in language**, but compared to its English-speaking counterparts, Italian **feminism** has given little importance to language.

Further reading

De Mauro, T. (1963) *Storia linguistica dell'Italia unita*, Bari: Laterza (a standard reference).

Fiorato, A. *et al.* (1992) *L'insegnamento della lingua italiana all'estero*, Turin: Fondazione Giovanni Agnelli (a factual description and critical discussion of Italian teaching in nine countries).

Schino, F. (ed.) (1987) *Cultura nazionale, culture regionali, comunità italiane all'estero*, Rome: Istituto dell'Enciclopedia Italiana (discussion of issues in the promotion of Italian language and culture abroad, by academics and Italian functionaries).

Vignuzzi, U. (1986) 'Why Study Italian? A Survey of the English-Speaking World', in C. Bettoni (ed.), *Altro Polo: Italian Abroad*, Sydney: University of Sydney, Frederick May Foundation (results of a large-scale survey).

JOHN J. KINDER

Lanza, Mario
b. 31 January 1921, Philadelphia;
d. 7 October 1959, Rome

Tenor

Mario Lanza found fame as the star of numerous Hollywood musicals of the 1950s, which provided an ideal showcase for his impressively robust voice. He was born Alfredo Arnold Cocozza, the son of Italian immigrants to America, and obtained his stage name from his mother, who had been born Maria Lanza. After early singing tuition had revealed him to possess considerable talent, he was signed up by Columbia Artists Management with a view to a career as a concert singer. However, these plans were shelved when Lanza was conscripted into the US Army in 1943. His army singing career led to his acquiring the nickname 'the Service Caruso', and during this time he appeared frequently in army shows, including the triumphal *Winged Victory*.

On demobilization, Lanza settled in New York where he began to give concerts and to appear on radio. He auditioned as a recording artist for RCA, but by chance the tape of his audition came into the hands of Louis B. Mayer, then head of MGM Film Studios. As a result, one of Mayer's producers, Joe Pasternak, signed Lanza to a seven-year film contract. In 1948, Lanza made his operatic stage debut at New Orleans with *Madam Butterfly*, but he was to avoid such work in favour of the popular musicals that made his name at MGM. These typically contained a mixture of light operatic excerpts and popular standards such as the million-selling *Be My Love* (from *The Toast of New Orleans*, 1950) and *The Loveliest Night of the Year*. Lanza's starring role in the biopic *The Great Caruso* (1951) prompted further comparisons with his idol, and resulted in increasing public demand for his live appearances. During this time, Lanza began to be troubled by problems with alcohol and drugs, and his weight increased to around 280 pounds. He walked out on *The Student Prince* in 1954 following a row with the director, and this severed his relationship with MGM. After a period as a recluse, Lanza made a tentative return to television in 1956, miming to his old recordings, and soon returned to the film studios under a new contract with Warner Bros. The film *Serenade* (1956) proved a critical and popular success, but Lanza was disenchanted with Hollywood and soon left to settle in Rome. He made his last two films, *The Seven Hills of Rome* (1958) and *For The First Time* (1959) in Europe, and undertook a tour of the continent. He died unexpectedly of a heart attack in a Rome clinic, prompting speculation that he had been the victim of a mafia plot.

Lanza's influence has been acknowledged by such figures as José Carreras and Placido Domingo, who narrated the television biography *Mario Lanza: The American Caruso* (1981). He was undoubtedly instrumental in the popularization of operatic music, but detractors point to his conservative repertoire and limited accomplishments, perhaps belying his genuine abilities.

Further reading

(1991) *Lanza: American Caruso*, VHS video, Kubicek and Associates.

JOHN KERSEY

Lattuada, Alberto

b. 13 November 1914, Milan

Film director

Lattuada's long and eclectic career as a film director saw him associated with most of the important genres of Italian cinema, from **neorealism** to the *commedia all'italiana* (comedy Italian style), and earned him a leading place in Italian cinema.

Before becoming a film-maker, in the 1930s Lattuada worked as architect, photographer and writer. He directed his first film in 1942, an adaptation of De Marchi's *Giacomo L'idealista*. Lattuada's taste for literary sources, ranging from D'Annunzio, Bacchelli, Machiavelli, Verga and Brancati to Gogol and Pushkin has in fact remained consistent throughout his career; the director's investment in literature is a passion which is also reflected in his own literary production. In the 1940s, along with **Zavattini**, **Flaiano** and Luigi **Comencini** (with whom he co-founded the Cinemateca Italiana), Lattuada actively participated in the conceptualization of a new Italian cinema constructed against fascism's petit-bourgeois ideals and concerned with social reality and psychological truth.

One of the forefathers of neorealism, Lattuada was also one of its masters and even though his contribution is perhaps less celebrated than **Rossellini**'s or **De Sica**'s, its originality deserves to be remembered. With such films as *Il bandito* (The Bandit) (1946) and *Senza Pietà* (Without Pity) (1948), Lattuada mixed the aesthetics of neorealism with the violence of Hollywood's 'film noir'. Such an unusually syncretic approach perfectly conveyed the ideological and aesthetic tensions inherent in neorealist film-making while, incidentally, exploring the possibilities of a generic and cultural hybridity that anticipates **Italian-American cinema**.

In 1950, Lattuada co-directed **Fellini**'s first film, *Luci del varietà* (Variety Lights), and during the 1950s, driven by decidedly ambivalent aesthetics, he alternated blockbusters and more personal films (*Il Cappotto* (The Overcoat), 1952, and *La Spiaggia* (The Beach), 1953, both based on Gogol; *Amore in città* (Love in the City) 1953, in which Lattuada crossed paths again with Fellini; and *La Tempesta* (Tempest) 1958), always intriguingly combining elements of the European and the American film tradition.

In the 1960s and 1970s Lattuada contributed to the evolution of the Italian comedy, at once within and going beyond the *commedia all'italiana* tradition, with films like *Mafioso* (1962), which analyses the clash between postwar modernity and customary traditions in the often revisited opposition between northern and southern Italy, or *Venga a prendere il caffè da noi* (The Man Who Came for Coffee) (1971), a caustic portrait of provincial life. Notable in Lattuada's cinema, especially in the films of this period, is an interest in female subjectivity and representation. Such a concern not only yielded strong female characters endowed with depth, but it also launched or confirmed the career of many actresses, including Giulietta **Masina**, Catherine Spaak, Nastassja Kinski and Dalila Di Lazzaro.

In the 1980s, Lattuada's cinema seemed to return to a more romantic vision and to melodrama, with films like *La Cicala* (The Cricket) (1982) and *Una Spina nel cuore* (A thorn in the Heart) (1986). At the same time he indulged his taste for large-scale spectacle by making a four-episode *Christopher Columbus* for Italian television in 1985. Though he has not directed any films in the 1990s, Lattuada has remained active in the film world, notably as the president of the Cinemateca Italiana. Aged eighty, he even acted in *Il toro* (Bull) (1984), directed by Carlo **Mazzacurati**.

Further reading:

Cosulich, C. (1985) *I film di Alberto Lattuada*, Rome: Gremese (a detailed study of Lattuada's film production).

DOROTHÉE BONNIGAL

Lega Nord

The Lega Nord, or Northern League, was formed in 1990 by Umberto **Bossi** through the unification of various northern regional parties. It has been a sometimes secessionist, sometimes federalist, but always strongly devolutionist party with a right-of-centre, free market economic policy. It has also always been heavily coloured by Bossi's personality as well as his politics, which one author called a 'charismatic centralism' (Diamanti, 1993), and, for the first time in postwar Italy, managed to shift politics away from its previous foundations of class, religion and secularism. In the new Italian politics, Bossi works from a basis of blue collar (or singlet) populism, in contrast to Berlusconi's double-breasted starched blue shirt populism.

The leagues began in the late 1970s as an expression of northern discontent with Roman politics. They appealed to a strictly local culture, and until 1987 had scant success outside the Veneto. In the 1990 regional elections, however, the Lombard League polled 18.9 per cent in Lombardy. The League's success mirrored the decline of the established **political parties** and

the system which supported them. The fall of the Berlin wall and then the Soviet Union meant that the centrist northern voter no longer had to follow Indro **Montanelli**'s advice ('hold your nose and vote DC') in order to stop the communists. And at the same time, the smell emanating from the **DC** and the **PSI** became unbearable for many due to **mafia** involvement and corruption scandals (see *Mani pulite*; *Tangentopoli*).

The Northern League's platform was always stridently anti-Rome (expressed in the frequent cry of *Roma ladrona* (thieving Rome)) and anti-South. In a period of massive **immigration** to Italy from Eastern Europe and the developing world, especially from North Africa, the League never made xenophobia or racism part of its official rhetoric, but it was often very close to the surface with electors and supporters, becoming blatant when Bossi supported Slobodan Milosovic's Anti-Kosovar Albanian policy. In 1992 the League won 8.6 per cent of the vote and was the fourth largest party in **Parliament**. Over the next two years it also won power in a number of northern cities including Milan, though this also meant that the party's contradictions as an 'anti-system party' began to show since it had to come to terms with real administration. These contradictions surfaced even more clearly in 1994 when the League formed an electoral alliance with **Berlusconi**'s **Forza Italia**. They won 8.4 per cent of the proportional vote (see **electoral systems**), and because of the alliance this translated into 18.6 per cent of seats, but it was clear that many of Bossi's supporters had voted Forza Italia. The League maintained an internal opposition to the **Polo della Libertà** – particularly against **Fini**'s 'post-fascist' **National Alliance** – throughout the electoral campaign as well as in the subsequent government. In December 1994, the opposition became external as Bossi helped to bring down the Berlusconi government.

As a result, the League went back to being an opposition party with symbolic media events like the 'declaration of independence of Padania' (September 1996) and a 'referendum' on secession (May 1997), though they did distance themselves from the mostly symbolic armed takeover of Saint Mark's Tower in Venice in May 1998. Despite the new electoral system, the League has refused to make alliances; it lost the mayoral elections in

Milan in April 1997. In 1996 it had maintained 10.1 per cent and 59 seats in the Chamber of Deputies.

Further reading

Diamanti, I. (1993) *La Lega. Geografia, storia e sociologia di un nuovo soggetto politico* (The League: Geography, History and Sociology of a New Political Subject), Rome: Donzelli.
—— (1996) 'The Northern League: From Regional Party to Party of Government', in S. Gundle and S. Parker (eds), *The New Italian Republic: From the Fall of the Berlin Wall to Berlusconi*, London: Routledge.

JAMES WALSON

legal system

Italy, like most of the continental European countries, has a legal system based on codified legislation – the so-called 'civil law' tradition – in contrast with the 'common law' tradition developed in England. This system distinguishes between public law (both international and domestic) and private law, the former being concerned with legal relationships in which at least one of the parties is the government or the state (or some body of it) while the latter deals with rules which regulate relationships among individuals or groups of individuals.

As in most civil law countries, in Italy each type of law is based on a legal text setting out the related norms which are administered by specialized courts. The Italian legal system is thus divided into separate jurisdictions. Constitutional law contains the basic legal norms of the state; it is implemented by a **Constitutional Court**, established in 1956, which is charged with ensuring the adherence of all laws to constitutional norms. Administrative law is a separate body of rules which regulates the legal relationships between the state, regional and local organs of public administration, and between those and the citizens; since 1971 these have been enforced by a separate system of special administrative courts, the Tribunali Amministrativi Regionali (Regional Adminis-

trative Courts). Criminal law is contained in the 1930 Penal Code (see **Codice Rocco**); in the immediate postwar period some of its harsher provisions, such as the death penalty, were abolished but the Code's authoritarian essence deriving from its Fascist origins remained basically unchanged, thus heavily compromising relations between the newly established democratic state and its citizens (see **police**). Criminal law is administered by separate courts according to a particular Code of Criminal Procedure. Finally, private law is based on a unified Civil Code promulgated in 1942, which assimilated laws relating to commercial matters. Since then, private law is no longer divided into civil law and commercial law and both are now administered by the Civil Court. Unlike the Penal Code, the Civil Code was only marginally influenced by Fascist legal thought and thus comprises a set of norms which fit in well with both the liberal tradition of Italian legal culture and the most advanced civil laws of other European countries.

The republican **constitution** of 1948 sought to established the judiciary as an important and independent check on both legislative and executive powers. The judiciary is thus controlled by an independent body, the Consiglio superiore della magistratura (Higher Judicial Council), which oversees magistrates' recruitment, promotion and discipline. The Council, presided over by the **President of the Republic**, is made up of thirty judges, lawyers and legal experts, twenty of whom are chosen by the magistrates themselves, the other ten being appointed by the **Parliament**. Nonetheless, throughout the whole Republican period the judiciary has been deeply permeated by political influence. Behind a formalist and apparently neutral façade, it was the government – and indirectly the ruling **DC** – which after 1945, through the Ministry of Justice, held sway over the magistrates by both controlling their careers and allowing them extremely favourable salaries. The Higher Judicial Council only came into operation in 1959, and its scope was effectively reduced by the government.

The situation changed dramatically during the 1960s and 1970s when the traditional 'one-way politicization', which largely aligned magistrates with the law-making majority, began to be checked by an increasing pluralism within the judiciary itself. This ceased being a compact, opaque body when factions within the magistrates openly emerged, with autonomous organizations, independent strategies, distinct legal cultures and different political attitudes which roughly corresponded to the categories of Left, Centre and Right. Nor was this was the only way through which the judiciary began to play a different political role. A national ordinary free-standing legislation, set apart from the norms prescribed by the Codes, gained momentum especially in the 1970s. Then the Parliament passed several bills which deeply changed the legal framework of a large number of matters – the most far-reaching being the **divorce** and **abortion** legislation, the Statuto dei lavoratori (the Workers' Statute, which set out the rights of workers in their workplaces) and a number of laws concerned with urban, financial and environmental crimes. Such new social issues, supported by **trade unions** and pressure groups, required protection and active promotion from the judiciary in order to overcome the widespread opposition from the affected interests, so much so that magistrates who actively implemented the new legislation acquired the nickname *pretori d'assalto* (assault judges).

At the same time, threats stemming from political **terrorism** and organized crime (see **mafia**) induced the Parliament to pass a series of 'emergency' security laws which enormously enhanced the discretionary powers of police, prosecutors and judges, and severely restricted citizens' civil rights. New and ill-defined crimes such as 'terrorist association' and 'mafia association' were introduced, which were aimed at prosecuting not only suspects of crimes but also their alleged associates in whatever way possible. Consequently, the earlier Fascist practice of allowing a suspect to be interrogated in the absence of an attorney was reintroduced, preventive detention was extended and much, often unscrupulous, use was made of **pentiti** or 'repenters', who enjoyed reduced penalties, or even freedom and police protection, in exchange for implicating others. All of this pushed the judiciary into a situation of role overload and high political exposure, further enhanced by the emergence in the 1970s and 1980s of widespread political corruption which often put magistrates and ruling politicians at odds.

Catch-all politicization, together with some gross miscarriages of justice – the most famous being the case of popular television presenter, Enzo Tortora, who was unjustly tried and sentenced after having being falsely implicated by *pentiti* with the Neapolitan Camorra – weakened people's confidence in the independence and impartiality of magistrates and led to a questioning of their very legitimacy. This was confirmed in 1987, when a referendum for removing judges' indemnity from civil liability resulted in a massive consensus, thus leading to the creation of a system for determining civil liability of judges accused of 'grave errors'. Even more importantly, a new Code of Criminal Procedure was introduced in 1989, which adopted some elements from the Anglo-Saxon common law. A new figure, the *giudice per le udienze preliminari* (judge for preliminary hearings) was created to determine, on the basis of an adversarial hearing, whether a prosecution should proceed, with defence attorneys and public prosecutors being given an equal role in all phases of the process and the defence being allowed to cross-examine witnesses.

The roles of judges and prosecutors thus came to be separated (although often more in theory than in fact), and the balance of interest between the accused person and the state was partly redressed, even though the transition to the new system proved controversial and the mix of old-style inquisitorial and new adversarial methods led to some initial confusion. At the same time, attempts by the ruling parties to bring the *pubblici ministeri* (public prosecutors) more tightly under government control failed because of the dogged resistance by a large part of the judiciary itself, strongly supported by the Left.

Fierce political confrontations regarding the judiciary's role have become even more heated in recent years, after the ***Tangentopoli*** investigations brought to light the existence of systemic political corruption within traditional parties, and Silvio **Berlusconi**, the media tycoon turned political leader, was also subjected to a number of investigations. There has also been strong criticism of the widespread use of preventive custody by prosecutors, a very sensitive matter given that illustrious party notables and top level managers of both state and private big business experienced long periods of custody. Harsh rows have continued to flare regarding the political use of judicial powers, and some proposed reforms of the judicial system (such as the full separation of careers between prosecutors and judges) have undoubtedly contributed to the faltering of the proposals for institutional reform (*Bicamerale*). If not formally resolved, such a conflict of powers risks becoming endemic, thus weakening the legitimacy of the judiciary itself in the eyes of the ordinary citizen which, needless to say, would represent a major weakness for Italian democracy and a source of inherent instability.

See also: *Mani pulite*

Further reading

Guarnieri, C. (1997) 'The Judiciary in the Italian Political Crisis', in M. Bull and M. Rhodes (eds), *Crisis and Transition in Italian Politics*, London and Portland: Frank Cass (a series of articles that effectively illustrate major questions related to the political role of the judiciary in Italy in the 1980s–1990s).

Rodotà, S. (1998) 'The Judiciary and Politics', in M. Donovan (ed.); *Italy*, Aldershot: Ashgate-Dartmouth, vol. 1.

Volcansek, M. (1998) 'The Judicial Role in Italy: Independence, Impartiality and Legitimacy', in M. Donovan (ed.), *Italy*, Aldershot: Ashgate-Dartmouth, vol. 1.

Watkin, T.G. (1997) *The Italian Legal Tradition*, Aldershot: Ashgate-Dartmouth (a concise and updated presentation of the main features of the Italian legal system and its historical roots).

STEFANO BATTILOSSI

Legge Mammì

The Mammì law (named after the minister responsible, Oscar Mammì) was a belated attempt to impose some measure of regulation on a broadcasting system which had emerged within a legislative vacuum. It referred specifically to private television and radio, as public broadcasting was served by existing legislation (1975, law no. 103).

Rather than carrying out a fundamental over-haul of the regulatory mechanisms, Mammì enacted a statutory acknowledgement of a 'duopoly' between the public broadcasting corporation, Radiotelevisione Italiana (**RAI**), and the national commercial network owned by Silvio **Berlusconi**'s **Fininvest** corporation. Berlusconi's network had emerged through flouting the existing anachronistic legislation which restricted private broadcasting to the local level. The Mammì law established a minimum of quality controls to regulate private broadcasting. It established the post of il Garante (the 'Guarantor') to keep a register of stations, rule on libel controversies, report to Parliament, meet with a Viewers' Advisory Council and set up minimal regulations on accepted standards of decency in programming and scheduling.

PAUL STATHAM

Leone, Sergio

b. 3 January 1929, Rome; d. 30 April 1989, Rome

Film director and producer

Son of silent film director Roberto Roberti, Leone served his apprenticeship in cinema as assistant director to **De Sica** and Mario Bonnard. However, his international renown derives mostly from his association with the '**spaghetti western**', a hybrid genre that developed in the 1960s and which, with its stylized, exaggerated and humorous renditions of a derelict world ruled by merciless and vindictive outlaws, revolutionized the classical Western tradition. Leone's bemusedly self-conscious films are inseparable from the musical scores of composer Ennio **Morricone**.

Significantly, Leone's mastery over the genre is founded on only five Westerns, though these include the legendary *Il buono, il brutto, il cattivo* (The Good, the Bad and the Ugly) (1966), and the equally celebrated *C'era una volta il west* (Once Upon a Time in the West) (1968) starring Henry Fonda and Claudia **Cardinale**. With his last film, *C'era una volta in America* (Once Upon a Time in America) (1983), starring Robert De Niro, Leone also demonstrated his command of the epic gangster genre.

Further reading

Bondanella, P. (1994) *Italian Cinema*, New York: Continuum (see ch. 7: 'A Fistful of Pasta: Sergio Leone and the Spaghetti Western').

DOROTHÉE BONNIGAL

Levi, Carlo

b. 29 November 1902, Turin; d. 4
January 1975, Rome

Novelist and painter

A medical doctor with a passion and a talent for painting, Levi was also an active anti-fascist. Tried by the regime in the 1930s, he was sent to a small town in the Southern region of Lucania (Basilicata) where he remained for some years. The result was a number of paintings of the South and its people, and also one of the most potent works of fictional autobiography in Italian literature, *Cristo si è fermato a Eboli* (Christ Stopped at Eboli) (1945). The work presents a striking portrait of the misery, poverty and the atavistic fatalism pervading the southern peasant population, filtered through the intellectually alert eyes of an educated northerner. The book, moving but not sentimental, is characterized by a dense narrative and a sharp psychological dissection which does not spare the pettiness and the provincialism of the local bourgeoisie. The autobiographical mode also pervades other works by Levi such as *L'orologio* (The Watch) (1950), *Le parole sono pietre* (Words are Stones) (1955) and *Tutto il miele è finito* (All the Honey is Finished) (1964).

See also: peasants

PAOLO BARTOLONI

Levi, Primo

b. 31 July 1919, Turin; d. 11 April 1987,
Turin

Holocaust survivor, writer and chemist

Primo Levi is best known, and most admired outside Italy, as one of the most powerful witnesses of the Holocaust, although since his death scholars and readers have become increasingly conscious of the literary value of his work. His testimony – which begins with his first book of memoirs, *Se questo è un uomo* (If This Is a Man) (1947), continues with *La tregua* (The Truce) (1963), with stories, poems, essays and lectures, and is finally summed up in *I sommersi e i salvati* (The Drowned and the Saved) (1986) – is a lesson in commitment for the present and the future. Levi stresses that the memory of the death camps does not belong only to Jews, but to the whole of humankind, and the duty to remember also involves the duty to think historically, trying to recognize the danger signals.

Levi's writings, however, have dimensions and meanings that go beyond the Holocaust. An industrial chemist who worked in a paint factory for nearly thirty years, he looked at the cognitive and moral aspects of scientific and technological work, representing it as an individual testing ground as well as the source of political and moral conflict. His masterpiece, *Il sistema periodico* (The Periodic Table) (1975) is a series of twenty-one stories, mostly autobiographical, each named after one of the chemical elements in Mendeleev's table. The stories are narratives dealing with the lessons which Levi's autobiographical persona and other characters learn from experiences of direct contact with an element, and are also interconnections of discourses on history, science and Jewishness. *La chiave a stella* (The Wrench) (1978), fourteen stories centred around the globe-trotting adventures of a Northern Italian industrial fitter, is at once a celebration of the challenges of all skilled work, a reflection on the craft of narration and a linguistic experiment, recreating as it does the Italian of post-Second World War working-class culture. In the essays collected in *L'altrui mestiere* (Other People's Trades) (1985) Levi consistently, and often humorously, stresses the need for human beings to be 'curious about many things', to keep learning about and from history, science and technology, to apply this knowledge to their daily experiences and to communicate what they have learned.

A middle-class, assimilated Jew who was forced to rethink his identity when anti-Semitic laws were passed in Italy in 1938, Levi discovered the richness of European Jewish culture in Auschwitz. He subsequently made conscious efforts to retrieve elements of Jewish tradition and to pass them on to his Gentile readers, in his autobiographical works, his essays and his one novel, *Se non ora, quando?* (If Not Now, When?) (1982), the story of a unit of Eastern European Jews who carry out guerrilla actions across Nazi-occupied Europe and, at the end of the war, head for Palestine. A confirmed agnostic, Levi viewed his heritage in a strongly humanist light, emphasizing above all its love for learning and its principle of solidarity between human beings.

See also: Jewish writers

Further reading

Cicioni, M. (1995) *Primo Levi: Bridges of Knowledge*, Oxford: Berg (a general introduction to Levi and his writings for English-speaking readers, with a full bibliography).

MIRNA CICIONI

Levi Montalcini, Rita

b. 22 April 1909, Turin

Neurologist and medical researcher

One of Italy's few internationally recognized female scientists, Levi Montalcini graduated in medicine in 1936, going on to specialize in neurology and psychiatry. She was forced to flee Italy to escape anti-Semitic persecution, but returned after the Second World War to work as a research assistant at the Institute of Anatomy at Turin University. In 1947 she moved to America to teach and research at the Washington University of St. Louis, alternating with periods at the Rio de Janeiro Institute of Biophysics. She returned to Rome in 1969 to direct research into cellular biology for the CNR. Her own researches led to the discovery of the NGF (Nerve Growth Factor), for which she received the Nobel Prize for Medicine in 1986, sharing it with the American researcher Stanley Cohen. A respected and much-loved figure in Italy, she has published a number of divulgative scientific books as well as an autobiography, *Elogio dell'imperfezione* (In Praise of Imperfection) and a book of advice for young people called *Il tuo futuro* (Your Future) (1993).

Further reading

Levi Montalcini, R. (1988) *In Praise of Imperfection: My Life and Work*, trans. L. Attardi, New York: Basic Books.

GINO MOLITERNO

Levini, Felice

b. 1956, Rome

Painter

Levini was one of the artists represented in the exhibition *Nuovi-Nuovi: From Italy to Canada*, which toured North America in 1986–7. Renato **Barilli**, art critic and art historian at the University of Bologna, grouped Levini with five other 'young artists' under the label Nuovi-Nuovi (New-New) and situated them within the general phenomenon of postmodernism. In his painting, Levini combines both abstract and representational elements, juxtaposing imagery derived from the contemporary world with subject matter from the past. His iconic images are set against abstract and textured decorative motifs, and he experiments willingly with scale, always aiming at linear elegance. Levini's more recent work was celebrated within a retrospective of the Nuovi-Nuovi held at the Gallery of Modern and Contemporary Art at Turin in 1995, beside work by other Nuovi-Nuovi such as Luigi **Ontani** and Marcello Jori.

OLIVIA DAWSON

Liala

b. 31 March 1897, Carrate di Lario, Como; d. 15 April 1995, Varese

Novelist

The undisputed queen of Italian light romance, Liala (the pseudonym of Amalia Liana Cambiasi Negretti Odescalchi) published more than eighty titles during her long life. After her debut in 1931 with *Signorsì* (Yessir), her books enjoyed an unbroken popular success in spite of critical reservations from the literary establishment and even personal abuse and attack during the years of feminist agitation. Indeed until the 1980s she was the only Italian writer able to sell one million copies a year. The majority of her narratives recall, in one form or another, her tragic love for the marquis Vittorio Centurione Scotto, who died in a hydroplane accident in 1926. While this event is particularly the subject of *Ombre di fiori sul mio cammino* (Shadows of Flowers on My Path), it is re-evoked in the theme of aviation which is the recurrent motif of most of her novels. Indeed, Gabriele D'Annunzio created her *nom de plume* precisely with the intention of ensuring that *ala* (wing) would always constitute a part of her name. Untouched and unperturbed by any of the social changes that swept through Italy in the wake of 1968, she continued to write light romances which in the 1990s still sold 50,000 copies per year.

VIRGINIA PICCHIETTI

Libera, Adalberto

b. 16 July 1903, Villa Lagerina, Trento; d. 17 March 1963, Rome

Architect

Libera's career closely followed the most significant social and political changes in twentieth-century Italy. Originally he designed in a rationalistic style and later in the so-called monumental idiom favoured by the fascists. In 1927 he joined the so-called Gruppo Sette (Group Seven), and soon after organized major exhibitions in Rome, Budapest and Berlin with renowned architects **Piccinato** and Minnucci.

After 1945 Libera used decoration as an integral part of the architectural object rather than as mere addition, and his works from this period are manifestly successful in integrating decorative elements and architectural form.

In 1958, Libera consulted for the commission that evolved the master plan for Rome's Olympic Village, and in 1962 he participated in redesigning the university architecture curriculum, a move which eventually divided the architecture faculties of Rome and Florence. Libera's design career culminated in the villa built for author Curzio

Malaparte on the island of Capri, later the stunning setting of Jean-Luc Godard's film *le Mépris* (Contempt) (1963).

Further reading

Garofalo, F. and Veresani, L. (eds) (1992) *Adalberto Libera*, New York: Princeton Architectural Press (an illustrated anthology of Libera's built and unbuilt works, also contains biography, extensive bibliography and a list of projects and writings).

FASSIL ZEWDOU

Liberal

Founded in March 1995 by Ferdinando Adornato, who continued to be its editor-in-chief and its principal driving force, the magazine *Liberal* was born with the declared aim of instituting an active dialogue between Catholic and lay forces and generally to promote a spirit of true political liberalism in the 'new' Italy, outside party forma-tions. The magazine, originally an attractively illustrated large-format monthly, received strong support and collaboration from many important figures; the first issue, for example, took on the daunting theme of how to change both the Left and the Right, and also carried a discussion between the Archbishop of Milan, Carlo Maria **Martini**, and semiologist Umberto **Eco** on the subject of faith and ethics. Through its affiliated Foundation of the Friends of *Liberal*, whose members included august financial figures such as Cesare **Romiti**, the magazine also promoted intellectual exchange and dialogue through a series of high-level colloquia and conferences. The magazine was turned into a weekly in February 1998 and initially sold well, but sales soon declined to around 10,000, raising fears that despite its undoubted quality, the magazine might not survive into the twenty-first century.

GINO MOLITERNO

Linus

The first Italian magazine to focus on **comics** and to upgrade that marginalized medium to the higher ranks of the artistic avantgarde, *Linus* first appeared in 1965 and was backed by intellectuals such as Oreste Del Buono, Umberto **Eco**, Elio **Vittorini** and Vittorio Spinazzola. It was targeted at an educated adult readership who were likely to appreciate those comic strips which had fascinated them in adolescence. The most famous authors and characters of international comics were presented in correctly translated versions which revisited old hits or proposed new ones. Not only did one find *Dick Tracy* by Chester Gould, *Li'l Abner* by Al Capp, *Krazy Kat* by George Herriman and *Popeye* by E. Segar but also *Peanuts* by Charles. M. Schulz, *Pogo* by Walt Kelly, *The Wizard of Id* by Parker and Hart and *Barbarella* by Jean Claude Forest. The magazine also hosted many budding Italian talents among them Renato Calligaro, Guido Crepax, Hugo **Pratt**, Enzo Lunari, Altan and Sergio Staino. The choice of Schultz's peculiar character for the title of the magazine was highly significant: Linus, the neurotic and complex-riddled kid, thanks to his intellectual ability, manages to win out over the scheming Lucy and the clumsy Charlie Brown.

At the outset *Linus* was an elitist magazine, but its anti-conformist snobbery was to be accepted and diffused among the masses: its message was fundamentally left-wing. Its readership grew to include adolescent students, who were especially drawn to *Peanuts*, a cult which spread rapidly. Elegantly drawn in a sober two-dimensional style, the young characters of Schulz's mini-stories display, despite their age, all the typical adult middle-class neuroses and respond with comic irony, pathetic melancholy and sarcasm to their condition of existential loneliness. Readers whose need for socialization was left unsatisfied in their everyday lives could easily identify with them while keeping a critical distance. The magazine's success was also due to its eclectic juxtaposition of different and contrasting languages and styles. The concise, well-mannered, elliptic and allusive strips appeared alongside long erotic stories like those of *Barbarella* and the deeply polemical, and often coarse, discourse of the Italian satirists and their carica-tures. *Linus* opened the market for many magazines of, and about, comics, among them *Eureka*, *Sgt. Kirk* and many other emulations such as *Comics-rama*, *Smack*, *Okay*, *Tommy*, *Tilt* and *L'Asso di Picche* (Ace of Spades).

Towards the end of the 1970s, *Linus* increased its social and political commitment and dedicated more room to satire and social criticism, a formula which helped maintain its readership until the 1990s. From the outset, it ran supplements offering material which could not be included within the magazine itself. In 1974 one of these supplements became a magazine in its own right, *Alter Linus*. It published mainly adventure stories, which had always been sacrificed to some extent in favour of the short comic strips. Popularity increased when it started to publish material from the French vanguard comics periodical *Metal Hurlant* (especially the work by Moebius). In 1977, *Alter Linus* changed its name to *Alter Alter*. Under the new name it continued its quest for new expressive dimensions, and launched in 1983 a group of avantgarde authors, the 'Valvoline Motorcomics', who in their drawings made continuous reference to pictorial art, especially to the Bauhaus and the **transavantgarde**. Publication ceased in 1986 due to a general crisis engendered by the expansion of television and video.

FRANCO MANAI

literary journals

Literary journals in Italian contemporary culture fall into two basic groups: academic journals, strictly devoted to hosting scholarly articles, and literary reviews oriented towards general discussion of current artistic events, in their cultural, sociological and political context.

The roots of the non-academic journals stretch back to the beginning of the century, when intellectuals such as **Croce**, Pirandello, Prezzolini Papini, and Marinetti animated the cultural scene, discussing artistic, historical, political and social issues in periodicals like *La critica*, *La voce*, *Lacerba* and *Nuova antologia*. The connection between sociological and literary issues became predominant in the journals founded after the Second

World War. Amongst these reviews were *Il Politecnico* (1945–7), directed by Elio **Vittorini**, who promoted a cultural view closely connected with the social issues raised by **neorealism**, although he tried to maintain a theoretical separation between political activism and artistic production. This last goal was partially achieved in the more openly literary-oriented review *il menabò* (1959–67), founded by Vittorini and Italo **Calvino**. *Il menabò* was devoted to monographic subjects, and published new Italian authors as well as new critical theories already known and debated outside of Italy (those of Roland Barthes, for instance). Another important journal of the time was *Officina* (1955–9), where authors such as **Pasolini** and **Fortini** confronted the ideological fading of the neorealistic experience, and promulgated a return to a more realistic approach to literature based on the late nineteenth-century tradition. On the opposite side was *il verri*, founded by Luciano **Anceschi** in 1956 and still published today. In the early 1960s, *il verri* became the home ground for writers belonging to the neoavantgarde (**Eco**, **Sanguineti**, **Porta**, **Balestrini** and others) and so focused on the exploration of literature as an ever-changing phenomenon, publishing work often written specifically in order to subvert traditional literary forms. Another important and still active review hosting fiction, sociological surveys and theoretical articles is *Nuovi argomenti*, founded in 1953 by Alberto **Moravia** and directed at various times by Pasolini, Attilio **Bertolucci** and Leonardo **Sciascia**; the current editor-in-chief is Enzo **Siciliano**.

Most of the scholarly journals of Italian literature and culture are usually connected with one or more universities. Amongst the oldest and more prestigious publications oriented towards a rigorous critical and philological approach are the *Giornale storico della letteratura italiana*, founded in 1882 and still published in Turin; *Lettere italiane*, founded in 1949 and currently edited by Vittore **Branca** and Carlo **Ossola**, a journal traditionally open also to theoretical essays and to foreign contributors; and *La rassegna della Letteratura Italiana*, founded in 1953 by Walter Binni, a journal that offers a rich and systematic review section of articles and books on Italian literature, subdivided by century and by topic. *Belfagor*, founded in 1946

by Luigi Russo, traditionally hosts classical and philological essays as well as critical debates and cultural discussions on contemporary issues. Amongst more specialized journals, open also to analyses of foreign cultures and of different disciplines, are *Strumenti critici* and *Lingua e Stile*, both founded in 1966. The former focuses mostly on semiological studies, the latter on interdisciplinary approaches which combine linguistics and literary criticism. Other important journals are *Filologia e critica*, published in Rome, devoted mainly to philological discussions and analyses; *Italianistica*, founded in 1972 and published in Pisa, often centred on critical debates amongst different schools of criticism; and *Critica letteraria* and *Esperienze letterarie*, both published in Naples, and both devoted to classic and contemporary Italian literature. There are also numerous journals, in Italy and abroad, devoted to specific subjects (Renaissance, baroque, romanticism and so on), authors (Dante, Boccaccio, Petrarch) or to contemporary Italian culture (for example, *Studi novecenteschi*, published in Pisa). Outside Italy there are also some very active and established journals of Italian studies, such as *Italica* and *Forum Italicum* (USA), *The Italianist* and *Italian Studies* (UK) and the *Review des études italiennes* (France).

Further reading

Mondello, E. (1985) *Gli anni delle riviste: le riviste letterarie dal 1945 agli anni ottanta* (The Years of the Reviews: Literary Reviews from 1945 to the Eighties), Lecce: Milella (a systematic and contextual study of literary journals and reviews from the immediate postwar period to the mid-1980s, with details of over 170 publications).

ANDREA CICCARELLI

literary prizes

The number of Italian literary prizes has increased substantially in the postwar period and now is, literally, in the thousands. On the one hand, this is undoubtedly a sign of the fertility and the liveliness of the Italian cultural and literary landscape. The creation of prizes such as the Grinzane Cavour or the Montblanc, which aim especially at the discovery and the recognition of new young writers, is a stimulating enterprise and cannot be anything but beneficial to the Italian world of letters. On the other hand, however, it is also true that an excessive proliferation of prizes, some of which leave much to be desired both from a cultural and artistic point of view, risks devaluing for many readers the level of the most established and serious manifestations, such as the Premio Viareggio (Viareggio Prize), the Premio Strega (Strega Prize), the Premio Campiello (Campiello Prize) and the Premio Penna d'oro (Gold Pen Prize).

The Premio Viareggio was first created in 1929 by a group of intellectuals around Leonardo Rèpaci, who remained for many years the president of the jury, and now consists of three different prizes, one each for narrative, poetry and the essay. The books are judged by a jury which over the years has included figures such as Massimo Bontempelli, Giacomo De Benedetti, Natalino **Sapegno**, Giovanni Macchia and Geno Pampaloni. The award takes place in Viareggio during the first ten days of July.

The Premio Strega was designed and founded by Maria Bellonci and Guido Alberti in 1947. The prize is awarded to an Italian novel published between 30 March of the previous year and 30 March of the current year. The jurors are 400 friends of the founders, the Amici della Domenica (Sunday Friends), who represent various aspects of Italian culture. The books are chosen through two successive ballots: the first one takes place in June, at Bellonci's house; the final one is at the beginning of July, at the Ninfeo di Valle Giulia, in Rome.

The Premio Campiello was created in 1963 by the seven Venetian industrial associations which in 1958 gave life to the Fondazione Campiello (Campiello Foundation). The prize is assigned only to first-edition Italian narrative works, and emphasizes the active participation of some Venetian industrial groups in the cultural life of the country. The jury awards at the beginning of June the Premi Selezione Campiello (Campiello Selection Prizes) to five novels. Then 300 readers, representative of Italian society, choose the winner of the Campiello on 1 September, in Venice.

The Premio Penna d'oro was established by the presidency of the Council of Ministers in 1957 for those writers who have especially contributed with their work to the cultural progress of the country. The prize intends to witness the fundamental function and importance that the democratic government assigns to the free and autonomous development of cultural life in Italy.

Among the other more respected literary prizes are the Bagutta, instituted in Milan in 1926 and able to count Emilio **Gadda** amongst its winners, and the more recently created Campiello Giovani, which is restricted to young writers below the age of twenty.

Further reading

Tani, C. (1987) *Premiopoli: un indice ragionato dei premi letterari* (Premiopoli: A Reasoned Index of Literary Prizes) (an investigation of the seamier side of literary prizes).

Tralli, F. (ed.) (1987–) *Catalogo nazionale dei premi letterari* (National Catalogue of Literary Prizes), Bologna: Seledizioni (a catalogue of all the literary prizes available in Italy in a particular year).

ENRICO CESARETTI

literature in dialect

Works written in dialect are usually labelled as 'minor' in standard literary histories, although they have existed since the sixteenth century alongside writing in the **Italian language** itself. Throughout the centuries this creative inheritance has increased, with works in dialect becoming even more abundant in more recent times. Yet debate about the antagonism between Italian and the **dialects** continues to this day, with even the best commentators and linguists sidestepping the need to provide some explanation for the flourishing of literature in dialect.

There is a tendency to maintain that fascism, in the years preceding the Second World War, opposed the dialects and all their rich, cultural heritage (see also **fascism and neo-fascism**). This is only partly true, since one should remember that Mussolini himself ordered the publication of a complete edition of the works of Giuseppe Pitrè on the language, poetry and folklore of Sicily in 1939. Furthermore, there is no evidence that poets writing in dialect during the Fascist period were ever persecuted specifically for their choice of language. By the same token, it is clear that during this period poets were able to use dialects which were still widely spoken in order to address a middle-class readership in the great cities and in metropolitan regions such as the Veneto.

During this era, poets such as Virgilio Giotti from Trieste published their first works, but for the most part dialectal poetry during the first half of the century flourished along the Milan–Rome–Naples axis. It was based on a strong, almost overwhelming realism, and had Pascoli and D'Annunzio as a constant point of reference. The results range widely from the decadent impressionism of Delio Tessa, the musical impressionism of Salvatore di Giacomo and the consolatory folkloric documentarism of Ferdinando Russo and Raffaele Viviani to the elegies of Eduardo **De Filippo** and the fabulism of Antonio Salustri (Trilussa).

In narrative, Carlo Emilio **Gadda** published his first novel, *La Madonna dei filosofi* (The Madonna of the Philosophers), in 1931, followed in the postwar period by *Quer pasticciaccio brutto de via Merulana* (That Awful Mess in Merulana Street), which appeared originally in the review *Letteratura* (Literature) in 1947 and then as a volume ten years later. This work, a detective story set in Fascist Rome, is emblematic of Gadda's narrative method and his extensive experimentation with the use of dialects mingled with slang and technical and scientific jargon. Yet Gadda's linguistic experiments remained marginal in the immediate postwar period, which was instead dominated by neorealism and its polemics against the literature of the Fascist period (which it charged with a lack of commitment).

Nevertheless, neorealist narrative, aided and to some extent preceded by the work of several film-makers such as **Rossellini**, **De Sica** and **De Santis**, attempted to realize a new stylistic model which adhered to spoken language, including dialects. Among the most authoritative representatives of this current were Francesco **Jovine**, Carlo Bernari, Cesare **Pavese**, Domenico **Rea** and Vitaliano **Brancati**. In the theatre, the plays of

Eduardo De Filippo, already recognized in the prewar period, were confirmed as the only viable attempt to continue the tradition of nineteenth-century Neapolitan dialectal theatre.

With the end of neorealism, the use of dialect largely disappeared from narrative (the one notable exception being the novel by Stefano **D'Arrigo**, *Horcynus Orca* (1975), in which the author experimented with an interweaving of Sicilian dialect and Italian language). The use of dialect survived in some theatrical experiments of the work of Roberto de Simone and other young Neapolitans, but came to be used more extensively in poetry.

Within a year of the publication of the anthology *Poesia dialettale del Novecento* (Twentieth Century Dialectal Poetry) (1952), edited by Mario Dell'Arco and Pier Paolo **Pasolini**, the more advanced critics realized that an ideological division had opened up between older and newer experiences of dialectal poetry. The anthology, and especially Pasolini's introductory essay, manifested an awareness of the possibilities for a renewal of linguistic expression and the advent of a literature which showed itself willing to loosen itself from its ties to the popular, impressionistic and folkloric tradition of the first half of the century.

By the 1960s, Pasolini's stance – the demand for a refinement of the instrument of language to the point where dialectal poetry could stand on a par with poetry in Italian – had already affected the work of many of the leading poets. It is no mere coincidence that it was Pasolini's beloved Friuli region and soon the Veneto area more generally that produced the results which served as models for literature in the other dialects. The important figures here were Virgilio Giotti, Biagio Marin, Giacomo Noventa and Andrea **Zanzotto**, with a new poetry which, having accepted its break with tradition, pursued expressionistic aims and asserted itself as no less noble than any other literary form in the national tongue.

The 1970s saw an extraordinary proliferation of poetry in dialect and the emergence of new authors such as Franco Loi, Raffaello Baldini, Franco Scataglini, Amedeo Giacomini and many others. This poetry was expressed in marginal idioms, in some cases manifesting no link whatsoever to any literary tradition. It was written in a dialect which was being spoken less and less but which had thus become precious and more responsive to the text's essential expressive needs. It often stood out as a linguistic code reinvented by the speaker-poet (especially notable in Loi's work), adapted to his specific capacities and requirements.

In more recent years, the number of poets using dialect has increased immeasurably to the point where critics, such as Pier Vincenzo Mengaldo, note the practical impossibility of detecting common lines or currents that might serve to group the individual poets together. Attempts at ordering such a fluid mass of material have been made in several anthologies such as Franco Brevini's *Poeti dialettali del Novecento* (Dialectal Poets of the Twentieth Century) (1987) and Achille Serrao's *Via Terra*. However, the characteristics of the selected poets have been so strikingly dissimilar that the editors have generally limited themselves to highlighting the importance of such individual poets within the general phenomenon of dialectal poetry. In this sense, the most significant figures are undoubtedly the above-mentioned Franco Loi, Raffaello Baldini, Franco Scataglini and Amedeo Giacomini, together with Giose **Rimanelli**, Dante Maffia, Roberto Giannoni, Piero Marelli, Giancarlo Consonni and Marcello Marciani.

See also: narrative; poetry

Further reading

Bonaffini, L. (1997) *Dialect Poetry of Southern Italy: Texts and Criticism, a Trilingual Anthology*, New York: Legas.

Haller, H.W. (ed.) (1986) *The Hidden Italy: A Bilingual Edition of Italian Dialect Poetry*, Detroit: Wayne State University Press (a rich and comprehensive bilingual anthology with a general linguistic and cultural introduction plus individual introductions and bibliographies for each region).

Serrao, A. (ed.) (1992) *Via Terra* (Via Earth), Udine: Campanotto.

Stussi, A. (1993) *Lingua dialetto e letteratura* (Language, Dialect and Literature), Turin: Einaudi.

ACHILLE SERRAO

literature of emigration

In older Italian scholarship, literature of **emigration** has usually been used to refer to writing which focuses on migratory themes, produced outside Italy by Italian emigrants. This traditional approach has undergone major revision in more recent times, and is being transformed into a more comprehensive notion able to respond to the changing national and international cultural situation and the new multicultural dimension of countries which, like Italy, have only recently become permanent hosts to masses of foreign immigrants. Understanding the import of these changes and of the way in which they have transformed the very notion of a literature of emigration necessitates an initial clarification of issues.

Literature of emigration as an anthropological definition might be applied to a wide variety of cultural situations, and could include both works written in the original national language or in the many foreign languages acquired by the emigrants in their host countries and then naturally transmitted to their descendants. One major critical tendency has been to regard the latter as part of Italian 'culture' for the amount of anthropological, sociological and ethnological information which they preserve, but with a clear notion that they are really part of a specific cultural field *distinguished* from both Italian culture and the culture of the host country, even if the original emigrant status, with its implicit or explicit tales of emancipation and assertion of the new identity, remains a natural and understood background in most of these works. Typical in this sense are the English works of the prolific Italian-American literary world. After decades of being catalogued or dismissed simply as the product of Italian folklore, or as ethnic American literature in the most fortunate cases, it is nowadays clear that Italian-American literature is part of a broad and growing field of its own, not just classifiable as literature of emigration. This field, now formally known as Italian-American Studies, is strongly connected with both the Italian cultural heritage and the new, immense international cultural horizon opened up by the English language, with all the stylistic and ideological ramifications that such linguistic choice implies and offers. In other words, for quality, quantity, variety, and for its specific and recognizable development, Italian-American culture – as well as any other well-established ethnic culture in a cosmopolitan or multicultural society – is an area which must be approached for its own and in its own world, even if this world can refer to its original as well as to its host cultural background.

Turning to works written in Italian (or in a dialect or in a derivative of it), other issues arise. One of them is the theoretical problem concerning the cultural definition of an emigrant and consequently of an emigrant writer. While in other European countries such as Spain, France or England, the strong presence of a post-colonial literature or the political situation which forced hundreds of Eastern European intellectuals to leave their countries for the Western world have caused a continuous and keen critical attention to the matter, several historical circumstances have instead prevented Italian culture from addressing this issue more consistently. The fact that Italy has been for many decades a country of emigration rather than of **immigration** has heavily influenced the scholarly approach to the subject. The almost uninterrupted exodus whereby millions of people left the many underdeveloped areas of Italy for the sake of survival in the years between political unification in 1860, and the immediate postwar period resulted in the identification of the figure of the emigrant with poverty, desolation, linguistic incompetence and scant formal education. This influenced the scholarly definition of emigration literature in Italy, leading Italian academic culture to classify it as something pertaining mostly to the sociological sphere, with little or nothing to do with the modern and contemporary Italian literary tradition except in the cases of works devoted to the subject by well-known writers. Because of this distinction, even the connection between emigration and exile was largely neglected. The identification of literature of emigration solely with works written by emigrants who belonged to the underprivileged population driven to migration by poverty and not by ideological and political reasons, limited the concept of literature of emigration not only thematically, but also culturally. This critical assumption, in fact, encouraged a notional gap between emigration and exile, the latter being the cultural condition of authors forced out of the country for political motives, for instance, during Fascism (see also **fascism and neo-fascism**). Thus the connection between emigration and exile was reduced largely to a sense of nostalgia or a depiction of the pain and suffering involved in the migrational experience. It is significant in this regard that Italian authors who were exiled or chose to leave the country during Fascism were very rarely seen as 'emigrant writers'. Their books, as for example in the most famous case of Ignazio **Silone**, may have focused on sociological and political themes which sometimes had to do with emigration, but their real aim seemed to be the raising of anthropological and ideological issues. This double-faceted approach to the subject strengthened the separation between literature of emigration and literature of exile in modern Italy, the latter being the traditional product of educated intellectuals who fully belonged to the mainstream of Italian literature, while the former remained for decades almost entirely a matter of sociological surveys.

And yet, one could easily argue that Italian literary culture itself had long been the product of exile and emigration caused by the geo-political divisions and the foreign dominations which afflicted the peninsula for centuries, and obliged many Italian writers to be, feel and live like perennial emigrants within Italy itself. And this situation was not purely literary; on the contrary, the only common cultural thread which united Italians for the longest time was, in fact, the literary language which stemmed from the fourteenth-century Tuscan of Dante, Petrarch and Boccaccio. Authors who willingly and passionately struggled to learn and master the revered Tuscan literary language politically belonged to Italian states, often ruled by foreign countries, which could be at war with Tuscany herself! A telling example of the depth of this ambivalent cultural perception which created a distinction between being an Italian author and, simply, an Italian, is provided in the early nineteenth century by the case of the major poet, Ugo Foscolo (1778–1827) who, having been born on a Greek island of the Venetian republic, was registered by both the Milanese and the Florentine bureaucracy as a 'foreigner'. While no cultured Italian of the time would have dared to consider Foscolo's poems, novels and plays the work of a foreigner, it was clear that, for the official culture, Foscolo's only claims to being Italian were his literary language and his works while his biographical and historical status was officially that of a foreign 'emigrant'.

Paradoxically, the emphasis placed upon unity and nationalism during the struggle to unify Italy – a struggle which was as much cultural as political, and that indirectly fuelled the nationalistic rhetoric that favoured the rise of Fascism after the First World War – helped to obscure the secular and vital connection between exile, emigration and Italian culture. After the Second World War, the absence of a strong and widespread 'Italophone culture' (a term originally employed to indicate Italian-speaking regions of Switzerland) and the fortunate democratic status which ruled out the possibility of exile as a legal form of punishment or the necessity to leave the country for political reasons, kept the topic almost entirely out of the critical eye.

However, it has been precisely the fading of the socioeconomic conditions which had prevented literature of emigration from being integrated within the illustrious stream of the Italian literary tradition which has forced many critics to reconsider the limits and the definition of subject. Italy's spectacular economic growth and its consequent more central role in European politics, the ever-increasing percentage of well-educated Italians who in recent years have emigrated to take part in the growing international job market, the gradual transformation of Italy from a country of emigration into a country of immigration, have all impacted on attentive scholarship. These changes have created a new awareness of the growing multicultural nature of Italian literary culture leading to the questioning of other traditional and monocultural classifications, once accepted without reservations. Some of these debates have taken up the theoretical opportunity to examine Italian literature not only for its national but also for its 'transnational' characteristics and this has highlighted the need for more inclusive terms for contemporary Italian literary production such as, for instance, the substitution of the traditional definitions of 'Italian literature' and 'Italian authors' with more flexible terms like 'literature written in Italian' and 'authors who write in Italian'. A conspicuous number of African migrants who reside in Italy have in fact begun writing in Italian, entering the official literary scene as 'Italian writers'. In view of this literary output, some scholars have suggested a broadening of the concept of literature of emigration in order to indicate a field which contains both the works of immigrants who write in the new adopted language or of an emigrant who preserves his/her own written language, regardless of the topics of their works. This new definition would allow the works of the growing number of Italian authors who live and operate abroad, as well as the works of educated foreigners who have chosen to write in Italian – not necessarily the typical emigrant according to the old socioeconomic classification – to be considered in a new light. Such an attitude would make possible richer but more specific interpretations of authors such as Fleur **Jaeggy**, Giorgio **Pressburger**, Edith **Bruck**, Fulvio **Tomizza** and Enzo **Bettiza**, whose works reflect an artistic and intellectual pattern often mirrored in their original and multifaceted cultures. Even Italian authors who belong to the cosmopolitan colony of writers who live and work abroad – in the United States, for instance, one could name **Ferrucci**, **Valesio**, **Rimanelli**, **Fontanella**, Pasinetti – can ultimately benefit from a theoretical approach which considers the imagery of their works in a transnational light, deeply implanted in both the native culture and that of the host country.

See also: Italian and emigration; Italian outside Italy

Further reading

Biasin, G.P. (1995) 'Le periferie della letteratura' (The Margins of Literature), *Intersezioni* 3: 439–49.

Gnisci, A. (1992–3) 'Verso un nuovo concetto di letteratura nazionale-mondiale' (Towards a New Concept of National-World Literature), *I Quaderni di Gaia. Almanacco di letteratura comparata* (Gaia's Notebooks: Almanac of Comparative Literature) 5–7: 135–9 (includes indication of Italian works written by non-European immigrants).

Marchand, J.J. (ed.) (1991) *La letteratura dell'emigra-zione. Gli scrittori di lingua italiana nel mondo* (The Literature of Emigration: Italian-Language Writers Throughout the World), Turin: Fonda-zione Giovanni Agnelli (the most important volume on the subject to date, it includes an authoritative and wide-ranging introductory essay, plus a complete bibliography covering theoretical, historical and cultural issues, specific national identities and authors).

ANDREA CICCARELLI

Lizzani, Carlo

b. 30 April 1922, Rome

Writer, director, actor and scriptwriter

Lizzani began as a film critic but soon worked as an actor in Vergano's *Il sole sorge ancora* (The Sun Still Rises) (1946). After making a number of political documentaries, including *Nel mezzogiorno qualcosa è cambiato* (Something Has Changed in the South) (1947) and *Modena città dell'Emilia rossa* (Modena, Communist City) (1948), he collaborated as script-writer with Giuseppe **De Santis**, Roberto **Ros-sellini** and Alberto **Lattuada**. His first feature film, *Achtung banditi!* (Achtung Bandits!) (1951), depicts an episode of the **Resistance**, drawing out its historical and social implications.

In his long career, Lizzani has made a wide variety of films, often exploring crimes and social violence as in *Svegliati e uccidi* (Wake Up and Kill) (1966) but also producing successful adaptations of literary works such as *Cronache di poveri amanti* (Chronicles of Poor Lovers) (1954) and *L'amante di Gramigna* (Gramigna's Lover) (1968). He is also the author of a history of Italian cinema and teaches at the **Centro Sperimentale di Cinematogra-fia**. In 1995 he directed *Celluloide*, an interesting but ultimately disappointing attempt to portray the making of Rossellini's *Roma Città Aperta* (Rome, Open City) (1945).

CRISTINA DEGLI-ESPOSTI REINERT

local administration

Italy is the land of the *cento città*, the 'hundred cities' that can trace their origins to the self-governing communities of the Middle Ages. The fierce pride that many Italians have for the town and province of their birth posed a challenge to the nation-builders of a united Italy. Aspirations for local and regional autonomy were encouraged by the collapse of Habsburg, Bourbon and Church power in the nineteenth century, and, fearing the political fragmentation that federalist and autonomist demands might bring, Cavour and Giolitti were determined to impose the authority of the national state on the communes and provinces that constituted Italy's local administration. Although Article 5 of the 1948 **constitution** made provision for 'local autonomy', most of the local government legislation from the Liberal and Fascist eras remained in place. Luigi Einaudi's demand to 'get rid of the prefects' was ignored by **De Gasperi** and his successors, and Italy retained what was to be one of the most centralized systems of local government in Western Europe.

Italy's local government is characterized by its large number of territorial units, which can vary greatly in terms of their size of population. There are essentially three tiers of local government. The basic level of local administration is the *comune* or commune; the equivalent of a British or American county is the *provincia* or province; and since 1970 all of Italy's regions now have their own elected authority with limited legislative powers (see **regional government**). There are over 8,000 communes, ranging from just a few thousand inhabitants to several millions (in the case of Rome and Milan). Each commune elects its own council, and since 1993 concurrent direct elections for the post of mayor (*sindaco*) have been held. The *sindaco* is both the political figurehead of the municipality and a government civil servant who is charged with a number of important public functions (for example, organizing and scrutinizing all political elections). It is the task of the mayor to appoint the council's executive body (*la giunta*) which is composed of a number of *assessori* (equivalent to commissioners in US local government or depart-mental directors in the United Kingdom). *Assessori* may be drawn from elected councillors or from outside the council chamber. In either case, the *giunta* is independent of the elected council in so far as the operational and managerial work of the commune is concerned. However, the council as a whole has the power to approve or reject the *giunta*, its programme and its proposed budget.

Italy has some ninety-four provinces which, as with the communes, elect a council by proportional representation. The councillors then elect a *giunta* headed by a president, which operates in a similar way to that of the commune. Historically, provincial government has been the least significant tier of local government in Italy, having few direct responsibilities (apart from the upkeep of minor roads, some public buildings, aspects of water supply, and limited community health and social services) and limited expenditure. With the advent of the 'ordinary' regions, the situation improved for provincial administrations, which found themselves the beneficiaries of delegated regional responsibilities such as transport, agriculture, commerce and tourism. The 1990 local government reform also gave the provinces greater administrative responsibilities in environmental protection, intercommunal public transport, public health, and education and training, and the provinces' traditional intermediary function in the area of land use and planning was also strengthened. However, the rationalization of local administration in the form of self-governing metropolitan areas has remained a vague aspiration which perhaps confirms the persistence of historic ties to territorial identities that no longer possess an administrative rationale.

See also: regions

Further reading

Dente, B. (1991): 'The Fragmented Reality of Italian Local Government', in J.J. Hesse (ed.), *Local Government and Urban Affairs in International Perspective: Analyses of Twenty Western Industrialised Countries*, Nomos: Baden-Baden, 517–49 (explores the variety of local government in Italy and the problems this entails).

Hine, D. (1993) *Governing Italy: The Politics of Bargained Pluralism*, Oxford: Oxford University Press (ch. 9 'Regional and Local Government', provides a concise account of substate govern-

ment since the institution of the 'ordinary' regions).

SIMON PARKER

Longhi, Roberto

b. 28 December 1890, Alba, Cuneo; d. 3 June 1970, Florence

Art historian

An eminent art historian who taught at the universities of Bologna and Florence from 1934 to 1961, Longhi exerted a strong influence not only on art critics and writers but also on film-makers such as **Pasolini**. Longhi assiduously practised connoisseurship and the careful study of the formal aspects of works of art, all expressed in an elegant literary style. His early work was on Caravaggio, Piero della Francesca and Venetian painting, but he also supported some contemporary art, recognizing Giorgio **Morandi** as a pioneering modernist and one of Italy's best living painters.

In 1950 Longhi founded the journal *Paragone* (Comparison) with his wife, Anna Banti. He also fought a long and bitter feud with Lionello **Venturi**, another eminent art historian, who kept Longhi out of a prized post at the University of Rome. Nevertheless, Longhi did well out of art, particularly through his promotion of seventeenth-century art to dealers and collectors, and he endowed the Fondazione di Studi di Storia dell'Arte 'Roberto Longhi', an institute for the study of art history, which was established in Florence in 1971.

MAX STAPLES

Longo, Luigi

b. 15 March 1900, Fubine Monferrato, Alessandria; d. 16 October 1980, Rome

Politician

A founding member of the **PCI** as a leader of its youth movement, Luigi Longo was in the front line during the Spanish Civil War, where he gained military and political experience subsequently invaluable to him as party leader in northern Italy throughout the **Resistance**. He became party secretary in 1964 upon the death of **Togliatti**, with whom he had been a close collaborator in developing the 'Italian road to socialism'. He continued Togliatti's revisionist process and rejection of anti-clericalism. Unlike most of the PCI leadership, Longo took a positive view of the challenge to the social order launched in 1968 by the **student movement** and sought to promote dialogue between the party and the movement, although without particular success. Known for his organizational skill rather than strategic or political innovation, he was effectively a caretaker secretary, succeeded by **Berlinguer** in 1972.

CLAIRE KENNEDY

Longobardi, Nino

b. 1953, Naples

Painter and installation artist

Longobardi lives and works in Naples in the sphere of the **transavantgarde**. His first solo exhibition was in 1978 at the Studio Giovanni Pisani in Naples, and he subsequently participated in numerous group shows including 'Italian Art Now: An American Perspective' at the Guggenheim Museum, New York, in 1982, and the 'Avanguardia e Transavanguardia' (Avantgarde and Transavantgarde) exhibition at the Galleria Mura Aureliane in Rome in 1983.

Although originally influenced by **conceptual art** and *arte povera* (poor art), particularly through the work of **Kounellis** and **Paolini**, Longobardi distanced himself from these influences in the 1980s, developing a stylistic eclecticism and a cultural nomadism which then became his hallmark. The critic Achille **Bonito Oliva** identifies in him a typically Mediterranean sensibility, oscillating between the representation of movement (reminiscent of futurists from Balla to **Schifano**), and baroque still-life, where the recurring images come from both the high culture and popular iconography of Naples: fountains, coffee machines, skulls, boats, marine fossils and nude figures. An archaic element in his later paintings suggests a concern with humanity's link to nature and history.

OLIVIA DAWSON

Loren, Sophia

b. 20 September 1934, Rome

Film actress

While Sophia Loren has often been celebrated as the sexiest woman in the world, her sex symbol status hardly accounts for the depth and intelligence of her acting skills, amply recognized by a number of Academy and Golden Globe Awards. Once Sofia Scicoloni, a sixteen-year-old extra playing a slave girl in Leroy's *Quo Vadis* (1951), Sophia Loren became famous overnight in 1953 thanks to her performance as the leading lady in a film adaptation of Verdi's *Aida*. More momentous for the history of cinema was Loren's encounter in 1954 with Vittorio **De Sica**, the director who was to give her some of her greatest roles. In the same year, Sophia Loren met the other major influence in her life, film producer Carlo Ponti, who became her husband.

From her collaboration with De Sica (five films), Sophia Loren won an Academy Award in 1961 for her outstanding performance in *La ciociara* (Two Women). She was often paired with Marcello **Mastroianni**, forming one of Italian comedy's most legendary couples. In 1998 she was awarded a Golden Lion at Venice for her career in cinema.

Further reading

Harris, W.G. (1998) *Sophia Loren: A Biography*, Hemel Hempstead: Simon and Schuster.

DOROTHÉE BONNIGAL

lotteries

The traditional Italian propensity for lotteries was strengthened after the war by the spread of greater affluence. During the period of reconstruction and the so-called '**economic miracle**', along with the revival of traditional lotteries such as Lotto and

Enalotto (both of them drawn in twelve towns), Italy saw the birth of several new forms of mass gambling. These were closely related to the main symbols of success, such as football and television, and their immense popularity can be considered an aspect of Italy's modernization. Totocalcio, a skills game based on the results of Serie A matches (see **football**), was launched by a private company, SISAL, in 1946 and then nationalized by the government in 1949, due to its unexpected success. Totocalcio rapidly became a national mania and its *schedina* (coupon) systematically provided CONI, the national Olympic committee (see **Olympics**), with remarkable revenue. In the 1960s and 1970s another mass phenomenon – and a major revenue for the state as well – became the New Year's Eve lottery, aligned with one of the most popular television programmes, ***Canzonissima*** (renamed *Fantastico* in the 1980s), a variety show mixed with a song contest. After a period of relative decline, lotteries have achieved a revival in recent years, when SISAL – which has continued to manage Totip and Tris (based on results of horse racing) – took over the flagging Enalotto from the state in 1996 and turned it into a national jackpot, Superenalotto, which again succeeded in seducing Italians with dreams of multi-billion lira wins.

STEFANO BATTILOSSI

Loy, Nanni (Giovanni)

b. 23 October 1925, Cagliari; d. 1995, Rome

Actor and film director

Graduating from the **Centro Sperimentale di Cinematografia**, Loy began his directorial career as assistant to Luigi **Zampa**. One of his first feature films as sole director was *Audace colpo dei soliti ignoti* (Brave Robbery by the Usual Suspects) (1959), an obvious attempt to repeat **Monicelli**'s success with *I soliti ignoti* (Big Deal on Madonna Street) (1958). Loy achieved national and international renown with *Le quattro giornate di Napoli* (The Four Days of Naples) (1962), a film in the neorealist style recounting the insurgence of the people of Naples in September 1943 against the occupying German forces. For the following three years, however, Loy was engaged in a television project called *Specchio segreto* (Secret Mirror), a candid camera type of programme which attempted to secretly record the reactions of ordinary people as they were placed in unusual situations, thus bringing out the ingrained habits, idiosyncrasies and taboos of Italian society. Loy's ironic commentary on Italian society continued in later films such as *Detenuto in attesa di giudizio* (Waiting to be Sentenced) (1971) and *Mi manda Picone* (Picone Has Sent Me) (1983).

CRISTINA DEGLI-ESPOSTI REINERT

Loy, Rosetta

b. 1931, Rome

Novelist, essayist and short story writer

Loy made her debut in 1974 with the collection of short stories *La bicicletta* (The Bicycle), winner of the prestigious Viareggio Prize. In many subsequent novels, among them *La porta dell'acqua* (Water's Door) (1976), *L'estate di Letuqué* (Letuqué's Summer) (1982) and *All'insaputa della notte* (Unknown to the Night) (1984), she fashions characters and their milieu through detailed psychological exploration. Milieu also plays a particularly important role in the successful novel *Le strade di polvere* (Dust Roads of Monferrato), the saga of a family of Piedmontese farmers which in 1987 won both the distinguished Campiello and Viareggio Prizes (see **literary prizes**). In her fictional works, Loy has also focused on women's experiences, most notably in the novel *Sogni di inverno* (Winter Dreams) (1992), which investigates the relationship between a mother and daughter in Rome. More recently, with *La parola ebreo* (The Word Jew) (1997), she has also dealt with the theme of the Holocaust.

Further reading

Amoia, A. (1996) *Twentieth-Century Italian Women Writers: The Feminine Experience*, Carbondale, IL: Southern Illinois University Press (see ch. 7 on Loy).

VIRGINIA PICCHIETTI

Luchetti, Daniele

b. 26 July 1960, Rome

Film and theatre director

One of the representatives of the so-called **New Italian Cinema**, Luchetti received his cinematographic training at the Gaumont film school, which he entered in 1980. In 1983 he directed *Nei dintorni di mezzanotte* (Around Midnight), one of the six episodes later included in *Juke-Box*, a collective film made out of the Gaumont experience. He then spent four years making commercials and working as assistant director to Nanni **Moretti** on several of his films. It was Moretti's new production company, Sacher Films, that in 1988 produced Luchetti's first full-length feature, *Domani accadrà* (It Will Happen Tomorrow). *Il portaborse* (The Factotum), released in 1991, starred Moretti in the lead role as a corrupt socialist politician and seemed to anticipate many of the revelations of *Tangentopoli*, just as Luchetti's next film, *Arriva la bufera* (The Storm Arrives) (1993), seemed to anticipate the legal clean-up of *Mani pulite* (Clean Hands). A director committed to political and social issues, Luchetti returned to the theme of the **Resistance** in 1998 with *Piccoli maestri* (Little Teachers), adapted from a novel by Luigi **Meneghello**.

ANTONELLA FRANCINI

Luzi, Mario

b. 20 October 1914, Castello, Florence

Poet and essayist

One of Italy's foremost poets, Luzi has maintained a constant and influential presence in Italian literature for over seven decades with a poetry characterized by its intensity and by an extraordinary wealth of themes and stylistic subtleties.

Highly influenced by French symbolism and Catholic modernism, which he had studied at the University of Florence while earning a degree in French literature, Luzi made his first appearance on the Italian cultural scene in the 1930s. He actively participated in the hermetic movement by contributing to the Florentine journals *Frontespizio*, *Letteratura* and *Campo di Marte* and through his friendship with Carlo **Bo**, Piero **Bigongiari** and Romano **Bilenchi**, among others. In his early collections of poems, from *La barca* (The Boat) (1935) to *Un brindisi* (A Toast) (1946), the poet's search for a transcendental truth is rendered by means of obscure language and images. In his poetry of the 1950s, in collections such as *Primizie del deserto* (First Fruits of the Desert) (1952) and *Onore del vero* (Respect for the Truth) (1957), Luzi would express on the one hand, the existential desertification and temporal disruption caused by the war, and on the other, the persistence of the 'human' in the most humble and least ideological aspects of everyday life. In this context, he highlighted the notion of Christian *caritas*, also understood as social solidarity amongst people.

The contradictory coexistence of motion and stasis in both the individual and the collective human experience, the flow of time and history conflicting with the revelation of the eternal, became the leitmotifs of Luzi's poetry in the 1960s and 1970s. His participation in the ongoing cultural and political debate was documented in *Nel magma* (In the Magma) (1963), while in *Su fondamenti invisibili* (On Invisible Foundations) (1971) and *Al fuoco della controversia* (Within the Fire of Controversy) (1978) Luzi began to consistently fragment his language suggesting that poetry could no longer reassemble the scattered pieces of reality but only express a plurality of voices. The religious reflection underlying Luzi's later collections – *Per il battesimo dei nostri frammenti* (For the Baptism of our Fragments) (1985), *Frasi e incisi di un canto salutare* (Phrases and Interpolations of a Hailing Song) (1990) and *Viaggio terrestre e celeste di Simone Martini* (Earthly and Celestial Journey of Simone Martini) (1994) – testifies to his never-ending search for a metaphysical origin of human existence.

As well as poetry, Luzi wrote several essays on literature – those on Stéphane Mallarmé and Dante's *Commedia* are particularly important – collected in *L'inferno e il limbo* (Hell and Limbo) (1949), *Studi su Mallarmé* (Essay on Mallarmé) (1952), *Tutto in questione* (Everything in Question) (1965), *Vicissitudine e forma* (Vicissitudes and Form) (1974) and *Discorso naturale* (Natural Discourse) (1984). His essays, together with verse drama like the *Libro di Ipazia* (Book of Ipazia) (1978), *Rosales* (1983) and *Hystrio* (1987), complemented his lyric poetry by exploring history and tradition in order to trace the origin of the present time.

Further reading

Jewell, K. (1992) *The Poeisis of History: Experimenting with Genre in Postwar Italy*, Ithaca, NY: Cornell University Press (a study on Pasolini, Luzi and Attilio Bertolucci focusing on the representation of history and temporality in their poetry).

Panicali, A. (1987) *Saggio su Mario Luzi*, Milan: Garzanti (overview of Luzi's poetics).

Specchio, M. and Luzi, M. (eds) (1993) *Luzi. Leggere e scrivere* (Luzi: Reading and Writing), Florence: Nardi (interview with Luzi on his poetics, highlighting Luzi's interest in European and non-European authors and their influence on his poetry).

FRANCESCA PARMEGGIANI

M

Maderna, Bruno

b. 21 April 1920, Venice; d. 13 November 1973, Darmstadt, Germany

Composer and conductor

A composer and conductor noted for his promotion of new music, Maderna entered the Conservatorium Giuseppe Verdi in Milan after early lessons on the violin. This course of study was cut short when he was sent to fight in the Second World War. On his return he resumed his studies in Milan, and then in Rome, Venice and finally Darmstadt, where he later lectured in new music and led the International Chamber Ensemble. He also taught at the conservatorium in Rotterdam and at summer courses in Tanglewood. An enthusiast of the possibilities of electronic music, Maderna founded an electronic music studio with Luciano **Berio** at Milan Radio Station in 1955. This interest in electronic music is strongly manifest in much of his later work.

Further reading

Fearn, R. (1990) *Bruno Maderna*, Contemporary Music Studies 3, New York: Harwood Academic Publishers (a detailed study in English of Maderna's work and influence).

ANDREW SCHULTZ

mafia

The term 'mafia' first appeared in popular and police usage in Western Sicily in the 1860s to name a new type of local criminal association. Today, any form of organized crime inside and outside Italy is likely to be called 'mafia', and the popularity of films (such as those by Coppola and **Damiani**) and novels (see **Sciascia**) testify to the topic's widespread and enduring fascination. Indiscriminate use of the term and media mythologizing have helped to complicate an already controversial topic. Whether the Neapolitan Camorra, the Calabrian 'Ndragheta, America's Cosa Nostra and gang activities in Colombia, Russia and Japan deserve to be called mafias depends on what 'mafia' is taken to mean in Sicily itself, but fundamental disagreements over its name and nature are as old as the thing itself.

Problems in defining mafia

Mafiosi use violence; but so do many other criminals. What, if anything, distinguishes mafia from other forms of organized crime? Cultural, economic and political answers have been given. Some interpreters (Hess, 1973; Duggan, 1989) accept that there are mafiosi but deny that they belong to any kind of genuine organization: 'mafia' is just a loosely-coupled network of independent local gangs (*cosche*), held together by personal links of kinship and friendship, whose members gain respect by using violence in accordance with

Sicilian values in pursuit of their own wealth and power. Other writers insist that mafia is a criminal organization but disagree over the kind of organization it is. Is its core business more like that of a *firm*, or a *state*? If it is best described as a firm, is its distinctive feature the company *method* – the use of violence to turn a profit from legal and illegal activities (Arlacchi, 1986) – or its *market* – specialization in the supply of protection for property rights and economic transactions which the state itself has never managed to provide (Gambetta, 1993)? If, instead, 'mafia' is best seen as a quasi-political organization, is it a *competitor* or an *accomplice* of the Italian state itself – an alternative territorial system of justice and order, or a private militia used by political elites to extract consensus and repress social protest (Blok, 1974)? Or perhaps, as Lupo (1996) argues, its truly distinctive feature may be precisely its *fusion* of economic and political functions.

For more than a century after the mafia was first named, little reliable evidence was available to resolve those questions. However, since the mid-1980s, successful judicial investigations based on the first insider accounts (see **pentiti**), accompanied by detailed historical research, have helped to establish a broad, if not complete, consensus on the nature and evolution of mafia. It now appears as an organization with strict formal boundaries, considerable continuity in its internal structure and long-standing reliance on economic and political connections outside Sicily. Recent evidence has made it much more difficult to write the history of mafia as the degeneration of a popular organization defending the weak into a brutal gang of racketeers. From the very outset, mafiosi have dealt in extortion, violence and the consequent reluctance of victims and witnesses to collaborate with police and judges (*omertà*).

Social and economic origins

The fundamental rationale for mafia lies in low levels of trust in fellow citizens and state institutions. From the mid-nineteenth century, the increasing number of Sicilians who acquired land did not trust the police and judiciary of the new Italian state to defend effectively their new property rights or punish damage. The protection

offered by mafiosi – initially former soldiers and hired retainers who were well-trained in violence – was regarded as more reliable. However, credible threats of violence reduced the level of trust between Sicilians still further, increasing the demand for mafiosi skills and allowing protection to be imposed where it was not solicited. Mafia strongholds were first created in three economic sectors where disputes were endemic: the landed estates (*latifundi*) of Western Sicily, owned by absentee landlords who relied on ambitious local men to manage their properties; the profitable fruit and vegetable markets in Palermo, where opportunities for price fixing and for destruction of orchards and crops encouraged cutthroat competition; and illegal activities (notably contraband and animal rustling) in which agreements between participants could only be ultimately sanctioned by violence. From these nineteenth-century bases, mafia methods spread out to dominate the distribution of the most profitable twentieth-century resources in Sicily: construction and commercial licences, public works contracts, industrial development funds and hard drugs.

Connections and refuge, first in the USA and then further afield, were provided by the extended networks of social relations created by a century of Sicilian **emigration**. The competitive advantage provided by the readiness to use violence has therefore enabled mafia to flourish at the leading edge of postwar Sicilian development, and severe unemployment has helped to ensure a supply of initiates (*picciotti*) seeking wealth and reputation as entrepreneurs in violence. As their interests have become more diverse and more valuable, mafiosi have protected themselves by ensuring the complicity of politicians, judges and policemen with the power to discourage competitors, block investigations and influence court decisions. Arlacchi (1996: 92) claims that 40 per cent of all West Sicilian MPs elected to Parliament between 1958 and 1979 were actively – and probably decisively – supported by Cosa Nostra. Allegations of the exchange of political favours for mafia electoral support have long been levelled at the ruling Christian Democrat party, in particular the **Andreotti** faction whose Sicilian leader, Salvo Lima, was murdered in 1992 for his failure to organize the quashing of verdicts against the leading mafiosi in the Palermo 'maxi-trial' of 1987 by the Court of Cassation.

Territorial organization and conflicts

The basic mafia unit remains the 'family', a group of men who claim a monopoly over the supply of protection for a particular territory. Each family is run by a single boss with the help of a small staff of advisers and professionals in violence. The un-skilled labour is provided by young men whose ritual initiation into the organization takes a form already described a century ago.

In the mid-1990s, Western Sicily had some 6,000 mafiosi, organized in about 150 families, each with between half a dozen and a hundred members, controlling territories mostly no bigger than an urban neighbourhood. Attempts to sub-ordinate families to even a province-wide supreme 'Commission' have always been short-lived, frus-trated by the rivalry within and between families over reputation and resources. However, in the early 1980s a group based in the town of Corleone and led by Salvatore (Totò) Riina attempted to achieve absolute control by the systematic physical elimination of its rivals, thereby flouting the traditional preference for keeping the actual use of violence below levels likely to provoke wide-spread public concern and compel the political elite to react. Defeat in the ensuing war prompted mafiosi from the losing side to retaliate by defying the rule of *omertà* and collaborating with police and magistrates. Many mafia leaders, including Riina himself, were arrested but not before they had managed to organize the murder of the family members of many *pentiti* as well as the policemen and magistrates responsible for investigative success (see **Falcone**).

Political and public responses

The mafia's entanglement with Italy's political, economic and judicial institutions has long under-mined attempts to extirpate it. Before 1945, the most direct effort at combat was made by Mussolini whose prefect Cesare Mori, despatched to Palermo in 1925, arrested many mafiosi but could not eliminate the social and economic circumstances which continued to produce them.

Thereafter, apart from the institution of a Parlia-mentary Commission of Inquiry prompted by the murder of seven policemen in 1963, little con-sideration was given to a serious anti-mafia strategy. Only when the systematic murder of politicians (Mattarella, La Torre), policemen (Dalla Chiesa, Cassarà) and judges (Costa, Terranova, Chinnici, Livatino, Falcone, Borsellino) began after 1980 – and political **terrorism** ceased to mono-polize public concern with violence – did mafia come to be generally seen as a national, rather than a merely Sicilian, problem.

The resulting state initiatives were inspired by the determination to identify and isolate mafiosi ever more rigorously. Laws passed in 1982 and 1992 gave greater precision and wider application to the definition of specifically mafia crime, and efforts to create new and more effective institutions of prevention and repression were made. In 1982 a High Commissioner of Anti-Mafia Affairs was appointed, but the position was ineffective and soon replaced by a Direzione Nazionale Antimafia (National Antimafia Bureau). A permanent Parlia-mentary Commission of Inquiry was also estab-lished to co-ordinate public action, and vastly more incisive judicial investigations were achieved by the creation of specialist teams of local magistrates for all mafia cases. Serious attempts were then made to sever the links between mafia and politics. In 1991 the Minister of the Interior was empowered to dissolve local councils suspected of infiltration by mafia interests – a power invoked in ninety-one cases between 1991 and 1996 – and extortion of votes was made a specific mafia offence in 1992. Measures to prevent mafiosi competing for public works contracts, using banks to launder money and accumulating wealth from suspect activities were passed: between 1982 and 1996, property worth more than 6 billion lire was impounded (Violante, 1997: 161). Defection was also encouraged: reduc-tions in sentences for mafiosi who turned state's evidence and witness protection programmes for their families became available in 1991, and covered about 6,000 people in the mid-1990s.

As state commitment to repression became more visible, so popular anti-mafia protest in-creased. In 1984, in revulsion against the growing number and importance of mafia victims, a coordinating group for grassroots initiatives was formed in Palermo, where an outspoken anti-mafia mayor, Leoluca Orlando, was elected by landslide in four successive elections between 1985 and 1997. The party La Rete (The Network), which he had created in 1993, became a significant force in Sicilian politics. Women, including the widows of victims and the mothers of children destroyed by involvement in the mafioso-run drug trade, were a novel and powerful presence in anti-mafia mobilization. Even the Church – whose local leadership had long been reticent to the point of apparent tolerance – began to furnish examples of young parish priests prepared to risk their lives by open denunciation of mafia. By the late 1990s, such political and popular initiatives had not succeeded in eradicating the organization, but they made it appear decisively less 'Sicilian' and more merely criminal than it had seemed at any time since its appearance in the 1860s.

Further reading

Arlacchi, P. (1986) *Mafia Business: The Mafia Ethic and the Spirit of Capitalism*, trans. M. Ryle, New York: Verso.

—— (1996) 'Mafia: The Sicilian Cosa Nostra', *South European Politics and Society* 1 (1): 74–94.

Blok, A. (1974) *The Mafia of a Sicilian Village*, Oxford: Blackwell.

Capponnetto, A. (1992) *I miei giorni a Palermo* (My Days in Palermo), Milan: Garzanti (indispensable account by senior colleague of Falcone and Borsellino).

Catanzaro, R. (1992) *Men of Respect: A Social History of the Sicilian Mafia*, trans. R. Rosenthal, New York: Free Press.

Duggan, C. (1989) *Fascism and the Mafia*, New Haven, CN: Yale University Press.

Gambetta, D. (1993) *The Sicilian Mafia: The Business of Private Protection*, Cambridge, MA: Harvard University Press.

Hess, H. (1973) *Mafia and Mafiosi: The Structure of Power*, trans. E. Osers, Lexington, MA: Lexington Books.

Lupo, S. (1996) *Storia della mafia. Dalle origini ai giorni nostri* (History of the Mafia From its Origins Until Today), Rome: Donzelli, 2nd edn.

Schneider, J. and Schneider, P. (1994) 'Mafia, Antimafia, and the Question of Sicilian Culture', *Politics and Society* 22 (2): 237–59.

Stille, A. (1995) *Excellent Cadavers: The Mafia and the Death of the First Italian Republic*, London: Jonathan Cape.

Violante, L. (ed.) (1997) *Mafia e società italiana. Rapporto '97* (Mafia and Italian Society: 1997 Report), Bari: Laterza.

DAVID MOSS

Magazzini Criminali

An experimental theatre company formed in Florence by four young art students (none with theatre training), this company went by the name Il Carrozzone (The Big Cart) until 1979. The change in name to Magazzini Criminali reflected developments both within the group and in the wider field of avantgarde performance, where the original avantgarde movement of the late 1960s and early 1970s (Carmelo **Bene**, Memé Perlini, Giuliano Vasilicò) had given away to what was termed *postavanguardia* or *transavanguardia* (see **transavantgarde**).

While their early work reflected the visual arts background of the group members, its dominant features were ritualistic, and can be included under the rubric of *teatro-immagine* (image theatre). In the mid-1970s the group moved to a mode of performance which linked a cerebral exploration of performance sign-systems (space, time, lighting, performers' bodies) with an obsessive and visceral focus on real, autobiographical (and sometimes violently abusive) repetitive action. These elements were deliberately united in a loose structure which ensured the uniqueness of any one performance.

Further reading

De Marinis, M. (1983) *Al limite del teatro* (At the Limits of Theatre), Florence: Usher, 101–5 (locates the group in the European avantgarde tradition).

Sinisi, S. (1983) *Dalla parte dell'occhio*, (From the Eye's Point of View), Rome: Kappa, 131–49 (a detailed description of the group's productions).

TIM FITZPATRICK

Magistretti, Vico

b. 6 October 1920, Milan

Architect, furniture and interior designer

Magistretti studied architecture at the Polytechnic of Milan, completing his training in 1945. On graduating he joined his father's studio and worked on architectural and design projects during the years of reconstruction. His collaboration with the Cassina furniture manufacturing company dates from 1960. Key designs for them include his 'Chair 892' of 1963. For Artemide, he produced an early set of plastic furniture items, namely the 'Stadio' table and the 'Selene' chair.

By the mid-1960s Magistretti was established as one of Italy's leading designers, and he went on to produce classics such as his 'Sinbad' chair for Cassina of 1981 which was inspired by a horse blanket. His work in lighting has also been seminal and includes the 1967 'Eclisse' table lamp by Artemide. Magistretti has been at the forefront of Italian design for half a decade, and remains one of its key figures. He prefers to work alone, with the assistance of a draughtsman.

Further reading

Pasca, V. (1990) *Vico Magistretti Designer*, New York: Rizzoli.

PENNY SPARKE

Magnani, Anna

b. 7 March 1908, Rome; d. 26 September 1973, Rome

Actress

One of the most celebrated film actresses of the early postwar period and universally regarded as the diva of neorealist cinema, Anna Magnani began her career on the stage in the late 1920s and achieved renown as a revue artist in the mid-1930s. After a supporting role in **De Sica**'s *Teresa Venerdì* in 1941, she went on to play the most famous of all her many roles, that of Pina in **Rossellini**'s *Roma città aperta* (1945). During a short-lived sentimental relationship with Rossellini she performed the extraordinary monologue of *La voce umana* (The Human Voice), one of the two episodes in Rossellini's *L'amore* (1948), and then went on to work with **Visconti** in *Bellissima* (1951) as well as with Jean Renoir in *Le carrosse d'or* (The Golden Coach) (1953). She made several films in Hollywood, amongst them Daniel Man's version of Tennessee Williams' *A Rose Tattoo* (1955), for which she won an Oscar, but returned to Italy to create one of her most memorable roles in **Pasolini**'s *Mamma Roma* (1962).

GINO MOLITERNO

Magrelli, Valerio

b. 1957, Rome

Poet

Among the most promising poets of the new generation, Magrelli signalled himself to the critics' attention with *Ora serrata retinae* (Closed Openings of the Retina), published in 1980. The dominant theme of these poems is the poet's attempt to rediscover meaning in the process of writing and in the reconstruction of one's world through memory. His second collection, *Nature e venature* (Natures and Venations), was awarded the prestigious Premio Viareggio (see **literary prizes**) in 1987. Together with Magrelli's third book, *Esercizi di tiptologia* (Tip-Tapping Exercises), it continues his search for meaning in poems that are 'crumbs' to find the way back through 'the woods of years' although increasingly the fear arises that 'finches will come/to erase the tracks … and devour you'. Magrelli, who writes for *Il Messaggero*, has also published essays and a travel reportage.

Further reading

Magrelli, V. (1991) *Nearsights: Poems*, trans. A. Molino, St. Paul, MN: Graywolf Press.

VALERIO FERME

Majorino, Giancarlo

b. 7 April 1928, Milan

Poet and writer

A high school teacher by profession, Majorino was also the founder of the journal *Il Corpo* (The Body) as well as a contributor to magazines such as **Quaderni piacentini** and **il verri**. His first book of poetry, *La capitale del Nord* (The Capital of the North) (1958) showed a propensity for the linguistic experimentation that would continue throughout his work. Yet, following in the tradition of Lombard poetry, his own presence in his work remains thematically secondary to the external world's social and moral concerns. The collections that followed, *Lotte secondarie* (Secondary Struggles) (1967) and *Sirena* (Siren) (1976), reveal in their titles the poet's progressive disillusionment with a world in which a sense of civic duty and the desire for social change have been lost. In his more cryptic recent work, Majorino, having assessed the impossibility of effecting change through poetry, shifts his attention to his own impending death, as the title of his last two collections, *Ogni terzo pensiero* (Every Third Thought) (1990) and *Tetrallegro* (Darkandhappy) (1995) attest. Majorino has also edited an anthology of twentieth-century poetry titled *Poesia e realtà 1945–1975* (Poetry and Reality, 1945–1975) (1977).

VALERIO FERME

Malaparte, Curzio

b. 9 June 1898, Prato; d. 19 July 1957, Rome

Novelist, poet, playwright, polemicist, journalist film-maker

During the Fascist era, Malaparte (real name Kurt Erich Suckert) wrote for a number of newspapers, and was chief editor of **La Stampa** from 1929 to 1931. Multi-talented but mercurial – and always strongly polemical – he published several pro-fascist works, and in 1926 joined the ultranationalist *strapaese* movement in advocating fascism's return to *squadrismo* (street gangs) and to Italy's

agrarian tradition (see also **fascism and neo-fascism**). However, he also violently opposed the bureaucratization of fascism and so was sent into internal confinement to Capri in 1933, where he remained for the rest of the war. By 1943 he was writing for the Communist **L'Unità**.

After the war, Malaparte published three books set in occupied Naples, including the international best-seller *Kaputt* and *La pelle* (The Skin), later adapted for film by Liliana **Cavani**. In 1950 he wrote and directed one interesting, if highly rhetorical, film, *Il Cristo proibito* (The Forbidden Christ). His late essays, written in a beautiful villa on an isolated promontory of Capri, were collected in *Maledetti toscani* (Those Cursed Tuscans) and continue to advocate Italy's return to regional agrarian life.

Further reading

Martellini, L. (1977) *Invito alla lettura di C. Malaparte*, Milan: Mursia (an introduction to the author's work with a complete bibliography).

VALERIO FERME

Il Male

Originating from an idea by cartoonist Pino Zac, *Il Male* (Evil) lasted barely three years but passed into history as the most famous, or infamous, satirical magazine of the postwar period. Beginning as a fortnightly tabloid in February 1978 under the editorship of Tommaso Chiaretti, the magazine soon became a weekly, but at the same time the editorial collective changed with alarming speed. The most frequent contributors to the magazine were cartoonists Vincino (Vincenzo Gallo), Angese (Sergio Angeletti), Vincenzo Sparagna, Andrea Pazienza, Giuliano Rossetti, Riccardo Mannelli and Roberto Perini, and writers Angelo Pasquini (under the pseudonym 'Marlowe') and Jacopo Fo (son of Dario **Fo**) who signed his pieces 'Karen'.

The counterculture of post-1968 had spawned a large number of satirical magazines, newspapers and broadsheets, but these had generally articulated clear, if extreme, left-wing political views. The great novelty of *Il Male* was precisely the absence of any definite or coherent political stance beyond the dadaist desire to lampoon everyone and everything, including itself. The full frontal irreverence of the magazine's cartoons and commentary was directed at all persons and institutions which took themselves seriously including, of course, the **Vatican** and the Italian Communist Party (see **PCI**) which at this stage was attempting its '**historic compromise**' with the Christian Democrat Party (see **DC**). Emblematically, the cover of the first issue, designed by Zac, depicted a bedpan full of excrement, ornamented with the crumbling sculptured heads of the leaders of all the main political parties. A month later, the kidnapping of Aldo **Moro** by the **Red Brigades** handed *Il Male* an opportunity for even greater irreverence. Whilst the serious press treated the matter as a national crisis, *Il Male* published scurrilous photomontages of Moro in the 'people's prison' making sardonic comments such as 'If they don't get me out soon, I'll be washing dishes forever'.

The magazine became most notorious for its meticulous and convincing counterfeits of the front pages of respected national newspapers. Just when the Communist Party was supporting the Christian Democrats in a government of national solidarity, *Il Male*'s special issue of the Communist Party organ, **L'Unità**, published photographs of a twenty-eight hour rally attended by seven million people at which party secretary Enrico **Berlinguer** had pronounced the historic words: 'We've had it up to here with the Christian Democrats!' A similarly faked front page of the **Corriere della sera** seriously reported the landing in Mexico of a spaceship from Mars together with realistic photographs and an explanatory article written by Umberto **Eco**. The most famous fake of all, however, remained the special issue of *Paese Sera* which sported a photograph of the famous comic actor Ugo **Tognazzi** held by **carabinieri** (police) beneath the giant headline 'Ugo Tognazzi Arrested: He is the Leader of the Red Brigades'.

Members of the magazine also organized public happenings and dadaist street theatre. The magazine's irreverence and sexual explicitness appealed to the post-1968 counterculture, but it offended all the political parties and national institutions which unfailingly responded with attempts at legal suppression, thus making the magazine even more

sought after. Nevertheless, internal frictions between the editorial collective, which in any case had never been united, soon led to the magazine's demise in 1981 and all attempts at reviving it proved unsuccessful. Surviving members of the collective attempted to relaunch the magazine in the run-up to the national elections of 1994 as a gesture against the advance of Silvio **Berlusconi** but this also failed dismally, confirming that the best days of *Il Male* had been consigned to history.

Further reading

Chiesa, A. (1990) *La satira politica in Italia* (Political Satire in Italy), Bari: Laterza (see ch. 11, 'La rivoluzione del Male').

GINO MOLITERNO

Malerba, Luigi

b. 11 November 1927, Berceto, Parma

Novelist, screenwriter and journalist

Malerba (real name Luigi Bonardi) employs a surrealistic style in both his novels and screenplays. His early work owes its thematic influence in part to the **Gruppo 63**, a group of experimental artists and writers to which Malerba belonged. Perhaps his most famous novel is *Il pianeta azzurro* (The Blue Planet) (1986), a work which depicts a political assassination and well illustrates Malerba's typical sarcastic approach as he examines the corrupting influence of hatred. Other notable works include the detective fiction *Salto mortale* (Deadly Leap) (1968), in which all the suspects have the same name, and *Itaca per sempre* (Ithaca Forever) (1997), which recounts the return of Ulysses to Ithaca but from Penelope's point of view. In 1990, *Il fuoco greco* (The Greek Fire) won Malerba the prestigious Flaiano Prize for narrative, though his failure to win the Strega Prize when he was shortlisted in 1996 led to the publication of a fiery pamphlet *Che vergogna scrivere* (How Shameful to be a Writer). His film work includes co-writing the screenplays for Lattuada's *Il cappotto* (The Overcoat) (1952), *La lupa*

(The She-Wolf) (1952) and one episode of *Amore in città* (Love in the City) (1953).

LAURA A. SALSINI

Manfredi, Nino

b. 22 March 1921, Castro dei Volsci, Frosinone

Actor

Eventually to become one of the best-known and best-loved faces of Italian postwar cinema and a constant presence in the films of the so-called *commedia all'italiana* (comedy Italian style), Nino Manfredi was formally trained at Rome's Academy of Theatre from which he graduated in 1947. His film career was launched by two collaborations with Mauro **Bolognini** in 1956, and his talent was then impressively confirmed in 1958 with the first of the six films he made with director Dino **Risi**, *Venezia, la luna e tu* (Venice, the Moon and You). He co-starred in a number of classic comedies with Alberto **Sordi** and Vittorio **Gassman**, and gave what is considered one his very best performances in Ettore **Scola**'s *C'eravamo tanto amati* (We Loved Each Other So Much) (1974). Although he continued making films into the 1990s, he is perhaps best remembered for his performance in what is regarded as the most brilliant and representative film of the *commedia all'italiana*, *Pane e cioccolata* (Bread and Chocolate), directed by Franco **Brusati** in 1973.

DOROTHÉE BONNIGAL

Manganelli, Giorgio

b. 15 November 1922, Milan; d. 28 May 1990, Rome

Literary and art critic, short story writer, novelist and translator

A prolific and multi-talented personality, Manganelli's activities and interests as a writer spanned diverse fields. With a doctorate in political science, he nevertheless worked for a time as tutor in the Department of English Literature at the University of Rome. He participated in the **Gruppo 63**, contributed to various publications including *Il Corriere della sera* and *Epoca*, and acted as editorial consultant for several publishing houses. He also translated works by O. Henry, T.S. Eliot and Edgar Allen Poe, published essays of art criticism including *Salons* (1987), and wrote travel literature such as *Cina e altri orienti* (China and Other Orients) (1974). Manganelli was also a theorist of the postmodern movement and published works of literary criticism, including *La letterature come menzogna* (Literature as Falsehood) (1967) and *Laboriose inezie* (Industrious Nonsense) (1986). His fictional prose is distinguished by a complex, postmodern syntactical style coupled with a science fiction or visionary content, as exemplified in *Hilarotragoedia* (The Tragicomic Play) (1964), *Amore* (Love) (1981) and *Tutti gli errori* (All the Errors) (1986).

VIRGINIA PICCHIETTI

Mangano, Silvana

b. 21 April 1930, Rome; d. 16 December 1989, Madrid

Film actress

Silvana Mangano became a star in 1949, thanks to her performance in Giuseppe **De Santis**'s neorealist masterpiece *Riso amaro* (Bitter Rice) though, paradoxically, contrary to the film's original purpose (which was to denounce the corrupting influence of Hollywood glamour), Mangano thereby became a pin-up and a sex symbol.

However, thanks to Pier Paolo **Pasolini** with whom she made three films, the plastic purity of Silvana Mangano's features came to symbolize an aristocratic beauty reminiscent of Renaissance representations of the Madonna. Wife/mother of Oedipus in Pasolini's *Edipo re* (Oedipus Rex) (1967), she applied her aesthetic sophistication to portray an upper-class wife and mother in Pasolini's next film, *Teorema* (1968). Not surprisingly, in *Il Decameron* (The Decameron) (1971), she was cast as the Madonna in Pasolini's cinematic reconstruction of a fresco by Giotto. Thus from the pin-up to the Madonna, Silvana Mangano has with equal talent explored the whole spectrum of the female iconography.

DOROTHÉE BONNIGAL

Mani pulite

Mani pulite (Clean Hands) is the shorthand term for the extensive series of investigations into major political, administrative and business corruption conducted by group of magistrates in Milan from 1992 onwards. Their results ended the careers of many members of the local and national political elites, made a public hero of a key member of the magistrates' team (see Antonio **Di Pietro**) and helped to reshape the Italian political system. The investigations also exacerbated the running conflict between politicians and magistrates over the extent and accountability of judicial power, provoked by the key role played by magistrates in the struggle against political violence in the 1970s and against the **mafia** in the 1980s.

The unfolding of *Mani pulite*

Mani pulite grew out of separate prosecutions of corruption in, Milan's local government in the late 1980s, which suggested the existence of systematic bribery and extortion linking political parties, the public administration and business. In early 1992 Mario Chiesa, the manager of an old people's home and leading figure in Milan's Socialist Party, was trapped into arrest as he was actually receiving a bribe. His subsequent confessions confirmed that most political parties and senior politicians supported themselves largely from the bribes paid by firms to ensure the award of public contracts, particularly in the public works and health sectors. Further arrests produced immediate confessions from men who who were surprised to discover that neither their political power nor their entrepreneurial prestige could preserve their immunity from investigation. By the end of 1994, about one thousand politicians, public administrators and businessmen had been investigated by the *Mani pulite* team, two hundred had been sent for trial and five hundred were under arrest pending trial. More than 30 billion lire was retrieved from the guilty,

and fines amounting to 14 billion lire were imposed. Indictments for bribery and extortion in relation to public contracts and tax audits, violation of the law on party finance, and illegal accounting practices were brought against leaders of all the governing parties, senior managers of Italy's largest public and private firms and senior ministerial bureaucrats. Few institutions, from the fashion industry to the financial police themselves, escaped unscathed. Some especially conspicuous figures (Cagliari from **ENI**, Gardini from **Ferruzzi**) committed suicide rather than face the courts: others, such as the former Prime Minister Bettino **Craxi**, chose exile. Pursuing the evidence uncovered by *Mani pulite*, magistrates in other cities began similar investigations, revealing networks of systematic corruption across Italy. Only the communist-administered **Third Italy** was relatively, if not completely, exempt although members of the **PCI** and some party-managed cooperatives were implicated in corruption elsewhere.

Obstacles to investigation

Investigations of corruption did not proceed without controversy or opposition, particularly when in 1993 they reached the person, business associates and media empire of the first elected Prime Minister of the post-Christian Democrat era, Silvio **Berlusconi**. Every act and pronouncement of the *Mani pulite* team was attacked by Berlusconi's media, ministers and defence lawyers; intimidatory ministerial inspections were ordered into its work and one magistrate from the team, later elected an MP for Berlusconi's party **Forza Italia**, resigned, charging her colleagues with political bias in their investigations. Di Pietro was exposed to particular pressure, simultaneously wooed with the offer of a ministerial job and threatened with the revelation of details of his allegedly discreditable personal financial dealings. However, although in 1994 he resigned to contest, successfully, a series of trumped-up charges against him, the investigations directed by the remaining core prosecutors (Borrelli, Colombo, Davigo) did not slacken. The governing parties also attempted to protect themselves, proposing in 1993 retroactively to decriminalize violations of the laws on party funding and in 1994 to eliminate pre-trial detention on corruption charges. Both proposals provoked the immediate public opposition of the *Mani pulite* magistrates, who received unprecedented displays of popular support, and the proposals were therefore withdrawn. However, accusations that unelected magistrates were using their investigative powers to bring down elected politicians for political advantage rather than to simply uphold the law continued to be voiced, particularly once Di Pietro himself had entered politics in 1996.

The success of *Mani pulite*

Since the early 1970s, recurrent scandals had indicated the existence of significant political corruption, yet no prosecution had reached party leaders or damaged their parties electorally, let alone discredited an entire political elite. What factors, therefore, enabled the prosecutors of *Mani pulite* to make a dramatically greater impact on corruption than their predecessors had managed? In the first place, the new code of penal procedure (1989) offered improved co-ordination and protection for judicial enquiries. Second, the model of judicial teamwork which had been vital in prosecuting **terrorism** and **mafia** was extended to the problem of corruption. Third, computer skills enabled the *Mani pulite* team to track and assemble essential data from an otherwise unmanageably large array of separate local and national contexts. Fourth, open popular support encouraged prosecutors to pursue their enquiries in the face of the political elite's resistance. In Northern Italy, the successes of the **Lega Nord** after 1990 were already revealing the collapse of the consensus hitherto enjoyed by the parties, notably the **DC** and **PSI**, from which the first defendants came. Their detailed confessions, which provided the chance for prosecutors to bring charges to court before the evidence could be destroyed or the time limits for prosecution expired, signalled the disengagement of the political and business elites themselves from the increasingly complex bargaining, bribery and blackmail of systemic corruption.

See also: clientelism; legal system; political parties; *Tangentopoli*

Further reading

Chubb, J. and Vannicelli, M. (1988) 'Italy: A Web of Scandals in a Flawed Democracy', in A. Markovits and M. Silverstein (eds), *The Politics of Scandal*, New York: Holmes & Meier (scandals in Italian politics before *Mani pulite*).

Colombo, G., Davigo P. and Di Pietro, A. (1993) 'Noi obbediamo alla legge non alla piazza' (We Obey the Law, Not the Street), *MicroMega* 5: 1–20 (the Milanese pool's description of its work).

Nelken, D. (1996) 'A Legal Revolution? The Judges and *Tangentopoli*', in S. Gundle and S. Parker (eds), *The New Italian Republic: From the Fall of the Berlin Wall to Berlusconi*, London: Routledge.

Patrono, M. (1996) 'Fra toghe e politica' (Between Prosecutors and Politics), in M. Fedele and R. Leonardi (eds), *La politica senza i partiti* (Politics Without Parties), Rome: SEAM (a critical account of the increasing politicization of *Mani pulite*).

Pederzoli, P. and Guarneri, C. (1997) 'The Judicialization of Politics, Italian Style', *Journal of Modern Italian Studies* 2 (3): 321–36.

Tate, N. and Vallinder, T. (eds) (1995) *The Global Expansion of Judicial Power*, New York: New York University Press.

DAVID MOSS

il manifesto

A highly-regarded communist daily founded in 1971, *il manifesto* offers an alternative source of news and opinion to that of mainstream newspapers, presenting itself as libertarian, antibureaucratic, critical, reflexive and independent. Its origin and evolution constitute one of the most interesting facets of Italian political life in general and of the publishing industry in particular.

In 1969, a group of **PCI** leaders published a monthly periodical, *il manifesto*, in which they criticized their party for not taking a firm enough stance against the USSR's violent military repression of the Czechoslovak reform movements. Expelled from the party, they continued to publish the periodical, which became a national daily paper as of 28 April 1971. At the outset, *Il manifesto* consisted of only four pages devoted exclusively to politics with no general, local, book, society, crime or sports news and no advertising. Its success (with sales increasing from 15,000 to 40,000 copies daily) contradicted general opinion, which presumed the death of political ideologies and foresaw the disappearance of a purely political press. The paper filled a space neglected by the historical left-wing parties (the **PCI** and the **PSI**) and their newspapers *L'Unità* (Unity) and *L'Avanti!* (Forward!), and provided a forum for expressing and discussing ideas concerning political and social renewal related to worker and student agitation of 1968. Articles in *il manifesto* were written in very elegant, often difficult language, emphasizing theoretical considerations but always inviting the reader to assume an active role without feeling manipulated because the topics dealt with were given ample background through short informative articles. This appealed to a readership made up of political leaders and politicized intellectuals more than to one of students and workers. It also attracted readers of differing political opinion or those in search of one.

The paper always dedicated much space to international politics, and was especially critical of the Soviet policy of isolation and military power. It headlined all instances of opposition, such as the renewal and reform movements in Eastern Europe, and also linked communism and freedom. The Chinese Cultural Revolution and Third World struggles for independence were used as prime examples. The paper's critique of authoritarianism and universalism extended its concern to sexual politics, and feminism became one of the newspaper's basic interests both as a social movement and as a new critique of knowledge.

The main thrust of the paper's domestic politics was to propose an alternative to the rule of the Christian Democrat Party (**DC**). It expressed this in daily attacks on government decisions and in strong campaigns such as those against **Fanfani** (1971), against restrictive **divorce** laws (1974) and against the PCI's **historic compromise**. Social issues that were addressed emphasized struggles against the organization of capital: in factories and universities, in hospitals and prisons.

From the late 1970s onwards, confronted with social and political fragmentation and the diminu-

tion of left-wing values, *il manifesto* changed its editorial policies, dedicating more and more pages to cultural topics such as general news, philosophy, literary criticism, popular culture and computer science. Unremunerated contributions were made by well-known Italian and foreign intellectuals such as Remo **Ceserani**, Cesare Cases and Noam Chomsky. By 1985 it had become a major informative and political newspaper, and in the 1990s its daily circulation reached 50,000.

It has maintained its critical stance by promoting political and cultural struggles. In the 1980s it gave strong support to the anti-nuclear movement and dealt daily with issues of justice, the environment, peace, non-violence, the rights of new immigrants and the problem of drug addiction. Never having been supported by either a political party or a big lobby interest, the paper has often encountered considerable problems, but has survived to date due to strong financial support from its readers.

See also: newspapers

Further reading

Bruno, V. (1985) 'Cambia "il manifesto"' ('The Manifesto' Changes), *L'Editore* 8 (81): 26–7 (a comment on the alterations of style, content and format the paper undertook in 1985).

FRANCO MANAI

Manzoni, Pietro

b. 13 July 1933, Soncino, Cremona;
d. 6 February 1963, Milan

Artist

Manzoni began in traditional figurative painting, but in the mid-1950s he changed to oil paintings featuring the impressions left by paint-dipped objects and became influenced by the *spazialismo* of Lucio **Fontana**. This resulted in a series of whitish paintings whose surface was built up from rough gesso and then scratched or marked. He continued to produce these 'achromes' throughout his career. As Manzoni's art moved rapidly towards the conceptual, he drew lines of varying lengths and conserved them in canisters, signed living bodies as artworks, sold boiled eggs signed with his thumbprint, or inflated balloons containing *Fiato d'artista* (Artist's Breath). His most notorious work, ninety tins of *Merda d'artista* (Artist's Shit), was sold by weight for the equivalent of the current price of gold. A forerunner of the *arte povera* movement, Manzoni thus presented a challenge to the artificial politeness and sterility of bourgeois culture at the very moment when the **economic miracle** was generating a new affluence.

See also: conceptual art

LAURENCE SIMMONS

Manzù, Giacomo

b. 22 December 1908, Bergamo;
  d. 17 January 1991, Rome

Sculptor

Manzù's work, including bronze figures, still-lifes and biblical and mythological scenes, is strongly informed by Greek and Roman influences and other classicist examples, especially Donatello. It is a figurative and representational art, yet distinctly modern and original in its simplification of form and geometric effect.

Like the painter Renato **Guttuso**, Manzù used the imagery of the crucifixion in a series of bas-reliefs from 1939 to 1946 in order to symbolize suffering under Fascism. Another long-running theme was his series of Cardinals, begun in 1937. An example from 1977–82, *Il Cardinale Seduto* (The Seated Cardinal), shows how the basic elements have become angular and stylized.

Although an atheist and a communist, Manzù received major commissions for bronze doors of cathedrals, most notably the *Doors of Death* for St Peter's in Rome, completed in 1964. He also designed stage sets and costumes. In 1966 he was awarded the Lenin Peace Prize.

See also: sculpture

MAX STAPLES

Maraini, Dacia

b. 13 November 1936, Florence

Journalist, novelist and poet

Perhaps the Italian female writer most widely recognized abroad in recent times, Maraini is not only a prolific novelist and short story writer, but also a respected critic, poet, journalist and the playwright who established la Maddalena, the first Italian theatrical group composed exclusively of women. The themes of limitation and oppression in Maraini's writings have their earliest roots in her childhood years, spent first in a concentration camp in Japan and then in what she later described as an equally oppressive setting, Sicily. Her works clearly align themselves with the ideological concerns of the Italian feminist movement (see **feminism**). They aim toward self-awareness and self-expression and focus directly on specific feminist issues such as **abortion**, sexual violence, prostitution, the mother–daughter relationship, and personal and collective history. Many of her works are autobiographical, utilizing the form of diaries and letters, as in *Lettere a Marina* (Letters to Marina) (1981) and *Dolce per se* (Sweet On Its Own) (1997). Maraini has won a number of literary prizes, including the Fregene Prize in 1985 for *Isolina* and the prestigious premio Campiello in 1990 for the historical novel, *La lunga vita di Marianna Ucria* (The Long Life of Marianna Ucria).

Further reading

Wood, S. (1994) 'The Silencing of Women: The Political Aesthetic of Dacia Maraini', in S. Wood (ed.), *Italian Womens' Writing 1860–1994*, London: Athlone.

BERNADETTE LUCIANO

Mari, Enzo

b. 27 April 1932, Novara

Designer

Enzo Mari is best known for the children's games, puzzles and plastic artefacts that he designed for

Danese from 1957. Educated initially as an artist at the Academy of Fine Arts of Brera in Milan, Mari went on to work on a range of objects for the Danese company. From 1959 he worked in plastics; memorable designs include his 1962 cylindrical umbrella stand and his reversible 'Vase' in ABS of 1969. Like many of his colleagues, he succeeded in turning plastics into a set of 'chic' sophisticated materials executed in striking colours. His forms are all strong, and he played a significant role in establishing the internationally recognized 'Italian style' of the 1960s. He has continued to teach and design since that period, and clients include Zanotta, Driade and Artemide.

See also: interior design

Further reading

Mari, E. (1970) *Funzione della ricerca estetica* (The Function of Aesthetic Research), Milan: Comunità.
Pedio, R. (1980) *Enzo Mari Designer*, Bari: Dedalo.

PENNY SPARKE

Mariani, Carlo Maria

b. 25 July 1931, Rome

Painter

A highly competent technician who paints in the neoclassical style of Mengs and David, Mariani has elevated himself above the throng of copyists by the audacity of his vision. Not only has he painstakingly depicted Andy Warhol, the prince of banality, as Napoleon Bonaparte (1986) but, in what he calls confronting great art head on, he has actually produced 'improved' or 'corrected' versions of Leonardo and Raphael.

Mariani argues that he is more than a mere copyist because he understands the ideas and the aesthetic of neoclassicism and lives them out. In the 1970s he was derided for working in painting, a medium many at the time considered dead, but Mariani recognized a parallel between the conceptual nature and melancholy for the past of neoclassicism and the art of his own day. By the 1980s Mariani was part of a trend of reusing motifs

and styles from the past with a revived attention to technique, a current variously known as 'new romanticism', *pittura colta* (cultivated painting), 'hyper-mannerism' or *la Nuova Maniera* (The New Style).

Further reading

Christov-Bakargiev, C. (1987) 'Interview with Carlo Maria Mariani', *Flash Art* 133: 60–3.

MAX STAPLES

Marini, Marino

b. 27 February 1901, Pistoia; d. 6 August 1980, Viareggio

Sculptor

Working in bronze, stone, terracotta and gesso, Marini's favourite themes were the horse and rider, the female nude, the dancer and portraits, which included those of Kokoschka and Stravinsky. Rather than creating or destroying, Marini saw the artist as transforming matter to display new forms. His great achievement was to create a modern art which did not deny the past but rather was deeply influenced by it, from archaic Greek sculpture and Etruscan figures to Tang statuettes and the bronze horses of St Mark's. Much of his work has the appearance of ancient and weathered remains, with more emphasis on volume and mass than finish.

After the Second World War, Marini became concerned with the possibility of nuclear disaster and the extinction of the human race, expressing his sense of foreboding through the theme of the horse and rider. Over the next twelve years, his increasing sense of apocalypse is displayed as the rider grows weaker and control over the horse decreases. The *Miracoli* (Miracles), executed between 1951 and 1954, show the horse lose balance and the rider pitch forward over its head. By 1962, with *Il Grido* (The Cry), the rider lies on the ground.

See also: sculpture

Further reading

Hunter, S. (1993) *Marino Marini: The Sculpture*, New York: Harry N. Abrams (ample discussions of works; illustrated).

MAX STAPLES

marriage

Whatever their social class, their age or the region in which they live, the great majority of Italians only inaugurate their own household and family after marriage in church. Since men do not usually take this step until their late twenties, 80 per cent of unmarried Italians below the age of thirty live with their parents, partly by preference, partly because finding independent affordable accommodation is difficult. The very limited mortgage market makes children dependent on their parents' savings to buy an apartment. Only 5 per cent of couples live together without marrying, of whom one-third are widows and widowers or people unwilling or unable to divorce their former partners. Such *de facto* unions are not legally recognized, and thus partners have very limited claims on each other or on public services.

Notwithstanding the considerable **immigration** since the late 1970s, Italians continue to choose their spouses among fellow Italians. In the mid-1990s, no more than 4 per cent of marriages each year were 'mixed', most consisting of marriages between Italians and North Europeans or between members of different immigrant communities.

Getting married – celebrated in church by four of every five couples – is likely to be very expensive: in Naples in the mid-1990s, even lower middle-class parents were spending around 230 million lire on the ceremony, reception, honeymoon and new home for the bride and groom (Piselli, 1996: 90–4). Despite such a spectacular investment, Italian marriages are ever less frequently stabilized by the partners' common interest in children or property. Procreation rates are among the world's lowest, and most spouses opt for individual property arrangements against the default presumption of common property established in 1975. **Divorce** became possible in 1970 but, despite an easing of its stringent conditions in 1987, it remains much less common than legal separation. Both endings are twice as common in the North as in the South, but for most Italians their first marriage is for life.

See also: family

Further reading

Pinnelli, A. and De Rose, A. (1995) 'Italy', in H-P. Blossfeld (ed.), *The New Role of Women: Family Formation in Modern Societies*, Boulder, CO: Westview.

Piselli, F. (1996) 'Esercizi di network analysis a Napoli' (Exercises in Network Analysis for Naples), *Rassegna italiana di sociologia* 37 (1): 83–106.

Saller, R. and Kertzer, D. (eds) (1991) *Families in Italy*, New Haven, CN: Yale University Press.

DAVID MOSS

Marsilio

Founded in the early 1960s by a group of professors from the University of Padua, Marsilio soon moved to Venice where, under the direction of Cesare De Michelis, Professor of Italian at the local university and a group of specialists of different disciplines, it grew from a small scholarly enterprise to become one of the most renowned and widely distributed publishing houses in Italy. A very positive and commendable aspect of Marsilio's commercial growth has been the maintenance of its high-quality essay series in many different disciplines (film studies, Italian literature, sociology, art history and so on) as well as its continued production of scholarly editions of the classics of ancient and modern literatures. Marsilio also devotes several different series to narrative, aiming to promote new writers as well as maintaining already established and critically acclaimed authors.

See also: publishers

ANDREA CICCARELLI

Martinazzoli, Mino

b. 30 November 1931, Orzinuovi, Brescia

Politician

A lawyer and local politician in Brescia, Mino Martinazzoli entered the Senate for the **DC** in 1972. He became prominent as chair of the bicameral committee which lifted two ministers' parliamentary immunity, thus allowing corruption allegations to proceed against them. He progressed rapidly to senior ministerial office, benefiting from his membership of the 'Base' faction and the secretaryships of **Zaccagnini** and **De Mita**. In October 1992 he became party secretary following **Forlani**'s resignation, his distance from clientelist politics, his devout Catholicism and his generally recognized honesty being seen as valuable assets for his party's relegitimization. Strategically, Martinazzoli reasserted the DC's centrist identity, attempting to exercise the balance of power in the new party system. However, in the 1994 election the newly named **PPI** fared disastrously, and Martinazzoli resigned. Thereafter he supported the PPI's leftward tendency, becoming mayor of Brescia for a centre–left coalition which foreshadowed the **Ulivo** (Olive Tree) alliance.

MARK DONOVAN

Martini, Cardinal Carlo Maria

b. 15 February 1927, Turin

Cardinal archbishop

Jesuit scholar and Cardinal Archbishop of Milan, Carlo Maria Martini is effectively the leader of the liberal opposition to **Pope John Paul II** in the Italian church. Martini entered the Jesuit order 1944 and was ordained at twenty-five, an unusually early age for a Jesuit. His doctoral theses in theology at the Gregorian University and scripture at the Pontifical Biblical Institute were so brilliant that they were immediately published. He was first dean of the Faculty of Scripture at the Biblical Institute, rector from 1969 to 1978, and then rector of the Gregorian University. He was appointed Archbishop of Milan in December 1979 and was made a cardinal in February 1983. He has published over fifty books since 1980, mostly pastoral letters, with annual sales of over a million copies worldwide. In contrast to John Paul II, he is 'soft' on sexuality and strong on ecumenism. He is widely regarded as a possible successor to the papal throne, though perhaps too liberal to ultimately succeed.

JOHN POLLARD

Martone, Mario

b. 20 November 1959, Naples

Theatre and film director

Martone made his debut in the theatre in 1977. He earned his reputation by creating the avantgarde theatre group **Falso Movimento** (False Movement) in 1979 and the ensemble Teatri Uniti (United Theatres) in 1987, both of which staged a number of significant works in the 1980s. Having worked in video from 1980 on and produced *Nella città barocca* (In the Baroque City), a 16 mm film on sixteenth-century Naples in 1984, Martone directed his highly-acclaimed first film, *Morte di un matematico napoletano* (Death of a Neapolitan Mathematician) in 1991, winning the Special Jury Prize at the Venice Film Festival. In 1995 he produced a second powerful and much-acclaimed film, *L'amore molesto* (Troublesome Love), based on the first novel of Neapolitan author, Elena Ferrante, which explores a complex mother–daughter relationship against the pulsating, sensual background of Naples. In 1998, Martone brought together his experience in both theatre and cinema in *Teatro di guerra* (Theatre of War), a film which uses the eventual failure of a Neapolitan theatrical company to take a production of Aeschylus's play, *Seven Against Thebes*, to war-torn Sarajevo as the vehicle for exploring social violence in even apparently 'civilized' societies.

ANTONELLA FRANCINI

Marzotto

Luigi Marzotto founded his wool-making business in 1836 in Valdagno Veneto, a region with a rich tradition in the textile trade. The small family-run mill eventually expanded into a spinning plant which, under the direction of Gaetano Marzotto, Jr, evolved into a minor textile empire. Surviving the crises of the lira and of Wall Street in the late 1920s, Gaetano turned his business into a community by surrounding the industrial plant with residences and other amenities for the workers and their families. Fascism's restrictions on the import of wool as well as direct political pressures forced Gaetano into exile in 1944, but he returned after the war to greatly expand the company, much aided by free trade policies. In the mid-1980s Marzotto entered a period of international growth as it acquired a number of companies both in Italy and abroad, including Lanerossa (1987) and Hugo Boss (1991). Today, with sales in more than eighty countries, the family business has become a world-class textile and clothing manufacturer, specializing in wool yarns and fabrics and fine linens as well as in classic men's wear, women's wear and sportswear. Despite its expansion abroad, the philosophy of Marzotto remains family-centred with a strong attachment to the community where it was born.

BERNADETTE LUCIANO

Masina, Giulietta

b. 22 February 1921, Giorgio di Piano;
d. 23 March 1994, Rome

Film actress

Often referred to as the 'female Chaplin,' Giulietta Masina started her career in theatre and radio in the 1940s. She then appeared under **Lattuada**'s direction in *Senza pietà* (Without Pity) (1948) and *Luci del varietà* (Variety Lights) (1950), the latter co-directed by Federico **Fellini**, whom she had married in 1943. Although she would also work with other directors, her screen and public persona would from then on be tied to Fellini and his cinematic creations. The characters she brought to life under his direction are unforgettable and vital

to an understanding of Fellini's work: Gelsomina, the fragile heroine of *La Strada* (The Road) (1954), Cabiria, the cartoon-like prostitute destroyed by her petit-bourgeois romantic ideal in *Le notti di Cabiria* (The Nights of Cabiria) (1956), the oppressed and tormented Giulietta in *Giulietta degli Spiriti* (Juliet of the Spirits) (1965) and the ageing yet flamboyant Ginger/Amelia revisiting her past in *Ginger e Fred* (Ginger and Fred) (1985). Significantly, she died only months after Fellini's own death.

DOROTHÉE BONNIGAL.

Mastroianni, Marcello

b. 28 September 1924, Fontana Liri,
Frosinone; d. 19 December 1996, Paris

Film actor

With 170 films to his credit, Marcello Mastroianni easily ranks as the most prolific and most accomplished actor in Italian postwar cinema. Although he also worked well with almost all the other major directors, from **Visconti**, **Antonioni** and **De Sica** to Pietro **Germi** and the **Taviani brothers**, he became particularly inseparable from Federico **Fellini**, with whom he made seven films and for whom he became the recognized alter ego. Convincingly personifying the weariness and the doubts of a whole generation in his first Fellini film, *La Dolce vita* (1960), Mastroianni also became famous for his performances as a comic actor, along with Sophia **Loren**, his ideal co-star from the mid-1950s.

Often regarded as the quintessential 'Latin lover', especially outside Italy, Mastroianni's boundless range of talents as an actor also allowed him to expose this persona to fruitful subversion, as in the impotent husband in **Bolognini**'s *Il bell'Antonio* (1959) or the anti-fascist homosexual in **Scola**'s *Una giornata particolare* (A Special Day) (1977). Mastroianni's death in 1996 inevitably marked the closure of a long chapter in the history of Italian cinema.

DOROTHÉE BONNIGAL.

Mattei, Enrico

b. 29 April 1906, Acqualagna;
   d. 27 October 1962, Milan

Industrialist and entrepreneur

Of humble and provincial origins, Enrico Mattei was to become universally acknowledged as the most powerful man in Italy in the immediate postwar period. After commanding a squad of Catholic partizans during the **Resistance**, Mattei became at the end of the war a leading member of the national council of the Christian Democrat Party (**DC**) and sat in the Chamber of Deputies from 1948 to 1953 (see also **Parliament**). Known as an efficient industrialist, Mattei was appointed vice-president of AGIP, the Italian Petroleum Agency, with a brief to wind the company up since it was regarded as unviable. Contrary to instructions, Mattei used the discovery of small quantities of petroleum and methane in the Po region not only to relaunch AGIP itself but also to lobby for an expanded national agency with monopoly control over fuel exploration and marketing throughout all of Italy. Against strong opposition from within his party, including from the party's founder, Don Luigi **Sturzo**, Mattei nevertheless managed to carry the day and in 1953 became president of the newly constituted Ente Nazionale Idrocarburi (**ENI**).

Although scrupulously honest in his private life, Mattei proceeded to utilize the public finances of the company for bribing politicians of all political persuasions to support a massive expansion of ENI's operations, both nationally and internationally. An energetic and astute entrepreneur, he strongly resented the market influence and high prices of the major American oil companies and so moved quickly to explore other sources for Italy's oil supplies. He initiated secret discussions with the Algerian National Liberation Front and, although these proved unsuccessful, in 1955 he signed an accord with Egypt which granted that country an unprecedented share of profits from oil revenues. In 1957 Mattei went further in breaking all the rules by signing an exclusive agreement with Iran, whereby ENI financed all oil operations but took only a quarter of the profits. There followed a similar accord with Morocco and, in 1960, ENI

began to import Russian oil. This increased the hostility of the American oil companies, who were seeing their profits continually undermined, and also prompted alarm at the highest levels of the American government which feared that Mattei's machinations would eventually lead to Italy's withdrawal from NATO.

At the very height of his power and influence, Mattei was killed when his private plane crashed just outside Milan. His death has remained one of Italy's many unsolved mysteries. In 1972, Francesco **Rosi** made a disquieting documentary-fiction entitled *Il caso Mattei* (The Mattei Affair) which brought together all the suspicious evidence regarding the crash, including eyewitness accounts that the plane had exploded in mid-air before plunging into an open field. A parliamentary inquiry in 1976 heard evidence which suggested **mafia** involvement in the crash but, inexplicably, the matter was shelved indefinitely. In June 1995 the case was re-opened in two separate investigations prompted by information from mafia super-informer, Tommaso Buscetta, but no further light was shed on the untimely disappearance of this key figure of the Italian **economic miracle**.

Further reading

Frankel, P.H. (1966) *Mattei: Oil and Power Politics*, London: Faber & Faber.

Lawton, H. (1996) 'Enrico Mattei: The Man Who Fell to Earth', in C. Testa (ed.), *Francesco Rosi: The Poet of Civic Courage*, Westport, CN: Greenwood Press (an analysis of Rosi's film but with much useful information and discussion about Mattei's life and politics).

GINO MOLITERNO

MaxMara

The MaxMara company was founded in Reggio Emilia in 1951 by Achille Maramotti as the first good quality yet affordable women's ready-to-wear manufacturer in Italy, specializing in coats and suits. By the end of the 1960s MaxMara had established a new co-ordinates label called Sportmax, and had begun to employ a succession of 'consultant designers', including Luciano Soprani and Kurt Lagerfeld. At the same time, they developed an image-conscious philosophy, an expanding export market and a retail network. Although the high-quality tactile coat remained the backbone of the business, MaxMara concentrated on creating different collections through autonomous companies. Sixteen clothing lines were established including Marella, Weekend and Marina Rinaldi, with a flagship store on Madison Avenue, but no licences were issued, not even for perfume. Generally, MaxMara's international success derived from an understated style, careful market targeting, advanced technology and excellent relations with the Italian textile industry.

See also: fashion

NICOLA WHITE

Mazzacurati, Carlo

b. 2 March 1956, Padova

Director

Mazzacurati began his career in 1979 by making *Vagabondi* (Vagabonds) in 16mm. After numerous collaborations in television productions, he made his directorial debut in 1987 with *Notte italiana* (Italian Night), a powerful and disturbing psychological thriller produced, significantly, by Nanni **Moretti**'s then newly formed company, Sacher Film. An unsuccessful second feature, *Il prete bello* (The Handsome Priest) (1989), was followed by the impressive *Un'altra vita* (Another Life) (1992). Here Mazzacurati displayed his full potential as the film, with its nocturnal and desperate atmosphere, presents all the uneasiness of a society in transition within which the love story of a Roman dentist and a Russian girl unfolds to its ill-fated end. A reversal at the level of the plot – as the journey moves from Italy to Hungary – but a repetition at the level of the story can be found in *Il toro* (The Bull) (1994). His *Vesna va veloce* (Vesna Runs Fast) (1996) is in many ways a creative reprise of the 1992 movie, as a young Czech woman struggles to find a new life in Italy.

MANUELA GIERI

Mediobanca

Established in 1946, Mediobanca is Italy's leading industrial bank. Its main original shareholders were **IRI**'s three deposit banks, Banca Commerciale, Credito Italiano and Banco di Roma, which also acted as its agents for the placement of long-term bonds.

During the 1950s Mediobanca typically provided long-term finance and assisted client companies in bond and equity issue. It was only with the nationalization of the electric power companies in the early 1960s (see **ENEL**) that Mediobanca, led by one of Italy's legendary financial figures, Enrico **Cuccia**, acquired an undisputed leadership as industrial bank and provider of sophisticated schemes of financial engineering. Its critics argue that, through such schemes, Mediobanca was instrumental in perpetuating Italy's outdated corporate governance system, based on holding companies which allowed a handful of families with relatively little capital to control a disproportionately large share of big businesses. Its supporters stress the positive role played by Mediobanca in upholding the private sector at times of overextension of public-owned companies and of state intervention in the economy, in creating positive externalities and cost-cutting integrations (both vertical and horizontal) within the industrial sector and in providing sorely needed industrial banking services.

GIANNI TONIOLO

il menabò

Published irregularly between 1959–67 by **Einaudi** and edited by Italo **Calvino** and Elio **Vittorini**, the cultural journal *il menabò* equalled in importance the earlier and very different periodical edited by Vittorini, *Il Politecnico*. The choice of title – the print trade term meaning a 'paste-up' – indicated an attitude to literature as process rather than product. Featuring fiction and poetry by the postwar generation of Italian writers, canvassing 'issues' (such as the **'Southern Question'**), and even inventing them (as in the case of the famous 'Literature and Industry' question in nos 4–5), *il* *menabò* adopted an international perspective with issue no. 7 (1964), hosting texts by Roland Barthes, Maurice Blanchot and Hans Magnus Enzensberger.

The division of editorial input remains unclear. The publication did not outlast Vittorini, except for the final commemorative issue (no. 10) in the year following his death, entirely devoted to his work. Calvino later described his own contributions to the journal as minimal, although he published some of his most important essays there.

Further reading

Fiaccarini Marchi, D. (ed.) (1973) *Il menabò (1959–1967)*, Rome: Edizioni dell'Ateneo.

SUZANNE KIERNAN

Mendini, Alessandro

b. 16 August 1931, Milan

Designer

A key member of Italy's radical design fraternity from the 1960s onwards, Mendini has been closely involved in Italian avantgarde architecture and design, and design journalism since the 1960s. He was a partner in the architectural studio of Marcello Nizzoli until 1970, the director of **Casabella** magazine from 1970 to 1976, the director of **Modo** magazine from 1977 to 1981, and the director of **Domus** magazine from 1979 to 1985. He has created a wide range of objects, furniture, environments and installations with international clients such as Alessi, Zanotta, Elam, Philips and Swatch, and has collaborated extensively with **Studio Alchimia**. His designs always challenge the status quo and suggest new ways forward. Some of his works are held by the Museum of Modern Art, New York, and the Centre Pompidou, Paris. In 1989, together with his brother Francesco, Mendini opened the Atelier Mendini in Milan which is responsible for designing, among others, Alessi House, a tower in Hiroshima, the Groningen Museum in Holland and a theatre in Arezzo.

See also: anti-design

Further reading

Bonito Oliva, A. *et al.* (1989) *Alessandro Mendini*, Milan: Giancarlo Politi Editore.

PENNY SPARKE

Meneghello, Luigi

b. 1922, Malo, Vicenza

Academic and novelist

After participating in the **Resistance** movement as a partizan and earning a degree in philosophy at the University of Padua in 1947, Luigi Meneghello left Italy for England. At the University of Reading he founded the Italian department and taught Italian literature for several years. His novels, from *Libera nos a malo* (Deliver Us From Evil) (1963) through *I piccoli maestri* (The Little Teachers) (1964, partially rewritten and translated into English as *The Outlaws* in 1967) to *Il dispatrio* (Leaving the Homeland) (1993), display his particular interest in language as a flexible tool of communication and expression. By ingeniously mixing his native Veneto dialect with standard Italian and English, Meneghello not only revives memories of his own childhood and of the recent historical past, but also records and comments on the social and cultural changes of Italy from the Fascist era to the postwar years.

FRANCESCA PARMEGGIANI

Menichella, Donato

b. 23 January 1896, Biccari, Foggia; d. 23 July 1984, Rome

Banker

As governor of the Bank of Italy (see **Banca d'Italia**) from 1948 to 1960, Menichella deeply influenced and often directed economic policy of Italian governments during the period of reconstruction, thus laying the foundations of the subsequent economic boom. Fiercely independent of both political parties and economic lobbies, and with a high sense of his office as a civil servant, he bravely defended the central bank's autonomy. A man of extraordinary integrity, he had spent his prewar years at the Bank of Italy and then at **IRI** as general manager. Having experienced bank failures and financial disasters at first hand, he always considered financial stability the safest condition for lasting economic growth. Although a strong believer in the market economy, he also thought of currency and credit as public goods to be safeguarded by the state. In 1960, during Menichella's last year as governor, the *Financial Times* proclaimed the Italian lira 'star currency of the year', thus marking both a great historical achievement and the culmination of a most distinguished career.

See also: economic miracle

STEFANO BATTILOSSI

Menotti, Gian Carlo

b. 7 July 1911, Cadegliano

Composer

In 1927, the sixteen-year-old Menotti, speaking no English, left Italy to begin compositional studies in America. Less than a decade later he was poised to become one of the most significant and financially successful composers of his generation.

The sixth of ten children, Menotti demonstrated musical talent from an early age, writing two operas before his thirteenth birthday. As an adolescent he was taken by his mother to meet Toscanini, a friend of the family, who advised Menotti to travel to America to study composition with Rosario Scalero at the Curtis Institute in Philadelphia. There he was soon befriended by another young student, Samuel Barber. They became close friends, collaborating musically and living together for many years.

Initially, Menotti's career was the more illustrious. His first published opera, *Amelia al Ballo* (Amelia at the Ball) (1935) was performed in the 1937 season at the Metropolitan Opera, and Menotti joined a select number of living composers to have their work staged at the Met. Based on the success of *Amelia*, the broadcaster NBC commissioned an opera for radio, *The Old Maid and the Thief*

(1939). Written in the belief that opera should be as accessible and immediate as a play or film, Menotti's next two operas, *The Medium* (1946) and *The Consul* (1950), changed the notion of what opera could mean for twentieth-century audiences. Against advice from the musical establishment, he sought financial backing to stage *The Medium* on Broadway rather than in an opera house. His instincts proved correct: between 1947–8, it ran for 211 performances and was enormously successful in both musical and financial terms. *The Consul*, his first full-length opera, also had an extended Broadway run and was awarded the Pulitzer Prize and the Drama Critic's Circle Award. A year later he was commissioned to write the first opera specifically for television, *Amahl and the Night Visitors* (1951). Requiring only modest orchestral forces and a talented boy soprano, it remains one of the most frequently performed operas in the United States.

Menotti has made significant contributions as a librettist, not only for his own works but for those of colleagues (he wrote the libretto for Barber's *Vanessa* in 1964). He is also a respected director for stage, television and film. His strong sense of theatre has often come at the expense of appreciation for his talents as a composer; enormous initial success has been followed by decades of disinterest and, at times, disdain from the musical establishment. In 1958, at the height of his fame he founded the **Spoleto Festival** of Two Worlds, in Spoleto, Italy. With Menotti's contacts in the visual arts and ballet, the Festival quickly became a focus for a stimulating confrontation between the established and the avant-garde. Artists invited to design their annual poster give an indication of Festival's calibre: Robert Motherwell, Willem de Kooning, David Hockney, Leonardo Cremonini and Henry Moore have each contributed over the years. Nineteen years later (1977), Menotti founded the sister festival in Charleston, South Carolina. While internecine tensions resulted in Menotti's resignation from the Charleston Festival, he continues to direct the Spoleto Festival in Italy, which in 1997 hosted Luciano **Pavarotti**, flamenco dancer Joaquin Cortés and the Dance Theatre of Harlem.

For the past three decades, Menotti has lived to see his work marginalized in favour of idioms more adventurous and less ingratiating. In the past few years, however, there are intimations of change. Recent productions of his operas *The Saint of Bleecker Street* (1954) and *Maria Golovin* (1958) have been received with enthusiasm. He was awarded the Kennedy Center Honor for lifetime achievement in 1984, and in his eightieth year was chosen 'Musician of the Year' by *Musical America*. In 1993 he was appointed Director of the Rome Opera, underscoring his distinguished reputation as a director of both opera and theatre. In 1995 he was invited to contribute a 'Gloria' as part of a Mass to celebrate the 1995 Nobel Peace Prize, and future plans include several new productions of his operas. The 1998 film of *Amahl* (the second film version in two decades, in addition to countless television productions) suggests Menotti is still revising the relationship between music and image. Indeed, Menotti's film, kinescope and video legacy remains one of the most comprehensive of any composer and paves the way for a systematic reappraisal of his contribution to twentieth-century music at some point in the future.

See also: opera

Further reading

Ardoin, J. (1985) *The Stages of Menotti*, New York: Garden City.

Barnes, J. (1994) 'Television Opera: A Non-History' in J. Tambling (ed.), *A Night in at the Opera: Media Representations of Opera*, London: John Libbey.

Gruen, J. (1978) *Menotti: A Biography*, New York: Macmillan.

JENNIFER BARNES

Merini, Alda

b. 21 March 1931, Milan

Poet and writer

Beginning in the early 1950s, Merini emerged as one of the most interesting lyric voices in Italian poetry. Her books are characterized by a spiritual and psychological search, sometimes opposed by, though more often fused with, an openly erotic streak and expressed in a direct, fervent and powerful style. Merini's major collections seem to follow either one or the other of her two lyric themes without a precise chronological trend. *Paura di Dio* (Fear of God) (1955), *Tu sei Pietro. Anno 1961* (You Are Peter. Year 1961) (1961) and *La Terra Santa* (The Holy Land) (1983) are anguished religious explorations, while other collections more clearly reflect her erotic and psychological quest, as in the case of *La presenza di Orfeo* (The Presence of Orpheus) (1953), *Delirio amoroso* (Delirious Love) (1989) and *Il tormento delle figure* (The Tormented Figures) (1990).

Merini was afflicted by a debilitating nervous disease which forced her into long poetic silences during almost two decades spent in mental institutions; these are recounted in *Diario di una diversa. L'altra verità* (Diary of a Different Woman: The Other Truth) (1986), a powerful book about the feelings, fears and aspirations of an intellectual forced into an internal exile.

Further reading

Merini, A. (1998) *Fiore di poesia: 1951–1997* (Flower of Poetry), Turin: Einaudi (complete collected poems).

ANDREA CICCARELLI

Merz, Mario

b. 1 January 1925, Milan

Artist and writer

While his art has a conceptual base and he has worked widely with installations, Merz is concerned with creating art objects which are ordered, complete and whole. In 1968 he produced *Igloo di Giap* (Giap's Igloo), made of mud brick with a metal frame and adorned with a neon slogan. This was the first of a series of igloos in various materials, the igloo striking Merz as an ideal organic form, representing at once both a small domestic shelter and the whole world. He has also been drawn to the idea that the mathematical progression of numbers known as the Fibonacci series is a manifestation of the underlying order of nature. Thus, some installations combine igloos with neon signs and Fibonacci. With his ethnographic leanings and his search for archetypes, Merz has, like the German artist Joseph Beuys, proved doggedly eclectic and has given his work a human element at a time when much other art has seemed mechanical and soulless.

Further reading

Celant, G. (1989) *Mario Merz*, New York: Solomon R. Guggenheim Foundation (illustrated exhibition catalogue).

MAX STAPLES

Messina, Francesco

b. 15 December 1900, Linguaglossa, Catania; d. 13 September 1995, Naples

Sculptor

A traditionalist who was apprenticed to a stonemason at the age of eight, and held his first exhibition at fifteen, Messina worked in marble, bronze and terracotta, and believed that a thorough knowledge of one's material was necessary to arrive at a lasting style. He produced religious works such as *Adam and Eve*, a recurring theme, and the Memorial to Pius XII in the Chapel of Saint Sebastian, in St Peter's, completed in 1964. He also created portraits, images of the female form, and horses, notably the *Dying Horse* outside the **RAI** building in Rome.

Stylistically, Messina ignored most of the trends of modernism. His ideal was the sculpture of the Florentine Renaissance, and he took as the point of departure for his own experimentation the more expressionist portrait busts and the harrowing *Penitent Magdalen* of Donatello. Messina was honoured by the Biennale of Venice with a prize for sculpture in 1942, and a retrospective in 1956.

See also: sculpture

MAX STAPLES

Methnani, Salah

b. 1963, Tunisia

Immigrant writer

Methnani came to Italy from Tunisia in 1987 with a university degree and a knowledge of the Italian language. He discovered that Italians felt threatened by his linguistic ability, and came to realize that he posed less of a threat if he could be identified solely as an immigrant, without any individual identity. In *Immigrato* (Immigrant), co-written with Mario Fortunato, Methnani describes the difficulties of retaining a sense of self apart from the mass of immigrants. His revealing autobiography is unique among the many testimonies of immigrants to Italy. It recounts his controversial choice of becoming a drug addict and a friend's decision to become a male prostitute as ways of acquiring an identity beyond the imposed role of a cultural and racial alien. Methnani is now a writer and a translator.

See also: immigrant literature

Further reading

Methnani, S. (1990) *Immigrato*, Rome and Naples: Theoria.

GRAZIELLA PARATI

Michelucci, Giovanni

b. 2 January 1891, Pistoia; d. 1 January 1991, Florence

Architect

The foremost Tuscan architect of the twentieth century and a renowned architectural pedagogue, Michelucci began in private practice in 1916. Although his style fluctuated somewhat during his remarkably long and fruitful career, expressionistic and organic elements tied together various phases of his work. Michelucci's Santa Maria Novella train station in Florence (realized in 1936 with collaborators) is an outstanding work of Italian rationalism and a stunning piece of modern architecture. Juxtaposed with the nearby Renaissance church of Santa Maria Novella, it embodies Michelucci's recurrent themes: the relationship of a single element with its larger context, whether urban, environmental or historical. Active in postwar city reconstruction, he also initiated and edited the journal *La città nuova* (The New City) from 1945 to 1956 (see **architectural and design magazines**). Always a craftsman, his classic works include the churches of Larderello, Saint John the Baptist of Arzignano (also known as 'of the Autostrada'), a memorial church piazza at Longarone, postal banks in Pistoia and Florence and apartments on via Guicciardini in Florence.

GORDANA KOSTICH

Milan Triennale

What became the Milan Triennale, a three-yearly exhibition of design held in Milan, began life as the Biennale Internazionale dell'Arte Decorativa (International Biennial of Decorative Art) in Monza in 1923. Its brief was to display the products of the Italian decorative art industries – ceramics, glass, furniture, metalwork, textiles and so on – alongside those of other countries. Two more Biennale were held in 1925 and 1927, after which the exhibition was organized every three years from 1930 onwards. Henceforth it was known as the Triennale Internazionale dell'Arte Decorativa. In 1933 it was moved to Milan to occupy a purpose-built building, where it has been held ever since.

Since the 1930s, the Triennale has been the place where Italian innovations in the decorative arts and design have first been seen, and all the leading designers of the day have displayed work there. It was particularly famous in the 1950s when design played such an important role in the cultural regeneration of so many countries. It was at the Triennale, for instance, that countries such as Germany and Finland first gained a reputation for innovation in this area. More to the point, however, it was also at this venue that the Italian designers of the postwar years demonstrated their creative skills and where companies such as **Olivetti** made such a mark for the design that they fostered.

The Triennales of 1951, 1954 and 1957 were particularly memorable in this respect. The Eighth Triennale of 1947 had a strong social emphasis, focusing on the problem of the postwar home. From 1951 onwards, however, this perspective was less in evidence and the 'Form of the Useful', the name of the display of the Italian goods in the Ninth Triennale, was overtly aesthetic in nature, showing how beautiful the design of functional goods could be.

The 1954 Triennale put an even more deliberate emphasis upon the visual rather than the social impact of design, and this time the display of Italian goods was called 'The Production of Art' to mark this fact. The influence of organic surrealism was in evidence and, in addition to the evocative nature of the display itself, the objects on display demonstrated what was called a spirit of 'abandoned playfulness'. The 1957 exhibition developed this emphasis, but by the 1960s the impact of the Triennale was becoming less forceful. The show of 1968 was closed prematurely due to the student uprisings of that year. Since then the Triennale has continued to take place, but with a significantly lower profile than it had in the 1950s.

See also: interior design

Further reading

Pansera, A. (1978) *Storia e cronaca delle Triennale* (History and Chronicle of the Triennale), Milan: Longanesi.

PENNY SPARKE

Milani, Don Lorenzo

b. 27 May 1923, Florence; d. 26 June 1967, Florence

Priest and social activist

Don Milani was one of the first priests of the Catholic *dissenso* (dissent), and his *Lettera a una professoressa* (Letter to a Schoolmistress) (1967) became an influential text during the 1968 student agitations and was translated into many languages. Born into an upper middle-class family, he was ordained as a priest in 1947. His first parish was an industrial suburb of Florence, and his experience of the poverty there led him to reject the policies of the Christian Democrat Party (see **DC**). In 1958 he was sent to Barbiana, a remote country parish, where he wrote *Esperienze pastorali* (Pastoral Experiences), which was censured by the Holy Office. In 1965, he was put on trial for his public attack on military chaplains who opposed conscientious objection. He died prematurely at the age of only forty-four, and his most important publication remains the *Lettera*, in he which attacked the class basis of the Italian school system.

See also: education

Further reading

Fallaci, N. (1977) *Dalla parte dell'ultimo. Vita del prete Lorenzo Milani* (On the Side of the Last: The Life of priest Lorenzo Milani), Milan: Libri Edizioni.
Lancesi, M. (1980) *Dopo la 'lettera'. Don Milani e la contestazione studentesca* (After the 'Letter': Don Milani and the Student Contestation), Bologna: Cappelli.

JOHN POLLARD

Milva

b. 18 July 1939, Goro, Ferrara

Popular singer

Seen at the start of her career as a rival to **Mina**, Maria Ilva Biolcati adopted the pseudonym 'Milva' after an **RAI** official announced that her name sounded like 'ploughed earth and agricultural labour'. Her career also saw a move away from her origins in popular song towards more prestigious activities. After participating in the **Sanremo Festival** in the early 1960s, Milva branched out into interpretations of the songs of Brecht and Weil, *engagé* singer-songwriters, gospel music and tango, performing in theatres in Berlin, Paris and London. With her lean, decadent appearance, mane of red hair and dark husky voice, she mined similar territory to the later Marlene Dietrich and Ute Lemper. Although she came to be seen as a singer for intellectuals, she did not cut herself off entirely from the popular market. In the 1980s she

made several rock-oriented albums written and produced by the Sicilian singer-songwriter Franco Battiato. Her signature tune, 'La rossa' (The Redhead), was written for her by Enzo **Jannacci**.

Further reading

Manfredi, G. (1982) *Mina, Milva, Vanoni e altre storie* (Mina, Milva, Vanoni and Others), Rome: Latoside.

STEPHEN GUNDLE

Mina

b. 25 March 1940, Busto Arsizio, Varese

Popular singer

Mina (the stage name of Anna Maria Mazzini) burst on to the Italian musical scene in 1959 with her first hit song 'Nessuno' (Nobody) and remained an important figure into the 1990s. Although she made her last television appearance in 1974 and was not seen in public after 1978, the release of her annual album has continued to be regarded as a great event. Endowed with a rich voice better fitted in some respects to the big band tradition than to the pop idiom, she has been compared to Barbra Streisand. She established, for the first time in Italy, the primacy of voice over text; her vocal range was reputed to extend over eight octaves. Mina scored many hits in the 1960s and 1970s, including 'Il cielo in una stanza' (The Sky in a Room) and 'Città morta' (Dead City). A girl of the 1960s who wore a mini-skirt, she appeared regularly on television shows such as *Il Musichiere* and *Studio Uno*. In 1963 she caused a scandal by becoming pregnant by a married actor, Corrado Pani. Her children, Massimiliano Pani and Nicoletta Mazzini, who grew up in the public eye, also work in the entertainment industry.

Further reading

Manfredi, G. (1982) *Mina, Milva, Vanoni e altre storie* (Mina, Milva, Vanoni and Others), Rome: Latoside.

STEPHEN GUNDLE

minority languages

Within the Italian nation, one finds a considerable web of minority or alloglot languages, compounding the already impressive plurilingualism resulting from the wealth of Italian **dialects** which continue to flourish side by side with the Italian language. Without taking into account here the significant number of new immigrant languages (African, Asian, East European and so on) and their more than one million speakers, across the peninsula more than 2,800,000 individuals in thirteen administrative regions speak a mother tongue other than Italian. These figures are approximate, due to factors such as continued internal and external migrations, and to fear of stigmatization in declaring linguistic minority status.

Most of the alloglot languages can be traced to historical immigrations. Italy's linguistic minorities are found mainly in border areas (Piedmont, Valle d'Aosta, Friuli and so on), or in scattered enclaves. Sociolinguistic stratification exists in alloglot communities, and while cultivated people tend to support the preservation of minority languages, they are also the first to abandon them. In general, little has been done by the state to stem erosion of these languages, and pluralism tends to be an abstract concept, long after the intolerance exerted by the Fascist regime. In fact, a law to protect Italian minority languages was passed in 1991 only by one chamber of Parliament, and the political debate is ongoing. These factors explain the generally low prestige which minority languages hold even within their own speech communities, where the standard languages and local dialects are generally given preferred status (see **language attitudes**). An abundant literature has engaged in the debate and study of the extremely complex situations of minority language groups from different vantage points, political and geographical, historical and anthropological, sociological and linguistic. Despite strong fluctuations from one context to the other, the situation of most minority languages with a lengthy historical tradition tends to be precarious. Still, the demographics can be impressive. Sardinian is spoken most widely (1,500,000 people), followed by Friulian (700,000), Provençal and Franco-Provençal (300,000), German dialects (280,000), Albanian-Italian dialects

(100,000) and a sprinkling among the other languages.

If we follow Italy's minority languages from the north-west to the north-east, the south and the islands, we come across Provençal in Piedmontese valleys such as the Stura, Gesso or Grana valleys; with the absence of a roof-language, Provençal functions as the low register next to Italian. Provençal is also found in Apulia and Calabria due to a secondary migration of Waldensians to the south in the fourteenth century; despite religious persecutions and a genocide in 1561, the language is still spoken by several hundred people living in Guardia Piemontese (province of Cosenza). Franco-Provençal, on the other hand, is used extensively in the province of Turin, in the Valle d'Aosta – the region holding special status since 1945 – where both French and Italian constitute the high register, and in the towns of Faeto and Celle di San Vito in the Apulian province of Foggia.

German dialect varieties sporadically line the Alpine range from Piedmont to the Veneto. Established in the South Tirol in the tenth century, the Alto Adige community with its close to 300,000 speakers in the province of Bolzano represents the most important Germanic region of Italy and enjoys significant protection in the public sector, despite the limited competence of the population in standard German. Unlike the Tirolian origin of these dialects, the speech of the four German enclaves in the Trentino and Veneto regions is of Bavarian origin. While the *mòcheni* (from German *machen* 'to make, do') community in the Fersina Valley today counts several thousand speakers, the German dialects in the isolated town of Luserna, on the highlands of Asiago, and in thirteen Veronese villages are either extinct or eroding rapidly. The German dialects are better preserved in the tourist town of Sappada/Plodn (province of Belluno), and in the Carnian linguistic islands of Sauris, Timau and Val Canale. Finally, Alemannic dialects are spoken by the Waldensian colonies who settled in the Eastern Valle d'Aosta area (Gressoney Saint Jean and Gressoney la Trinité) and in the provinces of Novara and Vercelli in the Middle Ages.

Friulian is among the most homogenous of the linguistic minorities, with a common variety, based on that of Udine, recognized by many of its 700,000 speakers. Following the 1976 earthquake, Friulian consciousness was revitalized and the language was recognized as autonomous *vis-à-vis* the Italian dialects, even though it is used with less integrity by younger generations. Ladin, the central Rhaeto-Romance variety, is spoken in the Dolomite valleys of Fassa, Gardena, Badia, Livinallongo, Boite and Piave by some 30,000 people.

In the provinces of Gorizia, Udine and Trieste, some 60,000 people speak Slovenian as their mother tongue, and the Adriatic coast from the Marche to the Molise was until the nineteenth century sporadically populated by Slovenian and Croatian minority groups who fled the Turkish invasions of the fifteenth century. Today, only three Croatian Italian groups survive in the province of Campobasso (Acquaviva Collecroce, San Felice Slavo and Montemitro).

Known as *arbarèsh*, the Albanian *tosco* variety is still used in some forty-five towns across south–central regions from Abruzzo to Sicily, together with the local dialects and Italian. The slight difference between this variety and the standard *shqip* may explain why some prestigious Albanian poets such as Giuseppe Variboba and Girolamo De Rada originated in Calabria.

Neo-Greek communities are found in the Salentine peninsula around Lecce and in the Calabrian towns of Condofuri, Bova and Roccaforte; however, language erosion in these communities is now at an advanced stage.

According to linguistic typology, the Logudorese and Campidanese varieties in Sardinia constitute an autonomous Romance language group. Given the lack of a generally accepted Sardinian standard and the importance of Italian, diglossia tends to be the norm here, despite many autonomist claims to the contrary. Sardinia also numbers two small linguistic communities: the Catalan community of Alghero (some 20,000 people), which is the remainder of a colony established by the Aragonese in 1354, and the Ligurian group, which came from the Tunisian island of Tabarca in 1738 to settle in Carloforte and Calasetta.

Finally, the Gipsy languages Sinti and Rom have been spoken in Italy by a considerable multilingual nomad population represented in the north and south–central regions since the fifteenth century;

their different internal varieties can be ascribed to the various dialect superstrata. Jewish Italian speech, flourishing in the peninsular diaspora since the Roman Empire, has been extinct since the mid-twentieth century. On the other hand, residues of Gallo-Italian dialects are still found in Sicily (Piazza Armerina, Nicosia, Sperlinga and so on) and Basilicata (Tito, Picerno, Trecchina, etc.), even though they have been strongly dialectalized. Samples from the Gallo-Italian dialect of San Fratello have found their way into a novel by Vincenzo **Consolo**, *Il sorriso dell'ignoto marinaio* (The Smile of the Unknown Sailor) published by **Einaudi** in 1992.

See also: Italian language; language policy

Further reading

Francescato, G. (1993) 'Sociolinguistica delle minoranze', (The Sociolinguistics of Minorities) in A.A. Sobrero (ed.), *Introduzione all'italiano contemporaneo. La variazione e gli usi* (Introduction to Contemporary Italian: Variation and Use), Bari: Laterza (an excellent survey with particular attention to the sociolinguistic issues involving minority language speakers and communities).

Telmon, T. (1992) *Le minoranze linguistiche in Italia* (Linguistic Minorities in Italy), Turin: Edizioni dell'Orso.

—— (1994) 'Aspetti sociolinguistici delle eteroglossie in Italia' (Sociolinguistic Aspects of Italy's Heteroglossia), in L. Serianni and P. Trifone (eds), *Storia della lingua italiana* (History of the Italian Language), vol. 3, Turin: Einaudi.

HERMANN W. HALLER

minority religions

Largely due to the efforts of the Counter-Reformation papacy which, through the Inquisition and the Index of Prohibited Books, worked tirelessly to extirpate heretical sects from the peninsula, until the 1970s Italy remained an overwhelmingly Catholic country. Only the Waldensians of Piedmont survived the persecutions of the Duke of Savoy (immortalized in the words of the English poet, Milton: 'Avenge oh Lord thy slaughtered saints whose bones lie scattered on the Alpine mountains cold') so that today the Waldensians and Methodists (united since 1989) count some thirty thousand members. There are now also Baptist and Anglican churches in most of Italy's major cities, the latter having a largely expatriate following.

Other major non-Catholic groups are the Seventh Day Adventists, the Mormons and the Pentecostalists, with roughly 170,000 adherents. These groups, and the Jehovah's Witnesses (reputedly 150,000 followers) were introduced into Italy (especially the South) by return migrants from America in the interwar years. The Rome telephone directory attests to the enormous success of the Pentecostalists and the Jehovah's Witnesses in the last two decades.

The oldest Italian non-Catholic community is the Jewish. The Italian Jews were the most integrated of all Europe's communities and have played a prominent role in public – and especially cultural – life since the Risorgimento. Originally granted a special statute by Mussolini in 1931, they were later victimized by his Racial Laws introduced in 1938, and eight thousand of the forty thousand indigenous Italian Jews were deported to their deaths in concentration camps by the Germans between 1943 and 1945. A further five thousand emigrated to Israel after 1945 (see **Jewish writers**; Primo **Levi**).

However, Italy's largest – and newest – religious minority is undoubtedly the Muslim community, the result of massive migration in the 1980s and 1990s from North Africa, especially from Morocco, Algeria, Tunisia and Egypt, and to a lesser extent from the Indian subcontinent. The largest Muslim community is in Rome, where there is now a major mosque and a thriving Islamic cultural centre. The leaders of Italy's 300,000 Muslims have decided to exercise their power by asking for the right to choose that .008 of their income tax be dedicated specifically to the religious, cultural and charitable activities of their own community.

As in other European countries, a number of Eastern religious cults such as the Krishna, Saia Bai and the Buddhists have also established themselves in Italy since the 1970s. Increased enthusiasm for Buddhism, in particular, was generated by Bernardo **Bertolucci**'s film *The Little Buddha* (1993).

A new Concordat between the **Vatican** and the Italian state, signed in 1984, has assured greater freedom and security for all non-Catholic religious groups living in Italy. The restrictions imposed on officially tolerated non-Catholic religious cults which were introduced by Mussolini in the wake of the 1929 Concordat have finally been replaced, in some cases by 'mini-concordats' between individual groups and the Italian state, which guarantee their rights and property before the law. In addition, there is now something approaching a spirit of ecumenism between Catholics and the mainstream Protestant groups, as well as Jews and Muslims. Other Protestant sects remain firmly separatist. However, it seems that generally the majority of Italians practise no religion at all, even if for the most part they remain nominally 'believers' in some way of the Catholic religion, rather than openly professing atheism or agnosticism.

See also: church, state and society; Second Vatican Council

Further reading

Riccardi, A. (1994) 'La vita religiosa' (The Religious life), in P. Ginsborg (ed.), *Stato dell'Italia* (State of Italy), Milan: Il Saggiatore (a wide-ranging, though not completely comprehensive survey of religion in Italy).

JOHN POLLARD

Missoni

The first collection by Ottavio and Rosita Missoni was produced for the Rinascente stores in 1953, but it was the Missoni label, introduced in 1958, which became internationally famous for imaginatively coloured knitwear. A workshop and factory were established in 1968 at Sumirago. The first boutiques were set up in Milan and New York in 1976, and the Missoni Uomo and Missoni Sport labels came into existence in 1981. Missoni achieved popular fame for its Spring 1967 collection in Florence, in which the models wore no underwear beneath their very fine knit dresses. Missoni's subsequent association with Milan helped to establish that city as an international fashion centre, despite the company's self-conscious dismissal of the fashion system. While modern technology remained central to the production of the Missoni knits, it was design, colour, imagination and, ultimately, practicality that sold them.

See also: fashion

NICOLA WHITE

MLD

Founded in 1969, the Movimento di Liberazione della Donna (Movement for the Liberation of Woman) was one of the many organized women's groups which emerged in the feminist wave which swept Italy in the late 1960s and early 1970s. An anti-authoritarian radical collective, it espoused socialist ideals and fought for the liberation of women and against their economic, psychological and sexual oppression. One of the feminist groups in federation, for a time, with the **Radical Party**, its most important battles were over the legalization of **abortion**, the liberalization of birth control and the establishment of childcare centres.

See also: feminism

Further reading

Bono, P. and Kemp, S. (eds) (1991) 'Manifesto and Document of the MLD, 1978/1979', *Italian Feminist Thought: A Reader*, Oxford: Blackwell.

BERNADETTE LUCIANO

Modigliani, Franco

b. 18 June 1918, Rome

Economist

A professor at the Massachusetts Institute of Technology, Modigliani was born in Italy but is an American economist in both education and culture. Widely regarded as one of the leading macroeconomists of our era, he received the Nobel Prize for Economics in 1985. Originally a Keynesian, in the 1960s–1970s he pursued a theoretical synthesis of the Keynesian and the neoclassical tradition and constantly focused on the relation between monetary phenomena and economic activity. Progressively drawn to monetarist theory, he made seminal contributions to areas ranging from monetary policy to the inflation–unemployment trade-off. Amongst specialists, he is best known for his so-called 'life cycle' theory of saving and consumption and his study of the firm's choice in financing investments (the so-called Modigliani–Miller theorem). He has also often contributed to debate on economic policy in Italy, supporting the incomes policy and repeatedly warning of the dangers of inflation and high national debt.

STEFANO BATTILOSSI

Modo

Founded in 1977 in Milan by Alessandro **Mendini** after his experience with **Casabella**, Modo was initially sponsored by product manufacturers such as Alessi, Cedit, Centrocappa, Elam, Flos, Poltranova, Stilwood and Zanotta but soon became a mouthpiece for the entire New Design Movement. In 1982 its editorship passed from Mendini to Franco Raggi, and subsequently to Andrea **Branzi** (from 1984) and then to Cristina Morozzi (from 1987) who brought the magazine closer to the problems of design production. Originally intended as an alternative to the canonical and official design culture, *Modo*'s greatest achievement was to bring Italian design to international notice. Its editorial policy was to widen the theoretical context of design, connecting it with issues such as ethno-anthropology and ecology as much as with industrialized processes, marketing and craftsmanship. It excelled during the debates on the new domesticity, consumerism, the unavoidability of the 'age of information' and the question of difference.

See also: architectural and design magazines

GORDANA KOSTICH

Modugno, Domenico

b. 9 January 1928, Polignano a Mare,
Bari; d. 6 August 1994, Lampedusa

Singer, film and stage actor

Born in small town on the Adriatic coast, 'Mr Volare', as Modugno came to be known throughout the world, moved to Rome in 1950 and studied acting at the **Centro Sperimentale di Cinematografia**. Although he would become best known as a singer, cinema was his acknowledged first love and even before graduating with honours from the Centro he had appeared in Eduardo **De Filippo**'s film version of *Filumena Marturano* (1951). He subsequently acted in numerous films, as well as on the stage, and worked with many of the major Italian directors including **Blasetti**, **Lizzani**, **Zampa**, **De Sica**, **Bolognini**, **Comencini** and with Giorgio **Strehler** at the Piccolo Teatro of Milan. In 1963 he directed his one and only film, *Tutto è musica* (All is Music).

In 1958 Modugno competed in the **Sanremo Festival** singing 'Volare, nel blu dipinto di blu', a song and an event that would mark a milestone in the history of Italian popular music and Italian popular culture generally. The song, inspired by a painting by Marc Chagall and written in collaboration with Franco Migliacci, won first prize and achieved immediate national and international renown. Selling an unprecedented 800,000 copies in Italy, it also remained first in the American charts for thirteen weeks, earning Modugno three Grammy Awards and his nickname 'Mr Volare'. It would eventually sell more than 22 million copies worldwide, be sung by artists as different as Bobby Rydell, Ella Fitzgerald, Dean Martin and David Bowie, and become the second best-selling song of all time, behind Bing Crosby's classic, 'White Christmas'.

While continuing his film and stage career, Modugno went on to win the Sanremo Festival three more times with songs that became classics of the Italian popular repertoire – 'Piove' (It's Raining) (1959), 'Addio, Addio' (Goodbye) (1962) and 'Dio, come ti amo' (God, How I Love You) (1966) – as well as also coming second three times and selling more than 60 million records worldwide.

Tragically, in 1984, while still at the height of his acting and singing career, he suffered a debilitating stroke and was forced to spend the last ten years of his life in reduced activity. Nevertheless, during this period he was also elected as a deputy for the **Radical Party** and recovered well enough to make a brief comeback in the early 1990s, recording a number of songs with his son, Massimo.

See also: cantautori; pop and rock music

GINO MOLITERNO

Mollino, Carlo

b. 5 May 1905, Turin; d. 27 August 1973, Turin

Architect, photographer, inventor and educator

Portrayed by Manfredo **Tafuri** as the *enfant terrible* of Italian architecture, Mollino was an eclectic 'inventor' from Turin, a city associated with Mollino's own curious pursuits of aeronautics and the occult. Like his friend Giò **Ponti**, Mollino assumed various roles: first and foremost, architect and photographer, but also inventor, designer, professor at Turin's Polytechnic, pilot of stunt planes and racing cars, and author of works on architecture, photography, art, aesthetics and sport. In all these restless pursuits, the frenetic Mollino tested the limits of human experience with utmost care and attention for what he regarded as the most enduring and vital foundation of humanity: the intimate relationship between individuals and their environments.

Further reading

Brino, G. (1985) *Carlo Mollino: Architecture as Biography*, Milan: Idea Books.

KEITH EVANS GREEN

Momigliano, Arnaldo

b. 5 September 1908, Caraglio, Cuneo; d. 1 September 1987, London

Historian

Arnaldo Momigliano was one of his century's most distinguished historians of Greece and Rome. Born into a Piedmontese Jewish family of liberal traditions and intellectual renown, he was appointed to the Chair of Roman History at the University of Turin in 1936. In 1938, anti-Jewish laws forced his dismissal and departure for England. After Oxford and Bristol, his academic home became University College London (1951–75), with lasting affiliations to the Warburg Institute, University of Chicago and the Scuola Normale Superiore in Pisa. His historical and historiographic studies of antiquity, marked by vast erudition and encyclopaedic range, defy simple summary. Two of his principal themes fit, however, with features of his own life. Experience of fascism reinforced a lifelong concern with liberty, ancient and modern. Likewise, his part-outsider status, as a Jew in Italy and an Italian in England, illuminates his interest in cultural translation: how European antiquity understood its neighbours and how later historians (notably Gibbon) understood that same antiquity. His subject matter was ancient; his preoccupations remain contemporary.

See also: historiography

Further reading

Brown, P. (1988) 'Arnaldo Dante Momigliano, 1908–87', *Proceedings of the British Academy* 74: 404–42.

Momigliano, A. (1975) *Alien Wisdom: The Limits of Hellenisation*, Cambridge: Cambridge University Press.

DAVID MOSS

monarchists

The June 1946 referendum, held simultaneously with the election of the **Constituent Assembly**, established a **Republic** and thus gave birth to a monarchist movement. Monarchism was strongest in the South, where support for the monarchy in the referendum reached nearly two-thirds (65.8 per cent) despite being a minority (45.7 per cent) in the country as a whole. Although the movement was divided into two parties for most of the 1950s and the parliamentary vote peaked in 1953 at a mere 6.9 per cent, its concentration in southern Italy gave it local strength and throughout the 1950s the Catholic Right sought to pressure the **DC** into coalition with it (and the **MSI**). The monarchists appeared to be gaining influence at the end of 1950s, but negative reaction to the centre–right **Tambroni** government and the subsequent **opening to the Left** marginalized them. Social change and the sheer passage of time rendered them anachronistic and they disappeared, being absorbed into the MSI in the 1970s.

MARK DONOVAN

Mondadori

Located at Segrate, Milan, Mondadori is one of the biggest and most successful **publishers** in Italy. The company began in 1923 when Arnoldo Mondadori founded the Società Anonima Arnoldo Mondadori, later transformed simply into Mondadori. Notwithstanding the dubious role that the company and its founder played during Fascism (for example, publishing the works of Mussolini), the publishing house assumed great importance in the postwar period. One significant achievement was acquiring the Italian rights for Micky Mouse (see **Topolino**) but a bigger breakthrough came with the inauguration of its paperback series *Oscar Mondadori* in 1965 which, from then on, provided a wide range of modern Italian and foreign literary texts at an affordable price. Another paperback series, the *Giallo Mondadori*, published weekly with a characteristic yellow cover, became synonymous with crime and detective novels to the point where *giallo* (yellow) became the general term for all crime novels (see **detective fiction**). Mondadori played a crucial part in the formation of a critical public by participating in the founding of the weekly *Panorama* and the daily *La Repubblica*. Although the Mondadori family still retain a strong influence in the company, since 1991 it has been part of the Berlusconi empire.

JAN KURZ

Il Mondo

Founded in February 1949 by Mario Pannunzio and a group of liberal democrats, *Il Mondo* (The World) achieved, in its short eighteen-year history, the status of a legend as one of the best examples of intelligent, independent and progressive journalism. With Pannunzio as chief editor and attracting the collaboration of some of the finest writers and intellectuals of the time (including **Brancati**, **Moravia** and **Croce** but also publishing articles by Thomas Mann and Truman Capote), *Il Mondo* became the committed standard bearer of Italian civil rights throughout the 1950s and early 1960s, publishing penetrating and critical analyses of the government and its clientelistic practices, the Catholic Church and other aspects of Italian culture and society. It closed in 1966 after the death of Pannunzio. Although relaunched by Arrigo **Benedetti** three years later, it was unable to regain ground against competitors like *L'Espresso* and *Panorama*, and in 1976 it was transformed into an economic journal of minor significance.

JAN KURZ

Monicelli, Mario

b. 15 May 1915, Viareggio

Film and theatre director, scriptwriter and critic

Although most commonly celebrated as the father of *commedia all'italiana* (comedy Italian style), Monicelli has been a versatile and a prolific director-scriptwriter who has worked successfully across a wide range of genres. While studying history and philosophy at the University of Pisa, Monicelli began writing film criticism for a number of minor journals. In 1934, together with his cousin Alberto Mondadori, he began making amateur films in 16mm. In 1935, their *I ragazzi della via Paal*

(The Boys in Paal Street), a silent short adapted from a novel by Ferenc Molnar and acted by family and friends, won the first prize in its category at the Venice Festival and opened the doors of the film industry to the young Monicelli. In the next fifteen years he worked as assistant to many established directors, including Machaty, Genina, Freda, Mattoli, **Camerini** and Bonnard, and wrote or collaborated on some fifty screenplays.

By the late 1940s, having already established a close screenwriting partnership with Steno (Stefano **Vanzina**), Monicelli co-directed *Totò cerca casa* (Totò Looks for a House), the first of eight films he and Steno would write and direct together in the next six years, four of them starring the inimitable comic, **Totò**. After several more light comedies on his own, in 1958 Monicelli directed *I soliti ignoti* (literally 'The Usual Unknowns', but generally known in English as 'Big Deal on Madonna Street'), the film that would make him famous and inaugurate the entire genre of the so-called comedy Italian style. Recounting a fumbled bank robbery by a motley group of inept small-time thieves, the film was something of a parody of the American gangster genre but the atmosphere reflected all the darker aspects of the so-called **'economic miracle'** and the characters, especially those played brilliantly by Vittorio **Gassman** and Marcello **Mastronianni**, were characteristically Italian in their self-centred, if lovable, eternal adolescence. The film became an overwhelming box office hit both in Italy and abroad, and received an Oscar nomination for Best Foreign Film. This was followed by *La grande guerra* (The Great War) (1959), a comic but fierce indictment of Italy's participation in the First World War, which sparked much controversy in official circles but which was ultimately awarded the Golden Lion at Venice, shared with **Rossellini**'s *Il Generale Della Rovere* (General Della Rovere).

Over the next four decades Monicelli continued to make a distinctive contribution to Italian cinema with works that were often humorous but always sharply alert to the tragic weaknesses and contradictions of the Italian character. As well as writing or co-writing the screenplays of his own films, he also collaborated on scripts for other directors and in the 1980s also ventured into theatre. With four Oscar nominations and a dozen 'classic' films to his credit, Monicelli was awarded a Golden Lion for lifetime achievement at the Venice Festival of 1991. Ever indefatigable, he thereafter went on to make the caustic comedy *Parenti serpenti* (Relatives and Snakes) in 1992 and then in 1999 *Panni sporchi* (Dirty Clothes), an outrageous farce that satirized the new entrepreneurial spirit in an Italy already caught up in globalization.

Further reading

Della Casa, S. (1987) *Mario Monicelli*, Florence: La Nuova Italia (a comprehensive survey of Monicelli's career up to the mid-1980s, together with filmography and a selected bibliography).

GINO MOLITERNO

Montaldo, Giuliano

b. 22 February 1930, Genoa

Actor and film director

Originally a stage actor, Montaldo moved into cinema by playing a partizan in **Lizzani**'s *Achtung! Banditi!* (1951). He then worked as assistant director to Lizzani, **Pontecorvo** and **Petri** while also making a number of short documentaries. His first feature film, an attempt to analyse fascism entitled *Tiro al piccione* (Pigeon Shoot) (1961), was not well received, but Montaldo went on to distinguish himself with more impressive films such as his critique of the **economic miracle**, *Una bella grinta* (Some Pluck) (1965) and his recreation of the famous trial in America of the two Italian anarchists in *Sacco and Vanzetti* (1970). His next attempt to denounce intolerance by recreating the life and martyrdom of the Renaissance philosopher, *Giordano Bruno* (1973), was interesting but ultimately failed to rise above the level of a mediocre biopic. After a competent adaptation of Viganò's famous **Resistance** novel, *L'Agnese va a Morire* (Agnes Goes to her Death) in 1976, Montaldo directed the mega-spectacle *Marco Polo* for Italian television in 1982. Though continuing to make films for television, in the 1990s he has worked extensively in opera.

GINO MOLITERNO

Montale, Eugenio

b. 12 October 1896, Genoa;
d. 12 September 1981, Milan

Poet

Universally acknowledged as one of the greatest Italian poets of the twentieth century, Montale spent his childhood in the Ligurian landscape that would be one of the inspirations of his first collection of poetry, *Ossi di seppia* (Cuttlefish Bones) (1925). In 1927 he moved to Florence, where he worked as an editor for the Bemporad publishing company and became the director of Gabinetto Viesseux until 1938, when his refusal to join the Fascist party led to the loss of that position. During this period he produced his second major collection of poetry, *Le occasioni* (The Occasions) (1939). In 1948 he moved to Milan where he spent the rest of his life, working for the daily newspaper **Corriere della sera**. A long silence followed his third major collection of poetry, *La bufera e altro* (1955), which was finally broken with the publication of the new and innovative collections of *Satura* (1971), *Diario del '71 e del '72* (Diary of 1971 and 1972) (1974) and *Quaderno di quattro anni* (Four-Year Notebook) (1977). In 1975 he received the Nobel Prize for Literature.

Montale's poetic beginnings are marked by a fertile dialogue with both his contemporaries and with the canonized Italian tradition. Thus, D'Annunzio's poetics are understood and absorbed but ultimately left behind in the search for a new Italian verse, less eloquent and closer to the ideal of a colloquial poetic voice. In his search, Montale looks to other Ligurian poets (Sbarbaro above all, but also Ceccardi), and to some of the so-called crepuscular poets such as Guido Gozzano. However, he also moves outside the borders of the Italian tradition to devote particular attention to the French and English fathers of modern poetry, especially Baudelaire and Robert Browning. Nevertheless the major reference point for a poetics of modernity remains the poetry of Leopardi, of which Montale is at once a legitimate inheritor and a sophisticated contrapuntal voice.

A stoic attitude, reminiscent of Leopardi, appears in the first collection of *Ossi di seppia*, represented in the dry and sharp natural landscape of this region, which in turn assumes allegorical meanings which recall the classical topoi of the closed garden and pleasant retreat. However, Montale emphasizes the negativity of existence by assuming an immanent perspective which is balanced by an agnostic attitude toward the metaphysical question of the beyond. The escape is possible, but not for the poetic self, who instead wishes that possibility for the silent interlocutor. The Other – a constant, although tacit, presence throughout Montale's poetry – is the only one who may be able to imitate the flight of birds and thus overcome the wall which encloses the sterile garden in which the self feels entrapped and separates it from the open space of which the sea is the climactic representation.

In *Le occasioni*, however, the Other acquires more definite features and becomes the feminine counterpart of the self, the 'visiting angel' who may bring salvation, thanks to her descent to earth. The first section of this collection, 'Mottetti', recounts the amorous relationship between the self and the angelic woman in a narrative where the love motif develops in a movement reminiscent of the poetics of Dante's *dolce stil novo* (sweet new style). The woman appears in a plurality of forms and names but all recognizable to the self who has invented them. The crucial episodes of the relationship are quotidian experiences which acquire the status of 'occasions' according to the particular sensibility of the self, who is able to perceive in the contingency of daily life the obscure reasons for the apparition of the emblems which carry the mark of the 'visiting angel'. Therefore, objects which come into contact with the self are able to create a correlation between the self and the Other, according to a redeeming interpretation of their presence; all of which is closer to T.S. Eliot's poetics of the objective correlative than to any poetics of alienation.

La bufera e altro (The Storm and Other Poems) is a collection whose very title denounces the tragedy of the Second World War, a tragedy commemorated in many of the poems and which in hindsight appears foreshadowed by certain of the female characters of *Le occasioni*. The Dantean allusion, however, opens no space to paradisiacal aspirations but rather tends to exalt the infernal certainty of the historical moment. In some of the poems, the religious question, which had previously received answers that recalled those of existentialism and negative theology, becomes more pressing and the angel-like woman is more strikingly represented as either heavenly or earthly, according to the mask that is evoked to name her.

This constant evolution of Montale's poetry of experience takes an inward and self-critical turn in the poems of *Satura*, many of which reflect on the themes of the previous collections and sometimes provide illumination of the hermetic enigmas of the early poems. It is also true, however, that this employment of irony, and indeed of satire as the title of the fourth collection suggests, leaves only the possibility of an extreme solution: the final acceptance of immanence, many times desperately expressed in eschatological terms. The infernal world prevails, full of ghosts that return to populate in vain an environment in which the self is left now alone to face the quotidian. The last two collections, *Diario del '71 e del '72* and *Quaderno di quattro anni*, reflect this effort to annotate the detailed facts of personal existence as the only defence against the overwhelming and invasive presence of the inexplicable, the numinous mystery to which Montale, to the end, refuses to attribute a specific divine identity. The lifelong coherent belief that, for humankind, it is impossible to open the gates that lead beyond, accompanies Montale's poetry throughout the rich and intense development of its resigned gnoseological standpoint.

Further reading

Biasin, G.-P. (1989) *Montale, Debussy and Modernism*, Princeton, NJ: Princeton University Press.

Cambon, G. (1982) *Eugenio Montale's Poetry: A Dream in Reason's Presence*, Princeton, NJ: Princeton University Press.

Cary, J. (1969) *Three Modern Italian Poets: Saba, Ungaretti, Montale*, New York: New York University Press.

Montale, E. (1984) *Tutte le poesie*, ed. G. Zampa, Milan: Mondadori, 1984 (a complete collection of all Montale's poetry).

—— (1982) *The Second Life of Art: Selected Essays of*

Eugenio Montale, ed. and trans. J. Galassi, New York: Ecco Press.

West, R. (1981) *Eugenio Montale: Poet on the Edge*, Cambridge, MA: Harvard University Press.

ERNESTO LIVORNI

Montanelli, Indro

22 April 1909, Fucecchio, Florence

Journalist and writer

Universally regarded – even by critics and adversaries – as the grand old man of Italian postwar journalism, Montanelli worked as foreign correspondent and then senior columnist and political commentator for the *Corriere della sera* from 1938 to 1972. After a brief period with *La Stampa* in 1974, he founded a new daily, *Il Giornale Nuovo* (from 1983, *Il Giornale*), for which he was general editor until the paper was taken over by Silvio **Berlusconi**'s group in the early 1990s. Personally conservative and regarded politically as to the right of centre, Montanelli became the target of an armed attack by the **Red Brigades** in 1977 but survived relatively unscathed. Recipient of many awards for his journalism, Montanelli is also a prolific author who has published numerous books on Italian history as well as several works for the theatre. In the 1990s, in addition to writing columns in newspapers and weekly magazines, he also appeared regularly on television as a respected political and social commentator.

GINO MOLITERNO

Montedison

A major industrial group, Montedison faithfully mirrored the changing balance of power between state-owned and private capitalism in Italy from the 1960s onward, when the chemical and petrochemical sectors emerged not only as a new frontier of industrial growth, but also as a favourite battlefield of big business. Montedison's history is a sort of Thirty Years War, marked by struggles and ceasefires and a number of scandals which revealed the sector as a privileged area of political corruption.

Montedison was established in 1966 through a merger of Montecatini, a chemical group with heavy debts and an ossified management, and Edison, once the most powerful private electric holdings before the 1962 nationalization. Through this merger **Mediobanca**, which stayed in the background, aimed to create a private giant to compete with **ENI** and other major European groups. However unresolved disputes between the two private partners cleared a path for **ENI**, then ruled by Eugenio **Cefis**, to successfully accomplish a takeover and win a strong position as shareholder of the private group. This sort of silent nationalization triggered off long-lasting underground battles, which nevertheless did not prevent Montedison from becoming a giant conglomerate whose chemical core business was paralleled by a number of unrelated companies in sectors such as textiles, food, engineering, electronics and even chains of hotels and department stores. Its political influence also grew stronger due to close relations between Cefis and the ruling Christian Democratic party (**DC**), which eventually allowed Montedison to gain control of the influential newspaper *Il Corriere della sera*.

However Montedison's fortunes were to decline. During the 1970s a severe blow was delivered by both a steep rise in oil prices and high inflation, so that profits turned into losses and debts began to rise quickly. This was just the beginning of an endless ordeal. In 1981, ENI abandoned Montedison by selling its shares to **Gemina**, a financial holding ruled by Mediobanca and **Fiat**. Five years later, disputes between Mediobanca and Mario Schimberni (Montedison's managing director, who wanted to turn the concern into a 'public company') cleared the way for a new owner, the **Ferruzzi** group, led by Raul Gardini, a dynamic but reckless entrepreneur whose dream was to reorganize Montedison and propel it again to a high international standing. In order to reach this goal, he proposed to amalgamate Montedison and ENI's chemical activities into a new giant joint venture, ENIMONT, but the prospective partners proved to be fierce enemies and even the ruling political parties became deeply involved. After wearisome negotiations, Montedison finally sold a large part of its chemical activities to ENI, while – as the **Tangentopoli** trials were later to prove – the main beneficiaries of ENIMONT ended up being the political parties themselves, since they were paid a gigantic bribe in order to facilitate a final resolution. In the meantime, enormous amounts of money had been used up and Ferruzzi was sinking into debt until it was rescued in 1993 by a banking pool led by Mediobanca. After the failure of a further attempt to amalgamate the chemical activities of Ferruzzi and Fiat under Gemina in 1995, Montedison was placed under the control of Compart, a financial holding owned by a large group of banks, and its chemical and electric power activities were reorganized and divided by creating two new subholdings named, again, Montecatini and Edison: an ironic ending to a long and contorted story.

Further reading

Marchi, A. and Marchionatti, R. (1991) *Montedison 1966–1989*, Milan: Angeli (a well-informed business history of the chemical group's strategy, structure and management).

STEFANO BATTILOSSI

Monti, Adriana

b. 1951, Milan

Video, film and documentary maker

During the 1970s, Monti was deeply involved in the feminist movement and worked mostly in television and experimental video art. In 1979 she began filming a group of housewives involved in a mature age education scheme called the '150 hours', a process that lasted several years and which eventually became the 16mm documentary *Scuola senza fine* (School Without End) (1983). In the early 1980s she also worked as assistant director to Luigi **Comencini** and directed her first feature, *Gentili signore* (Kind Ladies), in 1988. Less well known to the wider public than to other film-makers, she has nevertheless provided an impor-

tant contribution to women's cinema and to documentary film-making in Italy.

See also: feminist cinema

Further reading

Bruno, G. and Nadotti, D. (eds) (1988) *Off Screen: Women and Film in Italy*, London: Routledge (see especially the extended discussion of the 150 hours project and Monti's own introduction to the script of *Scuola senza fine*, pp. 21–107).

GINO MOLITERNO

Morandi, Gianni

b. 11 December 1944, Monghidoro, Bologna

Pop singer and actor

Young, only slightly aggressive and with a cleancut look that could still endear him to parents, Morandi was able from the beginning to mix the new sound of rock'n'roll with the Italian melodic tradition. Beginning in 1961 with his first major hit, 'Fatti mandare dalla mamma a prendere il latte' (Ask Your Mother to Let You Bring the Milk), Morandi has sold over 25 million records in his long career, becoming one of the mainstays of Italian popular light rock. As well as winning the highly-regarded **Canzonissima** three times, he also starred in a number of movies inspired directly by his songs. His fortunes declined somewhat in 1970s, but Morandi returned to studying cello and preparing his comeback, which he did as a singer in the 1983 **Sanremo Festival** and as an actor in a number of 1980s television films. In 1989 he toured internationally with Lucio **Dalla** and at the same time increased his social commitment by founding a national football team of singers which play twice a year for charity. In 1997, together with Bob Dylan, he sang in Bologna before the Pope, and in 1999 hosted his own television variety show on the RAI's first channel.

RICCARDO VENTRELLA

Morandi, Giorgio

b. 20 July 1890, Bologna; d. 18 June 1964,
Bologna

Artist

Throughout his life Morandi rarely left his native
city of Bologna, where he taught print-making and
etching at the Academy of Fine Arts. When he did,
it was often only to the small settlement of Grizzana
in the nearby Apennines, which furnished the
subjects for his many landscapes. Between 1918–
19, Morandi was influenced by Giorgio **de
Chirico**'s idea of metaphysical painting, but for
the rest of his life he consciously chose to limit his
pictorial vocabulary to still lives and landscapes.

He has been classified, perhaps too neatly, as a
simple painter of bottles, a provincial artist isolated
from the mainstream of twentieth-century painting
seeking to revive Old Master traditions. However,
Morandi's small paintings of collections of bottles,
jugs and containers, enveloped in neutral backgrounds and seemingly existing in a vacuum,
rigorously explore a poetics of form and structure,
and his work has continued to elicit widespread
interest and discussion. The city of Bologna
maintains a major museum devoted entirely to
Morandi's work.

Further reading

Klepac, L. (1997) *Giorgio Morandi: The Dimension of
Inner Space*, Sydney: Art Gallery of New South
Wales (a number of illuminating essays on
Morandi with a good selection of colour
reproductions, a full list of exhibitions and an
extensive English language bibliography).

LAURENCE SIMMONS

Morante, Elsa

b. 18 August 1912, Rome; d. 25 November 1985, Rome

Writer

Born in one of the poorer areas of Rome, Morante
was completely self-taught but went on to win two

of the most prestigious Italian **literary prizes**, the
Viareggio, with *Menzogna e sortilegio* (House of Liars)
(1948) and the Strega with *L'isola di Arturo* (Arturo's
Island) (1957). In her most popular novel, *La Storia*
(History: A Novel) (1974), as in earlier writings,
Morante often portrays intense and traumatic
relationships between parents and children from
the point of view of the child. *La Storia* epitomizes
the author's attitude towards history. Although the
novel has been criticized by some feminists for its
portrayal of women – in particular, the character of
the mother has been singled out as being ahistorical
– it is a powerful indictment of history as a brutal
process that crushes the weakest members of society
and an intense affirmation of Morante's broadly
humanistic values. It was eventually made into a
film for television in 1985, directed by Luigi
Comencini and starring Claudia **Cardinale**.

Further reading

Wood, S. (1995) 'The Deforming Mirror: Histories
and Fictions in Elsa Morante', in S. Wood (ed.),
Italian Women's Writing 1860–1994, London:
Athlone Press.

PIERA CARROLI

Moravia, Alberto

b. 28 November 1907; d. 26 September
1990, Rome

Writer, critic, journalist and playwright

Alberto Moravia is the pseudonym of Alberto
Pincherle. His psychological realist novels and
short stories address contemporary social problems
in a crisp narrative style stripped of rhetoric. He
confronts the themes of alienation and ennui, the
degeneration of the bourgeoisie and the inability of
human beings to communicate authentically and
profoundly. Moravia's early success and prolific
output throughout his long career has made him
one of Italy's foremost twentieth-century writers.

Born into an wealthy family (with a Jewish
father and a Catholic mother), Moravia's adolescence was marred by chronic tuberculosis of the
bone. However, the forced inactivity of nine years

spent in various clinics fostered Moravia's story-telling skills and exposed him to European literature as he undertook to read all the classic nineteenth-century works. His first novel, *Gli indifferenti* (The Time of Indifference) (1929), proved a *cause célèbre* for the twenty-two-year-old author. The novel, which traces the spiritual collapse of a middle-class family, was greeted warmly by many literary critics, but harshly criticized by the Fascist regime, which saw in it an anti-family, amoral perspective.

Many of Moravia's works are permeated by a strong element of sexuality, as he often traces the erotic awakening of young men and women. This theme is evident in *Agostino* (1945) and *La disubbidienza* (1948, translated under the title Luca), two novels which follow sensitive young boys as they emerge from adolescence. Other works which address sexuality include *L'amore coniugale* (Conjugal Love) (1949) and *Il conformista* (The Conformist) (1951) a novel later adapted by Bernardo **Bertolucci** to create what undoubtedly remains his greatest film.

Moravia's early but also most critically esteemed works are his short stories set in Rome, minutely detailing the lives of the working classes. These are collected in *Racconti romani* (Roman Tales) (1954) and *Nuovi racconti romani* (More Roman Tales) (1959). His novel *La ciociara* (Two Women) (1957), a powerful and intimate portrayal of a mother's misfortunes, set against the horrors of the Second World War, was also highly acclaimed and in 1960 was adapted by **De Sica** into an equally powerful film which starred Sophia Loren in one of her best screen performances.

In later years, Moravia turned to more contemporary issues, writing essays on the social and political movements of the 1960s. His fiction during this period included stories about marital infidelity, lesbianism, nuclear proliferation and unconventional sexual behaviour. Many of these short stories are collected in *La Cosa* (Exotic Tales) (1983) and *La villa del venerdì* (The Friday Villa) (1990).

Moravia also edited and contributed to a number of newspapers and periodicals, including the literary review *Nuovi Argomenti*, the weekly **L'Espresso** and the newspaper **Il Corriere della sera**. He also published children's stories, travel narratives describing his trips to Africa, and

several plays, including *Il mondo è quello che è* (The World Is What It Is) (1967), *Il dio Kurt* (The God Kurt) (1968) and *La vita è gioco* (Life Is a Game) (1969). He was married to the author Elsa **Morante** from 1941 until 1962 when they separated, and he also had a long-term relationship with feminist writer Dacia **Maraini**. In 1985 he married Italo-Hispanic writer Carmen Llera.

Further reading

Capozzi, R. and Mignone, M.B. (eds) (1993) *Homage to Moravia*, Stony Brook, NY: Forum Italicum (essays written on the death of Moravia).

Kozma, J. (1993) *The Architecture of Imagery in Alberto Moravia's Fiction*, Chapel Hill, NC: University of North Carolina Dept. of Romance Languages.

Moravia, A. (1966) *Man as an End: Literary, Social and Political Essays*, New York: Farrar, Straus & Giroux.

Peterson, T.E. (1996) *Alberto Moravia*, New York: Twayne Publishers.

LAURA A. SALSINI

Moretti, Luigi Walter

b. 2 January 1907, Rome; d. 14 July 1973, Isola di Capraia

Architect, urban planner and editor

Moretti's activities revolved around his native Rome, where he studied and then practised extensively. His prewar work as a leading member of Giovinezza Italiana (Italian Youth) includes the masterplan for the Foro Mussolini (Italico), the outstanding Fencing Academy and the Gymnasium for the Duce. His postwar projects include both luxurious residences (for example, the so-called Sunflower house on Viale Buozzi in Rome and the Watergate residential quarter in Washington) and low-cost housing such as Case-Albergo, an extraordinarily vigorous office and apartment complex in Milan.

As director and editor of the review *Spazio* (1950–6), Moretti openly voiced disagreement with functionalism and the international style. However, his emphasis on the emotive potential of form and his preference for sophisticated abstraction and refinement in composition and surface was not fully appreciated at the time. A controversial, isolated and difficult figure, particularly as regards his ideology, Moretti was excluded from serious discussion in postwar architectural culture for over forty years.

GORDANA KOSTICH

Moretti, Nanni

b. 19 August 1953, Brunico, Bolzano

Film director, actor and producer

Though born in Brunico, Moretti was raised in the middle-class suburbs of Rome, whose left-wing youth culture would give birth to his onscreen persona, Michele Apicella, and furnish the subject matter for his eight feature-length films. Beginning with *Io sono un autarchico* (I am Self-Governing) (1976) and followed by the clamorously successful *Ecce bombo* (1978), Moretti's cinema would take the pulse of the post-1968 generation as it confronted psychological and spiritual crises (*La messa è finita* (The Mass is Ended), 1985), political disillusionment (*Palombella Rossa* (Red Lob), 1989), alienation and mortality (*Caro diario* (Dear Diary), 1993) and biological paternity and political rebirth (*Aprile*, 1998). *Autarchia*, the subject of Moretti's first feature, can be seen as the trademark of an entire career dedicated to artistic independence and alternative film practice. To help other like-minded directors get a start, Moretti established his own production company, La Sacher Film, in 1987.

See also: New Italian Cinema

Further reading

De Bernardinis, F. (1993) *Nanni Moretti*, Pavia: Editrice il Castoro (overview of career and analyses of individual films through *Caro diario*).

Marcus, M. (1996) '*Caro diario* and the Cinematic Body of Nanni Moretti,' *Italica* 73 (2): 233–47 (an interpretation of the film in the context of his previous production).

MILLICENT MARCUS

Moro, Aldo

b. 23 September 1916, Maglie, Lecce; d. 9 May 1978, Rome

Politician and academic

One of the central figures of Italian political Catholicism in the postwar period, Moro held the post of Prime Minister five times between 1964–8 (the crucial years of the centre–left) and again between 1974–6. Most importantly, he was also secretary of the Christian Democrat Party (see **DC**) from 1959–64, a period in which he laid the foundations of the **'opening to the Left'** which eventually led to the inclusion of the **PSI** in government. He would later be kidnapped, 'tried' and 'executed' by the **Red Brigades**, paradoxically because he was once again opening to the Left and preparing the ground for the **PCI**'s entry into government. Intellectually able, meticulous and careful, he was nevertheless unable to take decisions quickly and was often justly caricatured as a Hamlet. His political speeches were always long and contorted and sometimes barely intelligible, although they generally succeeded in galvanizing support. During the Tambroni crisis of 1960, for example, he suggested in a speech that the DC and PSI should initiate a 'parallel convergence' – impossible in geometry, of course, but quite practical in politics – and a course which he successfully followed as Prime Minister.

As a young man, Moro was active in Catholic university politics, being amongst the founders of the DC itself and also close to the charismatic leader Giuseppe **Dossetti**. After serving in various ministries, Moro became party secretary and mediated between **Fanfani** and the powerful centrist faction, the **Dorotei**. At the DC's Eighth Congress in Naples in 1962, in a speech which lasted six hours, Moro formally launched the idea of a centre–left government, reassuring the party and the Church of the policy's 'novelty in continuity'. It was more this diplomatic ability to mediate and conciliate rather than any solid majority support in the party that allowed him to sometimes lead and always strongly influence the DC from then until his death.

In the mid-1970s after the Christian Democrats had suffered defeat in both the **divorce** referendum and the 1975 regional elections, Moro again took over from Fanfani as party secretary with the intention of initiating what he called 'the third phase' of Italian political life, namely cooperation between Catholics and communists. Together with Communist Party secretary Enrico **Berlinguer**, he became the architect of governments of 'national solidarity' between 1976 and 1979, the closest the country came to the realization of the so-called **historic compromise** between communist and Catholic forces. The policy was highly criticized by both the Right of the DC and the USA on the one side and by the fringes of the Left, who saw it as an adulteration of the PCI.

It was ostensibly because of this that Moro was kidnapped by the extreme left-wing terrorist group, the Red Brigades, in March 1978. After being held hostage for fifty-five days and interrogated and tried in a 'people's tribunal', he was killed and his body left in Via Caetani, symbolically halfway between the DC and PCI headquarters in Rome.

Puzzling aspects of the kidnapping and the staunch refusal of the DC to negotiate with the Red Brigades for Moro's release have continued to generate suspicion of at least implicit conspiracy on the part of others. The various criminal trials and the extensive parliamentary enquiry into the so-called 'Moro affair' have done little to allay public disquiet about the rapid and violent elimination of one of the most powerful politicians in postwar Italy.

See also: terrorism

Further reading

Drake, R. (1995) *The Aldo Moro Murder Case*, Cambridge, MA: Harvard University Press (the best book on the Moro case in English; includes a biographical chapter as well as a close examination of all the circumstances and documents).

Sciascia, L. (1987) *The Moro Affair and the Mystery of Majorana*, trans. S. Rabinovitch, Manchester: Carcanet (an illuminating attempt by the famous Italian writer and essayist to analyse the Moro affair soon after it occurred).

Wagner-Pacifici, R.E. (1986) *The Moro Morality Play: Terrorism as Social Drama*, Chicago: University of Chicago Press (the Moro case analysed within its complex social and political context).

JAMES WALSTON

Morricone, Ennio

b. 10 November 1928, Trastevere, Rome

Composer

With an estimated 400 film scores to his credit, Morricone is the most prolific, respected and renowned film composer of the twentieth century. In spite of such an overwhelming identification with film music, Morricone received a thorough training in classical music at the Conservatory of Santa Cecilia in Rome, which he entered at the age of fourteen and where he studied trumpet, orchestration, choral music and composition under Goffredo **Petrassi**. In order to support himself in the 1950s and 1960s, he worked extensively as arranger and conductor for a number of popular singers including Gianni **Morandi**, **Mina**, Charles Aznavour and Mario **Lanza**. In the mid-1960s he was also part of Nuova Consonanza (New Consonance), an avant-garde musical improvisation group formed in Rome by Franco Evangelisti and strongly influenced by the ideas of American composer John Cage.

Much in demand in Italy for his imaginative arrangements, Morricone came to international prominence in 1964 with his boisterous and captivating score for Sergio **Leone**'s first **spaghetti western**, *For A Fistful of Dollars*. He subsequently scored all of Leone's films, including the gangster epic *Once Upon a Time in America* (1983) as well as working with all the major Italian directors from Gillo **Pontecorvo** and Marco **Bellocchio** to Pier Paolo **Pasolini** and Bernardo **Bertolucci**. As Bertolucci himself once remarked in an interview, there was a period in the 1970s when practically every Italian film, with the possible exception of those of Fellini, carried the Morricone name.

Although Morricone had previously also worked with American and British directors on films as different as John Boorman's *Exorcist II* (1977) and Terence Malick's *Days of Heaven* (1978), for which he had received an Oscar nomination, he became especially known in the USA for his haunting and moving soundtrack to Roland Joffe's historical epic, *The Mission* (1986), a score which was again nominated for an Oscar as well as winning a Golden Globe. He went on to work on a multitude of other international films including Brian De Palma's *The Untouchables* (1987), Roman Polanski's *Frantic* (1988) and Pedro Almodovar's *Tie Me Up! Tie Me Down!* as well as contributing a very lyrical touch to Giuseppe Tornatore's Oscar-winning *Cinema Paradiso* (1988). All his scores also became available on CD, leading to over twenty gold and five platinum albums as well as a countless number of other prestigious awards.

Although he remains best-known for his film and television scores, Morricone has continued to produce a considerable body of symphonic and chamber music which he himself conducts, such as his *Cantata for Europe* (1988) or *UT*, a composition which he later permitted to be used for a television tribute to mafia crime fighter, Giovanni **Falcone**. As a sign of his pre-eminence in 1998 Morricone was commissioned by the **Vatican** to compose the official hymn for the Holy Year 2000, the result being a choral work for six choirs and fifty voices lasting ten minutes but using only the word 'Amen'.

See also: film composers

Further reading

Morricone, E. (1995) 'Music at the Service of the Cinema: An Interview with Ennio Morricone', *Cineaste* 21 (1–2): 76–80 (an extensive and revealing interview covering most aspects of Morricone's music).

GINO MOLITERNO

Morselli, Guido

b. 15 August 1912, Bologna; d. 31 July 1973, Varese

Novelist and essayist

A reclusive and solitary man, Morselli had written nine novels, four plays, three film scripts and a large number of short stories, critical essays and a diary before he took his own life at the age of fifty-one. Ironically, although his posthumously-published work shows a novelist of rare talent and intellectual sophistication, during his lifetime his manuscripts were invariably rejected for publication by all the major Italian publishers and editors, amongst them writers of the calibre of **Calvino** and **Moravia**. Following his death, three critical works and seven of his novels have been published, and several have also been translated into English.

Morselli's carefully-crafted novels are generally concerned with either the investigation of society, as in *Roma senza Papa* (Rome Without a Pope) (1974) or of the mind, as in *Un dramma borghese* (A Bourgeois Drama) (1978). While in *Roma*, Morselli's witty imagination allows him to take a close look at the Catholic Church and its function in contemporary society, in *Un Dramma borghese* he dissects the complex and incestuous relationship between a man and his eighteen-year-old daughter. Relentless psychological analysis, combined with subtle irony and an original representation of time and memory, renders Morselli's novels compelling and yet resistant to simplistic literary categorization.

Further reading

Morselli, G (1986) *Divertimento 1889*, trans. H. Shankland, London: Chatto & Windus (one of Morselli's few translated novels, preceded by a brief but useful biography).

PAOLO BARTOLONI

Moschino

'Warning: fashion shows can be dangerous to your health', was just one of the many provocative Moschino slogans that suggested the fashion designer's anti-fashion industry attitude. Committed to social issues such as the environment and human rights, Moschino warned his audience about media manipulation and the potentially homogenizing effect of fashion on culture. Franco Moschino started out as an illustrator for Gianni **Versace** and struck out on his own in 1983 in the jeans and casual wear line, followed by shoes, lingerie, evening wear and finally a perfume. Examples of the Moschino touch are the fried egg and plastic windmill buttons adorning his classical jackets, or the winter hat made up of a mass of cuddly teddy bears. He was also known for his bright vests, purses, T-shirts and black satin evening gowns. Moschino died in 1994 at the age of forty-three, provoking a sense of loss in Italy's fashion world.

BERNADETTE LUCIANO

motor car industry

A sector of outstanding importance in postwar Italy, the motor car industry grew at a tremendous pace from the 1950s onwards and became a major symbol of the Italian '**economic miracle**'. Car production, which had amounted to only 100,000 cars a year in 1952, had gone beyond one million per year just ten years later, while exports had also increased considerably. This phenomenon not only had important economic effects, but it was also epoch-making in terms of social and cultural change. In being able to buy a car – such as Fiat 500 or 600 – at an affordable price, alongside other durable consumer goods such as refrigerators or motorbikes – the latter a very Italian specialization with a worldwide success (see **motorscooters**) – a number of Italians experienced for the first time the potential benefits of industrial growth on their own living standards. Individual mobility increased enormously, as did geographical and social integration.

Fiat played an undeniable leading role in that process, since it won a high standing among European producers, effectively boosted the domestic market and succeeded in keeping leadership of it even in 1970s and 1980s, when foreign car makers won ever larger market shares. The Turin group ultimately monopolized national production by taking over most of the other Italian automobile producers such as Lancia (an old family-owned company which was specialized in high-powered luxury cars, but proved unable to enter mass production), Autobianchi and finally Alfa Romeo (a competing company controlled by **IRI**, with very successful models such as the Giulietta and Alfetta). Fiat also retained its traditionally close links with **Ferrari**, the famous racing car maker.

The company also benefited from strong political support whereby high custom duties made foreign cars more expensive and foreign producers were prevented from either opening plants in Italy or gaining control over Italian companies: in 1986, in fact, political pressures led IRI to sell Alfa Romeo to Fiat, although Ford had offered to take over the company at very favourable conditions.

However, the economic crisis of 1970s and early 1980s marked a real turning point. Market growth slowed and then reached saturation point in all developed countries, thus forcing the American and European motor car industries to restructure. As a consequence, during the 1980s and 1990s Fiat periodically reduced its labour force, introduced technological innovations and renewed its models. Focusing mainly on the domestic market, it won back a strong leading position in Italy, in spite of market maturity (with a structural low demand), the full market liberalization of 1992 and the gradual penetration of new competitors such as the Japanese producers. In particular, Fiat strengthened its advantage in low segments of the market (small utility cars), even if it continued to suffer competition for its high-powered cars in Italy and, even more, in the rest of Europe.

Further reading

Enrietti, A. *et al.* (1980) *La ristrutturazione dell'industria metalmeccanica: il caso dell'auto e dei componenti* (The Restructuring of the Metalwork Industry: A Case Study of Automobile and Components), Milan: Angeli (a study of restructuring strategies of the Italian motor car industry after the 1970 crisis).

Laux, J.M. (1992) *The European Automobile Industry*, New York: Maxwell Macmillan International (a description of the main European car makers and their position on the international markets).

STEFANO BATTILOSSI

motor racing

Italian car makers such as Alfa Romeo, Bugatti, Maserati and **Fiat** were among the pioneers of motor racing. Alfa Romeo was very successful in the period before the Second World War, but since the late 1950s **Ferrari** has been the catalyst for the passion Italians display for motor racing. Several television programmes are dedicated to pre- and post-race analysis; a victory by Ferrari often prompts dancing in the streets and the front page of *La Gazzetta dello Sport* will relegate even **football** to secondary status. The Mille Miglia (One Thousand Mile) race – until 1957 – and the Monza and San Marino Formula One Grand Prix are amongst the most awaited events of the sports season.

Alfa Romeo's achievements continued after the Second World War. In 1947, Alfa Romeo took the Mille Miglia. In 1950 the Alfetta won all eleven races it had entered, clinching the second manufacturer's world title and making Giuseppe (Nino) Farina the first Formula One world champion. The next year, racing great Manuel Fangio repeated the exploit, taking the world title for himself and for Alfa Romeo. However, at the end of the 1951 season Alfa Romeo announced its withdrawal from Formula One and in 1957 Maserati also abandoned Grand Prix competitions, although for some years it continued to provide engines for other teams.

The time was now ripe for Enzo Ferrari and his team to take centre stage. Ferrari, in fact, was responsible for the creation of what has become the ultimate dream car and a cultural icon. He started his career as a driver and then directed racing operations for Alfa Romeo, where he established the first Scuderia Ferrari. After the Second World War, he began manufacturing his own cars at the Maranello plant outside Modena. On 11 May 1947, the first car carrying the Ferrari logo participated in an official competition. That first car never completed the race, but in 1948–9 Ferrari cars won the Mille Miglia and the Targa Florio (the most prestigious uphill race, held in Sicily). 1949 also brought the first victory at Le Mans (the world's best known twenty-four-hour endurance contest), thus firmly establishing Ferrari's reputation outside Italy.

Among the sport events that were reinstated after the war was the now legendary Mille Miglia, a race of roughly one thousand miles, run only on public roads. Large crowds gathered on the sides of the roads to cheer their favourite drivers. However, the engines were now more powerful (and the cars much faster) than those of pre-1945, but no greater safety measures had been taken. In 1957, Marquis Alfonso de Portago lost control of his Ferrari during the final miles of the race, killing himself, the navigator and eleven roadside spectators. An official investigation followed and Enzo Ferrari was charged with manslaughter (even the **Vatican** issued a denunciation against him). The race was suspended and although Ferrari was acquitted after a long trial, the Mille Miglia was considered too dangerous and discontinued.

At that point, Monza's Formula One Grand Prix (already a hugely popular race) became the main event of Italian car racing. The Monza autodrome, among the world's oldest and most challenging, is situated in the former royal park just outside of Milan. Every year, thousands of people arrive days before the race, camp in the park and wait in long lines or pay scalpers ten times the face value of a ticket. Others choose more creative ways to view the Grand Prix and build their own (often precarious) stands or sit in the trees that line the course. The drivers usually reward this show of enthusiasm with fierce competition, knowing that a victory at Monza in front of the home crowd will guarantee a lifetime of adulation.

Another Formula One Grand Prix takes place in Italy, at Imola, though its official denomination is Grand Prix of San Marino (a tiny independent republic completely surrounded by Italian territory). During the trials for the San Marino Grand Prix in 1994, Austrian driver Roland Ratzenberger lost control of his car and died. The next day, a similar fate befell three-time world champion Ayrton Senna. The accidents were eventually attributed to mechanical failure, and the FIA (Federation Internationale de l'Automobile) imposed a series of regulations aimed at limiting the power of Formula One cars.

Italian motor racing had a number of famous drivers, though none greater than Tazio Nuvolari. This extraordinary driver (also known as 'the flying Mantuan' and 'the red devil'), had worked for Alfa Romeo's Scuderia Ferrari before the war, and returned under the direction of Enzo Ferrari in July 1947. Unlike that of his impeccable companion and rival Achille Varzi, Nuvolari's driving style was very unorthodox and he took more risks than anyone else, which is what made him a legend in the eyes of the public. Furthermore, experts like Enzo Ferrari and his technicians also saw that Nuvolari could push cars to their limits without destroying them and could thus offer precious technical information on how to improve them. Nuvolari retired in 1950.

Lorenzo Bandini, Andrea de Cesaris, Vittorio Brambilla, Michele Alboreto, Riccardo Patrese, Alessandro Nannini and Elio De Angelis are among the drivers who tried, without much fortune, to repeat the successes of Ascari and Nuvolari. The foreign drivers who have won world titles for the Italian colours are Manuel Fangio (who triumphed on Alfa Romeo and Ferrari), Mike Hawthorn (also a world champion in motorcycle racing for Italian-made MV-Agusta), Phil Hill, John Surtees, Niki Lauda and Jody Scheckter, the last driver to win a world title on a Ferrari, in 1979. All these world champions won titles for Enzo Ferrari, who died in 1988 at the age of ninety-one. However, the name and the legend he created lived on, though under the control of Fiat and the **Agnelli family**.

Italy's most successful make in rally racing has been Lancia. It won the manufacturer's title in 1972 and 1974–6. In 1977–8 and 1980, the title was secured by Fiat but Lancia won again in 1983 and also from 1987 to 1992, a period which included two world titles for best driver to M. Biasion, 1988–9.

In motorcycle racing, Nello Pagani, Tarquinio Provini, Carlo Ubbiali and Umberto Masetti were amongst the first Italian champions, but Giacomo Agostini and Renzo Pasolini were the ones who ensured the sport's success in Italy. Agostini won fifteen world championships: 1968–74 in the 350cc category, and 1966–72 and 1975 in the 500cc. He won a total of 122 races, most on an MV-Agusta. Agostini was the only man to win world titles in separate categories in five consecutive years. Renzo Pasolini raced in the same years as Agostini and their duels were regarded by Italian sports fans as true epics. In fact however, due to MV-Agusta's superiority, Pasolini never posed a serious challenge to Agostini. Pasolini's tragic death on 20 May 1973 at the Monza track placed him forever among the modern heroes of Italian sport. In following years, Marco Lucchinelli won the world title in the 500cc in 1981 and Franco Uncini repeated in 1982.

Italian bike maker Aprilia and world champions Loris Capirossi (the youngest world champion in the history of the sport at the time he won his first title in the 125cc in 1991), Luca Cadalora and Max Biaggi (250 cc, 1994) continue the winning tradition originated by their predecessors.

Further reading

Raffaelli, F. (1994) *Emilia-Romagna e Marche: terra di piloti e di motori*, Modena: Artioli (Emilia-Romagna and Marche: a land of cars and pilots – a book dedicated to the motor racing industry and pilots of these two bordering regions of Italy).

PAOLO VILLA

motorscooters

In the immediate postwar period Italy's great leap forward into modernization came to be both effected and symbolized by the motorscooter, a vehicle which provided cheap and easy transportation as well as exhibiting a penchant for style that would henceforth be associated with the 'Made in Italy' label. As the **economic miracle** bore its fruits in the 1950s, providing Italians with more spending power, loyalties divided fiercely between two major rivals: the Vespa (so-called because its sound and shape suggested a wasp), designed by aeronautical engineer Corradino D'Ascanio for the Piaggio Company in 1946, and the Lambretta (named after the Lambro river near Milan where it was first assembled), launched in 1947 by the Innocenti Company. More innovative and stylish in terms of design, the Vespa conquered a greater share of the market and by the late 1990s had sold over 15 million worldwide. The Lambretta, less sophisticated in its design, nevertheless also had its enthusiasts and by 1998 had sold more than 3.5 million. Already immortalized by Gregory Peck and Audrey Hepburn in the film *Roman Holiday* (1953), the Vespa was also more recently celebrated by Nanni **Moretti** in his 1993 film, *Caro Diario* (Dear Diary).

GINO MOLITERNO

Moussa Ba, Saidou

b. 1964, Senegal

Writer and actor

Saidou Moussa Ba migrated to Italy from Senegal in the late 1980s. His first book in Italian, *La promessa di Hamadi* (Hamadi's Promise) (1991), written in collaboration with Alessandro Micheletti, is a fictional autobiographical narrative which recounts the experiences of two Senegalese brothers in Italy, their encounter with Italian organized crime and the death of the older brother. Ba's second book, *La memoria di A.* (The Memory of A.) (1995), also written in collaboration with Micheletti, deals with discrimination and racism, focusing on anti-Semitism as seen by a young Italian man who moves to Germany.

Teacher, writer and actor, Ba has worked on films such as *Waalo Fendo* (Where the Earth Freezes) (1997) and his play, *Nessuno può coprire l'ombra* (No One can Cover the Shadow), was staged by the group Ravenna Teatro (Ravenna Theatre). Ba has also collaborated with Ravenna Teatro in establishing a performing centre in Dakar.

See also: immigrant literature

Further reading

Moussa Ba, S. (1991) *La promessa di Hamadi*, Novara: Istituto Geografico De Agostini.

GRAZIELLA PARATI

Movimento di Comunità

The Movimento di Comunità (Community Movement) began as a cultural initiative, accompanied by an eponymous journal and publishing house, established by Adriano **Olivetti**. Responding to the social tensions created by the rapid industrialization of the early 1950s, Olivetti attempted to apply sociological expertise to humanize relations within his firm and to shape its impact on local society. Among the intellectuals closely associated with Olivetti's effort to modernize simultaneously industry and culture were the literary critic Pampaloni, the novelists **Volponi** and **Ottieri**,

and the sociologist Ferrarotti. Olivetti's communitarian ambitions led Comunità into politics; but in its only electoral contest (1958), the Movement won just 173,257 votes (0.6 per cent) and elected a single MP (Olivetti himself, who subsequently resigned in favour of Ferrarotti). That failure, and Olivetti's subsequent early death, ensured the Movement's disappearance.

Further reading

Olivetti, A. (1960) *Le città dell'uomo* (Man's Cities), Milan: Comunità.

DAVID MOSS

Movimento Nucleare

The Movimento Nucleare (The Nuclear Movement) was a group of artists founded in 1951 by Enrico **Baj** and Sergio Dangelo. The first manifesto expressed opposition to the rules and traditions of academic art and to the then prevailing avantgarde style, geometric abstraction. Instead, the participants favoured gestural and abstract expressionist art (similar concerns to **L'Informale** group), and the use of chance and automatism as had been practised by some of the surrealists. Early works were characterized by the technique of spilling paint.

In 1957, Piero **Manzoni** published his manifesto 'Towards an Organic Painting', which called for a move beyond impression and memory to a free painting which continuously reinvented itself. These were similar ideas to the Movimento Nucleare, and in the same year Manzoni, along with Giò **Pomodoro** and Yves Klein, was a signatory to the group's manifesto 'Contro lo stile' (Against Style), which denounced style and argued for a painting that was always new, without conventions or repetition, a presence rather than a representation.

Further reading

Celant, G. (1994) *The Italian Metamorphosis 1943– 1968*, New York: Guggenheim Museum, 718–

19 (English translation of some of the group's manifestos).

MAX STAPLES

MSI

The MSI (Movimento Sociale Italiano, or Italian Social Movement) was a neo-fascist party (see **fascism and neo-fascism**) occupying the far right of politics for most of the postwar period. Founded in 1946, the party became the MSI–DN (National Right) in 1972 and, reflecting the ambiguities of fascism itself, included both legally oriented ultra-conservatives as well as anti-constitutional radicals. Considered illegitimate by most of the other **political parties** which had cooperated to found the **Republic** on the basis of **anti-fascism**, the MSI was permanently excluded from government during the 'First' Republic. However in 1995, under the leadership of Gianfranco **Fini**, it dissolved itself into the AN (**National Alliance**), having already formed, under the AN flag, part of the **Berlusconi** government in 1994.

The MSI's original inspiration was the Italian Social Republic (RSI), a puppet fascist mini-state set up and supported by the occupying German forces from 1943–5 and centred on the northern town of Salò. Republican fascism was critical of the Fascist regime established after 1924, harking back to earlier forms of fascism with their anti-monarchist, anti-bourgeois and socialistic dimensions. Even within the MSI, however, these radical aspects were rapidly subordinated to the more legal tendency, in part because otherwise the party risked being made illegal and in part because its electoral successes were largely concentrated in the conservative south. In 1948, all six of its MPs were elected there and, accordingly, the party's leadership shifted to the moderates. Under Augusto De Marsanich (1949–54) and Arturo Michelini (1954–69), the parliamentary electoral approach to politics was reinforced. Hostility to NATO, the epitome of the western liberal capitalism which had humiliated Italy, was abandoned and the party sought to ally itself with the **DC**, the **monarchists** and the Liberals (**PLI**), all previous enemies. This strategy almost worked until the Tambroni crisis demonstrated the impracticability of right-wing governments. In 1963, in fact, the DC turned away and initiated an **opening to the Left**.

The new centre–left government formula marginalized the right-wing parties, rendering the MSI's conservative strategy of seeking cooperation with the DC irrelevant. This reinforced the radical wing of the party, and the growing social tensions of the 1960s strengthened this shift. When De Marsanich died in 1969, the leadership returned to Giorgio Almirante, one of the party's ex-RSI founding fathers, who led the party until 1987 when Gianfranco **Fini** took over. Almirante revamped the conservative strategy of seeking to unite the country's divided parliamentary Right and attempting to draw the DC away from cooperation with the Left. He thus formed the National Right (MSI–DN), opening the party to prestigious conservative candidates. For the sake of party unity, however, Almirante maintained links with the radical – and, in this period, violent and subversive – Right. This fatally undermined the National Right strategy. The collapse of terrorism in 1982 and the subsequently transformed political climate led to political depolarization which embraced even the MSI. The party, however, was not prepared for this and reconfirmed its fascist identity. Its anachronistic irrelevance was now marked, but the party avoided the lacerating identity crisis which, on the Left, engulfed the **PCI** (see also **PDS**). Fini's able exploitation of the opportunities opened up by the collapse of the 'First' Republic meant that the rebaptised party made considerable progress towards finally achieving full legitimacy. The orientation of the new political context of the 'Second' Republic was towards the future, not the past, and to the practical governing capacities of parties rather than their outmoded ideological histories.

Further reading

Chiarini, R. (1991) 'The "Movimento Sociale Italiano": A Historical Profile', in L. Cheles, R. Ferguson and M. Vaughan (eds), *Neofascism in Europe*, London: Longman.

Ferraresi, F. (1996) *Threats to Democracy: The Radical Right in Italy after the War*, Princeton, NJ: Princeton University Press.

Ignazi, P. (1993) 'The Changing Profile of the Italian Social Movement', in P.H. Merkl and L. Weinberg (eds), *Encounters with the Contemporary Right*, Boulder, CO: Westwood Press.

MARK DONOVAN

Il Mulino

Founded as a 'review of politics and culture' by a group of young Bolognese intellectuals in 1951, *Il Mulino* has become a well-established if still slightly unorthodox presence on the Italian cultural scene thereafter. *Il Mulino* is in the first place a cultural association, which oversees the activities of a bi-monthly review, of a publishing company regarded as a major outlet for high quality research in the humanities and the social sciences, and of a prestigious research centre, the Istituto Cattaneo. In its earliest years, along with a few other intellectual innovators like enlightened industrialist Adriano **Olivetti**, *Il Mulino* was instrumental in introducing empirical social science to a cultural milieu which had been dominated by historicism and idealism. Based in the Emilia-Romagna region, an area politically dominated by the communist Left but with a strong presence of Catholic organizations, and with liberal intellectuals also heavily involved in its steering group, *Il Mulino* has constantly operated as a bridge between different cultural and political traditions in the country (see Ezio **Raimondi**).

MARIO DIANI

Munari, Bruno

b. 24 October 1907; d. 10 October 1998, Milan

Sculptor, painter, film-maker and graphic designer

Munari's artistic career began as an artist of the second generation of futurists in 1927, and he continued to exhibit with them into the 1930s. From 1939 onwards, especially in his sculpture, Munari tended towards a constructivist aesthetic culminating in a series of 'Useless Machines', three-dimen-sional abstract forms constructed from painted cardboard and other lightweight materials. After the Second World War, Munari concentrated on industrial design. An early example is 'X Hour' (1945), an alarm clock with rotating half-discs replacing the hands. In 1963, X Hour was produced as a multiple and there followed the mass production of other not strictly utilitarian objects by Munari such as the Flexy, a flexible metal wire structure that could be set in any number of positions. In 1950 he also began to experiment with film, producing his first coloured-light film with electronic music, *I colori della luce* (The Colours of Light) in 1963. During a long and busy career, Munari continued to promote the principle of public access to the means of visual communication, believing that anyone can produce objects of aesthetic value if given adequate techno-logical resources.

Further reading

Tanchis, A. (1987) *Bruno Munari: Design as Art*, Cambridge, MA: MIT Press (a comprehensive, generously illustrated account of Munari's achievement in artistic design).

OLIVIA DAWSON

Muratori, Saverio

b. 1910; d. 1973, Rome

Architect, town planner, and historian

A leading figure in twentieth-century Italian culture, Muratori confronted the principal question of contemporary Italian thought, namely the relationship between civilization and nature, through the analogous relationship between architecture and the environment. In his formative period, he sought an amalgamated solution to experiments in expressionism and rationalism. After 1945 he worked on reconstruction projects, especially the INA–CASA neighbourhood housing project in Rome. In *Vita e storia delle città* (Life and History of Cities) he retraces the principles guiding these projects, developing a philosophical frame-work for his later notions of 'city as living organism'. He formulated his ideas systematically in his courses at the University of Venice from 1950–5 and in Rome thereafter. In the 1970s, he equated the crises of architecture with those of civilization. His theoretical writings on the city as a living organism later found enthusiastic audiences elsewhere, especially in North America, where they are still being taught.

FASSIL ZEWDOU

Mursia

Founded in Milan by Ugo Mursia in 1955, Mursia soon developed into one of the most prestigious names in publishing in postwar Italy. A large part of its editorial success has been due to its series of classics of Italian and other national literatures aimed at a broad readership, but always edited and annotated by renowned scholars in the field. Another useful and successful enterprise has been its agile critical series 'Invito alla lettura di' (An Invitation to the Reading of), devoted to providing accessible and wide-ranging interpretations of a large number of modern authors. Throughout the years, Mursia has built up a reputation both as a scholarly publisher connected to many university editorial projects and as a cultural publisher able to target and reach out to a wider non-specialized audience.

See also: publishers

ANDREA CICCARELLI

music festivals

Festivals exist in almost every town and village in Italy and cover the presentation of an enormous range of music from **opera** and contemporary classical music to rock, jazz and world music. Many of the most famous festivals take place annually in the summer and autumn months, and become tourist attractions in their own right through the quality of the international artists they attract. Festivals often receive support from local and national government sources in recognition of the artistic and commercial benefits that flow from such events.

Occasions such as the Bergamo Baroque Music Festival last for only a few days and consist of only a handful of specialist concert presentations, whereas other festivals, including the Florence Maggio Musicale (May Music Festival) last several months (in spite of its name) and involve numerous concert and opera performances. A special theme or artistic emphasis lends distinctiveness to some festivals: the events in Montepulciano (near Siena) and at the **Spoleto Festival** often counterpoint intriguing combinations of artists and programmes from different parts of the world. For other festivals such as the Aosta International Organ Festival, an associated event, such as an international competition held concurrently, attracts the attention of musicians and audiences with a particular interest.

The birth of famous composers in particular towns and cities provides the occasion for events such as the Verdi Festival in Parma (near his birthplace in Roncole) and the Rossini Opera Festival in Pesaro. Puccini wrote some of his most famous operas, including *Tosca*, at Torre del Lago, so an annual festival of his work is held there, featuring performances in an open-air theatre.

Capitalizing on scenic and historic landscape and buildings often provides an interesting focus for Italian festivals. The medieval town of Salerno on the coast south of Naples hosts its Musica per Velia festival in archaeological sites around the town. In Taormina, Sicily, the historic amphitheatre provides the setting for the Taormina Arte, while in Rome the ruins of the third-century Baths of Caracalla provide a venue for ballet and opera. In Lombardy in Northern Italy *Il Canto delle Pietre* (The Song of the Stones) is a festival of choral and dramatic music associated with the Christian liturgy occurring over eight or nine weekends in various churches in and around Bergamo, Como and Cremona. As with various other festivals, the nature of the event encompasses other artistic work that links to the Festival's themes. The famous summer festival held in the enormous outdoor theatre at Verona continues to attract large audiences to a staple of spectacular operatic potboilers.

The standard of the festivals varies but the best-known often present artists of the highest international calibre. Events such as the Autumn Music Festival in Como, the Ravenna Festival, the Estate Musicale Chigiana and Music Week in Siena and

Turin's Musical September are examples of festivals that usually feature very high-quality performers. Jazz festivals in Bessano and Corridonia, rock festivals in Arezzo, Cremona and Umbria and the festival of world music in Rome complete a picture of great musical diversity in the Italian musical calendar.

See also: arts festivals

Further reading

Brody, E. and Brook, C. (eds) (1978) *The Music Guide to Italy*, New York: Dodd & Mead.

Gottesman, R. and Sentman, C. (eds) (1992) *The Music Lover's Guide to Europe: A Compendium of Festivals, Concerts, and Opera*, New York: John Wiley.

ANDREW SCHULTZ

music institutions

Italy's rich musical heritage has given rise to a lively contemporary musical culture in which institutions play an important role. Since the Second World War, there has been a recognition in Italy that governments have a responsibility to provide funding to support and encourage cultural life and to see that institutions meet the aspirations of artists and the needs of the public. In general terms, music institutions can be divided into performing and educational bodies.

In the late 1940s the Italian government took a number of steps to foster and protect musical theatre traditions. **Opera** was thought to be worthy of government subsidy, since Italy was internationally recognized as a centre of excellence in this field. Producing quality singers and encouraging the performance of Italian music were seen as priorities, and so the Ministry of Tourism and Entertainment, through a Music Commission, was given the brief to control subsidy of opera and other performing activity.

State-subsidized theatres were officially designated in major cities such as Bologna (the Communale), Milan (**La Scala**) and Venice (La Fenice). In the mid-1970s the thirteen designated theatres and organizations became the joint responsibility of the national and regional governments, and were given the title of National Institutions. At the same time, other theatres were reviewed and fifteen were given grants because they were considered to be of artistic or historic significance. These *teatri stabili* (established theatres), including those in Parma, Mantua and Pisa, are usually located in provincial areas and are often a focal point for the varied cultural activities of the area. In addition, there are over forty opera houses in Italy that are neither National Institutions nor Established Theatres but privately funded organizations which regularly present musical activities. Similarly, there is a mixture of government sponsorship and private funding of orchestras and ensembles in Italy. The **RAI** supports four orchestras – in Naples, Rome, Turin and Milan – which present public concerts as well as recording for radio and television broadcast.

Music education institutions in Italy can be categorized into four types. The most highly esteemed are the national conservatoria, which are located in the major cities. The curriculum in the conservatoria is strictly regulated so that the same diploma is available from each. Consequently, each state conservatorium has equivalent entrance requirements, course structure and graduation levels. The curriculum in the national conservatoria is divided into main and supplementary courses. The main courses are the ones in which students specialize, such as piano or voice, whilst the supplementary courses are those which are designed to give breadth to the students' general knowledge of music. Instead of dividing the courses into years, study programmes are separated into levels such as lower, intermediate and advanced. Students who pass the advanced level of their course are awarded the diploma, while those who complete only the lower levels are awarded a study certificate. The advanced level can take up to ten years to complete.

While these conservatoria strive to produce equivalent curricula, it is interesting to note that their history has made them all very distinct. The Conservatorio di Musica Giuseppe Verdi in Milan is unique in housing a number of rare collections of fifteenth-century French and Italian songs in its library. In Genoa, the Conservatorio di Musica Niccolo Paganini houses a statue of Paganini and also Paganini's violin, which distinguished musicians are occasionally invited to play. The Conservatorio di Musica Benedetto Marcello in Venice conserves eighteenth-century manuscripts from the Venetian school of sacred music and opera, and has an impressive museum of instruments. The Conservatorio di Musica Claudio Monteverdi in Bolzano is a multi-lingual campus – a necessity given its proximity to the Austrian border – and Pesaro's Conservatorio di Musica Gioacchino Rossini holds the composer's manuscripts as well as those by Donizetti and others.

Another type of institution, the 'equalized institutes', are recognized by the state and monitored by the Ministry for Public Education. Each institution in this category has been through a process of accreditation so that the diploma it offers is equal to that offered by the conservatoria. The equalized institutions are subsidized to cater for students who cannot attend a conservatorium in a large city. Equalized institutions also provide a stimulus and act as a centre for rural musical activity.

A third type of musical training occurs in universities, where advanced courses in musicology and music education are offered. However, while over thirty universities offer music courses, very few offer complete degrees in music.

Lastly, there are innumerable local music schools and also summer schools, where courses are fairly short and specific and quality is varied. These range from excellent and specific programmes to generic summer workshops for beginners. The Stradivari School of String Instrument Making in Cremona is an example of a high quality institution. It trains and awards diplomas to makers of string instruments. The school is government-sponsored, as Cremona is recognized internationally as a centre of excellence in this field. Another outstanding music school is the Pontifical Institute of Sacred Music, which trains its students in the history and practice of Gregorian Chant. At the other end of the scale one finds the six-week 'Vacanza Musicale' – musical vacations – that tourists can take in Venice. These are designed for foreigners and although courses cover conducting, voice and musicology, the main aim of the course is to learn more about Italian music and musical life generally.

Numerous other institutions exist which contribute to musical life in Italy. They include academies (which support performance and study), museums and libraries (often with important historical collections of manuscripts and instruments), radio, television and other media outlets, music publishers, private concert promoters, **music festivals** landmarks and churches.

Further reading

Brody, E., and Brook, C. (1978) *The Music Guide to Italy*, New York: Dodd & Mead (for specific details of each institution).

Uscher, N. (1988) *The Schirmer Guide to Schools of Music and Conservatories Throughout the World*, New York: Schirmer (for details and a commentary on each school of music).

ANDREW SCHULTZ

Muti, Riccardo

b. 28 July 1941, Naples

Conductor

Muti is noted for his musical intelligence and accomplished technique. He graduated in piano from the Naples Conservatory and began a degree in philosophy. A chance invitation to conduct led him to abandon his degree, taking instead a five-year course in conducting at the Milan Conservatory. In 1967 he won the Guido Cantelli Competition, and soon after made his international debut. He was principal conductor of the Florence Maggio Musicale from 1969–81, and in 1973 succeeded Klemperer at the New Philharmonia Orchestra, a post which he relinquished in 1982. In 1980 he was appointed musical director of the Philadelphia Orchestra. Equally active in **opera**, he became musical director at **La Scala** in 1986, where he restored five Mozart operas to the repertoire.

Muti preserves an admirable balance of head and heart in his interpretations of the symphonic classics, but he has also been effective in introducing new works by such composers as Ligeti, **Petrassi** and **Dallapiccola**.

JOHN KERSEY

N

Nannini, Gianna

b. 14 June 1956, Siena

Popular music artist and composer

One of Italy's foremost popular music artists, Nannini first studied piano at Lucca and subsequently read composition and philosophy at the University of Milan. Her first recording, *Gianna Nannini* (1976), achieved wide popularity, and in the ensuing years she produced another fourteen albums. Although Nannini's style remains within the mainstream of European popular music, her wide intellectual interests have produced some intriguing artistic projects. In 1982 she composed the music for Gabriele **Salvatores**'s film of *A Midsummer Night's Dream*, in which she also played the part of Titania. Her short operas *Eberhard Schöner* (1996) and *Palazzo dell'Amore* (Palace of Love) (1997) reveal a conscious search for an audience beyond the popular music field, while her hit 'Fotoromanza' was made into a video-clip by no less than Michelangelo **Antonioni**. In 1994 Nannini was awarded the degree of D.Phil. by the University of Siena for a thesis on Tuscan traditional music.

JOHN KERSEY

Napolitano, Giorgio

b. 29 June 1925, Naples

Politician

Napolitano joined the Italian Communist Party (see PCI) in 1945 and always represented its moderate wing. He served as parliamentary deputy from 1953–63 and again from 1968–96, was president of the PCI Parliamentary Group from 1981–6 and Speaker of the Chamber of Deputies between 1992 and 1994. He was also PCI/**PDS** Shadow Minister for Foreign Affairs between 1989 and 19992 and was subsequently appointed Minister of the Interior in the **Prodi** government (1996–8).

In the 1960s, Napolitano worked closely with Giorgio **Amendola** to encourage cooperation and close ties with the Socialists. Always in favour of European integration and NATO, he served as a Member of the European Parliament from 1989–92, as President of the Italian Council of the European Movement from 1995 and a member of the Italian delegation to the North Atlantic Council 1984–9 and again 1994–6.

Further reading

Napolitano, G. (1977) *The Italian Road to Socialism*, trans. J. Cammet and V. DeGrazia, London: Journeyman Press (a series of interviews with Eric Hobsbawm in which Napolitano discusses all major aspects of PCI thought and strategy).

JAMES WALSTON

narrative

Scholars have usually analysed the postwar narrative in the context of the radical social, political and economic changes that Italy experienced in the second half of the century. The turn from monarchism to republicanism in the 1940s (see **Republic**), the rapid development from an agricultural to an industrial economy in the 1950s (the so-called **economic miracle**), the increasing literacy of the Italians and their linguistic unification all deeply affected Italian cultural life. These developments brought about important changes in the means of production and reception of the literary work, from its conception in the writer's mind to its marketing by the publishing industry. By the mid-1940s, narrative had come to be privileged over other literary forms such as poetry, for an alleged capacity to present its social, economic and political context. Much fictional and non-fictional narrative of the period aimed, often by a combination of expressionist and realist modes with linguistic and structural experimentation, to represent the writer's relationship with reality.

Yet, while cultural critics have been able to establish rather confidently both the temporal duration and the cultural functions of literary currents and movements such as **neorealism** and the neoavantgarde, they have proceeded with more caution when discussing the narrative of the last twenty years, as though continually reminding themselves, as they approach the present, of an inevitable lack of historical perspectivism. Nevertheless, the major thematic and stylistic trends in more contemporary Italian narrative have been mapped from a number of theoretical viewpoints, and now include not only the emergence in the 1970s and mid-1980s of voices traditionally marginalized, such as homosexuals and women (see **women's writing**), but also the discourses of different ethnic groups, mainly coming from Africa and Asia, in the late 1980s and 1990s (see **immigrant literature**).

In the years of the **postwar reconstruction** (1945–55), the dominant neorealist narrative became an expression of social commitment seeking to carry out both a pedagogical function (to educate the people) and a faithful, if at times ironical, documentation of the war experience and contemporary social conditions. Remembrance of the events of recent history and political engagement were deeply permeated by the optimistic belief in a perfect coincidence between 'reality' and

'truth'; in other words, to recount stories in order to represent reality meant to tell the truth. At first, it was the truth of the resistance to fascism; then, it became the truth of the lives of ordinary workers and **peasants** in northern and southern Italy, and the process of their social and political emancipation. Realist narrative sought to express the voices of ordinary people by recording their everyday language, slang and dialect, thereby finally dismantling fascist rhetoric. The increasing economic exploitation of the working classes, however, and the increasing hardening of Marxist ideology into political authoritarianism in the mid-1950s proved how illusory had been the claims to truth of literary representation. Significantly, in 1955 **Pratolini**'s novel *Metello*, the story of a young worker set in the context of the social conflicts of the late nineteenth century, gave rise to much controversy among left-oriented critics, with only some reading the novel as a true expression of a new-born realism, while others saw its representation of the working class as populist and consolatory. The critical debate on Pratolini's *Metello* together with the subsequent controversy over the publication of Tomasi di **Lampedusa**'s *Il Gattopardo* (The Leopard) (1958) manifested an erosion of faith of the writer's claim to be able to represent the truth.

From this point on, postwar narrative registered the disintegration of the rationalistic belief of antifascist intellectuals in the social and moral revival of the country together with a profound sense of disillusionment with the official position of the Communist Party (**PCI**). At the same time, it documented the birth of a different cultural attitude that privileged a more ethical commitment to representing and understanding reality in the place of political engagement. Giving voice to this new attitude, at the turn of the decade Elio **Vittorini** and Italo **Calvino** founded the cultural journal **il menabò** (1959–67). In its pages, they launched the notion of a new literature, neither escapist nor compromised with socialist realism, but highly aware of the most pressing issues of the time and, as a consequence, expressive of the common commitment to oppose the **status quo** without cherishing false hopes, as had happened in the recent past.

The transition from the 1950s to the 1960s, and later into the 1970s, was highly influenced by the appearance of phenomenology, psychoanalysis and structuralism. These soon became the main theoretical frames for all debate on the role of narrative discourse in contemporary society and provided the writers with new heuristic models and a new language to express insight into the human subject and social dynamics. By dismantling such traditional novelistic conventions as character, plot and linear narrative, writers sought to refine the notion of a political and cultural commitment to understand and change reality. For example, the neoavantgarde's iconoclastic mood, which survived the breaking up of its founding group (see **Gruppo 63**) turned into radical political activism. Roberto **Roversi**, Francesco Leonetti and Nanni **Balestrini**, among others, aimed at subverting the cultural and political establishment, particularly by means of a documentary narrative (assemblage of excerpts from newspapers and people's interviews). At the same time, the ongoing debate within the Roman Catholic community, urged to keep up the pace with the contemporary world, inspired the realistic narratives of Pier Paolo **Pasolini**, Luigi **Santucci** and Mario **Pomilio** to name a few, who attempted to reconcile Christian values with Marxist ideals by highlighting the notions of human *caritas* and social solidarity. No longer a way to convey *the* truth, literature became the symbolic space where women and gay could express *their own particular* truth and voice their demand for equal rights while also demanding to be acknowledged as political, social and cultural subjects. Novels by Anna Maria **Ortese**, Natalia **Ginzburg**, Elsa **Morante**, Lalla **Romano**, Gina **Lagorio**, Francesca Sanvitale and Dacia **Maraini** were critically acclaimed and won favour with both male and female audiences. Furthermore, in what had become the atomic era, novelists such as Giuseppe **Berto**, Guido **Morselli**, Paolo **Volponi** and Stefano **D'Arrigo** fictionally staged the end of the world and the subsequent meaningless survival of the individual. By drawing attention to environmental issues, they also denounced technology's potential for self-destruction.

The very notion of a realistic language, mirroring reality by reproducing its human variety, was carried to extremes, to the point of threatening its own communicative function. In the wake of Carlo Emilio **Gadda**'s stylistic expressionism and plurilingualism, the experimental narratives of authors such as Antonio Pizzuto, Alberto **Arbasino**, Giovanni **Testori**, Edoardo **Sanguineti** and Giorgio **Manganelli**, among others, rejected the notion of the cognitive power of a language compromised with tradition and culture while presenting the gap opening up between language and reality, words and things, as the most apparent sign of the individual's alienation from the self, society and history.

In the 1970s and the 1980s, writers seemed to retreat into their private workshops as a result of the general distrust in literature as a vehicle for knowledge as well as a radical disillusionment with social reality resulting from the tragic outburst of **terrorism**. Literary creation became then a mere display of narrative strategies to underscore the self-referential nature of art. Having failed to explain reality, literature resorted to representing only itself, and writing turned into a ludic interplay with the reader, wittily challenged to solve unsolvable riddles. Particularly successful at the time was the detective story, in which the reader also came to be inextricably involved in the characters' fictional search for the truth. Yet in narratives such as Calvino's *Se una notte d'inverno un viaggiatore* (If on a Winter's Night a Traveller) (1979) and **Eco**'s *Il nome della rosa* (The Name of the Rose) (1980), to name only the most internationally acclaimed, neither the author nor the characters nor the reader safely escape the intricate narrative plotting which, in the end, deconstructs any cognitive tool or system of thought in order to mislead human reason. Alongside this literature of clever entertainment and skilful technique, there also developed, in the works of Sebastiano **Vassalli** and Roberto **Pazzi**, a narrative which expressed the individual's obsession with time and an uncanny sense of the end of history.

In the context of the increasing power of the culture industry and the impact of media and computers on culture and society, the Italian narrative in the 1990s has displayed a multifaceted nature. Particularly popular among young readers, and controversial among critics, is the hyperreal fiction of young authors such as Niccolò Ammaniti and Aldo Nove, the so-called pulp or splatter literature. Influenced by Stephen King's horror stories and Quentin Tarantino's cult movie, *Pulp Fiction*, these writers recount the everyday life of ordinary people using a language which is a combination of slang and jargon, mostly derived from the language of the media (particularly television and comics). Contemporary society is represented in its most obsessive and shocking aspects, unreasonably violent and paradoxical.

The documentary and autobiographical writings by North African immigrants, in collaboration with Italian journalists, testify to Italy's development into a multiethnic society. Works such as *Io, venditore di elefanti* (I, Vendor of Elephants) (1990) by Pap Khouma and Oreste Pivetta, *Chiamatemi Alì* (Call me Alì) (1991) by Mohammed Bouchane, Carla De Girolamo and Daniele Miccione, *La memoria di A.* (Memory of A.) (1995) by Saidou Moussa Ba and Alessandro Micheletti, to mention only a few among the most successful, have had a strong impact upon the Italians' perception of their own identity in an era of economic and political globalization. By telling their stories of discrimination, exploitation, violence and suffering, these narrators uncover the tensions arising in the Italian society at the turn of the century, and a sense of general mistrust in political institutions. At the same time, however, they confirm that a process of social and cultural integration of diverse ethnic groups has been set in motion and that a new, global society can perhaps be forged.

See also: immigrant literature

Further reading

Amoia, A. (1996) *20th Century Italian Women Writers: The Feminine Experience*, Carbondale, IL: Southern Illinois University Press.

Baranski, Z. and Pertile, L. (eds) (1993) *The New Italian Novel*, Edinburgh: Edinburgh University Press.

Barilli, R. (1995) *La neoavanguardia italiana* (The Italian Neoavantgarde), Bologna: Il Mulino (critical overview of the neoavantgarde movement, its protagonists and literary journals).

Brolli, D. (ed.) (1996) *Gioventù cannibale* (Young Cannibals), Turin: Einaudi (a collection of Italian horror stories).

Cannon, J. (1989) *Postmodern Italian Fiction: The Crisis of Reason in Calvino, Eco, Sciascia, Malerba*, London and Toronto: Associated University Press.

Ceserani, R. (1990) *Il romanzo sui pattini* (The Novel on Rollerskates), Ancona: Transeuropa (essay collection on contemporary Italian writers).

Ferretti, G.C. (1974) *Introduzione al neorealismo* (Introduction to Neorealism), Rome: Editori Riuniti.

Lucente, G. (1986) *Beautiful Fables: Self-Consciousness in Italian Narrative from Manzoni to Calvino*, Baltimore: Johns Hopkins University Press.

FRANCESCA PARMEGGIANI

Natalini, Adolfo

b. 10 May 1941, Pistoia

Architect

In 1966 Natalini graduated from the University of Florence, where he has subsequently lived, worked and taught in the Faculty of Architecture. In the same year he began to be involved as a theoretical spokesman for **Superstudio**, one of the most representative groups of the so-called 'radical architecture'. Since 1979 he has also worked independently, designing among other things a series of urban projects for historical cities and some office buildings (Zola Pedrosa in Bologna, Alzate Brianza in Como), all of which have displayed both his interest in exploring the dialectical relationship between architectural projects and their specific contexts, and his personal obsession with time, memory and the traces through which these manifest themselves in places. Heideggerian phenomenology, Leon Battista Alberti, Louis Kahn, Le Corbusier, Stirling, Ungers and **Rossi** are some of his admitted points of reference.

MAURO BARACCO

National Alliance

The term 'National Alliance' (AN) was hijacked by Gianfranco **Fini**, leader of the **MSI**, in 1993. As the **DC** disintegrated in the wake of the *Tangentopoli* investigations, the MSI, repackaged as the

MSI-AN, showed its ability to replace the DC in southern Italy. In 1994 Fini's party formed part of Silvio **Berlusconi**'s government, and in 1995 the MSI dissolved itself into the AN, leaving a small splinter group, the MS-FT (Social Movement – Tricolour Flame or, more simply, Flame) to contest the party's fascist heritage (see also **fascism and neo-fascism**).

From the time of De Gaulle's triumph in France, Italy had a Gaullist political current, but Italian presidentialism had always been illegitimate and condemned as crypto-fascist. In the 1990s the idea was revived – not least by President **Cossiga** – and a neo-conservative presidential project was mooted by political scientist Domenico Fisichella, who coined the term 'National Alliance'. The speed of the collapse of the governing parties in 1993 left conservative voters open to mobilization on a party basis, and this was ably exploited by Fini. Taking advantage of Berlusconi's public declaration of support in the middle of his campaign for the mayorship of Rome, Fini quickly appropriated the idea of a 'National Alliance'. The move was backed by Fisichella, but very few non-MSI figures joined the new movement. Nevertheless, in the 1994 national elections the MSI-AN all but tripled its vote (to 13.5 per cent) and, most significantly, it went on to participate in government with five ministers and twelve undersecretaries. The taboo on government participation was finally broken, even though the coalition did not last, being brought down by the defection of **Bossi**'s **Lega Nord**.

The AN's founding congress was held at Fiuggi in January 1995, by immediately following by the MSI's last congress which saw the old party dissolve itself into the AN: into, that is, more or less itself. Virtually the entirety of the MSI elite and its membership transferred into the new party, taking with them the organizational machinery and culture of the MSI. In many respects, the organizational style of the new party, of which Fini became president (rather than secretary), was less democratic and more 'top down' than that of the MSI, which meant that, ironically, the new Gaullist conservative orientation of the leader could be enforced against fascist regurgitations. Nevertheless the real possibility of the return of the party's fascist inheritance fuelled both domestic and international

alarm at its growing legitimacy. As if to neutralize such fears, the party styled itself as 'post-fascist' and its new statutes condemned racism and recognized the historic value of anti-fascism. This was an advance on oral statements to that effect by the former MSI leader Giorgio Almirante.

However, what was condemned was not fascism *per se*, but the statist regime-fascism which the MSI's radical founders had condemned from the outset. Thus while many, even on the Left, accepted the AN's supplanting of the MSI as signalling the normalization of Italian politics, many suspended judgement until the party's personnel had changed and, more importantly, its culture had been fundamentally transformed.

Further reading

Adler, F.H. (1996) 'Post-Fascism in Italy: From MSI to AN', *Italian Politics and Society* 46: 35–43.

Ruzza, C. and Schmidtke, O. (1996) 'Toward a Modern Right: Alleanza Nazionale and the "Italian revolution"', in S. Gundle and S. Parker (eds), *The New Italian Republic: From the Berlin Wall to Berlusconi*, London: Routledge.

Woods, D. (1998) 'Looking for a Center of Gravity: The Reconstitution of the Italian Right', in F.L. Wilson (ed.), *The European Center-Right at the End of the Twentieth Century*, New York: St. Martin's Press.

MARK DONOVAN

national anthem

The words of the Italian national anthem, variously known as Fratelli d'Italia (Italian Brothers) or Inno di Mameli (Mameli's Hymn), were written by a young patriot, Goffredo Mameli, in 1847 and put to music a few months later by Michele Novara. A highly rhetorical call to arms set to a rather simple marching tune, it became widely used during both the movement for unification (the Risorgimento) as well as after unification in 1860–1, although the official national anthem remained the march of the ruling House of Savoy. In 1946 the Council of Ministers suggested that Mameli's Hymn be adopted 'provisionally' as the national anthem, but this temporary arrangement became permanent. In spite of repeated calls which surface regularly in the media and elsewhere to replace it with something less florid and more modern, Mameli's Hymn remains the Italian national anthem.

GINO MOLITERNO

La Nazione

One of Italy's leading regional dailies, *La Nazione* (The Nation) is also one of the oldest, founded in Florence by Bettino Ricasoli in July 1959. Strongly independent, it voiced open opposition to fascism in the early years of the Fascist regime before being forcibly brought to heel. Throughout the postwar years it has maintained a conservative tone and style and has concentrated its attention on issues affecting Tuscany and the centre–north of the country, where most of its readership is located. At the end of the 1990s *La Nazione* is published by the Poligrafici Editoriale Group, which is owned by the Monti Rifesser family, and boasts an average daily circulation of 250,000.

GINO MOLITERNO

Nenni, Pietro

b. 9 February 1891, Faenza, Forlì;
   d. 1 January 1980, Rome

Politician

Pietro Nenni was the most prominent figure in the **PSI** (Italian Socialist Party) from the 1920s until the 1970s. In the postwar years, he maintained the party's effective subordination to the **PCI** until the USSR's invasion of Hungary in 1956. He then launched a policy of cooperation with the **DC**, which led to the **opening to the Left** and his party's entry into government. These strategic choices provoked two splits: the **PSDI** to the right in 1947 and the **PSIUP** to the left in 1964. As Deputy President of the **Council of Ministers** in DC–PSI governments from 1963 to 1968, he bore some responsibility for their failure to achieve reforms, seemingly more preoccupied with simply

staying in government. As foreign minister, he was an early proponent of normalization of relations with China and a keen supporter of European integration and East–West detente.

CLAIRE KENNEDY

neorealism

Neorealism is a label applied to a group of fiction films from the immediate postwar period featuring socially progressive themes and unadorned documentary techniques. Since neorealism never constituted a formal movement, with a manifesto and a list of bylaws to which its adherents actively subscribed, its status as a critical category has remained open to question. Nonetheless, French critic Georges Sadoul claims that neorealism meets all the requirements of a school: masters and disciples, a set of working rules and clearly delineated geographical and temporal boundaries. Taking Sadoul's guidelines as a point of departure, we can assert that the practice of neorealism was largely confined to Rome in the period extending from the mid-1940s to the early 1950s. Its masters were Roberto **Rossellini**, Luchino **Visconti** and Vittorio **De Sica**; its disciples were Giuseppe **De Santis**, Aldo Vergano, Luigi **Zampa**, Renato **Castellani** and Pietro **Germi**, while its rules included on-location shooting, non-professional actors, lengthy takes, unobtrusive editing, natural lighting, a predominance of medium and long shots, respect for the continuity of time and space, use of contemporary, true-to-life subject matter, rejection of conventional dramatic structure, open-ended plot, working-class characters, dialogue in the vernacular, active viewer involvement and implied or overt social criticism.

These attributes, however, are not meant to be understood in a totalizing or prescriptive way, since the stylistic differences among neorealist directors are often greater than their conformity to any agreed-upon set of rules. Rossellini, for example, has more in common with Fascist documentarists than with fellow neorealist De Sica, whose lyric humanism in turn is a far cry from Visconti's paradoxical blend of Marxism and aestheticism. Therefore, when analysing this period of Italian film history, it is perhaps more accurate to speak of neorealism*s*, of the way in which directors with very diverse backgrounds and ideological agendas participated in this common effort to film the story of Italy in the wake of the Second World War. On the other hand, it would be wrong to deny the strong sense of shared purpose which animated neorealist directors, for whom film-making had an urgency that went beyond aesthetics or profit. '*Sciuscià*', said Vittorio De Sica of his first postwar film, 'was a small stone, a very small stone, contributed to the moral reconstruction of our country' (Marcus, 1986: xiv).

In making such films as *Paisà* (Rossellini, 1946), *Ladri di biciclette* (Bicycle Thieves) (De Sica, 1948) and *La terra trema* (Visconti, 1948), neorealists were committed not just to the rebuilding of a film industry discredited by Fascism and dismantled by war, but to the making of a new national identity based on the historical precedent of the **Resistance**. Rossellini's 1945 film *Roma, città aperta* (Open City), commonly considered the inaugural film of neorealism, was a spontaneous attempt to chronicle the recent events of the Nazi occupation, and took as its subject matter the clandestine activities of an anti-Fascist priest and a group of Roman children. Neorealism may thus be seen as the cinematic fulfilment of the Resistance aspiration not only to overthrow the Nazi–Fascist regime, but to replace it with a new order based on the ideals of social justice and economic fair play. Hence neorealist cinema's emphasis on denunciation of social ills: from the horrors of the juvenile incarceration system of *Sciuscià* (Shoeshine) (1946), to the intractable problem of urban unemployment in *Ladri di biciclette*, to the workers' exploitation by capitalist middlemen in *La terra trema* and *Riso amaro* (Bitter Rice) (De Santis, 1949), to the social and personal plight of the elderly in *Umberto D* (De Sica, 1952).

Neorealism, however, did not spring fully-formed in 1945 like Minerva from the head of Jupiter. The term began its career as a literary designation, coined by Arnaldo Bocelli to describe the style that would eventually embrace the writings of Alberto **Moravia**, Elio **Vittorini**, Cesare **Pavese** and Vasco **Pratolini** amongst others. Umberto Barbaro was the first to apply 'neorealism' to the sphere of the cinema in an article published in 1943, but his referent was the French realist production of the 1930s. Prewar Italian cinema, dominated by historical super-spectacles, bourgeois melodramas and 'white telephone' films, featured very few realist works; notable among them were Nino Martoglio's *Sperduti nel buio* (Lost in the Dark) (1914), Alessandro **Blasetti**'s *Sole* (Sun) (1928) and *1860*, as well as Mario **Camerini**'s *Rotaie* (Rails) (1929). The theory of neorealism, later to be formulated by Cesare **Zavattini** in his famous essay 'Alcune idee sul cinema' (Some Ideas on Cinema) (1952) was already being adumbrated in a series of important editorials by Giuseppe De Santis and Mario Alicata in the journal *Cinema* as early as 1941. In 'Verità e poesia: Verga e il cinema italiano' (Truth and Poetry: Verga and the Italian Cinema), De Santis and Alicata issued a plea for a cinema of realism based on the model of nineteenth-century writer Giovanni Verga, in which the camera might be allowed to leave the narrow confines of the film studio and explore the neighbourhoods, fields and factories that comprise the set locations of everyday life. Visconti, who was to become the standard-bearer of the *Cinema* group, made *Ossessione* (Obsession) in 1942, based on James Cain's novel *The Postman Always Rings Twice*. Visconti's 1942 film is commonly held to be the precursor of neorealism in its focus on working-class characters, its technique of on-location shooting and its attention to a popular social context.

The reasons for neorealism's decline in the early 1950s are many and complex. With *Umberto D*, the story of a lonely pensioner who has no more reason to live, neorealism reached terminal purity, fulfilling the movement's impetus toward uncompromising social commentary and technical austerity. In denouncing social injustice, neorealist cinema constituted such a threat to Italian officialdom that *de facto* censorship was imposed. Reviling De Sica's 'pessimo servizio alla sua Patria' (wretched service to his fatherland), Undersecretary of Entertainment Giulio **Andreotti** instituted policies which would deny export to films that portrayed Italy in an unflattering light. Without access to foreign markets, neorealist film-makers could never recover their production costs. Nevertheless, despite the official demise of the movement in the early 1950s, neorealism has continued to exert a powerful influence on all postwar Italian film production, as proven not only by the affectionate tributes found in Ettore Scola's *C'eravamo tanto amati* (We All Loved Each Other So Much) (1974), Maurizio Nichetti's *Ladri di saponette* (Icicle Thief) (1988), and Carlo Lizzani's *Celluloide* (1995), but more importantly by contemporary film-makers' insistence on keeping alive the *impegno civile* (social commitment) of their neorealist heritage.

Further reading

Armes, R. (1971) *Patterns of Realism*, New York: Barnes (a good introduction to neorealism, followed by production histories and analyses of individual films).

Bondanella, P. (1991) *Italian Cinema from Neorealism to the Present*, New York: Continuum (see ch. 2, 'The Masters of Neorealism: Rossellini, De Sica, and Visconti', and ch. 3, 'Exploring the Boundaries of Neorealism').

Liehm, M. (1984) *Passion and Defiance: Film in Italy from 1942 to the Present*, Berkeley and Los Angeles: University of California Press (chaps 1–5 chronicle and analyse the neorealist trend from 1942–53).

Marcus, M. (1986) *Italian Film in the Light of Neorealism*, Princeton, NJ: Princeton University Press.

Overbey, D. (ed.) (1979) *Springtime in Italy: A Reader in Neorealism*, Hamden, CN: Archon (writings by directors and critics of the neorealist period).

MILLICENT MARCUS

Nervi, Pier Luigi

b. 21 June 1891, Sondrio; d. 1979, Rome

Architect and engineer

Nervi had an extraordinary talent for inventing building techniques and poetical structures. He lectured on technology and techniques at Rome University and formed a partnership with his sons Antonio, Mario and Vittorio in Studio Nervi in 1960. His Communal Stadium in Florence (1932) was immediately published by the most controversial magazines and served as a paradigm for the structural aesthetics of the modern movement. Studying natural forms (shellfish, insects and flower calixes), he translated patterns of infinite smallness into large structures. Aiming to make structures lighter and simultaneously mastering the medium of reinforced concrete, he came to excel in long-span buildings in the early 1960s, as in the Turin Exhibition Halls and the Palazzetto dello Sport built for the Rome Olympics. He was often a contractor for his own design projects, and also worked as a structural engineer for other architects such as on the UNESCO Building in Paris in 1957 with Brauer and Zehrfuss, and the Pirelli skyscraper in Milan in 1958 with **Ponti**. He has received numerous prizes, including eight honorary doctorates.

GORDANA KOSTICH

New Italian Cinema

The term 'New Italian Cinema' came to be used in the 1990s in order to acknowledge what was widely seen as a resurgence of creative energies in the Italian film industry, after the period of relative stagnation which had followed the crisis of Italian cinema in the mid-1970s. Although the expression had been used earlier in a tentative way to indicate the work of a number of younger film-makers who had made their debut in the early 1980s, it was the overwhelming success of Giuseppe **Tornatore**'s *Nuovo Cinema Paradiso* (New Cinema Paradiso) in 1989, in winning both the Grand Jury Prize at Cannes and an Academy Award for Best Foreign Film, that appeared to seal the return of Italian cinema to the world stage. The similar success of Gabriele **Salvatores**'s *Mediterraneo* three years later seemed to definitively confirm that Italy was producing a new generation of world-class film-makers who were creating, in fact, a new Italian cinema.

Although the signs of this renaissance were undeniable, the precise features of the new cinema proved more difficult to define. The many directors who came to be associated under its umbrella (Nanni **Moretti**, Gianni **Amelio**, Maurizio **Nicchetti**, Mario **Martone**, Daniele **Luchetti**, Francesca **Archibugi**, Silvio **Soldini** and others) were of different ages and from diverse backgrounds and their films often appeared to have little in common with each other. Nevertheless, even if manifesting no common ethical or political vision nor any shared aesthetic project, these films all appeared to be responding in a variety of ways to the more complicated and fragmented social reality around them where the old ideologies had crumbled and all previous certainties had disappeared with them. The road movies of Salvatores, in particular, expressed the profound disillusionment of members of the post-1968 generation who read **Corto Maltese** and continued to dream of flight from that intolerable society which they had long contested but into which they had ultimately become integrated. Other films such as Marco **Risi**'s *Mery per sempre* (Mery Forever) (1989), Aurelio Grimaldi's *La Ribelle* (The Rebel) (1990) and Vito Capuano's remarkable first film, *Vito e gli altri* (Vito and the Others) (1990) attempted to report in an honest and almost dispassionate way the institutionalized marginalization and the social degradation of the big cities, especially as they affected the younger generation, without, at the same time, being able to propose any solutions. Amelio's *Ladro di bambini* (The Stolen Children) (1992), one of the most accomplished achievements of this new cinema, successfully renewed the aesthetic paradigm of neorealism whilst recording the ultimate defeat of its aspirations to social progress through human solidarity. Luchetti's *Il portaborse* (The Lackey) (1991), on the other hand, was able to brilliantly use caricature and comedy to present a clear picture of the corruption and clientelism institutionalized in Italian politics which the **Mani pulite** investigations would soon confirm in all their detail.

Although the New Italian Cinema had no particular centre, Nanni Moretti came to be one of its major points of reference, not only because of his eccentric and always independent film-making and his willingness to act in films by other young directors but also because of his foresight in setting up Sacher, a production company which allowed him to have complete control over his own films and which was able to finance quite a number of the first films of other promising young film-makers.

Further reading

Gieri, M. (1995) *Contemporary Italian Filmmaking: Strategies of Subversion*, Toronto: University of Toronto Press (see especially Chapter 6, 'The New Italian Cinema: Restoration or Subversion', for an extended discussion of the major directors and their relation to earlier Italian cinematic tradition).

Sesti, M. (1994) *Nuovo Cinema Italiano: Gli autori, i film, le idee* (New Italian Cinema: The Directors, Films and Ideas), Rome-Naples: Theoria (an attempt to characterize the principal aspects and tendencies of the new cinema; also includes biographies and interviews with many of the major directors and scriptwriters).

GINO MOLITERNO

newspapers

The characteristics of the Italian newspaper can be considered under three headings: (1) types of paper according to geography and ownership; (2) readership profile, and (3) journalistic tradition.

Newspapers can be divided into categories by area of distribution. There are the national ones, such as **Il Corriere della sera** or *Il Sole-24 Ore*, that can be bought at kiosks in any part of the peninsula and are available abroad. There are pluri-regional and regional papers, such as **Il Resto del Carlino** or **La Nazione**, which are bought largely in the sizeable cities where they are based and in the surrounding area (Bologna/Reggio Emilia for the former). Smaller cities tend to support their own dailies, and often these have long histories, as with *Il Piccolo* of **Trieste**. However, even the national papers are often associated with a particular region, as is the case with **La Stampa** and *Il Corriere della sera*, and Italy does not have the equivalent of the *New York Times* or *Le Monde*. The local pages are important in the national dailies, reflecting the way Italians identify strongly with their city or locality. This gravitational pull, moreover, is not offset by a metropolis comparable to New York or Paris. But while in northern and central Italy there is a lively press, the South and islands are much more poorly served; *Il*

Mattino of Naples cannot compete with publications based in Milan or Rome.

The geographical distribution of newsprint is closely related to the economics and politics of ownership. Interestingly, it is the papers which owe their existence to non-commercial organizations, such as *L'Unità*, formerly the organ of the **PCI**, and *L'Osservatore Romano* of the **Vatican**, that have been most 'national' in circulation. By comparison, dailies founded by entrepreneurs have been more closely tied to their city of origin. Until the 1970s, commentators referred to the distinction between the commercial and the party papers as one of the defining features of the Italian press. However, little of the party press now remains. Alleanza Nazionale (**National Alliance**) sustains *Il Secolo d'Italia* and the **PDS** has continued faithfully to fund *L'Unità*, but continuing financial losses seem to point inevitably towards either privatization or a complete sale of even this venerable party organ. The local papers financed by the Church manage to survive without facing the same market demands thanks to their alternative system of distribution, but otherwise commercial ownership prevails.

The readership profile of newspapers in Italy testifies to regional imbalances. A survey in the late 1980s found that the ratio was one paper per 6.6 inhabitants in the North, one per 7.1 in the centre and one per 16 in the South. If Lombardy is taken in isolation, then the statistics on readership compare well with those of other European countries. If, however, the figures for Italy as a whole are used, then the position is nearer to that of Greece at the bottom of the league table. Ever since the beginning of the century, anxieties about nationhood have focused on the low consumption of newsprint. It is often remarked that between 1915 and today the readership of the daily press has remained fairly constant at around five million. Periodically, the press itself carries reports on what is called a national scandal. In the past, explanations of this phenomenon centred on high rates of illiteracy and semiliteracy, on the non-user-friendly language of articles, and on the fact that the newspapers did not have to have readers because they could rely on state aid in times of financial difficulty. More recently, attention has turned to the exclusion of the female readers and to the displacement of the press as a source of information by other media, notably television. Certainly the daily press in Italy has failed over the decades to expand its social base and therefore to broaden the base of its advertising revenue. No popular mass circulation papers equivalent to the *Bild-Zeitung* or the *Sun* have emerged. Arguably, only the sporting press has occupied a sector of this market. As a consequence, newspapers have by and large remained the preserve of the university-educated middle classes.

Traditions of journalism in Italy are related to this readership. Unlike the situation in English-speaking countries, there is no real tradition of popular newspaper journalism. Nor is there the equivalent of the muckraker and chequebook journalist. On the contrary, the journalist has a relatively high social status. In law and in the public eye, he or she is a member of a profession. To become a journalist, one has to take a number of examinations under the aegis of the Ordine dei Giornalisti, which is a corporate body that regulates the profession. Membership brings a number of privileges, including publicly subsidized travel. Obviously, most journalists work for a local paper rather than for a prestigious national one, but it is significant nonetheless that the popular image of the journalist in Italy is that of a famous columnist like Giorgio **Bocca**.

Paradoxically, journalists enjoy a measure of public respect but themselves often have a low opinion of journalism as practised in Italy. In particular, it is argued that the press is not properly independent due to a number of factors: dependence on owners who use it to pursue their own political agendas; tendency to conflate opinion and information; vulnerability to business interests, especially in financial reporting; the demise of the tradition of investigative journalism; and readiness to give priority to entertainment values under the influence of television. This situation is contrasted with American journalism, which is said to truly represent freedom of opinion. This perspective, however, leads the debate into largely spurious comparisons, as the shortcomings mentioned above are by no means exclusive to Italy. Many Italian journalists can also be rightly proud of their record in exposing the **Piazza Fontana** bombing cover-ups and maintaining democratic debate despite pressure to follow an official line.

Further reading

Castronovo, V. and Tranfaglia, N. (eds) (1994) *La stampa italiana nell'età della tv, 1975–94* (The Italian Press in the Era of Television, 1975–94), Bari: Laterza (a comprehensive and wide-ranging volume with analyses of different aspects of Italian publishing by a number of specialist authors).

Lumley, R. (1996) *Italian Journalism: A Critical Anthology*, Manchester: Manchester University Press.

Parnell, A. (1991) 'The Press in Postwar Italy', in A.M. Brasloff and W. Brassloff (eds), *European Insights*, New York: Elsevier Science Publishers (a brief but informative survey of the Italian press up to the early 1990s).

ROBERT LUMLEY

Nichetti, Maurizio

b. 8 May 1948, Milan

Director and actor

Mime, actor, scriptwriter, director of features, animated films and commercials, Nichetti is an eclectic and exuberant personality. After his debut with the short *Magic Show* in 1978, he gained public acclaim with his first feature *Ratataplan* (1979), a silent generational filmic tale of Milanese youth living at the borders of consumerist Italy. He soon became one of the most prominent directors of the **New Italian Cinema** as he pursued a fertile contamination of comedy and drama, mime and slapstick, realist narrative and animation. He has frequently produced exhilarating critiques of a society suffering from a general feeling of loss and estrangement, which are at the same time original and witty self-parodies characterized by the surreal juxtaposition of multiple levels of reality in films such as *Ladri di saponette* (Icicle Thief) (1989), *Volere volare* (1991) and *Stefano Quantestorie* (Stefano Many-Stories) (1993).

MANUELA GIERI

Nono, Luigi

b. 29 January 1924; d. 8 May 1990, Venice

Composer

Nono studied at the Venice Conservatory under Gianfrancesco Malpiero and Bruno **Maderna**, and was deeply influenced by the music of Schoenberg. During the Second World War he served in the **Resistance** as a member of the **PCI** (Italian Communist Party). After the war, his social commitment and espousal of communism gave his work its dramatic edge. *Il canto sospeso* (The Suspended Song) (1955–6) is a setting of excerpts from the last letters of members of the European Resistance condemned to death by the Nazis. *Suite: Intolleranza* (Intolerance Suite) (1960), one of his earliest works to utilize recorded material, is a passionate denunciation of both fascism and intolerance, which provoked a violent reaction from neo-fascists at its premiere in Venice (see also **fascism and neo-fascism**). Working from Germany in the early 1960s, Nono became recognized as one of Italy's leading composers of electronic and serial music and, in keeping with his political commitment, he created many portable tape works suitable for recitals in factories and small halls. He crowned his career of socially committed music with *Prometeo* (Prometheus), composed in 1985 and widely regarded as one of the twentieth century's most moving spiritual works.

LAURENCE SIMMONS

Nuova Compagnia di Canto Popolare

Founded in 1967 by singer-songwriter Eugenio Bennato and Carlo d'Angiò, the Nuova Compagnia di Canto Popolare (New Company of Popular Song) brought together a number of talented musicians (Giovanni Mauriello, Patrizio Trampetti, Peppe Barra, Fausta Vetere and Nunzio Areni and others) in a project aimed at reanimating the long and rich tradition of Neapolitan folk song. Joined in 1972 by ethnomusicologist and theatre director Roberto De Simone, the group achieved wide recognition for their genuine recreation of forgotten forms of Neapolitan song such as the villanelle and the moresche of the fifteenth and sixteenth centuries. Their grand musical spectacle, *La gatta Cenerentola* (Cindarella, the Cat), directed by De Simone and performed at the **Spoleto Festival** in 1976, was hailed as a milestone by both audiences and critics alike and increased what was already a strong international reputation. During the 1980s many members of the ensemble returned to solo performance and other individual activities but, with the participation of several of the original members, the Compagnia was reconstituted in the 1990s. It recorded a number of successful new albums including *Medina* (1992) and *Tzigari* (1995) and appeared at several editions of the **Sanremo Festival** to much renewed critical acclaim.

GINO MOLITERNO

Occhetto, Achille

b. 3 March 1936, Turin

Politician

When Occhetto became general secretary of **PCI** in 1988, the party had been losing ground for over ten years. Occhetto initiated a 'new course', proclaiming an affinity with Western European social democratic parties and promoting greater internal democracy and feminist and environmentalist concerns. Then, in November 1989, claiming that the collapse of communism in Eastern Europe removed the basis for divisions on the Left in Italy, he announced his intention to dissolve the PCI to make way for a new, unified left-wing party. While this operation split the party, with many leaving to found Rifondazione Comunista (**RC**), the majority joined Occhetto's **PDS** (Party of the Democratic Left) in 1991. This remained the dominant left-wing party and was more 'respectable' than the PCI as a candidate for government. Occhetto resigned following the defeat of the left-wing coalition at the 1994 election, and thus it was his successor **D'Alema** who actually took the PDS to government in 1996.

CLAIRE KENNEDY

olive oil

Produced over the centuries in Italy and other Mediterranean countries, olive oil is extensively used in Italian cuisine: in fact, the healthiness of the so-called 'Mediterranean diet' has been attributed in part to this type of mono-unsaturated oil. Olive oil is used for cooking and as a condiment, but also to preserve vegetables such as eggplants, tomatoes, olives, mushrooms and even herbs. Many types of **bread** and focaccia owe their softness and flavour to the presence of olive oil in the dough.

Like all other oils, *olio d'oliva* is obtained by a pressing of the fruit, followed by processes of settling, centrifugation and filtering. The percentage of fat and acid contained in each oil influences and characterizes its flavour, nutritional value and preservative capacity. Extra virgin olive oil includes only 1 per cent of oleic acid, while the virgin olive oil contains 2 per cent of it. Other varieties are obtained through a refining process of the virgin olive oil, or mixing several varieties. Olive oil is no higher in calories than any other oil. The types of oil used depend on the dish being cooked. Salads and steamed vegetables are generally dressed with lighter oils. More tasty oils are preferred for minestrone, legumes, artichokes and bruschetta. Delicate-tasting oils are selected for frying purposes.

MARIELLA TOTARO GENEVOIS

Olivetti

An industrial group of electronics and telecommunications based at Ivrea, Olivetti is traditionally regarded as the anomaly of Italian big business. Established by Camillo Olivetti in 1908 as the first Italian maker of typewriters, Olivetti was in the vanguard of managerial culture from the 1930s on, when Adriano, the founder's son, restructured the family business by introducing scientific management and Taylorism.

Adriano Olivetti was a unique figure. He emerged in the postwar period as a progressive entrepreneur with a socialist vein, who was regarded by his conservative colleagues as a rather eccentric character. He strongly supported modern industry (that is, rationality and efficiency) as a means of modernizing society but, in his enlightened view, a company needed to be managed democratically, not only by accepting a role for the unions but also by making a major contribution to the progress of the local community, i.e. by organizing social services and city planning. 'Community' was Adriano's keyword. '**Movimento di Comunità**' was, in fact, the name of a political movement he created in 1950s, which was totally independent of political parties, won a large popular support in Ivrea and ruled local government for a long time. His publishing group was also named 'Comunità' as Olivetti attempted to play a fundamental role in promoting modern enlightened culture. By financing young scholars such as Franco Ferrarotti, Luciano Gallino and Alessandro Pizzorno – who later became the founders of contemporary Italian sociology – to research the impact of industrialization and technological development on rural communities, workers and the young, Olivetti contributed enormously to the renewal of Italian culture by facilitating the spread of the more progressive trends of American sociology. Intellectuals and writers such as Franco **Fortini** and Paolo **Volponi** were also deeply influenced by their experience as employees in Olivetti's research and social relations department. Above all, by enlisting the services of imaginative architects such as **Figini and Pollini** for Olivetti's own buildings and innovative designers such as **Sottsass** and **Bellini** to design its office products, Olivetti came to be a byword for postwar Italian design culture.

Adriano's death proved to be a real watershed in the company's history. Thanks to a management wedded to its tradition of dynamism and innovation, Olivetti quickly entered the computer sector, established a joint venture with Bull, a French group, and tried to redress the wide technological gap with American companies. However, this move was not successful. Such a small concern could not compete with the American giants, and the Olivetti family refused to admit any strong outsider shareholders until a grave financial crisis in 1963 forced them to give up control to a private group led by **Mediobanca**, **Fiat** and **Pirelli**. Research costs soon skyrocketed, and Olivetti quit the computer sector to fall back on typewriters. This was to prove a crucial strategic mistake, since the computer sector grew tremendously and American giants such as IBM and Honeywell soon conquered the Italian market while Olivetti, after its false start in the electronics race, plodded along in its traditional activities.

A successful trend seemed to start again in early 1980s under the dynamic management of Carlo **De Benedetti**. Thanks to an effective restructuring plan, Olivetti dramatically improved its productivity and economic performance and in 1983 formed an alliance with AT&T, the US telecommunications giant, in order to enter the fast growing personal computer market. This, however, proved a bad marriage, which ended in 1989 with a separation by mutual consent.

In the 1990s, with the group's standing in the international personal computer market continuing to decline and personnel drastically reduced, telecommunications became the major challenge. In a clever move, Olivetti established a strategic partnership with the German group Mannesmann, and successfully entered the market for mobile phones and fixed-line service through its subsidiaries Omnitel and Infostrada, thus effectively biting into Telecom's former monopoly (see **STET**). At the beginning of 1999, in alliance with a group of Italian entrepreneurs and leading banks under the financial co-ordination of Mediobanca, Olivetti sold Omnitel and Infostrada to Mannesmann and successfully launched a hostile takeover bid for Telecom. This was the biggest ever hostile takeover bid in Europe and an unprecedented innovation for Italian business style, which suddenly transformed Olivetti once again into a leading force in the Italian economy and a group of great international standing.

See also: industrial design

Further reading

Kicherer, S. (1990) *Olivetti: A Study of Corporate Management of Design*, New York: Rizzoli (a comprehensive history of the company and its role in Italian design culture; also contains a useful bibliography).

STEFANO BATTILOSSI

Olmi, Ermanno

b. 24 July 1931, Bergamo

Film director

After making almost forty short documentaries in the 1950s, Olmi made his first feature film *Il tempo si è fermato* (Time Has Stopped) in 1959. Acutely observant and with quiet, subdued tones, the film accurately presents the daily life of two ordinary individuals in the mountains of northern Italy. In *Il posto* (The Job) (1961) and *I fidanzati* (The Fiancées) (1963), Olmi continued to use a documentary style which would characterize most of his later films, while *E venne un uomo* (A Man named John) (1965) is a sensitive and respectful portrait of **Pope John XXIII**. Olmi came to international renown, however, with *L'albero degli zoccoli* (The Tree of the Wooden Clogs), a moving epic of peasant life in Lombardy in the late nineteenth century which won the Golden Palm at Cannes in 1978. His later *La leggenda del santo bevitore* (The Legend of the Holy Drinker) (1988), adapted from a novel by Joseph Roth, was also awarded the Golden Lion at Venice.

CRISTINA DEGLI-ESPOSTI REINERT

Olympics

Although Italian athletes participated in the second edition of the modern Olympic games, held in Paris in 1900, it was only after the establishment of CONI (the Italian National Olympic Committee) in 1914 that Italian participation in the games become a concerted effort. In 1996, Italy won thirty-five medals at the Atlanta Olympic Games, an accumulation of victories second only to those of 1932 and 1960. Performances of this kind established Italy's role as a major player in the world of sports (see also **winter sports**).

The 1952 Helsinki games was the site of Italy's first outstanding postwar achievement. Placing fifth overall in the medal count, Italian athletes took eight gold medals, nine silver and four bronze. Giuseppe Dordoni won the 50-km walk, establishing a new world record, while fencer Edoardo Mangiarotti continued the series of wins he had begun four years earlier. At the London Olympic games of 1948, Mangiarotti was part of the foil and épée teams which took silver medals, and achieved third place in the individual épée. In Helsinki, Mangiarotti won two gold medals (individual and team épée) and two silver (individual and team foil). In Melbourne in 1956, Mangiarotti added a gold medal in the team foil, a gold in team épée and a bronze in individual épée.

Italy was again fifth in Melbourne, this time with eight gold, eight silver and nine bronze medals. Five of these medals came from cycling and seven from fencing (including first, second and third place in individual épée). In 1956, due to Australian quarantine laws, the equestrian events were held in Stockholm. Brothers Raimondo and Piero D'Inzeo received silver and bronze in the individual jumping event, and when teamed up with Salvatore Oppes, took the team silver medal as well. Raimondo and Piero's Olympic success continued until 1972 for a total of twelve medals.

Rome, chosen to host the Olympic Games of 1960, underwent a series of transformations. Most of the sporting venues were built for the occasion, including the stadium and the Olympic village. A new road, the Via Olimpica, was added to facilitate the flow of traffic within the city. The 1960 Olympics were especially significant because they were the first to be broadcast via television. Italy finished as third nation overall in terms of medals. As it did in 1948, the Italian water polo team was able once again to thwart Hungary's supremacy in the sport (with the exception of 1948 and 1960 Hungary took all the gold medals in water polo from 1932 to 1964). Livio Berruti's gold medal in the 200 metres was the first ever for an Italian sprinter. Rome also marked the international debut of boxing sensation Nino Benvenuti. The most enduring memory of the Rome Olympics, however, remains that of barefooted Ethiopian Abebe Bikila, who won the men's marathon, setting a new the world record in the process.

At Tokyo in 1964, Italy took ten gold, ten silver and seven bronze medals. The cycling team did its part as always, finishing with eight medals. Abdon Pamich, third in Rome in the 50-km walk, managed to win the event, setting a new Olympic record. Franco Menichelli's gold medal in the floor exercise came more than thirty years after Italy's previous Olympic success in gymnastics, and Klaus Dibiasi's silver medal was the first ever for Italy in diving events. Dibiasi went on to become the most successful diver of all time, winning a total of five Olympic medals in diving events from 1964–76. In 1968 he took gold in men's platform and silver in men's springboard. Dibiasi repeated his victory in the men's platform at the 1972, following with two gold and two silver medals at World Championships in 1973 and 1975. He then took gold for the men's platform again at Montreal in 1976, becoming the only diver in the sport's history to win the same event in three consecutive Olympic games.

As a team, Italy did not perform well at the Olympic games of Mexico City in 1968, Munich 1972 or Montreal 1976. The combined medal count of these three games was lower than that of Rome alone. In 1972, victories came from Novella Calligaris, Italy's first woman swimmer to step on the podium (silver in the 400-metre freestyle, bronze in the 800-metre freestyle and the 400-metre individual medley), and runner Pietro Mennea, third place in the 200-metre sprint. Mennea competed in Montreal as well, with no success. His major breakthrough was in 1979, when he set the world record for the 200 metres with the time of 19.72s (it took almost seventeen years before Michael Johnson bettered that mark). In Moscow in 1980, at his third participation, Mennea finally won an Olympic gold medal in the 200 metres. High jumper Sara Simeoni, the first Italian woman to break the 2-metre barrier, also won her event. In 1980, many nations (including the USA) did not participate to protest against the USSR's invasion of Afghanistan. CONI decided to send to Moscow only those athletes who were neither government employees nor military. Italy ended the 1980 expedition in fifth place overall (eight gold, three silver and four bronze medals).

The XXIII Olympic games took place in Los Angeles, in 1984. This time, it was the Soviet Union's turn to boycott the games, along with the rest of the communist countries except for China, Romania and Yugoslavia. Italy took full advantage of these absences to win an unprecedented fourteen gold medals, some in sports such as pentathlon and weightlifting traditionally ruled by the athletes of the former eastern block. Runners Alberto Cova (men's 10,000 metres) and Gabriella Dorio (women's 1,500 metres) obtained first-time victories for Italy. Vincenzo Maenza's gold medal in Greco-Roman wrestling (48 kg category), was followed by another gold in 1988, and silver in 1992. Brothers Giuseppe and Carmine Abbagnale (with coxswain G. Di Capua) began their own string of victories in 1984, capturing the men's coxed pair's gold medal; the same crew won again in Seoul in 1988, and finished second in Barcelona four years later. If not comparable to the accomplishment of 1984, the Seoul and Barcelona expeditions produced satisfactory results for Italy, including the first victory in an Olympic marathon, obtained by Gelindo Bordin in 1988.

The downward trend of 1988 and 1992 was reversed at the Atlanta Olympic Games of 1996. Twelve of Italy's thirty-five medals came from **cycling** and fencing. Equally impressive were the performances of the competitors in rowing and skeet and trap competitions, while gymnast Yuri Chechi added an Olympic gold to his world title in the rings event.

PAOLO VILLA

Ontani, Luigi

b. 24 November 1943, Vergato, Bologna

Artist

Highly innovative in his use of figuration, before the **transavantgarde** heralded the figurative revival, Ontani also in some ways prefigured Francesco **Clemente** in the erotic imagery of his work, his Indian influences and his concentration on himself as subject matter. Ontani's hand-tinted photographic works include elaborate staged tableaux, featuring himself in various guises, such as Dante, Pinocchio and Leda, complete with swan. The ceramic sculpture *Panontale*, from 1994, uses an agglomeration of tourist kitsch to support an upside down shape of Italy. Even exhibition spaces come in for the Ontani treatment, transformed with lush drapes as if to dispel every trace of the mundane.

Ontani was voted one of the most popular artists at the 1995 **Venice Biennale**. However in 1996, he caused an uproar with his commissioned design of a 'mascot' for Milan. A clever collage of thoroughly Milanese elements, it was nevertheless stridently rejected by many who described it as a deformed Frankenstein and an offence to the city.

Further reading

Weiermair, P. (ed.) (1996) *Luigi Ontani*, Kilchberg/Zurich: Edition Stemmle (illustrated exhibition catalogue, with various essays).

MAX STAPLES

opening to the Left

The so-called 'opening to the Left' – proposed in the mid-1950s and consummated in 1963 – signified the move towards government collaboration between the **DC** and **PSI** which was intended, but failed, to deliver substantial social reform. Politically, the alliance was essential: the DC could no longer rely on its weakening coalition partners (**PLI**, **PRI** and **PSDI**) or support from the **MSI**. However, Church and American hostility to political collaboration between Catholics and socialists had to be overcome and here the liberalizing influence of **Pope John XXIII** and President Kennedy proved decisive. Moreover, the Soviet invasion of Hungary (1956) drove deeper divisions between PSI and **PCI** and repaired relations between PSI and PSDI. Finally, **Fanfani**, **Moro** and **Nenni** slowly persuaded their parties that their reformist ambitions for the changing Italy of the **economic miracle** would be neither radicalized (DC) nor compromised (PSI) by a centre–left government.

Further reading:

Ginsborg, P. (1990) *A History of Contemporary Italy*, London: Penguin (see ch. 8, 'The Centre–Left, 1958–68').

DAVID MOSS

opera

The importance of opera to Italian composers in the twentieth century has been reflected less in formal trends or conventions than in a culture of individuality allowing a wide variance of approach. At the beginning of the century, the Verdian ideal of Romantic opera was dominant to the exclusion of most foreign influences, with the exception of Wagner. The characteristics of Romantic opera were a pronounced sense of theatrical effect, strong, dramatic plots and a melodic prominence designed to reflect the utmost vocal virtuosity. From this style developed *verismo*, an attempt to attain a greater naturalism and to address those areas, particularly of working-class life, which the plots of Romantic opera had largely ignored. *Verismo* was typified in the literary work of Giovanni Verga, whose novella *Cavalleria rusticana* was accorded operatic treatment by Mascagni in 1890, and in such operas as Leoncavallo's *I Pagliacci* (1892), in whose prologue the key phrase 'uno squarcio di vita' (a slice of life) appears. Such a life was increasingly to embrace the seamier side of human behaviour, with plots that concentrated on criminal activity and crimes of passion.

The growth of one-act opera in this period was to provide an ideal vehicle for *verismo*, producing, in addition to the two examples quoted above, Puccini's *Il trittico* (1918) (in particular its first part, *Il tabarro*), Giordano's *Mala vita* (1892) and Sebastiani's *A San Francesco* (1896). Puccini (1858–1924) was to widen the horizons of *verismo* to produce a broader and more convincing emotional range in his operas, although accusations of sentimentality may be justly levelled at his work. Nevertheless, his most important compositions for the stage, amongst which must be counted *La bohème* (1896), *Tosca* (1900) and *Madam Butterfly* (1904), have attained a lasting place in the repertoire.

The influence of Puccini proved to be far-reaching, both in his native country and throughout Western Europe, especially France. In particular, the concept of an overall dramatic vision largely replaced the former ideal of opera as a vehicle for vocal display. Younger Italian composers such as Pizzetti (1880–1968) and Malipiero (1882–1973) sought to further regenerate opera as a vital artistic conduit in their bid to create a coherent national style. This style typically eschewed the atonality of the Second Viennese School in favour of native baroque and folk influences. Pizzetti's operas, such as *Debora e Jaèle* (1923) and *L'assassinio nella cattedrale* (Murder in the Cathedral) (1958), display some particularly fine writing for the chorus and are generally successful in their attempts at dramatic integration. Malipiero's style proved to be considerably more eclectic, avoiding contrapuntal developments such as serialism while maintaining a sharply radical outlook. His opera *Giulio Cesare* (Julius Caesar) (1936) was partially a celebration of the achievements of Mussolini, and was to be the first in a series of classically inspired heroic treatments. Later, Malipiero was to adopt a more surreal, fantastic style, as in *L'allegra brigata* (The Cheerful Brigade) (1950) and *Mondi celesti e infernali* (The Worlds of Heaven and Hell) (1961), which would have a lasting influence on the Italian avantgarde.

In the years following the Second World War the work of **Menotti**, who was of Italian birth but was primarily domiciled in America and Scotland, rose to prominence. Menotti achieved an immediacy of appeal that was indebted partly to a reliance on the backward-looking techniques of *verismo* and partly to a simplicity of musical language. His early success with *The Medium* (1946) and *The Telephone* (1947) showed a sure instinct for both the serious and the more comic demands of the theatre, and this was to lay the foundations for his popular television opera *Amahl and the Night Visitors* (1951). Menotti's dramatic command, however, was largely unallied to significant musical development and the naïvety of his style meant that his achievements were less influential among the composers of his homeland.

Among the avantgarde during this period, opera was largely secondary to instrumental music. The two operas of **Petrassi** mark an attempt to bring a determined musical radicalism to the operatic medium. In *Il cordovano* (The Man from Cordova) (1949, revised 1959), the voices and instrumental parts go some way to achieving parity, although the libretto was widely lambasted for its supposedly pornographic nature. *Morte dell'aria* (Death in the Air) (1950) is more artistically successful, with a strong plot that treats a birdman's unsuccessful flight from the Eiffel Tower. The operas of Luigi **Nono**, a pupil of Malipiero, were a more consistent reflection of a renewed interest in the demands of the theatre, with *Intolleranza* (Intolerance) (1960) provoking a fascist-organized riot at its première. Nono's style incorporates a number of European influences, notably in his use of serial techniques. During the 1970s he sought to reflect the prevailing concerns of the time within an operatic structure; this resulted in *Al gran sole carico d'amore* (To the Great Sun Charged with Love) (1975), which deals with the ideals of the Paris Commune. The work of the fellow Malipiero pupil Bruno **Maderna** was similarly coloured by an interest in the European serialists, this interest being complemented by his activities in the revival of Renaissance music. His *Satyricon* (1973) shows a sure instinct for drama within a highly complex musical language.

Since the 1980s, a number of young Italian composers have undertaken operatic work of increasing diversity. The neo-tonalist Lorenzo **Ferrero** has been imaginative in his assimilation of contemporary multimedia techniques into the operatic form, as may be seen in *Marilyn* (1980), and has also sought to fuse the classical tradition with musical features derived from pop music. In the work of Paolo **Arcà**, this search for a new relevance has led to the continuation of the elements of myth and fantasy seen in Malipiero's later work. The recent operatic work of Salvatore **Sciarrino** develops the tendencies towards the European avantgarde found in Nono and Maderna, with *Vanitas* (1981) and *Lohengrin* (1982–4) suggesting a strong link with past models while at

the same time maintaining a determinedly progressive outlook.

See also: La Scala

Further reading

Bianconi, L. and Pestelli, G. (eds) (1987) *Storia
dell'opera italiana* (The History of Italian Opera),
Turin: EDT/Musica.
Kimbell, D. (1991) *Italian Opera*, Cambridge:
Cambridge University Press.

JOHN KERSEY

Orelli, Giorgio

b. 1921, Airolo, Canton Ticino,
Switzerland

Poet, novelist and essayist

The most important Swiss poet writing in Italian,
Orelli writes with formal precision and great
erudition, focusing thematically on the landscape
and life of Lombardy and the Canton Ticino. With
time, however, Orelli has displayed the ability to
move from the epigrammatic and gnomic quality of
his 1944 collection *Né bianco né viola* (Neither White
Nor Purple) to the narrative and dialogic airiness on
display in *L'ora del tempo* (Time's Hour) (1961) and
Sinopie (Outlines) (1977). His later work, such as
Spiracoli (Spiracles), published in 1989, continues the
poet's evolution by linguistically resorting to
instances of local dialect and German and by
thematically reaffirming the poet's puritan and
methodical Swiss background. Orelli's collection of
short stories, *Un giorno della vita* (A Day of Life) (1960)
and his critical essays also display the writer's great
linguistic control and attention to style.

VALERIO FERME

Orengo, Nico

b. 1944, Turin

Novelist and poet

Although residing in Turin, where he was born,

Orengo has elected the Liguria region as his artistic
home and this emotional and cultural attachment is
evident in most of his writings. In the novel *Ribes*
(1988), for instance, Orengo narrates the transformation of a rural community – based on the Ligurian
town of Dolceacqua (in the novel, 'Acquadolce') – as
a result of the introduction of television. Similar
geographical settings characterize the novels *Mir-
amare* (1976) and *Dogana d'amore* (The Customs House
of Love) (1986). His tribute to Liguria takes a
different form in the collection of poems *Cartoline di
mare* (Postcards of the Sea) (1986) where the
protagonists are the animals and the plants inhabit-
ing the region. This poetry celebrates the liminal
zone between the sea and the earth by exploring its
ecological habitat through a language which is an
interesting combination of scientific knowledge and
humble reverence. Orengo is also known for his
colourful and captivating children's literature: *A-ulí-
ulé. Filastrocche, conti, ninnenanne* (A-ulí-ulé: Nursery-
Rhymes, Limericks and Lullabies) (1972) and *Andare
per mare. Storia del Capitan Rebissu e della sua barca
Gianchettu* (1975), translated as *The Sea Voyage*.

PAOLO BARTOLONI

Ortese, Anna Maria

b. 13 June 1914, Rome; d. 11 March
1998, Rapallo

Novelist

Ortese began her writing career by contributing to
such publications as *Oggi*, **L'Europeo**, and **Il
Corriere della sera**. She has lived in different
cities, mostly in Southern Italy, the setting of
several of her works. In 1937 she published her first
collection of short stories, influenced by magic
realism. Later narratives, however, are distinguished by neorealist themes, and reflect her
journalistic writing as well as her interest in the
fantastic. The collection of short stories *Il mare non
bagna Napoli* (The Sea Does Not Touch Naples)
(1953), winner of the Viareggio Prize, and *Silenzio a
Milano* (Silence in Milan) (1958) portray the
economic problems of the South and the alienating
existence of the developed North. At the same
time, novels such as *L'iguana* (The Iguana) (1965),

Poveri e semplici (Poor and Simple) (1967), which won the Strega Prize, and *Il porto di Toledo* (Port of Toledo) (1975), and the short story collection *La luna sul muro* (The Moon on the Wall) (1968) recount her life experiences. Later works include *In sonno e in veglia* (In Sleep and In Wake) (1987), winner of the Elsa Morante Prize. She was honoured by the Italian Republic with the equivalent of a knighthood (commendatore).

Further reading

Wood, S. (1995) "'Such stuff as dreams are made on": Anna Maria Ortese and the Art of the Real', in S. Wood (ed.), *Italian Women's Writing 1860–1994*, London: Athlone Press.

VIRGINIA PICCHIETTI

L'Osservatore Romano

Originally founded in July 1861 with the blessing of Pope Pius IX, *L'Osservatore Romano* (The Roman Observer) is now the recognized organ of the **Vatican** and, as such, conveys its official comment on national and international current affairs. It publishes a weekly supplement on Sundays, *L'Osservatore della domenica* (The Sunday Observer) as well as also appearing in a weekly edition in French, English, Spanish, German and Portuguese and as a monthly in Polish. By the late 1990s it had put several of its foreign language editions online and made them available on the Internet.

See also: Catholic press and publishing; newspapers

GINO MOLITERNO

Ossola, Carlo

b. 1945, Turin

Literary critic and essayist

Previously Professor at the University of Geneva and now Professor of Italian at the College de France, Ossola is one of the most active and respected scholars in Italian Studies today. His works on the Renaissance, *L'autunno del Rinascimento* (Autumn of the Renaissance) and *Dal 'Cortegiano' all' 'Uomo di mondo'. Storia di un libro e di un modello sociale* (From the 'Courtier' to the 'Man of the World': History of a Book and of a Social Model), are considered critical cornerstones in the field. Ossola has also worked extensively on twentieth-century Italian poetry, in particular on the work of Giuseppe **Ungaretti**, on which he has written what is generally regarded as the most important monographic work to date. Together with Vittore **Branca**, Ossola edits the prestigious journal *Lettere Italiane* (Italian Letters), and he is also the director of the renowned Summer Seminars on High Culture sponsored by the Giorgio Cini Foundation in Venice.

ANDREA CICCARELLI

Ottieri, Ottiero

b. 29 March 1924, Rome

Novelist, poet and playwright

In his first book of fiction, *Memorie dell'incoscienza* (Memories of Unconsciousness) (1954), Ottieri dealt with the traumatic experiences of war, but his subsequent works up to *Donnaruma all'assalto* (Donnaruma on the Assault) (1959) analyse the alienation and disenfranchisement of a whole generation of southern peasants forced to migrate north where they are required to learn different social rules and professional conventions. Ottieri's later fiction is characterized by a stylistic concern whose main feature is dialogic experimentation. In *I due amori* (The Two Loves) (1983), for instance, the continuous, heterogeneous and disorderly accumulation of sounds and voices results in a polysemous, clownish and hyperrealistic effect reminiscent of some of **Fellini**'s movies. This experimental trait is explored even further in the collections of poems in prose, *Il palazzo e il pazzo* (The Palace and the Lunatic) (1993), *Il poema osceno* (The Obscene Poem) (1996) and *Diario del seduttore passivo* (Diary of the Passive Seducer) (1995), in which Ottieri's writing, using a mixture of archaic, literary and graphic language, investigates the themes of love and madness.

PAOLO BARTOLONI

P

P2

P2 (Propaganda 2) was a secret Masonic lodge, established under the aegis of the larger of Italy's two Masonic families, the Grand Orient of Palazzo Giustiniani. It was dissolved by Parliament as a criminal association in 1981.

P2's real history begins in 1970 when a Tuscan businessman, Licio Gelli, was granted responsibility for the lodge and power to initiate new members privately. Gelli's suspiciously recent conversion to Freemasonry (he was initiated in 1965) and his political obscurity suggest that his role, designed by others, was to infiltrate the organization and convert an influential segment of the P2 into a clandestine centre of anti-communist influence. His wartime experiences, which included service to Fascists, Germans and Americans, had given him entry into both moderate and extreme conservative circles in Italy and abroad, and his links with leading members of the Italian secret services enabled him to obtain the dossiers they had compiled on 300,000 Italians in the 1960s. Gelli was able to turn such resources to good effect in recruiting for the P2. The list of 511 members which was made public in 1981 included ministers and MPs, magistrates and judges, senior officers in the armed forces and security services, and high-ranking state officials. Other powerful affiliates included Angelo Rizzoli, then owner of the **Corriere della sera**, and two bankers who were to meet violent deaths, Michele Sindona and Roberto Calvi. The revelation that even leading politicians were ready to join a secret association suspected of plotting against the state forced the resignation of the Christian Democrat government in 1981 and its replacement by the first postwar government to be led by a member of another party (Giovanni Spadolini from the **PRI**).

What purpose did the P2 serve? Its structure, based exclusively on direct links between Gelli and affiliates whose involvement was not widely known to other members and who met only in small groups, certainly militated against any clear collective goal. Some accounts portray it as little more than an underground **salotto**, organized by Gelli to make participants aware that their fear of the advance of communism, and sympathy for some kind of authoritarian response, was shared by people in other influential positions. Others, including several Italian courts, have identified it as an active agent in the right-wing conspiracies of the 1970s, detecting its hand in the neo-fascist strategy of tension (see **strategia della tensione**) and in a deliberate decision to allow **Moro**, supposedly soft on communism, to be murdered by the **Red Brigades**. Senior P2 members, notably from the armed forces, were fond of illegality, but it remains unclear whether their actions had a common origin in P2 strategy.

Further reading

Cecchi, A. (1985) *Storia della P2* (History of the P2), Rome: Editori Riuniti.

Cornwell, R. (1983) *God's Banker*, London: Victor Gollancz (the career of Robert Calvi and his links with the P2).

Ferraresi, F. (1996) *Threats to Democracy: The Radical Right in Italy After the War*, Princeton, NJ:

Princeton University Press (the political environment of the P2).

DAVID MOSS

Paci, Enzo

b. 19 December 1911, Ancona; d. 21 July 1976, Milan

Philosopher

Paci studied with Antonio **Banfi** at Milan and was heavily influenced by the phenomenology of Husserl and by historical materialism. His synthesis of the unlikely pair, phenomenology and Marxism, led him to formulate a philosophy of history which privileged events over entities and made the processes inherent in relatedness more important than substance itself. With a rapid succession of works and through the phenomenological orientation of the journal *Aut aut*, which he founded in 1951, Paci inspired the return to Husserl that animated Italian philosophy of the 1960s. His influence is due, at least in part, to his wide range of interests which included poetry, music, science and architecture.

Further reading

Dallmayr, F. (1973) 'Phenomenology and Marxism: A Salute to Enzo Paci', in G. Psathas (ed.), *Phenomenological Sociology*, New York and London: John Wiley and Sons, 305–56.

THOMAS KELSO

Padre Pio

b. 25 May 1887, Pietrelcina, Benevento; d. 23 September 1968, San Giovanni Rotondo, Foggia

Franciscan friar

One of the greatest foci of modern Italian popular piety and the principal cause of a religious revival in southern Italy in the postwar period, Pio entered the Franciscan order in 1905 and was ordained in 1910. In 1918 he first manifested signs of the *stigmata* (the wounds which Christ suffered on the Cross) and as a result his monastery at San Giovanni Rotondo, Puglia, became a centre of pilgrimage for the next sixty years. In spite of mystical leanings, Padre Pio showed great concern for the living and for working conditions of the local people, and in 1956 he opened a major hospital. For a long time the Church's general attitude towards the Padre Pio phenomenon was one of scepticism and distance, but in December 1998 his miraculous works were confirmed and in May 1999 he was officially beatified.

Further reading

McKevitt, C. (1991) 'San Giovanni Rotondo and the Cult of Padre Pio', in J. Eade and M.J. Sallnow (eds), *Contesting the Sacred*, London: Routledge.

JOHN POLLARD

Pagliarani, Elio

b. 25 May 1927, Viserba, Forlí

Poet

After completing his degree in Political Science in 1951, Pagliarani taught in several high schools in Milan and worked on the editorial staff of the socialist newspaper *Avanti!* (Forward!). He also contributed to literary journals such as *Nuovi argomenti*, *il verri*, *Quindici* and, finally, *Periodo ipotetico* which he also founded. His poems appear in the neoavantgarde anthology *I novissimi* (1961), and he belonged to the **Gruppo 63**, a group of poets and intellectuals who sketched the theoretical background for neoavantgarde poetry itself. His poetry, prosaic and chronicle-like, is often filled with the imagery and characters of an urban landscape. His verses, especially the later ones, are characterized by a strong innovative and experimental tension which aims at undermining the structures of language and discourse.

Further reading

Pagliarani, E. (1985) *(La ragazza Carla – Lezione di fisica e Fecaloro – Dalla ballata di Rudi)* (Poems for

Recitation: The Girl Carla – The Physics Lesson and Fecaloro – From Rudi's Ballad), ed. A. Briganti, Rome: Bulzoni (a representative collection of Pagliarani's poetry).

ENRICO CESARETTI

Pajetta, Giancarlo

b. 24 June 1911, Turin; d. 13 September 1990, Rome

Politician

One of the most popular and prestigious leaders of the **PCI** (Italian Communist Party), Giancarlo Pajetta was first jailed for subversive activities at the age of sixteen. During the **Resistance**, as a leader of the CLNAI (National Liberation Committee), he was responsible for agreements in which the Allies and the caretaker Italian government recognized the CLNAI as their representative in the North, in return for a guarantee to relinquish authority after Liberation. While Pajetta claimed that it had been impossible to achieve more, the socialists considered this price for support of the partisan struggle too high. A member of parliament from 1945 onwards, as well as editor of *L'Unità* and *Rinascita* for long periods, Pajetta was known for his corrosive wit and fiercely combative spirit. Within the party, he played a key role in organizational affairs and foreign policy development.

CLAIRE KENNEDY

Paladino, Mimmo (Domenico)

b. 18 December 1948, Paduli, Benevento

Artist

Paladino was part of the Italian **transavantgarde** and the return to the use of figurative elements in painting in the 1970s and 1980s. His interest in drawing is shown by the compositional nature of his works which, like those of other artists identified with the transavantgarde, make use of a wide range of sources, including ancient art and mythology. Paladino's work is somewhat more mysterious, however; it alludes to the past, to states of life and death and to the unknowable, without attempting to impose fixed meanings. *On the Edge of Evening* (1983) is composed of human and animal shapes built up to suggest a dreamlike state where matter is in flux. Paladino has held numerous exhibitions since 1976, moving beyond painting to mixed media, print-making and sculpture.

Further reading

Bonito Oliva, A. and Rosenthal, N. (1993) *Mimmo Paladino*, Milan, Fabbri Editori (exhibition catalogue with some colour illustrations).

MAX STAPLES

Palazzeschi, Aldo

b. 2 February 1885, Florence; d. 18 August 1974, Rome

Poet and novelist

As one of the founding members of the Italian avantgarde, Palazzeschi (the pseudonym of Giurlani Aldo) not only revolutionized Italian literature earlier in the twentieth century with his anti-literary work but, through his writing's ironic and self-reflexive parody, also offered an early example of postmodern sensitivity in Italian culture.

Having trained briefly as an actor before starting his career as a writer, Palazzeschi published his first book of poetry, *I cavalli bianchi* (White Horses) in 1905. In this as well as in other early books, Palazzeschi parodies and attacks the leading poetic schools of the time by transforming D'Annunzio's Nietzschean celebration of the poet's Dionysian powers and the 'tubercular' resignation of *decadentismo* (the decadent school) into what one critic has called 'l'occasione per l'irriverenza, la malizia, la metamorfosi in manichini dei personaggi tipici di tali luoghi e spazi' (the occasion for irreverence, for malice and for the metamorphosis into puppets of the typical characters represented in such works) (Barbèri Squarotti, 1994: 704 (my translation)). Having joined the futurists' revolt against the status quo, Palazzeschi continued to attack the literary establishment with the narrative works *Codice di Perelà* (Perelà's Codex) (1911) and *La Piramide* (The

Pyramid) (1926), whose fantastic and sarcastic humour signal a pessimistic abandonment of the rhetorical and self-centred artistic representations of the previous Italian tradition. Prior to the Second World War, Palazzeschi also published his most successful novel, *Le sorelle Materassi* (The Materassi Sisters), which was made into film in 1943 and adapted for Italian public television in the 1960s. On the surface level, the novel narrates the emotional and financial swindling of two sisters by a nephew with whom they have fallen in love. However, it is also meant as the occasion for a scathing indictment of the Florentine bourgeoisie and its provincial morality.

Following a period of inactivity that coincided with the Second World War, Palazzeschi returned to writing in the late 1940s and early 1950s with the novels *I fratelli Cuccoli* (The Cuccoli Brothers) (1948) and *Roma* (1953), books that do not maintain the biting originality and cohesive attacks on the system of his previous works. More interesting are the short stories collected in *Bestie del Novecento* (Twentieth-Century Beasts) (1951), where the elaboration of a modern bestiary provides the occasion for an attack on the vices of his contemporaries. After another lengthy interruption, the 1960s saw a renewed flurry of activity on Palazzeschi's part. Of significance are the poems collected in *Cuor mio* (My Heart) (1968), which display novel linguistic experimentation side by side with the usual polemics against the intellectual establishment. Palazzeschi was moreover the author of numerous autobiographical works, chief among them *Tre imperi ... mancati* (Three Empires ... Lost), in which Fascism's imperial policy is divested of its false rhetoric of power and heroic virtue, and exposed as the source of all the suffering and civic unhappiness that followed.

Further reading

Barbèri Squarotti, G. (1994) 'Palazzeschi', in G. Barbèri Squarotti (ed.), *Storia della civiltà letteraria italiana* (History of Italian Literary Culture) Turin: UTET.

Tamburri, A. (1990) *Of Saltimbanchi and Incendiari: Aldo Palazzeschi and Avant-Gardism in Italy,* London: Associated University Press.

VALERIO FERME

Pannella, Marco (Giacinto)

b. 2 May 1930, Teramo

Politician and civil rights campaigner

For more than twenty years, Marco Pannella acted as conscience of the Italian Left, a professional outsider who was in fact part of the establishment, the joker in the political pack and in practice the leader of the anti-clerical non-Marxist liberal left. He was among the founders of the **Radical Party** as a pressure group in 1955, and its *de facto* leader when it became a parliamentary party in 1974. Pannella and the Radicals fought in favour of **divorce**, legal **abortion**, conscientious objection to conscription and decriminalization of illegal drugs. In the 1980s they fought for increased famine relief and aid to the developing world. The main weapons used were civil disobedience, hunger strikes and **referenda**. In 1994 he left the left-wing Progressive Alliance and gave ambiguous support to Silvio **Berlusconi** (bearing out Teodori's characterization of Pannella as 'schizophrenic'). He was a deputy in the Italian Parliament from 1976–92 and the European Parliament from 1979, either as a Radical or standing under the banner of the 'Club Pannella' or 'Riformatori'.

Further reading

Tedori, M. (1996) *Marco Pannella. Un eretico liberale nella crisi della Repubblica* (Marco Pannella: A Liberal Heretic in the Crisis of the Republic), Venice: Marsilio.

JAMES WALSTON

Panorama

Launched in October 1962 by publisher Arnoldo **Mondadori** in association with the American Time–Life group, *Panorama* was originally a generic monthly presenting cultural and entertainment features with little or no space dedicated to politics. Poor sales soon led the Time-Life group to abandon the project. The magazine was taken over by Arnoldo's son Giorgio, who transformed it into a weekly newsmagazine modelled on the

American *Newsweek*; by 1968 it was selling over 100,000 copies per issue. In a climate of accelerating political and social change, the magazine came to focus ever more on news and current affairs, significantly adopting the subtitle 'I fatti separati dalle opinioni' (the facts separated from opinions). As the 1970s progressed, *Panorama* became more politically active, denouncing **terrorism** and government corruption, uncovering scandals and supporting progressive liberal campaigns in favour of **divorce** and **abortion**.

Given its new direction, the magazine soon became locked into fierce competition with its rival newsmagazine, *L'Espresso* (by 1980 both magazines were selling close to 300,000 copies each). A series of financial takeovers in the late 1980s brought *Panorama* under the control of television and media magnate Silvio **Berlusconi**. During the 1990s the magazine became ever more closely identified with his political line, in the later 1990s waging an open campaign against both the **Ulivo** centre–left governments and Berlusconi's nemesis, Antonio **Di Pietro**.

GINO MOLITERNO

Paolini, Giulio

b. 5 November 1940, Genoa

Artist

Paolini briefly exhibited under the rubric of **arte povera** in the late 1960s. From his debut in 1961, his activity explored the structures and rationale of making art, working on the rudimentary materials – canvas, frame, pots of paint – rather than on representations. He then focused on the figure of the artist and the viewer. His *Young Man Looking at Lorenzo Lotto* (1967) – a photograph of the portrait – wittily reversed the position of artist and spectator. It anticipated a career-long dialogue with art history in which canonic works appeared in photographs or plaster reproductions, suggesting a circularity whereby the past is continuously reinterpreted. Often associated with **conceptual art**, Paolini's historicism displays a European if not an Italian sense of artistic language. His interests also draw him to stage and costume design.

Further reading

Bonito Oliva, A. (1984) *Dialoghi d'artista* (Artists' Dialogues) Milan: Electa.

ROBERT LUMLEY

Pareyson, Luigi

b. 4 February 1918, Piasco, Cuneo

Philosopher

Professor of philosophy at the University of Turin since 1964, Pareyson was one of the first interpreters and commentators of existentialism in Italy. From existentialism, Pareyson develops an original elaboration of an ontology of the self which permeates his most seminal work, *Estetica* (Aesthetics) (1954). In opposition to the Crocean aesthetic based on ideal intuition (see **Croce**), Pareyson proposes an aesthetic based on the actual process of 'making', of transforming matter into artefact. It is only by focusing on the different stages and moments of this process, he argues, that one can gain insight into the essence and meaning of the aesthetic object itself. This processual knowledge is arguably subjective and changes according to the agent of creation. Subjectivity is fundamental to Pareyson's philosophy and central to his discussion of interpretation which is based on the capacity of the individual to decode meanings. It follows that interpretation, and the meanings arrived at through interpretation, are plural and multifarious and forever susceptible to change. The influence of Pareyson's philosophy of interpretation is clearly visible in the works of some of his most illustrious students, among them Gianni **Vattimo** and Umberto **Eco**.

PAOLO BARTOLONI

Parise, Goffredo

b. 8 December 1929, Vicenza;
  d. 31 August 1986, Treviso

Novelist and journalist

The literary career of Goffredo Parise (born

Goffredo Bertoli) began with the 1951 publication of *Il ragazzo morto e le comete* (The Dead Boy and the Comets). Given the prevailing neorealist imperative at the time, the fairy-tale qualities of the novel marked Parise as eccentric and affiliated to no recognizable literary school. After the success of *Il prete bello* (The Handsome Priest) (1954) and the less popular *Il fidanzamento* (The Engagement) (1956), Parise published the satirical *Il padrone* (The Boss) (1965), which abandoned the provincial settings of his earlier works in order to broach the broader theme of alienation in a metropolis of the '**economic miracle**'. His journalistic writings were collected in *Cara Cina* (Dear China) (1966) and *Due, tre cose sul Vietnam* (Two or Three Things on Vietnam) (1967), while his two *Sillabari* – alphabetically arranged vignettes on love and life – also found great critical favour, the second winning the coveted Strega Prize in 1982. *L'odore del sangue* (The Smell of Blood), a study of sexual jealousy written in 1979, was published posthumously in 1997.

Further reading

Crotti, I. (ed.) (1997) *Goffredo Parise*, Florence: Olschki.

DAVE WATSON

Parliament

For practically the entire postwar period, Parliament, together with the **political parties**, has been the source of power in Italy or rather, Parliament has been the main stage where the parties' power has been exercised. The **Republic** has seen thirteen legislatures from 1948 to 1996, in addition to the original **Constituent Assembly** (1946–8) which acted as a single chamber legislature.

The Italian Parliament is composed of two chambers: the upper house or Senate is located in Palazzo Madama while the lower house, the Chamber of Deputies, is in Palazzo Montecitorio. Both houses have equal legislative powers so that bills have to be passed with the identical text by both houses before becoming law. Originally the number of deputies and senators was proportional

to the electorate, but since 1963 the number has been fixed at 630 for the Chamber and 315 for the Senate. The retiring **President of the Republic** automatically becomes a life senator, and presidents may create up to five life senators from men or women of distinction in the arts (Eduardo **De Filippo** and Eugenio **Montale**), in industry (Gianni Agnelli – see **Agnelli family**) or in politics (Giulio **Andreotti**).

Until 1975, the age of voters for the Chamber of Deputies was set at twenty-one years but was then lowered to eighteen. Deputies are elected for five years and candidates must be at least twenty-five. Originally the Chamber was elected through a system of proportional representation with preferential votes, but in 1993 it was changed to a mixed system with three-quarters of the seats allotted on a first past the post basis and one-quarter allotted proportionally with a 4 per cent threshold.

Senate electors must be twenty-five and candidates at least forty. Originally the Senate had a six-year mandate, changed to five years in 1963. In practice, the Senate electoral system has followed that of the Chamber. The Speaker of the Senate is the second highest office in the land, with the Senate Speaker taking over if the **President of the Republic** is unable to carry out his functions. Despite this, and in spite of theoretically equal powers, the Chamber has more prestige than the Senate and almost all prime ministers have come from the lower house.

The speakers of both houses are expected to show fairness but are not required to be completely above party politics; they are elected as part of the power-sharing mechanism for the distribution of posts in government and the public service. Given the lack of a strong executive, at least until 1994 – and in practice later – this has meant that parliamentary business was not controlled by government as in most other parliamentary democracies but by the Speaker together with party secretaries, parliamentary group chiefs and faction leaders.

There are two other characteristics of the Italian Parliament which distinguish it from most others and which have coloured its work. The first is that if Parliamentary groups agree, bills may be passed by a committee rather than the whole assembly; second, until 1988, most votes were secret. The first provision has resulted in a high number of sectorial and micro-sectorial laws (*leggine* or 'little laws') while at the same time, given the lack of clear leadership and parliamentary direction for most of the Republican period, major issues were rarely debated. The secret vote was intended to free parliamentarians from the iron grip of the parties, but in effect allowed secret dissenters or so-called *franchi tiratori* (sharpshooters) to block a measure or even bring down the government without having to bear any responsibility.

Debate in the chambers can often appear heated but in fact, especially from the early 1980s to the mid-1990s, the tension between government and opposition was more apparent than real since the **PCI** (later the **PDS**) supported the majority of bills passed. This was known as 'consociationalism', a term which by the mid-1990s had become an insulting epithet associated with the 'First' Republic and indicating underhand, perhaps criminal, compromises. Characteristic of the period was the high number of both government and private members' bills tabled and the high number actually passed, often with also a high number of amendments.

As part of the general fear in allowing any single individual, party or state organ to gain too much power, the Italian Parliament has never developed satisfactory ways of dealing with obstruction either in form of filibusters or quite simply tabling thousands of amendments. This has meant that government business has suffered relative to private members' business and has left successive governments with little option but to issue decree laws which need to be converted into parliamentary laws within sixty days. If this is impossible then the decree is reissued, possibly many times, and finally converted into law with a vote of confidence on the whole measure so that no discussion actually takes place. This procedure has been severely criticized since the early 1980s but has continued to be used by governments, even after the 1994 reforms.

The question of decree laws shows how inherently unchanging the Italian Parliament has been. The reforms which have taken place to both it and the parties have been brought on almost entirely by judicial action, as in the ***Mani pulite*** (Clean Hands) and **mafia** investigations, and by popular initiative, mainly through the use of **referenda**. In 1991, a referendum reduced the preference votes for the Chamber from four to one, a minor change

to the system but one which attacked the basis of clientelism and corruption. Two years later, another referendum converted the Senate electoral system to first past the post, forcing Parliament to change the Chamber as well. Rather than the single elements of the electoral engineering, voters were rejecting a whole system, and indeed 1994 did see the beginnings of a two-party system.

Parliament has made various further attempts to reform itself and the **constitution**. In 1997, a seventy-member Bicameral Commission was established with the intention of reducing the number of both houses and introducing a federal element into the Senate. However, the Commission was terminated after two years with no agreement reached on any reform.

See also: electoral systems

Further reading

Cotta, M. (1994) 'The Rise and Fall of the "Centrality" of the Italian Parliament: Transformations of the Executive–Legislative Subsystem after the Second World War', in M. Donovan (ed.), *Italy*, Aldershot: Ashgate, vol. 1.

JAMES WALSTON

Parmiggiani, Claudio

b. 1 March 1943, Luzzara, Reggio Emilia

Artist

Lecturer in painting and drawing at the Academy of Fine Arts in Bologna, Parmiggiani is also editor of the review *Tau Ma* and winner of the Premio Bolaffi in 1976. His early works made extensive use of photography, but subsequently his art took a more conceptual turn, often using sculpture to examine the process of dismantling and reinterpretation involved in cultural memory. His work typically contains a mass of references and quotations, a strategy exemplified in works such as *Lo studente di lettere* (The Student of Letters), which presents a series of interventions and 'corrections' of a painting by Rembrandt of the same title. Also typical of Parmiggiani's conceptual art are his 'de-locations', a series of installations whereby absence itself is made present and significant. Often he has accompanied his three-dimensional works with delicate preparatory drawings which have a fascination of their own.

LAURENCE SIMMONS

Partito d'Azione

The Partito d'Azione (Action Party) (1942–7) was created out of the active resistance to Fascism by non-communists, but was destroyed by the post-fascist obligation to choose between liberal and socialist allegiances. Inspired by the Giustizia e Libertà movement of Nello and Carlo Rosselli, its founders included intellectuals (**Venturi**, **Bobbio**, Lussu) and future leaders of the **PSI** (Lombardi), **PRI** (La Malfa) and **PSDI** (Parri, Prime Minister in 1945 in the single Action Party-led government). Without pre-fascist roots, the Action Party's emphasis on politics as an individual moral commitment rather than a professional career did not equip it to create a mass party: it won just seven seats in the **Constituent Assembly**. The Cold War split between the **DC** and **PCI/PSI** exacerbated conflicts in the Pd'A over the design of post-Fascist institutions: once the liberal wing had defected, the socialist rump merged with the **PSI** in 1947.

See also: Resistance

Further reading

De Luna, G. (1997) *Storia del Partito d'Azione 1942–1947* (History of the Action Party 1942–1947), Rome: Editori Riuniti.

DAVID MOSS

Pasolini, Pier Paolo

b. 5 March 1922, Bologna;
   d. 2 November 1975, Ostia, Rome

Poet, novelist, essayist, playwright,
scriptwriter and film-maker

During his troubled lifetime, Pasolini was Italy's most prolific and most controversial intellectual artist. His life and work were affected profoundly by his homosexuality and by what some have suggested was an unresolved Oedipus complex. Following his brutal murder, his works, liberated from the burden of his public persona, have become the object of renewed interest both in Italy and abroad.

Pasolini grew up in the cities of Northern Italy where his father, an army officer and a fascist, was stationed, and among the peasants of his mother's native Friuli. Encouraged by his doting mother, he began painting and writing poetry at an early age. By the time he was twenty, Pasolini had published a volume of poetry in the difficult Friulan dialect. His formal education at the University of Bologna was abruptly ended by the Second World War. Because of his sympathy for the Friulan farm labourers and, incongruously, because of the murder of his younger brother by Yugoslav communist partisans, he moved towards the left and began to read Antonio **Gramsci** and other Marxist authors.

Following the end of the war, upon receiving his degree in Italian literature in 1946, Pasolini began to teach in a junior high school. He also became increasingly involved in leftist activities, and in 1947 he joined the Italian Communist Party (**PCI**). In 1949 he was accused of corruption of minors and of obscene acts. Convicted on 28 December 1950, he was fired from his position as teacher and expelled from the party. On 8 April 1952, when Pasolini was absolved of all charges for lack of evidence, he had been living with his mother in abject poverty in the slums of Rome for over two years.

Confronted by a world which was alien to his petty bourgeois upbringing, Pasolini began a study of the inhabitants of the borgate and their dialects. The novels that resulted, *Ragazzi di vita* (The Ragazzi) (1955) and *Una vita violenta* (A Violent Life) (1959), depicted a brutal milieu that was unknown to the Italian middle class and brought Pasolini both notoriety and work. Between 1954 and 1962 he contributed to the scripts of fifteen films by directors such as Mario **Soldati** (*La Donna del fiume* (The Woman of the River), 1954), Federico **Fellini** (*Le notti di Cabiria* (The Nights of Cabiria), 1956), Mauro Bolognini (*La notte brava* (The Bold Night), 1959) and Franco Rossi (*Morte di un amico* (Death of a Friend), 1960). In 1961 Pasolini began his own career as a director with *Accattone*, the story of a two-bit Roman pimp and hustler who eventually dies in a motorcycle accident. Following this, and while continuing to write volumes of poetry, novels, tragedies in verse, essays on subjects ranging from Dante to semiotics, and translating Greek and Latin plays, he also directed twenty-one films.

The response to Pasolini's work during his life was in large measure a function of the political attitudes of his critics and of the controversy that constantly swirled around him. His earliest films, which seemed to foreshadow a rebirth of Italian **neorealism**, were welcomed initially by leftist critics. However, they began to have second thoughts when they perceived the political irrelevance of the characters and their Christian symbolism. Pasolini's notoriety reached new heights when he was arrested and given a suspended sentence for blasphemy for his *La ricotta* (The Ricotta Cheese), one of the episodes of *RoGoPag* (1963), a composite film with contributions by Roberto **Rossellini** (Ro), Jean-Luc Godard (Go), Pasolini (Pa) and Ugo Gregoretti (G). Thus the announcement that Pasolini was going to film the *Vangelo secondo Matteo* (Gospel According to Matthew) (1964) caused apprehension. However, the film, which adhered closely to the text of the Bible, was an international success praised, with few exceptions, by Catholic and Marxist critics alike.

In Pasolini's next film, *Uccellacci e uccellini* (Hawks and Sparrows) (1966), a talking crow attempts to educate politically a man (**Totò**) and his son (Ninetto Davoli) and is eaten by them for his troubles. This frequently funny and always intellectual commentary on the passing of faith in grandiose ideological solutions to the problems of humanity contains, amongst other things, a highly entertaining disquisition on the semiotics of the languages of birds.

In the late 1960s, Pasolini raised his intellectual indictment of capitalism to new levels of abstraction with *Teorema* (1968), in which a strangely Christ-like figure seduces and destroys the members of a rich bourgeois family. During the same period he reinvented prehistory in *Edipo Re* (Oedipus Rex) (1967) and *Medea* (1969). These two trends came together in a little-known, difficult but fascinating film called *Porcile* (Pigsty) (1969) that

favourably compares cannibalism and bestiality to capitalism. However, while the director received the plaudits of progressive critics, he alienated the general public.

Unlike so many other left-wing intellectuals of the time, Pasolini regarded the 1968 student uprisings (see **student movement**) as little more than temper tantrums by spoiled brats. At the same time he began to question the political validity of avantgarde cinema as a means of reaching the masses. Thus he turned away from his earlier difficult films in favour of a more popular and accessible cinema based on three narrative masterpieces. In these films, *Decameron* (1971), *I racconti di Canterbury* (Canterbury Tales) (1972) and *Il fiore delle mille e una notte* (Arabian Nights) (1974), Pasolini once again recreated the past by analogy, and once again he intended it to be a metaphor for the present. As he had already done on several occasions, in these films Pasolini foregrounds his favourite weapon, sex, the more unconventional the better, in his attack on what he considered to be the cornerstone of bourgeois capitalism, the family. According to some, these films, which Pasolini collectively called his 'Trilogy of Life', revealed a new optimism on his part. According to others, they barely concealed a profound pessimism which found its fullest manifestation in his last film, *Salò o le 120 giornate di Sodoma* (Salò) (1975). This very controversial film is loosely based on De Sade's novel. It is set in Salò, the Northern Italian town on Lake Garda where Nazi Germany established the Fascist republic after Mussolini was deposed in 1943. As in all his historical films, Pasolini depicted the past to comment on the present, a present which he had come to consider intolerable. *Salò* depicts the gruesome, graphic torture and murder of a number of young persons by representatives of the establishment. It is an extremely disturbing, almost unwatchable work that has been the object of legal proceedings for obscenity in Italy, the United States and Australia.

Pasolini's violent murder in 1975 has continued to generate controversy in spite of the confession of a young Roman hustler who was charged and subsequently imprisoned for the crime. Because a number of odd features of the crime were never resolved, rumours that Pasolini may have been the victim of a right-wing conspiracy have continued to circulate since his death and have resulted in several books and films.

See also: literature in dialect

Further reading

Greene, N. (1990) *Pier Paolo Pasolini: Cinema as Heresy*, Princeton, NJ: Princeton University Press (a very intelligent and readable study of Pasolini's films).

Pasolini, P.P. (1988) *Heretical Empiricism*, trans. B. Lawton and L.K. Barnett, ed. L.K. Barnett, Bloomington, IN: Indiana University Press (the only English language translation of Pasolini's major essays on language, literature and film).

Schwartz, B.D. (1992) *Pasolini Requiem*, New York: Random House (this fascinating biography of Pasolini reads like a mystery novel).

Siciliano, E. (1982) *Pasolini: A Biography*, trans. J. Shepley, New York: Random House (for over a decade this absorbing, impressionistic work was the definitive biography of Pasolini).

BEN LAWTON

pasta

Pasta, or more precisely in Italian *pasta alimentare*, is the generic modern term, by now international and widely used, to indicate a range of 'pasta' types (spaghetti, lasagne, tagliatelle, rigatoni, bucatini and so on). The origin of *pasta* appears uncertain. Some Etruscan mural paintings show tools that can be connected to pasta making, but there is little evidence of, or reference to, pasta eating among the Romans. However, a description of *lagana* found in *De re coquinaria* (The Art of Cooking) (230 AD) by Celius Apicius, suggests a close similarity with modern lasagne. It has also been argued that the spread of pasta in Italy could be linked to the Arabs, who conquered Sicily in 827 (Robb, 1996: 76–7). On the other hand, it has been shown that noodles, the Italian tagliatelle, were widely used in China from the eleventh century onwards, and Marco Polo's *Il Milione* (1298) reports the existence in China at that time of a food similar to lasagne. The obvious conclusion would be that both the Chinese and the Italian civilizations created a product which in time evolved and is by now the modern pasta.

Whatever its origins, pasta has long been a staple food throughout the peninsula and it has remained the key and most characteristic element of the Italian diet. Furthermore, Italian pasta has gained international renown and is an extremely successful export product (around 1,700 billion lire annually). A contribution to the diffusion of pasta has certainly been made by Italian emigrants who have taken their culinary traditions – among which a love of pasta – to their host countries. Pasta thus came to be widely imitated and manufactured outside Italy, though not always successfully because, according to the experts, too often the wheat varieties used are not appropriate so that the consistency of the pasta obtained is not comparable with that made in Italy.

Until the invention of pasta-making machines in the first decade of the nineteenth century, pasta was made by hand, at home, by skilled women. The homemade or handcrafted varieties of *pasta fresca* (fresh pasta) are made with a type of soft wheat semolina, while industrially manufactured pasta (which involves a complex series of operations, for example, a lengthy drying procedure) predominantly uses durum wheat semolina to obtain *pasta secca*.

The cooking of pasta does not require special skills. It needs boiling water – approximately 1 litre per 100 gr of pasta – and when the water reaches its boiling point salt must be added, before the pasta is also added two minutes later. Stirring gently while cooking helps to prevent the pasta from sticking together. Cooking times vary, depending on the pasta type; tasting is probably the wisest way to satisfy personal preferences. Overcooking pasta is a major culinary (and cultural) heresy for Italians; the expression *al dente* identifies the ideal consistency of the pasta in whatever recipe is presented. After being cooked, the pasta must be carefully drained. *Pastasciutta* (the term derives from the elimination of all water) is a general label covering dishes of pasta cooked as described above and then seasoned with various sauces. Widely popular and always in demand, both in the motherland and abroad, are dishes such as *pasta alla bolognese*, *pasta alla marinara*, *penne all'arrabbiata* and *pasta all'amatriciana*, all of which originated in the rich traditions of **regional cooking.**

Lasagne deserves its own special attention and, as already mentioned, is a very old variety of pasta, which can be homemade using light flour and eggs. Of course there are also excellent manufactured lasagne, which only require a longer amount of time in boiling water. Cut into large rectangular strips, after boiling and draining at the *al dente* stage, they are placed in buttered oven dishes, covered with sauces and layers of other ingredients such as meat balls and mozzarella cheese and are then baked and eaten hot, after a settling period of approximately ten minutes. The recipes for lasagna are numerous and may vary from region to region. There is an original but hardly known variety created for the Bourbon royal family, in eighteenth-century Naples, which uses a bechamel sauce (of French ancestry), egg yolks and artichoke hearts. However, in the North, lasagna sauces almost always include meat.

There exist literally hundreds of dishes based on pasta, each region having its own specialities. New recipes are also constantly being created and, at times, new fashions dictate contingent rules (for example, the trend for fresh pasta dishes flavoured with cream-based sauces combined with other ingredients, or the craze for old recipes of rural ancestry). However, the witty remark that the most conspicuous sign of Italy's unification was not language, but the ceremony taking place every day when in all the kitchens of the peninsula, around midday, pasta is plunged into the boiling water, probably reveals more than a touch of truth about the Italian identity.

Classic recipes for pasta dishes are known to travel across mountains and oceans and have acquired worldwide approval. This phenomenon, however, conceals potential dangers: the genuine recipe is filtered through the interpretation of its cooks, who may add or subtract some ingredients and make the kind of changes that are likely to please his/her clients, with the result that the same name is given to a different dish. An example of this phenomenon is the amount of meat used in *pasta alla bolognese*. While in the original dish the meat in the sauce (and the sauce on the pasta) are used in a discrete, almost frugal, manner, outside Italy a plate of *spaghetti alla bolognese* implies a towering layer of a thick meaty sauce, surely nutritious but quite different in the balance of flavours when compared with the same dish on Italian soil.

Further reading

Cattaneo-Jarrat, E. and Jarrat, V. (1969) *230 modi di cucinare la pasta* (230 Ways of Cooking Pasta), Milan: Mondadori (see in particular the introduction by Italian writer and journalist Paolo Monelli).

de' Medici Strutti, L. (1993) *Pasta*, Sydney: RD Press.

Penta de Peppo, M. (1996) *La nuova cucina mediterranea* (The New Mediterranean Cooking), Rome: Newton & Compton Editori.

Piccinardi, A. (1993) *Dizionario di Gastronomia* (Dictionary of Gastronomy), Milan: Rizzoli.

Robb, P. (1996) *Midnight in Sicily*, Sydney: Duffy & Snellgrove (for a number of insights into pasta and Italian food in general).

MARIELLA TOTARO GENEVOIS

patron saints

Patron saints protect places, professions and people in every kind of physical and spiritual condition, according to a complex but rarely exclusive division of spiritual labour. Italy has three national patron saints (Bernardino of Siena, Catherine of Siena and Francis of Assisi) and has produced more saints (eighty-two) than any other nation. Best-known among those canonized since 1945 is Santa Maria Goretti, a twelve-year-old peasant girl murdered during a rape attempt in 1902, whose piety provided a model for many postwar upbringings. In cultural response to African immigration, mayor Leoluca Orlando has placed Palermo under the extra protection of Sicily's only black saint, Saint Benedict the Moor, patron saint of American blacks and now also joint guardian of the city with Santa Rosalia.

Most patron saints have large and assorted caseloads. The especially popular Saint Anthony of Padua is the patron saint of barren women, lost articles, political prisoners, the shipwrecked, the starving and travellers. Saint Mark, who protects Venice, watches over lawyers, notaries, prisoners and glaziers and provides defence against impenitence and scrofulous diseases. Saints are generally preferred to the Virgin Mary and Christ as community protectors, but the popularity of individual saints varies from region to region. In the continental South, Nicholas of Bari and Rocco are the most favoured: Joseph ranks a lowly nineteenth there, but emerges as the top choice in Sicily. Sanctuaries, statues and relics continue to attract devotees. A spectacular example is the blood alleged to have come from Saint Januarius, patron of Naples, which liquefies on three commemorative occasions each year in the presence of eager spectators.

The celebration of the local patron saint provides an annual focus for community identity and collaboration: in the South many saints' days have been moved to summer when emigrants can return on holiday and participate. Simultaneous celebrations are often organized by concentrations of emigrés abroad. Since patron saints intercede with Mary, Christ and God on behalf of their human supplicants, they provide a spiritual model for relations between human patrons and clients. Like earthly patrons, they are expected to perform: those who fail to respond to prayers, entreaties and gifts may be replaced without compunction.

Further reading

Carroll, M.P. (1992) *Madonnas that Maim: Popular Catholicism in Italy since the Fifteenth Century,* London: Johns Hopkins Press.

Galasso, G. (1982) *L'altra Europa* (The Other Europe), Milan: A. Mondadori (religious practice and belief in Southern Italy).

Orsi, R.A. (1985) *The Madonna of 115th Street: Faith and Community in Italian Harlem, 1850–1950,* New Haven, CN: Yale University Press.

Tentori, T. (1976) 'An Italian Religious Feast: The Fujenti Rites of the Madonna dell'Arco, Naples', *Cultures* 3 (1): 117–40.

DAVID MOSS

Patroni Griffi, Giuseppe

b. 27 February 1921, Naples

Director and playwright

As playwright, Patroni Griffi's work ranges from wordy pedestrian realism to the broad vivacity of the Neapolitan comic tradition. Artistic director of Rome's Teatro Eliseo since 1978, Patroni-Griffi is best known as a meticulous theatrical director, balancing close attention to text, design and performance. He has mounted prestigious works of high literary calibre, both within and outside the Italian tradition, by such playwrights as Goldoni, Brecht, Alfieri, T.S. Eliot, Chekhov, Jean-Paul Sartre and Alberto **Moravia**. His revival of plays by fellow Neapolitan Raffaele Viviani, and his staging of Pirandello's metatheatrical trilogy, using the same actors and exercising a strong and consistent directorial vision, have especially served to establish his reputation. His cinematic direction of half a dozen films, including film versions of two of his own plays, has been more sporadic and uneven in quality.

WILLIAM VAN WATSON

Pavarotti, Luciano

b. 12 October 1935, Modena

Tenor

Pavarotti won the international competition at the Teatro Reggio Emilia in 1961 and made his debut as Rodolfo there in the same year. His international career developed swiftly, with operatic performances at Covent Garden in 1963 and tours of Australia (1965) and the USA (1968). Acclaimed for his robust, energetic style, he became particularly identified at this time with the roles of Edgardo, Tonio (The Daughter of the Regiment), Cavaradossi and Arturo (*I puritani* (The Puritans)), and was often partnered with Joan Sutherland. Pavarotti's prominent international reputation increased as a result of his involvement in Italy's 1990 World Cup festivities. Together with José Carreras and Placido Domingo, he appeared in a gala concert that was billed as 'The Three Tenors', and his performance of Puccini's *Nessun dorma* (None Shall Sleep) was adopted as the official anthem of the tournament. His showmanship and flair ensure his continued popular appeal, but musical connoisseurs may prefer, perhaps, to remember him by his notable recordings of the 1960s and 1970s.

Further reading

Kesting, J. (1996) *Luciano Pavarotti: The Myth of the Tenor*, trans. S. Hay, Boston: Northeastern University Press (an examination of the mass marketing of the Pavarotti 'phenomenon').

Pavarotti, L. and Wright, W. (1995) *Pavarotti: My World*, London: Crown Publications (Pavarotti's own story).

JOHN KERSEY

Pavese, Cesare

b. 9 September 1908, Santo Stefano Belbo; d. 27 August 1950, Turin

Novelist, poet, translator and essayist

One of the century's most prolific authors, Cesare Pavese influenced subsequent generations of writers even though his activity as a writer was cut short by suicide. Early in his life, he read extensively from the classics and from contemporary authors, developing an intense interest in American film and literature. Between 1930 and 1943, Pavese translated novels by Anderson, Faulkner, Lewis, Melville, Stein, Joyce, Dickens, Defoe and others, and was one of the first Italian intellectuals, with Elio **Vittorini**, to appreciate the influence of American culture in Italy. In 1936, while Pavese was confined to Brancaleone Calabro for allegedly helping the communist underground, *Lavorare stanca* (Hard Labour) was published, a collection of poems whose narrative structure was influenced by Walt Whitman's free verse. During the war Pavese became an editor for **Einaudi** and in 1941 published his first novel, *Paesi tuoi* (The Harvesters), a book considered to be an early example of literary **neorealism**. Although sym-

pathetic to the cause of the **Resistance**, Pavese did not join the partisans, an omission that haunted him after the war. Instead, he wrote a number of short stories that were published in the 1946 collection *Feria d'agosto* (Summer Storm) and, posthumously, in *Notte di festa* (Festival Night).

At the end of the war, Pavese joined the Italian Communist Party (**PCI**) and returned to work for Einaudi where, as one of the chief editors, he introduced the work of Carl Jung and Károlyi Kerényi on ethnography to the Italian public, and helped promote the writing of Italo **Calvino** and Beppe **Fenoglio**. Between 1945 and 1950 Pavese wrote at a feverish pace: among the books that Einaudi published in those years are *Il Compagno* (The Comrade), Pavese's only outspokenly political work, and *La casa in collina* (The House on the Hill), the anguished reflections of an intellectual's plight during the Resistance which is frequently considered his best novel. Yet, it was only with *La luna e i falò* (The Moon and the Bonfires), published a few months before his death, that Pavese finally achieved both critical acclaim and financial success. The end of his short-lived relationship with American actress Constance Dowling – the last in a long list of amorous failures – and the subsequent bout of chronic depression led Pavese to commit suicide in August of 1950. After his death, Einaudi continued to publish Pavese's manuscripts. The most important was the diary *Il mestiere di vivere: 1935–1950* (The Burning Brand: Diaries 1935–1950), which remains the clearest documentation of a generation's struggle to reconcile its aversion to fascism with its populist aspirations as the country returned to democracy in the postwar years.

Further reading

Lajolo, D. (1983) *An Absurd Vice*, trans. M. Pietralunga and M. Pietralunga, New York: New Directions (a somewhat idealized biography that includes a useful bibliography of Pavese's work).

O'Healy, A. (1988) *Cesare Pavese*, Boston: Twayne Publishers (a general introduction to the life and works of Pavese).

Pavese, C. (1990) *The Moon and the Bonfires*, trans. D. Walder, Milton Keynes: Open University Press (most recent translation of what is often regarded as his most accomplished novel).

—— (1979) *Hard Labor*, trans. W. Arrowsmith, New York: Ecco Press (Pavese's early collection of poetry which is still considered among his highest achievements, especially in English-speaking countries).

—— (1961) *The Burning Brand: Diaries 1935–1950*, trans. A.E. Murah, New York: Walker.

VALERIO FERME

Pazienza, Andrea

b. 23 May 1956, San Benedetto del Tronto (Ascoli Piceno); d. 16 June 1988, Montepulciano

Cartoonist, visual artist

A veritable legend among Italian cartoonists, Pazienza often claimed to have begun drawing at the age of eighteen months. What is certain is that, in the early 1970s, while still in high school in Pescara, he participated in various artistic activities and exhibited numerous paintings and drawings with the *Convergenze* collective. In 1974 he enrolled in the DAMS (School of Art, Music, Spectacle and Dance) at the University of Bologna, soon becoming involved in the student movement which would explode into the tragic events of 1977 (see **Radio Alice**).

In 1977, together with fellow cartoonists Filippo Scozzari, Stefano Tamburini and Tanino Liberatore, he initiated the magazine *Cannibale* whilst having his first of his *Le straordinarie avventure di Pentothal* (The Extraordinary Adventures of Pentothal) published in the prestigious *Alter-Alter* (see **Linus**). In 1978 he began collaborating on the satirical journal, *Il Male*, and by the time it had folded in 1981 Pazienza had already co-founded a new illustrated magazine, *Frigidaire*, in whose pages the wicked, sharp-nosed Zanardi first made his appearance before spreading to the pages of *Alter-Alter* and *Comic Art*. He had also designed numerous album covers and film posters, including a memorable poster for **Fellini**'s *La città delle donne* (The City of Women).

In 1985 he moved to the small Sienese town of Montepulciano and a year later married Marina Comandini. From 1986 onwards, as well as continuing many of his previous collaborations, he also contributed to **Tango**, the new satirical supplement of the **PCI** daily, *L'Unità*, as well as designing the *Agenda Verde* for the ecological group *Legambiente* (see **environmental movement**) and posters for *Amnesty International*.

However in June 1988, at his home at Montepulciano, a heroin overdose would give the lie to what had been one of his favourite and often-repeated maxims: 'La pazienza ha un limite; Pazienza no!' (Patience has a limit but not Pazienza).

Following his untimely death at the age of only thirty-two, the town of Cremona instituted the Centro Fumetti Andrea Pazienza (Andrea Pazienza Centre for Comic Art) to commemorate his art and memory, and in 1997 Bologna hosted a huge retrospective of his work, much of which has now been made available on CD ROM.

Further reading

Benvenuto, M. (ed.) (1997) *Andrea Pazienza: l'antologia illimitata* (Andrea Pazienza: the Unlimited Anthology), CD ROM, Profile Multimedia and Ponderosa Arte (a digital multimedia journey through his life and works; includes two complete versions of *Le straordinarie avventure di Pentothal and Gli ultimi gioni di Pompeo*).

Pazienza, A. (1992) *Sturiellet* (Short Stories), Montepulciano: Editori del Grifo/La Nuova Mongolfiera (a good collection of some of Pazienza's best shorter pieces).

GINO MOLITERNO

Pazzi, Roberto

b. 18 August 1946, Ameglia, La Spezia

Professor, poet and novelist

A native of Liguria, Roberto Pazzi has elected to live and work in Ferrara. After several collections of poetry, in 1985 he published his first novel *Cercando l'imperatore* (Searching for the Emperor), which was critically acclaimed both in Italy and abroad and received the prestigious Campiello Prize. There have followed a number of other novels, including

La principessa e il drago (The Princess and the Dragon) (1986), *La malattia del tempo* (The Illness of Time) (1987), *La stanza sull'acqua* (The Room on the Water) (1991) and *Incerti di viaggio* (The Hazards of Travelling) (1996). Pazzi's fiction is characterized by an evocative treatment of time whereby the historical past is suspended in an atemporal present, thus provoking loss and disruption of both collective and individual memory. While successfully continuing to write poetry and fiction, Pazzi also contributes to a number of magazines and newspapers.

FRANCESCA PARMEGGIAN

PCI

The PCI (Partito Comunista Italiano, or Italian Communist Party) was founded in 1921 through secession from the Socialist Party. Outlawed by the Fascist regime in 1926, it played the leading role in the **Resistance** in 1943–5 and became the largest communist party outside the Soviet bloc and China by the mid-1970s. In 1991, still a major force in Italian politics, it dissolved itself. The Party's history shows many paradoxical features. It declared national redemption as its mission, although its most loyal following was concentrated in a few regions of central and north-central Italy; it pursued the dictatorship of the proletariat, but found more members and voters in the middle classes than among industrial and agricultural workers; it was committed to defending the weak and the powerless, but attracted greater support in the rich heartlands of the **Third Italy** than in the poor regions of the South; and it proclaimed the value of democracy while remaining highly undemocratic in its internal organization and hostile to mass culture. Even these idiosyncrasies, however, did not enable it to find the distinctively 'Italian route to socialism' sought by its most influential postwar leader, Palmiro **Togliatti**. Nevertheless, the Party *did* play an essential role in establishing Italy's postwar democracy in the late 1940s, in defending it against **terrorism** in the 1970s and, generally, in promoting the ideals of social justice and equality.

Inventing the new party and the new Italy, 1944–7

Returning to Italy from Moscow in 1944, **Togliatti** declared that the PCI must become a mass democratic party rather than the semi-clandestine revolutionary sect created by Leninist ideology and Fascist persecution. Sixty thousand sections and factory cells were established, and Party membership rapidly rose to almost two million. Collaboration with Catholic and socialist leaders during the Resistance was extended into postwar government coalitions with the **DC** and **PSI**. In pursuit of national reconstruction and Party legitimacy, Togliatti was prepared to sacrifice class interests and communist ideals to the maintenance of government unity. His strategy, for which he claimed the intellectual authority of party founder, Antonio **Gramsci**, enabled Italy to replace the monarchy with the **Republic**, adopt a new **constitution** and deal with the Fascist legacy without paralysing conflict. But for many Party faithful, the PCI made too many concessions to the Church and conservative interests; and radical members continued to believe that the Party's popularity and Resistance armoury could – and should – have been used to force through a social revolution. In 1947, however, under Cold War pressures, the PCI was first ousted from government and then defeated in the 1948 elections. Tainted by association with Soviet communism, the Party was never again regarded as a legitimate partner in power.

The long march through the institutions, 1948–79

Defeat encouraged the PCI to expand its presence in Italian society. Party influence was spread through a daily newspaper (**L'Unità**), a journal (**Rinascita**) and a publishing house (Editori Riuniti), by strong ties with **trade unions** (the CGIL), the major women's organization (**UDI**) and **co-operatives** (National League of Co-operatives), by the setting up and maintenance of intellectual centres (Gramsci Institutes) and recreational associations (**ARCI**) and by annual festivals (**Festa dell'Unità**). These cultural networks remained firmly under the control of the PCI leadership (see **Amendola**; **Berlinguer**; **Ingrao**; **Napolitano**; **Pajetta**), enabling the Party to increase its vote at each election between 1948 and 1976 and thus to play an essential role in negotiating government legislation. Despite the emergence of a hostile **extraparliamentary Left** in 1968–9 and the internal dissent of *il manifesto*, the Party actually gained from the accompanying prolonged wave of industrial, social and cultural conflict. In 1975 the PCI came to power in every major Italian city, and in the national elections of 1976, one in three Italians voted communist. Profiting from widespread dissatisfaction with scandal-ridden DC governments incapable of reforming Italy's archaic institutions, the PCI also benefited from its '**historic compromise**' proposal, from its willingness to acknowledge middle-class and even employer interests and by its gradual detachment from Soviet influence. However, the Party's seemingly unstoppable advance towards power went no further, culminating simply in support for the 'national solidarity' DC-government of 1977–9.

Several factors account for the check. The need to combat high inflation and **terrorism** associated the Party with unpopular conservative policies; municipal responsibilities forced inexperienced local Party leaders to neglect politics in favour of administration; implementing the 'historic compromise' alienated many local branches from national policy; and the murder of Aldo **Moro** by the **Red Brigades** in 1978 removed the Party's leading DC interlocutor. In 1979, the PCI abandoned the pursuit of an alliance with the DC and openly criticized the Soviet invasion of Afghanistan, thus definitively eliminating – without obvious replacements – the Party's national and international policy co-ordinates.

Wandering in the wilderness, 1980–91

In the 1980s, the organization and ideology which had earlier been so effective in mobilizing support for the PCI proved a serious liability. The Party's autocratic structure and class rhetoric made it unattractive to Greens (see **Verdi**), feminists or civil libertarians; its lingering suspicion of 'American' mass culture denied it much appeal to youth or the consumption-oriented middle classes, who

preferred the **PSI** under **Craxi**; its lasting fondness for state control put it out of step with enthusiasms for 'market forces' and resurgent European integration; and the decline of Italy's industrial working-class and trade union movement drained a traditional reservoir of support. Party membership not only fell by 20 per cent between 1977 and 1989, but it also aged rapidly: by 1990, the average age of a PCI member was fifty-two, and one in four members was a pensioner. The Party's electoral support fell as inexorably in the 1980s as it had risen in earlier decades, signalling a policy vacuum and a loss of any clear political identity or social vision for the Left. Claims to stand for a new public morality failed to impress voters or to halt the spread of corruption. Even before communism collapsed on a global scale after 1989, therefore, the last leader of the PCI, Achille **Occhetto**, had determined to transform its name, organization and ideology. Although the PCI was still easily the second largest party and was supported by one in four Italians, Occhetto pushed through his proposal to dissolve it at the Party's Twentieth Congress in 1991. A small minority created a new party to preserve the name and symbol of communism, but the larger successor organization, the Democratic Party of the Left (**PDS**), used the leaders, organization and support which it had inherited from the PCI to win power in 1996 as the leading force in the **Ulivo** coalition of centre–left parties.

Further reading

Bull, M. (1991) 'Whatever Happened to Italian Communism? Explaining the Dissolution of the Largest Communist Party in the West', *West European Politics* 14 (4): 96–120.

Hellman, S. (1996) 'Italian Communism in the First Republic', in S. Gundle and S. Parker (eds), *The New Italian Republic: From the Fall of the Berlin Wall to Berlusconi*, London: Routledge (clear summary of changing PCI strategies and the issues they raised).

Kertzer, D. (1980) *Comrades and Christians: Religion and Political Struggle in Communist Italy*, Cambridge: Cambridge University Press (anthropological description of communism and Catholicism in working-class Bologna).

Sassoon, D. (1992) 'The Rise and Fall of West

European Communism 1939–48', *Contemporary European History* 1 (2): 139–69 (examines the impact of the Cold War on the development of communism, comparing Italian and other European experiences).

DAVID MOSS

PDS

A transitional post-communist party, the PDS (Partito Democratico della Sinistra, or Democratic Party of the Left) inherited most of the leaders, members and political culture of the **PCI** but was destined to give way to a broader left-wing formation less constrained by the PCI inheritance.

After a fifteen-month spell as *La cosa* (The Thing), in which the name, ideology and structure of the new party were widely debated at the grassroots, the PDS was formally established in February 1991. Achille **Occhetto** was elected leader but a significant minority of true believers headed by Armando Cossutta, who refused to jettison communism, left to form **Rifondazione Comunista**. Uncertainty about the PDS programme, open conflict between its factions and diminished activism on the part of its falling, if still substantial, membership of 700,000 led to severe punishment at the national elections in 1992: the party achieved only 17 per cent of the vote, as against the 26 per cent won by its predecessor in 1987. Nonetheless, the PDS provided three ministers in the new **Ciampi** government, although they resigned after three days when the Chamber of Deputies (see **Parliament**) refused to waive the parliamentary immunity of the **PSI** leader, Bettino **Craxi**, under investigation for corruption on a grand scale. Despite its success in getting many of its candidates elected mayors at the local elections of 1993, the coalition in which the PDS was the dominant member was decisively defeated by the **Polo della Libertà**, headed by Silvio **Berlusconi**, in the national elections of 1994. Achille Occhetto resigned, to be replaced by Massimo **D'Alema** who narrowly defeated Walter **Veltroni** for the position of general secretary.

In the next elections in 1996, D'Alema paid much greater attention to the arts of coalition building and tactical voting, assembling a thirteen-party formation (named **l'Ulivo** or Olive Tree) around the PDS. His skill paid off in an unexpectedly decisive victory, and the PDS became the leading party in the **Prodi** government. However, the party failed to attract new voters, the electorate being largely put off by the party's evident continuity in personnel and style with its communist past. At the Second Congress in February 1997, therefore, D'Alema proposed a radical solution: that the PDS, along with its smaller partners under the Olive Tree, dissolve itself into an inclusive social democratic formation. D'Alema's proposal carried the day, and consequently in February 1998 the PDS was transformed into a broad grouping of former communists and socialists called the Democratici di Sinistra (the Left Democratic Party). In homage to this unity, a pink rose replaced the hammer and sickle in the emblem of the new group.

Further reading

Baccetti, C. (1997) *Il Pds*, Bologna: Il Mulino.

Bull, M.J. (1996) 'The Reconstitution of the Political Left in Italy: Demise, Renewal, Realignment and Defeat', in R. Gillespie (ed.), *Mediterranean Politics*, vol. 2, London: Pinter.

Gundle, S. and Parker, S. (eds) (1996) *The New Italian Republic: From the Fall of Communism to the Rise of Berlusconi*, London: Routledge.

Kertzer, D. (1996) *Politics and Symbols: The Italian Communist Party and the Fall of Communism*, New Haven, CN: Yale University Press.

DAVID MOSS

peasants

At the time of Italian unification in 1860–1, **agriculture** was the predominant form of economic activity in the peninsula, with 90 per cent of the population engaged in it. For post-1860 Liberal Italy, the peasantry, both because of its allegiance to a Catholic church opposed to unification and its rootedness in traditional communitarian ways, represented the main impediment to forming a strong national identification, and the potential reserve army of clerical reaction and anarchistic revolutionism. Fascist policy sought to 'nationalize' the peasants through propaganda, while keeping them on the land or settling them in the colonies. In the 1943–5 **Resistance**, most peasants in the centre and north of Italy concentrated on survival, limiting their active participation to withholding food from enforced collections and supplying the black market, on which most of the urban population came to depend.

In 1945, peasants still comprised almost half the working population of the country. Their relationship to the land was highly differentiated geographically: in the northwest, parts of the northeast, and the Marches, there were mainly small family farms, only marginally viable, and tenanted farms. In Tuscany, Veneto and parts of Puglia, most were sharecroppers; in the Po Valley, and in the South they were generally agricultural labourers, usually landless. The wartime experience of survival strategies, and the long tradition of management of family resources by small farmers and sharecroppers, provided an apprenticeship in microeconomic management which enabled a critical proportion of the sharecroppers and small proprietors of the central and northern regions to make the transition, during the **economic miracle**, to participation as independent producers in small and medium-sized **industry**, particularly in the 'industrial districts' of the **Third Italy**. The younger generation of peasants moved directly into paid employment in such industry, the women often as home-workers, while maintaining their links with the family holding.

In the South, however, where agricultural production in 1945 was still concentrated upon the great estates, unemployment often approached 40 per cent and the only solution for many was **emigration**. In the absence of the culture, infrastructures and internal market needed for industrialization there was little development of entrepreneurial attitudes. From 1944, repeated mass occupations of uncultivated lands prompted postwar governments to introduce piecemeal agrarian reforms, followed in 1950 by the **Cassa per il Mezzogiorno** (Southern Development Fund). The aim was to create a class of independent, prosperous peasant farmers with access to roads, irrigation works and a clean water supply, but the Cassa was essentially a paternalistic technocratic organization inspired by a universal model of large-scale development with little reference to the local conditions and cultures of the peasantry.

This attempt, over three decades, to rescue the South from economic underdevelopment largely failed. There was a mass exodus of adults of working age to northern industry, and, especially after the creation of the EEC in 1957, also to other countries in Europe. Agricultural jobs fell by 60 per cent, in spite of a doubling of agricultural production due to improved technology and applied crop science. The relative failure of the attempt to implant industry and enterprise emerges clearly from the disparity between the increase in new industrial jobs: two million in the North as against only 370,000 in the South. The relocation of millions of peasant migrants to the bleak suburbs of the northern cities, where they competed for unskilled work in factories and sweatshops, left the South severely drained of enterprise and easy prey to corruption and organized crime. More significant still, however, was the corresponding scissorseffect in relation to small businesses: while in the North during this quarter-century, artisan family firms employing fewer than ten people rose by 25 per cent, in the South they fell by 20 per cent. While the number of employees in these small and medium manufacturing firms rose by 70 per cent in the centre and North, in the South there was no increase at all, clearly signalling the inability of the southern economy and its workforce to respond to the market challenges of an unprecedented period of rising demand.

A particularly significant feature of this development was the absence of any large-scale internal migration from the South to the 'Third Italy', compared with the massive flow of almost three million unskilled southerners to the established factories of the 'industrial triangle' in the northwest by 1963. The recruits to the small and medium-sized industries of the Third Italy came from urban hinterlands where, for generations, extended peasant family farms had long had economic links with the towns through piecework done at home and local seasonal employment. Generations of low and discontinuous wages, compensated by the capacity to survive by collective effort and coupled with comparable generations of flexible manual skills and human resources management within the family productive unit, were the basis for a self-propelling advance into industrial forms of production. Such peasant families were already an integral part of the 'moral' as well as the material economy of the town-dwellers with whom they shared the industrial district, which thus avoided the additional external social and administrative costs of taking in large numbers of migrants from other parts of Italy.

The strong local political cultures of these areas also supported the spread of the micro-capitalism of the family enterprise though the micro-capitalists, for their part, continued to vote, even at the height of the Cold War, for those who proclaimed anti-capitalist doctrines at election times. The economic strength of these industrial districts lay in the flexibility which stemmed directly from the structural characteristics of the family firm, which could set wages and conditions without reference to national norms laid down by authority or in collective bargaining, and invest in new technology from high rates of saving involving sacrifices of living standards. In the period of the 'economic miracle' over 40 per cent of the corporate income of small and medium-sized enterprises was reinvested.

The far less positive counterpart to the real prosperity attained within networks of strong local identity by millions of Italian peasants of the North and centre, who had emerged from a poverty-stricken agriculture only a few years earlier, was the much stonier path to participation in the benefits of industrialization that southern peasants had to tread, and the continuing relative deprivation of the South today.

Further reading

Bell, R.M. (1979) *Fate and Honor, Family and Village: Demographic and Cultural Change in Rural Italy since 1800*, Chicago: University Of Chicago Press.

Holmes, D.R. (1989) *Cultural Disenchantments: Worker Peasantries in Northeast Italy*, Princeton, NJ: Princeton University Press.

Kertzer, D.I. (1984) *Family Life in Central Italy, 1880–1910: Sharecropping, Wage Labour and Coresidence*, New Brunswick, NJ: Rutgers University Press.

Pitkin, D.S. (1985) *The House that Giacomo built: The History of an Italian Family 1898–1978*, Cambridge: Cambridge University Press.

Pratt, J. (1994) *The Rationality of Rural Life: Economic and Cultural Change in Tuscany*, Amsterdam: Harwood Academic Publishers.

ROGER ABSALOM

Penna, Sandro

b. 12 June 1906, Perugia; d. 23 January 1977, Rome

Poet

After a restless youth and a short period spent in Milan during which he held a series of different jobs (accountant, bookstore sales clerk, proofreader) Penna moved to Rome, where he was to spend most of his life. His friendship with the poet Umberto **Saba**, and the success of his first book of poetry helped him begin collaboration with several literary journals, such as *Corrente, Letteratura, Frontespizio, L'Ambrosiano, Primato, Poesia, La Rassegna d'Italia* and *Paragone*.

Penna's first poetry collection, *Poesie* (1938), is the only work which predates the Second World War, even though most of his poems could be qualified as 'atemporal'. The collection shows an existential slant, a physicality and an authenticity that immediately set it apart from, and go beyond, the anti-rhetorical tendencies of the coeval poetics of *ermetismo* (hermetism), characterized instead by an expressive research for the essential and the absolute, for the *poesia pura* (pure poetry). It would be incorrect, however, to affirm that Penna is completely extraneous to the hermetic experience. The apparent simplicity and the general descriptive and narrative tone of his poetry shows the direct influence of Umberto Saba, especially for its anti-modernism, for its taste and preference of traditional words and its regular verse structure. But Penna's poems sometimes present also a bold allusivity and rapid sequences of images which may well recall those of the hermetic poetics. The successful combination of these two stylistic and formal aspects, together with a thematic which is inspired significantly by the poet's homosexuality, is what gives Penna's poetry its originality and poignancy. His writing is not tainted by any superfluous intellectualism, and it is simplified to the extreme. It aims at seizing a particular moment or presenting a picture frozen in the flux of time. His poetry is thus rich in images of streets, inns, movie theatres, public urinals and young boys.

Nevertheless, the common language and simple rhymes, as well the sometimes troubled and controversial content of the poems, do not prevent his poetry from reaching a higher and more rarefied atmosphere where a profound and calm existential coherence emerges. The publication and subsequent critical review, in 1957, of a collection of all Penna's poems written between 1927 and 1955, under the title of *Poesie*, has suggested the possible existence of a third stage of his poetry, after the initial influence of Saba and the hermetic experience. This would be characterized by a renewed vital energy and an almost expressionistic quality which, nonetheless, directly stems from the fundamental anxiety and melancholy that constitute the original roots of his lyrical enterprise.

See also: poetry

Further reading

Penna, S. (1950) *Appunti* (Notes), Milan: Edizioni della Meridiana.
—— (1956) *Una strana gioia di vivere* (A Strange Joy of Living), Milan: Scheiwiller.
—— (1970) *Tutte le poesie* (All the Poems), Milan: Garzanti.
Nava, G. (1991) 'La lingua di Penna' (The Language of Penna), *Paragone* 42: 52–69 (an examination of Penna's poetic language).
Vaglio, A. (1993) *Invito alla lettura di S. Penna* (An Invitation to the Reading of S. Penna), Milan: Mursia (a handy general introduction to Penna's work).

ENRICO CESARETTI

pensiero debole

More of an intellectual approach than a doctrinaire movement, *il pensiero debole*, or 'weak thought', emerged in the 1980s as a common reaction on the part of some Italian philosophers and thinkers to the perceived 'crisis of classical reason', a crisis usually regarded as having been announced by Nietzsche in the late 1800s but which underlies much of twentieth-century thought and which was graphically summed up in Italy by the influential anthology of critical essays, *Crisi della ragione* (Crisis of Reason) edited by Aldo Gargani and published by **Einaudi** in 1979.

Since weak thought was a reaction rather than a philosophical programme, its adherents varied widely in their positions and it would be inaccurate to think of them as a school. What linked those who came to be associated with the label, however, was an open acknowledgement of the 'postmodern condition' and an acceptance of the fact that, in spite of all the successes of science and technology, Western rationality, on the basis of the rigorous requirements it itself had established, could no longer justify its exclusive claims to absolute Truth. In the light of the impossibility of henceforth making a 'strong' claim to truth, weak thought sought to avoid a total collapse into irrationalism by falling back on a 'weaker' claim, which would firstly, recognize the validity of a multiplicity of possible interpretations of the world, and secondly, propose models of understanding founded on 'reasonableness' rather than Reason. The application of such models would, of necessity, vary widely, but a sample of such approaches was published in 1983 as an anthology titled, in fact, *Il pensiero debole*, which was edited by philosophers Gianni **Vattimo** and Pier Aldo Rovatti (who, in their preface, explained their use of the term) and included essays by both editors as well as by Umberto **Eco** and other leading Italian thinkers. The anthology and the approach were widely discussed, and the tag was used often in the late 1980s though by the late 1990s it had fallen into disuse.

Further reading

Rosso, S. (1990) 'Postmodern Italy: Notes on the "Crisis of Reason", "Weak Thought" and *The Name of the Rose*', in *Exploring Postmodernism*, ed. M. Calinescu and D. Fokkema, Amsterdam and Philadelphia: John Benjamins.

GINO MOLITERNO

pentiti

The term *pentiti* (literally 'those who have repented') first came into popular use in 1980 to designate the members of left-wing terrorist groups who renounced political violence, turned state's evidence and qualified for the reduced sentences envisaged by part of the anti-terrorist 'emergency legislation'. Despite misgivings over its identification of motive (repentance) and action (supplying evidence), the term was subsequently used for all participants in any crime or criminal association, including the **mafia**, who collaborated with prosecutors and police. Their testimony became an essential element in the successful repression of political violence, organized crime and political corruption, but the impact of heavy reliance on evidence provided by self-confessed criminals about their former comrades or enemies remained controversial for the judicial system. Furthermore, the volatile mix concocted from the repudiation of solidarities, remorse for victims and pursuit of personal advantage – in continuous, often compelling, display in courtrooms, television studios and autobiographies – has given the practice of secular 'repentance' and confession a central place in contemporary Italian culture, sustained by the very familiarity of Catholic rites of absolution.

Reductions of sentences had long been available to criminals whose collaboration helped to avert some of the damage of their *actions*. The novelty of the 'emergency legislation' was to make benefits conditional on the public reconstruction of the collaborator's *identity*. The so-called 'Cossiga' law of 1980 required a truthful confession, full collaboration, explicit rejection of violence and abandonment of all links to terrorist organizations in order to qualify for sentence reductions for the most serious crimes, short of bomb massacres. Laws in 1982 and 1987 extended similar benefits to lesser offences and to collaborators (*dissociati*) who confessed their own responsibilities but refused to name others. Further discretionary benefits of financial help, changes of name and protection from betrayed comrades were available to the most important *pentiti*. The rewards for collaboration undoubtedly helped to encourage defections by members of armed political groups who had already lost their faith in violence, but the specific ideological motivations behind political terrorism made Parliament wary of extending similar legally prescribed benefits to collaborators from non-political criminal associations. It took not only the verified confessions of senior mafiosi but also the retaliatory murders of many of their kin (thirty-seven of Tommaso Buscetta's relatives were killed in revenge for his confessions to the prosecutor **Falcone**) for Parliament in 1991 to acknowledge collaboration as an extenuating circumstance for mafiosi and to introduce a formal witness protection programme which by 1996 covered 5,361 family members of 1,231 collaborating ex-mafiosi.

Permitting cases and convictions to rest substantially on evidence provided by self-confessed criminals has given rise to fierce controversies inside and outside the judicial system. *Pentiti* have been denounced for making false or incomplete confessions to settle old scores, secure their own immunity or achieve public notoriety. Prosecutors have been accused of neglecting to search for more reliable or confirmatory evidence once they have elicited a confession; complaints have also been made about their use of the rewards for collaboration to put unreasonable pressure on suspects to confess, demolishing in practice the right to remain silent. Courts, faced with the demand to assess the overall credibility of *pentiti* and therefore to accept or reject their testimony in its entirety, have sometimes seemed too ready to overlook discrepancies and ignore counter-evidence from defendants who have not collaborated. Calibrating sentences according to the defendant's readiness to collaborate can produce strikingly unequal punishments for identical offences and thus undermine the principle of equality before the law. Victims have had to accept that their 'repentant' aggressors may go virtually unpunished. Repeated pronouncements by Italy's highest court that confessions by *pentiti* are admissible as proof provided they can be supported by other evidence or by clearly independent testimony from other collaborators has not succeeded in dispelling doubts about their impact on the certainty and impartiality of judicial processes.

Of the many controversial cases involving *pentiti*, three stand out due to the status of the defendants. In 1983 a popular television personality, Enzo Tortora, was arrested for drug trafficking and

Camorra membership, solely on the basis of the testimony of collaborators from the Camorra itself. His conviction was overturned on appeal in 1986, which not only threw general suspicion on the use of confessions in prosecution cases but helped to ensure popular support for the referendum of 1987 to increase the civil liability of prosecutors for professional mistakes. In 1993, charges of mafia membership, resting on testimony by eight collaborating ex-mafiosi, were laid against Italy's former Prime Minister, Giulio **Andreotti**. Whether accepted in court or not, the confessions contributed to the discrediting of the pre-*Tangentopoli* political class and narrowed the perceived distance between politics and crime in postwar Italy. Lastly, in 1988 Adriano Sofri, a leading figure in the long-defunct Lotta Continua was arrested for having ordered the political murder of a police officer in 1972, on the basis of a highly contentious confession provided by a belatedly 'repentant' member of the alleged murder squad. The alternating verdicts of conviction and acquittal of Sofri and his fellow defendants in successive trials between 1990 and 1997 demonstrated very clearly how courts could reach completely opposite conclusions once they were mainly required to assess the motivations, character and credibility of *pentiti*. The three cases fuelled the criticisms of the judicial system for its inclination to accept intrinsically unreliable evidence as a way of compensating for chronically inefficient organization. They also provide a warning against allowing contemporary history to rely too heavily on evidence and interpretations accepted in the courtroom.

See also: terrorism

Further reading

Chelazzi, G. (1981) *La dissociazione dal terrorismo* (Dissociation From Terrorism) Milan: Giuffré (analysis of the 1980 law).

Foschini, M.V. and Montone, S. (1997) 'Il caso Tortora' (The Tortora Case), in L. Violante (ed.), *Storia d'Italia: Annali 12: La criminalità*, Turin: Einaudi.

Ginzburg, C. (1990) *Il giudice e lo storico* (The Judge and the Historian), Turin: Einaudi (historian's scrutiny of the evidence and outcome of the first trial of Sofri).

Laudi, M. (1984) *Terroristi 'pentiti' e liberazione condizionale*, ('Repentant' Terrorists and Conditional Release) Milan: Giuffré (analysis of the 1982 law).

Padovani, T. (1981) 'La soave inquisizione: osservazioni e rilievi a proposito delle nuove ipotesi di ravvedimento' (The Gentle Inquisition: Observations and Remarks on the New Rules for Repentance) *Rivista italiana di diritto e procedura penale* II: 529–45 (the novelty and implications of the 'repentance' legislation).

Peci, P. (1983) *Io, l'infame*, (I, The Abominable) Milan: Arnaldo Mondadori (autobiography of the first Red Brigades defector to turn state's evidence).

DAVID MOSS

Pertini, Alessandro (Sandro)

b. 25 September 1896, Savona;
d. 24 February 1990, Rome

Politician

Unusually popular for a politician, Sandro Pertini was known universally as *il nonno degli italiani* (the grandfather of Italians). A committed socialist who had spent most of the Fascist period in prison, Pertini incarnated the spirit of the **Resistance**. From 1943 to 1945 he was a leader of the CLNAI (National Committee for the Liberation of Upper Italy), but after the war his political career languished and his presidency came more as the reward for failure than success. Nonetheless, Pertini gave the office a new relevance, and his probity and commitment to humane values assisted the Republic to recover from the crises of the 1970s. Ironically, however, Pertini's term coincided with the rise of Bettino **Craxi**, another socialist, but one who embodied not probity and **anti-fascism** but scandal and corruption.

R.J.B. BOSWORTH

Petrassi, Goffredo

b. 16 July 1904, Zagarolo

Composer

Petrassi studied at the Conservatory of S. Cecilia in Rome under Alessandro Bustini and subsequently received much guidance from Alfredo Casella. In 1932–3 he won several competitions with his orchestral *Partita*, and this work was consequently taken up by conductors abroad. He was professor of composition at the Conservatory of S. Cecilia (1939–59) and then succeeded Pizzetti at the Accademia S. Cecilia until 1974. His pupils include Maxwell Davies, **Clementi** and Cardew.

Petrassi's highly diverse compositional style has occasioned comparisons with Stravinsky. Early works display an incisiveness and energy that draws strength from Italian composers of the seventeenth century as well as from contemporaries such as Hindemith. With the coming of war, Petrassi's style became darker and more austere (for example, *Coro di morti* (Choir of the Dead), 1940–1) and tonality was to become increasingly strained in the ensuing years. The opera *Morte dell' aria* (Death in the Air) (1949–50) and the cantata *Noche oscura* (Dark Night) (1950–1) were to provide evidence of his mastery of extended forms, and the works of the 1960s were to renew his highly personal allegiance to the predominant trends of the postwar avant-garde. Notable among these are *Propos d'Alain* (1960), in which a baritone soloist declaims a philosophical text against an instrumental accompaniment of great complexity, and the *Seventh Concerto for Orchestra* (1961–2, revised 1964) which exploits the forces of the orchestra at their most extreme and intense.

Further reading

Annibaldi, C. (1971) 'Goffredo Petrassi: catalogo delle opere e bibliografia' (Catalogue of Works and Bibliography), Milan.

JOHN KERSEY

Petri, Elio (Eraclio)

b. 29 January 1929, Rome;
d. 10 November 1982, Rome

Film director

After working as a journalist for **L'Unità**, and as a screenwriter (particularly for Giuseppe **De Santis**), Petri made his directorial debut in 1961 with *L'assassino* (The Murderer). A French-influenced police thriller, it displayed the mixture of symbolism and realism which, along with a concentration on politics and the exercise of power, was to characterize all of Petri's films. His blend of biting satire and political commitment is most explicit in the 1970 *Indagine su un cittadino al di sopra di ogni sospetto* (Investigation of a Citizen Above Suspicion), a caustic critique of the untouchability of corrupt police. *La classe operaia va in paradiso* (also released as *Lulu the Tool*), a treatise on industrial exploitation, won the Palme d'Or at Cannes in 1971. *Todo modo* (*One Way or Another*) (1976), adapted from a novel by Leonardo **Sciascia**, mercilessly exposes the rotten core of the ruling Christian Democrat Party.

Further reading

Rossi, A. (1979) *Petri*, Florence: La Nuova Italia.

DAVE WATSON

photography

In his introduction to *Fotografia 1943*, published by **Domus**, Ermanno Scopinisch wrote:

> The Italian photographer is reluctant to engage in technological research and is still not fully aware of the necessity of becoming fully proficient with photographic technology. The Italian photographer manages by the skin of his teeth. He gets by in the studio with make-shift lighting, and in the dark room with primitive equipment; he compensates for the poverty of his instruments of work with his cunning.
> (quoted in Zannier, 1979: 280 (my translation))

If the cultural autocracy of the Fascist regime, with its stifling of intellectual creativity and experiment, could be held partly responsible for this lamentable situation, a general diffidence towards the immediacy of photographic language and its basis in mechanical devices was also symptomatic of a culture dominated by a more ancient humanistic tradition. In Italy, there had always been a widespread tendency to dismiss photography either as an artistic practice for amateurs or as a commercially based handicraft. Such a persistent marginalization marked Italian photography with a sense of provincialism.

Changes were initiated in the 1940s by the **Gruppo degli otto** and by Domus, both promoting innovation to bring Italian photography up to date with the European avantgardes. Also in the immediate postwar years, a number of new publications were launched including *Tempo Illustrato*, *Oggi*, *L'Europeo* directed by Arrigo **Benedetti** and, in 1950, *Epoca* by Mondadori. Yet while developments in journalism and neorealism in cinema (**Rossellini**, **De Sica**, **Zavattini**) aroused the enthusiasm of certain photographers who recognized the sociological significance of photography, the Bussola Group, founded by Giuseppe Cavalli in 1947, was rejecting documentary photography and prolonging the diatribe, based on Crocean aesthetics, of photography as art. This polarization between documentary and artistic photography would continue to characterize the activity of Italian photographers for decades. In the 1950s the magazine *Ferrania*, written by the photographers Guido Bezzola, Alfredo Ornano and Luigi Veronesi, was the point of reference for Cavallian neo-formalists, while Pannunzio's magazine *Il Mondo* and Elio **Vittorini**'s *Il Politecnico* were publishing documentary social realist images.

In this period, Italian publishing and illustrated journalism reached European levels and, encouraged by the **economic miracle** which promoted a new market in visual advertising, talented photographers like Mario De Biasi, Carlo Bavagnoli and Ugo Mulas came to light. In Venice, rising stars of new Italian photography such as Paolo Monti, Gianni Berengo-Gardin and Fulvio Roiter – who are still working today – were emerging and formed the group La Gondola. Their individual work differs greatly, ranging from the documentary, historicizing approach on the one hand through to the expression of a purely personal and ahistorical sensibility on the other. Berengo-Gardin (b. 1930), who worked as a freelance reporter, was much admired by Cesare Zavattini. The most eloquent examples of Berengo-Gardin's work are his images of Venice, his series of photographs from India, and his pictures of Luzzara, the village he visited two decades before Strand. Roiter (b. 1926) is famous for his evocative images of Venice, most of which have been published in books, such as *Essere Venezia* (1977) – an all-colour volume which sold 150,000 copies in three years in English, French, German and Italian.

In the 1960s there was increasing acknowledgement of the existence of a 'culture' of photography and photographers finally emerged from what had been a peripheral ghetto. The international magazine *Camera*, directed by Romeo Martinez, acted as an intermediary between foreign masters – Haas, Cartier-Bresson, Steichen, Weston – and Italian photographers. Within this ferment of ideas and styles, it was the work of Berengo-Gardin, Franco Fontana, Mario Giacomelli and Giorgio Lotti, all with a background in photojournalism, which displayed the greatest formal resolution. Giacomelli (b. 1925) and Fontana (b. 1933) developed landscape photography in particular, playing with the relationship between precise representation and abstraction. Their work is exemplified by the early black and white, deeply contrasted images of the Marche by Giacomelli, and by Fontana's later colour landscapes of Basilicata, which at first glance often appear to be abstract patterns of colour and geometric shapes. Of the two, Fontana has been the most commercially and internationally successful, exhibiting constantly worldwide throughout the 1970s to the 1990s. Giacomelli's work is of a more documentary nature, but is formally highly crafted nonetheless. Always in black and white, and printed on high-contrast paper, his images are the result of the photographer's close connection with his native country, and of his investigation of its inner reality.

In the late 1970s the fashion explosion and the success of Italian designers provided another outlet for photographers in what could be considered a second Italian miracle, bringing to the fore the talents of adventurous fashion photographers like Oliviero **Toscani**. Elisabetta Catalano, later to become more widely known for her portraits, extensively photographed the work of conceptual artists like **Pistoletto** and **Pisani**. This period also saw a renewed interest in nineteenth-century photography, and 1979 marked the great historical photographic exhibitions in Venice and Florence. Although younger photographers such as Gabriele Basilico, Giovanna Borghese and Isabella Colonnello are currently photographing the post-industrial landscape, in spaces along the edges of the urban redevelopments and in the silent spaces of empty industrial plants, there nevertheless remains a strong attachment to the classic photographic style of the turn of the century.

The Italian photographic scene in the late 1990s is dominated by the 'heavyweights' of the older generation such as Romano Cagnoni (b. 1935), a photojournalist, whose images from the wars of Biafra, Vietnam and Afghanistan set a standard for Italian photojournalism: his last individual exhibition, 'War in Yugoslavia', was shown at the Italian Institutes of Culture in New York, Los Angeles, Chicago and Washington DC in 1993. Lisetta Carmi (b. 1924) is best known for her book *I Travestiti* (Transvestites), a particularly controversial subject in Italy. Mimmo Jodice (b. 1934), from Naples and influenced by Frank, Klein, and Strand, works in a documentary fashion and has focused largely on the contrasting faces of his native city. Pepi Merisio (b. 1931), from Bergamo, has made most of his work in and about that area, showing the country life and deeply felt religious devotion of a people confined to the borders of history. Ferdinando Scianna (b. 1943) achieved renown with the book, *Religious Festivals in Sicily* (1965), with texts by **Sciascia**; his work has much of the static, emblematic quality of Strand's images, and he is the most loved and imitated photographer in Italy. Marialba Russo (b. 1947), an ethnographer, works in the south of Italy where she has investigated the religious festivals and the archaic rites of the peasant community. Her interests are both anthropological and psychological, and her photographs move away from an objective documentary style, focusing instead through the use of sequence, movement and angle

of view on a far more objective response to events unfolding before her.

Other photographers working in the documentary tradition are Franco Grignani, Frank Harvart, Cesare Leonardi, Enzo Ragazzini and the original 'paparazzo', Tazio Secchiaroli, who in fact soon abandoned the sensationalist photography that had made him famous in order to work on film sets, photographing, amongst others, all of **Fellini**'s films. More formalist, postmodern concerns inform the work of Vasco Ascolini, who photographs sculpture, architectural structures and theatre, and whose images have a metaphysical quality; Luigi Ghirri (b. 1943), a conceptual photographer with a taste for colour, trompe l'oeil, the industrial image and the snapshot; and Paolo Gioli (b. 1942), who is primarily interested in experimenting with modern technology but is a debunker of the photographic medium and ironic about its technicality.

Further reading

(1988) *Italy: One Hundred Years of Photography*, with introductory texts by S. Sontag and C. Colombo, Florence: Alinari.

Zannier, I. (1979), in *Venezia'79: La Fotografia*, Milan: Electa.

—— (1986) *Storia della fotografia italiana* (History of Italian Photography), Bari: Laterza (see especially Chapter 6).

OLIVIA DAWSON

Piano, Renzo

b. 14 September 1937, Genoa

Architect, engineer, teacher and theoretician

Born into a family of builders, Piano has become the master of well-crafted, large-scale 'organic' structures, inspired by a constant search for lightness in both a physical and a figurative sense. A deep fascination with harbours, ships, airports, airplanes and historical centres returns insistently throughout his work, while a technological virtuosity forms his personal signature. Piano's contribution is substantial both in volume and significance, and ranges from a restructuring of Potsdamer Platz in Berlin to Osaka airport, from a Centre for Kanak culture in New Caledonia to apartment blocks in Sydney, Australia. His buildings tend to expand their formal programme in response to their context thus making larger social statements as, for example, in the Parisian multicultural centre Beaubourg, designed with **Rogers** in 1971 and conceived as a factory for making culture while presenting an ironic look at technology. He has been awarded numerous prizes and awards for building excellence.

Further reading

Piano, R. (1997) *Logbook*, New York: The Monacelli Press (an excellent, updated overview of Piano's work presented by the architect himself, together with biographic and bibliographic data).

GORDANA KOSTICH

Piazza Fontana

On 12 December 1969, in the wake of the student protests and worker revolts of 1968–9, a bomb exploded in a bank in Piazza Fontana in Milan, killing 17 people and injuring 90. The unprecedented act of violence inaugurated nearly two decades of political bombings, murders and woundings. Blame for the bomb was immediately attributed to anarchists, one of whom (Pino Pinelli) fell to his death while in police custody. The conservative press and politicians united to condemn trade unions and the Left for their encouragement of radical social conflict. Dogged judicial enquiries, however, revealed that the bomb was in fact the work of an extreme right-wing group in the Veneto, headed by Franco Freda and Giovanni Ventura, helped by members of the security services who intended the Left to be blamed and discredited. The power of highly-placed sympathizers to obstruct investigations was sufficient to ensure that, despite thirty years of investigations by different magistrates and eight trials in various cities, the ultimate responsibilities for the planning and execution of the massacre still remain obscure. 'Piazza Fontana' thus became

shorthand for the unacknowledged links between power and violence in Italy's 'First' Republic.

DAVID MOSS

Piccinato, Luigi

b. 30 October 1899, Legnago, Verona; d. 1984, Rome

Architect and town planner

A graduate of the Scuola Superiore di Architettura of Rome in 1923, Piccinato was to become one of the most influential town planners and architects of Italy. He was among those who, from the 1950s onwards, played a significant role in promoting wide discussion of issues connected with **urban planning**, and later helped to found modern Italian town planning as an autonomous discipline.

Piccinato's interest in modern town planning pays homage to the notion of local cultural setting, an idea he explored from 1925 onwards and which he presented in projects for North Africa at the 'Oltremare' (Overseas) exhibition in Naples in 1940. He developed the notion further in projects for cities in Argentina (1948–50), Turkey (1956–9) and Israel (1960–5). He was also the founder of *Metron*, a magazine he co-edited with architect Mario **Ridolfi** between the years 1948–58.

FASSIL ZEWDOU

Pietrangeli, Paolo

b. 29 April 1945, Rome

Singer, film director and television producer

A militant member of the Communist Party (see **PCI**), Pietrangeli was active in the 1968 **student movement** while also working as assistant director to **Visconti**, **Fellini** and **Zurlini**. His first film, *Bianco e nero* (White and Black), a long and detailed documentary on the collusion between neo-fascism and the **DC** in postwar Italy, was released in 1975, and in 1977 he filmed an adaptation of *Porci con le ali* (Pigs with Wings), a notorious novel set within the student movement, which had became something of a cause célèbre. In the 1980s, without abandoning his political militancy, he became producer of the Maurizio **Costanzo** show, while continuing to tour Italy singing protest songs. In the national elections of 1996 he stood unsuccessfully for the House of Deputies (see **Parliament**) as an independent candidate supported by **Rifondazione Comunista**. In spite of his many other considerable achievements, he will probably be most remembered as the author and singer of *Contessa* (Countess), a passionate song that became the anthem of left-wing contestation in the 1970s.

GINO MOLITERNO

Piovene, Guido

b. 27 July 1907, Vicenza; d. 12 November 1974, London, England

Novelist and journalist

Piovene's fiction is characterized by disparate themes which are linked together by an overall preoccupation with human psychology and religious faith as in *Lettere di una Novizia* (Confession of a Novice) (1941), *Gazzetta Nera* (Black Gazzette) (1943) and *Pietà contro pietà* (Piety Versus Piety) (1946). The latter is a detailed and sometimes painful documentation/confession of Piovene's political adherence to fascism (see also **fascism and neo-fascism**). While his plots encompass a variety of interests, Piovene's style is consistent, obviously influenced by his career as a journalist writing for *Il Corriere della sera* and *La Stampa*. This translates into a narrative which is simultaneously necessary and informative, simple and direct. An illustrative example of Piovene's condensed and yet highly intriguing narrative is offered by the posthumous collection of short stories *Inverno d'un uomo felice* (The Winter of a Happy Man) (1977). Here, psychological investigation is supported and permeated by an eerie atmosphere whose masterly construction brings to mind novelists such as Poe, Hawthorne and Henry James.

PAOLO BARTOLONI

Pirella, Emanuele

b. 1940, Reggio Emilia

Comic strip writer, critic and novelist

After graduating from university, Pirella moved to Milan where he became the artistic director of an advertising agency which he had helped to set up. In 1972, he began to collaborate with Tullio Pericoli with whom he wrote political comic strips published in the satirical magazine *Linus*, and he also wrote literary reviews in comic strip form for the *Corriere della sera*. In 1976, after the Left's failure to defeat the Christian Democrats (see **DC**) in national elections, he declared that he would stop creating comic strips because they obviously lacked persuasive power. Eventually, Pirella and Pericoli did resume their collaboration and Pirella also published what he called he called 'a post-**Gruppo 63**' novel about a young copywriter and ad-man. In the novel, by the use of heterogeneous linguistic and literary modes, woven into a traditional novelistic structure, Pirella effects a critique of the relation between contemporary literary discourse and the reality it attempts to represent.

OLIVIA DAWSON

Pirelli

A leading industrial group of the rubber sector, Pirelli is the oldest of Italian big businesses, having being founded in Milan by Giovanni Battista Pirelli in 1872. Tyres and cables have remained its traditional core business, and since the 1920s Pirelli has made a name for itself as a leader on international markets, becoming one of only a few Italian multinationals, with a number of foreign branches all around Europe, Asia and Latin American. The Pirelli family has always retained control of the group, although only as minority shareholders and thanks to longstanding alliances with other families of the Italian entrepreneurial elite such as the **Agnelli**, the Orlando and the strong support of **Mediobanca**.

Alberto Pirelli, who ruled the company together with his brother Piero from the interwar period to the 1960s, was an entrepreneur of high international standing. Having played a major role in the economic diplomacy of the Fascist regime, he remained a most influential figure after the war but preferred to relinquish public office in order to remain in the background. His legacy then passed to his son Leopoldo in 1965, but thirty years later the family's entrepreneurial continuity was broken with the appointment of Marco Tronchetti Provera as an external managing director. Nevertheless, unlike other industrial dynasties such as the Agnelli, the Pirelli never aroused press curiosity. They continued to maintain a low profile in the public eye, adhering to a tradition of reserve and understatement; even in private, their style of life always shunned magnificence and pretence, leading some critics to describe it as calvinistic behaviour.

The mass motorization of 1960s led to a boom in the tyre industry and opened up the most successful period of Pirelli's business. However, keen competition in Italy and abroad in new products – such as radial tyres, where Michelin, a French group, won the leadership – slowed Pirelli's growth. In 1971 a strategic alliance with the British group Dunlop was set up in order to achieve a stronger position on world markets. The persistence of a competitive and technological gap and difficulties in amalgamating management made this marriage a total failure, and it was wound up ten years later. This was the first of many defeats. In 1988 Pirelli failed to take over Firestone, the third largest rubber group in the world, in spite of massive financial support from major Swiss banks. Later on, in 1990–3 the group attempted to wrest control of Continental, a leading German group, but again was defeated after an exhausting financial struggle.

Pirelli's setbacks are an emblem of the difficulties confronting Italian big business in the international arena. Like Agnelli and other entrepreneurial families, the Pirelli are still facing a difficult dilemma: how to relaunch the group's fortune – which inevitably means entering a strategic partnership with some international concern in order to prepare for global competition – while not, at the same time, relinquishing family control.

See also: motor car industry

STEFANO BATTILOSSI

Pisani, Vettor

b. 1934, Naples

Sculptor, playwright and conceptual artist

Pisani started architectural studies in Naples in the late 1950s but abandoned them to immerse himself in Rosicrucianism. In Rome, Pisani studied the work of Robert Motherwell (1960–5) and Marcel Duchamp (1965–70). The result was the exhibition 'Maschile, femminile e androgino: Incesto e cannabilismo in Marcel Duchamp' (Male, Female and Androgyne: Incest and Cannibalism in Marcel Duchamp) (1970), in which he presented 'psychoanalytically-informed' objects such as the 'Chocolate Cast of Suzanne Duchamp', for which he won the Premio Prino Pascali. In the same year he began to participate in *arte povera* and to collaborate with Michelangelo **Pistoletto**. Pisani saw parallels between artistic and alchemical activity, aligning himself with Duchamp, Yves Klein and Joseph Beuys, the latter becoming the subject of the performance 'The Rabbit Does Not Like Joseph Beuys' (1975). Other performances included 'R.C. Theatrum' (held at Pisani's own warehouse theatre), in which performers included a rabbit and a stripper, and 'Oedipus and the Sphinx after Fernand Knopff' (1981), set in the Protestant cemetery in Rome.

OLIVIA DAWSON

Pistoletto, Michelangelo

b. 23 June 1933, Biella

Artist

A highly theatrical painter whose work continually veered towards performance, Pistoletto broke up the picture surface and achieved both extreme figuration and audience involvement with his 'mirror paintings', made up of figures painted on cloth, glued to reflective sheets of stainless steel and, later, photographic transparencies on plexiglass. Each work consisted of these fixed images as well as the chance reflection of the viewer. *Voyeurs*, from 1971, played further on this device by depicting two men as if looking at the art object.

Pistoletto responded to **arte povera** with his *Oggetti in meno* (Absent Objects), which were in fact everyday objects, and he also created things from balls of newspaper. *La coda dell'arte povera* (The Tail-End of *Arte Povera*) from 1980 is a particularly witty piece consisting of a trail of rags knotted together.

Further reading

Celant, G. (1989) *Pistoletto*, New York: Rizzoli (a comprehensive illustrated anthology with details of exhibitions, performances and a full bibliography).

MAX STAPLES

pizza

The term 'pizza' is of uncertain etymology, but in its present form the pizza may be traced back to the early nineteenth century when Neapolitan pizza came to be the most celebrated in the Italian tradition. Its fame outside Italy spread increasingly after the Second World War, making it a symbol of Italian cooking. Official figures suggest that, in the mid-1990s, Italians were consuming one million pizzas a day throughout the peninsula, roughly 400 million per year.

In its originally small, round version, pizza was sold on the streets of Naples. Significantly, it was also called *il cibo dei poveri* (food of the poor), because its modest price made it affordable by all. However its size and variety increased as time went by. The *pizza Margherita* is said to have been created by an unknown patriotic *pizzaiolo* (pizza maker) in honour of the then Queen of Italy and, topped with tomatoes, basil and mozzarella, it reproduces the red, white and green colours of the Italian **flag**. Other renowned Neapolitan varieties are the *pizza marinara* and *pizza quattro stagioni*. A food of humble origin, the original pizza hardly resembles in texture and flavour of its richer, but perhaps less tastier, counterparts which are now spread all over the world.

Further reading

Serao, M. (1973) *Il ventre di Napoli* (The Stomach of

Naples), Naples: Delfino (see ch. 3: 'Quello che mangiano' (What They Eat)).

MARIELLA TOTARO GENEVOIS

PLI

Although liberals dominated the Italian state until the crisis of the First World War, they failed to build a mass party, founding a formal party only in 1922. In the Republican period, mass political mobilization was dominated by the socialists and communists on the one hand and the **DC** on the other. The vote of the PLI (Partito Liberale Italiano, or Italian Liberal Party) peaked at 7 per cent in 1963. It was saved from irrelevance only by the DC's coalition strategy, which generally preferred alliance with one or more of the lay centre parties (the PLI, **PRI** and **PSDI**) than with either the Right (**monarchists** and **MSI**) or the Left (**PCI** and, before 1963, **PSI**). A right-liberal party, unlike the left-liberal PRI, the PLI adopted a 'free market/strong state' orientation prior to the 1970s, and was very close to the **Confindustria**, the major business employers' association. The PLI was swept away by the turmoil of the early 1990s.

Further reading

Donovan, M. (1996) 'The Fate of the Secular Centre: The Liberals, Republicans and Social Democrats', in S. Gundle and S. Parker (eds), *The New Italian Republic: From the Fall of the Berlin Wall to Berlusconi*, London: Routledge (an overview of the nature and role of the PLI and the two other 'lay' parties in the 'First' Republic).

MARK DONOVAN

POA

A nationwide, Church-run charitable organization which operated into the 1950s, the POA (Pontifica Opera di Assistenza, Pontifical Works of Assistance) had been set up during the Second World War in order to bring relief to populations in or close to the war zones and in cities affected by the bombing. After the war, the organization turned its attention increasingly to poor children and teenagers, providing welfare, education (chiefly nursery schools), and sporting and recreational facilities, especially in the form of summer holiday camps. In 1952, for example, the POA provided assistance in some form or another to one and a half million children and young people. Indirectly a political influence in favour of the **DC** among the poor, it was controlled from the **Vatican** by the all-powerful Cardinals Canali and Galeazzi, both close to **Pope Pius XII**, and was largely financed by contributions from American Catholics.

Further reading

Falconi, F. (1956) *La Chiesa e le organizzazioni cattoliche in Italia 1945–1955* (The Church and Catholic Organizations in Italy 1945–1955) Turin: Einaudi.

JOHN POLLARD

poetry

In the aftermath of the Second World War, Italian culture was caught up in an intense debate about the scarcity of realism, both in the literary and figurative arts. This critical discussion went hand in hand with the development of **neorealism**, especially in the films and novels of the late 1940s and early 1950s. Poetry, although almost by definition the most conservative and least public of the artistic genres, was also engulfed by the disputes which pressed for a more realistic style reflecting public concerns against the private lyrical themes prevalent in Italian poetic tradition. In the fascist prewar period, Italian poetry had been largely – but not totally – influenced by French symbolism's search for the purity of poetic form and its interest in the evocative power of the lyrical word. The pursuit of music and sound over meaning in the development of twentieth-century Italian poetry was also partly inspired by the immediate critical success of poets as diverse as **Ungaretti** and **Montale**, whose early works immediately became icons for the poetic generation of the 1930s.

The poems of Ungaretti's *Allegria di naufragi* (The Happiness of the Shipwrecked) (1919) and of Montale's *Ossi di seppia* (Cuttlefish Bones) (1925) were far from mere attempts at pure form but Ungaretti's intense concern for a lyrical word which could express the feeling of life and Montale's more realistic content but consigned to highly musical texts, served to insert the symbolist experience into Italian culture. This trend developed within what came to be known as 'hermeticism', or the 'hermetic school', according to Francesco Flora's famous but questionable definition coined in the thirties to address certain obscure characteristics of the poetry of Ungaretti and **Quasimodo**. It would be more accurate, however, to talk about a hermetic current than a school, because if hermeticism did exist, it was in the works of a varied group of poets only generically connected by their preference for a refined language and, in a few cases, obscure style. While Ungaretti's second book *Sentimento del tempo* (The Feeling of Time) (1933) and some of Montale's poems from *Le Occasioni* (Occasions) (1939) especially the section called 'I Mottetti' (the Motets), show traces of what are commonly considered stylistic traits of this period, the hermetic current was most actively represented by poets who began publishing in the 1930s or early 1940s, such as **Luzi**, **Betocchi** and **Bigongiari** on one side, and Quasimodo, Gatto and **Sinisgalli** on one other. The first group operated in Florence, the second mostly in Milan. With the advent of neorealism, some of the previously hermetic poets, such as the Nobel laureate Quasimodo, openly and successfully converted to a realistic, sometimes almost documentary style. Others poets confronted the cultural crisis caused by the war in a more critical way, filtering the hermetic and symbolist inheritance toward new existential and anthropological stances.

Luzi, in particular, was at the centre of the debate between the ex-hermetic current and the realistic one championed by **Pasolini** and others in the early 1950s. Luzi, in the journal *La chimera* (The Chimaera), and Pasolini, in the pages of *Officina* (see **literary journals**), debated the possible future direction of contemporary Italian poetry. Both considered the neorealistic inspiration largely exhausted by the early 1950s, but while Pasolini proposed a new realism to fill the vacuum, as in his mature 1957 collection *Le ceneri di Gramsci*

(The Ashes of Gramsci), Luzi, even if also aware that the hermetic experience was over, advanced the possibility of building further on it. Moving from the poetics of early and somewhat neglected twentieth-century authors such as Clemente Rebora (1885–1957) and Dino Campana (1885–1932) and re-evaluating the Dantean legacy of the Italian tradition, Luzi admitted that the war represented a watershed which had changed the course of Italian literary culture, forcing it to confront reality; but he also cautioned against confusing realism with a simple and facile change of style. Realism for Luzi meant, above all, to embrace the Dantesque resolve to scrutinize the metamorphic evolution of life without abandoning the hope and the will to follow its often painful but inevitable transformations. This position is well embodied in Luzi's major books after the war, *Onore del vero* (To Honor the Truth) (1957) and *Nel magma* (In the Magma) (1963), and was retained, with subtle but continuous changes in style, even in his last collections published in the 1990s.

Most poets who belonged to the hermetic generation or who published their first books immediately after the war were forced in some way to confront the crisis of hermeticism and the new interest for neorealism, both debates carrying over well into the 1960s. Yet beyond the critical exchanges and theoretical positions on poetic matters, it was the lyrical production of major authors such as Luzi and Pasolini themselves which set the tone for further developments. First of all, Ungaretti and Montale, preserving their independent and leading roles within the poetic scene, kept publishing cornerstone books for the development of Italian poetry, such as Ungaretti's *Il taccuino del vecchio* (The Old Man's Notebook) (1960) and Montale's *La bufera e altro* (The Storm and Other Things) (1956) and *Satura* (1971), these two latter volumes being especially influential on the poets of the 1960s and 1970s.

Other poets either confirmed their steady presence in the 1950s and early 1960s or emerged in the wake of the critical debate which emancipated Italian poetry from the postwar literary disputes. Among the first group were **Caproni**, **Bertolucci** and **Penna**, who had published their first works in the 1930s. Penna's poems, highly lyrical and somewhat disconnected from the Italian cultural tissue of his times, occupied an isolated position, in part because of their homosexual themes, which contributed to making unique what were already fresh and original texts. Caproni and Bertolucci, two central poetic figures of the second part of the century, demonstrated some affinities with the former hermetic poets in their early books. However, they soon established independent and original positions which were, in the long run, equally distant from hermeticism and from neorealism, and they both found a balance between a sincere and deep analysis of reality and their own lyrical interests. Caproni in particular worked at successfully combining a common idiom with the high style of the Italian tradition, never betraying his independence and his strenuous commitment to existentialist themes.

Other major poets like **Sereni**, **Fortini** and **Zanzotto**, who had published their first books during the hermetic period, also followed fruitful, independent directions. Sereni, acclaimed as the major poet of what **Anceschi** defined as the *linea lombarda* (the Lombard line), demonstrated a capacity for a genuine and objective exploration of daily life, projected within a sincere and fresh lyrical world which absorbs and recreates in a personal way the images perceived from the external world. More ironic, and above all linguistically more experimental, was Zanzotto's fundamental stylistic achievement, especially in his later books, *La beltà* (Beauty) (1968), *Galateo in bosco* (Etiquette in the Forest) (1978) and *Fosfeni* (1983). Zanzotto's plurilinguism, including his interest in the use of the Venetian dialect, embodies a fundamental step forward for both the experimental and the realistic current of the second part of the century. Fortini's works, beginning with his *Poesia ed errore* (Poetry and Error) (1959), attest instead to the validity of the realistic trend, especially if emancipated from the cultural polemics connected with neorealism and re-elaborated into a vivid, personal style.

Some of the new poets of the 1960s surfaced as part of the *Neoavanguardia*, an avantgarde cultural movement which intended to renew the entire way of conceiving literature (see **Gruppo 63**). Poets such as **Porta**, **Balestrini**, **Pagliarani**, **Giuliani** and **Sanguineti** opposed the neorealistic current and asserted a new interest in lyric language and experimental forms, even in the shape of visual poetry. What realism entrusted to content, these poets entrusted to the language itself, regarded as the only corrosive element which could oppose and modify the lyric tradition. While the artistic value and poetic weight of these individual authors differ substantially from one another, at least in their early collections (for example, in the anthology *I novissimi*) (1961, edited by Giuliani), these poets showed traces of their common attempt to distance themselves from any traditional line, be it the hermetic or the realistic one.

On the other side of the poetic spectrum at this time, the traditional current of Italian poetry continued, inspired mostly by the works of poets like Umberto Saba (with Montale and Ungaretti, the other influential poet of the generation between the two wars), and represented by authors from different backgrounds and with diverse poetic goals. Saba's preference for a traditional poetic language and his rejection of any form of experimentation had isolated him during the avantgarde and the hermetic period. Except on a few occasions (for example Montale's early praise), Saba's simple, lyrical and potent language (or 'honest', according to his own definition of what poetry should be), did not receive due attention until after his death in 1957, but many poets who began publishing in the late 1950s and early 1960s reappropriated Saba's style, in some cases combining it with the more ironic but somewhat compatible Montalian streak.

Some of these poets, although they did not gather in groups or schools and did not produce aesthetic manifestos like their counterparts in the neoavantgarde, were very influential in the development of poetry in the 1960s, sometimes through theoretical writings, but mainly for the validity of their lyrical production. Amongst them were Giovanni **Giudici** and Giovanni **Raboni**. Giudici engaged in an original mediation between existentialism and his own ironic and realistic expectations, as in *La vita in versi* (Life in Verse) (1965) and *Autobiologia* (Autobiology) (1969), demonstrating a predilection for the grotesque which exorcises the poet's existential anxiety. Raboni's sober compositions are closer to the realistic stream that led back, from Saba to the ethical teachings of Alessandro Manzoni (1785–1872) and Giuseppe Parini (1729–

99), as evident in early collections like *L'insalubrità dell'aria* (The Unhealthiness of the Air) (1963) and corroborated by later publications such as *Cadenza d'inganno* (Deceiving Cadence) (1975). The works of Maria Luisa **Spaziani** are characterized by a strong lyric vein which makes her one of the most distinct voices of the second part of the century. Spaziani's poetic production stretches from the 1950s to the present, and her poems are highly recognizable for their elegant language and defined form. Another poet who can be considered at the crossroads between the traditional, the realistic and the experimental lines, all three unified within a complex spiritual and poetic search, is Giovanni **Testori**.

The postwar period also witnessed a continuation and a development of poetry written in dialect (see **literature in dialect**). The poetic use of the dialects often aims at very different aesthetic goals: sometimes to establish a sociological connotation (mostly with a realistic intent), and sometimes to express a specific culture which would lose its original freshness if adapted into Italian, for instance, Pasolini's highly lyrical *La meglio gioventù* (The Best Youth) (1956), devoted to the Friuli region and people. On other occasions, writers experiment with dialect to increase their stylistic and aesthetic repertoire (for example, Zanzotto). There are also authors who choose their own dialect as their main, or only, linguistic code, amongst them Biagio Marin (1891–1985) writing in the dialect of his hometown of Grado (near Trieste), Franco Loi (b. 1930), writing realistic and innovative poems in Milanese, often set against a dramatic city background, and Albino Pierro (1916–96), whose mature collections are in the dialect of his hometown Tursi in Basilicata. Each of these poets, in choosing his respective dialect, reaches back to an abandoned and neglected cultural world, which is recovered and presented to the reader in new and powerful poetic images.

The events of 1968 (see **student movement**) interrupted poetic debate until the late 1970s when, thanks to a series of editorial enterprises, old and new poets were brought back to public attention. As in the early 1960s, so too in the 1970s the new poetic projects were presented through a number of anthologies, most notably *Il pubblico della poesia* (The Public of Poetry) (1975), edited by

Alfonso Berardinelli and Franco Cordelli, and *La parola innamorata* (The Word in Love) (1978), edited by Enzo di Mauro and Giancarlo Pontiggia, which presented a number of new poets, amongst them Milo De Angelis, Maurizio Cucchi and Dario **Bellezza**. The entire decade was also represented in a broad collection edited by Antonio Porta, *Poesia degli anni settanta* (Poetry of the Seventies) (1979).

Besides new and strong poetic voices such as that of Valerio **Magrelli**, whose poetry is suspended between a highly metaphoric structure and a more discursive style, the last two decades have seen the confirmation of authors now regarded as classics of twentieth-century Italian poetry, from Luzi to Zanzotto, from Bertolucci to Sanguineti. They have also witnessed a spectacular increase in women poets, who, up to the late 1970s, were represented almost only by Spaziani and Amelia **Rosselli**, whose stylistic and linguistic solutions carved out an original space within the experimental current. Amongst the most active and recognized women poets who began publishing in the late 1960s and in the 1970s are Biancamaria **Frabotta**, Patrizia **Cavalli**, Patrizia **Valduga** and Annalisa **Cima**. While it was inevitable that at the beginning of their careers some of these poets presented themselves as part of a cultural movement (see Frabotta's anthology *Donne in poesia* (Women in Poetry)), most of them are today considered amongst the best and most original contemporary poetic voices. Their lyrical works span both the experimental and the formalistic current, and while sometimes they seem comfortably inserted within the previous tradition, in most of their poems they revisit, rewrite and revitalize the poetic trends of the century.

Further reading

Hainsworth, P. and Tandello, E. (eds) (1995) *Italian Poetry Since 1956*, Reading: University of Reading Press (a general but comprehensive anthology with good introductions to each author).

Spatola, A. and Vangelisti, P. (eds) (1982) *Italian Poetry, 1960–1980: From Neo to Post Avantgarde*, San Francisco: Red Hill Press (a useful and well-thought-out anthology of the poetry of the 1960s and 1970s).

ANDREA CICCARELLI

polenta

Italian polenta is enshrined in the Oxford English Dictionary as a type of 'porridge'. In medieval times it was made from broad beans cooked and crushed in a mortar, then fried with onions and sage or – for a sweet variation – figs and honey. Since the eighteenth century, polenta has been made by pouring cornflour into boiling, salted water and stirring until it reaches a thick consistency.

In the past, polenta was the main food of the poor and rural people, especially in northern Italy where it was often a substitute for more expensive bread. Later, it became customary to eat polenta as an accompaniment to other foods such as game, meat and cheeses. Northern Italians appear to prefer a firmer polenta, while in central Italy it tends to be creamier. Cooked polenta can be sliced and baked in a variety of recipes. There are several dishes expressly prepared to accompany polenta, their ingredients varying from region to region (see **regional cooking**).

MARIELLA TOTARO GENEVOIS

Poletti, Ugo
b. 19 April 1914, Omegna, Novara;
d. 24 February 1997, Rome

Cardinal

A leading figure in the Italian Church and reputed to be a confidential adviser to **Pope John Paul II**, Poletti was widely regarded as the most likely candidate for the papal crown in the 1978 conclave, though his bid proved ultimately unsuccessful.

After an early career as a seminary teacher and rector in his own diocese, he entered the Roman curia in 1958 and was made head of the Pontifical Missionary Societies in 1964. In 1967 his career changed direction when he was appointed Bishop of Spoleto. In 1972 he was given the most important pastoral job in the Italian Church – the pope's Vicar for the Diocese of Rome – and a year later he was made a cardinal. In 1991 he became head of the Italian Conference of Bishops. A constant critic of local government in Rome, even when it was in the hands of the **DC**, Poletti was especially concerned about the inadequacy of housing and other public and social services in the city. As a result, he was accused by some of opening the way to the **PCI** conquest of the capitol, although he was very popular with ordinary Romans.

JOHN POLLARD

Poli, Paolo

b. 23 May 1929, Florence

Actor, singer, writer and satirist, Poli takes classical and modern, known and unknown texts and reworks them with a devastatingly hilarious effect by presenting their unintentional comic substance. After working in radio and university theatre, he gained wider recognition in Aldo **Trionfo**'s experimental theatre in Genoa. From the early 1960s, most of his shows were written with Ida Omboni; later, sets and costumes were designed by Lele Luzzatti but musical collaboration has been consistently with Jacqueline Perrotin. Generally the shows have been performed with small companies, with Poli playing a wide variety of roles, some in drag and some straight.

A philologist and an expert of popular song, Poli combines satire with affection for his material. This has ranged from Roman literature (Apuleius's *Golden Ass*) and medieval hagiography (*Rita da Cascio*) to F.T. Marinetti's 'Il suggeritore nudo' (The Naked Prompter). Some shows have just been collections of songs and texts on a theme, as with 'Feminilità' (Femininity), performed with his sister Lucia. All have been extensively revived.

JAMES WALSTON

police

Italy boasts a number of different police corps, the main ones being the *polizia di stato* (state police) the **carabinieri** and the *guardia di finanza* (finance officers). Since, historically, their relative roles and jurisdictions have never been satisfactorily differentiated, these organizations are often in each others' way. In spite of superficial differences, however, the general notion of the police in Italy has remained that of a 'police of the government' which defends the political order against social opposition. In fact, the police forces in the postwar period largely continued the tradition of fascist and pre-fascist times. Even after the Second World War, the police were strongly militarist in style: they lived in barracks, were subjected to strong discipline and were prohibited from joining **trade unions** and political parties. Only very slowly after the war were some elements of a 'citizens' police', which protects citizens' rights, introduced into the self- and public perception of the *polizia di stato*.

First attempts at reform in the postwar period were in fact blocked by the Cold War, which saw the Communist Party and worker organizations characterized as the major threat to public order and therefore the criminal enemy. In fact, during this time police organizational structure and training were mostly focused on crowd control and containment of riots. In the 1940s and 1950s, the most common image of the police was that derived from their often brutal suppression of protest marches and public gatherings. About one hundred protesters and bystanders were killed in this way during this period.

The various police corps, overlapping in responsibilities but lacking in coordination, were nevertheless centralized in the Ministry for Home Affairs, a Ministry that from 1947 to 1994 was firmly under the control of the Christian Democratic party (**DC**). Notwithstanding a steady increase in the number of officers, the level of professionalization remained very poor. Low salaries and miserable living conditions, including the isolation from the population, made joining the police a sort of last resort for the less educated. At the same time, police powers were extremely wide. Following a tradition of strict control and preventive intervention, the police had the right to impose restrictions on the movement, residence and activities of Italian citizens. It was only beginning in 1956 that the newly created **Constitutional Court** started to declare illegitimate some provisions of the police law, many of which dated back to the Fascist regime.

The first indications of a possible change in police culture emerged in the early 1960s, when the Socialist Party's entry into government initiated hopes for a reform. The political transformation was reflected in a less brutal control of political protest, and between 1963 and 1967 there were no fatal casualties during police attendance at demonstrations. This evolution towards a different perception of the police role, however, came to a brisk stop when a long cycle of protest – starting in 1967–8 in the universities, and then spreading to the factories in the so-called 'Hot Autumn' of 1969, and, later on, to the most different social and political groups – again polarized the political culture (see **student movement**). Demands for major reforms produced a backlash from the governing elites. A series of bomb attacks by right-wing terrorists and attempted coups by conservative generals helped to radicalize many groups of the opposition, some of them ending up in the underground (see **terrorism**; **extraparliamentary Left**). In a situation characterized by strong demand for 'law and order', the police forces were again deployed to repress protestors, and demonstrators again lost their lives during police interventions. In the second half of the decade, emergency laws to fight terrorism and organized crime increased police powers and reduced the rights of citizens and defendants.

However, the 1970s were not only years of escalation. A most unexpected outcome of the protest cycle of the late 1960s and early 1970s was the emergence inside the police forces themselves of demands for long-delayed reforms. Already in the early 1970s, against the will of their superiors, police officers started to denounce their poor living conditions and miserable training and the arbitrariness of the command structure. The protest cycle catalysed this discontent in two ways. On the one hand, working conditions deteriorated even further when policemen were sent from one end of the peninsula to the other, kept waiting for days in police

wagons, and made to face the growing hostility of the population. On the other hand, the mobilization of various social groups – including those that, a few years before, would have never gone onto the streets – contributed to a legitimization of protest, even inside the police. At the same time, the struggle against terrorism increased an appreciation of professionalism. Demands for police reforms, however, did not find support among those political forces traditionally considered 'police friendly', and almost a decade elapsed before a police reform bill was passed in Parliament in 1981. The main effects of the reform were the demilitarization of the police (though not of the *carabinieri* or the *guardia di finanza*) and the unionization of the corps. The force also became open to women, who entered *en masse*. The salary as well as the self-respect of the police increased, and so too did the educational level and social background of the new recruits.

The development towards professionalization continued in the 1980s with the creation of special bodies. After the struggle against terrorism, the struggle against the **mafia** gave new legitimization to the police, contributing to their wider acceptance in the population. The escalation of violence during the 1970s initiated learning processes both among protesters and among the police forces, and efforts at de-escalation from both sides considerably reduced the radicalism of protest. The image of the police as 'citizens in uniform' emerged, with a growing sensitivity towards a 'legitimization from below'.

This democratization of the police forces is not yet complete, however. First of all, while the state police is demilitarized and more responsive to social needs, the *carabinieri* and *guardia di finanza* remain military, and very secretive, bodies. Second, the police reform was a reform moved from within, which focused more on the living conditions of police officers themselves than on police accountability towards society. The police remain extremely centralized, with the Ministry of Home Affairs still in full control and no devolution of powers to the **regions** or the city governments.

Further reading

Della Porta, D. and Reiter, H. (eds) (1998) *Protest Policing: The Control of Mass Demonstrations in Contemporary Democracies*, Minneapolis, MN: University of Minnesota Press (see especially chaps 6, 9 and 10 which deal extensively with Italy, and the introductory chapter which locates the Italian case in a cross-national perspective).

DONATELLA DELLA PORTA

Il Politecnico

Overseen by Elio **Vittorini** as commissioning editor, with Franco **Fortini** as co-editor, *Il Politecnico* was committed to disseminating cultural news in a popular form. It began as a weekly on 29 September 1945, becoming a monthly from 6 April 1946. Originally a broadsheet, it moved to magazine format as a monthly, when it also became more a journal of review and 'agenda setting' than of news. Given economic conditions in the immediate postwar years, few of the magazine's target readership could afford the 15 lire cover price, so the move to a monthly appears dictated, in part, by financial considerations. For the remainder of its life – whose extreme brevity now seems inversely proportional to its significance in postwar culture – the magazine appeared more often bi-monthly and sometimes quarterly.

Vittorini's aims with the publication were pluralist, interdisciplinary and divulgative; its tone was enthusiastic, its attitude a youthful irreverence and curiosity not entirely out of keeping with the editor's age (thirty-seven), nor with his intention to commemorate in its pages those who had died in the recent war and **Resistance**. The project had originated, in fact, in 1943–4 in clandestine discussions within the Resistance regarding the need for a 'new culture' that, in contrast to fascist culture, was open to ideas propounded in other parts of the world and was some advance on the liberal–humanist culture that had proved insufficient to combat the rise of European fascism (see **fascism and neo-fascism**). Significantly, the name was modelled on the nineteenth-century periodical devoted to promoting culture and social improvement, published by Milanese republican and federalist Carlo Cattaneo in the period leading up to the struggle for national unification.

Within the limits of its low budget, the publication was graphically interesting, innovative and original, particularly in the use of photographs and illustrations (including cartoons and comic strips) and in its moderately 'experimental' page design. Among the new fiction and essays it showcased were some sent in by *un semplice lettore* (a mere reader) and first-time writer, Italo **Calvino**. At the end of the first series, Vittorini estimated a readership of 80,000 based on sales of 22,000.

While Vittorini had strong moral affiliations with the Left in the *Politecnico* period, his assertion of a principle of imaginative and creative autonomy could not coexist with the **PCI** imperative at the time that culture must serve political ends. In mid-1946, PCI leader Palmiro **Togliatti** instigated a debate on this issue in the periodical *Rinascita*, as well as in a letter which Vittorini published in *Il Politecnico* 33–34 (1946) and to which he responded in no. 35 (1947). As a result, the publication was unable to survive the opening up of ideological differences between its broad-minded editorial policy (implicitly a libertarian politics) and the political force that could have been expected to be its chief support and constituency. No. 39 (December 1947) was (unofficially) the last issue; its lead article, significantly, dealt with the aporias of the anti-fascist culture.

Further reading

Gundle, S. (1989) 'The Communist Party and the Politics of Cultural Change in Postwar Italy, 1945–1950', in N. Hewitt (ed.), *The Culture of Reconstruction: European Thought, Literature and Film*, Macmillan: Basingstoke.

Il Politecnico (1975), Turin: Einaudi; facsimile reprint.

Zancan, M. (1984) *Il progetto 'Politecnico'. Cronaca e strutture di una rivista* (The Politecnico Project: History and Structures of a Magazine), Venice: Marsilio.

SUZANNE KIERNAN

political parties

As Sergio Romano, ex-ambassador and political analyst, once pointed out:

Italy is the only western democracy in which a

party secretary has more influence than a minister and in some cases, even more than the Prime Minister. Italy is the only large western democracy where a party's parliamentary group is less influential than its secretariat.

(*La Stampa*, 5 January 1997: 1)

This particularly Italian phenomenon has been known as *partitocrazia* or 'rule by parties', a term coined by Giuseppe Maranini in 1960s and much used to characterize the failures of the so-called 'First' **Republic**, another term used to indicate the intricate system of party dealings which typified Italian politics until the earthquake represented by the 1992 elections and their aftermath. Romano's observation is hardly less valid for the so-called Second Republic.

The other keyword closely associated with both *partitocrazia* and the First Republic is *lottizzazione*, literally the breaking up into lots, or more generally, dividing up the spoils. Not only were government posts regularly divided up according to the electoral share of the coalition partners – a normal and essential element of coalition democracy – but great swathes of the Italian public sector were also carved up between the parties. The posts of chief executive and membership of the boards of state agencies and companies like the **RAI**, State Railways, the Southern Development Fund (see **Cassa per il Mezzogiorno**), **IRI** and **ENI** were all filled according to party power first and competence second, if at all. For as long as government controlled the chief executives and boards of major banks, the same mechanism applied. At a regional and local level, *lottizzazione* was the usual way of filling personnel in utilities and municipal agencies from bus companies to hospitals and the local health units (USL). It goes without saying that civil service and municipal jobs, and subsequent promotion or làck of it, were all dependent on party loyalty. Even the magistrature, supposedly independent and in many ways much more so than other parts of the state, was divided largely along party lines with the groups in the High Council of the Magistrature (CSM) reflecting the parties albeit in a blurred way.

Beyond the state and other parts of the public sector and well into civil society, the parties also maintained a pervasive influence. Associations as diverse in purpose and size as a village bowls club and national **trade unions** with millions of members all came, more or less, under the aegis of a political party. With very few exceptions, until the 1990s there were no free-standing single-issue pressure groups but there were groups within the parties which fought for feminist issues and gay or housing issues. Professional groups also had their party representative, so that there would be Christian Democrat and Communist (and sometimes others as well) groups for small farmers, craftsmen and so on. So it was too for recreation: young people either played table tennis in the parish hall or in the local Communist headquarters.

The march of political parties into both the state and civil society began when the first successful mass party, the National Fascist Party (PNF), made explicit efforts to take over the state and, by implication, civil society. After the demise of the PNF, the idea and the structures remained, even if Italy was no longer a one-party state. As Montanelli wrote in 1976, 'They [Fanfani and other Christian Democrat leaders] did not say "Everything in the party and nothing outside the party" because Mussolini had already proclaimed that. But they thought it' (Montanelli, 1976: 109). The growth of a number of mass parties after the Second World War, in particular the **DC**, the **PCI** and the Socialist Party, ended the power of local notables thereby itself increasing the parties' power.

The corruption investigations (see *Mani pulite*; *Tangentopoli*) and the collapse or reorganization of all the traditional parties in the early 1990s meant that the mechanisms of *lottizzazione* faltered for a time; resources could no longer be distributed through the parties, since many of those parties had effectively ceased to exist. Nonetheless, as was shown by **Berlusconi**'s immediate rush to fill the RAI with his own nominees when he came to power, the desire to use party to control public resources was naturally carried through to the 'Second' Republic.

As a result of the proportional electoral system in the First Republic, electoral alliances tended not to work since parties attempted to increase their share of the vote by accentuating differences rather than similarities (in organization, policies and style) even where those differences were minimal. In the

'Second' Republic, by contrast, alliances became essential in order to win seats in single-member constituencies. Yet, even if clear alliances have been formed and – since 1994 Italy has indeed moved towards a system of two big blocs – the actual number of parties has not decreased. **L'Ulivo** and the **Polo della Libertà** are made up of a varying number of separate parties, even more numerous than in the First Republic's proportional system. Ironically, in spite of all the changes, a very small political party could still bring down an entire government, as often happened in the First Republic and as the Refoundation Communist Party (see **Rifondazione Comunista**) was able to do with the **Prodi** government in 1998.

Ideologically, the Italian parties belonged to four main streams: a socialist one (the PCI, the **PSIUP** which split, largely as a reaction to the Cold War, into the **PSDI** and the **PSI**, with the PSDI soon moving into the secular centre and the PSI following in the 1980s); a Catholic one (the **DC**): a secular orientation (right and left, **PLI**, **PRI**, PR) and a Fascist successor (**MSI**, later AN). In the late 1980s, the separatist Northern League (see **Lega Nord**) was added to the four but, despite the reshuffling of names and the borders between centre–right and centre–left, the parties of the 'Second Republic' maintained the same categories as before: **PDS** (later becoming DS) and Rifondazione Comunista (RF) on the Left, the PPI, CCD–CDU for the Catholics, **Forza Italia** succeeding the secular centre and Alleanza Nazionale (**National Alliance**) providing a name change for the MSI.

See also: constitution; Parliament

Further reading

Bull, M. and Newell, J.L. (1997) 'Party Organisations and Alliances in Italy in the 1990s. A Revolution of Sorts', *West European Politics* 20 (1): 81–109.

Carter, N. (1998) 'Italy: The Demise of the Postwar Partyocracy', in J.K. White and P.J. Davies (eds), *Political Parties and the Collapse of the Old Orders*, Albany, NY: State University of New York Press.

Farneti, P. (1985) *The Italian Party System, 1945–1980*, ed. S.E. Finer and A. Mastropaolo, London: Pinter (a detailed study of all aspects of the Italian party system).

Golden, M. (1998) 'Interest Representation, Party Systems, and the State. Italy in Comparative Perspective', in M. Donovan (ed.), *Italy*, Aldershot: Ashgate, vol. 1.

Hine, D. (1996) 'Italian Political Reform in Comparative Perspective', in S. Gundle and S. Parker (eds), *The New Italian Republic: From the Fall of the Berlin Wall to Berlusconi*, London: Routledge.

Montanelli, I. (1976) *I protagonisti*, Milan: Mondadori.

Pasquino, G. (1997) 'No longer a "Party State"? Institutions, Power and the Problems of Italian Reform', *West European Politics* 20 (1): 34–53.

JAMES WALSTON

Polo delle Libertà

The Polo delle Libertà was the last of a series of centre–right electoral alliances engineered by Silvio **Berlusconi** between 1994 and 1996, often known simply as Il Polo, and usually translated as 'Freedom Alliance'. By 1997 it had become firmly based on two pillars, **Forza Italia** and Alleanza Nazionale (see **National Alliance**), and less firmly on a third formed by the small centre–right parties that had emerged in the wake of the dissolution of the **DC**.

In 1994, Berlusconi created Forza Italia (FI) and negotiated two separate electoral alliances to cover the single-member constituencies across the country. In the North, most seats were divided between FI and the **Lega Nord** (Northern League), and the alliance was called Polo della Libertà. In most constituencies, a candidate of the right-wing Alleanza Nazionale (AN) also stood against the Polo and other candidates. In the South, there was an arrangement between FI and AN, who put up a common candidate for each seat under the name of Polo del Buon Governo (Alliance for Good Government). In both alliances, there were candidates from the right-wing ex-Christian Democrats (**CCD**), the Lista Pannella and the Unione del Centro (Union of the Centre) under the ex-Liberal, Raffaele Costa. After the election, the term 'Polo' was used to refer to the government coalition led by Berlusconi and made up of FI, AN, LN, CCD and the smaller groupings. From April to December 1994, the divergences between Berlusconi and Umberto **Bossi**, the outspoken leader of the Northern League, became increasingly apparent until the government coalition dissolved. Over the same period, Berlusconi, **Fini** and Casini of the CCD developed a separate alliance. In January the following year they were joined by half of a further breakup of the ex-DC when the **PPI** split into the right-wing **CDU** under Rocco Buttiglione and the left-wing under Gerardo Bianco. In opposition and in the regional elections in 1995, during the elections of 1996 and in opposition afterwards, the label Polo came to refer to an operational alliance made up mainly of FI, AN, CCD–CDU and some smaller groups. They contested the election together with a common candidate in all the single member constituencies and normally voted together in **Parliament**. However, they maintained separate Parliamentary groups and did not present a common manifesto at the 1996 elections.

There are important ideological and structural differences between the Polo's three main components – Forza Italia, Berlusconi's company party, Alleanza Nazionale, described by its leader Gianfranco Fini as 'post-fascist' or 'social right wing', and the successor parties of the DC – which make the alliance both unwieldy and unstable. There have been crucial differences on fundamental policy choices such as the extent of privatization necessary to free up the public sector (see **privatization and nationalization**) and the kind and amount of constitutional reform desirable (including electoral reform and devolution). The smaller elements which have made up the Polo, like **Pannella** and Costa, are even more disparate amongst themselves. The only clear notion which all components of the alliance share is a common opposition to the Communist Party and its successors, the **PDS** and the DS, and it was this orientation that won it a relative majority of votes in the 1996 elections, although this was not effectively translated into seats.

See also: political parties

Further reading

Bull, M. and Newell, J.L. (1997) 'Party Organisations and Alliances in Italy in the 1990s: A Revolution of Sorts', *West European Politics* 20 (1): 81–109 (the Polo in the context of more general changes in Italian politics in the 1990s).

JAMES WALSTON

Pomilio, Mario

b. 21 January 1921, Orsogna, Chieti; d. 3 April 1990, Naples

Novelist, critic and essayist

From his first appearance on the literary scene in 1954 with the novel *L'uccello nella cupola* (The Bird in the Cupola), Mario Pomilio expressed his particular interest in ethical and religious themes. He would continue to explore them in later novels such as *Il quinto evangelio* (The Fifth Gospel) (1975), winner of the Best Foreign Book award in Paris in 1978, and *Il Natale del 1833* (The Christmas of 1833), winner of the Strega Prize in 1983, as well as in many newspapers articles, later collected as *Scritti cristiani* (Christian Writings) (1979). Pomilio also participated in the intense cultural and political debates of the 1960s, on the one hand by representing the crisis of the postwar leftist ideology in the novel *La compromissione* (Compromise) (1965), on the other by strongly opposing the neoavant-garde movement, as documented in his essays *Contestazioni* (Protests) (1966) and short stories *Il cane sull'Etna* (The Dog on Etna) (1978).

FRANCESCA PARMEGGIANI

Pomodoro, Arnaldo

b. 23 June 1926, Morciano di Romagna

Sculptor

Arnaldo Pomodoro produces abstract sculptures based on geometric forms, such as cubes, cylinders and pyramids, with smooth outer surfaces. Sections of the skin and segments of the shapes are then cut away to reveal complex insides which may look like anything from organic forms to the internal structures of machines or computers. His works can be seen in public places in Cesena and in Rimini, where he grew up.

Asse di movimento (Axis of Movement), from 1983–7, is a square pyramid of bronze. A major, jagged horizontal slice has been taken out, like a gaping mouth, which, with some vertical jags, seems precariously poised, as if about to clamp shut. There is the sense that these are subtractions, complete forms with some vital part removed, but that of course is illusion. Arnaldo has struck upon a very rich vein of abstract imagery, which he mines with talent.

See also: sculpture

Further reading

Barilli, R. (ed.) (1995) *Arnaldo Pomodoro*, 2 vols, Cesena: Il Vicolo (illustrated catalogues of exhibitions at Cesena and Rimini, with text in Italian and English).

MAX STAPLES

Pomodoro, Giò

b. 17 November 1930, Orciano di
  Romagna

Sculptor

Giò Pomodoro's technical background is evident in his abstract sculptures, which experiment with the possibilities of materials and form. *Grandi contatti* (Big Contacts) of 1962 shows his interest in giving a rigid material like bronze the unusual appearance of having been folded. From the 1970s onwards, Pomodoro intentionally worked against the fashion of ephemeral art created for private display by producing works in marble and bronze for exhibition in public places, and which encouraged community participation. Unlike his brother and fellow sculptor, Arnaldo **Pomodoro**, who tends to base works around one monumental geometric form, Giò's works are more a combination of many geometric shapes. *Sole-serpente* (Sun Serpent) of 1988–9 has the appearance of a jumble of three-dimensional letters of the alphabet.

See also: sculpture

MAX STAPLES

Pontecorvo, Gillo (Gilberto)

b. 19 November 1919, Pisa

Film director

After studying chemistry at the University of Pisa, Pontecorvo turned to journalism and became a left-wing correspondent in Paris. In 1941 he returned to Italy, joined the **PCI** and fought as a partisan. After the war he spent several years as assistant to Mario **Monicelli**. His first feature film, *La grande strada azzurra* (The Long Blue Road) (1957) was an adaptation of a novel by Franco Solinas, who collaborated on many scripts of Pontecorvo's later films. *La battaglia di Algeri* (The Battle of Algiers) (1966), Pontecorvo's most famous film, was awarded the Golden Lion at the Venice Film Festival in 1966. Financed by Algerian government money and starring actual members of the liberation movement, it adopts a semi-documentary style to meticulously recreate historical events. The international success of this film – except in France, where it was banned for many years – paved the way for Pontecorvo's move to Hollywood where he made *Queimada/Burn!* (1969), a film about the self-destructive nature of colonialism starring Marlon Brando. This was followed by *Ogro* (The Tunnel) (1979) dealing with Basque terrorism. In 1992 Pontecorvo was appointed Director of the Venice Film Festival, and set about engineering its return to world significance.

LAURENCE SIMMONS

Ponti, Giò (Giovanni)

b. 18 November 1891, Milan;
  d. 16 September 1979, Milan

Architect

An 'architect-artist' true to his name, Ponti created connections between architecture, culture and industry, both inside and outside Italy. In bridging various expressive tendencies, Ponti assumed a number of roles for himself: architect, industrial designer, set designer, painter, editor, academic and organizer of the **Milan Trienniale** exhibitions.

Ponti's autonomy allowed him to make such connections effortlessly. Although he developed a sympathetic rapport with creative individuals like **Mollino** and **de Chirico**, he distanced himself from exclusive membership of any artistic or political group. Consequently, Ponti's expression, freely drawn from far-reaching sources, was personal, pluralistic and poetic.

For over forty years, Ponti was editorial director of *Domus*, the journal he founded in Milan in 1928. In writing for *Domus*, Ponti and his contributors sought the means to realize the quintessential 'home'. Also founded in the same city, in the same year, was the journal *Casabella*. These two Milanese journals served as the expressive vehicles for two opposing but not mutually exclusive attitudes within Italian architecture: the artful, inclusive and international attitude of *Domus* and the polemical, self-reflective stance of *Casabella*.

The inclusive attitude forged by Ponti in *Domus* was made evident in his Milanese works, buildings that were both light and dynamic. For the early SIVEM/Torre project (1933–4), Ponti designed two dissimilar buildings for one site – one in the decorative 'novecento' (twentieth-century) style, the other according to the 'rationalist' tenets advocated by *Casabella* – not to endorse either of the two competing Milanese tendencies but rather to suggest the legitimacy of both. For the **Pirelli** tower (Milan, 1956–61), Ponti, together with engineers Nervi and Danusso, artfully combined building form and structure to craft an expressive prism that reflected the international fashion for glass towers. The counterpart to the 'light' Pirelli tower was the 'weighty' Velasca tower, realized in Milan at the same time. Unlike the outward-looking Pirelli – a physical articulation of Ponti's postwar *Domus* – the Velasca tower designed by Belgiojoso, Peressuti and **Rogers** was meant to bear the cultural history of its city, a position advocated by Rogers, then editor of *Casabella*. The coexistence of two different architectural expressions was once again facilitated by Ponti.

While completing the design of the Pirelli tower, Ponti also published *Amate l'Architettura*, a plea to architects, patrons and the wider public to 'love architecture'. Ponti defined this collection of personal reflections, thoughts and aphorisms concerning architecture as an 'autobiography' and in it, in his typical way, he characterized architecture as a 'precise fantasy' that itself reveals the 'fantasy of precision'.

Ponti's most exemplary achievement remains, perhaps, his butterfly-like residence for the Planchart family (Caracas, 1955). Ponti envisioned this house to be like his life: an encompassing artistic project containing and transforming fundamental life-lessons. Architecture nevertheless remained for Ponti an unrequited love, an unfinished house, a dream yet to be realized.

See also: architectural and design magazines

Further reading

Ponti, L.L. (1990) *Giò Ponti: The Complete Works 1923–1978*, Cambridge, MA: MIT Press.

KEITH EVAN GREEN

Pontiggia, Giuseppe

b. 25 September 1934, Como

Writer and critic

Pontiggia's career as a writer began in 1959 with the publication of the novel *La morte in banca* (Death in the Bank), in which the influence of prestigious models such as Svevo and Kafka is traceable not only at the level of plot, but also in the polished literariness and the balanced style of the book. Pontiggia's work is also generally characterized by a preference for a 'classical' type of literature, that is, not only a passion for Latin writers such as Sallust and Lucan, but a writing which is itself pondered and extremely attentive to its formal and stylistic aspects. The other pole of his poetics is an experimental and innovative tension, one which took him close to the neoavantgarde (see for example his *L'arte della fuga* (The Art of Escape), 1969). His later novels successfully manage to merge the 'classical' and the 'experimental' into a relaxed and affable narrative. His critical essays similarly range effortlessly and widely across both classical and modern authors.

Further reading

Pontiggia, G. (1984) *Il Giardino delle Esperidi* (The Garden of Hesperides), Milan: Adelphi (a collection of critical essays on authors as varied as Lucan, Plutarch, Gadda and Borges).
—— (1989) *La grande sera* (The Great Evening), Milan: Mondadori (winner of the Strega prize).

ENRICO CESARETTI

pop and rock music

Italian pop music may be taken to begin at the **Sanremo Festival** of 1958 with perhaps the most famous Italian song of all time, 'Volare, nel blu dipinto di blu'. Written and performed by Domenico **Modugno**, a young singer-songwriter from Puglia, the song marked a definite line of separation from the older melodic tradition represented by singers like Nilla Pizzi and Claudio **Villa**. In spite of its novelty, however, 'Volare' was indebted, at least in part, to young American music, in particular to the sounds of the Platters, and Italian pop music in the postwar period would continue to be a fusion of certain native elements and imported British and American influences.

The more swinging style of the so-called *urlatori* (screamers) followed in the early 1960s with singers like Peppino Di Capri, together with the more aggressive rock'n'rollers like Adriano **Celentano**, who scandalized the Sanremo audience in 1961 by turning his back as he sang his '24 mila baci' (24 Thousand Kisses).

The 'beat' period, from 1963 to 1970, can be divided into three major strands. The first two, the individual pop singers and then the development of groups, were variously influenced by the new music coming mostly from Britain, especially that of the Beatles (who appeared live in Rome in 1965) and the Rolling Stones. These included singers like Gianni **Morandi** and Rita Pavone, and bands like Equipe 84, I Camaleonti (The Chameleons), The Dik Dik and The New Trolls. Young and angry, Morandi and Pavone captivated their audience

with a style which was both aggressive and soft. 'Datemi un martello' (Gimme a Hammer), sang the 'yeah-yeah girl' Rita, but also 'Come te non c'è nessuno' (There's Nobody Like You). With his baby face, Morandi conquered both teenagers and their parents, and his songs were also immediately made into successful movies. In the same style, Caterina Caselli, with her characteristic blonde hairdo, recorded songs like 'Nessuno mi può giudicare' (Nobody Can Judge Me) and 'Perdono' (Forgive Me). Radio programmes like *Bandiera Gialla* and clubs like The Piper in Rome became the sanctuaries for this type of music. The Piper was the birthplace of many future Italian legends including Patty Pravo, another blonde singer who was to make an indelible mark on Italian Pop. Inevitably, there was also a crowd of Elvis Presley imitators such as Bobby Solo ('Una lacrima sul viso' (A Tear On Your Face)) and Little Tony ('Riderà' (She Will Laugh)).

The first rock bands were formed in the wake of the success of the Beatles, using the classic voice, guitar, bass and drums line-up. Equipe 84, from Modena, followed the model closely, with both original songs and translated covers of British groups (like 'Blackberry Way' from The Small Faces). Similar bands were I Nomadi (The Nomads) with their leader Augusto Daolio, and the Dik Dik who covered the anthem 'California Dreamin' by the American Mamas and Papas. The New Trolls, from Genoa, introduced a more guitar-driven, Hendrix style. There were also British pop singers who achieved success in Italy using an odd linguistic mix such as Mal of The Primitives and Shel Shapiro, from The Rokes; Shapiro also acted in Mario **Monicelli**'s film *Brancaleone alle Crociate* (The Crusader Brancaleone).

The third strand in those early years was represented by artists who wrote their own songs in the French 'chansonnier' tradition. Luigi Tenco, with a troubled personal life which would tragically end in suicide (see *cantautori*), was a sort of founder of this style, and his melancholic songs effected a whole generation of Italian young people. Gino Paoli contributed a romantic touch ('Il cielo in una stanza' (The Sky In a Room)), while Fabrizio De Andrè took more intellectual detours ('La canzone di Marinella' (The Song of Marinella)). Special mention should be made of **Mina**, an excellent interpreter of all genres, from melodic to rock style, from samba to jazz, and Lucio **Battisti** who together with the lyricist Mogol created some of the most memorable songs of the period, such as 'Acqua azzurra, acqua chiara' (Blue Water, Clear Water) and 'I giardini di marzo' (The Gardens In March).

At the beginning of the 1970s, new influences from the United States (the hippie movement) and the birth of 'progressive rock' brought changes to the Italian music scene. The more 'classic' individual singers like Morandi declined in popularity while the rock bands drew greater public interest, encouraged by music magazines like *Ciao 2001*. Groups such as Le Orme (The Footprints) or Premiata Forneria Marconi, inspired by Pink Floyd and King Crimson, mixed rock and classical music. With a taste for a carefully crafted pop sound, the Pooh topped the charts and extended their success during the 1970s. The band Area occupied a unique position: linked to the political movement of the 1970s and present at the Re Nudo (Naked King) mass gathering at Parco Lambro in Milan, the Area was led by its Greek-born singer Demetrio Stratos and played a special fusion of free jazz and progressive rock. Politics also inspired bands that were closer to the folk tradition, like the Stormy Six who sang about workers strikes or historical events like the Battle of Stalingrad. This was also the time of garages, and groups would join together to play in dark cellars as much as on the Sanremo stage. Matia Bazar became the most famous group of the late 1970s, with pop anthems like 'Solo tu' (Only You) and sophisticated but old-fashioned songs like 'Vacanze romane' (Roman Holidays).

The punk era also exerted its influence, and in Bologna after 1977 a new generation of aggressive bands made their noisy debut. Skiantos, led by oddball Freak Antoni, mixed ironic lyrics with devastating guitar riffs, and Gaznevada anticipated the new wave revolution. In Florence at the beginning of the 1980s, a darker sound began to emerge with bands like Litfiba, led by powerful singer Piero Pelù, and Diaframma, with its obscure, poetic lyrics. In the middle of Emilia, Giovanni Lindo Ferretti created CCCP, a strange ensemble of musicians and dancers, celebrating in an electronic and sarcastic way the alienation of modern life and the orthodox communist ideal ('Fedeli alla linea' (Faithful to the Line), 1985). Predictably, the group changed its name to CSI after the dissolution of the Soviet Empire, and became producers helping young emerging bands.

The 1990s witnessed the **rap music** revolution, born from a political context in the urban centres with combos like 99 Posse, Onda Rossa Posse and Sangue Misto as well as a varied underground scene, influenced by different currents, from grunge to British pop revenge. Marlene Kuntz were the Italian Sonic Youth ('Catartica', 1994), while the Massimo Volume (Maximum Volume) from Bologna worked with a peculiar conception of musical poetry ('Lungo i bordi' (On the Borders), 1994) and Casino Royale from Milan explored techno ('CRX', 1997). The linguistic dialectal tradition, mixed with dub influences inspired bands like Almamegretta, from Naples ('Sanacore', 1995) while a more theatrical experience led Avion Travel to original and refined songwriting. Neri per Caso (Black by Chance) revived the tradition of 'vocal only' groups while Afterhours and Negrita repeated the rock lesson of Rolling Stones.

See also: American influence

Further readings

Arbore, R. (1989) *Il nuovissimo dizionario del rock* (The New Dictionary of Rock), Rome: Pandalibri.

Castaldo, G. (1994) *La terra promessa. Quarant'anni di cultura rock (1954–1994)* (The Promised Land: Forty Years of Rock Culture 1954–1994), Milan: Feltrinelli.

Ceri, L. and De Pasquale, E. (1993) *Mondo beat. Musica e costume nell'Italia degli anni sessanta* (The World of Beat: Music and Custom in the Italy of the 1960s), Bologna: Thema.

Pasquali, A. (1997) *Dizionario della musica italiana* (Dictionary of Italian Music), Rome: Newton Compton.

Riccio, G. (1980) *Percorsi del rock italiano* (Roads of Italian Rock), Milan: Il Formichiere.

Rizzi, C. (1993) *Enciclopedia del rock italiano* (Encyclopedia of Italian Rock), Milan: Arcana.

RICCARDO VENTRELLA

Pope John XXIII (Angelo Giuseppe Roncalli)

b. 25 November 1881, Sotto il Monte, Bergamo; d. 3 June 1963, Rome

Pope, 1958–63

Warm and open, John XXIII was universally regarded as 'the people's pope', and the one who initiated the process of bringing the Catholic Church into modern times. Of humble peasant origins, Angelo Giuseppe Roncalli was a product of the northern Italian Catholic milieu, which has produced five popes during the twentieth century. He was educated at the Bergamo and Roman seminaries, ordained on 10 August 1904 and became secretary to the Catholic social reformist Bishop Radini-Tedeschi. His first pastoral experience was as a medical orderly/chaplain with the Italian army from 1915–18.

In 1920 Roncalli entered the missionary congregation Propaganda Fide (Propagation of the Faith), becoming archbishop and apostolic delegate to Bulgaria in 1925 and to Turkey (with responsibility for Greece) in 1935. These difficult postings gave him an experience of diplomacy and an ecumenical perspective, and when the Second World War came he also became involved in saving Jews. In 1944 he was appointed nuncio to France with the task of dealing with the problematic worker priests and with De Gaulle's demand for the removal of thirty-three bishops who had collaborated with Vichy. In the end, only eight bishops were removed.

In 1953, he was made a cardinal and appointed patriarch of Venice, where he showed much concern for the poor of the city's industrial hinterland and maintained cordial relations with the socialists. At his election as pope in 1958 he was initially seen as a compromise or stopgap candidate, but he quickly dispelled such illusions by taking the radical step of summoning the **Second Vatican Council** in 1960.

The Council was John XXIII's greatest achievement, especially since he faced systematic obstructionism on the part of curial conservatives. His pontificate was also notable for his attempts to mediate in the Cuban Missile Crisis of 1962 and the first tentative steps in the direction of 'Ostpolitik',

an opening to the east which was reciprocated by the visit of Khruschev's son-in-law to the Vatican in 1963. Two major encyclicals, *Mater et Magistra* (Mother and Teacher) of 1961 and *Pacem in Terris* (Peace on Earth) of 1963 set new directions in papal social teaching, and the fundamental distinction drawn between the falseness of Marxism as a philosophy on the one hand and the practical policies of parties like the Italian Socialists, on the other, gave the signal for the launching of the first centre–left government in Italy, with peace and the problems of the Third World being placed firmly on the Catholic social agenda.

John XXIII's critics accused him of selling out to communism and of destroying the theological and liturgical unity of the Church, but at his death in June 1963 he was mourned as no other pope has been in the twentieth century. His extraordinary spiritual stature was officially confirmed in 1999 when he was set down for beautification in September 2000.

Further reading

Falconi, C. (1967) *The Popes in the Twentieth Century: From Pius X to John XXIII*, London: Weidenfeld & Nicolson (excellent biographical essays; see especially last chapter).

Hebblethwaite, P. (1984) *John XXIII: Pope of the Council*, London: Geoffrey Chapman (the definitive biography in English).

JOHN POLLARD

Pope John Paul I (Albino Luciani)

b. 17 October 1912, Forno di Canale, Belluno; d. 28/29 September 1978, the Vatican

Pope, 1978

The pontificate of John Paul I was one of the shortest in history, just thirty-three days. Educated in his diocesan seminary, Luciani was ordained priest on 7 July 1935. Acting Vicar-general of Belluno in 1948, he was appointed Bishop of neighbouring Vittorio Veneto ten years later and in 1969 he was promoted Patriarch of Venice. He was elected pope on the opening day of the conclave which followed the death of Paul VI in August 1978. It is still unclear whether he was the compromise candidate between the 'serious contenders', cardinals Benelli and Siri, or was chosen as a 'pastoral' pope after the intensely 'political' Paul VI. His humility and simplicity led him to abolish the papal coronation and change his title from 'Supreme Pontiff' to 'Supreme Pastor'.

Further reading

Cornwell, J. (1989) *Like a Thief in the Night: The Death of Pope John Paul I*, London: Corgi (convincingly debunks the theory of Yallop, below).

Yallop, D. (1984) *In God's name: An Investigation into the Murder of Pope John Paul I*, London: Viking (argues that John Paul was murdered because he was about to clean up various messes left by his predecessor, and thus upset powerful figures inside and outside the Vatican).

JOHN POLLARD

Pope John Paul II (Karel Jozef Wojtyla)

b. 18 May 1920, Wadowice, Poland

Pope, 1978–

John Paul II is the first Slav pope and the first non-Italian since Pope Hadrian VI (1522–3). The pontificate of this former actor has been characterized by a mixture of conservatism and charisma. Born into a poor family, Karel Wojtyla was educated at the Jagellionian University and the Archbishop's Seminary in Cracow, clandestinely in the latter case due to the Nazi occupation. He was ordained in 1946 and after a period at the Angelicum University in Rome, he served as parish priest and university chaplain. In 1958 he was appointed an auxiliary bishop of Cracow, archbishop in 1964 and cardinal in 1967. He became known outside of Poland thanks to his participation in the **Second Vatican Council** and a number of lecture tours in the USA.

He was elected pope after the death of John Paul I on 16 October 1978, a compromise candidate between the strongly conservative Cardinal Siri

and his liberal opponents. Since his election, he has carried forward the implementation of Vatican II in a conservative key. International synods of bishops have been held under tightly controlled conditions, and national ones have been used to 'tame' hierarchies regarded as too liberal, such as the Dutch and the Americans.

Wojtyla has also held the line firmly on doctrinal and disciplinary matters. The appointment of Cardinal Joseph Ratzinger as head of the Congregation for the Doctrine of the Faith has led to a crackdown on radical Catholic theologians and publications, and a denunciation of liberation theology. In his public pronouncements, Wojtyla has firmly rejected married priests and the ordination of women, and he has followed an uncompromising line in continuing to oppose contraception, abortion and homosexuality. In 1994, the Vatican made itself extremely unpopular at the Cairo Conference on Population and Development for its stand on these issues, and a year later it took an equally intransigent stand on 'female reproductive rights' at the Beijing conference.

His encyclical *Veritatis Splendor* (The Splendour of Truth) and the *Catechism of the Catholic Church*, both in 1993, epitomize his conservatism in matters of theology and morals. But there can be no doubt about the powerful effects on Catholics of his own personal warmth and charm, typified by the blessing which he gave to the crowds in St Peter's Square early in January, 1979: 'God bless you; and your umbrellas.'

Under a Polish pope, the Vatican's 'Ostpolitik' (relations with the Eastern bloc) changed somewhat, but its architect, Cardinal Casaroli, remained John Paul's Secretary of State from 1979 to 1991. Wojtyla is regarded as having played a significant role in the downfall of communism, and there are allegations of Soviet involvement in the attempt on his life in 1981. On the other hand, the Pope has repeatedly attacked the decadence of Western capitalist materialism, most notably in his encyclical *Centesimus Annus* (1991). During John Paul's reign, Vatican diplomacy has expanded enormously in both numbers and prestige, even if it ultimately proved to be ineffective in avoiding the 1991 Gulf War, or in intervening in the troubled affairs of the former Yugoslavia.

John Paul II's impact upon Italy has not been

substantially different from that on other countries, the most momentous events in his pontificate being the signing of the new Concordat in 1983 (see **church, state and society**) and his direct intervention in politics at the birth of the **PPI**.

See also: Vatican

Further reading

Bernstein, C. and Politi, M. (1996) *His Holiness: John Paul II and the Hidden History of Our Time*, Auckland and London: Doubleday (particularly concerned with Wojtyla's alleged collaboration with Ronald Reagan and with the pope's role in the victory of the Solidarnosc movement and the collapse of communism).

Willey, D. (1992) *God's Politician*, New York: St Martin's Press (a broad survey of John Paul II's policies, by the BBC's 'man in Rome').

Williams, G.H. (1981) *The Mind of John Paul II: Origins of His Thought and Action*, New York: Seabury Press.

JOHN POLLARD

Pope Paul VI (Gianbattista Montini)

b. 26 November 1897, Concesio, Brescia; d. 6 August 1978, Castelgandolfo, Rome

Pope, 1963–78

Paul VI was pope during one of the most difficult periods in the recent history of Roman Catholicism and of Italy. Gianbattista Montini was born into a middle-class family; his father, Giorgio, was heavily involved in the Catholic movement. Delicate health necessitated a partly private education and exemption from military service in 1916. He was ordained priest in 1921 and was sent to the Academy of Noble Ecclesiastics as a prelude to a career in the **Vatican** diplomatic service. In October 1924 he entered the Secretariat of State, where he remained for thirty years.

Alongside his curial duties, he carried on a pastoral ministry in FUCI, the Catholic University Students Federation, and in ML, the graduates' association, and lived an intense intellectual life. He immersed himself in French Catholic thought, including the works of Marc Sangnier and Jacques Maritain, and soon acquired a reputation as an anti-fascist and as a 'dissident' in the Vatican. In 1937 he was appointed Substitute to the Cardinal Secretary of State, and his role in wartime became very important, especially after Cardinal Maglione's death in 1944.

In 1954 he was appointed Archbishop of Milan, a move engineered by his opponents in order to get him away from the Vatican. Consequently, although head of Italy's most important metropolitan see after Rome, he was not made a cardinal until after the election of **Pope John XXIII** in 1958. He became heavily involved in John's project for a **Second Vatican Council** and thus became his 'designated' successor. Against strong curial opposition, he was elected pope in June 1963.

Bringing John's council to a successful conclusion was probably Montini's greatest achievement as pope, but there were others: he reformed the Roman curia, making it more international and abolishing much of the unnecessary pomp, including the Noble and Palatine Guards. In his encyclical *Octogesima Adveniens* (Eightieth Anniversary) (1971) he developed further John's social teaching, and put it into practice through his travels to the Third World (he was the first pope since the early nineteenth century to travel outside of Italy) and the pursuit of an understanding with the Eastern bloc nations. In particular, he repeated a condemnation of nuclear war, sought to bring the Vietnam War to an end and also pushed forward the cause of ecumenism, especially with the Anglican Communion. Ironically, however, he will probably be most remembered for the encyclicals *Humanae Vitae* (On Human Life) (1968), which condemned artificial methods of birth control, and *Personae Humanae* (The Human Person) (1975), which argued that homosexual acts were 'intrinsically disordered', a stance strongly resented by the Italian gay community.

In the Italian context, he will be remembered for his difficult relationship with the leadership of the Christian Democratic party (see **DC**), many of whom he had nurtured during his years with the university student associations. In his declining years he felt the bitterness of defeat in the divorce referendum of 1974 and, despite his attempts in his 'Letter to the **Red Brigades**', he suffered the pain of being unable to save Aldo **Moro** from death at their hands in April 1978.

Futher reading

Hanson, E.O. (1987) *The Catholic Church in World Politics*, Princeton, NJ: Princeton University Press (see especially the sections on 'Ostpolitik' and The Third World).

Hebblethwaite, P. (1993) *Paul VI: The First Modern Pope*, London: HarperCollins (the definitive biography in English).

JOHN POLLARD

Pope Pius XII (Eugenio Pacelli)

b. 2 March 1876, Rome; d. 9 October 1958, Castelgandolfo, Rome

Pope, 1939–58

Chiefly remembered for his silence over the Holocaust, in postwar Italy Pius XII presided over, and epitomized, a short-lived but oppressive period of Catholic 'triumphalism'. From a family of minor Roman nobility in papal service, Eugenio Pacelli was ordained priest in 1899 after education at the Collegio Capranica and the Gregorian and Rome universities. In 1901 he entered the Vatican Secretariat of State at the beginning of a brilliant career. Nominated Secretary of Extraordinary Affairs in 1912, he was appointed nuncio to Bavaria in 1917 and nuncio to Berlin in 1920, where he remained until appointed Secretary of State in 1929.

As relations between the **Vatican** and Germany deteriorated, and as Europe became increasingly polarized between the democracies and the dictatorships, Pacelli established closer links with the former and also visited the USA in 1936. By the time Pius XI died in February 1939, Pacelli had clearly become his heir and was quickly elected pope in March of that year. By 1945, he had steered the Vatican through the vicissitudes of war and established a close relationship with the USA.

The Soviet takeover of Eastern Europe, and the subsequent persecution of the Church there, led Papa Pacelli to mount an anti-communist crusade. He responded to the challenge of the communist parties of France and Italy, the two largest outside the USSR, by a decree of the Holy Office that excommunicated communists and their collaborators. And though in formal diplomatic terms the Vatican maintained a steadfastly neutral stance in the developing Cold War, he was dubbed 'chaplain' of the Atlantic alliance.

In ecclesiastical matters, Pius XII was no great innovator, though his liturgical reforms in the early 1950s anticipated the greater changes of the **Second Vatican Council**. His encyclical *Humani Generis* (1950) was a warning against the 'new' theology emerging from France, and his infallible definition of the dogma of the Assumption of Our Lady in 1950 estranged non-Catholics further from the Church.

Even though the postwar period saw the emergence of Christian Democratic parties of government in most countries of Western Europe, Pius XII was initially sceptical of the prospects for the Italian Christian Democrats (see **DC**), preferring a more authoritarian mode of government on the Portuguese or Spanish model. After the DC victory in 1948, Pius XII and some of his collaborators still sought to keep the party on a short leash, and he never forgave **De Gasperi** for preventing the formation of an electoral coalition of Catholics and the extreme right in Rome in 1952 in order to defeat the communists. And, until the very end, the pope officially forbade the much hoped-for governmental alliance of the Socialists and DC, the so-called '**opening to the Left**'.

On the positive side, Pius XII exploited his charisma very effectively among crowds and on the electronic media. He has frequently been referred to as the last 'real' pope, that is, the last with absolute power.

See also: church, state and society

Further reading

Cornwell, J. (1999) *Hitler's Pope: The Secret History of Pius XII*, London: Viking (a controversial study of Pacelli's relations with Nazi Germany).

Cross, S.L. and Livingstone, E.A. (eds) (1997) *The*

Oxford Dictionary of the Christian Church, Oxford: Oxford University Press.

Falconi, C. (1967) *The Popes in the Twentieth Century: From Pius XI to John XXIII*, London: Weidenfeld & Nicolson (see ch. 4, the only useful biographical essay in English).

JOHN POLLARD

population

Beginning at the end of the Second World War, Italy began a phase of major development that would transform it in less than fifty years from a largely agricultural country into an advanced industrialized capitalist economy. In the process Italy came to record patterns of both demographic and class structure characteristic of most other advanced Western nations.

Especially since the 1970s, Italian demographics, once typically Mediterranean, have come increasingly to resemble those of north Europeans. A rapid decline in birthrate – from 18.5 per 1,000 in the early 1950s to less than 10 per 1,000 in the late 1990s – has been reflected in the dramatic slowdown of natural population growth. Resident population grew from 47.1 million in 1951 to 57 million in 1985, but thereafter slowed dramatically with the 1991 census recording only 56.8 million. In fact the growth rate, measured as yearly and national average compound rate, fell to 0.3 per cent from the 1970s to the1990s in comparison with 0.7 per cent in the previous decades, with the rate in the northern regions actually becoming negative.

Change in population structure has been even more dramatic. Due to a marked decline in fertility, the average number of children per woman has fallen from 2.4 in the early 1970s to just 1.2 in the early 1990s on national average (slightly higher in the South), a value that puts Italy amongst the group of European countries which experts consider having crossed the 'danger threshold' towards negative growth and ageing. As a consequence, the youngest generations have declined continuously. Under-15s accounted only for 15 per cent of total population in the early 1990s – a figure below the average of advanced countries – while the old (over 65) have risen above 14 per cent.

Another major feature of recent demographic change in Italy – traditionally a country of emigrants – has been its transformation into a country with an active migration balance. **Emigration** abroad reached its peak during the 1950s–1960s, when more than 5.6 million people (mostly from the southern regions) expatriated, either seasonally or permanently. However, expatriations declined substantially in the 1970s–1980s and were beginning to be offset in the late 1980s by **immigration**, mainly from eastern European countries (Poland, Rumania and Albania) and African and Asian developing countries (Morocco, Tunisia and the Philippines). A large part of such immigrants – named *extracomunitari* (coming from non-EEC countries), a term which implies a sense of exclusion from the national community – remained clandestine. In 1991 there were about 410,000 *extracomunitari* officially registered at the Ministry of Domestic Affairs, but a similar number were estimated to be clandestine. Numbers of immigrants living officially in Italy have risen continuously throughout the 1990s, reaching 1,250,000 at the end of 1998 (to this number should be added nearly 400,000 more who expect to regularize their position according to the immigration law of 1998). Nevertheless, the total number of residents from countries outside the European Union still lies below 3 per cent of total population, a figure well below that of other European countries, such as France or Germany.

In the years of the '**economic miracle**', massive internal migration from the South – which recorded a negative population balance of about 3.5 million – and from rural areas generally also produced a dramatic redistribution of population towards the industrialized northern regions and urban areas all around the country. This trend substantially weakened from the mid-1980s as an increasing number of people began to move out of congested, heavily polluted and costly metropolitan areas into more provincial areas in search of a better quality of life.

Economic development has also determined a profound change in class structure. Rural classes sharply declined, to such an extent that the traditional basis of rural Italy, still extremely strong at the end of the Second World War, vanished in less than thirty years. Peasant proprietors and rural working classes, accounting for 44 per cent of total working population in 1951 (much higher than any other European countries, excluding those of the Mediterranean basin), were dramatically reduced to 18 per cent twenty years later and to just 9 per cent in the early 1990s. Industrial working classes, after having reached a peak in 1975 with 31 per cent, suffered a substantial reduction during the restructuring processes of the 1980s and came to account for just 25 per cent in mid-1990s, since the increasing numbers of medium-sized to small firms could not offset the effects of massive downsizing of large firms. By contrast, the urban middle classes emerged definitively as the backbone of the Italian population. Traditional middle class (shopkeepers and craftsmen) continued to account for a much larger part of the workforce than in other European countries (17 per cent in the mid-1990s). Particularly significant, however, has been the rapid growth of white-collar employment (from just 13 per cent of the total workforce in 1951 to nearly 30 per cent in mid-1990s). This trend, though in line with transformations occurring in all advanced countries, has revealed a strong peculiarity in composition since, especially from the 1980s onwards, public sector employment growth has outstripped that of the private sector.

Further reading

Ginsborg, P. (1990) *A History of Contemporary Italy*, London: Penguin (a good general overview with a number of extremely useful statistical appendices showing changes in population, employment patterns and migratory flows).

—— (1994) *Stato dell'Italia* (The State of Italy), Milan: Bruno Mondadori (demographic, economic and social indices of Italy in the mid-1990s).

STEFANO BATTILOSSI

Porcinai, Pietro

b. 1910, Settignano; d. 1986, Florence

Landscape and garden architect

One of the very few professionally-trained Italian landscape architects of the prewar period, Porcinai obtained a degree in agriculture from the Florence Agrarian Institute in 1928 and then continued his formal training in Germany (Berlin) and Belgium, since Italy did not have an academic landscape programme until the 1980s. This resulted not only in a network of lifelong professional contacts but also in a certain 'northern' atmosphere in his work, often described as 'mystical'.

By bringing together the approaches of the Greco-Roman *hortus* and Persian-Oriental *paradeisos*, and by recreating the beneficent tranquillity of Renaissance *orti*, Porcinai underlined the profound impact of the garden on the humanities. In over 1,300 projects, he has covered every aspect of landscape design: private residences, public and recreational parks, piazzas, highways and ports, industrial and rural complexes. His well-deserved international reputation celebrates his gift for combining the traditional and the modern into harmonious creations, enchantingly refined, thoughtful, tactful and witty. The elegance and propriety of his work stem from the simplicity of his basic design approach, a belief that the design solution is already contained in the landscape to which it relates just as a poem is inherent in the words of the language from which it emerges. Ephemeral spatial elements such as light, and daily and seasonal changes and aromas, are the fundamental design tools that Porcinai uses with care and mastery to achieve surprise and delight. An imaginative treatment of pools, ponds, artificial lakes, waterworks and corresponding aquatic plants became his trademark. While not shunning the occasional application of ecologically compatible exotic plants (bamboo being his favourite), he preferred to work with the indigenous, well-adjusted, low-maintenance species.

Porcinai acted as landscape consultant on many projects which became famous for their extraordinary integration of architecture and surroundings and the use of landscape in design, including Brion Tombs (with **Scarpa**) and the Brion-Vega factory (with **Zanuso**), projects in Saudi Arabia (with Albini-Helg and with Gino **Valle**), Parco Sempione (with **Viganò**, 1954), the garden in Saronno (1958) and Cappo Stella (with **BPR**, 1960), the **Olivetti** plant (with Luigi Cosenza, 1962), the Parco di Pinocchio in Collodi, Pistoia (with **Zanuso**, 1964), the Beaubourg (with **Piano** and **Rogers**) and the ecological park in the new headquarters of **Mondadori** (with Oscar Niemeyer, 1974). His design for the 'villa Apparita' in Siena is a paradigm of inventive historic landscape recreation.

In 1948 Porcinai was among the founding members of the Associazione italiana degli architetti del giardino e del paesaggio (the Italian chapter of IFLA, the International Federation of Landscape Architecture). In 1957 he moved his office to the prestigious location of villa Rondinelli in Fiesole, previously a *foresteria* (guest lodge) of the villa Medici, with the intention of organizing an international centre for the study of landscape architecture on the principles of the Renaissance *convivium*; unfortunately, this project was never realized.

Further reading

Matteini, M. (1991) *Pietro Porcinai: architetto del giardino e del paesaggio* (Pietro Porcinai: Garden and Landscape Gardener), Milan: Electa (the only thorough presentation of Porcinai's opus).

Seddon, G. (1991) 'The Brion Cemetery, S. Vito, Italy 1970–72', *Landscape Australia* 13 (2): 146–53 (a clarification of Porcinai's role and the symbolic aspect of plants in this celebrated design).

GORDANA KOSTICH

pornography

Article 529 of the Italian Penal Code defines obscenity as 'those acts or objects which, according to general opinion, offend public decency', although it explicitly excludes from prosecution 'acts or objects of artistic or scientific value on condition that they are not offered, sold, or put at the disposal of minors under the age of eighteen for reasons other than study'. This wording has allowed widely differing interpretations, which have taken into account not only the actual acts or objects, but also the context of sexually explicit material which might be deemed pornographic and the personal conditions of its consumers.

While the text of the penal law facilitated the emergence of a more tolerant attitude with respect to pornography in the 1980s and 1990s, in response to a greatly changed notion of what might be considered offensive to common decency, in the 1940s and 1950s the notion of *pudore* (public decency) was seen as coinciding with the feelings of the 'normal' law-abiding citizen whom the law needed to protect against a rising tide of sexual obscenity. According to this view, the law defended a given set of moral values which, as such, were perceived as an integral part of Italian national identity. Starting in the 1980s, however, magistrates became convinced of the necessity to adapt the interpretation of the laws to changes in **sexual mores**. Prosecution did not stop altogether, but was based on links between pornography and other crimes such as the exploitation of prostitution or the corruption of minors.

Notwithstanding severe repression during the 1950s and 1960s, an illegal network catered for clients interested in the acquisition of porno films in super8 format, often produced abroad. A more pronounced eroticism also gradually made its way into normal cinemas, often under the form of sexy documentaries which purported to illustrate the nightlife or curious sexual practices in foreign capitals, usually in a falsely moralizing tone. The first of them, *Europa di notte* (Europe by Night) by Alessandro **Blasetti**, dates back to 1959.

New developments also took place in the world of **comics** and other visual material aimed at adults. For example, until the early 1960s references to sexuality had been virtually absent in romantic stories published in **fotoromanzi** like **Grand Hotel**, *Sogno* and *Bolero film*. The publication of *Barbarella* in France in 1962 inspired many Italian imitations like *Selene*, designed by Marco Rostagno, *Alika* and *Uranella*, and the erotic possibilities of cartoons were further developed in the second half of the 1960s with new magazines like *Gesebel*, *Isabella*, *Messalina* and *Iolanka*, which were overtly pornographic and which often illustrated sado-masochistic practices. These magazines were a major commercial success: at the zenith of its popularity, between 1967 and 1970, *Isabella* sold as many as 80,000 copies. Interestingly, picture stories like *Supersex* had relatively less success.

Among the outcomes of the sexual liberation movement, and coinciding with the period of radical student and workers' protest around 1968, was a rapid increase in the production and consumption of pornography. The appearance of numerous new magazines *per soli uomini* (for men only), like *Playmen*, *Ore d'amore* and *Supermessalina*, made inroads into the market for adult comics without substituting them completely. Furthermore, the heroes and heroines of the cartoons at times inspired new forms of erotic entertainment: for example, *Flash Gordon* re-emerged in a 1974 movie as *Flesh Gordon*.

Pornography acquired even more visibility and acceptability in 1977 with the opening of the first cinemas *a luci rosse* (red-light cinemas), which specialized in hardcore. These quickly expanded, and in the early 1980s they numbered more than 200. Most of the films shown were American, but Italian productions, with directors like Joe D'Amato, soon followed their example.

The products of the thriving Italian porno industry were characterized by the fact that they were not 'all-sex' and paid some attention to narrative aspects. Another characteristic was the creation of a star system based on the popularity of actresses like **Cicciolina**, Moana Pozzi, and, more recently, Selen, Jessica Rizzo and Eva Henger. Many of them imitated Riccardo Schicchi, the owner of Italy's main porno business Diva futura, in presenting pornography as a form of sexual liberation.

With the rapid diffusion of videorecorders, owned in 1995 by 47.4 per cent of Italian families, the commercialization of pornography shifted massively to the sale of video cassettes. The main sales points were video shops and newsstands; the number of porno shops in Italy remained extremely limited.

Thanks to the gradual disappearance of the social disapproval of pornography, a porno star like Moana Pozzi (1961–94) could become a regular guest star on television, not only in the late night talkshow of Maurizio **Costanzo**, but also in the Saturday evening family programmes conducted by Pippo **Baudo**. The gradual blurring of the distinction between pornography and other forms of eroticism led to an ever greater acceptability of pornography and opened new markets, where, in some cases, the transgressive dimension of pornography could be almost completely subsumed by the commercial dimension. Thus in 1997–8, a winter catalogue for shoes was advertised as 'a guide to porno and good shoes', exalting the qualities of both footwear and porno stars.

In public debate, the anti-pornography position remained weak: while books in defence of pornography were rapidly translated, the works of anti-pornographic campaigners like Andrea Dworkin and Catherine MacKinnon attracted little interest. By the 1990s, the laws against pornography were only being rigorously applied in cases involving minors. In 1997 a bill was introduced for the more severe punishment of the production, commercialization and distribution of explicit sexual material involving minors, such exploitation being defined as a form of slavery. The proposed bill made special reference to the use of the Internet, but failed to clearly define pornography and thus left open the continuing possibility of contrasting interpretations.

See also: censorship

Further reading

ISPES (1989) *La pornografia in Italia* (Pornography in Italy), Rome: Merlo Editore (a detailed overview of various aspects of pornography in Italy in the second half of the 1980s).

Spinazzola, V. (1995) *L'immaginazione divertente. Il giallo, il rosa, il porno, il fumetto* (Entertaining Imagination: Detective Stories, Romance, Pornography, Cartoons), Milan: Rizzoli (a collection of essays about mass culture).

Stella, R. (1991) *L'osceno di massa. Sociologia della comunicazione pornografica* (Obscenity for the Masses: The Sociology of Pornographic Communication), Milan: Angeli (an analysis of the production and consumption of pornography in Italian society).

BRUNO P.F. WANROOIJ

Porta, Antonio

b. 6 November 1935; d. 1989, 12 April Milan

Poet, novelist and critic

Born Leo Paolazzi, Porta began his literary activity

in the 1950s by collaborating on important journals such as *Malebolge* and *il verri*. He was one of the five 'experimental' poets published in the seminal anthology *I novissimi* (The Very New), edited by fellow poet Alfredo **Giuliani**, and together with Giuliani and others he was also one of the founding members of the neoavantgarde movement, **Gruppo 63**. He contributed to the magazine *Quindici*, edited by Nanni **Balestrini**, before being amongst the founders of the cultural journal *alfabeta*.

Fundamental to Porta's poetics is a refusal to identify with the lyrical self of the poet, which has its creative counterpart in the recognition of the importance of the external event and no longer only the persona of the isolated poet. As well as poetry, Porta also published several novels and a theatrical work.

Further reading

Porta, A. (1986) *Invasions*, ed. P. Vangelisti, trans. A. Baldry, P. Verdicchio and P. Vangelisti, San Francisco: Red Mill Press (last collection of poetry; originally appearing as *Invasioni*, Milan: Mondadori, 1984).

ERNESTO LIVORNI

Portoghesi, Paolo

b. 2 November 1931, Rome

Architect

Renowned for combining architectural practice with teaching architectural history, Portoghesi first trained at Rome's Scuola Superiore di Architettura. From 1962–6 he taught History of Architecture and Criticism in Rome, and from 1967–77 he was professor of the History of Architecture at the Politecnico of Milan. In 1963–4 he won the Italian Institute of Architecture's national prize and the Manzù Foundation gold medal. In 1966 Portoghesi became a member of the prestigious Accademia di San Luca. Author of a number of monographs, he also contributed to many periodicals, as well as editing the *Quaderni dell'Istituto di Storia dell'Architettura* (Notebooks of the Institute of the History of

Architecture) and running the architectural section of the cultural journal, *Marcatrè*. From 1969–83 he directed **Controspazio**, and in 1983 he became editor of the journal *Eupalino*. His fascination for the 'Orient' as a recurring architectural theme began with early research on the Origine group and led to international design work in Sudan (1973), Jordan (1974) and the Mosque and Islamic Cultural Centre in Rome (1976–93).

Further reading

Pisani, M. (1992) *Paolo Portoghesi*, Milan: Electa (an anthology of his buildings from 1965–90).

FASSIL ZEWDOU

postal services

The Italian preference for the spoken over the written word is illustrated by the contrast between telephone and mail culture. Italy shows a similar telephone density and use to Northern Europe. However, each year Italians post only half the number of private letters per capita that the French, Germans and British post, and they spend only one-tenth of what Northern Europeans spend on mail-order products. In a public sector renowned for its inefficiency, the postal service's indifference to its customers has been as legendary as the protection enjoyed by its employees. Compared with the EU average, the letters that Italians do write cost one-third more to send, move towards their destinations at only one-third of the speed and require significantly more postal workers per item to get them there. Clientelist and trade union pressures have made the attempts to increase the productivity of the service conspicuously less successful in Italy than elsewhere.

DAVID MOSS

postmodernism

The term 'postmodernism' refers both to the theory that the 'modern' period has ended and been replaced, and to a practice in contemporary art and literature which seeks self-consciously to generate 'post' modern features. Since 'modern' is generally understood to mean simply 'the present moment', the term 'postmodern' immediately generates some confusion. To understand how something could be considered more recent than 'modern', it is necessary to approach modernism as a relative term, referring to a specific style and a clearly defined historical period.

According to most of its exponents, the defining characteristic of modernism was its novelty. Unlike traditional art, which was valued according to how much it resembled the work of other accepted masters, modern art was valued by how much it rejected everything that had come before. This rejection was led by a small elite band, the self-consciously avantgarde, who courageously ventured into as yet unexplored possibilities of artistic expression ahead of others, despite lack of approval from the conservative masses. However, once a new and avantgarde style had gained wide acceptance, it necessarily became conventional and was therefore rejected as 'passé'. Consequently, the history of modernism is marked by a succession of short-lived movements. Moreover, since the avantgarde made such a point of rejecting the past, many modernist artists were self-taught, and technical skill itself was not considered necessary.

Modernism, like social Darwinism, claimed a logic of progression. The past should be rejected because it *was* the past and therefore, by definition, not as up to date as the present, whereas the present was valuable of itself and would lead to a better future. At its extreme, modernism could lead to totalitarianism. So, for example, although Hitler detested abstract art, the state he created was thoroughly 'modern', supported by the latest technology and guided by scientific planning, stripping away of all superfluous ornament and traditional (i.e. non-modern) humanist emotion in an overriding adherence to modern, abstract values.

Yet modernism outlived Hitler. After the Second World War, new suburbs and apartment blocks sprang up. By the 1960s, major Italian cities had their outgrowth of residential towers, justified by their designers according to the modernist mantra of Walter Gropius and the Bauhaus in which 'form follows function'. Rejection of the past fitted conveniently with the commercial needs of the developers. Individuality, craftsmanship and dec-

orative effect were abandoned as old fashioned, in favour of mass production and uniformity. It is ironic that the features of modernist architecture and design, which at first seemed so rebellious, were cheap to produce and to reproduce and so came to be repeated everywhere: monochrome concrete, curtain walls, rectangular forms and an absence of eaves or, indeed, of any relieving detail.

By the end of the 1960s, modernism had reached a crisis point in many of its forms. In art and literature, it appeared that the possibilities for innovation had been exhausted. More significantly, the myth of the value of progress was shattered by widespread student and worker protests. Western culture had delivered material gains, but failed to satisfy other human needs. In architecture, millions had been housed in the new quarters, but in conditions which, at their worst, were social disasters. Italy, in the past home to the world's greatest architecture, now also boasted some of the poorest. Simplicity and repetition crushed any sense of individuality out of the occupants. Where planned variety was introduced, it was sterile, and could not match the organic richness of cities which had evolved over centuries.

'Postmodernism' thus began to be used as term to indicate a new way of thinking in which style did not have to be new, the past could be revisited, elements from different codes could be mixed, and progress was not a linear trajectory. Architecture was quick to articulate such a style, which borrowed at will from many sources. Postmodern buildings are thus typically eclectic and a pastiche of elements, such as a tower block with a touch of Greek temple on top. In what Charles Jencks referred to as dual coding, buildings could speak on two levels: one to the general public, in terms of their immediate appeal, and the other to adepts in the field, who could admire the ironic wit of the architectural references.

The postmodern freedom of expression spread through visual art as a theoretical approach and range of strategies, not as a single style. Much of the art produced in Italy after the 1960s displayed postmodernist tendencies, one of which was eclecticism. Artists such as **Clemente** felt they could look to the past, and to diverse cultures and media for their inspiration, rather than reacting only to the latest trend. Another postmodernist tendency was that of 'appropriation', the incorporation of recognizable elements or even entire works of others into one's own work. So **Paolini**, for example, used plaster casts of classical sculptures and reproductions of old master paintings as his own works, and **Mariani** painted in the style of the French neoclassicists. A third aspect, resulting from eclecticism and appropriation, is pastiche: postmodern works may be formed as an assembly of pre-existing elements, as in the tableaus of **Ontani**. One further general tendency that characterized postmodernism in painting was the rejection of the modernist notion of 'unschooled' art. This led to a renewal of learning and, given the necessity of training, an understanding of the history of art for the purposes of citation and copying; it also led to a reappreciation of technique. In painting, the return of figuration, the re-emphasis on technical skill, and the awareness of the history of art displayed by the **transavantgarde** are all indications of the same rejection of modernism and thus marks of a certain postmodern tendency.

In both literature and the visual arts, however, the postmodernist licence to appropriate the past also needed to avoid being simply 'old' or unfashionable, and this was done through a constant and overriding use of irony. In his postscript to *The Name of the Rose*, Umberto **Eco** discusses the dilemma of the postmodern lover who is anxious to tell his beloved that he loves her madly, but realizes that he will sound like someone from a pulp romance. So he frames his declaration as a quote: 'As Liala would say, I love you madly', thus communicating his feelings at the same time as he signals, through irony, his own sophistication. In other terms, copy at will, but acknowledge; and Eco was careful to employ this device himself.

Nevertheless, in spite of all its vigorous rejection of its own immediate past, it is still uncertain whether postmodernism is in fact completely distinct from modernism or whether, perhaps, it is no more than an ironic and clever re-utilization of the same progressive, avantgarde myths of modernism itself.

Further reading

Calinescu, M. (1987) *Five Faces of Modernity*,

Durham, NC: Duke University Press (discusses the features of modernism, and postmodernism as a reaction).

Eco, U. (1984) *Postscript to the 'Name of the Rose'*, trans. W. Weaver, New York: Harcourt Brace Jovanovich (contains Eco's definition of postmodernism).

Jencks, C. (1977) *The Language of Postmodern Architecture*, New York: Rizzoli (an early, defining work).

MAX STAPLES

postwar reconstruction

The term 'postwar reconstruction' is commonly used to indicate the period from immediately after the Second World War to the mid-1950s when, especially in the crucial areas of agriculture and industry, production was restored to prewar levels.

The destructive impact of the Second World War on the European territory was indeed quite massive, far worse than that of the First World War. As well as the cost in human lives – around 45 million people – there was extensive damage to the productive and communications infrastructure, and to housing. Scene of some of the bloodiest battles of the war for almost two years, Italy was especially affected – the most troubled sector being transport, where infrastructure was almost completely destroyed – by the fury of two opposing armies and a ferocious civil war at a time when the Italian peninsula constituted one of the most strategically important fronts of the entire war.

The agricultural sector, brought to almost a complete standstill in some areas, was also in deep crisis. Fortunately, much of the industrial infrastructure was located in the northeastern 'industrial triangle' which, as the hostilities ceased almost unexpectedly in April 1945, was discovered to have sustained less damage than originally feared. Bank of Italy estimates of war damage to industry suggested around 8 per cent of total value, even if areas such as metallurgy, iron and steel and heavy industry were more seriously affected than others.

Nevertheless, the real economy could only be expected to pick up within a reasonable time if a solution were found to the other overwhelming problem which had been inherited from the war and from the financial superstructure: inflation. In fact, the inflation already existing in Italy before the fall of Mussolini was aggravated by the devastating monetary policies carried out during the rest of the war years. Both occupying armies, but particularly the Anglo-American one, had financed the upkeep of their troops by issuing large quantities of banknotes (the so-called AM liras). That currency was still circulating and, given the extreme shortage of consumer goods, was pushing inflation to a level which risked bringing down the entire price system.

Identifying the best solution to the serious problem of inflation became the focus of heated debate among political parties, scholars and economists. The Left was in favour of changing the currency, as was happening in other countries, while the liberals and conservatives, led by Luigi Einaudi, were vehemently opposed to the measure. For the Left, changing the currency seemed the simplest, the most radical but also the most equitable solution, since the intention was to follow it with a progressive tax on capital and a state-generated loan aimed at drying up the profits of the war. The liberal-conservatives, however, were especially opposed to this new tax, which they thought would indiscriminately penalize the middle class which had invested its savings in public deficit shares. While the different sides argued, inflation became ever more the central problem of the economy. In 1944 inflation had reached 345 per cent, and the following year it increased by a further 108 per cent. 1938 prices had increased tenfold by 1945 and by 1947 they had increased thirty-two times.

With regard to employment, repatriation from the ex-colonies and the blocking of overseas migration had created a critical situation. In 1946, despite the opposition of trade unions, dismissals were de-regulated. By the end of the year more than two million people were registered with unemployment offices, although there were many other unemployed who had not registered. It is also worth noting that in northern Italy alone, more than one million workers had been employed in companies which were directly or indirectly linked to the arms industry, and these companies were now inactive and awaiting conversion.

The gravity of the situation, of which inflation

and unemployment were only the two most obvious facets, forced the ruling politicians to implement a number of temporary measures in order to face the most pressing priorities although, in so doing, they lost sight of an overall strategic plan which alone could have ensured a lasting success. Moreover, as already mentioned with regard to monetary policies, the contrasting ideological positions of the government coalition members (Christian Democrats, Liberals, Radical Actionists, Socialists and Communists) led to interminable delays in taking important decisions. The situation became somewhat clearer between 1946 and 1947, when Italy's position within the zone of Western influence was assured.

The indisputable hegemony of the United States in the market economy was signalled by the retreat of the pound sterling and the rise of the US dollar as an international currency. In accordance with the principles of economic co-operation and integration (principles which after the Second World War were followed much more vigorously than after the First World War), Italy, together with the other major Western European countries, participated in the creation of international institutions such as the International Monetary Fund, set up through the Bretton Wood agreements. The establishment of the Fund was dictated by the need to end monetary devaluation as a tool of trade competition and to promote a process of trade liberalization by overcoming the clearing system. This was to some extent facilitated by the political changes which saw the ousting of the communist and socialist Left from the executive when **De Gasperi** formed his fourth government in May 1947, in which liberal politician – and later President of the Republic – Luigi Einaudi figured prominently. At this point, the position of Italy in the international context became clear, and it was able to benefit from the Marshall Aid Plan (which was announced in June 1947) and to adopt an unambiguous economic policy. Such choices appeared appreciated by the electorate when a year later, in the elections of April 1948, the Left suffered a massive defeat.

Among the first measures to be taken by the De Gasperi–Einaudi government were those relating to the Italian currency. New rules aimed at regulating compulsory payments set aside by banks with the issuing institution were established, and the official discount rate was drastically increased. A credit squeeze and a careful policy of containing the public deficit allowed the country to defeat inflation and to pave the way towards the so-called **economic miracle** of the 1950s.

However, even if the government generally favoured a free market economy, there was also state intervention. In fact, the most peculiar feature of the Italian case was probably the combination of free market measures, aimed at gradually removing the few forms of control introduced by Fascism, with measures aimed at consolidating the impressive apparatus of public enterprises which had been established after the 1929 economic crisis. The Institute for Industrial Reconstruction (**IRI**) continued to play an important role and fully participated in the reconstruction activity, giving the state a direct presence in the process. The international economic growth ignited by the Korean war at the beginning of the new decade found the Italian economy with the right conditions needed in order to benefit from the international boom and to initiate what would become known as the 'economic miracle'.

See also: economy; housing policy; industry; railway system

Further reading

Aldcroft, D.H. (1978) *The European Economy: 1914–1970*, London: Croom Helm.

Becher, V. and Knipping, F. (eds) (1976) *Power in Europe: Great Britain, France, Italy and Germany in a Postwar World, 1945–1950*, Berlin: Walter de Gruyter (see especially the essay by V. Zamagni, 'Betting on the Future: The Reconstruction of Italian Industry, 1946–1952').

Mildward, A. (1984) *The Reconstruction of Western Europe: 1945–1951*, London: Methuen.

Woolf, S.J. (ed.) (1972) *The Rebirth of Italy: 1943–1950*, New York: Humanities Press.

PIETRO CAFARO

PPI

The PPI (Partito Popolare Italiano, or Italian Popular Party) was officially born in January 1994 as a 'refoundation' of the disintegrating Christian Democratic party (see **DC**). The attempt by Rosa Russo Jervolino and Mino **Martinazzoli** to save the DC from the tempests of the *Tangentopoli* ('Bribesville') scandals by returning to the name and principles of the original Italian Catholic party, the Partito Popolare Italiano of Don Luigi **Sturzo**, failed due to the deep disagreement regarding the future of political Catholicism in Italy. Despite the strong support of the Church, which was expressed in a letter of **Pope John Paul II** calling, once again, for the 'political unity of Catholics', there was a veritable diaspora of the party as elements of the former DC leadership sought to assure their own futures in a variety of political groupings.

In the national elections of March 1994, against the logic of the recently introduced first past the post system for three-quarters of the seats, the Popolari insisted on maintaining an independent, centrist position in alliance with Mario Segni and his Patto per l'Italia (Pact for Italy) group. The result was that the party won only 11.1 per cent of the vote and was thus out of government.

In March 1995 there was a split in the party between the supporters of the then Secretary-General, Rocco Buttiglione, and pretender Gerardo Bianco. Buttiglione set up the **CDU** (Cristiani Democratici Uniti, or United Christian Democrats) and, after a protracted court battle, the PPI party badge went to the CDU, the newspaper *Il popolo* went to the PPI and the traditional headquarters, Palazzo Gesù, was divided evenly between them.

The outcome of the by-election in Padua in 1995 caused by the appointment of **Forza Italia** MP Emma **Bonino** as European Fisheries Commissioner prefigured the general elections of a year later. A centre–left candidate supported by the PPI, the **PDS** and the local diocesan curia won against a pro-abortion, **Forza Italia** politician. In 1996, under the leadership of Gerardo Bianco, the PPI entered the **Ulivo** electoral alliance with the PDS and other centre–left 'progressive' forces. Inevitably, it won a smaller share of the vote in both the

Chamber and the Senate, but three PPI members became ministers in the government of Romano **Prodi** in April 1996 and the vice-premiership of the D'Alema centre–left government of 1998 also went to the PPI.

JOHN POLLARD

PR

The Partito Radicale (PR) or Radical Party was formed in December 1955 when the left wing of the Liberal Party (see **PLI**), which included many of the intellectuals and writers connected with Marco Pannunzio and his weekly magazine *Il Mondo*, broke away in protest against what they saw as the PLI's increasing accommodation to the politics of the **DC**. The orientation of the new party, which included, as well as Pannunzio, Ernesto Rossi, Arrigo **Benedetti**, Elio **Vittorini**, Eugenio **Scalfari** and the young Marco **Pannella** amongst others, was strongly secular and liberal democratic, pro-NATO on the international front and highly critical of the government's clientelistic policies at home. In particular, the party supported the immediate implementation of all the democratic provisions of the constitution and the abrogation of all Fascist laws.

The egalitarian and democratic ideals of the new party were reflected in its non-hierarchical and decentralized structure which allowed all members of the party to exercise their own special expertise in various fields in order to competently criticize governmental decisions. However commendable in intellectual terms, this lack of centralization and discipline nevertheless proved to be a weakness in political terms and the party, which presented itself united with the Republicans in the 1958 elections, performed extremely poorly at the ballot box. The DC's '**opening to the Left**' also soon divided Radical opinion, and in 1962 Pannunzio and his group abandoned the party, which thereafter remained on the edge of dissolution throughout most of the 1960s. Neither the party's third 'refoundation' congress held in 1967 nor the explosion of the **student movement** in 1968, with its similar libertarian orientation, managed to significantly revive its fortunes.

Together with a number of other political and feminist groups, the Radicals campaigned strongly for the **divorce** legislation which was finally passed by the Italian Parliament in 1970, but it was ultimately the active and highly visible role which the Radical Party – and in particular Marco **Pannella**, who had by then become one of its most charismatic leaders – played in the defeat of the referendum to abrogate the divorce law which lifted the party to prominence in the 1970s. Although its success at the ballot box would remain modest – it received 1.1 per cent of the vote at the 1976 elections, the first at which it presented itself on its own, 3.4 per cent in 1979 and 2 per cent in 1983 – the Radical Party's greatest successes from then on would be tied to its effective strategic use of **referenda** in order to change Italian society. In 1975, the Radicals took a leading role in attempting to bring about a referendum to abrogate the Fascist law against **abortion**, a measure which ultimately forced the Italian Parliament to pass its own law legalising abortion in May 1978. In the same year, the Radicals were able to institute a referendum against public financing of political parties, a measure which was technically defeated but which proved that almost 44 per cent of the Italian population were against parties being financed from the public purse.

During the 1980s, the Party continued to fight for progressive political and social measures, often using civil disobedience, as in the attempt to decriminalize soft drugs, and publicity strategies such as hunger strikes to highlight the international problem of world hunger and to demand some positive response from Italian authorities. At its 1988 Congress, the Party decided to no longer even contest elections as an Italian political party as such, but to function from then on as a transnational 'trans-party' organization which would fight for human and civil rights everywhere. As such, in the 1990s the Radicals have remained active and visible in Italian politics, but at election time individual currents have presented themselves separately in lists under their own name.

GINO MOLITERNO

Prada

Granddaughter of a high fashion name in Italy since the beginning of the century, Miuccia Prada revitalized the family's leather accessories business in 1979. Best known for her signature nylon backpack of the late 1980s, Prada's success story is also partially due to her marriage with Patrizio Bertelli. Prada and Bertelli are the two sides of the Prada coin: she is the creative soul behind the company and he is the business strategist. Since the company took off, they have expanded from women's and men's wear into a number of product lines including accessories, shoes and ready-to-wear. Once aspiring to a high fashion clientele, creations of the Miu Miu youth line and a Prada Sport line are meant to appeal to a more mass market. There are plans to expand into lingerie, perfume and functional but optimally designed kitchenware. The Prada philosophy revolves around her favourite adjective *trasversale* (transversal) which suggests a way of living and dressing that crosses the boundaries of age, social class, race and continents. Confident enough to attempt a **Gucci** takeover, Prada and Bertelli continue to attribute their success to their complementarity: her tranquillity versus his aggressiveness; her passion for art, which results in the sponsoring of art shows and artists worldwide, versus his for sailing, which has resulted in a 90 billion lire investment in a leading America's Cup contender which 'wears' the name of the great success story.

BERNADETTE LUCIANO

Pratolini, Vasco

b. 19 October 1913, Florence;
   d. 12 January 1991, Rome

Novelist

A self-taught member of the urban proletariat who began his working life at the age of twelve, Pratolini wrote at all times with a consciousness of class and a direct knowledge of social struggle. While his early works belong to a vein best defined as that of affectionate and sometimes overidealized local recollections – the most artistically successful of these being *Il Quartiere* (A Tale of Santa Croce) (1945) – Pratolini will be remembered for *Cronaca familiare* (Family Chronicle) (1947), an intimate monologue addressed to his dead brother, and *Cronache di poveri amanti* (A Tale of Poor Lovers) (1947), later filmed by Carlo **Lizzani**. He divided critical debate over **neorealism** in 1955 with the publication of *Metello*, the first volume of a historical trilogy which moves away from local reflections and attempts to paint an affresco of Italian life from the 1870s onwards.

Further reading

Russo, F. (1989) *Vasco Pratolini*, Florence: Le Monnier.

DAVE WATSON

Pratt, Hugo

b. 15 June 1927, Rimini; d. 20 August
   1995, Lausanne, Switzerland

Cartoonist, painter and writer

Perhaps the most internationally renowned of all Italian cartoonists, Pratt is best remembered as the creator of **Corto Maltese**. Italian-born, Pratt nevertheless spent most of his life outside Italy, travelling the world and visiting exotic locations in a way not unlike his most famous fictional character. He grew up in Africa in the late 1930s, where his father had migrated to work for the Italian Colonial Administration. At the end of the Second World War he returned to Venice, where he began collaborating with a group of other writers and illustrators on a cartoon magazine published by an Argentinean company. In its pages he gave life to his first famous character, a masked avenger in tights in the style of Lee Falk's Phantom named Asso di Picche (Ace of Spades), which was soon adopted as the name of the magazine itself. In 1950 he moved to Argentina and thereafter lived in Brazil and various parts of the Americas and England before returning to Italy in the early 1960s. Here he contributed to the *Corriere dei piccoli*, a Milan weekly for young people, illustrating, amongst other things, several of the classic adventure stories by Robert Louis Stevenson and giving birth to the character of *Ombra* (Shadow).

In 1967, on the pages of an adventure magazine called *Sgt. Kirk* (the name of one of his earlier creations) he first introduced the character of Corto Maltese in a long story called the *Ballad of the Salt Sea*. In 1970 he moved to Paris, where he invented numerous further adventures for Corto Maltese in the pages of the French magazine *Pif Gadget*. In 1984, widely renowned and having already achieved something of a cult status, he moved to Lausanne in Switzerland, from where he continued to contribute to a variety of publications including a cartoon and adventure magazine which had now taken on the name of his famous adventurer-hero.

Although best known for his cartoons and illustrated adventure stories, Pratt was also a fine painter and writer. Two novels featuring Corto Maltese were published shortly after Pratt's death, and an exhibition of his splendid watercolours was held at the Galleria Nuages in Milan in 1996.

Further reading

Hugo Pratt: il disegno dell'avventura (Hugo Pratt: Drawing the Adventure), CD-Rom, Profile Multimedia (a comprehensive multimedia presentation of Pratt through a detailed biography and reproductions of his work).

GINO MOLITERNO

presepe

Although many European countries have a long tradition of staged Nativity scenes, Italians are especially devoted to it and both assembled *presepi* (representations of Christ's Nativity), made of models and statues, and real-life re-enactments of the birth of Christ can be seen everywhere throughout Italy at Christmas time. Not only large cities such as Rome and Milan but also most small towns and provincial churches will display at least one *presepe*, often ingenious constructions with miniature running brooks and twinkling starry skies surrounding the hut where the Christ-child lies in a manger, flanked by his parents and adored

by the three wise men and shepherds with their assembled flocks.

Said to have originated with Saint Francis of Assisi – though the custom is probably older – the tradition was carried on by master craftsmen throughout the centuries and many *presepi*, such as the one made of fine red coral, now in the Museum of San Martino in Naples, are magnificent works of art of the highest calibre.

See also: patron saints

Further reading

Wills, G. (1996) 'The Art and Politics of the Nativity', *The New York Review of Books*, 19 December: 75–82 (an extensive, in-depth survey with a highly informative bibliography).

GINO MOLITERNO

President of the Council of Ministers

The President of the Council of Ministers is the Italian equivalent of the Prime Minister in the Westminster system. In theory, he is nominated by the **President of the Republic**, although in practice, especially during the 'First' **Republic**, his name only emerged after often long and exhaustive consultations between the President and party secretaries and faction leaders.

Rather than being the effective leader of the executive, or even the co-ordinator of the cabinet, the President of the Council was usually the representative of the most powerful party factions at the time and as such was in fact controlled by them (see **political parties**). Since the other ministers were appointed in the same way, their ministries were more independent fiefs rather than departments co-ordinated by the prime minister. In fact, the underlying function of the system was actually to maintain the weakness of the prime minister's position.

Following the general collapse of the major parties in 1992, the President of the Republic exercised considerable power and influence though after the change of electoral system in 1994, the leaders of the winning coalition (**Berlusconi** and **Prodi**) were automatically elevated to premier. At one point during this period, because of the return of uncertainty and a power vacuum, the prime minister (Lamberto **Dini**) was chosen by the President of the Republic but the choice was supported by a majority in the Parliament. Both Prodi and Berlusconi had declared their intentions to be prime ministers who led and co-ordinated their cabinets and policies and, given their legitimization by the ballot box rather than party secretariat, they largely succeeded although clearly the continuing influence of party leaders, such as **D'Alema** in the case of Prodi's Prime Ministership, was considerable.

In the 'First' Republic (from 1946 to 1992), there were 48 governments in 46 years, or an average of 350 days each, although the apparent instability is belied by the continual return of certain powerful individual leaders to the post. Seven prime ministers governed for more than half the period, and **De Gasperi** was prime minister for almost eight years without a break. Given the power of the parties, it is not surprising that the prime ministers who lasted longest and contributed most were or had been party secretaries, such as De Gasperi, **Fanfani**, **Moro** and **Craxi**. At about a year, the average prime ministerial life from 1992 to 1998 was only slightly longer than had been the case in the 'First' Republic.

Further reading

Hine, D. and Finocchi, R. (1998) 'The Italian Prime Minister', in M. Donovan (ed.), *Italy*, vol. 1, Aldershot: Ashgate.

JAMES WALSTON

President of the Republic

The President is the head of state who, as well as representing the country generally, also nominates the prime minister (see **President of the Council of Ministers**), is chief of the armed forces and chairs the High Council of the Magistrature (Consiglio Superiore della Magistratura). In theory the presidency is non-political; in practice, the President is elected by a political assembly and reflects its balances and divisions.

The President is elected for a seven-year term by members of both houses of **Parliament** and representatives of the regions, and has his offices in the Quirinale Palace (often used as a synonym for the Presidency). A President may serve a second term, although none have to date. Leone and **Cossiga** resigned before the end of their terms, the first due to private and family matters and because he was accused of involvement in the Lockheed bribery scandal, while the second was formally accused (by the **PDS**) of not being impartial and of 'interference with other state powers' but resigned before either Parliament or the **Constitutional Court** could pronounce on the matter.

The President's power is closely circumscribed by the **constitution** and only becomes apparent when there is a vacuum in one of the other powers of the state. He appoints the prime ministers which, for most of the postwar period, has meant mediating between party secretaries and faction leaders and then registering their conclusions. Sandro **Pertini** had a much more hands-on approach and pushed for non-**DC** prime ministers, although this was made possible at the time by the DC's internal dissension. The President is also supposed to nominate the other ministers in the Council on the prime minister's recommendation, although here again, a President like **Scalfaro** has sometimes been able to exercise a determining influence. The President signs legislation into law. This is normally a formality, although he may return bills to Parliament when financial cover is not guaranteed or if they are deemed unconstitutional: Cossiga returned twenty-one bills, Pertini seven. The President also appoints senators for life. The constitution allows five, but Pertini and Cossiga both interpreted this as meaning five per president not five in total. This was of slight importance until the majority system was introduced in 1993; in 1994, the life senators held the balance of power, and their number became crucial again in 1996.

Until Cossiga's presidency, the President's role as chair of the High Council of the Magistrature (CSM) was purely formal, but for a time Cossiga really did take charge of the Council. He was severely criticized for doing so, and his successor, Scalfaro, did not continue the practice.

Since Pertini, presidents have increasingly developed a commentating and advisory role; in Cossiga's case, this became a veritable *potere di esternazione*, or a capacity for 'externalizing' on all manner of subjects. This development was due partly to the personalities of individual presidents, but also to the growing intrusiveness of the media and the confusion of the other state powers. As Parliament and government lost credibility in the 1990s corruption scandals (see **Mani pulite**; **Tangentopoli**), so the office of the President gained in influence and power.

The 1997 Bicameral Commission proposed a change to a popularly-elected presidency with responsibility for foreign affairs and defence but, in the continued absence of political unanimity, no move has yet been made to bring this to effect.

Further reading

Hine, D. and Poli, E. (1997) 'The Scalfaro Presidency in 1996: The Difficult Return to Normality', in R. D'Alimonte and D. Nelken (eds), *Italian Politics: The Center-Left in Power*, Oxford: Westview Press (a discussion of the changing role of the Presidency in the crisis of the 1990s).

Pasquino, G. (1993) 'Electing the President', in G. Pasquino and P. McCarthy (eds), *The End of Postwar Politics: The Landmark 1992 Elections*, Oxford: Westview Press (a discussion of the office and powers of the President through a specific analysis of the election of Francesco Cossiga).

JAMES WALSTON

Pressburger, Giorgio

b. 1937, Budapest

Novelist, playwright and director

After an early career as a playwright, Pressburger made his debut as a novelist in 1986 with the short story collection *Storie dell'ottavo distretto* (translated as Homage to the Eighth District: Tales from Budapest) and the novel *L'elefante verde* (The Green Elephant), both written in collaboration with his twin brother Nicola who died in 1985 (they had both emigrated to Italy in 1956 after the Russian invasion of Hungary). In these and in subsequent works, Pressburger balances the humanistic values of European literature and the Jewish tradition with an acute sense of the tragic grotesque of everyday life. He has continued to publish novels – most recently *La neve e la colpa* (The Snow and the Guilt) (1998) – but also works as a theatrical producer in Italy.

ANDREA RICCI

PRI

Founded in 1895, the Italian Republican Party (Partito repubblicano italiano, PRI) had a radical anti-monarchist, anti-clerical and later uncompromisingly anti-fascist tradition. It was at that time a left-liberal party, unlike the **PLI**. Furthermore, although pro-US and pro-market, it believed in a reformist capitalism, regarding Italian 'historical capitalism' as in need of state intervention, especially with regard to the South. The party benefited from the **DC**'s centrist coalition strategy and became an influential government party. Strategically, its leaders, notably the Sicilian Ugo La Malfa, exploited the party's hinge position between the Centre and Left in order to support the governmentalization of the **PSI** and the attempted integration of the **PCI**. In 1981, Republican party leader Giovanni Spadolini became the first non-DC premier. The party was largely destroyed in the early 1990s crisis, but a rump survived as one of the several tiny parties in the new party system.

Further reading

Donovan, M. (1996) 'The Fate of the Secular Centre: The Liberals, Republicans and Social Democrats', in S. Gundle and S. Parker (eds), *The New Italian Republic: From the Fall of the Berlin Wall to Berlusconi*, London: Routledge (an overview of the nature and role of the party in the 'First' Republic).

MARK DONOVAN

private television

Private television came late to Italy but when it did, it thoroughly transformed the television model which had been created by the public broadcaster, the RAI, during its two decades of monopoly under Ettore **Bernabei**. Private television began modestly in 1972 with Tele Biella, a cable channel in a little town near Turin broadcasting locally to about 100 subscribers. Invoking the RAI's presumed monopoly over all broadcasting, the government moved to close the station down, but a legal wrangle ensued and the matter eventually came before the **Constitutional Court**.

At that time, the legislative situation regarding television was something of a desert (see **broadcasting**). In 1952, a decree by the Minister for Post and Telecommunications, Giuseppe Spataro, had assured the RAI a monopoly over television broadcasting for the next twenty years. However, when the Tele Biella case came before it in July 1973, the Constitutional Court ruled against the legality of the decree and thus opened the floodgates to private broadcasting. Many private television channels opened in 1974 and 1975: TeleFirenze started to relay programmes from Tele Capodistria and ORTF, the second French channel, and **Telemontecarlo** began transmitting into Northern Italy from Monaco. Then, with Law 103 of 1975, the government effectively deregulated all radio and television. For a relatively small licence fee, any Italian (or European) citizen could now set up a private radio or television channel, although transmission was still restricted to local areas with severe prohibitions against networking in order to avoid any rival national coverage. The number of channels grew rapidly: in 1976 there were ninety private broadcasters but by 1978 the number had increased to 360 and by 1983 RAI estimates put it at almost 800. In spite of all this growth, however, the government proposed no legislation in order to regulate the new phenomenon.

In its early period, the private television system was organized in three different ways. The 'independent televisions', such as Antenna 3 in Milan produced their own programmes and collected advertising revenues. The 'circuit' channels delivered programmes and advertising to many different television stations, whilst the 'networks', exploiting a legal loophole and imitating the American model, transmitted programmes simultaneously through the use of videotapes and by aerial systems to ever wider areas. The real penetration of private television remained a mystery until 1979, when a report revealed that the private channels had accumulated 20 per cent of the share, a real revolution in Italian television viewing habits. This meant that private television had become big business and, accordingly, the giants stepped in.

In 1979 Silvio **Berlusconi**, a building magnate and successful entrepreneur, founded Rete Italia and Publitalia, to develop programmes, buy movies and sell advertising. TeleMilano, his first cable channel, became **Canale Cinque** as it networked with seventeen other private channels and acquired technical facilities equal to those of the RAI itself. In a final brilliant move, Berlusconi attracted the legendary Mike **Bongiorno** away from the RAI, followed a year later by popular presenters Raimondo and Corrado Vianello, thus creating a real alternative to public television.

The Berlusconi story, with all its links to Italian politics and to foreign capital, was certainly the most striking and the most successful in the long term, but Berlusconi was not alone: the new television business attracted quite a number of large investors and, especially, the interest of the great publishing houses. Angelo Rizzoli founded Prima Rete Indipendente, **Mondadori** founded **Rete Quattro** and Rusconi established **Italia Uno**. Rizzoli abandoned television in 1981 following the **P2** scandal as the first shots began to be fired in the great 'private television war' between Canale Cinque, ReteQuattro, Italia Uno and Euro TV (the latter being a network founded by Calisto Tanzi, owner of the dairy giant Parmalat, and close friend of **DC** secretary and sometime Prime Minister, Ciriaco **De Mita**). The decisive battles were won by Berlusconi's **Fininvest** company, which acquired Italia Uno in 1983 and ReteQuattro in the following year. This effectively created a dualistic system with political implications, with the Christian Democrats at the helm of the RAI and the Socialist Party aligning itself with Fininvest. A crucial point was reached in October 1984 when several judges and magistrates moved to close down Berlusconi's channels in some cities, claiming that the Fininvest network breached legal restrictions on broadcasting nationally. A few days later, however, a decree by the Socialist Prime Minister, Bettino **Craxi** (followed by another in February 1985), re-opened Berlusconi's channels. The absence of any clear laws regulating television broadcasting was again highlighted as Berlusconi now established a *de facto* 'duopoly' with the RAI.

The late 1980s thus saw an intensification of the television wars between Berlusconi's Fininvest network and the RAI as **Auditel** began to publish its daily analyses of audience share. In 1987, after many years at the RAI, Pippo **Baudo** moved to Fininvest as artistic director. The RAI replied by increasing investments, especially in the third channel, which was largely the province of the Communist Party. Under the direction of Biagio Agnes, the public network regained some ground and Pippo Baudo came back to the RAI in April 1989. Berlusconi also lost the first round of a contest with De **Benedetti** for the property of Mondadori, and with Tanzi for Euro TV, which was soon transformed into a new network named OdeonTV.

A certain peace in the television wars came with the 'Mammì law' in 1990 although, following hard on several years of bitter political wrangling, the law itself turned out to be a compromise which largely worked in Berlusconi's favour. RAI and Fininvest could both retain three channels. Fininvest would have to divest itself of some of its newspaper interests, but in recompense it would now be allowed to legally interconnect stations and broadcast live, thus achieving its aim of becoming an alternative national television network to the public broadcaster. Needless to say, Berlusconi's successful campaign for Prime Minister in 1994 passed through all the television screens controlled by Fininvest.

In 1995, a referendum to abrogate the Mammì law failed, and in the following year Fininvest was transformed into Mediaset, a listed holding company with shares held by, among others, Rupert Murdoch and Leo Kirch. Thus in the late 1990s, the Italian television sky is effectively a 'duopoly', divided almost equally between the RAI and Mediaset, with the Cecchi Gori Group and its Telemontecarlo network attempting, with little success, to create a 'third pole'.

Further reading

Fiori, G. (1995) *Il venditore. Storia di Silvio Berlusconi e della Fininvest* (The Salesman: A History of Silvio Berlusconi and Fininvest), Milan, Garzanti.

Giacalone, D. (1992) *La guerra delle antenne* (The Broadcasting War), Milan: Sperling & Kupfer.

Grasso, A. (1992) *Storia della televisione italiana* (The History of Italian Television), Milan: Garzanti.

Monteleone, F. (1992) *Storia della radio e della televisione in Italia* (The History of Radio and Television in Italy), Venice: Marsilio.

Noam, E. (1991) *Television in Europe*, Oxford: Oxford University Press (for Italy, see ch. 9).

Wolf, M. (1989) 'Italy from Deregulation to a New Equilibrium' in *The European Experience*, ed. G. Nowell-Smith, London: BFI.

RICCARDO VENTRELLA

privatization and nationalization

As a means of reforming corporate ownership, privatization entered the Italian political agenda in the early 1990s, but actual privatizations only began from 1992–3 onwards. Thus, since state-owned banks and enterprises represented a major part of Italian economy since the interwar years, the early 1980s might be considered the beginning of a new epoch.

The expansion of state-owned enterprises in Italy was a result both of deliberate political decisions and historical accidents, and followed different organizational patterns. Railways were nationalized after a long political debate in 1905 and a state company, Ferrovie dello Stato (State Railways), was created as an autonomous organization within the public administration under the control of the Ministry of Public Works (see **railway systems**). INA (Istituto Nazionale delle

Assicurazioni/National Insurance Institute) was created in 1912 to manage a state monopoly of life insurances (never actually enforced) and marked a major innovation: it was established as a state concern but had an autonomous legal status and operated as a private business outside the public administration. In the interwar period, the Fascist regime adopted the INA formula to establish new banking institutions such as IMI (Istituto Mobiliare Italiano) in 1931, in order to finance private big business with long-term industrial credit. This approach was further developed with the setting up of **IRI** (Istituto per la Ricostruzione Industriale, or Institute for Industrial Reconstruction) in 1933, a new state-owned holding which took over banks shattered by the Great Depression (**Banca Commerciale Italiana**, Credito Italiano, Banco di Roma) and all their industrial securities, thus becoming the leading shareholder of a heterogeneous group of large enterprises (shipping, steel, mechanics and shipbuilding, telephones, electricity) which accounted for a major part of Italian industry.

In the early postwar period, IRI was reorganized and it then successfully carried out the modernization of strategic sectors such as steel (see **Italsider**), telecommunications (through **STET**), electromechanics and motorways (see **autostrada network**). Stemming from AGIP (Azienda Generale Italiana Petroli, or General Italian Petroleum Agency), which had been created in 1926 by the Fascist regime as a state–private joint venture, **ENI** was created in 1953 as a state monopoly of natural gas after an epic dispute with American oil multinationals (see Enrico **Mattei**), and it quickly became an international oil giant, playing a leading role in the Italian '**economic miracle**'. A new form of political control over the state-owned system took shape in 1956, when a Ministry for State Shareholdings was established; the chain was further strengthened during the 1960s through a number of interministerial committees, so that state-owned enterprises became officially a means of enforcing economic planning and southern industrialization. Finally, in 1962 the centre–left government nationalized electricity (which had been managed by five powerful private groups) and **ENEL** (Ente Nazionale Energia Elettrica), a giant company which monopolized production and distribution, was set up as a state company outside the state shareholding system.

The economic crisis of the 1970s forced the state to play an anticyclical role, mainly by nationalizing sick private concerns, maintaining high levels of employment and investing heavily in declining capital-intensive sectors (such as steel and petrochemicals), especially in the South. At the same time, other state holdings such as EFIM (Ente per il Finanziamento dell'Industria Meccanica, or Agency for Financing Mechanical Industry) and EGAM (Ente per la Gestione delle Aziende Minerarie, or Agency for the Management of Mineral Firms) emerged as terminal care hospices for mechanical and mining enterprises. By this time the state-owned system had become a giant conglomerate with disastrous economic and financial performances, a situation further worsened by mediocre (if not worse) managers, usually loyal only to political parties of the government coalitions which had become 'hidden shareholders' of such enterprises. As a result, a large part of the state-owned system was increasingly dependent on government endowments, which burdened the national budget with heavy losses and drew sharp criticism from Italy's European partners.

1992 thus marked a turning point as IRI, ENI and ENEL were transformed into limited companies owned by the Ministry of Treasury, and the **Amato** government endorsed a general plan for public holdings and banks to be privatized. In the following years, subsequent governments stressed the importance of privatization as a means of reducing the national deficit and spreading shareholding to small savers. However, privatizations might more accurately be seen as a major result of the political changes brought about by *Tangentopoli* and the collapse of traditional parties in 1992–4. In fact a number of public managers proved to have been involved in corruption (see *Mani pulite*), so that privatization appeared the easiest way of breaking relations between economy and politics once and forever. Public opinion pushed this change forward energetically in 1993 by giving overwhelming support to a referendum which proposed abolishing the Ministry for State Shareholdings. Nevertheless, several crucial questions about how to privatize remained unsolved. Supporters of the public company model (the British way of privatizing through a severe fragmentation of shareholding) looked to privatizations as a form of economic democracy and a way of enlarging the Italian stock exchange, while supporters of the French model considered a stable command group a better strategy. The long-winded dispute produced no clear winner, and Italian governments have privileged a case by case approach.

As a result, pragmatism has become the keynote of Italian-style privatizations. Credito Italiano (Italian Credit) and Banca Commerciale Italiana (Italian Commercial Bank) had to be officially transformed into public companies, but just after their privatization in 1993–4 strong controlling groups emerged, the former was drawn into the circle of Allianz, a German insurance group, while the latter fell under the control of a group bound to **Mediobanca** and its allies. In other cases, such as INA and IMI, privatizations simply implied conveyance to San Paolo di Torino, another public bank (although linked to major private partners) to form a leading banking and insurance group. Other major banks to be privatized were Banca di Roma and Banca Nazionale del Lavoro in 1997–8. The largest privatizations proved to be those of ENI and Telecom Italia (see **STET**), completed in 1997. Both found overwhelming favour with retail and institutional investors. However, the state kept a golden share in both companies which still gives the Treasury a major influence in appointing directors and determining strategy. In fact, the real lesson from Italian privatizations seems to be that changing ownership is not an economic reform in itself.

As directives from the **European Union** enforced a liberalization of electricity, telecommunications, banking and transport markets, monopolies, both privatized (such as ENI) and still state-owned (such as **ENEL** and the State Railways) will have to confront competition within a different regulatory framework determined by new independent authorities on public utilities (such as the Authority of Electricity and Gas, established in 1995, and the Telecommunications Authority, established in 1998), set up to foster competition and efficiency and to safeguard consumers' rights. Such structural change has only just begun and the final result is very difficult to predict.

Further reading

Baldassarri, M., Macchiati, A. and Piacentino, D. (eds) (1997) *The Privatisation of Public Utilities: The Case of Italy*, London: Macmillan (a collection of papers on actual and ongoing privatization of public utilities).

Macchiati, A. (1996) *Privatizzazioni tra economia e politica* (Privatizations Between Economics and Politics), Rome: Donzelli (a general picture of the economic and institutional change triggered by privatization policy in the 1990s).

STEFANO BATTILOSSI

Prodi, Romano

b. 7 August 1939, Reggio Emilia

Economist and politician

A graduate of the Catholic University of Milan, Prodi became professor of industrial and political economics at Bologna University. He was Minister for Industry under **Andreotti** (1978–9) and president of **IRI** (1982–9 and 1993–4), where he carried out some controversial privatizations and radical restructuring.

In February 1995, Prodi launched **L'Ulivo** (The Olive Tree Alliance) a centre–left coalition which aimed to compete for government against Silvio **Berlusconi**'s **Polo della Libertà**. Prodi was in an ideal position to lead such a coalition: he was on the Left but was neither an ex-communist nor ex-socialist, and he was a Catholic but was not too closely identified with the **DC**. In economic policy terms, he was a privatizer and one of the few successful state managers. In 1996, l'Ulivo won the elections and, in record time, Prodi set up a government which aimed at restructuring Italian welfare and pensions, introducing some form of federalism and bringing the economy up to EMU criteria. Prodi succeeded in bringing Italy into line for the single European currency and avoided parliamentary defeat for two and a half years, despite regular threats from **Rifondazione Comunista** which gave his government external support. However, in October 1998 he lost a budget division by one vote and so resigned. The following year, together with Antonio **Di Pietro**, he founded a new party called I Democratici (The Democrats), and was also nominated President of the European Commission.

JAMES WALSTON

prosciutto

Prosciutto is pork leg, salted and dried. These few words, however, summarize a series of complex operations in which climatic conditions, environmental factors and, of course, professional expertise play a crucial part. The selection of the meat, for instance, requires specific skills.

After exposure to the air for two to three days, the chosen pork legs go through a skilful fat-trimming procedure. The drying process, before the salting, is carefully monitored with strict controls on temperature and airing. After this, the *prosciutti* are carefully washed and sun exposure then ensures natural drying. The result is the exquisite *prosciutto crudo*, not to be confused with *prosciutto cotto*, where the pork leg is de-boned, cured, pressed and steam-cooked. Among the most famous Italian *prosciutti crudi* are the San Daniele from Friuli and the *prosciutto di Parma* from the famous town in Emilia. *Prosciutto crudo* and rock melon have earned an international reputation as a delightful hors d'oeuvre.

MARIELLA TOTARO GENEVOIS

PSDI

The PSDI (Partito Social Democratico Italiano, or Italian Social Democratic Party) was founded when the right wing of the **PSIUP**, led by Giuseppe Saragat, broke away in January 1947 at a famous meeting at Rome's Palazzo Barberini. The new party was initially called the PSLI, but this was soon changed to PSDI. Its orientation was centrist and pro-NATO, and as such it was present in most governing coalitions from its foundation in 1947 to its demise in 1993. On average it polled around 4.5 per cent of the vote, with a maximum of 7.1 per cent in 1948 and a minimum of 2.7 per cent in

1992. It was characterized by similar policies and methods to the Christian Democrat Party (see **DC**), differentiating itself only in specifically religious or moral matters like **abortion**. In 1966 the party reunited with the **PSI** under the banner United Socialist Party (PSU). They polled 14.5 per cent, 5 per cent less than the two parties had received separately in 1963, so the parties split again in 1969. Like the other parties of the 'First' Republic, the PSDI sank in 1993 in a sea of debts and legal writs.

JAMES WALSTON

PSI

In opposition from 1947 to 1963, and in government for much of the rest of its life until 1994 when it was officially dissolved, the PSI (Partito Socialista Italiano, or Italian Socialist Party) was characterized in the first period by strong internal ideological dissension between reformist and revolutionary wings, in particular between those who wanted to work with the **PCI** and those who wanted autonomy. In the second period, until **Craxi**'s leadership, the divisions were between the pragmatists who wanted to work within the government and the Left which wanted to maintain an ideological purity. These divisions led to a number of splits and mergers. In the final period, despite an apparent initial success, the PSI became uniformly centrist and increasingly corrupt, until it finally sank in a sea of debts and arrest warrants resulting from the **Tangentopoli** investigations. For fifty years before that, the PSI had navigated a course between the **DC** and the PCI, at times risking being overwhelmed by one or the other and at times able to exploit its pivotal position between the two.

The old pre-Fascist Socialist Party had very little in the way of underground organization at the time of the fall of Fascism (see **fascism and neofascism**), but in August 1943 the Socialist old guard came together with two new groups, the Milanese Movimento di Unità Proletaria (Movement of Proletarian Unity) led by Lelio Basso and the Roman Unione Proletaria Italiana (Italian Proletarian Union) led by Giuliano Vassalli, to form the Partito Socialista Italiano di Unità Proletaria (see **PSIUP**) with Pietro **Nenni** as its leader. In the 1946 elections for the **Constituent Assembly**, it figured as the biggest party of the Left, leading the PCI by a small margin. However, in 1947 the social democratic wing of the party broke away to become the PSLI (changed in 1952 into the PSDI), while what was left became the PSI (Italian Socialist Party). In the national elections of 1948, the PSI went into an electoral alliance with the PCI as the Popular Democratic Front (FDP). The move proved massively unsuccessful for the Left (they won much less in 1948 than the two parties had won separately in 1946) and absolutely disastrous for the PSI, which was overwhelmed by the Communist Party's organization. The setback pressured the party first into striving for organizational independence and then, increasingly after the Twentieth PCUS conference and the Soviet invasion of Hungary in 1956, into ideological independence as well. Partly because of these changes and partly because of the DC's electoral decline, the PSI began negotiating with the Catholics in 1960 for places in local government, which eventually led to the first centre–left national government in 1963 with Nenni as deputy prime minister.

However, the left wing broke away the following year, again taking up the name of PSIUP; this weakened the PSI's influence in government, but nonetheless some elements of their programme were realized, including the nationalization of **ENEL**, an increase in the school leaving age and later, the Workers' Statute, **divorce** law and, in the 1970s, various civil rights measures. As a result of the experience of government and of the PSI's general move towards the centre, the PSI and the PSDI reunited in 1966. In the polarized climate of the late 1960s, the result was again disastrous electorally, and so in 1969 they parted company once more.

The early 1970s was a period of confusion for the PSI, with some in the party enthusiastically taking part in government – which also meant in clientelism and corruption – and some attempting to remain faithful to socialist principles and traditions. As the *Times* put it, when the PSI had made a poor showing in the 1975 regional elections, the Socialists had 'disappointed their supporters by the eagerness with which they leapt onto the gravy train and the mess which some of their leaders made while spreading it about' (18 June 1975).

The party left government, although it continued to support the so-called 'governments of national unity'. Then in 1976, Bettino **Craxi** was elected secretary. Initially a compromise candidate, he soon consolidated his position within the party, maintaining a clear distance from the PCI and emphasizing the PSI's European social democratic vocation. In 1980 the Socialists were back in the governing coalition, and in 1983 Craxi was able to exploit the decline of the DC's fortunes in order to become prime minister for the next four years. From then until his political death and legal exile in 1993, Craxi completely dominated the party. Other factions gradually disappeared and the PSI became a machine for managing power and public resources (see **clientelism**), effectively a technological, modernized and media-friendly version of the old DC.

The policy brought some electoral gain, but never the overwhelming success that Craxi and his supporters had expected. Like the DC, the PSI stood over the changing Communist Party like a vulture waiting for titbits from the corpse, but in the event it was the **Lega Nord** (and the **PDS** and **Rifondazione Comunista**) which fed off what remained of the PSI. In February 1992, the arrest of Mario Chiesa, PSI leader in Milan and Craxi's close associate, initiated what came to be known as the *Mani pulite* (clean hands) investigations. Craxi would later maintain that it was the whole Italian political system which was corrupt, not just the PSI, but this did not help save either the party or its leader. The immediate result of Chiesa's arrest was that Craxi was no longer prime minister after the April elections; the next result, following soon after, was that instead of celebrating its centenary in 1992, the PSI prepared for its own funeral. This took place in 1994 when the rump divided into the Laburisti on the Left, led by Valdo Spini, and the Socialisti Italiani (SI) on the right led by Ottaviano Del Turco. Other ex-Socialists moved to either the PDS or **Forza Italia**. In 1998, some of Craxi's supporters tried to refound the party but with scant success.

See also: De Martino; opening to the Left

Further reading

Di Scala, S. (1988) *Renewing Italian Socialism: Nenni to Craxi*, New York: Oxford University Press (informative and comprehensive but rather biased in favour of Craxi).

Gundle, S. (1996) 'The Rise and Fall of Craxi's Socialist Party', in S. Gundle and S. Parker (eds), *The New Italian Republic: From the Fall of the Berlin Wall to Berlusconi*, London: Routledge.

JAMES WALSTON

PSIUP

The PSIUP (Partito Socialista Italiano d'Unità Proletaria, or Italian Socialist Party of Proletarian Unity) was the official name of the relaunched Socialist party between 1943 and 1947. However, it became better known as the name taken up again by the left wing which split from what had by then become the Italian Socialist party, or **PSI**, when the latter was drawn into government by an alliance with the **DC** in 1964 (see **opening to the Left**). Although the PSIUP survived the 1968 election with 4.5 per cent of the vote, this plunged to 1.9 per cent in the 1972 elections, despite the party having anticipated many of the themes of the New Left; which, however, largely preferred extraparliamentary action (see **extraparliamentary Left**). Consequently most PSIUP activists joined the PCI, often occupying its extreme Left. While the PSIUP's leaders accurately foresaw that the new 'centre–left' coalition could not effect a transition to socialism, the 1964 split contributed to the PSI's subordination to the DC and also deprived the socialists of their organizational linkages with the working class, thus speeding the party's transformation into a southern clientelist and northern 'yuppie' party.

MARK DONOVAN

psychoanalysis and psychiatry

Psychoanalysis in Italy has long struggled against powerful cultural, religious and political opposition: Freud's declaration that his visit to Rome in 1901 was 'the crucial point of my life' was not locally reciprocated. The Catholic Church was hostile to confessional competitors; Crocean idealists dismissed it as a 'pseudo-science; Marxists had no time for a 'bourgeois science'; and the Fascist regime was suspicious of the Jewishness of its leading exponents. Not surprisingly, by the mid-1960s the Italian Psychoanalytical Society (Freudian, created in 1925), the Association for the Study of Analytical Psychology (Jungian, 1961) and the Italian Centre for Analytical Psychology (Jungian, 1966) could count a mere forty analysts, concentrated in Rome and Milan. Only after the 'cultural revolution' of 1968–9 and the subsequent expansion of psychology as a university discipline could psychoanalysis and its therapies begin to find a significant market. By 1991, 726 Freudian and 495 Jungian analysts were at work, managing roughly 12,000 patients. Outside these traditional institutions even more spectacular growth occurred, so that some 30,000 psychotherapists of varying persuasions and respectability were treating 350,000 patients. Doubts about the nature of some therapies led in 1989 to the establishment of a professional register for psychologists and restriction of a licence to practice psychotherapy to those with a psychology degree and four years' postgraduate training.

The demand for psychoanalysis in the 1980s was greatly increased by psychiatrists in search of a new professional knowledge base. Since the nineteenth century, emphasis on the biological basis of mind and evolution – exemplified by Cesare Lombroso and his followers – had aligned psychiatry with medicine: people diagnosed as mentally ill were consigned to long stays in asylums. In Italy as elsewhere, the 1960s brought a widespread challenge to all forms of institutionalization, producing major changes in psychiatric practice. Already by 1960 patient stays in asylums were becoming shorter, and in some cities (Gorizia,

Trieste, Arezzo, Perugia) the writings and practice
of Franco Basaglia had inspired the replacement of
custodial regimes by community care programmes.
In 1978, the deinstitutionalizing trend was accelerated by law 180, which ordered a halt to all
admissions to mental hospitals. The law remained
controversial, partly because its critics confused
problems of design with problems of implementation, and partly because evidence from north,
centre and south produced quite contrasting
assessments. Critics underlined the lack of professional preparation for the reform in many parts of
Italy, particularly the south; but in the centre and
north the reforms worked well and the improvements they brought were not outweighed by
negative side effects (for example, the suicide rate
did not increase).

Further reading

David, M. (1982) 'La psychanalyse en Italie'
(Psychoanalysis in Italy), in R. Jaccard (ed.),
Histoire de la psychanalyse, Paris: Hachette.

Scheper-Hughes, N. and Lovell, A. (1986) 'Breaking the Circuit of Social Control: Lessons in
Public Psychiatry from Italy and Franco Basaglia', *Social Science and Medicine* 23 (2): 159–78.

Trasforini, M. (1988) 'I silenzi di un mestiere. La
professione di psicanalista in Italia' (The
Silences of an Occupation: The Profession of
Psychoanalyst in Italy), *Polis* 2 (2): 323–55 (the
development of psychoanalysis since 1970).

DAVID MOSS

publishers

Publishing in Italy is a huge industry, with total
sales estimated at over 3.5 billion lire per year.
Although many of Italy's most prestigious and
successful publishing firms can boast a long
established tradition, the postwar period witnessed
a continual mushrooming of new publishers,
sometimes as many as five per month, so that by

1998 the total number of registered Italian publishing houses approached 5,000.

Publishing and Italian law

Publishing in postwar Italy was originally regulated
by law 47 of 1948 which attempted to give effect to
Article 21 of the constitution, which paradoxically
sanctioned freedom of speech but at the same time
prohibited the publication of anything that went
against the common sense of decency (*contrario al buon
costume*). The 1948 law thus required all publishers to
be legally registered, for the names and addresses of
editors to be lodged and for all journalists to belong
to the national association and to be registered on
the Journalists Roll (*Albo dei giornalisti*).

In response to both the multiplication of
publishers and an increasing process of concentration of the press, a new law was proposed in the
mid-1970s, although it had a troubled passage and
was not fully approved until August 1981. Known
as Legge dell'editoria (Law on Publishing) it
contained specifications regarding press company
structure and levels of acceptable concentration,
and prescribed the publication of official annual
reports. A second section of the law also contained
regulations for the subsidiaries of publishing
companies and, most importantly, established the
position of a 'guarantor', a magistrate who would
effectively 'guarantee' the proper application and
observance of the law by presenting a report to
Parliament every six months. Even after its long
period of gestation in the Parliament – or, perhaps
because of it – the law proved to still have a
number of fundamental deficiencies which continued to come to light in the following years,
resulting in its being amended several times in the
1980s. Although the law stated that no publishing
group could control more than 20 per cent of the
national daily press and 50 per cent of the press in
well-defined regions, the ongoing media concentrations of the late 1980s continued to prove the
law inadequate, and it was finally abandoned and
superseded in 1990 by the Mammì law. Although
the Mammì law has also been subsequently

criticized as deficient, it does include antitrust clauses, and it also extends the functions of the guarantor to the **radio** sector, permitting direct intervention as well as the imposition of sanctions.

Major bodies

As well as the publishing companies themselves, there exist a number of important national interest and lobby groups. The major and most influential groups are: the Federazione italiana editori giornali (Italian Federation of Newspaper Publishers), which is the parent organization of all Newspaper publishers; the Associazione italiana editori (Associ-ation of Italian Publishers), a voluntary publishers' interest group; the Società italiana degli autori ed editori (Italian Society of Authors and Publishers), the group concerned with the protection of copy-right; the Ordine dei giornalisti, Albo dei giornalisti (Order and Roll of Journalists), the official national association of all Italian journalists, and the Associazione Italiana Editori Piccoli (Italian Asso-ciation of Small Publishers), the most important independent association of small editors in Italy.

Major events

The major events for the publishers are the various book fairs. For Italians, as for most European publishers, the Frankfurt Book Fair is still the most important occasion to present one's products on an international stage. The first genuinely Italian book fair took place in May 1988 at the Salone di Torino (Turin Fair). Organized by the city of Turin and the region of Piedmont, it included theatrical perfor-mances, recitals, round table discussions and a range of other cultural activity in various locations throughout the city. The historical roots of the fair lay in a tradition of Piedmontese printers which went back to the sixteenth century, and its revival proved to be so successful, both with the publishers who participated and with the population at large, that the event has continued to be held throughout the 1990s with the annual participation of over 900 publishers.

Another important event for publishers is the yearly award of the numerous **literary prizes**. Companies participate either by direct sponsorship of prizes or, less visibly, by their presence on the judging panels, a situation which often leads to bitter controversy. The motivation for most publish-ers would appear to be less the economic benefits deriving from higher sales and more the increase in reputation and the opportunity to spot new talent, although these cannot always be held distinct.

Trends towards concentration

As in other European countries (Hachette in France, Bertelsmann in Germany) in Italy the trend has been towards a concentration of increasing portions of the media market under the control of fewer companies. Traditional and well-respected publishers like **Mondadori**, **Ei-naudi**, Rizzoli, Bompiani and Sonzogno have now been incorporated into Silvio **Berlusconi**'s **Fin-invest**, which controls, through a complicated system of interlocking shareholdings, more than ten different publishing houses (Einaudi Editore, Electa, A. Mondadori Editore, Società Europea di Edizioni, Editrice Penta, FIED, R. Riccardi Editore, SAGE-Seregni Grafica, SEL-Editrice Lombarda, SGN-Grafica Novarese, SIES, Sorit-Rotocalcografia Italiano). The RCS group is in second place. It controls well-known publishers like Rizzoli Libri, Rizzoli Periodici (which includes prestigious newspapers like *Il Corriere della sera* and *Il Giornale*), Fabbri, (including Bom-piani, ETAS Libri, Sonzogno), Fabbri-Rizzoli Edizione Periodiche and De Agostini-Rizzoli Periodici. Editoriale *L'Espresso* is in third place, but with its thirteen regional newspapers, its dominant position in the private **radio** system, and its control of the second largest national daily, *La Repubblica*, as well as the influential weekly *L'Espresso*, the company plays a major role in the Italian information system.

Major publishers

The landscape of Italian publishing is thus characterized by a wide variety in the size of the different companies. The massive presence of huge and influential conglomerates, like the three mentioned above, leaves little room for newcomers or for traditional publishers to extend their reach beyond well-defined borders unless they become part of a larger company. Consequently, traditional and more independent publishers like G. Ricordi & C. (Milan, 1808), Sansoni Editrice (Florence, 1873), Casa Editrice Leo S. Olschki (Florence, 1886) or Casa Editrice Felice Le Monnier (Florence, 1837) have tended to focus more and more on special fields like Dante (LeMonnier), Italian composers (G. Riccordi & C.), scholarly and university publishing (Olschki) or dictionaries (Sansoni). Art prints and art in general are the province of several small but well-known companies. One of the leading publishers for the arts is Umberto Allemandi & C. (Turin, 1982) with books and journals in both Italian and English (for example, *Il giornale dell'arte* (Art Newspaper)). Medium-sized publishers like **Feltrinelli** continue to attempt to provide their readers not only with information, but also with fragments of a collective identity constructed around left-wing traditions.

Further down the scale in terms of size are vestiges of the alternative press which emerged in the wake of the **student movement** of 1968 and the counterinformation movement of the 1970s. Although in reduced form, two important companies have survived: **il manifesto** (founded in Rome, 1969) and Stampa alternativa (also founded in Rome, 1975). Stampa alternativa became famous for its publication of a handbook on how to cultivate and use soft drugs in an attempt to prevent young people from moving to harder drugs (see **drug culture**). Its more recent publications on ecology, alternative food, the Third World and the well known series Millelire (selections of classic or contemporary authors for the price of 1,000 Lire) – often used instead of change in bookshops – have had considerable success. The dire economic straits of *il manifesto*, however, demonstrate the constant danger that such small publishers continue to face in the hostile environment of media concentration.

See also: newspapers

Further reading

Castronovo, V. and Tranfaglia, N. (1994) *La stampa italiana nell'età della tv, 1975–94* (Italian Publishing in the Era of Television, 1975–1994), Bari: Laterza.

Giglioli, P.P. and Mazzoleni, G. (1991) 'Concentration Trends in the Media', in F. Sabetti and R. Catanzaro (eds), *Italian Politics: A Review*, London: Pinter.

Parnell, A. (1991) 'The Press in Postwar Italy', in A.M. Brassloff and W. Brassloff (eds), *European Insights*, Amsterdam: Elsevier Science Publishers.

Peresson, G. (1990) *Passaggio a nord ovest. I cambiamenti della produzione consumo e distribuzione del libro negli anni ottanta* (Northwest Passage: Changes in the Production, Consumption and Distribution of the Book in the 1980s), Milan: Sogedit.

JAN KURZ

Pucci, Emilio (Marchese di Barsento)

b. 20 November 1914, Naples; d. 1992, Florence

Fashion designer

Pucci has often been described as 'the first Italian innovator of the postwar years'. After participating in the 1934 Winter Olympics, he attended college in the USA and realized that there was an international market for playful, flattering and simple sportswear. He became famous for his eclectic use of swirling surface pattern and fluid fabrics to create extraordinary colour combinations such as fucshia, lime and turquoise. His tight ski pants, loose shirts and dresses were worn by an international elite, from Jackie Kennedy to Audrey Hepburn. For the rest, there was a wide array of accessories, including the famous Pucci scarf. The Pucci style enjoyed a fashionable renaissance in 1991, when its body-hugging lycra and overshirts became immensely popular with a new young audience.

See also: fashion

NICOLA WHITE

Purini, Franco

b. 1941, Isola del Liri

Architect

In 1971, Purini graduated from the University of

Rome, where he is currently living, teaching in the Faculty of Architecture and working professionally with Laura **Thermes**. He has defined himself as a 'visionary rationalist'. Influenced by elements indirectly derived from both the futurist and the metaphysical movements, Purini has pursued a line of theoretical research which, under the disguise of a kind of surrealistic 'drawn architecture', has sometimes reached a dimension of Piranesian 'excess'. His projects, characterized by pure, 'frozen' geometrical forms and pervaded by a sense of memory which evokes a dimension somewhere in between reality and the imaginary, exalt a complexity entirely composed of simple elements. Among some of his built works are la Casa del Farmacista (the Pharmacist's house) and a system of five squares, both in Gibellina, a Chapel in Poggioreale and apartment housing in Naples-Marianella.

MAURO BARACCO

Q

Quaderni Piacentini

What would become *the* most influential and widely-read journal of the New or **extraparliamentary Left** and later of the 1968 **student movement**, Quaderni Piacentini (Piacenza Notebooks) began life modestly as a cyclostyled magazine in March 1962. Edited for most of its twenty years by its founders, Piergiorgio Bellocchio and Grazia Cherchi, at its height it achieved national sales of 12,000 (although its actual readership was much wider). In its pages it hosted political and cultural writing by some of the best left-wing intellectuals outside the Communist party (see **PCI**), providing high-level sociological and political analyses, reporting on what was happening on the American campuses and, during the 'leaden years' of the 1970s, encouraging wide-ranging debate on **terrorism** and political violence. The journal closed in the early 1980s but, as a testimony to its importance, was extensively reprinted in three anthologies, the first two published by Gulliver and covering the periods 1962–8 and 1968–72; the third, a more general anthology titled *Prima e dopo il '68* (Before and After 1968), was published by Minimux Fax editions in 1998.

GINO MOLITERNO

Quaderni Rossi

Founded at a time of renewed working-class militancy, *Quaderni Rossi* became a highly influential publication for the nascent New Left in Italy. Its contributors, such as Raniero Panzieri and Vittorio Foa, were mostly ex-members of the Socialist Party who identified a radical separation between contemporary Marxist theory and practice and the realities of a Fordist factory system. They proposed a re-reading of Marx and return to a revolutionary politics based on democracy at the workplace. Capitalism, it was argued, could no longer be equated with unbridled competition; a changed relationship between capital and the state had created a planned 'neo-capitalism' that attempted to integrate workers into the system by a policy of welfare and controlled wage increases. However, differences over the role of **trade unions** and Panzieri's premature death meant that the experience ended in the factionalism that had long characterized the Italian Left.

ROBERT LUMLEY

Quaroni, Ludovico

b. 28 March 1911, Rome; d. 22 July 1987

Architect, urban planner and educator

In the late 1930s, Quaroni worked on exhibitions, luxurious residential buildings and designs for the Foro Mussolini. After spending five years in India as a prisoner of war, his interests shifted towards low-cost housing projects such as his exemplary Tiburtino quarter, designed in 1950, and the La Martella housing development at Matera from 1952. His churches in La Martella, S. Franco at

Francavilla al Mare and the Holy Family in Genoa are modest in scale but conceptually stunning. His winning collaborative competition design for the pedestrian passage for the New Termini Railroad Station in Rome is often considered a turning point for Italian postwar modernism. As one of the major figures of Roman postwar realism, Quaroni contributed to the intellectual integration of populist themes and the use of regional materials. In **urban planning** he addressed the issues associated with the North–South dichotomy, especially after joining the Continuità movement in 1956. His last project was a 'basilical' completion of the Opera House in Rome from 1983, which he characterized as 'post-antique'.

GORDANA KOSTICH

Quasimodo, Salvatore

b. 20 August 1901, Modica, Sicily;
   d. 14 June 1968, Naples

Poet, translator and critic

The 1959 Nobel poet laureate Salvatore Quasimodo has left a complex, powerfully evocative poetic corpus that continues to elude any easy definition. Dense, fulminating compositions such as the famous 'Ed è subito sera' (And Suddenly it's Evening) alternate with longer poems which, while continuing to weigh every syllable before the spiritually charged surrounding white space of the page, exude a lyricism that merges with emblematic natural images. The natural world is filtered through myth, Christian history, traditional Italian poetic influences (Leopardi, Dante, Pascoli and d'Annunzio, among others), and the memories of the poet, who sings an enigmatic, 'submerged' music from his place in exile, far from his Edenic native Sicily. His early poetic voice, which has been rightly described as hermetic in the fullest sense of the term, modulated through collections more indebted to French symbolists (Baudelaire, Rimbaud and so on) to express, after the Second World War, a view of poetry which he shares with others such as T.S. Eliot, as a consolation for historical reality.

Born in Modica, Sicily, Quasimodo attended technical schools in Palermo and Messina, where he founded the short-lived monthly *Nuovo Giornale Letterario* (New Literary Journal), before transferring to the Polytechnic University of Rome in 1919 to study engineering. Financial hardship forced him to take various jobs as draftsman, clerk in a hardware store and employee at the department store La Rinascente, from which he was fired for organizing the last Italian strike on the day before the adoption of Fascist legislation banning labour protests. During these difficult years, Quasimodo nonetheless managed to study Greek and Latin, and married his 'Emilian lady', Bice Donetti.

In 1926 Quasimodo was hired by the Ministry of Public Works and transferred to Reggio Calabria. Three years later he followed his brother-in-law Elio **Vittorini** to Florence, where he was introduced into the city's literary milieu and began collaborating on the journals *Solaria* and *Letteratura*. In 1930 he published his first volume of poetry, *Acque e terre* (Waters and Lands), which excited a good deal of critical attention for its nurtured 'secret syllables' that, in essentialized verse, expressed a yearning to return to mythical origins.

The split of Quasimodo's life between his government job and his poetry continued when he was transferred by the Corps of Engineers to Imperia in 1931. He meanwhile formed friendships with the poets Adriano Grande, Angelo Barile and Camillo Sbarbaro in Genoa, and contributed to the journal *Circoli* (Circles). *Oboe sommerso* (Submerged Oboe) was published in 1932 and won the Antico Fattore poetry prize. This collection built on the previous one, stylistically in its continued use of elliptical syntax, allusion and analogy, and thematically in its tortured, Christological/orphic/existential expression of the word by syllables that 'de-flesh' the poet in search of 'virginal roads' that may lead him back to his source.

After a short period in Sardinia, Quasimodo's work in the Corps of Engineers brought him to Milan and in 1935 his illegitimate daughter Orietta was born. The third collection of poems, *Erato e Apòllion*, named after the muse of love poetry and the angel of destruction in the Apocalypse, appeared in 1936. Two years later Quasimodo definitively abandoned his government job, opting instead to work in publishing under the author and film-maker Cesare **Zavattini**. The first important anthology of Quasimodo's poems under the title *Poesie* (Poems) was published in 1938 with an introduction by Oreste Macrì, who emphasized Quasimodo's 'poetics of the word'. Quasimodo's translation of *Lirici greci* (Greek Lyric Poets), published in 1940, caused an immediate sensation 'almost unparalleled in the history of translation' (G. Finzi) as both a poetic success and academic scandal, in part given its publication by the journal *Corrente* (Current), which maintained a critical attitude toward the Fascist regime.

In 1941 Quasimodo was named, due to his 'great renown', Professor of Italian Literature at the Giuseppe Verdi Conservatory of Music in Milan, where he taught until his retirement in 1968. While the poet did not take an active role in the partisan **Resistance** during the final years of the War, he was nonetheless denounced in the state media as an anti-fascist and suffered at least one 'nocturnal incident', as he himself described it, with the blackshirt patrols. In the meantime, the definitive edition of *Ed è subito sera* was published along with the 'new poems' written between 1936 and 1942. Quasimodo also translated the *Gospel According to John*, Catullus's *Songs* and excerpts from Homer's *Odyssey*, which were published after the end of the war.

Having joined the Communist Party in 1945, Quasimodo inaugurated a new phase of more politically oriented verse in a recognizably epic tone with *Con il piede straniero sopra il cuore* (With the Foreign Foot over My Heart), later enriched by two poems and republished under the title *Giorno dopo giorno* (Day After Day) (1947). *La vita non è sogno* (Life is Not a Dream) (1949), *Il falso e vero verde* (The True and False Green) (1956) and *La terra impareggiabile* (The Incomparable Land) (1958) soon followed. During these years, Quasimodo was awarded numerous prizes, including the San Babila, the Etna-Taormina, which he shared with Dylan Thomas, and the Viareggio Prize. After the death of his first wife, Bice Donetti, in 1948, Quasimodo married the dancer Maria Cumani, who bore him a son.

Quasimodo suffered a heart attack in 1958 while on a trip to the Soviet Union, and during the long recovery in Moscow wrote some of the poems

included in *Dare e avere* (To Give and To Have), his last collection of poems, published in 1966. The conferring of the 1959 Nobel Prize, supported by letters of recommendation by Francesco Flora and Carlo Bo, was not, however, without bitter polemics in some literary circles. The poet also received an honorary degree from Oxford University in 1967. These final years witnessed a copious production of translations of ancient as well as modern poets (including Euripides, Shakespeare, Pablo Neruda and e.e. cummings) in addition to critical articles on literature, art, and theatre.

Further reading

Dutschke, D. (1969) 'Salvatore Quasimodo', *Italian Quarterly* 47–8: 91–104 (gives a brief overview of Quasimodo's life and works and presents a selection of not previously translated poems in English).

Loriggio, F. (1994) 'Modernity and the Ambiguities of Exile: On the Poetry of Salvatore Quasimodo', *Rivista di Studi Italiani* 12 (1): 101–20.

Quasimodo, S. (1964) *The Poet and the Politician and Other Essays*, trans. T. Bergin and S. Pacifici, Carbondale, IL: Southern Illinois University Press.

—— (1960) *Selected Writings*, trans. A. Mandelbaum, New York: Farrar, Straus & Cadahy.

—— (1983) *Complete Poems*, trans. J. Bevan, London: Anvil Press Poetry.

SHERRY ROUSH

Quelli della notte

Broadcast live on the second **RAI** channel between 11 p.m. and about midnight on Mondays to Fridays for a period of less than three months in 1985, *Quelli della notte* (The Night Crowd) became more than just a cult programme; rather, it marked a revolution in Italian popular culture.

Building on some elements of his earlier and extremely successful ***L'altra domenica*** (Another Side of Sunday), musician-presenter Renzo **Arbore** created a hybrid programme where late night viewers were invited into his chaotic, kitschy and slightly arabesque living room, peopled by a circus of odd characters, all affecting different television styles and talk show stereotypes. These amusing and eccentric figures included Riccardo Pazzaglia, a Neapolitan philosopher obsessed with the 'primal soup', Arbore's fictional spinster cousin Marisa Laurito, always frantically awaiting a boyfriend who never appeared, Nino Frassica, a monk who spoke a peculiar language full of neologisms, Massimo Catalano, Expert of the Obvious, Harmand, Arbore's mysterious Arabic brother, and a host of others, with the New Pathetic Elastic Orchestra providing the musical numbers, several of which became independent best-selling hits.

Attracting only a modest 800,000 viewers during its first week, the programme soon became the main point of reference of late-night viewing, and by its seventh week had gained 51 per cent of total share. Wisely terminated by Arbore at the height of its popularity and before it began to repeat itself, the programme achieved legendary status as many of its tics and neologisms became absorbed into Italian popular culture.

RICCARDO VENTRELLA

R

Raboni, Giovanni

b. 22 January 1932, Milan

Poet, critic and journalist

A lawyer by training, Raboni soon abandoned his profession in favour of literature and journalism. He has worked for *Il Corriere della sera* and has edited the series *I quaderni della Fenice* (The Phoenix Notebooks) for Guanda. In line with a Lombard tradition that ultimately harks back to Manzoni and Parini, Raboni reduces to a minimum the presence of the lyrical 'I' in his early poetry and, in a conscious reprise of Eliot's and Pound's objective correlative, lets city, history and political events narrate themselves. Raboni's later poems, especially those of the 1982 collection *Nel grave sogno* (In the Deep Dream), continue to privilege a detached narration, although they are permeated by a greater moral tension and existential angst.

Further reading

The Coldest Year of Grace, trans. S. Freibert and V. Rossi, Middletown: Wesleyan University Press (an anthology of Raboni's poetry with a brief introduction to his work).

VALERIO FERME

radio

Having begun in the mid-1920s, Italian radio broadcasts were soon expanded by the Fascist regime, which recognized their potential for propaganda and consensus building. After the end of the Second World War, the radio system was restructured and centralized in the state-controlled **RAI** (which after 1954 became RAI-TV), a state monopoly which lasted until the 1970s when a multitude of illegal local radio stations were established and, eventually, achieved legal status. This emergence of other participants and political interests put pressure on the system, leading to new balances and interconnections between the more than 2,000 private and local radio stations and the major broadcasting companies. Finally, after two decades of rapid and often chaotic change, at the end of the 1990s the Italian radio system had settled into twelve national networks (led by RAI Radiouno but closely followed by the commercial Radio Dimensione Suono), some 1,500 local stations and an estimated daily audience of 35 million.

Italian public radio

The history of Italian radio in the immediate postwar period is largely the history of the RAI which, as public broadcaster, was overwhelmingly under the influence of the government of the time. The reconstruction of the heavily-damaged transmitting stations and studios started with the aid of US troops in the army of occupation, and in October 1944 the EIAR (Ente Italiano per le Audizioni Radiofoniche, or Italian Commission for Radiophonic Broadcasting) was transformed into RAI. Mussolini himself had greatly expanded radio in Italy, and his famous words, 'Voglio una radio in ogni villaggio' (I want a radio in every village), had been largely implemented during the war. Over two million receivers had been installed in market places, factories, schools and military facilities, and after the war the number of receivers in private households increased rapidly to over seven million.

Ironically, in view of the way in which the Fascist regime had controlled radio for propaganda purposes, the early postwar period came to be characterized by a systematic ban of political opinions other than that of the governing Christian Democrat party (see **DC**). In fact, as a reaction to the government's use of radio during the Cold War as its own political megaphone, the Communist Party (see **PCI**) tried to find a place in the medium by broadcasting from foreign countries. In the early 1950s, for example, the programme *Oggi in Italia* (Today in Italy) was transmitted daily but from Radio Prague 3.

At the same time, due to the intensive diffusion of radios in the countryside and particularly in the South, where illiteracy was still rife, radio effectively became the first real mass medium. Especially during the period between the end of the war and the first positive effects of the '**economic miracle**', the radio was one of the most important elements keeping the nation mentally together. Regular reporting of progress in programmes such as *Cronache della ricostruzione* (Chronicles of Reconstruction) or *L'Italia com'è* (How Italy Is) created uplifting collective moments for the multitudes in bars, offices and factories, as well as enabling spiritual fraternization with the pain and suffering of the whole nation. Consequently, more than any of the other traditional mass media at the time, the radio brought Italy together as a geographical and spiritual entity.

In the intention of its makers, radio was to have less of an entertainment and more of an educational function. Spreading standard Italian as a common language (see **Italian language**) in the southern regions, increasing literacy and strengthening national identity were the major aims, and all were partly achieved. By 1955, over 19 million Italians listened for an average of four hours a day to the three RAI programmes, Nazionale, Secondo and Terzo, which were generally meant to privilege information, entertainment and educa-

tion respectively. By 1958 there were seven million active subscribers, although the familiar North–South divide was clearly visible even in the distribution of listeners: four million in the North, 1.5 million in the centre and 1.5 million for the whole South, including Sicily and Sardinia.

The first real challenge to radio came from the introduction of regular television broadcasts in 1954. Significantly, RAI became RAI-TV and the popularity of the new medium quickly increased. In response, the three radio programmes focused more on their special functions and attempted to exploit some of the major advantages of radio, in particular its ability to be integrated into the fixed daily habits of the audience without disrupting work and other activities. New radio plays were introduced and prominent musicians like Luigi **Nono**, Bruno **Maderna** or Luciano **Berio** were inducted into the RAI. Live reports were also increased and developed, but the medium continued to lose ground to television.

Nevertheless, technical innovations such as the transistor made the radio portable and thus more common everywhere. As a status symbol in the early 1960s, the portable radio was much in evidence during holidays on the beaches or in the mountains. Other novelties also helped to hold the line against television: for example, direct phone contact with the audience was initiated in 1969 with the famous programme *Chiamate Roma 3131* (Call Rome 3131). The targeting of particular groups such as the young was reinforced after 1966 when Radiomontecarlo, the first competitor to RAI, began broadcasting from the principality of Monaco into northwest Italy (see **Telemontecarlo**). Through the voice of Herbert Pagani, Radiomontecarlo won the hearts of the Italian listeners overnight; Pagani's way of presenting music, his humour, the selection of the music and the general unconventionality of the station immediately attracted a large audience. Interestingly, this possible infringement of the RAI's broadcasting monopoly went unnoticed, or at least unchallenged, and the question only surfaced in the aftermath of 1968 with the determination of the **student movement** and the **extraparliamentary Left** to provide their own 'counterinformation' to that of the political establishment.

Private radio

In spite of sporadic previous experiments, independent radio stations were only effectively established in 1975. In the beginning officially defined as *radio pirate* (pirate radios), the stations called themselves *radio libere* (free radios) alluding to both the constitutional right to freedom of opinion and to freedom of trade. Radio Libera in Florence, Radio Parma, Radio Emmanuel in Ancona, and Radio Milano International and Radio Canale 96 in Milan were forerunners in a trend that brought over 1,600 new radio stations into the Italian broadcasting system within the next three years, increasing to 4,400 ten years later

It was obvious from the beginning that the new radio stations had different interests from each other. On the one hand there were the 'commercial radios' (*radio commerciali*) which were motivated by financial interests. Radio Parma, for example, was clearly founded by a local businessman for its economic and advertising potential. In 1976, Gamma Radio became the first ambitious attempt by Milan tycoons to build up a wider network, followed by other networks like Radio Italia, Rete 105 and Radio Dee Jay. The programmes mostly consisted of Italian and international pop music, light entertainment and advertising, with serious information and background analysis playing a decidedly minor role.

On the other hand, there were the politically engaged 'democratic radios' (*radio democratiche* or *radio di classe*) which constituted the counterpart to commercial radios. The initial aim of most of the democratic radios was to reveal the 'reality' of the strained political and social situation of the country through unfiltered information, thus providing a service of 'counterinformation' against the RAI which, as even the **Constitutional Court** agreed in 1974, had manipulated the news in favour of the leading parties. The democratic radios thus aimed to provide interest groups, youth cultures, workers, women and unionists with 'objective' information. However, it was only in July 1976 that the Constitutional Court confirmed the legal right of regionally confined stations to broadcast, providing the contents were not against the constitution itself. Radio Città Futura, Radio Popolare, Radio Bra Onde Rosse, **Radio Alice**, Controradio and

Radio Radicale all soon rose to prominence, but their obvious political leanings brought nearly all of them into conflict with the police. Provocative symbolic action like starting and ending all programmes with the Marxist hymn, the *Internationale*, as Radio Bra Onde Rosse did in Piedmont, was a dangerous demonstration of radical sympathies in the context of frequent terrorist attacks. This, and an openly pro-drug stance, were often used as arguments to close down some of the stations. Sometimes, as in the famous case of Radio Alice, the radio was used by leaders of leftist groups to actually incite and co-ordinate demonstrations and street actions.

With the decreasing mobilization of the political mass movements in the 1980s, the democratic radios entered into a state of crisis. The concept of counterinformation became dull and the weak finances of most of the radios resulted in the exodus of many poorly paid employees. Criticism of institutions, once an effective weapon, now became merely boring ritual and the audience declined. Some democratic radios survived by transforming themselves into local stations (for example, Controradio in Florence, or Città del capo in Bologna). Others tried to integrate themselves into the new broadcasting system after the passing of the Mammì law in 1990. Radio Popolare, for example, tried to establish a new network after 1990. The station had been founded in 1976 in Milan by members of different unions as well as representatives of the **PSI** and the extraparliamentary Left. Committed to a self-declared workers 'reality' in the streets and factories, it became famous for its live coverage of endless political discussions in bars or in front of industrial plants. Its financial crisis at the end of the 1970s led to a solidarity campaign to save the station from economic ruin. In 1990, however, Radio Popolare became a limited company, its restructuring and its professionalization financed by advertising revenues.

The history of Radio Radicale shows another response to changing times. Founded in 1976 as the local station of the **Radical Party** in Rome, Radio Radicale delivered live information, mainly from the **Parliament** or, during important trials such as those of terrorists or the **mafia**, directly from the court room. Fiercely libertarian, in 1986 it began transmission of live and uncensored comments from anonymous listeners about anything they cared to talk about, from politics to racism, from sexist stories to complaints about the mother-in-law. The programme proved to be highly controversial and came to an end after only two weeks when the police confiscated answering machines and tapes. Nevertheless, Radio Radicale managed to continue to expand and in 1990 provided information to a network of nearly 100 stations throughout the country. In spite of its chequered past, in 1994 Radio Radicale was chosen by the government to officially broadcast live sessions of Parliament – an obligation of the Mammì law that the RAI was apparently not able to discharge – and the income from this service together with its subsidy as an organ of the Radical Party continued to keep it financially viable.

If the introduction of **private television** in the early 1980s and the high profile of the ensuing 'television wars' appeared again to relegate radio to a secondary position, this has largely changed in the 1990s and radio has regained much of its lost ground. Audiradio, the radio counterpart of **Auditel** which monitors television audience share, has estimated a steady growth since the early 1990s of one million new listeners per year. According to Audioradio data, in 1997 an average of 35 million Italians were listening to a radio sometime during the day. It thus appears that the inherent advantages of portability and flexibility of radio over television are likely to continue to make it one of the most important of the mass media in Italy well into the new century.

See also: broadcasting

Further reading

Eco, U. (1994) 'Independent Radio in Italy', in R. Lumley (ed.), *Apocalypse Postponed*, London: BFI.
—— (1983) 'New Developments in the Mass Media of Contemporary Italy', in R. Bosworth and G. Rizzo (eds), *Altro Polo: Intellectuals and their Ideas in Contemporary Italy*, Sydney: Frederick May Foundation for Italian Studies.
Monteleone, F. (1992) *Storia della radio e della televisione in Italia. Società, politica, strategia, programmi 1922–1992* (History of Radio and Television in Italy: Society, Politics, Strategies, Programmes 1922–1992), Venice: Marsilio.

JAN KURZ
GINO MOLITERNO

Radio Alice

The most famous of the 'free radios', Radio Alice was founded in Bologna in 1975 by a collective of students and feminists connected with the **Autonomia** movement. In February 1976 it began broadcasting its anarchic and playful format, which included pranks such as on-air trick phone calls to important politicians and counterfeit news, thus initiating the practice of dadaist politics later taken up by the satirical magazine *Il Male*. Although Bologna had a communist administration, the radio soon came under attack from local authorities who accused it of inciting civil disobedience. The conflict came to a head in March 1977 during large-scale demonstrations in the centre of Bologna, provoked by the death of a student at the hands of police. Functioning as a point of relay of information and tactics, the radio was able to help demonstrators to anticipate and counter police moves. When this was discovered, the station was physically dismantled by police and the broadcasters arrested on air, several eventually receiving substantial prison sentences. Despite these upheavals, the station itself survived until 1980 when many of its collaborators moved to other stations and the collective effectively dissolved.

See also: radio

GINO MOLITERNO

RAI

Relative to its Western European counterparts, the Italian broadcasting system was a slow developer. Trapped like many aspects of Italian culture and society within an incomplete process of modernization, the broadcasting system was unsophisticated and rudimentary. Television was the only 'mass' medium in the sense that it addressed the entire population, but national television coverage was monopolized by a large state-run broadcasting institution, the RAI (Radiotelevisione Italiana). Furthermore, until the mid-1970s, the RAI television news reported uncritically the government activities of the day, provided little space for opposing political views, and excluded the Communist Party (**PCI**) from public visibility.

In the early 1970s, a **Constitutional Court** ruling ended the RAI's monopoly of broadcasting by asserting the need for a more pluralist mass media. The resultant legislation (law no. 103, 1975) presented the first challenge to the old concept and practice of broadcasting as a centralized public service delivered and controlled by the state. This triggered a phase of internal organizational reform within the RAI as well as allowing the emergence of the first privately owned local television networks. The legislation had two major consequences. First, it strengthened and institutionalized party political control over the state broadcaster, since an administrative council was created whose members were nominated by Parliament on a 'representative' basis in proportion to the number of seats of each party. This made the RAI, like other major state institutions in the First Republic, subject to the practice of *lottizzazione* whereby the ruling political parties divided the organization into 'pillars' of control, each party holding patronage of appointment over a 'pillar' of the network. Competition between the state channels reflected competition between the political parties, as the major channel Rai Uno became a fiefdom of the Christian Democrats (**DC**), Rai Due came under the patronage of the Socialists (**PSI**), and Rai Tre, the channel initiated to extend the plurality of coverage, belonged to the Communist Party. The second consequence of the legislation effecting the RAI's monopoly was the opening up of broadcasting to the market, so that from the mid-1980s onwards the privileged and protected position of the RAI came to be increasingly challenged by competition from an emerging and innovative private network at the national level. The public broadcaster's ability to innovate through commercial activities in this technologically driven sector were constrained by an organizational 'logic' that prioritized the interests of the political parties, and this left

significant commercial opportunities open to the private sector.

Between 1975 and 1990, Italian broadcasting developed within a legislative vacuum but under the influence and control of the political parties, and it became increasingly influenced by the challenge of Silvio **Berlusconi**'s private broadcasting to the state monopoly. The overriding political logic of appointments to the RAI made the state industry a hugely inefficient enterprise that was increasingly unable to justify the large-scale public funding through the licence fee. Crippled by inefficiency and financial crisis, the RAI tried to compete with the entertainment-based transmissions of the Berlusconi group. It subsequently lost distinctiveness and credibility as a public service, and in any case was more likely to pander to the demands of politicians than serve the public interest. Like many other state organizations, the RAI became a victim of the inability of the 'partycratic' political system to regulate and make rational decisions for the future of the industry. The so-called Mammì law, the 1990 Broadcasting Act (law no. 223), entrenched a RAI/Berlusconi 'duopoly', but did very little to reduce political party stranglehold over the state broadcaster. Reform of the RAI remained a hotly debated political issue over which the parties were unable to reach a consensus.

The collapse of the political system in the early 1990s in the wake of the ***Tangentopoli*** corruption scandals weakened the control of the 'old' political parties over the RAI, but the reorganization of the RAI and the entire broadcasting sector remained a sharply contested political issue, as a new set of political parties competed to exert control over the broadcasting system. The situation was complicated and further 'politicized' by the entry of Silvio Berlusconi into party politics at the head of **Forza Italia** and by his appointment as Prime Minister for eight months in 1994. Berlusconi retained control of his private broadcasting empire despite repeated proclamation of an intention to divest himself of this conflict of interests, as in the proposed sale of Mediaset to Rupert Murdoch in 1998. In sum, all attempts to reorganize the RAI have remained stifled by a new type of political competition over broadcasting, which, once more, has worked against the creation of a rational contextual framework for a mixed private/public industry to serve the public.

Data on the programming of the RAI networks shows that competition from the private sector has increased the amount of programmes that are bought relative to those produced by the RAI, and that there has been a 'convergence' between the proportion of entertainment, cultural programmes, and news and current affairs shown by the public and private sectors. Commercialization of the industry has, in fact, brought the RAI into the 'infotainment' era. Nevertheless, despite competition, the RAI remains a dominant actor in Italian broadcasting. By 1993, in the important evening band of viewing (20.30–22.30), the RAI networks had a combined 48 per cent of the audience, compared to the 44 per cent of Berlusconi's channels and the 8 per cent of the other networks. Between the three RAI networks, Rai Uno accounted for 20.5 per cent of the audience, Rai Due 15.7 per cent and Rai Tre 11.8 per cent. It should also be noted that whereas Rai Uno and Rai Tre screened relatively more news and current affairs, Rai Due served more fiction and **television talk shows**.

See also: broadcasting; private television; radio

Further reading

Annuario Rai 1994 (1995), Turin: Nuova Eri (RAI's data report on broadcasting, with information on viewing figures, programming and legislation in Italy).

Mazzoleni, G. (1994) 'Italy', in J. Mitchell and J.G. Blumler (eds), *Television and the Viewer Interest: Explorations in the Responsiveness of European Broadcasters*, Media Monograph no.18, London: John Libbey (an account of the development of the regulatory system for broadcasting in Italy).

Richeri, G. (1990) 'Hard Times for Public Service Broadcasting: The RAI in the Age of Commercial Competition', in Z.G. Baranski and R. Lumley (eds), *Culture and Conflict in Postwar Italy*, London: Macmillan.

Statham, P. (1996) 'Television News and the Public Sphere in Italy: Conflicts at the Media/Politics Interface', *European Journal of Communication* 11 (4): 509–54 (an account of

the history of the 'politicization' of broadcasting with comparative data on public/private news coverage).

PAUL STATHAM

railway system

Italy's railways emerged heavily damaged from the Second World War and were reconstructed quite slowly, a fact which increased the technological and organizational gap compared with the more advanced systems in Europe and long inhibited the FFSS (Ferrovie dello Stato, or State Railways), the state company established in 1905 after nationalization of the railways, from meeting the large demand for modern transport triggered by the economic development of the country. The heyday of the railways came only in the 1960s, when the modernization of their infrastructures was set as a priority of both economic planning and direct state intervention to boost economic development of backward southern regions. New double-track railways were then established along the North–South axis, as massive migration from the South placed a huge demand on long distance transport; at the same time, electrification of main lines was completed, signalling systems were technologically upgraded and trains became faster and more comfortable.

Nevertheless, improvement also brought contradictions. The railways' budget recorded chronic deficits, mostly due to low fares and a disproportionate number of employees (from 150,000 in the 1950s to over 200,000 in the 1980s), with the lowest productivity in Western Europe. Moreover, development strategies also turned out to be rather contradictory. While the core of passenger transport demand was on short or mid-distance – that is, metropolitan and regional networks linked to the main urban centres and mostly used by daily commuters – investments were focused on long distance traffic and privileged the modernization of the Rome–Milan line, the capacity of which was quadrupled in order to compete with the emerging highway system (see **autostrada network**). Building or modernizing other North–South lines (namely the coastal Tirrenian axis from Turin to

Rome and the southward leg from Rome toward Naples and Sicily) was neglected, so that growing traffic found itself compressed into a bottleneck at the Apennines crossing. At the same time, regional traffic was disregarded with the result that ageing trains offered a growing number of customers an increasingly worse service, while no effort was made to provide southern regions with an efficient short-distance network. Furthermore, FFSS also neglected to develop goods transport, which in other European countries had proved both a profitable business and a strategic means of economic competition. Consequently, decline of efficiency of service came to be matched only by increase of losses, as during the 1980s FFSS turned into a clientelistic caravan under managers selected by ruling parties, whose main business was distributing rich contracts to supply firms in order to benefit their political patrons (see **clientelism**).

Financial deficit eventually led FFSS to the verge of bankruptcy, while disorganization, unremitting strikes and finally the eruption of bribery scandals – the most famous of which was named *lenzuola d'oro* (golden sheets) – put the railways under intense scrutiny from unfavourable public opinion. Then, suddenly, there was an unexpected resurrection, which seemed to gain momentum from the late 1980s on. Ruled by Lorenzo Necci, an unscrupulous but dynamic manager (later to come under investigation), FFSS underwent radical changes and its economic performance improved astonishingly. The number of employees dropped to 125,000 after over 80,000 took advantage of an early retirement programme funded by the government; losses were gradually reduced and productivity was brought closer to European average.

The most remarkable move of all was the launch of the so-called 'High Velocity Project', which aimed at modernizing the railways network in order to introduce European-style high-speed transport in Italy. Funded jointly by the European Community, the Italian government and a pool of leading national and foreign banks, High Velocity proved the biggest business of public works of the 1990s, and all the main state-owned and private groups (such as **IRI**, **ENI** and IAT) took part in it as general contractors, each leading large consortia

of firms. Unfortunately, this has also proved to be one of the railways' biggest failures. Though high-velocity trains (the so-called 'Pendolino') have begun to run, not a kilometre of new track has in fact been built and the project has been hampered by bureaucratic inefficiencies, the paralysis of public works after *Tangentopoli* and the opposition of environmentalist organizations. Consequently, thousand of billions of lire provided by the European Union for modernizing the Italian network have remained idle, and Italy now risks being excluded from the European high-velocity network for passengers and goods, a fact which might have serious economic consequences. In addition, in 1997–8, most likely due to the ageing of track and signalling infrastructure and cuts in maintenance, several high-velocity trains were involved in a series of accidents resulting in many deaths and injuries.

At the same time, FFSS was also being faced with the challenge of strong competition from foreign railway companies, which were permitted to run trains on the domestic network from 1999 onwards. Plans for partial privatization also continue to be rumoured, but the crucial question remains how to rapidly modernize the Italian railways in order to match efficiency with safety.

STEFANO BATTILOSSI

Raimondi, Ezio

b. 22 March 1924, Lizzano in Belvedere, Bologna

Literary critic and essayist

After teaching for many years at the University of Bologna, Raimondi is currently the Cultural Superintendent of Emilia-Romagna. He is one of the few scholars of his generation who has written profoundly and substantially on all aspects of Italian literature, from Dante and Petrarch to many contemporary authors. His constant and preferred subjects have been literary developments during the Renaissance and Baroque periods, the works of Tasso and Manzoni and contemporary literary theory. In his numerous critical works, Raimondi has demonstrated the rare ability to intertwine the most daring literary theories with solid historiographical knowledge and a penetrating anthropological approach to authors and texts. His books include *Poesia come retorica* (Poetry as Rhetoric) (1980), *Il romanzo senza idillio. Saggio sui 'Promessi sposi'* (The Novel Without Idyll: Essay on Manzoni's 'Betrothed') (1974), *Scienza e letteratura* (Science and Literature) (1978) and *Le poetiche della modernità* (Poetics of Modernity) (1990).

ANDREA CICCARELLI

Rame, Franca

b. 18 July 1929, Parablago, Milan

Theatre artist

Wife of and co-performer with Dario **Fo**, Italy's most famous man of the theatre, Rame was a member of a family touring company, and her career and that of Fo became inextricably entwined. He began his career writing farces for the company, and subsequently they both left the mainstream in the years of political turmoil following the 1968 student uprising to form Associazione Nuova Scena (New Scene Association) and Collettivo Teatrale La Comune (La Comune Theatrical Collective). During this period Rame evolved from usually playing the *soubrette* to taking on more demanding parts, and she also shouldered an important political and administrative role in running the companies. Her most impressive work as playwright and performer has been in the monologues on women's issues co-written with Fo. *Abbiamo tutte la stessa storia* (We All Have the Same Story) and *Il risveglio* (Waking Up) are scabrous and farcical, but carry out serious and coherently argued social critiques.

Further reading

Fo, D. and Rame, F. (1983) *Theatre Workshops at Riverside Studios*, London: Red Notes (valuable outlines of their working processes).

TIM FITZPATRICK

Ranieri, Massimo

b. 3 May 1951, Pallonetto, Naples

Popular music artist and composer

The wide range of Ranieri's creative activities reveals a progressive artist who has sought to transcend the limitations of mainstream popular music. Born Giovanni Calone, he assumed his stage name in tribute to Prince Rainier of Monaco, making his debut at the New York Academy at the age of thirteen. In 1967 his performance of 'Pietà per chi ti ama' (Mercy On He Who Loves You) brought victory in Cantagiro and provided Ranieri with his first entry in the hit parade. There followed eight years of consistent success with numerous number one hits. In 1971, Ranieri met Leonard Bernstein and planned an album of Neapolitan songs with the London Symphony Orchestra. His activities in this area resulted in the award of a gold disc for *O surdato 'nnamurato* (The Soldier in Love) in 1972. From the late 1970s, Ranieri succeeded in pursuing a parallel career as an actor, working extensively in film and theatre throughout Europe, though he also found the time to compete in, and win, the **Sanremo Festival** of 1988.

JOHN KERSEY

rap music

Although house, ska, hip hop and raggamuffin had already appeared as musical styles in Italy during the 1980s, rap music only surfaced in a distinctive way in the early 1990s. It then quickly exploded into a major phenomenon. Pop singer Javanotti (Lorenzo Cherubini) has often claimed to have been the first to introduce rap to Italy, but this primacy has always been strongly contested by more militant Italian rappers, many of whom prefer to locate the first signs of truly Italian rap in the rough-edged music of the Onda Rossa Posse broadcast by the Roman underground radio station Radio Onda Rossa in the summer of 1990. Others suggest that the real genesis of Italian rap lay in the Ghetto Blaster evenings at Bologna's occupied drop-in centre, Isola del Kantiere, between 1988 and 1990, when it was forcibly closed down by the authorities.

Inevitably modelled on American examples in the first instance, Italian rap quickly took on very distinctive characteristics. The first – and in direct contrast to its earlier manifestations in the mid-1980s, when Italians had tried to sing in English – was a strong tendency to manifest a resolutely local identification, using not only regional Italian but often even more restricted dialects in order to communicate local issues and concerns. Far from being a sign of provincialism, this localization manifested a desire both to remain close to the grassroots of daily life and to distance itself from official homogenized Italian culture. The second and often aligned characteristic of much Italian rap has been the close connection of many of the Italian groups – in particular the Italian 'posses', who have been practitioners of the so-called 'combat rap' – with the *centri sociali* (drop-in centres often occupied illegally) of the big cities of Naples, Rome, Milan, Turin and Bologna. This close association with marginalized youth and the socially disaffected prompted rap to naturally assume the function of social protest and opposition to the status quo, thus reintroducing a political dimension into popular music which, much in evidence in the 1970s, had almost completely disappeared during the hedonistic 1980s. This commitment to oppositional culture was a strong characteristic of most of the well-known groups including the Sud Sound System, Isola Posse All Stars, Onda Rosse Posse (Posse Red Wave) and 99 Posse and, significantly, when Gabriele **Salvatores** attempted a return to more politically committed film-making in 1993 with *Sud*, the soundtrack bristled with rap, from Assalti Frontali (Frontal Assault) and 99 Posse to Papa Ricky from the Isola Posse All Stars.

In the late 1990s, the aggressive tone of rap has mellowed somewhat with some of the posses disbanding and others choosing to join more mainstream performance and distribution circuits. However rap, especially in the more commercial form of *rap leggera* or light rap, remains extremely popular and continues to sell well, with Javanotti's last album *L'Albero* (the Tree) having already exceeded 600,000 copies.

Further reading

Mitchell, T. (1996) 'Questions of Style: The Italian Posses and their Social Contexts', *Popular Music and Social Identity*, New York: Leicester University Press (an extensive discussion of Italian rap and its social and political context).

Pacoda, P. (1996) *Potere alla parola. Antologia del rap italiano* (Power to the Word: An Anthology of Italian Rap), Milan: Feltrinelli (a number of informative essays, followed by a representative anthology of texts by all the major rappers, each with its own introduction).

GINO MOLITERNO

Rasy, Elisabetta

b. 1947, Rome

Novelist and essayist

Roman by birth, Rasy spent much of her childhood in Naples before returning to live and work in her native city. She is a writer of both fiction and criticism, and has written some key feminist works, among them the long essay *La lingua della nutrice* (The Nurturing Tongue) (1978), a text praised by Julia Kristeva for its innovative theoretical prose, *Le donne e la letteratura* (Women and Literature) (1988) and *Ritratti di Signora* (Portraits of a Lady) (1995), which examines the lives and works of three other female writers, Grazia Deledda, Ada Negri and Matilde Serao. Rasy has been a key figure in theorizing women's writing and analysing major shifts in Italian feminist thinking. Her first novel, *La prima estasi* (The First Ecstasy), was published by Mondadori in 1985, followed by *L'altra amante* (The Other Lover) (1990). She has also written an autobiography, *Posillipo* (1997), as well as art criticism, essays and stories which have appeared in many periodicals.

BERNADETTE LUCIANO

Rea, Domenico

b. 8 September 1921, Nocera Inferiore,
  Naples

Novelist, poet and short story writer

Generally regarded as a neorealist writer, Rea
consistently used the colourful world of Naples as
the backdrop for his novels and his numerous short
stories. His works avoid stereotypical representations of the poor in order to more convincingly
portray the hardships and deprivations of provincial life. Almost completely self-taught, Rea's own
works reveal the influence of Russian and American authors, whose books he read widely. His short
stories, which have generally been more critically
acclaimed than his novels, are collected in
Spaccanapoli (The Spaccanapoli Quarter) (1947),
Gesù, fate luce (Jesus, Shed Your Light), which won
the Viareggio prize in 1951, and *Quel che vide
Cummeo* (What Cummeo Saw) (1955), amongst
others. *Una vampata di rossore* (A Blush of Shame)
(1959) is widely regarded as his most accomplished
novel, while *Due Napoli* (Two Naples) is a critical
work which outlines the motivations behind his
narrative style. Rea has also published poetry and a
Diario napoletano (Neapolitan Diary) (1971), which
includes essays on his native city.

LAURA A. SALSINI

realism

Realism, in a variety of forms, was the dominant
trend in immediate postwar Italian art. However,
adopted and constrained by the Communist Party
(see **PCI**), it soon became a backwater as artists
turned away from didactic messages towards
abstraction and only re-emerged in the return to
figuration of the 1970s.

Realism and social realism in postwar Italian art
need to be clearly distinguished from earlier forms
of these trends. Realism had been a mid-nineteenth
century French movement associated with Courbet, who rebelled against the fantasies and
emotionalism of the Romantic movement. Courbet's realism was a style which sought to depict
things as they 'really were', that is, painted directly
from life without exaggeration or embellishment. It
also came to have a political aspect in that, for the
first time, labourers and peasants were considered
worthy subjects for large-scale canvasses.

In Courbet's day, realism was new and radical
but inevitably over the next century it became part
of establishment art. Avantgarde art became
increasingly abstract, and realism came to be
considered passé. In fact, many modern movements measured their own worth by the extent to
which they actively departed from realism.

In the 1930s there arose fierce argument about
what constituted revolutionary art. The German
expressionists, the dadaists and the surrealists all
had programmes of social renewal, and argued that
a new and experimental avantgarde style could
best convey this message. The Mexican muralist
Diego Rivera, on the other hand, argued that
because realist art was true to life and without
artifice, it could be immediately understood and
read by an uneducated audience. Stalin agreed
with him, and the style of flat, linear, illustrative art
that resulted came to be known as social (or
sometimes socialist) realism, because it combined
truth in representing objects with political truth in
representing the class struggle. In Germany, Hitler
also favoured simple, graphic, narrative art and
despised all the -isms of avantgarde art, which he
regarded as perversions. All agreed on the broad
idea that art is a vehicle for ideas, and a control
over the production of art means some control over
the political agenda.

In Fascist Italy, however, there was less policing
of artistic styles. Official architecture and sculpture
was monumental and classicist in a dry, modernist
way, but Mussolini expressed no desire to censor
the styles of individuals. Hence Il Corrente (The
Current), an artists' movement formed in 1939,
included both formalists and realists, who were
united more by opposition to Fascist politics than
by stylistic concerns. The solidarity among artists
increased during the last years of the Second World
War, when many participated together in the
Resistance. However, as with the democratic
political parties, often all they had in common was
their opposition to Fascism, so it was not surprising
that their unity soon crumbled.

Some artists, such as the Forma (Form) group,
quickly declared themselves for abstract art,

arguing that it was possible to be both formalist and Marxist. Even among those who supported realism, there was a considerable range of opinion. The most orthodox communist view was put forward by writer Antonello Trombadori, who favoured a flat, pictorial style with aesthetic qualities clearly subordinate to the expression of the political message. Trombadori praised the didactic nature of **Guttuso**'s *Gott mit uns* (God With Us), from 1945, which depicted a historical episode of German brutality, but was unable to see how more personal or abstract art could also express positive political values. De Micheli, on the other hand, spoke out against veristic or naturalistic realism, which he saw leading to the error of social realism. In their manifesto *Oltre guernica* (Beyond Guernica) from 1946, Morlotti and **Vedova** made the same claim, suggesting that realism was a shared state of mind rather than a style, which shows just how broad the Italian sense of realism could be. Indeed, elsewhere the term 'figurative' (dealing with the recognizable shape of objects) would be used, as it allowed for a lesser or greater degree of abstraction. Guttuso himself adopted a neo-cubist style. Thus when Birolli, Morlotti, Vedova, Santomaso, Corpora and Guttuso came together in 1947 in the Fronte nuovo delle arti (New Front of the Arts), they could speak of themselves as representing a *realismo nuovo* or new realism, even though collectively they ran the gamut of figurative styles.

In 1948, the ideal of a unity between political action and art was shattered when Communist Party leader Palmiro **Togliatti** condemned modernist art, including the work of Forma and the Fronte, as rubbish, in terms remarkably similar to those which had been used by Hitler fifteen years earlier. At the same time, growing tension between America and USSR dashed hopes of a rapprochement between liberalism and socialism. This presented a crisis for the realist tendency. There were artists who decided they were simply not interested in delivering any sort of message, preferring to pursue the formal and technical aspects of their craft. Others came to see that abstraction was the language of the international avantgarde and that by persevering with representation they would be left out in the cold. Writer Elio **Vittorini** argued that whatever an artist's commitment to political and social progress, there should be no obligation to 'suonare il piffero' (play the pipe) for the revolution by adopting any particular style.

Nevertheless, realism became the official style of the Communist Party and Guttuso its figurehead, adopting a popular, narrative style exemplified in his *Occupazione della terra incolte in Sicilia* (Occupation of Uncultivated Land in Sicily) (1950). However, Guttuso's followers were described by Vittorini as minor dilettantes, and the whole experience was seen as a mere revival. In 1956, *Realismo*, the official journal of the movement, closed down just as the Soviet Union invaded Hungary and the revolution finally lost its gloss. Later, in the 1960s, Guttuso himself would say that both abstract art and art which sought to be mistaken for reality were a product of the imagination, and therefore not truly realist. True realism should honestly bear the marks of what it is: a painting, a sculpture, a work of art.

Further reading

De Micheli, M. (1989) 'Realism and the Post-war Debate', in E. Braun (ed.), *Italian Art in the 20th Century*, Munich: Prestel-Verlag.

MAX STAPLES

Red Brigades

The Brigate Rosse (Red Brigades) were the largest, longest-lived and most damaging of the left-wing groups which used clandestine political violence as a 'revolutionary' political strategy in the 1970s and early 1980s. Between their first appearance in 1970 and their last murder in 1988, the Red Brigades attracted some 450 members and carried out more than 500 attacks on people and property. Their attacks were mostly concentrated in the four cities of Milan, Turin, Genoa and Rome, and included 81 murders, 75 woundings and 17 kidnappings.

The BR signature was invented in Milan in an extreme left group led by Curcio, Cagol and Franceschini. Embarking on 'armed struggle' for socialism, they argued, could be justified on several grounds. The Vietcong had shown how effective clandestine violence by small groups could be against larger forces; the **PCI** was irremediably 'reformist' and had betrayed the radical inheritance of the **Resistance**; the mass protests of the Hot Autumn showed that the working class was ready for revolutionary change; and the incapacity of the **extraparliamentary Left** to resist the increasing neo-fascist violence demonstrated the need for armed defence of working-class interests.

Between 1970 and 1975, the BR restricted themselves to the intimidation of factory staff and kidnappings of symbolic 'class enemies', designed to publicize the group's revolutionary commitment and show that violence could achieve what non-violent protest under political party or trade union direction could not. Few were convinced. Shunned as 'provocateurs' by the Left, unable to attract recruits or prevent its leaders' arrests, the BR all but disappeared. After 1975, however, new en-thusiasts for violence emerged from the ruins of the extraparliamentary Left (see **Autonomia**). The BR, identified in the acts and anathemas of their early members on trial in Turin between 1976 and 1978, attracted new nuclei of support across central and north Italy. The problems of welding these dispersed groups into an effective political force were met by raising the level of violence and the status of its targets, a strategy designed to display an ability to attack the 'heart of the state' and attract members from other, less ambitious armed groups. 1976 saw the first deliberate BR murder, inaugurating attacks on politicians, journalists, magistrates, police and factory personnel which culminated in the fifty-five-day kidnapping and eventual murder of the prime minister and **DC** leader, Aldo **Moro**, in 1978. However, every serious attack provoked internal disputes over its political importance, followed by defections. In 1980 the confession of a disillusioned BR activist, Patrizio Peci, led to widespread arrests and encouraged other members, many by now con-vinced that violence could be neither effective nor popular, to follow his example (see **pentiti**). Thereafter the rapidly declining membership battled for exclusive rights to the BR's 'revolu-tionary inheritance', publicly disowned by the

group's founders, but promoting their claims by sporadic murders until 1988.

See also: Curcio; terrorism

Further reading

Catanzaro, R. (ed.) (1991) *The Red Brigades and Leftwing Terrorism in Italy,* London: Pinter Pub-lishers.

Wagner Pacifici, R.E. (1986) *The Moro Morality Play: Terrorism as Social Drama,* Chicago: University of Chicago Press.

DAVID MOSS

referenda

The Italian **Republic** owes its very existence to the referendum of 2 June 1946, which saw republicans triumph over monarchists by the narrow margin of 54 to 46 per cent. The **Constituent Assembly**, elected at the same time, was sufficiently impressed by the plebiscitary mechanism to include the right to initiate referenda in the **constitution** of 1948. However, Italians cannot call a referendum to *make* a law; a 'yes' vote can only serve to abrogate existing legislation. In order to achieve this objective, a number of obstacles have to be overcome. The referendum's sponsors must assemble 500,000 registered voters' signatures on a petition, or win the support of five regional councils. The referendum proposal is then scrutinized by the Court of Cassation (and ultimately the **Constitutional Court**), which must rule on its legality. Once the approval of the courts has been secured, a date is set, but if this falls after a dissolution of parliament has been called, the referendum must wait until after a new legislature has been sworn in and another govern-ment formed. Assuming all the necessary condi-tions have been met, at least 50 per cent of the electors need to turn out to vote, and a majority of valid votes must be secured before the measure can be approved.

In practice, this has meant that few referenda survive the course, but those that do tend to have important political, social or economic conse-quences. Of these, the 1974 referendum on the

divorce law was one of the most celebrated. The referendum mechanism was used in this case by the Catholic right in an attempt to overturn the divorce legislation passed four years previously. Nearly three-fifths of those who turned out voted against the abrogation of the law and in favour of the right to divorce. It was a landmark event in Italian political life, and was followed by the failure (following a dissolution) to institute an anti-abortion referendum in 1976, which jolted parliament into approving new abortion legislation in 1978. These events were seen as litmus tests for Italy's growing secularization and liberalism, although the failed attempts to repeal anti-terrorist legislation and to preserve wage indexation in the 1980s showed that the referendum device does not always favour anti-conservative causes.

Nevertheless, it has generally been the radical Left rather than the Right that has championed the referendum as an instrument of popular democracy. Indeed, the former **Radical Party** under its leader Marco **Pannella** has been the leading force in many of the referenda initiatives since the 1970s. Chief among them has been the campaign to reform the Italian voting system, with the aim of instituting a majoritarian system which might result in less corruption and break the stranglehold of the party system. A rare success in the courts allowed a lay–Catholic coalition of electoral reformers to call a referendum on the abolition of the preference vote in parliamentary elections. To outsiders, the 1991 referendum seemed a trivial measure, but the fact that over 60 per cent of Italian voters turned out with over 95 per cent voting for the abolition of the preference vote meant that the political establishment had suffered its first serious defeat. Two years later, after much judicial wrangling, an even bigger campaign succeeded in altering the electoral system for the Senate, thus forcing a by now discredited parliament to introduce 'first past the post' elections for three-quarters of parliamentary seats. Thus it could be said that the popular referendum has been both the midwife and the executioner of the 'First Italian Republic'.

See also: electoral systems

Further reading

Ambrosini, G. (1993) *Referendum*, Milan: Bollati Boringhieri.

Caciagli, M. and Uleri, P. (eds) (1994) *Democrazie e referendum* (Democracies and Referendums), Rome: Laterza.

Donovan, M. (1995) 'The Referendum and the Transformation of the Party System', *Modern Italy* 1 (1): 53–69 (discusses the key referenda on voting reform of the early 1990s).

SIMON PARKER

regional cooking

It has been remarked that Italy, an ancient country but a young nation, finally managed through political unification in 1860–1 to bring together a wide range of regional states, all different from each other and all with strong individual identities. This observation might serve equally well to underscore the unity in diversity of Italian regional cooking, for a large part of the originality and richness of Italy's great culinary tradition derives from its twenty diverse **regions**, which are characterized by different geographical and climatic features, varying ethnic ancestry of the natives, individual agricultural products and diverse histories. Another factor in the culinary equation is that, on the whole, two parallel eating traditions have survived for centuries as a reflection of the social divide between the rich and the poor. The first is documented in detail by books on gastronomy written by experts, the second is borne out by traditions passed down through generations. In addition, one needs to keep in mind the obvious but important fact that the poorer classes were inevitably forced to rely on what was available and affordable to them in the areas where they lived.

A review of historical influences can also aid an understanding of the variety of Italian regional cooking. The expansion of the Roman empire dramatically expanded its citizens' previous frugal diet, though early Christian customs signalled the return of a severe approach to food. Fifth-century contact with barbarians left legacies such as the raw-meat steak tartare, while the splendour of the

Renaissance was similarly reflected in a cuisine characterized by the use of new spices, fruits, vegetables and cereals arriving from recently explored lands.

Political unification accelerated the spread of local culinary customs beyond regional boundaries, thus initiating an ongoing process of mingling and cross-fertilization. For example, after the heroic phase of the Risorgimento was over in 1870, the use of fresh tomatoes to make *pasta al sugo* (pasta with tomato sauce), spread from the South, where tomatoes had been cultivated almost exclusively, to the whole of the peninsula. Furthermore, although the distinction between the cuisine of the affluent classes and that of *il popolo* (the working classes) continued, the gradual process of democratization slowly modified this relationship to the point where, as economic wealth spread, the diet of the working classes came to include food previously out of their reach, while rustic, simple peasant foods came to be also appreciated by the more affluent and served on more sophisticated tables. The rapid modernization in the postwar period and the spread of modern technology further facilitated this blending; in particular, improved transportation made products readily accessible to all, while also bringing together diverse traditions and experiences and accentuating interchange and reciprocities. Yet, notwithstanding this process of inveitable homogenization, the spectrum of Italian regional cooking remained, and remains, extraordinarily varied.

Regions in the northeast of Italy, blessed with abundant water from the river Po, share the common denominators of rice and corn. The first has inspired the creation of a whole range of risotti from the Venetian *risi e bisi* (rice with peas) to the risotto with mussels or crab, risotto nero with cuttlefish ink or the risotti paired with vegetables: pumpkin, asparagus, beans, radicchio and fennels. From corn are derived the range of **polenta** dishes, with game or sausages, pork stews, cod or fresh and salt-water fish. In Friuli-Venezia-Giulia are produced the world-renowned **prosciutto** *di San Daniele* and the local fish soup, called simply brodetto, is justifiably famous. In Trentino Alto Adige, a mountainous and wooded area, the basic components of the local diet are, predictably, meat and game preparations. Well-known and much exported is *speck*, a local smoked meat product.

On the northwestern side, Liguria with its dramatic marine landscape but scarce arable land is well known for both fish and vegetable recipes. The fragrant pesto sauce originated here. In the spectacular but harsh mountainous area of Val d'Aosta, soups based on meat broth are appropriately reinvigorating. *Polenta concia* (polenta baked in alternate layers with *fontina*, butter and finely sliced **tartufi**) is another well-known speciality of this region. From Lombardy come *risotto alla milanese* and *cotolette alla milanese* plus an impressive range of **cheese**s (stracchino, gorgonzola, robiola) and the Christmas cake, *panettone*. Piedmont prides itself on an exclusive combination of meats (turkey, beef, pork, veal, chicken and goose) and vegetables (potatoes, lentils, onion and cabbage) plus sauces (mustard, pickles, green sauce) which all together produce the *bollito misto*, lengthy in preparation but deliciously satisfying. *Fonduta*, another Piedmontese speciality, consists of a cream made with *fontina*, butter, milk and white *tartufo* and served piping hot.

In Central Italy, the enchanting variety of the landscape of its five regions is matched by a panorama of gastronomic wonders. The Tuscan cuisine, based on excellent natural ingredients meticulously prepared, features the succulent *bistecca alla fiorentina*, white bean soups and stuffed *cannelloni*. Roman gastronomy offers unrivalled vegetable dishes, lamb or mutton preparations and a whole repertoire of spaghetti (*alla carbonara*, *all'amatriciana*, *al cacio e pepe*). Umbria produces and makes use of its excellent olive oil; local *tartufo nero* used on spaghetti or trout transforms them into refined specialities such as *spaghetti alla nursina* or *trota al tartufo*. The cuisine in the Marche region has recipes dating back to Roman times. The local white lasagna dish named *vincigrassi* is justly defined as incomparable, and the Marche version of *brodetto*, requiring between twelve and twenty varieties of fish to make properly, is also renowned for its exquisite taste. We come then to Emilia, where Bologna is regarded as the gastronomic capital of Italy. Ravioli, tortellini and cappelletti originated here. The stuffing of these homemade

pasta determines subtle differences in taste and constitutes almost an art. From Emilia, *parmigiano reggiano* and pork products are exported everywhere in the world. In the Romagna area, along the sea, *brodetto alla romagnola* is a celebrated dish based on local fish.

Moving to southern Italy, Naples is the predominant gastronomic force in the Campania region. The wealth of its dishes, both from the aristocratic and the plebeian traditions, offers examples such as **pizza**, *parmigiana di melenzane*, *polpi affogati*, *carne alla genovese* and the famous *ragu alla napoletana*, a lengthy preparation of meat whose superb sauce is used on pasta. Abruzzi compensates the difficult mountainous geographical position with the quality of its products and the creativity of its experienced cooks. One of the famous local specialities is *maccheroni alla chitarra*, fresh pasta resembling guitar strings, with a *ragu* sauce and tiny veal meat balls. L'Aquila is renowned for its *panarda*, which consists of forty different dishes served in one single meal. In Puglia, the regional cuisine makes skilful use of vegetables and also pairs them with pasta, creating original *minestre* (varieties of soup). The oil here is strong in flavour, and this region is also renowned for abundant seafood used in many traditional recipes. In Basilicata, a geographically isolated region, culinary traditions have remained unchanged for centuries under the local families' custody. Popular meat dishes are based on lamb and pork; vegetables are baked in delicious combinations with a generous use of hot chilli. Calabria is not a wealthy region, however, and its cuisine finds its roots in the ancient Mediterranean civilization. Local olive oil is used to cook most foods. Eggplants are used in a rich variety of recipes: *in agro dolce*, *a funghetto* or grilled with anchovies, *alla parmigiana*. Based on cod, the celebrated *baccalà alla castrovillari* includes cod and sweet or hot peppers, and there is an extensive range of hand-made pasta.

Sicilian cuisine reflects the stratification of the many cultures that have settled on the island over the centuries. In particular, the Arabic culture seems to have left a most definite mark. The renowned cake *cassata*, from Palermo, is an example of this lineage. Out of the innumerable vegetables dishes *caponata*, based on eggplants, is elaborate in preparation but unforgettable in taste. *Pasta con le sarde* (pasta with sardines) is another gastronomic landmark of Palermo. Sweets and cakes *di tradizione conventuale* (originally made by nuns) are mostly based on almond paste; brightly coloured and shaped like fruit, these sweets are a traditional feature of most Sicilian *pasticcerie* (cake shops). The other large Italian island, Sardinia, offers two types of bread, unusual in shape and texture: *carasau* and *carta da musica*. The many local sauces for pasta (with walnuts, with ricotta, with lamb and pork) give this food its unique Sardinian flavour. Meats are grilled and flavoured with myrtle leaves. In seafood, Cagliari offers its famous fish soup, *buridda*, which is inherited from Liguria.

The wide variety of its regional cuisine is no doubt one of the most fascinating features of Italian culture. However, the only effective way to understand and truly appreciate its appeal and complexity is through an exploration via tastebuds. As Italian novelist Italo **Calvino** perceptively suggested, a genuine voyage involves a radical change of diet, an ingestion of the visited country's fauna and flora, and thus of its very culture.

Further reading

Cattaneo-Jarrat, E. and Jarrat, V. (1969) *230 maniere di cucinare la pasta* (230 Ways of Cooking Pasta) Milan: Mondadori (see in particular the introduction written by writer and journalist Paolo Monelli).

de' Medici Strutti, L. (1988) *Italy, The Beautiful Cookbook: Authentic Recipes from the Regions of Italy*, Sydney: Child & Associates.

Gentile, E. (1997) *La grande Italia* (The Great Italy), Milan: Mondadori (see in particular: 'Parte prima, La patria degli italiani' (Part I: The Italians' Homeland)).

Piccinardi, A. (1993) *Dizionario di gastronomia* (Dictionary of Gastronomy), Milan: Rizzoli.

Roden, C. (1989) *The Food of Italy: Region by Region*, London: Vintage.

MARIELLA TOTARO GENEVOIS

regional government

Regional government is a comparatively recent development in Italian political life, but a strong association with the culture and history of a *territorio* has been an enduring feature of society in the peninsula and islands of the contemporary Italian state.

Because Fascism had destroyed what little autonomy the provincial and communal administrations had once enjoyed, the **Constituent Assembly**, in its determination to make Italy a democratic **Republic**, placed a strong emphasis on decentralization in the provisions of the 1948 **constitution**. In 1948, four 'special' regions were created in Sicily, Sardinia, the Aosta Valley, and in Trentino-Alto Adige (the South Tyrol), to which was added Friuli-Venezia-Giulia in 1963. The so-called 'ordinary regions' were created in 1970, including Calabria, Basilicata, Puglia, Molise, Abruzzo, Lazio, Umbria, Marche, Tuscany, Emilia-Romagna, Liguria, Veneto, Lombardy and Piedmont. The twenty-year delay in implementing regional government had much to do with the Christian Democrats' fear of conceding political space and institutions to the Left. Yet it would be unfair to single out the DC as the sole obstacle to regional reform, since many leaders on the Left were hostile to the idea of creating a 'balkanized' republic. Thus it was that Italy's experiment in regional government began *sotto voce*.

Every five years, each region elects its own assembly which varies from 30 to 80 members, depending on the size of the regional population. The regional council then elects a president and a *giunta*, which is constituted in a similar way to the provincial and communal authorities (see **local administration**). Unlike 'lower' tiers of government, the regions have the power to draw up their own statutes and to pass legislation which applies within the regional territory. These powers may be exercised so long as they do not conflict with the constitution or with national statutes. An early important legislative initiative was to formally recognize the existence and activity of neighbourhood councils which had been pioneered in Emilia-Romagna in the 1960s. However, only in 1972 did the funds finally arrive from central government, together with the administrative personnel and the delegatory powers necessary for the regions to begin their work.

Yet if regional politicians and electorates had expected to see a swift devolution of power from Rome to Italy's regional capitals, they were to be disappointed. Funding, which had never been generous, was frozen until the mid-1970s while central government spending continued to grow. It was clear that national politicians and the senior civil servants who headed the powerful spending ministries were resolutely opposed to giving regional governments real powers. Regional advocates realized that they faced an uphill battle to implement in full the decentralization measures that the constitution had promised.

A change in the national balance of power in 1975 and 1976, during which the Italian Communist Party (**PCI**) won control of several major Italian cities and further extended its influence over regional government, coincided with the period of the '**historic compromise**'. With the Christian Democrats reliant on the PCI's external support, **Andreotti**'s government agreed to a number of concessions which speeded up the transfer of powers and funds to regional government. The Interparliamentary Committee for the Regions also played a key role by helping to secure the passing of law 382 in 1976, giving **Parliament** greater powers in relation to governmental decrees concerning the regions. The following year saw the first concrete moves to transfer personnel and resources to the regions. The so-called '616 decrees' saw the relocation of 20,000 offices from the national bureaucracy and the transfer of primary responsibility for planning, social services and health. Health care is now the most important and costly service that the regions administer, and by 1989 it accounted for over a half of the regional budgets (see **health service**). Largely as a consequence of the health reforms, by the early 1990s one-tenth of Italy's GDP was being spent by regional government. However, many regional politicians were to complain that their role was limited to passing on central government funds to the local health authorities, while health policy as a whole continued to be decided in Rome. This complaint was amply borne out by the De Lorenzo corruption scandal at the height of *Tangentopoli*, which revealed how easy it was for one minister to dictate extortionate terms to the whole pharmaceutical industry.

Regional politicians' attitudes towards regional autonomy, their relations with Rome and with their national party hierarchies since the 1970s have been analysed by Robert Putnam. His research suggests that regional politicians have become more independent of their national party leaderships and are more willing to enter regional coalitions. As the decentralization of powers to the regions has continued, elected councillors in regional governments have also been less ready to criticize central government interference, suggesting that an appreciation of their mutual roles is developing. Central government has been less happy about regions establishing direct links with the institutions of the **European Union**, but this has not prevented Italian regions opening offices in Brussels. Indeed, so important are highly industrialized regions such as Lombardy to the transalpine economy that strong links have been established with neighbouring regions such as Bavaria in Germany and Rhones-Alpes in France in order to discuss issues of mutual concern such as transport infrastructure, labour markets and multinational investment plans.

Inevitably, the success of dynamic and affluent regions such as Lombardy and the Veneto is caught up with the problems associated with Italy's historic economic and social divide between North and South. Whereas Lombards have a higher average income than most Germans, Calabrians exist on approximately half the average income of other EU citizens. To the extent that regional government is able to tackle such disadvantages, it is widely conceded that the efficiency and the transparency of southern regional administrations leaves much to be desired. Nevertheless, observers such as Putnam do concede that, as institutions of civic development, regional governments have succeeded in nurturing a more professional, pragmatic and less self-serving class of politicians and administrators. *Tangentopoli* revealed that 'civic mindedness' had not been uppermost in the minds of many regional politicians in the North who fell foul of the judicial authorities, leading in some cases to the paralysis of local government (a process that was exacerbated by the collapse of the **PSI** and DC, who had governed many regions

in coalition in the 1980s and early 1990s). The Northern League (**Lega Nord**) and the **National Alliance** have been strengthened as a result, although both parties have diametrically opposed views on the subject of federal autonomy (the former being strongly in favour, the latter mostly against).

Since its election in 1996, the centre–left **Ulivo** government has committed itself to the reform of subnational government in a federal direction, and regional government expects to be the main beneficiary. However, the regionalist lobby will have to contend not only with the 'centralizers' in Rome, but will also have to deal with the powerful association of communes and provinces and the increasingly influential big city mayors who will be loath to see their own powers absorbed into what many consider to be politically weak and inexperienced regional administrations. But, although the prospects for regional government continue to appear uncertain, there is no doubt that they represent a rare example of successful institutional reform in postwar Italy.

See also: regions; Southern Question

Further reading

Hine, D. (1993) *Governing Italy: The Politics of Bargained Pluralism*, Oxford: Oxford University Press (see ch. 9, 'Regional and Local Government').

Levy, C. (ed.) (1997) *Italian Regionalism: History, Identity and Politics*, Oxford: Berg (an informative collection of essays on regionalism in Italy since unification).

Putnam, R. (1993) *Making Democracy Work: Civic Traditions in Modern Italy*, Princeton, NJ: Princeton University Press.

SIMON PARKER

regions

Italy's regional diversity is proverbial, yet 'region', 'regionalism' and 'regional identity' remain elusive as concepts and problematic as social realities. In fact, in spite of the widespread myth, the Italy of the regions is no more the 'real' Italy, nor is it markedly more stable or more socially cohesive, than the national framework.

The geography of the peninsula is extremely varied, ranging from the Alps, to the flood-prone alluvial valley of the Po, to the bleak deforested hillsides of the South and Sicily. Furthermore, between the fall of the Roman empire and political unification in 1860–1, different parts of Italy lived very different histories. Sicily, to take perhaps the most extreme example, passed through the hands of virtually every dominant power in Europe and the Mediterranean. Italy also offers a wide variety of minority languages and **dialects**, which in places differ between neighbouring towns. The divide in living standards between Italy's richest and poorest areas (see **Southern Question**) is the widest of any major European state.

Since the war, considerable power has been devolved to sub-national tiers of government. Yet the regions remain problematic entities. The map of Italy's administrative structure shows the peninsula neatly divided into five 'special statute regions', established in 1948 (Sicily, Sardinia, Trentino-Alto Adige, Friuli-Venezia-Giulia and Valle d'Aosta), and fifteen ordinary regions, established in 1970 (Piedmont, Lombardy, Veneto, Liguria, Emilia-Romagna, Tuscany, Marche, Umbria, Lazio, Abruzzi, Molise, Campania, Apulia, Basilicata and Calabria). Yet, despite the range of powers arrogated to all of these regions on paper in the **constitution**, they are perhaps the least powerful tier of authority, as is evinced by their very limited financial autonomy, and by the far greater numbers of people employed in municipal, provincial and national government. Nor is the regional sub-division systematically mapped over dialectal or linguistic areas, except in the peripheral cases of Valle d'Aosta, Trentino-Alto Adige and, to some extent, Friuli-Venezia-Giulia. Venice has certainly shaped the historical identity of the Veneto, as the comparatively progressive Grand Duchy did that of Tuscany before unification, but Italy's regions cannot all be said to be the product of sedimented historical realities dating back to the pre-unification period. For example, the old Kingdom of the Two Sicilies was centralized in Naples and embraced Sicily and the mainland Mezzogiorno (South). Nor are these regions all territories powerfully rooted in the imaginations of their inhabitants. The pattern of geographical loyalties varies widely between the administrative regions: any 'Campanian' identity is dwarfed by that of Naples. Indeed, local identities tend to be centred on the city, town or village, producing historical rivalries – such as those between Modena and Bologna, or Pisa and Livorno – far stronger than regional sentiments.

'Regionalism', a term which historically has tended to be employed to abuse 'unpatriotic' enemies rather than for social scientific purposes, also sometimes refers to the whole issue of sub-national geographical identities inasmuch as they are deemed to impede the spread of an Italian identity and undermine the legitimacy of the national state. The fact that the regions were set up so late in Italy's history is indicative of the strong sense of the new state's fragility which influenced the 'unitarian' perspective of its national ruling classes up to and including Fascism. But it may also be taken to betray the surprising lack of centrifugal regional movements 'from below' in Italian history even after the war: the **Lega Nord** is in this respect an anomalous product of recent years. Local interests have traditionally preferred to preserve margins for autonomy within the existing machinery of government. Politicians become mediators managing complicated exchanges of resources, favours and votes between the local and the national levels.

Italy displays other 'regional divides' which, while they are not recognized administratively, describe the country's social contours and historical transformations at least as well as the twenty regions listed above. The villages and towns of rural Lombardy and the Veneto were, until recently, the heartland of a 'white' (i.e. Catholic) subculture. The central 'red' belt of Tuscany and Emilia-Romagna, particularly the latter, was the domain of a rooted Communist subculture. There is the northwestern 'industrial triangle' of Milan, Turin and Genoa, and now the **Third Italy** characterized by specialized, family-run light industries in the centre and northeast. There is, of course, the North–South divide (see also **Southern Question**), although one must be careful not to forget the great diversity internal to each of these areas. The South has never been a banner for a political movement, although in the postwar period the state devoted huge resources to a special **Cassa per il Mezzogiorno** (Southern Development Fund) in an effort to alleviate the region's 'backwardness'. Stereotypical constructions of the South as a metaphor for corruption and parasitism have been a constant in Italian history. The North had no institutional or political meaning until the early 1990s and the emergence of fanciful Lega Nord plans for a 'Republic of the North' or 'Padania'. Italian political opinion remains divided over the degree of decentralization the country needs, and over the most appropriate level at which regional government should operate.

See also: minority languages; regional government

Further reading

Ginsborg, P. (ed.) (1994) *Stato dell'Italia* (The State of Italy), Milan: il Saggiatore (pp. 114–223 contain useful short portraits of each of the regions).

Levy, C. (1996) 'Introduction: Italian Regionalism in Context', in C. Levy (ed.), *Italian Regionalism: History, Identity and Politics*, Oxford: Berg (a well-documented analysis of the entire range of problems which come under the heading 'regionalism').

Hine, D. (1996) 'Federalism, Regionalism and the Unitary State: Contemporary Regional Pressures in Historical Perspective', in C. Levy (ed.), *Italian Regionalism: History, Identity and Politics*, Oxford: Berg (deals specifically with the political and administrative problems of the Italian regions).

Mack Smith, D. (1974) 'Regionalism', in E.R. Tannenbaum and E.P. Noether (eds), *Modern Italy: A Topical History since 1861*, New York: New York University Press (a survey of the problem of regional identities since unification).

JOHN DICKIE

La Repubblica

A novel idea in Italy, where newspapers were traditionally identified with their city of provenance, *La Repubblica* was founded in Rome in 1976 by Eugenio **Scalfari** with the specific intention of being a national daily. Its declared political orientation was left-wing but not party-aligned ('independent but not neutral', as it characterized itself in its first issue). In tabloid format – also unusual in Italy at the time – it originally appeared only six days a week with its twenty pages dedicated overwhelmingly to commentary of national and international news, a central double page devoted to culture and several other pages of economic discussion. Its succinct style (shorter, well-defined articles, clearer language) and its smaller, more manageable format made it attractive, especially to members of the post-1968 generation, and within three years it reached national sales of 145,000. The paper gradually grew in size and influence, and eventually came to include sports and entertainment as well as magazine supplements. In 1986 it finally succeeded in overtaking *Il Corriere della sera* and although *Il Corriere* subsequently regained a slim lead in the 1990s, *La Repubblica* was firmly established in the front rank of Italy's daily press.

GINO MOLITERNO

Republic

Modern Italy became a Republic in June 1946 through a popular referendum, which chose an elected republican form of government over the hereditary reigning monarchy which had, amongst others things, appointed and supported the Fascist regime and thus become tainted with all its faults. Italy had previously had brief experiences of republican government: there had been republics in Rome in 1798–9 and then, more notably, in 1849, led by Giuseppe Mazzini. Between 1943 and 1945 the German occupying forces had supported the Fascist Italian Social Republic, also called the Republic of Salò (see **MSI**), which had governed Italy, at least nominally, until Liberation. The modern Republican **constitution** was drafted by the **Constituent Assembly** in 1946–7 and came into effect on 1 January 1948. All the subsequent dramas of postwar Italian political life, from the centrism of the 1950s and the '**opening to the Left**' of the 1960s, the response to the threat from terrorism in the 1970s and the consolidation of the 'partitocracy' (see **political parties**) of the 1980s, took place against the backdrop of this Republican constitution and within this form of governance.

From the 1980s onwards, constitutional reform became a serious issue, and following the debacle of the 1992 elections and the subsequent *Tangentopoli* and *Mani pulite* (Clean Hands) investigations, there came to be much talk of a 'Second Republic' which it was hoped would inaugurate a new era in Italian political life, ending the rule by the parties and the **clientelism** and corruption which appeared to have characterized the 'First' Republic. For the first time since the war, thoroughgoing constitutional change, and in particular a more differentiated function for the two houses of **Parliament** and a stronger role for a possibly directly elected **President of the Republic**, appeared on the political agenda. A Bicameral Commission to explore the possibilities was set up; however, given the complexity of rewriting the 1948 constitution and the mutual vetoes of the numerous parties, the original charter was not changed.

Some have argued that nevertheless, the material constitution *had* been transformed and that Italy had *de facto* become a 'Second' Republic. Certainly, in terms of political culture, the exposure of systemic corruption and the effect it had on the old parties was a major warning to the new and transformed parties which emerged in the mid-1990s not to follow the same path. Institutionally, the new electoral system introduced in the wake of a 1993 referendum, which replaced proportional representation with a three-quarters plurality vote (see **electoral systems**) encouraged the formation of two stable alliances of parties (the **Ulivo** or Olive Tree Alliance and the **Polo delle Libertà** or Freedom Alliance) each competing to govern in what was called a party system of 'imperfect bipolarism'. If, as Italy crosses over into the new millennium, such a bipolarism were to be consolidated to become less 'imperfect', it would most likely end the phenomenon of permanent government facing permanent oppositions which has been such a major feature of Italian politics since unification.

Further reading

Hine, D. (1981) 'Thirty Years of the Italian Republic: Governability and Constitutional Reform', *Parliamentary Affairs* 34: 63–80.

Pasquino, G. (1998) 'Reforming the Italian Constitution', *Journal of Italian Studies* 3 (1): 42–54.

MARK DONOVAN

Resistance

Between September 1943 and April 1945, Italy became the battleground between diehard fascist supporters of the Republic of Salò, backed by the Germans, and opponents of the regime. Eventually, tens of thousands of armed partisans would fight against the Nazis and fascists in the belief that they were attempting to create a new Italy.

The communist wing was the best organized and numerically largest segment of the partisan movement but socialists, Christian Democrats and liberals also participated in what came to be called, simply, the Resistance. Indeed, a key motive for opposing Mussolini in his last days was often nationalism, or rather, a patriotism which considered that the military disasters of the Fascist regime and its current subservience to Nazism had humiliated Italy and threatened the whole national project. Members of the Resistance in fact often spoke about the need for a 'new Risorgimento' or political re-awakening.

In 1945, the liberal democrat section of the Resistance briefly came to government under Prime Minister Ferruccio Parri and his **Partito d'Azione** (Action Party). The Actionists, however, possessed a minimal popular base and the **Republic** was eventually constructed by the Christian Democrats and in the atmosphere of Cold War rather than through the more radical ideas of the Resistance. Contemporaries spoke about the 'wind from the North', where the Resistance had been regionally concentrated, being treacherously 'diverted' by Rome and the South, where liberation had come at the hands of the Allied armies.

Nevertheless, in the following decades, a certain 'myth of the Resistance' came to play an important part firstly in cultural and then in political life. By the 1970s, it was frequently argued that the Republic was indeed heir to the Resistance and that **anti-fascism** both provided its moral base and grounded its political practice. In the same decade, however, left-wing terrorists took to defining themselves as the 'New Resistance' and justified their violent acts, including the murder of Aldo **Moro**, by appeal what had once been done by partisans.

The brutality of the terrorists' treatment of Moro in turn provoked a conservative counter-offensive. This led to a major re-assessment of the Resistance experience in the 1980s and 1990s, in which historians and other commentators tended to emphasize the mixture of motives which turned people into partisans and the ambivalence, at best, of peasant support for the Resisters. Conservatives, especially, claimed it was difficult to distinguish ethically between the violence of the Resistance fighters and that of the *repubblichini* (Salò republicans), and also pointed out that the killing itself did not completely stop with the end of the war. Even a moderate leftist historian like Claudio Pavone was led to suggest that the period from 1943–5 might best be regarded as a time of 'civil war'. Present-day Italy is no longer sure about the legacy of the Resistance.

Further reading

Pavone, C. (1991) *Una guerra civile: saggio storico sulla moralità nella Resistenza* (A Civil War: Historical Essay on the Morality of the Resistance) Turin: Bollati Boringhieri (the most important book written on the Resistance since 1945).

R.J.B. BOSWORTH

Il Resto del Carlino

Bologna's daily newspaper, *Il Resto del Carlino*, was founded on 21 March 1885 by four law graduates. Its name is attributed to the fact that the newspaper was first sold in tobacco shops and the original price of the paper was roughly the change (*il resto*) that one received when one bought a cigar with a coin of the local currency (the *carlino*). From 1886 to 1907 it was regarded as one of the most modern of Italian newspapers due to the variety of information it provided and the calibre of its writers. Among its most prestigious literary collaborators were Carducci, Pascoli and D'Annunzio. After the liberation of Italy, the daily changed its name to *Il giornale dell'Emilia* (The Newspaper of Emilia) for a brief period, but reclaimed its original name in 1953. Giovanni Spadolini and Enzo Biagi have been among its best-known editors, and since 1995 the paper has been under the direction of Giovanni Castagnoli.

BERNADETTE LUCIANO

Rete Quattro

The publishing group **Mondadori** inaugurated Rete Quattro in January 1982, in order to compete with Silvio **Berlusconi**'s **Canale Cinque** by providing higher quality information and cultural programmes. The policy failed to attract audiences, however, and the subsequent flop of the expensive serial, *Venti di guerra* (Winds of War), left the network in dire financial straits. Debt-ridden, in 1984 it was acquired by Berlusconi's **Fininvest**, thus setting the seal on the magnate's national television empire.

Rete Quattro immediately began targeting the female audience, in particular housewives. Screening an abundance of **telenovelas** and soap operas like *Sentieri* (The Guiding Light), it soon became the most watched channel throughout Italy. In the wake of the provisions of the Mammì law of 1991, it initiated its own national live news programme, TG4. Presented by the eccentric and rather histrionic Berlusconi supporter, Emilio Fede, the programme was characterized from the beginning by a melodramatic tendency to sensationalize the news and a continual attempt to 'scoop' the other news programmes. After Berlusconi's entry into politics in 1994, TG4 openly and consistently celebrated the exploits of his party, **Forza Italia**.

RICCARDO VENTRELLA

Ricci, Franco Maria

b. 2 December 1937, Parma

Publisher

Born in Parma in 1937, Ricci started his publishing house in his native city in 1965, his first manuscript being a facsimile of Giambattista Bodoni's *Typographic Manual of Parma*. The unexpected success of that reprint set the tone for the future of Ricci's enterprise. His flair for the beauty of a text, for the proportion and harmony of its layout, and for everything that adorns it lies at the core of his books. Among his most memorable series are *I segni del tempo* (The Signs of Time) and *La Biblioteca di Babel* (the Library of Babel), edited by Jorge Luis Borges. Other notable publications include the reprint of the *Encyclopedie* of Diderot and d'Alembert (18 volumes, 1970) and the *FMR Enciclopedia dell'Arte* (15 volumes, 1990). In 1982 Ricci founded an exceptional art Magazine, *FMR*, published simultaneously in English, Spanish, French and Italian. He has achieved international fame as both graphic designer and editor, and his books and his magazine continue to evoke a unique and unmistakable artisan style which has greatly influenced the way art is perceived by Europe's cultural elite.

BERNADETTE LUCIANO

Ricciarelli, Katia

b. 18 January 1946, Rovigo

Soprano

Katia Ricciarelli's career has demonstrated particular strengths in the *bel canto* repertoire. Her studies in Venice led to a stage debut as Mimi in Mantua in 1969. A year later she won the Verdi Award and appeared in Rome as Joan of Arc to considerable acclaim. Her American debut in 1972, as Lucrezia (*I due foscari*) in Chicago, launched a successful worldwide operatic career. She sang at **La Scala** in 1973 (Angelica) and at Covent Garden the following year (Mimi), and made her debut at the Metropolitan Opera in this latter role in 1974. The 1970s were dominated by the major Verdi and Puccini roles, which she went on to record for companies including RCA and CBS. From 1981 to 1989, Ricciarelli performed many of the Rossini operas at Pesaro. Her admirers point to her effectiveness as a direct, communicative actress and to her expressive and flexible voice.

Further reading

Blyth, A. (1990) 'Katia Ricciarelli', *Opera* 41: 28–33.

JOHN KERSEY

Ridolfi, Mario

b. 5 May 1904, Rome; d. 1984, Piediluco

Architect

A leading member of the Movimento Italiano per l'Architettura Razionale (Italian Movement for Rational Architecture), Ridolfi was influenced both by German Expressionism and by the Roman School of Giovannoni, Del Debbio and Aschieri. After the Second World War, he shifted from rationalism to 'organic architecture', expressing his views in *Metron*, which he co-edited with its founder, renowned urban planner and architect Luigi **Piccinato**. Ridolfi's fascination with architecture as 'organic' is linked to Giovannoni and to Bruno **Zevi**, both of whom also promoted 'organic architecture' in Italy.

After 1945, Ridolfi participated actively in the debate concerning the reconstruction of the city: while emphasizing the necessity to standardize building materials and construction principles, he also stressed the need to protect the historic centres. In his 1946 *Manuale dell'Architetto* (Architect's Manual), Ridolfi proposed design guidelines later incorporated into Italy's government-subsidized housing. His study of the house also contributed fundamentally to Italian culture and his extensive research on vernacular architecture was particularly praised for its appropriateness to postwar Italian conditions.

See also: urban planning

Further reading

Rebecchini, M. (1990) *Architetti italiani, 1930–1960: Gardella, Libera, Michelucci, Ridolfi*, Rome: Officina (the chapter on Ridolfi covers his important buildings and unbuilt projects).

FASSIL ZEWDOU

Rifondazione Comunista

When the **PCI** broke with its Marxist past in 1991 and reinvented itself as the Democratic Party of the Left (**PDS**), a number of dissident delegates led by Amando Cossutta broke away and, together with other leftist groups like Proletarian Democracy (see **Democrazia Proletaria**), established Rifondazione Comunista (Communist Refoundation). The new party maintained the symbols and ideology of Marxism and was dismissed by many as a 'Stalinist' fringe with no future, but it won 5.6 per cent of the vote in the 1992 national elections, and was similarly successful in local elections. Fausto Bertinotti, whose background was in the **trade unions**, joined in 1993 and soon became leader. The RC vote rose to 6.0 per cent in the 1994 elections, and to 8.6 per cent in 1996. With this vote it held the balance of power in the Chamber of Deputies (see **Parliament**), but it showed itself unable to reconcile its instinctive quest for ideological purity with its desire to support **Prodi**'s leftist coalition. It briefly brought the government down in October 1997 over a proposed reform of the pension system, then offered support to the reconstituted government before splitting into two factions in late 1998, one headed by Bertinotti and keeping the name, the other led by Cossutta and now called simply Comunisti Italiani (Italian Communists).

JOSEPH FARRELL

Rimanelli, Giose

b. 28 November 1925, Casacalenda

Novelist, poet and literary scholar

Rimanelli is Professor Emeritus of Comparative Literature at State University of New York at Albany. His first and most successful book, *Tiro al piccione* (translated as *The Day of the Lion*), based on his Second World War experiences, was published in 1953 to much critical acclaim. Largely due to Cesare **Pavese**'s favourable interpretation, the book came to be regarded as a classic of Italian **neorealism**, while in retrospect it now appears more as an anthropological analysis of human behaviour, inspired by tragic cultural circumstances. The original critical misunderstanding of Rimanelli's literary vein was partially responsible for his dissatisfaction with the Italian cultural scene, which prompted his permanent move to the United States. Throughout the years, Rimanelli has continued to write fiction both in Italian and in his native Molise dialect, and he has also enriched his literary production with a fresh and idiosyncratic English style, as exemplified in his novel *Benedetta in Guysterland* (1993), winner of the 1994 American Book Award. Amongst his other titles are *Moliseide* (1990), *Detroit Blues* (1996) and *Alien cantica* (1994).

ANDREA CICCARELLI

Rinascita

A 'journal of politics and culture', *Rinascita* (Rebirth) was founded by Palmiro **Togliatti** in 1944 with the stated aim of providing ideological direction for the communist movement. Initially a monthly publication, it became a weekly in 1962. Although owned by the **PCI**, and playing a significant part in the education of its cadres, *Rinascita* was more than a party organ. It sought, often successfully, to play a significant role in political and cultural debate within Italy and internationally. It was in *Rinascita* that **Gramsci**'s letters from prison were first published, as well as Togliatti's Yalta memorial and **Berlinguer**'s formulation of the **historic compromise**. The journal reached its highest circulation during the period of the party's greatest success, the mid-1970s, with average sales of 60,000–80,000. Circulation subsequently dropped and publication was suspended in 1989 due to financial constraints. Relaunched in a new format in 1990, *Rinascita* survived another year, closing just after the PCI transformed itself into the **PDS**.

CLAIRE KENNEDY

Risi, Dino

b. 23 December 1916, Milan

Film director

Brother of poet Nelo **Risi** and father of one of the most impressive representatives of the **New Italian Cinema** in the 1990s, Marco **Risi**, Dino Risi graduated in psychiatric medicine, but soon tired of that profession and at first made a living by contributing to the satirical journal *Bertoldo* (founded in Milan in 1937). He then entered the film industry as assistant to directors Mario **Soldati** and Alberto **Lattuada**. After a period as film critic, he made his directorial debut with a series of realistic documentaries, one of which, *Buio in sala* (Darkness in the Movie Theatre) (1950), was appreciated enough by film producers to invite him to Rome.

Since the inception of his career, Risi has always been a director with a great feeling for actuality and contemporary issues, and has incessantly recorded each new phenomenon in Italian society with promptness and accuracy. In the 1950s he participated in the so-called *neorealismo rosa* (pink neorealism) with his *Pane, amore e ...* (Bread, Love and ...), (1955) and *Poveri ma belli* (Poor But Beautiful) (1956). Together with Luigi **Comencini**'s *Pane, amore e fantasia* (Bread, Love and Fantasy) (1953) and *Pane, amore e gelosia* (Bread, Love and Jealousy) (1954), Risi's films dealt with poverty in postwar Italy but in a comic fashion, stretching the boundaries of **neorealism**. Tied too closely to the optimism of the 1940s and early 1950s, 'pink neorealism' was soon dismissed as facile and, under the heading of comedy, Italian directors began producing increasingly pessimistic critiques of contemporary society. Thus in the 1960s Risi shifted to impressive yet grim portrayals of Italy in the throes of the **economic miracle**, thereby creating some of the undisputed masterpieces of the so-called 'comedy Italian style' (see **comme-**

dia all'Italiana, films such as *Una vita difficile* (A Difficult Life) (1961), *Il sorpasso* (The Easy Life) (1962) and *I mostri* (The Monsters) (1963) which always to some extent expanded and modified the genre.

With *I mostri*, Risi also initiated a trend in Italian film production called 'film a episodi' (films in several episodes made by different directors), a fashion which proved successful at the box office and attracted the participation of directors as diverse as **Rossellini**, **Fellini**, **Pasolini** and even the French director Godard in *RoGoPag* (1963).

In the 1970s, Risi's humour darkened as his cinema came to reflect the ever more difficult times of Italian society. His themes became more utterly and explicitly dramatic: corruption and speculation in *Nel nome del popolo italiano* (In The Name of the Italian People) (1971), illness and suicide in *Profumo di donna* (Scent of a Woman) (1974) and **terrorism** in *Caro papà* (Dear Dad) (1979). Although Risi habitually treated his themes with detachment and scientific precision, with *Profumo di donna* and *Caro papà* his cinema became coloured with a tenderness that would eventually mark a regression during the 1980s with films such as *Scemo di guerra* (War Idiot) (1985).

MANUELA GIERI

Risi, Marco

b. 4 June 1951, Milan

Film director

Son of Dino **Risi**, one of the masters of the **commedia all'Italiana** (comedy Italian style), and nephew of director and poet Nelo **Risi**, Marco Risi came to the silver screen early in life as assistant director and scriptwriter. After a lacklustre apprenticeship with commercial film comedies, from *Vado a vivere da solo* (I am Going to Live on My Own) (1982) to *Soldati 365 all'alba* (Soldiers 365 Days Before Discharge) (1987), Risi's cinema found its own voice in a retrieval of **neorealism** and its ethos of social critique. His later films also owe much to Francesco **Rosi**'s 'cinema of denuncia-tion' and Pier Paolo **Pasolini**'s investigation of the subproletariat, both amply evident in his diptych on the underground world of Sicilian cities, *Mery per sempre* (Mery for Ever) (1989) and *Ragazzi fuori* (Boys Out) (1990). Among his later films, are *Muro di gomma* (Rubber Wall) (1991), *Nel continente nero* (In the Dark Continent) (1992), and *Il branco* (The Herd) (1994).

MANUELA GIERI

Risi, Nelo

b. 21 April 1920, Milan

Poet and film-maker

Originally a medical graduate, Risi has never exercised his profession. In the immediate postwar period he made a number of documentary films, especially in Africa, and in the 1960s he also produced films for television and continued publishing poetry. Risi's poetry is a poetry of content in which political and social issues take centre stage with a determination which is the cipher of his political and stylistic allegiance. In his numerous collections, from *L'esperienza* (Experience) (1948) to *Amica mia nemica* (My Friend My Enemy) (1976), the protagonists are often simple workers who are juxtaposed to unscrupulous capitalists and corrupt politicians, and even the more personal and autobiographical passages which recall childhood memories are interspersed with social critique. Notwithstanding the apparent focus on content over form, his poetry is informed by a poetic tradition which runs from Surrealism to Montale to the Italian avantgarde movement of the 1960s (see **Gruppo 63**). While remaining a fully engaged poet and director – among his more renowned films are *Diario di una schizofrenica* (Diary of a Schizophrenic) (1968) and *Una stagione all'inferno* (A Season in Hell) (1971) – Risi also acknowledges that literature and art are often inadequate and powerless in the face of political oppression and injustice.

PAOLO BARTOLONI

Rogers, Ernesto Nathan

b. 16 March 1909, Trieste;
d. 7 November 1969, Gardone

Architect, editor and educator

Influential editor of **Casabella** and partner in Studio BBPR (see **BPR**), Rogers recognized a 'continuity' between past and present and strong associations between architectural traditions, the city, the academy and everyday life. For Rogers, even Italian 'rationalism' could be continued as a tradition if cleansed of associations with the same fascism that had taken the life of one of the partners of BBPR itself. In fact, surviving members of BBPR re-established their architectural practice through the 'Monument to the Dead in the Concentration Camps in Germany' as both a continuation of rationalism and a memento of fascist terror. Rogers thereafter conceived of a 'house of man' that sought to forge a collective architectural culture, exemplified in his writings for *Casabella* and by such 'historicist' buildings as BPR's Torre Velasca.

Further reading

Ockman, J. (1993) *Architecture Culture 1943–1968*, New York: Rizzoli.

KEITH EVAN GREEN

Romano, Lalla

b. 11 November 1906, Demonte, Cuneo

Novelist, poet, critic and translator

Romano's intimate and lyrical narratives perceptively depict the interior lives of her female protagonists. While bringing realist detail to the social and familial portraits she creates, Romano also illustrates each character's internal condition, as in her first novel, *Maria* (1953), which convincingly portrays a poor woman's rich interior life. The function of memory is also an important motif in her texts, especially in works such as *La penombra che abbiamo attraversato* (The Half-Light Through

Which We Have Come) (1964), which describes the author's upbringing near Cuneo, and *Il tetto murato* (The Walled-Up Roof), which draws on Romano's partisan activities and which earned her the Pavese Prize in 1957. Her later texts, including *Lettura di un'immagine* (Reading an Image) (1975) and *Romanzo di figure* (A Novel Made of Figures) (1986), intertwine images and text to create innovative narratives. Romano has also published poetry, collected in *Fiore* (A Flower) (1941), *Giovane è il tempo* (Time is Young) (1974) and *Le lune di Hvar* (The Moons of Hvar) (1991). Recipient of many awards and recognition during her long career, Romano was awarded the prestigious Strega Prize in 1969 for what is generally regarded as her best novel, *Le parole tra noi leggere* (Words Light Between Us).

LAURA A. SALSINI

Romiti, Cesare

b. 24 June 1923, Rome

Industrial manager

Managing director of **Fiat** from 1976 on, Romiti has been depicted by both supporters and detractors as a ruthless man with a strong taste for power. Widely regarded as the real leader of Italian entrepreneurs, he earned his reputation on the industrial battlefield in 1980 by crushing union opposition to his restructuring plan and by his later success in extricating Fiat from its deep crisis. In the mid-1980s he clashed with Vittorio Ghidella, another managing director of Fiat, who supported a car-centred strategy. Romiti appeared the loser in 1987 when Gianni Agnelli (see **Agnelli family**) publicly invested his brother Umberto and Ghidella as Fiat's future leaders, but Romiti ultimately succeeded in eliminating his rivals and imposing his own strategy of diversification. With **Mediobanca** on his side, he was even admitted to the exclusive circle of Fiat family shareholders, an unprecedented privilege for an outsider.

In 1993, as Fiat's managing director, Romiti was implicated in some of the **Tangentopoli** inquiries, which eventually led to a conviction for fraudulent accounts and illegal funding of political parties. In 1999, however, he was finally acquitted of the charge of bribing public officials regarding contracts for the building of the Rome underground. Meanwhile, in 1998 he resigned as chairman of Fiat, but immediately assumed the presidency of the powerful RCS editorial group which controls both the Rizzoli publishing house and the influential Milan daily, *Il Corriere della sera*.

STEFANO BATTILOSSI

Ronconi, Luca

b. 8 March 1933, Sousse, Tunisia

Theatre director

Later to become an acclaimed director of theatre and opera at some of Europe's most prestigious theatres, Ronconi's most important contribution to contemporary Italian theatre remains some of his earliest productions, most significantly *Orlando Furioso* (1969). Throughout his career, his work has been characterized by an emphasis on spectacularly designed use of non-dedicated theatre spaces, anti-conventional spatial relationships between actor and audience, and an almost iconoclastic, yet always revealing, attitude to classical texts.

Ronconi trained and worked as an actor until 1963, when he directed a production of Goldoni's *La buona moglie* (The Good Wife). In 1966 he directed *I lunatici*, an adaptation of Middleton's *The Changeling*, but it was his 1969 production of **Sanguineti**'s adaptation of Ariosto's Renaissance epic poem, *Orlando Furioso*, which marked him as an extraordinarily innovative, inventive and influential figure in the Italian theatre avantgarde.

The impact of the mid-1960s Italian tour of The Living Theatre was evident in this and many productions at the time, in terms of style if not in political content. The work of Jerzy Grotowski's Theatre Laboratory was also a visible influence. The two most significant characteristics of this production, which excited not just Italian audiences but also those of Europe and the United States on its 1970 tour, were its use of non-theatrical spaces for the performance, and a multifocal and spatially fluid production style. Most often performed in open spaces such as *piazze* or town squares, its premise was not the normally static and highly codified actor–audience relationship of the proscenium arch theatre. Instead the audience was encouraged, even constrained, to mingle with the actors in the performance space: the actors performed on large moveable platform stages, and astride large steel horses and other machines, with action often taking place at a number of points simultaneously. Sanguineti's adaptation of Ariosto's narrative stressed its leaps from one strand of action to another, and the audience experienced these shifts physically, being moved from one place to another to accommodate the changing requirements of the moveable performance spaces. This was an entirely new and exciting experience for Italian audiences, since the flexible staging experiments which had dominated British and North American theatre design in the wake of such visionaries as Edward Gordon Craig, Max Reinhardt and Tyrone Guthrie had largely bypassed Italy, with its extensive legacy of traditional proscenium arch theatres. Used to sitting in orderly rows all looking in the same direction (and interpreting what they saw synoptically in much the same way), the spectators at *Orlando Furioso* were forcefully disrupted from their usual habits and made aware that they were necessarily experiencing the production in a fragmentary and highly personalized manner, and that their choices as to where to be and in which direction to look would determine their interactive and interpretative relationship to the production. Though reminiscent of theatrical techniques which go back to the Middle Ages, and which have survived in popular theatrical forms such as the *commedia dell'arte*, vaudeville or variety theatre (something which did not escape the attention of the Italian futurists), the hegemony of proscenium arch culture assured that many audience members would be shocked and even outraged at losing the illusion (for illusion it is) that everyone was seeing and experiencing the same thing.

Ronconi continued these lines of exploration in later productions. *XX* used a labyrinthine series of performance spaces through which the audience

moved, and *The Oresteia* was produced not in a theatre (though its actor–audience relationship was in fact quite traditional), but in a huge disused warehouse in Prato, outside Florence. This led to the setting up in 1976 of Ronconi's Prato Theatre Laboratory, which explicitly recalled Grotowski's Theatre Laboratory and the programme of Grotowski's disciple Eugenio **Barba**, at whose Odin Theatre Ronconi taught.

In the 1980s and 1990s Ronconi held positions at the **Venice Biennale** and with the Turin resident theatre company. In parallel with his theatre productions he forged an equally daring and often contested career as opera director, directing nearly fifty productions in Italy, France and Germany.

See also: theatre directors

Further reading

Quadri, F. (1970) 'Orlando Furioso', *The Drama Review* 14: 116–24 (description and discussion of the production).

Milanese, C. (1973) *Luca Ronconi e la realtà del teatro*, (Luca Ronconi and the Reality of Theatre), Milan: Feltrinelli (source materials, interviews with Ronconi).

TIM FITZPATRICK

Rosi, Francesco

b. 15 November 1922, Naples

Film director, scriptwriter and actor

One of Italy's most socially committed film-makers, Rosi has consistently blended the aesthetic and the political in films which attempt to uncover the inner workings of power, both legal and illegal, and to investigate the networks of complicity and intrigue through which it is exercised.

Growing up under Fascism, Rosi's earliest artistic experiences were in theatre during his university days. His first and fortuitous involvement with cinema came in 1948 when he became assistant director to **Visconti** for the Sicilian epic, *La terra trema* (The Earth Trembles) (1948). He continued his apprenticeship in the next ten years by assisting a number of established directors, amongst them Luciano Emmer, Mario **Monicelli**, Ettore Giannini and the young Michelangelo **Antonioni**, as well as Visconti again on *Bellissima* (1951) and *Senso* (1956).

In 1957 he directed his first feature film, *La sfida* (The Challenge), the first of many films set in southern Italy and dealing with illegal power networks, in this case the Neapolitan Camorra. In 1961 he established himself definitively as a significant new director with *Salvatore Giuliano*, a brilliant and disquieting documentaristic inquest on the death of the famous Sicilian bandit (see **Giuliano**). This was the first in a trilogy of biographical films that would include *Il caso Mattei* (The Mattei Affair), which explored the suspicious circumstances surrounding the death of the powerful Italian industrialist (see **Mattei**) and was awarded the Cannes Grand Prix in 1972, and *Lucky Luciano* (1973) which was less a portrait of the notorious gangster himself than of the violent world which surrounded and imprisoned him. Further investigation of corruption and the links between legal and illegal power was carried out in *Le mani sulla città* (Hands Over the City) (1963), a powerful film which vehemently denounced the criminal evasion of proper building codes during the so-called '**economic miracle**', in many cases producing disastrous and deadly consequences (see also **housing policy**; **urban planning**). *Cadaveri eccellenti* (Illustrious Corpses) (1976), adapted from a novel by Leonardo **Sciascia** and made in a period when the '**historic compromise**' was in the air, hinted at levels of complicity between political, legal and illegal power that defied penetration from even the most committed criminal investigator.

Running parallel to Rosi's interest in the exercise and morality of power has been his attention to the problems of the South (see **Southern Question**), a theme present in many of the films already mentioned but given its fullest treatment in his moving but unsentimental adaptation of Carlo **Levi**'s novel *Cristo si è fermato a Eboli* (Christ Stopped at Eboli) (1979).

Adaptations of the opera *Carmen* (1983) and Gabriel Garcia Marquez's novel *Chronicle of a Death*

Foretold (1987) temporarily lured Rosi away from political cinema during the 1980s, but he returned to more committed film-making in the 1990s with *Dimenticare Palermo* (To Forget Palermo) (1990) and *Diario napoletano* (Neapolitan Diary) (1992).

Further reading

Klawans, S. (1995) 'Illustrious Rosi', *Film Comment*, January–February: 60–5 (a concise but comprehensive assessment of Rosi as auteur, followed by an interview with Rosi himself).

Michalczyk, J. J. (1986) *The Italian Political Filmmakers*, London and Toronto: Associated University Presses (see ch. 1, 'Francesco Rosi: The Dialectical Cinema', for a chronological discussion of Rosi's major works to the mid-1980s).

Rosi, F. (1984) 'The Audience Should Not Be Just Passive Spectators', in G. Georgakas and L. Rubenstein (eds), *Art, Politics, Cinema: The Cineaste Interviews*, Chicago: Lake View Press.

Testa, C. (ed.) (1996) *Poet of Civic Courage: The Films of Francesco Rosi*, Wiltshire: Flicks Books (an anthology of illuminating essays on Rosi's work by leading film scholars; includes a detailed filmography and a comprehensive bibliography of material in English).

GINO MOLITERNO

Rosselli, Alberto

b. 1921, Palermo; d. 1976, Milan

Architect and industrial designer

An important architect and designer of furniture and industrial products in the years of the **postwar reconstruction**, Rosselli studied engineering and architecture before forming Studio PFR with Giò **Ponti** and Antonio Fornaroli in 1950. Their most notable design was the 1956 **Pirelli** tower in Milan. In 1955 Roselli opened his own design office producing, among other things, furniture for Arflex and Kartell and a range of small domestic items for Fontana Arte. He founded the journal ***Stile Industria***, which he edited from 1953 to 1963. One of his best-known designs was the fibreglass 'Jumbo' chair for Saporiti (1970) which became an icon of the 1970s.

See also: interior design

Further reading

Fossati, P. (1972) *Il design in Italia* (Design in Italy), Turin: Einaudi.

Klaus Koenig, G. *et al.* (1981) *Stile Industria: Alberto Rosselli*, Parma: Artegrafica Silva.

PENNY SPARKE

Rosselli, Amelia

b. 28 March 1930, Paris; d. 11 February 1996, Rome

Poet, essayist, translator and musician

Daughter of exiled anti-fascist Carlo Rosselli, Amelia spent her early years first in England and then the United States, only returning to Italy in 1946. After studying musical composition and working as a translator, she published her first collection of poems, *Variazioni belliche* (Variations on War), in 1964. Her innovative prosodic style and her continual attempts to free words from linguistic conventions makes it difficult to distinguish between her prose and her poetry. Her style is also characterized by the use of the *lapsus* as creative error, a process which, as many critics have pointed out, makes it impossible to classify Rosselli's works in any pre-set category. The multilingualism, the fragmentation and formal experimentation of her writings challenge the order of syntax and reflect both her lifelong struggle with mental illness and her profound mistrust of predetermined ideological positions. Recipient of many of Italy's most prestigious literary prizes, she is widely regarded as a poet's poet and is highly esteemed by the poetic community itself.

ANDREA RICCI

Rossellini, Roberto

b. 8 May 1906, Rome; d. 3 June 1977, Rome

Film director, screenwriter and television producer

Long regarded in international circles as the key figure in the cinema movement known as **neorealism**, in Italy Rossellini is almost as famous for his fierce intellectualism, his famous romances – lover of Anna **Magnani**, husband of Ingrid Bergman – and his *bon vivant* lifestyle. Indeed, while his importance for Italian cinema in the 1940s and 1950s is beyond doubt, this was only one distinct episode of his long career and he is, for example, also considered to be the godfather of French New Wave cinema as well as a pioneer of Italian television.

Born in Rome in 1906 to an upper-class family and inheriting a substantial fortune in his teens, the young Rossellini knew little of the other classes or even of the incipient fascism throughout the 1920s. His education provided little guide for his future and it was only his interest in the thought of Benedetto **Croce**, a major influence in Italy at the time, that inspired him to critical and mostly anti-theoretical stances. From Croce, Rossellini learned to value the power of the human will to construct itself within history and the need for perpetual cultural renewal, notions which would underpin much of Rossellini's artistic commitment to a new postwar culture.

A rather frivolous lifestyle gave way in the late 1930s to the making of short films, scriptwriting and assisting Goffredo Alessandrini on *Luciano Serra pilota* (The Pilot Luciano Serra) (1938), a film supervised by Mussolini's son, Vittorio. This was followed by three rather conventional war films, amongst which was *La nave bianca* (The White Ship) (1941), and some involvement in a few minor features. With the end of the war came the films that made his reputation, the so-called 'neorealist trilogy': *Roma città aperta* (Rome, Open City) (1945) *Paisà* (1946) and *Germania anno zero* (Germany Year Zero) (1947). Due in part to the economies of wartime shooting, the 'on location' style looked then perhaps more innovative than it now does, masking in the first film a rather conventional family melodrama, regardless of the desperate setting of an occupied city. *Paisà* is perhaps more successful in its blend of location and character used to explore the issues of the Allied liberation of Italy and the devastating effects of civilization turned to inhumanity, while war-devastated Berlin provides a contrapuntal image to Rome in the last film of the trilogy. In these films, many aspects of European family life are shown as utterly forlorn and with little future hope.

Rossellini's status as a great neorealist really rests on these three films, and yet he would increasingly abandon the style, evolving in the late 1940s along a parallel pathway to **Antonioni**'s somewhat later attempt to explore the cinematic medium itself with an equal focus on alienation and mental breakdown. *La macchina ammazzacattivi* (The Machine that Kills Bad People), made in 1948 but not released until 1952, is about a camera as a killing machine, while films such as *L'amore* (Love) (1948), starring Anna Magnani, tend to explore psychological breakdown, especially in women.

In the 1950s his star vehicle was Ingrid Bergman, with many of the storylines of the films appearing as attempts to work through aspects of their private lives. The scandal surrounding *Stromboli, terra di Dio* (Stromboli) (1950), with its theme of adultery, led to the film's being released in a heavily cut version. Subsequently Rossellini and Bergman married and had a daughter, Isabella, who would later also become a film actor. Although their next few films were critically acclaimed – indeed the French New Wave directors and the influential critic, André Bazin, greatly admired *Viaggio in Italia* (Journey to Italy) (1954) – the films failed at the box office.

Rossellini attempted to revive his career with several more conventional films such as *Il generale Della Rovere* (General Della Rovere) (1959), which starred Vittorio **De Sica**, and *Anima nera* (Black Soul). These proved less than successful, and in the 1960s he turned to television, abandoning the cinema completely with the single exception of *Anno Uno* (Italy Year One) (1974), a biography of the Christian Democrat leader Alcide **De Gasperi** (see also **DC**). Regarded as his most famous production, *La Prise du Pouvoir par Louis XIV* (The Rise to Power of Louis XIV) was made atypically

for French television in 1966. This was only one of a long series of historical documentaries exploring the general unfolding of Western history largely through dramatized biographies such as *Socrate* (Socrates) (1970), *Blaise Pascal* and *L'età di Cosimo de' Medici* (The Era of Cosimo de' Medici), both 1972, and *Cartesius* (Descartes), made in 1974. *Louis XIV* marks Rossellini's continuing interest in the Crocean *ricorso* (recurrence), and a constant commitment to a renewal of culture. In this light, *Anno Uno* may appear as a continuation of the television productions and his other work rather than merely as an attempt to revive his cinematic career. Typically, most of these docudramas were made in association with **RAI** and had little impact outside Italy, despite Rossellini's desire to penetrate international markets and in spite of his legendary status.

At the time of his death he was preparing a television biography of Karl Marx, tentatively subtitled *To Work for Humanity*, while a number of agencies were still striving to tempt him back to making films, even though the subjects, such as a version of Stendhal's *Charterhouse of Parma*, and a RAI commission on Saint Peter, must have been attractive to him. However, the newer medium appeared to take precedence even if the treatment of the subject matter and the social commitment was unchanged.

Further reading

Aprà, A. (ed.) (1987) *Rosselliniana*, Rome: De Giacomo (most thorough bibliography with interviews and other writings).

Bondanella, P. (1990) *Italian Cinema: From Neorealism to the Present*, New York: Continuum, 2nd revised edn (survey of postwar film placing Rossellini in a national context).

—— (1993) *The Films of Roberto Rossellini*, New York (critical study placing select films in a national context).

Brunette, P. (1987) *Robert Rossellini*, New York: Oxford University Press (a thorough biography and critical study).

Gallagher, T. (1998) *The Adventures of Robert Rossellini: His Life and Films*, New York: Da Capo Press (major biography and critical study).

Ranvaud, D. (ed.) (1981) *Roberto Rossellini*, British

Film Institute Dossier no. 8, London: BFI (basic introductory studies).

JEFF DOYLE

Rossi, Aldo

b. 3 May 1931, Milan; d. 4 September 1997, Milan

Architect

Educator, practitioner and important contributor to *Casabella* (see **architectural and design magazines**), Rossi sought to renew a waning relationship between architecture and urbanism. For Rossi, architectural work provided something more than a programmatic function: it also had the capacity to reflect and to perpetuate the history and culture of the city in which it was sited.

Rossi's interest in architecture and urbanism furthered the 'continuity' of architectural tenets of prewar Italy that his mentor **Rogers** had earlier established as editor of *Casabella*. Teaching with **Quaroni** in Arezzo and **Aymonino** in Venice allowed Rossi to cultivate further his theories of architectural morphology and urban typology. Rossi articulated these themes in *The Architecture of the City* (1966), a hugely influential book both inside and outside Italy. In it, Rossi argued that although the city is formed by buildings, it is more a repository for collective memories than a mere collection of disparate images. Consequently, rather than designing buildings according to functional requirements, Rossi sought a basis for architectural design in what he called a 'timeless typology'. 'Type', for Rossi, was not an architectural image to be copied but an architectural 'idea' which results in building forms that may be dissimilar but which, nevertheless, together, can perpetuate the collective memory of the city.

In projects such as Gallaratese 2 in Milan and the Cemetery of San Cataldo in Modena, Rossi thus conceived architectural works which were themselves urban forms. For the Gallaratese 2, a residential complex for a Milanese suburb, Rossi and Aymonino designed not a repetitive cluster of dwelling units, but a complex of four buildings – a city itself – shaping and containing all of the richness and associations offered by the city. The Cemetery in Modena replicates the forms of the Gallaratese 2, this time to create a city of the dead. These 'cities' of life and death are demonstrations of what Rossi called an 'analogous city', an architectural poetic in which each single work shares formal elements with other works in an associative play of private and collective memory.

Rossi's self-reflective design practice and theory was also elaborated in his whimsical drawings and in a second book, *A Scientific Autobiography* (1981), which combined his cultural interest in architecture and the city with his personal, compulsive search for primary forms. Beginning in the 1960s, in fact, Rossi had sought to combine primary elements such as the triangle, the cube and the cone in dramatic assemblages. An enduring and obsessive practice, this seemingly haphazard combination of simple, familiar elements – the ceaseless transformation of almost 'nothing' – was meant to reveal something fundamental about form.

Curiously, the one consistent decorative feature of Rossi's architectural work is the mysterious reappearance of the clock set within a triangular pediment, much as in the paintings of **de Chirico**. In the Teatrino Scientifico, Rossi's 'little scientific theatre' of 1978, the clock was fixed at five o'clock for the life of the building, to enigmatically suggest, perhaps, that the time for architecture had passed.

Further reading

Tafuri, M. (1989) *History of Italian Architecture, 1944–1985*, trans. J. Levine, Cambridge, MA: MIT Press.

KEITH EVAN GREEN

Rota, Nino

b. 31 December 1911, Milan; d. 10 April 1979, Rome

Composer

Rota was born in Milan into a musical family, and from an early age demonstrated an extraordinary capacity for composition. At the age of eight, after only one year of formal tuition, he was composing at will, filling pages upon pages of musical score. He began his studies at the Milan conservatory at the age of eleven. He later studied in Rome and went on to study music at the Curtis Institute in Philadelphia. While well-versed in twentieth-century developments in music and a great admirer of Stravinsky, whom he knew personally, Rota's own work can be considered more nine-teenth century. His music reflects his philosophy that compositions should be spontaneous, melo-dious and rhythmic. Rota's opus is abundant and encompasses almost every musical genre. He composed music for theatre productions, lyric operas and ballets, as well as chamber music. He is most remembered, however, for his many soundtracks for films by **Visconti**, **Zeffirelli**, Coppola (winning an Oscar for *Godfather II*, 1974) and above all **Fellini** (*Lo sceicco bianco* (The White Sheik), *La strada* (The Road), *La dolce vita*, *8½*, *Amarcord*). Rota died during the troubled filming of Fellini's *City of Women* in 1979.

See also: film composers

BERNADETTE LUCIANO

Rotella, Mimmo (Domenico)

b. 17 October 1918, Catanzaro

Artist

Rotella studied at the Academy of Art, Naples, and at the University of Missouri. His earliest works were phonetic poems, but from the early 1950s he developed and refined a collage technique first practised by the cubists and then the French *affichistes* known as 'decollage' (double collage). Rotella stripped posters from walls, reduced them or decomposed them by further mutilation and then transferred these 'manifesti lacerati' (torn posters) to canvas. The resulting compositions were carefully balanced but vibrant, colourful and dramatic. In the mid-1960s Rotella's work changed to involve the use of single newspaper images, reproductions of magazine covers, photographic portraits more as a form of photo-reportage. These works heralded the new photorealistic school of

painting, and Rotella was invited to join the French Nouveaux Realistes in 1961. He coined the term 'mecart' to encompass both the mechanical nature of the process of his art and also its connections with mass media.

LAURENCE SIMMONS

Rotunno, Giuseppe

b. 19 March 1923, Rome

Cinematographer

Regarded as Italian cinema's most authoritative colourist, Giuseppe Rotunno started his career in 1955 with Dino **Risi**'s *Pane, Amore e ...* (Bread, Love and..., also known as Scandal in Sorrento) and has photographed no less than fifty films ranging from Luchino **Visconti**'s *Il Gattopardo* (The Leopard) (1963) to Bob Fosse's *All That Jazz*. To Rotunno, establishing the most immediate relation between the audience and the director's project is the cinematographer's responsibility. As a result, cinematography is an art that reinvents itself with each film, in accordance with the story that is being told. Such a talent for adaptability and reinvention is certainly exemplified by Ro-tunno's extended collaboration with Federico **Fellini**, a partnership which continued almost without interruption between 1968 and 1983. The audacity of Rotunno's framing and lighting strategies has been consistently and colourfully attuned to the baroque and surreal idiosyncrasies of Fellini's world, as *Fellini Satyricon* (Fellini's Satyricon) (1969) and *Il Casanova* (Casanova) (1976) most masterfully reveal.

DOROTHÉE BONNIGAL.

Roversi, Roberto

b. 28 January 1923, Bologna

Poet and novelist

After beginning as a lyric poet in 1942, Roberto Roversi became more involved in postwar cultural and political life by not only contributing to Pier

Paolo **Pasolini**'s magazine, *Officina* in the late 1950s, but also founding in Bologna the Marxist-oriented literary journal *Rendiconti* (1961–77). Subsequently in his poetry, and in novels like *Dopo Campoformio* (After Campoformio) (1962), *Materiale ferroso* (Ferrous Material) (1977) and *I diecimila cavalli* (Ten Thousand Horses) (1976), Roversi sought to document the degradation of peasant culture by industrialization as well as the explosion of youth protest in 1968 (see **student movement**) with its legitimate claims but numerous contradictions. In order to both criticize and undermine the dominant cultural industry, Roversi resorted to distributing his poems in cyclostyled copies and performing in cabaret shows.

FRANCESCA PARMEGGIANI

Rubbia, Carlo

b. 31 March 1934, Gorizia

Nuclear scientist

Later to become Italy's most celebrated nuclear physicist, Rubbia graduated from the Scuola Normale Superiore di Pisa in 1956 and then spent four years in America at Columbia University. In 1960 he became a full-time researcher in physics at the CERN (European Organization for Nuclear Research) laboratories in Geneva, and from 1970 to 1988 divided his time between teaching at Harvard University and continuing research at CERN. In 1984 he shared the Nobel Prize for Physics with Simon van der Meer for the discovery of the new subatomic particles, the W and Z bosons. Between 1989 and 1993 he served as Director-General of CERN, and subsequently took up appointment as professor of physics at the University of Pavia while continuing to be a member of many CERN commissions and other scientific bodies. He has received numerous awards, including the Order of Merit of the Italian Republic and the French Legion of Honour as well as honorary degrees from a number of prestigious universities.

GINO MOLITERNO

Rubini, Sergio

b. 21 December 1959, Grumo Appula, Bari

Actor and director

Rubini began his artistic career acting and directing for the stage. He also appeared in movies, his first big starring role being in Federico **Fellini**'s *Intervista* (Interview) (1987). He acted in several generational films such as Giuseppe Piccioni's *Il grande Blek* (The Great Blek) (1987) and *Chiedi la luna* (Ask for the Moon) (1991) and, more importantly, in Giuseppe **Tornatore**'s extraordinary existential thriller, *Una pura formalità* (A Mere Formality) (1994). Rubini made his impressive directorial debut in 1990 with *La stazione* (The Station). Although a close adaptation of a play by Umberto Marino with the same title, *La stazione* was far from just 'filmed theatre', and the film's greatest originality is in fact its investigation of original avenues for a reciprocal contamination of filmic and theatrical discursive strategies. Among his later films are *La bionda* (The Blonde Woman) (1992), *Prestazione straordinaria* (Extraordinary Service) (1994) and *Il viaggio della sposa* (The Journey of the Bride) (1997).

MANUELA GIERI

Ruini, Camillo

b. 19 February 1931, Sassuolo (Reggio Emilia)

Cardinal

As the Cardinal Vicar of the Rome diocese and president of the Italian Bishops' Conference (CEI), Ruini is the second most powerful man in the Italian Church after the Pope himself. Ruini was born and brought up in the region of Emilia, 'Don Camillo' territory, where he also served his first pastoral ministry. He was made secretary of the CEI in 1985. In January 1991 he was made pro-Vicar of Rome and six months later, Vicar and cardinal. His absolute authority over the Italian Church was demonstrated by his orchestration of its decennial gathering at Palermo in 1995. He was also a strong supporter of the **DC** and tried to stave off splits in the Catholic party when it re-founded itself as the **PPI** in January 1995 by persuading the pope to intervene with an open letter invoking the political unity of Italian Catholics. Since then, accepting the reality of Catholic political pluralism, he has advocated 'a Christian cultural project' to unite the Catholic political diaspora through its common values and priorities.

JOHN POLLARD

S

Saba, Umberto

b. 9 March 1883, Trieste; d. 25 August 1957, Gorizia

Poet

The poetry of Umberto Saba (real name Umberto Poli) traverses the first half of the twentieth century, indifferent to the influence of the various cultural tendencies, literary fashions and different expressions of the avantgardes and remains instead substantially faithful and coherent to its own principles and inspiring motifs. It is a poetry of intimacy, characterized by a traditional metrics and common vocabulary, depicting a series of melancholic and yet serene daily life experiences.

Saba's cultural formation was similar to that of other intellectuals (like Svevo or Slataper) who lived in **Trieste** between the end of the nineteenth and the beginning of the twentieth century. This 'mitteleuropean' city was free from provincialism and receptive to the most diverse international influences. Against this background, however, his life was marked from its earliest stages by traumatic experiences which profoundly affected him emotionally and psychologically: his father's abandonment of the family; the conflict between the maternal figure and that of his nanny; his 'different' Jewish heritage in a country that was soon to enforce racial laws; his chronic neurosis and his fundamental need for emancipation and integration. He was helped in coping with this situation in part by Freud's psychoanalytical doctrine which, over and above the therapeutic use made of it by his doctor, E. Weiss, became an integral part of his culture, and in

part by the passionate study of Nietzsche, whom he found especially fascinating because, as he puts it, 'parla all'anima e di cose dell'anima' (he speaks to the soul and about things of the soul).

Saba's poetics clearly reflects these cultural stimuli. Poetry materializes, according to Saba, through the delicate and balanced combination of a child and an adult. It draws from the past, from that obscure and remote taboo that, for the poet, is the world of childhood, a world which, through poetry, may redeem itself, become socially acceptable and sublimate itself in the forms of civilization. Through his poems, then, Saba descends towards the origins of his human nature. His poetry becomes a search for existential clarifications and for a cathartic liberation from the unavoidable pain that always accompanies human life, a goal which he hopes to accomplish through the evocation of, and the encounter with, those same 'objects' – the people, the most humble things, the animals – which give shape to his life.

His *Canzoniere* (Songbook), from its first edition in 1921 until the posthumous one in 1961, gathers all the twenty-two collections published by the poet in the course of the years. Its overall interpretation comes from Saba himself in his *Storia and cronistoria del 'Canzoniere'* (History and Development of the *Canzoniere*) (1948), written in the third person, which is both a reconstruction of his own poetic and psychological itinerary and a guide to the most important topics of the book. What emerges from it is the emblematic story of a man who, from the traumas and the conflicts experienced during his childhood, to the contradictions and the anxieties of his mature age, is desperately looking for a final clarification of his own self. The *Canzoniere*, therefore, becomes a sort of poetic autobiography in the shape of a psychoanalytical novel. The *Versi militari* (Military Verses), *Il piccolo Berto* (The Young Berto) and *Autobiografia* (Autobiography), for example, are all concerned in different ways with his mother's need for emancipation and his own attempts to get over his inhibitions and infantile regression. However, the collection also transcends this psychoanalytical pattern. Many of the poems in *Casa e campagna* (Home and Country) and *Trieste e una donna* (Trieste and a Woman), in particular, are a celebration of warm domestic values, often centred around the beloved character of his wife, Lina. It needs to be emphasized that the human warmth and especially the simplicity that these verses convey, are not synonymous with obviousness and triviality, but are instead the conquered fruit of an intense research into the depth of the poet's soul.

Theoretically independent from European symbolism and the contemporary hermetic experimentations, Saba has a 'classical' measure. He is not interested in experimenting with forms and structures, or in the creation of new expressive means. He continues to prefer traditional lyrical forms, regular metre, and almost aulic rhythmical and syntactical solutions. On the other hand, and in contrast to this, on the lexical level there is the recurrence of an imagery constituted by humble objects, daily affections, intimate and modest surroundings, and the universal sorrows shared by men and animals alike.

This, however, does not immediately include Saba in the prosaicism of the so called *crepuscolare* (twilight) poetic current. His austere existential meditation and his constant autobiographism, in fact, mark a profound difference between *Il Canzoniere* and the decadent-ironical descriptivism of the 'twilight poets'. The representation of scenes of daily life, of common men and women in the background of 'his' Trieste, is always connected to intense personal experiences. The objective world refers to and reflects the vicissitudes of the self; it only makes visible the poet's need to find an identification and an integration in the world.

Saba's illustrious poetic career was crowned by many literary prizes. In 1946 he received the Viareggio Prize and in 1951 he was awarded the Feltrinelli Prize by the Accademia dei Lincei. In 1953 the University of Rome awarded him an honorary degree in letters, and in 1957 he shared the Marzotto Prize with fellow poet Mario **Luzi**.

See also: poetry

Further reading:

Aymone, S. (1971) *Saba e la psicoanalisi* (Saba and Psychoanalysis), Naples: Guida (an attempt to explore how psychoanalysis affected Saba's writing).

Cary, J. (1993) *Three Modern Italian Poets: Saba, Ungaretti, Montale,* Chicago: University of Chicago Press (a general analysis of Saba's poetry that reaffirms his place in modern Italian literature).

Gilson, E. (1993) *The Stories and Recollections of Umberto Saba,* Riverdale on Hudson, NY: Sleep-Meadow (a selection of Saba's poetry and prose translated into English).

Magris, C. (1986) 'Things Near and Far: Nietzsche and the Great Triestine Generation of the Early Twentieth Century', trans. T. Harrison, *Stanford Italian Review* 6 (1–2), 293–9 (a comparative study of Saba's relationship to Nietzsche, Svevo and Slataper).

Saba, U. (1961) *Il Canzoniere* (complete edition), Turin: Einaudi.

ENRICO CESARETTI

salotti

Salotti (drawing rooms or parlours) are regular private meeting places for select VIPs, mostly organized by women of aristocratic descent or marriage, mainly found in the two cities – Milan and Rome – with the densest concentrations of status rivalry among both hosts and guests. Wielding names, manners and menus, the hosts compete for attendance by members of the political, economic and cultural elites. Invitations add social prestige to the professional reputations of guests, who can exhibit and cultivate their connections, their culture and their culinary knowledge. A genuine, successful *salotto* demands a pleasurable and productive encounter between status and power: mere gatherings of men and women of letters, no matter how well-known or convivial, do not count.

Further reading

Cederna, C. (1984) *Vicino e distante: gente, ambienti, salotti, usi, costumi: impressioni sull'Italia di ieri e di oggi* (Near and Far: People, Circles, Salons, Usages, Customs: Impressions of Italy Yesterday and Today), Milan: Mondadori (insider account by Milanese observer of the pretensions and abuses of power).

Pardo, D. (1997) 'Metti un inciucio a cena' (Imagine a Little Hugger-Mugger at Dinner), *L'Espresso*, 28 May: 78–81 (*salotti* in the 1990s).

DAVID MOSS

Salvatores, Gabriele

b. 20 July 1950, Naples

Theatre and film director

Winner of the 1992 Oscar for the Best Foreign Language Film with *Mediterraneo* (Mediterranean), Salvatores had already emerged in the 1980s as one of Italy's most promising young directors with his *Marrakech Express* (1989) and *Turné* (Tour) (1990). His popular success continued with *Puerto Escondido* in 1992 and *Sud* (South) in 1993. Born in Naples, Salvatores grew up in Milan where he studied drama and served his apprenticeship as theatre director. In 1972 he co-founded the Teatro dell'Elfo (The Elf's Theatre) producing experimental works such as a musical version of Shakespeare's *A Midsummer Night's Dream*, a spectacle which then became his first full-length film in 1983 starring the female rock singer, Gianna **Nannini**. Using more or less the same cast in most of his films, Salvatores has painted an autobiography of his post-1968 generation, in a style often regarded as a contemporary version of the ***commedia all'Italiana*** (comedy Italian style). In all his films, including the 1997 science fiction *Nirvana*, his characters are confronted with an exceptional experience which disrupts their ordinary lives and relaunches the recurrent motif of his desire to escape.

ANTONELLA FRANCINI

Samonà, Giuseppe

b. 8 April 1898, Palermo; d. 1983, Rome

Architect

Equally renowned as practitioner and educator, Samonà was director of the **IUAV** from 1945–71, where he gathered together the major exponents of Italian architectural culture, thus making it one of the most important schools in Europe. He emphasized an unbroken unity between region and building. For Samonà, the city was something to be unravelled in an open reading where autobiographical and literary passions contended with the managerial concerns of town planning. His own work was caught in powerful tensions between antiquity and modernity, form and disintegration, the particular and the universal, all evident in his INAIL (National Institute of Insurance against Workplace Injury) Headquarters (1952–6) and further typified by his Bank of Italy building in Padua (1968–74), a singular construction with strikingly heterogeneous facades, each attuned to the differing urban situations they face. Also representative are his competition project for the Chamber of Deputies Building in Rome (1967) and the Public Theatre of Sciacca (1974–9).

Further reading

Samonà, G. (1985) *L'urbanistica e l'avvenire della città* (Urban Planning and the Future of the City), Bari: Laterza (his most important theoretical statement).

ROSS JENNER

Sandrelli, Stefania

b. 5 June 1946, Viareggio

Film actress

Stefania Sandrelli started her career in the 1960s in

two films by Pietro **Germi**, *Divorzio all'italiana* (Divorce, Italian Style) (1961), starring Marcello **Mastroianni**, and *Sedotta e abbandonata* (Seduced and Abandoned) (1964), both comic depictions of Sicilian society. In 1968, she met Bernardo **Bertolucci** for the film *Partner*, an encounter which was decisive for her career. With Bertolucci, she made three further films: *Il conformista* (The Conformist) (1970), in which she portrayed the giddy upper-class wife of a fascist agent, *Novecento* (1900) (1976), in which she was a socialist teacher, and *Io ballo da sola* (Stolen Beauty) (1996), where she embodied a mature specimen of upper-class decadence. In the 1970s and 1980s, she also collaborated with Ettore **Scola**, to whom she owes some of her greatest roles, as in *C'eravamo tanto amati* (We Loved Each Other So Much) (1974) and *La famiglia* (The Family) (1987). Even though she has often been cast as the average Italian bourgeois wife in both comedies and dramas, Sandrelli also explored more transgressive aspects of her femininity, as in Giovanni Soldati's *The Lie* (1984), or Bigas Luna's *Jamon Jamon* (1992).

DOROTHÉE BONNIGAL

Sanguineti, Edoardo

b. 9 December 1930, Genoa

Poet, novelist, critic and translator

A leading representative of the postwar literary avantgarde, Sanguineti had already published his first collection of poetry and several extended critical studies of Dante, Gozzano and **Moravia** before achieving renown as one of the five poets included in the landmark *I novissimi* anthology of 1961. He was subsequently a prominent member of the **Gruppo 63**, publishing, amongst other things, arguably the most interesting experimental novel to emerge from the movement *Capriccio Italiano* (Italian Caprice) in 1963. He also began writing theatrical works, and in 1969 adapted the Renaissance epic *Orlando Furioso* for the legendary production by Luca **Ronconi**. In the 1970s, while continuing to exert a strong cultural presence, he also took part in mainstream politics and was elected a deputy for the **PCI** in 1979. A prolific

and militant literary critic and historian, Sanguineti has also published translations of Petronius, Aeschylus, Sophocles and Seneca as well as composing lyrics for music by Luciano **Berio** and others.

GINO MOLITERNO

Sanremo Festival

For one week every February since 1951, the Italian media dedicate much time and space to a song competition which is held annually in the Ligurian city of San Remo. The songs themselves arouse little interest or enthusiasm today and, with relatively few exceptions, the singers who participate are ageing has-beens or young unknowns. However, the Festival keeps alive the mythology of Italy as the land of song, and a victory by anyone other than a melodic singer is regarded as a matter of some controversy.

The Festival began as a publicity exercise for the municipal casino of San Remo, but thanks to radio and television interest it grew to be an event of national importance. In the conservative climate of the 1950s it offered an important forum for reassertion of the national melodic tradition (which draws from both **opera** and from Neapolitan popular song) after the intrusion of jazz and swing during the immediate postwar years. Although Italy was changing rapidly, bland nostalgic tunes praising village life, motherly love and chaste romance found a ready audience. It was 'the triumph of nothing, framed by violins and rose petals', as Gianfranco Baldazzi has written (Baldazzi, 1989: 77) Singers of humble origins, like the Bolognese Nilla Pizzi and Claudio **Villa**, a Roman from Trastevere who dominated the Festival in its early years, achieved great national popularity. Thanks to their remarkable voices and forceful personalities, they contributed to a revival of the Italian melody as a core component of a shared culture.

Domenico **Modugno**'s international hit 'Nel blu dipinto di blu' (also known as 'Volare') brought a breath of fresh air to the Festival in 1958, and in the following years domestic rock'n'roll and pop singers did battle with the old guard. Instead of slightly different executions of the same song, the public was presented with alternative versions: up-tempo and melodic. However, the emergence of committed singer-songwriters (see **cantautori**) and beat groups produced more diversity than the festival could handle. The suicide of Luigi Tenco in 1967 following the exclusion of his song from the final at the expense of one entitled 'You, Me and the Roses' marked a watershed. In the 1970s the festival declined in popularity, and in 1973 **RAI** television only broadcast the final evening.

The successful revival of the Sanremo Festival in the 1980s owed everything to a coincidence of interests between RAI and the record companies. However, the Festival ultimately failed to harness the talents of the best-selling Italian artists, though it did contribute to the success of some significant new performers, amongst them Eros Ramazzotti and Laura Pausini, two young singers from the melodic mould who achieved popularity abroad as well as at home. The Festival achieved renewed popularity with television audiences in the 1990s and its status as an innocuous, if slightly onanistic, national event was underscored in 1997 when it came to be presented again, for the tenth time in his career, by no less an *éminence grise* of Italian television than Mike **Bongiorno**.

See also: pop and rock music

Further reading

Baldazzi, G. (1989) *La canzone italiana del Novecento* (Italian Popular Song in the Twentieth Century), Rome: Newton Compton.

Borgna, G. (1980) *La grande evasione: storia del festival di Sanremo – 30 anni di costume italiano* (The Great Escape: History of the Festival of Sanremo: 30 years of Italian Popular Culture), Rome: Savelli.

Settimelli, L. (1991) *Tutto Sanremo* (All Sanremo), Rome: Gremese.

STEPHEN GUNDLE

Santoro, Michele

b. 2 July 1949, Salerno

Television presenter and journalist

A former Maoist and journalist on the communist daily *L'Unità* who joined **RAI** in 1980, Santoro achieved prominence in the early 1990s as the anchorman of current affairs programmes on RAI 3. *Samarcanda* was a new type of 'people show' which led to accusations of left-wing bias but which caught the public imagination just as the old political system collapsed. The programme's black set and the moralistic tone Santoro adopted in treating matters such as corruption, the **Gladio** affair, the **mafia** or the **Ustica** case, made it an actor and not merely a forum in the political crisis. The follow-up programme, *Rosso e nero* (Red and Black), enjoyed similar success but after 1994 Santoro's star began to wane. He failed to win control of RAI 3 news, to take his brand of populist reporting to RAI 1 or RAI 2 or to realize his ambitious but vague dream to take over the management of one of Berlusconi's channels. In 1997 he presented *Moby Dick* for Mediaset, a programme using extensive opinion polling but scoring only a very modest success.

STEPHEN GUNDLE

Santucci, Luigi

b. 11 November 1918, Milan

Novelist and essayist

After graduating at the Catholic University in Milan with a thesis on children's literature, Luigi Santucci worked as high school teacher in Gorizia and Milan until 1962, when he retired to devote himself exclusively to literature. In early novels such as *In Australia con mio nonno* (In Australia with My Grandfather) (1947), *Lo zio prete* (The Uncle Priest) (1951) and *Il velocifero* (The Stage Coach) (1963), Santucci displays a rich inventiveness in narrating the characters' travels and family sagas. In the later *Orfeo in paradiso* (Orpheus in Paradise) (1967) and *Il bambino della strega* (The Witch's Child) (1981), set in an atmosphere of fable, he explores the individual's lifelong search for Christian love and joy, highlighting the significance of childhood as the metaphorical place of innocence and protection in the human journey to explore the self and understand history.

FRANCESCA PARMEGGIANI

Sapegno, Natalino

b. 10 November 1901, Aosta; d. 11 April
1990, Rome

Literary critic and essayist

One of the most respected figures in twentieth-
century Italian literary studies, Sapegno taught at
the University of Palermo before taking up the
chair of Italian Literature at the University of
Rome, La Sapienza, which he held from 1937 to
1976. His cultural background was shaped by an
early encounter with the liberal thought of Piero
Gobetti and the aesthetics of Benedetto **Croce**,
later filtered through the Marxism of Antonio
Gramsci. After the war, his Marxist beliefs led
him to participate in the Italian Communist Party
(see **PCI**), which he abandoned along with many
other Italian intellectuals in the wake of the
invasion of Hungary by the Russian army in
1956. His fame is particularly tied to his meticulously annotated edition of Dante's *Divine Comedy* (in
three volumes 1955–7) and to the manual of Italian
literary history, *Compendio di storia della letteratura
italiana* (three volumes, 1936–47, re-issued 1990),
both extensively used as textbooks by several
generations of Italian students. He published many
books of criticism on all the important Italian
authors from Jacopone da Todi to Leopardi and
Manzoni, and was also a life member of the
prestigious national Accademia dei Lincei. In his
honour, and to continue his pedagogical work, his
native region of Valle d'Aosta set up a Centre for
Historical–Literary Studies in his name.

ANDREA RICCI

Sassu (Sassù), Aligi

b. 17 July 1912, Milan

Painter and sculptor

Sassu's expressionist, figurative style, combining
elements of social realism and the Italian Baroque,
foreshadowed the more general return to figurative
art of the transavantgarde in the late 1970s. A
committed socialist, Sassu had been imprisoned
before the Second World War for his political
activism. After the war he continued to paint
contemporary subjects, such as his 1968 portrait of
Che Guevara, and he also worked on Biblical and
mythological themes. Between 1980 and 1986 he
illustrated Dante's *Divine Comedy*, describing his
approach as an inspired manifestation of Dante in
visual form. In 1996 he donated a collection of his
work including paintings, drawings, and sculptures
of mythological themes, women, horses and cyclists
to the city of Luino, to enable the establishment of
a Foundation in his name.

MAX STAPLES

Satanik

Satanik is the heroine of the comic book by the
same name which appeared in 1964 following the
editorial success of *Diabolik*. The authors, Bunker
and Magnus, added a grotesque touch to the figure
of the criminal hero popularized by *Diabolik*,
proposing a negative, Italian-made version of the
American superhero with some deeper psychological insights. Satanik is alone in a violent and
corrupt society, having been rejected by her father
and scorned by her sisters because of her deformed
face. Unlike the beautiful, good, passive and
conformist popular heroines of the *fotoromanzo*,
the prey of heroes and villains, Satanik nevertheless
transforms herself into a beautiful and sensual
woman with a magic potion. She becomes a
criminal with neither morals nor sexual inhibitions,
and she turns her repressed anger into open
revenge. Satanik strongly appealed to male and
female teenage and adult readers, who were drawn
by her anarchic and violent rebelliousness and
enjoyed Magnus's expressionistic and parodic style,
which allowed them to keep a moral distance from
the stories. Publication ended in 1974 due to harsh
competition from American superheroes and
Italian comic book porno-heroines, which employed a graphic eroticism not found in *Satanik*.

See also: comics

FRANCO MANAI

Saviane, Giorgio

b. 16 February 1916, Castelfranco
Veneto, Treviso

Lawyer and novelist

From his literary debut in the late 1950s with the
novel *Le due folle* (The Two Crowds), critics have
highlighted Saviane's increasing attention to ethical
and social issues as well as to religious themes –
attention which originates from his Catholic
education in Veneto and his activity as attorney
in Florence. In his prolific and highly original
fiction, Saviane represents the individual's search
for identity and freedom in the contemporary
world, the need for love and solidarity, and, in a
novel such as *L'inquisito* (The Accused) (1961),
presents a passionate demand for social justice. In
spite of a general religious orientation, his work has
also questioned the presence/absence of God in
everyday life and the role of the Catholic Church
as a political and cultural institution, as in his early
Il papa (The Pope), 1963.

FRANCESCA PARMEGGIANI

La Scala

The Teatro alla Scala was built in Milan in 1778
on the site of the medieval church of Santa Maria
della Scala, to replace the Teatro Reggio Ducale
which had burned down two years earlier. It
established its reputation as a centre of national
importance in the first half of the nineteenth
century as Milan became dominated by a prosperous bourgeoisie. During the period 1806–97, La
Scala was jointly owned by the city of Milan, the
box holders, impresarios and patrons. In 1897 the
city of Milan withdrew its financial support, and
consequently Duke Guido Visconti di Modrone
headed an independent board which took over the
administration of the theatre. One of the first
actions of this board was to appoint Arturo
Toscanini as artistic director in 1898, and Toscanini was to serve for three influential terms in this
post (1898–1903, 1906–10 and 1920–9). Toscanini's rule at La Scala saw a rise in musical standards
and a more adventurous choice of repertoire, with

many appearances by the world's leading singers.
In 1929, Toscanini left after quarrelling with the
Fascists and was replaced as musical director by
Victor de Sabata (1930–57, artistic director 1953–
57). The theatre was bombed in August 1943, and
reopened in May 1946. The most important of
Sabata's successors as musical director have been
Claudio **Abbado** (1971–80, artistic director 1977–
9) and Riccardo **Muti** (1986–), although Carlo
Maria Giulini has also been closely involved with
La Scala since his 1951 debut and served briefly as
chief conductor (1953–6). Herbert von Karajan
was also a frequent visitor during the years 1948–
68. Giulini's tenure in the early 1950s saw an
important relationship develop between the theatre
and the soprano Maria Callas.

The director Luchino **Visconti** was inspired by
Callas's portrayal of Norma to undertake an
acclaimed period of collaboration between 1954
and 1958. His productions included *La Sonnambula*
(1955), *La Traviata* (1956) and *Anna Bolena* (1957).
Influential artistic directors have also included
Antonio Ghiringelli (1948–53, director 1946–72)
and Francesco Siciliani (1957–67, 1979–82).

During the postwar period, a number of
significant premières have taken place. These have
included Poulenc's *Dialogues des Carmelites* (Dialogue
of the Carmelites) (1957), Pizzetti's *L'assassinio nella
cattedrale* (Murder in the Cathedral) (1958), **Donatoni**'s *Atem* (1987) and Bernstein's *A Quiet Place*
(1984). La Scala also saw the premières of Stockhausen's *Licht* (Light) sequence, beginning with
Donnerstag (Thursday) in 1981.

Since the 1970s, La Scala has undertaken a
search for a greater accessibility at the same time as
seeking to expand its already extensive repertoire.
Its seating capacity now stands at 3,000. In 1955
the Piccola Scala (capacity 600) was built beside the
theatre to provide a performing venue for early
opera and chamber-scale contemporary works. It
was abandoned in 1983. The La Scala company
has undertaken many successful foreign tours in the
postwar era, following the pioneering example of
Toscanini's tours to America and Germany in the
1920s. These have included London Covent
Garden (1950, 1976), Japan (1981), Berlin (1987),
Korea (1988) and the Soviet Union (1989).

See also: music institutions; opera

Further reading

Long, G. (ed.) (1982) *La Scala, vita di un teatro* (La Scala, Life of a Theatre), Milan: Mondadori (an informative and colourful overview of La Scala up to the 1980s).

JOHN KERSEY

Scalfari, Eugenio

b. 6 April 1924, Civitavecchia

Journalist, editor and writer

A law graduate with a passion for journalism, Scalfari collaborated on the influential postwar magazines *Il Mondo* and *L'Europeo* as well as being amongst the founders of the **Radical Party** in 1955. In the same year he also helped found the weekly magazine *L'Espresso*, assuming its direction from 1963 to 1968. As a journalist he was especially active in investigative reporting, uncovering illegal right-wing activities and major government cover-ups. In 1968 he was elected to the House of Deputies as an independent aligned to the **PSI**. His greatest exploit, however, was to found the newspaper *La Repubblica* in 1976. Few believed such a venture could succeed in the already crowded marketplace, but under Scalfari's skilful editorship *La Repubblica* prospered to the point of rivalling the prestigious *Corriere della sera* in both sales and status as a national daily. Scalfari relinquished his directorship in 1995, but remained active both in *La Repubblica* and *L'Espresso*. He has also published a number of books including *L'Autunno della Repubblica* (Autumn of the Republic) (1969) and the novel *Il Labirinto* (The Labyrinth) (1998).

See also: newspapers

GINO MOLITERNO

Scalfaro, Oscar Luigi

b. 9 September 1918, Novara

Politician and statesman

A law graduate from the Catholic university, Oscar Luigi Scalfaro was elected for the **DC** to the 1946 **Constituent Assembly** and to the Chamber of Deputies at every election from 1948 to 1992. A junior minister from 1959, he obtained full ministerial rank in 1966. In 1992 he was elected **President of the Republic** in the wake of **Cossiga**'s sudden resignation. A defender of parliamentary rather than presidential government, Scalfaro's tenure nevertheless saw the president's role greatly reinforced. The crisis of the traditional parties led to a series of so-called technocratic or presidential governments, those of **Amato**, 1992–3, **Ciampi**, 1993–4, and **Dini**, 1995–6. While the first two were relatively uncontroversial, Scalfaro's refusal to dissolve parliament in early 1995 led to acrimonious disputes between the President and **Berlusconi**, the outgoing premier. Also controversial were Scalfaro's alleged favouritism towards the Catholic centre parties and the centre–left coalition, and his outspokenness across a range of issues.

MARK DONOVAN

Scaparro, Maurizio

b. 1932, Rome

Theatre director

A prominent left-wing theatre critic (from 1960 he was reviewer for the communist newspaper *Avanti* and editor of the theatre journal *Teatro nuovo*), Scaparro's career as director began in 1965 with a production celebrating the Italian **Resistance**. This was followed by a production at the **Spoleto Festival** of the anonymous sixteenth-century play, *La Veneziana* (The Venetian Lady), which established him as an important newcomer. After periods as director with theatre companies in Bologna and Bolzano, he founded Il Teatro popolare di Roma in 1975, which he headed until 1983; he then became artistic director of the Rome Theatre Company.

His productions tended to be rigorous and simple in their staging, betraying a thoughtful and even anti-spectacular attitude to theatre. However his contribution to Italian theatrical culture was broader: he came to international attention in 1980 when he masterminded a 'Theatre Carnival' as part of the **Venice Bienniale**, an innovation which subsequently became an important element of the biennial event. In 1982 he was nominated co-director of the Théâtre de l'Europe in Paris, alongside Giorgio **Strehler**.

See also: theatre directors

TIM FITZPATRICK

Scarpa and Scarpa

Following in the footsteps of his father, renowned architect Carlo **Scarpa**, Tobia Scarpa (b. March 1935, Venice) studied architecture and design at the **IUAV** in the late 1950s where he met and married fellow student and freelance designer, Afra Bianchini (b. 1937, Montebelluna). In 1960 they set up a studio in Montebelluna, and thereafter worked professionally as a couple. Early designs were for the Venini Glassworks in Murano (Venice), but the couple went on to create many innovative product, furniture and lighting designs for numerous prestigious companies including Cassina, B & B Italia, Gavina and Flos. Their (armless) 'Soriana' armchair was awarded a Golden Compass in 1970, and is now permanently housed in the New York Museum of Modern Art. The couple have also helped to ensure the success of the **Benetton** company by a long collaboration which has included designing its prototype store.

GINO MOLITERNO

Scarpa, Carlo

b. 2 June 1906, Venice; d. 28 November 1978, Sendai, Japan

Architect

Recognized only after his death as one of the great architects of this century, Scarpa was for much of his career an isolated and detached figure. His work is characterized by a virtuosity of light, colour and texture, an extraordinary refinement of detail and complex manipulations of materials and geometry.

Scarpa made a major contribution to postwar Italian architecture by reconstructing several his-

toric buildings as museums, most notably the Palazzo Abbatelis (Palermo, 1953–4), the Museo di Castelvecchio (Verona, 1956–64), and Quirini-Stampalia (Venice, 1961–3). He also designed numerous exhibitions in London, Paris, Rome and Milan and many for the **Venice Biennale** (1946–61). Rejecting the neutral spaces of mainstream modernism, Scarpa created settings which highlighted the uniqueness of objects, where container and content interacted across history, manifesting for the first time a new attitude to the past and a break with modernism's utopian concerns. In his works, historical objects and contexts were no longer simply assimilated, juxtaposed or contrasted but rather were interpreted by the architecture itself.

Each of Scarpa's projects tended to be approached without a fixed concept in mind, resulting instead from personal interactions with client, craftsmen and pre-existing context. The designs were developed as processes of making, particularly in his unique mode of drawing which proceeded, like the structure of the final building itself, in strata and palimpsests, and with meticulous attention to the smallest details. In this sense, the works were both occasional and decorative: they were befitting celebrations or commemorations of occasions and persons, equally alien to both contemporary functionalist and later neorationalist approaches.

Scarpa was influenced by Frank Lloyd Wright, but the sumptuous visual density of his work is rooted in the traditions of Venetian craftsmanship and Viennese ornamentation. It is regional without a fixation on local identity and ornamental without applied decoration, arising from a complex poetics of differentiation and junction by nodes and seams. Hermetic and labyrinthine, the work demands to be deciphered at every level. Other outstanding works include the **Olivetti** Showroom (Venice, 1957–8), the Gavina Showroom (Bologna, 1961–3) and the posthumously completed Banca Popolare di Verona (Verona, 1973–5) which suggests the directions he might have followed with large-scale projects had he not died prematurely. It is, however, the Brion-Vega Tomb and Cemetery (San Vito d'Altivole, 1970–2) for Giuseppe and Onorina Brion that best typifies both Scarpa's enigmatic quality and his tendency to push form to a condition of process.

Scarpa was director of the **IUAV** from 1972–8.

Further reading

Dal Co, F. and Mazzariol, G. (1984) *Carlo Scarpa: The Complete Works*, New York: Electa (the most comprehensive of all the numerous works devoted to Scarpa).

ROSS JENNER

Scelsi, Giacinto

b. 8 January 1905, La Spezia

Composer

Born into an aristocratic family, Scelsi showed early evidence of musical talent but received no formal training until his mid-twenties. After some years of European travel, he studied under Egon Köhler and later worked with Viennese serialist, Walter Klein. Scelsi's early works show a wide-ranging interest in the prevailing trends of the avantgarde; thus *Rotative* (1929) is cast in a mechanistic style akin to that of Antheil. However, the improvisatory work for piano, *Poemi* (Poems) (1937), recalls the heady exoticism of Scriabin, a tendency that would prevail from the 1950s onwards as Scelsi turned increasingly to the philosophy of the East for inspiration. In *Quattro pezzi* (Four Pieces) (1959) the attention of each piece is focused on a single pitch, around which minuscule changes are wrought, suggesting the effect of a mantra. Scelsi's later compositions, at times venturing into the realms of *musique concrète* (a combination of live instruments with electronics), have served to underscore the essential radicalism of his highly individual style.

JOHN KERSEY

Schifano, Mario

b. 1934, Homs, Libya; d. 26 January 1998, Rome

Painter, photographer and collagist

From a period of minimalism in the early 1960s, Schifano moved into a pop style which drew on street signs, advertising billboards and the mass media. Recognizing that film and television have greater reach than fine art, Schifano produced paintings that resembled a television screen, covering some of them with coloured plexiglass, as well as venturing into experimental cinema. By the 1980s he was producing landscapes, but still in a schematic, pop vein. Throughout his career, which encompassed a multitude of styles and media, Schifano often alluded to the history of art without mimicking it, as in *A de Chirico* (To de Chirico) of 1962, a minimalist tribute to the master of imagery (see **de Chirico**). His works are very representative of their times.

MAX STAPLES

scholarly publishers

The historical absence in Italy of a direct university press system has created the need for the various Italian universities to form links with local publishing firms. Due to the strict correlation between the academic world and socio-political life in Italy, all major commercial publishers, dealing in everything from fiction to journalistic surveys, have also instituted special series devoted to various scholarly and scientific disciplines. These publications usually aim at a broader audience, and host works and series which target a non-specialized and/or academic audience. These series usually focus on the social sciences, and, in the case of humanistic subjects, concentrate on biographies, monographic presentations of classics and the re-reading of historical topics and periods. In specific cases, some of these publishing series preserve a very academic and scholarly connotation despite the more openly commercial goals of the publishing houses. This is the case of **Feltrinelli**, Garzanti, Rusconi and other major publishing enterprises, which still entrust their non-fictional editorial decisions to editorial boards mostly composed by university professors or specialists of the various subjects. There are also publishing houses which began largely as scholarly enterprises but have grown to be overall editorial businesses, with a broad and varied readership, such as **Einaudi**, Laterza, **Marsilio** and **Mursia**.

In the case of more specific scholarly and scientific works, the academic system has had to turn to local and less commercial publishers – many of them internationally acclaimed in their specific fields – which organize their editorial activity mostly around the local or the national university system. The series, established in different disciplines, are directly controlled by editorial boards composed of professors and scholars active in Italian universities. Many prestigious and internationally known critical and scientific works, or highly reputed journals, have been and are published by these small unofficial university presses.

Some of these scholarly publishers have become so tied to their local academic environment as to have practically become the local university presses, working almost exclusively on publications suggested and financed by the local universities. Others, such as Olschki (Florence), Bollati-Boringhieri (Turin), **Il Mulino** (Bologna) or, on a lesser scale, Bulzoni (Rome) or Liguori (Naples), have in different capacities established a nationwide distribution and a strong scholarly reputation for many or all of their publications.

Other publishers have specialized in the critical editions of classics, and have achieved a very prestigious scholarly status. This is the case, for instance, with UTET (Turin), or Sansoni and Le Monnier (Florence). Others, like Vallecchi (Florence), Marietti (Genoa) and Sellerio (Palermo) move easily between the most scholarly and academic level and a selected and refined fictional and journalistic production. Finally, there are some that have a more openly scholastic approach, and they address their scholarly activity mostly towards a pedagogical market, like Zanichelli (Bologna), Loescher (Turin) or La Nuova Italia (Florence).

ANDREA CICCARELLI

Scialoja, Toti

b. 16 December 1914, Rome; d. 1 March 1998, Rome

Artist and poet

A significant exponent of *l'informale*, Scialoja

taught scenography and was a director of the Academy of Fine Arts in Rome. He first witnessed action painting in New York in 1956, and took up the technique of dripped paint. His *Impronte* (Impression) series, produced between 1957 and 1968, used a piece of paper or fabric as a stamp to produce repeated impressions across the canvas in graduated bands of colour. He also produced dozens of books of poetry beginning in 1952. His works for adults, which he described as lyric prose, tended towards minimalism. The works for children, which are self-illustrated, are more playful, and have been compared by Italo **Calvino** to the English tradition of nonsense poems and limericks.

Further reading

Scialoja, T. (1975) *Una vespa! Che spavento: poesie con animali*, (A Wasp! What a Fright: Poems With Animals) Turin: Einaudi (a collection of illustrated poems for children).

MAX STAPLES

Sciarrino, Salvatore

b. 4 April 1947, Palermo

Composer

Sciarrino's precocious talent led to the performance of one of his works during the 1962 International New Music Week in Palermo, when he was aged fourteen. He discarded the music that he had written between 1959 and 1965 as the work of immaturity, however, and in 1969 attended the course in electronic music under Evangelisti at the Accademia S. Cecilia. Already considered a leader of the Italian avantgarde, he went on to win a number of significant international awards during the 1970s. Sciarrino's mature work begins with the radical *Atto II* (1965) for speaker, three trumpets and percussion. This was followed by *Quartetto II* (1967), which shows a confident mastery of the form born of study of the late works of Beethoven. His style has remained constant and, notwithstanding occasional excursions into aleatoricism (*Sonata for two pianos*, 1967), is founded on the Beethovenian elaboration of fragmentary ideas into large-scale structures. The one-act opera *Amore e Psiche* (Cupid and Psyche) (1973) shows a tendency towards symbolism and fantasy, while later works (*Lohengrin*, 1982–4; *Vanitas*, 1981) reassert his allegiance to the past.

Further reading

Chiesa, R. (1998) *Salvatore Sciarrino*, Milan: Targa Italiana (a biographical study).

JOHN KERSEY

Sciascia, Leonardo

b. 8 January 1921, Racalmuto, Sicily;
d. 20 November 1989, Palermo

Writer and essayist

Sciascia's writing typically confronts the problems afflicting Sicily and considers how far logic and reasoning can be used to improve social conditions. His style locates itself somewhere between the essay and fictional narrative: it is essay in its depiction of social problems – though these are sometimes composite rather than exact – while its use of fictional narrative leads the reader through the character's coming to conscious realization of these social facts.

His early work, *Le parrocchie di Regalpetra* (The Parishes of Regalpetra) (1956) was a thinly veiled documentary account of daily life in his own birthplace, Racalmuto. Sciascia used an autobiographical model in recounting his childhood in Sicily under Fascism, as he grew to understand the realities of the regime. However, his greatest popular success came in 1961 with *Il giorno della civetta* (The Day of the Owl), which was soon translated into English (as *Mafia Vendetta*) and also made into a film by Damiano **Damiani**.

In this work, Sciascia adopts the form of the classic English detective story in which crime is an aberration with respect to the norm, and the detective needs only to identify the perpetrator in order to gain a confession and, consequently, the restoration of order. In Sciascia's clever reworking of the formula, the culprits are soon identified, but this has no practical effect because they remain safe and untouchable behind political protection, which suggests that society itself is out of joint. Furthermore, within the apparently fictional narrative Sciascia produces a highly accurate and realistic portrayal of how the **mafia** operates, and of the mentality of its members and supporters.

As **Eco** would later prove with *The Name of the Rose*, the murder-mystery was an ideal form for rational inquiry, and Sciascia followed *Il giorno* with three more detective stories. In interviews, he admitted using the genre as a structuring device to engage the reader while conveying information about Sicilian society. At the same time, he also rejected the idea that crime can generally be analysed and solved through reason, and indeed his later narratives came to shed less light and make less sense. Sciascia took the French Enlightenment as his icon of rationalism, and it appears in his novels *Il Consiglio d'Egitto* (The Council of Egypt) (1963) and *Candido* (Candide) (1977), but throughout his life his attitudes wavered, from the emphatic optimism he expresses in his first works to his 'serene despair' that Italy would never change, expressed shortly before his death.

Despite his popularity and success, Sciascia wrote only part-time until 1970, while continuing to work as a teacher and civil servant. Later he served as member of local government and then in the Italian and European Parliaments. His final works examined the law, civic and moral responsibilities, and justice. He campaigned against capital punishment, which he regarded as murder sanctioned by the state, laying out his arguments in *Porte aperte* (Open Doors) (1987), a fictionalized account of a magistrate who must decide whether or not to impose a sentence of death. *Il cavaliere e la morte* (The Knight and Death) (1988) serves as a summing up of his reflections on life, reason, and madness, in preparation for death.

Further reading

Farrell, J. (1995) *Leonardo Sciascia*, Edinburgh: Edinburgh University Press (a substantial discussion of Sciascia's themes and works, showing how his philosophies are given literary form).

Sciascia, L. (trans. 1963) *Mafia Vendetta*, London: Jonathan Cape.

—— (trans. 1993) *Open Doors and Three Novellas*,

trans. J. Ravinovitch and M. Evans, New York: Vintage Books.

MAX STAPLES

Scola, Ettore

b. 10 May 1931, Trevico

Director and scriptwriter

Scola is one of Italy's most visually and intellectually exciting film-makers. A number of his films such as *C'eravamo tanto amati* (We All Loved Each Other So Much) (1974) and *Una giornata particolare* (A Special Day) (1977) have received international acclaim, while others like *Trevico-Torino: Viaggio nel Fiat-Nam* (Trevico-Turin: Voyage to Fiat-Nam) (1973) have generated aesthetic and political controversy. And yet, perhaps because his personal life has not lent itself to scandal and because his approach to film-making has been entirely competent and professional, he has not been the object of the frequently morbid media and the critical interest that has surrounded better known Italian filmmakers like **Rossellini**, **Fellini**, **Pasolini** or **Bertolucci**.

Born into a middle-class family in rural southern Italy, Scola moved to Rome when he was four. At an early age he discovered a talent and passion for drawing caricatures, sketches and cartoons. Against the wishes of his family, who wanted him to follow his father in becoming a physician, Scola approached the editors of the satirical magazine, *Marc'Aurelio*, with samples of his work. Initially rejected, his work was eventually published and he continued to contribute to the magazine while still in high school. During his four years with *Marc'Aurelio* (1949–53) Scola met several young men who were to become prominent as filmmakers (Cesare **Zavattini**, Francesco **Rosi**, Federico Fellini, Mario **Monicelli**) and scriptwriters (Vittorio Metz, Marcello Marchesi, Steno, Ruggero Maccari and Furio Scarpelli).

Beginning his career in the film industry in the 1950s by writing gags for more established scriptwriters, Scola went on in the next three decades to co-author over fifty scripts, mostly of *commedia all'Italiana* (comedy Italian style). In 1964, with little practical experience, he directed his first film, *Se permettete, parliamo di donne* (If You Don't Mind, Let's Talk About Women), a light comedy which was critically well received but which provoked Lina **Wertmüller** to reply in kind the following year with her *Questa volta parliamo di uomini* (This Time We Talk About Men). In the years that followed, while continuing to write scripts for other directors, Scola also directed over twenty-five films of his own.

Scola's first films already demonstrated an evolution beyond the value-free humour of the *Marc'Aurelio* towards the more trenchant social criticism of Italian mores being articulated by the better directors and scriptwriters of the comedy Italian style. In his subsequent films, his major interest shifted to the fate of the individual overwhelmed by forces which can be neither controlled nor understood. In many films Scola, also continued to explore a theme which had fascinated him from the beginning, not only social reality but the very nature of representation in film.

Further reading

Bondanella, P. (1995) *Italian Cinema: From Neorealism to the Present*, New York: Continuum (an analysis of Scola's career and films).

Gieri, M. (1995) *Contemporary Italian Filmmaking: Strategies of Subversion*, Toronto: University of Toronto Press (see pp. 157–97 for an analysis of Scola's place in Italian cinema).

Marcus, M. (1986) *Italian Film in the Light of Neorealism*, Princeton, NJ: Princeton University Press (see in particular pp. 391–421 for an analysis of *C'eravamo tanto amati*).

BEN LAWTON

sculpture

Like painting, contemporary Italian sculpture has found itself divided between figurative and abstract tendencies. Traditional Italian art, along with the more recent examples of **Marini** and **de Chirico**, provided a figurative model, but the entire thrust of modernism and the avantgarde was towards experimentation and the denial of representation.

Unlike painting, which returned to a refreshed figuration in the 1980s, sculpture continued to find its scope eroded by the changing market and the emergence of new genres of mixed media and installation, with perhaps only public sculpture remaining a vital area of activity.

Italian sculpture dominated Western art, in Imperial Rome and again during the Renaissance, the Baroque and beyond, with masters such as Brunelleschi, Michelangelo, Bernini and Canova. At its height, sculpture was set up in public places in order to impress the ordinary passer-by with the deeds and power of the rich and famous. The modern state, however, does not need sculpture as propaganda since it has more sophisticated and wide-reaching forms of image building at its disposal such as the press and television. This is one reason why the idea of sculpture has become disassociated from the notion of statues.

Since the Second World War, art in Italy has been characterized by a succession of movements all claiming to be innovative and challenging. In addition, there has been a struggle between figurative and abstract styles. This contestation has been largely played out in the medium of painting since, in its representation of three-dimensional objects on a two-dimensional surface, painting encapsulates the artfulness of artistic representation. Self-consciously modern painting initially shocked its audience precisely because it renounced this vocation in order to revel instead in its own surface, as for example in the works of Alberto **Burri**. Sculpture, however, being a three-dimensional medium representing three-dimensional things, was never quite as central to the debate. Significantly, when Lucio **Fontana** chose to explore the deep space of art, he did it in part with rents and gashes on the surface of a two-dimensional canvas.

Some postwar sculptors continued to work in a figurative style. Marino **Marini** throughout the 1950s produced an expressive series of horse and rider, which he used to reflect the human condition. Giacomo **Manzù**, a professed atheist, was nevertheless able to attract major religious commissions for figurative works, most notably the bronze Doors of Death for St Peter's in Rome.

Ranged against this figurative current were 'assemblers' such as Ettore **Colla**, who organized recognizable found objects in new abstract shapes, and the rather more whimsical Fausto Melotti and Leoncillo Leonardi, who worked with terracotta. Such sculpture, however, despite its modernist credentials, was not highly sought after either by private collectors or by museums. In fact, abstract sculpture had its greatest successes when commissioned for public places. Here, it played on the great Italian tradition of public display of art, though it tended to be located in newly created quarters or those bereft of more traditional sculpture, with the doctrinaire purpose of bringing culture to the people.

Recent public sculpture has been inclined to use large, geometric shapes, and to display new materials and technologies in a positive light. Such are the geometric forms of Arnaldo **Pomodoro**, displayed in Rimini and Cesena, and the formal jumbles of his brother Gio **Pomodoro**, combinations of regular shapes which actively encourage community participation.

At the same time, sculpture has found its domain eroded by two new genres, installation and mixed media, which are less oriented to aesthetic effect and more towards a message. Installation is a temporary arrangement of objects in a three-dimensional form in a room or other space. Mixed media is more an extension of painting, usually beginning with a flat surface but to which can be added all sorts of objects created or found to make it three-dimensional.

In the 1960s, installation was non-commercial, temporary and closely tied to the statements it sought to make. However, since then it has become largely commodified. Much installation today is sponsored by, and set in, galleries and there are even a few private collectors who are buying entire installations and setting them up in their homes, thus shifting the emphasis from the message back on to the object. Moreover, since the 1960s it has become difficult to distinguish between what has been intended as sculpture and what as installation, though a rule of thumb may be that sculpture more often consists of objects genuinely created by the artist. For example, Giulio **Paolini**'s *Mimesis* (1975) may look very much like sculpture – the Medici Venus in fact – but it is not. It merely uses plaster copies of sculpture to form an installation; the artistic input lies in the combination of the elements and the intent. Pino Pascali displays a full-size cannon in Cannone 'Bella Ciao' of 1965, an ironic comment on the machines of war, not an invitation to admire the workmanship of the armourer. His *Rinoceronte e giraffe* (Rhinoceros and Giraffes) of 1966 is labelled an installation, but is apparently the work of the artist and has aesthetic qualities, which suggests it is sculpture. This difficulty of classification becomes extreme in the work of Jannis **Kounellis**, whose *Cavalli* (Horses) (1969) consists of real horses. Here there is no mimesis or figuration because Kounellis has taken the signified to represent the signifier, but this leads to the question of whether this is 'living' sculpture, installation, art or merely a material joke.

Given the increasing precariousness of earning a living as a full-time sculptor, sculpture is now more often produced by artists active in other fields. The painter Giorgio de Chirico created his *Hector and Andromache* in terracotta in 1940, but this was posthumously enlarged and cast in 1986 in order to exploit de Chirico's greater reputation at this time. This signals the same return to figuration as *Scultura andata, scultura storna* (Sculpture Gone, Sculpture Averted), a bronze fountain featuring a Renaissance-style angel produced by Enzo **Cucchi** and Sandro **Chia** in 1982. However, such large-scale works are a commitment of time, technique and materials that few artists today can afford to produce.

See also: art movements

MAX STAPLES

Second Vatican Council

Called by **Pope John XXIII** in January 1959, the Second Vatican Council transformed the Roman Catholic Church worldwide and had profound effects on Italy. Consisting of most of the Roman Catholic bishops of the world, experts on canon law and theology, and many Catholic and non-Catholic observers, the Council met in three sessions from October 1962 to December 1964. The early stages were notable for the fierce battles over the conduct of sessions and the drafting of schema and declarations between the conservatives in the Roman curia and progressive bishops,

especially from Belgium, France and North America. In the end, the progressives won most of the battles.

The most important outcomes of the Council were as follows:

1. The Constitution on the Sacred Liturgy, which replaced Latin by the vernacular in the services of the Church, and introduced mass facing the people.
2. The emergence of the concept of 'collegiality', whereby all bishops share in the responsibilities of the pope and the consequent summoning of synods of bishops every two or three years.
3. The declaration exculpating the Jews for the death of Christ which, though welcomed by the Jews themselves, did not lead to an immediate improvement in relations between the Vatican and the state of Israel.
4. The declaration on religious liberty and the relaunching of Catholic ecumenism with a consequent warming of relations with Orthodox, Anglican, Methodist, Lutheran and other Christian churches.
5. A new emphasis on the role of the laity in the Church.
6. A stress on the importance of individual conscience as against the absolute authority of the teachings of the Church.
7. The Constitution on the Church in the Modern World, which accelerated the increasing concern on the part of the Church for the countries of the Third World.

The work of the Council was generally welcomed inside the Church, but it was also criticized for subverting traditional Catholic belief and discipline, most notably by the French archbishop Lefebre and his followers, who set up a schismatic church in protest.

The influence of the Council undermined the traditional Italian Catholic culture of obedience, giving rise to the *Cattolici del dissenso*, groups of Catholics at loggerheads with the hierarchical church over such things as the liturgy, mixed lay–clergy communities and questions relating to sexuality. Most spectacularly, the Council made it possible for some leading Catholic intellectuals to defy the Church hierarchy and advocate a 'no' vote in the referendum against divorce in 1974. In broader terms, the Council also resulted in the undermining of traditional forms of Catholic associationalism in Italy and weakened the political influence of the Church, thus making it possible for increasing numbers of Catholics to vote for parties other than the **DC**.

See also: Catholic associations; church, state and society; Vatican

Further reading

Hastings, A. (1991) *Modern Catholicism: Vatican II and After*, London: SPCK.

JOHN POLLARD

sectorial languages

Sectorial languages (also called sectional varieties, special languages, technical languages or subcodes) are the varieties of Italian used in specific sectors of society, such as the language of the bureaucracy, of chemistry, of politics. More precisely, 'sectorial' languages refer to less specialized areas without a specific terminology and addressing the wider audience through the mass media, such as politics and advertising. 'Specialist' or 'scientific' languages, on the other hand, refer to highly specialized disciplines with their own terminology and precise rules governing it, such as chemistry, linguistics or physics.

Specialist and sectorial languages are rapidly expanding as a result of the creation of new fields and subfields of specialization, which in turn create new linguistic needs. Consequently, two major issues concern the actual number of languages that can be identified and the boundaries between them.

Of major interest is the formation of their lexicon. Specialist and sectorial languages draw upon ordinary language to create their own terms, but they also have an impact on ordinary language, especially through the media. This is particularly noticeable for some sectorial languages, such as sport or advertising. As to specialist languages, their penetration into ordinary language has been attributed to the high prestige enjoyed by scientific terms. Overall, current trends point to an increas-ing impact of these languages on ordinary language.

Both specialist and sectorial languages fluctuate between the need to further specialize and the need to reach out to the wider public. It is recognized that, compared to other countries, Italy still lacks a suitable language for the wide diffusion of scientific material. Among sectorial languages that have been studied most are the languages of sport, politics, bureaucracy and advertising; among specialist languages, the languages of economics, science and computers.

In the lexicon of sectorial languages, words are taken from everyday language and given a new meaning: for example, in sport, *porta* 'door' to indicate the goal area, and *panchina* 'bench' to refer to the coaches; in politics, *linea* 'line' to mean 'political orientation'. Archaisms or learned words are also very frequent: for example, in the **bureaucracy**, *dirimere* 'to settle' and *codesto* 'that' continue to be used although obsolete everywhere else. Sectorial languages abound in rhetorical figures: in the language of politicians, *crisi strisciante* 'creeping crisis' and *manodopera disponibile* 'available workforce' refer to unemployment and the un-employed, for the double purpose of catching the audience's attention and being deliberately ob-scure; in the language of sport, *novanta minuti di furente battaglia* 'ninety minutes of raging battle' may describe a match. Frequently new words are created: in advertising, *amarevole* 'bitter', instead of *amaro*, and *cioccolatarsi* 'to have oneself a chocolate' try to have a special impact on their audience; in politics, ***Tangentopoli*** 'corruption city' refers to the uncovering of political and bureaucratic corruption by the Italian magistrates. Many of these new words, however, have a very limited life-span. Words are also borrowed from other languages: in sport, *pivot*, *play-maker* and *tie-break* are imported from English. Some borrowings may take on Italian endings, such as *dribblare* from 'to dribble'. Sectorial languages frequently use rou-tines and formulas: in the bureaucracy, *nel caso che* 'in case that' and *non si esclude che* 'it is not excluded that' attempt to moderate the general tone of the statements, and *entro e non oltre il giorno* 'within and not beyond the day', when setting deadlines, creates an effect of 'precision' by being redundant. Interestingly, sectorial languages also tend to borrow terms from each other: the language of politics draws upon economics, as in *gestione* 'management' and *bilancio* 'budget'; upon sport, as in *rilanciare la palla* 'to resend the ball'; upon medicine, as in *diagnosi* 'diagnosis' and *terapia* 'therapy'; and upon technology, as in *freno* 'brake' and *acceleratore* 'accelerator'.

At the grammatical level, sectorial languages display a number of features which include (1) a very frequent use of prefixes or suffixes such as *super-*, *ultra-*, *bio-* and *mini-* in advertising, *-ista* and *-ino* in politics, to form for example *leghista* 'member of the **Lega Nord**' and *pidiessino* 'member of the **PDS**'; and (2) a preference for nominal structures, so that verbs tend to be substituted with a verb plus noun structure: for example, in bureaucracy, *prendere in esame* 'to take something into consideration' instead of *esaminare* 'to examine', and *opporre un rifiuto* 'to give a refusal' instead of *rifiutare* 'to refuse'.

The lexicon of specialist languages differs from that of sectorial languages as they need to refer to entities with maximum precision and clarity; hence, each term has one meaning only and cannot be substituted by a synonym but at the most by a definition, in order to avoid any possible ambiguity. Their terms often have everyday equivalents: for example, *acido cloridrico* 'hydrochloric acid' versus *acido muriatico* 'muriatic acid'. Furthermore, new terms are created by using a few standard mechanisms: in medicine, the suffix *-osi* is used to refer to a chronic disease, as in *scoliosi* 'scoliosis', and *-oma* to refer to types of tumours, as in *carcinoma* 'carcinoma'. Thus, a great number of new terms can be formed through a limited number of endings. Specialist languages also employ everyday terms with a totally different meaning – in mathematics, *campo* 'field' refers to an algebraic system with particular properties – and they borrow or translate words from other languages: for example, 'pace maker' in medicine, and 'fiscal drag' and *drenaggio fiscale* in economics.

At the grammatical level, texts in specialist languages also display a strong preference for nouns and more generally for nominalization, whereby a verb is turned into a noun, such as *l'aumento del metabolismo* 'the increase of metabolism' instead of *il metabolismo aumenta* 'metabolism increases'. Other features include a narrow range of verbal tenses and moods, a reduced use of prepositions, as nouns are juxtaposed or separated with a dash, (*la spirale prezzi-salari* 'the price-salary spiral'), and a frequent use of the passive voice and of impersonal forms. Furthermore, these texts are characterized by a linear structure of the sentence, with very few subordinate clauses. All these features contribute to create texts that are both lexically very dense, that is, with a high number of words compared to the number of sentences, and rather neutral and impersonal. The textual structure is also very rigid, with precise and obligatory stages in the presentation and the frequent use of few connectors: for example, *dato che* 'given that', *ammesso che* 'admitting that' and *ne segue* 'it follows'. With the rapid increase of scientific publications, many new types of text, such as the abstract or the report, are also being introduced.

With regard to the impact on everyday language, it has been noted that, due to the popularity of sport, many sporting expressions are now in common use: examples include *serie B* 'second rate', *salvarsi in corner* 'to get off by the skin of one's teeth', and *prendere in contropiede* 'to catch someone off balance'. Likewise, some advertisements tend to become set phrases, such as *Il signore sì che se ne intende!* 'Sir really knows what's what', from an advertisement for a brandy. Advertising has also had an impact at the grammatical level: it has reinforced the use of adjectives in the place of adverbs, as in *parcheggia facile* 'park easy', where the adjective *facile* 'easy' is used instead of the adverb *facilmente* 'easily', and it has reduced the use of prepositions through formations such as *alimenti-natura* 'food from nature' instead of *alimenti della natura*, and *modello-famiglia* 'family model' instead of *modello per la famiglia*. With respect to the popularization of scientific terms, the press has played a fundamental role by presenting them accompanied by their explanation: for example, *ipertermia, cioè la febbre alta* 'hypothermia, that is, high fever'.

It is recognized that, in order to satisfy the need to reach out to the wider public, each language, including specialist languages, operates at various levels according to the type of interlocutors and the specific purpose. The language used by scientific researchers to talk about their field will vary if they are writing for an academic journal, for a high school textbook or for a newspaper.

See also: advertising; Italian language; Italian lexicon; Italian morphology; sport and society; varieties of Italian

Further reading

Beccaria, G.L. (1973) *I linguaggi settoriali in Italia* (Sectorial Languages in Italy), Milan: Bompiani (essays on specific sectorial languages and their relationship to ordinary language).

Dardano, M. (1981) *Il linguaggio dei giornali italiani* (The Language of Italian Newspapers), Part II, Roma-Bari: Laterza (the lexicon of some sectorial languages through the Italian newspapers).

—— (1994) 'I linguaggi scientifici' (Scientific Languages), in L. Serianni and P. Trifone (eds), *Storia della lingua italiana* (History of the Italian Language), vol. 2, Turin: Einaudi (a historical account of the rise of scientific languages up to the present day).

Sobrero, A.A. (1993) 'Lingue speciali' (Specialized Languages), in A.A. Sobrero (ed.), *Introduzione all'italiano contemporaneo. La variazione e gli usi* (Introduction to Contemporary Italian: Variation and Usage), Bari: Laterza (the differences between sectorial and specialist languages at various linguistic levels).

ANTONIA RUBINO

Segni, Mariotto

b. 16 May 1939, Sassari

Politician

Son of a former **President of the Republic**, Mario Segni was politically inactive until elected as a deputy in 1976 in the **DC**'s attempt at self-renewal. A conservative technocrat, Segni opposed any accommodation with the **PCI**, preferring institutional and party reform. DC–**PSI** resistance to electoral reform led to his championing the referendum as an instrument to force change on an inadequate political class. The overwhelming success of the 1991 and 1993 referendums, which he had done so much to bring about, made him a potential prime ministerial candidate in this volatile period, but Church hostility to the challenge he presented to his party – which he left in March 1993 – and his flirtation that summer with the PDS – the only effectively organized reformist force – alienated his natural backers. Hostile to **Berlusconi** yet lacking any allies other than the **PPI**, the quasi-majoritarian 1994 election ironically proved to be a disaster for him. Although he aligned himself openly with the centre–left in 1995–6, his campaign for presidential government reinforced his identification with the Right and continued to keep him in a political no man's land.

MARK DONOVAN

Segre, Cesare

b. 4 April 1928, Verzuolo, Cuneo

Academic and literary critic

Professor of romance philology at the universities of Trieste and Pavia, Segre has served as president of the International Association for Semiotic Studies and editor of the journals *Strumenti critici* and *Medioevo romanzo* and the series *Critica e filologia* for the **Feltrinelli** publishing house. Segre's philological contributions are particularly significant in the study of the Old French *Song of Roland* and the *Orlando Furioso*, the Italian Renaissance chivalric poem by Ludovico Ariosto. He is also responsible for editing a critical edition of Italian thirteenth-century prose works and directing an edition of the complete works of Ariosto. A more historiographical emphasis is apparent in other books by Segre, which bring to the study of literary language and style considerations of the influences of society and experience. Segre's enthusiastic promotion of structuralist methodologies in the late 1960s, together with his foundational work in linguistic theory, evolved to produce *Strutturalismo e critica* (Structuralism and Criticism), a collective work that Segre edited, and which is generally considered the first Italian text devoted to the semiotics of literature.

Further reading

Segre, C. (1988) *Introduction to the Analysis of the*

Literary Text, trans. J. Meddemmen, Bloomington, IN: Indiana University Press.

SHERRY ROUSH

semiotics

The study of signs is as old as the divinatory
practices of ancient cultures, but semiotics as the
science of signs and the academic discipline that
analyses the process of signification is usually taken
to originate in the early 1960s in France within the
ambit of structuralism. However, despite its French
origins, semiotics also exerted a very strong
influence in postwar Italy where, from the early
1960s onwards, theorists and critics like Umberto
Eco, Gillo **Dorfles**, Cesare **Segre**, Maria **Corti**,
Ferruccio Rossi-Landi and others used semiological
analysis to both undermine the overwhelming
influence which the thought of Benedetto **Croce**
had exercised over most aspects of Italian culture
since the early 1900s, and to develop new
theoretical tools for understanding and appreciat-
ing the irresistible spread of popular culture.
Within ten years of the publication of Barthes's
Elements of Semiology, usually taken as one of the
discipline's founding texts, the University of
Bologna had instituted a chair of semiotics, which
was immediately filled and held for the next two
decades by the prolific and ubiquitous Umberto
Eco.

The desire to escape the cultural parochialism
fostered by the Fascist regime was, in part,
responsible for the rise of semiotics in Italy. The
rapid diffusion of television and the development of
postwar Italian cinema were also crucial for the
discipline, whose beginnings contested the dominance of Croce's philosophy and Marxist historicism. The Frankfurt school's variation on Marxist
theory was imported to Italy in the late 1950s, and
it shared with Croce's aesthetics a tendency to
radically separate mass or popular culture from the
exalted sphere of Art. Semiotics undermines this
division by considering the various forms of
cultural activity all as rule-bound signifying practices. This stance implies that a work of art should
be seen neither as an isolated expression of artistic
intuition, nor as the determined reflection of a
particular historical situation. Against historicism,
the critical activity of semiotics seeks to discover the
internal logic of the construction of cultural
artefacts, and against Croceanism, semiotics insists
that cultural artefacts are meaningful because they
refer to signifying systems operating in the larger
field of the culture itself. In fact, Eco has even
proposed that *all* cultural phenomena can and
should be studied as a set of communication
processes founded on systems of signification (Eco,
1976: 22)

Thus, despite the fact that many semioticians
were explicitly engaged in aesthetics, their quest for
new aesthetic criteria contributed to a re-evaluation of the opposition between high and low
culture. This trend was evidenced in early semiotic
studies of **advertising** by Gillo Dorfles and
Umberto Eco, and in fact, were it not so
exceptional, Eco's career, with its trajectory from
the offices of **RAI** television to international
academic and literary stardom, could be seen as
paradigmatic of the progressive fortunes of the
discipline itself. And if Eco and other semioticians
have seen fit to take an interest in popular culture,
the reverse could also be said to be the case. Since
1965, Eco has written a column entitled 'La
bustina di Minerva' in the magazine ***L'Espresso***,
which he has used to divulge information about
semiotics as a discipline as well as to disseminate
semiotically informed cultural commentary. The
stature and credibility of semiotics in Italian culture
is also illustrated by the participation of Eco and
Paolo Fabbri in the Aldo **Moro** affair, when
government authorities saw fit to solicit their
assistance in order to verify the authenticity of
letters written by Moro while he was being held in
a terrorist hideout.

Perhaps more mundanely, semiotics has also
made the rounds of the various academic and
critical disciplines. In Italian literary studies, Cesare
Segre and Maria Corti have been instrumental in
unifying semiotics and the various threads of
twentieth-century literary theory. Film theory has
a rich Italian history, and semioticians such as
Gianfranco Bettetini and Emilio Garroni have
made important contributions to the discipline.
Meanwhile, anthropology and folklore have been
influenced by Eco's *La Struttura assente* (The Absent

Structure) (1968) and by Antonino Buttita's *Ideologia e folklore* (Ideology and Folklore).

Theatre, art, architecture, non-verbal communication, television, fashion, journalism, game theory and even cartoons have been similarly studied by semioticians. Semiotics also plays an important role in one of Italy's newest and most exciting educational opportunities at the university level. In 1996, more than 2,100 students competed for only 140 openings for the degree programme in 'Sciences of Communication' at Bologna. The programme is considered to offer excellent employment prospects, and, as befits the information era, it includes coursework in semiotics, sociology, law, computer science, psychology, advertising and journalism. Currently, the programme is also offered at the universities of Turin, Siena, Trieste, Padua and Rome.

The place of semiotics in postwar Italian culture has been summed up by Thomas Sebeok, one of the foremost American semioticians: 'Italy is the country where the European renaissance of semiotics has its roots and whence some of its best work continues to resonate worldwide' (Sebeok in Segre, 1988: vii).

Further reading

Bettetini, G. and Casetti, F. (1986) 'Semiotics in Italy', in T. Sebeok and J. Umiker-Sebeok (eds), *The Semiotic Sphere*, New York: Plenum, 292–321 (the most comprehensive English-language history of Italian semiotics to date).

Corti, M. (1978) *An Introduction to Literary Semiotics*, Bloomington, IN: Indiana University Press (a useful introduction to semiotics with emphasis on its literary applications).

Danesi, M. (1994) *Messages and Meanings: An Introduction to Semiotics*, Toronto: Canadian Scholar's Press (an outstanding general introduction to a variety of perspectives on semiotic issues).

De Lauretis, T. (1978) 'Semiotics in Italy', in R. Bailey, L. Matejka and P. Steiner (eds), *The Sign: Semiotics Around The World*, Ann Arbor, MI: Michigan Slavic Publications (a conveniently succinct summary of the development of Italian semiotics).

Eco, U. (1976) *A Theory of Semiotics*, Bloomington, IN: Indiana University Press.

—— (1994) *Apocalypse Postponed*, ed. R. Lumley, Bloomington, IN: Indiana University Press (an excellent selection of Eco's occasional writings on Italian culture).

Segre, C. (1988) *Introduction to the Analysis of the Literary Text*, trans. J. Meddemmen, Bloomington, IN: Indiana University Press.

THOMAS KELSO

Sereni, Vittorio

b. 27 July 1913, Luino, Varese; d. 10 February 1983, Milan

Poet, essayist and translator

The son of a customs officer, Sereni was born on the Lago Maggiore (one of the great northern lakes), which remains a constant landscape in his poetry. In 1937 he published his first poems in *Il Frontespizio* (The Frontispiece) and founded the literary journal *Corrente* (Current), although it was not until 1941 that his first volume of poetry, *Frontiera* (Frontier), was published, which suggested to some critics the influence of **Ungaretti** and **Montale**. However, the thematic focus on Lombard landscapes, the musicality of the verse and a colloquial language that resembles the poetic diction of **Saba** underscored from the beginning Sereni's own originality. Called up to join the Italian army that same year, Sereni served on the African front. He was captured in 1943 and spent two years in prisoner of war camps in Algeria and Morocco, an experience that is central to his second book, *Diario d'Algeria* (Algerian Diary). Here, the personal experience of captivity becomes the lyrical counterpoint for the grander historical drama of the war, and reveals the poet's shame and sense of futility at being a helpless spectator of historical events.

After the war, Sereni returned to Milan, where he taught high school before going to work in the advertising branch of industrial giant **Pirelli** and, later, as literary editor for **Mondadori**. *Gli strumenti umani* (Human Instruments), published in 1962, begins with the poems that closed *Diario*, revealing Sereni's desire to present his poetry as a lifelong continuum. The discussion of moral and social concerns begun in the previous volume is continued, although it is transferred to the familiar landscape of the great industrial city. But in observing this world, the poet gradually suggests that his hopes for social reconstruction after the war have fallen by the wayside. Considered to be Sereni's most important collection, *Gli strumenti* experiments heavily with dialogue and everyday spoken language, and thus reflects the poet's desire to abandon his literary world in order to actively denounce the injustices of capitalism

Sereni's pessimism continues and increases with *Stella variabile* (Variable S), the volume of poetry published two years before his death. No longer buoyed by the hope that 'human instruments' will guide him, Sereni confides in the 'variability' of the stars to lead him through his later years, as hopelessness and despair close about him.

A candidate for the Nobel Prize in literature in his later years, Sereni also wrote a number of essays, collected in *Letture preliminari* (Preliminary Readings) and the short stories *L'opzione* (The Option) and *Il sabato tedesco* (The German Saturday). He is also known for his translations of Apollinaire, Char, Pound and W.C. Williams, collected in *Il musicante di Saint-Merry* (The Musician of Saint-Merry).

Further reading

Baffoni Licata, M.L. (1986) *La poesia di Vittorio Sereni: alienazione e impegno* (The Poetry of Vittorio Sereni: Alienation and Commitment), Ravenna: Longo (a discussion of Sereni's movement from the aesthetic to the social sphere in his poetry).

Sereni, V. (1990) *Selected Poems of Vittorio Sereni*, trans. M. Perryman and P. Robinson, London: Anvil Press Poetry.

VALERIO FERME

Severino, Emanuele

b. 26 February 1929, Brescia

Philosopher

Emanuele Severino teaches at the university of Venice and contributes regularly to *Il Corriere della Sera* and various periodicals. His writings

contest the tradition of Western metaphysics as a whole. Severino's crucial insight concerns the opposition of post-Platonic philosophy to the static conception of the universe that is associated with Parmenides. His proposed 'return to Parmenides' is predicated upon the possibility of undoing the fundamental alienation from Being that he sees as inherent in the Western metaphysical paradigm, insofar as it views beings as entities that emerge and return to the void after a transitory existence. He has defended this thesis in a three-volume history of philosophy, but he has also written extensively on the nature of technology, aesthetics and ideology.

Further reading

Borradori, G. (1988) 'Introduction', in G. Borradori (ed.), *Recoding Metaphysics: The New Italian Philosophy*, Evanston, IL: Northwestern University Press, 1–26.

THOMAS KELSO

sexism in language

Questions related to gender discrimination and stereotyping through language play a lesser role in Italy than they do in English-speaking countries. In Italy, such debates generally tend to address more philosophical and ideological aspects, and focus less on specific points of usage. There are two main reasons for this. The first concerns the nature of the language itself: grammatical gender affects not only all Italian nouns, but also their pattern of agreement with articles, adjectives, pronouns and participles (see also **Italian morphology; Italian syntax**); if Italian were to leave unspecified the sex of the person, saying for example, 'I have gone' (in Italian inevitably either *sono andato* or *sono andata*), then it would become a completely different language. The second reason concerns language usage: Italian has suffered a long tradition of prescriptivism based on purist, and in this century also fascistic, grounds (see also **Italian language**); hence, any official attempt to tamper with spontaneous use and enforce a language policy meets with scepticism, if not downright resistance.

However, even if the debate on sexist language in Italy developed less forcefully and later than in other Western countries, when it did, progressive ideas obtained prompt endorsement by the government. In the 1980s a Commissione Nazionale per la Realizzazione della Parità fra Uomo e Donna (National Commission for the Implementation of Parity between Man and Woman) was set up in the Office of the Prime Minister, under whose auspices *Le raccomandazioni per un uso non sessista della lingua italiana* (Recommendations for Non-Sexist Use of the Italian Language) were written by Alma Sabatini. Its proposals were numerous and varied, but include the following. First, words referring to males, which are usually masculine in form, should not be used as general terms denoting both men and women; for example, *i diritti dell'uomo* (the rights of man) should become *i diritti umani* (the human rights) or *i diritti della persona* (the rights of the person). Second, masculine agreement should be avoided when both sexes are involved; for example, *Ragazzi e ragazze furono visti* (Boys and girls were seen/masc.) should become *Ragazzi e ragazze furono viste* (Boys and girls were seen/fem.), or *Ragazze e ragazzi furono visti* (Girls and boys were seen/masc.), where the agreement is made with the latter, closer item. Third, when referring to women, terms for professions, titles and so on should be used in the feminine, and this should be expressed in its simplest form if more than one is available; for example *Maria Rossi, direttore* (director/masc.) should be replaced by *Maria Rossi, direttrice* (director/fem.), and *la studentessa* (the student/ fem.) by *la studente* (the student/fem.).

Despite these official recommendations, common usage has changed only slightly, partly for the two reasons mentioned above, and partly because some of the proposals are not sufficiently sensitive to the history of the language and the implications they entail. Thus, for example, Italians may call a woman who is a chief constable *questore* (masc.), *questora* (fem.) or *questrice* (fem.), and make whatever agreement they like, i.e., *il questore Maria Rossi è arrivato* (the chief constable Maria Rossi has arrived/masc.) or *il questore Maria Rossi è arrivata* (the chief constable Maria Rossi has arrived/fem.).

See also: feminism; Italian lexicon; language education; language policy

Further reading

Lepschy, G. (1991) 'Language and Sexism', in Z.G. Baranski and S.W. Vinall (eds), *Women in Italy. Essays on Gender, Culture and History*, Moundmills: Macmillan (a review of Sabatini's *Raccomandazioni* and a balanced survey of some of the problems they entail).

Sabatini, A. (1986) *Raccomandazioni per un uso non sessista della lingua italiana*, Rome: Presidenza del Consiglio dei Ministri.

CAMILLA BETTONI

sexual mores

As with many other countries, Italy witnessed a radical transformation of sexual mores beginning in the 1960s. although low rates of **divorce** and the survival of a predominant role for the **family** into the 1990s both suggest a fair amount of continuity and testify to the survival of at least some traditional values.

In the immediate postwar period, the widespread fear of moral disorder was closely linked with the idea of national decline. The presence of American troops and the popularity of American movies showing independent women and angry young men favoured the process of moral liberalization. Moreover, secularization seemed to threaten social stability and the proposal to introduce divorce raised fears about the disintegration of family life. In an attempt to save the traditional family, Catholic mass organizations like the Azione Cattolica (**Catholic Action**) launched a strong campaign for moral 'rearmament', which obtained the support of the **DC** politicians in power.

The combined efforts of religious and political authorities were aimed at preventing a radical change in sexual mores. Censorship, social pressure and police measures served to combat bikinis, striptease and obscenity in the attempt to safeguard national customs. Repression, however, was not the only characteristic of the 1950s, for during the same years reformist movements obtained the elimination of some of the more glaring social inequities: for example, the legal position of illegitimate children was improved and the 1958 legislation promoted by Lina Merlin abolished 'closed houses' for prostitution.

Convinced that better information about sexual life before marriage and sexual harmony after marriage were necessary to avoid the break-up of marriages, Catholic priests like Don Paolo Liggeri organized courses of sexual education and created the first family advisory agencies in Italy. In a different way, the public discussion of scandals tore through the veil of silence, although a moralizing tone was always prevalent.

After an attempt by left-wing politicians to abolish the legal obstacles to birth control, the Italian Association for Demographic Education (AIED) was created in 1956. For many years, however, the efforts of the AIED remained without success, and those speaking up in favour of the legalization of contraception risked legal persecution (see **feminism**).

The '**economic miracle**' of the late 1950s and the rapid transformation from a rural to an industrial society were at the roots of the change which occurred in the following decades. Mass migration from the South to the North, urbanization, secularization, the higher standard of living, improved **education** and increased social and geographical mobility all contributed to undermine parental authority and the role of the local community and created new opportunities for women and young people to conquer higher levels of personal freedom and autonomy.

Sexual themes now appeared more often in popular literature and in cartoons such as *Kriminal* and, at a more sophisticated level, Guido Crepax's Valentina (see **comics**). In the early 1970s, magazines like *Cosmopolitan* and *Liberal* tried to exploit the commercial opportunities offered by the general interest in sexual issues, soon followed by other women's magazines which offered their readers a 'scientific' approach to sexuality, while condemning **pornography**. The film industry both reflected the changes in sexual morality and tried to promote change, as with Pietro **Germi** denouncing the male code of honour and the absurdities of Italian legislation in films like *Divorzio*

all'italiana (Divorce, Italian Style) (1961) and *Sedotta e abbandonata* (Seduced and Abandoned) (1964).

The transformation of sexual mores in these years emerges clearly from court cases. After a long debate, kissing in public was declared legal in 1969. In the same year a Roman Court declared that miniskirts, although of dubious taste in aesthetic terms, were not contrary to public decency. Finally in 1982 the Court of Cassation made a similar decision about women going topless at the beach. Gradually, legislation regarding sexual behaviour was adapted to the changed reality. Still, in 1965 the **Constitutional Court** had ruled that detailed information about contraceptives should remain illegal because it offended public morality, and that only generic pleas in favour of birth control could be allowed. The law prohibiting propaganda in favour of birth control, however, was declared anti-constitutional in 1971. In 1969 the Court had already abolished the crime of adultery, and a year later divorce had been introduced.

The year 1975 marked a watershed in the transition from repression to an attitude more respectful of personal values and civil liberties. The new family law finally recognized the principle of equal rights for men and women. In the same year, public family advisory agencies were set up with the aim of assisting singles and couples to solve problems regarding sexuality, procreation and related matters. When **abortion** became legal in 1978, family advisory agencies became responsible for providing the necessary information.

The more active role played by public authorities in issues relating to the intimate life of citizens created problems for the Catholic Church, which in the past had enjoyed a virtual monopoly in this sector. Hopes for a major liberalization in questions of sexuality and birth control had been dashed in 1968, when **Pope Paul VI** published the encyclical letter *Humanae vitae* which confirmed the traditional teaching of the Church. In the attempt to strengthen Catholic influence, in 1975 the Italian Conference of Bishops made the attendance of courses preparing for matrimony mandatory for young people who opted for a religious ceremony.

Equally critical of the changes in sexual mores – albeit from a different point of view – was Pier Paolo **Pasolini**, who denounced the predominance of the values of a consumer society which had halted a more authentic process of liberation. Sexual liberation in the 1960s and early 1970s was clearly male-oriented and this may explain why many women in this period complained of an unsatisfactory sexual life. Moreover, at least initially, the movement had a strong heterosexual bias and shared the general attitude of repressive tolerance with regard to homosexuality. Only in 1972 did the **gay movement** FUORI make its first public appearance during a conference of sexologists.

Not surprisingly, the major efforts for further changes in sexual mores and for the recognition of alternative lifestyles since have emanated from gay, lesbian and feminist groups. Their requests have been only partially satisfied due to continuing Catholic opposition, but also to the substratum of Italian society, which continues to be characterized by a strong institutionalization of marriage and a generally conservative attitude.

See also: censorship; gay writing

Further reading

Sabatini, R. (1988) *L'Eros in Italia. Il comportamento sessuale degli italiani* (Eros in Italy: The Sexual Behaviour of Italians) Milan: Mursia (a survey of the sexual mores of Italians in the 1980s).

Wanrooij, B. (1996) 'Back to the Future: Gender, Morality and Modernisation in Twentieth-Century Italy', *Italian History & Culture* 2: 41–59.

BRUNO P.F. WANROOIJ

Sgorlon, Carlo

b. 26 July 1930, Cassacco, Udine

Writer and critic

Sgorlon's early study of the Austrian author Franz Kafka infused his work with grotesque and oneiric undertones, most apparent in his first works, which include *La poltrona* (The Easy Chair) (1968). Sgorlon's devotion to the culture of his region and his love of the Friulian dialect is also already evident in these early works, for the short work entitled *Prime di sera* (1971), written in Friulian, later

evolved into the novel *Il vento nel vigneto* (The Wind in the Vineyard) (1973). His later works are typified by narratives rich in magic and myth, influenced perhaps by a period of study in Germany as well as by his study of the author Elsa **Morante**. Sgorlon lyrically depicts his native Friulian region in such novels as *Gli dei torneranno* (The Gods Will Return) (1977), *L'armata dei fiumi perduti* (The Armada of Lost Rivers) (1985) and *La fontana di Lorena* (The Fountain of Lorena) (1990). In 1973 he won the Campiello prize for his novel *Il trono di legno* (The Wooden Throne), which portrayed a Friulian community torn between the past and present. His short stories are collected in *Il quarto re mago* (The Fourth Wise Man) (1986).

LAURA A. SALSINI

Siciliano, Enzo

b. 27 May 1934, Rome

Writer and literary critic

An eclectic left-wing figure in the Italian cultural scene, Siciliano has served as president of Italian Public Television (**RAI**) as well as contributing to newspapers, magazines and literary journals such as *La Stampa*, *L'Avanti*, *Il Corriere della Sera*, *L'Espresso*, *Paragone*, *Tempo presente* and *Nuovi Argomenti*. Like Pasolini, an intellectual he particularly admired, Siciliano also experimented with film directing. His literary production tends to be qualitatively uneven and includes several collections of short stories, (*Racconti ambigui* (Ambiguous Tales), 1963, and *Dietro di me* (Behind Me), 1971), and a novel, *La coppia* (The Couple, 1966). His critical activity, on the other hand, has always been particularly innovative and stimulating. With *Prima della poesia* (Before Poetry) (1965), he constructively polemicizes against an established and fossilized idea of literature, and then with *Autobiografia letteraria* (Literary Autobiography) (1970), he successfully manages to combine a Marxist and a psychoanalytical approach into a creative essay form.

Further reading:

Siciliano, E. (1982) *Pasolini: A Biography*, trans. J. Shepley, New York: Random House.

ENRICO CESARETTI

Silone, Ignazio

b. 1 May 1900, Pescina dei Marsi;
d. 22 August 1978, Geneva,
Switzerland

Novelist

A Communist official who broke with the Party in 1931, Silone (born Secondo Tranquilli) was to call himself a 'socialist without a party and a Christian without a church'. Persecuted by fascists and communists alike, he published his first novels in Switzerland, where he lived in exile from 1929. *Fontamara* (1933), his strongest work, deals with the exploitation of peasants by fascist landowners, while *Pane e vino* (Bread and Wine) (1936) and its sequel, *Il seme sotto la neve* (The Seed Beneath the Snow) (1942), blend the themes of social struggle and Christianity. After returning to Italy in 1944, Silone published *Una manciata di more* (A Handful of Blackberries) (1952), which reworks *Fontamara*, this time with communist oppressors, and *Il segreto di Luca* (The Secret of Luca) (1956).

Further reading

Martelli, S. and Di Pasqua, S. (1988) *Guida alla lettura di Silone* (A Reader's Guide to Silone), Milan: Mondadori.

DAVE WATSON

Sinisgalli, Leonardo

b. 9 March 1908, Montemurro, Potenza;
d. 31 January 1981, Rome

Poet, editor and industrial engineer

After graduating in electronic and industrial engineering, Sinisgalli worked for the **Olivetti** and **Pirelli** companies, and between 1953–9 also edited *Civiltà delle macchine*, sponsored by Finmeccanica. As a poet he enjoyed the friendship and support of Giuseppe **Ungaretti**, and his first poetic anthology, *Vidi le Muse* (I Saw the Muses), received critical approval from Gianfranco **Contini**.

Sinisgalli's poetry derives some of its themes from Ungaretti and **Quasimodo** and, ultimately, from Leopardi, but in terms of style and experiment Sinisgalli looks to Surrealism, and not only to the literary avantgarde of Breton and Aragon but also to a painter such as Libero de Libero. With *I nuovi Campi Elisi* (The New Elysian Fields) Sinisgalli's poetry changes to reveal affinities with **Montale**'s poetics of the 'occasions', and the epigrammatic style of the fragments of his first collections, which recalled modes of Oriental poetry, led him to experiments using the dialect of Lucania, transformed by the poetic elaborations of the Italian language.

Further reading

Sinisgalli, L. (1982) *Selected Poems*, trans. W.S. Di Piero, Princeton, NJ: Princeton University Press.

ERNESTO LIVORNI

social welfare

In the postwar period, Italy developed a welfare system comparable to its European neighbours. Social expenditures went through a continuous and spectacular growth and allowed Italian welfare to completely recover its lag in adjusting to the international average of protection. However, four main features stand out as peculiar to welfare Italian-style. First, unlike the British/Scandinavian model (based on the egalitarian principles of universalism and uniformity of services, and financed through taxes), it offered citizens a wide diversity of services according to their profession. Second, it was based on the principle of compulsory insurance, so that contributions by both employers and employees represented its main source of financing. Third, it consisted almost exclusively of social security (pensions and social insurance) and **health services**, while **unem-**

ployment and housing policies were always considered fringe sectors. Finally, like other continental countries (namely France and Belgium), it provided mainly cash incomes rather than public services.

Beginning in the 1950s, minimum pension levels were extended from state and private employees to many non-wage and salary earning categories (farmers and sharecroppers, craftsmen, shopkeepers and all the professions), with each category creating an autonomous fund or pension board, mostly managed by **INPS**, the state body also responsible for other social security. Crisis loomed after the pension reform of 1969, which improved the benefit level of old age pensions (in part by linking it to the official cost of living index), introduced the so-called 'social pensions' (granted to all over the age of sixty-five with neither income nor sufficient contributions, irrespective of any previous salary) and enlarged the disability insurance programme as a means of income redistribution in underdeveloped regions, especially in the South, where unemployment was higher and political consensus was largely based on clientelistic relationships (see **clientelism**). Moreover, besides traditional old age pensions, the system spread to provide many others, such as the so-called 'seniority pensions' (given mostly to civil servants or employees of state-owned companies, who were allowed to retire early, after only twenty years of service) and disability pensions (paid to workers with physical or psychological handicaps). As a consequence, the pension system became an inextricable labyrinth of privileges and disparities. Finally, in the 1970s the Cassa Integrazione Guadagni (Earnings Integration Fund, a government-funded system of benefits to workers temporarily dismissed by their employers) was used extensively to ease social tensions which stemmed from the crisis of industrial firms. As the number of retired grew enormously (in the early 1990s almost 40 per cent of working-age Italians were over sixty years old, compared to just 23 per cent in the 1950s) employment shrank (in 1960 there were 2.6 employees for each pensioner; in 1990 this had diminished to 1.2 employees per pensioner), and

contributions began to cover an ever-decreasing part of social outlays with the resulting deficit financed at the expense of the national budget. Thus, given the inability of both governments and Parliament to pass reform bills and the fierce opposition to change from many categories of workers, social security became, together with the wages of state employees, the main item of the recurrent state expenditure and, as a result, in early 1990s the system approached collapse.

The increasing unsustainability of the national deficit and heavy pressures from both European partners and international financial organizations eventually forced change. After long negotiations, a reform was initiated in 1995–6 aimed at slowing down the growth of pension expenditure by raising the retirement age, reintroducing a generalized system of capitalization and increasingly integrating state pensions with private pension funds.

In the 1990s, reform was also instituted in the health system, which was the second main item of Italian social welfare. Since 1978 Italy had been one of the few countries of continental Europe (along with Denmark, Spain and Portugal) to have a national health system. The establishment of an NHS was aimed at overcoming the serious disorganization of hospitals and health services, which had been provided until then by a plethora of insurance funds, with heavy disparities of treatment among different categories of workers. The NHS improved the average assistance received by citizens but also produced new inequalities. The health budget was funded largely by contributions from private employees (more than 65 per cent of total contributions at the mid-1990s) and to a much lesser extent by state employees (17 per cent) and autonomous workers (13 per cent) but the system soon proved financially unsustainable. Fast-growing demand of treatment and prevention, ageing of population, emergence of new mass diseases (tumours, cardiopathies and chronic pathologies) and social problems such as drug addiction, caused a steep increase in expenditure. Furthermore, the burden was made even heavier by serious wastage of resources through widespread bureaucratic inefficiencies, heavy intrusion of

political parties in management and clientelistic use of health expenditure. Finally, since the state invested little and badly in hospitals and health infrastructures, it had to turn increasingly to expensive arrangements with private nursing-homes so that a substantial part of the private health system developed merely as a subsidized sector with poor controls on its quality and efficiency. This obliged governments to ask citizens to pay ever more for worsening services or to rely increasingly on very expensive private hospitals.

Then, as local health services continued to incur enormous deficits, the **Tangentopoli** investigations revealed massive bribery, corruption and schemes for the private enrichment of the ministers and civil servants who had ruled the Ministry of Health in the 1980s. These shocking revelations led to extensive reform in 1993. Controls on expenditure were tightened, local authorities were asked to assume direct responsibility for health services and to adopt a managerial approach and, at the same time, private health insurance funds were introduced. Subsequent changes both in the pension and the health system partially succeeded in stabilizing expenditure so that Italian welfare appeared reasonably balanced and financially sustainable in the medium term, although critics still maintain that it has some way to go before being truly equitable and efficient.

Further reading

Ascoli, U. (1996), 'The Italian Welfare State Between Incrementalism and Rationalization', in L. Balbo and H. Nowotny (eds), *Time to Care in Tomorrow's Welfare Systems: The Nordic Experience and the Italian Case*, Vienna: European Centre for Social Welfare Training and Research, 107–41 (a concise outline of postwar trends in welfare policies and the main features of the Italian system such as particularism, clientelism, non-progressiveness and persistence of poverty).

Cazzola, G. (1994) *Lo stato sociale tra crisi e riforme: il caso Italia* (The Welfare State between Crisis and Reform: the Italian Case), Bologna: Il Mulino (a broad picture of the challenge to reform facing the Italy welfare system in the 1990s).

Ferrera, M. (1997) 'The Uncertain Future of the Italian Welfare State', *West European Politics* 20 (1): 231–49.

STEFANO BATTILOSSI

Solbiati, Alessandro

b. 1956, Busto Arsizio

Composer

Solbiati's compositional style turns the language of the avantgarde to poetic ends, revealing a close familiarity with the traditions and aesthetic concerns of Italian music of the past. His early studies under Sandro Gorli culminated in the award of a diploma from the Milan Conservatory in 1982, after which he went on to study under Franco **Donatoni** at the Accademia Chigiana in Siena. He won recognition in a number of competitions, and was soon receiving commissions from the **RAI** and the Teatro alla Scala (see **La Scala**) in Milan. Subsequently his compositions were performed at the **Venice Biennale** and at the festivals of Lille and Avignon. Solbiati has consistently produced work of high quality for a wide variety of instrumental forces. His concerto for violin and orchestra *Di luce* (Of Light) (1982) shows a marked feeling for timbre and texture, while *Studi* (Studies) (1983) for chamber orchestra explores further realms of colour and emotional expression.

JOHN KERSEY

Soldati, Mario

b. 17 November 1906, Turin; d. 19 June 1999, Tellaro, Liguria

Writer, art critic and film director

Soldati's early years studying in a Jesuit college and his experiences living in the United States form the thematic basis for much of his literary output. Indeed, his works, often psychological in nature, reveal a strong element of autobiography, written in a style characterized by a witty urbanity, an unabashed sensuality and an unstudied freshness.

Many of his novels and short stories explore the contradiction between the urge to give in to natural human impulses and the religious strictures that forbid doing so, a dichotomy he ascribes to his own exposure to a repressive religious education. Soldati's characters, often belonging to the sophisticated upper classes, are caught in a bind as they attempt to satisfy their own desires while obeying the social and moral laws condemning such behaviour. The impossibility of reconciling these two desires typically leads to a profound and debilitating sense of guilt. The novels *La confessione* (The Confession) (1955), and *La busta arancione* (The Orange Envelope) (1966) both depict the negative effects of a harsh religious upbringing.

Soldati's experiences as an art student at New York's Columbia University from 1929–31 are documented in *America, primo amore* (America, First Love) (1935). Although this work captures Soldati's fascination with life in the United States, the fascists pointed to its more critical sections as proof that America was morally degenerate.

His most famous work, the novel *Le lettere da Capri* (The Capri Letters), follows the experiences of two American expatriates living in Rome, Capri, Paris and Philadelphia. The book, which garnered immense public and critical support, also won the 1954 Strega Prize (see **literary prizes**). Other works include *La verità sul caso Motta* (The Truth about the Motta Case) (1941), a psychological thriller, and *A cena col commendatore* (Dinner with the Commendatore) (1950), a collection of three long stories set in the world of art and music. The autobiographical novel *Le due città* (translated as *The Malacca Cane*) (1964) portraying a young man interested in a film career, is set in both Turin, which represents purity, and Rome, a symbol of decay. *L'attore* (The Actor), about a television director, was awarded the Campiello Prize in 1970. In a more psychological vein are novels such as *Il vero Silvestri* (The Real Silvestri) (1957), in which a dead man's lover and his best friend analyse his persona, and *L'Architetto* (The Architect) (1986).

A talented and multifaceted personality, Soldati has been involved in a wide variety of artistic activities, and has been at various times a journalist, art critic, radio lecturer, television producer, an actor and has also written knowledgeably on food and wine. In the 1930s he collaborated with Mario **Camerini** on the screenplays of many of his best

films including *Gli uomini, che mascalzoni!* (Men, What Rascals!) (1932) and *Il Signor Max* (Mister Max) (1937), both starring Vittorio **De Sica**. Between 1938 and the late 1950s he also directed over thirty films, including elegant adaptations of two novels by the nineteenth-century author Antonio Fogazzaro, *Piccolo mondo antico* (The Little World of the Past) (1940) and *Malombra* (1942), and a moving film version of **Moravia**'s novel, *La provinciale* (The Woman from the Provinces) (1952).

Further reading

Heiney, D. (1964) *America in Modern Italian Literature*, New Brunswick, NJ: Rutgers University Press (for a discussion of Soldati's works, see pp. 29–34 and 87–104).

Mauro, W. (1981) *Invito alla lettura di Mario Soldati* (Invitation to the Reading of Mario Soldati), Milan: Mursia (a critical overview of Soldati's works).

LAURA A. SALSINI

Soldini, Silvio

b. 1958, Milan

Film director

One of the most impressive representatives of the **New Italian Cinema**, Soldini made his directorial debut with a short entitled *Drimage* (1982), the title being a collage of three words: dream, image, and age). In 1983 he created *Paesaggio con figure* (Landscape with Shapes), but it is with his 1985 fifty-eight minute production, *Giulia in ottobre* (Julia in October) that his cinema finally acquired its distinctive form, as Soldini found his own particular characters in those individuals who live alienated lives in a desolate urban environment. This is the characteristic landscape of his first feature, *L'aria serena dell'Ovest* (The Serene Air of the West) (1990). Then, with *Un'anima divisa in due* (A Split Soul) (1993), a startling and dazzling film in which a neurotic Milanese falls desperately in love with an enigmatic gypsy, Soldini confronts a foreign culture and tries to follow alternative existential and cultural paths as the tale is, at first, formally and stylistically divided into two and then merges differences into one narrative and stylistic flow. In 1997 he directed *Le acrobate* (The Female Acrobats).

MANUELA GIERI

Solmi, Renato

b. 27 March 1927, Aosta

Editor, translator and literary critic

Solmi, like his father Sergio **Solmi**, has left behind ample testimony of his dedication as translator and literary critic. Renato Solmi's interests, however, have centred more on political–economic theory and on contemporary German philosophy, in particular the work of Adorno, Lukács, Benjamin and Brecht, which he edited and translated and thus helped to disseminate in Italy. Solmi also helped to found the journal *Discussioni* (Discussions), and from 1951–63 was editor at the **Einaudi** publishing house. He subsequently taught history and philosophy at the Liceo Scientifico Galileo Ferraris in Turin.

SHERRY ROUSH

Solmi, Sergio

b. 16 December 1899, Rieti; d. 7 October 1981, Milan

Poet, art and literary critic

After graduating in law from the University of Turin, Solmi founded the Crocean-inspired journal *Primo tempo*. His earliest critical contributions were on French literature and included studies of Alain and Montaigne. During the Second World War Solmi fought in the **Resistance** movement and was captured and imprisoned in the jail of San Vittore, which served as the backdrop for much of the poetry of his 1950 collection, titled *Poesie*. This was followed in 1956 by *Levania* and *Dal balcone* (From the Balcony) (1968). Solmi's visions of cosmic isolation, especially in these last two volumes, link his lyric work to the critical attention he dedicated to the genre of science fiction. An art

critic and translator (of among others, Valéry, Machado, W.H. Auden and Hesse), Solmi also published perceptive studies of Leopardi.

SHERRY ROUSH

Sordi, Alberto

b. 15 June 1919, Rome

Film actor

Having appeared in almost 150 films, Alberto Sordi is one of the most familiar and best-loved faces of Italian screen comedy, featuring most commonly as the protagonist of comedies 'Italian style' (see **commedia all'Italiana**) in which he typically embodies the hopelessly immature and mediocre Italian male. With many years of experience on stage and radio – and having previously worked in films both as an actor and as the Italian voice of Oliver Hardy – Sordi was already well-established as a comic actor and a box office draw when **Fellini** offered him the starring role in his first film, *Lo Sceicco bianco* (The White Sheik) (1952). The film's success led Fellini to cast Sordi as the funniest but most pathetic of the five eternal adolescents in arrested development in his next film, *I Vitelloni* (Spivs) (1953). Sordi subsequently went on to work with all the great Italian comic directors from **Monicelli** and **Comencini** to Steno and Dino **Risi**, and also directed himself in more than a dozen feature films, though none were as memorable as those in which he was directed by others.

Further reading

Fava, C.G. (1993) *Alberto Sordi: An American in Rome*, Rome: Gremese International.

GINO MOLITERNO

Sorge, Bartolomeo

b. 25 October 1929, Rio Marina, Livorno

Priest, writer and editor

One of the most influential Jesuit intellectuals in

postwar Italy, especially during the reign of **Pope Paul VI**, Sorge had a particular impact on Sicilian Catholics involved in the battle against the **mafia**. Educated in both Italy and Spain, he became a Jesuit in 1966 and edited the prestigious Jesuit fortnightly magazine, *La Civiltà Cattolica* (Catholic Civilization), from 1978 to 1985. A prolific author, his most notable works are *Capitalismo, scelta di classe e socialismo* (Capitalism, Class Choice and Socialism) (1976) and *Uscire dal tempio* (Leaving the Temple) (1989). Since 1985 he has been director of the Istituto di Formazione Politica 'Pedro Arrupe' (Institute of Political Training Pedro Arupe) and of the Centre for Social Studies in Palermo, where initially he had a powerful influence on Leoluca Orlando, the ex-DC mayor who created the breakaway party, La Rete, to fight the mafia but with whom he has since fallen out.

Further reading

Sorge, B. (1993) *I Cattolici e l'Italia che verrà* (Catholics and the Italy which is Coming), Milan: Oscar Mondadori.

JOHN POLLARD

Sottsass, Ettore

b. 14 September 1917, Innsbruck, Austria

Architect and designer

An Austrian/Italian architect designer, Sottsass, more than any other, has challenged the meaning and forms of modernism and introduced a radical note into Italian design from the 1960s onwards. He was the son of a successful rationalist architect active in Italy in the 1930s, Ettore Sot-Sas, who moved to Turin in 1928. The younger Sottsass studied architecture at the Polytechnic of Turin from 1935 to 1939. In 1947, after several years' involvement with the war effort, he established a practice in Milan, working on interiors and furniture in the first instance. The **Olivetti** company employed him in 1957 to head the design of its computer division, and he subsequently moved into the area of typewriter design. He created some of Olivetti's most notable machines at that time, among them the 'Praxis' of 1963 and the 'Tekne 3' of 1964.

As well as working on these modern technological goods, Sottsass simultaneously created ceramics and prototypes of furniture items which were influenced both by Indian mysticism and American Pop Art. These radical personal exercises strongly influenced the **anti-design** movement of the late 1960s and early 1970s, and Sottsass was regarded by many as the founder of that movement. In the late 1960s he produced an exhibition of giant ceramics and a set of furniture pieces which he called his 'Grey' series.

While his reputation as a radical designer grew apace, Sottsass continued to work for Olivetti, concentrating both on office furniture and systems in which his pop-derived ideas began to become visible as well. By the 1970s he had worked with a wide range of manufacturing companies – among them Poltronova – but at the end of that decade he made the greatest international impact of all through his work, first with **Studio Alchimia**, and subsequently with the 'Memphis' group (see **Studio Memphis**) which he set up in 1981 with a group of younger colleagues and friends from his design firm, Sottsass Associati (established a year earlier with Aldo Cibic, Marco Zanini, and Matteo Thun), and elsewhere.

The impact of the 1981 Memphis exhibition was enormous both inside and outside Italy. It showed a new, radical way forward out of the cul-de-sac of modernism and inspired many to emulate its work. Sottsass became an international figure and the hero of young designers across the globe. Memphis continued to hold annual exhibitions until 1988, while Sottsass expanded his links with international companies even further. During the 1980s he worked prolifically in the area of product design and also built a house in the USA. He continued to travel extensively and to assimilate many eclectic influences into his work. Now over eighty years old, Sottsass is still active in Milan. The length of his career is such that he has moved through the whole period of postwar Italian design and has consistently played a key, and highly individual, role within the dramatic changes that have occurred since the 1940s.

See also: interior design

Further reading

Di Castro, F. (ed.) (1976) *Sottsass' Scrap-book*, Milan: Casabella.

Radice, B. (1993) *Ettore Sottsass: A Critical Biography*, New York: Rizzoli.

Sparke, P. (1982) *Ettore Sottsass Jnr*, London: Design Council.

PENNY SPARKE

Southern Question

In essence, what has come to be known as the 'Southern Question' consists in the analysis of the economic, political, social, cultural and ethical differences between North and South and the ensuing debate on how to reduce these differences. The role of an apparently backward and economically underdeveloped South within a united Italy has always been in question, and has remained for almost a century and a half 'the most intractable issue facing the development of the Italian state and society' (Davis, 1996: 53). However, in the 1990s, the phrase 'Northern Question' has been used to describe a distorted mirror image of the Southern Question, while the Southern Question itself has undergone considerable redefinition, partly due to new studies and partly due to the growing demand for some form of federalism.

Approaches to the Southern Question have changed considerably since the 1980s, largely due to the work of the journal *Meridiana* and its associated research institute, IMES (Istituto Meridionale di Storia e Scienze Sociali, or Southern Institute of History and the Social Sciences). In these studies, the conventional image of the South as uniformly agricultural and economically backward has been gradually dismantled and a much more complex reality built up. The new studies have argued that, far from suffering from lack of economic change, the South has had too much. Furthermore, those two archetypes of a 'traditional' and even 'feudal' South, the *latifondo* (large estate; see **agriculture**) and **mafia** have been presented not as inherent southern blights but as specific modern responses to the economic problems produced by unification. These new studies have also shown how, together, the market and

state intervention as well as original conditions have created a number of very diverse 'souths'.

Nonetheless, despite the validity of these new studies and new ways of interpreting the problem, objective and major differences remain. **Unemployment** in the South at 23.6 per cent is almost double the national average of 12.4 per cent (North 6.0 per cent, centre 9.7 per cent) (ISTAT, January 1999) and thus investment and job creation in the South remain as high on the agenda of governments of the 'Second' **Republic** as they were in the 'First'. A major attitudinal change, however, has taken place in the North.

For the first time there now exists a political party, the **Lega Nord** (Northern League) which is hostile to the uncontrolled redistribution of resources from North to South and to the 'southernization' of the civil service. Furthermore, there is a growing voice of northerners in the other parties who accept many of the Northern League's premises, albeit less stridently. The economic aspect of the question has also become strongly coloured by a perception of a 'lawless' South with different cultural norms from the North and centre, a belief not based solely on the existence of organized crime (mafia, 'Ndragheta, Camorra, and so on) but on more widespread and capillary illegality, for example in the building industry and in the general distribution of public resources (see **clientelism**).

This contrasts with the way in which the Southern Question was generally perceived in most of the postwar period, during which scholars and politicians agreed that the problem was primarily economic. In their different ways, writers like Carlo **Levi**, agriculturalists and economists like Sereni, Rossi Doria and Compagna argued that once the economic imbalance between North and South had been righted, social, cultural and ethical differences would automatically be reduced, a view shared by the politicians. In fact, from the **Constituent Assembly** onwards, there came to be a consensus among Italy's political class that resources had to be transferred from North to South, although they did not always agree on how it should be done.

Already in 1944 the Communist Minister of Agriculture Fausto Gullo, himself a Calabrian, had passed a series of decrees aimed at transforming the southern peasantry. The decrees produced enormous mobilization but ended in failure because of the hostility of the **DC** and Liberals. The unrest in the southern countryside continued after the war, and the subsequent Christian Democrat-led government was forced to face agricultural reform despite opposition from the right of the party and the **PLI**. In 1950, agrarian reform laws were passed affecting Sicily and Calabria as well as parts of the centre and North. Almost half a million hectares were appropriated and distributed to landless peasants. In practice, many of the plots were not economically viable, but the reform did provide many with the necessary capital to emigrate as well as being a powerful instrument for building up electoral support for the DC.

Also in 1950, the **Cassa per il Mezzogiorno** (Southern Development Fund) was founded. Until 1957, it concentrated on creating infrastructure, including water mains and sewers, electricity, roads and railways. It then started a policy of industrialization, ambitiously aimed at the creation of 'development poles' in activities such as petrochemicals (Gela) and steel (Taranto). Though billions were spent on preparation (for example, the Gioia Tauro steelworks) many were never finished or utilized, and the abandoned projects were soon labelled 'cathedrals in the desert'. The Fund's stated brief was to provide 'extraordinary' financial support for economic development but, in the event, even more than the land reform agencies, the Fund merely developed a clientelistic network of patronage which utilized public resources for the consolidation of DC power. In 1986 the Fund was changed into the Agenzia per la Promozione e Sviluppo del Mezzogiorno (AGEN-SUD, Southern Promotion and Development Agency) but this produced no better results and in 1993 'extraordinary' intervention was finally integrated with 'ordinary' development, meaning that state funds went through the various ministries rather than a special agency. In January 1999, in line with the policy of privatizing what were formerly completely public agencies, a new company called Sviluppo Italia (Italian Development) was formed, with the task of promoting development in depressed areas throughout Italy and not just the South.

That other litmus test of the South, migration, had also changed in the meantime. Between 1946 and 1976 more than 4 million people had left the South for the North and abroad (mainly Europe). In the 1980s, the South, along with the rest of Italy, has become a place of **immigration**, mainly but not exclusively from North Africa.

The Southern Question has thus persisted, although it has changed more since the Second World War than it did since unification. It is no longer a question of rural misery and a quasi-feudal ruling class, since problems such as imbalances of wealth distribution or urban decay are not so different from the rest of the Italy, as with many other statistical indices. Furthermore, the problems of the South are coming to be analysed within a wider European context. Nevertheless, beyond the economic questions, many of which are being solved, there remain the cultural and ethical differences which provide evidence of the continuing existence of a Southern 'question'.

Further reading

Bevilacqua, P. (1993) *Breve storia dell'Italia meridionale dall'Ottocento a oggi* (Brief History of Southern Italy from the 1800s to Today), Rome: Donzelli.

Davis, J.A. (1996) 'Changing Perspectives on Italy's "Southern Problem"', in C. Levy (ed.), *Italian Regionalism: History, Identity, Politics*, Oxford: Berg.

Lumley, R. and Morris, J. (eds) (1997) *The New History of the Italian South: The Mezzogiorno Revisited*, Exeter: University of Exeter Press.

JAMES WALSTON

spaghetti westerns

'Spaghetti westerns' was the label applied by American critics, often pejoratively, to a large number of Italian versions of the western genre, which appeared between 1963 and the mid-1970s. Around 400 such films were made during this period, mostly as co-productions with other European or American companies and using, for the most part, the **Cinecittà** studios in Rome and external locations in southern Italy and Spain. The films achieved enormous popularity and box office success in Italy as well as being widely distributed abroad, encouraging not only many other local variants (Hong Kong westerns, 'curry westerns' in India, even 'borscht westerns' in Soviet Russia) but also contributing to a revival of the fortunes of the genre in the United States. In a conscious effort to appear more genuinely American, both for the US market and for local consumption, the films typically included one or two recognizably American actors while at the same time disguising the European origin of their directors and other actors under Anglo-Saxon aliases.

Some twenty westerns had already been produced at Cinecittà during 1963, but it was Sergio **Leone**'s *Per un pugno di dollari* (A Fistful of Dollars), made in 1964, that definitively launched the genre to local and international success. Departing conspicuously from the formula of the 'classic' American western, which clearly distinguished good from evil and ultimately reasserted the values of society and civilization, Leone created a much more cynical and self-serving gunslinger hero who inhabited a violent, amoral universe in which only the clever and the ruthless survived. Using long silences and extreme closeups to heighten the tension, and the powerful and haunting music of Ennio **Morricone** to punctuate the comic-strip violence, Leone created the model that he himself would use in his subsequent and extremely popular *Per qualche dollaro in più* (For a Few Dollars More) (1965), *Il buono, il brutto, il cattivo* (The Good, the Bad and the Ugly) (1966) and *C'era una volta il West* (Once Upon a Time in the West) (1968), and which would be repeated, constantly but with surprising variation, by many others who came to work in the genre. Directors such as Sergio Corbucci, Enzo Barboni, Duccio Tessari and Gianfranco Parolini created new but recognizable versions of Leone's gunslinger with no name, all of whom reappeared in a number of films so as to almost become subgenres of their own (Django, Ringo, Sartana, Trinity).

Although often regarded as mere escapist fantasy, and in some cases censored for an extreme indulgence in explicit violence, the genre also developed a more politically conscious strand such as in Damiano **Damiani**'s *Quién sabe?* (released in America as *A Bullet for the General*) (1967), written by Marxist scriptwriter Franco Solinas, and Carlo

Lizzani's *Requiescant* (1967) in which Pier Paolo **Pasolini** appeared, memorably, as a revolutionary priest.

After dominating the film industry for a decade the genre faded away in the later 1970s, although the more slapstick Trinity version, starring Terrence Hill and Bud Spencer, continued to appear sporadically well into the 1990s.

Further reading

Beatrice, L. (1996) *Al cuore, Ramon, al cuore: la leggenda del Western all'italiana* (Go for the Heart, Ramon, the Heart: The Legend of the Western Italian-style), Florence: Tarab (a thorough study of the genre which includes interviews with some of the major actors and directors).

Bondanella, P. (1983) 'A Fistful of Pasta: Sergio Leone and the Spaghetti Western', ch. 7 of *Italian Cinema from Neorealism to the Present*, New York: Ungar (a brief but comprehensive appraisal of the place of the genre in postwar Italian cinema and the key role played by Sergio Leone).

Frayling, C. (1981) *Spaghetti Westerns: Cowboys and Europeans from Karl May to Sergio Leone*, London and Boston: Routledge & Kegan Paul (the most exhaustive study of the genre available; includes a critical filmography and select bibliography).

GINO MOLITERNO

spas

A tradition which dates back to the ancient Roman era, Italian spas are internationally renowned. Italy is the European country richest in mineral and thermal springs, mostly concentrated in the North and centre (from Veneto to Emilia-Romagna and Tuscany) but with important locations also in the South, especially in Lazio, Campania and Sicily. Some *città d'acque* (water towns), such as Montecatini, Chianciano and Fiuggi, and thermal centres, the most famous of which are Abano, Salsomaggiore and Ischia, acquired their international reputation around the turn of the twentieth century. It was only in the postwar period, however, that spas gained momentum as an industrial business. Some of the most famous springs (among them Fiuggi, Sangemini, Recoaro and San Pellegrino) became leading trademarks of the emerging mineral water industry. At the same time thermal therapy, once a rather elitist privilege, was included among the health benefits either provided or subsidized by the state, thus becoming a mass phenomenon. Spas therefore quadrupled in number from 100 in the early 1950s to 400 forty years later, and came to play an important role in the tourist industry, attracting some 18 million visitors a year in the early 1990s, one-quarter of which came from abroad (especially from Germany, France and Northern Europe). In recent years, however, spa tourism has become much more sophisticated, focusing on centres that offer a wider range of opportunities – such as bathing or visits to art cities – while spa-only localities have recorded a substantial decline.

See also: tourism

STEFANO BATTILOSSI

Spatola, Adriano

b. 4 May 1941, Sapjane, Yugoslavia;
   d. 23 November 1988, Parma

Poet, novelist and critic

An active participant in the literary neoavantgarde of the 1960s, Spatola was a member of the **Gruppo 63** and collaborated on several influential journals including *il verri*, *Malebolge* and *Quindici*. His first novel, *l'Oblò*, published in 1964, won the Ferro di Cavallo prize and exemplified the new experimental approach to writing. In 1966 he published his first collection of poems, *L'ebreo negro* (The Black Jew) and in the following years he continued to experiment with visual and performance poetry, much of which was collected in *La composizione del testo* (The Composition of the Text) in 1978. In his *Verso la poesia totale* (Towards a Total Poetry) (1978), Spatola theorized what he had practised for many years: a dynamic and 'total' poetry that willingly moved beyond the limits of the word on paper to become a form of visual and performance art.

Further reading

Spatola, A. (1978) *Various Devices*, ed. and trans. P. Vangelisti, Los Angeles: Red Hill Press (a representative sample of Spatola's poetry).

GINO MOLITERNO

spazialismo

Spazialismo (spatialism) is a movement founded by Lucio **Fontana** in 1947 which stressed that space, movement and time were as important as colour, perspective and form. Fontana issued numerous manifestos for *spazialismo*, anticipating it in his *Manifesto Blanco*, published in Buenos Aires in 1946, through to his *Manifesto tecnico dello spazialismo* (Technical Manifesto of Spatialism) in 1951, and he was subsequently to refer to his own paintings of lacerated and punctured canvases as *concetti spaziali* (spatial concepts). Spatialism went beyond the surface of the canvas or the volume of a statue to include the surrounding space. In 1947, in a move that predated later environment art, Fontana painted an entire room black and entitled it *Black Spatial Environment*. On other occasions he extended the colour and form of a canvas out into the surrounding space by using new materials such as neon in something akin to later installation art.

LAURENCE SIMMONS

Spaziani, Maria Luisa

b. 7 December 1922, Turin

Poet, essayist, literary critic and translator

Professor of French literature at the University of Messina and recipient of many literary prizes, Spaziani was nominated for the Nobel Prize in 1990 for her rich poetic production. Early in her career, she founded the literary journal *Il dado* (The Die) and she later turned to poetry, publishing her first collection, *Le acque del sabato* (The Sabbath's Waters), in 1954. Spaziani's poetry is highly crafted and marked by an introspective reflection of the self and its relationship to nature and to the poetic universe. Among her many poetry collections are

Primavera a Parigi (Spring in Paris) (1954), *Geometria del disordine* (Geometry of Disorder) (1981), and *La stella del libero arbitrio* (Star of Free Will) (1986). She has also published numerous critical works on French literature, and in particular on the history of French theatre, together with Italian translations of works by, among others, Gide, Yourcenar and Cocteau. She is president of the prestigious Centro Internazionale Eugenio Montale and has been a regular contributor to the newspaper *La Stampa*.

VIRGINIA PICCHIETTI

Spazio e società

An international, bilingual (Italian/English) quarterly review for architecture and urbanism, *Spazio e società* (Space and Society) was founded in Milan in January 1978 by Giancarlo **De Carlo** – still its director/editor – and has reflected his belief that architectural issues need to be understood in both their immediate and their broader social context. Conspicuously a non-product-oriented magazine with minimum space allotted to commercial advertising, the review has sought to explore and encourage cultural diversity in architecture. The magazine's singular editorial policy, expressly announced in the first issue, has been the raising of questions much more than the provision of answers. This, together with its devotion to 'new concepts, approaches, tools and their interrelations', has set it apart from most architectural magazines, as has its stance 'against pseudo-problems and narcissistic divertissements'. A wide variety of consultants and foreign correspondents have provided intriguing and varied articles, including De Carlo's colleagues from Team X who are among the magazine's regular contributors.

See also: architectural and design magazines

GORDANA KOSTICH

Spoleto Festival

Also known as the Festival dei due mondi (The Festival of Two Worlds), the Spoleto Festival was inaugurated by composer Giancarlo **Menotti** in 1958. Since then, every June and July the small Umbrian town of Spoleto becomes the stage for an international artistic festival which includes a plethora of shows, concerts, operas and improvisation. Along with the lyric music, theatre and dance performances, there are also shows dedicated to cinema and to the visual arts. The events all take place in the welcoming spaces of the city and the festival always closes with a much awaited symphony played in the Piazza del Duomo. Concern for the future of the festival has recently been voiced by Menotti, who fears for the Duomo (cathedral) which has been threatened by the recent round of **earthquakes** which have struck the Umbria region and which have also caused considerable damage to the Basilica of St Francis in Assisi.

BERNADETTE LUCIANO

sport and society

During the last three decades there has been a steady increase in the number of active participants in Italian sports, due to Italy's improved economic status and the global trend towards a more active lifestyle, and there are now more than seventy thousands sport clubs (*società sportive*) throughout the country. The majority of these clubs function thanks to a network of volunteers, and belong to specific federations which, in turn, are under the control of CONI (the Italian Olympic committee), the central organization that promulgates all the regulations.

It was during the Fascist regime that the first attempts were made to make sporting activities part of everyday life, a move typical of authoritarian rulers who conceive of sport in terms of identification with the regime and as a tool of social control. To this end, CONI was integrated into the Fascist party, and in 1927 an academy was founded to train teachers of physical education who would promote a mixture of gymnastic and military drills in the school system. These efforts produced mixed results. It is true that Italy obtained some great successes in international competitions, such as the Olympic Games of 1932 and 1936 (second and third nation overall, respectively), and the victories in **football**'s World Cup in 1934 and 1938. Nevertheless, in spite of all official efforts, widespread popular participation in sport did not really take root during the Fascist regime.

After the Second World War, following a decree that sanctioned the elimination of the Fascist party and of all fascist organizations, Giulio Onesti was given the task of liquidating CONI. However, Onesti soon understood that the absence of a central ruling organization could jeopardize the future of organized sports in Italy. Onesti was able to convince the new political powers of the need to save CONI and was subsequently elected CONI's president, a position he held until 1977. During his mandate, he reorganized the entire structure of Italian sports and contrived a system of lotteries linked to the week's football scores, which to this day provide much of the financial support for the activities of CONI.

A renewed effort to make sports an integral part of the school curriculum led to an agreement between CONI and the Ministry of Education (Ministero della Pubblica Istruzione). Through the Gruppi Sportivi Scolastici (School Sporting Groups), competitive sports were introduced into secondary schools. In 1969, a sort of Olympic Games for secondary schools, called Giochi della Gioventù (Youth Games) were instituted, soon becoming a showcase for the best junior athletes. Once again, though, the success of the school programme was limited, primarily because of a lack of proper facilities along with the limited time allotted for out of class activities (until the late 1970s–early 1980s Italian schools operated only in the morning). Thus, for the great majority of Italians, involvement with organized sports activities begins and continues outside the school system. Catholic organizations have been very active in the promotion of sports, through the network of the *oratori*. The *oratorio* is an enclosed and supervised space attached to most churches which typically includes football fields, basketball and volleyball courts, along with a number of indoor activities. In most cases, especially in the years prior to the 1960s, these were the only sports facilities available to young people in Italy.

Since 1944, the various leagues and tournaments that are part of the *oratori* system have been organized by the CSI (Centro Sportivo Italiano). The functioning of both the *oratori* and the non-Catholic sport clubs is made possible in part by the commitment of an estimated 500,000 volunteers who serve as coaches, referees, judges and administrators. The various military organizations (the **armed forces**, **police**, *carabinieri*, *guardia di finanza*) have also played an important role in the Italian sports panorama. Athletes specializing in those Olympic disciplines which do not have a popular following often find in the military the means of support that allow them to continue their careers. It is an investment that has consistently paid dividends: more than half of the medals obtained by Italy in the Olympic Games between 1960 and 1994 came from athletes belonging to one of the military or police forces.

According to statistical data released by CONI, which took into consideration the ten most popular sport and leisure activities (football, hunting, fishing, **basketball**, **volleyball**, **tennis**, **winter sports**, *bocce*, track and field, and motorcycles), as of 1990 more than four and a half million Italians were registered members of sports clubs. In terms of numbers, football remains by far the most popular sport in Italy, involving 25 per cent of total active participants, the great majority of whom are males. The increase in female participation in the last decades, however, has been particularly significant. The percentage of women practising sports moved from less than 10 per cent of the total in the late 1950s to over one-third in 1985. Female participation is especially concentrated in volleyball, basketball, tennis and track and field, a factor that contributed to the exponential growth of these sports (from just over 200,000 official combined members in 1974 to well over a million in 1990). This increase in the number of participants and spectators determined an increase in the revenues generated by all those businesses that, in one way or the other, revolve around Italian sport. In the decade 1979–89, the finances linked to sport activities such as ticket sales, sports apparel, membership in fitness club and so on increased by 60 per cent.

The coverage of sports by the media is another area of continuous growth. The three sports dailies (see **sports publications**) achieve a distribution of at least one million copies, which accounts for one-fifth of all daily newspapers. Until the late 1970s, **RAI** (the state television) had a complete monopoly on all television broadcasting and its sports offerings were very limited (see **sports broadcasting**). The situation changed with the advent of private televisions, mainly controlled by Silvio **Berlusconi**'s **Fininvest** group. Berlusconi challenged RAI's exclusive right to broadcast sport events nationally (particularly football and cycling) and began to diversify the programming of his three television channels to attract new audiences. As a result, sports that were either only practised by an elite or completely unknown to Italian audiences (such as golf or American football), are now part of the typical broadcast of Italian televisions.

Further reading:

Porro, N. (1995) *Identità, nazione, cittadinanza. Sport, società e sistema politico nell'Italia contemporanea* (Identity, Nation, Citizenship: Sport, Society and Political System in Contemporary Italy), Rome: SEAM (a study of the use made of sport and sports organizations by the Italian governments).

PAOLO VILLA

sports broadcasting

The first live radio broadcast of a sporting event in Italy was that of a boxing match held in Milan in 1928. Although coverage has always been guaranteed for the main events of almost every sport (especially **boxing**, **tennis** and **motor racing**), broadcasting in Italy has always been primarily dedicated to **football** matches and, during the Giro d'Italia and the Tour de France, to **cycling**.

Television broadcasting in Italy made its official debut on 1 January 1954. *La domenica sportiva* (Sunday Sports News) appeared just two days later, and today remains one of the main sports programmes. In the beginning, *La domenica sportiva* consisted mainly of the highlights of the day's football matches. In addition, every Sunday evening the national channel of the **RAI** (Italy's only national television channel until 1961), also broadcast a recording of half of a football match.

Both programmes went on air well after the end of the matches, so the only chance for millions of eager football fans to follow the exploits of their favourite teams in real time was to turn to the **radio**. Men carrying small battery-operated radios during Sunday outings with their families became a very common sight in Italy. The radios were tuned to *Tutto il calcio minuto per minuto* (All the Football, Minute by Minute), a programme which offered live coverage of the second half of every Serie A match and of the most important Serie B matches. In 1970, another Sunday television programme, *Novantesimo minuto* (90th Minute), began showing the goals and highlights of the day's Serie A matches only a few minutes after their conclusion. Until the mid-1990s, however, no Italian league football match could be broadcast live. Live coverage of football was provided only for the national team's matches and for matches in the various European competitions for club teams. The most famous names connected with the reporting and broadcasting of football throughout the period were Niccoló Carosio, Nando Martellini, Bruno Pizzul, Sandro Ciotti, Enrico Ameri and the legendary Gianni **Brera**.

Cycling has also been an important feature of Italian sports broadcasting, with radio and television coverage of every main race, be it on Italian territory or abroad. Usually the live broadcast starts within an hour of the finish and continues after the race with interviews of the day's protagonists. Broadcaster Adriano De Zan, a legend in his own right for his ability to recognize without fail all the racers and recite their full biographical data and career accomplishments, has been entertaining and informing cycling aficionados for over forty years.

As for other sports, motor racing, track and field, **basketball**, boxing and **winter sports** are among those that receive steady attention from the Italian media. Until the late 1970s and early 1980s, RAI, the Italian government-controlled radio and television organization, held a monopoly over television broadcasting. With the advent of privately owned television networks, sports offerings also increased, including the broadcasts of previously neglected foreign events (American NBA and college basketball and NFL football among the most popular ones) along with alternatives to RAI's coverage of Italian sports. Eventually, private networks were able to cut into RAI's exclusive deals with Italy's major sport federations (such as FIGC) to secure their own live and taped coverage and even pay-per-view broadcasting.

PAOLO VILLA

sports publications

There are more than 300 sports publications in Italy. They range from three nationally circulated dailies to specialized periodicals in every imaginable sports and leisure activity: **football**, **cycling**, **tennis**, rugby, squash, chess, hiking, fishing, billiards and so on.

La Gazzetta dello Sport, founded 1897, is the oldest of the sports dailies. Published in Milan, it covers all major sports, but devotes substantial coverage to the town's two Serie A football teams, to the Ferrari racing team (see **motor racing**), and to cycling. *La Gazzetta dello Sport* is the organizer of the Giro d'Italia, and the winner of the Giro wears *la maglia rosa* (the pink jersey), the same colour as the pages of the *Gazzetta*.

The other two dailies (similar in format to *La Gazzetta*) are *Tuttosport* and *Corriere dello Sport-Stadio*. The first, published in Turin, focuses on the Piedmont and Liguria regions. The second (originally two separate papers, *Corriere dello Sport* from Rome and *Stadio* from Bologna) follows more closely the events of central and southern Italy. The combined circulation of these three sports newspapers reaches more than a million copies a day. The very presence of these dailies and their circulation numbers are a clear indication indicate that, for a great number of Italians, sporting news take precedence over politics and current events.

The weekly *Il Guerin Sportivo*, founded 1912, presents extensive summaries of all professional football matches, complete with colour photos of the most salient moments. Many periodicals are dedicated to football, including monthly publications which deal exclusively with the games, players and activities of a specific major soccer team. *I giganti del basket* (The Basketball Giants), a weekly publication started in 1966, contains articles on Italian, European and American **basketball**.

In addition to the coverage they receive from the dailies, cycling fans find information about races, athletes and the latest technological innovation in monthly periodicals such as *Bicisport* and *Bicicletta*. *Motociclismo*, founded 1914, offers news about two- and three-wheel motor vehicles, including races, test results and prices. *Gente Motori* provides a similar service for the automobile industry, along with articles on boats and boating. *Multisport*, directed by former marathon champion Marco Marchei, caters to the growing number of participants in multisport events such as duathlon and triathlon.

PAOLO VILLA

Squarzina, Luigi

b. 18 February 1922, Livorno

Theatre director

A prominent and influential figure in the postwar Italian theatre through his work as director (but also as playwright, critic, editor and translator), Squarzina's familiarity with contemporary American theatre made him a particularly important cultural conduit (he had been a Fulbright Fellow at the Yale Drama School in the early 1950s). He introduced Italian theatregoers to a number of American plays, but was also renowned for his productions of Brecht, and for reviving the work of Goldoni and of Pirandello (who had suffered from his identification with fascism in the prewar period).

Squarzina graduated from the National Academy of Dramatic Art in Rome shortly after the end of the war, and began by directing contemporary plays. After returning from America he began a long and distinguished career as director, first at the Teatro Stabile at Genoa (1962–76) and then at the Teatro di Roma (1976–83), where some of his most memorable productions, of contemporary and classic texts, were done.

In this period he also directed a number of his own plays, to considerable popular and critical acclaim. His 1959 play *Romagnola* (The Woman from Romagna) uses a large cast in a series of episodes which span the final fifteen years of fascism, and its treatment of large-scale social movements and use of songs to punctuate the action reveals the influence of Brecht on its playwright and director. Both his own plays and his other productions reflect a leftist political viewpoint; he is interested in the dialectical social forces at play in the historical process, and his characters reflect this in the emphasis placed on their positioning within the dynamics of historical process rather than on their individual psychological states and reactions.

Squarzina was also for a considerable period the chief supervizing editor of the comprehensive and influential *Enciclopedia dello spettacolo* (Encyclopedia of Theatre), for which he used to outstanding effect the theatre-historical research methodology he had been exposed to under Alois Nagler at Yale.

See also: theatre directors

Further reading

Squarzina, L. (1988) *Da Dionisio a Brecht* (From Dionysius to Brecht), Bologna: Il Mulino (Squarzina's view of theatre and its history).

TIM FITZPATRICK

La Stampa

Founded in Turin in 1867, *La Stampa*'s history and identity is closely bound up with that of the regional capital. The sole shareholder is a subsidiary of the **Fiat** motor company. While the paper is distributed throughout Italy and abroad, its readership of around 400,000 is concentrated in Piedmont and its attempts to create a more national image for itself have frequently met with resistance. During the 1950s and 1960s this *campanilismo* (provincialism) sometimes took racist forms. However, the politics of *La Stampa* did become more enlightened, and in later times it severely criticized both **Berlusconi** and the **Lega Nord** (Northern League). Significantly, later top appointments were to include former members of the **extraparliamentary Left** group, Lotta Continua. *La Stampa* has also maintained serious coverage of cultural matters, giving ample space to the activities of the Turin intelligentsia.

See also: newspapers

ROBERT LUMLEY

STET

A telecommunication holding of the state-owned group **IRI**, STET was established in 1933 in order to coordinate three companies which operated public telephone utilities in northern and central Italy. By 1955 STET was able to take over the last of the private companies and thus bring the whole national system under its financial control, while operating management would be later concentrated in SIP (a former electricity company which had been nationalized in 1962).

Under state monopoly, telephone services were totally reorganized. This proved an enormous task, as the system was technologically backward and telephone density was well below the European average. However, telephones took off spectacularly during 1960s, when private consumers increased from 1.5 million users to more than 4 million. STET and SIP invested heavily, aiming principally to develop the trunk network and fill the North–South phone gap. This proved to be a decision of overwhelming social significance, since long-distance calls had become a major means of maintaining family links between thousands of emigrants in the North and their relatives in the South (see **economic miracle**).

Phone services were further improved in the 1970s with the introduction of an integral direct dialling system for calls abroad (only the Netherlands and Germany had reached the same level at that time). In the 1980s, digital technologies were introduced and the network of optical fibre cables was extended so that, finally, in the 1990s, mobile phones became commonplace. In 1994 SIP was renamed Telecom Italia. It successfully promoted the mobile phone business (through its subsidiary TIM, Telecom Italia Mobile) and then was privatized in 1997 in the largest privatization to be ever carried out. At the same time, in compliance with the **European Union**'s directives regarding liberalization, competition was introduced, forcing Telecom Italia, now controlled by IFI (a financial holding of the Agnelli group –

see **Agnelli family**) and its private allies (a group of major banks and insurance companies) to give up part of its monopoly, although the Italian government retained a golden share with special voting rights. Finally, a new independent telecommunications authority was instituted in 1998 with the task of further liberalizing the market and regulating both telecommunications and other integrated business such as television, cable and digital communications.

At the beginning of 1999, Telecom Italia, now a diversified group operating in all sectors of the information business but entangled in managerial infighting and strategic confusion since its privatization, was taken over by **Olivetti**, its main rival both in mobile and fixed-line phones. It was the biggest ever hostile takeover bid in Europe, which Telecom attempted to resist by launching a merger plan with Deutsche Telekom, a state-owned German giant. The move, however, proved to be in vain.

STEFANO BATTILOSSI

Stile Industria

The magazine *Stile Industria* joined **Domus** magazine at a key moment in the history of modern Italian design. Edited throughout its relatively short life (1953–63) by Alberto **Rosselli**, it represented to an international audience the rigorous standards of Italian industrial design in the period of economic and cultural reconstruction. Its striking photographs, which treated even such mundane objects as plastic buckets as objects of sculpture worthy of a presence on a plinth in an art gallery, helped to spread the strong neomodern formalism and high cultural status that characterized Italian design at that time. The magazine's demise in the early 1960s was a sign of the end of an era in which designers had played a vital and unquestioning role within the Italian economic and cultural status quo.

See also: architectural and design magazines

Further reading

Klaus Koenig, G. *et al.* (1981) *Stile Industria: Alberto Rosselli*, Parma: Artegrafica Silva.

PENNY SPARKE

Storaro, Vittorio

b. 24 June 1940, Rome

Cinematographer

A 1960 graduate of Rome's **Centro Sperimentale di Cinematografia**, Vittorio Storaro is one of the most gifted cinematographers of his generation. His career was launched in 1969 when he began collaborating with his former fellow student at the Centro, Bernardo **Bertolucci**. Since then, Storaro's eye has consistently explored new territories, at once extending and renewing the excellence of his technical expertise and scholarship. Each of his films focuses on one particular aspect of his medium. The result has been a series of dazzling concertos: concerto for camera movement in *La strategia del ragno* (The Spider's Strategy) (1969), concerto for lenses and angles in *Il conformista* (The Conformist) (1970), concerto for colour in *Ultimo tango a Parigi* (Last Tango in Paris) (1972) and concerto for framing in *Novecento* (1900) (1976). After his brilliant contribution to Francis Ford Coppola's *Apocalypse Now* (1976), Storaro was seduced by the Hollywood sirens and has been working in the United States since 1980. However, his crew has remained entirely Italian as he attempts to disseminate the Italian aesthetic tradition at the heart of the Hollywood machine.

DOROTHÉE BONNIGAL.

strategia della tensione

The *strategia della tensione* (strategy of tension) is a term widely used to indicate the increased use of violence by extreme Right groups between 1969 and 1975 in an attempt to reverse the democratization achieved by the student and worker movements of 1967–9. Since at least the early 1960s right-wing extremism had attracted sympathizers of senior rank in the **armed forces** and security services, who claimed that the unrecognized advance of communism in every institution was undermining Italian society. The right-wing coup in Greece in 1967 added another authoritarian regime to Italy's Mediterranean neighbours (Spain and Portugal), and raised both hopes and fears that Italy might follow. The main right-wing groups such as Ordine Nuovo (New Order) and Avanguardia Nazionale (National Avantgarde) were endorsed by the leaders of the **MSI** who simultaneously encouraged the extremists' largely uncoordinated violence as a way of increasing social tensions and demanded an authoritarian response to the demonstrable collapse of social order. The most lethal elements of the 'strategy' were the bombs placed in cities and trains across Italy between 1969 and 1974 (see **fascism and neo-fascism**; **Piazza Fontana**; **terrorism**). Subsequently, most active conspirators used their high-level protection in Italy and abroad to frustrate judicial investigations and evade conviction.

Further reading

Borraccetti, V. (ed) (1986) *Eversione di destra, terrorismo, stragi* (Right-wing Subversion, Terrorism, Massacres), Milan: F. Angeli (panoramic account of right-wing groups and their responsibilities).

Ferraresi, F. (1996) *Threats to Democracy: The Radical Right in Italy after the War*, Princeton, NJ: Princeton University Press (chaps 3–6 analyse the origins and development of the strategy of tension).

DAVID MOSS

Strehler, Giorgio

b. 15 August 1921, Barcola, Trieste; d. 25 December 1997, Lugano

Theatre director

The most important theatrical figure to come out of Italy since the Second World War, Giorgio Strehler is renowned as a director (particularly of Goldoni, Pirandello, Shakespeare and Brecht) and as the inspiration of the company he founded. In a theatre-industrial context which had relied for three hundred years on touring companies, limited rehearsal periods and stock sets, Strehler set up the first *teatro stabile* or permanent resident company, the Piccolo Teatro di Milano, shortly after the end of the war. The company accumulated a long and rich history of productions, often reworked and returned to the repertory after long absences, and over the span of forty years brought a new level of excellence and professionalism to Italian theatre. Strehler's productions were marked by intellectual rigour and a brilliant use of design elements which, despite their overwhelming visual impact, contributed substantially to – rather than distracted from – the director's overarching vision.

Strehler was born into a musical family, and his childhood ambitions lay in the direction of music, but an interest in theatre led him to train as a drama student in Milan before the war. His early influences were French (fruit of his wartime exile in Switzerland), and towards the end of the war he founded a French-inspired company in Geneva. Returning to Milan after the war, he and Paolo Grassi set up the Piccolo Teatro di Milano in a disused cinema. He directed the company initially until 1968, insisting on the need for a permanent company of actors and proper rehearsal periods to achieve artistic integrity and high production values. He thus succeeded in turning the Piccolo into one of the most influential companies in Europe, directing a vast range of plays during this period. Some of his Goldoni, Pirandello, Shakespeare and Brecht productions justifiably became legendary: *Arlecchino servitore di due padroni* (Harlequin, Servant of Two Masters) was premièred in 1947 (and the production was revived and substantially revised a number of times after); *The Tempest* was first produced in 1948, Pirandello's masterpiece *Sei personaggi in cerca d'autore* (Six Characters in Search of an Author) in 1953, and Brecht's *Galileo* in 1963.

Underlying these theatrically stunning and intellectually rigorous productions was a view of theatre as – in Strehler's own words – the 'three Chinese boxes':

In the first box we approach the play on the level of reality: that is to say through the story of a family, its life at a particular moment; in the second we shift to a historical level and in the conflict and struggles of the individual characters we see reflected the social and political conflicts of the period; in the third we are operating in the context of universal – let us call them abstract – values.

(Strehler, *Il Corriere della sera*, 14 May 1974)

This concern with ordinary human affairs on three levels (as individual, as instances of wider political and social issues, and as emblematic of more general universal preoccupations) is the connecting thread which draws together his productions: the challenge he sets himself – and achieves more often than not – is to realize all three perspectives in equal depth.

Away from the Piccolo between 1968 and 1972, he founded the Gruppo Teatro e Azione (Theatre and Action Group), whose name indicates a mission of developing a more politicized and socially involved theatre. On his return to the Piccolo he produced his renowned *King Lear*, which re-examined the Shakespearean text in the light of Samuel Beckett: a simple, sparse staging centred on a circular enclosure of grey sand.

In 1982 Strehler's focus shifted to Paris, when he became one of the artistic directors of the Théâtre de l'Europe. Strehler had already opened the Théâtre in 1978 with a new production of *The Tempest* which provided stunning visual effects, but his more definitive move onto the European 'stage' was prompted, at least in part, by the difficulties he was having at this time persuading the Milanese authorities to contribute to solving what had become a perennial problem for the successful Piccolo: a permanent theatre that was big enough to cater for its audiences

A distinguishing feature of Strehler's career has been his persistent return to direct new productions of texts already in the repertoire of the Piccolo. The best case in point is *Harlequin, Servant of Two Masters*, which has punctuated, even dominated, Strehler's theatrical production. It has remained in the repertory of the Piccolo since the original 1947 production, being reworked and developed no less

than five times. In 1952 he developed more systematically the comic *lazzi* or gags from the *commedia dell'arte*; in 1956 he added a 'play outside the play', simply by having the performers not leave the stage between their scenes so the audience could witness their 'offstage' behaviour. For an open air production in 1963, this 'off stage' reality of the actors was further reinforced, the stage space being flanked by the two carts of the families who made up the 'company'. An entirely different fifth production in 1977 was suffused with decadence and decay, as the tired and ageing members of the 'company' performed in a dingy indoors venue. In the final 1987 production the 'cast' was rejuvenated and the action vivacious, in a simple, sparse setting that has become one of Strehler's trademarks.

His work on Brechtian texts is of particular interest. Strehler directed half a dozen of Brecht's plays, including two *Lehrstücke*, but of greater significance is the evidence of the influence of Brecht's theories of acting in his other productions such as *Coriolanus* or *King Lear*. Brecht's techniques of epic acting to create a detached intensity in the actor are in stark contrast to the emotive and passionate acting style which Strehler and his actors inherited from the Italian tradition, so the significance of this achievement is not to be underestimated.

Strehler has also been a prominent director of **opera** at **La Scala**; among his numerous productions (Mozart, Verdi, Wagner), Verdi's *Macbeth* and *Simon Boccanegra* have been the most favourably received.

See also: theatre directors

Further reading

Hirst, D.L. (1993) *Giorgio Strehler*, Cambridge: Cambridge University Press (an overview of Strehler's career and significance, with bibliography and list of productions).

Moscati, I. (1985) *Strehler, vita e opere di un regista europeo* (Strehler: Life and Works of a European Director), Brescia: Camunia (a biography concentrating on Strehler's theatrical career).

Strehler, G. (1974) *Per un teatro umano* (Towards a

Human Theatre), Milan: Feltrinelli (Strehler's views on theatre and its function).

TIM FITZPATRICK

student movement

Along with industrial workers, students were among the most crucial actors in the protest movements of the late 1960s and early 1970s. The earliest signs of student unrest in Italian universities became manifest in the mid-1960s. University buildings were occupied by students in Pisa (1965), Trento (1966) and Turin (1967). Protest activities also took place on other campuses across the country. These early mobilizations were largely reform-oriented and restricted to issues such as rises in tuition fees, poor quality of university estates and forms of student representation on university governing bodies. Even the organizational forms of the embryonic movement showed a certain similarity to established political organizations: for example, among the promoters and coordinators of the protests were many members of UNURI (Unione Nazionale Universitaria Rappresentativa, or Representative National University Union), a body which united and represented student organizations of all political persuasions.

It did not take long, however, for the movement to gain momentum and to spread from the universities to secondary schools. The bureaucratic model of traditional organizations like UNURI was soon rejected in favour of looser organizational forms. Emphasis was placed on the individuals' contribution to the movement and the *assemblea* (general meeting) came to be regarded as the only structure able to truly reflect students' will. A more radical agenda was also adopted, with established academic culture and the knowledge produced by universities coming under attack as purely functional to the interests of dominant groups. Decision-making procedures in the universities were labelled as authoritarian and student involvement was demanded in all decisions, including professorial appointments. Access to university was portrayed as class-biased, and demands were made for substantial 'rights to education' in the form of

grants, free accommodation and so on for members of the lower classes.

In a further step, these and related demands became part of a more organic critique of bourgeois society and of the bourgeois state. Issues of social inequality, and the critique of the relationship between education and class domination, quickly replaced anti-authoritarian and countercultural themes as the major focus of the movement's activities. Already in late 1968 and early 1969 the dominant language within the movement was the language of class struggle. Students were regarded as a specific social group, occupying a subordinate – albeit temporary – position in the social structure. This was held to be particularly, but not exclusively, true for students from the lower classes.

Consequently, as a result of the dominance of a class perspective within the student movement, new types of rigid, bureaucratic organizations, many of them close to radical versions of Marxism, developed and gradually took control of the movement's activities. Groups of the **extraparliamentary Left** – among others, Lotta Continua, Avanguardia Operaia, Potere Operaio – were largely inspired by a Leninist model of political organization, even if with varying degrees of rigidity. They increasingly took up coordination roles, and reduced students' general meetings to purely ritual exercises.

As a further consequence, exclusive emphasis was placed on the political and public dimension of student activism. Comparatively, little attention was paid to conflicts and changes in the private sphere, in striking contrast especially to the US movements, where the countercultural dimension was particularly strong. Intergenerational conflicts, relationships between gender groups, attitudes towards sexuality and so on, while central to the everyday life of movement activists, were largely ignored by New Left organizations and leaders. Countercultural groups like Re Nudo played some role in urban areas but their wider impact was limited. This was despite the fact that the student movement had originated out of a broader trend towards cultural innovation among the younger generations (as witnessed, for example, by changes in fashion, popular music and so on); and that major controversial issues had consistently included moral issues like teenagers' sexual conduct (a prominent example being the court action taken in 1967 against a few Milanese high school students, who had published an article in their student magazine addressing precisely that topic).

The student movement was also close to its working-class counterparts in its repertoire of action. Public gatherings, rallies and marches were all widely used by students. So was the occupation of schools and universities, once again by analogy with the occupation of factories by striking workers. However, there were also a number of innovations as, for example, in the widespread use of sit-ins which Italian students borrowed from the American civil rights and anti-Vietnam war movements. Significantly, although the degree of disruption and confrontation was high, mass violence was originally not an explicit tactical option for the movement, though its relative importance grew stronger as the cycle of protest entered its declining phase and students' mobilization potential decreased in 1972–3.

Recourse to violence was fuelled and legitimized in the eyes of many students by the violent repressive tactics adopted by **police** at that time. A taste of what was to come in the following years was the so called 'Valle Giulia battle' in March 1968, when students from Rome University not only successfully withstood a police baton charge but actually forced the police to retreat. Another reason for the escalation of violence was the increasing conflict between left-wing and right-wing organizations, much, if not all, generated by assaults on student meetings and left-wing activists by neo-fascist groups. Students' radicalization was also hastened by growing suspicion about complicities between sectors of the state – in particular the police, **intelligence services**, the military and sometimes even the judiciary – and elements of the extreme right. In particular, the Milan bombing massacre in December 1969 (see **Piazza Fontana**) and the state's response to it led many activists in the movement to fear for Italian democracy. The bombings also strengthened activists' view that a new **Resistance** struggle, similar to the one waged against Nazism and fascism by the 'old' Italian Left thirty years earlier, was looming ahead. Concern about state response and neo-fascist activities combined with the myth

of armed struggle and revolutionary violence, popular among significant sectors of the New Left, caused thousands of former members of the movement to gravitate towards fully-fledged **terrorism** by the end of the 1970s.

A peculiarity of the Italian student movement was that it lasted far longer than its counterparts in other Western countries. This was due, at least in part, to the presence of extraparliamentary organizations rather than to the intrinsic momentum of the more informal student mobilizations, which had run out of steam by 1970. It was also due to the fact that students' organizations had managed to establish significant, if often contentious, relationships with working-class organizations and traditional left-wing parties. Ever since the 'hot autumn' of 1969, when worker protest rose to unprecedented levels, student organizations were keen to play a supportive role in industrial action. In turn, they also tried to bring working-class points of view into university life. There were particularly intense contacts with, amongst others, the new grassroots working-class organizations connected to 'factory councils', which had developed in those years as a critical response to the moderatism and bureaucraticism of the traditional unions. Extraparliamentary groups actually reflected the joint presence of student and working-class cadres, the latter often having no previous experiences of industrial action in established **trade unions**. Ties between the student movement, New Left groups and the Communist Party were similarly strong, though often unacknowledged. In fact, despite criticism of the **PCI**'s alleged moderatism, the students, the New Left and the Communist Party all shared symbolic codes and fundamental values, as well as the perception of being part of a common effort to change the structure of Italian society. The debt of the student movement to the Catholic tradition should also not be overlooked. Many activists in student and New Left organizations had previously been active in Catholic organizations, including mainstream ones such as **Catholic Action**. Attention to the negative effects of colonial rule over Third World countries, to the persistence of poverty in areas untouched by the Italian **economic miracle** and to the role of education in reproducing social inequalities, was not restricted to left-wing parties and unions. Critical figures in the Catholic world, from Lorenzo Milani to Ernesto Balducci, contributed to fusing Catholic ideals and social criticism.

By the mid-1970s, the entire social movement experienced a deep crisis. Most activists demobilized and turned back to more mundane affairs; in a minority of cases, to drugs and self-destruction. Most of those who did not lose interest in politics became institutionalized, joining traditional left-wing parties and unions, or transforming extra-parliamentary groups into New Left parties, as in the case of **Democrazia Proletaria** (Proletarian Democracy), which went on to contest all national elections between 1976 and 1987. Other militants turned to terrorism, and only a handful remained active in movement organizations. The last major outburst of student revolt, before the country entered a different political phase in the 1980s, took place in 1977. Government proposals to reform higher education spurred a new wave of demonstrations on most university campuses. Confrontation quickly escalated into open violence and mass disruption. Students were killed by police during demonstrations in Rome and Bologna; in the latter case with devastating symbolic consequences, given Bologna's status as the capital city of communism 'Italian style.'

The 1977 movement differed from the post-1968 student mobilizations in a variety of ways. First of all, there was no linkage to traditional left-wing organizations. Following its resounding success in local elections in 1975 and national elections in 1976, the Communist Party was close to taking government and so, keen to avoid any shadow or suspicion of democratic unaccountability, it sought to sever its ties with the extraparliamentary Left. The need for such a distance had become ever stronger with the spread of terrorist activities. The PCI's support of police repression of the Bologna movement and its labelling of the whole radical Left as a liability for Italian democracy were inspired by just such preoccupations.

Even the linkage to traditional values of the Left was thin at best for members of the 1977 movement. For example, in direct contrast to the basic tenets of the workers' movements, work was dismissed as a source of oppression rather than

dignity. Concepts like party discipline and respect of hierarchy, so crucial to revolutionaries in the orthodox Left tradition, were similarly disregarded or overturned. While the post-1968 student movement stressed the role of students as a section of an enlarged – and no matter how much redefined – working class, the 1977 movement conceived of them as part of the most marginal social groups. The overlaps between student actions and the activities of alternative centres in the urban peripheries which organized marginal youth with no specific educational background bear this out. Even the forms of revolt reflected this shift. The 1977 movement repertoire, when not explicitly violent and contentious, consisted mostly of symbolic forms of challenge and irony and satire, and the adoption of lifestyles regarded as outrageous by the majority of citizens, including those with leftist sympathies, played a far greater role than in the post-1968 movements. These explicitly counter-cultural traits, combined with the unfavourable political situation created by the increase in terrorism and the greater integration of the Communist Party into institutional politics, prevented the consolidation of the movement along lines similar to those followed by the student movement of the previous years. The 1977 movement was in many respects more than a student movement; it was a youth movement with a strong countercultural component. It was also an opportunity to address themes (such as the relationship between public engagement and the pursuit of personal happiness; between private and public identities; between humankind and nature; between work and leisure; between individuals and organizations) which had been largely sidelined by the bureaucratic transformation of post-1968 organizations; and which were being elaborated in the same years by the women's or the **environmental movement**, albeit sometimes in very different ways. This was probably its strongest legacy.

See also: Radio Alice; universities

Further reading

Della Porta, D. (1995) *Social Movements, Political*

Violence, and the State, Cambridge: Cambridge University Press.

Lumley, R. (1990) *States of Emergency: Cultures of Revolt in Italy from 1968 to 1978*, London: Verso.

Melucci, A. (ed.) (1984) *Altri codici. Aree di movimento nella metropoli* (Alternative Codes: Social Movements in Metropolitan Areas), Bologna: Il Mulino (especially chapters by Grazioli and Lodi, and Melucci).

Tarrow, S. (1989) *Democracy and Disorder*, Oxford: Clarendon Press.

MARIO DIANI

Studio Alchimia

Established in 1976 by Alessandro Guerriero, Studio Alchymia (as it was first called) was an attempt to provide a forum for members of the **anti-design** movement of the late 1960s together with a new generation of radical designers who sought to use design as a form of cultural commentary and criticism rather than a hand-maiden for the capitalist status quo. As such, it allied itself to the world of fine art by using the gallery as a site for display. Early members included Donatella Biffi, Pier Carlo Bontempi, Carla Ceccariglia, Stefano Casciani, Tina Corti, Walter Garro, Bruno Gregori and Patrizia Scarzella, and the first years were spent on experimentation around the theme of the mass replication of images.

The studio first made an impact through two exhibitions, held in 1979 and 1980, which were called, ironically, BauHaus 1 and BauHaus 2 and which made use of kitsch, recycled objects and popular imagery to make its critique of modernism. It also exhibited a show in Linz. Famous icons from these years included Alessandro **Mendini**'s 'Poltrone Proust', which made visual reference to a painting by Seurat, and a number of pieces by Andrea **Branzi** which referred to classic Italian designs from the 1930s. These pieces shocked the Milanese design establishment and were published widely in the international press.

Studio Alchimia (as it later called itself) acted as an open forum, as well as an active studio, allowing several designers to associate themselves with it. In 1981 Mendini launched his 'Mobile Infinito' (infinite furnishing) at a 'happening' which coincided with the annual Milan Furniture Fair. Collaborating with fine artists, he attempted to remove the designer as all-powerful manipulator in the design process by developing pieces of decorative detailing which could be moved about by the consumer/user of the pieces. Michele de Lucchi also collaborated with Alchimia, showing his maquettes for a series of electrical domestic appliances which looked more like toys than tools.

Among other active collaborations, including ones with the designer Daniela Puppa, Paola Navone and the older architectural duo, the Hausmanns, perhaps the most significant one was with Ettore **Sottsass**, who saw the opportunity to start making radical design statements again. The second half of the 1970s had been relatively quiet ones for Sottsass, but he had an active spurt from 1979 onwards, producing a range of furniture pieces for Alchimia which used plastic laminate decorated with imagery derived from popular culture, especially that of the 1950s, the heroic period of Italian design. Alchimia faded from view in the later 1980s, eclipsed by the spin-off studio, **Studio Memphis**.

Further reading

Bontempi, P.C. and Gregori, G. (1986) *Alchimia 1977–8*, Turin: Allemandi.

Sparke, P. (1981) *Ettore Sottsass Jnr*, London: Design Council.

Studio Alchimia (1980) *Bauhaus Collection 1980–1*, Milan: Alchimia Editore.

PENNY SPARKE

Studio Memphis

Memphis was the name given to a group of designers working with Ettore **Sottsass** in Milan who presented a show in conjunction with the Milan Furniture Fair of September 1981, which shocked the international design establishment and influenced the course of '**anti-design**' through the rest of that decade. Based upon ideas that Sottsass had already developed during his long career (a rejection of 'Italian chic', anti-modernism, the importance of decoration and symbolism and the use of design in a gallery setting to provoke and challenge the status quo), a group of young designers who were all attached to him in one way or another – Aldo Cibic, Marco Zanini, George Sowden, Nathalie du Pasquier, Michele de Lucchi and others – presented a group show of furniture, fabrics, ceramics and glass. The name Memphis was chosen by Sottsass because it was both the birthplace of Elvis Presley, the father of pop culture, and the home of the Egyptian gods, the root of spirituality and mysticism, and therefore evoked all of his preoccupations in a single word. Memphis was a reaction to the intellectual approach of **Studio Alchimia** inasmuch as it stressed the roles of intuition and of the preconscious and prelinguistic associations that are suggested by images, colours, patterns, forms and so on. Thus the items on display emphasized image over object. To this end, craftsmanship was of secondary importance, as was the object's function which was vestigial rather than pre-eminent.

From the outset the annual Memphis shows, which continued until 1988, stressed the internationalism of the New Design movement, as it came to be called. This was represented by the inclusion of work by the Austrian, Hans Hollein; the American, Peter Shire; the Japanese, Arata Isozak; the Englishman, Daniel Weil (although of Argentinean and Israeli origin); and the Spaniard, Javier Mariscal. Thus Memphis signalled a shift in design thinking that was initiated by Italians but experienced globally as well.

The fame of Memphis spread through the agency of the glossy international design press, and its visual influence was soon felt in a wide range of design media, especially popular graphics where its patterned surfaces were widely reproduced. Only a few people, among them the fashion designer Karl Lagerfeld, who furnished his house in Memphis items, and museum curators, actually purchased pieces. It remained a gallery exercise for the most part, but one which had enormous impact in the world of popular style. Exhibitions of Memphis pieces were held in a number of international venues, among them London (1982) and New York. It served to make its collaborators international successes overnight and individuals,

such as Michele de Lucchi and George Sowden, went on to become internationally significant designers in the 1980s and 1990s.

Further reading

Memphis Milano in London (1982), London: The Boilerhouse Project.
Radice, B. (1984) Memphis, New York: Rizzoli.

PENNY SPARKE

Sturzo, Luigi

b. 26 November 1871, Caltagirone;
d. 8 August 1959, Rome

Priest and politician

After a long involvement in the Christian Democracy movement at turn of the century and in social activism in his native Sicily, Sturzo founded the Partito Popolare Italiano (PPI, Italian Popular Party) in 1919, which quickly mobilized all sections of the Catholic movement and as a result won 20 per cent of the vote in the national elections of 1919. However, the PPI was unable to govern alone and in November 1922 was forced into a coalition with the Fascists. Sturzo strongly opposed this and the **Vatican**, under pressure from Mussolini, forced him to resign as leader of the party in 1923. A year later he was sent into exile in England and later America, from where he continued to campaign against fascism. He returned to Italy in September 1946, but was unable to play an active political role until 1952, when he led an operation to prevent Rome from swinging to the Left. He is frequently evoked by present-day Catholic politicians to support their varying positions.

See also: DC

Further reading

De Rosa, G.(1977) Luigi Sturzo, Turin: UTET (the standard Italian biography of Sturzo).
Molony, J.N. (1977) The Emergence of Political Catholicism in Italy: Partito Popolare, 1919–1926,

London: Croom Helm (the first and the last chapters provide a concise biography of Sturzo).

JOHN POLLARD

Superstudio

An Italian architectural and design group based in Florence in the late 1960s, which played a key role within the 'anti-design' movement of those years, Superstudio was established in 1966 by Adolfo **Natalini** and Cristano Toraldi di Francia. Between 1970 and 1972 they were joined by four other architects, who were involved in teaching at the University of Florence. They allied themselves with the **student movement** of those years and sought to develop a strategy for what they called 'evasion design'. Their 1969 project 'Il monumento continuo' (The Continual Monument), for example, moved architecture into the realm of the conceptual rather than the real, thereby allying it with contemporary fine art practice. The group was active until the late 1970s.

See also: anti-design

Further reading

Raggi, F. (1973), 'Radical Story', in *Casabella*, no. 382.

PENNY SPARKE

T

Tabucchi, Antonio

b. 23 September 1943, Pisa

Professor, writer and translator

While pursuing an academic career as professor of Portuguese literature at the University of Genoa and contributing as literary and cultural critic to *La Repubblica* and *L'Espresso*, Antonio Tabucchi published several novels and short stories which were critically acclaimed both in Italy and abroad. In his inventive and exuberant fiction, characterized by intricate plots, contrasting narrative voices and unpredictable twists of fate, Tabucchi not only represents the mutability of reality with playful subtlety, but also ironically comments on Italian contemporary culture and society. Among his most successful works are *Piazza d'Italia* (Piazza Italia) (1975), *Notturno indiano* (Indian Nocturne) (1984) and *Piccoli equivoci di poca importanza* (Little Misunderstandings of No Importance!) (1985). His widely-acclaimed novel *Sostiene Pereira* (Pereira Declares) (1985) was made into a film by Roberto Faenza in 1996 and starred Marcello **Mastroianni** in one of his last roles.

FRANCESCA PARMEGGIANI

Tadini, Emilio

b. 5 June 1927, Milan

Artist and writer

A novelist and art critic, Tadini took up painting in the 1960s, though writing and literature remained important elements in his art. In his use of flat colour, precise drawing, heavy outlines and silhouetted figures, Tadini's early painting was influenced by the pop art movement, and it had a certain advertising feel to it. However, in contrast to the popular subject matter and figures of pop art, Tadini chose to focus on literary themes and figures, and his work shares some similarities with that of Valerio **Adami**, another artist working in Milan at the time. Tadini's paintings often explore the ways in which images and words co-exist and inform each other. His novels similarly mix literariness with the painterly and the everyday. *L'Opera* (1980) is a *giallo* (see **detective fiction**) based on the death of a painter, and *La tempesta* (1993) is a reworking of Shakespeare's *The Tempest*, set on the outskirts of contemporary Milan.

LAURENCE SIMMONS

Tafuri, Manfredo

b. 4 November 1935, Rome; d. 1994, Venice

Architectural historian

Tafuri achieved international prominence from the 1970s onwards as one of the most compelling and innovative historians in any field. His Marxist diagnosis of the historical avantgardes in *Architecture and Utopia* (1976) was bleak but rigorous, as was his critique of subsequent attempts to extend or refute the language of modernism in *The Sphere and the*

Labyrinth (1987). His *Modern Architecture* (with Francesco Dal Co, 1979) and the *History of Italian architecture, 1944–1985* have become standard reference works. Thereafter he turned his main attention to the Renaissance, with the intention of allowing the unresolved problems of the past to live on, and hence trouble the present.

Tafuri's complex intellectual constructions and writing style are elaborated from a vast array of sources and presented in a spirit of total disenchantment. As he put it: 'The real problem is how to project a criticism capable of constantly putting itself into crisis by putting into crisis the real' (Tafuri, 1987: 9).

Further reading

Tafuri, M. (1987) *The Sphere and the Labyrinth: Avantgardes and Architecture from Piranesi to the 1970s*, trans. P. d'Acierno and R. Connolly, Cambridge, MA: MIT Press.

ROSS JENNER

Tamaro, Susanna

b. 12 December 1957, Trieste

Writer

Tamaro, who declared in 1997 that she could live on 600,000 lira (about $US 500) a month, has earned billions of lire with her best-selling novel *Va' dove ti porta il cuore* (Follow Your Heart). Between 1994 and 1997 the book sold over two and half million copies in Italy and five and half million abroad, a success matched only by Umberto **Eco**'s *The Name of the Rose*. Like Eco's work, *Follow Your Heart* was also soon made into a film. While some prominent Italian literary critics accused her of writing populist, sentimental mush rather than literature, others praised her for reaching a public that seldom reads books as well as for her delicate portrayal of the generation gap. After such an unbridled success, her following novel, *Anima mundi* (1997) was closely scrutinized and again there was much division of opinion, especially over its ideological content, resulting in it being both condemned and praised for being staunchly anti-communist and conforming to Catholic orthodoxy. Ignoring her critics, Tamaro wrote a song for the 1997 **Sanremo Festival**.

PIERA CARROLI

Tambroni, Fernando

b. 25 November 1901, Ascoli Piceno; d. 1963, Rome

Politician

A member of the Christian Democrats (see **DC**), Tambroni was Interior Minister between 1955 and 1959, replacing Mario Scelba, and he became, briefly and notoriously, **President of the Council of Ministers** in 1960. By the late 1950s the centre-based government coalitions had become difficult for the DC to maintain. The **Vatican** and business interests vetoed co-operation with the Socialists (see **PSI**) while the DC's left-wing opposed initiatives on the Right. The impasse came to a head when Tambroni appeared to be constructing an authoritarian populist government supported by the neo-Fascist **MSI**. Strong police reaction to street demonstrations left several people dead, and Tambroni was consequently forced to resign, the clear lesson for the DC being that right-leaning governments were impossible. The government of so-called 'parallel convergence' which followed was based on the abstention in the government's inaugural vote of confidence of both the PSI and the **monarchists**, i.e. part of both the hitherto 'anti-system', Left and Right now converged on the democratic centre. The brainchild of Aldo **Moro**, the new government smoothed the path to the **opening to the Left** in 1963, and subsequently Tambroni was only remembered for the violent events over which he had presided.

MARK DONOVAN

Tangentopoli

The term *Tangentopoli*, translatable as 'Bribesville', was coined to describe the networks of systematic corruption linking businessmen, politicians and public administrators in which the payment of a bribe (*tangente*) was a standard requirement for the award of any kind of public contract. Milan, where extensive corruption was first uncovered in 1992 (see **Mani pulite**), was the original *Tangentopoli*. However, as judicial excavation revealed identically illegal foundations for politics in many other cities and areas of public activity, *Tangentopoli* ceased to refer to Milan alone and became the generic term for all large-scale corruption institutionalized in the 1980s throughout most of Italy.

See also: clientelism

Further reading

Hine, D. (1995) 'Party, Personality and Law: The Political Culture of Italian Corruption', in P. Jones (ed.), *Party, Parliament and Personality: Essays Presented to Hugh Berrington*, London: Routledge.

Sassoon, D. (1995) '*Tangentopoli* or the Democratisation of Corruption: Considerations on the End of Italy's First Republic', *Journal of Modern Italian Studies* 1 (1): 124–43.

DAVID MOSS

Tango

In an attempt to lighten the tone of the **PCI** daily *L'Unità* in 1986, cartoonist Sergio Staino was allowed to produce a four-page weekly supplement of satire and cartoons, called *Tango*. With the active collaboration of writers like Michele Serra and Gino and Michele, and cartoonists like Vincino, Angese and **Pazienza** who had all earlier been part of *Il Male*, the pink-coloured insert became a popular fixture as it irreverently lampooned all politicians and public figures, including those in or close to the Communist Party. Although this helped to increase sales, it also provoked considerable hostility from some members of the party, who professed to be appalled at what was happening in the pages of the paper that had been founded by Antonio **Gramsci**. Nevertheless, in early 1988 Staino was able to expand it to eight pages. However, by October of that year, in part as a result of internal criticism and in part due to the

death of Pazienza, who had been one of its major contributors, the magazine was discontinued.

GINO MOLITERNO

tartufo

The *tartufo* (truffle) is an underground fungus of a large family (*Tuberaceae*), which includes around thirty varieties. It grows in clayish-calcareous soil, in symbiosis with other plants. There are two highly valued varieties among the edible *tartufi*. The first, *tartufo bianco*, grows under oaks, poplars, hazel and lime trees. It is lumpy in shape, pale ochre in colour and characterized by an intense scent. It is found predominantly in northern Italy. The second, *tartufo nero*, is mostly found in the central regions, Tuscany and Umbria. Its dark brown colour presents purple reflections, and its surface is irregular and lumpy. *Tartufo bianco* is at its best when eaten raw, very finely sliced, for instance on a white risotto, or tagliolini (fine noodles), **polenta** or eggs gently fried in butter. *Tartufo bianco* should be layered on food, so that its flavour is not suffocated. *Tartufo nero* must be eaten cooked: its delicate aroma develops in the cooking process.

MARIELLA TOTARO GENEVOIS

Taviani brothers

Vittorio Taviani was born on 20 September 1929, and his brother Paolo on 8 November 1931, in San Miniato. Having gained international recognition in 1977 with *Padre padrone* (My Father, My Master), the Taviani brothers have since emerged as leading film directors, putting their stamp on a cinema which fuses realism, fantasy, myth and commitment.

Their early documentaries, *San Miniato luglio '44* (San Miniato, July '44), dealing with a Nazi atrocity in the directors' native village, and a full-length documentary on the Italian South, *L'Italia non è un paese povero* (Italy is Not a Poor Country) (1960), were greatly influenced by **neorealism**; but even by the time of their first feature in 1962, *Un uomo da bruciare* (A Man for the Burning), they were using flashbacks, stylized choreography and self-reflexive techniques which transcended the neorealist canon, and had more in common with contemporary French directors than with the Tavianis' national forebears. Tracing the career of a Sicilian trade unionist murdered by the **mafia**, the film incorporates the themes of idealism, destiny and resistance to authority which characterize the brothers' later films.

Over the next twelve years, the Tavianis explored a number of social issues. *I fuorilegge del matrimonio* (Matrimonial Outlaws) (1963) is a playful and sometimes grotesque take on the absurdities of Italian divorce law. *Sovversivi* (The Subversives) (1967) ironically traces four personal stories against the background of Palmiro **Togliatti**'s death and the crisis of the Italian Left. The violent clash between conservatism and utopianism is the theme of the mythical parable *Sotto il segno dello scorpione* (Under the Sign of Scorpio) (1969). *San Michele aveva un gallo* (St Michael Had a Rooster) (1971) examines the difficulty of maintaining individual faith in social revolution, while Fulvio Imbriani, the spineless protagonist of the uneven *Allonsanfan* (1974), epitomizes political vacillation and treachery.

At Cannes in 1977 the Tavianis won the Palme d'Or and the International Critics' Prize with *Padre padrone*, a confronting film which charts the itinerary of a Sardinian shepherd from a state of brutalized inarticulacy through the liberating trauma of military service on the mainland, to a professorship in linguistics. While the film tells one particular story, it remains a general reflection on, and critique of, a disabling patriarchal system.

After the 1979 failure of *Il prato* (The Field), a confused film about the struggle for utopia, the Tavianis returned to relative form with *La notte di San Lorenzo* (also released as *The Night of the Shooting Stars*) (1982), which tells of the flight from Nazi reprisals of a village community in 1944. *Kaos* (1984), a film based on Pirandello stories, is also stylistically accomplished, and found popular if not critical favour, while the would-be homage to cinema and Italian creativity, *Good Morning Babilonia* (titled *Good Morning, Babylon* in America) (1986), is disappointing for its lack of fluency and character development.

Il sole anche di notte (Night Sun) (1990) draws on familiar themes: self-sacrifice and the pitting of individual destiny against historical forces, a thread also woven through *Fiorile* (1992), a fable about the simultaneously liberating and damning consequences of wealth, told through several generations of one family's history. The Tavianis' 1996 adaptation of Goethe, *Le affinità elettive* (Elective Affinities), is their first love film proper, and suggests the impossibility of rationalizing emotional attraction.

Further reading

Malavolti, F. and Ugolini, K. (eds) (1994) *L'utopia, la poesia, il silenzio. Il cinema dei fratelli Taviani* (Utopia, Poetry and Silence: The Cinema of the Taviani Brothers), Rovigo: Tipografia La grafica.

Ranvaud, D. (ed.) (1987) *Good Morning, Babylon*, London: Faber & Faber.

DAVE WATSON

tavola calda

Tavola calda, in the Italian context, identifies a snack-bar. More accurately, *tavola calda* can be a section of a restaurant, bar or *rosticceria* (a takeaway food shop), where meals can be also eaten while standing at the counter. Generally at the *tavola calda* food is served all day, without interruption, with no closing hours over the lunch break or a rigid 8 p.m. closing. As the adjective *calda* (hot) indicates, at the *tavola calda*, hot food is available for clients. They may eat it standing or sitting on stools, at high benches placed along the walls or even at tables: people come in and out and the turnover is rapid. The concept encompasses fast meals, without long delay, and is not necessarily restricted to a bread roll with filling (*panino imbottito*) but the enjoyment of something tastier, more elaborate, and, of course, hot. Among foods found at the *tavola calda* are *arancini di riso* (stuffed rice balls), *pizzette* (little pizzas), omelettes, legumes, *cotolette* (cutlets) and many others.

While the most notorious icons of fast food have not spared Italy (for example, the Piazza di Spagna in Rome, embellished by McDonalds), Italians so far seem to prefer *tavola calda* food. Even the most likely clients of the fast food industry, teenagers living predominantly at home, appear less prone to fall captive to American-style fast food.

MARIELLA TOTARO GENEVOIS

taxation

Contrary to anecdotal evidence, the Italian tax system is reasonably efficient in gathering revenue, most Italians do pay taxes, and the tax design does not differ much from that of Italy's partners in the **European Union**. As is often the case, however, the devil is in the details.

Taxes were the object of a comprehensive reform in 1971–4. This was the point of arrival of a long debate on the modernization of the tax system, which had started in Parliament with a commission set up in 1962, chaired first by Cosciani and later by Visentini. Since the end of the Second World War, and particularly during the debate on the **constitution**, tax policy had been the object of a conflict between the liberalism of Luigi Einaudi, who advocated a tax system centred around the ideas of neutrality and market efficiency, and the redistributive social doctrine of Ezio **Vanoni**. Italy opted for the latter, and later in the 1960s the tax system was perceived by policy makers as Vanoni had conceived of it, that is, as an indispensable element of the national plan for economic development. Nevertheless, notwithstanding the impetus for modernization, until the 1970s Italy remained with a tax system which penalized instead of sustained economic activity and citizens with low incomes.

The 1971–4 tax reform improved the coherence of the whole tax system, introduced a modern European tax – the value-added tax – and gradually boosted revenue. In 1979 taxes and social contributions were only 26 per cent of the gross domestic product, against the 35.6 per cent of the European Community average, but in 1994 Italy reached the European average of 45 per cent. The tax reform of the 1970s had the merit of disposing of an archaic tax system, but was not without its own problems. During the 1980s it became clear that the heaviest burden of taxation had been placed on specific categories of citizens.

Small firms, the self-employed and agricultural rents were not only granted favourable tax regimes, but poor assessment criteria and an ineffective tax administration led to an extremely limited contribution of these categories to revenue gathering. In addition, estimates of tax evasion have almost invariably ranked Italy within the top positions. Accordingly, steeply rising marginal tax rates hit a rather narrow tax base, which consisted mainly of employees' labour income. At the same time, myriad tax exemptions, a maze of different tax regimes for alternative types of capital income (at the beginning of the 1990s there were thirty-seven different taxes on capital income and financial intermediation), the widespread use of tax amnesties (a short-term response to the need for more revenue), the pathological state of litigation (in 1994 more than three million cases were still pending), and the lack of simplification all contributed to create a widespread perception of unfairness in the tax system, epitomized by the expression *evasori e tartassati* (evaders and tax harassed). This was an unbearable burden for most taxpayers, amidst ample areas of exemptions and evasion. The situation was compounded by the tax wedge between taxes and expenditure: taxation was centralized, whereas spending power remained with **regional government**. The result was a politicization of tax issues in the 1990s, with the emergence of the **Lega Nord**, symptoms of tax revolt in the northeast, and a debate on fiscal federalism as a component of major proposed institutional reforms.

Economic integration within the European Union also helped to make the tax system a serious handicap for the Italian economy. High statutory corporate tax rates, the tax-induced bias for debt financing, high employer social security contributions, and the lack of efficient and simple rules for the taxation of capital income all made Italy a rather uninteresting place for multinationals. The liberalization of capital movement, following the 1988 directive of the European Community, and the proliferation of financial innovation exacerbated the inefficiencies of Italian tax policy in the context of the European single market. The absence of incisive reform of tax administration intensified the problems of the Italian tax system. The neglect of administrative reform (see **bureau-**

cracy), in line with a political culture more interested in macro-design than in the implementation and delivery of public policy, was a crucial failure. Not only would the modernization of tax administration be an essential component of better fiscal relations between the state, the citizen and the economy, but effective international tax enforcement and mutual assistance between tax administrations would require tax inspectors who were up to the job of managing the tax system in the global economy.

Not surprisingly, then, by the 1990s proposals for tax policy change reached the political agenda. In 1994 a White Paper was presented by the **Berlusconi** government but was never discussed in **Parliament**, and in 1997 the **Prodi** government obtained from Parliament the power to issue tax legislation. Following this, a new regional tax simplified the taxation of economic activity and corporate taxation was changed with the aim of aiding companies willing to reinvest profits or to use equity risk capital. Due to political obstacles to the reform of the welfare state, and the consequent impact on public expenditure, taxes remained a major element in the Italian strategy for coping with the criteria on public finance established by the Treaty of Maastricht. In 1996–7, a so-called 'tax for Europe' symbolized the determination of Italians to qualify for the single currency. However, the more fundamental problem of tax administration was yet to be tackled, with the attempt made in 1991 having yielded only scarce results.

Further reading

Ceriani, V., Frasca, V. and Monacelli, D. (1992) 'Il sistema tributario e il disavanzo pubblico: problemi e prospettive' (The Tax System and the Public Deficit: Problems and Perspectives), in E. Einaudi (ed.), *Il disavanzo pubblico in Italia: natura strutturale e politiche di rientro* (The Public Deficit in Italy: Structure and Adjustment Policies), Bologna: Il Mulino, 601–819 (a comprehensive presentation of the Italian tax system and its problems).

Guerra, M.C. (1993) 'Tax Policies in the 1980s and 1990s: The Case of Italy' in A. Knoester (ed.), *Taxation in the United States and Europe: Theory and Practice*, London: St. Martin's, 328–54.

Lupi, R. (1996) *Le illusioni fiscali. Risanare gli apparati per riformare il fisco* (Fiscal Illusions: Healing Administration to Reform Taxation), Bologna: Il Mulino (a non-technical discussion of tax administration by a scholar who has been personal advisor to several Italian Ministers of Finance).

OECD (1996) *OECD Economic Surveys: Italy*, Paris: OECD (ch. 4, 'Reforming the Tax System', contains a concise analysis of tax policy and policy recommendations for reform).

CLAUDIO M. RADAELLI

Telemontecarlo

Born in 1974, Telemontecarlo was the first legal private television channel after a judgement of the **Constitutional Court** allowed the broadcasting of foreign frequencies into Italy. Beamed from the municipality of Monaco, it originally transmitted in two languages, Italian and French, and only reached north and central Italy. From the early 1980s it went through a long series of financial changes. First the **RAI**, and then Brazilian television Rede Globo and the **Ferruzzi** group gained control. At the same time, lacking a strong identity and consistent programming, it suffered in competition with **Berlusconi**'s **Fininvest** channels. The situation improved when Telemontecarlo decided to privilege sport, especially **football**, which was highlighted in the popular programme *Galagoal* (presented by showgirl Alba Parietti), and skiing, celebrating the victories of Alberto **Tomba**. In 1995 the channel was acquired by the Cecchi Gori Group, who united it with the music channel **Videomusic**, then named TMC 2, in an attempt to create a 'third television pole' along with RAI and Fininvest. A year later, in a stunning coup, Cecchi Gori acquired the rights to prime football broadcasting, taking these away from RAI for the first time in television history. However, after a legal battle, the rights were shared between them and, still in financial trouble, the channel's future remains uncertain.

RICCARDO VENTRELLA

telenovelas

Appealing to the same taste for melodrama and romance which made the *fotoromanzi* so popular, telenovelas became an important launching platform for Italian commercial television and appeared in abundance on Italian television screens during the 1980s. Usually produced on low-budgets in South and Central America, these long-running serials could be acquired at reasonable prices and so became a staple of daytime programming. The Brazilian *Anche i ricchi piangono* (Rich People also Cry), screened on Rete A, was the first successful telenovela of the early 1980s. Networks like **Rete Quattro** subsequently based much of their programming on such serials in a successful effort to target housewives, especially in the morning period. The popularity of the serials also spawned a number of magazines, and actresses like Veronica Castro and Grecia Colmenares became superstars with regular fan clubs. Either from surfeit or merely as a sign of changing times, the number of telenovelas on Italian screens decreased markedly in the 1990s.

RICCARDO VENTRELLA

television talk shows

A genre well-known in the United States, the television talk show was something of a milestone in Italian television, initiating a new form of communication with the audience. The inventor of the Italian talk show was Maurizio **Costanzo** with his *Bontà loro* (With Their Kind Permission) in 1976. Previously there had only been *Processo alla tappa* (Stage Under Trial), a programme dedicated to **cycling** and to the Giro d'Italia, but for the most part this was no more than a clarification of the rules of the game. Costanzo's show was something different. Cleverly mixing important guests and ordinary people (a plumber, for example, on the first night), an interest for the private dimension of life and a touch of polemics, the television screen was soon transformed into lively forum where people could speak, confess and quarrel. Under the watchful eye of the camera, Costanzo allowed his guests – politicians, actors,

sportsmen, writers – to reveal all their virtues and their vices. A significant novelty for Italian television, *Bontà loro* also demonstrated the viability of programming after 10 p.m., a time slot which until then had virtually abandoned.

Having inaugurated it, Costanzo went on to become the master of the genre, with *Acquario* (1978–9), a slight variation on the previous format and then, from 1982, the never-ending *Maurizio Costanzo Show*, in which the television studio was replaced by a real theatre, encouraging the appearance of new characters and 'masters of improvised thinking' like Vittorio Sgarbi. Another of the early talk shows, *Pronto Raffaella* (Hello, Raffaella), presented by Raffaella **Carrà**, introduced viewer participation through the use of the telephone. Even extremely silly games ('Guess the number of beans in this jar?') were a huge success as the spectator's feeling of being part of the show both destroyed the screen as a barrier and confirmed television as a miracle object. More private, painful stories invaded later talk shows, from love affairs in *L'amore è una cosa meravigliosa* (Love Is a Many Splendoured Thing) to divorces and family life in *Stranamore* (Stangelove), youth problems in *Amici* (Friends), female matters in *Harem* and the news of the day mixed with games in *I fatti vostri* (Your Business).

The fundamental inspiration of the talk show is the idea of television as a meeting point for the spectators. Television becomes a virtual drawing room: one can sit on a sofa and just chat, as in *Tappeto volante* (Flying Carpet), sometimes about culture (*Parlato semplice* (Simply Speaking)) or even about television itself (*Telesogni* (TeleDreams)). The discussion can become heated and extremely polemical. A master of this type of Italian 'battle' talk show is Gianfranco Funari, with his *A bocca aperta* (Mouth Wide Open). Aggressively shouting in Roman dialect, Funari plays the intermediary between opposing factions. The duels on the show are extremely popular, and Funari, with his gruff, vulgar style, has become one of the most famous Italian television anchormen.

Given Italians' love of sport, many talk shows address particular sports, especially football, like the long-running *Il processo del lunedì* (Monday's Tribunal), which analyses the weekend games, and *Galagoal*, a Sunday afternoon football discussion which lasts seven hours (see also **sport and society**). In more recent times, especially after the explosion of *Tangentopoli*, justice has become the subject of talk shows: in *Forum*, for example, a real judge passes a real sentence. Political discussion (such as Bruno **Vespa**'s *Porta a Porta*) and current affairs (Enzo **Biagi**'s *Il Fatto*) also continue to attract a stable audience.

Catering to Italians' natural sense of curiosity and conviviality as well as to their addiction to television, the talk show has supplanted **telenovelas** as the most visible and popular television genre in the late 1990s.

RICCARDO VENTRELLA

tennis

After a pause of fifteen years (due to events preceding the Second World War), international tennis returned to Italy in 1950 with the championships on red clay played at the Foro Italico in Rome. In that year, Annalisa Bossi became the first player of the postwar period to win in front of her compatriots (she was also the only Italian female to be ranked in the top ten, 1949–50). Fausto Gardini took the podium for Italy in 1955, followed by Nicola Pietrangeli in 1957, who won again in 1961. During his exceptionally long career (1954–72), Pietrangeli became the most successful Italian tennis player of all time. In 1959–60, he won the French men's singles championships. Affectionately known as 'Mister Davis Cup', Pietrangeli still holds the record for the highest number of matches played (164) and won (120) in Davis Cup history. Pietrangeli also excelled in the doubles competitions. He and Orlando Sirola collected a series of victories which confirmed them as one of the most formidable pairs in tennis history. Together, they reached the men's doubles final at Wimbledon in 1956, which they lost but which remains the best-ever Italian performance at the English tournament. In 1959 they took the men's doubles in Paris, then the Italian championships in 1960, and played the Davis Cup finals in 1960–61 (losing it both times to the Australian team). In 1958, Pietrangeli also won the mixed doubles in Paris with Shirley Bloomer. Pietrangeli, the only Italian to have been

inducted into the Tennis Hall of Fame, was ranked in the top ten six times between 1957–64, climbing all the way to the number three spot in 1959–60.

After retiring from competition, Pietrangeli became the non-playing captain of the Italian Davis Cup team, leading Adriano Panatta, Corrado Barazzutti, Paolo Bertolucci and Antonio Zugarelli to victory in 1976 against Chile. The victory was tinged with bitterness as the fierce political controversy regarding the situation in Pinochet's Chile affected the tournament. Many, both in and outside of Italy, contended that Italy's success was possible only because other countries had previously refused to play against Chile. Nevertheless, the Italian team reached the Davis Cup final again in 1977, 1979 and 1980.

The success of the Italian team was due largely to the talent of Adriano Panatta, nicknamed 'the goalkeeper' for his frequent driving returns. His moment of glory (outside of Davis Cup competition) came in the summer of 1976, when he won the Italian championships after having survived a first-round match in which his opponent reached match point against him eleven times. Soon afterwards, Panatta triumphed in the French Open, beating the great Björn Borg in the semifinal and Harold Solomon for the title. These victories made him the number five player of 1976.

This string of successes helped to popularize what was once an elite sport, fostering new generations of tennis hopefuls. However, after the accomplishments of Panatta and his team, it took Italian players almost twenty years to return to international success. Andrea Gaudenzi was among the top ten in the mid-1990s, and Gaudenzi and Diego Narciso led the Italian team to second place in the Davis Cup of 1998.

PAOLO VILLA

Terra, Stefano

b. 1917, Turin; d. 1986, Rome

Novelist, poet and essayist

Forced to abandon Italy during the Fascist period because of his pacifist and democratic beliefs, Terra (real name Giulio Tavernari) moved to Egypt, where he published passionate denunciations of the regime. After the war Terra returned to Italy, where he worked as a journalist for the newspaper **La Stampa** while continuing to write novels and poetry. His prose manifests a taste for a neo-romantic style, while his poetry takes inspiration especially from the classical world and the Greek landscape which he had come to know through a long stay in Athens. In his novels, Terra combines the narration of simple daily events with the evocative power of remembrance of the exotic countries which he visited. Among his most memorable works are the novels *La generazione che non perdona* (The Generation that Does not Forgive) (1942) and *Alessandra, Le porte di ferro* (Alexandria, The Iron Doors) (1979) and his collection of poetry *Quaderno dei trent'anni* (Notebook of the Thirty Years) (1956).

ANDREA RICCI

terrorism

Terrorism, understood as clandestinely organized damage to people and property to achieve broadly political objectives, has been a recurrent feature of Italian public life since 1945, though its antecedents go back much earlier. In fact, each of Italy's three political regimes since 1860 has been closely linked to the exploits of armed groups: Garibaldi and his Thousand forcing completion of the Risorgimento; Fascist *squadrismo* in 1920–2, followed by the March on Rome and the establishment of an authoritarian state; and the **Resistance** in 1943–5 as the anti-fascist foundation of the postwar **Republic**. The Italian state itself has not been reluctant to use violence to suppress protest: military campaigns against southern peasants in the 1860s, the army's assault on rebellious working-class neighbourhoods in Milan in 1898, the intimidation and coercion of the Fascist regime, and the deaths at the hands of police of more than 200 demonstrators, especially in the South again, after 1945. This history has provided a rich store of models and myths for activists who want to believe that controlled violence can be successfully used to accelerate or obstruct political change.

Terrorism in the borderlands

Postwar terrorism first appeared in the German-speaking South Tirol where, in 1957, the Befreiungsausschuss Südtirol, a conspiratorial group based in Austria, began a bombing campaign in an attempt to overturn the 1919 division of the Tirol between Italy and Austria and to ensure autonomy for its German population. Altogether, 227 bomb attacks took place, resulting in 37 deaths and 556 injuries, mostly of Italian **police**. The violence ended in 1969 with an agreement between the Italian and Austrian governments which granted special rights to the German-speaking population of the province of Bolzano.

At the other end of Italy, the routine low-level violence of the **mafia** has regularly been punctuated by acts of terrorism to discourage insider defection or outside interference. Murders of left-wing politicians, trade unionists and public antagonists have served warnings against attempting to change the social and political order. Slain high-ranking policemen such as General **Dalla Chiesa** testify to the dangers of investigative zeal and the long series of 'excellent cadavers' (judges and politicians) since 1980, accompanied by bombings of trains and public buildings across mainland Italy, have asserted mafia power and reminded sections of the political elite that withdrawal of its protection will not be tolerated. Local politics in many parts of southern Italy have been deeply corrupted by the threat of violence and intimidation.

Terrorism at the centre

The most sustained terrorist assault on postwar political institutions was launched by the neo-fascist Right (see **fascism and neo-fascism**) with a bomb massacre in Milan in 1969, and ended with the murder of a Christian Democrat intellectual by the leftwing **Red Brigades** in 1988. For two decades, Italy's political parties and institutions resisted the convergent violence of both political extremes, dominated first by the Right (1969–74), then by the Left during the *anni di piombo* (years of lead, 1975–80), then once again by the Right (1980–84). The militants of the extreme Right, helped by conspirators in the parliamentary **MSI**, the **armed forces** and the security services, pursued a so-called 'strategy of tension' (see **strategia della tensione**), a campaign of bombs and murder designed to make Italians regret and reverse the democratization of workplace and society initiated by the student and worker movements of 1968–9. At the other political extreme, some members of the **extraparliamentary Left** wanted to push that democratization further, impatient with the insufficiently revolutionary pace and direction of change. First responding in kind to right-wing violence, the semi-clandestine left-wing groups in Rome and the major industrial cities of the North began a systematic assault in 1975 on major political and economic institutions, their representatives and defenders: politicians, industrial managers and factory personnel, police, magistrates and journalists. Between 1969 and 1982 the attacks from both political wings cost nearly 400 lives and more than 700 serious injuries: damage to property was estimated at $1,360 million. In the late 1970s, the scale of the assault on Italian democracy can be gauged from the seven attacks recorded per day and the more than 500 group signatures adopted by the assailants.

The impact of the attacks was, however, diminished by the public disagreements among the users of violence about what their primary targets and aims should be and whether violence ought to accompany or replace ordinary political activities. Eventually the failure of even the most dramatic attacks (the kidnapping and murder of **Moro** in 1978 and the bombing of Bologna railway station in 1980) to show that violence by clandestine groups could achieve what negotiation by **political parties** and **trade unions** could not provoked widespread disillusion among militants who, after 1980, began to abandon their groups and turn state's evidence in increasing numbers. Laws rewarding confession (see **pentiti**) with greatly-reduced prison sentences encouraged defection, and mass trials of the 3,000-odd former activists became a public spectacle of the 1980s. Revelations of the ramshackle nature of even the apparently best-organized terrorist groups and the haphazard selection of their targets encouraged the longstanding suspicion that terrorism had been deliberately encouraged, or at least allowed to develop undisturbed, by powerful groups in or outside Italy for their own political or strategic advantage.

The consequences of violence

Most of the consequences of the violence of the 1970s for Italian politics and society were unintended. The terrorists' hopes that their actions would drive public opinion into a polarization between right-wing reaction and left-wing radicalism were disappointed. However equivocal they might be about defending a clientelist and corrupt state, Italians showed no enthusiasm for the prospect of civil war. Electoral allegiances even in the cities most directly under attack were barely altered, and demonstrations against violence, organized mainly by the **PCI** and trade unions, attracted substantial support. Responses by governments to terror did not result in any serious curtailment of civil liberties, partly because the major parties disagreed about its political origins and real aims, making it impossible to assemble sufficiently broad support for draconian antiterrorist measures. Although Italy's dominant party, the **DC**, suffered the most direct damage, violence also had a substantial impact on the PCI. In defence of the **historic compromise** and the state which the party aspired to direct, the PCI was driven into a conservative stance unpopular with its supporters. Moreover, coming to power in 1975 in the cities where violence was most intense, the PCI had to divert vital administrative energies and personnel to the mobilization against any acceptance of violence as a legitimate political tactic. Among magistrates, the need to prosecute groups operating in several jurisdictions produced new forms of collaboration which were later copied in the successful investigation of mafia (see Giovanni **Falcone**) and political corruption (see *Mani pulite*).

Further reading

Della Porta, D. (1995) *Social Movements, Political Violence and the State*, Cambridge: Cambridge University Press (comparative study of the origins and development of political violence in Italy and Germany after 1969).

Ferraresi, F. (1996) *Threats to Democracy: The Radical Right in Italy after the War*, Princeton, NJ:

Princeton University Press (the nature, political responsibilities and cultural contexts of extreme right-wing violence).

Moss, D. (1989) *The Politics of Leftwing Violence in Italy 1969–1985*, Basingstoke: Macmillan (the organization of left-wing violence and the responses by its political, trade union and judicial opponents).

—— (1997) 'Politics, Violence, Writing: The Rituals of Armed Struggle in Italy', in D. Apter (ed.), *The Legitimization of Violence*, Basingstoke: Macmillan (analysis of the co-evolution of right-wing and left-wing violence).

Wagner-Pacifici, R. (1986) *The Moro Morality Play*, Chicago: Chicago University Press (the substance and semiotics of the kidnapping and murder of Moro).

DAVID MOSS

Testori, Giovanni

b. 12 May 1923, Novate Milanese, Milan; d. 16 March 1993, Milan

Writer

After completing his degree in philosophy at Milan's Catholic University, Testori began his career as a writer with 'Il Dio di Roserio' (Roserio's God) (1954). This story was later included in the collection *Il ponte della Ghisolfa* (Ghisolfa's Bridge) (1958), the first part of a series of works (novels and plays) collectively named *I segreti di Milano* (Milan's Secrets), which have the Milanese lumpenproletariat as its main topic and inspiring motif. His plays often combine religious thematics with grotesque representations of classical masterpieces. However, Testori's initial and original revitalization of a certain literary **neorealism** achieved through, on the one hand, his widespread use of Milanese dialect and, on the other, the almost exclusive presence of 'low characters' (thieves, whores and so on) tends to degenerate in his later works into a mannered style and an excessively elaborated writing which loses its liveliness and poignancy.

Further reading

Urgnani, E. (1994–5) 'Intervista con Giovanni Testori' (An Interview with Giovanni Testori), *Gradiva: An International Journal of Italian Literature* 6 (1): 12–13, 51–3.

ENRICO CESARETTI

Tex Willer

One of the most popular and long-lived Italian cartoon characters, Tex Willer was created in 1948 by Gian Luigi Bonelli and illustrated for many years by Aurelio Galleppini (usually known simply as 'Gallep'). Other illustrators have subsequently contributed to drawing the stories, amongst them Ferdinando Fusco, Giovanni Ticci, Claudio Villa and Roberto Raviola (the legendary 'Magnus').

A government agent/ranger on a Navajo reservation, Tex is respected and loved by the Indians, who regard him as a wise white brother whom they call Night Eagle. A friend of another legend, Kit Carson, Tex is often accompanied in his exploits to do good and to right wrongs by his son Kit and Indian Tiger Jack.

In spite of its slightly dated Western storyline, the comic continues to sell 400,000 copies monthly and also appears in translation in Finland, France, Turkey, Croatia and Brazil. Tex's first appearance on film, *Tex e il signore degli abissi* (Tex and the Lord of the Depths), in 1985 failed to impress fans, but his fiftieth birthday in 1998 was extensively celebrated with numerous events and the publication of a Tex Willer encyclopedia.

See also: comics

GINO MOLITERNO

theatre

The end of the Second World War left Italy in desperate need of reconstruction, both physically and in terms of a cultural and national identity which fascism, despite its boasts, had failed to create. In the immediate postwar years, this national identity was created through a strong rejection of the fascist past, which was general throughout the population at a socio-political as well as cultural level.

The situation of Italian theatre during these years reflected Italian society as a whole, being considerably more backward and poorer, in authors and new plays, than most other Western European countries. Twenty years of fascist censorship and closure to foreign influences did not benefit most forms of art, least of all the theatre, which since the beginning of the century had produced only one major playwright with an international reputation, Luigi Pirandello. The general view for many years had also been that theatre was primarily entertainment rather than art (Richards, 1991: 278). This limited the possibilities for innovation and, above all, restricted theatre to a middle-class, bourgeois audience, avoiding any serious social commitment.

This would soon change after the end of the war: in fact, opposition to the traditional style of acting and staging plays, with primary attention focused on the main actors and the literary value of the text, arose as soon as Mussolini's dictatorship ended. A new notion suggesting that theatre should get closer to the masses soon began to circulate. The first proponent of the new concept of 'people's theatre', influenced by Jean Vilar and the Théâtre National Populair in France, was Vito Pandolfi. He envisaged the creation of new theatres subsidized by the state and based in every town with more than 100,000 inhabitants (Richards, 1991: 281). The main advantage of such a publicly funded theatre network would have been to make performances accessible to a wider audience, and the fostering of more experimentation. Pandolfi's ideas appeared to be realized in 1947, when Giorgio **Strehler** and Paolo Grassi founded the Piccolo Teatro in Milan. This was the first of the state-subsidized theatres, later called *stabili*. The aims of the Piccolo Teatro and of the *stabili* were mainly to foster the participation of people from every social class, moving away from elite traditions and embracing a commitment to contemporary social issues. The Piccolo, under the direction of Strehler, became a great success and established a high reputation for itself, both in Italy and abroad. One of its greatest contributions to the development of Italian contemporary theatre was the introduction of works by foreign authors, notably those of Bertold Brecht who, together with Samuel Beckett, Eugene Ionesco and Harold Pinter,

became the major influences on new Italian drama.

In the decade after the establishment of the Piccolo Teatro, another ten *stabili* were created. Despite the good intentions that motivated the foundation of these theatres, and although a few of them, such as the Teatro Stabile di Torino and Teatro Stabile di Genova, achieved an international status, the majority led troubled lives and failed to achieve their main aims. Their distinguishing characteristic, namely that of being subsidized by the state, also worked against them since funds and support often derived from political rather than artistic considerations (Cairns, 1992: 112–13). In this way the state was able to control productions, minimizing or even eliminating opportunities for ideological opposition and expansion of social awareness of particular issues, which the then conservative Christian Democrat governments wanted to avoid. Their conservative nature also tolerated a firm system of **censorship**, which had been introduced by the fascists but continued to operate until 1962. These factors explain the ultimate failure of the *stabili* in the 1950s, as well as the small number of plays related to contemporary controversial social issues and minimal experimentation with new forms and language for the theatre.

Nevertheless, by the end of the 1950s Italian theatre had moved forward compared to the situation fifteen years earlier: it had opened up to important foreign influences, and had revised its repertoire almost entirely. It had also seen the development of new directors and authors, some of whom would eventually become internationally renowned, including Strehler and Diego **Fabbri**, Gianfranco De Bosio, Luigi **Squarzina**, Silvio Bompiani and Vitaliano **Brancati**. Among the major plays of this period were Fabbri's *Processo a Gesù* (The Trial of Christ) and *Il seduttore* (The Seducer), and *Tre quarti di luna* (Three Quarters of the Moon) and *Romagnola* (Romagnese) by Luigi Squarzina. Vitaliano Brancati's *La governante* (The Governess) explored the controversial issues of homosexuality and became one of the most famous cases of censorship. But perhaps the greatest name in Italian theatre during the 1950s was Eduardo **De Filippo**, who represented a unique case with his combination of a strong Neapolitan tradition, the still pervasive influence of *commedia dell'arte* and, from 1945 onward, of more contemporary social issues. His most famous plays, *Napoli Milionaria* (Millionaire from Naples) and *Filumena Marturano*, present the reality of postwar Italy in a style clearly influenced by neorealist cinema (see **neorealism**). However, at the end of the 1950s Italian theatre was still not regarded as a real art form and, above all, had not attracted wider and more differentiated audiences as intended.

During the 1960s, the social and political climate of the country moved from a phase of relative optimism, deriving from the economic boom of the late 1950s (see **economic miracle**), to a real social revolution during 1968–9 (see **student movement**). The social unrest and political battles had a common denominator, which was the social demands of the working class. Theatre, too, lived the 1960s in a state of crisis. The introduction of plays of the absurd was enlightening for many Italian intellectuals: the language responsible for the lack of communication in the plays of the absurd was equally accused of being responsible for the crisis of theatre in Italy. Writers like Pier Paolo **Pasolini** denounced the language adopted by mainstream theatre for being academic, artificial and distant from the language as commonly spoken (Richards, 1991: 284). This was also believed to be a reason for the increasing popularity of plays written in **dialects** during these years, such as the very successful plays of De Filippo. Plays written in dialects rather than in standard Italian were not new in the panorama of theatre and had been flourishing for centuries in the peninsula, where language unification only became a reality after the introduction of national television in 1954 (see **Italian language**). Thus the use of standard Italian on the stage, at a time when it was still relatively little spoken in everyday situations, easily attracted the charge of artificiality. The problem of language was also linked to a second factor, highlighted in extensive discussions in theatre journals like *Sipario*, namely the lack of a real interest on the part of people who were unfamiliar with the theatre and therefore unable to understand the many forms of experimentation that started to appear in the second half of the 1960s.

Once again, these experimentations emerged under foreign influences, especially the American Living Theatre and the new British drama. The strong impact that the Living Theatre in particular had on Italian drama is witnessed by the number of small, mainly self-financed groups that made experimentation their main aim. These new groups worked in direct opposition to the *stabili*: they often lacked financial and political support, but their productions were extremely innovative in both content and form. Their experiments often involved the text itself, which was modified on an ad hoc basis during performances. These companies, calling themselves *collettivi* (collectives), adopted an entirely collective approach to all aspects of theatrical production, rejecting the traditional star system under which the leading actors exercised primary control and aiming specifically at expanding the social and political commitment of the theatre. It is true that most of their productions proved ephemeral, but they made an important contribution to Italian theatre, especially in opening the way for figures such as Carmelo **Bene**, Dario **Fo** and Luca **Ronconi**, who in different ways introduced new concepts and artistic forms. The common denominator became the rejection of the literary dimension which had been such a strong characteristic of previous Italian theatre. Bene's *Pinocchio*, for instance, is the director's own interpretation of the story and started a practice whereby fixed roles and traditional aesthetic conventions were caricatured and often overturned. Ronconi's first major production, *Orlando Furioso*, was innovative in its use of five different stages on which the same story was performed but from different perspectives, as well as in its greater use of the figurative arts and puppets. Dario Fo, on the other hand, revived the older tradition of *commedia dell'arte* but used it to criticize and satirize most venerated institutions, including the Pope and the Vatican, as in *Mistero buffo*.

The proliferation of different forms of this **avantgarde theatre** would eventually lead, during the 1970s, to a public recognition of this new artistic expression which came to be known as 'alternative theatre' because it chose a different circuit for its performances, distinct from that of the established public and private theatres. Instrumental in the promotion of this alternative theatre were the communist recreational associations such as ARCI, which provided the various *collettivi* with the alternative venues and helped to bringing theatre to the masses. The alternative circuit was more effective than the established theatre in at least one aspect, in that it had a more widespread presence in the national territory. This led the *stabili* themselves to tour some of their productions outside the city centres in order to reach peripheral areas and population, where there was now a greater interest in theatre. A second major achievement of the alternative theatre was the creation of new audiences, witnessed by the doubling of theatre attendance between 1970 and 1990 to twelve million.

During the 1970s the frequently postponed legislation on regional devolution was finally passed and it affected the funding system for theatre. **Regions** were now supposed to allocate funding for cultural activities, but their functions were not clearly defined, and indeed local authorities had no legal requirement to provide funding, although many did. The procedures for applying for public funds were also very bureaucratic and time consuming, making state funding not easily accessible.

By the end of the 1970s, feminist issues started to be recognized in theatre as artistic expression of a movement that had grown during the decade. Among exponents of this feminist group were Dacia **Maraini**, Franca **Rame** and Natalia **Ginzburg**. Dacia Maraini set up her own theatre company, La compagnia blu (The Blue Company), later called Teatroggi, which was linked to the ARCI circuit, and the theatre workshop Teatro della Maddalena, for women writers, which was closed in 1990 due to lack of public sponsorship (Wood, 1995: 90). Franca Rame, working with Dario Fo, gave voice to women's issues in monologues like those in *Parti Femminili* (Female Parts), such as *Tutta casa, letto e chiesa* (All Home, Bed and Church) and *Una donna sola* (A Woman Alone). Natalia Ginzburg, better known as a novelist, explored in her plays the lost communication between people, focusing most of her plays on the character of the 'Mother'.

After the turmoil of the 1970s, the new decade started with newfound optimism in the wake of greater economic prosperity. In the arts, the 1980s will be remembered for law 163 in 1985, which regulated funding to the performing arts. Among

other features, this law promoted private investment and tax concessions. What did not change was touring. With the main theatre companies located in major cities and with only eleven permanent regional theatres, the issue of decentralization, so important for Italian theatre, was partly solved by the touring of many and varied companies throughout the country.

The many experimental groups of the 1970s gradually disappeared and Italian theatre during the 1980s became more interested in the quality of the plays rather than in the quantity of the productions. One important director who first appeared in the 1970s but who made his career during the 1980s was Gabriele Lavia, who was interested in textual research and in a neonaturalistic approach to classic works.

The Italian theatre of the 1990s has focused again on the use of language. The Odin Theatre of Eugenio **Barba**, based in Oslo, with its concentration on performance as an event disconnected from the outside world, has exercised an important influence especially on the way in which language is used in theatre. Artistic and linguistic aspects of performance have become more important than any realistic meaning the play may project. In the same vein, Mario Ricci, has created a new 'Theatre of Images', where every aspect of the theatrical experience, from lighting to scenography to actors, is carefully integrated in order to highlight the spectator's own perceptions of the experience itself (Vallauri, 1994: 525). It is this 'Theatre of Images' which has emerged as a major influence on Italian theatre at the very end of the twentieth century.

See also: avantgarde theatre; theatre actors; theatre directors

Further reading

Allen, J. (1981) *Theatre in Europe*, Eastbourne: John Offord Publications.

Bernard, E. (ed.) (1991) *Attori e drammaturgi. Enciclopedia del teatro italiano. Il dopoguerra (1950–1990)* (Actors and Playwrights: Encyclopedia of Italian Theatre: Postwar Period 1950–1990), Rome.

Cairns, C. (1992) 'Italy', in R. Yarrow (ed.), *European*

Theatre 1960–1990: Cross-Cultural Perspective, London: Routledge.

Cowan, S. (1977) 'Theatre, Politics and Social Change in Italy since the Second World War', *Theatre Quarterly* 29: 7–27.

Richards, L. (1991), 'Drama, Politics and Society in Postwar Italy: Theatre in Search of a role', in A.M. Brassloff and W. Brassloff (eds), *European Insight: Postwar Politics, Society, Culture*, Amsterdam: Elsevier Science Publisher.

Tessari, R. (1988) 'Actor training in Italy', trans. S. Bassnett, *New Theatre Quarterly*, 4 (14): 181–92.

Vallauri, C. (1994) 'Italy', trans. D. Santerano and R. Buranello, in D. Rubin (ed.), *The World Encyclopedia of Contemporary Theatre*, vol. 1, London: Routledge.

Wood, S. (1995), 'Women and Theatre in Italy: Natalia Ginzburg, Franca Rame and Dacia Maraini', in E. Woodrough (ed.), *Women in European Theatre*, London: Intellect Books.

FEDERICA STURANI

theatre actors

In the wake of the traditional role of the *capocomico* first established within the *commedia dell'arte* during the sixteenth century, actors in Italy have always had an important, and sometimes overwhelming, influence on the style of theatre productions. However, despite their importance, Italian actors traditionally did not receive professional training but merely followed the acting style of the main actor or actors in the company, which thus tended to limit the possibilities for personal and artistic development.

At the end of Second World War in Italy, there existed only one state school for actor training, the Accademia Nazionale di Arte Drammatica in Rome, established in 1935 by the critic Silvio D'Amico. It was to remain the only facility for producing professional actors until after the events of 1968, when the turmoil among students and workers spread (see **student movement**), to unsettle old practices and tradition in almost every sector of social and public life. A younger generation of actors with an interest in investigating new styles in theatre emerged, giving rise to new demands for more and diverse schools for actor training.

The Accademia Nazionale di Arte Drammatica, renamed after Silvio D'Amico when he died in 1957, tried to maintain its detachment from particular trends, but in later years, and particularly after the appointment of Aldo **Trionfo** as its director in 1980, moved towards a greater diversification of its training, attempting to avoid directing its students into one particular mode.

Following the increasing demand for qualifications in drama, in the early 1960s some state-subsidized theatres set up acting schools attached to their repertory companies. The most successful examples are the school linked to the Piccolo Teatro in Milan (see **Strehler**) and that of the Teatro Stabile in Genoa. Both schools have a similar focus on the development of the actor, which is obtained through various acting activities including mime and dance and re-evaluating the body as an essential instrument of expression.

From the end of the 1980s the issues related to actor training have acquired an ever more central position in the panorama of Italian theatre. There has also been a flourishing of small, often occasional, private courses which itself is proof of the strong demand for such training, rarely met by public institutions, particularly the universities. Other important schools for actor training are those which were founded by several prominent theatre actors at the end of the 1970s: Gigi Proietti's Rome Performance Laboratory and Vittorio **Gassman**'s Florence Theatre Workshop mirror the different views that the two actors have of theatre: the actor's versatility of expression is fully explored in Proietti's school, while Gassman's workshop tends to develop more specific skills.

Despite these new initiatives for a full professional training for actors, detached from any particular style, the old tradition of the great actor, the so-called '*mattatore*', has survived in Italian theatre, largely through major figures like Carmelo **Bene** and Dario **Fo**. Both have developed a very distinct style which makes each of their productions unique but always strongly dominated by the personality of the artist. Bene's approach has been ruthlessly iconoclastic. Moving away from conventional aesthetic taste, his theatre has attempted to overturn all traditional relationships between text and performance by relying on his own extraordinary acting ability to bend traditional roles like

Hamlet to his own purposes. Fo, on the other hand, has created a theatre which is a blend of clownesque improvization and social satire but, in spite of strongly-marked social and political concerns, the work's success is predicated largely on Fo's own highly personal style.

Thus, although highly original artists, Bene and Fo have perpetuated the actor star-system which has long dominated Italian theatre and characterized theatrical productions. Amongst the most famous and influential actors of the immediate postwar years were Ruggero Ruggeri, who specialized in roles from Pirandello's plays, and Gino Cervi, who preferred to interpret classic authors from Sophocles and Shakespeare and who consolidated his reputation by also working in cinema and television. Anna **Magnani**, Marcello **Mastroianni** and Vittorio **Gassman** also achieved their first great successes on the stage, although later they all also moved to cinema and, of the three, only Gassman has regularly returned to performing in the theatre.

Other prominent Italian actors who achieved fame on the stage before also, often, moving to film and television are Romolo Valli, Rossella Falk, Anna Proclemer, Valeria Moriconi, Mario Scaccia and Mariangela Melato, while the actor who was instrumental in bringing Strehler's *Arlecchino, servo di due padroni* (*Harlequin servant of two masters*) to international success was Marcello Moretti. Many of these actors are still an important presence in contemporary theatre, whilst younger actors such as Monica Guerritore, Gabriele Lavia and Elena Sofia Ricci have also earned a respectable reputation on the theatrical scene.

Further reading

Tessari, R. (1988) 'Actor training in Italy', trans. S. Bassnett, *New Theatre Quarterly*, 4, 14:181–92.

FEDERICA STURANI

theatre directors

The director made a late and much resisted entry into Italian theatre in the 1920s and 1930s, long after the role had been undisputably recognized in other European theatres. As late as 1945, the critic Silvio D'Amico had to resist the view that the director was a creature of Fascism, and should be jettisoned with the regime. Fortunately, developments in the postwar years consolidated the director's position. The growth in popularity of cinema, where the director had been the lynchpin from the outset, helped to increase prestige, while the establishment of the *teatri stabili* (state-subsidized theatres) in all the principal cities – the real revolution in Italian theatre in the postwar period – gave the director crucial control over programming and casting. These developments marked the end of the traditional actor-centred theatre, and gave the director the right to impose his or her own critical vision on the script and to make actorial flair secondary to the realization of that vision.

The aims and tendencies of the new Italian directors became clearer with a number of epoch-making productions in the immediate postwar period, most notably the 1945 Roman production of Jean Cocteau's *Les parents terribles* by Luchino **Visconti** and Giorgio **Strehler**'s 1947 production in Milan of Gorky's *The Inn of the Poor*.

Visconti – as was to be true of many Italian directors – was equally at home in theatre and cinema. His 'style' has been the subject of much analysis, since he combined in varying measures a professional rigour, a languid, aristocratic taste for decadence and aestheticism, a cult of the image, a taste for *verismo* and a torrid eroticism. He was equally at ease with the domestic dramas of Arthur Miller or Tennessee Williams, where families were torn apart by internal dissension, as with such classical tragedies as Shakespeare's *Troilus and Cressida* or Alfieri's *Oreste*.

Strehler's biography is inseparable from that of the Piccolo Teatro (Little Theatre) in Milan, which he co-founded in 1947 and directed until his death in 1997, with a brief break in 1968. His desire to recreate the original style lay behind his use of *commedia dell'arte* techniques and routines in his celebrated production of Goldoni's *Harlequin, Servant of Two Masters*. Pirandello and Brecht were, together with Goldoni, the authors he staged most frequently. His productions of Goldoni's *Villeggiatura* (Holiday) Trilogy concentrated on the social background, unlike his more openly poetic *Campiello*, while with Brecht's *Threepenny Opera*, staged with the assistance of the author, he revealed the more radical aspect of his beliefs and pointed the way to a political theatre founded on song, word and choral movement. Strehler's Pirandello, by contrast, was pre-eminently the metaphysical Pirandello of the myths, as evidenced by his several productions of *The Mountain Giants*.

Although he employed various assistant directors at the Piccolo, there was no Strehler school, whereas Franco **Zeffirelli** and Giorgio De Lullo can be regarded as disciples of Visconti. Zeffirelli directed in English as well as Italian, producing **De Filippo** at the National Theatre in London, as well as a *Life of Saint Francis* and a *Romeo and Juliet* for the cinema. His Italian stage version of the same play had a youthful freshness and sensuality, as did his *Hamlet* with Giorgio **Albertazzi** in the title role. Zeffirelli brought Edward Albee to the Italian stage, while De Lullo can claim credit for introducing Giuseppe **Patroni Griffi**, several of whose plays he produced.

Rarely, however, have Italian directors seen it as incumbent on them to encourage and foster new playwrights, or to make the staging of new plays an integral part of their professional duty. In consequence, Italian playwriting has largely languished in the postwar period. The director's role was viewed as being primarily concerned with reshaping, rereading, reassessing the script in accordance with his own vision. This convention gave many second-rate directors licence to present versions of plays which were unrecognizable but which could be justified in the name of experimentation, although with the very best directors this led to some highly applauded, insightful productions.

Few directors produced more visually stimulating productions than Gianfranco de Bosio, director of the Turin *stabile*, who worked with Dario **Fo** on Fo's *Comica finale* (Happy Ending), and who, with a series of scrupulously researched and theatrically invigorating versions of Ruzante's work, reintroduced the Venetian Renaissance playwright to the Italian stage. Luigi **Squarzina** was director at the *stabile* in Genoa and later in Rome, and perhaps more than any other similar director, was able to take advantage of his position to assemble a quality company with an identifiable style. Squarzina may have lacked the purity of vision of Strehler and Visconti, but he was the consummate professional,

combining social realism and pure theatricality in his production of a trilogy of works by Goldoni, and allowing individuals like Alberto Lionello to excel in Shaw's *Man and Superman*.

The 1960s produced new names like Giancarlo Cobelli, Mario Missiroli, Aldo **Trionfo** and Massimo **Castri**. Some were self-conscious exponents of the avantgarde, but all were new iconoclasts, determined to break with the past and sweep away the tradition of the 'well made' production. The director was undisputed king, his aim to identify a 'subtext' which might have been unknown to the author, now relegated to a subsidiary position. Cobelli produced a controversial *Anthony and Cleopatra* almost in the style of a farce, while Castri produced a version of Pirandello's *Right You Are If You Think So*, in which the raisonneur Laudisi remains wordlessly playing a piano at the back of the stage throughout. Their contemporary, Luca **Ronconi**, carved his own path. After early productions of some Jacobean authors, he astonished Italy with a large-scale, promenade production of *Orlando Furioso*. Later, as director of the *stabile* in Turin, he produced a similar scale version of Karl Kraus's *Last Days of Mankind* in a disused steel plant.

Eduardo De Filippo and Dario Fo continued to represent the more traditional strain of Italian theatre, being actor-author-directors with their own company. The 1968 movement brought a rebellion against the power of the director, which found its expression in the founding of theatrical co-operatives. La nuova scena (The New Scene), with which Fo was involved between 1968–70, and the Cooperativa di Parma were the most productive, but their impact was short-lived. The director was now firmly established as the ruling figure in Italian theatre.

JOSEPH FARRELL

Thermes, Laura

b. 1943, Rome

Architect

A leading figure in contemporary Italian architecture, Thermes has maintained both a personal and professional partnership with Franco **Purini** since 1966 and they have collaborated extensively. Her innovative designs, ranging from small houses to large-scale urban projects, were featured at the **Venice Biennale** in 1978 and 1980, at the Architectural Association, London, in 1984 and at the **Milan Triennale** in 1987. Thermes's works are renowned for their high level of architectural sophistication, in particular for their capacity to interiorize the social drama of architecture, achieved through the analogous relationship of construction details to the building as a whole. She expressed her views and the intellectual dimension of her work in numerous professional journals, among them *Controspazio*, for which she also served on the editorial board. She has been a Visiting Professor at the Syracuse University of New York, and is a standing faculty member of Rome's Scuola Superiore di Architettura where she teaches and conducts research on the history of architecture.

FASSIL ZEWDOU

Third Italy

The term 'Third Italy' was coined by the sociologist Bagnasco in 1977 to identify the socio-economic distinctiveness of central and northeast Italy (mainly Emilia-Romagna, Tuscany, Marche and the Veneto), by contrast with the 'First Italy' (the industrial triangle between Milan–Turin–Genoa, dominated by large, early leader firms such as **Fiat**, **Pirelli** and **Olivetti**), and the 'Second Italy' (the South, with its economy heavily dependent on state subsidies).

The originality of the 'Third Italy' – which contains some of Italy's richest provinces – rests on the concentration in 'industrial districts' of technologically advanced, innovative production in small and medium-sized firms. Work organization is distinguished by three kinds of close relations (1) between firms and clients to produce short runs of customized goods, (2) between employers and workers, so that workers have the opportunity to learn the skills to establish their own artisan businesses, and (3) between local firms themselves, which are often linked by alternating relations of collaboration and competition. Today's market rival is tomorrow's ally; today's fellow worker is tomorrow's employer. The Third Italy produces mainly high-quality consumption goods, notably textiles, footwear, ceramics and furniture but may also include sophisticated light engineering products such as machine tools and motor-bikes. In the 1970s, the export success of these stylish products established a market niche for the 'made in Italy' label.

The combination of economic success, ability to respond rapidly to new demands and egalitarian work organization on a human scale has made the Third Italy seem a highly desirable model for the future of industrial organization. But is it the product of a unique concatenation of local, historical and social factors, or can policy-makers deliberately engineer its reproduction elsewhere? Theorists have disagreed. Some identify regional historical factors as decisive: traditions of share-cropping (see **agriculture**) which encouraged entrepreneurial skills and family collaboration; the influence of long-standing urban craft traditions and training institutions; and the dominance of a single political culture (Catholicism in the Veneto, replaced in the 1990s by the **Lega Nord**; Communism in Emilia and Tuscany), which glues together political and economic institutions and ensures the trust necessary to sustain simultaneously competition and collaboration. Others emphasize the consequences of the decentralization of production by large firms in the 1970s to escape the union militancy of the Hot Autumn (see **student movement**), the existence of a large pool of female and young employees available for flexible work commitments, and the active support of town and regional governments. The enthusiasm for detecting breakthroughs in industrial organization should not, however, disguise the diversity within the Third Italy nor the role of gender and worker exploitation in making some parts economically viable.

Further reading

Bagnasco, A. (1977) *Le tre Italie* (The Three Italies), Bologna: Il Mulino (basic sketch of the distinctiveness of the 'Third Italy').

Goodman, E. and Bamford, J. (eds) (1989) *Small*

Firms and Industrial Districts in Italy, London: Routledge.

Leonardi, R. and Nanetti, R. (eds) (1994) *Regional Development in a Modern European Economy: The Case of Tuscany*, London: Pinter (see especially Part II: 'The Tuscan Economy and its Industrial Structure').

Pyke, F. and Sengenberger, W. (eds) (1992) *Industrial Districts and Local Economic Regeneration*, Geneva: International Institute for Labour Studies.

DAVID MOSS

Tiezzi, Federico

b. 13 December1951, Lucignano, Arezzo

Theatre actor and director

Together with Sandro Lombardi and Marion D'Amburgo, Tiezzi founded Il Carrozzone (The Big Cart) which, beginning in 1972, created a number of highly refined spectacles characterized by languorous atmospheres mixing dream imagery and art nouveau. In 1980, having become **Magazzini Criminali**, the group turned towards darker themes, leading to a production of Beckett's *Comment c'est*, for which the theatrical critic Franco Quadri acted as dramaturge. A tendency to fragmentation and dreamlike images enveloped by a musical saraband, as with the obsessive and all-embracing rhythms in *Sulla Strada* (On the Road), adapted from the Kerouac novel in 1984, explicitly recalled the American neoavantgarde of Bob Wilson and Richard Foreman as well as neo-dada conceptualism. Both direction and performance often succumbed to the temptation to shock the audience through violent gestures such as symbolic mutilations or the actual slaughter of a horse in *Genet a Tangeri* (Genet in Tangiers) in 1984. As such youthful radicalism waned, Tiezzi turned between 1989 to 1991 towards more traditional material such as Manzoni and Dante, further reappropriating the primacy of language in texts of Eduardo **Sanguineti**, Mario **Luzi** and Giovanni **Giudici**.

Further reading

Mango, L. (1994) *Teatro di poesia. Saggio su Federigo*

Tiezzi (Theatre of Poetry: Essay on Federigo Tiezzi), Rome: Bulzoni.

PAOLO PUPPA

Tobino, Mario

b. 16 January 1910, Viareggio; d. 11 December 1991, Agrigento

Novelist and psychiatrist

A prolific and successful writer as well as a practising psychiatrist, Tobino has won both the prestigious Strega and the Campiello prizes (see **literary prizes**). Tobino's writing is often permeated by strong autobiographical elements. In his novels *Le libere donne di Magliano* (The Women of Magliano) (1953) and *Per le antiche scale* (Up the Old Stairs) (1971), his own experience as director of a psychiatrist hospital becomes the subject of a powerful and compelling narrative. In *Il manicomio di Pechino* (The Peking Madhouse) (1990), the autobiographical tone is increasingly foregrounded by a diaristic style in which the narrator, Tobino's alter ego, recounts his medical experience, the relationship with his patients and the personal dilemma of an individual divided between an allegiance to his profession and a passion for literature. If investigations of the self and a preoccupation with the mystery of the human mind are central themes in Tobino's literary works, he nevertheless does not ignore broader social issues which take priority in novels like *Il clandestino* (The Underground) (1962). A strong attachment to his native region, Tuscany, is another of Tobino's recurrent motifs, and appears in most of his writings.

PAOLO BARTOLONI

Togliatti, Palmiro

b. 26 March 1893, Genoa; d. 21 August 1964, Yalta, Russia

Politician

As undisputed head of the Italian Communist Party (see **PCI**) for the first two decades after the Second World War, Togliatti was, together with his great adversary, the Christian Democrat leader Alcide **De Gasperi**, one of the two most important political figures in immediate postwar Italy. His death in 1964 definitively marked the end of an era in Italian political life.

Born in Genoa of schoolteacher parents, Togliatti completed his high school in Sassari, Sardinia, and then won a scholarship to Turin University where he studied philosophy and law. In 1911 he met Antonio **Gramsci** and soon became part of the socialist group which edited *Ordine Nuovo* (1919). He participated in the campaign for factory councils in 1920, was a foundation member of the Italian Communist Party in 1921 and in 1926 went to the Communist International in Moscow, where he remained until 1944. From 1934 onwards he was a major architect of the united front against Fascism and Nazism. In 1937 he became the third leader of the PCI, and remained general secretary until his death in 1964.

Although Togliatti fell out with Gramsci in 1926 over Togliatti's support for Stalin's attack on Trotsky, both men came to share a strong conviction that Italian national traditions needed to be taken into account when planning revolutionary policy. Togliatti's *Lessons of Fascism* (1935) bear out his willingness to work with other anti-fascist forces, and in fact, after returning to Italy in 1944, Togliatti built the 'new' Communist Party on a policy of cross-class alliances, particularly with Roman Catholics, in order to achieve a progressive parliamentary coalition. Thus by 1947 the Communist Party had over 2 million members, and it remained the second-largest party in Italy in terms of voters, members and parliamentary representation throughout Togliatti's life. Following the Russian invasion of Hungary in 1956, an event which provoked a strong reaction in Italy, Togliatti firmly committed the party to an Italian road to socialism and, after a long period of hostility with the Socialist Party (see **PSI**) which had placed the Communists in a political ghetto, he also re-established links with the Socialists and their leader Pietro **Nenni**.

Togliatti's long residence in the Soviet Union and his leading position in the Communist International has led to much debate about his possible complicity in the Stalinist purges and to accusations of having played a double game. However, after the war he gave ample proof of his support for a polycentric communist movement freed from Moscow's control, and made major statements (in *Nuovi Argomenti* in 1956 and in his *Memorial from Yalta* in 1964) about the defects of Stalinism and about Khruschev's attempts to divorce that experience from the structural and social problems of the USSR. In the *Memorial* he also suggested that a non-violent and democratic road to socialism was the most appropriate for all countries. Nevertheless, his cautious, cold and indecisive academic style, coupled with his extreme authoritarianism within the party itself, did create a constant suspicion of his motives while at the same time provoking opposition from hardliners such as Pietro Secchia.

Togliatti was prominent in promoting the **intellectuals**' role in Italy through *Rinascita* and other journals. While conservative in his literary and artistic tastes, he encouraged debate on such matters. Despite some delays, he had Gramsci's prison notes smuggled out of Italy, to be returned and published in full between 1947 and 1951. He thereafter became the major interpreter of Gramsci, portraying him as a loyal party man and a Leninist whose ideas had inspired the policies of the 'new party'.

Demonstrating their esteem for one of the founding fathers of the Italian **Republic**, one million Italians attended Togliatti's funeral in Rome in 1964.

Further reading

Agosti, A. (1996) *Togliatti*, Turin: UTET.

Sassoon, D. (1981) *The Strategy of the Italian Communist Party*, London: Pinter.

Togliatti, P. (1979) *On Gramsci and Other Writings*, ed. and introduced D. Sassoon, London: Lawrence & Wishart (a representative selection of Togliatti's writings translated into English).

ALASTAIR DAVIDSON

Tognazzi, Riccardo (Ricky)

b. 1 May 1955, Milan

Film director

Son of actor Ugo **Tognazzi**, one of the great

protagonists of Italian postwar cinema, Ricky began in the movies as assistant to directors such as Pupi **Avati**, Luigi **Comencini** and Sergio **Leone**. After starring in **Scola**'s *La famiglia* (The Family) (1987), he directed an episode of the series *Piazza Navona* entitled 'Fernanda' (1987) and *Piccoli equivoci* (Small Misunderstandings) (1988). However, it was with *Ultrà* (Ultras) (1991) and *La scorta* (The Bodyguards) (1993) that Tognazzi re-evoked the ethical style and social commitment of **neorealism**. *Ultras* unquestionably displays powerful visual and thematic tones as it follows a group of subproletarian Roman youth in their 'violent life', eventually ending in tragedy and death during a soccer game. *The Bodyguards* is a tight-paced and engaging political thriller which draws its inspiration and strength from contemporary Italian events related to the fight against political corruption and the **mafia**. Tognazzi's 1996 *Vite strozzate* (Strangled Lives) is the disheartening tale of a true plague of contemporary Italian society, usury.

MANUELA GIERI

Tognazzi, Ugo

b. 23 March 1922, Cremona;
d. 27 October 1990, Rome

Film actor

Together with Alberto **Sordi** and Vittorio **Gassman**, Tognazzi was one of the most prominent faces of Italian film comedy. His name became inseparable from the *commedia all'Italiana* (comedy Italian-style), the comic genre prevailing in the 1960s and 1970s in which he was consistently cast as the eternal adolescent, whose appalling selfishness and sexism are, nevertheless, pathetically funny.

In one of the classics of the genre, **Risi**'s *I mostri* (The Monsters) (1963), an episode film in which Tognazzi stars with Gassman, he plays the multifaceted embodiment of the era's moral monsters. Twenty years later, Tognazzi was to work under Ettore **Scola**'s direction in *La terrazza* (The Terrace), a sharp criticism of the very genre he epitomized. Tognazzi also collaborated with more

auteurist film-makers like **Pasolini** (*Porcile* (Pigpen), 1969), **Ferreri** (*Non tocare la donna bianca* (Don't Touch the White Woman), 1974) and **Bertolucci** (*La tragedia di un uomo ridicolo* (The Tragedy of a Ridiculous Man), 1982).

DOROTHÉE BONNIGAL.

Tomba, Alberto

b. 19 December 1966, Bologna

Skier

Tomba took the world by surprise at the Winter Olympic Games in Calgary in 1988 by winning both the men's slalom and the giant slalom. Four years later in Albertville, Tomba won the giant slalom again, becoming the first skier ever to take the same event in consecutive Winter Games (see **winter sports**). Tomba's unique style combines great power and technique which has led many to consider him as the greatest slalom skier of all times. Nevertheless, he has managed to win the overall World Cup only one time, in 1995. Early in his career he promised his mother that he would never compete in the dangerous men's downhill event, and this decision has deprived him of the precious extra points to be gained for the combined event, meaning he often finishes the season behind skiers such as Zurbriggen and Girardelli who have taken full advantage of the combined events. What has made Tomba a truly international star, however, is that, in addition to his sporting talents he enjoys the limelight of the media and is willing to play to it, a rarity in a sport whose protagonists are often very reserved and averse to the public gaze.

PAOLO VILLA

Tomizza, Fulvio

b. 26 January, 1935, Materada, Istria;
d. June 1999, Trieste

Novelist, journalist and dramatist

The geographical instability of Tomizza's childhood, which saw Italy and Yugoslavia battle for his native Istria, was later played out in his literary works. The uprooting of thousands of Istrians is documented in his first three novels, later published together as the *Trilogia istriana* (Istrian Trilogy) (1967) which also strongly depict the resulting alienation and the lasting emotional trauma. Even more autobiographical is a series of novels tracing the maturation of a young man as he marries, experiences both post-invasion Prague and the literary circles of Rome, and finally returns home. Perhaps Tomizza's most successful work, however, is the novel *La miglior vita* (The Better Life), winner of the Strega Prize in 1977 and which, in the tradition of Manzoni and Verga, portrays the lives of humble folk near the Italo-Yugoslav border against the backdrop of larger historical and political events.

LAURA A. SALSINI

Tondelli, Pier Vittorio

b. 1955; d. 1991, Correggio, Reggio Emilia

Novelist and literary critic

One of the new generation of Italian writers to emerge in the 1980s, Tondelli made a spectacular literary debut with his *Altri libertini* (Other Libertines) (1980), a collection of short stories that was immediately officially censured as 'obscene', although it was subsequently absolved due to widespread critical acclaim for its provocative themes and tragi-comic style. This was followed in 1982 with *Pao Pao* (Bang Bang), a semi-autobiographical novel which parodies barracks life as it depicts a year of obligatory military service, with all of its daily routines, subversive pranks, visits to discos and homosexual liaisons. His next novel, *Rimini* (1985), is complex and multilayered, telling a number of stories concurrently, all of which in some way eventually cross with a journalist's attempt to solve the mysterious suicide (or murder?) of a prominent political figure. *Camere separate* (Separate Rooms) (1989), published only two years before the author's death from AIDS, is much more dramatic and muted in tone and seems to presage Tondelli's own premature disappear-

ance. Literary critic for the weekly *L'Espresso*, Tondelli also edited the series *Giovani blues* (Young Blues), dedicated to publishing the works of young authors.

GINO MOLITERNO

Topolino

Topolino, the Italian version of Mickey Mouse, was launched in the early 1930s as a comic book character. After the war Topolino, a periodical featuring only Disney characters (with Italian names: Paperino/Donald Duck, Zio Paperone/Uncle Scrooge, Pietro Gambadilegno/Peg-Leg Pete) became the most widely diffused comic book in Italy. Initially targeting children and adolescents, it increased its adult readership to six million per week by the 1990s. Since 1948, Italians have begun to write and draw stories for these characters following the basic narrative structure of the American model but introducing references to Italian culture and thus intensifying both the readers' interest and the processes of identification. The 'Great Parodies', like *L'inferno di Topolino* (Mickey Mouse's Hell) and *I promessi paperi* (The Betrothed Ducks), stories in which the classics of Italian and Western literature are adapted to the world of Disney characters, are a characteristic of the Italian version, along with the creation of new characters like Brigitta and Trudy, the fiancées of Paperone and Gambadilegno.

See also: comics

FRANCO MANAI

Tornatore, Giuseppe

b. 27 May 1956, Bagheria, Palermo

Film director

Self-taught cineaste and photographer, Tornatore became internationally-known with *Nuovo Cinema Paradiso* (New Paradise Cinema), winner of the 1990 Oscar for Best Foreign Language Film. His earlier work had included documentaries and television programmes featuring aspects of the popular tradition and culture of his native Sicily. His first cinematographic experience was also linked to Sicily, as in 1984 he had been assistant director to Giuseppe Ferrara on *Cento giorni a Palermo* (One Hundred Days in Palermo), and generally his major works are all of Sicilian inspiration, including *Cinema Paradiso*, his 1990 road movie *Stanno tutti bene* (Everybody is Fine) and his 1995 Academy Award-nominated *L'uomo delle stelle* (The Star Maker). However, with *Una pura formalità* (A Simple Formality) made in 1993, Tornatore created a radically different film which starred Gerard Depardieu and Roman Polanski in a powerful and complex metaphysical detective story set largely in one single room. In a further departure, in 1998 Tornatore adapted a theatrical monologue by Alessandro **Baricco** into the megaproduction *La leggenda del pianista sull'Oceano* (The Legend of the Pianist on the Ocean), with Tim Roth as the pianist and a musical score by Ennio **Morricone**.

ANTONELLA FRANCINI

Torrini, Cinzia

b. 15 May 1954, Florence

Film director

Cinzia Torrini is the first Italian female director to reach an international audience after the successes of Lina **Wertmüller** and Liliana **Cavani**. After working as a news photographer, Torrini studied at the Munich Film School where she directed several short films, one of which, *Ancora una corsa* (One More Race), toured extensively on the festival circuit. Her first feature, *Giocare d'azzardo* (Gambling) (1982) is an intriguing film about a gambling housewife, gambling being a recurrent theme in Torrini's work. Following several documentaries produced for television, in 1987 she directed an international feature, *Hotel Colonial*, starring Robert Duvall and Massimo **Troisi**, the story of an Italian political refugee in Central America in the1980s. Between 1990 and 1994 she directed several other shorts and features for television including *La colpevole* (The Guilty Woman), *Dalla notte all'alba* (From Night to Dawn), *L'aquila della notte* (The

Night Eagle) and *Un taxi la nuit* (Night Cab). In 1995 she directed *Caramelle* (Sweets), her first erotic film.

ADRIANA MONTI

Toscani, Oliviero

b. 22 February 1942, Milan

Photographer

Italy's most notorious fashion photographer and widely regarded as the 'enfant terrible' of the advertising industry, Toscani studied photography in Zurich in the early 1960s. His work soon appeared in prestigious international magazines such as *Elle* and *Vogue*. He continued photographing for established fashion houses such as **Valentino** and **Fiorucci** but first raised controversy with an advertising campaign for Jesus Jeans, which coupled the erotic image of the behind of a girl in cut-down jeans with the caption, 'whoever loves me should follow me'. He achieved even greater notoriety during the 1990s with his advertising campaigns for **Benetton** which utilized arresting photographs of subjects like mafia murders and AIDS sufferers which many found shocking and in bad taste. The ads were nevertheless effective, and Toscani subsequently became one of the pillars of the Benetton group's publicity machine, acting as both editor of their trimestral glossy journal, *Colors*, and director of Fabrica, an exclusive high-class art college initiated and funded by Benetton.

GINO MOLITERNO

Totò (stage name)

b. 15 February 1898, Naples; d. 15 April 1967, Rome

Comic actor, songwriter and poet

Already established as a comic stage act by 1922, Totò (the stage name of Antonio De Curtis) topped the bill in innumerable variety shows (memorably with Anna **Magnani**) until his last stage performance in 1956. He made the first of his almost 100 films in 1937, *Fermo con le mani* (Hold Your Hands

Still) and by 1948 he was famous enough to have his name in the title of a film – *Totò al Giro d'Italia* (Totò and the Tour of Italy) – the first of thirty-four to bear his name, including the first Italian film in colour (*Totò a colori* (Totò in Colour), 1952). He published a volume of Neapolitan poetry, *A livella* (1964), of which he was justly proud, and in his last years he also made a number of television shorts. He often worked with Nino Taranto and Mario Castellani as his straight men, but also performed with other famous comics such as the Neapolitans Edoardo, Peppino and Titina **De Filippo** as well as Vittorio **De Sica** as an actor and director, the Roman Aldo Fabrizi and the Turinese Macario. He was almost always flanked by one or more of the most beautiful starlets of the time. Many of the films, such as *Totò Tarzan* (1950), *Che fine ha fatto Totò Baby?* (What Ever Happened to Baby Totò?) (1964) and *Totò d'Arabia* (Totò of Arabia) (1965), were parodies of current successes, but others were completely original comedies.

The roles he played were always founded on the persona he had developed from his early days in variety theatre and which had its roots in the *commedia dell'arte* tradition. He was part Pulcinella (Punch) and part Harlequin, and not unlike Charlie Chaplin in some ways; but Totò's character was nevertheless a very individual creation. A funny little Neapolitan in a bowler hat and baggy trousers, slap shoes and coloured socks, a shoelace for a tie and a tail coat too small for him, he typically fights against the big, the bullies and the bureaucrats and wins through with a combination of innocent anarchy and of not so innocent guile. His classic division of the world was between 'men' (real people) and 'corporals' (officious asses), a quip that he had picked up during the First World War but which he then made his own, incorporating it in the title of one of his best-known film comedies, *Siamo uomini o caporali?* (Are We Men or are We Corporals?) (1955). Gifted with a naturally funny but disarming face, he used mime techniques and puppet movements together with virtuoso displays of puns and tongue-twisters which he mostly improvised on the set.

To his chagrin, his films were sneered at by highbrow critics despite constant popular success, so he was very gratified to work with 'intellectual' directors like **Pasolini** and Nanni **Loy** in the last few years of his life.

Much loved and revered by ordinary Italians, he was nevertheless a profoundly contradictory character. He was both generous and jealous, ironic and iconoclastic, both on and off the set. He was also fiercely proud of his aristocratic title and always insisted on being addressed as 'Principe' (he was the unacknowledged illegitimate son of a Marquis De Curtis, and spent much effort proving his noble descent). Politically, he was both a socialist and monarchist. Married to Diana Rogliani, with whom he had had a daughter, Liliana De Curtis, in 1933, he lived with Franca Faldini from 1952 until his death. Since then his popularity has continued to increase to the point where he now enjoys cult status.

Further reading

Caldiron, O. (1980) *Totò*, Rome: Gremese (a comprehensive illustrated survey, includes a full biography and a detailed presentation of all his shows and films).

Governi, G. (1980) *Vita di Totò. Principe napoletano e grande attore* (Life of Totò: Neapolitan Prince and Great Actor), Milan: Rusconi (includes filmography and theatre).

JAMES WALSTON

Touring Club Italiano

The aim of the Touring Club Italiano (TCI) is to promote and assist **tourism** in Italy, especially through a series of publications that focus on the natural and artistic beauties of the country. Founded in Milan in 1894 as TCCI (the second 'C' standing for *Ciclistico* (Bicycling)), its first function was the organization of trips, excursions and non-competitive bicycle races. Soon the emphasis switched to the needs of the automobile driver. TCI now produces studies and surveys to determine and improve the condition of the roads, supplies accurate road maps and roadside assistance in conjunction with ACI (Automobile Club d'Italia), and provides the necessary documents for Italian drivers travelling abroad. TCI is also involved with the hotel industry, for which it publishes manuals and sponsors hotel management classes and training programmes. Hotels, restaurants, campgrounds and other establishments that display the TCI logo have been inspected and approved by the organization.

PAOLO VILLA

tourism

Italy offers a diverse range of tourist products, from cultural tourist attractions based on art, culture, music and religion, to coastal tourism, mountains, hot springs and **spas**, natural resources, theme parks and special events. It has been estimated that at least 40 per cent of the world's cultural and historical heritage (including 50 per cent of the world's artistic heritage) is concentrated in Italy (Bonini, 1993). However, such concentration presents the Italian government and the tourist industry with a conundrum: Italy's cultural heritage will inevitably help to maintain that country's attractiveness to domestic and international travellers but, at the same time, large numbers of tourists present complex visitor management problems, which ultimately threaten the sustainability of tourist resources.

Domestic tourism is the mainstay of Italy's tourist industry, with domestic travel highly seasonal and heavily concentrated in the traditional holiday months of July and August. Tourism is also concentrated geographically. Northern Italy contains five of the leading tourist destination regions in terms of visitor arrivals and bed-nights, reflecting the economic differences between the wealthy north and the poorer south. The major destination areas in Italy continue to be Rome, Florence and Venice. These cities, with lengthy tourism histories, have experienced recent declines in their tourist market shares because, among other things, their hotels are old and overly expensive, restaurant prices are excessive, transportation is inefficient and many cultural attractions keep irregular hours (for example, opening only in the morning or in the afternoon), are closed on Sundays and public holidays, or are open only on special request. In addition, the Naples–Capri–Sorrento area was one of Italy's largest tourist destinations until the mid-1970s, when social problems, pollution and degradation led to declines in its share of tourist travel (Bonini, 1993). Conversely, former minor historical and cultural sites (attributes which appeal to the growing numbers of discerning tourists) concentrated in central and northern Italy (such as Assisi, Pisa, Siena and Verona) have steadily increased their shares of the tourist market. This area too, however, especially the Umbria region, suffered extensive physical damage in the disastrous 1997 earthquakes, the consequences of which were extremely severe and wide-ranging.

Italian tourism itself has had a long, significant but turbulent history. During the Roman Empire, 'state official travel offices' provided travel permits incorporating maps with information on accommodation and transportation services. With the fall of the Roman empire and the coming of the 'dark ages', tourism was largely restricted to pilgrimages. From the seventeenth century onwards, Italy regained its position as one of the world's leading tourist destinations, with the Italian peninsula the core destination within the 'Grand Tour'. In the nineteenth century, Thomas Cook's career as a travel agent began when increasing numbers of English people took an active interest in travelling to the beaches of the Italian Riviera (Formica and Uysal, 1996). From 1860 to 1960, tourism was Italy's biggest and most lucrative industry (Bosworth, 1996).

In 1912, Bonaldo Stringher made dubious claims that tourism contributed invisible assets which kept the national balance in budget and thereby contributed to Italy's development and prosperity (see Bosworth, 1997). However, the onset of the First World War created a sense of urgency to develop a national tourism policy. Although many Italian tourist resources were either destroyed or extensively damaged in the two world wars (during the Second World War, 40 per cent of hotels were destroyed and another 20 per cent were damaged), there was recognition that the management of postwar tourist attractions and sites (such as battle sites) would require public sector intervention and planning. Subsequently, the Ente Nazionale per le Industrie Turistiche (ENIT) was established in 1919, mainly as a result of F.S. Nitti's commitment to rational economic planning. By

October 1922, as Fascism came to power, this body was inevitably still feeling its way, and the Fascist regime, beginning in 1923, had the major responsibility for developing a detailed policy for ENIT's future and for international and domestic tourism planning and promotion (Bosworth, 1997). Despite the well-documented failings of ENIT, a second government tourist agency (the Compagnia Italiana Turismo, CIT) was established in 1927, followed in 1934 by the Direzione Generale per il Turismo (DGT, which fell under the authority of the Ministry of Press and Propaganda) and then the Ente Provinciale per il Turismo the following year. The charters of these and other independent agencies (for example, the Royal Italian Automobile Club, RIAC) created considerable overlap in tourism policy and administration, thereby generating much postwar debate about which of the administrations should be retained and how it should be structured domestically and internationally (see Bosworth, 1997).

The problems in the public administration of Italian tourism aside, by 1950 Italy had become the world's third most popular tourist destination after the United States and Canada. Although Italy's tourist facilities were modest, its prices for accommodation, transportation and meals were internationally competitive. Between 1951 and 1965, tourism growth in Italy averaged 11.5 per cent per annum, and tourism's share of exports rose from single figures to 19.3 per cent. However, during this period the international tourism scene changed dramatically as population growth and demographic changes (such as the baby boom), technological innovations (such as jet aircraft) and socioeconomic developments (such as reductions in working hours) encouraged international travel and competition, and as tour operators began to invest heavily in the comparatively cheap coastal areas of the Mediterranean (especially Greece, Spain, Turkey and Yugoslavia). These areas competed successfully with Italy mainly on the basis of price and sustained marketing and promotion programmes.

This competition was all the more damaging since the public organization of tourism in Italy had long been ineffective. Public tourist organizations lacked strategic foci and appropriate institutional frameworks. The Ministry of Tourism and Performing Arts, abolished in April, 1993, was previously responsible for all leisure-related public policy, but it did not have a separate tourism portfolio and it patently demonstrated little concern with the sustainability of the Italian tourist industry. The Ministry was transformed into a Tourism Department of the Presidency of the Council of Ministers, and is now responsible for international tourism policy and for coordinating tourism development and promotion. Until the early 1990s, most public sector activity had been concerned with funding large events such as the 1990 World Soccer Championships and the 1992 500th anniversary of the discovery of America. Simultaneously, the Ente Nazionale Italiano del Tourismo (ENIT, Italian National Tourism Board) performed poorly. ENIT promoted Italy by way of images that been in use for more than fifty years, while its delegates, assimilated with diplomatic personnel, were generally experts in public relations generally rather than tourism marketing and promotion specifically. The burden of tourism marketing and promotion was relegated to a network of twenty regional tourist and promotion boards which discharged those responsibilities with mixed success (Bonini, 1993).

In an important and recent turnaround in tourism planning and promotion, ENIT has established foreign partnerships, regularly participates in international travel, trade fairs and congresses, and has supported a series of interregional projects with diverse cultural and environmental themes, mainly by way of providing regional authorities with financial backing. These projects demonstrate a more coordinated approach within and among the different levels of tourism public sector administration in Italy, and reflect a wider concern with the broad relations and global dimensions of the tourism industry. Such developments perhaps have also helped to deflect suggestions that ENIT should be privatized.

It is also worth noting other negative factors limiting Italy's ability to attract tourists from the 1970s to 1990s, amongst them Italy's lack of quality accommodation and transport services, negative publicity stemming from natural disasters and pollution (such as an oil spill off the coast of Liguria), crowding and congestion in major tourist centres, petty crime and the algae problem in the

Adriatic Sea, which discouraged seaside visiting from the late 1980s. As a result, international travel and visitor bed-nights in Italy declined considerably throughout the 1980s and early 1990s.

The 1992 recession and continued stagnation of the Italian economy created inflation in tourism services and hotel prices, thereby compounding the problems outlined above, and further threatening the competitive position of Italy's tourist industry. However, the devaluation of the lira in September 1992, and the unstable political situations in the former Yugoslavia, the Middle East, Egypt, Turkey and Spain had positive impacts on international travel to Italy. These factors combined to allow the Italian peninsula to re-establish itself as a major tourist destination in 1993 and 1994, and led to a significant rise in international visitor bed-nights. By 1995, Italy was fourth in the list of the world's top ten tourist destinations (29.2 million visitors, a 9.2 per cent rise on 1994), and was the world's third largest tourism earner, with international tourism receipts rising 13.1 per cent in 1994–5. In 1994, the main origins of international visitors were **European Union** residents (approximately 50 per cent, around half of whom were Germans), followed by the United States (approximately 10 per cent) and then the Japanese (approximately 5 per cent). In 1996, approximately 4.5 per cent of Italy's workforce (1,063,000 people) was employed directly and indirectly in tourism. 'These results seem to augur well for the future of tourism, although Italy is prone to periodic economic, political, social and even meteorological vagaries which have repercussions on the sector' (Francescone, 1997: 5).

Clearly many domestic and global factors have impacted upon the development of the Italian tourist industry, and that country's competitiveness as a tourist destination. Interestingly, as suggested above, global forces largely beyond the control of the Italian government and the local tourist industry have contributed to Italy regaining its status as a leading international tourist destination. Projections to the year 2000 are promising, indicating that Italy will receive an average annual rise of 5.2 per cent per annum in international tourists (Francescone, 1993), with increasing arrivals from Eastern Europe and Asia. The greatest growth potential in tourist attractions is likely to come from the cultural, health, rural and sport tourism sectors.

The Italian tourist industry has access, admittedly limited with respect to some cultural attractions, to an enormous wealth of natural and cultural resources whose tourist potential has not yet been fully tapped and which far exceeds that of many other nations. However, the sustainability of the industry will require greater proactive public and private sector attention if Italy is to successfully compete in the increasingly discerning and competitive global tourist market. Recent public sector policies and programmes and the publication of extensive information dealing with many aspects of the Italian tourist industry by the Department of Tourism, ENIT and several public and private agencies are a start in the right direction. However, major challenges requiring greater attention from industry and government are the conservation of heritage and managing visitors at heritage sites, the coordination of tourism planning, development and promotion, and the provision of facilities at an appropriate standard.

Further reading

Bonini, A. (1993) 'Tourism in Italy', in W. Pompl and P. Lavery (eds), *Tourism in Europe: Structures and Developments*, Wallingford, UK: CAB International.

Bosworth, R.V.B. (1996) *Italy and the Wider World*, London: Routledge (see ch. 8: 'Visiting Italy: Tourism and Leisure 1860–1960').

Bosworth, R.V.B. (1997) 'Tourist Planning in Fascist Italy and the Limits of a Totalitarian Culture', *Contemporary European History* 6 (1): 1–25.

Francescone, P.M. (1997) 'Italy', in G. Todd (ed.), *International Tourism Reports* 1: 5–25.

Formica, S. and Uysal, M. (1996) 'The Revitalisation of Italy as a Tourist Destination', *Tourism Management* 17 (5): 323–31.

JOHN M. JENKINS

trade unions

The so-called 'hot autumn' of 1969 is still widely regarded as the principal watershed in the evolution of postwar Italian trade unionism, since it was only after that troubled period that the Italian unions became powerful protagonists in both industrial relations and the political system, and therefore either feared antagonists or respected partners of firms and governments alike.

Italy's free trade unionism had been reconstituted by the Pact of Rome, concluded among the anti-fascist parties in 1944, as a unitary, class-oriented, centralized movement. However, the unitary Confederazione Generale Italiana del Lavoro (CGIL), or Italian General Confederation of Labour was internally divided into partisan factions. The breakdown of unity – which stemmed largely from the Cold War climate – came about in 1948–9, when the Christian democratic, reformist socialist and republican factions withdrew from the single trade union confederation, largely dominated by communists and socialists, and formed two further main confederations, the Confederazione Italiana Sindacati dei Lavoratori (CISL), or Italian Confederation of Worker's Unions, and the Unione Italiana del Lavoro (UIL), or Italian United Labour. As well as their division along ideological lines, a key element of weakness for the trade unions was the unfavourable situation of the labour market, characterized by major layoffs, high unemployment and the labour-saving character of capital accumulation.

The situation began to change only in the years straddling the 1950s and 1960s, mainly due to the more favourable labour market conditions produced by the 'economic boom' (see **economic miracle**) and to the first cautious political dialogue made possible by the end of the Cold War. These conditions permitted a certain unity of action by the unions and acceptance of some company-level bargaining, and also encouraged some attempts to set up shopfloor organizations in the factories. However, this was too little to enable the unions to harness the growing discontent of broad sectors of the labour force, a discontent which bred a period of severe conflict culminating in the 'hot autumn' of 1969. In the period 1968–75, the strike volume reached an average rate of 11.55 working hours lost per employee per year (with a peak of 23 hours in 1969), a significant increase with respect to the already high rate of 7.26 hours during the period 1959–67. Furthermore, workers' mobilization assumed much more radical forms than those traditionally envisaged by the unions, and the claims advanced – egalitarianism and rejection of the Taylor–Fordist organization of work – were highly innovative. Most importantly, the conflict was highly charged with ideology.

Despite the unions' initial difficulties in controlling the collective mobilization, they eventually drew considerable benefit from it. They managed to strengthen themselves organizationally, and they used the mobilization to install themselves as indispensable participants in negotiations with the employers and the government, thereby increasing the degree of recognition accorded to them by both. This organizational success meant that the unions' principal concern gradually became that of conserving the power that they had acquired, while they also sought to prevent any harmful macroeconomic consequences. This concern led to the decision – symbolized by the 'EUR turning point' of 1978 (a document which the majority trade union, CGIL, approved at its Congress held in the EUR Congress Centre in Rome) – to moderate wage demands in exchange for benefits in the political sphere. Consequently, the second half of the 1970s and the early 1980s were characterized by a central importance being assigned to consensual incomes policies and to tripartite negotiation of economic and social policies more generally.

On the other hand, during the 1980s Italian firms fully recovered the key position that they had lost in the previous decade. It was on the ability of firms to restructure, in fact, that the economic adjustment of the entire country depended; and the firm consequently became the locus of not only technological, but also organizational and social innovation. The Italian unions responded to these changes in an apparently contradictory manner. While the central bodies mostly restricted themselves to ritual reaffirmation of adversarial positions, in the workplaces forms of cooperation arose between management and local unionists which were based on pragmatic acceptance of the new situation and of its consequences. These developments concerned the industrial sector and a large part of the private services sector. In the public services, on the other hand, the 1980s saw widespread and fragmented conflict, as well as the marked particularization of protest, which gave rise to a scattering of representation and a proliferation of small 'autonomous' unions or radical rank and file organizations, such as the well-known Comitati di Base (COBAS), shopfloor committees. However, despite forecasts to the contrary, this form of sectoral conflict did not spread beyond the public sector.

The deep political crisis of the early 1990s forced the top levels of the trade union confederations to adopt a more collaborative stance, by engaging again in tripartite negotiation. The most significant events in this resurgence of political bargaining were the laws informally negotiated between the government and the unions in 1990 and 1992–3 to bring public sector employment more closely in line with the overall model of Italian trade union relations; the tripartite agreements on incomes policy and the collective bargaining structure signed in 1992 and 1993; the negotiated law that in 1995 reformed the Italian pensions system; and the achievement of a tripartite 'pact for employment' in 1996 and of a 'social pact' in 1998. In 1993, a major reform of the representational system was also carried through, which led to the formation of Rappresentanze Sindacali Unitarie (RSU), or Unified Union Representation, an institution similar to the German 'works councils' elected by all workers, but at the same time officially recognized by the trade unions as their own organizational level in the workplaces.

Italian trade unions have, therefore, slowly regained a key role in public policy formation as well as in collective bargaining and cooperation with employers. Although they no longer enjoy the prestige and the large following of the 1970s, they maintain an important position in the economic, political and even cultural spheres of Italian life.

See also: economy; industry

Further reading

Franzosi, R. (1995) *The Puzzle of Strikes: Class and State Strategies in Postwar Italy*, Cambridge: Cambridge University Press (an analysis of strike behaviour, which provides a more general insight into trade unions' changing strategies).

Lange, P., Ross, G. and Vannicelli, M. (1982) *Unions, Change and Crisis: French and Italian Union Strategy and the Political Economy 1945–1980*, London: Allen & Unwin (the most detailed account of trade union behaviour in the 1950s and 1960s).

Pizzorno, A., Reyneri, E., Regini, M. and Regalia, I. (1978) *Lotte operaie e sindacato: il ciclo 1968–1972 in Italia* (Workers' Struggles and the Unions: The Period 1968–1972 in Italy), Bologna: Il Mulino (the most comprehensive and illuminating analysis of the causes and consequences of the 'hot autumn').

Regalia, I. and Regini, M. (1998) 'Italy: the Dual Character of Industrial Relations', in A. Ferner and R. Hyman (eds), *Changing Industrial Relations in Europe*, Oxford: Blackwell (an overall analysis of the evolution of Italian trade unions within the context of changing industrial relations).

MARINO REGINI

transavantgarde

The transavantgarde (*transavanguardia*) was a notional grouping of artists championed by the critic Achille **Bonito Oliva** in the 1980s. Bonito Oliva initially identified five: Sandro **Chia**, Francesco **Clemente**, Enzo **Cucchi**, Nicola **De Maria** and Mimmo **Paladino**. With Bonito Oliva's clever promotion – the title itself was a masterstroke, suggesting a transcendence of modernism – the group achieved an enormous success at the 1980 **Venice Biennale**. Consequently the artists became well-entrenched and are represented today in art museums around the world.

The term 'transavantgarde' plays on the modernist idea of a small, elite group of 'avantgarde' artists who boldly precede the conservative majority and, by constant experimentation and originality, finally drag others with them. Modernism itself is 'Darwinistic' in its belief that art evolves and progresses toward a more advanced stage, and that its newness is the measure of its worth. In Italy, futurism had been the outstanding avantgarde movement. The futurists joyfully proposed destroying the art of the past, and with unusual consistency, predicted that their own art would soon become obsolescent. It was much more common, however, for avantgarde movements to assume that their own art would somehow be preserved from the general process of change.

Another aspect of modernism was the belief that changes in art run parallel to transformations in society, and that art can play a positive social role in forging a new sort of person. This was the belief of the futurists, and it also came to be the motivation of **arte povera** and conceptual art of the 1960s and 1970s, when the physical artwork was reduced to a pretext for political or ideological messages. However, once art was reduced to a slogan or external meaning, it became dependent on its cause and when, in the late 1970s, popular protest subsided and ideological models lost their appeal, modernism and conceptual art both declined. According to Bonito Oliva, this was the historic moment when the myth of progress and the blind worship of novelty were overturned and art rediscovered subjectivity.

In a densely-worded manifesto in **Flash Art** in 1979, Bonito Oliva outlined the crisis in modernity. However, he noted, a few recent artists had gone back to the real process of picture making, feeling no need to be always new or practising in the latest style but instead travelling in their own various directions. Their art had broken away from the need to express social concerns in order to depict an imaginary, artistic world, and it was a happy 'catastrophe', the result of unplanned accidentality. As these artists 'bypassed' or 'crossed' (the geography is not clear) the avantgarde idea of art as a problematic which confronts the viewer, Bonito Oliva labelled them the transavantgarde.

There was still an artistic elite. If anything, it was reinforced because technical ability was revived as a positive value. But this was no longer a unified group dragging art towards a particular future. Instead, it consisted of individuals: Chia, with his technical skill and variety of styles; Clemente, who also mixed styles and techniques; Cucchi, with works bursting with energy; de Maria, with his geometric and organic forms; and Paladino and his surfaces.

Above all, the transavantgarde did not ignore the history of art but simply refused to regard it as linear. Artists were free to pick and choose from any style or period. This was not done, Bonito Oliva hastened to add, as slavish copying. The past is used as a general model, not a precise quote, and it is used ironically so the reference is obvious to artist and viewer.

The transavantgarde was recognized as the first Italian art movement of international significance since the futurists. However, unlike futurism and despite the success of the label, it was not a formal movement, with fixed membership or a common declaration of aims. The theorizing was done by critics and was more polemic than description. Bonito Oliva initially sought to identify a geographical movement, rooted in Italian culture, but contemporary art is notoriously trans-national, and genuine local movements are hard to find. Technically the work of Clemente, Cucchi, and Chia is akin to German neo-expressionism. Furthermore, it seems clear that these artists would have been produced their work even without the label that came to be attached to them.

Bonito Oliva does offer a useful explanation for the return of figuration to Italian painting, arguing that the figures now act as rhetorical devices rather than standing as literal representations. However, in arguing that the role of the avantgarde has ended, to be replaced by a sort of 'after,' Bonito Oliva does no more than echo the central theme of **postmodernism**, that the modern period and style have been replaced by an 'after-modern'. Thus, in sociological terms, the 'discovery' of the transavantgarde can be seen as Bonito Oliva's attempt to carve out his own particular Italian version of postmodernism.

See also: art movements

Further reading

Bonito Oliva, A. (1979) 'The Italian Transavant-garde', *Flash Art* 92/3: 17–20.

—— (1981) 'The International Transavantgarde', *Flash Art* 104: 36–43.

—— (1982) *Transavantgarde international*, Milan: Giancarlo Politi Editore (the second part deals with 'new painting', with the disclaimer that not all new painting can be identified as transavant-garde).

MAX STAPLES

Trieste

From the late eighteenth century, when the Habsburgs established the city as an international port, Trieste provided a harbour for political and religious exiles from Europe and the Levant. It has since earned a controversial place on the international map as the site of a series of international boundary disputes.

Before the First World War, Trieste, still under Austrian tutelage, was coveted by Italy as 'unredeemed' Italian territory. Along with the Istrian peninsula, Trieste officially entered the Italian fold in 1921. By this time it had already earned a reputation as a regional fascist stronghold. After the Second World War the city was the epicentre of Cold War tension between Italy and the newly-communist Yugoslavia. In the period 1945–54 Trieste came under the administration of a British-American military government while it awaited a decision on its future, whether it would be Italian, Yugoslav or a free territory. When the Western Allies returned Trieste to Italy, the city continued to be the focus of discontent expressed by Italian nationalists and exiles from Istria, who regretted the loss of the Istrian peninsula to Yugoslavia.

The transformations of Trieste's political status have affected its relations with neighbouring territories, but its linguistically and ethnically diverse population (most notably its Slovene minority), and its 'frontier' identity have continued to make it an important centre of international culture. In the early twentieth century, Trieste was the temporary home of James Joyce. One of Joyce's most admired writers was his Triestine contemporary, Italo Svevo (a pseudonym emphasizing the writer's Germanic and Italian origins and masking his Jewish surname Schmitz). Svevo wrote the Triestine landscape into a number of novels that were to earn him fame, and popularized the idea of a Central European culture. It was through Trieste's Viennese connections that Freudian psychoanalysis was first disseminated in southern Europe (see **psychoanalysis and psychiatry**). This 'international' cultural legacy was an inspiration to the postwar generation of writers such as Ernesto Sestan and Umberto **Saba**, whose nom de plume suggested Jewish, Catholic, Slovene, Austrian and Italian undercurrents. Claudio Magris's writing has consolidated Trieste's 'cosmopolitan' or trans-national, as well as Italian, identities.

In 1963, Italy made Trieste the capital of the new autonomous region of Friuli-Venezia-Giulia and its minority groups thus gained the right to preserve their cultural diversity. The 1975 Treaty of Osimo between Italy and Yugoslavia was meant to resolve Cold War differences over territory between the two states. However, the treaty's attempt to create an interregional economy to deal with the links that had been unofficially maintained across Trieste's national frontier proved to be ineffectual.

Local politicians and businessmen have attempted to tackle the postwar perception of Trieste as a dying city with an ageing population by rebuilding Trieste's international networks. The creation of Alpe Adria, an economic and cultural unit embracing the neighbouring frontier towns of Italy, Austria, Germany, Slovenia and Hungary, was relatively successful in this respect. However, with the breakup of Yugoslavia in 1992 the question of the 'frontier' resurfaced, and the past of Italian fascism and Yugoslav communism have been revisited locally as a means of coming to terms with the territorial and cultural obligations of both Italy and its eastern neighbours.

See also: foreign policy; regions

Further reading

Ara, A. and Magris, C. (1987) *Trieste, un'identità di frontiera* (Trieste: A Frontier Identity), Turin: Einaudi.

GLENDA SLUGA

Trionfo, Aldo

b. 10 February 1921; d. 6 February 1989, Genoa

Theatre director

Following an apprenticeship in acting and mime with Alessandro Fersen, in 1957 Trionfo founded the cabaret theatre Borsa d'Arlecchino (Harlequin's Bag) in Genoa, where for the next three years he staged avantgarde texts. He subsequently alternated between musical and prose theatre, demonstrating a devastating wit in approaching the classical texts as well as a talent for discovering minor or unusual works, from Salgari to the Elizabethan repertoires, from Hubay to Dreyer, from **Pavese** to Svevo, from **Roversi** to Patti. Often original scripts are contextualized more widely, in satirical collages representative of the bourgeois imaginary. His overall strategy is a celebration of grotesque registers and vaudeville counterpoint, creating vertiginous associations between high and low culture. Exemplary in this sense are the *Festa per la beatificazione di Margherita Gautier, la Signora delle Camelie, santa seconda categoria* (Feast for the Beatification of Margherita Gautier, Lady of the Camelias and Second-Rate Saint) of 1972 and his *Faust-Marlowe-Burlesque* of 1976. In spite of his subversiveness and irreverence, he was appointed head of the Turin State Theatre in 1972 and the Roman Academy in 1980. His work often crossed paths with the elegant fairy-tale scenography of Emmanuele Luzzati and the whimsical dramaturgy of Tonino Conte.

Further reading

Groppali, E. (1977) *Il teatro di Trionfo, Missiroli, Cobelli* (The Theatre of Trionfo, Missiroli, Corbelli), Venice: Marsilio.

PAOLO PUPPA

Troisi, Massimo

b. 19 February 1954, San Giorgio a Cremano, Naples; d. 4 June 1994, Ostia, Rome

Actor and film director

Troisi made his debut at age fifteen in the theatre of his native town. In 1969 he co-founded the group La Smorfia (The Grimace), which gained national attention in 1970s through appearances on popular television shows. He broke box office records as both leading actor and director of his first feature film, *Ricomincio da tre* (I'm Starting

From Three) in 1981. With *Non ci resta che piangere* (Nothing Left to Do but Cry) (1985), a medieval fantasy made with Roberto **Benigni**, and *Le vie del Signore sono finite* (God's Ways Are Finite) (1987), Troisi confirmed a very personal comic style which combined elements of traditional *commedia dell'arte* with uninhibited use of Neapolitan dialect. His role as a neurotic character afflicted by indolence and uncertainty, reluctant to accept conventions and social integration, returned in the 1991 *Pensavo fosse amore invece era un calesse* (I Thought It Was Love But It Was A Carriage) and in several other comedies directed by Ettore **Scola**. Suffering from birth from a serious heart ailment, he died shortly after the completion of Michael Radford's *Il postino* (The Postman), where he played the role of the Neapolitan friend of the exiled Pablo Neruda.

ANTONELLA FRANCINI

Trussardi, Nicola

b. 17 June 1942, Bergamo; d. 14 April 1999, Milan

Fashion designer

Trussardi came from a family of designers, inheriting a well-established glove company from his father in 1970. As a first move in expanding the company, he hired expert technical staff to help him set up a tannery and to perfect procedures for treating and refining leather. His research into the treatment of leather led to his development of many softer leather products. Choosing an elegant and dynamic greyhound as the trademark for his product, Trussardi began to produce purses, luggage and other small leather goods. The success of his first collection resulted in further expansion into belts, shoes, umbrellas, foulards and ties and finally into ready-to-wear leather garments. The first Trussardi shop opened in Milan in 1976, and today his boutiques are found throughout Italy and abroad. His look has been labelled classic but innovative. Expanding beyond the fashion market, Trussardi created the Palatrussardi outside Milan, an arena which has staged pop and rock concerts featuring international stars including Frank Sinatra, Liza Minelli and Sammy Davis, Jr. At the time of his death in a car accident, Trussardi was at work designing a 'Fashion City' which would include fashion schools, an area for fashion shows, a hotel and other features. The project is scheduled to continue.

BERNADETTE LUCIANO

U

UDI

The rebirth of Italian feminism after its virtual demise under Fascism came about in September 1944, only several months after the liberation of Rome, with the foundation of the UDI (Unione Donne Italiane, or Union of Italian Women). The Union of Italian Women was initially made up of southern women and partisan women of the North, and came into being as an autonomous organization within the framework of the political Left. The impetus for its formation come from **PCI** leaders, particularly Palmiro **Togliatti** who encouraged women within the party to form a national women's organization that would unite all existing groups. Members of the original organising committee of the UDI included Rita Montagnana and Egle Gualdi (PCI), Bastiana Musu (**Partito d'Azione**/Action Party), Giuliana Nenni and Maria Romita (**PSI**) and Marisa Rodano Cinciari and Luigia Cobau representing the Catholic communists. Although emerging from grassroots, the UDI developed into an extremely hierarchical organization with local circles, provincial committees and a national executive with elected officers. Nevertheless, it was largely responsible for winning the women's right to vote in 1945 and thereafter campaigned heavily to ensure women's fundamental needs including maternity leave for women workers and protective legislation for women working in factories and on farms. By 1949, the organization had expanded its structure, boasted one million members and its periodical *Noi donne* (We Women) had a distribution of 200,000.

By the mid-1950s the UDI initiated a battle for birth control (strongly opposed by the Catholic Church) and adopted causes such as revising the family law and securing rights for illegitimate children. In its ongoing struggle to safeguard women in the workforce, it fought for equal salaries and increased representation in workplace organizations as well as proposing a salary for housewives. In the 1960s the organization campaigned for strong laws to prevent the common practice of women being fired from their jobs when they married thus helping to increase women's access to careers and public office. The UDI produced **abortion** legislation in 1978, while working for women's health clinics and attempting to initiate a referendum to change laws relating to sexual violence. At the same time it continued its interest in humanist as well as feminist issues; having petitioned for the disarmament of the atomic bomb in 1947, it also participated actively in the 1986 Chernobyl demonstrations (see **environmental movement**).

In the turbulent climate of 1968, UDI members split over the ongoing issue of alliance to the Italian Communist Party. Some members distrusted the larger political machines and questioned the link between feminism and principles that seemed incompatible with the feminist theory of difference. After a long period of discussion, the UDI finally acted to put an end to what had become an increasing subordination to the parties of the Left. Moving ideologically away from politics toward cultural concerns of neofeminists, it declared itself an autonomous organized movement in May 1982, its new aims being to expand the feminist movement so as to embrace women who were concerned with feminist issues but who were not necessarily ideologically aligned with the PCI. In fact, central to the new UDI was the acknowledgement of multiple feminist perspectives which made it possible for women to differ ideologically while working together on a variety of women's issues such as lesbianism, female sexuality, a union for prostitutes and so on. Thus, evolving from fairly traditional and male-centred forms of political militancy, the UDI became instrumental in developing what has become a widely diffused women's consciousness in Italy today.

See also: family; feminism; marriage

Further reading

Birnbaum, L.C. (1986) *Liberazione della donna: Feminism in Italy*, Middletown: Wesleyan University Press (the UDI within the larger context of Italian feminism).

Slaughter, J. (1997) *Women and the Italian Resistance*, Denver: Arden Press (for the roots of the movement).

BERNADETTE LUCIANO

UDR

The UDR (Unione Democratica per la Repubblica, or Democratic Union for the Republic) was founded in the summer of 1998 by the volatile former **DC** prime minister and **President of the Republic**, Francesco **Cossiga**, in an attempt to re-create the old Christian Democratic centre grouping. It failed to win over the **PPI** but effectively absorbed the **CDU** of Rocco Buttiglione, split the **CCD**, with one of the latter's leading lights, Clemente Mastella, joining it, and also attracted several disgruntled personalities from **Forza Italia**, including Carlo Scognamiglio, ex-president of the Senate, and Tiziana Parenti, magistrate and ex-member of the *Mani pulite* team. Thus, in spite of holding only 5 per cent of the seats in the Chamber of Deputies, it occupied a strong strategic position and so was able to play a crucial role in the formation of the new centre–left government of

Massimo **D'Alema** in October 1998. In consequence, the UDR obtained three cabinet posts.

JOHN POLLARD

Ulivo

The change to a mainly single-member constituency **electoral system** in 1993 obliged parties and groupings to form electoral alliances in order to contest elections with any hope of success. Thus, later that year the Left came together as the Progressisti (Progressives), led by Achille **Occhetto**, who seemed confident of victory. The Progressive alliance, however, was countered by **Berlusconi**'s **Polo della Libertà** which actually did win, and it thus became clear that a broader left-wing alliance was necessary to match the Polo. By August 1994, Romano **Prodi** began to be identified as a possible counter-leader to Berlusconi, and in March 1995, Prodi launched the Ulivo (Olive Tree) as a centre–left coalition of Catholics and ex-communists.

The deputy leader of the **PDS** and editor of *L'Unità*, Walter **Veltroni**, became deputy leader of the Ulivo, and Prodi and Veltroni toured the country launching the new political movement. The core of the Ulivo was obviously the PDS, but there were hopes that the **PPI**, essentially the centre–left of the old **DC**, might also become part of the alliance. Opinion in the PPI differed and in fact, soon after Prodi announced the formation of the Olive Tree, the PPI split over whether it should support the Polo or become part of the new centre–left grouping. The Left of the PPI, led by Gerardo Bianco, kept the name and supported the Olive Tree, but the Right, under former secretary Rocco Buttiglione, formed the **CDU** which confederated with Casini's **CCD** and joined the Polo. In the lead-up to the 1996 elections the then prime minister, Lamberto **Dini**, declared his intention of founding a new movement in the centre. After some hesitation, especially with regard to who might be the future prime minister should the alliance win, Dini accepted Prodi's leadership and his Rinnovamento italiano (Italian Renewal) became part of the Ulivo. For the first time, there was a single programme (published in December 1995) underwritten by all the components of the alliance.

An agreement was also reached with **Rifondazione Comunista** (Communist Refoundation) by which Ulivo and RC candidates would not contest the same seats. RC did not subscribe to the manifesto, but said that it would support a possible Ulivo government on an issue-by-issue basis.

The results of the 1996 national elections gave the Olive Tree alliance (together with RC) a majority in both the Senate and Chamber of Deputies (see **Parliament**). Its policies came to be summed up in the title of a collection of Prodi's essays *Il capitalismo ben temperato* (Well-Tempered Capitalism). Specifically, in 1995, and when in government the following year, substantive constitutional reform, a massive reduction of the public deficit to reach the Maastricht criteria for European monetary union, pension reform, continuation of the privatization process initiated by the **Ciampi** government (see **privatization and nationalization**), introduction of fiscal federalism and a reduction of the number of laws and of **bureaucracy**.

The Olive Tree government pursued these aims, though not without some tension both between Prodi and **D'Alema**, leader of the biggest party in the coalition, and also between those who supported the Olive Tree as a broad confederation of centre–left groupings including Catholics and centrists (Prodi and Veltroni) and those who wanted a single left-wing party for ex-communists, socialists, Christian socialists and Greens. The future of the Olive Tree Alliance was put under severe strain when D'Alema succeeded Prodi as Prime Minister in October 1998.

Further reading

Bull, M. and Newell, J.L. (1996) 'Party Organisations and Alliances in Italy in the 1990s: A Revolution of Sorts', *West European Politics* 20 (1): 81–109 (the Ulivo alliance in the wider context of party change in Italy in the 1990s).

JAMES WALSTON

unemployment

Although Italy came out of the Second World War with unemployment rates above 30 per cent (in line with other European countries directly affected by the war), after a fitful start it experienced two decades of high growth, and consequently Italians did not perceive the existence of a problem of unemployment of the labour force until the end of the 1970s.

During the 1950s and 1960s, internal migrations from the southern regions ensured an almost unlimited supply of labour to the factories in the North. As a result, the unemployment rates in the two regions began to converge, leading politicians and economists to hastily predict the disappearance of the North–South divide. However, at the beginning of the 1980s Italy experienced a process of industrial reorganization and restructuring, which mainly affected the North of the country where the industries were concentrated. The extent of this change was enormous: the industrial sector lost almost one million jobs in four years (1981–4), which represented one-fifth of dependent employment in the sector. As in other OECD countries, the Italian economy did not return to the growth rates experienced during the golden age of capitalism, and this was reflected in a slower growth of employment. At the same time, the cultural change induced by rising enrolment in school produced an increase in participation rates of women, and women began entering the labour market in force. The combination of low growth in employment and rising participation rates, only partially counterbalanced by longer stay at school, almost doubled unemployment levels. In addition, the employment growth was concentrated in the Northern regions, thus exacerbating the unemployment in the South. Furthermore, a crucial feature of the unemployment problem has remained its concentration in specific segments of the labour force. So, for example, while the average unemployment rate in 1996 was calculated as 12.1 per cent, this becomes 33.8 per cent for young people aged 15–24 and reaches a maximum of 64.9 per cent for young women in the South. Undoubtedly some of the regional differences are still related to cultural roles: thus one can compare women's participation in employment in the North (35 per cent) with the corresponding figure for the South (19 per cent), but if one takes into consideration that the average number of children per woman are respectively 1 and 1.5, it becomes clear that the northern labour market corresponds to an indus-

Growth and Unemployment Rates: Italy 1951–96 (percentages)

	Italy: growth rate	Italy: unemployment	North and centre: unemployment	South: unemployment	South/North: unemployment
1951–60	6.3	9.7	7.6	14.5	1.8
1961–70	6.3	5.1	4.7	6.0	1.3
1971–80	3.8	7.2	5.5	11.1	2.0
1981–90	2.4	12.0	8.1	21.0	2.6
1991–96	0.1	14.2	8.4	26.4	3.2
1951–96	4.3	9.3	6.7	14.6	2.1

Figures from statistical appendix of Bank of Italy report

trial (or post-industrial) society, while in the South there remain wide areas of agricultural society.

Another peculiarity of the Italian labour market is that pressure from **trade unions** , made possible by the tight labour market conditions during the 1970s, provided the already employed workers (the so-called 'insiders') with legal protection against unfair dismissal their employers. This contributed to the creation of a dual labour market: in the primary labour market, a job might last for almost the worker's entire life, with wages regulated by national contracts; in the secondary market, jobs would be temporary, fiscal evasion widespread and wages often below minimum levels.

Significantly, most of the Italian unemployed work in the secondary market. In 1996, irregular work positions were estimated to exceed 10 per cent of regular positions. Labour legislation was also under revision, in an attempt to increase temporary jobs so as to facilitate entry into the labour market for young people. Great hopes were also raised by the prospect of a legislated reduction of working hours. However, many economists doubted the wisdom of such a move, based on fear that firms would be unable to hold their own against foreign competition due to increased costs, and thus the eventual outcome might very well be a reduction rather than an increase in total employment.

The Italian welfare system supports unemployed people in differentiated terms, according to their previous employment status: for workers previously employed in firms with more than 50 employees, there exists a temporary lay-off (named CIG, or Cassa Integrazione Guadagni, corresponding to 80

per cent of previous pay), for a maximum of two years, at the end of which the worker may either be fired (and in this case the subsidy is extended for a period varying from 2–4 years) or goes back to work. Temporary lay-off subsidies do not exist for people working in small business: if fired (but not in cases of voluntary dismissal), such workers obtain only a six-month subsidy (equal to 30 per cent of previous pay). By contrast, first-job seekers are not entitled to any kind of social support. Since the vast majority of young people fall within this group, their only option is living with their **family** of origin, which explains why the family leaving rates are lower than in other European countries, and the **marriage** age is higher and rising.

The social perception of the unemployment experience is therefore rather different according to the age of the people involved. For young people, especially those living in the South, there is little or no social stigma attached to the condition of being unemployed and economically supported by someone else, usually the family. The condition of older workers fired after a working life of 20–25 years is rather different. In most cases these are blue-collar workers, with a low level of **education** and even lower probability of re-employment. In this case, the unemployment experience may be dramatic, both in terms of self-perception and with respect to economic resources, since in the older generation the household head would most likely have been the only person earning an income for the family. The practical impossibility of finding a regular job often leads to a loss of self-esteem, a lack of contact with friends and relatives which thus closes down all information channels about potential vacancies, and sometimes also exacerbates poor health conditions. It is not surprising, then, that suicide rates have been highest among unemployed.

See also: agriculture; economic miracle; peasants; social welfare

Further reading

CEPR (1995) *European Unemployment: Is there a Solution?*, Cambridge: Cambridge University Press (an analysis of the effect of labour market rigidity on unemployment in an European perspective).

ISTAT (1997) *Rapporto Annuale – La situazione del Paese nel 1996*, Istituto Poligrafico di Stato (especially ch. 3 which presents a detailed analysis of Italian unemployment).

DANIELE CHECCHI

Ungaretti, Giuseppe

b. 10 Bebruary 1888, Alexandria, Egypt;
d. 1 June 1970, Milan

Poet

After childhood and adolescence in Egypt, Ungaretti went to Paris in 1912, where he stayed for two years, before entering to the Italian army to fight in the First World War. In the French capital, Ungaretti met the most important members of the avantgardes of the period: the futurists (F.T. Marinetti, Boccioni, Severini, but above all Giovanni Papini, Ardengo Soffici and Carlo Carrà), the cubists (especially Picasso) and Apollinaire. After several poems had appeared in *Lacerba* and *La Diana*, Ungaretti was able to enlist the help of Ettore Serra to publish his first collection of poems, *Il Porto Sepolto* (The Buried Harbour) (1916) in a small edition. In 1919 he added some new poems and variations on some of the old poems and published it again under the new title of *Allegria di naufragi* (Joy of Shipwrecks). This would become Ungaretti's characteristic way of working, and all his collections would be marked by a constant return to earlier verse in order to file and perfect it to the point of silence. Such a poetics of the word redeploys some of the stylistic tenets

proposed by the avantgarde movements and pushes to the limit some of the experimentation that had already fascinated the poets of French symbolism (Baudelaire and Mallarmé especially, but also Rimbaud). At the same time Ungaretti, in reaction to the eloquent lyric of D'Annunzio, embraced the Italian romantic tradition of Giacomo Leopardi and experimented with the metre by dismantling the compact unity of the hendecasyllable. The result was a poetry that emphasized the value of the sounds, especially the smallest elements of the word itself. The very short poems which Ungaretti included in his first collection are phonic particles embedded in the white of the page, the blank space being homologous to the silence in which the word resonates and to which it returns. This gesture, a manifest expression of the poetics of the fragment, left a distinctive mark on hermeticist poetry. The collection, moreover, presents itself as a sort of war diary, with the exact specification of dates and places and with an internal chronological organization to the sections.

Working as a correspondent for Mussolini's newspaper, *Il popolo d'Italia* – a collaboration that, magnified by the innocuous preface written by Mussolini for the 1923 edition of *Il Porto Sepolto*, would create problems for the poet after the war – Ungaretti moved to Italy in 1921 and lived first in Rome, then at Marino. After working for some years for the Foreign Ministry, in 1931 he became as correspondent for the Turin newspaper *La Gazzetta del Popolo*. While publishing new editions of his first collection (*Il Porto Sepolto* in 1923, and *L'Allegria* in 1931), he worked on a new book of poetry (*Sentimento del Tempo*) (Feeling of Time) (1933, 1936) which marked a return to more traditional poetic forms, the most striking one being the reconstruction of the hendecasyllable. The new collection also bore witness to a spiritual crisis which afflicted the poet until 1928, when it was partially resolved by his return to Catholicism. Furthermore, in *Sentimento* Ungaretti attempts to reconsider the epistemological tenets that lay at the basis of his early poetry (foremost the philosophy of Henri Bergson, whose lectures he attended at the Sorbonne during his Paris years). Poetry must be both new and classic at the same time. Ungaretti's second collection is thus a continuous meditation articulated as a number of illuminations, organized in a series of small strophes which themselves evoke and recall the fragments of the first collection. But this time it is memory that, more efficaciously and pervasively than before, leads the poetic expression. By crossing Leopardi's poetics with Bergson's philosophy, Memory has become a psychological rendition of lost innocence and the Christian myth of Eden and the Fall can be resurrected through its power. A concern with time remained a constant motif of Ungaretti's poetry, so much so that in 1942, when the publisher Mondadori began publication of his collected work, the poet insisted on having them appear under the general and comprehensive title of *Vita d'un uomo* (Life of a Man).

In the meantime, during a congress organized by the Pen Club in South America, Ungaretti had been offered the chair in Italian Language and Literature at the University of São Paulo in Brazil and had accepted. After six years in Brazil, he returned to Italy in 1942 and, on the basis of his great renown, was given a professorship in contemporary Italian Literature, a position he temporarily lost at the end of the Second World War due to his collaboration with the Fascist regime.

The period in Brazil had been a time of personal suffering. Far from the war itself (which, however, had found its place in the poet's echo of collective lamentations and invocations of peace), Ungaretti had lost his brother and his son Antonietto. This time of sorrow interrupted the project of the third book of poems, overwhelmed by the outburst of *Il Dolore* (The Sorrow) (1947). Only in 1950 was *La Terra Promessa* (The Promised Land) published, a collection whose title is purposefully deceptive, since it explicitly recalls the Jews' Exodus from Egypt, but it actually celebrates Aeneas's voyage to Italy. At this point, the reflection on poetry and memory had been completed not only in light of his own personal experiences of loss, but also in the study of Plato and Neoplatonic philosophy. Aeneas, the hero of the quest who conquers the promised land, is never named and left out of the collection as the absence par excellence, in line with the symbolist tradition from Mallarmé to D'Annunzio, from Valéry to hermeticist criticism.

With a poetic life already fulfilled, there followed the publication of other small collections of poetry,

such as *Un Grido e Paesaggi* (A Cry and Landscapes) (1952) and *Il Taccuino del Vecchio* (The Notebook of the Old Man) (1960), some critical writings, such as the travel notes *Il Deserto e dopo* (The Desert and Afterwords) (1961) and his important translations from Gongora, Shakespeare, Mallarmé and St John Perse.

Further reading

Brose, M. (1977) 'Ungaretti's Promised Land: The Mythification of *L'Allegria*', *Italica* 54 (3): 341–66.

Cambon, G. (1967) *Giuseppe Ungaretti*, New York: Columbia University Press.

Cary, J. (1969) *Three Modern Italian Poets: Saba, Ungaretti, Montale*, New York: New York University Press.

Jones, F.J. (1977) *Giuseppe Ungaretti: Poet and Critic*, Edinburgh: Edinburgh University Press.

Perella, N.J. (1979) *Midday in Italian Literature: Variations on an Archetypal Theme*, Princeton, NJ: Princeton University Press.

Ungaretti, G. (1969) *Vita d'un uomo. Tutte le poesie*, ed. L. Piccioni, Milan: Mondadori (a complete collection of all the poems).

—— (1971) *Selected Poems*, introduction and notes by P. Creagh, Harmondsworth: Penguin.

ERNESTO LIVORNI

L'Unità

Official daily of the Italian Communist Party (**PCI**) and subsequently of the **PDS**, *L'Unità* (Unity) has reflected the changing nature and fortunes of the party. It was founded by **Gramsci** in 1924 as a tool for fostering unity between workers and peasants and North and South. Suppressed under Fascism and refounded by **Togliatti** in 1942, it thrived as the organ of the postwar mass party, thanks largely to militants' door-to-door distribution and **Festa dell'Unità** (Festival of Unity) fundraising. While the decline in militancy in the 1980s brought a reduction of sales, *L'Unità* remained one of Italy's most significant dailies. During the same period, greater freedom of debate within the party was reflected in the spawning of satirical magazines **Tango** and **Cuore**. Under

Veltroni's editorship from 1992 to 1996, the paper broadened its appeal by dedicating a complete section, '*L'Unità due*', to culture and sport, inviting greater contributions from intellectuals outside the party and regularly including free books, video and music cassettes. Although sales improved somewhat and the paper became much less identifiable with the party, these changes were not sufficient to overcome its severe financial difficulties, making its sale to private interests increasingly probable.

See also: newspapers

CLAIRE KENNEDY

universities

The recovery of freedom after the Fascist period was characterized, almost symbolically, by the recovery of autonomy in the appointment of academic authorities. In September 1944, while half of Italy was still under German occupation, a decree gave back to professors the right to elect the rector of the university (previously named by the minister) and the deans of the faculties (previously chosen by the rector). The decree also instituted a new academic authority, the Corpo Accademico, formed by all professors; however, no powers were given to it, and in fact in most universities it has never even convened. This situation is quite emblematic for at least two reasons: first, as would happen in many other cases, innovation in university rules remained on paper; second, the institution proved to be based on individualism, and to be inclined to react against any introduction of collegiate bodies.

In the years immediately following 1944, higher education was not a national priority. **Postwar reconstruction** absorbed most resources, and since even the lower levels of the educational system were still subject to heavy class selection, the progressive parties and movements concentrated their attention on compulsory schooling and professional training. In the **constitution**, higher education is barely mentioned: there is only a reference to the autonomy of universities within the limits of state law and to the right of the 'capable and worthy' young to reach the highest levels of schooling, with the aid of scholarships if need be.

For a long time, these theoretical principles did not have any practical effects; for more than a decade, the university situation was extremely stable, both qualitatively and quantitatively. However, around 1958 the situation began to change. The number of students began rising, increasing by 2.5 times over ten years. No substantial transformations accompanied this expansion: the elitist structure of the university system seemed unchangeable.

The main features of the Italian university system had been established in 1923 by the Minister for Education and renowned idealistic philosopher Giovanni Gentile in his educational reform, and included a dominant role for the humanities with little attention – if any – to technology and professional training. The administrative structure was extremely centralized; conversely, at the local level each institute, usually consisting of a single chair, was run on a totally individualistic basis. The situation was reminiscent of the feudal system and prompted the widespread use of the expression *baroni delle cattedre* (chair barons). Only in some scientific sectors – mainly physics, where the Fermi school was active – was there any evidence of teamwork and international connections. Consequently, the proposal for a new organization based on departments, in itself not much more than a technical measure, appeared almost revolutionary.

The contradictions between an archaic academia and a society which was undergoing rapid expansion and modernization (see **economic miracle**) quickly became evident. As soon as a center–left government took power (1962–3), a parliamentary committee drew up a report proposing significant reforms. In 1965, a draft law based to a large extent on these proposals was sent by the government to **Parliament**. It represented a rather cautious compromise between tradition and innovation, but the debate on this draft law, which became known by its number, 2314, lasted three years and was extremely heated. Those in academic power opposed even the suggestion of collegiate management of universities, whereas a new generation of younger scholars called for more radical steps toward reform. In fact, in order to maintain their privileges, full professors had blocked any increase in their number; therefore, to cover the needs of the increased number of students, more and more assistants and other teaching staff were hired to teach regular courses. With the same duties as full professors but with a totally dependent status, they became the protagonists of a rather strong movement, leading to strikes and widespread unrest.

Thus, the 1967–8 student revolt, which hit Italy like many other European countries, fell upon an already troubled situation. Both leftist political parties and the organizations representing university teachers with non-professorial status found themselves split. Some wanted to take advantage of the new situation to overcome conservative resistance to reforms; others raised the stakes, claiming that any reform within the existing institutions would be a hoax. Unavoidably, in such a situation, the draft law 2314 was withdrawn.

In 1969–71 a new Parliament seemed ready to give some positive answers, through a more advanced law, to students and to those among the junior teaching staff who were fighting for a new university system and not merely looking for career benefits. Almost as an advance payment, while the comprehensive Reform Law on the University System was moving forward, at the end of 1969 a law concerning student access and curricula came into force with immediate effect. This 'Liberalization Law' guaranteed access to any university faculty from any long-cycle (five-year) higher secondary school and also permitted any student to submit to faculty committees a proposal for a personal curriculum, even if quite different from those officially established. At the time, both liberalization measures were announced as temporary and were considered to be almost provocative, since it was claimed that the comprehensive reform would soon be in place; in fact, they turned out to be the enduring product of the events of 1968, as even the Parliament which lasted from 1968 to 1972 did not succeed in passing the reform law. Progressive movements, as suggested earlier, were split and so unable to exert any effective pressure; furthermore, at the end of that period the political balance moved to the Right.

Thus, while the quantitative expansion of higher education continued, political authorities dealt only with emergencies. To address the problem of the teaching staff who had been hired and continued to be hired with an ambiguous status (or without any status at all), university legislation concentrated for almost two decades on personnel matters, ignoring pedagogical problems and instituting organizational changes which overall proved rather ineffective. Two laws passed in 1973 and in 1980, and slightly revised up to 1985, reorganized the teaching staff. A second level of professorship, *professore associato*, was added to the first level of full professor; a new position, *ricercatore*, was introduced for teaching staff without full responsibility for a course.

The 1973 law also tried to deal with university management issues, and gave a role to representatives of all those involved in the university including teaching staff, administrative staff and students. This undoubtedly constituted a change as compared to the past, when only full professors were represented, and apparently satisfied the requests for democratization; in practice, it produced very limited effects. The structure of central administrative bodies was not much affected; as far as the teaching staff was concerned, the transformation of faculty councils was a more radical measure. However, even this change did not lead to a substantial renewal of policies, as no power was given to student representatives, whereas teachers with career problems turned out to be rather dependent on full professors. Thus, all in all, the scepticism which had been originally expressed with regard to *cogestione* (the participation of all representatives in the management process), proved in the end quite well-grounded.

A faint echo of the 1968 controversies about academic power may be recognized in the 1980 law, which allowed universities to set up departments. However, this was not compulsory, and moreover, decision-making power remained in the traditional faculty structure, as departments had mainly an organizational function, or at most some responsibility for research projects. The law stated that after four years of such an 'experiment', a final decision should be taken with regard to university government and structures but, predictably, this failed to happen.

Thus at the end of the 1980s, the possibility of a major reform along the lines discussed for a quarter of a century had lost all credibility. Events did start moving, but in a different direction. The major topics under discussion became more and more the differentiation of curricula, which had been violently refused by the 1968 movement, and the autonomy of universities, which had been scarcely considered beforehand. The political trend towards **European Union** heavily contributed to concentrating attention upon such topics, which were at the centre of debate in other countries.

With regard to autonomy, a first result came in 1989, when universities were allowed to adopt statutes departing from the national rules previously in force. In 1993, budget autonomy was established; previously, each line of expenditure was separately funded by the Ministry, but now each university would receive a lump sum to be spent at its own discretion. As regards curriculum, a law of 1997, implemented during 1999, replaced the detailed national curricula, which previously were set centrally for each study programme, with 'guidelines', within which each university will be able to define its own curriculum. This process of didactic autonomy is just starting and, in fact, even the processes of institutional and financial autonomy begun in 1989 are not completed. However, the trend appears quite clear.

As far as differentiation is concerned, the Italian tradition was always alien to it. Except for established institutions in the Arts (Accademie di Belle Arti, Conservatori di Musica), there has never been a system of non-university tertiary education. Concrete proposals to initiate such a system have only surfaced in the late 1990s and still remain mere proposals; in reality, only isolated activities usually classified as post-secondary schools courses are being carried on. At the end of the century, it is still true that – apart from fine arts and music – to talk about the Italian higher education system is to talk about the university.

Even within the university, only one degree, the *laurea*, approximately corresponding to a Masters degree, used to exist on a generalized basis (the exceptions were specialization courses in the medical field). A first change came in 1980 when Ph.D. programmes were introduced; there are still ambiguities, as the labour market is not very interested in such degrees, and as a result Ph.D. programmes are perceived as leading mainly to an academic career, but gradually things are being clarified. A second change came about in 1990

through a law that has been implemented since 1992: this concerns a first degree (*Diploma universitario*), corresponding to completion of a three-year programme. In this case too, there are ambiguities: in some instances, the curriculum almost coincides with the first part of the curriculum leading to the *laurea*, while in other cases it is completely separate. The goal in introducing the *Diploma* was to reduce the high number of university dropouts (only one-third of the students who start university obtain the *laurea*). After five years, in 1996–7, fewer than 10 per cent of first-year students are entering programmes leading to the *Diploma*: thus, the situation is changing very slowly. The guidelines for the renewal of university teaching, which are presently under discussion, will most likely increase the speed of the changes since universities are being asked to make the first-level degree a compulsory step in long-cycle programmes. However, a conflict may be expected in the coming years between the new tendency towards flexibility and tradition-bound rigidity. Whereas a reform law would have resulted in just one winner, it is likely that in a system of increasing autonomy there shall be, across the country, universities or even university sectors, where innovation wins and universities or university sectors where it fails miserably.

See also: education; student movement

Further reading

Clark, B. (1977) *Academic Power in Italy*, Chicago: Chicago University Press ('baronage' as it was, and still is in some places; an excellent guide to most of the postwar system).

Luzzatto, G. (1988) 'The debate on the University Reform proposals in Italy and its results', *European Journal of Education* 23(3): 237–47.

—— (1996) 'Higher Education in Italy 1985–95: An Overview', *European Journal of Education* 31 (3): 371–8.

Marsiglia, G. (1993) 'L'università di massa: espansione, crisi e transformazione' (Mass University Expansion, Crisis and Transformation) in *Fare gli Italiana* (Creating Italians), vol. 2, Bologna: Il Mulino (on mass higher education and the 1968 movement).

Martinelli, A. (1992) 'Italy', in *The Encyclopedia of Higher Education*, Oxford: Pergamon, vol. 1, 355–69.

Moscati, R. (1993) 'Moving Towards Institutional Differentiation – The Italian case', in *Higher Education in Europe*, London and Philadelphia: Jessica Kingsley Publishers.

—— (1998) 'The Changing Policies of Education in Italy', *Journal of Modern Italian Studies* 3 (1): 55–72.

Miozzi, U.M. (1993) *Lo sviluppo storico dell'università italiana* (The Historical Development of the Italian University), Florence: Le Monnier (a historical sketch of the development of university since 1860, the year Italy became a unified country).

Santoni Rugiu, A. (1991) *Chiarissimi e Magnifici*, Florence: La Nuova Italia (the professorship in the history of Italian university).

GIUNIO LUZZATTO

L'Uomo Qualunque

L'Uomo Qualunque was a short-lived populist movement (1944–8), which bequeathed the derogatory term *qualunquismo* (distaste for politics, ideology and public life) to Italy's political vocabulary. Its founder was an exuberant journalist and playwright, Giuglielmo Giannini (1891–1960) who, in the pages of the weekly paper, *L'uomo Qualunque* (The Ordinary Man), which he founded in December 1944, attacked all politicians as indifferent to the desire of ordinary war-weary people for work, order and freedom from government meddling. Exploiting conservative fears about the communist-dominated 'wind from the North' (see **Resistance**) while simultaneously defining himself as 'anti-anti-fascist', he transformed his paper into a political movement in 1945. In the **Constituent Assembly** elections, the UQ attracted 1,211,956 votes (5.3 per cent), mainly in the South but, forced to convert anti-political slogans into parliamentary strategies, the leadership divided over attitudes towards fascism and the **DC** government, while the larger centre–right parties drew away its grassroots support. The movement disappeared after its dismal failure in the 1948 elections.

Further reading

Satta, S. (1995) *L'uomo qualunque 1944–1948* (The Uomo Qualunque 1944–1948), Bari: Laterza, 2nd edn (definitive history of the movement and its leaders).

DAVID MOSS

urban planning

Italian urban planning since 1945 has traditionally been viewed as an enormous series of errors, failures and missed opportunities. The challenges presented by **postwar reconstruction**, economic expansion and then de-industrialization have not been met with adequate answers at either a local or national level. Urban planning in Italy has classically been a mixture of urban plans (drawn up by local politicians, council technicians, planners and architects) and political negotiation, which has led to interminable changes, adaptations and delays in all the major cities. Much of this has been blamed on national delays and (lack of) political reform. The rebuilding necessary after 1945 was carried out via fascist plans and with fascist planning legislation still in operation (especially the law of 17 August 1942). As such, the opportunities presented by large amounts of open space at Milan, Turin and Genoa, for example, were largely wasted in a series of ad hoc projects aimed at providing housing for immediate needs rather than rational plans for urban development. Some of the areas left derelict by wartime bombings were still unused even in the 1990s, such as the huge Varesina wasteland in Milan.

With the economic upturn, speculation and mass migration imposed with even greater intensity the need for coordinated urban plans. Milan passed a plan in 1953, but Turin and Rome only followed suit in the late 1950s and early 1960s. Even these (often innovative) plans were left largely unfulfilled, with private (and often corrupt) interests winning out over public need. This period was one of enormous damage to cities like Rome, Palermo, Turin and Milan. Building speculation and lack of control over construction and demolition led to the so-called 'sack of Rome' and 'sack of Palermo' under Christian Democrat (**DC**) rule and often with corrupt **mafia** influence, a process illustrated vividly for Naples in Francesco **Rosi**'s film *Le mani sulla città* (Hands Over the City) (1963). A few isolated voices, such as Antonio Cederna and his Italia Nostra (Our Italy) movement, founded in 1957, and the magazines *Il Mondo* and *L'Espresso* spoke out amidst a general rush to profit. At Rome, the campaign against the construction of the Hilton Hotel at Monte Mario (approved in 1958, opened in 1962) became an emblematic defeat.

Nationally, the opportunities presented by the Sullo reforms of 1962 for control of urban growth and planning were swamped by a wave of hysterical propaganda from the Right and a lack of will from within the centre–left government. Similarly, in 1967 any positive effects of the Mancini laws, passed as a response to the urban disasters at Agrigento (where illegal housing collapsed near the Valley of the Temples in 1966) and Florence (massive flooding in 1966 destroyed houses, churches and millions of books in the national library) were counteracted by a year-long moratorium. In that year, one million building permits were granted. Further attempts were made to better the situation in 1977 (Bucalossi laws) and 1985 (Galasso), but by then it was too late.

Italy has no green belts, no new towns and no coherent national planning policy. All too often, incredible amounts of money were spent on extraordinary but largely superfluous motorways while whole areas were left without public services or green space. The lack of parks is a constant problem: Milan has the lowest level of green space per person in Europe and the parks that do exist are often virtual no-go areas. Genoa's green space in its historic centre is measured in centimetres per person. Over large parts of Italy the landscape has become a monotonous urban sprawl, constructed without any indication of form or content, ruled by the motor car and commercial interests.

The problems of traffic (there were 26 million cars on the road by 1989) and the destruction of the urban 'historic centres' led to a number of policy decisions in the 1980s and 1990s. City centres were closed to traffic in Milan, Bologna and Florence. Parking was made difficult and very expensive. Attempts were made to maintain residents in these areas (at least in Bologna).

However, these policies have not worked. Milan's city centre was re-opened to traffic in 1997. The ring roads of all these cities are centres for pollution and gridlock. The cities with the greatest problems – Rome and Naples – have done very little. Another tactic was to decentralize business and industry into so-called *centri direzionali*. Naples's *centro direzionale* is designed by Kenzo Tange, and is as incongruous as it is empty. Other cities have simply caved in to conservative commercial interests. Milan built the extension to its trade fair near to the city centre in 1996–7. The whole northern part of the city is now paralysed by traffic jams whenever a trade fair is on. All attempts to decentralize services have met with massive opposition. One example will suffice: Milan began building its customs and road freight centre outside of the city in the 1960s. It was still nowhere near to being opened in 1997.

The South is no better off. Illegal private housing, often funded by wages sent back by migrants or returning migrants, is a feature of every small town and village right across the South, Sicily and Sardinia. Typically, one or two floors of each house have been finished, but the buildings are usually unpainted and large metal poles stretch out towards the sky. The effect on the landscape is not difficult to imagine. Constant amnesties (called *condoni*) for these illegal private builders have simply made the situation worse, encouraging further illegality. Occasionally, this situation comes to public attention, such as with the illicit housing on the side of an exploding Etna volcano, or the villas built near precious temples near Agrigento, but in general little is done and many southern politicians defend the illegal builders. The problem is not confined to housing. One famous example was a hideous, enormous white hotel built (illegally) on the coast near Salerno in the early 1970s. Only a campaign by intellectuals finally led to the destruction of the hotel – which became known as Il Mostro (The Monster) – in 1999. Tourist-linked construction (roads, holidays homes, hotels) has devastated whole regions – Liguria, the Adriatic coast, northern Sardinia – and threatens the natural havens of Trentino and Valle d'Aosta.

However, there have been some important and innovative examples of urban planning in Italy since 1945. Piero Bottoni's plans for an experimental neighbourhood at Milan – QT8 – are perhaps the most impressive examples of urban design from the 1940s. Bottoni incorporated a hill into the plan, using the rubble from the wartime bombings, which he named Monte Stella after his wife. The happy combination of green space, mixed housing, squares and gardens was to remain an isolated example in the city which has perhaps lost the most through speculation. Usually, however, the most positive experiences have been located in 'red' Italy and in smaller provincial towns. Bologna attempted to preserve residents in its city centre through planning controls and operated an innovative decentralization programme. Giancarlo **De Carlo**'s work in Urbino (1962–6) and Terni (1969–74) is seminal. Lodovico **Quaroni**'s designs for Rome and Venice and experiments at Matera have remained as innovative examples of Italian urban design. Unfortunately, as with so many plans where Quaroni has had an input (above all his influential collective plans for San Giuliano at Mestre, 1959), these ideas have been left largely unrealized. Often, plans have been massacred during the political process, such as at Palermo where there were six hundred 'variations' to the 1959 plan under the auspices of mafia-controlled assessors Salvo Lima and Vito Ciancimino, or at Rome in the 1950s. Perhaps the most interesting combination of work by architects, intellectuals, urbanists and industrialists took place at Ivrea from the late 1930s onwards, where Adriano **Olivetti** inspired and financed a whole series of studies and projects (for houses, factories, schools, individual products and even an asylum) which remain unique in Italy and probably in the world. The most common charge levelled at Olivetti has been a familiar one, namely, his utopianism. Olivetti was active in setting up the Istituto Nazionale di Urbanistica, an important forum for debate and collective pressure. The INU produced an important Urban Planning Code as a guide for planners and architects.

Debates raged in innovative magazines like *Casabella*, **Domus**, *Urbanistica*, *Edilizia moderna*, *Edilizia Popolare*, **Controspazio** and *La nuova città*. Architects, planners and designers drew up battle lines over neo-liberty, or modernism or brutalism, often through the wholesale (acritical) importation of non-Italian models. The issues at stake differed.

Often, the argument was about form. Usually there were attempts to come to terms with the Italian historical tradition, both in terms of urban form and architecture. Often these debates focused on single, important, buildings, most notably the Torre Velasca and the **Pirelli** Tower in Milan, both completed in 1958. While the former, designed by the **BPR** group in a combination of traditional and modern styles, was heavily criticized by both traditionalists and modernists, the latter became a symbol of the unparalleled development of the **economic miracle**. Occasionally, the debates became political and radical, especially in the wake of 1968. Nonetheless, very few of these ideas had more than a marginal impact on the actual form of the cities in question. The impotence of the planners and the architects in Italy is far greater than elsewhere. However, these debates did influence whole generations of students and architects in Italy and elsewhere, and certain key texts have remained as important reference points: Carlo **Aymonino**'s *Il significato della città* (The Meaning of a City) (1975), Aldo **Rossi**'s *L'architettura della città* (The Architecture of a City) (1966) and Quaroni's *La Torre di Babele* (The Tower of Babel) (1967).

In the 1990s, money flooded into urban areas for the World Cup, but only left its mark in two enormous stadiums with bad views at Bari and Turin and the enlargement of those of Milan (where the grass refused to grow on the pitch) and Naples. Renzo **Piano**, who designed the best new stadium at Genoa, was also involved in the ill-fated re-organization of the city's port for the so-called Colombian anniversaries. Planners increasingly took refuge in formulas as the fragmentation of decision making (especially with the setting up of regional governments in the 1970s) made co-ordinated planning even more difficult. Intercommunal plans were replaced by metropolitan cities, which were replaced in turn by post-industrial scenarios. Thousands of monographs and research projects were produced, with local or national funding, to investigate the feasibility of plan A or plan B. Meanwhile, the real decisions were left to the politicians. Inertia and compromise were the outcome, and Italy's cities are both contracting and expanding at the same time. Residents leave the immediate urban centres to move to the provinces, creating huge sprawling megalopoli which stretch from Bologna to Ravenna, from Naples to Caserta, from Milan to Turin.

The future of Italian urban planning is marked by opportunity, although much of the damage done cannot now be reversed. Huge areas are available for development into parks, universities and housing as industries close down and move out. The debate in Milan, Turin and Genoa is now dominated by the fate of the so-called *aree dismesse* (abandoned areas). Yet, any hope for change in the whole process must be tempered by the knowledge of the damage done to Italian cities over the last fifty years by planners, architects and, above all, speculators and politicians. All too often, the lure of the 'grand project' is too much for local leaders, notwithstanding any possible damage to the fragile urban environment.

Futher reading

Cederna, A. (1991) *Brandelli d'Italia. Come distruggere il bel paese* (Scraps of Italy: How to Destroy the Beautiful Country), Rome: Newton Compton (a selection of urban planning horror stories collected by one of the founders of the Italian environmental movements).

Muratore, G. (1988) *Guida all'architettura moderna. Italia, gli ultimi trent'anni* (A Guide to Modern Architecture: Italy in the Last Thirty Years), Bologna: Zanichelli (good introduction summarizing a series of architectural debates, followed by a comprehensive review of individual projects and buildings with photos and maps).

Quaroni, L. (1983) 'I principi del disegno urbano nell'Italia degli anni '60 e '70' (The Principals of Urban Design in Italy in the 1960s and 1970s), *Casabella* 47 (487/488): 82–9.

Secchi, B. (1984) *Il racconto urbanistico. La politica della casa e del territorio in Italia* (The Urban Planning Story: The Politics of Housing and Territory in Italy), Turin: Einaudi.

Tafuri, M. (1989) *History of Italian Architecture, 1944–1985*, Cambridge, MA: MIT Press (translation of *Storia dell'architettura italiana, 1944–1985*, Turin: Einaudi, 1982).

JOHN FOOT

Ustica

On 27 June 1980, an Italian civilian airliner on regular flight from Bologna to Palermo fell into the sea near the island of Ustica, north of Sicily, with the consequent loss of all eighty-one lives on board. The original official explanation blamed it on a structural fault, but in the years that followed a number of parliamentary inquiries found disquieting signs of failure to examine relevant evidence, tampering with records and a cover-up at a number of levels, including the highest ranks of the Italian Air Force. This encouraged a wide variety of hypotheses to surface, ranging from that of a terrorist bomb in the toilet to a stray missile. Despite repeated attempts to get to the truth of the matter, the cloak of 'national interest' and 'security concerns' continued to be used to obstruct investigations so that, at the end of the 1990s, the case remained unsolved with many informed commentators crediting the bizarre, but nevertheless plausible, explanation that the aircraft was accidentally hit by a missile launched in a covert battle between American NATO warplanes and Libyan fighters.

Further reading

Salvatori, G. (1993) 'Ustica: The Unending Investigation', *Italian Politics: A Review*, vol. 8, ed. S. Hellman and G. Pasquino, London: Pinter.

GINO MOLITERNO

V

Vacca, Roberto

b. 1927, Rome

Electrical engineer, novelist and essayist

With a technical background and degree in
engineering, Roberto Vacca taught at the University
of Rome, worked as managing director and was
computer expert at the Polytechnic of Milan. He
also contributed to a number of journals, published
several successful essays such as *Esempi avvenire*
(Samples To Come) (1965) and *Medioevo prossimo
venturo* (The Coming of Dark Age) (1971) and various
works of political and science fiction. In his novels,
from *Il robot e il minotauro* (The Robot and the
Minotaur) (1963) to *La morte di Megalopoli* (The Death
of Megalopolis) (1974) Vacca forces the reader to
contemplate apocalyptic visions of a world in the
near-future where human survival is constantly
threatened by technological and social dysfunctions.

FRANCESCA PARMEGGIANI

Valduga, Patrizia

b. 20 May 1953, Castelfranco Veneto, Treviso

Poet and translator

Regarded by many as one of Italy's most interesting
contemporary female poets, Valduga's poetry has
been noted for its striking mixture of eroticism and
a darker, almost mortuary, lexicon. She develops
her contents by borrowing poetic forms from the
contemporary and classical Italian literary tradition

though with a strong stylization that sometimes
breaks the balance of the verse. More generally for
Valduga, poetry seems to be a way to survive the
banalities and the absurd routine of everyday life.
She has translated Molière, Mallarmé, Valéry,
Céline, John Donne and Shakespeare and written
a number of dramatic monologues, which include
Dama di dolori (The Queen of Pain) (1991) and *Corsia
degli incurabili* (The Ward of Incurable Patients)
(1996). Her first poetry collection was published in
1981 under the title *Almanacco dello specchio* (Almanac
of the Mirror), followed by *Medicamenta* (Medica-
ments) (1982) and *La tentazione* (Temptation) (1985).

ANDREA RICCI

Valentino

b. 11 May 1932, Voghera, Pavia

Fashion designer

Valentino (full name Valentino Garavani) became
assistant to French couturier Jean Dessés in 1950,
and established his own high fashion business at
the centre of Italian couture in Rome in 1960. He
showed his first ready-to-wear in 1962, and by the
early 1970s had already added interiors, textiles,
gifts and men's wear collections, as well as
international boutiques. A signature fragrance
appeared in 1978, followed by more subsidiary
products such as eyewear and underwear. Valentino became particularly renowned for his trouser-
suits, the short dresses of his 1968 White
Collection, and his fondness for red. His work

was essentially grand and colourful, with luxurious combinations of texture and pattern. Valentino's glamorous lifestyle was frequently featured in the glossy magazines of the world, and his vision of opulence continued to attract a faithful private clientele, which in turn bolstered the keen market for his accessories.

See also: fashion

NICOLA WHITE

Valesio, Paolo

b. 14 October 1939, Bologna

Literary critic, poet and novelist

Professor of Italian and Comparative Literature at Yale University, Valesio's critical production is characterized by an intense attention to the stylistic construction of literary texts, as well as by an anthropological interpretation of rhetoric. This double approach to literature is evident in his theoretical books – *Novantiqua: Rhetoric as a Contemporary Theory* (1980) – as well as book-length essays such as *Gabriele d'Annunzio: The Dark Flame* (1992). In his poetic and narrative production, Valesio's lyrical eye scrutinizes the submerged and suffered spiritual values of day-to-day existence, and also focuses on the existential paradoxes caused by the contemporary intellectual migration between Europe and North America. He has published novels (*L'ospedale di Manhattan* (Manhattan Hospital), 1978), short stories and numerous poetry collections, amongst them *Dialogo del falco e dell'avvoltoio* (Dialogue Between the Hawk and the Vulture) (1987) and *La campagna dell'Ottantasette* (The Campaign of Nineteen Eighty-Seven) (1990), which won the Tagliamento Prize for Poetry.

ANDREA CICCARELLI

Valle, Gino

7 December 1923, Udine

Architect, teacher and urban planner

After graduating from the **IUAV** in 1948 Valle studied in America as a Harvard Fulbright scholar (1951–2). After returning to Italy, and in partnership with his father and brother, he established the Studio Architetti Valle in 1955 and proceeded to design mostly industrial buildings in the area of Udine. His **Zanussi** offices in Porcia, Pordenone (1959–61), first brought him to international attention. His achievement lay in projecting a multivalent image of industry, stressing structures while at the same time concentrating on detail and the overall quality of the object. In fact, Valle's work always reflects precision, even in a work like the Monument to the **Resistance**, a sophisticated fountain and town square in Udine, designed for competition in 1958. In the 1970s, colour became ubiquitous in Valle's formal expression. His main projects during the 1980s, such as the offices of the Italian Commercial Bank in Manhattan, the IBM buildings at la Défence in Paris and the **Olivetti** offices in Ivrea, although large-scale buildings, are all concerned with the demands of human dimension and humanistic values, Valle's most recurrent philosophical theme.

GORDANA KOSTICH

Valli, Alida

b. 31 May 1921, Pula, Yugoslavia

Film actress

With over 100 films to her credit, Alida Maria Altenberger, better known as Alida Valli, is one of the most acclaimed dramatic actresses of Italian cinema. A native of former Yugoslavia, Valli moved to Rome as a child and started her film career in the 1930s, collaborating with some of the most important film-makers of the period (**Camerini**, among others). The 1940s were equally productive years for Valli whose career became international, as her presence in Carol Reed's *The Third Man* (1949), along with Joseph Cotten and Orson Welles, illustrates. In 1954, her sophisticated beauty had already been celebrated in over forty films when Luchino **Visconti** cast her as the unforgettable Countess Livia Serpieri in *Senso*. She subsequently worked with directors as prominent as **Antonioni** (*Il grido* (The Cry), 1957), **Pasolini**

(*Edipo re* (Oedipus Rex), 1967) and **Bertolucci** (*La strategia del ragno* (The Spider's Stratagem) 1969), and also directed a film (*L'Amore in tutte le sue espressioni* (Love in All its Expressions), 1968). In 1997, she was awarded a Golden Lion at Venice for her life contribution to cinema.

DOROTHÉE BONNIGAL.

Vanoni, Ezio

b. 3 August 1903, Morbegno, Valtellina;
d. 16 February 1956, Rome

Economist

An important figure in Italian **postwar reconstruction**, Vanoni is best remembered as the architect of the 'Vanoni Plan', a socially progressive economic strategy for postwar development which was presented in 1954 but never implemented, due to trenchant opposition from conservative government forces. He was also the first Italian finance minister to introduce a taxation system based on individual income declaration (the form, first introduced in October 1951, was popularly known as the 'Vanoni form').

Originally from a socialist background and a militant anti-fascist in his youth, Vanoni was a brilliant student who, largely through the support of Luigi **Einaudi**, was able to study abroad on a Rockefeller Foundation scholarship and thus create an international reputation as a fine economist. An early friendship with Alcide **De Gasperi** eventually brought him into the Christian Democrat Party (see **DC**) and in 1948 he became Minister for Finance. Esteemed by all for his honesty and financial acumen, he was nevertheless unable to overcome internal opposition to his plans from influential members of the DC, and the taxation system which he set in place – fair in principle but open to abuse – also failed in its objectives and was eventually replaced in 1974.

See also: taxation

GINO MOLITERNO

Vanzina family

Son of film director Stefano Vanzina (also known as Steno), Carlo Vanzina (b. Rome, 1951) started his film career as assistant to **Monicelli** on a number of his films before collaborating with his father on several comedies featuring Alberto **Sordi**. Carlo's first film, *Luna di miele in tre* (Honeymoon for Three) (1976) was made with the script collaboration of his brother Enrico, with whom he went on to produce a long series of rather superficial films that focus on youth culture and attempt some social criticism but never quite reach the quality of the Italian comedies of the 1950s, many of which were directed by their father. Among Carlo and Enrico's films are many of the vacation sagas like *Sapore di mare* (Seaside Holidays) (1983), *Vacanze di Natale* (Christmas Holidays) (1983) and *Vacanze americane* (American Holidays) (1984).

Belonging to the previous generation, Steno Vanzina (1915–88) started as a writer in the 1940s for the satirical review *Marc'Aurelio* but was soon working with Monicelli as co-scriptwriter and co-director on several of the **Totò** films: *Totò cerca casa* (Totò Looks for a House) (1949), *Guardie e ladri* (Guards and Thieves) (1952) and *Totò e i re di Roma* (Totò and the Kings of Rome) (1951). He went on to make a number of popular comedies which employed the proven talents of Alberto Sordi, Vittorio **De Sica**, Nino **Manfredi** and Ugo **Tognazzi**, amongst which *Un americano a Roma* (An American in Rome) (1954) and *A noi piace freddo* (Some Like it Cold) (1966). Unfortunately his later films achieved little success.

CRISTINA DEGLI-ESPOSTI REINERT

varieties of Italian

The term 'Italian' is conveniently used to cover a great many language varieties, as is the case with all major national languages. These varieties are geographic, social and situational, as well as historical, but in the case of Italian, the chequered linguistic and political history of the peninsula has determined more marked variation than in the other Romance languages. This means that, beside the basic general features (sounds, words, rules and so on) used by everybody in all circumstances, which constitute the common core of Italian, there are other particular features which, when grouped together, form a variety.

Standard Italian is the variety which comprises the basic common features. It in turn exists in two varieties: a high standard, and a low standard. The former is the variety traditionally described in grammar books, prescribed at school and taught to foreigners, that which is most stable and functions as a reference model for all considerations of correctness. This high standard has a rather literary character, is used by the upper, more learned classes, in formal situations, and is realized more often in writing than in speaking. By definition, it is neither geographically nor socially marked. It is widely used by modern writers, especially those who choose to write most carefully and elegantly, such as Italo **Calvino**. In its oral form, the high standard sounds artificial and bookish and, although considered prestigious, it is not an ideal to which Italians strive to conform (see also **language attitudes**).

The low standard is used most by the middle and upper classes, and is realized more in speaking than in writing. It is called also the new standard because it is highly unstable, as colloquial and informal features, still considered substandard in writing, are gradually being accepted in speaking. In this variety the modernization of the old elitist literary language is most evident. Unlike the high standard, where the norm is determined by authoritative literary and school canons, with this low standard the norm is established by usage. The most unstable level is grammar, especially that of pronouns and verbs. Some common features are (1) the loss of the subject pronouns *egli* 'he' and *ella* 'she', *essi* 'they/masc.' and *esse* 'they/fem.', replaced respectively by *lui* 'he', *lei* 'she' and *loro* 'they'; (2) an extended use of *che* for example, *il giorno che ci siamo conosciuti* 'the day in which we met', and *vieni che ti faccio un regalo* 'come, I'll give you a present'; (3) a reduced use of the historic past, for example, *l'anno scorso andai* 'last year I went' replaced by the perfect *sono andato*; and (4) a greater use of the imperfect, for example, *se lo sapevo non ci venivo* 'if I had known I would not have come') where the high standard would have *se lo avessi saputo non ci sarei venuto*. At the lexical level, words

are accepted which only slightly previously were considered substandard: the high standard *adirarsi* 'to get angry' becomes *arrabbiarsi* in the low standard, but even *incavolarsi* is now common. At the phonological level, there is a general tendency towards reproducing in speech the common nationwide features of the spelling: for example, the original Tuscan seven-vowel system tends to be gradually replaced by a five-vowel system, as spelling does not distinguish between open and closed vowels in such words as *venti* 'winds' with an open *e* versus 'twenty' with a closed *e*, and *botte* 'blows' with an open *o* versus 'barrel' with a closed *o*. Like the high standard variety, this low variety of Italian is also widely used by modern writers, especially those who wish to imitate most closely the spoken language, such as Natalia **Ginzburg**.

Regional Italians are the local varieties of Italian. These are not substandard forms living in the shadow of the national standard, they are what constitutes Italian. The borders between them coincide with those between the main **dialect** groupings. Thus broadly speaking, there is a northern variety, which further includes Gallo-Italian varieties in Piedmont, Lombardy, Liguria and Emilia-Romagna, and northeastern varieties in the Veneto; a central variety, including Tuscan Italian; a southern variety, including the two important varieties of Campania and Puglia; an extreme southern variety, with Sicilian Italian and Calabrese Italian; and a Sardinian variety. The differences among these varieties are greatest in phonology, but are still noticeable in the lexicon and in the syntax. At the level of pronunciation, each regional Italian has its own rules for sounds, intonation and rhythm, so that when one hears Italian one can easily recognize the speaker's region of origin. Thus regarding consonants, for example, northern Italian tends to reduce double ones and pronounce them as single: the standard *è tutto bello* 'it's all beautiful' becomes *è tuto belo*; in central Italian double consonants are usually (for example, in Tuscany and Umbria) the same as in the standard; while in southern Italian some single consonants are doubled between vowels: *la bella gente* 'the fine people' becomes *la bbella ggente*. At the lexical level, regionalisms abound, especially for everyday objects produced locally: a 'coat hanger' is called *ometto* in northern Italy, *gruccia* in central Italy and *stampella* in southern Italy; and in the absence of a single national term, the small piece of thick cloth used to hold hot handles of pots and pans is variously called *presina, pattina, chiappino, pugnetta, cuscinetto* and so on. At the syntactic level, for example, northern Italian replaces the standard historic past with the perfect: *l'ho conosciuto dieci anni fa* 'I met him ten years ago' versus *lo conobbi.* Central Italian uses *te* instead of *tu* in sentences like *vieni anche te?* 'are you coming too?'. Southern Italian generalizes the use of the historic past – *lo vidi stamattina* 'I saw him this morning' – and uses transitively many intransitive verbs: *ho uscito il bambino* 'I let the child out'. Even within the same region, the specific features of regional Italian vary a great deal and are seldom found all together: in actual speech, they are consistently more present and regionally more extreme the more informal the situation, the less educated and the older the speaker, and the more expressive the intention. Thus, as with the standard, we can distinguish between high and low varieties of regional Italian: the former are similar to the standard except for certain dialectal phonetic choices, the latter are richer in dialectal features. For example, standard Italian [kwanti anni avevi kwando ti sei spozato?] 'how old were you when you married?' may be in Puglia respectively [kwandi anni avevi kwando ti sej sposato?] or [kwandi anni tenevi kwando ti aj sposato?].

Popular Italian is a substandard variety, which is marked socially as belonging to lesser educated speakers of the lower socioeconomic classes. Its main feature is a reduced and simplified morphology, due to the fact that it is used mainly by native speakers of the dialects with limited access to the standard. Yet, precisely because in this variety the local dialects surface quite strongly, popular Italian is always marked regionally as well, both in pronunciation and in the lexicon, so much so that it can be seen as an extreme form of low regional Italian. On the other hand, its defining morphological traits are constant thought Italy, since they depend more on intrinsic complexities of Italian than on the external contact with the dialects. Some common tendencies of popular Italian are: (1) the regularization of inflectional morphology, whereby such nouns as the standard *moglie* 'wife', *mani* 'hands' and *camion* 'lorries' become respectively *moglia, mane* and *camioni,* and such verbs as the

standard imperatives *vada* 'you/sing. go' and *vengano* 'you/plur. come' become respectively *vadi* and *venghino*; (2) the fragility of complex systems, such as that of the unstressed personal pronouns, whereby *ci* tends to be used not only for *a noi* 'to us' as in the standard but also for *a lui* 'to him', *a lei* 'to her' and *a loro* 'to them'; (3) the extension of the use of *che,* which we have already noted as a feature of the new, low standard. This last tendency shows how difficult it is to draw a clear borderline between the new, lower standard and popular Italian. Traits like the overextension of *che* can define one or the other variety depending on whether they are used orally by well educated upper-class young people in the most informal situations, or in writing by old uneducated persons who are trying to do their best linguistically.

Beside these clearly labelled geographical and social varieties of Italian, there are many other situational varieties, among which the **sectorial languages** are most prominent. Other varieties are bound to the degree of formality of the situation in which they are used, others again to the oral and written media. All these varieties become more difficult to distinguish as most of their features cut across not only these subdivisions but also the geographical and social ones. Thus, for example, the use of *mica* after the verb instead of *non* before it (*son mica scemo!* 'I'm not stupid!') is at the same time a typical oral, informal and northern Italian feature; while the anacoluthon in sentences like *perché io Palermo la mia città mi piace moltissimo* 'I love Palermo, my own city, very much' may be puristically considered as belonging to popular Italian or more tolerantly to a most informal, oral subvariety of the new, low standard.

See also: dialect usage; Italian language; Italian lexicon; Italian morphology; Italian phonology; Italian syntax; language attitudes

Further reading

Berruto, G. (1989) 'Main Topics and Findings in Italian Sociolinguistics', *International Journal of the Sociology of Language* 76: 7–30.

Lepschy, A.L. and Lepschy, G. (1977) *The Italian Language Today,* London: Hutchinson (a description of contemporary Italian preceded by a long introduction examining 'some aspects of its history which have often led people to wonder whether an "Italian" language really existed').

Sobrero, A.A. (ed.) (1993) *Introduzione all'italiano contemporaneo. La variazione e gli usi* (Introduction to Contemporary Italian: Variation and Usages), Bari: Laterza (especially chaps 1 and 2 by G. Berruto, and ch. 3 by Telmon).

CAMILLA BETTONI

Vassalli, Sebastiano

b. 25 October 1941, Genoa

Poet, novelist and critic

Sebastiano Vassalli's first appearance on the cultural scene dates back to his participation in the neoavantgarde movement in the early 1960s. After witnessing its end in the 1970s, he turned from experimental narrative and poetry to the historical novel. By setting his stories in clearcut temporal frames (such as the life of poet Dino Campana in *La notte della cometa* (The Night of the Comet) (1984), or the persecution of an eighteenth-century alleged witch in *La chimera* (The Chimera), 1990), Vassalli has attempted to explore the collective memory of the Italian people and to trace the formation of its national identity. In addition to poetry and narrative, Vassalli has also published a number of essays on Italian culture (*Sangue e suolo* (Blood and Soil), 1985) and language (*ll neo-italiano* (Neo-Italian), 1989). Alien to any current literary trend or intellectual group, he has lived in relative isolation in the country between Vercelli and Novara since the early 1980s.

FRANCESCA PARMEGGIANI

Vatican

The term 'Vatican' designates the power centre of the Roman Catholic Church, also called the Holy See or the Papacy. This short-hand term essentially dates from 1870 when, as a protest against the occupation of Rome by northern Italian troops, Pope Pius IX withdrew into the Vatican, declaring himself to be its 'prisoner'. Excommunicating

Italy's rulers, the Pope and his successors continued their protests about the 'Roman Question' by forbidding Italian Catholics to vote in elections and strove to enlist the support of foreign powers for its solution. By 1929, however, relations between the Papacy and the Italian state had improved immensely and with characteristic boldness, Mussolini was finally able to resolve all outstanding issues between them through the Lateran Pacts.

From the view of the Papacy, the key feature of the Pacts was the restoration of a portion of its former 'temporal power' in the shape of the one hundred-acre state of the Vatican City. Since its emergence, this tiny state has evoked ambivalent responses from Italians. Mussolini himself lamented the interference of what he described as a 'foreign state' in Italy's internal affairs when Pius XI resisted his will over issues such as **Catholic Action**, Catholic youth and labour organizations and the racial laws of 1938. However, postwar democratic 'secular' politicians have often voiced similar complaints, particularly when popes like **Pope Paul VI** and **Pope John Paul II** have criticized Italian legislation on **divorce** and **abortion**. On the other hand, there was an incestuous relationship between the Vatican and the Italian Catholic political leadership during the reign of Paul VI, when his *prediletti* (favourites) in the prewar Catholic student movement – **Andreotti**, Colombo and **Moro** – became the leaders of the Christian Democratic Party.

The presence of the Vatican and its subordinate organizations, universities and seminaries scattered throughout the city obviously has a powerful impact on the economy and prestige of Rome. The 'sacred character of the city', as the Lateran Pacts described it, is no longer defended as zealously by the local authorities as it was in the immediate postwar period, but Rome remains a great beneficiary of the pilgrimages and tourism which that presence generates, and it is in the interests of the Roman authorities to collaborate closely with the Vatican in preparations for 2000, the year of the 'great jubilee'.

The presence of the Vatican affects Italy in two other important ways, the first financial and economic, the second in the area of international relations. Ever since Bernardino Nogara shrewdly invested the cash and government stock which the

Lateran Pacts gave to the Papacy in compensation for the lost revenues from the former Papal States, the Vatican has been a major player in the Italian economy, owning wholly or in part a number of banks and manufacturing industries, and controlling large swathes of the property market, especially in Rome itself. In recent years, Italy's financial relations with the Vatican have been soured by arguments over taxation of profits from these investments and, above all, by the operations of the Vatican bank, the quaintly-named 'Institute for Religious Works'. The latter's involvement in the Sindona and Banco Ambrosiano scandals in the 1970s and 1980s (see **P2**) eventually led to judicial action in Italy against the president of the Vatican bank, Archbishop Paul Marcinkus.

No Italian government can afford to ignore the fact that the Vatican has one of the largest diplomatic establishments in the world, maintaining relations with some one hundred and sixty states and international organizations, including all the great and medium-sized powers except China, and all the Islamic states except Saudia Arabia. Mussolini himself attempted, largely without success, to harness the Vatican's diplomatic influence in order to further the objectives of Fascist foreign policy in the 1930s and 1940s. With the collapse of the regime in 1943, the balance of power between the Vatican and Italy shifted radically. Since Italy had effectively ceased to exist as an autonomous international entity, the Vatican was able to exercise a great deal of influence over its future. Pius XII used his 'special relationship' with the USA, largely mediated by his friend Cardinal Spellman of New York, to win American backing for **De Gasperi** and the Christian Democrats (see **DC**) and to mitigate the terms of the Allies' peace treaty with Italy in 1947. The pope was also chiefly instrumental in persuading the Christian Democratic party to support De Gasperi and Sforza in taking Italy into NATO in 1949, despite concerns about the neutrality of the Vatican in the event of war, and he also strongly endorsed Italy's participation in European integration in the 1950s.

Since then, there have been interesting and not unconnected parallels in the development of the foreign policies of the two states. The change from the intransigent hostility of Pius XII towards the Communist bloc in the initial Cold War period to the 'opening to the East' of **Pope John XXIII** and the subsequent development of the Vatican's 'Ostpolitik' was paralleled by Italy's attempts to establish more cordial political and trading relations with the Soviet Union in the early 1960s, attempts that were clearly out of step with US policy. Italy, like the Vatican – though for ostensibly different reasons – has also been cooler in its relations with Israel and warmer in those with the Arab states than most Western Powers. During the 1991 Gulf War, John Paul II's appeals for peace were supported by an alliance of Catholics and Communists (**PDS**) inside Italy. More recently, the Serbs have accused Italy of pandering to the Vatican's hegemonic aspirations in Europe by recognizing Croatia and Slovenia in 1991 and thus helping to precipitate war in the former Yugoslavia.

See also: church, state and society

Further reading

Kent, P. and Pollard, J.F. (1994) *Papal Diplomacy in the Modern Era*, New York: Praeger (see the essays on Ostpolitik, Israel, Palestine and the Vietnam War).

Pompei, G.F. (1994) *Un Ambasciatore in Vaticano: Diario 1969–1977* (An Ambassador in the Vatican 1969–1977), Bologna: Il Mulino (an account of the tortuous and byzantine relations between the Italian government and the Vatican in the latter part of the reign of Paul VI).

Raw, C. (1992) *The Money Changers: How the Vatican Bank Enabled Roberto Calvi to Steal $250 Million for the Head of the P2 Masonic Lodge*, London: Harvill.

Reese, T.J. (1996) *Inside the Vatican: the Politics and Organisation of the Catholic Church*, Cambridge, MA: Harvard University Press (the finest analysis of the institutions and the politics of the Vatican).

JOHN POLLARD

Vattimo, Gianni

b. 4 January 1936, Turin

Philosopher

Professor of Theoretical Philosophy at the University of Turin and one of the most imaginative and influential philosophers of the later postwar period, Vattimo was also highly visible as regular commentator on Italian society in the popular press. In the 1950s, Vattimo studied at the University of Turin with Luigi **Pareyson**, who is credited with having introduced existentialism into Italy in the 1940s, and then worked with Hans-Georg Gadamer at the University of Heidelberg. Vattimo's early work was on theories of aesthetics in classical antiquity, but he came to be particularly known for his theories on postmodernism and *il pensiero debole* (weak thought). In *Le avventure della differenza* (The Adventures of Difference) (1979) and *La fine della modernità* (The End of Modernity) (1985) Vattimo argues that the thought of Nietzsche and Heidegger prepared the way for the more recent proclamations of the notion of difference and the end of the modern era. In a later volume, *La società trasparente* (The Transparent Society) (1989) he maintains that the postmodern condition is linked to the development of the mass media, but rejects the belief that this will produce a more enlightened and 'transparent' society. Vattimo's subsequent writings have dealt with the theme of religion.

LAURENCE SIMMONS

Vedova, Emilio

b. 9 August 1919, Venice

Painter

Vedova is the outstanding Italian exponent of *l'informale*, akin to American abstract expressionism, and one of the few to develop a personal and recognizable style in his great, swirling, chaotic action paintings of the 1950s and early 1960s, such as *Ciclo '62 B.B.9* (Cycle '62 B.B.9) and the explosive *Scontro di situazioni -I-I* (Conflicting Situations -I-I). The *Plurimi* series uses the same painting style, on various flat surfaces arranged seemingly at will in three dimensions, which somewhat dissipates the effect by breaking up the picture plane. The *Tondi* paintings, from the 1980s, are circular.

Vedova arrived at his own style via geometrical cubism, and participated in avantgarde groupings

such as Corrente, the Fronte Nuovo delle Arti (New Front of the Arts), and the **Gruppo degli otto** (Group of Eight). Always deeply committed politically, Vedova thought that social justice could be brought about with a radical avantgarde style of art rather than through the didactic, illustrative style favoured by the Communist Party. His works thus deal with social protest, time (in a generic sense) and conflict.

MAX STAPLES

Veltroni, Walter

b. 3 July 1955, Rome

Politician and journalist

Following the victory of the **Ulivo** coalition at the 1996 elections, Veltroni became Deputy President of the Council of Ministers, the first member of the **PCI/PDS** to hold that office. He was also appointed minister for culture and **sport**. The party's chief expert in mass communications and propaganda, Veltroni had been a member of parliament since 1987 and editor of *L'Unità* since 1992. As the most liberal democratic of the PDS leadership, and an admirer of certain leaders of the Democratic Party in the USA, he led the minority within the PDS who favoured the evolution of the Ulivo coalition towards a single 'democratic party' encompassing the broad centre–left area of Italian politics. He was a strong candidate for the PDS leadership upon **Occhetto**'s resignation in 1994, but was defeated by **D'Alema**. Film critic for *Il Venerdì*, the television guide in *La Repubblica*, he is also the author of several books on television, politics and political figures, including studies of Robert Kennedy and Enrico **Berlinguer**.

CLAIRE KENNEDY

Venezia, Francesco

b. 28 September 1944, Lauro

Architect

Venezia's work became prominent in the 1980s in the context of an architectural scene generally lacking in direction. It stems from a keen under-standing of the natural landscape of Sicily and the Naples region which allows him to incorporate geological strata and subterranean and hydrologi-cal elements into the architecture itself. As well as building several urban landscape works, he has also continuously produced outstanding competition projects.

Venezia's intense meditation on the traditional Mediterranean values of light, shadow and geo-metry, together with his tendency to recycle pre-existing elements, is outstandingly typified by his Museum in Gibellina Nuova, where he installed the fragmented façade of a palazzo from the old earthquake-devastated city inside the walled court-yard of the new museum thus creating a place of lyrical silence and resolution.

Further reading

Francesco Venezia (1990), Barcelona: Gustavo Gili (a catalogue of his works to 1987).

ROSS JENNER

Venice Biennale

The Venice Biennale was founded in 1895 by a group of Venetian intellectuals who wanted to encourage artistic activity in their city. The frequently controversial international arts festival has been held regularly every two years beginning in 1910 and interrupted only twice during the years of the two world wars.

Until the First World War, the festival was dominated by academic art typical of world expositions in the nineteenth century. Following the war, the Biennale assumed a more modern orientation. In 1930 the Biennale became an autonomous state-funded body and no longer the responsibility of the Venice City Council. The exhibition was expanded to include fields other than figurative arts, taking in music, cinema, theatre and, for a limited period, also poetry. In 1932 the Lido of Venice put on the first Mostra Internazionale d'Arte Cinematografica (Interna-tional Exhibition of Cinematographic Art), the first international film festival of its kind. In 1934, the

staging of the Merchant of Venice added a theatrical festival to the Biennale which takes place in the various squares of the city.

After the Second World War the Biennale was once again restructured with contemporary artists displaying not just single works but presenting entire shows. In addition, retrospective exhibitions were encouraged focusing on major avantgarde movements of the century (impressionism, expres-sionism, metaphysical painting). In the 1960s the Biennale hosted new movements such as pop art. In 1973 the organizational structure of the Biennale was again changed, and its goals became specifically the representation of recent trends in the fields of art and art theory with a focus on research, documentation and experimentation. In 1976 ASAC (the Historical Archive of Contem-porary Arts) was relocated to the prestigious Palazzo corner of the Regina palace to include a print library (with a special periodical and news-paper section), a film library, a photographic library and a recorded music library, as well as an archive.

During the 1980s many of the controversies which had buffeted the Biennale in the turbulent protest period of the late 1960s and early 1970s were quelled and a section entitled 'Aperto 80', focusing on the work of younger artists, was instated in the International Art Exhibition. While the 1970s had offered occasional exhibitions of architecture organized by the Visual Arts Section, the architecture section came into its own in 1979.

Since then the Biennale has further expanded its scope to host, among other things, a number of competitions for the reshaping and restoring of Venice. The centenary of the Biennale's foundation was celebrated in 1995 with a series of exhibitions: the 34th International Theatre Festival, the 46th International Festival of Contemporary Music, the 46th International Art Exhibition, the 52nd International Exhibition of Cinematic Art, and in 1996, the 6th International Architecture Exhibi-tion.

Today, each country contributing to the Biennale has its own pavilion centred around the original one, named the Italian pavilion. The twenty-seven pavilions are monuments to the work of internationally acclaimed architects. The Bien-nale is also supported by other cultural events such as annual international theatre and prose shows, and film and contemporary music festivals which all coincide with Biennale events.

See also: arts festivals

BERNADETTE LUCIANO

Venturi, Lionello

b. 25 April 1885, Modena; d. 14 August 1961, Rome

Art historian and critic

Venturi had established his reputation as a leading art historian before the Second World War. Refusing to swear allegiance to the Fascist government, he left Italy for the United States, but returned in 1945 to take up a post at the University of Rome. He produced studies on artists of the Italian Renaissance, including Leonardo, Botticelli, Giorgione and Caravaggio, and traced a line of progression from them through Cézanne and the School of Paris to the art of his own day. Recognizing the limited market for contemporary art in postwar Italy, Venturi used his reputation to promote artists as diverse as the neo-realist Renato **Guttuso** and the abstract **Gruppo degli otto** (Group of Eight) to a wider, international audience.

See also: art criticism

Further reading

Venturi, L. (1956) *Four Steps Toward Modern Art: Giorgione, Caravaggio, Manet, Cézanne,* New York: Columbia University Press.

—— (1964) *History of Art Criticism,* New York: Dutton.

MAX STAPLES

Verdi

The formation of a Federazione delle Liste Verdi (Federation of Green Lists) in November 1986 was the outcome of co-operation between numerous Green political organizations and signalled the arrival on the political landscape of a national political party with a primary focus on environmental issues. The Italian **electoral system**, which until 1993 was based on proportional representation, provided genuine opportunities for minority parties to gain seats, and Green political organizations had already emerged in the early 1980s to contest municipal elections. In 1985, Green groups secured 636,000 votes (2.1 per cent) in regional elections, and in 1988 the Federazione delle Liste Verdi polled an average of 3.7 per cent in local, regional and provincial elections. In the national election of 1987, Green groups received around one million votes (2.5 per cent) and gained 13 seats in the Lower House and 2 in the Senate. The result was similar in 1992 (2.8 per cent, 16 seats in the Lower House and 4 in the Senate), in 1994 (2.7 per cent and 9 seats) and in 1996 (2.5 per cent and 14 seats in co-operation with parties like the **PDS**). Their share of seats in the Senate was 7 out of 325 in 1994 and 14 out of 325 in 1996.

In the 1989, European elections the Liste Verdi achieved 3.8 per cent of the vote and a coalition of Green associations, Verdi Arcobaleno (Rainbow Greens), gained a further 2.4 per cent. The latter represented and reflected the connection between environmental issues and left-wing groups, and included several 'red-red' groups as well as Green groups with left leanings. In fact, many activists and local groups of Verdi Arcobaleno came directly from **Democrazia Proletaria** and were without any ecological experience whatsoever. In the next elections to the European Parliament held in 1994, the Liste Verdi attracted over a million votes (3.2 per cent of the ballot) and secured 3 out of 87 seats.

As in many other European countries, supporters of Green groups have tended to be young, well-educated and affluent. A key issue that contributed to the rise of Italian Green groups was a plan, announced in 1975, to establish numerous nuclear power stations in Italy. The plan drew strong opposition from prominent scientists and intellectuals, and was challenged by organizations like Friends of the Earth (Amici della Terra) and by the **PCI**. In the wake of the 1986 nuclear disaster at Chernobyl in the Ukraine, Italian environmental groups initiated a campaign in 1987 for a referendum in which a majority voted against plans by the government to develop nuclear power and for decisions to be made at the local level.

In terms of programmes, the various Green political organizations have experienced difficulty in agreeing on a common approach. Some, like the Liste Verdi, have tended to focus on purely environmental issues, while others include a broader programme of social justice, peace and disarmament and the rights of minorities. The reform of the electoral system, away from proportional representation, has presented further difficulties and forced the Liste Verdi to join in coalitions of left-wing and socialist groups like the Progressive Alliance.

See also: environmental movement; environmental policy

Further reading

Diani, M. (1989) 'Italy: the "Liste Verdi"', in F. Müller-Rommel (ed.), *New Politics in Western Europe: The Rise and Success of Green Parties and Alternative Lists*, Boulder, CO: Westview Press, 113–22 (a survey of the early development of 'Green Lists' including electoral bases and organizational structure).

O'Neill, M. (1997) *Green Parties and Political Change in Contemporary Europe: New Politics, Old Predicaments*, Aldershot, Hampshire: Ashgate (a wide-ranging comparative analysis, but see especially pp. 215–36 for a very up-to-date analysis of the Italian situation).

Rhodes, M. (1995) 'Italy: Greens in an Overcrowded Political System', in D. Richardson and C. Rootes (eds), *The Green Challenge: The development of Green parties in Europe*, London and New York: Routledge, 168–192 (an analysis of the Greens in the context of the Italian political system).

ELIM PAPADAKIS

Verdone, Carlo

b. 17 November 1950, Rome

Actor and director

Son of film historian Mario Verdone, Carlo studied at the **Centro Sperimentale di Cinemato-**

grafia in Rome, worked as a theatre and television actor until his directorial debut with *Un sacco bello* (Really Cool) (1979), a film produced by director Sergio **Leone**, for which Verdone wrote the script and played leading role. He continued to score popular success in his following films, which include *Bianco, rosso e verdone* (White, Red and Verdone) (1984), *Troppo forte* (Too Much) (1986), *Io e mia sorella* (My Sister and I) (1987), *Perdiamoci di vista* (Let's Not Keep in Touch) (1994) and *Sono pazzo di Iris Blonde* (I am Crazy about Iris Blonde) (1996). Role playing characterizes most of Verdone's films as he transforms himself into a series of similar comic characters who function as obnoxious, though not wholly unsympathetic 'types', whose merciless portrayal is always more important than the stories. Verdone's films are a parodic representation of reality permeated by a cynicism that never quite becomes satire.

CRISTINA DEGLI-ESPOSTI REINERT

il verri

Founded in Milan in 1956 by Luciano **Anceschi**, and thereafter published quarterly under his direction, *il verri* became the most influential literary and cultural journal of the 1960s and 1970s, with most members of the neoavantgarde passing through its pages. Hosting theoretical and critical articles, experimental writing and literary and cultural reviews, the journal promoted both aesthetic and cultural reflection and active artistic experimentation, thus becoming a major focus for serious cultural discussion in Italy. As well as regularly presenting a mixture of both creative and critical texts, the journal also published special issues dedicated to particular themes such as phenomenology, the new poetry, engagement and the avantgarde, and linguistic and literary structuralism. The journal survived the death of its founder in 1995 and is still published regularly, continuing to offer a creative mixture of critical reflection and cultural practice.

GINO MOLITERNO

Versace

Later to become known as both 'Lorenzo de Versace' and a 'bourgeois prince', Gianni Versace was first exposed to the world of fashion in his mother's atelier in Reggio Calabria in the early postwar period. Puzzled by the fact that southern women had to conceal their sexuality behind black clothing and heavy shawls, in a land where garments of silk chiffon and velvet more accurately represented the warmth and sensuality of the Mediterranean, Versace left his homeland in search of greater freedom. He moved north to Milan, and in 1978 the first collection bearing his name appeared on the fashion scene. He was not alone in his venture. His sister Donatella, after graduating in languages from the University of Florence, joined him in Milan and soon became his indispensable muse and adviser. His brother was later to become the managerial mind behind the Versace label.

Gianni's American dream began in 1979 when he was asked to design a line of sportswear for men. Although it did not succeed, Gianni continued to pursue the American market, where he soon became visible because of his unique ability to unite European taste and the American spirit. Soon, GV boutiques and perfumes emerged. In 1982 he was crowned best fashion designer for his collection of that year, which displayed the famous metal garments which became a Versace trademark. His miniskirt suits with wide shouldered jackets were even more successful. Eventually the Versace label expanded beyond clothing to include glasses, watches and perfume. Not only did Gianni revolutionize design, but he transformed the dynamics of the fashion show by having his models parade not alone on the catwalk but in the company of other models, constantly crossing paths and interweaving.

Gianni's artistic sense spilled over from fashion into a passion for the arts. He collaborated with internationally renowned photographers and held a number of museum shows all over the world. In addition, he designed costumes for numerous ballets and operas. His love for art overflowed into his homes in New York and Miami, which he filled with Picassos, Andy Warhols and Murano glass, as well as commissioned art which included a two-ton bronze bed.

Versace's life came to a tragic premature end with his murder on 15 July 1997. Eyewitnesses report that the killer approached Versace on the doorstep of his Miami Beach villa, uttered a few words, and shot him twice in the head. The man responsible was thought to be Andrew Cunanan, a serial killer who had murdered several other men but who committed suicide only days after Versace's death. The brutal murder came on the heels of several other dark moments in the Versace fairy tale. A few years previously Versace, together with a number of other fashion houses including **Krizia** and **Ferrè**, had been found guilty of paying off the Finance Ministry. In 1994 he had been linked to the Calabrian mafia, and in 1995 a rare tumour had been discovered in his right ear. The illness took its toll on Gianni, who prepared himself for death and rumours spread that the gay designer had contracted AIDS.

It was during his illness that Donatella assumed control of the business. As advisor, Donatella's influence had always been strong. She maintained the Versace image while he occupied himself with his passion for theatre, art and music. While he designed his costumes she vacationed with Sting, had lunch with Elton John, and went to the party celebrating the birth of Madonna's child. As art director, she was in charge of the publicity campaigns and the publication of the lavish books issued under the symbol of the Medusa, the symbol that Gianni had selected for the company because, like the Versace style, it seduces on sight.

Since her brother's death, Donatella has maintained the strongly sexual and colourful style that recalls Gianni. Versace's seductive woman remains the opposite of the Armani androgynous business type. In the new millennium, the Versace woman will continue to dress provocatively in low-cut blouses, slit skirts, spiked heels and transparent evening gowns. The sensuality which Gianni first sensed in his mother's atelier led him finally to Miami, a town whose eroticism was both a source of inspiration and the occasion of his death. Ironically he did not die serenely, as he had hoped, but as a victim of a violence all too reminiscent of his native city from which he had escaped twenty years earlier.

BERNADETTE LUCIANO

Vespa, Bruno

b. 25 May 1944, L'Aquila

Journalist and television anchorman

Working for the national broadcaster, the **RAI**, since 1968, Vespa has successfully weathered different seasons of television journalism. His ability to explain in simple terms the complicated games of Italian politics has always drawn him an audience as he progressed from rank and file journalist to executive producer of the RAI's main news presentation on its first channel (1989 to 1992). Vespa's greatest individual scoop was in 1978 when he was the first journalist on the scene of Aldo **Moro**'s kidnapping by the **Red Brigades**. Ever obsequious to the powerful and generally linked to the Christian Democrats, he nevertheless presented the current affairs programme *Porta a porta* (Door Against Door) in the early 1990s, documenting the troubled path of the **Tangentopoli** investigations and the end of the so-called First **Republic**. With his talk show technique and his ability to simplify, he democratized politics for the average spectator. He is known also as a writer of 'instant' political books like *Il duello* (The Duel) (1995) or *La svolta* (The Turn) (1996).

RICCARDO VENTRELLA

Videomusic

MTV came to Italy in 1984 when **Rete Quattro** screened the first programme of videoclips. Subsequently the Marcucci group, through their company Beta Television, set up Videomusic, a channel targeted at the 20–30 age group and screening videoclips in rotation twenty-four hours a day, interspersed with music specials and live concerts. In 1991 the channel inaugurated its first regular programme, *Roxy Bar*, conducted by Red Ronnie,

which mixed live music and entertainment. The programme was a great success, but by the mid-1990s the channel came to face serious challenges to its musical monopoly. In 1995 Telepiù3 (and then Rete A) began to relay the signal of MTV Europe into Italy. In the same year the film producer, Cecchi Gori, who had also bought **Telemontecarlo**, purchased Videomusic and changed both its name to TMC2 and its style of programming to less music and videoclips and more movies and sports. Red Ronnie remained in the team with *Roxy Bar* and a new daily programme, *Help!* but the channel's overall popularity with the younger audience was never the same.

RICCARDO VENTRELLA

Viganò, Vittoriano

b. 14 December 1919, Milan; d. 5 January 1996, Milan

Architect, teacher, urban and industrial designer

After graduating from the Milan Politecnico in 1944, Viganò became involved in the **postwar reconstruction** of Milan. His work includes residential, sports, educational and healthcare buildings as well as Milan's Parco Sempione. However, Viganò is best known for his youthful project, the Marchiondi Spagliardi Institute in Milan-Baggio (1957) which, with its emphasized structure, heavy massing, and exposed and untreated reinforced concrete, is considered the paradigm of the Italian variation of brutalism. From the early 1960s Viganò taught in the Faculty of Architecture of the Milan Politecnico, for which he also designed the campus in 1974. In his teaching, he stressed the ethical side of design and its relation to aesthetics and fine art.

Further reading

A come architettura: Vittoriano Viganò (A as in Architecture: Vittoriano Viganò) (1992), Milan: Electa (exhibition catalogue presenting a good comprehensive review of his work).

GORDANA KOSTICH

Villa, Claudio

b. 1 January 1926, Rome; d. 7 January
1987, Padua

Singer

Born Claudio Pica, the son of a shoemaker in the
poorer Roman quarter of Trastevere, Villa went on
to become one of the most renowned and
financially successful singers of postwar Italy,
coming to be known simply as *il reuccio* (the little
king) and *il fenomeno* (the phenomenon). Having
only partially recovered from tuberculosis contracted during the war years, Villa began singing
on the radio in 1945; by the mid-1950s he had
become a household name. During a dazzling
career he was awarded literally hundreds of prizes,
trophies, medals and diplomas. He sold more than
42 million records, and won the **Sanremo
Festival** four times and the **Canzonissima**
twice. His overwhelming success was due in large
part to his fine tenor voice and his ability to sing
traditional melodies, but it was also aided by astute
marketing and self-promotion through an extended
network of American-style fan clubs.

GINO MOLITERNO

Villaggio, Paolo

b. 31 December 1932, Genoa

Actor and writer

A popular comic actor better known to Italian
audiences in the guise of his fictional persona, Ugo
Fantozzi, Villaggio abandoned his job at the
Italsider steel mill to try show business. While
doing comic monologues on stage in Milan in 1968
he was noticed by Maurizio **Costanzo**, who
invited him to Rome and eventually to appear on
the **RAI**'s variety show *Quelli della domenica*, where
Villaggio created the first version of what would
eventually become the grotesque figure of Fantozzi.
Servile, eternally flustered and a born loser,
Fantozzi was a perceptive caricature of major
common defects in the Italian character, and he
became an immediate hit both on television and in
print. There followed a number of Fantozzi films,

most of which were also huge box office successes,
thus firmly establishing the character in the Italian
imagination.

In spite of being overwhelmingly identified with
this tragicomic persona, Villaggio has given proof
of great versatility in his acting talent by playing
leading roles both on stage (for example, in
Strehler's production of Molière's *L'Avare*) and
on screen (**Fellini**'s *La voce della luna* in 1990 and
Olmi's *Il segreto del bosco vecchio* in 1993). In 1992,
he was awarded a Golden Lion at Venice in
recognition of his career.

GINO MOLITERNO

Visconti, Luchino

b. 2 November 1906, Milan; d. 17 March
1976, Rome

Film director and opera producer

Visconti's early years were marked by an upper-
class upbringing during which he developed an
intense interest in music, something to which he
would return in his later films and in his work in
opera. In his late twenties, his interest in film saw
him move to Paris where, after being in the French
film-makers' circle for some years, he assisted Jean
Renoir on *Une Partie de campagne* (A Day in the
Country) in 1936. They collaborated again in
Rome when he worked with Renoir on *La Tosca* in
1940, a production which had been arranged
under the invitation of Mussolini despite the
previous banning in Italy of Renoir's *Grande Illusion*
(1937). In the event, *La Tosca* proved not to be a
successful project and, due to the increased German presence in Italy, Renoir abandoned Rome,
leaving Visconti to finish the film with the help of
assistant director Carl Koch.

After a short visit to Hollywood, Visconti
returned to Rome and became one of the group
around the film journal *Cinema*, who were developing theoretical foundations for a new film
realism evolved from *verismo*, the style of many
nineteenth-century novels, particularly those of
Giovanni Verga. Indeed, for his first film Visconti
turned directly to Verga's *L'amante di Gramigna*
(Gramigna's Lover), but his script was rejected by

the Fascists, and so in 1942 he made *Ossessione*, an adaptation of James Cain's novel *The Postman Always Rings Twice*. The film, using locations in the Po valley and naturalistic depictions of character, made his reputation among the neo-realists. The success of the film, however, was not helped by his anti-fascist politics and he found himself detained by the Gestapo in 1944.

A short postwar period in the theatre was followed by a return to cinema. The Italian Communist Party (see **PCI**) commissioned three films on the Sicilian working class, but only the one concerning fishermen was released, as *La terra trema* (The Earth Trembles) in 1948. This was also based on a Verga novel, *I Malavoglia* (The House by the Medlar Tree), and, with its use of location shooting and non-professional actors, became a classic of neorealism. Indeed the local fishermen who appeared in the film spoke such a strong dialect (see **dialects**) that Visconti was obliged to add a voiceover in standard Italian to make the dialogue comprehensible to non-Sicilians. Such critical purity met with box office failure, and Visconti was forced to turn to apparently more mundane fare for his next film, *Bellissima*, in 1951. From a script by Cesare **Zavattini**, which he disliked, and with Anna **Magnani** as the star, he created a fine satirical attack on **Cinecittà** itself.

Like most of the neorealist directors, Visconti had to this point avoided shooting in colour, preferring the stylish crispness and verité effects of black and white. However, with *Senso* in 1954, he not only embraced colour but seemed to some to abandon all of the values of neorealism. The film was a lavish historical recreation of the Italian aristocracy during the period of the Risorgimento and even exploited the star system by featuring guaranteed box office stars Farley Granger and Alida **Valli**. Both in *Senso* and in the 1963 adaptation of Giuseppe Tomasi di **Lampedusa**'s *Il gattopardo* (The Leopard), which explored the same historical setting and starred Burt Lancaster, the broad sweeping plots and the opulent, spectacular settings seem at odds with Visconti's earlier style, and more in keeping with his own patrician background. Nevertheless, some critics defended this apparent shift as an evolution of Visconti's interest in critical realism. Indeed it might be argued that, rather than wallowing in a superficial aesthetic beauty, Visconti's meticulous counterpoising of setting and narrative demonstrates the disjunction between the apparent tastes of the patrician class and their spiritual and political failures.

Manifesting his interest in the development of the modern nation state, Visconti's focus on the late nineteenth century as a time of ideological crisis merely shifts his commitment to realism from a neorealist contemporary setting to its historical antecedents, with all their attendant spectacle. The detail and scope of the film frame is still precise, although the subject matter's surface has changed. The spectacular decadence of an aristocracy confronting its own ideological crises and its imminent demise is the subject in varying degrees of his major internationally acclaimed films, *La caduta degli dei* (The Damned) (1969) a narrative of the Krupp family's support for the Third Reich, and *Morte a Venezia* (Death in Venice) (1972), an adaptation of Thomas Mann's novella which stars British actor Dirk Bogarde as the aristocratic von Aschenbach in a story which allegorizes the denials, crises and decline of the patrician class in Europe. Both *Ludwig* (1972), the story of the mad Bavarian king (the 1980 re-release is longer and truer to the director's intent) and *Gruppo di famiglia in un interno* (Conversation Piece) (1974), again starring Burt Lancaster, also explore the sense of a generation out of touch with its ideological foundations.

Illness had intervened in many of these films, and Visconti's output was never prodigious due to the extended production effort involved and time diverted to other interests in **opera** and **theatre**. His last film, an adaptation of another realist novel, D'Annunzio's *L'innocente* (The Innocent) (1976), continues the theme of the aristocratic class losing its reasons for social and political existence.

Regarded as one of the most important of all Italian film-makers, Visconti's influence can be seen in the work of Bernardo **Bertolucci**, Franco **Zeffirelli**, Liliana **Cavani** and Stanley Kubrick.

Further reading

Bacon, H. (1998) *Visconti: Explorations of Beauty and Decay*, Cambridge: Cambridge University Press (an essential critical and biographical study of the entire output which focuses on Visconti's narrative continuity with nineteenth-century *verismo*).

Bondanella, P. (1990) *Italian Cinema: From Neorealism to the Present*, New York: Continuum, 2nd revised edn (a survey of postwar film in Italy placing Visconti, among others, in a national context).

Miccichè, L. (1996) *Luchino Visconti. Un profilo critico*, Venice: Marsilio Editori (one of the essential critical responses).

Sorlin, P. (1996) *Italian National Cinema 1896–1996*, London and New York: Routledge (another survey with a strong emphasis on a cultural studies reading of nationalism).

Stirling, M. (1979) *A Screen of Time: A Study of Luchino Visconti*, New York: Harcourt Brace Jovanovich (an important early study).

JEFF DOYLE

Vitti, Monica

b. 3 November 1931, Rome

Film actress

Under the pseudonym of Monica Vitti, Maria Louisa Ceciarelli started her career as a film actress in the 1960s thanks to her association, both professionally and personally, with Michelangelo **Antonioni**. Her singular beauty, at once sophisticated and abstract, suited the originality of Antonioni's vision, as epitomized in his famous 1960 trilogy, *L'avventura* (The Adventure), *La notte* (The Night), *L'eclisse* (The Eclipse) and then in *Deserto rosso* (Red Desert) (1964), which all starred Vitti. In the 1970s, thanks to films such as **Scola**'s *Dramma della gelosia* (Jealousy, Italian Style) (1970) and **Sordi**'s *Polvere di stelle* (Stardust) (1973), she became a popular figure of the **commedia all'Italiana** (comedy, Italian style) while pursuing an international career, collaborating with Luis Bunuel (*The Phantom of Liberty*, 1974) and appearing in American productions like *An Almost Perfect Affair* (1979). In 1983, she received a Silver Bear in Berlin for her outstanding performance in *Flirt* (1983), a film she co-wrote with the director Roberto Russo and Silvia Napolitano. An accomplished actress and a writer, Vitti also directed her first film,

Scandalo segreto (Secret Scandal) in 1989. In 1995, she was awarded a Golden Lion in Venice for her life achievement.

DOROTHÉE BONNIGAL

Vittorini, Elio

b. 23 July 1908, Siracusa; d. 12 February 1966, Milan

Novelist, essayist, editor and journalist

The son of a Sicilian railway worker, Vittorini had become at the time of his death one of the most influential Italian writers of the twentieth century, not only for his contributions to Italian literature but also for his active participation in the political and cultural life of the nation. Indeed, his ability to bring together the worlds of politics and of literature set an example for the generation of literati that became politically active in the 1960s (see **Gruppo 63**).

After running away from home several times and working in a variety of jobs, in 1927 the self-taught Vittorini married **Quasimodo**'s sister, Rosa, and began his literary career by contributing articles on art and literary criticism to *Il Mattino*, **La Stampa** and **Il Resto del Carlino**. Concurrently, he openly embraced fascism (see **fascism and neo-fascism**), drawn by its trade unionist and populist propaganda. However, refusing to accept the autarchic provincialism of the Fascist intelligentsia, in 1929 Vittorini joined the editorial staff of *Solaria*, a Florentine journal that embraced European literary developments such as those proposed by Proust and Joyce. In *Solaria*, Vittorini published his first volume of short stories, *Piccola borghesia* (Small Bourgeoisie), where he discarded the prevailing realism of the time for a lyrical and allegorical type of narration. Also in *Solaria*, Vittorini first published in instalments *Il garofano rosso* (The Red Carnation), a work that caused the suppression of the journal by the Fascist censorship in 1934, ostensibly because of the plot's sexually explicit themes but more probably because of Vittorini's emerging socialist and populist beliefs. Meanwhile, Vittorini had been studying English and when, in 1934, he was forced to abandon his typesetting activity following a case of lead poisoning, he began a productive career as a translator and editor of literary anthologies.

With the outbreak of the Spanish Civil War, Vittorini realized there existed a conflict between his personal beliefs and Fascist policy. In 1937, an article he wrote condemning fascism's involvement on the side of the anti-republican army led to his expulsion from the Fascist party. He then moved to Milan to work as an editor for Bompiani, all the while continuing to oppose fascism and increasing his literary activity of implicit and explicit subversion. Between 1938 and 1940, he translated widely from American literature – Poe, Faulkner, Steinbeck and Saroyan – because he was convinced, like Cesare **Pavese**, that contemporary American literature could offer useful models for – as he was later to put it on the front page of *Il Politecnico* – a culture that would protect the weak from the abuses of the powerful rather than simply console them. During this time he also wrote his most accomplished novel, *Conversazione in Sicilia* (Conversation in Sicily). First published in instalments between 1938 and 1939, *Conversazione* is an allegorical rendition of the struggle to awaken a political reaction to fascism which relies on the combination of myth and history in a Sicilian landscape to represent the suffering and outrage of the lower strata of the Italian population under fascism. The book caused a sensation when it appeared, and elevated Vittorini to a position of prominence among anti-fascist writers although, inexplicably, it was not actually censored until 1942. What was immediately censored, however, was the anthology *Americana* (1942), a historical overview of American writing edited by Vittorini and for which he had written the introductory notes to each author. The anthology, even with Vittorini's original comments expunged and replaced by a negative evaluation of American culture by Emilio **Cecchi**, documents the interest and fascination of an entire generation of Italians for the youthful and exuberant culture of the United States.

During the war Vittorini was arrested for his participation in the clandestine Communist Party (see **PCI**). Once freed, he joined the **Resistance** in Milan as editor of its underground press and, in 1944, he wrote *Uomini e no* (Men and Not Men), a book inspired by the partisan resistance and often considered – though, perhaps, too restrictively – as one of the best examples of literary **neorealism**. With the liberation of Italy, Vittorini first took over the Milanese branch of *L'Unità*, then began an intense activity as an editor. His most important project was the editorship of *Il Politecnico*, a broadly literary and cultural journal in which Vittorini wished to continue in his project of approaching culture from a humanistic viewpoint that would bridge the gap between intellectuals and the masses. Initially approved by the Communist Party, Vittorini's weekly eventually fell foul of the party's official line when, in reply to an article by party intellectual Mario Alicata in **Rinascita**, Vittorini initiated a very public debate with Palmiro **Togliatti** about the relationship between politics and culture. Vittorini strongly resisted Togliatti's suggestion that the weekly should toe the party line and publish only those authors whose ideals furthered the progress of communism. Eventually, however, under constant political pressure from the party and from other opponents of his project, Vittorini terminated the weekly's publication in 1947.

In the following two years, Vittorini published his last complete novels, *Il Sempione strizza l'occhio al Frejus* (translated as *The Twilight of the Elephant*) (1947) and *Le donne di Messina* (Women of Messina), before concentrating his attention on editorial work and family matters (in 1950 he was divorced from Rosa, and five years later his son Giulio died). Between 1942 and the time of his death, Vittorini edited a number of literary series for Bompiani, **Einaudi** and **Mondadori**, through which he actively made available and promoted the work of both great foreign authors and new Italian writers. His strong support for new writing was indefatigable although spectacularly, as editor for Einaudi, he made the mistake of rejecting Tommasi di **Lampedusa**'s *Il gattopardo* (The Leopard) in 1958, a work that was soon picked up by rival publisher **Feltrinelli**, and has since become an Italian classic.

In 1957, Vittorini published *Diario in pubblico* (Public Diary), the first of two important collections of essays that document the difficult relationship between the writer's literary world and the ever-changing political and cultural reality of postwar

Italy. The second volume, *Le due tensioni* (The Two Tensions), brings together and expands on the articles Vittorini wrote for *il menabò di letteratura* (The Literary Printer's Proof), which he co-directed with Italo **Calvino** and in which he discussed the often difficult rapport between the literary and the industrial world in Italian society. Diagnosed with an incurable illness in 1963, Vittorini continued to work until the time of his death in 1966.

Further reading

De Nicola, F. (1993) *Introduzione a Vittorini* (Introduction to Vittorini), Rome: Laterza (a broad analysis of Vittorini's work that includes a complete bibliography).

Lupetti, F. (1975) *La polemica Vittorini-Togliatti e la linea culturale del PCI nel 1945–1947* (The Polemic between Togliatti and Vittorini and the cultural direction of the PCI between 1945–1947), Milan: Lavoro liberato (an in-depth look at the public debate between the two men in the pages of *Il Politecnico*).

Potter, J. (1979) *Elio Vittorini*, Boston: Twayne Publishers (a general introduction, in English, to the life and works of the Sicilian author).

VALERIO FERME

volleyball

Italy is home to one of the most competitive volleyball leagues in the world, as was proven by the men's national team dominance in the last decades of the twentieth century, which includes victories in the World League in 1990–2, 1994–5, 1997 and 1999. Before the expansion of professional beach volleyball in North America, Italy was also the favourite destination for many top US players, who lacked a professional outlet after their college careers, and for players from countries such as Brazil who were attracted by better contracts. Professional volleyball teams are divided into Serie A1 (first division) and Serie A2 (second division). A system of playoffs determines not only the national champion but also the teams which move from A1 to A2 and vice versa. As is the case for **basketball**, the name of the sponsor becomes the official name of the team and this can change from one season to the next, thus creating some confusion for the less than dedicated fan.

PAOLO VILLA

Volonté, Gian Maria

b. 9 April 1933, Milan; d. 6 December 1994, Florina, Greece

Actor

Graduating from Rome's Accademia d'arte drammatica in 1957, Volonté started in theatre and never gave up the stage completely, in spite of his extraordinary range of involvement in the cinema. In 1962 he landed his first starring role in *Un uomo da bruciare* (A Man for the Killing), directed by the **Taviani brothers** and throughout the 1960s he became a familiar figure in **spaghetti westerns**, both under his real name and under the pseudonym of John Welles. However, his most productive years were the 1970s, during which Volonté committed himself to Italy's cinema *engagé*, collaborating with all the major political film-makers such as Giuliano **Montaldo** (*Sacco e Vanzetti*, 1971), Francesco **Rosi** (*Il caso Mattei* (The Mattei Case), 1972, and *Lucky Luciano*, 1973) and above all Elio **Petri** (from the Oscar-winning *Indagine su un cittadino al di sopra di ogni sospetto* (Investigation of a Citizen Above Suspicion), 1969, to *Todo Modo* (One Way or Another), 1976). After almost a decade of 'exile' in France in the 1980s, marked by awards both at Cannes and at Venice, Volonté returned to Italy to join the **New Italian Cinema** and work with the younger generation of political film-makers, in particular with Gianni **Amelio** (*Porte aperte* (Open Doors), 1991). Volonté died of a heart attack in 1994 while filming Theo Angelopoulos's *Ulysses' Gaze* in the Balkans.

DOROTHÉE BONNIGAL.

Volponi, Paolo

b. 6 February 1924, Urbino; d. 23 August 1994, Ancona

Lawyer, poet and novelist

While pursuing a managerial career in such firms as **Olivetti** and **Fiat**, Volponi fostered his interest in literature and published both poetry and narrative. In early novels such as *Memoriale* (My Troubles Began) (1962) and *La macchina mondiale* (The Worldwide Machine) (1962), Volponi represented the difficult process of the individual's social and cultural integration into the newly born industrial society, resulting in alienation and self-destruction. Volponi's linguistic and stylistic invention, owing much to the expressionism of Carlo Emilio **Gadda**, registers a dysfunctional social reality and its violence upon the individual, despite any attempt to adhere to nature. From the grotesque and parodic treatment of historical events in *Il sipario ducale* (Last Act in Urbino) (1975) to the apocalyptic representation of a final explosion in *Il pianeta irritabile* (The Irritable Planet) (1978), Volponi lucidly dissected the ills of Italian postwar society while powerfully constructing a visionary fictional world.

Further reading

Papini, M.C. (1997) *Paolo Volponi: il potere, la storia, il linguaggio* (Paolo Volponi: Power, History, Language), Florence: Le Lettere.

FRANCESCA PARMEGGIANI

W

Wertmüller, Lina

b. 14 August 1928, Rome

Director and scriptwriter

'I feel stronger when I stick to the popular side' said Lina Wertmüller who has been described as an aristocratic but moderate anarchist (her full name is Arcangela Felice Assunta Wertmüller von Elgg Spanol von Braueich). It was largely due to her passion for popular culture that in the 1970s she gained an unexpected international success by writing and directing a series of grotesque social satires, one of which, *Pasqualino settebellezze* (Seven Beauties) (1975) – a story about a prisoner in the concentration camps during the Second World War – received four Oscar nominations.

Wertmüller graduated from Pietro Sharoff's Theatrical Academy, and for the next ten years she worked in theatre, radio and television, writing scripts for comedians Garinei and Giovannini, producing puppet shows and directing the famous musical television show **Canzonissima** for **RAI**. During a holiday in the region of Puglia, she conceived her first film as a way of showing life in some areas of southern Italy. Back in Rome she became assistant director to Federico **Fellini** and in 1963, with Fellini's crew, she shot *I basilischi* (The Lizards). The film was critically well received but did poorly at the box office. Wertmüller returned to more popular entertainment with *Questa volta parliamo di uomini* (This Time We Talk About Men) (1965), an open rejoinder to **Scola**'s previous *Se permettete parliamo di donne* (With Permission, Let's Talk About Women) (1964). This was followed by

Rita la zanzara (Rita the Mosquito) (1966) and *Non stuzzicate la zanzara* (Don't Tease the Mosquito) (1967), two musicals starring Italian pop singer Rita Pavone but directed under the pseudonym of George H. Brown. Returning to the theatre, she met the sculptor Enrico Job, who became her husband and the set designer for many of her films.

In 1972, she directed *Mimì Metallurgico ferito nell'onore* (The Seduction of Mimì), a love story between Fiore, a beautifully emancipated Milanese Trotskyist, and Mimì, a Sicilian blue-collar worker. The film is set within the exciting atmosphere of the 1968 student protest permeated by political idealism and free love; however Mimì eventually allows himself to fall into the clutches of the **mafia** and so Fiore leaves him. The overwhelming success of this feisty tragicomedy allowed her to shoot a film every year with her favourite actors, Mariangela Melato as the northern Italian liberated woman and Giancarlo Giannini as the deeply conservative southern man: *Film d'amore e d'anarchia* (Love and Anarchy) (1973), *Tutto a posto niente in ordine* (All Screwed Up) (1974), *Travolti da un insolito destino* (Swept Away) (1974–5).

During the 1980s, her films moved to deal with even more complex social themes such as kidnapping, drug addiction, organized crime and AIDS. She also continued working in theatre and, amongst other things, directed the **opera** Carmen for the San Carlo Theatre in Naples. Naples became for a while her favourite setting, where she filmed the very moving *Sabato domenica e lunedì* (Saturday, Sunday and Monday) (1990), adapted from a play by Eduardo **De Filippo** and starring Sophia **Loren**. In 1988 she was appointed

Commissario Straordinario (Independent Commissioner) for the **Centro Sperimentale di
Cinematografia**.

In the 1990s she found other targets for her
strong popular satire with *Io speriamo che me la cavo*
(Ciao, Professor) (1992), a story about a northern
teacher, played by Paolo **Villaggio**, sent to Naples
to teach to a bunch of streetwise kids, and *Meccanico
e parrucchiera in un turbine di sesso e politica* (Mechanic
and Hairdresser in a Tornado of Sex and Politics)
where she ridicules the **Lega Nord** (Northern
League) and the parties of the new left, RC
(**Rifondazione Comunista**) and **PDS** (Partito
democratico della sinistra).

See also: feminist cinema

Further reading

Bondanella, P. (1983) *Italian Cinema from Neorealism to
the Present*, New York: Ungar (on Wertmüller, see
ch. 10, 'The Contemporary Scene and New
Italian Comedy').

Marcus, M. (1986) *Italian Film in the Light of
Neorealism*, Princeton, NJ: Princeton University
Press (see ch. 14, 'Wertmüller's *Love and Anarchy*:
The High Price of Commitment').

Michalczyk, J. (1986) *The Italian Political Filmmakers*,
London and Toronto: Associated University
Presses (see ch. 7, 'Lina Wertmüller: The Politics
of Sexuality').

ADRIANA MONTI

wine

The function of wine in Italian culture is extremely
complex, for wine is simultaneously a dietary
staple, an important commodity and an aesthetic
philosophy. Consequently, an account of Italian
wine needs to weave together three competing
narratives: wine for the people, wine for the palate
and wine for the market.

The first narrative concerns the historic wine
culture of Italy or wine as a dietary staple. As the
old saying, 'bread, wine and olives', suggests, wine
has historically been regarded as food. Thus wine is
grown both as an economic crop and an
agricultural necessity throughout Italy, from northern Piedmont to the southern islands of Sardinia
and Sicily. Although the majority of wine today is
sold through wine stores, rural families still have
demijohns of regional wines delivered to their
homes. Likewise, urban dwellers still drive to rural
co-operatives (*cantine*) to purchase demijohns that
they bottle themselves upon return to the city.

Since, historically, wine drinking has been
widespread through all classes of the population,
it has created the custom of drinking wine from
one's own region and even the advent of *enoteche*
(specialized stores that sell wines from elsewhere in
Italy and Europe) has not really changed this
practice. Although the custom ultimately derives
from the lack of navigable rivers and the historic
difficulty of travel between provinces, it continues
today as an established part of a cultural system in
which, for example, dishes of one region are
usually paired only with the wines from that region.

Furthermore, since regional wines are produced
by farmers and small producers usually for local
and personal consumption, wines are made in and
for the immediate area and some wines are thus
virtually unknown outside their DOCs (accredited
areas of origin). Because of the low yields, these
wines are frequently sold before they are even
bottled. Customarily, families in the region negotiate to buy these wines in twenty-five to fifty-litre
increments, or enough wine to drink over the year.
Throughout the 1960s these wines could still be
found in unlabelled bottles; however, subsequent
DOC legislation has done much to eliminate this
practice.

With grapes grown and wine made throughout
the peninsula, some experts estimate that Italy
produces over 3,800 wines, an achievement which
makes Italy the most diverse wine producer in the
world. However, only a portion of these wines have
actually been successfully exported to the Anglo-
American world. From 1945 through to the 1960s,
Italy's exports consisted mainly of bulk wines for
blending and the straw-basketed flasks of chianti
popular in Italian restaurants. This popular chianti,
moreover, has little to do with the DOC-classified
chianti of Classico, Colli Senesi, Colline Pisane,
Ruffina, Colli Fiorentini, Aretini, and Montalbano.
In fact, the exported chianti has created a cultural
identity of wine for the market which is at odds
with the actual wine produced in the Chianti

region. Thus, as chianti has become the classic accompaniment to pizza and spaghetti, it also has become a cultural icon for the Anglo-American world's imagination of Italian culture.

The successful marketing of chianti proves, however, that wine for the market – and here we move to the second competing narrative in Italian wine-making – has been an important concern since the 1970s. Eager to transform wine into a commodity and to elevate Italy's status in the Common Market, exporters began to target the United States. With the popular eclipse of chiantis, exporters were forced to imagine new forms of wine which could be uniformly produced in mass quantities and marketed abroad. During the 1970s, wines like lambrusco from Emilia-Romagna and soave from the Veneto displaced the once en-trenched chianti as the most popular exported Italian wine.

Lambrusco, perhaps, has done the most damage qualitatively and the most good quantitatively in establishing wine as a viable commodity. The wine's export success has been largely due to its lack of all specifiable attributes associated with the varietal. It's blandness encouraged the notion that good wine should not divert attention away from food. In its heyday, lambrusco even came in colourless and non-alcoholic versions to satisfy what Italians imagined as the American palate, a palate which only tolerated a softer, rounder, sweeter and lighter wine.

The export success of lambrusco led many Italian winemakers to see it as the 'magic liquid' of Italy's international economic resurgence, but lambrusco also changed the way Italians them-selves perceived wine. The popularity of lambrusco overseas and the gradual acceptance in Italy of foreign wines provoked a similar revolution in the Italian palate, which came also to demand a softer and rounder wine. In fact, the success of the lambrusco well illustrates the conflict between Italians' own perception of wine and how they have historically marketed their wines to the Anglo-American world. In Italian culture, wine complements a meal so that flavours, textures and fragrances are enhanced even in the most basic of dishes. The pairing of montepulciano d'Abruzzo, a simple red from the Abruzzi, for example, with porchetta, requires that the wine complements and

amplifies the flavours present in the dish as a whole. By contrast, in the US, wine has been perceived as cumbersome if it appears too distinctive in relation to food or if it requires too much thought. Thus wine should not warrant too much reflection; as an accompaniment to pizza, wine should be consumed quickly. As a result, some of Italy's great wines are still virtually unknown in many parts of the Anglo-American world.

This fact poses a problem for Italian wine exporters, who see their mission to the Anglo-American market as primarily an educational one. In fact, some exporters feel it is necessary to introduce the less demanding wines of valpolicella, bardolino, pinot grigio, and amarone to the American palates in order to create an interest in the more querulous wines, whose flavours might not emerge quite so straightforwardly. The opu-lence and elegant austerity of the Piedmont's barolos and barbarescos are cases in point. These aged wines are primarily the expression of the nebbiolo grape; the difference between the two is the respective time that they are left to age in oak barrels. They are classic cellaring wines and embody the soul of Italian winemaking; they are truly 'philosophies in a bottle'. When barolos are drunk too young, however, they are tight, tannic chores, which require real patience from the consumer, if the consumer is at all interested in the wine's complexities. The third competing narrative in Italian winemaking, wine for the palate, suggests that premium wines require time and reflection in order to understand and imagine their nuances.

Even connoisseurs, accustomed to the legendary wines of California, France and Australia's Grange Hermitage, have no analogue for the many kinds of local premium wines produced in Italy. This problem is compounded when one realizes that over two thousand grape varietals are alleged to exist in Italy and that the internationally recog-nized cabernet is just a small percentage of wines in that eclectic mix. In fact, Italian cabernet only emerged as a varietal to be taken seriously in its own right during the 1980s. Likewise, the back-bone of Italian varietals, barbera, is almost unknown in the United States, except through the efforts of some of the Cal-Ital winemakers.

However, barbera holds an esteemed place in

relation to two other principal varietals, sangiovese, the primary grape in chianti, and nebbiolo, the primary grape in barolo. Depending on the wine, the varietals can be hot and spicy, or reminiscent of wild berries, tar and leather. Although these three varietals produce red wines (*rosso*), white wines (*bianco*) are also commonplace in Italian culture. The best-known varietals derive primarily from pinot, riesling and tokai stocks and can be either as dry as stone and slate, or as fragrant as wildflowers and freshly cut herbs. Rosé (*rosato*) and sparkling wines (*spumante*) are likewise produced in many areas. Moreover, all of these types of wines vary in style according to the residual amounts of sugar after vinification; thus they can be very dry (*secco*), semi-dry (*semi-secco*) or sweet (*dolce*).

Another style of wine, *vin santo*, is a *passito* wine also extremely popular with Italians. *Vin santo* is known as a dessert wine but can be vinified in a sherry-like style. As a *passito* wine, it is usually sweet and made from semidried grapes. *Vin santo* is culturally understood as 'the holy wine' because it is made historically between Christmas and Easter.

Since the 1970s, almost all Italian wines have been influenced by lambrusco's success with mass production. What was once consigned to fate – how various varietals would fare season by season – has now been superseded by technology and science. Indeed, technology has ensured that Italian wines reach consistently high levels of quality throughout the vintages. Moreover, new wine technology has changed the making of some white wines altogether. For example, the historic practice of leaving white varietals 'on their skins' has been permanently displaced by more efficient methods. Likewise, the presence of oenology has transformed the red wine industry. The teroldego of the Trentino-Alto-Adige appears to the watchful eyes of oenologists to be one of the most impressive vinological transformations of the nineties and its recent showing at Vinitaly, the foremost wine fair in the world, heralds it as the symbol of Italian winemaking for the twenty-first century.

Nevertheless, Piedmont with its barolos, barbarescos and gattinaras, and Tuscany with its chiantis and brunellos, have long held a place of primary importance both legislatively with the DOC, and popularly with Italian wine connoisseurs. However, as the example of teroldego demonstrates, every province falls under the legislative gaze of the DOC; therefore, every province either has already or hopes to have in the near future specific wines included in the DOC's hierarchical system of classification.

Known as No. 930, the Denominazione di Origine Controllata (DOC) system stipulates that winemakers must prove that their wines derive from specified or controlled areas. In this way, the Italian government attempts to legislate the wine industry. In 1993, 42 DOC areas existed within Italy's 20 regions. Primarily done for the sake of the European Common Market consumer, the DOC provides legislative protection. Prior to the DOC's inauguration in 1963, in fact, and as early as 1924, consortia of producers had attempted to designate controlled areas for the production of chianti, Italy's historically popular wine. The consortium, Chianti Classico, organized the producers of that region and were able to get lawmakers to approve the zone in 1932. However, after the Second World War, the Italian courts could not devote attention to the problems of the emerging wine trade and so producers from all over Italy could produce wines labelled chianti. Similarly, some wines from the designated zone, even from the same vineyard, were radically different from each other so that the consumer had no guarantee that a wine labelled chianti actually was chianti. The DOC legislation made it illegal to call a wine chianti unless it was produced from sangiovese grown in the DOC's Chianti zones.

However, No. 930 initially promised consumers that wines so labelled were also made according to a minimum standard of quality. Thus the DOC appended 'Guaranteed' (*Garantita*) to Italy's classified wines. In other words, the DOCG determines that Italian wines produced in DOC regions have to uniformly and consistently guarantee their quality as well as their origin. In 1992, law No. 164 altered the previously all-encompassing DOCG to indicate only premium wines of a superior level. The more recent law ensures that producers do not overproduce this special class of wine. Although the effect of this legislation has been a consumer's dream, the government's desire to standardize the operations and the quality of Italian wines is at odds with the soul of the winemaking industry. This cultural caesura escalated into what has become the *vino da tavola* (table wine) revolution in Tuscany.

On the one hand, Tuscany is the historic producer of some of Italy's most legendary reds: chianti, brunello di Montalcino and vino nobile di Montalcino. These wines are all DOC-recognized wines. On the other hand, Tuscany produces grapes for winemaking in areas outside its fourteen legislatively recognized DOCs. In fact, the production of premium non-DOC wine, an earlier winemaking scandal, has become a symbol of the creativity and individualism of the Italian winemaking industry. These 'Super Tuscans' emerge from areas not only unrecognized by the DOC, but even previously unknown for premium wine in Italian popular culture. Under Italian law, these wines can only be sold under the label of table wines (*vino da tavola*). However, Italian table wines had always been cheap and, whether bought at a wine store, a cooperative or from a farmer, they were notable only because they were affordable necessities, available in great quantity.

Thus the 'Super Tuscans' have transformed the humble image of Italian table wine into a symbol of oenological rebellion against governmental attempts to standardize Italian creativity. The idea that Italian wine reflects the individual winemaker's palate and creativity emerges, moreover, in direct opposition to the image of an homogenous, standardized, consistent product for a standardized European consumer. In other words, the 'Super Tuscans' have thwarted the DOC's attempt to rehabilitate Italy according to the rubrics of an imagined European palate. Thus table wines have become a manifestation of some of the greatest achievements in Italian winemaking. Ironically, the prices to be paid for these new wines must reflect then not the legislation's assessment of them, but rather the winemaker's personal style and qualities, a significance at odds with the lexical definition of table wines.

The significance of wine in Italy suggests, then, a culture both heterogeneous and creative, necessarily fraught with contradictions. The morass of legislation prompts winemakers to take innovative risks while, at the same time, they revel in a tradition that is singularly theirs. Even with the changes in palate, wine continues to be a critical component holding together disparate sectors of society. Whether through the Marxist co-operatives of lambrusco or the aristocratic producers of barolo, wine remains a cultural as well as a dietary staple of Italy.

Further reading

Anderson, B. (1994) *Wines of Italy: Vino, The Quality of Life*, Rome: Italian Institute for Trade/ICE.
Gleave, D. (1989) *The Wines of Italy*, London: Salamander.
Hazan, V. (1982) *Italian Wine*, New York: Knopf.
Pedrolli, F. and Sola, P. (1994) *Vias Wines*, Trento: Alvin Service.
Robinson, J. (1995) *Oxford Companion to Wine*, London: Oxford University Press.

KITTY MILLET

winter sports

Encircled by the Alps along its northern edge and with the Apennine range running the length of the peninsula, Italy has many mountain regions which offer many possibilities for recreational and competitive winter sports. Italy was one of the original sixteen countries which participated in the first Olympic Winter Games held at Chamonix, France, in 1924, but almost thirty years passed before an Italian stepped onto the podium. The first medals for Italy came in 1952 in Oslo, where Zeno Colò won the men's downhill ski race and Giuliana Minuzzo took bronze in the women's downhill (competing under the married name Chenal-Minuzzo, she won another bronze in the women's giant slalom in the games of 1960, the only medal taken by Italy that year).

In 1956, it was Italy's turn to host the games. The site chosen was Cortina d'Ampezzo, an exclusive resort and picturesque village nestled in the Dolomite range of the eastern Alps. More nations (32) and athletes (820) than previously took part, and for the first time ever, television cameras were present to broadcast the games, a factor which greatly increased the number of spectators and consequently the popularity of winter sports. Among other things, the cameras broadcast images of the first Olympic team representing the USSR.

It became immediately clear that the Soviet Union was a force to be reckoned with, as its team went on to dominate the 1956 games, winning sixteen medals overall, including seven gold.

Italy won three medals in front of the home crowd, its best performance to that time. All three came from bobsledding competitions, beginning a tradition of Italian strength in the sport. In Cortina, Lamberto Dalla Costa guided Italia 1 to victory in the two-man bobsled race, and Eugenio Monti in the Italia 2 took the silver medal in the same competition. Monti, who won another silver medal in the four-man bobsled in Cortina, there began his quest for Olympic gold as part of a long career that made him one the world's all-time great bobsledders.

Since the Winter Games of 1960 did not include bobsled competitions, Monti's next chance came in 1964, in Innsbruck, Austria, where however he only managed two bronze medals. Monti finally achieved his goal in 1968, at the age of forty. At the tenth Winter Olympics in Grenoble, France, he climbed the highest step of an Olympic podium for both the two-man and the four-man bobsled, topping his previous Olympic silver and bronze medals and adding to his nine titles as world champion.

1968 proved to be a particularly good year for the Italian contingent, which won more gold medals in Grenoble than in all the previous Winter Olympics combined. After an investigation that revealed foul play on the parts of the two East German lugers, who placed first and second, Italian luger Erica Lechner's third place was transformed into a gold medal. More shocking yet, and this time completely of his own doing, was the gold medal clinched by twenty-seven-year-old Franco Nones. Never in the previous nine Winter Games had a non-Scandinavian won a cross-country ski race; Nones broke that tradition when he won the 30 kilometre event.

In the years between 1971 and 1976, a group of Italian skiers known as *la valanga azzurra* (the blue avalanche) managed to claim most of the available trophies. Gustavo Thoeni was the foremost among this group of champions. As was the case for many who lived in remote Alpine villages, skiing was Thoeni's means of transportation from very early age, which accounted for the naturalness and efficiency of his inimitable style. During his career, he won four Alpine World Cups, four overall World titles (1971–3 and 1975), one Olympic gold medal (men's giant slalom in 1972) and two silver medals (men's slalom in 1972 and 1976). Just one step below Thoeni was Piero Gros, gold medallist in 1976 in the men's slalom and overall world champion in 1974. They were joined, among many others, by Gustavo's brother Roland, who came in third in the slalom at the 1972 Winter Olympics, by Claudia Giordani, silver medallist in 1976 in the women's slalom, and by Herbert Plank, who took the bronze medal for the men's downhill in 1976. The successes of the *valanga azzurra* were also a great vehicle for the promotion of the ski industry; it was in this period that ski resorts started to expand in order to cater to an ever increasing number of skiers.

Thoeni and friends were a difficult act to follow, but at the 1980 and 1984 games more glory was in store for the Italian team. In 1984, Paoletta Magoni prevailed in the slalom, becoming the first Italian woman to win an Olympic gold medal in alpine skiing. Paul Hildgartner, already a gold medallist in 1972 in the men's double luge, won a silver in 1980 and a gold in 1984 in the men's singles. Combined with the silver medal in men's doubles in 1980, this was the start of a series of victories in luge competitions which continued on to the 1994 games in Lillehammer, Norway. In 1994, Italian lugers, men and women, won four of the six available medals, including two out of three golds.

The spectacular performance of the lugers in Lillehammer was matched by many other representatives of the Italian team, which accumulated an astounding twenty medals, finishing in fourth place overall. In a twelve-day span, Manuela Di Centa performed a miracle of her own, capturing two gold medals and two silver in the four cross country individual ski races she entered. She then helped the Italian women's team to the bronze medal in the cross-country relay competition. Stefania Belmondo finished third in the 15 kilo-metre cross-country pursuit. The men's cross-country team responded with the gold medal in the 4×10 kilometre relay and two third places in individual races. Manuela Di Centa was the most decorated athlete of the Lillehammer games, and

Italian skiers obtained a total of nine medals, more than any other nation.

In Alpine skiing, Deborah Compagnoni took first place in the women's giant slalom (two years before, at the Albertville Winter games, she had won the Super G), and teammate Isolde Kostner gained two bronze medals, one for the women's downhill and one for the Super G. But the Italian skier everyone expected to perform well was Alberto **Tomba**. Tomba established himself as the man to beat in Calgary in 1988, where he won both the slalom and the giant slalom. Four years later in Albertville, while teammate Josef Polig triumphed in the alpine combined competition, Tomba won the giant slalom again. No other skier before him had managed to take the same event in consecutive Winter Olympics. Tomba, possibly the greatest slalom skier of all time, won another silver medal in 1994. If his performance at Lillehammer was somewhat disappointing for his numerous fans, Tomba made it up to them by returning the overall world title to Italy in 1995, exactly twenty years after the last won by Thoeni, now one of his coaches.

Further reading

Chamonix to Lillehammer (1994), An Official Publication of the US Olympic Committee, Salt Lake City: Commemorative Publications (an illustrated volume with a brief overview of all editions of the Winter Sports until Lillehammer and a complete medal list as appendix).

PAOLO VILLA

women's writing

Italian women's writing of the postwar period has employed diverse genres to explore themes that include women's subjectivity, disenfranchisement and the female voice in Italian society. While not all works are feminist in purpose, many within the literary and theoretical fields give voice to and illuminate women's marginalized experiences and investigate themes of creativity, motherhood and female desire. Others explore the author's personal and artistic vision, creating a unique perspective within mainstream literary convention. Together, these writings contribute to the landscape of women's expressions and to cultural tradition that dates back centuries.

Women's writing has flourished in diverse periods of Italian history. In the medieval and Renaissance periods, for example, poets such as Gaspara Stampa and Veronica Franco produced lyrics of generic and thematic sophistication, dealing with such concerns as poetic voice and desire. During the nineteenth century, writers such as Erminia Fuà Fusinato and Vittoria Aganoor Pompili contributed to the Risorgimento and to the decadent movement, respectively, while authors such as Matilde Serao produced works documenting women's socio-cultural conditions. The twentieth century, however, has witnessed an impressive rise in women's literary production across all genres.

In the first half of the twentieth century, authors such as Grazia Deledda and Sibilla Aleramo produced influential accounts of women's lives. With few exceptions, however (for example, the writing of Nobel-Prize winning Deledda), these authors' works were often considered too personal and, consequently, remained marginalized. With the advent of the postwar women's movement, Italian women's writing achieved both an international audience and recognition as an invaluable contribution to Italian culture.

Italian women's writing in the second half of the twentieth century has been greatly influenced by the feminist inquiry into women's identity and subjectivity. Feminist theoreticians such as Carla Lonzi and the members of the Milan Women's Bookstore Collective have theorized a project for women's liberation, which calls for a reversal of women's historical marginalization and dispossession. Women's lives and daily experiences, they note, have traditionally been shrouded in silence and, consequently, have not shaped our sense of our historical heritage. These theorists propose, therefore, the exploration of women's lives and the recuperation of female subjects in history. While this can serve immediately to uncover the realities of women's experiences in history, it ultimately also creates a cultural legacy for women.

Establishing a legacy of subjectivity represents one of the chief undertakings and recurring themes of postwar Italian women's writing. Indeed, numerous works profile female subjects in Italian history, among them Anna Banti's *Artemisia*, a fictionalized biography of the seventeenth-century painter Artemisia Gentileschi, Elsa **Morante**'s novel *La storia* (History) (1974), about the trials and tribulations of a mother in Second World War Italy, and Dacia **Maraini**'s novel *La lunga vita di Marianna Ucrìa* (translated as *The Silent Duchess*) (1990), a reconstruction of the life of an eighteenth-century deaf-mute woman. In presenting what has been elided in conventional accounts of history, these works reconstruct a historical framework for women.

While revising their heritage through their writings, Italian women writers in the postwar period have also maintained a distinctive position *vis-à-vis* mainstream literary movements such as **postmodernism**. While postmodernist theorists question the validity of the authorial voice and of the referentiality of language, many women authors have felt compelled to preserve their unique voices and to subjectively recount their experiences as both women and artists. They have also often, though not exclusively, joined the feminist tradition of uncovering the realities of women's lives and constructing the world of their characters out of lived episodes. In order to achieve this aim, these authors have typically favoured the autobiography and confessional, represented through diverse literary genres such as prose, poetry and theatre. Perhaps the most significant work hailed today as a historical reference point for postwar writers is Sibilla Aleramo's account of her own experiences in turn of the century Italy, the novel *Una donna* (A Woman) (1906). In the latter half of the twentieth century, this autobiographical tradition makes an important contribution to the feminist notion that the private is indeed a political and public concern. The resulting personal or fictionalized accounts often depict previously obscured elements of the domestic sphere. Serving as metaphors for women's conditions, quotidian elements of this sphere are central to such works as Alba **de Céspedes**' novel *Quaderno proibito* (Forbidden Notebook) (1952), Armanda Guiducci's autobiographical essay *La mela e il serpente* (The Apple and the Serpent) (1974), Franca **Rame**'s

play *Tutta casa, letto e chiesa* (translated as *Orgasmo Adulto Escapes from the Zoo*), and Clara Sereni's autobiographical novel *Casalinghitudine* (Houseworkness).

While many authors have employed, and continue to employ, the autobiographical style to create a space for female voices and to depict women's experiences in Italian culture and society, other writers have purposefully adopted more literary styles to express their visions. The poet Maria Luisa **Spaziani**, for example, creates an introspective reflection of the self and of her poetic vision in a highly crafted conventional form. Meanwhile, the novelist and short story writer Paola **Capriolo** fashions fictional works that tackle philosophical issues and feature the fantastic and the mythical. Other writers still have fashioned a cultural theory that examines women's literary productions and their socio-historical contexts. In critical essays, Elisabetta **Rasy** and poet Biancamaria **Frabotta**, for example, explore the way Italian women's writing responds to, challenges and/or revises literary tenets to expand the context of its social and cultural vision. However, regardless of the genres and styles they employ and the themes and issues they explore, Italian women authors enjoy continued success in their endeavours to express their visions, to create a space for female voices, and to give shape to a historical heritage which includes such important postwar novelists as Natalia **Ginzburg** and Francesca **Duranti**, poet Giulia Niccolai, and theorists Adriana Cavarero, Luisa Muraro, and Silvia Vegetti-Finzi.

See also: feminism

Further reading

Blelloch, P. (1991) 'Postmodernism and Italian Women Writers', *NEMLA* 15: 183–200.

Lazzaro-Weis, C. (1993) *From Margins to Mainstream*, Philadelphia: University of Pennsylvania Press.

Wood, S. (1995) (ed.) *Italian Women's Writing 1860–1994*, London: Athlone.

VIRGINIA PICCHIETTI

Z

Zaccagnini, Benigno

b. 17 April 1912, Faenza; d. 5 November 1989, Ravenna

Politician

After being a leader in the **Resistance** movement, Benigno Zaccagnini was elected for the **DC** to the **Constituent Assembly** and thereafter to successive parliaments. Associated with the DC-left and a strong supporter of Aldo **Moro**, he became party secretary between 1975–80, replacing Amintore **Fanfani** in the aftermath of the **divorce** referendum debacle. Known affectionately as 'honest Zac', he rebuilt the youth movement which Fanfani had dissolved and improved the image of the party, not least in the Catholic world. The 1976 election saw a substantial influx of new faces into the party. However, although the party's Left became organizationally dominant for the first time at the 1976 congress, Zaccagnini was unable to rebuild the party programmatically. Following the end of the national solidarity experiment (1976–8) in which the **PCI** had backed DC governments, his pro-PCI line was overturned at the 1980 Congress.

MARK DONOVAN

Zampa, Luigi

b. 2 January 1905; d.15 August 1991, Rome

Film director

After graduating from the **Centro Sperimentale di Cinematografia** in 1935, Zampa wrote screenplays for **Soldati** and **Camerini**, and began directing in 1941. His 1946 film, *Vivere in pace* (To Live in Peace), was considered a neorealist masterpiece (see **neorealism**), though Zampa's burlesque treatment of war themes places this film, like most of his others, in the realm of the closely observed comedy of manners. More engaging is the trilogy of films written by Vitaliano **Brancati**, *Anni difficili* (Difficult Years) (1948), *Anni facili* (Easy Years) (1953) and *L'arte di arrangiarsi* (The Art of Survival) (1954), scathing depictions of society under both fascism (see **fascism and neo-fascism**) and Christian Democrat (see **DC**) rule. The Neapolitan melodrama *Processo all città* (The City Stands Trial) (1952) is unique in Zampa's output for its seriousness, while *Una questione d'onore* (A Question of Honour) (1966), about Sardinian crimes of passion, and the mordant satire on the venality of health service doctors, *Il medico della mutua* (The Health Service Doctor) (1968), reveal a similarly genuine preoccupation with social concerns.

DAVE WATSON

Zanuso, Marco

b. 14 May 1916, Milan

Architect and designer

Zanuso is one of the generation of 'designer heroes' whose reputation is linked to that of the modern Italian design movement that was born in the years after 1945. Marco Zanuso graduated in architecture from the Polytechnic of Milan in 1939. He was a professor at that institute from 1945–86. In 1945, he also set up his own design studio in Milan. His experience as an academic and as a practitioner enabled him to become one of the key spokesmen of his era, and he was involved in Italian design across a wide spectrum of activities including organizing the **Milan Triennale**, editing *Domus* and *Casabella*, and designing a range of important furniture pieces and products. He was especially well known for his 'Lady' armchair for Arflex of 1951, in which he used foam rubber in an innovative way, and for his use of plastic in the design of a child's stacking chair for Kartell in 1964. He also worked extensively for Brionvega.

Further reading

Dorfles, G. (1971) *Marco Zanuso: Designer*, Rome: Editalia.

Fossati, P. (1972) *Il design in Italia 1945–1972* (Design in Italy:1945–1972), Turin: Einaudi.

PENNY SPARKE

Zanussi

Based in Pordenone, the Zanussi company was originally formed in 1916 by Antonio Zanussi. At that time it was a workshop for repairing stoves but by the interwar years it was producing cookers, refrigerators and other household appliances in the 'streamline' style, heavily influenced by design trends in the USA. In the 1950s the company set up a design department, headed by Gino **Valle**, who was responsible for the sophisticated, unobtrusive appearance of its products. In the 1980s Zanussi rejected the minimal look in favour of a more ostentatious 'postmodern' approach to de-

sign. Seminal designs included that of the 'Wizard' refrigerator, created by Roberto Pezetta, who led the design department in those years.

Further reading

Issue 2 (1989) London: Design Museum.

PENNY SPARKE

Zanzotto, Andrea

b. 10 October 1921, Pieve di Soligo, Treviso

Poet and essayist

A high school teacher in his hometown, Zanzotto is considered by critics Stefano **Agosti** and Gianfranco **Contini** to be the foremost living Italian poet and an important, albeit independent, precursor to the literary experimentation of the neoavantgarde (see **Gruppo 63**). After participating in the Second World War, Zanzotto lived in France and Switzerland before returning to his birthplace, where he has remained. His early poetry was influenced by the Florentine hermetic group, by Giuseppe **Ungaretti** and by the surrealists' stream-of-consciousness techniques. Then, with *Vocativo* (Vocative), published in 1957, Zanzotto began a series of experiments that juxtapose the poetic search for an aesthetic, pure language, and the stream-of-consciousness intrusion of everyday language that forever displaces this search. In the subsequent collections, *IX Ecloghe* (IX Eclogues), *La beltà* (Beauty) and *Pasque* (Easters), Zanzotto's excavation of language, affected by his reading of post-structuralism, deconstruction and Lacan's psychoanalytic theory, led to very abstract poems where the language and its formal constraints commingle and diverge on a variety of registers. Thematically, in these collections Zanzotto's wordplay is grafted onto the images and mythological background of the Veneto region, as it moves from its traditionally agrarian past into the age of mass media and pop culture.

In 1976, the book *Filò* signals a new phase in the poet's development. Written in Venetian dialect and containing the ballads Zanzotto wrote for Federico

Fellini's film *Casanova, Filò* coherently continues the linguistic experimentation of his previous work and explores the expressive possibilities of dialect to create meaning. This search for linguistic coherence is explored in *Galateo di bosco* (A Forest Book of Etiquette) (1978), the first volume of a trilogy that includes *Fosfeni* (Phosphenes) (1983) and *Idioma* (Idiom) (1986). In *Galateo*, Zanzotto continues to deconstruct language and the unified self by juxtaposing linguistic registers that shift from the aulic, codified language of 'civilized' society to the vulgar and unruly language of dialect and contemporary language. *Fosfeni* shifts Zanzotto's search for linguistic coherence to the language of scientific logic, although the new idiom also fails to impart clarity and unity to the poet's world vision. It is only with *Idioma*, published in 1986, that Zanzotto suggests a possible return to coherence by using dialect and effacing the poetic self. Here the poems, written for the most part in dialect, recapture metric structures long abandoned by the poet and intimate that the integrity which the contemporary world's fractured language cannot provide is to be found in one's roots. Moreover, because the poet's lyrical self is effaced to celebrate both local and literary icons, Zanzotto seems to imply that memory and community can become substitutes in the self's search for coherence.

Zanzotto is also the author of short stories and essays that further document his interest in modern language and in contemporary literary theory.

Further reading

Zanzotto, A. (1993) *Poems*, trans. A. Bennett, Lewes: Allardyce Books.

VALERIO FERME

Zavattini, Cesare

b. 20 September 1902, Luzzara, Reggio Emilia; d. 31 October 1989, Rome

Journalist, critic, scriptwriter, novelist, painter and film-maker

Although often remembered merely as one of the founding fathers of cinematic **neorealism**, and mostly for his collaborations with **De Sica** on such landmark films as *Sciuscià* (Shoeshine) (1946), *Ladri di Biciclette* (Bicycle Thieves) (1948) and *Umberto D* (1952), Zavattini was a genial and polymorphic figure who overflowed with creative talent in many different fields and took an active and enthusiastic role in all aspects of Italian culture for over six decades.

After living and teaching in Parma for several years and contributing to several small provincial magazines, Zavattini moved to Milan in 1930 where he met, among others, the publisher Valentino Bompiani with whom he began a lifelong friendship. In Milan he worked at a number jobs with different publishers, contributed to a variety of popular magazines and founded several new magazines of his own. At the same time he also published two playful novels permeated by a light, surreal sense of humour, as well as co-writing the screenplay for Mario **Camerini**'s immensely successful film, *Darò un milione* (I'll Give a Million) (1935).

In 1940 he moved to Rome and, while continuing to write – and having in the meantime also taken up painting – he gravitated more towards the cinema, soon collaborating on the script of **Blasetti**'s *Quattro passi fra le nuvole* (A Walk through the Clouds) (1942). There followed the beginning of his decisive partnership with De Sica, with whom he made *I bambini ci guardano* (The Children are Watching Us) (1943), a precursor of the classic neorealist films of the late 1940s and early 1950s.

In the postwar period, while continuing his partnership with De Sica and becoming the most vocal proponent of neorealism, Zavattini also scripted numerous films for other directors, including **Visconti**, **De Santis**, **Blasetti**, **Lattuada**, **Germi** and **Castellani**. For the next thirty years he continued to work as a scriptwriter while also painting, publishing novels and poetry, contributing to popular magazines, conducting talkback radio programmes and organizing a wide variety of cultural encounters and events.

After having collaborated with other directors on an estimated 120 films, in 1982 Zavattini finally directed himself in his first solo film for television, *La Veritàaaa* (The Truthhhh), a gentle pacifist tale which, in its anarchic and slightly demented sense of humour, perfectly reflected his sunny disposition and summed up his philosophy of life.

Only a year after his death, his wide and varied contribution to European culture was celebrated in a four-month retrospective at the Georges Pompidou Centre in Paris. His literary works, his screenplays and his writings on the cinema have now been extensively published or republished by Bompiani, and in 1998 all his paintings were also exhibited in a comprehensive retrospective.

Further reading

Gili, J.A. and Bernardini, A. (eds) (1990) *Cesare Zavattini*, Paris and Bologna: Centre National Georges Pompidou/Regione Emilia-Romagna (a number of essays in a lavishly-illustrated volume ranging over diverse aspects of Zavattini's creative genius).

Strand, P. and Zavattini, C. (1981) *Un Paese: Portrait of an Italian Village*, trans. M. Shore, New York: Aperture (a portrait of Zavattini's native village of Luzzara and a fine example of his artistic collaboration outside the cinema).

Zavattini, C. (1953) 'Some Ideas on the Cinema', *Sight and Sound*, trans. P.L. Lanza, October: 64–9 (Zavattini's passionate manifesto of neorealism).

GINO MOLITERNO

Zeffirelli, Franco

b. 12 February 1923, Florence

Director

With Maria Callas and erstwhile lover Luchino **Visconti**, Zeffirelli revolutionized **opera** production at **La Scala** during the 1950s. His knowledge of English led to an early interest in Shakespeare, whose plays he directed both in Italy and in Great Britain. His second Shakespearean film, *Romeo and Juliet* (1968), set box office records for Paramount and launched an international career. Known for spectacularly monumental productions and a keen attention to realistic detail, Zeffirelli has dedicated virtually his entire career on both stage and screen to Italian and English works. Entering politics and marrying, both very late in life, Zeffirelli has

become notorious for his reactionary positions, his Catholic conservatism and his homophobic views.

Further reading

Watson, W. (1995) 'Shakespeare, Zeffirelli and the Homosexual Gaze', in D. Barker and I. Kamps (eds), *Shakespeare and Gender*, London: Verso.

Zeffirelli, F. (1986) *Zeffirelli: An Autobiography*, New York: Weidenfeld & Nicholson.

WILLIAM VAN WATSON

Zeri, Federico

b. 12 August 1921, Rome; d. 5 October 1998, Mentana

Art historian

Zeri's talent for accurate attribution and dating of artworks made him the natural successor to Roberto **Longhi** as the leading connoisseur of Italian art following the Longhi's death in 1970. Working mainly on art of the past and strongly resistant to fashionable trends in art theory, Zeri has appeared retrograde to some but, in fact, these very qualities have made him one of the most influential figures in Italian art. The monetary value of an artwork derives above all else from its accurate identification, which is where Zeri excelled. Dealers and collectors relied on his word, while at the same time certain institutions and sellers were piqued by his refusal to confirm a prestigious attribution, or by his demotion of a work from the master to the 'school of'.

Zeri's craft was based on possessing both an excellent eye and an encyclopaedic knowledge. After having studied 'hard sciences', in the form of botany and chemistry, he turned to philology and came under the influence of Longhi, with whom he collaborated on the journal *Paragone*. In the 1950s he worked in Rome, where he reorganized the collections of local galleries. During the next two decades he worked in the United States, where he published a highly regarded series of catalogues such as the *Census of Italian Paintings in North American Collections*, and descriptions of Italian paintings in the Metropolitan Museum of New York and the

Walters Art Gallery in Baltimore, the latter often considered his masterpiece. At the same time he consulted for major collectors such as Vittorio Cini, J. Paul Getty, Sr and Kesters. In Italy, Zeri helped to edit the 13-volume Einaudi *Storia dell'arte italiana* (History of Italian Art) between 1979 and 1983, and also wrote for the popular press.

His ideas are set out in *Behind the Image*, where the work of the art historian is compared to that of the detective. Zeri highlights the need to balance consideration of formal qualities with assessment of subject matter, style and quality, all together. He makes the effort to write clearly, and criticizes the obscurity of much art writing in Italy which renders it accessible only to initiates and untranslatable into other languages. In his own very substantial series of studies, Zeri tends to begin with a specific problem and moves from this to a consideration of more general issues.

Zeri's labours brought him both recognition and financial success. He lived in a villa at Mentana with his private library of 70,000 books, and in the 1990s he was appointed vice-president of the National Council for Cultural and Environmental Heritage. In 1997 he published, with Carmen Iarrera, a murder mystery, *Mai con i quadri* (Never With Paintings), about the assassination of a Professor of Art History.

See also: art criticism

Further reading

Zeri, F. (1987) *Behind the Image: The Art of Reading Paintings*, trans. N. Rootes, New York: St Martin's Press.

Zeri, F. and Iarrera, C. (1997) *Mai con i quadri*, Milan: Longanesi.

MAX STAPLES

Zevi, Bruno

b. 22 January 1918, Rome; d. 9 January 2000, Rome

Architect, architectural critic, historian and editor

Having graduated from Harvard in 1941, Zevi returned to Rome in 1944 where he joined the **Partito d'Azione** (Action Party) and founded the APAO (Association for Organic Architecture). Inspired by Wright's organic architecture and American models in general, Zevi insisted on establishing a functionalist tradition in Italy as a basis for modern architecture but, while advocating an uncompromising battle against rationalism, he neglected to acknowledge the importance of its modern component. His theoretical stands were inseparable from envisioned principles of action, and so after APAQ he went on to found the National Institute for Architecture in 1959 and then the Institute of Operative Criticism in Architecture in 1970. He collaborated on the magazine *Metron* from 1945 until 1955 when it became *L'Architettura – cronache e storia* under his sole directorship. One of the best-known architectural critics and writers in Italy, he has published numerous books and articles, organized many exhibitions and won various distinguished awards for his teaching and criticism.

Further reading

Oppenheimer Dean, A. (1983) *Bruno Zevi on Modern Architecture*, New York: Rizzoli.

GORDANA KOSTICH

Zorio, Gilberto

b. 21 September 1944, Andorno Micca, Vincenza

Artist

Closely identified with *arte povera*, Zorio studied at the Scuola di arte e di ceramica (School of Art and Ceramics) and then at the Accademia delle Belle Arti (Academy of Fine Arts) in Turin, the city where he continued to live. His first solo exhibition at the Sperone Gallery in 1967 led to his adoption by Ileana Sonnabend and Leo Castelli in New York. From 1967 to 1972, his work appeared in pioneering group exhibitions such as 'When Attitudes Become Form' in Berne. Zorio began his artistic experimentation using materials from his father's building sites, creating structures made of scaffolding, polystyrene, cement mixes and rubber. His work explores the energy in materials and their interaction, sometimes involving the spectator as catalyst: in *Tent* (1967), salt water dries on canvas leaving deposits; in *Burnt Writing* (1969), words in invisible ink appear for an instant on combustion of a piece of paper; in *To Purify Words* (1969–84), chemical substances react to human breath. For Zorio, art is a corporeal experience embracing all the senses and does not require prior knowledge to be understood. Like those of Penone and Mario **Merz**, Zorio's creations are accompanied by his own philosophical commentaries.

Further reading

Gilberto Zorio (1988), Florence: Hopefulmonster.

ROBERT LUMLEY

Zucchero

b. 25 September 1955, Adelmo, Reggio Emilia

Singer

One of Italy's most popular and commercially successful rhythm and blues singers, Zucchero (Sugar; real name Adelmo Fornaciari) began forming pop bands during the 1970s. In the early 1980s, always sporting the distinctive hat and feather which became his trademark, he appeared several times at the **Sanremo Festival** with only modest success. In the mid-1980s, however, he visited the USA and returned to Italy with a new band, which included American musicians and was more strongly focused on the blues. He began writing more of his own songs and was soon recognized as one of the new generation of *cantautori*. His album *Blue's*, released in 1987, reached record sales both in Italy and abroad, and

gave Zucchero an international reputation which continued to grow during the 1990s.

Singing in a guttural style which has sometimes prompted comparisons with Joe Cocker, Zucchero has performed with musicians as different as Miles Davis, Eric Clapton, B.B. King and Luciano Pavarotti, achieving both impressive record sales and international renown. In 1994 he was the only Italian musician invited to the second Woodstock Festival, and in 1995 his image was adopted by the United Nations to celebrate its 50th anniversary.

GINO MOLITERNO

Zurlini, Valerio

b. 19 March 1926, Bologna; d. 27 October 1982, Verona

Film director and art critic

After graduating in law from the university of Bologna, Zurlini began his career in cinema in the late 1940s with a number of short urban documentaries. His first feature film, *Le ragazze di San Frediano* (The Girls of San Frediano) (1954), from a novel by Vasco **Pratolini**, was the first of several fine adaptations of literary works that would mark his career and which would include *Cronaca Familiare* (Family Diary) (1962), also by Pratolini, and *Le soldatesse* (The Female Soldiers) (1965) from a novel by Ugo Pirro. In 1968 he made *Seduto alla sua destra* (Seated at his Right, more commonly known as *Black Jesus*), a powerful indictment of white colonialism in Africa and a fierce parable of man's inhumanity to man. Zurlini is probably best remembered, however, for the more delicately wrought and intellectually complex *Il Deserto dei Tartari* (The Desert of the Tartars) (1976), his highly successful adaptation of Dino **Buzzati**'s brilliant novel of the same name.

GINO MOLITERNO

Index

Page numbers in **bold** indicate references to the main entry.